Black Progress: Reality or Illusion?

BLACK PROGRESS: Reality or Illusion?

AN EDITORIALS ON FILE BOOK

Editor: Carol C. Collins

Assistant Editor: Tracey Dewart

Facts On File Publications

New York, New York • Oxford, England

Black Progress: Reality or Illusion?

Published by Facts On File, Inc.
460 Park Avenue South, New York, N.Y. 10016
© Copyright 1985 by Facts On File, Inc.

Library of Congress Cataloging in Publication Data
Main entry under title:

Black progress.

   Includes index.
   1. Afro-Americans—Politics and government.   2. Afro-Americans—Education.   3. Afro-Americans—Economic conditions.   4. Afro-Americans—Civil rights.   I. Collins, Carol Chambers.
E185.615.B547   1985   305.8'96073   85-6994
ISBN 0-87196-968-8

International Standard Book Number: 0-87196-968-8
Library of Congress Catalog Card Number: 85-6994
9 8 7 6 5 4 3 2 1
PRINTED IN THE UNITED STATES OF AMERICA

Contents

Preface

"There are those who are asking the devotees of civil rights: 'When will you be satisfied'? We can never be satisfied as long as the Negro is the victim of unspeakable horrors of police brutality. . . . We can never be satisfied as long as the Negro's basic mobility is from a smaller ghetto to a larger one. We can never be satisfied as long as our children are stripped of their selfhood and robbed of their dignity by signs stating 'For Whites Only'.

We cannot be satisfied so long as the Negro in Mississippi cannot vote and the Negro in New York believes he has nothing for which to vote. No, no, we will not be satisfied until justice rolls down like water and righteousness like a mighty stream."

Martin Luther King, Jr.
August 28, 1963
Washington, D.C.

When Dr. King delivered his ringing "I have a Dream" speech at the Lincoln Memorial, the Civil Rights Act of 1964 and the Voting Rights Act of 1965 had yet to be passed. Much has changed in the intervening two decades. The "For Whites Only" signs that were once ubiquitous in the South have long since disappeared. Desegregation and affirmative action programs have opened education and employment opportunities to black students and workers. Blacks have won elections as mayors, state legislators and members of Congress; a prominent black civil rights leader, Jesse Jackson, sought the Democratic nomination for President in 1984.

But beyond these obvious indications of change, there is considerable disagreement about the progress that has been made in civil rights, and even greater disagreement over how to measure that progress. Many Americans believe that the civil rights battle has largely been won, pointing to individual achievements by blacks and an apparent absence of overt discrimination as evidence of a now colorblind society. Some feel that the march for equal justice has gone beyond its legitimate goals, charging that the preferential treatment accorded minorities under some affirmative action programs is a new kind of race-consciousness that violates the principle of equal opportunity as grievously as the old discrimination.

Others feel that the nation has not truly incorporated the principle that all Americans, black or white, are entitled to equal opportunities and equal treatment under the law. They point to studies showing that the socio-economic gap between blacks and whites is as wide now as it was in 1963, and that the disparity is growing rather than increasing. The statistics cited in these studies document high levels of poverty, unemployment, poor housing and ill health in much of the black community. This yawning 'color gap', current civil rights leaders argue, cannot be attributed to the effects of historical discrimination alone, but to continuing,

vii

pervasive discrimination that although subtler than that practiced twenty years ago is no less damaging. Reports of continuing housing discrimination, or of inequities in the criminal justice system, fuel fears that the hard-won advances of the 1960's are being eroded. In the conservative political climate ushered in by the Reagan Administration, many civil rights advocates feel, the struggle for black equality has become a low priority.

The use of statistics is itself the subject of debate in some of the editorials reprinted on the following pages. It is pointed out that bald numbers—whether quantifying income levels, occupational choices, criminal arrests and convictions, or divorce rates—do not in themselves support conclusions that link the lower socio-economic status of blacks with discrimination. Opponents of federally-funded social programs and affirmative action plans argue that these programs do not treat the root causes of poverty among blacks. These causes, they say, are to be found in the social pathology of the ghetto: high rates of teenage pregnancy, chronic unemployment, poor schooling and high dropout rates—much the same factors that make it difficult for any disadvantaged group to break out of the cycle of poverty. Government aid, they claim, merely creates a dependency upon outside financial support, rather than helping to lift its recipients out of poverty. It may be due to the nation's racist past, they concede, that blacks came to constitute a disproportionate share of ghetto inhabitants. But they are adamant that the ills of the black community can no longer be blamed upon white racism, claiming that the evidence for such a cause-and-effect relationship is not provided by the statistics and is not borne out by a dispassionate examination of the nation's present attitudes and practices.

Another objection to statistics is that they exacerbate an inevitable tendency, when discussing any group, to speak of its members collectively, as of a monolithic entity with shared desires and goals. Certainly it is misleading, if semantically convenient, to refer to 'the black vote' or 'the black family'. It is important to remember, however, that statistics are an irreplaceable tool in assessing the conditions affecting any large group. Numbers can sometimes mask important developments, but it is the task of the researcher to analyze statistics intelligently. The numbers themselves do not lie, but neither do they provide their own explanation.

Because most of the editorials contained in this book were written between 1979 and the present, bracketing President Reagan's first term and the beginning of his second, they are primarily concerned with the many changes in government policy touching civil rights that have characterized the Reagan Administration. They examine the Administration's enforcement of existing civil rights laws, its reconstitution of the U.S. Civil Rights Commission, and its steadfast opposition to affirmative action quotas. They address the "fairness" issue associated with Reagan's economic policy, and the impact upon blacks of cutbacks in social programs such as food stamps, AFDC (Aid to Families With Dependent Children) and college tuition assistance. They evaluate the effects of busing programs, minority business contracts and loans, and the Jesse Jackson presidential campaign. Taken from major newspapers across the nation, these editorials can be compared to superimposed images that provide a kind of composite snapshot of black Americans today. Their selection was guided by the belief that every viewpoint adds depth to the final picture.

April, 1985   Carol C. Collins

Introduction: Looking Back

King Holiday Debate Examines Civil Rights Leader's Hero Status

The U.S. Senate voted, in 1983, to make Dr. Martin Luther King Jr. the second American, after George Washington, to be honored by a federal holiday. (The House had approved similar legislation two months earlier.) The vote, 78 to 22, followed acrimonious debate in the Senate, primarily between Sens. Jesse Helms (R, N.C.) and Edward M. Kennedy (D, Mass.). Helms made several attempts to delay and amend the bill. In addition to objecting to the holiday on economic grounds, Helms charged that the black civil rights leader had been a Marxist-Leninist influenced by "elements of the Communist Party USA." When John F. Kennedy was President, with Robert F. Kennedy as his Attorney General, Helms contended, they had authorized wiretaps on King. Helms also sought access to sealed Federal Bureau of Investigation files on King, but the request was denied by a federal judge. The records had been ordered sealed for 50 years in 1977 in order to protect the privacy of King's family. Sen. Kennedy accused Helms of conducting a "smear campaign."

In a news conference the day of the Senate vote, President Reagan, who had initially opposed the bill, said he "would have preferred" setting aside a day which individual states had the choice of observing or not, "but since they seem bent on making it a national holiday, I believe the symbolism of that day is important enough that I'll sign that legislation." Asked if he agreed with statements by Helms on the Senate floor that King had had communist associations or was a communist sympathizer, Reagan responded, "We'll know in about 35 years, won't we?" Aides later said this was meant as a joke. Reagan went on to defend Helms' sincerity in wanting the records revealed, saying: "I think that he's motivated by a feeling that if we're going to have a national holiday named for any American...we should know everything there is to know" about him.

The following year, in March, 1985, black leaders and civil rights activists participated in a commemoration of the famous 1965 voter-registration march from Selma to Montgomery, Alabama. The 600 marchers led by King in 1965 had been met and turned back by 200 law enforcement officials armed with nightsticks, whips and tear gas. The bloody confrontation occurred as a result of Gov. George C. Wallace's determination to enforce a ban against any march to protest the denial of voting rights to blacks in Selma. (The march was later completed by thousands of protesters under the protection of National Guard units called out by President Johnson.) The march helped lead to passage of the Voting Rights Act later that year. (See pp. 226-235.)

THE LOUISVILLE TIMES
Louisville, Ky., November 4, 1983

Sometime in his Hollywood days, Ronald Reagan must have had a lesson from Fred Astaire in how to dance on a ceiling and get away with it. The President performed the political equivalent this week when he signed the bill creating a national holiday in honor of Dr. Martin Luther King Jr.

His praise for Dr. King was 180 degrees removed from his refusal to defend Dr. King at a news conference last month. If anything, the President then had seemed to side with North Carolina Sen. Jesse Helms, who had attacked Dr. King as a "Communist sympathizer."

"We'll know in about 35 years, won't we," Mr. Reagan quipped when asked if he agreed with Sen. Helms. His reference was to the fact that records of FBI surveillance of Dr. King have been sealed until 2027. Sen. Helms wanted them opened in hopes they would substantiate his belief, thus trashing Dr. King's reputation.

At first, aides insisted Mr. Reagan had blown his lines at the news conference. He had rehearsed a response to a question about the King holiday that was designed not to offend anyone. Instead, he blurted out what was meant to be a quip. However, later it came out that the President was not ad-libbing. He had drawn guffaws in the dress rehearsal with the 35-year line. None of his aides, according to reports, thought he would be so insensitive as to use the line in public. But it went over so well, he could not resist using it again.

None of those right-wing notions of Dr. King as a dangerous radical were on display in the Rose Garden, though. Instead, Dr. King was a man who stood for a "just cause" and who, in just 39 years, "had changed America forever."

This, remember, is the same President who only last week junked a very carefully worked out compromise designed to preserve the Civil Rights Commission as an independent and effective watchdog. The commission had angered him by being too zealous a watchdog over those changes advocated by Dr. King.

That was the ideological side of Ronald Reagan. The political side was on its best behavior for the Rose Garden ceremony attended by Dr. King's widow and many of his close associates. Sooner or later, the law of gravity will catch up with Mr. Reagan's act, and he will fall off that ceiling. But with his luck it will be later rather than sooner.

THE SAGINAW NEWS
Saginaw, Mich., October 23, 1983

Congress has made the third Monday in January, starting in 1986, a national holiday in honor of Martin Luther King Jr. At this point, the Saginaw City Council might as well follow suit and formalize the occasion on the municipal level.

Why reverse our stand against a paid holiday? For one thing, obviously, the issue is settled. But most of all, the powerful House and Senate majorities voting for a holiday, after annual rejection of the proposal ever since King's murder in 1968, suggest that there is a greater chance of giving the day real meaning.

Unquestionably Dr. King deserves a formal national tribute. By stirring word, example and courage, he awakened the conscience of the country.

Only 30 years ago, the color of one's skin made a world of difference in the United States — really two worlds, separate and unequal, in the notorious phrase. Personal prejudice, even hate, all too often was written into the law, to our national shame and today, to our deep regret. Thanks largely to King, legal racial discrimination now is unthinkable. And even though there is still a long way to go on the individual level, it is a real sign of progress that few can be found who will defend the past. In that sense, King worked and was martyred on behalf of all Americans.

So why object to a holiday at all? Our major concern was that a paid holiday, as opposed to a Sunday, would amount to little more than another day off for, in most cases, public employees. We doubted that those getting the day off would spend it contemplating King's life and purpose any more than they reflected upon Christopher Columbus a couple of weeks ago. Perversely, a Monday holiday would prevent many of those who care most deeply from honoring King on the day set aside for that purpose. It would be almost entirely symbolic.

But as King's stature has grown, so has the value of that symbolism. As proponents have contended, anything less than the full tribute would make King's day a second-class holiday in ugly parallel of precisely what he struggled to overcome.

Congress finally accepted that argument. Now the task is to make the day a true national reminder not only of King, or of the civil rights movement, or of the growing influence of the black vote — itself an outgrowth of King's movement — but above all, of the principles of equality and justice he espoused.

Perhaps, as Sen. Jesse Helms predicted, there are embarrassments within the sealed government files on King. But we already know he wasn't spotless. Neither were most of our other national heroes. And we foresee no disclosure that could erase the public record of the enduring good that he achieved.

A Martin Luther King Day, then, seems to be the sense of the Congress and of the country. It is one more example of how an inspired man who strived to free us all can still overcome.

The Washington Times
Washington, D.C., October 18, 1983

As America's symbol for the civil rights struggle of the 1950s and 60s, the myth of Martin Luther King Jr. is larger than life. King was no saint, nor did he claim to be. A national holiday in his name will honor the country's ideal of equality.

But because a holiday for King will confirm him as a model for Americans of all creeds and colors, the FBI's files and tapes — all of them — should be disclosed and debated. And the Senate vote on the holiday bill, scheduled for tomorrow, should be postponed.

The 25,000 documents released from the bureau's files last week include vague but disturbing charges that King and his Southern Christian Leadership Conference were aided and abetted by communists. Names and data have been deleted by the FBI in many documents, apparently to protect informants and investigative methods.

The 1977 federal court order sealing FBI surveillance tapes of King should be lifted. The bureau should provide complete copies of all documents where important national security values will not be harmed.

Many of King's admirers would rather the tapes be erased, the papers burned. One commentator notable for his insistence on full disclosure of his adversaries' sins large and small has confessed that years ago he refused to report FBI information critical of King; he "saw nothing . . . that would warrant publishing a story." That he now chooses to write about it proves just how wrong he was.

King's supporters say there's nothing of substance in the FBI files. If that's so, and we hope it is, then we all have everything to gain, nothing to lose, by bringing those files into daylight.

THE SACRAMENTO BEE
Sacramento, Calif., October 28, 1983

It was entirely predictable that Sen. Jesse Helms of North Carolina would try to sabotage the move in Congress to designate a new federal holiday in memory of the late Martin Luther King Jr., and that Helms would resort to any procedural stratagem to block action in the Senate. What was less obvious, and is even more distressing, is that President Reagan would be so graceless in dealing publicly with the matter, notwithstanding the controversy the King holiday proposal touched off.

"We'll know in about 35 years, won't we?" answered the president, with an almost audible smirk, in response to a reporter's question about whether King was a Communist sympathizer. In the 15 years since King's tragic death, not a shred of evidence has been produced that the black civil rights leader held any pro-Communist sentiments. Moreover, persons who have seen the still-sealed FBI records on King, to which Reagan alluded, have stated publicly that nothing in the documents led them to conclude that any such accusation — insinuation would be more accurate — was justified.

Beyond his initial tasteless remark, though, the president, during his news conference last week, seemed to bend over backward to sympathize with Helms' motives in trying to obstruct the Senate vote on the holiday, and seemed incapable of saying anything even mildly gracious — never mind complimentary — about the slain leader. During a rambling and not altogether coherent explanation of why he would still sign the holiday legislation, the president alluded to "a stormy period in our history" and "a very real crisis in our history . . . and the part that he (King) played in that" without ever making it clear whether he

held King responsible for causing the crisis or helping to resolve it.

That ambiguity was all too reminiscent of Reagan's response to King's murder in 1968, when he remarked that "the murder of Martin Luther King began the first day some of us in this country began to decide it was all right to choose the laws we wanted to obey."

The president's subsequent telephone call to Coretta Scott King, widow of the late civil rights leader, might have made at least partial amends. But afterward, the White House refused to characterize Reagan's explanation of his news conference remark as an apology. Still worse, it was revealed that only two weeks earlier Reagan had written sympathetically to former New Hampshire Gov. Meldrim Thomson, who had objected to the King holiday on the ground that King was "a man of immoral character whose frequent association with leading agents of communism is well-established." In his reply to Thomson's letter, the president wrote, "I have the same reservations you have, but here the perception of too many people is based on image, not reality. Indeed, to them the perception is reality."

There was a valid argument to be made against creating a national holiday commemorating any American, at least until a long period of time could allow a fuller assessment of that person's contributions. Unfortunately, the negative argument was made — by Helms — in such a reprehensible way that, not only was the good name of Martin Luther King called into question, but the debate itself was robbed of much of the dignity that should have attended it. Sadly, the president's graceless handling of the situation only added to that lamentable tone.

The Philadelphia Inquirer
Philadelphia, Pa., October 6, 1983

Now comes Sen. Jesse Helms (R., N.C.) to warn the Senate that, even in death, the Rev. Dr. Martin Luther King Jr. deserves no honor. The Senate appears on the verge of dedicating a new national holiday to the memory of the slain civil rights leader. Ah, but does the Senate realize, proclaimed Mr. Helms, that Dr. King was a wolf in sheep's clothing, that he espoused "action-oriented Marxism" and "radical political views" not compatible with the American ideal?

Mr. Helms' American ideal, of course, is not everyone's. Mr. Helms' ideal, for example, romanticizes a South of juleps and linen suits, a nation of Christian values — read "state-mandated prayers" — and universities where those with unpopular political views would have no podium. He presumes — and he presumes mistakenly — that his sense of morality appeals to the majority when, in fact, it appeals narrowly to the Moral Majority.

Federal holidays, argued Mr. Helms, are an occasion for "shared values." And on that, at least, he was quite correct. Trouble is that in the crucible of protest and response where democracies are tested, it has been Mr. Helms' values — his knee-jerk anti-communism, his militaristic foreign policy, his self-righteous stands against women's rights and court prerogatives — that have been losing ground while those of Dr. King, thank goodness, have been gaining. The low-key, commemorative march on Washington a few weeks ago was noncontroversial for the very fact that the values of equal opportunity and racial harmony that Dr. King preached 20 years ago have found acceptance among a broad spectrum of Americans.

It is not, as Mr. Helms declared, Dr. King's name that remains a source of tension, "a deeply troubling symbol of a divided society." It is the name of Jesse Helms, an unreconstructed racist who would seek — as he has ever since masterminding a vicious whispering campaign against North Carolina's progressive Frank Porter Graham — to generate political funds with crude slanders. "Red smear" tactics, is what Sen. Edward M. Kennedy (D., Mass.) rightly called Mr. Helms' outburst.

Those such as Mr. Helms add weight to the argument favoring a holiday for Dr. King. Their vindictive narrow-mindedness calls for rebuttal both symbolic and tangible. It calls for celebration of an American ideal large enough to embrace those who once tested its sincerity, celebration of reconciliation and the efficacy of nonviolence. It calls for a tribute to courage and to a dream that men and women can learn to live together — most of them anyway. Unfortunately, there always will be those such as Mr. Helms, who will never learn.

Rocky Mountain News

Denver, Colo., October 22, 1983

EVER since he was felled by an assassin's bullet 15 years ago, friends and admirers of the Rev. Martin Luther King Jr. have fought to have the civil rights leader's Jan. 15 birthday commemorated as a legal public holiday.

With the Senate's overwhelming passage of the bill to honor King and President Reagan's promise to sign it, the fight has been won. The question no longer is should there be such a holiday but how to observe it.

It will be a shame if the holiday, which will fall on the third Monday in January starting in 1986, is treated like just another free day in winter — with much of America, beer can in hand, watching football on the tube.

Conversely, the day will prove valuable if many Americans reflect on King's life and work and rededicate themselves to what he stood for: human rights, racial equality, social justice achieved through nonviolence.

Also it will be fair to use the holiday to acknowledge black Americans' contributions to this country, which have not received the recognition they deserve.

Some of the opposition to honoring King, such as that of Sen. Jesse Helms, attempted to smear him as a communist sympathizer. But some raised valid questions: Should federal workers and others get a tenth paid holiday? What will be the effect on the economy?

Reagan would do well to appoint a presidential commission to look into the matter of holidays. It might find, for instance, that King, Washington and Columbus should be honored on their birthdays, not on designated Mondays which become commercialized.

It also could decide that 10 national holidays are too many and that the country would benefit from more production. In that case Memorial Day and Veterans Day could be combined, since both honor those who sacrificed in war.

AKRON BEACON JOURNAL

Akron, Ohio, October 20, 1983

POOR JESSE HELMS. He's still fighting the Civil War, living in the 19th century, and going down in flames again contending that there was something subversive about the Rev. Dr. Martin Luther King.

For those unfamiliar with the track record of the Southern Republican senator, this is an old refrain of his — dating back many years in North Carolina.

As a political figure in that state, Mr. Helms has always sided with those opposed to civil liberties and opposed to an end to discrimination.

As an editorial broadcaster before he ran for the U.S. Senate, Mr. Helms numbered Dr. King and the civil rights movement among his favorite targets. His views on race and racial equality have long been a modern-day, dressed-up version of the vile, racist lingo of the Bilbos of old.

Now the U.S. Senate has seen in full flower this throwback to the days when laws in the South decreed a society that was separate and anything but equal. And on the issue of a national holiday for the man who helped lead Americans out of the evil of state-sanctioned discrimination and second-class status for blacks, the Senate has rejected vehemently the codewords of racism. The country can be thankful for that.

As for Senator Helms, he faces a potentially tough reelection fight in North Carolina next year. The issue will be whether the old slogans designed to stir racial fears among white voters still work.

As has been the case in the U. S. Senate with the holiday for a great and gentle fighter for American equality, one hopes not.

St. Petersburg Times

St. Petersburg, Fla., November 4, 1983

"I have a dream!" cried out Martin Luther King Jr., and a roar arose from the vast crowd standing before the statue of Abraham Lincoln, the great emancipator.

"... That one day this nation will rise up and live out the true meaning of its creed: 'We hold these truths to be self-evident, that all men are created equal.' I have a dream ..."

Like great rolls of thunder, the crowd roared again and again as King's spellbinding oratory galvanized the civil rights movement and awoke the conscience of the nation.

That was 20 years ago on Aug. 28, 1963 — but the crowd's thunder and King's challenge echoed anew in Washington Wednesday, as President Reagan signed the bill to establish a federal holiday honoring the great black emancipator who pursued American justice through nonviolence.

WITH DIGNITY and restraint, the historic ceremony was performed in the White House Rose Garden before blacks and whites, Republicans and Democrats, liberals and conservatives — joined for a few moments of reconciliation.

The most compelling political issue of 1984 will be a political agenda of equal justice for Americans of all colors and all ages who believe that the United States stands for nothing, if it does not stand for decency to all its people.

Mr. Reagan paid warm tribute to King, saying his words and deeds had "stirred our nation to the very depths of its soul." With Coretta Scott King at his side, the President acknowledged that "traces of bigotry still mar America" and called for all citizens, each year on Martin Luther King Day, to rededicate themselves to "the just cause he stood for."

After the bill was signed, many in the crowd began singing *We Shall Overcome*, the moving anthem of the civil rights movement. Though rarely heard in the nation these days, the great anthem grew in volume and deep emotion as Mr. Reagan and Vice President George Bush moved through the Rose Garden. They shook hands with guests, but did not join in the singing.

Still, the anthem soared, capturing the irony of those historic moments — as a President, who wages a relentless campaign to turn back the civil right progress inspired by Martin Luther King, so eloquently espoused brotherhood, love, equality and justice.

The singing seemed rich in symbolism — almost a solemn declaration that the civil rights anthem and Dr. King's dream again will ring across the nation with renewed determination — galvanized not only by the nation's honor for King's cause, but by the Reagan administration's attempt to turn back time and justice.

PERHAPS, the Rose Garden ceremony raised Mr. Reagan's consciousness of American blacks' long struggle for freedom and equality. He spoke of that struggle with great sincerity.

Perhaps, his eloquence was not merely a political expediency, a well-staged attempt to improve his image among blacks for the 1984 campaign.

But Mr. Reagan's philosophies have been steadfast, as though frozen in past attitudes many Americans have now surrendered.

If Mr. Reagan really has undergone some transformation, it will be well tested in his re-election campaign. The challenge, already posed by white Democratic presidential candidates, was strengthened Thursday by Rev. Jesse Jackson's symbolic bid for the Democratic nomination.

Although acknowledging that he does not expect to win, Jackson's candidacy will be constructive in the campaign as he pursues the goal of awakening blacks, Hispanics, other minorities, the poor and women, to their political power.

"If we come together around our common economic plight and a humane political agenda, we won't be poor and powerless anymore," Jackson declared Thursday.

IF HIS CANDIDACY inspires massive voter registration among blacks and other minorities, the democratic process will be strengthened — and that may be Jackson's great contribution to the civil rights movement.

Some may view the flamboyant Jackson as an opportunist, trying to capitalize on the growing power of black voters by advancing a political agenda for blacks and the poor. But there is no black voting bloc and no coalition of the poor in this nation, and Jackson's candidacy alone cannot create them.

The most compelling political issue of 1984 will not be simply a black agenda for freedom, justice and equality, or economic justice for the poor. It will be a political agenda of equal justice for Americans of all colors and all ages who believe that the United States stands for nothing, if it does not stand for decency to all its people.

Equal justice. Simple human decency. Those were the dreams that Martin Luther King lived and died for.

The Providence Journal

Providence, R.I., October 10, 1983

Is Thomas Jefferson any the less revered because there is no national holiday in his name? Or John Adams? Or a multitude of others in the two-century-long pantheon of outstanding Americans? Of course not. And neither would Martin Luther King Jr.,

The Kansas City Times

Kansas City, Mo., October 20, 1983

The ugly campaign waged by Jesse Helms, Republican senator from North Carolina, ought not to diminish national satisfaction in a holiday celebrating the birthday anniversary of Dr. Martin Luther King Jr. Mr. Helms has embarrassed his party and his state and hurt himself. He has not hurt Dr. King.

In a sense all such observances are recognition of the human spirit personified in an individual. History makes heroes. Washington's birthday symbolizes the struggle of a people for self-rule and representative government. Columbus Day reminds us of courage, discovery and initiative. Independence Day takes us back to small, brave beginnings that changed the direction of mankind.

The King holiday does the same. It will remind the nation of a people who surmounted two and one-half centuries of outright slavery and another century of active prejudice, neglect and oppression that was written in the tradition of the land and the laws of some states. Until Dr. King and men and women like him faced the sheriffs, jails, police dogs and water hoses of brutal custom, the fact of racial injustice in the United States was far too easy for too many to ignore or even condone. And by such omission or action, the value of American citizenship was debased for everyone. The Public Accommodations Act, the Voting Rights Act, the other laws that underlined rights the majority took for granted, and upheld the meaning of citizenship, were essential. But most of all the shame and guilt, the facing up to injustice that Dr. King and his colleagues and followers evoked, transformed the conscience of America.

The contents of the raw FBI documents Mr. Helms is panting to disclose have nothing to do with the cause, whatever they may concern. Few among any of us are paragons of copybook virtues; as for political influences real or imagined, well, desperate times can bring strange but usually temporary alliances. Before he died Dr. King had embarked on the correction of economic hardship and injustice. It seems evident that political freedom is not of much use to the ignorant, hungry and idle, unless that freedom can be used for self-betterment. In any event, the files are irrelevant except as gross material for small minds.

Dr. King's cause was nothing less than the cause of liberty and opportunity in the United States; in short, to give full value to that quality called American citizenship as defined in the Constitution. His dream is not fully realized. But Americans can rejoice in the reminder of King Day and what he and people like him have done for all of us.

the martyred black civil rights leader, be reduced in popular esteem should Congress and the President not memorialize him with a national holiday on his birthdate, Jan. 15.

Were such a designation needed to show proper respect for Dr. King, it would imply that his reputation could not stand by his deeds alone as has been the case with a whole roster of equal greats in U.S. history. And this is not true. Dr. King measures up with the best of them. Let's face it. The notion in Washington that enactment of the King-holiday bill is a must arises principally from the politicians' fear that failure to pass it will result in their loss of black votes.

Besides such self-serving cravenness, the idea that black Americans (more than other large ethnic groups, each with their own heroes) have to be placated by such a gesture is to patronize them — and the day for that fortunately has gone by in this country. The best tribute to Dr. King is that increasingly paid him on a voluntary basis annually by whites and non-whites alike, and by the nation's constant move toward ending all forms of bigotry. No formal holiday is necessary to advance this process and none need be created.

Were such a designation needed to show proper respect for Dr. King, it would imply that his reputation can't stand by his deeds alone

---

Indeed, adding another to the already lengthy list of workdays off would hardly improve the nation's economy. And its improvement is the best favor that blacks, suffering from an inordinately high unemployment rate, could receive. Dr. King himself, who was slain while campaigning for job betterment for blacks in Memphis, would surely agree with that.

The Detroit News

Detroit, Mich., October 21, 1983

Congress has now voted to make the third Monday in January a federal holiday honoring Martin Luther King Jr. Whether it will be a meaningful national holiday or just another "day off" for federal workers depends on what we make of it.

We know what we should not make of it. We should not treat it simply as a monument to political expedience. The best argument of those who opposed the holiday was that it was still too early to assess Mr. King's place in history. They painted the movement for a King Day as mere election-eve politics. But ultimately the question of a man's place in history comes down to a question of political judgment. Our political process has now rendered judgment. It does our country and that process no honor to belittle that judgment.

Nor should we treat the holiday as simply an honor to a great black man, as if all that happened was that the pantheon of national heroes had been integrated by some sort of affirmative action program. That would doom the new federal holiday to the apathy that yearly greets Columbus Day, which has shrunk to an "Italian-American Day" in too many minds and is celebrated by only 38 states. That would be a shame.

A truly national holiday must honor Rev. King not as a black man but as a model for future generations of all races, an embodiment of national ideals.

Clearly among those ideals was Mr. King's commitment to civil rights. When he spoke of his "dream," of a nation where his children would "not be judged by the color of their skin but by the content of their character," he was describing more than a black dream. He was affirming the American dream: equal rights, equal justice, and equal opportunity regardless of accidents of birth like race, sex, or national origin.

Yet Martin Luther King was more than a civil rights leader, and the holiday in his honor is really more than a "national civil rights day," as some would describe it.

Mr. King was even more impressive because he sought to "overcome oppression and violence without resorting to oppression and violence." He saw nonviolent political action as the only alternative to passive acceptance of injustice on the one hand and a resort to violent intimidation and retaliation on the other. Certainly, King's example provides a national model of how to achieve great political and social change by working within the democratic system.

Finally, Mr. King represents a personal idealism and courage worth emulating. Despite his own experiences with poverty, brutality, and injustice, he remained optimistic about improving the human condition. He refused to succumb to self-defeating cynicism or apathy or fear. As he once told a Detroit audience, "If a man hasn't discovered something that he will die for, he isn't fit to live." That is a profound truth we all need to remember, especially in the nuclear age.

The difference between Mr. King and so many others is that he really meant what he said, living and dying in the service of high ideals.

And if we really mean it, if we make this new holiday a recognition of Martin Luther King's ideals and example, then King Day will transcend the petty concerns of race and politics to become a meaningful national holiday.

THE INDIANAPOLIS NEWS

Indianapolis, Ind.,
October 22, 1983

Now that it appears a national holiday honoring Martin Luther King will become a reality, a comment is in order about the "opposition," Sen. Jesse Helms, R-N.C.

There were sound reasons to oppose such a holiday. Many argued that King should not have a holiday if Americans such as Thomas Jefferson and Abraham Lincoln do not have one in their honor. They said that Congress should wait 50 years in order to gain a historical perspective on King's greatness. Others argued the holiday would be too expensive. Still others argued that honoring King as a tribute to blacks and the civil rights movement would undermine the principle for which King stood: A racially integrated society.

Unfortunately, Sen. Helms responded by questioning King's loyalty. He called him a Communist, a traitor and un-American.

It seems strange that J. Edgar Hoover never confronted King with these allegations, if they were true. King's "crime" seems to be that he looked at several subjects in a different manner from others. Denying a man the right to think differently is what is un-American.

King was confronted during his life by many who disagreed violently with him and his ideas, but he did not respond with hate or name-calling.

Sen. Helms would have done well to follow King's example.

Detroit Free Press

Detroit, Mich., October 9, 1984

THE EFFORT to honor Dr. Martin Luther King Jr. with a national holiday has been long and hard-fought. For too many people, Dr. King remains a controversial figure; not all the dust from the abrupt collapse of officially sanctioned segregation has settled. All the more reason America needs to be reminded anew, every year, of Dr. King's message, that eloquently expressed dream of equality for blacks and whites, young and old, brother and sister, North and South.

Despite the opposition, the House has approved a bill designating the third Monday in January as a holiday in honor of Dr. King. In the Senate, the bill has been stalled by Sen. Jesse Helms, who began his public career as a segregation-spouting radio announcer. But last week word came down that in return for timely consideration of the tobacco subsidy bill, the senator from North Carolina would cease to oppose the King holiday.

A vote will be taken in mid-October, and there is a strong likelihood the bill will pass. The man who forced a nation into a historic confrontation with its conscience will get his holiday, courtesy of the tobacco lobby — surely a classic case of the right thing being done for the wrong reasons. Dr. King, a Baptist minister, would probably have pointed out that if the Lord can work in mysterious ways, so can Congress.

THE PLAIN DEALER

Cleveland, Ohio, October 20, 1983

On the third Monday of January 1986, taxpayers will pay their 2,888,957 federal workers a total of about $259 million to do nothing. The workers, because of action taken in the Senate yesterday, will get the day off in honor of the late Dr. Martin Luther King Jr.

Martin Luther King Day becomes the 10th federal holiday. In addition to the federal workers who will be able to take the day off to ski, shop, sleep, watch television or whatever else is done on a day off, millions of teachers will have an additional holiday (many but not all states now close their schools on the anniversary of King's birth). The new holiday also will be recognized by millions of union members.

The resulting productivity loss will cost billions of dollars. So you may wonder, as have we, whether another national holiday is worth it. But think for a moment about the enormous cost of the racism that persisted in this country before King marched the civil rights movement into the political forefront. Think about the millions of people whose talents would be unrealized; about those people who would be unable to contribute fully to the nation's economy.

With a black unemployment rate of about 20%, the country still has far to go. But few would deny that life has been improved by the 1965 and 1968 Civil Rights Acts and the Voting Rights Act of 1964.

One of those few is Sen. Jesse Helms, R-N.C., who waged a gutter-level battle against creation of the King holiday. Helms, who faces a tough re-election fight next year, unabashedly played to the racist lobby by dredging up the tired old rumors about King's alleged Communist ties—ties which, as Joshua Muravchik points out on the opposite page today, never have been substantiated.

What a contrast: King the gentle man; Helms the savage supremacist. But while King no doubt would have been pleased to have seen the Senate stand up to Helms, he would have been disturbed by Congress' honoring him with a federal holiday while refusing to keep alive the federal commission charged with monitoring civil rights progress. The Senate, in a dispute with the president over the independence of the commission, has failed to authorize the body to continue its work.

Sen. Arlen Specter, R-Penn., has proposed to expand the committee by two members in what looks to be a sensible compromise to the current appointments deadlock with the White House. If Specter's fellow senators and the president really want to do honor to King's name, they will act to ensure that the Civil Rights Commission has the independence, as well as the authority, to do its job.

The Chattanooga Times

Chattanooga, Tenn,. October 24, 1983

It was a tribute to the Senate's conscience that it voted by such a wide margin on Wednesday in favor of a national holiday in honor of Dr. Martin Luther King Jr., the charismatic preacher whose efforts were instrumental in helping black Americans achieve racial equality. The vote was all the more valuable as a repudiation of the revived smear campaign waged against the martyred leader by several senators, notably Jesse Helms, Republican of North Carolina.

It was typical of Sen. Helms' opposition that in a news conference following the 78 to 22 vote, he charged that the holiday had been pushed through Congress "in an atmosphere of intimidation and political harrassment. It's a tyranny of the minority."

It's ironic that Sen. Helms would charge proponents of the holiday with exercising intimidation and political harrassment, for those are precisely the tactics he employed in vainly trying to torpedo the effort. He went to court to attempt to persuade a federal judge to release documents about Dr. King gathered by the FBI and sealed by court order in 1977 for 50 years. To its ever-lasting credit, the Reagan administration staunchly opposed that maneuver, arguing among other things that it would not be a party to violating the federal government's word with the King family by releasing the documents. Sen. Helms had contended that release of the documents was necessary so that senators could cast "informed" votes on the holiday issue. But that was a transparent ploy. The real reason was to release for public consumption the raw data gathered during the FBI's scurrilous invasion of Dr. King's privacy, and thereby one last time to destroy his reputation. That campaign ordered by former Director J. Edgar Hoover, whose hatred of Dr. King was well-known.

Equally well-known are the tired old objections to Dr. King's activism, objections that center on the confrontational yet non-violent tactics he used to break down walls of blatant racial segregation, his alleged immorality and his reported association with Communists. Of the three, the last is the most reprehensible. It implies that the progress in the civil rights struggle sprang not from Americans' inherent sense of fairness, compassion and belief in equality before the law, but merely from subversive elements that tried to attach themselves to Dr. King.

The Senate's vote Wednesday is a welcome and long overdue repudiation of the effort to besmirch Dr. King's reputation, and by extension the value of his contributions to all Americans, black and white.

THE DAILY OKLAHOMAN

Oklahoma City, Okla., October 21, 1983

THE DEED is all but done. Congressional action on a bill to create a federal holiday in memory of Martin Luther King Jr. has been completed and President Reagan says he will sign it into law.

But such a *fait accompli* will not necessarily bring the reconciliation its promoters fondly hope for it, simply because of the polarizing nature of the man being honored.

Now the battleground will move to the states that have not already established King birthday memorials. Technically speaking, there are no national holidays; each state designates its own, although in practice most observe the federal legal holidays.

The president demonstrated by his responses to questions at his news conference the other night that his acquiesence is less than enthusiastic. He explained he had preferred something other than a full-fledged holiday to recognize the slain civil rights leader. But he said he understands the importance of the symbolism to the black community.

What was really understood by the president — and the 78 senators who earlier in the day voted for the measure — was the political risk of voting against something so ardently pursued by the civil rights lobby.

Oklahoma's two senators split on the issue: Democrat David Boren expressed reservations about King's actions and his personal life but said he was voting for the "cause of reconciliation and equal opportunity." Republican Don Nickles earned the ire of black activist Clara Luper and probably others by voting "no" with 21 fellow senators. Yet even he pitched his dissent on economic grounds while praising King as a man of vision.

Whether or not sealed FBI files contain, as opponents of the bill insisted, concrete evidence of King consorting with known communists, the public record should be sufficient to reveal the stridency of his attacks on American policy during the Vietnam War. True, he was not alone in this, but his partisanship is hardly calculated to promote unity among the American people.

Still, neither this nor the accusations regarding his personal life should have been the overriding issue. Only one other American — George Washington, the father of our country — has been honored with a national holiday in his name. Many other great people, including blacks, have not been singled out for such high national tribute, not even Abraham Lincoln, who is credited with holding the country together in perhaps its greatest crisis.

But now the gate is open; a precedent has been established. Sooner or later other ethnic groups, such as Hispanics or Indians or Orientals, will be demanding a similar honor for one of their heroes. And how can they be denied?

San Francisco Chronicle

San Francisco, Calif., October 26, 1983

IT HAS TAKEN 15 years since it was first proposed to enact legislation making the birthdate of the late Dr. Martin Luther King Jr. a national holiday. The Senate vote, 78-22, a better than two-to-one majority, is probably a quite accurate gauge of public sentiment on the matter. Most Americans, we believe, even those who did not fully agree with him, believed that Dr. King, a man of international stature, should be given proper national honor.

Dr. King deserved this recognition not only for his non-violent civil rights' leadership but also because his name is a powerful symbol of an entire era.

It was the era not only of black assertion and claim for justice long denied but also of white awareness of that denial and of significant white participation in change. The college students went south to register voters and to be beaten, jailed and, in some instances, to be killed. It was the time of extraordinary courage by individual blacks in all sections of the country in laying claims to rights which had been denied for the entire century after the abolition of slavery.

IT WAS THE era when "We Shall Overcome" was accompanied by legislation to make the way easier. But it was also the era when individuals had to make lonely stands to ensure that the legislation was enforced. The march on Washington, the march on Selma, the Birmingham bus boycott, the desegregation of Central High School in Little Rock, the opening of the doors of public facilities in both South and North are, today, all part and parcel of one great movement that changed the face of the land.

THE ONE DOMINANT figure who symbolizes this vast and historically-important movement— even though he was not present at many significant times and places — was Dr. King for he became the movement's spiritual and philosophical leader.

The designation of the third Monday in January is an honor that was resisted vigorously only by those who do not recognize that the nation has changed. The day should remind the rest of us that Dr. King's great dream is not yet attained fully.

The Hartford Courant
Hartford, Conn., October 6, 1983

Having had his day in the media sun, North Carolina Sen. Jesse A. Helms on Tuesday stopped filibustering against the idea of creating a national holiday to honor the Rev. Martin Luther King Jr. The final Senate vote is expected to come Oct. 19, and President Reagan reportedly has agreed to sign the bill. The House approved the measure in August.

Sen. Helms' opposition would have been defensible — albeit misguided — had he confined his argument to asserting that the nation couldn't afford another holiday. The King holiday, to be observed on the third Monday in January, beginning in 1986, will cost about $18 million in lost federal work, and schools, banks and many other businesses will close for the day. Dr. King's birthday is now a state holiday in Connecticut.

But Mr. Helms went far beyond a call for fiscal prudence. He accused the slain civil rights leader of espousing "action-oriented Marxism" that is "not compatible with the concepts of this country," adding that "I think his whole movement included Communists at the highest possible levels."

President Reagan's recent indication that he would sign the bill, together with informal persuasion and a threatened movement by Senate leaders to invoke cloture, may have persuaded Mr. Helms to give up his attack. But a senator with a greater sense of responsibility, and a greater sense of Martin Luther King's place in history, would not have uttered such words to begin with.

THE ATLANTA CONSTITUTION
Atlanta, Ga., October 31, 1983

The mud has settled from the congressional debate which led to the enactment of a national holiday honoring Martin Luther King Jr. Most of the mud has stuck, not to King, but to Sen. Jesse Helms (R-N.C.), and the few others like him who threw it.

The nation now knows — Helms and his sort to the contrary notwithstanding — that the sealed FBI file on King does not show that the civil-rights leader was a Communist, Soviet agent or Comintern dupe. Former federal officials who read the file, and others high officals who were briefed on it, report that.

The one person who went unheard-from in the ugly little spasm of race- and Red-baiting that was excited by the holiday legislation was King himself. Yet his book "Strength To Love," a 1963 collection of sermons, bears witness. One piece begins, "Let me state clearly the basic premise of this sermon: Communism and Christianity are fundamentally incompatible. A true Christian cannot be a true Communist, for the two philosophies are antithetical and all the dialectics of the logicians cannot reconcile them."

The sermon's conclusion is no less uncompromising: "Our hard challenge and our sublime opportunity is to bear witness to the spirit of Christ in fashioning a truly Christian world. If we accept the challenge with devotion and valor, the bell of history will toll for Communism, and we shall make the world safe for democracy and secure for the people of Christ."

Inter alia, King unloads on humanism and "ethical relativism" in ways that would stoke even the most hard-bitten of today's fundamentalist preacher-politicians, but he also offers:

"Communism will never be defeated by the use of atomic bombs or nuclear weapons. Let us not join those who shout war and who through their misguided passion urge the United States to relinquish its participation in the United Nations . . . We must not call everyone a Communist or an appeaser who recognizes that hate and hysteria are not the final answers to the problems of these turbulent days.

"We must not engage in a negative anti-Communism, but rather in a positive thrust for democracy . . . After our condemnation of the philosophy of Communism has been eloquently expressed, we must with positive action seek to remove those conditions of poverty, insecurity, injustice and racial discrimination which are the fertile soil in which the seed of Communism grows and develops."

Twenty years before Helms and his pack took to yelping, Martin Luther King Jr. had already had the last word.

The San Diego Union
San Diego, Calif., October 21, 1983

The bill establishing a new federal holiday commemorating the birth of Martin Luther King is on its way to the White House. President Reagan's promise to sign it carries the same tone of resignation that we detected among many of the senators who put the bill across with a vote of 78-22. "Well, what choice is there?"

The King bill picked up the kind of momentum on Capitol Hill that is accorded to issues generally described as motherhood and apple pie. A good many of those 78 senators had figured that voting against the bill would be voting against black America, which no senator wants to do.

We suspect that Sen. Jesse Helms and the 21 senators who stood with him in opposition to the bill did not want to be recorded as voting against the aspirations of an important segment of our population. They deserve some credit for sticking by their convictions, right or wrong, in the face of the political steamroller that bowled over a majority of their colleagues.

They were insisting, for various reasons, that a federal holiday honoring Martin Luther King is not necessarily the best way to honor black people or to commemorate the civil rights movement that brought them out of second-class status as Americans.

Mr. Helms was willing to state on the floor what was heard mostly in the Senate cloakroom during the debate — that there are unknown areas in the life of Dr. King that might become more clear with the passage of time and might later be pertinent to whether he should be the symbol which the new holiday promises to make him. President Reagan acknowledged the existence of such concern when he mentioned at his news conference Wednesday night that questions about Dr. King's associations will have to wait another 35 years, until an FBI file now sealed for the protection of his family, will be opened.

Dr. King, felled by an assassin's bullet 15 years ago, is a hero to millions of black Americans, and should represent to those of all races what can be accomplished by pursuing a dream with courage and conviction. The arguments about whether his name should or should not be attached to a national holiday can now be put behind us.

Like other holidays, the new one to fall on the third Monday in January will mean to each of us what we choose to make of it. We can hope that the image of Dr. King will rise above the ambiguities which still surround it, and that his birthday will become associated with those ideals of justice and equality which were brought to realization in the last generation.

the Charleston Gazette
Charleston, W. Va., October 18, 1983

PUT us down as supporting the suggestion that Congress enact law stipulating that a century must elapse before establishment of national holidays memorializing individuals — subject only to the condition that the law be adopted after Congress approves and the president signs legislation authorizing a national holiday in memory of the Rev. Martin Luther King Jr.

It is essential for the spirit and for the soul of America that this courageous leader of a greatly oppressed minority be honored. Thus, in turn, will our society correct an enormity and honor a people who through no fault of their own but wholly because of skin color experienced centuries of persecution.

Some opposing the holiday argue that King was a Communist and in addition had numberless undesirable character faults. King on occasion did mix with Communists. He mixed with anybody concerned about the unjustified outrages perpetrated against his race. King, a devout Christian, was no Communist, however. Neither was he a god, not even a demigod. Being mortal, he was, like all mortals, flawed.

King's frailties should surprise nobody. His weaknesses, far overshadowed by strengths, hardly disqualify him from having a national holiday dedicated to him. Name any hero whose daily life, once subjected to the kind of microscopic and intimate scrutiny the Federal Bureau of Investigation on illegal orders from its racially bigoted director gave King's life, would be found to be spotless in all particulars.

Other critics of providing King a holiday don't argue that he was a splendid American and perhaps deserving. Their opposition is based upon the conviction that it's too soon to commemorate a day to him.

In principle we agree. It is early to be honoring King. National holidays should be rarely bestowed, lest they become too plentiful and therefore meaningless, and fixed years after a person has lived and died. Let all dust settle and let a record be accumulated, as the Catholic Church does with its saints.

But from this sensible and desirable rule we except King for the reasons that black Americans want a holiday, need a holiday and, the Lord knows, are entitled to a holiday. And if not King, who? No human, since Lincoln, has done more to liberate American blacks.

Symbolically the Rev. Martin Luther King Day is important and in a very minor way will correct an obscene record that for years ahead will continue to be this society's great abiding shame.

The Burlington Free Press
Burlington, Vt., October 7, 1983

Few Americans will quarrel with the idea of honoring Martin Luther King as a hero and martyr in the black struggle for equality.

He perhaps did more than any other black leader of his time to draw attention to the plight of his people and to awaken the consciences of those white people who stubbornly resisted efforts to attain equal rights for all. Charismatic and courageous, King lived by the noble principles he preached and became a living symbol of non-violence for all Americans. That he was gunned down before his dream was realized was at once a tragedy and a disgrace. He truly deserves a niche in the pantheon of American heroes.

Yet the idea of declaring a national holiday in his honor raises some nagging questions about the purpose of such observances. Of the nation's presidents, only Abraham Lincoln and George Washington are so honored. Christopher Columbus, credited with the discovery of America, is the only other person who claims a national holiday. The remainder of the federally-proclaimed calendar of holidays commemorates events — Thanksgiving, Memorial Day and Christmas — or honors groups of people, such as veterans and workers. Creating another holiday to honor an individual would depart from the tradition that is weighted toward remembrances of events.

Adding King's birthday to the list of holidays would cost government and business an estimated $250 million dollars in extra pay. Celebrating it on the third Monday in January would mean a long weekend for state and federal employees who observe legal holidays and would mean a shortened work week for business that closed for the observance.

Rep. James M. Jeffords, R-Vt. who opposes the bill to create the holiday, has suggested that King's birthday be observed on Sunday when churches could recognize him as a religious and civil rights leader.

Indeed that seems to be more appropriate than the idea of a legal holiday on a weekday and might avert the clamor that can be anticipated from other groups seeking to honor their heroes.

King should be remembered in the type of observances which focus on his spiritual commitment to the goal of equality for all and a national holiday would seem to distract attention from that aspect of his life.

THE SACRAMENTO BEE
Sacramento, Calif., March 5, 1985

The symbolism was irresistible. There was Joe E. Smitherman, longtime mayor of Selma, Ala., and, in times past, a diehard segregationist, sharing a hymnal with the Rev. Jesse Jackson, as — together — they commemorated the 20th anniversary of the voting rights march from Selma to Montgomery.

In the "segregation now, segregation forever" days of 1965, Joe Smitherman would not have allowed Jesse Jackson into his office, except maybe to empty the wastebasket or wash the windows. Two decades ago, it was the temerity of some 500 blacks, marching to dramatize their exclusion from the polling place, that brought out the state troopers — all of them white, of course — who attacked the kneeling demonstrators with billy clubs and bullwhips.

One measure of a successful revolution is how completely it transforms our frame of reference, making it almost inconceivable that things could ever have been any different. "Try as you can," one Selma black teenager said, "you can't believe that white people once treated black people that way." Selma's Bloody Sunday played a powerful part in this transformation. The indiscriminate official violence aimed at innocent and righteous individuals shocked the nation. That event was a major impetus for the passage of the 1965 Voting Rights Act, which outlawed the threats used to deny the ballot to blacks.

The evidence of change is apparent in the enfranchisement of blacks — the number of registered blacks in 11 Southern states more than tripled, from 1.4 million to 4.3 million, between 1960 and 1980 — and in the correspondingly greater role that blacks play in the political life of the region. It is apparent, too, in countless incidents of daily life, in the desegregated schools and the expanded job opportunities. Old insults, such as "white only" drinking fountains, have become museum exhibits of a bygone era.

The message of Selma isn't that the task of perfecting relations between the races has been accomplished, that the "American dilemma" can now be put behind us. As a banner carried during Sunday's march proclaimed, this task is still "unfinished." During the march, there was criticism aimed at whites, for withholding genuine economic power from blacks; and criticism as well of black politicians, for attaching themselves — "like limpets," a local black columnist put it — to a popular but superficial cause.

But that should not obscure the reality of the achievement. "Everything has changed, and nothing has changed," declared the Rev. Joseph Lowery, president of the Southern Christian Leadership Conference. The ceremonies in Selma celebrate the fact of change — not as an event of history but as a present challenge.

The State
Columbia, S.C., March 10, 1985

ONE OF our readers asked the other day what good it did to revive memories of the 1965 racial conflict in Selma, Ala., with press coverage of the re-enactment of the historic civil rights march to Montgomery.

Our caller was white, and we guess was among those who still would turn the clock back to the days before anybody worried about "civil rights." Some folks still feel threatened by changes in our society which they never imagined happening in their lifetime.

A host of young Americans, white and black, who were not born 20 years ago, are the generation which in a few years will become the nation's opinion makers, its leaders and custodians of our values and standards. It is important to America's soul that they know the meaning of "Bloody Sunday" at Selma and the historic changes in our national life which resulted.

The day may come when we will not need to be reminded of Selma. But it is not yet.

DAYTON DAILY NEWS
Dayton, Ohio, March 7, 1985

It's been a long road from Selma.

More than 1,800 people went to that little Alabama town Sunday to celebrate the 50-mile march to Montgomery two decades ago. The march of 1965 was historic not only for what it said in the cause of voting rights, but for the hatred it brought onto the news pages and television screens of this nation as whites jeered, as state troopers beat the demonstrators, black and white, Christian and Jew.

Racism is so much easier to accept when it is hidden, when it is confined to slurs and jokes and unspoken contempt and the convenience of ghettos. Racism is more subtle when it quietly keeps blacks out of white neighborhoods (look around) or private clubs (look around) or social and professional opportunities (look around).

The 1960s were a watershed. The nation at last recognized the demands of courageous decency, if not in every facet of life at least in public rights and law. Since that Selma march, this nation has traveled far. The current mayor of Selma, who 20 years ago opposed the marchers, welcomed the return of those demonstrating now for civil rights. For at least this much symbolic distance traveled, take heart.

But not every road that needs to be walked has asphalt where the spit and the taunting dry in the heat of the sun and solidarity. Not every river has a bridge across which waits the symbol of brutality, uniformed and well defined. Not every walk is in the eye of a camera that plays back, almost instantly, for all to see, the savage handiwork of that belief in separation, place, inferiority.

It's a long road from Selma. Look around.

The Miami Herald
Miami, Fla., March 4, 1985

HUNDREDS of civil-rights activists will return to Selma, Ala., today to commemorate the 20th anniversary of the day in 1965 when club-wielding sheriff's deputies attacked 600 civil-rights marchers as they tried to make their way from Selma to Montgomery. The confrontation made Selma a household word and provided the impetus that Lyndon Johnson needed for passing the Voting Rights Act. It became law later that year and altered the South forever, politically and socially.

That bloody Sunday bared to the world the disfranchisement of blacks in the South and the lengths to which Southern whites would go to deny them the basic rights of citizenship.

From 1960 to 1980, the number of black registered voters in the South rose to 4.3 million from 1.4 million, far outpacing the increase in white voters' registration. Having blacks on voting rolls has led to having blacks in elected offices. In the 10 Alabama counties that have black majorities, blacks hold more than half the elective offices. Nationwide, the number of black elected officials grew to 5,700 in 1984 from 1,469 in 1970.

Those figures speak of real achievements. However, reflecting on Selma affords an opportunity to take stock of how far this country still has to go. Blacks *have* made remarkable legal and social gains since the heyday of the civil-rights movement, but by and large those gains have not been translated into economic and political leverage. Blacks still are plagued by high unemployment and unequal education. Prospects for near-term improvements in either of those spheres appear slim.

As blacks look forward from the 20th-anniversary commemoration of the Selma march, it is imperative that they use their votes more effectively locally and in state and national politics. And as they look back, they should remember that many still might not have full voting rights but for the courage of those marchers in Selma 20 years ago.

BUFFALO EVENING NEWS

Buffalo, N.Y., March 6, 1985

IT IS important to remember Bloody Sunday, March 7, 1965. That was the fateful day 600 supporters of equal voting rights for blacks began their march from Selma to Montgomery, Ala., only to be driven back with tear gas and clubs wielded by state police in a brutal racist spectacle as the non-violent marchers crossed the Edmund Pettus Bridge.

It is important to remember Selma because the bloody incident galvanized public support for adoption by Congress of the 1965 Voting Rights Act, a monumental gain for voting freedom in this nation. The Voter Education Project reports that the number of blacks registered to vote in 11 southern states 20 years ago amounted to 2.1 million. Last year, the number was 5.6 million. Most of that gain can be traced to the 1965 law.

So, too, can the election to public office across the South of hundreds of blacks in the last 20 years, as well as the moderation of many white candidates who, because of the enfranchised minority members, must court their votes at the ballot box.

Remembering Bloody Sunday is important, as well, because of altered attitudes. Joe T. Smitherman, then as now the mayor of Selma, said the other day he was "shocked" when the Rev. Martin Luther King Jr. came to Selma 20 years ago. But today, he acknowledges: "The city's hands were not clean. We were wrong to try to stop blacks from voting."

Time and new habits should deepen the changes in attitudes that the impact of Bloody Sunday fostered. No one believes that racism has vanished 20 years later or that the march for equality has reached its final destination. But there have been changes, fundamental ones, and these represent hope for the future as well as progress from the past.

Solid reasons, all, for recalling Selma's Bloody Sunday. And for pondering future steps along the road from Selma to a society of full equality for all Americans.

Birmingham Post-Herald

Birmingham, Ala., March 8, 1985

Celebrating the anniversaries of historic events serves a useful purpose. It encourages us to take a broader view than we normally do in our concern with day-to-day matters. The contrast between society as it was and what it is now can be encouraging, even as it reminds us of what remains to be done to build a more perfect society.

So it is with this week's re-enactment of the 1965 Selma to Montgomery civil rights march.

Twenty years ago, marchers feared for their lives. Local and state law enforcement agencies were rightly seen as enemies to their cause, as was most evident in the events of Bloody Sunday when state troopers attacked marchers on the Edmund Pettus Bridge. The governor of Alabama, the mayor of Selma and other public officials were doing everything in their power to resist not just the march, but the social and legal changes that were being sought.

This week, the mayor of Selma, the same Joe Smitherman who was in office then, joined in kicking off the re-enactment. Alabama has the same governor, too. But the public stance of George Wallace on racial matters today is in marked contrast to his stance 20 years ago.

The tension that marked the original march was gone this time, although one reminder of the past came with the discovery of an apparent explosive device along the march route. We have not eliminated the lunatic fringe. But its members no longer enjoy tacit public support.

Evidence of the changes brought by the civil rights movement is all around us.

Attitudinal surveys of the American public reveal a steady decline in racism among all age groups.

Black Americans have enjoyed considerable economic progress in the past two decades. The percentage of black families who own their own homes, attend college and live in the suburbs is far higher than in the early 1960s.

Since 1970 alone, the number of black accountants has more than tripled; black engineers have also tripled, doctors and dentists doubled, school administrators multiplied nearly fourfold and computer specialists increased by at least that rate. And those advances have been matched in many other professions.

Indeed, civil rights activists succeeded in opening doors of opportunity far faster than historical precedent gave them reason to expect.

Of course, most blacks are not every black. Some observers insist a "pulling away" has occurred between the middle class and the poor, in which the latter are left ever farther behind.

These are the people who aren't reached by affirmative action because they are entirely unskilled. They can't go to college because they don't finish high school. They inhabit depressed central-city communities where broken families, violence, drug abuse and government dependency have become the norm. In this state, rural poverty remains a major problem.

In large part, this week's march was intended to call attention to these continuing problems. Problems that have no easy or readily apparent solutions.

But it also reminds us that we have already moved far toward solving problems that seemed equally intractable 20 years ago.

Houston Chronicle

Houston, Texas, March 6, 1985

They were shot in 1965, but the old news photos have the eerie quality of something that happened much more than a lifetime ago: There are pictures of police bullwhipping, clubbing and teargassing marchers; pictures of blacks kneeling together in prayer under the shadow of a gun; pictures of streams of people, black and white, pouring across a little bridge in Selma, the Alabama cotton town that became that year the symbol of a dream that wouldn't die.

Of all the towns held in segregation's iron fist, why Selma? Because it lay in Dallas County, where fewer than 500 of 15,000 eligible blacks were registered to vote. Because voter registration drives in Selma and other towns in Alabama's Black Belt had provoked violent clashes in January and February that year; because in Marion, near Selma, Jimmie Lee Jackson, a young black protester, had been shot to death for the cause.

Other lives — that of Viola Liuzzo, a Detroit housewife, and the Rev. James J. Reeb, a Unitarian minister from Boston — would be lost near Selma before the struggle was finished. And 600 civil rights marchers would be beaten and routed by police on the Edmund Pettus Bridge in Selma on March 7, the Black Sunday on which the marchers began their 50-mile walk to Montgomery to insist on full inclusion in the civil life of the nation.

They were turned back temporarily by the violent law of Dallas County Sheriff Jim Clark and Alabama's then-segregationist Gov. George C. Wallace; two weeks later, though, armed with a U.S. court order and protected by federal marshals, they completed their march.

Veterans of the historic confrontation gathered this month to make the journey again. This time it was different. At the start of the march, Joe T. Smitherman, the white man who is mayor of Selma as he was 20 years ago, ceremonially gave the keys of the city to Coretta Scott King, the Rev. Jesse L. Jackson, the Rev. Joseph E. Lowery, president of the Southern Christian Leadership Conference, and other black leaders commemorating the event. This time, there was no violence.

The marchers carried signs that read, "Finish the Unfinished Task." Although what happened in Selma 20 years ago awakened a nation, inspired a generation and culminated in passage of the sweeping federal Voting Rights Act of 1965, the struggle for freedom and dignity has not ended.

A group of civil rights advocates held a twilight vigil on the steps of the nation's Capitol last week to ask for swift passage of the Civil Rights Restoration Act of 1985, which would guarantee federal protection against discrimination based on race, sex, age or physical disability.

Their vigil was a small but timely echo of Selma, and a reminder that the work begun there isn't yet finished.

Diverse Crowd Reenacts 1963 March on Washington

More than a quarter of a million people participated in a celebration in Washington in August, 1983 to commemorate the 1963 march led by the late Dr. Martin Luther King, Jr. Twenty years before, demonstrators had been mobilized by labor, religious and black civil rights leaders to marshal support for sweeping civil rights legislation. King had delivered his famous "I have a Dream" speech at the Lincoln Memorial.

In 1983, the reenacted March on Washington II, which had an official theme of "Jobs, Peace and Freedom," did not have the singleness of purpose that characterized the original event. The causes touted by banners, chants, songs and speeches ranged from support for a nuclear freeze to gay rights. Environmental issues and women's rights were championed by many participants; the most widespread sentiment appeared to be opposition to the Reagan Administration, fostered by disagreement with its policies on a number of domestic issues. Many observers felt that the multitude of interests represented by the demonstrators weakened the focus of the reenactment, and reflected a lessened fervor concerning the rights of minorities that the civil rights movement could ill afford.

Passage of the 1964 Civil Rights Act, following the remarkable march on the nation's capitol in 1963, marked the beginnings of legislative progress in removing barriers to minorities in schools, jobs and public facilities. The 1964 legislation was enacted by Congress in direct response to dozens of sit-ins and other protests, mostly in the South, to which law enforcement officers often reacted with brutal violence. This period in the civil rights movement followed naturally upon the courtroom battles fought for two decades before by the NAACP. Dr. King's non-violent methods, as blacks transferred these battles to the streets in mostly peaceful mass protests and demonstrations, gained wide sympathy for the goals of civil rights groups. Under King, the Southern Christian Leadership Conference made black civil rights a national priority.

But the end of an era in civil rights was around the corner. Even before the assassination of King in 1968, the civil rights movement underwent a transformation. The nascent "black power" movement signaled a stepping away from the emotional appeal of the 1960's and a growing emphasis upon political power. Dissatisfaction with congressional failure to remedy continuing discrimination against black Americans was often expressed in bitter anger rather than reasoned rhetoric. Racial riots in the nation's cities attested to growing despair with the insufficient power or will of the government to eliminate abuses. Today, as reflected in the commemoration of the famous 1963 march, civil rights groups appear to have grown, following the nation's mood, into a less idealistic, more diverse force.

THE MILWAUKEE JOURNAL
Milwaukee, Wisc., July 3, 1984

Twenty years ago this week, President Lyndon Johnson signed the Civil Rights Act of 1964, climaxing a struggle to ensure the enjoyment by black Americans of the elementary rights that most citizens long had taken for granted. The signing ceremony was an appropriate means at an appropriate time to bring renewed attention to this nation's historic ideals of freedom and justice.

The Civil Rights Act that came to Johnson's desk had originally been proposed by his martyred predecessor, President John Kennedy, who had warned of "fires of discord" burning in the land.

Kennedy's bill largely grew out of demonstrations for the startlingly simple right to eat in a restaurant or sleep in a hotel (or just to use a service-station restroom). The high point of demonstrations was the mammoth gathering before the Lincoln Memorial in August, 1963, at which the Rev. Martin Luther King Jr. eloquently proclaimed his dream.

Johnson, succeeding Kennedy, told a grieving Congress that "no memorial oration or eulogy could more eloquently honor President Kennedy's memory than the earliest possible passage of the civil rights bill." Johnson brought his own considerable energies to that task, in which he was joined by such Democratic stalwarts as Sen. Hubert Humphrey of Minnesota and by the golden-tongued Illinois Republican, Sen. Everett Dirksen. That participation by Dirksen and other congressional Republicans seemingly marked the last hurrah of the party of Lincoln in the civil-rights sphere. The days of bipartisan leadership in this vital cause regrettably seem a dim memory.

Today, when the civil rights battles are fought with words, some people may be hard put to recall or understand the bloody and bitter path the nation walked to achieve the Civil Rights Act. That struggle must not be forgotten. That commitment must not be abandoned.

The Miami Herald
Miami, Fla., August 31, 1983

THEY came from far and wide, 200,000 or more of them, drawn to the Mall for reasons as disparate as the hopes that produced them. The weekend's march in Washington, D.C., was more than a commemoration of the Rev. Dr. Martin Luther King, Jr.'s ringing "I Have a Dream" speech there 20 years earlier. It was, as one observer put it, "a bazaar of slogans and strategies" too.

A great deal has changed in America since August 1963, and much of that change was wrought in the crucible of moral force for which Dr. King's philosophy of nonviolent protest was — and remains — the unquenchable flame. There were only about 300 black elected officials in the United States then; today there are nearly 5,200, according to the Joint Center for Economic Studies. Blacks have gained in median years of school completed and in white-collar employment. Schools, stores, voting booths, and residential areas that once were closed to them now are open.

Yet despite those encouraging gains, blacks today are unemployed at significantly higher rates than whites. Blacks' median income in 1982 was only about $13,000 per family, slightly more than half the $24,000 median earnings of white families. And although the number of black families living below the poverty line has declined dramatically — from about 47 per cent in 1962 to about 35 per cent in 1982 — the proportion of impoverished white families has remained relatively constant at around 12 per cent.

These data reflect the enduring difficulty of achieving in fact the equality of opportunity that Dr. King's dream has seen realized in law. The concept of equality is accepted without challenge in every school, court, and other institution in the land. To translate that concept into reality will require the unflagging commitment of all those institutions for decades to come.

Saturday's march was not for or about black causes alone. The original march was a gathering of individuals united principally in their determination to end racial discrimination. Saturday's commemoration brought organized groups representing all manner of causes, from nuclear disarmament to gay rights. Fear was common among those who came to hear Dr. King's electrifying speech, for none knew what reaction the first march might provoke. Fear was absent from the Mall 20 years later.

"We still have a dream," Dr. King's widow, Coretta Scott King, told the multitude on the Mall, "and we've come here today to reaffirm our commitment to justice, peace, brotherhood, and equality." Even if the gathering had served no other purpose, it would have been worthwhile as a massive testament to the reverence that millions of Americans still have for those commendable goals.

Richmond Times-Dispatch
Richmond, Va., August 27, 1983

He stood there, on an August day two decades ago, to describe a dream to tens of thousands who had poured into Washington from all corners of the nation. In his dream, he saw the United States becoming a nation where racial justice prevailed, a nation that practiced the maxim that "all men are created equal," a nation whose citizens would be judged not "by the color of their skin, but by the content of their character."

So the Rev. Dr. Martin Luther King Jr. eloquently described the America he envisioned to the civil rights marchers who massed around the Lincoln Memorial 20 years ago. Today, thousands will gather in Washington to mark that event and, in the words of one civil rights leader, to launch "substantive initiatives to make the yet unfulfilled portions of Dr. King's dream living realities." In truth, however, the underlying purpose of today's march is to encourage continuation of the process of perverting his dream into a nightmare.

It was Dr. King's mission to lead black Americans from the debilitating and demeaning shadows of segregation into the sunlight — to paraphrase him — of racial equality and fairness. His objective, as he described it, was a society in which men and women would neither lose nor gain solely because of their race. But in the years since he delivered his speech in Washington, the civil rights movement has veered from the course he outlined toward a society in which race, again, often does determine the way a citizen is treated.

So we have affirmative action programs, under which blacks are favored because of their race and whites may suffer because of theirs. We have the forced busing of school children solely for racial reasons. We have the official gerrymandering of election district boundaries to produce certain desired racial results at the polls. And so it goes. Is this the kind of society for which Martin Luther King yearned? Racial justice did not prevail when laws and customs deprived black citizens of rights and gave white citizens advantages. Is it just today to treat black and white citizens differently?

Today's march is not about racial justice. It is about racial favoritism. It is about social and economic liberalism. The organizers of the march have a potpourri of objectives that have nothing to do with "racial justice." They want more federal jobs programs, greater emphasis on affirmative action and more lavish federal welfare programs. Prominent among the marchers are elements that favor peace at the risk of imperiling the nation, elements that are sympathetic to the Marxist rebels in El Salvador and elements that are rabidly critical of Israel. This rally will be a parody of the original event.

From dream to nightmare in 20 years.

THE SACRAMENTO BEE
Sacramento, Calif., August 27, 1983

On a steamy August day 20 years ago, a quarter of a million Americans, white and black, gathered in Washington, D.C., to share Martin Luther King's dream that "one day this nation will rise up and live out the true meaning of its creed." That dream was as old as the republic itself, but King revived it, endowing it with a sense of moral rightness — and moral inevitability — that powerfully moved the nation.

As hundreds of thousands gather today in Washington to commemorate this event, it's worth remembering just how much has changed since 1963. In 11 states south of Mason's and Dixon's line, blacks and whites could not use the same restrooms or drink from the same water fountains. Fewer than two Southern black children in a hundred attended school with even a single white youngster. There were almost no Southern black public officials and very few anywhere else. Indeed, there were precious few black voters, for in the cotton-belt states registering to vote was an act of courage that could have cost the individual his job — or his life.

America's most prescient observer, Alexis de Tocqueville, remarked more than a century ago that evil suffered patiently as inevitable "seems unendurable as soon as the idea of escaping from it is conceived." That was the impact of King's speech, which sought dignity and a measure of simple justice for black Americans.

That much has largely been achieved, through changes both in the law of the land and in the behavior of the citizenry, changes which have restored to blacks the full protections of the Constitution and, in the process, restored the South to the nation.

Part of the hope of that day was that assuring dignity and legal equality to blacks would also bring about a more tangible economic equality. As Lyndon Johnson, a Southerner who as president rendered King's dream into national policy, declared in 1966, "We seek not just freedom but opportunity — not just legal equity but human ability — not just equality as a right and a theory but equality as a fact and a result."

That equality, of course, has not come to pass. Just this week, the Census Bureau confirmed the depressingly familiar fact that the 1980s recession had "brought to a halt the momentum of overall social and economic improvement for black Americans." The black unemployment rate remains double the rate for whites, and median family income for blacks is just about half of that for whites.

Narrowing this gap — somehow — is the challenge for civil rights in the 1980s, but there is no consensus on how to accomplish that, no enthusiasm on the part of this president to make civil rights something other than a rhetorical cause. Yet perhaps, just perhaps, a speech delivered today at the Washington rally — or in the future, somewhere else — will again seize the American conscience, even as a preacher's sermon captivated and helped transform his countrymen two decades ago.

THE CHRISTIAN SCIENCE MONITOR
Boston, Mass., August 26, 1983

In the 20 years since Martin Luther King's March on Washington the US has advanced impressively toward the dream he enunciated so dramatically — a dream of equality and freedom for blacks as well as whites.

Since then segregation has been banished in employment and blacks have gained access to management positions and highly visible jobs. Millions of black Americans have been registered to vote and have made their political power felt. Housing segregation has been substantially ended. And schools have been widely desegregated, a process begun in 1954. Considered against the background of more than 300 years of discrimination, this is progress of astonishing speed.

Yet Dr. King's dream is not yet fully realized. Unemployment for black teen-agers is 45 percent — twice the rate for white teens. The quality of education is sinking in predominantly-black public schools of inner cities. Good housing seems increasingly out of the reach of many blacks, as many whites. The number of Americans living in poverty has begun to increase, with grave concern raised that many single-parent households with children, especially minority households, are in danger of becoming a permanent economic underclass.

Most challenging of all, the driving energy which formerly fueled a national commitment to achieve equality for all Americans now seems diminished. It is as if white Americans now are less aware — or uninterested — that the promise of equal opportunity remains to be fully filled.

Black Americans know better and make the point frequently, outlining the need both in general and specific terms. Needed now is for major US political leaders — including the President, members of Congress, and governors — to call publicly, consistently, and vigorously on the nation to be true to its ideals and make all of Dr. King's dream come true. The words need to be followed steadfastly by such government action as is necessary to aid the process; but mostly it is the climate for progress which again must be set forth.

This is the way the United States achieved its greatest civil rights progress, in the 1960s. President Kennedy's enunciations of the goals were followed by President Johnson's successful insistence that Congress bring them about.

In individual states the situation was similar. In the early '60s substantial civil rights progress began in Georgia under the leadership of Gov. Carl Sanders; backsliding appeared in the late 1960s when Lester Maddox, perceived as antiblack, was governor.

Today many black Americans are concerned that national backsliding has begun in civil rights and that much progress made in the past 20 years could be negated. No one believes there will be a return to segregation and the state and local laws that enforced it. Rather the concerns focus on the amount and quality of education, employment, and housing.

It is on the leadership of its elected officials that the US now must depend to see that there is no backsliding of hard-won gains, and that proper progress continues. And to ensure that, in Dr. King's words, "we will be able to transform the jangling discords of our nation into a beautiful symphony of brotherhood."

The Morning News

Wilmington, Del., August 27, 1983

TODAY, THOUSANDS OF PEOPLE will descend on the nation's capital trying to recapture both the spirit and the powerful impact of the legendary March on Washington in the summer of 1963.

In the two decades since Dr. Martin Luther King Jr. dramatically challenged this nation to confront its racist attitudes, to eliminate discriminatory laws and to live in brotherhood, much of what he called for has been accomplished. But much remains undone, too.

There was magic in the air on that steamy August afternoon when Dr. King described to the nation his dream of freedom and equality. Martin Luther King Jr. had already achieved prominence in the civil rights movement in his crusades against discrimination in the South. But when he told the hundreds of thousands gathered at the Lincoln Memorial — "I have a dream . . ." — the crusade became national and he became its undisputed leader.

Who will ever know why, at that moment, the nation was willing to listen to pleas and arguments it hardly acknowledged, let alone considered, for decades? But, listen it did. Dr. King's powerful, persuasive preaching was a factor, certainly. The multi-racial marchers — a quarter-million strong — impressed the politicians with their display of strength and solidarity if not their convictions.

Laws were passed. Conditions improved. A black is among the handful of serious presidential candidates this year. Still, the job is not complete. Discrimination still exists — more subtle, perhaps, but it still exists. Blacks and other racial minorities have achieved freedom in this land, but true equality still eludes them in any significant numbers. For every black corporate executive there are still thousands of illiterate, unemployed.

The anniversary march today will try to refocus the nation's attention on the concerns of the minorities and the poor — among other things. Those actively supporting the march represent virtually every liberal cause in the United States from old-line, civil rights activists to anti-nuclear protesters and radical feminists. They will gather under the banner of jobs, peace and freedom to proclaim that "we still have a dream."

Will the self-interest of these disparate groups keep the march from having the dramatic effect its precursor had 20 years ago?

Many of the voices calling for "rights" today are strident — lacking in the understanding and compassion that Dr. King expressed even for his enemies. He did not shrink from action, he did not hesitate to disobey a law he viewed as immoral. But, even in his most dramatic confrontations one perceived his devotion to the fundamental Christian principle of forgiveness.

These are harsh times. And, those who govern — conservative and liberal alike — need to be reminded of the plight of those who still must claw and fight for basic human dignity. If today's march achieves this, if it forces those with wealth and power to recognize that thousands of Americans have neither, it will be a success.

San Francisco Chronicle

San Francisco, Calif., July 4, 1984

THE 208TH ANNIVERSARY of the Declaration of Independence comes two days after the 20th anniversary of the signing of the Civil Rights Act of 1964. The declaration said all men are created equal. The civil rights act said, in effect, that bigotry still stood in the way of the truth and the goal and must be fought.

The anniversaries remind us that this is a nation which has been in the forefront of social change and remains so today. We still pursue the dream of equality and opportunity for all.

There are those among us who will angrily deny this is so. While admitting blemishes and failures, we ask that they simply look elsewhere and study the grim pictures of the result of racial, religious and political hate in so many parts of the world today.

THE CIVIL RIGHTS Act of 1964 was a national admission that opportunity had been denied millions of Americans. But it was a powerful step toward correcting this. National attention was, at the time, centered upon racial segregation and the act outlawed the practice in places of public accommodation. These were defined as hotels, motels, restaurants, theaters and sports arenas. The law also established the Equal Employment Opportunity Commission to help eliminate discrimination in hiring. And it prohibited racial discrimination in any program or activity which received any federal funding.

THIS WAS AN important expression of the national conscience and of the national will. The Fourth of July is an appropriate day to reflect upon it.

The Hartford Courant

Hartford, Conn., August 26, 1983

The legacy of the Rev. Martin Luther King Jr. has been scattered and diluted, claim those civil rights traditionalists who wouldn't give their active support for Saturday's March on Washington.

Twenty years ago, the Great March had a focus — jobs and freedom for black people; the commemoration, however, has been widened to include practically every activist cause, they complain.

Dr. King's progeny are going to Washington bound more by a common legacy than by a single goal. That is because Dr. King's dream of freedom and equality and belief in peaceful protest have inspired practically every social movement of the past two decades: antiwar activists, environmentalists, feminists, and nuclear freeze advocates.

The new marchers are going to the capital to recapture Dr. King's courage and confidence that a dream of social justice could be achieved — peacefully. "With this faith we will be able to transform the jangling discords of our nation into a beautiful symphony of brotherhood," he told people desperate to believe.

Today's marchers, rallying under separate banners, are even more desperate to believe.

In 1963, a march on Washington was a novel — and radical — way to compel attention and congressional reaction. A young and powerful civil rights coalition forced change from the outside in.

The president, John F. Kennedy, supported the protest and observed, on the day of the march, "If satisfaction with the status quo had been the American way, we would still be the 13 small colonies straggling along the Atlantic Coast."

Today, civil rights leaders are on the inside: lobbying, filing lawsuits and writing legislation. They are mayors, city council members, and state legislators all over the country. They are congressmen, and one offers himself as a presidential candidate.

The policies of the president, Ronald Reagan, have become the object of protest, for he would weaken the federal civil rights commission, lessen efforts to achieve school integration, eliminate social programs and deny constitutional rights to women.

Peace has been added to the call of the 1983 march because, the new activists say, there will be no jobs or freedom — the theme 20 years ago — so long as the federal budget is dominated by defense spending.

But peace was on Dr. King's agenda — both as a tactic and a goal. His opposition to the Vietnam War drew criticism at the end of his life. Civil rights leaders chastised him for diverting attention from the cause of black Americans.

Still, he pressed on in the antiwar movement and later with a new vision of poor people united by economic circumstance and not by race, a vision in which "you've got to have a reconstruction of the entire society, a revolution of values."

The spectrum of participants in Saturday's march mirrors that evolution in Dr. King's thinking and his willingness to embrace an unpopular cause.

The loose coalition that will go to Washington tomorrow is still in search of that unity which only one man — one speech — could forge.

The Virginian-Pilot

Norfolk, Va., August 29, 1983

It's hardly surprising that Saturday's march in Washington seemed so flat. The sequel is almost never as good as the original. The shadow of the '63 march and of Dr. Martin Luther King's eloquence hung over Saturday's affair and made it appear lifeless by comparison.

The 1963 march was a pivotal event in modern American history. The 1983 march became almost a non-event within 24 hours: On the Sunday news shows it was relegated to also-ran status, behind Israeli politics, the settlement of the telephone strike and a hurricane.

Why? There are probably a dozen reasons, but one stands out: The 1963 march was a protest against a centuries-old system of racial discrimination. It had a moral message that appealed to the entire nation. The theme of Saturday's march turned out to be a protest against Ronald Reagan. It was a political rally, and much of its appeal was limited to those who question the wisdom of the president's policies.

When 250,000 people vent their displeasure with a politician, that's certainly a major event. But it doesn't carry the weight of the crusade that Dr. King waged two decades ago. The 1963 march helped raise Americans' consciousness about important national issues. Saturday's march was designed to do the same, but the spark just wasn't there.

Roanoke Times & World-News

Roanoke, Va., August 31, 1983

THE idea behind the first March on Washington was to press the Kennedy administration into pushing civil-rights legislation more vigorously. But what is remembered 20 years later — and will be remembered for many more years to come — is the timeless vision proclaimed by the late Martin Luther King Jr.:

I have a dream ... deeply rooted in the American dream. I have a dream that one day this nation will rise up and live out the true meaning of its creed, "We hold these truths to be self-evident, that all men are created equal." I have a dream ... (of) that day when all God's children, black men and white men, Jews and Gentiles, Protestants and Catholics, will be able to join hands and sing in the words of the Negro spiritual: "Free at last. Free at last. Thank God Almighty, we are free at last."

One measure of King's greatness is the way in which he imbued political struggles with a moral authority that transcended specific issues. While calling black America to action, he also called white America to heed the principles on which the nation is built. He called Americans of both races to freedom, and he looked to the day when talk of two Americas would be the stuff of history rather than of contemporary reality.

Martin Luther Kings are rare, and they are not produced on demand. Perhaps it was inevitable that, two decades later, his successors have failed to match the power of his vision. But failed they have, and it was evident Saturday when 250,000 people descended on Washington for a second march to commemorate the first.

The Reagan administration, goodness knows, is open to criticism for its attitude on civil rights and for its insensitivity to the concerns of minorities. But for the leaders of the second march to evoke the memory of King's speech by citing grievances against the current administration was to trivialize that memory.

King enunciated a profound moral vision. Saturday's program was little more than a political rally for the defeat of Reagan in the 1984 election. King's words of 20 years ago will continue to echo long after those of Saturday — and, for that matter, those of the Reagan administration — are forgotten.

Ironically, events that King helped set in motion have worked against the emergence of a successor with similar moral authority. By and large, overt barriers to equality have tumbled. In retrospect, given their seeming rigidity at the time, those barriers collapsed with remarkable speed.

In the '50s and early '60s, the struggle for racial justice required a physical courage that's not easy to imagine in 1983. In other ways, though, the struggle today is harder, because the issues are more complicated. While the death of Jim Crow enabled millions of blacks to join the American mainstream, millions of others have been left behind in poverty and despair. Racial inequality remains, but its connection to the moral foundation in the idea of racial justice is more amibiguous.

How do you widen the bridges that span a cultural gulf created by 350 years of formal discrimination? How do you root out and eliminate subtle, unobvious forms of discrimination? For how long can remedies for past discrimination be implemented without creating a permanently dependent underclass — and without encouraging a resurgence of racist thinking among the majority?

Twenty years ago, the task was still to secure the most basic of rights: to vote, to enjoy equal access to public accommodations, to speak freely without fear of violent retribution. Because an assassin's bullet killed King in 1968, nobody can say for sure how he would have answered the more complex questions that have arisen since. Worrisome as are the implications of some current civil-rights thinking, even more annoying are efforts (often by those who opposed King when he was alive) to yank his vision out of context and use it as an excuse for inaction.

Whatever the answers, they won't work very well unless King's dream continues to be dreamed. To conclude Saturday's event, they played a recording of the speech of 20 years earlier. By then, only a fraction of the crowd was still around, and that's a shame.

The Orlando Sentinel

Orlando, Fla., August 30, 1983

Last weekend's march on Washington might have lacked the historical significance of the civil rights march on the capital 20 years ago, but it will find its place in contemporary politics. Emerging from the dissonance of issues was one theme — the marchers' unhappiness with Ronald Reagan.

It is unlikely that Mr. Reagan will change his policies because a quarter-million demonstrators demanded *Jobs, Peace and Freedom.* But how he handles these issues will shape the 1984 election.

The president seems calmly confident in tax cuts to create jobs and a military buildup to keep the peace. And he seems to reckon that freedom was pretty much perfected a few years ago. But if he stands pat on these issues, it may well be bad politics and bad policy.

On jobs, more than 10 million Americans who want to work are jobless, and blacks are twice as likely as whites to be among them. Saturday's marchers wanted Washington to create a million new jobs, a debatable approach that doesn't have majority support in Congress.

But the president is naive to think the current economic upturn by itself will make things right. Two-hundred-billion-dollar deficits are like playing Russian roulette with the recovery. And it's clear that even if the economy gets through next year without a new recession, a hardened corps of Americans — millions of them — still won't have enough money to meet basic needs.

On peace, it's a different story despite the rhetoric Saturday, the death of two Marines in Lebanon Monday, and the tensions in Central America. America is at peace. The spectacle of American hostages in Tehran has ended; the specter of our dependence on foreign oil is out of sight and mind.

A quarter-million protesters decry spending a quarter-trillion dollars for defense, and indeed the White House seems to equate security with big spending. Though the marchers' demands for a nuclear freeze may be unrealistic, the president's commitment to arms talks certainly appears reluctant at best. Yet if the country can stay out of a war, the "peace" issue won't work the way critics expect. And should there be an arms limit agreement, Mr. Reagan could own that issue.

It is the last third of the slogan, "freedom," where the president has failed clearly. In his words to Republican women Friday, in his statement on civil rights Saturday, he doesn't seem to understand how flawed the freedom of racial minorities and women has been. Just as he stood "on principle" against the major civil rights legislation of the '60s, he opposes the ERA today and claims he'll guarantee women's equality with laws.

To the "rainbow coalition" of blacks and whites, unionists and environmentalists, men and women who marched against his policies, the president's stance on freedom is unacceptable. He seems far more excited about defending it overseas than fulfilling it at home.

The attitude that freedom can be somewhere over the rainbow for any American is intolerable. If that doesn't change, those who reject that attitude may yet be the majority in 1984.

THE SUN
Baltimore, Md., July 3, 1984

Congress passed a law 20 years ago extending to black Americans the right to secure a room in a public hotel or eat a meal in a public restaurant. The Civil Rights Act of 1964 marked the beginning of the end of an era of "Jim Crow" laws that mandated a rigid separation of races in many towns and many states. It was landmark legislation in a nation that allowed separate drinking fountains, separate bathrooms, separate elevators, separate waiting rooms, separate entrances and exits in buildings, separate schools and separate cemeteries to keep the races apart.

The ban on discrimination in public accommodations has become so much a part of American folkways that it is hard to recall today the passions that preceded its passage. The law rejected the concept of separate-but-equal, which had been supported by the Supreme Court in an 1896 decision that paved the way for the "Jim Crow" era in the South. It recognized that separate had always been unequal and said that henceforth it would be illegal.

"It was not merely that Negroes could not enter a theater or get a cup of coffee or ride in comfort on public transportation," notes historian John Hope Franklin. "It was also that as a degraded and despised people, without a semblance of political power and no one obliged to listen to their case, they could not wield any influence to get jobs, to get justice in the courts, to secure a decent education for their children, and adequate housing for their families."

Mr. Franklin calls the public accommodations act a modest achievement which extended the basic rights that any civilized nation should offer its citizens. He is right. But that achievement — and others — has led to a major transformation in the American way of life.

There are still serious inequities between the majority of blacks and the majority of whites in this country. One need only to look at the black unemployment rate, which is consistently twice the rate for whites, to know that problems still exist.

But this country has come a long way from where it was just 20 years ago, and the changes have lifted the burdens of overt discrimination from both black and white Americans. The historic steps of the 1940s, 1950s and, especially, the 1960s laid the foundation for the progress of the 1970s and 1980s. They also are the foundation from which any future progress will grow.

THE ANN ARBOR NEWS
Ann Arbor, Mich., August 29, 1983

Saturday's massive rally in Washington D.C. commemorating the famous march on Washington 20 years ago led by the late Rev. Martin Luther King Jr., was a wave of deja vu for the many who participated in or watched film footage of the impressive event.

But in the aftermath of all the speeches, all the condemnations of Reaganomics, the buildup of nuclear weapons and continuing high unemployment, one comment stands out.

"It's great to see so many folks put forth so much effort," said the Rev. Herbert Lowe, pastor of Ann Arbor's Church of the Good Shepherd, "but the important thing is going to be what we do when we get home."

Indeed. What will come of the issues of peace, jobs and civil rights that were on the lips of so many?

It's unlikely landmark legislation, such as the Civil Rights Act of 1964, will result from the march. That probably wasn't the aim of those who marched, save those who favor passage of the Equal Rights Amendment.

It's debatable whether the peace movement will gather much momentum from Saturday's march. Only legislation calling for funds for jobs and job training programs might receive a boost from the rally.

It seems to us there are more intriguing political questions in the aftermath of the huge rally at the Lincoln Memorial. Will the fervor of the march carry over into voter registration of poor people and minorities? Will it encourage the independent candidacy of the Rev. Jesse Jackson, which in turn could split the Democratic party? Will it move the Reagan administration a bit closer to the political middle as the 1984 election approaches?

But far more importantly, will the march prick the conscience of America once again, a conscience that needs to be reminded that the economic gap between blacks and whites still remains great, that unemployment among black youth still hovers around 50 percent, that racism still exists in this country?

AKRON BEACON JOURNAL
Akron, Ohio, August 27, 1983

AS PETER, Paul and Mary pointed out at Blossom last Sunday night, the answers are indeed still "Blowin' in the Wind" — in many ways just as elusively and frustratingly as they were that day 20 years ago when the Rev. Dr. Martin Luther King Jr. fired the emotions of a quarter-million freedom marchers with his "I have a dream" speech in front of the Lincoln Memorial.

And maybe that's reason enough to assure success — whatever "success" is for this kind of event — for today's "20th Anniversary Mobilization for Jobs, Peace and Freedom," in which a crowd even bigger than 1963's has piled into Washington to assemble on the same spot.

But laudable as are the intentions and ideals of those who have spent two years organizing the commemorative demonstration, it seems unlikely that its flame can match the heat of 1963's.

The event was sure to be big; the organizers this time lined up more than 4,000 buses — almost three times the number used in 1963 — to bring participants, some from as far away as Utah. Lots of prominent people are there, among them Ohio's governor and many members of the Congress (but nobody from the administration, it appears).

A string of well-known rights leaders, among them the fiery Rev. Jesse Jackson, will make five-minute addresses to the throng. Many top entertainers who took part in the 1963 march will be performing again.

Peter Yarrow, Noel Paul Stookey and Mary Travers — now edging into the "walker set," as Peter kidded at Blossom, but as hotly indignant as ever over violations of human rights — will repeat the Bob Dylan *Blowin'* song that their 1963 performance helped make an anthem of the 1960s protest movement.

And despite the improvements that have come since Dr. King's speech, much racism still blotches the face of American society. So do sexism and other forms of discrimination against certain segments of that society. Unemployment is far worse than it was then; poverty and hunger still fester. And more people are dying in more wars around the world than then.

But there's a difference working against the excitement of this demonstration as compared with 1963's, all the same.

The purpose then was clear, unified, coherent. Legal stratagems and other devices still blocked a vast number of blacks and members of other minority groups from equal access to ballots, educational facilities and job and promotion opportunities, and a hot congressional fight was in progress over the principles in what later became the landmark Civil Rights Act of 1964.

The aim of the demonstration was to dramatize the need for such a 20th century "Bill of Rights" to compel the opening of something closer to true equal opportunity for all.

This time, by contrast, the aims of the more than 715 groups that have endorsed "March II" seem as scattered as the buckshot from a sawed-off shotgun. There is no sharp, single focus.

Jobs are surely needed. And peace. And freedom. But despite the vows of the sponsors that this event will not be merely a jangle of single-issue pleas, in advance it has that look.

The interest groups are even assembling under differently colored balloons and signs — pink for senior citizen activists, blue for women's rights groups, brown for those seeking to stop discrimination against homosexuals, orange for environmentalists, maroon for elected officials.

Some Jewish groups have withdrawn support after seeing what they perceived as anti-Israel overtones. The Gay Rights National Lobby has protested because the organizers scheduled no homosexual or abortion-rights speakers.

The dynamics of anything this large have a life of their own, and out of them some unpredictable coherence may emerge. And one central purpose, of course, is clear: deserved honor to the memory of Dr. King. But otherwise it looks as if it may be hard, after the fact, to say just what-all this was about.

The Burlington Free Press
Burlington, Vt., August 27, 1983

"I have a dream that one day on the red hills of Georgia the sons of former slaves and the sons of former slave-owners will be able to sit together at the table of brotherhood...that one day even in the State of Mississippi, a state sweltering with the heat of injustice, sweltering with the heat of oppression, will be transformed into an oasis of freedom and justice...that my four little children will one day live in a nation where they will not be judged by the color of their skin but by the content of their character." The Rev. Martin Luther King's address to civil rights marchers in Washington, Aug. 28, 1963.

The State
Columbia, S.C., August 31, 1983

IT IS TOO soon to assess the historical or political significance of Saturday's massive rally at the Lincoln Memorial in Washington, the 20th anniversary of the memorable march led by the Rev. Martin Luther King Jr.

Understandably, those who participated in Sunday's event in the 100-degree heat, traveling great distances to and from the nation's capital, came away convinced that this, too, was a turning point for America. In the wake of the 1963 march, Congress enacted the 1964 Civil Rights Act abolishing segregation in public facilities, and discrimination in jobs and voting.

A year after, the 1965 Voting Rights Act was passed to ensure the registration of blacks, mainly in Southern states. To these landmark laws can be traced what has been called the "black revolution" in America.

At this time and distance, however, we do not discern such monumental results from Saturday's event, although it attracted 250,000 people, an impressive number.

The 1983 march was not so distinctly focused as the 1963 march, which was on a national redress of black grievances of discrimination and blacks' petition for equality as Americans. This time, the march's slogans embraced the causes of a number of groups — senior citizens, organized labor, women, nuclear freeze advocates and gays, among others — and more than 50 speakers addressed the crowd.

It became an anti-Reagan rally. Speaker after speaker attacked the President's policies. Executive Director Benjamin Hooks of the National Association for the Advancement of Colored People, for instance, exhorted the crowd to chant "Reagan no more in 1984."

The 1984 Presidential election, therefore, may very well be the first litmus test of the historic impact of the 1983 march in Washington. The President has not yet said whether he will run for re-election. But should he run, he now knows the coalition of opposition. Mr. Reagan, however, was not driven from office last Saturday.

Another measure of the march's impact politically should be the strength of the support the Rev. Jesse Jackson may receive from the coalition in his flirtation with a Presidential race. Mr. Jackson was one of the most popular speakers Saturday. He was in the forefront of the march with Mrs. Coretta King, Walter Fauntroy and the Rev. Joseph Lowery. But it didn't turn out to be a runaway political rally for Mr. Jackson's candidacy.

Finally, the 1983 march represented a "New Coalition of Conscience," a coalition of diverse groups whose causes have displaced black civil rights as the foremost activists' cause. It remains to be seen whether it can hold together in supporting disparate political aims — other than the overriding one of getting rid of Mr. Reagan.

This march has been characterized as a revival of the activist left in America. If so, the movement may help Americans to clarify their own places in the political spectrum. The marchers may not have been certified Democrats, but they surely weren't Republicans.

For two centuries, American blacks were treated as second-class citizens in a country that prided itself on being the ethnic melting pot of the world.

Even though they had been liberated from physical bondage by President Abraham Lincoln's Emancipation Proclamation, they were victims of the more insidious bondage of discrimination, subjected to indignities that stripped them of their rights to have a voice in their government. In the North and the South, they were consigned to ghettoes with the most appalling living conditions. Their children were forced to attend sub-standard schools that were established for them by the white power structure under the flawed separate but equal educational doctrinethat was nothing more than an instrument of segregation in its worst form. They were exploited by their employers, harassed by the police and intimidated by politicians. In short, segregation was a shameful disregard of human rights for the most specious reason.

Even now, 19 years after the passage of the Civil Rights Act of 1964, there are those whites who would cancel the gains that blacks have made in there past two decades by barring them from schools, excluding them from neighborhoods and denying them the chance to compete for jobs. The law may be color blind but many citizens are not.

What progress has been made must be credited largely to the Rev. Martin Luther King's persistence and his willingness to lead his people to the "mountain top." He led the effort to contest segregation on public buses in Montgomery, Alabama; he was arrested in Atlanta in 1960 for protesting segregation at a department store lunch counter; he led the 1965 civil rights demonstration in Selma, Alabama; and he opposed the war in Vietnam in which many black soldiers died.

But perhaps his most effective step toward prompting Congress to pass legislation to put an end to violations of blacks' civil rights was the Aug. 28, 1963, demonstration which drew 200,000 marchers, black and white, to the nation's capital to demand equal justice for all citizens under the law. In his address to the marchers, he stressed the Christian message of brotherhood in the often-quoted "I have a dream" speech.

A year later, he was awarded the Nobel Peace Prize, an honor which was based on his struggle for equal rights in this country. He not only had led demonstrations but also had written several books in which he dealt with the strategy of non-violence in effecting change.

On April 4, 1968, he was gunned down by James Earl Ray outside a Memphis motel. The night before he delivered what was to be his final address to an audience in the city. "I don't know what will happen now, we've got some difficult days ahead," he said. "It really doesn't bother menow, because I've been on the mountain top. I won't mind. Like anybody I would like to live a long life. Longevity has its place. But I'm not concerned about that just now. I want to do God's will and he's allowed me to go up on the mountain, and I've looked over and I've seen the Promised Land. I may not get there with you, but I want you to know tonight that we as a people will get to the Promised Land..."

In observing the 20th anniversary of that march today, participants in Washington and the people of the country should ask themselves what they can do to insure that the black people of the country will soon reach that Promised Land.

THE RICHMOND NEWS LEADER

Richmond, Va., August 26, 1983

He had, he said 20 years ago, a dream:

I have a dream that one day this nation will rise up and live out the true meaning of its creed: "We hold these truths to be self-evident, that all men are created equal." I have a dream that one day on the red hills of Georgia the sons of former slaves and the sons of former slave-owners will be able to sit down together at the table of brotherhood.... I have a dream that my four little children will one day live in a nation where they will not be judged by the color of their skin, but by the content of their character.

Has the day about which the Rev. Dr. Martin Luther King, Jr., dreamed arrived? Yes, surely. And no.

Surely, as the Census Bureau testifies, in certain measurable categories blacks are making great strides: in health, in education, in economic well-being. Surely, at law, countless statutes and judicial rulings have given them the full legal equality they fully deserve. In many ways, the Supreme Court's 1954 *Brown v. Board of Education* decision setting aside the separate-but-equal doctrine — one of the Court's finest moments — made realization of King's dream possible after a far-too-long black sojourn in the American wilderness. The subsequent years have brought impressive gains.

They have brought obstacles and excesses, too.

The obstacles have come primarily in the form of federal laws and practices supposedly aimed at black betterment, such as occupational licensing and the minimum wage that restrict blacks' freedom of movement into — and within — the economy. They do much to explain the deplorable rate of black unemployment, for instance. And the half-a-trillion federal dollars spent during the past two decades to increase the economic independence of blacks (and others), have left lamentably large numbers of blacks below the official poverty level because of the sense of economic dependence those initiative-sapping dollars instill.

The excesses have come primarily from the federal courts and the federal enforcers. Are Americans today, black and white, "judged by the content of their character"? Were he alive, the late Rev. Dr. King might agree that too frequently they are "judged by the color of their skin." In the name of rectifying past injustices we tolerate retributive "remedial discrimination" in the whole panoply of quotas and targets, guidelines and goals, ratios and parities, compulsory busing and racially-drawn voting districts, affirmative action and minority set-asides. Urged to be color-blind, we dwell in a maze forcing us to be color-conscious — a maze constructed through continuous concessions by politicians and bureaucrats to black leaders.

Sometimes those leaders lead drives in directions contrary to the interests of blacks. How can this be? UCLA's Professor Thomas Sowell, a black, explains:

"Black leaders share a social vision common among the white Liberal elite with whom their lives are intertwined and from whom they receive the favorable publicity and financial support essential to their roles as black leaders." Moreover, he says, they have not been selected by blacks to represent the black community, but rather have been "regarded by the white news media, white philanthropy, and white politicians as 'spokesmen' for the black masses. [Hence] much of the black leadership is not in the business of leading blacks but of extracting what they can from whites, and their strategies and rhetoric reflect that orientation."

❖ ❖ ❖

Most of the pernicious inhibitions the Rev. Dr. King catalogued in his speech reprinted elsewhere on today's page no longer exist. The past 20 years have seen a dissipation of the deadening prejudices of race. Most of the grim wrongs and "unspeakable horrors" are over. Blacks have full freedom of access to quality education. There is, today, equal opportunity for all. King's dream has been fulfilled to an extent far greater than anyone might have dared expect just two decades ago.

Now the questions are these:

Having by and large — albeit painfully — achieved "equality of opportunity," will the nation embark on the road toward an unattainable "equality of condition"? Will we permit the principle of racial neutrality to be blurred? In the name of integration, will we allow busing to continue to produce (or hasten) segregated school systems? Purportedly striving for — in James Baldwin's phrase — "the evanescence of color" — will we ever more vigorously accentuate race as the crucial criterion for choice? Will we continue to abide governmental policies and practices that close blacks out of the market? Marching behind the banner of "civil rights," will we suffer excesses to be done in its name?

Perhaps it is not too much to hope (or, as King did, to dream) that the next 20 years will provide the right answers, each of which — in a nation grounded in liberty — should be... No. For to answer any of those questions in any other way would render this nation — contrary to King's admonition — "guilty of wrongful deeds" as it failed to "live out the true meaning of its creed."

The San Diego Union

San Diego, Calif., August 30, 1983

When the late Dr. Martin Luther King dramatically articulated his dream of freedom and brotherhood before a quarter-of-a-million people in Washington, D.C., 20 years ago, American blacks were victims of institutionalized racism. They were barred from numerous restaurants, hotels, and other public facilities. In some states, they were kept from voting.

Considerable progress has been made since then, thanks to civil rights legislation and the fact that a great majority of Americans have come to realize that racial discrimination is immoral and has no place in the United States.

Two decades after Dr. King's "I have a dream" speech, more than 5,000 blacks have been elected to public office and significant advances have been made in other areas. In 1980, for example, nearly 80 percent of blacks were graduated from high school, compared to 53 percent 10 years earlier. Approximately 3.7 million blacks owned their own homes, an increase of 1.1 million since 1970.

Nevertheless, substantial problems remain. The rate of black unemployment is double the jobless rate for whites. Blacks account for half of all domestic help and a third of all trash collectors, but only three percent of lawyers and engineers.

Broadening opportunities for blacks caught in poverty is a goal that is shared by all, not just the estimated 250,000 persons who attended the "Jobs, Peace, Freedom" march and rally held Saturday in Washington to commemorate the 20th anniversary of the historic demonstration led by Dr. King.

But the agenda advocated by the leaders of Saturday's rally clearly fails to offer much hope for blacks or others who are unemployed or poor. The proposals for government job programs, a nuclear freeze, and American disengagement from Central America echo a familiar left-wing litany.

As revealed by speaker after speaker, the main purpose of the rally had little to do with civil rights. Instead, its goal was to foment support for a campaign to defeat President Reagan and his supporters in next year's elections. Under the guise of promoting civil rights, the speakers mainly were concerned with returning to the big spending philosophy that prevailed in Washington until Mr. Reagan entered the White House.

The rally's leaders and others who advocate more spending for social programs ignore the convincing evidence of the failures of government largesse. Federal spending has not enabled significant numbers of people to break out of the poverty cycle. Moreover, simplistic proposals for more spending fail to consider such factors as the connection of poverty and welfare programs with the increasing number of families headed by women who are single parents.

In stimulating the creation of private sector jobs, Mr. Reagan's economic program offers far more to the poor and unemployed than anything heard Saturday. The recent encouraging economic news shows the President's program is beginning to work.

Moreover, it was hypocritical for the rally's leaders to proclaim support for civil rights when they would abandon Central America to Marxists who already have established a totalitarian regime in Nicaragua. Mr. Reagan's commitment to assist the democratically elected government of El Salvador and to restore American military strength are essential for the protection of freedom and civil rights.

Twenty years ago, Dr. King stood on the steps of the Lincoln Memorial and issued a majestic call for freedom that stirred the nation and the world. On Saturday, those who claim his mantle called only for a return to flawed domestic policies and a dangerous retreat to isolationism.

The Boston Globe

Boston, Mass., August 27, 1983

When Martin Luther King Jr. described his dream for America 20 years ago before a crowd of 250,000 at the Lincoln Memorial he was a 34-year-old father of four. As fathers often do he talked of the future that he wanted for his children: "I have a dream that my four little children will one day live in a nation where they will not be judged by the color of their skin, but by the content of their character."

At the time, King's son Martin 3d was six. Like many children, he wanted to go to a local amusement park in Atlanta. Like all black children, he could not. Funtown was "for whites only." Martin Luther King 3d mentioned that barrier during a recent news interview. The signs have come down but statistics indicate that discriminatory barriers remain, if not in many public accommodations, in jobs and housing.

That is why hundreds of thousands will march again today in Washington. The force of their numbers will remind the nation that many Americans will tolerate nothing less than equality and that millions, black and white, need jobs. As the new coalition of labor, women, religious groups and minorities focuses on economic inequities as well as racial inequalities, much of the jobs, peace and freedom message will be directed to the Reagan Administration, against its civil rights reversals and policies that have harmed minorities, women and the poor.

Just as leaders of the first march sought to influence civil rights bills pending before Congress, leaders at today's march will attempt to influence legislation which would create one million jobs for the longterm unemployed; establish a mutual reduction in nuclear weapons; strengthen fair housing; provide equal rights and economic parity for women; ban new business investments in South Africa and any information or technology that would allow that country to accelerate a nuclear program; and promote peaceful negotiations in El Salvador. One bill that will receive special attention needs only Senate approval and President Reagan's signature; it would make King's birthday a national holiday.

Children will be on the minds of many at the march. "We must make sure that the future generation, the children under 10, continue to progress," a black student from Ole Miss – which the federal government integrated forcibly the year before the first march – told a reporter. College students were at best toddlers during the first march. Most of them have no memory of the civil rights leader who was assassinated 15 years ago. Their involvement is crucial. The major march-related function of King's 26-year-old son, Martin 3d, has been to involve youth. They must become the new strategists, the youngest keepers of the dream.

In some ways, their lives are better than the lives of their parents. Twenty years ago, the majority of black Americans could not vote. King addressed that violation of rights at the first march. "We cannot be satisfied as long as the Negro in Mississippi cannot vote and the Negro in New York believes he has nothing for which to vote." Two years after the march, Congress passed the Voting Rights Act, which suspended the literacy tests that had been used to exclude black Americans from the voting booths, and established criminal penalties for those convicted of interfering with voting rights. Congress extended those protections last year, despite Reagan Administration opposition until a last minute flip-flop. The law was needed this summer during statewide elections in Mississippi.

Political progress is cutting through some of the despair of Northern blacks. Chicago elected a black mayor this year. Black mayors lead six other major cities: Atlanta, Detroit, Los Angeles, Newark, New Orleans, Washington, D.C. and 220 other municipalities. In upcoming elections, candidates have a chance in Boston and a stronger chance in Philadephia.

On another political front, Rev. Jesse Jackson, one of King's aides, is contemplating a run for President. King's son Martin is considering a future run for the US House. Currently, 21 black representatives serve in the Congress – as contrasted to five in 1963 – but not one represents a district in any of the 9 Southern states, which are home to 53 percent of black Americans. More than 50 black federal judges sit on the bench. In fact, 5000 black officials – more than double the number 20 years ago – were elected last year, but unfortunately they represent one percent of the nation's total.

Twenty years ago, the majority of black Americans could not patronize most restaurants, hotels, motels, public libraries or parks in their communities. As seen through a child's eyes, those signs meant no trip to the amusement park, no lunch downtown, no day at the beach. During the first march, King promised that "devotees of civil rights" would "never be satisfied as long as our children are stripped or their selfhood and robbed of their dignity by signs stating 'for whites only . . .'" The next year, the Congress passed the 1964 Civil Rights Act, which barred discrimination in public accommodations.

The signs are down, but as A. Philip Randolph, a prominent black labor leader who was the march director 20 years ago pointed out then, ". . . those accommodations will mean little to those who cannot afford to use them."

Despite some spectacular individual progress most black Americans are losing ground. The income gap has widened between black and white Americans. Black joblessness at 19.5 percent is double that of an intolerable national rate of 9.5 percent. Americans are backsliding into poverty at the most alarming rate in 15 years. Black Americans are still disproportionately poor and one of every two black children is growing up in poverty.

The children have the most to lose and the most to gain.

"We've made some progress," said Benjamin Hooks, head of the National Assn. for the Advancement of Colored People. "But we still have a long way to go." So today's march must be more than nostalgia. The newly broadened coalition must motivate new laws and new freedoms as the first march did.

President Kennedy told the leaders of that first march that the cause of civil rights had been advanced. Today's march must also advance the cause. Again, a father's dream for his children, all children, will be back on the minds of millions.

THE DENVER POST

Denver, Colo., August 27, 1983

TODAY'S "March for Jobs, Peace and Freedom" in Washington celebrates the 20th anniversary of Dr. Martin Luther King Jr.'s epochal march. The observance is being echoed in smaller gatherings around the nation, including one in Denver.

Aug. 28, 1963, was the day hundreds of thousands of people of all races and religions showed their commitment to racial justice and equality. It was the day Dr. King said, "I Have a Dream" and compelled hundreds of millions of complacent Americans to listen.

The goal today, two decades later, is not to awaken the nation to the gaping wounds. That has been done; the wounds, if they are not healing as quickly as they might, at least are being attended.

This time the agenda is more evolutionary. Saturday's platform includes the by-now-familiar themes of unequal employment and hunger and education. It adds a topic, world peace, which was not in the spotlight at that 1963 march. These are not topics on which there is unanimity. The Reagan administration will be taken sorely to task for not doing the right things to solve these problems of economics and equality and peace. But that is not to trivialize today's events.

The added element — the official marriage of the peace and civil rights movements — is something of a test of the organizers' ability to rekindle the nation's sense of purpose. The organizers expect 3,000 buses and more than a quarter of a million participants. More than 700 organizations have endorsed the march. Countless people who attended the 1963 march are planning to return to retrace their footsteps and renew their commitments. It remains to be seen whether there will be a new mobilization on behalf of old goals.

These gatherings two decades later may not be able to capture the drama of their predecessor. That was, after all, a day of exceptional importance in the nation's moral history. But today's marches and speeches cannot help but remind us that there is much to be done yet — and that there are still a great many people committed to doing it.

Pittsburgh Post-Gazette

Pittsburgh, Pa., August 30, 1983

As expected, last weekend's 20th anniversary re-enactment of the march on Washington was a powerful testimony to the legacy of the man who declared that "I have a dream" and who died a martyr's death before seeing that dream fulfilled.

But the latter-day "March for Jobs, Peace and Freedom," which attracted 300,000 Americans to the capital, also dramatized the fact that Dr. Martin Luther King Jr.'s clarion call for simple justice has been replaced by a sometimes dissonant chorus of many voices.

Where Dr. King called down biblical judgment on the undoubted evil of legally mandated segregation, those who gathered in Washington last weekend took many — perhaps too many — texts for their sermonizing. There was unemployment, El Salvador, the arms race, the environment and the failings, and not only in civil rights, of the Reagan administration. ("We're here," Benjamin Hooks of the NAACP told the throng, "because we're committed to the elimination of Reaganism from the face of the earth.")

Even on the question of race, the solidarity in the streets and the addition of "jobs" to the litany of "peace and freedom" concealed fissures in black as well as white opinion about how to improve the situation of the so-called "underclass" in America, which is disproportionately black.

It is fashionable — and fair to some extent — to blame the depressed circumstances of much of black America on the conservative in the White House. But for all of his deplorable snipping of holes in the social safety net, President Reagan is miscast as the omnipotent nemesis of black hopes. As many black politicians and other leaders are now making bold to say, the poorest of the poor are trapped in a subculture of dependency that is not obviously amenable to quick fixes of any sort.

The complexity of the so-called "underclass" problem is no argument for Reaganism, of course. But it does underline the fact that, unlike the campaign to eradicate Jim Crow laws, the quest for "economic justice" for blacks points in no one direction.

To take only a few examples, some black leaders continue to see the public school as the repository of hopes for the younger generation and insist that tax support go only to public schools; some others, noting that there has been black as well as white "flight" to private and parochial schools, endorse tuition tax credits, voucher systems and other proposals to diversify educational opportunity.

The problem of black teen-age unemployment likewise does not command a consensus. The majority view is no doubt the one held by many of those gathered in Washington last weekend: that relief should take the form of government-created jobs. But an articulate minority of black economists suggest a different approach: repeal of the minimum wage for teen-agers, the creation of regulation-free "enterprise zones" and so on.

To remark on the complexity of the problem is not to minimize its roots in white racism (roots which provide the best argument for affirmative-action programs of one sort or another). It is to note that more than the passage of time distinguishes this year's march on Washington from its historic precursor.

The Atlanta Journal
AND
THE ATLANTA CONSTITUTION

Atlanta, Ga., August 27, 1983

Twenty years after the Washington March for Jobs and Freedom, our long night of enforced segregation has ended. Poll taxes have given way to voter-registration drives, we now drink from the same water fountains and ax handles are no longer respectable souvenirs. It is no small achievement: The old poisons have been neutralized, if not entirely purged.

Yet today's March on Washington promises to be a bittersweet observance.

Sweet? The memory of victories past, and their present legacies, will make it rich: the campaigns in Montgomery, Selma and Birmingham, the Freedom Rides, and of course, the 1963 march itself and the breakthrough civil-rights legislation it helped inspire.

Dominating today's observance, too, will be the sweet inspiration of Dr. Martin Luther King Jr. It was King who 20 years ago stood at the foot of the Lincoln Memorial and gave impassioned voice to the movement's goals and stirred the nation's conscience from a long, neglectful sleep.

Bitter? Contemporary events have stirred a strong measure of disillusionment. The issues no longer are simple matters of right and wrong, of racial inclusion vs. exclusion. Instead, we face complex questions of implementation. How do we complete the process of inclusion?

There is no national consensus. Having scrapped discriminatory laws, many want to leave things at that. But if we leave racial progress there, without erasing the *effects* of historic discrimination, our nation will face the same destructive racial divisions it has always faced. Only the terminology of this tension will change: This time, it will polarize "haves" and "have-nots," instead of blacks and whites. It is the same problem in a different context.

Sadly, the current national administration is not alone as it fails to grasp this crucial point. It mistakenly equates affirmative action with "reverse discrimination." Its support for private education (at the expense of public schools) and for reduced social programs seem to define the limits of America's taste for reform, at least in the short run.

A new direction, with a clear destination, is urgently needed. King's eloquent dream has not been realized yet.

Five years before the Washington March, King wrote: "History has thrust upon our generation an indescribably important destiny — to complete a process of democratization . . . How we deal with this crucial situation will determine our moral health as individuals, our cultural health as a region, our political health as a nation, and our prestige as a leader of the free world."

As yet, that process remains incomplete.

The Washington Post

Washington, D.C., August 28, 1983

NO ONE THOUGHT it would be—and it wasn't: yesterday's march was not the march of 1963. It was different. The march of Aug. 27, 1983, was less focused, less thematic, less morally intense and more diffuse. It was also more political in a particular sense. There were stretches, hearing the rhetoric—the boilerplate, really—that some of its speakers thought fitting for the occasion, when you might have imagined you were sitting through those preliminary, time-killing sessions at a Democratic National Convention when speaker after speaker jumps up and down on the Republican adversary.

Down with Reagan!—that was the message. We do not speak as particular admirers of this administration's attitude to civil rights. The administration itself will be pleased to tell you that. But we do think that so far as the fulfillment of Martin Luther King Jr.'s dream is concerned, anyone who believes that the Reagan government is the problem and its replacement the solution is living a different kind of dream: a pipedream. And in truth it is precisely because the terrain has become so much more complicated than it once was, because so many different interests and values and claims have come into conflict in the drive to fulfill the promise of racial justice, that a renewal of the essentially simple and unassailable moral proposition involved was a good and necessary idea. There were many speakers who, in various parts of their speeches, did handsomely recapture and rekindle the commitment that the 1963 march was all about.

The Rev. Jesse Jackson himself, speaking eloquently of progress made and new challenges yet to be overcome ("Apartheid—illegal segregation—is over. But 20 years later we do not have equality. We have moved in, now we must move up . . ."), called attention to the classic, mean irony. Progress inevitably reveals new barriers and troubles, or, more exactly, barriers and troubles that one did not even have the luxury of addressing before when so many stark, elementary injustices had yet to be addressed.

With or without romance and nostalgia, it is almost impossible to recreate the mood and condition of civil rights in 1963 with any fidelity. Few now remember and even fewer seem to want to remember the apprehension that seized both blacks and whites as to whether such a march could be peaceable at all. How much the nation was to experience and learn—much of it bloody and painful—about the politics of mass mobilization in the years to follow. And how innocent and gentle that march now seems in retrospect. It is almost as difficult to remember what life was like then in respect to national and local policy and practice on racial matters.

Our sense of yesterday's march is that—unsurprisingly, given the horrendous difficulties and great disappointments attending the current effort to achieve social and racial justice in this country—it revealed a movement that has yet to find its most persuasive theme and its voice. We also believe the act of assembly was essential and that the fundamental commitment it honored is as alive and compelling today as it was in the days when Martin Luther King Jr. lived.

THE COMMERCIAL APPEAL

Memphis, Tenn., August 27, 1983

HAS IT BEEN 20 years since Martin Luther King Jr. stood on the steps of the Lincoln Memorial and launched a civil rights revolution with his "I have a dream" speech?

Has it been only 20 years since this nation's black citizens were forced to ride in the back of buses, drink from "colored" water fountains and attend segregated schools?

Maybe it's only a matter of perspective, but it must seem like yesterday to white America that civil rights demonstrators were strutting up and down the streets demanding their rights. And it must seem like ages ago to black Americans that they first raised their voices in protest of the contempt and ridicule under which they were held by the law.

Just as the passage of time is measured differently by the young and the old, so must it be viewed differently by the nation's haves and have-nots, by white and black America. Time does pass quickly when you're having a good time. And it does creep along at a painful pace when you're in pain. Understand that and you understand black impatience with two decades of "progress." Fail to understand it and you fail to understand why there are still barriers between white and black America.

Much has been said about the lack of enthusiasm shown in the black community for the King commemoration taking place today in Washington. That's not really surprising, though, is it? While the King speech raised the spirits of black America — and gave the movement a flowing eloquence with biblical overtones — it was white America's reaction to the speech that made it a turning point in the civil rights movement.

Twenty years ago, the enemy was there for all to see. It was tangible. It could be touched, seen, heard in the brazen "hell, no" utterances of radical whites. The solution was simple: to strike down those laws that discriminated against blacks and to devise new laws to redefine the "blessings of liberty" as guaranteed by the Constitution.

Because the injustices were so visible, they were easy to attack. White America, after some vociferous soul-searching, took down the signposts of discrimination, reformed the law and then moved on to other things. Those black leaders who were part of the struggle also moved on to other things, at least many of them did. Those who did not were eventually branded as out-of-touch. Their rhetoric became dated, their faces aged, their battle cry lost on younger generations of blacks who never had to walk past "whites only" fountains to get a drink of water.

TODAY, blacks are worse off in many ways than they were when King made his famous speech. Black unemployment is higher, black poverty is greater and black households are less stable. Blacks have more equality under the law than they had 20 years ago, but less economic freedom. That is what frustrates today's black leaders.

White America can't see the injustices facing today's black generation, for they are more subtle than in years past. What it can't see, it can't be mobilized to combat. Those black leaders who speak of today's problems, using yesterday's rhetoric, are not only failing to reach white America, they are failing to reach those blacks who want more out of life than the right to drink from the water fountain of their choice.

Had he lived, maybe King would have found the words on the anniversary of his "I have a dream" speech to redefine the black struggle for equality. Maybe he would have been able to explain why blacks and whites have measured the 20-year interim with different clocks. Maybe, just maybe, he would have been able to explain — as he did in 1963 — why black dreams don't have to become the stuff of white nightmares.

The Birmingham News

Birmingham, Ala., July 8, 1984

When the Civil Rights Act of 1964 cleared the Congress and became law 20 years ago this week, blacks and many whites who had pressed so hard for full citizenship for minorities hailed it as a new day for America. It was and still is.

Others, including some members of the legal community, predicted a hundred years would pass before all of the implications of the act would be understood by the public and before its effects would be fully known.

Actually, the act has been far more effective than the framers ever dreamed. It has ushered in a virtual, mostly peaceful, revolution, not only in the law but in social attitudes as well. While feelings about minorities, be they black or other, vary widely, today every measurement in our social order says that there is only one law of the land and that it is to be applied equally to all persons, regardless of race, creed, sex, age, condition or national origin.

Americans can be proud of this state of the law and its acceptance by the vast majority. Southerners, though some may still resent the changes the act has wrought, can be especially proud of the distance they have come in validating the promise of the Declaration of Independence.

Black people, appropriately and especially in the South, have been quick to claim full citizenship under the law. Today, blacks in growing numbers are serving at nearly all levels of government, including the White House staff. They serve in the highest echelons of the military, in the FBI, CIA and in every agency of the federal government, as well as in most police and fire departments across the country.

They also are increasingly awarded management positions in a wide variety of private sector businesses and industries and in public-supported, as well as private institutions of higher education. They are active professionally — in medicine, law, architecture and journalism. They are present in world-class sports far beyond their percentage in the population.

But perhaps the greatest change wrought by the act is in the area of political power. Black leaders have been quick to recognize that, in a democracy, the key to real power lies in the ballot box. Not only is it the path to decision-making positions, it is the way one goes about changing the distribution of power so as to include black goals and aspirations on the national, state and local agenda.

But the Civil Rights Act has not come up all roses. Through no fault of its own, it has produced some negatives. Its impact on law, especially constitutional law, has been immense. In some cases, it has tended to bend some constitutional provisions out of shape. Activist judges have seized the opportunity to legislate new laws in all but name. It has encouraged some federal judges to intrude as never in history on state and local law and to violate accepted understandings of the separation of powers.

It has contributed to a trivialization of the law. Success in the courts over legitimate civil rights violations has encouraged an unprecedented tidal wave of litigation in almost every area of life, many on claims of "civil rights" violations. A spinoff has been legal actions, many of them unjustified, against almost every agency of government and against many professions and institutions in the private sector.

It has needlessly inflated the legal profession, as thousands of businesses have had to employ lawyers or law firms to protect themselves against "civil rights" piracy. The multitude of cases has encouraged some to believe they can be compensated for almost any real or imagined wrong, regardless of the seriousness of the offense, if they can get a lawyer to file suit in federal court.

Perhaps the greatest damage from uneven and many times wrong-headed interpretation of the act has been done to thousands of public schools and to the cities in which they are located. In large measure, public schools have borne the brunt through forced pursuit of a fictional racial balance, a procedure which the act itself outlawed.

Schools, in many cases, have been crippled to the point of being mere caretaker centers for children. The forced and illegal pursuit of racial balance and the deterioration of scholastic achievement has sent hundreds of thousands of middle-class families fleeing to suburbs, destroying for all time in some cases the very social mix which has been one of America's strengths. The upshot has been to segregate many cities and their schools and foster a new kind of black separatism.

However, it was not the act which was or is at fault, but the interpretation by an impatient and activist judiciary that obviously concluded that the act did not go far enough or compensate those who had been wronged in the past by discriminatory laws and practices.

With such judges still about, one cringes at the thought of the litigation and the senseless intrusion of the federal bureaucracy that will follow if the Civil Rights Act of 1984, already approved by the House, is ratified by the Senate.

Even so, the Civil Rights Act of 1964 will be viewed by future historians and philosophers as an awakening of the American conscience to the evils of destructive discrimination, as well as a deeper understanding of the "hidden" promises of the Great Declaration and the U.S. Constitution. Indeed, it incites wonder that a document nearly 190 years old could have such an impact in the last 20 years of a blase 20th century.

Part I: Education

Desegregation and Busing: Legacy of the *Brown* Decision

The *Brown v. Board of Education* Supreme Court decision constitutes a watershed in the history of race relations in the United States. This 1954 class-action lawsuit dealt with several related cases nationwide, but was named for Oliver Brown, who protested the busing of his daughter to a black elementary school when there was a white school within walking distance of their home. Thirty-one years later, the implementation of the *Brown* ruling remains one of the most highly controversial topics in education.

The Court, in its unanimous opinion, did not specify the methods to be used in desegregating the school systems in 21 affected states, but asserted that the question "presents problems of considerable complexity," and called for further argument the following year. Tangible results were thus slow to materialize; in many counties in the South, where the decision met with the fiercest opposition, more than fifteen years elapsed before blacks and whites were going to school together. During this time, court battles between recalcitrant school boards and civil rights adherents gradually established racial balance formulas and the transportation of students from one school to another as an effective way of achieving integration; that is, it was a strategy that could not readily be thwarted by schemes to continue segregation while pretending to eliminate it.

By the late 1960's and early 1970's, busing students from one school district to another was increasingly applied to achieve integration between metropolitan school districts and those in the surrounding suburbs. Opposition mounted in the North as well as the South. The phenomenon of "white flight" to the suburbs documents the attempts of white families to avoid newly integrated, mostly urban, school districts. Black parents objected to the disruption caused by busing, and to the time wasted in transporting their children to schools that in many cases were no better in quality than the ones they had been attending; many black schools were closed in the process. The wisdom of busing came under attack from black and white parents alike, who were increasingly concerned about the standard of education received by their children, independent of the racial balance of the classroom in which they received it. In addition, a growing body of parents began to object to all such "race-conscious" policies, pointing out that it was a quest to end unequal treatment for minority and white schoolchildren, a desire to eliminate differential treatment based on race, that had resulted in the *Brown* decision. (Thurgood Marshall, then special counsel to the NAACP and a chief architect of the litigation in the *Brown* case, had stated that his hope for a favorable ruling was that it would result in the establishment of school districts "on a natural basis, without regard to race or color.")

The fundamental change in government desegregation policy that marked the switchover from the Carter to the Reagan Administration and has continued into President Reagan's second term—an unwavering opposition to busing as a means of achieving integration in the nation's schools—is reflected in the content of the editorials on the following pages. One of the last acts of President Carter in office was to veto an anti-busing amendment that would bar the Justice Department from bringing any legal action to require school busing. In June, 1981, with a new Administration in place, the House passed a similar measure, barring the Justice Department from starting lawsuits to institute busing programs for school desegregation, by a vote of 265 to 122. (The amendment did not prohibit private groups from bringing suits to establish busing, nor did it affect busing programs already in operation.) In the Senate, a companion measure, which would not only prohibit federal courts from ordering schoolchildren to be bused more than five miles or 15 minutes from their homes, but would dismantle any such busing plans already in operation, was sponsored by Sens. J. Bennett Johnston (D, La.) and Jesse Helms (R, N.C.). Action on the issue was delayed nearly a year by filibusters, led by Sen. Lowell Weicker, Jr. (R, Conn.) and other

opponents, but the Senate did, in March, 1982, finally pass the proposed legislation, which contained the most restrictive anti-busing language ever passed by either house of Congress. The Johnston/Helms anti-busing rider then ran into strong opposition in the House, however, in large part because of the constitutional implications of limiting court power, rather than as a result of support for forced busing. The amendment was finally dropped when the appropriations resolution to which it was attached cleared Congress—in April, 1982, just in time to avert a shutdown of the government departments funded by the larger bill.

The Reagan Administration, meanwhile, had made no secret of its opposition to court-imposed busing schemes. In May, 1981, the Justice Department unveiled an unprecedented financial-incentive plan for encouraging school integration between St. Louis and its suburbs, as an alternative to the court-ordered busing that had begun the year before. If approved by the city's federal district court, the state of Missouri would award partial college tuition to white elementary or high school students who voluntarily transferred to predominantly black city schools, and to black students who transferred to predominantly white suburban schools. The plan also called for the creation of several "magnet schools" in the city, in order to attract students from different districts. When the 11-year St. Louis desegregation dispute was finally resolved, however, in February, 1983, the innovativv tuition payments were not included in the voluntary busing agreement reached by the school districts.

In another effort to devise desegregation programs that avoid busing, the Justice Department in 1984 engineered an arrangement for the Bakersfield, Calif. public schools that Administration officials called "a blueprint for the future." Under a consent decree proposed by the Justice Department to avoid litigation, Bakersfield would attempt to attract white students to predominantly black and Hispanic schools by creating special programs in science, computer training, and in the creative and performing arts. Four of the city's 25 elementary schools, where whites had accounted for no more than 8% of the enrollment, would be involved in the project. Bakersfield school authorities were to file progress reports with the courts yearly; the requirements of the decree would expire after three years if the city attained statistical goals for desegregating its schools.

In the judicial realm, two Supreme Court cases, decided in 1982 and 1983, narrowed the extent to which states and local districts could alter or restrict court-ordered busing programs. The first involved California's Proposition One and Washington state's Initiative 350, both statewide ballot measures. The high court upheld the constitutionality of Proposition One, finding that the proposition was "racially neutral," or not aimed at harming the rights of blacks or other minorities. Supporters of Proposition One had used the measure to dismantle a sweeping busing plan in Los Angeles in 1981, arguing successfully that intentional school segregation had not been shown, and that therefore the plan exceeded the Constitution's guarantees of equal protection. The high court struck down Washington's Initiative 350, however, finding that "despite its facial neutrality," there was little doubt that the initiative "was effectively drawn for racial purposes." Initiative 350 went further than Proposition One, in that it prohibited local boards from instituting voluntary busing programs. In the second case discussed by editorialists here, the Justice Department in 1982 asked the high court to overturn an appeals court ruling which ordered additional busing between Nashville and the surrounding Davidson County area. (The case had come to court because a federal judge had found that Nashville's original busing program, begun in 1971, had failed to adequately desegregate the district's schools and had prompted "white flight" from the district.) The Supreme Court declined, in January, 1983, to review the appeals court decision, leaving in effect the expanded busing program in Nashville.

The Charlotte Observer

Charlotte, N.C., December 7, 1980

Although President Carter has vetoed the $9 billion appropriations bill with the anti-busing rider, anti-busing sentiment is likely to raise its head again early next year as a new, more conservative Congress convenes.

That may please a lot of people. Busing is not a popular remedy, even among people who otherwise accept desegregation. But it will be unfortunate if Congress inflames all the old anti-busing emotions again, just as the nation is beginning to see some positive effects of busing and needs to turn its attention to more substantive educational issues.

The anti-busing rider, proposed by North Carolina Sen. Jesse Helms, would have prohibited the Justice Department from going to court to desegregate schools if busing was involved. After considerable debate, the bill made it through both houses of Congress to the president's desk.

President Carter vetoed the bill because of the anti-busing measure, and he was right to do so. Now that the executive branch can't withhold federal money to press for desegregation, the Justice Department, as Carter pointed out, is the sole remaining agency that can enforce desegregation as required by Congress in Title VI of the 1964 Civil Rights Act. And in many instances, busing is the only way — and a practical way — to achieve desegregation.

The Separation Of Powers

It is the executive branch's duty under the Constitution to enforce the laws of the land, Carter reminded Congress. For the legislative branch to stop the executive branch, in effect, from performing its duty violates the principle of separation of powers.

There are several other good reasons why the Justice Department should be allowed to push for school desegregation, using busing where necessary. School desegregation didn't get started in any massive way in this country until the last few years, and its positive social and educational consequences are only beginning to surface.

Last month, for example, the National Institute of Education released a two-year study which showed that school desegregation has promoted neighborhood integration in large metropolitan school districts, including Charlotte-Mecklenburg. The study's authors concluded that in those areas where parents couldn't escape busing by moving to the suburbs, they integrated neighborhoods so their children could go to neighborhood schools. The use of busing then declined — in some cases, dramatically.

Also last month, two University of Connecticut professors reported that in the 14 years Hartford has operated a voluntary desegregation plan, its inner-city students who were bused to suburban schools have gotten better jobs after graduation than their urban peers and have been more likely to continue their education beyond high school.

Goals Can Be Realized

What these studies hint at is that once school desegregation becomes established, it can achieve at least some of its goals, namely encouraging a multi-racial society and improving the education of minority students.

Anti-busing supporters said their measure wouldn't prevent individuals and civil rights groups from suing to continue the desegregation process. But such litigants don't have the money or clout to pursue as many cases as the Justice Department. When costs of desegregation cases, particularly in large cities, run into hundreds of thousands of dollars, the NAACP Legal Defense Fund, for example, can afford to press only a couple of cases at a time.

Moreover, if Congress withdraws its support of busing, some federal judges may think twice before ordering it. In communities where busing is a fact — as in Charlotte, for example — that could raise false hopes that busing might be terminated and stir up old conflicts.

Since the Justice Department started enforcing Title VI, it has been involved in 500 school desegregation cases, much of the time as the primary litigant. It now has about 75 active cases, most of them in the North and Midwest. The chaos that would result if it pulled out of those cases is almost unimaginable.

There Are Bigger Problems

But of course, the anti-busing supporters weren't worried about the implications of their idea. They were simply playing on emotions, some of them racist, that have been around a long time, and they got a lot of publicity along the way. The country would be better served if they would worry more about what children are learning, or aren't learning, in the classroom, and less about how the kids get there.

Chicago Tribune

Chicago, Ill., December 7, 1980

In what might be their last great spat, Congress and President Carter are facing off over whether the Justice Department should be forbidden from spending any money in seeking busing for school desegregation. President Carter says he will veto the appropriations bill containing such a provision. Congress, for its part, threatens not to pass any stopgap legislation to allow the Justice Department to function after Dec. 15 unless it has such a rider. The lame-duck Congress' recess may be long delayed by the controversy.

Congress might just as well forget the anti-busing provision and go home because the proper way to bring sense to the law of school desegregation is not through tacking restrictive riders onto appropriations bills.

Why tie the incoming Reagan administration's hands on this subject? The key to bringing some sense to school desegregation law is in the courts. And the Reagan Justice Department should be allowed maximum flexibility in pursuing a legal strategy to minimize the counterproductive use of busing.

Congress' anti-busing provision would not be interpreted by the courts to prohibit the executive branch from bringing any school desegregation case. That interpretation would raise serious constitutional questions about Congress' authority to tell the President what parts of the law and the Constitution he can and cannot enforce, and the courts would probably avoid such a constitutional show-down.

Consequently, the Justice Department could bring the cases and simply let other parties to the litigation—or the federal courts themselves—bring up the remedy of busing. In this respect, the anti-busing rider accomplishes nothing.

The proposal could, however, prevent the Reagan administration from participating in a helpful way in pending cases such as Chicago's. The most useful way the new Justice Department could behave in such cases would be to work with the local school board in drafting a plan that might be accepted by the courts and then to support the plan in court. The plan might involve some busing, but far less than might otherwise be ordered. If the Justice Department is forbidden from supporting any busing at all, then it might be prevented from being a voice of reason and moderation, even from being an ally of the school board.

Moreover, the new Justice Department has the opportunity to take positions before the U.S. Supreme Court encouraging the elimination of some of the most mindless elements of busing law. But if it is forced to support no busing at all, the Reagan Justice Department might be cornered into advocating a position that the Supreme Court will never accept.

The new administration has a great opportunity to channel the use of busing in constructive rather than destructive ways—through its authority to revise administrative regulations, to decide what new cases to bring, to advocate legal change before the Supreme Court, and to participate in the drafting of desegregation plans. But if it is to be effective, it will have to do so in a careful, unemotional, and sophisticated manner. It will have to persuade the courts, and this requires the greatest leeway in the way it fashions its arguments. The Congress' meat cleaver approach would do more harm than good to the movement to eliminate the excesses of court-ordered busing.

Chicago Defender

Chicago, Ill., Febuary 11, 1980

Every time the discussion gets around to desegregating public schools in the Chicago area, somebody yells: "You ain't talking about busing my kids, are you?" And the conversation comes to a screeching halt.

Opposition to busing seems to be one of the few things blacks and whites, rich and poor concur on these days. People automatically put school busing in the same category with leprosy, the black plague and venereal disease. So they never get around to looking at the pros and cons.

The evidence, which is coming to us from cities like Boston and Los Angeles, indicates the cons aren't as awful as everyone assumed. Not only have short bus trips in the L. A. system promoted racial balance and helped reading scores, the studies show they have been far better received by the students than any experts anticipated. In fact, one report showed many children looked forward to the bus ride; it was a pleasant, socially enriching experience.

We all know the cons on busing — the old argument about "neighborhood" schools and forced racial mixing and how much it all costs. But we also ought to think about the cons of our present separate-but-unequal school system. Black kids in Chicago aren't getting a decent education because their schools are understaffed, poorly equipped and shortchanged in a hundred other ways. Because they are all-black, they are low priority. This is how it has always been, is now and ever will be, as far as we can tell.

One alternative is to integrate — yes, to force integration by busing if need be — not to please Uncle Sam or satisfy the liberals, but in order to insure that no school is a potential dumping ground by reason of the color of the students.

Certainly, it will be difficult to convince black parents about the value of busing. On the other hand, it shouldn't be hard to convince anyone that damn little education is going on in the present "neighborhood" school system.

THE DAILY OKLAHOMAN

Oklahoma City, Okla., December 3, 1980

WHILE Justice Department lawyers continue to push forced busing as a remedy for racial segregation in the classroom, school boards all over the country are having to deal with its consequences. One of them is reduced pupil enrollments in metropolitan districts as families flee to the suburbs.

A dramatic example of that has occurred in Oklahoma City, where the board of education faces the unhappy choice of closing some schools or stretching an already tight budget to accommodate higher per-pupil operating costs.

Feverish activity in the Justice Department's civil rights division in the waning days of the Carter administration has resulted in the filing of a lawsuit charging Yonkers, N. Y., deliberately segregated its public schools and residential areas. A reported desegregation plan already in the works would involve some busing of students.

Under consideration is a suit seeking the end of segregation in Charleston, S. C., schools, possibly through cross-district busing. The whites are concentrated in suburban school districts and the blacks in the city schools.

The Justice lawyers and civil rights activists stubbornly refuse to acknowledge mounting evidence that forced cross-town busing of students simply to achieve racial balance has been counter-productive to good racial relations and generally has failed to improve the education of minority pupils.

Most often the result has been to send both white and black families packing to the suburbs. The exodus has left inner-city school districts with drastically reduced enrollments — and empty buildings. Granted, some of the enrollment decline can be attributed to the passage of the "baby boom" peak, but the hostility to forced busing cannot be denied.

The Oklahoma City district has seen its pupil population fall from 75,000 in 1966 to 41,000 this year. Not all of the loss has been "white flight"; black parents have moved to the suburbs, too, because their children have borne the burden of busing.

Superintendent Thomas Payzant has recommended closing five schools next year and three more in the near future for a savings of $350,000 a year. He believes this will be a prudent allocation of limited financial resources but concedes it means a further sacrifice of the neighborhood-school concept and parental involvement.

Des Moines Tribune

Des Moines, Iowa, December 12, 1980

Studies concluding that a school desegregation effort has had a harmful effect on education, housing patterns or some other aspect of community life attract far more attention than studies that find beneficial effects. So it is not surprising that a two-year study recently completed by the Center for National Policy Review of Catholic University, Washington, D.C., has been little noticed.

Researchers compared racial patterns in housing in seven metropolitan areas where area-wide school desegregation programs had been in effect for at least five years with housing in seven similar cities with no such programs.

Wichita, Kan., whose school district includes suburbs, was compared with Tulsa, Okla., where suburbs are separate districts. Charlotte, N.C., which is part of a county school district, was compared with Richmond, Va., where a federal court requiring busing between city and county school districts was reversed on appeal.

Researchers concluded that housing integration has been proceeding at such a brisk pace in metropolitan areas with area-wide school desegregation plans that the need for busing to achieve racial balance may soon be eliminated.

In some cities, busing plans that leave pupils already attending well-integrated schools in their own neighborhoods have made those neighborhoods attractive places to live. In other cases, the prospect of suburb-to-city busing appears to have countered the decades-old trend of families with children to seek suburban homes.

The fears of black families about moving into formerly all-white neighborhoods appear to be lessening. Black parents have become less apprehensive because their children have had opportunities to develop friendships with white children in desegregated schools.

Housing integration is not all that has shown improvement. Although this study deals only with housing, other studies have shown that pupil scores on standard tests improved in the Charlotte area after a few years of city-suburban busing.

The Supreme Court has ruled that suburban school districts cannot be compelled to enter desegregation programs with the city districts they adjoin. With rare exceptions, this has limited area-wide desegregation programs to cities with school districts extending into the suburbs.

The new study is no more the definitive study of the effects of desegregation and busing than those that preceded it, but it does indicate that broad-scale desegregation may be more beneficial than even its advocates suspected.

Houston Chronicle

Houston, Texas, September 21, 1981

The busing of school children for racial integration was a bad idea from the start. It takes children from their neighborhood schools and buses them perhaps miles and hours away from home; it discourages parents from taking an active part in school activities; entire cities have been emotionally torn apart by unrealistic busing programs; it puts more emphasis on numbers than on seeing that children have equal educational opportunities.

Even among those who are supposed to be helped, busing has many opponents. Busing might achieve a degree of temporary integration, but it upsets parents, children and teachers to the point of nullifying any good points that might have been made in its favor.

In short, busing simply does not work and will not work. One way to bring federal pressure for busing to a halt is through congressional limitations. Anti-busing legislation adopted by both the House and Senate in 1980 came to naught in a veto by President Carter. However, the public pressure continued, and the House in June, by a better than a 2-1 margin, adopted legislation that would bar the Justice Department from spending funds for "any sort of action to require directly or indirectly" busing beyond the school nearest a pupil's home.

Similar legislation came up for Senate consideration in June but opponents began a filibuster that tied up the legislation through the summer. Not until last week did the Senate muster enough bipartisan votes to end the filibuster and get the legislation moving again.

The cloture vote was 61 to 36, indicating a solid majority of senators favor a limit on busing. But the going won't be smooth. Opponents, led by Sen. Lowell P. Weicker Jr., R-Conn., already have vowed to use every rule in the Senate book to fight the legislation.

The Senate vote was a positive step toward acceding to the wishes of the people to end what Rep. James M. Collins, R-Texas, who introduced the anti-busing legislation in the House, so aptly termed "this costly and counterproductive forced school busing."

The Washington Star
and Daily News

Washington, D.C., June 22, 1981

"Busing," word and deed, stirs up just about everyone. That goes far to explain the attraction of the anti-busing rider recently passed by the House of Representatives. Unsurprisingly, the amendment to the Justice Department authorization, offered by Rep. James M. Collins, R-Tex., passed by better than a 2-1 margin. He and Sen. Jesse Helms, R-N.C., have tried to pass it before. They failed last fall only because the bill to which their rider was attached was vetoed by President Carter.

The mood in Congress is different now, but the measure, pending before the Senate, remains as dishonest as ever. President Reagan, who says he will sign the bill, opposes "busing" as a remedy for school segregation. But that is not the point. It never was the point of the Helms-Collins amendment.

The measure does not – it cannot – prohibit busing. Nor does it limit the authority of federal judges to order busing or the right of a private plaintiffs to sue. It does prohibit the Justice Department from participating in "any sort of action to require directly or indirectly" busing beyond the school nearest a pupil's home. An exception is made for handicapped students.

Those to whom this sounds straightforward should look again. At the heart of the measure is a dilution of the law-enforcement powers of the executive branch, and what this may auger for the future is anybody's guess.

For the present, of course, the amendment has little impact Attorney General William French Smith has said he opposes busing as a method of desegregating schools. It is administration policy to forbid the pursuit of busing through administrative measures. In fact, only 3.6 per cent of children who ride buses to school are being bused for desegregation purposes, according to the U.S. Civil Rights Commission. So if the Helms-Collins rider becomes law, almost no one will notice. After all, it appears to attack a desegregation "remedy" that is unsettling at best and probably counterproductive as well.

But the issue, as former President Carter observed last fall, is that the amendment "would impose an unprecedented prohibition" on a president's ability to govern. "Busing is not the real issue," Mr. Carter said in a letter to then-Majority Leader Sen. Robert C. Byrd. "The real issue is whether it is proper for the Congress to prevent the president from carrying out his constitutional responsibility . . ."

Just so. The Helms-Collins rider, which carries with it the illusion that a firm blow has been struck against busing, invites similar legislative devices by other congresses with different goals in mind.

The 97th Congress might wish to attach to a bill an amendment affecting, say, the enforcement of the Supreme Court's school prayer decision or another "social" question. A future Congress might wish to interfere with a president's ability to conduct foreign policy. Mr. Carter saw the danger when he said, "If a president can be barred from going to the courts on this issue, a future Congress could by the same reasoning prevent a president from asking the courts to rule on the constitutionality of other matters upon which the president and the Congress disagree."

What is at stake, then, is not busing, or racial "code words," or various concepts of what constitutes "equal justice." It is, as we, have noted before, law and order. In that respect, more than any other, Collins-Helms is a disturbing precedent.

THE CHRISTIAN SCIENCE MONITOR

Boston, Mass., September 22, 1981

Ways to better desegregated schools are fortunately being found just when schools are being challenged to observe desegregation law with lessened federal support.

The latest study of desegregation, a seven-year project embracing analysis of 1,200 other studies, reaches an unsurprising, persuasive conclusion: that to make a desegregated school a good school means improving administration, discipline, curriculum, and instruction in a comprehensive approach. Communities and parents should be involved both before and after desegregation. Opportunities for desegregated extracurricular activities should be maximized. Clear and consistent expectations for student behavior should be established. There should be such follow-through as analyzing reasons for any disproportionate suspension of minority students and providing in-school alternatives to keeping students out through suspensions.

Responding to questions at a news conference, study director Willis Hawley of Vanderbilt University said the Reagan administration appears to believe that the American people want to withdraw from desegregation. But he noted that, no matter what the administration says, hundreds of school systems and millions of children will be involved under court orders and other desegregation programs. Hence the basic need to make desegregation work – and work better, in line with Dr. Hawley's statement that "desegregation seems to have positive effects on children, particularly minority children, although it has not been as successful as its advocates hoped it would be."

Can positive effects be continued and increased without firm leadership in Washington? Do the American people really want to withdraw from desegregation?

Such questions are heightened by recent events in Congress and the administration. Last week the Senate finally broke a filibuster against legislation that would restrict both the courts and Justice Department in the enforcement of desegregation law through the means of mandatory busing. The American Bar Association has understandably thrown its weight against such constitutionally dubious efforts to circumscribe the other branches of government. Many Americans who are not opposed to desegregation have reservations about the manner busing has been used in some circumstances. But the appropriate way to limit it is not through the pending limits on the courts and, in effect, the president through the Justice Department. Delay of final action on the Senate legislation should permit a full airing of the matter.

Meanwhile, the Justice Department on its own is turning away from support of strong desegregation efforts. Last month it reversed itself and approved a Chicago desegregation plan it had previously called incomplete. This month it reversed itself and supported a Washington state antibusing law, thus in effect opposing even busing plans adopted voluntarily by school boards in three cities.

Which brings us back to the challenge mentioned at the beginning, to make desegregation work with reduced federal leadership.

St. Petersburg Times

St. Petersburg, Fla., June 15, 1981

"I don't think busing is popular anywhere," said Rep. Peter W. Rodino Jr., D-N.J., chairman of the House Judiciary Committee. "But to say it's unpopular doesn't mean that it's not right."

Rodino's appeal to reason — simply because busing to desegregate schools and promote equal educational opportunity is right — did not dissuade the House of Representatives last week.

By an overwhelming margin, 265 to 122, the House voted to prohibit the Justice Department from pursuing court cases that could lead to busing for desegregation.

A SIMILAR measure appears certain to be passed this summer by the Republican-controlled Senate and eventually become law, even though it is unconstitutional.

The 14th Amendment, guaranteeing the right of equal education, cannot be abridged by a simple statute; nor can the Congress violate the separation of powers by intruding into the provinces of the judiciary and executive.

But constitutional constraints, obviously, will not impede the Reagan administration's civil rights retreat, which threatens to wipe out 27 years of progress toward social justice.

That retreat has been clearly signaled by Attorney General William French Smith, who has said that mandatory busing and quotas in civil rights disputes have been overused and that the Reagan administration will take a more "practical" approach to equal educational and occupational opportunity.

"Practical," of course, means no help from the government to gain civil rights.

In one generation, blacks have made notable advances toward equal opportunity. Their hard-won gains coincided with a federal commitment to civil rights and affirmative action, school desegregation and preferential consideration in higher education and elsewhere.

Nationally, the proportion of high school graduates going to college is now roughly the same for blacks and whites, and the average income of young black couples equals that of whites.

BUT THE LEGACY of 300 years of discrimination and deprivation remains. Blacks make up a disproportionate number of the citizens dependent on public assistance. Unemployment rates among black males and teen-agers are twice as high as among whites.

To his discredit, U.S. Rep. C. W. Bill Young, R-St. Petersburg, joined the House majority in the anti-busing vote, even though he knows first-hand the success of busing and desegregation to provide equal educational opportunity in Pinellas County.

The House bill, however, does not prohibit private individuals or groups, such as the National Association for the Advancement of Colored People (NAACP) from bringing desegregation cases. Neither does it disturb existing busing plans, such as Pinellas' desegregation court order, won by the NAACP.

As the Reagan team sets out to dismantle 27 years of desegregation progress, the battle for social justice will depend upon broad public support for a revitalized NAACP and other civil rights groups.

If America is a humane society, it will honor its obligation to equality and justice by repudiating the Reagan retreat.

ST. LOUIS POST-DISPATCH

St. Louis, Mo., December 7, 1981

One of the myths of opponents of school desegregation is that it necessarily damages the quality of education. Another answer to that has come from a seven-year Vanderbilt University study based on test scores and other data from segregated and desegregated schools across the country.

The authors told a St. Louis audience that the test scores of black students who attend desegregated schools tend to increase over the scores of those who attend all-black schools. At the same time, the scores of white students in desegregated schools remain about the same as those of students in all-white schools. The most marked improvement in test scores of blacks occurred in kindergarten and the first grade; blacks who transferred later to desegregated schools did not show as much improvement. Obviously students should be able to attend desegregated schools from the very first.

The authors backed metropolitan desegregation because, they found, volunteer plans historically have not done enough to overcome core-city segregation. St. Louis city schools could corroborate that point.

The Virginian-Pilot

Norfolk, Va., October 25, 1981

This month the Reagan administration finally revealed what it officially thinks about busing for racial balance in the schools. Not surprisingly, the administration doesn't think much of it. But what may be surprising—especially to those who once cried that Ronald Reagan would "turn back the clock on civil rights"—is that the Justice Department is not simply against busing, period.

Last week's testimony on Capitol Hill by William Bradford Reynolds, the assistant attorney general in charge of civil rights, demonstrates that the administration has thought carefully and wisely about race and the schools. Mr. Reynolds surveyed the desegregation decisions starting with Brown, pointing out that when the Supreme Court first proposed forced busing—in 1971, in Swann—it rejected the idea of a "constitutional right" to a "particular degree of racial balance" in the schools and characterized busing as only one of a number of remedial devices.

What has happened in the past 10 years, of course, is that many, including many who sit on federal benches, have come to think of desegregation only in terms of "racial balances" and have viewed forced busing as the only true remedy for a finding of racial discrimination in the schools. The whole object of Brown—equal educational opportunity—has meanwhile seemed to drop out of sight.

Today there are plenty of reasons to oppose busing, the main one of which is that, as Mr. Reynolds pointed out, it hasn't advanced equal educational opportunity. But the task, as the administration sees it, isn't simply to quit a policy that hasn't worked. "Stating our opposition to busing," said Mr. Reynolds, "is but a starting point in developing just and sound policies to achieve the central aim of . . . equal educational opportunity."

Accordingly, the Justice Department is going to bring suit against those school systems it believes are not doing enough to provide equal educational opportunity in some of its schools—and it is going to do so, to quote Mr. Reynolds, "whatever the ultimate racial composition [might be]." Evidence of such discrimination would lie in the kind of educational offerings available at a school, in the quality and experience of the teachers, and in the size, age, and condition of the school buildings.

In all this the administration is on the right track. Busing hasn't worked, but the correct response to busing isn't simply to try to stop it and then sit back as though the issues that led to busing have been resolved. That has been the approach by many disgruntled conservatives. It was evident in the recent congressional drive to forbid the Justice Department from proposing busing as a desegregation remedy; it is evident now in the several bills pending in Congress that would either outlaw busing by constitutional amendment or prevent the lower federal bench from ordering busing. It is this wholly negative emphasis—however justified is the need to end busing—that has raised questions about the sincerity of some of those who are against the practice.

Congress usefully could consider a larger application of the administration's policy for the simple reason that the Justice Department is not the only one that files desegregation suits. In cases where private parties successfully sue a school district for racial discrimination, a court still would be free to order any remedy it wants—which means it could order busing for racial balance. But if, taking seriously its obligations under the Fourteenth Amendment, Congress were to specify feasible remedies for constitutional violations by a school district, it could exclude busing from this list and fill it instead with others—including those Justice has suggested. This way, courts could not order busing, but yet progress still could be made on enhancing equal educational opportunity.

A good measure of the influence of the administration's policy on desegregation thus will lie in whether Congress decides to make it, in effect, our national policy. Nevertheless, it is crucially important that the administration has adopted the policy it has. All along what has been missing from the busing debate has been some intelligent leadership on the issue. It is about time that someone in power proposed to quit busing in such a way that still pays honors to, and seeks to further, the idea of equal educational opportunity.

'Oh, come now — you can't expect us to have the answer to everything!'

Detroit Free Press

Detroit, Mich., Febuary 7, 1982

WHEN THE Senate votes to tell the courts they can't impose busing as a solution to discrimination in the public schools, it is tearing up the Constitution, as well as retreating from the cause of racial equality. The anti-busing activity in Congress, like the granting of tax exemptions to schools that discriminate, has taken on an importance that far transcends the number of students and schools affected.

Blacks cannot help but read it as a message that Congress is more concerned with protecting whites from integration than protecting blacks from discrimination. Bigots will read it as a sign they are on the ascendancy. But Michigan's Sen. Carl Levin, who joined Sen. Donald Riegle in voting against the busing ban, pointed out the real dimensions of the harm done.

"I'm not somebody who believes that busing is the only answer, but I am someone who believes in the Constitution," Sen. Levin said. "This sets a precedent. If we say the Supreme Court can't enforce the Constitution on busing, tomorrow we'll say it can't enforce the Constitution on free speech, or on some other area."

Busing often cracked the enforced isolation of the black community, but it is no secret it has not achieved all that was hoped for. The neighborhood school was more important as an anchor — to black and white communities alike — than was always recognized in the busing decisions. And white flight in the wake of busing was swifter and greater than anticipated, damaging the dream of stable, integrated neighborhoods in the cities affected.

In the context of the times, however, busing appeared to many people to be a difficult but necessary way to reverse decades of segregation deliberately created by school boards or local governments. It is not farfetched to suppose that busing will be less frequently relied on in the future, no matter what Congress does. The courts heard testimony from social scientists in the '60s and '70s that black children were adversely affected by segregation. If the times, the evidence and the aspirations of black parents have changed in the '80s, the courts will hear that, too.

In Detroit, where busing is slowly being wound down, the court-ordered programs to improve the quality of education may prove the most durable and valuable outcome of the busing case. The point to be made is that the court had the freedom and the flexibility to devise those solutions, on the basis of the law and evidence before it — as the Constitution intended.

Already, both houses of Congress have voted to bar the Justice Department from seeking busing as a remedy in discrimination cases. There is no question that is an undesirable constraint on government lawyers. But an amendment to curb the courts is far worse in its constitutional and practical implications. Sen. Lowell Weicker's planned filibuster is unlikely to prevent final passage by the Senate. But in the House, even those members who dislike busing should see the danger in assaulting the independence of the courts, and refuse to concur.

THE INDIANAPOLIS STAR
Indianapolis, Ind., Febuary 14, 1982

At least a dozen surveys around the nation have weighed the effects of court-ordered racial balance busing of school pupils, and the net of evidence is that it has not attained its stated goal of bettering educational skills.

This seems to justify congressional efforts to limit busing. The Senate has voted 58 to 38 for legislation that would prohibit federal judges who are handling desegregation cases from ordering busing for students who live more than five miles or 15 minutes from their schools.

A study of desegregation in Indianapolis high schools concluded that racial mixing does not have a significant effect on academic performance. Martin Patchen, a sociology professor at Purdue University, said in a new book, "Maybe we've spent a little too much time trying to use racial desegregation as a tool for improving academic performance."

Student achievement, he said, appears to be related closely to the expectations of school administrators and teachers and not to the racial composition of classes, he wrote. He suggested desegregation could be better justified for promoting better understanding and harmony between the races—social benefits.

His conclusions appear in "Black-White Contact in Schools: Its Social and Academic Effects." It is based on a study of about 4,000 high school pupils from 1970 to 1972 when Crispus Attucks and later the other Indianapolis high schools were being desegregated.

A major survey involving studies of some 5,000 pupils in grades one through 12 in six cities, testing educational results in pupils who were bused against those in pupils who were not, was conducted by David Armour, an associate professor of sociology at Harvard and former researcher for the Civil Rights Commission.

"None of the studies," he wrote, "was able to demonstrate conclusively that integration has had an effect on academic achievement as measured by standardized tests."

He also found that "pupils who were bused developed lower educational aspirations and a higher degree of racial antagonism than did those who weren't."

To these findings newer data was added in a later study by Jeffrey Leech of the Indiana University Law School who reported: "In every city studied, busing failed to reduce the gap between black and white achievement."

He continued: "In fact, most cities reported that the achievement gap had grown even larger after busing. Scholars who have reviewed the evidence . . . have concluded that busing has little if any effect on the academic achievement of either black or white children."

Thus, he wrote, "sociological evidence fails to confirm a basic premise underlying the rationale for court-ordered busing: i.e., that it will positively affect the academic performance of minority children."

Other factors of court-ordered busing are the immense cost, long-drawn-out legal proceedings, disruption of school systems and tremendous consumption of time.

The untold hundreds of millions of dollars and pupil-hours consumed by long-distance busing would be better spent on direct improvement of the quality of education and fitting young Americans for productive careers. The legislation pending in Congress might make this possible.

DESERET NEWS
Salt Lake City, Utah, March 8, 1982

AKRON BEACON JOURNAL
Akron, Ohio, March 5, 1982

JESSE HELMS, R-N. C., Bennett Johnston, D-La., and 55 of their Senate colleagues won their school busing battle this week, but they have not yet won the war.

Nor have they won any glory for themselves in their challenge to the Constitution and the courts.

The honor goes to Sen. Lowell P. Weicker Jr., R-Conn., perhaps more than any of the other 36 senators who joined him in a losing vote against a bill which, if finally approved by the Congress, would virtually end busing of school pupils to eliminate racial segregation in the schools.

It would prohibit federal judges from ordering students to be transported to schools more than 15 minutes or five miles from home for purposes of desegregation. It would prevent the Justice Department from bringing legal action that could lead to court-ordered busing for desegregation. And it would allow old busing cases to be reopened.

Sens. Helms and Johnston apparently have no problem with busing more than 15 minutes or five miles for religious or academic purposes so long as that does not make skin color a factor in the decision.

And they apparently are untroubled by the recasting of judicial and legislative roles rooted in the Constitution that their proposals would accomplish.

But it just may be that the power of the courts they are challenging will prove their undoing — assuming that House and Senate conferees can agree on a final version of the bill. The House earlier passed a Justice Department authorization bill with less-sweeping anti-busing provisions. It would prohibit the Justice Department from spending funds for any action to require busing beyond the school nearest a pupil's home for purposes of desegregating schools.

Against odds that were discouraging almost from the start, Sen. Weicker fought and filibustered from last June to last week to halt a vote. He deserves the appreciation of all those, black and white, who struggled so long to reach the level of school desegregation that has been achieved.

By itself, busing cannot make scholars and achievers of children. But if it offers no more than equal access to educational opportunities pupils must have to learn and achieve, it should not be denied.

Sen. Weicker understands that. It is sad that people like Sens. Helms and Johnston refuse to understand.

Unless a few die-hards somehow manage to thwart it, Congress seems to be on the verge of sending the federal courts an important message.

The message is that, despite its good intentions, mandatory busing as a means of achieving racial balance in the schools hasn't worked and should largely be scrapped.

That conclusion reflects the sentiments not just of a growing number of congressmen but of the public itself, including a majority of black school patrons.

Last week the Senate sent the House of Representatives the toughest anti-busing legislation ever approved. The bill would prevent federal courts from ordering students to be bused to any school more than five miles or 15 minutes from their homes. It also would forbid the Justice Department from seeking mandatory busing as a remedy to illegal racial discrimination in the schools. Though a similar measure previously passed the House, some observers warn the new bill could be held up in a House judiciary subcommittee.

Is the Senate's action, then, a vote in favor of discrimination, a vote to keep poor blacks concentrated in the most impoverished and worst schools?

If it is, that must come as a surprise to the thousands of blacks who voted to overturn mandatory busing in Los Angeles, the nation's second largest public school district. It must also come as a surprise to the majority of blacks who have told pollsters over the years they do not favor busing.

That sentiment is certainly understandable. No convincing evidence has yet been produced to show that busing helps black children as a group. Instead, busing diverts large sums of money from the business of teaching, makes it harder for students to participate in after-school activities, makes involvement of parents more difficult, and adds to disciplinary problems. That adds up to a powerful case for House passage of the Senate anti-busing bill.

Because of these problems, plenty of highly respected authorities who once supported busing now oppose it. One of them is Norman Cousins, who observes of mandatory school busing:

"There is no disgrace in having failed in an important social enterprise. The only disgrace is persisting with failure because we have made commitments without regard to the need for keeping an open mind."

"WHAT DO YOU MEAN **STOP**?! ARE YOU TRYING TO PUSH ME AROUND? ARE YOU TRYING TO ABUSE YOUR AUTHORITY?"

The San Diego Union
San Diego, Calif., July 3, 1982

The U.S. Supreme Court decision upholding Proposition 1 seems to say the last word on court-ordered busing to desegregate schools in California. The court finds no conflict with the U.S. Constitution in the anti-busing language put into our state constitution by voters in 1979.

Proposition 1 declares that California courts must follow federal court policy in ordering busing to integrate schools. In other words, mandatory busing can be employed only in communities where segregation has resulted from a deliberate act of state or local officials.

Busing cannot be required, as the California Supreme Court once ordered, in cases where segregation resulted from a concentration of whites and minorities in different neighborhoods.

Neither Proposition 1 nor the U.S. Supreme Court decision has a direct effect on the voluntary integration program in San Diego. The Carlin case here did not allege that white and minority children were deliberately segregated in our schools. Justice Lewis F. Powell, Jr. could have been speaking to San Diego when he wrote in his majority opinion:

"The state courts of California continue to have an obligation under state law to order segregated school districts to use voluntary desegregation techniques, whether or not there has been a finding of intentional segregation.

"The school districts themselves retain a state law obligation to take reasonably feasible steps to desegregate, and they remain free to adopt reassignment and busing plans to effectuate desegregation."

That leaves San Diego where it has been all along — with a legal and moral obligation to overcome any inequalities in educational opportunity that can be traced to racial isolation in some of our schools. Our voluntary integration programs have made measurable progress in that direction, and must continue to do so.

ARKANSAS DEMOCRAT
Little Rock, Ark., July 5, 1982

The Supreme Court has declared in two separate opinions that the people of a state can tell their own courts to limit racial-balance busing, but can't tell them not to bus at all. The first ruling comes out of a California case and the other out of a Washington state case. You might wonder what the Supreme Court's doing setting limits on what people can tell their courts to do.

Well, since the Supreme Court has made busing into a "constitutional right" — and since state courts, like federal courts, are empowered to rule on constitutional questions — the court can decide the constitutionality of what state citizens tell their state courts to do or not to do. Clear?

No. If a state court's constitutional power to rule on busing involves the power to prescribe remedies appropriate to a given case, how could California's "Proposition One," limit the busing remedies its courts can hand down? And if Californians can limit busing, then why can't Washingtonians go all the way and say, no busing at all? The power to prescribe busing remedies is either absolute or it is nothing.

Our own perverse feeling is that state citizens should be able to tell their courts to stay out of any constitutional field they care to specify — on grounds that the federal courts are doing enough mischief in that quarter and having trouble enough of their own interpreting what the ruling Supreme Court's decisions in the field mean.

An even better reason for posting fields like busing against state-court entry is that state-court rulings are subject to challenge in federal courts. That means nothing decided is certain to stand.

Nothing illustrates that fact better than the Supreme Court's own rulings in the California and Washington cases. These contradictory opinions ought to be proof enough that the high court itself doesn't have any settled opinion on the power of state courts to bus. The high court appears to be saying, leave it to us feds. We may not know our own minds but we do have the final say.

The Seattle Times
Seattle, Wash., July 1, 1982

YESTERDAY'S United States Supreme Court decision invalidating this state's Initiative 350 was welcome on two counts:

First, the 5-to-4 opinion reaffirmed the proposition that no law (in this instance a voter-approved initiative to block Seattle schools' desegregation busing) can make distinctions according to race.

Second, it reinforced the principle that the judiciary has the right of independent judgment on legislative acts regardless of popular sentiment.

The nation's highest court quickly perceived the principal shortcoming in Initiative 350, one that had been identified in lower-court decisions earlier: The only thing singled out for prohibition was busing for racial balance. Under the measure approved by Washington voters in 1978, mandatory busing could be used for any purpose unrelated to race.

The practical effect of the decision is to preserve Seattle's desegregation program, leaving to Seattle school directors and their counterparts in other districts the flexibility to devise desegregation remedies at the local level.

Seattle had started its busing program four years ago on its own volition, the first district in the country to do so without a court order.

The decision came at an opportune time for those concerned over recent shifts in attitudes on racial issues, such as the Justice Department's shocking policy switch last year away from legal actions against segregated schools.

Anti-busing forces now will look more than ever to Congress for relief — perhaps a constitutional amendment to permit racial distinctions, or statutes designed to end-run court decisions.

Supporters of the initiative have contended that the court should have heeded the measure's heavy, 2-to-1 margin of voter approval, saying in effect that the public's wishes should prevail regardless of constitutional questions.

But the record is full of instances where legislative statutes and popular initiatives have been struck down because of constitutional problems. A fresh example was this week's lower-court ruling in Tacoma against Initiative 394, to require voter approval of spending for nuclear energy plants.

If the courts ever began rendering decisions not according to the Constitution, but to the ballot box, the stage would be set for a dangerous unsettling of the delicate balance of powers within the American system.

The Pittsburgh
PRESS
Pittsburg, Penn., July 9, 1982

It isn't easy to sort out what the U.S. Supreme Court added to or subtracted from the school-busing controversy in its two latest decisions on this subject.

In one case, the court said the voters of California could stop a Los Angeles busing program.

In another, it said the voters of the state of Washington could not stop a Seattle busing program.

★ ★ ★

The California case was pretty clear-cut.

A state court there had ordered Los Angeles to undertake massive busing to achieve better racial balance in its schools — even though there had been no finding that local school authorities had intentionally discriminated against minorities.

The Supreme Court ruled, by a vote of 8 to 1, that the state-court order went beyond desegregation requirements of the U.S. Constitution.

Therefore, it held California voters had a right to restrain their state courts by amending the California constitution to bar court-ordered busing beyond that required by the U.S. Constitution.

The Washington case was more complicated.

There, the Seattle school board thought it should have a better racial balance in schools and voluntarily instituted a busing program to achieve it.

Voters throughout the state tried to overturn that program by approving an initiative which barred local school boards from transporting students beyond neighborhood schools except for health, safety or special-education needs.

The Supreme Court ruled, in a 5-to-4 decision, that the voters had created an unconstitutional discriminatory situation by prohibiting local boards from using busing to achieve racial balance but allowing them to bus for a variety of other purposes.

★ ★ ★

What the two cases seem to boil down to is this:

✓ The authority of courts to impose busing programs on localities has been somewhat diminished.

✓ The authority of local school boards to run schools as they see fit has been somewhat enhanced.

Most folks won't find fault with that.

THE TENNESSEAN
Nashville, Tenn., January 26, 1983

THE U.S. Supreme Court's refusal to review the Nashville school desegregation case presents the school board with the duty of coming up with a new plan that will meet constitutional requirements.

The high court's action leaves in place the U.S. 6th Circuit Court of Appeals decision last summer overturning a neighborhood schools plan approved by District Judge Thomas Wiseman for grades kindergarten through four. The Court of Appeals held that the plan would resegregate the system.

The decision said the District Court's choice of 15% members of either race as a minimum presence was unacceptable because it would leave 85% white or 85% black in some schools. The court said the composition of 68% white-32% black would be an appropriate place to start to obtain a new ratio.

The "education components" of Judge Wiseman's plan — remedial programs for children performing below the average for the system, or for those "where the majority of a school's population is made up largely of socio-economically deprived children"; the use of West End Junior High School as a magnet school, and an Afro-American studies program — were upheld by the appellate court and apparently remain in the plan.

However, board Chairman Kent Weeks said these steps were to be funded by savings realized through reduced busing under Judge Wiseman's plan and that these educational components may

now have to be re-examined.

The Supreme Court didn't say why it would not hear the Nashville case, but there may be a clue in the appeals court decision. "This much delayed school desegregation case...offers no new legal issues and can and must be decided by this court on the basis of final decisions of the United States Supreme Court," said that decision, written by Chief Judge George Edwards.

Thus, the Supreme Court may have agreed with the 6th Circuit Court of Appeals that it had already decided all substantive matters and that no new legal issues remained to be considered.

Metro's desegregation plans have been hashed and rehashed in the courts for many years, yet desegregation still has not been extended countywide. In the words of the Court of Appeals, "It...is clear that when the first 'comprehensive and potentially effective desegregation order' was entered in this case in 1971, the existing racial separation in the Nashville schools had resulted from de jure segregation. And despite the 1971 plan's potential, the record establishes and the District Court found that desegregation in the Nashville schools has never been achieved. Thus the effects of state imposed segregation have yet to be eradicated."

The Supreme Court's refusal to review the case seems to be the courts' final word in the matter and all that remains to be done is carry out the direc-

tive to desegregate Metro schools countywide. The decision presents the newly-elected board with its first crisis, but it should be nothing insuperable.

Nashville now has an elected school board, and many in the community have feared that some of its members might resort to demagoguery over the difficult effect of busing. It is hoped this board won't waste its time on useless rhetoric but will do its best to make Nashville's schools better in the face of the challenge ahead.

The board has pledged to act in good faith to carry out its duty under the law. Chairman Weeks, in commenting on the high court's action, said "...this board will meet its legal and educational responsibilities to the community. Our central business is the education of our young children."

No decision has been made, as to when a new plan will be ready. Some have estimated it will not be before the fall of 1984. However, it is likely the courts will have a say in that. It is hoped the plan can be put into effect in a way that will not disrupt the school system and involve it in massive planning at the last minute.

Any plan the board comes up with and the courts approve will likely involve more busing than is currently the case. How much additional money this will take remains to be seen. Whatever the board decides it will have to do to abide by the courts' orders, it will need the understanding and cooperation of the community, the council and other elected officials.

The Dallas Morning News
Dallas, Texas, January 29, 1983

The U.S. Supreme Court, in refusing to hear an appeal of a school-busing ruling, has again thwarted the will of the administration and the majority of the American people. The high court let stand a decision that means students in kindergarten through fourth grade have to be bused across Nashville, Tenn.

The high court's refusal to hear this case indicates that it may implicitly approve of the standard used by the appeals court, i.e., that the racial balance should approximate that of the district's population.

This is hardly good news to the Dallas School Board, which has appealed a ruling by Judge Barefoot Sanders.

There is ample evidence that, by helping to spur white flight from the central cities and into private schools, busing has actually increased segregation, the problem it was said to be a remedy for.

The only encouraging thing is that there are those in the Justice Department who know all this, and at long last are at least trying to minimize busing's ravages.

St. Louis Globe-Democrat
St. Louis, Mo., January 27, 1983

The U.S. Supreme Court may have a busy schedule but this can't excuse its refusal of the Justice Department's request to review using court-ordered busing to desegregate schools in Nashville, Tenn.

This was an opportunity for the Supreme Court to provide important guidance to the nation on a highly controversial issue. But the justices passed without even commenting on the case.

The Justice Department intervened in the Nashville case in November when it filed a friend-of-the-court brief asking the Supreme Court to review the case.

The administration had supported the ruling by a federal district judge in May 1980 that would have prevented the Nashville district from busing any pupil below the fifth grade for purposes of desegregation. The judge said the city's 10-year-old school desegregation plan had been undermined by white flight from the Nashville school system. He ordered that the money being used for busing be used instead to improve education for minority children.

The district judge's ruling was overturned by the 6th U.S. Circuit Court of Appeals in Cincinnati, which ordered him to

desegregate the younger grades, saying it was a "fundamental error" to allow neighborhood schools where there was a history of segregation.

The overwhelming majority of Americans — more than 75 percent according to most polls — oppose mandatory busing of school children in an attempt to combat segregation. Poor results in Nashville, in St. Louis and in cities all over the country have intensified heavy opposition to the undemocratic practice of ordering school systems to bus young children long distances to achieve arbitrary racial quotas.

Justices on the Supreme Court should feel a duty to accept a case on this important issue. They ought to render a definitive opinion rather than refuse to hear the appeal. By ducking out, the high court indicates it doesn't have the stomach to take on tough cases.

Refusal to accept responsibility has caused demands for other remedies, such as cutting off funds for Justice Department efforts to enforce busing orders, and legislation prohibiting busing beyond the neighborhood school as part of a court-ordered desegration plan.

The Union Leader

Manchester, N.H., January 27, 1983

Assistant Attorney General William Bradford Reynolds, the Justice Department's head civil rights enforcer, commenting on the U.S. Supreme Court's rejection of a challenge to the school busing plan in Nashville, Tennessee:

"(It) in no way indicates that the legal issue of mandatory busing is closed. It is not unusual for the Supreme Court to leave the development of this area of the law to lower federal courts."

Tommyrot! The court decision constitutes a stunning defeat not only for the Reagan administration, which had taken a strong position against forced busing and urged the court to use the case to reassess its controversial 1971 ruling, but also for every realist who recognizes that forced busing has been a miserable failure. It has harmed educational standards. It has more often than not increased racial tensions. It has wasted taxpayers' money. It has caused the flight of white children to private schools or to public schools outside forced busing areas. And it has not helped black children academically.

In Nashville, the result of court-ordered, cross-town busing has been "white flight" and the busing of black inner-city children.

Even as the court was turning its back on reality, a study commissioned by the Joint Center for Political Studies in Washington was pointing out that racial segregation in the nation's public schools has increased significantly over the past 15 years. In the report on trends in the 50 largest urban districts and 44 metropolitan areas including suburbs, it is revealed that two-thirds of the students in the 10 largest school districts in 1980 belonged to minorities —a ratio that is rising rapidly. Only in districts, mostly in the South, where there has been extensive court-ordered busing, has there been increased integration. But, generally, minority populations rose and white populations decreased in city schools, the report declares, turning them into "minority institutions."

The report's recommendation? Of course! More forced busing!

That "logic," it appears, has great appeal to the U.S. Supreme Court.

THE ATLANTA CONSTITUTION

Atlanta, Ga., January 29, 1983

case, it in effect upheld a lower-court finding that the school board still has a duty "to eliminate from the public schools all vestiges of state-imposed segregation." It also rebuffed administration arguments for consideration of the "educational, social and economic cost of busing" including "white flight."

But the increasingly conservative high court did so without comment, and without the participation of Thurgood Marshall, the only black justice, leading to speculation of a close vote. While four votes are sufficient to schedule a case for argument, a 4-to-4 decision automatically affirms a lower-court ruling.

Civil-rights advocates are troubled by evidence that racial segregation is on the rise in the nation's schools, amid the cooling of desegregation efforts under Reagan.

A report urging the administration to halt the "aggressive ostracism" of minority children in schools was released this week by the Joint Center for Political Studies, which found no improvement since 1968 in cities using voluntary desegregation programs. Minority populations rose and white populations decreased nationwide in city schools, which author Gary Orfield said are turning into "minority institutions."

The school districts that made the most progress in the past 15 years had extensive court-ordered busing programs that integrated suburban and city children, most of them in the South, the report said.

Tennessee civil-rights lawyer Avon Williams Jr. said after the Supreme Court acted Monday that he thought "all right-thinking people were or should have been shocked that the Justice Department, for the first time in several decades, intervened on the side of segregation and discrimination."

Unhappily, it promises to be the first of many such cases; in this, as in other matters, the administration seems senselessly determined to stay the course.

President Reagan didn't get his way in Nashville. The U.S. Supreme Court refused this week to hear a challenge to court-ordered school busing there, letting stand a 1971 plan for achieving racial balance amid cheers from civil-rights advocates.

But the cheering is premature. It's only a temporary setback for Reagan and Justice Department officials, who have lately intensified their campaign to wipe out mandatory busing as an instrument of desegregation.

A reopening of the Nashville case would have provided the arena they've been seeking since last September, when Assistant Attorney General William Bradford Reynolds infuriated civil-rights advocates by inviting school boards seeking to "modify" busing plans that are "not working" to contact him. But he considers the busing issue "in no way . . . closed" by the decision, he said, and "will not hesitate" to approach the Supreme Court again, "in an appropriate case."

The court's degree of commitment to busing as a means of achieving balance is also uncertain. In refusing to reopen the Nashville

Arkansas Gazette.

Little Rock, Ark., January 26, 1983

Certain encouragement may be found in a decision by the United States Supreme Court this week that the Reagan administration will not be allowed to scrap busing as a tool for school desegregation and substitute instead all-voluntary methods of desegregation.

The Supreme Court's ruling came without dissent in a case originating in Nashville. The justices left intact a lower court ruling that the law of the land still requires school officials to do everything possible — including busing — to achieve "the greatest degree of actual desegregation."

★ ★ ★

In November, the Reagan Justice Department had filed a "friend-of-the-court" brief in the Nashville case, urging an abandonment of court-ordered busing when its "educational, social and economic costs" are so high as to be "unacceptable."

The director of the department's civil rights division, William Bradford Reynolds, naturally makes the least of the Supreme Court's decision, contending that the decision "in no way indicates that the issue of mandatory busing is closed." The battle, in the administration plan, will be fought in the lower federal courts, where the administration will press for acceptance of voluntary methods as alternatives to court-ordered busing. The Supreme Court's ruling in the Nashville case, however, is strong indication that it is not about to allow the abandonment of busing as one tool to bring about the objective of desegregated educational opportunity.

It is of related interest that on the day after the Supreme Court ruled, the results of a study commissioned by the House Judiciary subcommittee on civil and constitutional rights offered some revealing insights into the effectiveness of voluntary desegregation methods of the sort now being promoted by the Reagan administration. The Joint Center for Political Studies, which examined the period from 1968 to 1980, found not only that racial segregation in the schools has increased significantly in this period but also that in cities trying voluntary desegregation of the kind the Reagan administration supports no improvement has been made toward integration. Even more to the point: School districts making the most progress in the period used court-ordered busing programs that integrated suburban and city children, most of them, it turns out, in the South.

The report's author, Gary Orfield, a political science professor at the University of Chicago, in addition identifies what would seem to be a direct conflict with the administration position: "We are being told now that desegregation efforts have not worked, so they are taking away what we have now * * * when what [we] really need is more. The problems related to segregation are getting worse. We just cannot continue to become more separate and more unequal."

★ ★ ★

Desegregation of schools in far too many communities will never be accomplished through purely "voluntary" efforts. The United States Supreme Court knows it and recognizes it. Despite its statements, the Reagan administration has to know the truth as well, but for reasons of its own denies the reality, choosing as it does to support justice for some but not for all

The Providence Journal

Providence, R.I., January 12, 1983

The eight-year experiment of running Boston's public school system out of a federal courtroom, immune to public accountability, has entered the final stage. Authority for monitoring compliance with court orders has been transferred from U.S. District Judge W. Arthur Garrity Jr. to the state Board of Education and Commissioner John L. Lawrence.

While final restoration of control by elected officials is still two years away, the curtain is starting to come down and the conclusion has to be reached, even by former supporters of the court's takeover, that the effort to advance desegregation was less than successful.

Like other cities across the country, Boston has experienced a significant drop in school enrollment. In 1974 when the court took over the system's day-to-day operation, the school population was 95,000. Today it is 57,200. The crucial factor, however, is not so much numbers of students as it is racial makeup of the student body. Eight years ago whites represented 70 percent of the students; today the figure is about 30 percent. At least some of that change (no one knows how much) has to be attributed to "white flight" to private and parochial schools and the suburbs.

Judge Garrity's takeover was never a desirable option. It was a last resort which he tried diligently to avoid. When the National Association for the Advancement of Colored People filed suit in behalf of a group of black parents in 1972, both the state Board of Education and the Boston School Committee had demonstrated clearly their intention to resist desegregation. With respect to the historic 1954 Supreme Court decision declaring unconstitutional so-called separate but equal school facilities for blacks and whites, both bodies were unmoved. The status quo of one of the nation's most segregated school systems was vigorously protected. Racial hostility seethed.

Judge Garrity saw it as his duty to uphold the Constitution with no feasible alternatives left other than to oversee the enforcement of his own orders. In terms of desegregation, education and the expenditure of tax revenues for transportation and administration, experience has shown that the effort in general failed.

That said, the focus now shifts to Chicago where a federal district court has approved a voluntary "desegregation" plan that eschews busing, strengthens the financing of 45 all black schools and reflects a contentment with educational enrichment as opposed to desegregation per se. "The case does not establish the principle that busing is an inappropriate remedy," said the special counsel to the Chicago Board of Education. What it does, is show that a plan that "maximizes desegregation" may be acceptable even though it uses only voluntary means.

Judge Milton I. Shadur who approved the voluntary plan based his decision on a fear that mandatory assignments and busing might "accelerate resegregation". In light of the Boston experience, it will be interesting to see whether in the first instance the flexible approach passes muster during higher judicial review given the Supreme Court's opposition to the principle of separate but equal, and in the second proves any more effective at equalizing the educational opportunities of all students regardless of race or color.

Newsday

Long Island, N.Y., March 12, 1983

There seems to be something to suit almost every taste in the desegregation agreement that St. Louis-area school districts reached recently:

● The agreement involves not only St. Louis schools but those of 22 suburban districts as well. That's promising; according to a recent integration study, interdistrict busing is by far the most effective way to desegregate schools.

● Although the St. Louis agreement depends on substantial numbers of transfers, students will change schools voluntarily. That means "forced" busing, which has been so heavily opposed, will not be necessary.

● The plan depends on superior "magnet" schools to attract suburban whites to city schools that are predominantly black. That should appeal to the Reagan administration, which has stressed the importance of improving schools with large minority student bodies.

What isn't clear yet, however, is whether the plan will work. It's not even very ambitious: Although 37 per cent of the region's students are black, suburban schools will be required to achieve only 15 per cent minority attendance.

In one important way, though, the St. Louis solution is encouraging: It's the first multidistrict integration plan entered into without a direct court order. Faced with the probability that a court would impose a desegregation plan, the 23 districts in the area came up with their own solution, thus eliminating the need for one to be mandated.

Meanwhile, the Reagan administration remains complacent about school segregation. It is so strongly opposed to busing that it joined the Nashville, Tenn., school board's effort to overturn a busing plan there. The U.S. Supreme Court rejected that appeal, as it should have.

However undesirable busing's side effects may be, it's often still the only effective method of achieving integration.

Long Island, N.Y., October 1, 1983

When federal officials agreed to Chicago's voluntary school desegregation plan in 1980, they pledged a real effort to help pay its costs. At the time, Washington had a ready way to do that: The Emergency School Aid Act provided money to help school districts carry out integration programs.

But in 1981, at the urging of the Reagan administration, Congress consolidated emergency aid and about two dozen other school-assistance programs into a single block grant, and gave state governments the job of distributing the money.

One result is that large urban school districts that must carry out costly desegregation orders or agreements are getting much less than they did before. That's a regrettable outcome, which a bill the House passed in June would help remedy. We hope the Senate passes a similar bill.

In most cases, districts with desegregation plans are belatedly working to live up to the constitutional requirement that all citizens be treated equally. It's important that Washington provide not only the motivation for recalcitrant school boards to act, but the resources to make sure the constitutional requirement is adequately met.

The House bill would authorize spending as much as $100 million a year for three years to help fund a variety of desegregation projects. To avoid controversy, the funds could not be used to finance busing programs.

As things stand now, the block-grant program is being used for such purposes as buying computers and improving school libraries. Those are surely worthwhile, but they lack the constitutional imperative of desegregation. When federal budgets are as tight as they are these days, combating segregation ought to be near the top of the list of Washington's education priorities.

ST. LOUIS POST-DISPATCH

St. Louis, Mo., September 15, 1983

When lawyers for opposing sides each claim to be pleased by a court's ruling, the public has good reason to be confused by what has transpired. Such is the case with the clutch of rulings handed down by the 8th U.S. Circuit Court of Appeals on the St. Louis school desegregation plan.

In such circumstances, the best question to ask is usually the most fundamental one. Hence, the first point to address is whether the appellate judges have placed the precedent-setting desegregation program on hold — or, worse, overturned it. The answer here is a reassuring No.

As the court noted unanimously, in rebuffing Attorney General Ashcroft's assertion that the implementation of the desegregation program would do irreparable damage to the state, to halt the transfers of students now would disrupt the lives of thousands of students and teachers. There is no reason to consider doing that until the court has had an opportunity to reflect upon the entire desegregation case, which it will take up in November.

Mr. Ashcroft and other enemies of the desegregation plan approved by U.S. District Judge William Hungate are encouraged by two components of the appellate decision: the temporary halting of further interdistrict transfers and the instruction to Judge Hungate to hold off raising city taxes. This first is inconsequential, inasmuch as it will have no effect on this year's desegregation efforts. What happens next will depend upon the result of the appellate court's full review.

As to the leash on Judge Hungate, the appellate order suggests that the court may well be taken aback by the astronomical estimates that Mr. Ashcroft and other officials have placed on the desegregation plan and is determined to study the financing problems in detail before permitting the district court to become involved in a tax-raising order that would set off a firestorm of public protest. Although the interdistrict remedy to segregation is essentially a creature of the appellate court, that body has not yet reviewed the particulars of Judge Hungate's pioneering solution. The question of a judicial order to increase taxes warrants careful appellate consideration.

Moreover, the green light that the 8th Circuit gave the desegregation program for this school year makes it seem unlikely that the major elements of the Hungate plan will be dismantled. St. Louis school children have been found to have suffered a constitutional injury and that wrong cannot be allowed to be perpetuated. One way or another adequate financing for desegregation must be assured. In this regard, it is significant that Judge Hungate was upheld in his order to use for desegregation purposes money from the Proposition C sales tax that otherwise would have gone to roll back property taxes.

The appeals court may well be hoping to be taken off the tax hook by initiatives from the city and state. Gov. Bond has reversed himself and now proposes new state taxes, revenue from which would go for desegregation. The St. Louis Board of Education will place a $63.5 million bond issue before the voters in November. It will be a difficult, uphill fight for both Mr. Bond and the board, for neither money-raising scheme will be popular. Yet if integration is to proceed, what alternative is there?

The answer, of course, is the courts. The appellate ruling is an understandable statement that the 8th Circuit would prefer to see other possibilities exhausted before deciding whether to cross that bridge.

The Washington Post
Times Herald

Washington, D.C., June 21, 1983

ST. LOUIS is your classic hard-case school desegregation city: 80 percent of its school population is black and most of the suburban school districts are white. After years of litigation over how best to integrate schools in the area, a settlement has been proposed to the federal court. The NAACP and the city school board have signed the proposal as have almost two dozen suburban school districts. The objective of the plan is to encourage the voluntary transfer of black students from the inner city to suburban schools and to provide incentives for white students to go to special magnet schools in the city. Suburban schools have agreed to increase black enrollment by 15 percent or to a total of 25 percent, whichever is less, during the next five years. For their part, the city schools would provide enriched programs, new specialty schools, creative early-education classes and other facilities designed both to attract suburban youngsters and to improve those city schools that will probably remain predominantly black. The key to the agreement is providing incentives that will lead to *voluntary* interdistrict transfers.

All this will cost money, of course. The parties to the agreement propose that the state of Missouri redistribute state aid and pay all transportation costs and that the city of St. Louis raise school taxes. Both state and city governments have thus far refused to accept this aspect of the settlement. But neither of the alternatives to a voluntary plan —continued racial segregation or mandatory court-ordered busing—is really practical.

If the St. Louis proposal is adopted and put into effect, other cities will have a chance to see if imaginative voluntary programs will work. Spending this money makes sense. In the long run the construction of such a useful model would be far less costly —financially, emotionally and socially—than continuing the bitter and divisive struggle over school desegregation.

Roanoke Times & World-News

Roanoke, Va., May 17, 1983

JESSE JACKSON is heir to Martin Luther King Jr.'s mantle as the premier orator of the civil-rights movement. Last Friday, he brought a message of rhyme and rhythm to Norfolk — and maybe some reason, too.

He came to oppose the city's proposal to eliminate busing as a means to assure racial balance in its elementary schools. In an eloquent speech following a march on Norfolk City Hall, he declared: "We want the mayor and council to know we would rather talk than walk, but that we will walk until we can talk." In vintage Jacksonian cadence, he declared that blacks are "going to go from the slum house and the outhouse to the courthouse, the statehouse and the White House." Jackson is contemplating a run for the presidency.

Jackson's remarks were at times off base, but they were delivered with a good humor that seemed not to exacerbate the divisions that now plague the city over the busing issue. His talk with Mayor Vincent Thomas at Norfolk International Airport seems to have laid the groundwork for a dialogue between black and white leaders of the city. It's a little late in coming, but it's needed.

Norfolk's schools began massive cross-busing in 1970. In 1975, federal courts declared that the city had achieved a "unitary" school system, meaning that it had eliminated *de jure* segregation — segregation under the law.

In the years since busing was introduced, the school population has gone from 60 percent white to 60 percent black. Norfolk leaders feared that when the black school population reached 60 percent, the tipping point would be reached and the city's schools would resegregate through the out-migration of white families.

The School Board proposed a plan that, on its face, seems reasonable. It would discontinue busing in the city's 35 elementary schools and assign children to schools closest to their neighborhoods. That would leave 10 schools with more than 95 percent black majorities. Eighteen would have 70 percent majorities of one race or the other. But a child who found himself in a school with more than a 70 percent majority of his own race could transfer to another school. Busing to high schools and junior high schools would continue.

The plan had some support in the black community. One of the three black members of the seven-member school board voted in favor of it. Then the leadership pulled a boner.

The school board decided to test the legality of its "unbusing" plan in federal court. It did so by filing suit against four people who had spoken against the plan at a public hearing. This was not a "friendly" test case. The four defendants were unwilling litigants.

The effect on the black community was devastating. Even though the suit has since been withdrawn, the black community's historical distrust for the white leadership has become deeper.

That is unfortunate. Norfolk's white leadership has generally shown a sincere concern for the interests of the minority race. That concern, though, has frequently been manifested through an attitude of *noblesse oblige*. Grass-roots black leaders had little involvement in policy formation.

After conferring with Jackson, Mayor Thomas announced that he was "prepared to convene white and black leaders in Norfolk to discuss the issues at large."

The unbusing plan may already be fatally wounded, but long-range race relations need not be. It's time for the two sides to talk, equals to equals. Norfolk's lesson should not be lost on other cities with problems stemming from racial distrust.

The Miami Herald
Miami, Fla., January 30, 1 1984

BECAUSE the Reagan Administration rejects many traditional civil-rights approaches to resolving social problems, it is obliged to produce solutions of its own. One idea that bodes well for easing school segregation is greater use of magnet schools.

The Justice Department announced such a plan the other day calling it a "blueprint for school desegregation in the future." That characterization is debatable, but magnet schools demonstrably offer good potential for improving the racial complexion in the nation's schools.

The Administration plan, being implemented under a consent decree, calls for voluntary attendance at four magnet schools in Bakersfield, Calif. Under the magnet-school idea, schools in minority communities are infused with desirable programs, special classes, and top faculty in order to attract a broader spectrum of students.

Bakersfield is a small school district, with only 18,194 students. Success there would not necessarily mean that magnet schools will work elsewhere, particularly in large urban communities where isolation is greater and resistance more entrenched.

The lure of magnet schools, however, is that first-rate schools strategically located will draw a better mix of students. In some cities, magnet schools are tremendously successful. Model magnet schools function in St. Petersburg, Boston, Milwaukee, and San Diego.

The Administration hopes that magnet schools will work so well that court-ordered busing to achieve racial balance may not be necessary. That has not been so in Boston, even at magnet schools. The Boston school district consequently has linked its magnet schools with mandatory busing.

Unfortunately, the Administration repudiates busing under any circumstances. Despite rigidity, the Administration's revival of the magnet-school concept is encouraging. Government is duty-bound to do more than say what it is against; it also must assert what it is for.

Magnet schools may not be the full answer to segregated schools, but they hold promise. If successful in other districts — Dade County, for instance, should reconsider the idea — magnet schools will improve the racial and ethnic balance in schools. More important, though, they would promote values of racial tolerance that the United States steadfastly should foster.

Richmond Times-Dispatch
Richmond, Va., February 1, 1984

"A model for the desegregation of schools in the future" is the way William Bradford Reynolds described the consent decree the Justice Department and the Bakersfield, Calif., school district recently agreed on to terminate the city's 15-year-old school desegregation case.

For the sake of quality education, we hope the words of the assistant attorney general prove prophetic, for the settlement appears to be an attractive alternative to compulsory busing.

Where busing strikes a negative and impersonal tone, the Bakersfield "magnet school" plan accentuates the positive. Students of different races come together in schools not because they have to, not because they are numbers on someone's racial balance sheet, but because they want to and because they are individuals with varying needs and interests.

Bakersfield has a school population that is 46 percent white, 36 percent Hispanic, 16 percent black, and 2 percent of other ethnic origin. To attract student bodies of diverse makeup, magnet schools will feature such appealing options as extended day-care for working families, computer-aided instruction, performing arts, special opportunities in science, and programs for the talented and gifted.

Will the magnets land students in the same racial ratio as exists for the school system as a whole? That's highly unlikely. But, then, rarely has busing in pursuit of racial balance ended with the intended balance. Much more often, in fact, it has unbalanced the school system's demographics. Whatever desegregation is achieved by the magnet approach should be durable, because it will be built on consent and commonality of interest.

May the magnets increase in number and strength throughout the school systems of the land.

THE MILWAUKEE JOURNAL
Milwakee, Wisc., Febuary 24, 1984

In one of the Reagan administration's more blatant efforts to undermine court-ordered school desegregation, the Justice Department has moved to restrict federal court supervision of desegregation plans once they are in effect.

The department filed legal papers in a Denver case calling for judges to stop monitoring court-ordered or approved desegregation once a city showed it had done all it was ordered to do. The department's civil rights chief, William Bradford Reynolds, argued that the change would help return control over schools to local authorities.

Now just a darn minute! In the vast majority of cases resulting in court-ordered desegregation, it was the local authorities who were found to have violated citizens' rights that are guaranteed by the US Constitution. That's a very serious form of lawbreaking.

Courts would be merely playing charades if they did not try to make their remedies stick. Abandoning or sharply curtailing the courts' monitoring process would imply a confidence in the violators' future good behavior that is rarely afforded other lawbreakers after their conviction.

THE SACRAMENTO BEE
Sacrramento, Calif., Febuary 1, 1984

With much fanfare, the Justice Department has just announced its brave new approach to desegregation. The plan, settling a suit brought against the Bakersfield schools, relies not on busing — a failed policy, in the administration's judgment — but instead on specialized magnet schools designed to entice black, white and Hispanic students into attending school with one another.

It's hard to quarrel with the proposition that busing is a problematic approach, but the Reagan administration hasn't offered even one of the plausible available alternatives in its stead. The Bakersfield "plan" isn't a plan at all, but only the vaguest of school district commitments, with little likely impact on either the racial mix or the educational quality of that community's schools.

Consider: Fifty-five percent of Bakersfield's students are non-white. In four of the city's 25 elementary schools (the district includes only kindergarten-through-eighth-grade schools), more than nine out of every 10 students are members of minority groups, while in two others, four-fifths are white. In such a community, redrawing school attendance boundaries can bring different racial groups together without creating the kind of logistical nightmares that have plagued Los Angeles. But Bakersfield has opted for a different strategy. It will put some special programs — in the arts, perhaps, or in computer-aided instruction — into effect in the four heavily minority schools, and will open enrollments throughout the district, with the aim of assuring that, in every school, at least one-quarter and no more than three-quarters of the students are white.

Will that come to pass? Not likely. Right now, there's only $60,000 earmarked in Bakersfield's budget for "integration activities" and no ready funds available in Sacramento or Washington; school officials hope that they can draw on their reserve accounts for a few years in developing a program. Nor has the district committed itself to doing anything specific: Computer-aided instruction sounds nice — at least if it's done well — but because it's costly there's no guarantee that it will be put in place. Indeed, if funding gets tight, Bakersfield school officials may be tempted to put a new name on an old school, call it a magnet, and hope for the best.

Desegregation by the numbers is what the Justice Department has criticized. What it has given us instead, in the Bakersfield case, is desegregation by press release. The proposed agreement has little to do with education, nothing at all to do with ending racial isolation or with creating a system where black and white youngsters can learn from one another. Bakersfield may do better than this; at least at the rhetorical level, the local commitment is there. But as national policy, this is just the latest saga in the Reagan administration's "emperor's new clothes" approach to civil rights.

Detroit Free Press

Detroit, Mich., April 27, 1984

THE FEDERAL court could not continue indefinitely as active monitor and manager of the Detroit Public School system, but it is with some misgivings that parents and people concerned about the schools will watch the demise of the Monitoring Commission.

The court has ordered the phasing out of the commission, at least in its present form, and told the school system to devise its own code of conduct and school-community relations program. The ruling sets a timetable for the end of the court's active involvement in the running of the schools. It begins the final winding down of the historic Detroit busing case. And it places on the school board and staff the burden of proof that they can administer the schools in safe, orderly, effective fashion, without prodding or oversight of the court.

Detroit's desegregation case was unique in that the remedies ordered by the court went far beyond busing for a better racial mix in the classroom, and to the very heart of what makes schools work. The integration of classrooms and teaching staff made it far less likely that black children would be relegated to inferior, inadequately equipped schools. But integration by itself was not enough to guarantee students the quality education they had been denied in a segregated system.

Thus Federal District Judge Robert E. DeMascio ordered a wide range of reforms beyond busing, including remedial classes, a student conduct code to establish a safe and orderly atmosphere in the schools, the construction of new vocational centers and an intensive community relations effort. The judge ordered the state to pay for part of the improvements and created the Monitoring Commission to oversee them.

Over the years, the Monitoring Commission gave the school mixed grades for compliance. What the commission reported was no secret to people with children in the Detroit public schools.

Discipline — the student code of conduct — is unevenly enforced from school to school; some high schools are bedlam, others have a cheerful and well-ordered atmosphere, depending upon the fibre of the principal and staff. The vocational schools were slow to get going and are still not serving as many students as they should. Guidance counselors were often used as attendance clerks. Community relations programs ranged from the successful to the sham, again depending upon the attitude of the principal. Bureaucrats often substituted compliance on paper for substantive reform.

The Monitoring Commission was valuable precisely because it gave the public, as well as the court, an unvarnished report on how things worked in the corridors and the classrooms. Although the commission's reports often bolstered Superintendent Arthur Jefferson's efforts to improve the schools, it is not surprising that superintendent, staff and school board have been chafing to get out from under its surveillance.

On Thursday, the three-judge panel that inherited the busing case ordered the eventual transfer of the monitoring commission's function to the state board of education. The monitoring will continue until 1987-88, when state funding for the court-ordered improvements ends; whether it will be as effective remains to be seen.

But at some point the school board does have to be the school board. The responsibility and accountability for the system ultimately does have to rest with the elected board and the administrators it chooses. Once the court's orders have been complied with, the court cannot and should not be the superintendent of schools. It has been extraordinarily useful to Detroiters to have the Monitoring Commission; maybe every big-city school system ought to have an independent, gadfly citizens' group. But with or without the court looking over their shoulders, the challenge to Mr. Jefferson and the school board is the same as it ever was: To make the public schools work.

Rocky Mountain News

A Scripps-Howard Newspaper · *Reg. U.S. Pat. Off.* · *Colorado's First Newspaper—Founded in 1859*

Denver, Colo., Febuary 15, 1984

THE first thing to admit about the U.S. Justice Department's intervention in the Denver school desegregation case is that it probably won't make much difference. District Court Judge Richard Matsch is not the type to get flustered by the legal muscle-flexing of a newcomer — even if the newcomer does happen to represent the executive branch.

The second thing to note is more positive: To the extent arguments in the Justice Department's "friend of the court" brief are addressed by Matsch, we might get a better idea of just how much he intends to demand of the school board before releasing it from his supervision. And we might also learn how much freedom of action the board is likely to have after the release.

The Justice Department brief argues that courts should consider two tests for deciding when to end a desegregation order: Whether school authorities have implemented a constitutionally acceptable desegregation plan, and whether school officials "have subsequently refrained from intentionally segregative acts."

Those tests can be variously interpreted, of course, but a full reading of the brief suggests the Justice Department's focus would be rather narrow and specific. And the justification for that focus is quite impressively argued.

The brief is interesting also for its emphasis on what the district has done, as opposed to what it is likely to do. The Justice Department contends, sensibly, that a court's authority ends when a district is in constitutional compliance. Apparently that would not mean a district had to sign off on a plan showing, for example, how it would maintain certain pupil assignment ratios into the foreseeable future.

Yet clearly some pressure exists for drawing up a fairly precise plan for Denver. A lawyer for the plaintiffs has gone so far as to argue that a school is "racially identifiable" when it deviates from the racial makeup of the district by more than 15 percent. Would that kind of specificity have to be incorporated into a plan satisfactory to Matsch? Perhaps at last we will see.

Los Angeles Times

Los Angeles, Calif., January 30, 1984

William Bradford Reynolds, assistant attorney general for civil rights, has described the minority-integration plan for the Bakersfield public schools as "a blueprint for desegregation in the future." He affirmed confidence that voluntary programs will prove effective.

His optimism is not widely shared. But at the same time it must be acknowledged that his abhorrence of mandatory integration programs, particularly forced busing, is widely shared. In the public perception, busing has caused as many problems as it has solved, and solved few. So there is a willingness to let the Bakersfield experiment go forward, to judge it by standards no less generous than those by which other efforts to erase the marks of racism from the schools have been judged.

The federal plan for Bakersfield relies primarily on the establishment of "magnet" programs in schools with predominantly black and Latino enrollment in the hope that these programs will attract white students and thereby help correct the racial imbalance that is evident in the school system. There is not much in the experience with magnet schools to suggest that they will prove attractive enough to correct the problem. But the increased investment in schools where enrollment is predominantly black and Latino will raise the potential for better teaching in those schools.

The federal plan will further reinforce the quality of education by continuing an existing program called Project Rise—racially isolated school enrichment—which has sought to improve reading and mathematical skills in schools with high minority enrollments. But those programs, if not accompanied by a significant change in enrollment patterns assuring better racial balance, will fail in the essential task because it is as true today as when the Supreme Court unanimously affirmed the principle in 1954 that separate schools cannot be equal.

The plan now approved for Bakersfield is the result of a combined community effort that included leaders of blacks and Latinos, according to the Justice Department. If this community endorsement is translated into community cooperation, the possibilities of success will be enhanced. But it would seem premature to conclude that mandatory desegregation actions are no longer needed in the nation—or, for that matter, in Bakersfield.

The Wichita
Eagle-Beacon
Wichita, Kans., May 14, 1984

It seems almost unthinkable now that only a couple of generations ago, even in Kansas, many children were bused to school for the express purpose of keeping them segregated. Blacks in many places were expected to be satisfied with schools that were "separate but equal," meeting a standard of educational fairness established by the U.S. Supreme Court in 1896. Thirty years ago this week, Linda Brown and a later Supreme Court changed all that.

One of the great social revolutions of the 20th century began in 1950 with a little black girl living in Topeka asking her parents why she had to be bused two miles to an all-black school while her white playmates were able to attend a neighborhood school only a few blocks away. Linda Brown's parents referred the question to the federal courts. Four years later, on May 17, 1954, the Supreme Court delivered its landmark decision.

Schooling that was racially "separate," the court said in its unanimous finding in the case of Brown vs. Board of Education of Topeka, was "inherently unequal." Chief Justice Earl Warren explained why: To separate black children "from others of similar age amd qualifications solely because of race generates a feeling of inferiority ... that may affect their hearts and minds in a way unlikely ever to be undone."

The next year, on May 31, 1955, the court spoke on the matter again, calling on local courts to require "a prompt and reasonable start toward full compliance" of its ban on racial segregation in education. It said local administrative problems should be resolved "with all deliberate speed."

Kansans accepted the Supreme Court's mandate gracefully. There was no unseemly resistance such as that exemplified by Arkansas Gov. Orval Faubus's 1957 schoolhouse door stand to try to keep nine black students from entering Little Rock's previously all-white Central High School.

Still, "deliberate speed" can be time-consuming. It took the Wichita Board of Education, motivated by the best of intentions, until 1971 to work out and implement a desegration plan that fully satisfied both federal authorities and the courts. This was despite legal challenges by citizens opposed to its cross-busing provisions.

The turnaround since 1954, when almost 40 percent of the nation's public schools were racially segregated, is truly worthy of celebration. Had not Linda Brown asked the right question and her family followed it up with legal action, millions of black children still might have to trudge across railroad yards, as young Linda once had to, to catch buses that would take them to their educational ghettos.

The Dispatch
Columbus, Ohio, May 16, 1984

It will be 30 years ago tomorrow that the U.S. Supreme Court handed down the landmark decision in *Brown vs. The Board of Education* — the ruling that declared racially segregated schools to be unconstitutional. The events flowing from that decision have been powerful and they are yet transforming the nation.

On May 17, 1954, the court ruled that the "separate but equal" doctrine that had been in place since 1896 could no longer be tolerated in a nation that professed equal rights for all. The doctrine was the basis for two separate school systems in some communities — one for whites and one for blacks. The court held in *Brown* that forcing blacks to attend their own schools was inherently racist because it "generates a feeling of inferiority . . . that may affect their hearts and minds in a way unlikely ever to be undone."

The ruling set off waves of emotions. Many officials in the South were determined to ignore the decision and continue their practices.

This initial resistance was soon demonstrated to be futile, and the schools in the South were opened for all, even though some less apparent methods to continue segregationist feelings were attempted.

The ruling also set the stage for the civil rights movement of the 1960s that resulted in the passage of sweeping equal rights legislation by Congress. This, in turn, resulted in the court challenges to various provisions of the legislation as the nation tried to determine exactly what the laws — and their consequences — meant. These challenges continue today, and it is likely to be many more years before the probing ends.

The ruling did not, of course, eliminate racism in this society. That is something that can only take place in the private deliberations of one's one mind. But the ruling — and the subsequent developments — demonstrated that this nation has the courage to attempt to improve the quality of life for all its citizens. It is an honorable effort and one that must succeed.

The Hartford Courant
Hartford, Conn., May 23, 1984

There are a few things that should always provoke a respectful skepticism in the public: One is any report of a "breakthrough" in science and another is any description of a court decision as a "landmark." Expectations from both tend to be overblown.

The "landmark" decision of Brown vs. Board of Education of Topeka (Kansas), for example, seemed to hold the promise of equal and racially integrated education 30 years ago with its uncompromising statement that "separate educational facilities are inherently unequal."

The case did serve as a precedent for the dismantling of many segregationist laws, particularly at public accommodations like buses and restaurants, but many public school systems and even colleges and universities are still far from adequately integrated.

The anniversary of the decision this month serves as a reminder not only of how far we have come in breaking down legal barriers, but how far we have to go to realize the full promise of Brown vs. Board of Education of Topeka.

Integration of schools has, of course, taken place in some areas with generally positive results for students. But in many other areas, especially in the Northeast, integration is as distant a goal as it has ever been. Hartford is no exception. Thirty years after the Brown decision and 15 years after Connecticut passed a desegregation law, some city schools — including Weaver and Hartford high schools — are virtually all minority.

Even without a conscious segregationist policy, segregation persists because of the growing concentration of blacks and Hispanics in the city, the movement of whites to the suburbs and the lack of a firm commitment by officials at every level to school integration.

Project Concern, which is being cut back, does benefit the several hundred minority students from the city who are bused to suburban schools, but the traffic goes only one way and does not help to integrate Hartford's schools.

Integration of colleges, further, has proceeded slowly over the past several decades. It was not until 1978, in fact, that the federal government ordered many states to develop desegregation plans or face the prospect of losing federal funds. Even that effort has waned in recent years.

Other factors, including the use of achievement tests biased against minorities and the threat of reduced federal aid to students, have worked to discourage minority enrollment. Though the number of blacks in higher education is increasing, they are underrepresented in fields where there is the most opportunity; the number of blacks in graduate and professional schools is declining.

Clearly, integration is not going to be attained in communities like Hartford until predominantly white suburban towns show a willingness to join in a regional plan to mix students of different races. Any such plan would encounter stiff political resistance in the name of local control, but that should not deter political and educational leaders in the state from pressing ahead in the name of equality.

Brown vs. Board of Education was a "landmark," but it didn't mark the end of the fight for school desegregation. It marked the beginning.

Black Colleges and Universities: Reverse Discrimination?

During the early 1970's, great strides were made by black students in colleges and universities, both in terms of enrollment and achievement. The number of blacks enrolled full-time in undergraduate programs almost doubled between 1970 and 1980, with most of the growth occurring by 1976. By 1975, the percentage of black high school graduates who had gone on to college, 32%, was the same as that for white high school graduates. Unfortunately, federal data on completed degrees broken down by race are not available until the late 1970's, when black enrollment had slowed. Data for the period between 1976 and 1981 indicate a slight decline in the total number of graduate degrees awarded to blacks, and an overwhelming decrease in the number at the master's level.

An important role in higher education for black students has been played by the traditionally black colleges and universities, established before the 1954 Supreme Court ruling which made racial segregation in public schools illegal. (See pp. 24-38.) These institutions, about a hundred in number, continue to enroll about a fifth of all black college students in the United States. It was not the historically black institutions, on the whole, that experienced the tremendous growth in black enrollment from 1970-1975. But after 1975, when nationwide college enrollment among eligible black students suffered a setback, the enrollment at these institutions remained stable, and the percentage of degrees awarded by them were disproportionately large. Ironically, the quality and purpose of many of these schools is now threatened not only by federal funding cuts but by the very Supreme Court ruling that was intended to address racial discrimination in education. Several lawsuits now contend that, because of the high proportion of blacks enrolled, they are in fact illegally segregated, and must begin enrolling white students in equal numbers. In addition, some of the black colleges and universities are suffering a decline in enrollment because of the efforts of neighboring schools to attract black students, in an effort to meet their own percentage requirements for black enrollment.

THE PLAIN DEALER
Cleveland, Ohio, May 31, 1981

When the federal Department of Education recently cited Ohio for violating the Civil Rights Act by maintaining Central State University as a predominantly black school, it raised the old question of whether Central State should be abolished, both to achieve better integration in other Ohio colleges and to save money.

We do not believe Central State should be abolished — now. But neither should it necessarily be kept as a black-oriented state college indefinitely. What is certain is that the issue needs to be aired.

The federal citation to Ohio on Central State should not come as a surprise. The old federal Department of Health, Education and Welfare made Central State a prime target of racial discrimination investigation beginning in 1978. The issue probably will be settled amicably, without closing Central State. Settlement of similar objections elsewhere usually have included plans to promote more integration and allocate more funds, but generally have left predominantly black or white colleges as they were.

Central State was formed when education courses were spun off in 1947 from Wilberforce University, a predominantly black liberal arts college in Wilberforce, near Xenia, supported by the African Methodist Episcopal Church. Wilberforce has about 1,000 students from 30 states and 15 countries. Central State has about 2,500 students, mostly from Ohio. The campuses adjoin, the students interact and the milieu produces a black perspective and culture-source supported by black Ohioans.

Until the creation in 1966 of larger Wright State University near Dayton, about 15 miles away, Central had a white enrollment of near 24%. It has dropped to 7.4%, with all the appearance of a deliberate state segregation policy. The state could merge Wright and Central, an old recommendation. That might satisfy the federal government and the urge to save money by consolidating small enrollments. But that would change the administration and student body, which is Central's reason for being.

Some people believe that Central State serves a necessary function by providing a place for black educators and by allowing minority students to learn and progress in an environment in which they are the majority. But is that the proper responsibility of a state school?

Some people feel that Central State is the only college open to many disadvantaged students. But if that is so, it should not be. It would be against the philosophy of a state admissions policy. Some people point out that Central State is integrated, only in reverse order and more equally than at many predominantly white state universities.

Retaining Central State as a predominantly black college in the long run promotes the separation, not the integration, of Ohioans. Despite denials, it puts the state in the business of maintaining a college based on race. And it would appear to violate the aims of the 1964 Civil Rights Act.

The other side of the coin is that prejudice is still alive and well; that many blacks feel the barriers of discrimination still exist — even if subtly — despite the elimination of segregation at predominantly white colleges.

As a social relief valve, a fount for black viewpoints and a crutch on a too long journey toward parity, a predominantly black Central State may still be needed in Ohio. But for how much longer?

THE INDIANAPOLIS STAR
Indianapolis, Ind., April 10, 1980

American parents and their children, in record numbers, accuse public schools of the sin of under-expectation.

A study of attitudes among teen-agers gathered in a Gallup poll recently conducted for the Charles F. Kettering Foundation revealed that 53 percent of teen-agers believe they are not being asked to work hard enough in school.

A striking finding was that black teen-agers (66.5 percent of them) feel more strongly than do the white teen-agers (50.4 percent) that public schools don't demand enough of them.

Dr. John M. Bahner of the Kettering Foundation interprets poll results as indicating public schools set expectations too low.

A growing number of black parents apparently agree with him. A phenomenon little known outside the black community is the growth of black private schools in New York City. A New York Times article sees the development as a quiet revolution in the same school districts that once rang with cries for integration and later for community control.

The Times article highlighted the case of a Board of Education social worker, Mrs. Jonnie Marshall, who had enrolled her 12-year-old son in a private school in Harlem.

"They couldn't develop my son's potential," she said of public schools, "and they were well on the way to damaging him as a student. It's an expense I can hardly afford but a parent has to make these sacrifices."

The black private schools are perfectly legal, according to Dr. Sterling S. Keyes, New York State coordinator of the Office of Urban Schools Services, as long as they provide "an educational program equivalent to public schools" in the same district.

The private schools all have waiting lists, even though they do not advertise, and all insist that their pupils perform better than their public school peers. A marked characteristic is an emphasis on discipline and most require the teaching of religious values, character and morality.

Some parents whose children attend such schools are middle-class professionals but the majority are working-class parents willing to sacrifice to pay the tuition which averages $50 a month.

Several such parents told the Times that although blacks and Hispanics comprise the majority of New York's public school population, the predominantly white Board of Education has given up on education and chosen instead to maintain an industry that exists mainly to support professional educators.

That is a strong charge to make but obviously many black parents feel it is justified.

The Virginian-Pilot
Norfolk, Va., July 24, 1983

The college integration bonuses aren't catching on yet.

Those are the $1,000 grants that were supposed to persuade black two-year community college students to transfer on to historically white, four-year universities and encourage their white classmates to go on to black schools.

So far, about 110 of the 500 grants, or 22 percent, have been handed out through the community colleges and the State Council of Higher Education.

As of last week, Tidewater Community College had awarded only 15 of the 71 scholarships it had been allocated.

The state was counting on these grants to help it achieve a more representative racial mix in its four-year public universities. The state is under a federal court order to get more blacks into traditionally white institutions, such as the University of Virginia, Virginia Tech, William and Mary and Old Dominion University, and more whites into the two mostly black schools, Norfolk State and Virginia State.

If the state doesn't meet the targets soon (you can call them "quotas" if you like, a word shunned by state and federal officials) then the feds might start cutting off millions of dollars in education aid that comes to Virginia.

So Virginia has a powerful incentive to succeed here. And the lack of enthusiasm for the $1,000 grants is discouraging to those officials who felt this would be an effective way to promote integration.

But all is not lost. Most of the state's four-year colleges seem to be on track — so far — in reaching their goals. That's because other recruiting methods aimed at high school seniors are having fair results. So the failure of one part of the overall strategy may not be fatal.

Why have the bonuses apparently flopped? Some experts say it's because only a fraction of the students at community colleges can pick up and move to the cities where the four-year universities are located. Many of them have jobs and families.

And the conditions attached to the grants may have led to a smaller eligibility pool in the community colleges than state officials figured: You must have a C-plus average, be accepted for admission to a four-year school in which you would be in a racial minority, and demonstrate a need for financial help.

There's also the problem of timing. Guidelines for the new program were issued this spring; many prospective transfer students had made their decisions for next fall by then.

And there's another factor: Many students are reluctant to go to schools where they will be in the distinct racial minority.

Barry M. Dorsey, associate director of the State Council of Higher Education, predicts that the grant picture will improve by September, in part because a number of applications are in the pipeline.

But if hundreds of thousands of grant dollars continue to sit idle, then the state should take a close look to figure out why. Community college students should be surveyed to determine what will, in fact, make them more inclined to become minority transfers.

Why is it important for this grant program to succeed? Because it is a relatively painless way to encourage voluntary college integration.

The alternatives, should Virginia continue to fall short of federally mandated goals, may be harsher: A loss of critically needed funds, more litigation in the federal courts, and possibly, more directives from Washington on how Virginia should run its colleges.

The Arizona Republic
Phoenix, Ariz., May 24, 1983

THE most prestigious black institution of higher learning in the United States is Howard University, and it's determined to retain that distinction.

Unfortunately for Howard, however, Title VII of the Civil Rights Act of 1964, which opened the door to black students and scholars in the nation's white institutions of higher learning, also opened the door to whites at black institutions.

And this has created a problem for the university administration.

If Howard were to abide faithfully by the Civil Rights Act, it might remain a prestigious institution but it eventually would cease being black.

Howard has chosen to ignore the act, and the result has been a spate of suits charging discrimination brought by whites, women, a black professor with a white wife, and a group of black African professors.

Howard has lost several of the suits and settled the others out of court.

Now the university has come up with a new defense.

A District of Columbia jury found that Howard had discriminated against a white professor of French, Gabrielle Turgeon, by failing to renew her contract and replacing her with a black.

Howard is appealing the verdict on the grounds that even if the charge of discrimina-tion is true, the university is not guilty of violating the act because black institutions should be judged by a different legal standard.

Black institutions do have valid reasons for dismissing a white professor on purely racial grounds, the appeal argues.

Among them:

✔ To provide role models for black students;

✔ To create "psycho-socially congenial settings" for black students; and

✔ "To contribute to the positive pluralism of the American higher educational system by providing a wider freedom of choice of institutions."

In effect, Howard is saying the Civil Rights Act does not apply to blacks, that whites can't discriminate against blacks but that blacks have *carte blanche* to discriminate against whites.

Howard also is saying that it puts color above ability in choosing its faculty.

Someone in the university administration should take a look at the 14th Amendment, which assures everyone in this country, even illegal aliens, "the equal protection of the laws."

It took a bloody civil war to open the way to enactment of the 14th Amendment.

Does Howard really want to remove its protection from whites?

St. Petersburg Times
St. Petersburg, Fla., May 4, 1983

Five years ago, Florida entered an agreement with federal authorities to try to attract more black students and teachers to public colleges and universities. Since then, black enrollment in Florida's nine state universities has declined every year from 10.4 percent to 8.3 percent.

State university presidents last week gave the Board of Regents a lot of excuses for the drop in black enrollment. They said fewer blacks were enrolling in Florida's two-year colleges, which feed the public university system. They cited aggressive recruiting by the military, which is a big employer in the Florida Panhandle and other parts of the state. They blamed cuts in federal financial aid. They claimed a declining number of black high school graduates hampered recruitment efforts.

University officials may be right that it has become more difficult to recruit black students. But their attitude is wrong. They have conceded defeat much too easily.

THE OFFICE of Civil Rights sent Gov. Bob Graham a letter Jan. 28 complaining that "for the most part, little progress toward desegregation has occurred." In response, Florida Education Commissioner Ralph Turlington said, "The Office of Civil Rights did not take into account these factors . . . The goals are just not realistic today. If we had known in 1977 what we know now, we would have taken another look at the agreement."

With that kind of attitude, it's no wonder Florida's public institutions of higher learning are drifting back into segregation. Instead of giving up, state officials should be pledging to work more diligently than ever to desegregate state universities. Without such a commitment, the drop in black enrollment will not be reversed.

Two years ago, the regent's equal opportunity officer commented, "We were going great when our desegregation plan was first in effect, but it almost seems as if everybody slacked off after that and said, 'Okay, that's behind us.' "

A lack of commitment would seem to be the real reason that black enrollment in Florida's universities has declined steadily. University officials should be searching for solutions to the recruitment problems, rather than making excuses. In a draft letter to the U.S. Office for Civil Rights, released last Thursday, the regents said, "The state university system reaffirms its commitment to equalizing educational opportunities." And the regents promised to make substantial progress toward desegregation by 1985.

TO KEEP that promise, the state will have to make a greater effort to recruit black students than it is now. Cuts in federal financial aid have discouraged many students from even applying to a university. The state can do something about that. Graham has recommended that state student financial aid be increased almost 28 percent next year and 56 percent the following year. The Florida Legislature should follow the governor's recommendation.

The University of Florida is one of three universities that has increased black enrollment slightly during the last year. UF President Robert O. Marston attributed the increase to more scholarships and recruitment programs for black students, especially National Merit and National Achievement Scholars.

With a renewed commitment to equal educational opportunities, all of Florida's universities should be able to reverse the drift back into segregation.

The News American

Baltimore, Md., January 26, 1982

Maryland's black institutions of higher learning did not fare well in some respects in the budget Governor Hughes unveiled last week. The reason is far from clear and will no doubt give rise to damaging speculation on the campuses involved and in the broader educational community they serve.

The situation is most obvious in the area of so-called "enhancement" funds. These are funds the state recently decided to provide the schools in an effort to overcome the effects of years of neglect and past underfunding by the state legislature.

In his budget message to the General Assembly, the governor proposed an allotment of $718,570 to be shared by Coppin and Bowie State colleges, the University of Maryland Eastern Shore, and Morgan State University. That is far from the $10 million that had been asked for and expected.

Delegate Howard "Pete" Rawlings (D. 40th), calls the proposed allocation a "mere pittance" compared to the "disparity" it is supposed to overcome. The arithmetic is easily on the side of Rawlings's argument.

The allocation is only 7 percent of the amount that had been recommended by a state-sanctioned task force and 11 percent of that recommended by the State Board of Higher Education.

How the governor managed to end up so far out of step with the people who supposedly whose job it is to advise him is mystifying. We are baffled as indeed the officials at the schools, the task force, and the state board of education, must be.

Two things make the governor's action especially perplexing. First, it is a sharp departure from his previous stance on the future of black colleges in the state. In the past, and on a number of occasions — during Morgan's internal upheaval and during debate over campus consolidation, for example — Mr. Hughes had vowed to preserve and strengthen minority institutions.

Second, the proposed state budget is not a "tight" one. Despite hefty federal cutbacks, the governor is calling for an operating budget 6.9 percent greater than this year's. Without raising state property taxes, sales or income taxes, it provides for salary hikes for state workers, new prisons, more aid for libraries and the mentally ill and retarded and even an increase in welfare grants.

By comparison, enhancement funds for predominantly black colleges and universities seem to have been singled out for shabby treatment. In its budget deliberations, the legislature should try to ferret out the reason for it and to bring the allocation back into line.

The Afro American

Baltimore, Md., March 1, 1980

First, there were efforts to desegregate black colleges out of existence. Then there were rumors of financial scandals which became the alleged basis for federal inquiries. Now some senators seem bent on eliminating the federal aid program that has literally kept some black colleges alive.

That aid program is officially known as Title III of the Higher Education Act. And all the Senate has to do to get rid of Title III is do nothing; for the act of Congress will soon expire of its own accord.

For this reason, the United Negro College Fund is spearheading an all - out campaign to have Title III extended. A lobbying effort is currently underway to coincide with action scheduled to be considered by a Senate subcommittee on education and the arts this week. The subcommittee is a part of the Senate Labor and Human Resources Committee.

Without a doubt, it is imperative that the Senate act immediately to continue federal funding under this program. There are 41 black institutions (out of more than 120 predominantly black colleges and universities) which depend on Title III funds for their very life - blood.

To fail to act now could mean that the number of such schools could be drastically reduced by as much as a third if no other funding is found. And such funding is hard to come by.

When Congress first passed Title III, admittedly, it did not expect to always be assisting such schools. But such a temporary measure was itself unrealistic.

Black colleges and white institutions alike have failed to even begin to make up for the lost years of discrimination which kept us from our rightful access to both jobs and schooling (which is the only sure route to good jobs). Congress must realize that it will be a long time — if ever — before such injustice will be remedied.

This is all the more reason why commitment to funding these colleges must be viewed as a permanent priority. Promotion of equal educational opportunity for poor and disadvantaged students is a national objective, and it must be strengthened.

There were those, of course, who once predicted that black schools would eventually lose their appeal and phase out as predominantly - white schools opened their doors to all races. But the opposite has occurred.

True, there are many more blacks attending white colleges (although only a percentage of these are successfully graduating). But enrollment at black institutions of higher learning has also increased to an all - time high.

The number of blacks graduating from these colleges has doubled since the program began. This is evidence of the program's success.

But half of all baccalaureate degrees earned by black students are still conferred by black colleges. A bare handful of black schools are graduating as many students as all the other thousands of white colleges and universities combined. This is evidence of the program's continued need.

Not only this, but if Title III were not to be renewed and extended, it is doubtful if other monies could be found. Gifts, donations, bequests, and similar private aid to higher education which have received Title III have all become scarce in recent years. With inflation rising (and a conservative backlash hindering all positive steps to aid the disadvantaged), other sources of income for colleges, black and white, have dried up.

This is all the more reason why Title III must be extended. We favor an approach currently being offered by Sen. Donald Stewart (D - Ala.), which would extend Title III indefinitely and minimize the number of management restrictions (including the meddling of the General Accounting Office) on the program.

As the United Negro College Fund so strikingly reminds us, "A mind is a terrible thing to waste."

The Boston Globe

Boston, Mass., July 25, 1981

There is unease in academia over a decline in the number of blacks seeking doctor of philosophy degrees, particularly in the fields of literature, the fine arts, history and philosophy. These branches of learning, called the humanities, are the wellspring of intellectual activity and the source of scholars who influence the direction of nonscientific higher education.

On the surface it may appear to be the result of a cooling attitude toward affirmative action objectives at the college level. However, new opportunities in business and industry also may be contributing, at least temporarily, to the decline in blacks seeking doctorates.

Ellen Jackson, the dean for affirmative action programs at Northeastern University, says that more black undergraduates are going directly to work after earning undergraduate degrees because they need the money and because they are sought. She believes, however, that some of them will return to colleges for advanced degrees within a few years, either because they need them for continued career advancement or because they have rectified financial problems and are ready to complete their development as professionals.

If Jackson is correct, the current decline may mean that blacks are turning away from education, theology and social sciences as favored fields of professional opportunity. It also means that, unless colleges and universities begin to make known their needs to students at the junior and high school level, to private financial supporters, and particularly to their own faculty appointment and tenure committees, the supply of black professors will begin to decline within a few years.

There was a time when, among blacks, a career as a professor – usually in a black college – was among the highest aspirations. It often meant an opportunity for social and economic advancement. Ironically, the desegregation of higher education that has diminished the role of black colleges has also diminished the role of black educators as career models for black youth. To compensate for that, colleges should promote the idea of academic careers more vigorously among black students at the secondary level.

Many of the old sources of funds for minority postgraduate education are drying up, both in the public and private sector. New sources will need to be cultivated, especially in the private sector, and there must be an effort to earmark a significant portion of these funds for students who wish to become scholars in the humanities.

Black college faculty members at predominantly white institutions are having increasing difficulties moving up within their disciplines. As in business and industry, many do not benefit from the old-boy and old-girl networks that are important for steady advancement. Many are finding they are either languishing at low professional levels or isolated in advanced levels without the support to survive internal intrigues.

Unless these deficiencies can be remedied, the goal of enhancing the American academic world with an increasing number of black scholars in a wide variety of fields will be frustrated and another opportunity to meet the rising expectations of racial minorities in the United States will have been squandered.

Pittsburgh Post-Gazette

Pittsburg, Penn., March 1, 1983

The people in Happy Valley should be unhappy about the record that Pennsylvania State University has made in attracting black students.

The statistics are stark. Since 1972, Penn State has increased its total black enrollment by exactly 90 students, during a period when its total student enrollment went up by 9,486 to 56,749. It has a student body that is 2.5 percent black in a state with a black population of 8.8 percent, ranking it in the bottom third of state-supported schools in Pennsylvania.

The excuses are easy to make. Penn State is located in rural Centre County, home of few blacks. Most Pennsylvania blacks come from the cities and therefore prefer an urban environment and its amenities.

Well and good. Clearly, one cannot push a person to enroll in a university where he feels he will not be at home. But, curiously, Penn State's record is no better at its outlying campuses, such as McKeesport and Ogontz, which are located near major metropolitan centers,

Furthermore, Penn State seems to have had no trouble recruiting black football players. Why would they be different from other blacks in their willingness to study in a rural environment?

Could it be because they are deliberately wooed and know that they are wanted?

Has the university made a sufficient financial commitment to recruiting blacks (there is only one fulltime black recruiter at the main campus)? To be sure, Penn State has established the Paul Robeson Cultural Center to promote black studies, created a Black Scholars scholarship program for students and the President's Opportunity Fund to attract black faculty by increasing salary offerings, established a special program for disadvantaged students and set up workshops to improve faculty sensitivity to other cultures.

But as Robert Coleman, chairman of the Pennsylvania Equal Rights Council, tellingly puts it, "You can't measure intention, but you can measure results."

The attitudes of some faculty and students toward black students have been cited as detriments by black students. There doesn't seem to be the easy-going acceptance of different kinds of people that one finds on campuses in more cosmopolitan areas. Here, clearly, is a problem worthy of some soul-searching by Penn State and the larger State College community, including churches, clubs and businesses.

Even more pertinent is the matter of black faculty. A recently published study of black enrollment in 743 university programs across the country concluded that the single most important key to attracting black students is having sufficient black faculty. There Penn State is woefully behind, with a proportion of black faculty members and administrators far below state and national averages (1.16 percent of faculty, 1.56 percent of administration and 2.15 percent of all employees). Worse, the faculty and administrator numbers have fallen in the past six years.

It is true that the overall number of faculty has dropped in the past decade. But with an enrollment growth of 9,486 during that time, there obviously has been more room for faculty expansion in some departments than in many another hard-pressed institution.

One can only conclude that any programs to attract black faculty and administrators have been pursued somewhat halfheartedly. The challenge for Penn State is not to settle for excuses but to fashion and push hard explicit policies and programs to attract black faculty and students. It cannot be considered a truly first-class university until it overcomes this shortcoming.

THE ANN ARBOR NEWS

Ann Arbor, Mich., May 29, 1983

For the U-M smaller (read fewer) isn't better when it comes to minority enrollment.

The record in recent years is one of disappointment and frustration: Disappointment over steady declines in black enrollment, frustration over retaining and graduating black students after they gain admission.

Financial aid programs for black students help both in terms of recruitment and dollar assistance. But then it seems there is a lack of follow-through and retention of the minority student becomes less of a priority.

There shouldn't be. U-M educators and administrators who say they are committed to educating more black students should be prepared to extend that commitment to its logical conclusion.

The percentage of black students has declined from 6.9 to 5.2 percent of the student population since 1978. Black students on campus dropped from 2,230 in 1978 to 1,603 in 1982, a decline of more than 28 percent.

The goal of the Black Action Movement (1970), agreed to in principle by the University, was 10 percent black enrollment. Michigan appears to be keeping half a promise.

Several explanations, no doubt some of them valid, were suggested for the U-M's troubles in recruiting and retaining minority students, among them: poor preparation in high schools and a social-cultural milieu which tends to isolate minority students on campus and in Ann Arbor.

The latest report documenting further decline in black enrollment will be used as a guide for developing minority enrollment, U-M officials say.

That remains to be seen. In the meantime, state Superintendent of Schools Philip Runkel pointedly said recently that one of the looming big issues in education will be access to high education, specifically, minority access as part of the overall plan for higher education in Michigan.

Greater access suggests, among other things, minority scholarship programs in higher education funding – a defensible use of tax dollars. On campus, that should mean a heightened commitment to not just recruitment efforts, but follow-through programs such as counseling, career planning and, of course, financial aid.

The U-M will just have to try again and try harder.

THE RICHMOND NEWS LEADER

Richmond, Va., May 27, 1983

The four Es — education, energy, the economy, the environment — tend to vie for top billing in domestic news. Currently education leads the list.

There have been the withering findings of the President's task force on educational excellence (and, in response, the educationist establishment's frantic efforts at self-justification). There has been the Supreme Court's Tuesday decision allowing the Internal Revenue Service, without congressional sanction, to penalize private schools and other tax-exempt institutions for unorthodox views. There has been the federal judiciary's continuing obsession with the yellow school bus. And, here in Virginia, there has been the decade-long effort of four Governors to deal amicably with ever-escalating federal demands for racial quotas in the state's publicly-supported colleges and universities.

Yet to deal *amicably* as a hostage or a rapee is frequently the only alternative one has — that, and resigning oneself to one's fate. Which is how we view these federal demands, whether from bureaucrats or judges, about college quotas: with resignation.

These days the lovely federal folks are putting it to Virginia this way: Comply on quotas or risk losing oh, $160 million in federal cash. That kind of "either/or" can get your attention in a hurry.

No one with any sense rejoices in that demand — or no one should. Virginia's predominantly white colleges don't like it because it will mean recruitment of students and faculty for reasons of race alone. Virginia's predominantly black colleges don't like it because it will mean more of their better students — or their potentially better students — will be enticed to predominantly white schools, meaning in turn that the predominantly black schools will suffer in terms of both their identities and their academic reputations.

Yet Virginia has agreed to try to meet these quotas because Virginia had no other realistic alternative. State Education Secretary John Casteen has acknowledged that the settlement on quotas is "intrusive and domineering." Barry Dorsey, associate director of the State Council of Higher Education, has said that in accepting quotas Virginia might not be able to meet, "We had no other choice." In effect, the federal gun was — and remains — at Virginia's head.

So let no one deny any longer that federal cash means federal control. In education, Virginia is but a federal province — a federal region. Even to suggest that Virginia's colleges are not effectively under federal control is the purest whimsy. And is it not ironic? On the one hand a presidential commission deplores the quality of American education across the board; it urges us to academic excellence. Yet on the other hand, our federal bureaucrats and our federal judges continue to impose demands on the states and localities — demands that postpone, perhaps for forever, the day when academic excellence might return.

Ironic indeed. But then, as we have noted before, irony is the first resort of the oppressed.

Roanoke Times & World-News

Roanoke, Va., January 21, 1983

THE GHOST of Virginia's segregated past continues to haunt the present — and no more so than in the struggle to integrate the state's colleges and universities. The fight will go on for at least another three years, which is how long federal officials have given the state to show statistical improvement under the Robb administration's revised plan.

It's still a struggle, but it's not the same kind of struggle that it used to be. For years after the U.S. Supreme Court's famous *Brown v. Board of Education* desegregation ruling in 1954, the battle was between those who sought to dismantle the vestiges of officially sanctioned racial discrimination and those who wished to maintain the status quo. As recently as the second gubernatorial administration of Mills Godwin, from 1974 to 1978, the commonwealth seemed not to recognize any responsibility for rectifying illegal policies of the past.

That attitude changed under ex-Gov. John Dalton, Godwin's successor. Accepting the legal (and, perhaps, moral) indefensibility of intransigence, Dalton and his aides made a good-faith start in the effort to end the racially dual nature of Virginia's system of higher education. Though tactics have been adjusted, Robb and his aides have shown similar good faith. Today, the struggle is to find techniques that will work.

Pressure from federal civil-rights officials for Virginia and other Southern states to speed college desegregation stems from a court case brought 14 years ago by the Legal Defense Fund of the National Associaton for the Advancement of Colored People. The principle — segregation imposed or sanctioned by the state is a constitutional violation, and the burden for erasing it falls on the state — is simple enough.

Not so simple is finding an *effective* remedy. State-supported colleges are different from public elementary and secondary schools. Attendance is voluntary. The role of official policies — the location of individual institutions, for example, or their curricula — in perpetuating segregation is indirect and often subtle. Moreover, many blacks want to preserve the racial identity of historically black institutions such as Virginia State and Norfolk State universities.

One result is that desegregation goals conflict with each other. Black enrollment at predominantly white institutions is to be increased, but at the same time the predominantly black institutions are to be strengthened. For the paradox to stop short of being a full-fledged contradiction, it must be assumed that racially identifiable black universities will not exist forever. It must be assumed that such institutions serve temporary special needs, that they are collapsible way-stations on the road to true integration.

Virginians, both white and black, may not be ready to face that truth. For the moment, they don't have to. Even as a temporary expedient, the twin goals obviously can't be met if the gap continues to widen between the college-going rates of white and black youngsters. Correctly, federal officials focus on that gap as a key to the problem. Correctly, state officials see higher expectations and better counseling for black students — as early as in the elementary years — as a key to the solution.

But it will take more than three years to turn that particular lock. Is there hope for a breakthrough in the interim?

Maybe, just maybe.

For one thing, the small gains in black enrollment registered by Virginia's traditionally white institutions look a bit better when measured against the decline in the college-going rate of all blacks. At the least, those gains suggest that a) intensified efforts by white colleges to attract black students can pay off, and b) an increasing number of black students are prepared to accept the challenge of getting an education in a predominantly white environment.

For another thing, hard economic times seem to fall hardest on the poor, and black families are likelier to be poor than white families. If the sour economy can be blamed for the widening gap between white and black college-going rates, it's a tragic irony. Historically, higher education has been the main road out of poverty.

But if the gap is due to the economy, it's also reason for hope: When the economy recovers, more black youngsters should be in a position to enter college. Meanwhile, the good-faith efforts must continue, even though the results are sometimes discouraging.

THE DAILY OKLAHOMAN

Oklahoma City, Okla., Febuary 14, 1983

ONCE again, the threat of federal sanctions arises because, in the opinion of federal civil rights officials, the University of Oklahoma doesn't have enough black faculty members.

OU regents have been informed by Walter Mason, affirmative action director for the university, that the U.S. Office of Civil Rights doesn't think OU has made enough progress over the last six years toward meeting its goals in recruitment of both minority students and faculty.

As a result, OU and other state institutions of higher learning committed to a long-range state desegregation plan could be hit with federal penalties, such as withholding of research grants and funds for various student-aid programs.

Despite the recent addition of black professors to the faculties of the law and business schools, Mason says "an aggressive minority recruitment and retention plan is needed to overcome the deficit."

What we have here is a classic example of meddlesome federal intrusion into the affairs of a university under the name of civil rights which fails to consider the realities of higher education recruitment.

The problem is not that OU officials haven't made a concerted effort to recruit and retain more black faculty members. They have.

What the feds apparently don't take into account are simple demographic facts and the highly competitive nature of faculty recruitment.

As OU Provost J.R. Morris explains, "this part of the country simply isn't as attractive to many blacks as the larger urban centers on the east and west coasts."

The result is that when OU undertakes a nationwide search to fill a faculty position, not many qualified minority candidates apply. This is explained by the fact that there simply aren't that many qualified minority doctoral degree holders in some of the academic disciplines in demand. And the few with the requisite qualifications tend instead to seek teaching or research positions in eastern or western schools.

Another factor is that when OU does manage to recruit a black faculty member, it has a hard time retaining that individual — particularly if he or she is an outstanding teacher or researcher — because of the constant lure of offers from other institutions that are more attractive in terms of both compensation and location.

Between the fall of 1975 and the fall of 1982, the numbers of black students and faculty at OU has remained relatively constant, despite the university's good-faith efforts to achieve its affirmative action goals.

There were 779 black students and 15 black faculty members on the Norman campus in 1975. The numbers for last fall were 808 and 14.

OU had committed itself under the state desegregation plan — a plan stemming from a federal class action suit against several states where de jure segregation formerly existed — to seek to have 32 black faculty members by 1982. Calling it an affirmative action "goal" is a euphemism that cannot hide the fact that it really is a quota system imposed by the weight of the federal government.

As for what the feds apparently think is insufficient progress toward achieving that goal, it is pertinent to remind them that there is no university in the Big 8 Conference that has more black faculty members than OU does.

The Register

Santa Ana, Calif., September 24, 1984

At the federal courthouse in Nashville earlier this month, the irony must have been almost palpable in the protest march of 600 Tennessee State University students and teachers.

All but two of them black, the marchers were protesting a 16-year-old, court-imposed desegregation order that would require that equal numbers of black and white students be enrolled at a campus of the university where enrollment traditionally has been 90 percent black.

Until the 1950s, of course, those students had no legal choice but to attend such schools as the Tennessee State campus. That impediment was removed beginning with the landmark *Brown* vs. *the Board of Education* decision by the U.S. Supreme Court in 1954. Later in the decade, civil-rights activists marched to have further such impediments removed from the law.

Since then, the campus has remained predominantly black, because, could it really be, of the free choices of Tennessee college students.

The protesters at Tennessee State say that blacks do better at the school because they feel welcome there and are offered special tutoring. The protesters were said to be emotional and sentimental over the prospect of "their school" being radically changed. They feel they have something good in reality that is about to be sacrificed in the name of abstract notions of educational equality.

That may not be good enough for the courts, who have not been satisfied to simply *remove* legal impediments to free choice but, egged on by all sorts of social engineers, have found it irresistible to use government power to introduce new injustices.

And so students march in protest once again.

Tennessee State, of course, is not "their school." Although the courts have also shown a willingness to dictate the terms under which private schools operate, the new protesters should appreciate the fact that all tax-supported institutions are uniquely susceptible to such coercion.

As Ramsay David Steele, of the Institute for Humane Studies in Menlo Park, wrote recently, public education "has long been seen as a method for homogenizing the population, indoctrinating it with common ideals. But once this potent force for imposing common values is constructed, a political struggle begins to determine *whose* values are to be the 'common' ones chosen for mass implantation.

"The fundamental problem is that once you politicize an institution, individuals are turned into members of rival gangs fighting to control that institution."

Once the segregationist gang controlled the schools. Now the integrationists dominate. Either way, because the ruling gang has the power of government to impose its notions, rights are trampled and injustice results.

The State

Columbia, S.C., April 1, 1983

LEGISLATION to add one member, presumably black, to each of the state's college and university boards of trustees is not desegregating those boards. It is tokenism.

In 1981, South Carolina was cited by the U.S. Department of Education for failing to eliminate segregation in its institutions of higher education, including the governing boards. The state responded by developing a desegregation plan for higher education. It includes shifting some curricula from white colleges to predominantly black S.C. State in Orangeburg to encourage more white enrollment. The Orangeburg school also got a large increase in appropriations for improvements.

But integration of the trustee boards is a much more complex — and emotional — issue in the Legislature. The old school ties are strong. The institutions' lobbies are influential at the State House. Last year, an effort to revise substantially the trustee boards made no headway in the Senate.

This year, the House Education Committee is sponsoring a bill to give the governor power to appoint one more member to the boards at the University of South Carolina, the Medical University, The Citadel, S.C. State and Winthrop, and to the small colleges' governing board.

The idea is obvious; the governor is expected to appoint a black citizen to each of these new positions. Supporters of the bill acknowledge it is a "good-faith effort" to show to the federal civil rights lawyers. The "effort" has the curious support of the Legislative Black Caucus, which is taking a benign position on what is clearly tokenism. We wonder about the *quid pro quo.*

The Legislature is deceiving itself that this is meaningful integration of the boards, but maybe the federal authorities will accept it as a step in the right direction.

The Miami Herald

Miami, Fla., July 22, 1983

POLLS show that Americans generally are still firm believers in progress. Most like to think that things are getting better and that their children will enjoy more opportunities than the older generation did. Despite occasional setbacks, such optimism persists — with regard to technology and even with regard to social justice.

So it's disquieting, to say the least, to observe a substantial degree of backsliding in an area as important as college attendance by minorities, notably blacks.

A study of enrollment patterns in Florida's nine public universities shows that black enrollment has fallen in the past four academic years after reaching a peak in 1978.

While white enrollment rose by 14,543 from 1978 through last fall, black enrollment declined by 1,139. The percentage of black enrollment in the university system thus dropped to 8.2 per cent from 10.2 per cent.

According to the 1980 Federal census, blacks composed nearly 14 per cent of Florida's population — and a somewhat higher proportion of its college-age population. The current level of enrollment is thus only slightly more than half what might be expected should blacks attend state universities in proportion to their numbers.

Analysts blame the decline on tighter academic standards and cutbacks in financial aid at a time when the economy was beset by rounds of inflation, recession, and persistent high unemployment.

Certainly those factors have played important roles. The money problem, in particular, has caused many black students to drop out of college. Sometimes their decision was not merely a matter of the high costs of college, but also of a need to help support their family.

More-generous programs of grants and loans to college students can help remove money as a barrier to a college education. Follow-up studies conducted after the original GI Bill show that such programs are among the best investments the public can make, repaying financial and social dividends many times over.

Removing the barriers posed by tighter academic standards may be a more-difficult task, however, and one not entirely within the province of the university system.

Indeed, most of the burden of preparing students for college-level work falls upon the public schools. In the long run, the improvements in elementary and secondary education mandated by this year's Legislature should have a favorable impact, if adequately funded in future years. In the short term, however, the university system may have to rethink its decision to phase out remedial instruction for students who may be deficient in one or more academic fields.

Lots of other factors no doubt affect black enrollment, but many are beyond the reach of the university system. All it can do is to renew its efforts in areas where it can have a positive effect on black enrollment. The alternative is to perpetuate a vicious cycle of social injustice and inequality.

THE ATLANTA CONSTITUTION
Atlanta, Ga., Febuary 13, 1984

In one educational category, Georgia stands practically — but shamefully — alone: the extent to which minority kids are programmed for failure.

The disproportionate dumping of black children into classes for slow learners and the "educable" mentally retarded — in which they receive little intellectual stimulation and from which there are no exits — doesn't happen in other parts of the country to the extent that it has been observed in the South. There is little or no inequity in New Hampshire, Michigan, Oregon or Idaho, for example.

But the Southern states are, according to a 1983 study by Georgia State University's Asa Hilliard, "scandalous in the great magnitude of their disproportion." And Georgia, assigning nearly *five times* as many minority kids as white kids to classes for the "educable mentally retarded," is surpassed by only one state, Florida. The practice smacks heavily of covert racism.

Indeed, *white* underachievers typically turn up in a newer, and more socially acceptable category: as candidates for "learning-impaired" classes, in which the emphasis is on remediation rather than discipline.

No wonder black parents are charging, in a dozen lawsuits, that classes are being segregated by race on "grounds" of ability, under the jurisdiction of predominantly white school boards, in what looks like a ploy to restore separate and manifestly unequal systems of public education in Georgia.

Not surprisingly, there's a lot of resistance to that view from educators, many of them wildly enthusiastic about the "ability groupings" or "tracks" that came into vogue in the 1960s. The sorting of students into neat, predictive categories — gifted, college-bound, average learner, underachiever, educable mentally retarded — relieves teachers of a historic headache: how to identify, and serve, the widely divergent needs of many students at one time. No need to blame themselves for little Johnny's failure to catch on, once there is a category for "kids like" Johnny.

But, studies now indicate, children so labeled at the age of 5, 6 or 7 are labeled for life. Given custodial care in lieu of remediation, discipline instead of stimulation and little or no encouragement to master new learning skills, they grow to see themselves — often inaccurately — as "unable" to tackle certain tasks or subjects.

Seventy percent of those failing the state-required basic skills test and almost two-thirds of those expelled from school are black, we're told. But to attribute those disturbing statistics to anything other than educational incompetence, or racism, in some school districts is to ignore the data from other states, where minority kids aren't programmed for failure — not to mention a chilling example, much closer to home:

In Bleckley County, one of 13 Georgia counties sued by the NAACP, blacks and whites were found to have entered school with similar achievement levels, blacks scoring only one-half grade lower than whites on tests. But by the time they left the sixth grade, they were nearly three grade levels apart. Even worse, several blacks were found to have been placed in "slow" tracks, despite their test scores — *higher* than those of some whites in the advanced track.

It's hard to see Georgia's predominantly white school boards, many of them appointed and made up of people who send their children to private schools and are committed to keeping property taxes down, as blameless in the matter.

Our first step must be to acknowledge that we're not educating all our children to their full potential, a horrible human waste and one Georgia can't afford. Clearly, too, elected school boards must be required statewide as a means of assuring that minority concerns are addressed. That will only be a beginning, but it can be an important beginning.

The Cincinnati Post
TIMES — STAR
Cincinnati, Ohio, March 5, 1984

Herbert Brown, one of the black members of the Cincinnati School Board, recently took an audience through the history of black education in the United States. His theme was the priority his people have always placed on education.

Speaking before the Christ Church Community Forum, Brown recalled that a strong white Christian influence attended the development of schools for black children in the 18th century. But he also cited the work of black pioneers from the early years, like Prince Hall, who launched the black fraternity movement in Boston.

He recalled the days before the Civil War when blacks were forbidden by law to educate themselves. And he quoted the Rev. Thomas Calahan, a Presbyterian missionary immediately after the Civil War, who described the former slaves' thirst for education.

"Go out in any direction and you meet Negroes on horses, on mules, by the wagon, cart, buggy load, on foot, men, women, children, in rags, frame houses, tents, and living on bare ground,...all hopeful, almost all cheerful, everyone pleading to be taught, willing to do anything for learning."

The freemen's schools of the South followed, and the black colleges: Howard, Fisk, Talladega, Atlanta University. But in the same period, segregated schools became a way of life, sanctioned in law by the Supreme Court's "separate but equal" decision in 1898.

Slow progress in the 20th century became faster progress after that doctrine was reversed in 1954. Today, Brown said, "blacks are holding jobs not available to us before. Blacks are attending schools and colleges where we were only permitted to sweep the floor in the past."

For all that, racial isolation persists in a city like Cincinnati, where most of the poorest schools are also black. Nearly 80 percent of black high school juniors and seniors are in vocational programs.

The settlement recently reached in Cincinnati's school desegregation suit, Brown said, is an important opportunity to tackle problems like these.

Wisely, he balanced a sense of the challenge before us with a sense of the distance we have come.

The News and Courier
Charleston, S.C., May 23, 1984

A change that substitutes "equal and fair" or "affirmative action" in an education spending plan is not merely toying with words, a fact that the South Carolina NAACP has drawn attention to with a misguided decision to withdraw its political support for it.

Whether the state is actually equal and fair in the selection of those whose jobs are to be funded under the plan or whether it subscribes to affirmative action depends to a large extent upon whether the spending will attain the goals at which it is aimed. Equal and fair access to jobs within school systems does not guarantee good teachers. "Affirmative action," in essence unfair and unequal, guarantees bad teachers, as will any system of selecting teachers that puts racial before professional considerations.

In spite of all the talk of quality education heard in Columbia in connection with the governor's bill and the taxes needed to finance it, it remains an open question whether the people of South Carolina will opt for business as usual in their schools except for higher taxes and increased spending.

Lip service to the cause of good education abounds. Actions speak louder than words. The actions of the NAACP in continuing to play race politics in the classroom speak for themselves.

Supreme Court Rejects Tax Breaks for Biased Schools

The Reagan Administration announced in January, 1982 that nonprofit institutions, including some private and parochial schools and colleges, would be accorded tax-exempt status regardless of their racial policies. The decision revoked a 12-year-old government policy of denying tax exemptions to racially segregated schools.

This Administration reversal aroused such a storm of protest that President Reagan very quickly called upon Congress to undo his policy change through legislation. Reagan insisted that he was opposed to racial bias but defended his tax exemption decision, saying that he was "also opposed to administrative agencies exercising powers that the Constitution assigns to Congress." The President said he would work with Congress "to enact legislation which will prohibit tax exemptions for organizations that discriminate on the basis of race."

Less than a year earlier, in papers filed with the Supreme Court, the Administration had defended a tax penalty for two particular schools with racially discriminatory admissions policies. Bob Jones University, in South Carolina, restricted black enrollments in its kindergarten-through-college program and banned interracial dating or marriage among its students; Goldsboro Christian Schools, in North Carolina, barred admission to blacks from kindergarten through 12th grade. Now, in announcing its policy change, the Justice Department asked that the Supreme Court dismiss a case brought by the two Christian fundamentalist schools and throw out a prior appeals court decision against them. (Both schools had challenged the IRS policy, saying that their racial practices were dictated by Biblical doctrine. The unsuccessful lawsuits were brought on the grounds that the IRS policy exceeded the agency's legal authority, and violated the schools' First Amendment rights to freely practice their religion.)

The Supreme Court declined to dismiss the case, however, and ruled in May, 1984 that the IRS did have the power to deny tax exemptions to private schools that practiced racial discrimination. Chief Justice Warren E. Burger, writing for the majority, said that "it would be wholly incompatible with the concepts underlying tax exemption to grant the benefit of tax-exempt status to racially discriminatory educational entities...Over the past quarter of a century, every pronouncement of this court and myriad acts of Congress and executive orders attest a firm national policy to prohibit racial segregation and discrimination in public education."

The Washington Post

Washington, D.C., January 12, 1982

THE CIVIL RIGHTS movement was pushed back to 1969 on Friday. The Treasury Department announced a reversal of a consistent 12-year policy of denying tax-exempt status to educational institutions that practice racial segregation. Citing the absence of clear statutory authority to withhold tax-exempt status, Treasury officials tossed this hot potato right to Congress, declaring that the benefits would be conferred unless Congress directs otherwise.

This is a deplorable step backward, and one that ignores not only existing laws but also a series of court decisions. The question has long been settled —or at least it had been—and if a good purpose is served by reopening it, no one has said what it is.

In fact, Congress has *already* acted. Title VI of the Civil Rights Act of 1964 specifically prohibits any kind of federal assistance to institutions practicing racial discrimination. Is tax-exempt status such a benefit? You bet it is. First of all, institutions that qualify are exempted from federal Social Security and unemployment taxes. Second, and more important, private contributions to such organizations are tax-deductible, so that gifts are in a real sense subsidized by the taxpayers. In both categories, the advantages that go with tax-exempt status can be measured in dollars and cents. Congress clearly meant to withhold them from segregated schools.

The courts have already spoken, too. Shortly after the 1964 act became law, civil rights groups in Mississippi sued to stop the government from granting tax-exempt status to Jim Crow schools. Even after the IRS conceded in 1970 that it "could no longer justify allowing tax-exempt status to private schools which practice racial discrimination," the Supreme Court affirmed a lower court's prohibition of the practice. In that case, *Voit v. Green*, the court affirmed Treasury's new policy as the only correct interpretation of the Internal Revenue Code. In light of this decision, it is difficult to understand Friday's announcement that tax authorities are powerless to apply a national interest test in these cases.

Finally, the Treasury's reversal of policy is wrong because it's too broad. To date, the Supreme Court has not decided the question of whether schools that discriminate can continue to enjoy tax-exempt status if that discrimination is the result of religious belief. This question was before the court until Friday, with the United States arguing, correctly, that while the government could not prohibit a religious belief that resulted in segregation, such belief need not be subsidized by the taxpayers through the granting of tax exemption. With its announcement Friday, Treasury not only reversed its position in the case of religious groups, it went much further, reinstating tax exemptions for all groups whether or not segregation was required by religious belief.

Now it's up to Congress. A number of members have already said they plan to reverse this new policy by clear and unequivocal statute. Support them.

Detroit Free Press

Detroit, Mich., January 12, 1982

THE REAGAN administration's granting of tax-exempt status to private schools that discriminate on racial grounds is not surprising, but it is morally repugnant. Indeed, across a broad front, the administration is reversing a commitment to end discrimination that had come to have at least bipartisan lip service over the last quarter-century.

The decision of the IRS that tax-exempt status cannot be denied to private schools, colleges and certain other non-profit institutions that practice racial discrimination is a sudden reversal of the policy of the last 11 years. The IRS has denied tax-exempt status to segregated schools under administrations as diverse as those of Richard Nixon, Gerald Ford and Jimmy Carter. Only last September the Justice Department argued before the Supreme Court that federal tax laws required the government to deny tax exemptions to racially discriminatory organizations.

Benjamin Hooks, executive director of the NAACP, has called it "nothing short of criminal" for the IRS to turn about on an issue as settled and established as this one has been. Actually, it is something far worse. It is, in the light of recent federal actions, no more than what should have been expected.

The Reagan administration has been steadily steering the federal government away from its historic role as an advocate of the civil rights of minorities. It has sought to dilute the Voting Rights Act of 1965. Under Mr. Reagan's influence, Congress voted to end court-ordered busing of students to desegregate public schools. The president removed Arthur S. Flemming, an aggressive champion of civil rights and affirmative action, from his chairmanship of the U.S. Civil Rights Commission and replaced him with Clarence Pendleton, a black conservative opposed to busing and affirmative action programs.

The dropping of tax penalties for schools that discriminate could have a more devastating effect that any of these earlier actions. It will signal the private, all-white schools that have sprung up in the South and elsewhere to avoid complying with court-ordered desegregation that they need no longer fear government intervention.

To the degree that such schools and their abhorrent racial policies flourish, we will have moved that much further from bridging the historical, cultural and economic barriers that divide blacks and whites in this country. No one in our Republic can rest easy — or boast of its democratic principles — so long as we remain a nation rent by racial antagonism. Moreover, if Congress now approves tuition tax credits for private schools, that could spell the end not only of the drive for integrated schools but for reasonably well-funded and established public schools altogether.

The administration's actions are not only illegal and divisive but immoral. Those with the clarity of vision to understand what is happening must carry on the fight for a just society. Otherwise, we may find ourselves being compared to another society that believes it can flourish despite segregationist policies that foster racial hate. But do we really want to be known as the South Africa of the West?

St. Petersburg Times

St. Petersburg, Fla., January 12, 1982

There is scarcely any precedent and no plausible excuse for the Reagan administration's sudden decision to award tax exemptions to private schools and colleges that practice racial discrimination.

A tax exemption is, after all, a subsidy. At the whole public's expense, the government will be contributing to the support of institutions that not only practice bigotry but make no secret of it. The question with regard to Bob Jones University, Goldsboro Christian Schools and some 100 other entities whose exemptions had been revoked or denied wasn't even whether they discriminate against blacks, but simply whether it matters that they do. The Reagan administration now says it doesn't matter. This is a profound tragedy and a national disgrace.

FOUR ADMINISTRATIONS — those of Richard Nixon, Gerald Ford, Jimmy Carter and, yes, even Ronald Reagan — had adhered to the position that Congress did not intend for segregationist institutions to qualify as "charitable" under the Internal Revenue Code. To hold otherwise offends not only the law but common decency and common sense. As recently as last September, the Justice Department had filed papers in the Supreme Court in opposition to the Bob Jones and Goldsboro petitions. What reason could have prompted so abrupt and so radical a change? America's historic commitment to racial justice, a high national principle shared by all three branches of government for nearly half a century, no longer prevails at the White House.

No one should be deceived by the crocodile tears shed at the Treasury and Justice Departments last week. They would have it believed that they yielded only reluctantly to the argument that the Internal Revenue Service had usurped Congress' lawmaking power. That's utter nonsense. A federal district court settled this question in 1971 when it ruled that the law requires denial of tax-exempt status to segregated private schools. The government did not contest that conclusion and the Supreme Court upheld it. Most significantly, Congress did not venture thereafter to change the law.

THE REAGAN administration is simply playing to racial prejudice. What possibly might they expect of it? Is this the first shot of the Far Right's "social agenda" offensive? Is it a backdoor attempt to mollify all those to whom Mr. Reagan had promised tuition tax credits? If the latter, it will backfire. Most private colleges and schools have nothing to gain financially from subsidizing bigotry because they don't practice it and already enjoy tax-exempt status.

The president of the 800-member National Association of Independent Schools deplored the Administration's change of position. "Not only is nondiscrimination a national policy, but we consider it a matter of conscience," he said.

One can only hope that the courts will compel the administration to respect the law. The Congress also has an opportunity to act and to act swiftly. In the absence of any countermove, the IRS is likely to be overwhelmed with exemption applications not only from established segregation academies but from new ones. Watch for them to boast of how low their tuitions are, while their tax-exempt "donations" mount up.

MANY MEMBERS of Congress have called for legislation to close the unconscionable loophole that the administration was so eager to open. The House Ways and Means Committee has already scheduled investigative hearings to begin Feb. 4. Floridians may want to pay particular attention to how Rep. L. A. "Skip" Bafalis' performs on this question. He is set to run for governor.

Congress does not enter the dispute with totally clean hands. For years, it has withheld money to stop the IRS from pursuing charges against private schools that deny they practice discrimination. In its shameless surrender to overt prejudice, the Reagan administration no doubt feels secure in the belief that Congress will not interfere. If Congress has any character, now is the time to display it.

The Charlotte Observer

Charlotte, N.C., January 14, 1982

President Reagan's announcement Tuesday that he will seek legislation denying tax-exempt status for schools that discriminate on the basis of race was welcome, particularly coming four days after his administration appeared to give its blessing to such institutions.

Last week Mr. Reagan approved a Treasury Department decision to stop denying tax exemptions for schools that discriminate. That decision deserved the cries of outrage and charges of betrayal it triggered, not only from civil rights groups but also from the president's top black aides and key supporters in Congress.

Mr. Reagan says the Treasury Department decision was based solely on his conviction that government agencies "cannot be allowed to govern by administrative fiat" without a mandate from Congress.

We tend to share the president's discomfort with the idea of the Internal Revenue Service, on its own initiative, using tax policy to punish institutions whose actions do not specifically violate any law.

The Will Of Congress

But the will of Congress regarding racial discrimination in schools is affirmed in laws that deny direct federal financial aid to such schools. Exempting such institutions from certain tax liabilities, and allowing tax deductions for contributions to such institutions, are forms of financial assistance. And the price of that assistance, in lost revenue, is borne by other taxpayers — black and white.

What's most troubling about Mr. Reagan's approval of the treasury decision last week is that he apparently didn't anticipate the angry reactions it produced. We don't doubt that Mr. Reagan is, in his own words, "unalterably opposed to racial discrimination in any form." But he apparently failed to realize that the treasury decision signalled at least passive acceptance of racial discrimination. That failure suggests an alarming insensitivity to what has been the most important issue in American society and government over the past two decades.

It isn't enough for a president to be personally opposed to discrimination, just as it isn't enough for him to favor clean air and water, safe consumer products, a healthy, safe workplace and food for hungry children. If those goals are not as important to him as deregulation or a leaner budget or more vigorous industry, his personal attitudes will be no comfort to those who suffer as a result.

Nevertheless, if Congress enacts the legislation the president says he will propose, the result of what has happened over the past few days should be an even clearer and stronger federal policy against discrimination in private schools, and Mr. Reagan will deserve credit for that.

The Issue Of Religion

Even that legislation is likely to be tested in the courts by institutions such as the Goldsboro Christian Schools in North Carolina, which does not admit black students, and Bob Jones University in Greenville, S.C., which forbids interracial dating or interracial marriages by its students. Both institutions say their discriminatory policies are based on religious convictions and contend that denial of tax exemptions violates constitutional guarantees of religious freedom.

The 4th U.S. Circuit Court of Appeals refused to accept that argument and ruled in favor of the government in both cases, which were being appealed to the U.S. Supreme Court when the Treasury Department announced its change of policy Friday and said it would allow tax exemptions to both schools.

While we find the issue of religious freedom worthy of serious consideration in those cases, we agree with the appeals court, which cited an earlier court ruling denying veterans' benefits to Bob Jones University and its students: "It is clear that the Free Exercise Clause cannot be invoked to justify exemption from a law of general applicability grounded on a compelling state interest."

Some Difficult Questions

These cases, and the prospect of federal law forbidding tax exemptions for institutions that discriminate, raise some other issues too complex to be discussed fully here:

What about institutions that refuse to admit women — or men — or otherwise discriminate on the basis of sex? What about social clubs that discriminate on the basis of race or sex and benefit from tax policies that allow their members tax deductions for business entertainment there?

Congress, in framing the legislation Mr. Reagan plans to request, ought to consider those questions, too.

THE CHRISTIAN SCIENCE MONITOR

Boston Mass., January 14, 1982

Who says that citizens are helpless in the face of a poor White House decision? As a result of a swift public outcry, President Reagan has shifted his view on tax exemptions for private segregated schools. His aides clearly failed to think through the consequences when the Treasury Department recently reversed a 12-year-old policy of denying such tax breaks to private institutions practicing racial discrimination. The new policy opened the President to a charge of promoting racism, and it is therefore to his credit that he has moved quickly to assure Americans that is not the case.

However, the new IRS policy of granting tax exemptions to nonprofit institutions which engage in racial bias will remain in force until Congress outlaws it. The President says he favors such a ban and will submit appropriate legislation. Splendid.

The administration maintains, justifiably, that the Internal Revenue Service should not have the authority to make social policy without legislative mandate. One can only imagine the mischief the IRS might get into if it began operating more and more solely by executive order.

It is now up to Congress to legislate guidelines for the IRS. This will not be easy, given the political pressures and the legal complexities of the issue. But the worthy goal warrants pushing ahead. Surely private schools and colleges should not be given tax benefits when they flout national policy. Church-related schools, above all, have a moral obligation to be responsive to antidiscrimination laws. They are free to practice racial segregation as a matter of religious principle if they choose, but in that event why should they be given government support in the form of tax exemptions? All Americans in such case would then be asked to pay for maintaining racial bias. Let's not forget, too, that individual contributions to nonprofit institutions are tax deductible; so segregated organizations benefit already even before being allowed tax exemptions.

President Reagan promises to work with Congress to disallow the latter type of tax benefits. Those who worried about the IRS decision can ask him to apply all the determination which he exhibited in getting his tax program through. The national goal of racial equality can use his proven political skill.

The Sun Reporter

San Francisco, Calif., January 21, 1982

President Ronald Reagan in his first 1981 press conference proclaimed "I am unalterably opposed to all forms of racism or discrimination based upon color, creed or sex. As President I will enforce the laws against discrimination, if necessary at the point of a gun."

Actor Reagan should receive applause for this rhetoric. However, Ronald Reagan, 40th President of the United States, reveals in his personal action, as well as in the behavior of the White House staff, that Reagan is an old racist wolf hiding in sheep's clothing. Attorney General Smith, the Justice Department and the Treasury Department requested the U.S. Supreme Court to repudiate the Internal Revenue Service's 11-year-old policy, begun during Richard M. Nixon's presidency, of denying tax exemptions to private institutions which racially discriminated. After four days and some bitter criticism by racial minority groups, civil liberatarians and politicians of both major parties, Reagan announced he would propose specific legislation authorizing the IRS to deny such tax exemptions.

While Reagan awaits Congressional action, two of the institutions involved—Bob Jones University in South Carolina and the Goldsboro Christian Schools in North Carolina—will be allowed tax exemptions, but if the Supreme Court rules against them, these two institutions would have to pay the tax retroactively. While Reagan tries to extricate himself from this dilemma, Ed Meese, former Assistant District Attorney of Alameda County, who has been Reagan's alter ego since the early years of the Reagan governorshp, and up until now Reagan's spokesman to Black America, admitted that he acted alone on the racial tax ruling.

The wire services carried a story in the 1980 Presidential campaign that Reagan had promised at Bob Jones University that he would stop the IRS from creating and administering public policy not established by Congress. Reagan kept this promise on Jan 8. Besides ordering the IRS to stop denying the tax exemptions, since the IRS would then be granting Bob Jones and Goldsboro their sought-after tax exemptions, the administration asked the Supreme Court to throw out the Bob Jones and Goldsboro cases on the ground that they would become moot.

Over the first 12 months of Reagan's administration, there have been low-keyed but definite movements against civil rights and civil liberties statutes passed over the past fifty years. Reagan's campaign promises to Southern Republicans and national racists seem to be surfacing. The U.S. Civil Rights Commission, under its retiring chairman, Arthur Fleming, condemned Reagan's action.

The Carter Administration worked closely with the Federal Communications Commision to establish an affirmative action policy in the granting and renewal of radio and television licenses; however, in November 1981 the Smith Justice Department wrote a memorandum to the FCC suggesting that the Commission quietly phase out all affirmative action plans.

Donald Devine, the recently appointed acting chairman of the Office of Personnel Management, prepared an executive order, now awaiting the President's signature, denying 9 or 10 national charity organizations the right to participate in the Combined Federal Campaign. The old Civil Service Commission and the United Way of America are under orders of the U.S. District Court of Washington, D.C., to open the combined Federal Campaign so that the 9 or 10 national charities can participate.

While these incidents of racism are isolated, a mosaic is being formed. Reagan is literally destroying the accomplishments of racial minorities, women and the aged in their 50-year long struggle to remove inequities existing under the federal umbrella of institutional racism and sexism.

Whenever these single forays of Reagan and his minions against civil rights and civil liberties cause momentary shock-waves in the body politic, the President declares, "I share with you and your colleagues an unalterable opposition to racism in any form; such practices are repugnant to all that our nation and its citizens hold dear, and I believe this repugnance shold be plainly reflected in our laws." At the same time, the President states: "Agencies such as the IRS should not be permitted, even with the best of intentions...to govern by administrative fiat, exercising powers that the Constitution assigns to the Congress." Because of the possibility of a long filibuster, Reagan knows his proposed legislation prohibiting tax exemptions to any school which discriminates on the basis of race will probably not pass in the U.S. Senate.

The truth of the matter is: U.S. Congress in the Civil Rights Bills of 1964 and 1965 passed statutes denying U.S. tax exemption to any organizations refusing to obey the '64 and '65 statutes. The Federal Courts, District, Appellate, and even the U.S. Supreme Court, have affirmed these statutes as constitutional.

The Evening Bulletin

Philadelphia, Pa., January 14, 1982

The Gipper didn't get to the White House by dragging his feet. Just as he did when his Social Security cuts ran into a buzzsaw of criticism last year, President Reagan this week quickly changed course on tax exemptions for racially-discriminatory schools. It was none too soon either. The flap promised to become a major election issue for Republican congressmen.

What the President did, basically, was to alter his earlier decision to pass the problem to Congress. Now he promises to work with Congress to outlaw tax exemptions for organizations that racially discriminate.

The change, however, does not deny tax exemptions to the two southern schools in question or more than 100 others in 11 southeastern states. That's a mistake, in our view.

What the Administration did last week was legally complicated. In simple terms, it asked the Supreme Court to allow it to reinstate one school's tax exemption and grant an exemption to the other. How could such a legal move be interpreted as anything but racist?

Is Reagan himself a racist? The President says he is not, that he is unalterably opposed to racial discrimination — and his record seems to support that.

But this does not mean that certain of his conservative southern supporters feel the same way, or that they had no influence in his initial decision.

Was he then simply unaware his decision would be seen as racist? Apparently so, which he said he regretted.

But Reagan is equally opposed to government intrusion in private life. In his zeal to strip the Internal Revenue Service or any other government agency of broad regulatory authority, he failed to recognize the political repercussions of his act.

In effect, he reversed a decision which goes all the way back to another Republican administration. In Nixon's first term, the White House decided that denying tax exemptions was the surest way to hamper the spread of all-white private schools in the south.

'Will the new law lift tax exemptions from racially-discriminating schools elsewhere?

How long will it take Reagan to send a bill to Congress? He didn't say. The question deserves an answer.

Will he give it the wholehearted support that he gave the tax cuts and the AWACS deal? Will he be able to overcome a Senate filibuster? No one knows. But sensing opposition, he wisely won support from leading conservatives in Congress. That's the way to head off opposition before it starts.

Will the new law be broad enough to lift tax exemptions from discriminating schools or other organizations elsewhere in the country? It should. At this point, only southern schools are excluded. They're not the only ones that discriminate.

THE DAILY OKLAHOMAN
Oklahoma City, Okla., January 26, 1982

PRESIDENT Reagan explained at his news conference last week that the change in his administration's stand on tax exemptions for private schools was intended as a procedural change, not a changed policy toward racial discrimination.

He intended to get away from having the Internal Revenue Service write law to support a particular social policy. As he stated it, a primary goal of his administration is to return lawmaking powers to the elected officials — i.e., the Congress — and take them away from the bureaucrats.

That is a goal most of us can only applaud. But the question involved is a social issue that requires attention.

Congress ought to turn its attention immediately to the writing of an acceptable policy on tax exemptions for schools that have racist rules.

Bob Jones University has been mentioned in news accounts of these events because it is involved in a current lawsuit with the IRS over its tax exemption. But that school accepts students of all races; it does not systematically exclude blacks or any other racial or ethnic group. It is a religious school, and its students must comply with its strict rules governing daily life. It bans dating and marriage between members of differing races, based on a religious belief that the races should not intermarry.

Neither Congress nor the IRS has any business getting involved·

The schools whose tax-exempt status is at issue, in contrast, are those that are clearly segregationist, and whose admission standards exclude blacks or those of other minority groups. They should not, as a matter of public policy, be entitled to tax-exempt status.

The administration is correct in saying that how such cases stand before the law should depend on what laws Congress has written, not on the whims of bureaucrats who are not, in any sense, answerable to the American people.

In our view, schools that make racial exclusions their policy have every right to exist, but not to be exempted from taxation on the basis of their status as educational institutions. Congress should say as much by enacting a law that will henceforth forbid a tax exemption to such schools.

The Seattle Times
Seattle, Wash., April 25, 1982

WE ARE pleased that the U.S. Supreme Court has agreed to rule on federal tax breaks for schools that practice racial discrimination.

A court ruling should remove this issue from the kind of political battering it has had lately.

For 12 years, the Internal Revenue Service has refused certain exemptions to schools that discriminate against racial and ethnic minorities. But it has been a matter of department policy, without roots in congressional edict or court action. As a result, the policy is subject to the whim of whoever is in power.

That absence of firm legal standing left the ban open to legal challenge from the offending schools. But three presidents did not object to the IRS exerting its power in that way. Then Ronald Reagan was elected.

Reagan believed, he said, that the IRS should not have so much power. In January, he announced his decision to lift the ban. He defended his action by saying it was Congress' responsibility to pass a law barring federal tax exemptions to schools with discriminatory policies, if that was the will of the lawmakers.

The president's explanation was greeted with much derision, particularly since he planned to allow the schools in question to benefit from the tax exemptions while Congress deliberated.

The administration soon caved in under the enormous political pressures that followed, and turned to the Supreme Court for help.

Congress has had ample time to override the IRS ban. The failure to do so must be interpreted as general agreement with the policy.

But regardless of Congress' attitude, and the president's meddling, the Supreme Court was going to become involved in the case because of challenges from Bob Jones University and Goldsboro Christian School.

The court should have no trouble recognizing the basic unfairness of requiring minorities, through their tax dollars, to subsidize schools that are not open to them or treat them differently than other students.

FORT WORTH STAR-TELEGRAM
Fort Worth, Texas, May 30, 1983

In decrying the U.S. Supreme Court's ruling that the Internal Revenue Service can withhold tax-exempt status for private schools that practice racial discrimination, the president of Bob Jones University inadvertently provided more justification for that ruling.

"The ruling will not change one thing we do in our school except that we will pay taxes," said Bob Jones III.

What he was saying was that Bob Jones University will continue to prohibit interracial dating and interracial marriage for its students. And he is correct in suggesting that the Supreme Court can do nothing about that. But the court did not rule that the university must change its racially discriminatory policies. Nor did the court say Goldsboro Christian School in Goldsboro, N.C., which does not admit black students, must begin doing so. All the court said, in effect, was that the American taxpayers will not subsidize those schools.

The issue of religious freedom, which Jones said was the crux of the matter, had no real bearing on the lawsuit that resulted from Bob Jones University's having lost its tax-exempt status in 1976 because of its policies. No one's right to believe and preach was abridged. While the U.S. Constitution guarantees freedom of religion, it nowhere provides that all religious institutions should be tax-exempt regardless of the religious beliefs and practices associated with such institutions.

The court ruled 8-1, with Justice William Rehnquist dissenting, that the Reagan administration erred in breaking with a 13-year-old IRS policy of denying tax-exempt status to schools that practice racial discrimination. President Reagan said the administration will abide by the Supreme Court ruling.

Chief Justice Warren Burger acknowledged that the ruling would be a serious blow to many private religious institutions, and some may even be forced to close because their financial supporters will be less inclined to contribute to them if their contributions are not tax-exempt. But he said:

"The governmental interest (in stamping out racial discrimination in education) substantially outweighs whatever burden denial of tax benefits places on (the schools') exercise of their religious beliefs."

By way of putting this matter in perspective, one has only to imagine what would have happened had the Supreme Court ruled in favor of Bob Jones University. Instead of many private schools facing hard times and possibly closing, a new era of prosperity for schools that practice discrimination would have begun. Indeed, many more such schools would be opened.

The Supreme Court stated correctly and unambiguously with this ruling that racial discrimination in education runs counter to the fundamental policy of the nation and it cannot be supported financially by the federal government. It was a Supreme Court that is considered overall to be one of the most conservative in recent history that said that.

THE INDIANAPOLIS NEWS
Indianapolis, Ind., May 28, 1983

The U.S. Supreme Court made two key mistakes in its recent ruling against two private schools that practice racial discrimination.

The court ruled in favor of the Internal Revenue Service decision to revoke the tax exempt status of Bob Jones University in South Carolina and the Goldsboro Christian Schools in North Carolina.

Justice William Rehnquist, the only dissenter, pointed out that Congress should have ruled on this matter, instead of turning it over to the IRS to make the rules. "This court should not legislate for Congress," he declared.

Congress shares some of the blame, for avoiding its responsibilities. But the court could have stepped aside from the issue, to keep the constitutional responsibilities of each branch of government properly balanced.

The court also failed to rule on these two schools separately. In the Goldsboro case, the school is openly practicing racial discrimination against black applicants. We think the Congress, not the Supreme Court, should explicitly write a tax rule declaring that this kind of institution should not have the blessing of government tax exemptions.

The Bob Jones case, however, is different. The school no longer refuses to admit blacks. Its admissions policies are not discriminatory.

However, the university does prohibit interracial dating in its rules for students. As unwise as this kind of rule may be, it does not warrant the interference of the IRS or the U.S. Supreme Court. Educational institutions should be able to make their own internal rules, without interference from the government and the courts.

The Providence Journal
Providence, R.I., May 27, 1983

It is clear now, as a result of Tuesday's ruling by the United States Supreme Court, that federal tax exemptions may not be granted to private schools that are racially discriminatory. The 1970 policy of the Internal Revenue Service has been vindicated and the administration's attempts to overturn that policy over the last 17 months have been defeated.

The 8-to-1 ruling is a triumph of reason. In January, 1982 when the Justice Department declared the IRS policy void because it had never been

---

Interpretations of the Bible could be cited by any private educational institution in defense of a tax exemption

---

spelled out in congressional legislation, it appeared to many that two things were happening: 1. a valid tax policy approved by three Presidents was being flouted for political reasons; and 2. the nation's battle against racial discrimination on private campuses was being stopped in its tracks.

If Bob Jones University of Greenville, S.C. could ban interracial dating and marriage on religious grounds and the Goldsboro Christian Schools of Goldsboro, N.C. could maintain a racially discriminatory admissions policy for the same reason, others could do the same. If these schools and the all-white academies formed to avoid desegregation could have received federal subsidies through tax exemptions, the fight for equal educational opportunity would have been dealt a telling blow.

Interpretations of the Bible could be cited by any private educational

institution in defense of a tax exemption. The Rev. Bob Jones, president of the university, pursued that argument in response to the court's decision. The ruling, he said, was "an assault on religious freedom." In fact, religious schools remain free to practice racial discrimination but not with federal sanction or the taxpayers' money.

"Over the past quarter century," wrote Chief Justice Warren E. Burger, "every pronouncement of this court and myriad acts of Congress and executive orders attest a firm national policy to prohibit racial segregation and discrimination in public schools."

What about the 13-year-old IRS code (Section 501c3) banning tax exemptions for schools that lacked a racially non-discriminatory policy? Bob Jones and Goldsboro, along with the administration, said the code lacked congressional authorization. Justice Burger held that the policy was "wholly consistent with what Congress, the executive and the courts had repeatedly declared prior to 1970." Moreover, since that time 13 bills designed to overturn the policy had been rejected by Congress.

Many will regret the advent of this dispute. It bore all the earmarks of major regression in a civil rights struggle of more than three decades. In a more positive sense, however, it may have served as a healthy reminder of the nation's commitment to racial justice and a reaffirmation of this country's inexorable march toward a more harmonious society.

The court has earned the nation's gratitude. It has spoken on this crucial issue with wisdom and clarity, reflecting the public's overwhelming — and, it is hoped, unending — opposition to official policies that tolerate bigotry.

TULSA WORLD

Tulsa, Okla., May 25, 1983

THE U.S. Supreme Court Tuesday ruled the Internal Revenue Service can deny tax breaks to private schools practicing racial discrimination. The decision gives President Reagan the opportunity to bury one of the worst civil rights decisions of his administration — his reversal of the federal government's 13-year policy denying tax exemptions to schools that discriminate.

Since 1970, the Internal Revenue Service has held that racially discriminatory private schools are not charitable institutions and, therefore, are not entitled to tax exemptions.

In January 1982, the administration foolishly ventured into a political minefield by challenging IRS' right to deny the tax breaks. At issue was tax-exempt status for Bob Jones University in South Carolina, a fundamentalist college which prohibits interracial dating, and Goldsboro Christian Schools in North Carolina, which refuse to enroll black students. The tax question was complicated by the schools' claim that their policy of race discrimination was a religious belief.

The administration contended that Congress never expressly authorized IRS to deny tax exemptions on discriminatory grounds; therefore, the schools were entitled to tax breaks.

The outpouring of feeling from blacks and whites alike surprised the administration, which belatedly developed a legalistic argument to justify its stance. The president claimed he had to challenge IRS to "rein in the federal bureaucracy."

Public criticism forced the administration to backtrack and ask Congress to explicitly authorize IRS to deny the exemptions.

The Supreme Court's decision makes the request irrelevant. The president's wisest course would be to pronounce the issue settled and extricate himself completely. Any other course risks compounding the administration's original blunder.

BUFFALO EVENING NEWS

Buffalo, N.Y., May 29, 1983

It is gratifying that the Supreme Court has now ruled that private schools practicing racial discrimination do not qualify for federal tax exemption. Both the lopsided, 8-to-1 margin of the decision and the cogency of the majority's arguments should dispel any ambiguities that had recently clouded this issue.

The case dates back to 1970 when the Internal Revenue Service removed the tax-exempt status from two private schools, Bob Jones University in South Carolina and Goldsboro Christian Schools in North Carolina. The two schools disputed the authority of the IRS to take such action under the law. Maintaining that their discrimination against blacks flowed from their religious beliefs, they also contended that denial of the special tax status violated their constitutionally guaranteed free exercise of religion.

Last year, reversing the policy of three prior administrations, the Reagan administration blundered into the case by saying that, while it abhorred racial discrimination, it found no legal basis for the 1970 IRS action. There followed a series of wobbly shifts of administration position.

But now the nation's highest court, in an unequivocal decision written by Chief Justice Warren Burger, has cut through these claims with convincing logic and forcefulness.

On the narrower question of whether the law entitled the IRS to withdraw the exemption from the two schools, Justice Burger ruled it did. The IRS action conformed to what Congress, the executive and the courts had often declared before 1970, he said, and Congress since then had repeatedly refused to reverse that well-established policy.

To us, the controlling argument about religious freedom has been that denial of the tax exemption did not foreclose observance of these beliefs, however repugnant they were, by the institutions involved. It simply and correctly denied them the public subsidy by a society whose values on racial discrimination are diametrically opposed to those of these private institutions.

As the majority opinion pointed out, "the government has a fundamental, overriding interest in eradicating racial discrimination in education, discrimination that prevailed, with official approval, for the first 165 years of this nation's history. That governmental interest substantially outweighs whatever burden denial of tax benefits places on petitioners' exercise of their religious beliefs."

Our constitutional system guarantees a diversity of religious belief and practice, and the authority of government must take care on issues touching these matters. Significantly, however, even Justice William Rehnquist, who dissented from the majority opinion on narrower grounds, did not object in terms of the church-state relationship.

This country should not extend special tax treatment to educational institutions that practice racial bias. That would mock human equality and justice under law. Now the nation's highest court has cut to the core of the argument, assuring that does not happen in these kinds of cases. Its judicious clarification eliminates the need for further action by Congress and ought to put an end to the dispute.

THE PLAIN DEALER

Cleveland, Ohio, May 27, 1983

It has been nearly three decades since the Supreme Court tore down the nation's historic sanctions on segregated schools, yet attempts to retain vestiges of racial barriers endure. So, in an unusually firm ruling this week, the court struck a financial blow against islands of American apartheid, upholding the Internal Revenue Service's authority to revoke the tax exemption of private institutions that practice racial discrimination.

While an estimated 100 schools will be affected, the immediate focus is on the two that appealed to the court. Bob Jones University in Greenville, S.C., barred enrollment of black students until the 1970s and still rejects interracial dating and marriage. The Goldsboro (N.C.) Christian Schools do not admit blacks. Both institutions argued that the restrictions are based on their interpretation of the Bible.

As the justices pointed out, numerous court opinions and congressional actions since 1954 have set a firm national policy against racial discrimination. Tax exemption is based on whether an institution promotes or benefits society in keeping with public policy. The court held that because taxpayers become indirect contributors to a tax-exempt institution, a school "must not be so at odds with the common community conscience as to undermine any public benefit." Further, the court said that the Bob Jones ban on interracial dating and marriage violates earlier court decisions against discrimination based on racial affiliation and association.

There is, indeed, a fine line between the constitutional guarantees of religious freedom and the overriding public interest. The court concluded that not all burdens on religions are unconstitutional. Although the denial of tax benefits will have a substantial impact on the private schools' operation, the ruling will not prevent those schools, their students and their officials from observing their religious tenets. The institutions simply cannot expect the public to help pay for them.

The court's 8-1 ruling was a stinging repudiation of the Reagan administration's controversial endorsement of the schools' position, a stand that threatened to undo some of the progress of the last 29 years. The personal insults hurled by Bob Jones III against the justices was the kind of rhetoric heard at each major step of the civil rights movement. However sincere the schools are in their religious beliefs, allowing tax exemptions would have reopened the door to the creation of countless havens of bigotry.

THE SACRAMENTO BEE

Sacramento, Calif., May 25, 1983

Had it not been for the Reagan administration's clumsy attempt to reverse 12 years of civil rights policy, yesterday's Supreme Court decision upholding the denial of tax exemptions to two racially discriminatory private schools would have been no more than a legal footnote.

In yesterday's decision, the court rejected, 8-1, the contention of Bob Jones University and the Goldsboro Christian Schools of Greenville, S.C., that since their racial policies are a matter of religious belief and practice, denial of their tax-exempt status violates the Constitution's guarantee of religious freedom. The court also specifically rejected arguments that in the absence of specific legislation authorizing its regulation, the Treasury Department had no power to deny tax exemptions to the two institutions.

"It would be wholly incompatible with the concepts underlying the tax exemption," wrote Chief Justice Burger for the court, "to grant the benefit of tax-exempt status to racially discriminatory educational entities, which exert a pervasive influence on the entire educational process. Whatever may be the rationale for such private schools' policies, and however sincere the rationale may be, racial discrimination in education is contrary to public policy."

Nothing in that is remotely new. It has, one way or another, been affirmed and confirmed in scores of other situations by virtually every court in the country. What was notable in this affair was the way the Reagan administration, beginning early last year, tried to undercut longstanding government policy. After two reversals of position, the administration permitted a 12-year-old Treasury Department rule, first adopted in the Nixon administration, to stand, but instead of supporting civil rights groups — and its own practice — it joined the segregated academics in arguing before the Supreme Court that the Treasury Department had no right to do what it did.

Thus, for the first time in more than a generation, the U.S. government went to court to defend what, in effect, was racial segregation. It's to be hoped that the whole thing will now be forgotten — though the episode hardly enhances the administration's claims about its devotion to civil rights. With some luck, it may also represent the last occasion in American history when the U.S. government went to court on the side of segregationists defending racist practices.

Pittsburgh Post-Gazette

Pittsburgh, Pa., May 26, 1983

A week after President Reagan went out of his way to deny that his administration was hostile to civil rights, the U.S. Supreme Court has reminded blacks and whites alike of a Reagan gaffe that has contributed mightily to that impression.

Overruling the administration's view of the law — which Mr. Reagan backed away from after a national furor — the high court ruled 8-1 on Tuesday that America's "fundamental national public policy" against racial discrimination justified the Internal Revenue Service in denying tax-exempt status to racist private schools. The ruling, which came in cases involving Bob Jones University in Greenville, S.C., and the Goldsboro (N.C.) Christian Schools, upholds a 12-year-old IRS policy that Mr. Reagan tried to overturn last year.

The court's decision represents a deserved rebuke for the Reagan administration.

To hear the president tell it, his original attempt to abolish the IRS rule was motivated by legal scruples about whether the agency, without explicit congressional direction, could deprive discriminatory private schools of tax-exempt status.

But Mr. Reagan's critics offered another — and more plausible — interpretation: that the president was simply obliging Southern conservative supporters who long have complained about the IRS rule. The same critics noted tellingly that Congress had made no effort over a decade to overturn the IRS rule, and, indeed, had relied on it in framing legislation to deny tax-exempt status to discriminatory private clubs.

This week's court decision confirms the status quo by ruling on the main question raised at oral arguments: whether the IRS exceeded its authority in denying tax-exempt status to institutions that explicitly discriminate on racial grounds. (Bob Jones University, while it admits black students, forbids interracial dating. The Goldsboro schools refuse to enroll blacks at all.)

In ruling that the IRS acted within its authority, the court has offered a resounding affirmation of the national commitment to racial equality, a commitment reflected in innumerable congressional enactments and court decisions. "There can no longer be any doubt that racial discrimination in education violates deeply and widely accepted views of elementary justice [and] a most fundamental national public policy," Chief Justice Warren E. Burger wrote for the majority.

The court acknowledged that both Bob Jones University and the Goldsboro Schools based their racial policies on their interpretation of Scripture. But it found no violation of religious freedom in the IRS's decision to give greater weight to the presumption against racism than to the schools' religious motivations for their violation of standards required of other tax-exempt institutions. (Contrary to fears expressed at the time the Bob Jones case was argued, this week's decision does not threaten the tax-exempt status of single-sex religious schools or those private schools whose natural constituency — for example, Jews or black Muslims — happens to be of one race. Like the IRS rule, the decision focuses narrowly on intentional racial discrimination.)

Discriminatory schools are free to continue in existence, as they certainly will; they are not free to benefit from the national policy of using the tax system to shore up charitable enterprises.

Chicago Defender

Chicago, Ill., May 18, 1983

In ruling to deny tax exemptions to private schools with discriminatory racial policy, the Supreme Court handed down a judgement that will stand as a landmark that transcends mere legal conformity. The decision establishes a social policy that adds strength to the democratic structure. This is the present court's finest hour since the Earl Warren court's school desegregation ruling of May 17, 1954. It set the climate for a reaffirmation of constitutional rights as the framers of that historic document had conceived them.

Chief Justice Burger was exercising Salmonic wisdom when he said, speaking for the court's majority, that it was "against public interest" to perpetuate racial bias in schools that contend they are entitled to tax exemptions. The ruling came on an appeal from the Internal Revenue Service which denied applications for tax exemptions to South Carolina's Bob Jone's University whose status in the academic community is yet undetermined, and to a religious school in Goldsboro, North Carolina.

Since 1970, the IRS has held that a racially discriminatory private school is not a charitable institution entitled to tax exemption from Social Security, withholding and unemployment taxes. The IRS has also refused to treat wills to such schools as charitable deductions for income tax purposes. The case was argued with eminence and distinction by one of the most brilliant attorneys in the District of Columbia, William T. Coleman, a Black civil rights activist, who was appointed by the high court. It was a great day for him, for the court and for civil rights on which President Reagan has been hard at work in the White House funeral parlor.

The Birmingham News

Birmingham, Ala., May 27, 1983

No one should be suprised that the Supreme Court ruled in favor of the Internal Revenue Service in denying tax-exempt status to Bob Jones University and Goldsboro Christian Schools in North Carolina (and other institutions which have racially discriminatory policies). The ruling is consistent with scores of others the court has handed down since the landmark *Brown vs Board of Education* in 1954.

The vote on the decision was 8 to 1, with Justice William H. Rehnquist dissenting. While the effect of the ruling is desirable, we doubt that it was proper. The court said the Reagan administration was wrong when it contended that Congress had never empowered the IRS to withhold tax-exempt status because of racially discriminatory policies.

That was the real issue before the court — not whether the school practiced forms of racial discrimination as a matter of policy and not whether religious freedom was violated in denying tax-exempt status.

And it was on the matter of the court's power that Justice Rehnquist dissented. He agreed that that Congress "could deny tax-exempt status to educational institutions that promote racial discrimination. . . But, unlike the court," he wrote, " I am convinced that Congress simply has failed to take this action and, as this court has said over and over again, regardless of our view on the propriety of Congress' failure to legislate we are not constitutionally empowered to act for them. . . I have no disagreement with the court's finding that there is a strong national policy in this country opposed to racial discrimination.

"I agree with the court that Congress has the power to further this policy by denying (tax-exampt) status to organizations that practice racial discrimination.

"But as of yet Congress has failed to do so. Whatever the reasons for the failure, this court should not legislate for Congress."

One cannot argue with the court's anti-discrimination sentiment or, as Rehnquist pointed out, that the policies of the government as a whole are overwhelmingly opposed to racial discrimination. But there is something to be said about the court's penchant for putting sentiment ahead of the law, and in effect, legislating that which has not been approved by Congress as law and for making policy where the court has no power to do so.

Congress has clearly had ample opportunity to express its will on the matter and, for one reason or another, has refused.

The decision, however much we may agree with its effect, is therefore flawed. Congress should not have been taken off the hook any more than the Reagan administration. The court should have ruled in such a way that Congress would be forced to take a stand to provide a clear legal base for withholding tax-exempt status to Bob Jones and other institutions which have similar discriminatory policies.

The State

Columbia, S.C., May 27, 1983

THE U. S. Supreme Court has finally decided conclusively that racial discrimination defies public policy as tacitly expressed by Congress.

The ruling dealt a financial blow to fundamentalist Bob Jones University, which contended that it is entitled to a tax exempt status as a charitable institution. It was also a defeat for President Reagan. He had contended that bureaucratic institutions like the Internal Revenue Policy should not fashion broad public policy. Such policy, he said, should be clearly spelled out by Congress.

But the court ruled that Congress, by its inaction, had "acquiesced" in the IRS rulings of 1970 and 1971.

The 13-year-old case is complicated. It was marked by many twists and turns up to the denouement in the land's highest tribunal.

The landmark case was rooted in an IRS decision during the Nixon Administration. In 1970, it decided that the Greenville institution's discrimination against blacks denied it the right of exemption from taxes. But it was not until May, 1975, that a court order forced BJU to admit unmarried blacks.

But BJU continued to deny admission to "any applicant known to be a partner in an interracial marriage." And it expelled students for interracial dating or for encouraging it.

IRS then revoked BJU's tax-exempt status. But the school contended its religious rights were violated and won a federal court ruling which the U.S. Circuit Court of Appeals for the 4th Circuit reversed. Then the case moved to the high court.

Under Mr. Reagan, the government first contended IRS' authority was derived from national policy as set forth in many federal laws and in the Constitution. Last year the Administration made two surprising turns. It revoked the IRS policy, claiming Congress had never clearly addressed the issue. Then Mr. Reagan asked Congress to deny tax-exempt status to institutions like Bob Jones. Congress never acted.

Thus, the question the court decided was not whether racial discrimination is wrong. Most responsible and fair people think it is. They agree with freedom of religion but don't think taxpayers should have to subsidize, indirectly, institutions that discriminate.

But the question before the court was what authority IRS has and whether Congress had clearly expressed its intent.

Indeed, many organizations which eschew the narrow tenets of Bob Jones, including one Jewish group, supported the school's cause.

Now the court, by an 8 to 1 vote, has decided the issue once and for all. The vehicle for the decision also involved Goldsboro Christian Schools in North Carolina, which refuses to admit blacks.

The ruling will cost Bob Jones in two big-money ways: Donors will no longer get tax breaks for their gifts. And BJU will now have to pay federal taxes.

But college President Bob Jones III, charging "religious freedom has been murdered" by the court, said the school will pay the taxes but won't change policy because "it's a Bible policy." But religious freedom, like other basic freedoms, are not absolute. They are subject to some curbs.

The court's ruling, which sanctions the long-accepted, but dubious, use of taxing to achieve social ends, certainly strikes a major blow against racial discrimination. We hope that the approval of such broad power to a bureaucratic agency does not become a troublesome precedent in the future.

Portland Press Herald

Portland, Maine, May 31, 1983

The U.S. Supreme Court has sent a clear message to the Reagan administration: This country is not about to back away from its national commitment to the concept of racial equality.

By a vote of 8-1 the court ruled that racially disciminatory private schools are not eligible for federal tax exemptions. Specifically, the ruling supported the Internal Revenue Service in its denial of tax-exempt status to Bob Jones University of Greenville, S.C., which prohibits interracial dating or marriage on grounds of religious belief.

The Reagan administration argued in favor of tax exemptions for the school and another private religious college which does not admit blacks. It was an attempt to reverse a 13-year-old IRS policy which has had the full support of three previous presidents: Nixon, Ford and Carter.

The Supreme Court, led by Chief Justice Warren E. Burger, made plain that it would not permit the current administration to break with recent civil rights policies. Educational institutions which practice racial discrimination, for whatever reason, "should (not) be encouraged by having all taxpayers share in their support by way of special tax status," said the court.

Freedom of religion is not at issue here; the schools are perfectly free to carry on their discriminatory practices in the name of religious conviction. They just cannot expect to reap the benefit of special tax breaks if they do so.

The court said that the government's "overriding interest in eradicating racial discrimination in education" is sufficiently compelling to justify whatever economic burden a school may suffer from the denial of tax-exempt status.

In a nation pledged to racial equality, there will be a penalty to be paid by those who seek its denial.

Roanoke Times & World-News

Roanoke, Va., May 27, 1983

IF WORDS were thunderbolts, the Supreme Court building in Washington would be zapped to its foundations. And if the fulminations of Dr. Bob Jones III had the force of divine decree, the coals of hell would be stirred in anticipation of eight new black-robed arrivals.

The smell of brimstone hovers over Greenville, S. C., home of Bob Jones University, where racial apartheid is practiced in the name of religion and fiery damnation is preached for those whose views waver from that orthodoxy.

The Supreme Court of the United States did more than waver. All nine of its members found that the Congress of the United States has the right to deny tax-exempt status to privately operated schools that practice racial discrimination. Eight of its members went further. They held that Congress has, in fact, denied such status and that the Internal Revenue Service was correct in concluding that Bob Jones University and Goldsboro Christian Schools in Goldsboro, N. C., were not entitled to it.

Jones, exercising his usual gift for understatement, called it the murder of freedom of religion in this country. Nonsense.

The court has not denied Bob Jones or Goldsboro Christian Schools the right to practice racial discrimination as part of their religion, or to teach it as part of their instructional program. It has ruled, simply, that the United States government doesn't have to subsidize that discrimination. It has a right to refuse to grant these schools and their supporters exemption from taxes that they would ordinarily have to pay.

The Civil Rights Act establishes as a national policy the elimination of racial discrimination. The tax code allows tax exemption for organizations of a literary, scientific, religious, educational or charitable nature. But the IRS took the position — backed by respectable legal opinion — that such organizations cannot claim such exemption if they are in conflict with national policy. It found that racial discrimination practiced by Bob Jones and Goldsboro Christian Schools placed them beyond the benefits of the tax code.

The two schools contended that the IRS was violating the intent of Congress. But if this was true, the Congress consistently passed up opportunities to prevent the violation through clarifying legislation.

"The actions of Congress since 1970 leave no doubt that the Internal Revenue Service reached the correct conclusion in exercising its authority," wrote Chief Justice Warren Burger in his majority opinion. The government, he held, has a "fundamental, overriding interest in eradicating racial discrimination." Congress had translated this interest into law, and the IRS had implemented the law through its policies.

Goldsboro Christian Schools will not admit blacks. Though Bob Jones has deigned to admit a few blacks — less than a dozen out of an enrollment of more than 6,000 — it does not permit interracial dating. Bob Jones concludes that this rule affects both races equally. But no one familiar with the history of this school can doubt which race is being "protected" from the other.

Some have said that the Supreme Court should have dealt with the constitutionality of this discrimination. That was neither necessary nor desirable. Government should not tamper with religious doctrine or privately held convictions so long as their effects are confined to their willing adherents.

But it does not need to bestow legislative grace on religious or private practices that contradict public policy. That is what the Supreme Court has said.

Religious freedom will prosper in the aftermath of this ruling. So, probably, will Bob Jones University and Goldsboro Christian Schools. It is doubtful that their supporters' commitments will waver in the face of the need to pay taxes on the money they contribute.

The Morning News

Wilmington, Del., June 2, 1983

THE UNITED STATES Supreme Court has reaffirmed this nation's commitment to ending racial discrimination.

In an unusually strong opinion, the court rejected the contention of two southern schools that racial discrimination based on religious beliefs should not make private schools ineligible for tax exempt status.

The court's opinion was a major embarrassment to President Reagan. For several years the Department of Justice had fought Bob Jones University and the Goldsboro Christian Academies on the tax question. Then, in an inept political blunder, the Reagan administration took the opposite view: It contended that Congress had never specifically granted the Internal Revenue Service the power to deny tax exempt status on grounds of racial discrimination.

Chief Justice Warren Burger rejected the administration's position: "There can no longer be any doubt that racial discrimination in education violates deeply and widely accepted views of elementary justice. It would be wholly incompatible with the concepts underlying tax exemption to grant the benefit of tax-exempt status to racially discriminatory educational entities." Congress refused 13 times since 1970 to overturn the IRS ruling, the chief justice noted, thus giving implicit approval to it.

The White House says the president is personally offended when he is viewed as being anti-black or anti-civil rights. The president's convictions may be pure, but his public actions are the basis for judgment. His position in the tax case sent a message. So did his decision to clean house at the U.S. Commission on Civil Rights. His unprecedented replacement of three members with three others who share his conservative views on racial quotas, busing and affirmative action could be viewed only as another slight by blacks and other minority group members.

The president has not been popular among black voters, who suffered most from his efforts to slash government spending programs first in California and now in Washington. The impact of the rising tide of blacks registering and voting has already been felt in Chicago and Philadelphia. If voter registration drives continue with the same fervor in the South, the political fallout for President Reagan and other Republican office seekers could be disastrous.

The Chattanooga Times

Chattanooga, Tenn., May 26, 1983

By ruling 8 to 1 Tuesday that racially discriminatory schools are ineligible for exemptions from federal taxes, the Supreme Court made two important contributions. It decisively reiterated the valuable principle that "racial discrmination in education violates deeply and widely accepted views of elementary justice." But it also effectively repudiated the Reagan administration's shameful — and often confused — attempts to curry favor with the religious right by defending the tax exemptions.

The court's powerful majority opinion, written by Chief Justice Warren Burger, systematically demolished arguments raised by Bob Jones University and Goldsboro Christian Schools — and, implicitly, by the Reagan administration. It would be "wholly incompatible with the concepts underlying tax exemption," the court ruled, "to grant the benefit of tax exempt status to racial[ly] discriminatory educational entities, which exert a pervasive influence on the entire educational process." Whatever the rationale for such policies, it added, and however sincere the rationale, racial discrimination is contrary to public policy. Such institutions cannot be viewed as conferring a public benefit within the "charitable" concept.

The court also held that the IRS had not exceeded its authority by denying in 1970 tax exempt status to schools which discriminate on the basis of race. Indeed, the "failure of Congress to modify the IRS rulings of 1970 and 1971, of which [it] was . . . constantly reminded . . . make[s] an unusually strong case of legislative acquiescence in and ratification by implication of the rulings." Significantly, since the 1970 ruling, not one of the 13 bills introduced to overturn it has been reported out of committee.

Finally, the justices agreed that the free exercise clause of the First Amendment has been held an absolute prohibition against governmental regulation of religious beliefs. But they quoted a prior Supreme Court opinion that "not all burdens on religions are unconstitutional . . . The state may justify a limitation on religious liberty by showing that it is essential to accomplish an overriding governmental interest." Thus it justified the government's interest in eradicating racial discrimination in education as outweighing "whatever burden denial of tax benefits places on petitioners' exercise of their religious beliefs."

Three presidents and six Congresses have served since the IRS made its initial ruling in 1970 and none questioned the premise of that ruling: that although private schools can discriminate on the basis of race if they choose, and even justify it on religious grounds, they are not entitled to have other taxpayers subsidize such bias. The Supreme Court's decision on Tuesday is all the more welcome for dragging the Reagan administration, kicking and screaming, into acceptance of the IRS ruling.

The San Diego Union

San Diego, Calif., May 29, 1983

There's real common-sense appeal in the Supreme Court's decision in the case of Bob Jones University and Goldsboro Christian Schools, announced Tuesday. The court said that the Internal Revenue Service has every right to deny those schools the tax exemption extended to other private schools and religious institutions, because both institutions practice racial segregation of one form or another. Whether grounded in religious principles or not, that's a dangerous and offensive belief to most members of the community. And that's exactly why the Supreme Court

should, instead, have protected the schools by overturning the IRS ruling against them.

The ruling was bad for other reasons, not the least of them the point raised by the Reagan administration and by Justice Rehnquist: Congress has never clearly defined what the IRS should do about institutions that are fundamentally religious and charitable, but whose beliefs come into conflict with "the common community conscience," as Chief Justice Burger wrote for the court.

This may seem a legalistic cavil in light of the overriding ur-

gency of fighting racism. It is, rather, of comprehensive importance. Legal shortcuts — like Supreme Court justices writing law where Congress has not — undermine the force of the laws and the public's respect for them. And it is the force of the laws and of due process that logically are, and historically have been, a minority's chief protection against the tyranny of the majority towards which democracy is prone.

The Supreme Court is not the place to define the relationship between the government and the churches. It should apply, not set, standards.

If the court is not the place, where is? Congress? Again, whether the government has the right to tax some churches and not others is a prior question of law having to do with what Congress can and cannot do. It resides in the Constitution. And the Constitution tells us that "Congress shall pass no law" respecting the free exercise of religion. Its framers, and our national consensus, suggest that the question of what some church believes is too touchy for the state to involve itself in usefully. The general presumption, then, is hands off.

Does that mean Americans are forced to subsidize the beliefs of other Americans who think blacks and whites should be separated? No, it doesn't. That argument was raised by William T. Coleman, whom the high court appointed to argue against Bob Jones. It was again rejected, as it has been in hundreds of similar rulings.

Tax exemption does not mean subsidy; if it does, then taxpayers are still subsidizing thousands of churches and other causes that taxpayers may find equally revolting. When the government says it won't tax the Roman Catholic Church, it isn't endorsing the church's refusal to allow women into the priesthood, or the bishops' letter on nuclear arms. It is saying, instead, that the Catholic Church is a *bona fide*, established religion — and as such, is entitled to immunity from the state's power to destroy it through taxation.

Americans decided a long time ago that the best defense against pernicious beliefs is not a powerful state, ever-ready to smash those beliefs when they conflict with what the court's majority calls "fundamental public policy." The common sense of free men, over time, will defeat them far more surely, and with none of the attendant dangers of a government that tries to intervene in religion, however selectively.

What makes Bob Jones's beliefs objectionable is that they suggest we can deny to some students the privileges extended others because of their skin. Is the principle any less damaging when we deny church schools because of their beliefs?

Arkansas Gazette.

Little Rock, Ark., May 26, 1983

The U. S. Supreme Court has done its duty by the Constitution in its decision Tuesday denying tax advantages to two Southern church schools that practice racial discrimination as a purported exercise in Christianity.

This was one of those overwhelming, 8-to-Rehnquist, decisions that reaffirm faith in the country's highest court as the guardian of constitutional rights. The question before the court posed a fundamental test of whether a government agency, the Internal Revenue Service, may deny tax breaks that in effect subsidize private schools whose practices violate the basic constitutional rules governing public institutions. Had the court held otherwise, it would have ravished governing precedents and licensed the public subsidy of bigotry.

The losers in the case were Goldsboro Christian Schools in Goldsboro, N. C., and Bob Jones University in Greenville, S. C., the latter being one of the more notorious citadels of right-wing extremism among private colleges in the country: Goldsboro Schools deny admission to blacks; Bob Jones University forbids inter-racial dating and inter-racial marriage. For 13 years the IRS denied tax advantages to colleges such as Bob Jones U. but that was before Ronald Reagan took office and challenged the established IRS policy. In this contest, as in others, the Reagan administration has painted only the thinnest veneer over policies that are patently racist.

The wisdom and rightness of the Supreme Court's decision was, in a sense, underscored in a wild reaction from Bob Jones Jr., chancellor and founder of BJU, railing against "eight evil old men and one vain and foolish woman" on the court. Mr. Jones did not even recognize the dissenting vote of Justice William Rehnquist, but, no matter, his diatribe was evocative of the darkest era of Southern reaction that followed the Supreme Court decision in the 1954 school case, *Brown v. Board of Education.*

The court's decision offered no surprises — including the Rehnquist vote — even if it was re-

assuring to note the near-unanimity of the tribunal on this issue. Mr. Justice Rehnquist has come down against the Bill of Rights with relentless consistency since he was nominated to the court by Richard Nixon, and it is safe to say that the constitutional rights we have known over the last 30 years would become unrecognizable if there were five Rehnquists on the court. God forbid!

Chief Justice Burger, in his turn, had his best hour in writing the majority opinion in the Bob Jones case. "There can be no doubt," he said, "that racial discrimination in education violates deeply and widely accepted views of elemental justice [and] a most fundamental national policy."

"The government has a fundamental, overriding interest in eradicating racial discrimination that prevailed with official approval for the first 165 years of this nation's history," the chief justice added.

★ ★ ★

Mr. Burger's sense of history is as clear in his vote and opinion as Mr. Rehnquist's is demonstrably lacking. Warren Burger knows that the Supreme Court of the United States made two frightful errors in judging issues of racial discrimination, one in the Dred Scott case and the second in *Plessy-Ferguson,* 1896, wherein was articulated the ingenious fantasy of "separate but equal" schools. The legacy of these decisions was the establishment of a second-class citizenry, a constitutional underclass, in what was supposed to be the world exemplar of democracy. The process of remedy was undertaken late, in 1954, and it is still under way, laboring now in a climate of public opinion that is less hospitable than in the great years of the civil rights revolution. Warren Burger, the chief justice of the United States, knows better than most of us that the Supreme Court cannot afford a third historic mistake in determining constitutional equality, nor does he want to be identified in any way with such calamitous error, should it ever again befall the country.

Lower Minority SAT Scores Raise Question of Fairness

The Scholastic Aptitude Tests have long been a subject of controversy. These standardized exams are intended as a measure of general intellectual ability, and are used by college admissions offices as one indicator of academic potential. In 1980, consumer advocate Ralph Nader released a report criticizing the SAT and other standardized aptitude tests given by the Educational Testing Service. Among the charges made in the report were that the tests excluded from consideration a "disproportionate number of minority applicants who are capable of succeeding" in school, and that the test scores bore a direct relation to family income, while college grades and accomplishments did not. Top scorers' parents had a mean income of $24,124, the report noted, as compared with $8,639 for the lowest scorers. The effect, Nader concluded, was to "perpetuate class distinctions in the name, ironically, of meritocracy."

In 1981, average scores on both the verbal and mathematical sections of the SAT rose very slightly for the first time in 19 years. In its report on the 1981 tests, the College Board for the first time released a breakdown of the test results by race and family income. Black students scored an average of more than 100 points lower than whites on both the verbal and mathematical sections of the tests, and there was a high correlation between family income levels and performance on the SAT, with both blacks and whites from affluent families outscoring lower-income students. But the College Board noted that the nationwide improvement on the scores was due in large part to the improvement by blacks and other minority groups over their 1981 averages, with black scores rising an average of nine points on the verbal test and four points on the math. (The national gain was two points on the verbal section, to 426, and one point on the math section, to 467.) There was also a high correlation between students' performance on the test and the level of education attained by their parents. Critics of the tests have maintained that the chronic gap in scores is a result of bias against ethnic and racial minorities in the test questions themselves, while supporters contend that the scores merely reflect, not create, deficiencies and inequalities in the educational system as a whole.

THE SAGINAW NEWS
Saginaw, Mich., January 21, 1980

Ralph Nader's muckraking studies of such institutions as banking, Congress and, most recently, educational testing, have a peculiar way of correlating 100 percent with his preconceived notions about the faults of those institutions.

For the past couple of years, for instance, Nader has been questioning the value and accuracy of the Educational Testing Service's well-known Scholastic Aptitude Test (SAT) and other materials supposed to predict whether students can succeed in college or graduate work.

Written by an economics student at Columbia University, last week's report asserts — predictably — that the ETS contributes little to the college admissions process that cannot be measured by grades or extracurricular activity.

That conclusion is, uh, predictable. Students who earn good grades and are active in school likely will score well on standardized ETS instruments.

The Nader report, responded ETS officials, said little that was new. They urge use of a variety of admissions criteria. ETS also questioned the statistical methods used to come up with such dramatic assertions that a roll of dice is almost as good a predictor as the SAT.

Whatever its faults or proclaimed virtues, Nader's work performs one undoubted public service. It forces examination of the institutions that deeply affect our lives. In the ETS case, Nader's key point is whether these tests help exclude the poor and minorities from equal opportunity for higher education.

The ETS reply, unchallenged by the Nader report, is that economic level does affect student test performance. They note there is little difference, however, between the average scores of poor whites and poor blacks — or between middle-class whites and blacks. The discrimination is economic, not racial or ethnic. As long as admissions officers know that, they can and should take it into account when judging applicants.

If there are so many "ifs" connected to the tests, why use them at all? — a question raised for decades by thousands of students who approach SAT time with fear and trembling.

There are at least two very good reasons, taken from opposite ends of the grade spectrum.

One is that the well-documented grade inflation has resulted in some students emerging from high school with good marks, yet inability to read or calculate adequately for college work. Test scores at sharp variance with transcripts may help such students by indicating the need for remedial work.

And the true potential of other students who, for some reason, failed to achieve top grades may be disclosed only through independent evaluation.

Nader is probably right that for many students, these tests are a waste of time and effort. But the relatively few for whom testing turns up unsuspected information are also the ones who can most benefit by it.

What Nader is really talking about is throwing out one of the few objective cross-checks on the performance of our educational system. Standardized testing may be as imperfect as Nader's investigative technique, but we need it just as we need him.

WORCESTER TELEGRAM.
Worcester, Mass.,
January 18, 1980

Ralph Nader has fired his long-awaited volley at Educational Testing Service and its Scholastic Aptitude Test (SAT). As usual, the reckless extremism of his charges tends to weaken his case.

That is unfortunate. It will be relatively easy for the Educational Testing Service to deny that it practices "mind control," that it is "siege conscious," that it is racially and culturally biased, that it deliberately caters to the rich and the elite and that it prevaricates in regard to the value of coaching for the tests. But, rhetoric aside, the SATs present some real difficulties that need to be dealt with.

As James Fallows points out in the current Atlantic, the college boards and similar tests are not all they claim to be. Despite constant effort, they still have built-in biases toward certain groups. They do not accurately measure intelligence. They can be manipulated.

Back in the 1920s, Fallows notes, the first IQ tests showed women consistently less "intelligent" than men. When the test was restandardized in the 1930s, questions about sports events and personalities were taken out and replaced by other questions written from a female point of view. The result was that women became as intelligent as men, on the average.

The SATs today show a similar bias against minority groups, the culturally deprived and the poor. But it is proving far more difficult to remove those biases without gutting the tests. That is what one of the big controversies is all about.

"The tests measure something," writes Fallows; "probably something of value — But whatever it is it's clearly a symptom of social advantage."

The colleges and universities have known of these problems for some time, and have been putting less emphasis on SAT scores. But the SATs still swing a lot of weight on many campuses.

The answer is not to eliminate the tests, as Nader and the black psychological associations want. Flawed as they are, they do provide important information. But they should be redesigned. They should open doors, not close them. They should enable the motivated and the gifted to climb up the ladder despite deficiencies in cultural and educational background.

The evidence is that the SATs are not doing those things nearly as successfully as they should. Like it or not, Ralph Nader does have a case. Behind his steamy rhetoric are arguments deserving careful answers.

St. Petersburg Times

St. Petersburg, Fla., February 5, 1980

Consumer advocate Ralph Nader, the career iconoclast, has smashed — or at least dented — many myths about the national establishment. He has challenged almost everyone — from the members of Congress to coal miners, from car manufacturers to chicken raisers.

Nader's latest target is the standardized testing industry — the powerful "gatekeeper" to American educational opportunity — and his work will benefit the nation if it moderates the inflated importance assigned to multiple-choice tests as a measurement of the human mind.

Every year, 7-million to 9-million people trying to advance through thousands of schools and 50 different occupations are judged by their scores on standardized tests.

THE CHIEF arbiter of access to educational and career opportunities is the Educational Testing Service (ETS), a non-profit, $94-million-a-year, tax-exempt corporation based in Princeton, N.J. ETS writes and administers most of the standardized tests used in undergraduate, graduate and professional school admission decisions. It also makes tests for more than 50 occupations and professions, including police officers, firefighters, the foreign service and the Central Intelligence Agency.

Its best-known product is the Scholastic Aptitude Test (SAT), given each year to 1.5-million college-bound high school students.

The Nader report, based on a six-year investigation, is primarily the work of Allen Nairn, a 24-year-old graduate student at Columbia University and Nader employee. The report challenges the widely-accepted belief that academic tests closely predict academic success and concludes that multiple-choice tests like the SAT are scarcely more reliable than a roll of the dice.

The SAT, says the Nairn-Nader report, indicates first-year college performance only 12 percent better than random prediction. High school grades and past achievements are a more accurate and equitable basis for prediction,

the report contends — yet most American students are subjected to the SAT yardstick and many institutions reject those with low scores.

ONE OF THE most subtle and damaging effects of the ETS test system is its impact on the way students think about their own potential. Ambitions are abandoned and lives are detoured when some impressionable, discouraged students change school and career plans because low SAT scores convince them that they do not have the "aptitude" or "mental capacity" to succeed — although their test scores may have little to do with school or job performance.

Also disturbing is Nader's finding of a direct correlation between SAT scores and family income — the more a student's family earns, the higher that student tends to score. "The tests were conceived by the upper class for the upper class," says Nader, charging that discrimination by race and class bars millions of minority and working class students from educational and career opportunities.

ETS officials deny Nader's major criticisms and charge that his researchers used faulty statistical methods to discredit their tests. "Nader and Nairn wrongly blame the tests for showing that minority students are less well-prepared in school than majority students," says ETS president William Turnbull. "The tests do not create the difference, they reveal it."

THE NADER report does not suggest that tests be abandoned but it does urge the ETS to be more modest in its claims and more open about its products. That is a constructive challenge to opportunity's gatekeeper and it should encourage more colleges to broaden their admission standards, making high school grades and past achievements a prime consideration.

Beyond that, public awareness that the testing process is imperfect is a forward step. Too many lives, careers and dreams have been diverted by paper, pencil and multiple-guess – a process that cannot begin to measure the human spirit.

ST. LOUIS POST-DISPATCH

St. Louis, Mo., January 28, 1980

Ralph Nader has joined the growing chorus of those questioning reliance on national standardized academic tests and their influence on students' futures. He recently released a report that concludes that for 88 percent of college applicants, a roll of the dice would be just as accurate a predictor of first-year grades as a Scholastic Aptitude Test (SAT) score. The report asserts that the standardized national tests (such as SAT) produced by the Educational Testing Service of Princeton, N.J., are really not much good at predicting anything. In fact, Mr. Nader said that ETS' claims of accuracy are discredited by "hundreds of its own studies."

The tests have long been criticized for being culturally biased and encouraging superficial thinking by reliance on multiple

choice questions. Even so, to a large extent, those tests, flaws and all, decide the futures of millions of young people every year. They not only determine which students attend college, they determine which college and how much financial aid a student receives.

Mr. Nader's conclusion may be somewhat overstated but there is no denying that far too many schools are placing too much emphasis on test scores alone. Other variables, such as high school grades and activities in sports, arts and sciences can provide useful insights. Pointing that out is perhaps the most valuable lesson of the report. It does not call for abolishing the tests, rather it advocates less reliance on them. It puts the value of the tests in perspective. Admissions officers would be wise to pay heed.

The Courier-Journal

Louisville, Ky., January 19, 1980

RALPH NADER'S assault on educational testing is only the latest of several intemperate campaigns that have tarnished the good causes he has promoted over the years. The newly published Nader study of college entrance examinations, conducted by a college undergraduate, deserves much less than the publicity that has been lavished on it.

More worrisome is a somewhat parallel criticism of testing by the nation's new Secretary of Education, Shirley Hufstedler. The Secretary, of course, is in a position to translate her view directly into action. Furthermore, her criticisms are more sophisticated and hence more difficult to answer than the Nader diatribes.

The Nader thesis is chiefly that college entrance examinations and the like are unfair to minorities, because they reveal that minority students *as a whole* score lower on tests of mathematical and verbal ability and general knowledge. Further, Mr. Nader says, quite correctly, that standardized tests don't measure "judgment, wisdom, experience, creativity, stamina, determination" and the like.

College degrees, for that matter, don't always guarantee possession of the qualities Mr. Nader cites. He could have pointed out that today's emphasis on degrees may be unfair to the likes of such people as the Wright brothers or Thomas Edison. The latter's formal education stopped with a few months of grade school.

But higher education *is* useful, and so are entrance examinations and other tests. They are not supposed to measure subjective qualities, which is why colleges and graduate schools don't use them as the sole criterion for admission. But they do measure knowledge, and so add significantly to the ability of colleges and graduate schools to determine whether a student is prepared for the high-level work he is seeking to undertake.

Mrs. Hufstedler is more convincing in noting from personal experience that testing, particularly group-administered tests, can give false results when applied to individual children. Labeling and assigning children to slots as a result of their test scores is a dangerous business.

But that doesn't justify the Secretary's phobia — one shared by a good many others, to be sure — toward the multiple-choice and true-false tests that are a staple of standardized testing. Those tests are one tool of education. They won't do the whole job. But a screwdriver is not to be despised because it's a poor substitute for a monkey wrench.

Secretary Hufstedler isn't the first to argue that such tests stress rote knowledge rather than thinking. As she remarks, the fact that the Battle of Hastings was fought in 1066 may, by itself, not be a particularly useful piece of knowledge for many people. But it's a sure bet that children who don't know the significance of 1492, 1776, 1865 and the like don't have much understanding of the sequence of events that shaped their country. To answer multiple-choice math questions, of course, students must be able to solve the problems, which requires more than rote knowledge.

Standardized testing is unpopular in some quarters largely because it reveals painful truths — that educational standards have been declining in some very essential areas, and that, in many instances, schools have done a miserable job of educating children who come from low-income families and racial minorities. The misuses of testing deserve criticism. But education will be ill-served if some critics succeed in removing one of the most useful gauges of performance.

Roanoke Times & World-News
Roanoke, Va., February 8, 1982

A PANEL of the National Academy of Sciences has injected a welcome measure of common sense into the debate over standardized tests used in education and employment.

If what the tests measure is irrelevant, then don't use them. But they can be helpful in predicting performance, the academy's Committee on Ability Testing said. And the fact that blacks tend not to score as well as whites does not necessarily mean the tests are racially biased. To say that, the committee said in effect, would be blaming the messenger for the message.

Though such things as civil-service exams and elementary-school testing are part of the debate, the argument usually focuses on college entrance examinations. There's reason for the focus: The Scholastic Aptitude Test, and others like it, are part of the process that determines who gets into the most prestigious colleges and thus has the best entree into a promising career after graduation.

Critics, including the author of a 1980 Ralph Nader report, have attacked the SAT as a way of limiting educational opportunity. But historically, testing has expanded educational opportunity: Before the advent of standardized tests, for example, it was much harder for graduates of public high schools to gain admission to top universities such as Yale and Harvard. The tests showed that some products of public education are as well prepared for a rigorous college curriculum as are graduates of posh Northeastern prep schools.

Moreover, critics tend to ignore the strong link between what the SAT measures — verbal and computational skills — and the ability to do well in the classroom. The link is logical and, over the years, has been borne out statistically as well. Indeed, reports John T. Casteen III, former admissions dean at the University of Virginia and now state secretary of education, declining secondary-school standards have made the SAT a better predictor of college performance than even high-school rank in class.

There's nothing inherently unfair about a college or university's choosing students according to how well they're expected to do in the classroom. (It's an unwise admissions officer, though, who makes that judgment from an SAT score alone: There are thousands of individual exceptions to the general rule of predictability.) If there's unfairness, it's in a society and an educational system that encourage some youngsters more than others to acquire the skills that make for academic success.

Unquestionably, the tests remain a barrier to minority access to higher education, as they were in 1971 when so noted by Fred E. Crossland in a report for The Ford Foundation. Not only is the average score of white youngsters higher than that of black students, Crossland observed then, but the pattern in which individual scores are distributed tends to magnify the difference when it comes to the practical matter of admission to even moderately selective colleges.

More than a decade later, the gap has not vanished. More, though, seems known about the reasons for it. Studies commissioned by the State Council of Higher Education, for instance, suggest that the difference in scores in Virginia may be a direct reflection of the disparity between what black and white youngsters study as early as the 8th grade. Researchers have discovered that black and white students who take the same high-school courses, and do equally well in them, score about the same on the SAT. The problem appears to lie elsewhere than in the test.

There's something of an unintended irony in all this. Test critics may believe they are acting in the interests of minorities. But to argue that the gap between white and black scores is proof of test bias is to deny the lingering effect of centuries of racial discrimination on the way at least some black youngsters perceive and prepare for their own futures.

In the name of civil rights, one of the greatest evils of discrimination — the persistence of its impact — is overlooked. And ammunition is given those who argue, falsely, that racial discrimination is now so far in the nation's past that the need for remedies no longer exists.

The Detroit News
Detroit, Mich., May 27, 1981

Standardized testing in schools infuriates certain interest groups, and in recent months the anti-test campaign has coalesced around three prominent organizations.

Especially conspicuous is the National Education Association (NEA). Representing nearly two million members, NEA is the largest teacher's organization in the United States. Nine years ago the big union called for a nationwide moratorium on standardized testing, asserting the tests malign the efforts of public educators because of declining national scores.

The NAACP, for its part, charged the tests are racist. Citing the inability of many black students to achieve adequate test scores, the NAACP said the questions reflect a cultural bias.

Finally, Ralph Nader's Public Interest Research Group joined the chorus, claiming the tests are unfair because they supposedly have an excessive influence upon college admissions. The Nader lobby also insists the tests are arbitrary and capricious.

The primary object of these groups' ire is the Scholastic Aptitude Test (SAT), which was introduced in 1926 as a national college entrance examination. Not allied to the content of any local curriculum or to any specific content domain, the SAT is a test of verbal and mathematical reasoning ability. If anything, the test provides college access to large numbers of poor students from differing cultural backgrounds, and without lowering college admissions standards.

The SAT, like other standardized tests, achieves constancy through the process of equating. Simply stated, equating involves the inclusion of samples of previously used questions on new editions of the test to assure the newer questions are comparable in difficulty to the older questions. Successive versions of the test are constant in fairness and provide a perspective against which several generations of test takers may be measured for intellectual progress, stability, or regression.

That intellectual measure has revealed some depressing figures of late. Extending back to 1951, there was a long period of stability during which mean scores fluctuated along a narrow range until 1963-64. It was then that the mean scores began a decline that continued for the next 15 years.

Too, there is powerful supporting evidence from the American College Testing program (ACT). This Iowa-based, nonprofit corporation confirms the declining test scores. The inescapable conclusion is this: Students entering college today are generally less prepared than were their counterparts in the 1950s and 1960s.

But the NEA, the NAACP, and the Nader group deny the obvious. They insist it isn't the schools or the youngsters who are at fault for fading test scores. No, the tests are to blame. Specifically they allege the tests: don't measure everything that matters; can't accurately predict success in school or life; and are biased against minorities and the poor.

Thousands of researchers concede that no test measures everything or can accurately forecast success. Their data, however, make clear that the only bias present in the tests favors people with verbal and mathematical skills. Incidentally, at least one minority (Oriental students) scores higher than does its black or white competitors. To conclude that the tests are weighted in favor of Orientals is as absurd as suggesting the questions are designed to exclude blacks and whites.

Tests are tools. That they are imperfect is no reason to dismiss their measurements.

Standardized tests are useful because they tell educators how they are succeeding as well as how they are failing to meet their students' needs. Notwithstanding the outcry against these tests, there has been a recent improvement in SAT scores, which leads us to suspect that classroom teachers are getting the message.

To brand standardized tests as unfair because they tell unpleasant truths is comparable to slaying the messenger who brings the bad news. Comparable, and equally irrational.

The Kansas City Times

Kansas City, Mo., November 9, 1982

Test results ought to be used for more than praise or blame. That applies equally to information available for the first time from the Scholastic Aptitude Test, indicating inner city schools need more attention and strengthening than they're getting.

Last month, the College Board released three separate sets of data, subtly related. First was the welcome news that averages started to inch up on college entrance exams. Black students scored an average of 110 points lower than their white classmates. However, the overall rise in SAT scores was due in large part to improvements by blacks and other minorities on the 1982 SAT, board officials said.

There has been an understandable reluctance on the part of College Board officials to release data about low minority scores. A hasty and simplistic conclusion could be made that minority students are to blame for falling national averages recorded since 1963. Officials chose to risk that for potential gain: That the scores, supplemented by other statistics, underline the educational deficit this nation still must overcome. The role of family income and parental education overshadows simple test scores. That is what the educators and policy makers must include in deciding the meaning of the gap between test scores.

The blacks' average family income was less than half that of their white classmates: $12,500 vs. $26,300. The national averages were 424 in verbal and 466 in math. For blacks, the averages rose from 284 to 319 for those with incomes under $6,000 to 414 to 433 for those with incomes of $50,000 or more. Among black students, 17.5 percent reported their parents made less than $6,000 compared with 2.2 percent of white students at that financial level.

A capsule analysis of the data by a University of Pittsburgh psychologist coincides with conclusions drawn by other professionals and College Board officials: "The tests are simply a reflection of the educational advantages that wealthy kids have," said Dr. Lloyd Bond. "I'd be suspicious if the tests didn't show these differences between wealthy and poorer kids. The quality of instruction is vastly superior in suburban schools as opposed to inner-city schools."

The fact is, this nation is going to be paying a long time for the institution of slavery and the neglect and injustice, not to mention direct repression, visited for so long on black Americans. The victims pay the heaviest price of all. How prevailing standards are set, and how and by whom they are measured, are stories in themselves. The fact remains that an individual lives one life at a time under certain conditions. The message is clear. The worst effect of dismissing the schools as hopeless, or neglecting public education in areas where the need is greatest, is that it is an assault against young people. But unless those deficiencies are corrected, raising the overall achievements of students, reflected in college exam scores or higher education success, is not possible.

The Washington Post

Washington, D.C., February 10, 1982

AFTER FOUR YEARS of work and often heated debate, a panel of the National Academy of Sciences has finally produced its report on the uses and abuses of standardized ability tests. This is one of the prickliest subjects around.

The study found that the tests are capable of predicting future performance in both the classroom and the work place. The degree of accuracy depends on many things. But if a test is properly developed, if it is shown to correlate with the particular job or course of study for which it is being used and if the limits of these tests are understood (they do not measure creativity, motivation, experience) then ability tests are, in the study's words, "important predictive tools for our society." This holds true for both achievement tests and so-called aptitude tests, which largely measure the same thing—what a person knows at the time he or she takes the test, not inherent ability to learn.

The report's most important conclusion is that ability tests are equally valid for whites and blacks. The tests do not, as has frequently been claimed, "underpredict" minority group performance. Studies of college and graduate school entrance exams and of a variety of employment tests show that test scores either predict performance equally well for whites and blacks or somewhat over-predict for blacks.

The evidence also shows, however, that blacks score less well than whites on these tests. In general, the spread in average scores is what statisticians call one standard deviation. This is a very substantial difference. It means, for example, that a cutoff score that included the top 50 percent of the whites on a certain test would include only 16 percent of the blacks. A cutoff that included the top fifth would include only 4 percent of blacks.

There are people who resist and quarrel with such findings because, in our view, they misread the implications of them. In fact, there is something condescending, even racist in its way, about those who protest that there is an anti-black message to be found in the conclusion that the tests don't lie. Their assumption seems to be that what the test discrepancies reveal is an innate racial difference—as distinct from a difference in background and opportunity. But the fact is that these tests are not measuring inherent ability. Nor do the differences in average scores say anything about individual potential. That more minorities than whites score poorly on ability tests means neither, as is so often claimed, that the tests are discriminatory nor that there is something wrong with the people taking the tests. It means that people differ, very often for reasons embedded in national and personal history.

Those who would throw out standardized tests because of poor minority group scores, and those (like the federal government at the present time) who try to rig tests so that they produce equal passing rates are doing no one—especially their theoretical beneficiaries—a favor. On the contrary, they are undermining the credible argument for a stronger effort to reconcile these disparities—and thereby doing those minorities and the society as a whole great harm.

The Commercial Appeal

Memphis, Tenn., February 12, 1982

DOWN THROUGH the ages, bearers of bad tidings have been regarded as unwanted guests. Now it seems a couple of modern-day bearers of bad tidings — the American College Test and the Scholastic Aptitude Test — have been singled out as unwelcomed guests of higher education.

Two reports released this week by separate research groups call for either the abolition of standardized tests such as the ACT and the SAT, or the downgrading of the tests to a second-class status.

The National Academy of Sciences, after four years of study, concludes that the tests are not biased against minorities, but the organization questions the use of the tests because they cause "unnecessary expense and inconvenience" to students.

The Higher Education Research Institute, on the other hand, recommends that the tests be modified in such a way as to measure "student growth or change," instead of how students rank "in relation to each other."

"Because current practices emphasize the screening and certification of students," says the institute, "tests and grades not only fail to contribute to the learning process, but also pose special obstacles to the development of minority students."

Instead of focusing efforts entirely on academic learning, the institute says, colleges should put more emphasis on personal development, interpersonal skills and self-esteem.

Although both organizations make a good case that colleges should do everything they can to encourage minority students to pursue a college education, they do the cause a disservice to target standardized tests as a hindrance to the education of minorities.

It is ludicrous to say that the tests should be abolished or modified simply because they are an inconvenience to students or don't measure student growth or change. It is one thing to question the validity of the tests for minority students, or to prove that the tests discriminate against minorities; but it is another thing entirely to level arbitrary, nonsensical charges against the tests.

Perhaps the tests are an inconvenience, but they are no more inconvenient than attending classes or poring over reference books in the library. And if the tests measure how students rank in relation to each other, that is as it should be. Growth and change matter little if the end result is academic failure.

PERHAPS UNWITTINGLY, a spokesman for the National Academy of Sciences put the matter in perspective: "If there is one lesson to be learned from our report, it is simply that ability tests should not be viewed as a panacea for deep-seated ills or as a scapegoat for society's ills."

It's a good point.

Standardized tests should not be viewed as a scapegoat or a panacea, but rather as an impartial measurement of where a student stands in relation to other students. In that sense, the tests are a valuable tool for educators and their use should be encouraged.

Chicago Defender

Chicago, Ill., March 30, 1982

The crusty old theories about black genetic inferiority are likely to be revived, now that race-differentiated results of Scholastic Aptitude Tests have been released for the first time. According to the College Board, which administers the tests to high school students all over the country who are hoping to go on to college, blacks on the average finished 120 points behind whites on the verbal parts and 135 points behind whites on the mathematics segment.

That's a significant difference and a disturbing one. Some may even say the College Board shouldn't have released such information, since it feeds the bizarre theories of people like Dr. Shockley. It also bothers a lot of blacks who, in the depths of their being, have always considered themselves and their black brothers and sisters as truly inferior.

So why pander to the racists and the neurotics on both sides of the racial divide? The answer is that we have nothing to fear from truth — only from the muzzling of truth, out of motives of maliciousness or misguided protection.

The College Board presented some additional data which helps illuminate the full truth. Almost 60 percent of the black students taking the test had a family income of under $12,000, while only 14 percent of the whites were in that category. That, combined with what is now known about cultural bias in such tests, more than counteracts any genetic argument raised by Shockley and his colleagues. Thus, what is most signtficant in the College Board report is not the score differential, but the economic one!

Oklahoma City Times

Oklahoma City, Okla., February 4, 1982

ONE OF the controversies raging in educational circles has centered on the use of standard tests to measure achievement in school and aptitude for college work. Arguments have branched off into whether the tests are biased against blacks and other minorities and whether pre-employment examinations discriminate against them, too.

Responding to public pressures, some states have sought to counter a long-term decline in college admission scores by installing competency tests as a requirement for graduation from high school.

Now a prestigious national group has entered the fray with the results of its four-year study on the use of tests in America. It came up with two interesting conclusions that seem logical and probably reflect the thinking of the educational mainstream. Certainly they reject the more radical views of the Ralph Nader disciples, who have been waging all-out war against the testing industry.

The Committee on Ability Testing, created by the National Research Council of the National Academy of Sciences, was composed of 19 professors from a variety of academic fields. Only a few of them were test experts.

One finding was that tests used for civil service employment, college entrance, in the classrooms and in the workplace are not systematically biased against minorities, who usually score below average on them. It said the tests can help predict performance for blacks as well as whites.

The other finding is that too much emphasis may be placed on test results for college admission in general. The panel recommended that college admission officers reconsider their mandatory use of entrance exams taken by nearly 2 million high school seniors each year. It said the exams — primarily the Scholastic Aptitude Test and the American College Test — may be an unnecessary expense and inconvenience for most students because the "vast majority" of colleges are not selective in their admission policies.

While it concluded the tests are not systematically biased against minorities, the committee urged schools, colleges and employers to take steps to mitigate the potential adverse impact of tests on them. This may seem contradictory but probably reflects the idea that the poor and minorities do fare worse on tests because they have not had the opportunity to develop the skills being tested.

Many educators believe tests are useful for diagnostic purposes but should not be relied upon solely to determine which students are admitted to college, or promoted to a higher grade, or graduated from high school. Tests can measure skills well, but how the skills are used may be more important to a student's success.

Motivation also is critical. Educators can relate examples of persons who did poorly on tests but turned out to be good students, and others who scored high on the SAT or ACT but couldn't make it academically over the long haul.

It's not likely the panel's findings will end the fight over testing but they should settle the dust somewhat.

Richmond Times-Dispatch

Richmond, Va., October 30, 1982

Somehow we'd never fancied the College Entrance Examination Board as a strip-tease artist. That's the prim-and-proper outfit that publishes the Scholastic Aptitude Test (SAT) taken by many of the nation's college-bound students each year. But lately the staid old College Board has been tantalizing the fans of its data by peeling off one layer of SAT-score information at a time, revealing a little more interesting picture each time. Gypsy Rose Lee would approve.

First to drop was word that national-average scores of high school seniors who took SAT during the 1981-82 school year (this year's college freshmen) had risen by 2 points on the verbal section and 1 point on the math section from the previous year. That was a bit of an eye-opener because it marked the first time since 1963 that the averages had gone up. But because the gains were so puny, and the cumulative declines over the past 19 years so large (52 points for verbal, 36 for math), release of this data was not enough to bring fans out of their seats, cheering lustily.

But next the College Board went further than it had ever gone before, shocking some in its audience. It published statistics that it had collected for 10 years, but had refused to disclose, breaking down SAT performance by race. This report showed that while whites were averaging 442 on the verbal section and 483 on math last year (on a scale ranging from 200 to 800), black students were averaging only 332 and 362 — a gap of more than 100 points on each portion of the test. Those who believe that such ugly differences ought to be covered up were heard to mutter at this point about the show's lack of taste.

After allowing its followers sufficient time to brood about the implications for democracy of such a yawning gap, the College Board stripped off its (presumably) final layer and filled the house with smiling eyes. It reported that strong gains by blacks and other minority-group students had been largely responsible for this year's overall improvement in SAT averages. Verbal scores of blacks had climbed by 9 points and their math scores by 4 points. Furthermore, since 1976, data indicate that "the gap between minorities and whites is narrowing at a fairly steady pace," a board spokesman said.

The data also revealingly establish a relationship between a student's SAT scores and several non-racial factors, including his family's income and educational level. Blacks were decidedly at a disadvantage in those areas: Median family income of white test-takers was $26,300, more than double the $12,500 reported for blacks. And white students reported their fathers had completed an average of 14.2 years of schooling, and their mothers 13.4, while blacks reported averages of 12.2 and 12.4 years.

What do we see at the conclusion of the SAT-Tease Show? Perhaps a glimmer of what can be accomplished if the public keeps pressing the schools to cut out the vacuous electives that have crept into the secondary curriculum since the 1960s, accept no spurious substitutes (black or otherwise) for correct English, re-emphasize science and mathematics instruction and generally to set high standards for learning and discipline. Perhaps it shows that minorities benefit most of all from that kind of no-nonsense instruction. Perhaps. But we'd like to see more.

The News and Courier
Charleston, S.C., February 14, 1982

In the nick of time, the National Academy of Sciences has come to the rescue of standardized hiring and admissions tests. Advocates of affirmative action had just about destroyed the good reputation of tests, but the academy reports, after four years of study that they serve a useful purpose in measuring the abilities of applicants for jobs and educational institutions. Test are not by nature biased against blacks and other minorities, the scientists say. They predict the performance of one group of people about as well as they predict that of another.

In an attempt to make their findings as palatable as possible to those locked into a view of standardized testing as a tool of racial discrimination, the scientists have had to throw in some disclaimers. Test results should not be the only grounds for accepting or rejecting an applicant. It may be desirable for social reasons to give test results less weight than some other criteria.

All those things are suggested by common sense. They do not come as news to those who have used such tests and found them to be, if not perfect, very reliable as predictors of future performance. They do not affect the conclusion to be drawn from the scientists' findings: it is foolish to manipulate tests to assure that as many blacks as whites get jobs or are admitted to college.

In arguing that standardized testing denies people opportunities, the enthusiasts for affirmative action are blind to the opportunities that testing creates. Tests may not be perfect but they offer the best insurance so far devised that those who have something to offer will get the consideration they deserve, in spite of race, creed or origin.

The Boston Herald American
Boston, Mass., February 20, 1982

A National Academy of Sciences research panel has studied tests used for Civil Service jobs and for college entrance and finds they are not biased against blacks or Latinos.

The academy's National Research Council studied the tests four years. It defended their use in the business world. The council added, however, that the tests shouldn't be relied upon too heavily because they cannot rate character traits, which contribute to individual success.

It also advised that employers and educational systems take steps to cushion the lower test scores of minority groups. The council urged a selection system that recognizes the dual interest of equal opportunity and productivity.

The council report said there is evidence that offspring of the well-to-do score higher on such tests because they are provided more opportunity to develop abilities than children of the poor —often minority group members. But, the council report added, "We find little convincing evidence that well-constructed and competently administered tests are more valid predictors for one population group than another."

The Providence Journal
Providence, R.I., November 17, 1984

People dedicated to the progress of minorities in American society have always been convinced that the path to advancement lay through the groves of better education. It's encouraging to see a federal agency report an upgrading of educational test scores by these groups in recent years.

Among the findings is one that seems especially significant. In the last couple of decades, black-white differences in reading ability have been cut in half.

One probable factor in the improvement of minority students is their increasing enrollment in what might be termed the more demanding courses such as mathematics and the physical sciences.

This indicates that the students and those who guide them are on the right track. The younger generation, whether from the minority or majority population, needs to be challenged by a rigorous curriculum, not floated along to a diploma on a sea of easy-to-pass courses.

Statistics can be suspect if the "progress" they imply is based on short-term data collection. In this instance, the agency, the National Assessment of Educational Progress (NAEP) seems to have done its homework. The black-white reading comparison is based on students who are 14 years old, with a group born in 1953, who are at the creaky old age of 31.

The NAEP says the older group's tests showed a 20 percent disparity between blacks and whites in reading ability. It is now 10 percent, which is still cause for concern, but shows a move in the right direction.

As would be hoped, black, Mexican-American, Puerto Rican and American Indian students have improved their scores in most categories of the Scholastic Aptitude and College Board Achievement Tests.

Gregory R. Anrig, president of the Princeton, N.J. service that administers these tests, says it is now clear what minority students can achieve "when they have access to high-quality instruction, and the educational support and encouragement they need." The authorities who approve the budgets for the nation's schools might do well to keep that assessment in mind.

Detroit Free Press
Detroit, Mich., March 18, 1984

WHILE OTHER students' scores were falling, the average Scholastic Aptitude Test scores of blacks rose by 22 points. That is the good news from the College Board, though the news is not quite as good as it may at first seem.

From 1976 to 1983, the national SAT verbal average decreased six points and the national math average dropped four points. During the same period, the black average went up seven points on the verbal test and 15 points in math.

The trend toward higher math scores among blacks suggests that the compensatory education programs proliferating since the '60s have paid off — along with the renewed emphasis on teaching the basics in many big-city school districts. But among blacks taking the test last year, those in private schools had average scores 43 points higher in verbal and 24 points higher in math than those in public schools. This suggests two things: For all sorts of reasons, public schools still are not doing all they should to motivate and prepare minority youngsters; and highly motivated and upwardly mobile black families often send their youngsters to private schools.

The SAT scores don't actually tell us much, though, about the sort of conditions that have to prevail for continued progress. We know that family income is a factor. Both whites and blacks from higher-income families tend to score higher than lower-income test-takers. So before black test scores begin reaching the national norm — and blacks still lag 86 points behind in verbal ability and 99 points behind in math — their family incomes and participation in the economic mainstream must rise.

That will not happen, though, unless we renew our commitment to the struggle for equal opportunity and education. When all is said and done, the progress of black youngsters hinges, more than anything, on the existence of a climate of hope.

Black children must believe they have a future and a place in the world if they are to continue striving for success. They cannot truly come into their own so long as funding for public education and the promotion of integration carry a low federal priority. Nor can they be expected to believe in the future when black unemployment remains twice the national average. The improvement in black youngsters' SAT test scores demonstrates that, among the college-bound at least, many continue to hope and to struggle. Their faith must be kept alive.

Black History Courses Celebrated, Debated

Until the late 1960's, most American children would have learned, in school, of only a few blacks who made major contributions to the nation's history; many school textbooks are still limited to references to Booker T. Washington and George Washington Carver. It was to rectify this omission that black history courses came into being, to celebrate the ignored heritage of the many black scientists, civil rights leaders, inventors, writers, artists, military leaders and other figures who helped shape American history. In 1984, the achievements of the "Father of Black History," Carter G. Woodson, were celebrated during February, designated as Black History Month in 1978. The tradition, aptly enough, was begun in 1926 as Negro History Week by Carter himself, a historian and author who founded the Association for the Study of Afro-American Life and History, and established a publishing house to provide textbook material about black Americans.

Although black history courses have become a standard part of the curriculum at many schools and colleges, disagreement remains over whether these courses should constitute a separate discipline. Proponents of separate black history courses and black studies programs argue that the added emphasis thus placed upon the subject matter is necessary to compensate for its complete omission in the past. Those who feel that the material in black history courses would be more appropriately learned in the context of other history courses maintain that such special treatment gives the subject matter more weight relative to the whole than it deserves, and that special courses could equally well be demanded by any other of the many groups—Japanese, Jews, American Indians, etc.—who have also come together to form the fabric of American history and society.

Post-Tribune

Gary, Ind., February 1, 1984

A new postal stamp was issued today. On it is a photograph of Carter G. Woodson, often called the "Father of Black History." Issuance of the stamp coincides with the beginning of black history month.

This Harvard-trained historian deserves a place in history himself — he founded the Association for the Study of Afro-American Life and History in 1915 and promoted the annual observance of Negro History Week starting in 1926. That observance became Black History Month in 1978. Woodson founded the Negro History Bulletin and set up a publishing house to provide textbook material about his race — material other publishers left out.

Black history now is told in many ways, including the use of television — Alex Haley's "Roots" being one significant example. The need for emphasis on black history does not reflect an ethnic narrowness, but the gap left in America's story by not putting the lives and contributions of blacks into an accurate perspective.

What about the black-studies program? Across the country, an estimated 226 centers or departments exist on American campuses, compared to about 600 in 1973. We aren't sure what that reflects.

A year ago, a black woman wrote in the Los Angeles Times that "blacks no longer celebrate their existence in February or at any other time of the year. Most have chosen to forget the past, and they are therefore neglecting to prepare their offspring for a future in white America." She said one group of black high school seniors didn't recognize the names of black leaders of the past, except for Martin Luther King Jr.

That casual approach to history is not peculiar to black students, we suggest. It is too common in America. Black history deserves respect and attention, because of the textbook omissions. But pride in black achievements must not be restricted to blacks, any more than white accounts of history should be taken as the whole truth.

The goal must be to write, and to read, history the way it unfolds, replete with human errors, selfishness, injustice — and with the human kindness, ingenuity, cooperative spirit and understanding that make America great. The promise of America belongs to all of us, and the past is part of all, too, because it points to where we are.

THE ATLANTA CONSTITUTION
Atlanta, Ga., February 26, 1982

It would be great if there were no need to set aside a special time to hail the achievements of black Americans. But for more than 60 years, it has been necessary to spotlight black history once a year, as a reminder that all is not well in America. Blacks have made valuable contributions to this society, but many of them cannot be found in the history books for reasons more complex than blatant racial prejudice.

So once again, the February tradition goes on. This has been the month of Black History celebrations. Each time, America learns that there were many talented blacks other than George Washington Carver and Booker T. Washington. Each time, America fails to learn that after hundreds of years, blacks and whites do not yet know each other.

What would America be like without ice cream? Would whites stop eating the most famous American dessert because it was invented by Augustus Jackson, a black man? Hardly.

Much of the progress in space exploration can be attributed to Dr. George Carruthers, one of the two Naval Research Laboratory people responsible for the Apollo 16 lunar surface ultraviolet camera-spectrograph, which was placed on the moon in April 1972.

Other inventions by blacks include the riding saddle, golf tee, detachable car fender, lawn mower, bicycle frame, air-conditioning unit, two-cycle gasoline engine, thermostat and temperature-control system, electric lamp, fire extinguisher, pencil sharpener, lawn-sprinkler design, horseshoe, fountain pen, multiple barrel machine gun, refrigerator, rotary engine, pipe connection, marine propeller, fire escape ladder, railway telegraphy and automatic safety cut-out for electric circuits. The list goes on and on.

And yet, there are theories which say that blacks are inferior. If that's so, perhaps the question that should be answered is this: By what standard is inferiority measured? Life in America has been made better because of inventions and contributions by blacks to this society.

It is not enough to point out achievements by blacks just once a year. The key to the survival of this country may well be to tell the whole story of black America.

One of the reasons that blacks have not been recognized, especially in the scientific arena, is that the individual inventor has been replaced by government and corporate research-and-development teams. In many cases, the individual has received less recognition — regardless of race. However, something continues to be wrong with America when such names as Bell, Edison and Marconi are placed in textbooks which fail to mention black inventors.

The time has come to correct America's schoolbooks to include the history of blacks. It is crucial that the people of this society get to know each other on a daily basis. Until we learn to coexist peacefully, America will never achieve her full potential.

THE ANN ARBOR NEWS
Ann Arbor, Mich., February 12, 1984

Today is Lincoln's Birthday and February is Black History Month. The two, it seems, are bound up together.

Black History Month actually began as Negro History Week. Black history courses and books are a recent phenomenon, not really becoming commonplace until the period of boycotts, freedom rides and protest marches. School textbooks tended to either gloss over or ignore the role of black people in the American experience.

Lerone Bennett Jr. is a black history scholar and senior editor of *Ebony* magazine. He says "we still do not have a fundamental transformation of the textbooks in this country."

We have to go back to the beginning, Bennett says, "and create a common American history — one that takes into account that America is not a creation of white people alone. In too many presentations we pop up suddenly as slaves, and Lincoln 'frees' us.

"We came here before the Mayflower, and . . . we were essentially involved in creating the economic settlement of this country. It's impossible for white people to understand themselves and this country without understanding black history."

And so events all across America are marking Black History Month. It is observed in Ann Arbor schools in creative ways, if Clinton School is any example.

At Clinton Feb. 22 is a special day. That's when each class will participate in a brief show integrating Black History Month with George Washington's birthday celebration.

Student participation runs from helping to write the script for the show to performing and singing in the songs, games, spirituals and African dances which will make the Clinton School celebration as one to remember.

Black History Month is set aside to dramatize achievement in all areas. It's just that we wish the contributions of such giants as Paul Robeson and W.E.B. DuBois were as well known (and as honored) as, say, the exploits of Julius Erving (Dr. J) and Hank Aaron. We wish Rosa Parks were as instantly recognizable as Diana Ross, and that is not to diminish Ross's fine singing career.

Basically, Black History Month is education and education, as Malcolm X said, is our passport to the future, "for tomorrow belongs to the people who prepare for it today."

Knowledge, too, liberates people from stereotypes and notions rooted in ignorance and fear. We need to ask ourselves: Are whites and blacks in America coming together through education and power-sharing? Is racism any less destructive just because it tends to take subtler forms? Can't the values to be gained from stressing church, home and family be the bridge that binds the races in common purpose?

Clearly, we have a way to go in this country before equality of opportunity is guaranteed. Black youth unemployment is tragically high; blacks are usually the first to feel the sting of joblessness and then the follows the potential for despairing of all hope.

Black History Month encourages us to honor great men and women of the past and present, but it positively *compels* us to improve the future.

TULSA WORLD
Tulsa, Okla., February 6, 1984

FEBRUARY is Black History Month in this country, the product of a seed planted in 1926 by historian Carter G. Woodson. Woodson advocated a Negro History Week observance each year to recognize the contribution of blacks to the building of America. In 1978, Black History Month was established.

It is ironic that during this month the National Council for Black Studies should report a marked decline in the number of black studies programs on American college campuses. The Council estimates that in 1973 there were about 600 such programs in the country. Today there are only 226.

But that may not be a bad thing.

In the late 1960s and 1970s, those seeking to study black history had a difficult time finding resources which chronicled blacks' contributions. As a result, the chapters on black history that should have been included in authoritative American history texts were published separately.

Since then, history books have been rewritten to take account of black achievements. To a great degree, the decline in black studies programs may indicate that black history is being included in American history programs — where it belonged all along.

Separate black history programs never made much sense. Including the the role of blacks in the history of their country is an act of integration that is long overdue.

THE INDIANAPOLIS STAR
Indianapolis, Ind., February 27, 1984

It is tonic adventure to explore the story of the black role in the making of America.

Alain Leroy Locke (1886-1953), Philadelphia-born, was an honor graduate with bachelor and Ph.D. degrees from Harvard, a Rhodes scholar, graduate student at the University of Berlin, chairman of the philosophy department at Howard University where he was on the faculty 40 years.

He was a literary and art critic, author, a force in the "Harlem Renaissance" cultural awakening of the 1920s, a spokesman for and champion of emerging Negro artists and an interpreter of their work to the nation.

His book, *The New Negro,* in 1925, on black accomplishments, was aimed at creating an atmosphere in which all people would be judged on merit.

DuBose Heyward (1885-1940) wrote *Mamba's Daughters,* poetry, a Civil War novel and *Porgy,* about life in his hometown Charleston's Catfish Row, and this was adapted to become George Gershwin's folk-opera, *Porgy and Bess.*

Frederick Douglass (1817-1895), born a slave, was the fiery abolitionist and fighter for justice for all regardless of race, who preached, "If there is no struggle, there is no progress." . . "Those who profess to favor freedom, and yet deprecate agitation, are men who want crops without plowing up the ground." . . . "Power concedes nothing without a demand."

Sgt. William H. Carney was a Union hero of the Civil War battle of Charleston; Gwendolyn Brooks won the 1950 Pulitzer Prize for poetry; John Stewart founded the first Methodist mission in America; John Swain rode and fought Comanches and badmen as one of the first cowboys in Arizona Territory, and Steward First Class Leonard R. Harmon, killed in action in the naval battle of Guadalcanal, was awarded the Navy Cross for valor, and a warship was named for him.

Black pioneers, explorers, war heroes, cowboys, engineers, physicists, chemists, surgeons, inventors, industrialists, frontiersmen, Western scouts, master researchers, army generals, educators, fighter pilots, astronomers, nurses, missionaries, artists and writers had powerful roles in the making of America.

Pride in these resilient, hardy, daring men and women is justified in black and white. Their stories are exciting. Their courage is inspiring. Many times the obstacles they faced seemed much higher and wider than the Rockies. Their fighting spirit should give heart to anyone going against heavy odds today.

This is, of course, Black History Month. It could be celebrated by reading Richard Wright's *Native Son,* Ralph Ellison's *Invisible Man,* Chester Himes' *Blind Man with a Pistol* or Langston Hughes' *The Weary Blues.* Edward Margolies' survey, *Native Sons,* and the Negro Book Club's *Guide to African-American Books* offer insights.

Anyone embarking on a exploration of black history — and the dynamics at work in the United States cannot be understood in the least without it — is in for an eye-and-mind-opening trip.

The Kansas City Times

Kansas City, Mo., February 15, 1984

Black history is actually a long and major thread in the history of the United States. Yet now it is also studied and celebrated in its separateness. Only a short generation ago, its facts were quite secret from most of society. At best, there were highlights, scantily covered and written by whites.

Fortunately, this is changing. And the field remains rich in its unfolding, full of men and women whose contributions to the human race and their country were valuable though not splashy. It merits deeper understanding of those whose singular accomplishments long ago seeped through layers of ignorance; structures that endured and why; the self-confidence and pride the young drink thirstily from the revelation of roots.

It is important to keep in mind that black history is not limited to accomplishments relating to civil rights, momentous though they have been. Indeed, if that were so, the issues would be history only secondarily. In the same way, interim cooling toward civil rights as a priority and lamentable areas of discrimination that hang on are only items in the black story. People who want something better for their country will continue the battle for harmony and equal rights. And, we are convinced, they will prevail ultimately.

The celebration this month includes scholarship, both research and education. It includes events in this city and across the country. Through them the remote past comes alive. So do heroes and heroines of history and their peers of this generation.

In the most recent space shuttle Challenger flight, we see appropriate progress being made in dealing with the modern makers of black history. Unlike the brittle light focused on Lt. Col. Guy Bluford, the first black astronaut, little special notice went to the second black spaceman, Dr. Ronald McNair. He has his place in the records, neither more nor less because of his color.

But hundreds of years of obscurity compel a concentration on other outstanding minority representatives, just to bring the subject up to par with other threads of this nation's legacy. It is part of the crusade to remove bias and discrimination from American life.

A special exhibit at the Truman Library presented by the Black Archives of Mid-America is an example of proper focus. As Dr. Robert M. Warner, archivist of the United States, remarked on opening night, 20 years ago documents and artifacts for the study of black history were not available. "But the civil rights movement," he said, "raised people's consciousness about black history."

Today, as much as ever, the former cannot be promoted without honoring the latter.

The Dispatch

Columbus, Ohio, February 2, 1984

Black History Month, which began Wednesday, once again focuses attention on the contributions of black Americans.

This year's observance honors Carter G. Woodson, a Harvard-educated black historian. A U.S. Postal Service stamp bearing his picture has been issued.

Often called the "Father of Black History," Woodson promoted Negro History Week, the forerunner to Black History Month. He was the author of several books on black history, was a dean at Howard University and set up Associated Publishers to provide textbook material about black Americans.

This year Black History Month arrives with causes for optimism and concern. There were at least three significant events since the last observance: the designation in November of the third Monday in January (beginning in 1986) as a federal holiday honoring slain civil rights leader Dr. Martin Luther King Jr., Air Force Lt. Col. Guion Bluford became the first black astronaut to orbit the Earth when he and fellow crew members aboard the space shuttle *Challenger* took off in August, and Vanessa Williams of Millwood, N.Y., became the first black Miss America in September.

These historic achievements are balanced against a decline in black studies programs, centers or departments on American campuses. There were 600 in 1973, a peak year, but now there are only 226, including the program at Ohio State University.

And there is apparently some room for improvement in the level of awareness among black students. Shirlee Smith, a black writer who addressed a class of high school seniors in Los Angeles last year, found that King was the only prominent black leader whose name they recognized.

Still, the contribution of blacks to American history is probably better known now than ever before. Alex Haley's best-selling novel, *Roots*, inspired two highly successful television series. The first, in 1977, continues to rank among the most widely viewed programs of all time. The Dr. Martin Luther King Jr. holiday observance will further underscore the historic role and continuing emergence of black Americans.

Detroit Free Press

Detroit, Mich., February 8, 1984

THEY WERE among the first to stretch and reshape America's notions of what it meant to be female. Forced to fight both racial and sexual barriers, black women — as a travelling Smithsonian exhibit clearly shows — were toughened by their troubles and learned to prevail over pain.

The Smithsonian show, "Black Women: Achievement Against the Odds," will surprise even people who think they know something about black history and culture. It spotlights the stories, photographs and dreams of 116 black women who triumphed over turmoil.

Some of the show is predictable: the dazzling dancers, the singers who groaned the blues, shouted the gospel and swung jazz, the educators who sweated to build schools. You expect to see a profile of Rosa Parks, whose refusal to give up her seat to a white man on a Montgomery, Alabama bus in 1955 began 12 years of non-violent protest against segregation. You may have forgotten, though, that Wilma Rudolph was the first American woman to win three Olympic gold medals. Or that Maggie Lena Walker became the first American female bank president in 1899 as executive secretary-treasurer of the Independent Order of Saint Luke, a fraternal society and insurance co-operative headquartered in Richmond, Va.

The women profiled in the exhibition at Detroit's Afro-American Museum this month also include Gertrude Rush, one of the founders of the National Bar Association, and Edmonia Lewis, the only black artist to exhibit in the 1876 Centennial Exposition. They include Pauli Murray, an Episcopal priest who was one of the co-founders of the National Organization for Women. And Alice Dunnigan, the first female sports writer in the District of Columbia. They include Harriet Tubman, the escaped slave who was the only woman in American history to plan and lead a military raid. And Mary Church Terrell, who at age 89 led picket lines to desegregate restaurants in Washington.

The exhibition could not include all the grandmothers who pieced elaborate quilts preserving African patterns and ideas of harmony in the new world. Nor could it do justice to the thousands of black women who formed the backbone of the black church and who participated in higher numbers than men in the civil rights movement. Or the hundreds of thousands more who brushed and babied other people's children and scrubbed floors to help create a better educated generation of blacks. By celebrating a few individuals, though, the exhibition pays tribute to them all.

Michigan School Ordered to Implement "Black English" Program

When valid explanations are sought for the disparities in achievement between black children and white children in the school system, it is usually found that a variety of interlocking cultural and economic factors must be taken into account. In the mid-1970's, one of these factors—the colloquial form of English spoken in many black families—became something of a popular cause. "Black English," it was suggested, should be accorded the status of a separate language and be treated as such in the school system, rather than simply being considered incorrect. It was pointed out that the difficulty for young black children who conversed in a different dialect at home, when learning to read and write standard English at school, could be compared to the difficulty experienced by Spanish or French students at an American school. Some proponents maintained that the many local versions of "Black English" were similar in their speech patterns to African languages, and should thus be regarded as a distinct language rather than a group of dialects spoken by parts of the black community. Opponents of establishing "Black English" as a separate language in the school system, many of them blacks, pointed out that all children in the American school system, regardless of their ethnic background, were expected to learn the grammatical rules and correct pronunciation of standard English, and that mastery of the English language was an important skill in gaining employment in the United States. Establishment of a dual standard, they argued, would only serve to widen the racial gap in educational and social achievement.

In 1979, the Ann Arbor, Michigan school board approved a $42,000 program to teach "Black English" to all 28 teachers at its Martin Luther King Elementary School. The program had been ordered by federal Judge Charles W. Joiner at the close of a landmark suit, brought on behalf of 11 black children who complained that they were not receiving adequate instruction in standard English because the teacher did not understand their conversational speech. The judge's opinion did not advocate the teaching of "Black English," stating that the dialect was not inherently a language barrier. It went on to say, however, that the dialect became a learning obstacle when teachers did not take it into account in their instructions for reading and writing standard English.

Chicago Defender

Chicago, Ill., Aug 21, 1979

The forces which have vowed to keep blacks poor and ignorant have scored another victory. This time it is the education factor.

A U. S. District judge has ruled that black kids in an Ann Arbor, Mich. school do not have to be burdened with learning good English and that the teachers there recognize black English and teach the kids accordingly. Now black English is defined as a dialect which thrives in low-income black communities. And the reason for this latest ruling is that the educators in that area claimed that all (not just some) of the black children in a housing project there did very poorly in school. They attribute this to the English factor.

They insist that the reason "Johnnie can't read" if he is black, is because he speaks a different language than the teacher is using. In ordering academic recognition of black English, the opinion was that the black kid just can't cope in an upper middle class area.

When white Europeans came to this country, unable to speak the language, there was no thought of resorting to their language. They were forced to learn English in order to make their way. Why is it assumed that after being on these shores for some 400 years blacks are incapable of learning English?

It is essential that blacks learn in order to get jobs, become familiar with community needs and to progress.

It is an insult to lower educational standards solely for black students. Blacks are a part of American past have and still can become qualified through learning. It is up to all blacks (parents, teachers, community leaders) to get into this controversy and find methods of helping our children to learn and come up to the set standards. This is a battle we must win.

The Cincinnati Post

TIMES ⇌ STAR

Cincinnati, Ohio, July 23, 1979

The opinion of a federal judge in Detroit notwithstanding, we can't buy the idea that "black English" is a legitimate language in its own right. Whatever origins it may have in African speech patterns, it is a variant of standard English, a dialect of the ghetto.

Nevertheless, millions of black youngsters do use this dialect in their everyday lives. And insofar as U.S. District Court Judge Charles W. Joiner's ruling can facilitate their learning of standard English—as well as other academic studies—we think it is a worthwhile decision.

In a suit brought by the parents of 11 black children, Joiner ordered the Ann Arbor, Mich., school board to come up with a program to identify children speaking black English as their "home language" and to use that knowledge in teaching standard English.

As we understand it, this by no means confers linguistic equality on black English, despite the judge's calling it a legitimate language. Students will not be taught black English, or taught algebra or history in black English, as some misguided people have advocated.

What the order is intended to do is break down a barrier that may exist between teachers and students, not because they can't understand each other, but because, as Joiner said in his opinion, "in the process of attempting to teach students how to speak standard English, the students are somehow made to feel inferior and are thereby turned off from the learning process."

Put that way, the ruling strikes us as a sensible step toward bringing black children into the mainstream of American culture. "Black pride" activists shouldn't carry it any further than that.

The Afro-American

Baltimore, Md., Aug 4, 1979

Amid all the widespread hassle about so - called "Black English," one thing stands out clearly:

If we, as blacks, want and expect to get into the mainstream of American life and business, we will have to do so by way of the English language.

This is the route that have been taken by the Irish, the Italians, Russian Jews and other immigrants who have come to the United States.

They crowded the public schools and moved upward to do remarkably well in most aspects of American life.

This does not mean that there are not enclaves of Americans, with non - English heritage, who preserve their language and other cultural roots. There are and some of them run our banks and other corporations, all levels of government and our universities — but their operating language is English, at least the American version of English.

American blacks who insist on using or cultivating what is touted as "Black English," must indulge in this luxury as a luxury, but they should not expect the entire society to finance them — at least not any more than the society supports other recreational and avocational pasttimes.

Most important, as said earlier, is the fact this "Black English" thing does mean further isolation of black Americans from the main thrust of reading and writing, from businesses and government and from the main seats of power.

In the United States, English is the language of governance, of control, of power, of opportunity. English!

We know of no European immigrants of the 19th century, and since, who tried to keep their children from mastering English. And the newly arrived South Koreans, and Vietnamese are learning fast.

Pittsburgh Post-Gazette

Pittsburgh, Pa., July 16, 1979

A few years ago, to the accompaniment of widespread media coverage, some linguists began arguing that "Black English," the dialect spoken by a large number of black Americans, ought to be regarded as a distinct language with its own conventions of grammar and pronunciation.

The scholarly genesis of this theory was the discovery of arguable connections between African patterns of speech and some features of Black English. Its *political* genesis was the resentment by many blacks of the suggestion that the way they and their children spoke was incorrect. The central argument of the Black English movement, that incorrect forms were really correct after all, but by their own standards, thus seemed to many blacks and whites an exciting and liberating revelation. There were even predictions that the educational establishment would eventually "legitimize" Black English.

Last week that prediction was fulfilled in Michigan, but in a way that will disappoint some Black English enthusiasts. In a suit brought on behalf of black children with reading problems, Judge Charles Joiner ordered the Ann Arbor public school district to recognize the existence of Black English — but for the purpose of assisting black children to learn to read standard American English.

The emphasis in the judge's opinion on mastering standard English will undoubtedly be viewed by some as the act of a cultural imperialist. But it is significant that he acted in response to a suit filed on behalf of *black* children, whose complaint, essentially, was that they were not adequately being taught standard English. They knew what some early evangelists for Black English, black and white, seemed to overlook: that however valuable the dialect might be as a form of cultural affirmation, a command of standard English is necessary for educational and economic advancement in this society.

The approach ordered by the judge in Michigan — recognition of the distinctiveness of Black English as a prelude to instruction in standard English — seems a sensible way to handle an extremely sensitive educational and social problem.

THE ANN ARBOR NEWS

Ann Arbor, Mich., June 17, 1979

THE MOST IMPORTANT aspect of the "black English" case against the Ann Arbor school system, now being heard in U.S. District Court, is not legalistic at all.

Plaintiffs in this case say that "black English" should be officially recognized as a separate language system requiring bilingual school classes.

Judgments as to what constitutes acceptable usage of any language are made by the majority who use it, not by governments. Russians wear "dzhinsy" (jeans) and drink "viski" while the youth paper Komsomolskaya Pravda rails against "torture of the Russian tongue". The French speak of "hot dogs" and "le drug store" even though a 1977 law forbids using foreign words in advertising.

*   *   *

GERMAN PROVIDES examples particularly relevant to the "black English" case, which calls for designating a variation on standard English as a separate but equal language.

A Berliner visiting Munich may be told by that city's residents (usually in a friendly way) that he or she talks "like a Prussian pig". A native of Hamburg who visits Nuremberg will not only enjoy a type of sausage made nowhere else in Germany, but also strain to understand a dialect spoken nowhere else in Germany. Residents of resort villages in the mountains of neighboring Austria can usually tell immediately if German tourists are Bavarians or north Germans. Any German visiting the German-speaking region of Switzerland will understand about 60 percent of a conversation among local residents. Phrases understood by some German-speaking persons simply don't exist for others.

All schools in Germany, Austria and Switzerland's German-speaking region, and all German broadcasting, are conducted in standard "high German". All German-speakers who progress in school beyond approximately the fourth grade can, when they wish, shift from their local dialects to high German.

Inability or refusal to make that shift handicaps any German-speaker who wishes to perform more than menial labor.

*   *   *

AN YPSILANTI READER, Rob Dameron, who served recently on the Army's Race Relations/Equal Opportunity Staff while stationed in Germany, has sent us an article he wrote in February for an Army magazine, with these pertinent observations:

"While the American education system is white-oriented, it is not a white system; however it will become one if minorities abandon it and allow it to become so . . .

"Some soldiers were monolingual in nonstandard English before receiving assignments overseas. It is a strange phenomenon that although seemingly incapable of communicating verbally in standard English, many of these soldiers rapidly became fluent in German or other languages. Is it possible that their apparent inability to learn standard English is caused by a combination of peer pressure by their friends to conform to speech patterns and an inner conditioning by environmental elements which tells them not to bother since it wouldn't help anyway?

". . .People of all racial and ethnic groups should be encouraged to understand the necessity of acquiring facility in standard English without rejecting their own language and culture."

That's sound advice, considering that English is spoken by about 400 million people, more than speak any other language except Mandarin Chinese.

*   *   *

VARIATIONS will always add to the basic language's interest, sometimes contributing new words or new meanings to old words. But to pretend that variations from sentence structures and word-endings used by a majority speaking a particular language add up to a separate language can't make it so. Such pretense with a variation associated with an ethnic minority would be a new form of racial segregation.

THE PLAIN DEALER
Cleveland, Ohio, Aug 18, 1979

A recent federal court decision requiring teachers at an elementary school in Ann Arbor, Mich., to learn so-called "black English" because of the failures of young black pupils is preposterous. And it could turn out to be counterproductive.

While being sensitive to environmental differences can be very beneficial in the teaching process, the requirement placed on the Ann Arbor teachers is a cop-out. There was no evidence that the failures of the young blacks were the result of teachers' inability to understand them. And even if there were such evidence, it would not be reason enough for the court remedy.

Somebody has it backwards. The idea is for schools to teach pupils how to get along in society, not the other way around.

The court decision requiring 28 teachers to study "black English" for 20 hours followed a lawsuit filed in behalf of 11 black children who, the judge ruled, spoke a dialect that includes colloquial speech used primarily by black persons in informal conversation. Examples given included "he be gone" for "he is gone," and "to sell wuf tickets," meaning "to challenge to a fight."

There is nothing inherently wrong in informal colloquial conversation, nor in learning to understand someone else's colloquialisms.

But the complaint that the Ann Arbor teachers did not understand the pupils' conversational dialect is a too-easy alibi for not learning.

Carl T. Rowan, whose syndicated column appears in The Plain Dealer, has done research on the Ann Arbor legal case. Rowan points out that there was no issue of inferior school facilities; there was no issue of segregation as about 80% of the pupils were white and about 10% of the teachers were black; the school had special programs for remedial reading and diction lessons and appeared to have made major efforts to help teach disadvantaged pupils' to learn to read and write, and there was evidence that black pupils used standard English well in school while using "black English" only in casual conversation.

Asked Rowan, why blame the teachers when the pupils were frequently absent from school and showed learning and emotional problems? Rowan said that it is more important to get black children to attend school, to persuade their parents of the value of reading at home, and to persuade their teachers of the value of forcing pupils to consistently read newspapers and magazines.

Ann Arbor's school superintendent, Dr. Harry Howard, was quoted this week as saying teachers would not be teaching "black English" as a result of the federal court decision. We certainly hope not.

Schools do not need to teach in "black English" or any other special dialect. There is a great need for just the opposite, remedial courses in reading and writing, as well as basic mathematics — special programs to help people learn how to communicate and figure.

How can people be expected to get along, to be successful and to rise from poverty if they cannot speak, write and read the language of the society in which they hope to succeed?

Detroit Free Press
Detroit, Mich., July 27, 1979

THE SLEW OF opinions, some contradictory, stirred up by the Ann Arbor "black English" decision only prove the need for more discussion of the subject. It will take much intense dialogue and study to pinpoint just what black English is and why it can be a barrier to some youngster's proficiency in grammar-book English. Meanwhile the misunderstandings abound.

The most common fallacy, often voiced by whites who spoke a foreign language at home, is that it should be as easy for blacks to learn regular English as it was for them. But, in some very fundamental ways, they are wrong.

Unlike Polish or Lithuanian or Maltese, black English is not a language. It is a dialect, a variety of spoken English differing from the standard in pronunciation, syntax and other ways, but understandable to both blacks and whites. Since they can communicate with it, black youngsters may feel little pressure to abandon their dialect.

Teachers, for their part, may find it difficult to treat an unwritten dialect as they would a full-fledged language with a coherent grammatical structure. And to compound the problem, black English may not even mean the same thing to different groups of blacks.

A teacher working one summer in a Detroit remedial program seeking to prepare recent high school graduates for fall college work found herself tossing away the text after only two weeks. The book translated examples of black English into standard English. But many black youngsters in the classroom either didn't speak black English or spoke it in ways that differed from the text. "Why don't you just teach us the right way," an exasperated youngster grumbled one day. The textbook vanished into a drawer.

In forcing Ann Arbor schools to devise a plan for teachers to consider dialect when teaching reading, the black English decision could force an examination of all these issues. Such an examination is crucial. Ideally, both black and white dialects ought to be socially and culturally acceptable, but in the real world standard English helps people get jobs and other opportunities. Until that changes, the dialogue, and the search for better answers, must go on.

The Evening Bulletin
Philadelphia, Pa., Aug 8, 1979

There has been some misunderstanding, unfortunately, about what Federal Judge Charles Joiner did and did not say in his decision about "black English" in the Ann Arbor, Michigan, public school district.

In ruling that teachers must "recognize the existence of a home language" used by some of their black pupils, Judge Joiner emphatically was not ordering that black English be taught or even that its use be encouraged.

Quite the reverse. The judge seemed to be fully aware that incompetence in English is a handicap to anyone's development. He wrote: "Full integration and equal opportunity require much more (than scatter housing and busing) and one of the matters requiring more attention is the teaching of young blacks to read standard English."

One of the great accomplishments of American education has been to take immigrants of many tongues — the "huddled masses" — and give them a single language. With that they could survive, compete, excel; without it we'd all be citizens of Babel.

Black English, with its ambiguities and botched grammar, is really no asset. Precision in language may be tough to learn but it is vital to understanding.

Let us rejoice, also, that we don't have a double-language problem like Canada's, with its resentments and expensive, ponderous English-and-French versions of everything from streets signs to government documents.

What Judge Joiner did tell the Ann Arbor schools to do is to recognize that black English is a reality in some kids' home environments and is a language they bring to school with them. It is a condition, he said, that the school district must help the teachers deal with.

On today's Op-Ed page, Carl Rowan takes issue with Judge Joiner's statement that "the unconscious but evident attitude of teachers toward the home language causes a psychological barrier to learning." Mr. Rowan argues that what is really important is to have black parents understand the value of reading newspapers and magazines at home.

Well, it could be. But what Judge Joiner was getting at, as we see it, was that if a teacher makes a kid feel stupid because he is talking black English, it's not going to get him into a receptive mood to be taught. We think that makes sense.

The judge in no way urged teachers to encourage the speaking or — Horace Mann forbid — the writing of black English, only that it be recognized as a fact of some pupils' home and street life so that it can be dealt with.

Black English is not a cause to be run up anyone's flagpole. It is a weakness to be overcome.

Part II: Economic Status

The Black Family: An Economic Crisis

Many researchers feel that the family unit should be the starting-point for any program aimed at improving the economic status of black Americans. The National Urban League found, in its 1982 annual report, that the median black family income was $13,598, compared with $24,593 for whites, and that nearly half of all blacks under 18 were living in poverty. But the most startling statistic in the League's report was that, as of 1980, 42% of black families were headed by single mothers, up from 31% in 1970; in families with children, this figure increased to 47.I%. Black female-headed households have the lowest median income of any family type. In data compiled by the League from national census figures for 1980, the median income for black married couple families was $18,593, as compared to $23,501 for corresponding white families, and the median income for black female-headed households was $7,425 in comparison to $11,908 for white households headed by females. The reasons for the much lower incomes of female-headed households among both races are apparent: a single parent trying to hold a job while raising children is often faced with the necessity of working part-time or using a large portion of income for child-care. When other factors, such as the inequities in women's salaries in most of the job force, and the historically higher unemployment rates and lower incomes of blacks as compared to whites are considered, the fact that the lowest incomes are found in black female-headed families is not surprising.

A recent study undertaken by the Alan Guttmacher Institute, a private foundation, highlighted another aspect of black family life that has contributed to low incomes: the problem of pregnancy rates among black teenagers. The institute, which had studied the incidence of pregnancy among teenagers from 15 to 19 years old in the United States as compared to other industrialized nations, reported in 1985 that American teenagers as a whole had a pregnancy rate of 96 per 1,000; the pregnancy rate for black teenagers was tallied at 163 per 1,000. This astronomically high figure contributes to a cycle of black poverty, both increasing the high rates of teenage unemployment and adding to the numbers of female-headed families. (Interestingly, the rates of teenage births in the U.S. have actually decreased somewhat in the last decade. Federal figures show that in 1975, the birth rates for 15 to 19 year olds were 46.8 per 1,000 for white women and 113.8 for black women.)

The so-called feminization of poverty, and the high nationwide rate of teenage pregnancies, are not "black problems," but they are trends that have had a disproportionately harmful economic effect on the black community. In 1984, in recognition of the correlation between problems in family life and lowered incomes, the NAACP held a conference to explore "the crisis of the black family." Recent studies have concentrated not only upon the many interlocking factors—high divorce and separation rates, low levels of education, unemployment, high illegitimacy rates, etc.—that have contributed to the problems of many black families, but upon the factors that have helped other, stable black families to climb the economic ladder, closing the gap in income with white families. (See pp. 76-83.)

THE MILWAUKEE JOURNAL
Milwaukee, Wisc., February 24, 1980

Daniel Patrick Moynihan took a lot of heat in the 1960s when he warned that a collapsing family structure threatened the well-being of many black Americans. But he had a valid point, one that can be demonstrated even more graphically now than it could then.

In the intervening years, individual black workers have made remarkable econom c gains, but the average income of black *families* has slipped further behind that of white families. How can that be? It's quite simple: There has been a sharp increase in the number of white households that have two breadwinners each and a sharp increase in the number of black families that have only one or none.

According to the National Urban League's latest annual report, the proportion of black households headed by women rose from 22% in 1960 to 39% in 1977. Among whites, the percentages changed from 8 to 12. In the cores of many large cities, females head half or more of the black families. And many of those family heads are not women, but teenage girls.

Children born into those situations often are handicapped not only by low income but also by a variety of related ills. Among them are inferior schools, inadequate job opportunities, the lure of quick earnings from crime, and insufficient motivation to acquire education and job skills. Absent is the inspiring role model of a father who has succeeded in the straight economic world. So the dismal social pattern has a way of perpetuating itself from one generation to the next, even as middle class blacks move closer to full equality with whites.

Unfortunately, no one has an easy answer to the problem, although certain steps do appear to hold promise. For instance, the Carter administration is pushing a plan to give functionally illiterate youths basic education combined with work experience and skill training. That could help, if the trainees see a clear connection between the program and future self-sufficiency.

However, if there are no gainful jobs at the end of the program, it isn't likely to be taken seriously.

Another thing that could help break the poverty cycle is welfare reform, if only someone could figure out a formula that would provide for families' necessities and at the same time hold families together.

St. Louis Globe-Democrat
St. Louis, Mo., April 5, 1982

As the debate continues to rage over which approach to helping the poor works the best — the big-spending liberal welfare approach or the conservative approach of promoting economic growth — it is instructive to take a look at the record.

Recently two widely respected authors on the subject, George Gilder and Charles A. Murray, did just that in articles in The Wall Street Journal. Gilder, author of the best-selling "Wealth and Poverty," points out that the "redistributional schemes, by eroding the incentive to work, save or support families, have created in our inner cities a tragic wreckage of demoralization, and have left more than half of black children without a father in a home."

He goes on to say, "When welfare destroys the breadwinner role of the fathers, by offering a package of benefits more than double the minimum wage, the liberal answer is to take the mothers out of the home as well by giving them government jobs and day care centers."

Gilder writes, "Growth and opportunity are the only ways to lift the prospects of the poor." But he says the Reagan administration effort to reverse the vicious cycle of dependency by promoting economic growth is being undermined and thwarted by the constituents and administrators of "the utterly failed programs of the past."

In comparing the two approaches, Murray, former chief scientist at the American Institute for Research, cites the fact that in the 15 years prior to the launching of the enormous Great Society spending in 1964, the percentage of Americans below the poverty level decreased about 1 percent each year — from 32.7 percent below the poverty level in 1949 to 19.5 percent in 1964.

Then came the unprecedented surge in welfare spending under President Lyndon B. Johnson in 1964. But a strange thing happened. The poverty level continued to decline at about only 1 percent a year until 1969, and then virtually leveled off and failed to decline any further all through the 1970s even though welfare spending was doubling, tripling and quadrupling. It did temporarily dip to 11.1 percent in 1973, but then started up again and in 1980 stood at 13 percent.

So when the Congressional Budget Office and congressional liberals trumpet that Reagan-proposed budget cuts will widen the gap between the rich and the poor, they are simply wrong. The record shows that the much-maligned economic growth policies that call for curbing the growth of federal spending, reducing excessive taxes and weeding out unneeded and overly costly federal regulations hold out the best hope for the poor.

When the economy grows at a healthy rate, the poor benefit significantly. When economic growth is stifled by massive welfare spending and high taxes, the poor suffer.

Chicago Tribune

Chicago, Ill., July 28, 1983

There are several encouraging trends in the new study of blacks' and whites' incomes by the Center for the Study of Social Policy. And they must be emphasized and appreciated lest they be overlooked in the report's other depressing findings.

The income of black families with two wage earners is increasing faster than that of similar white families. Blacks have almost caught up with whites in education; there is only half a year's difference between the median educational level reached by blacks and by whites. College enrollment among blacks has increased sharply. Black and white literacy rates are almost equal. The percentage of blacks with professional, technical, sales, management and craft jobs has risen sharply. An increasing number of black families have moved into the middle class.

The country must have been doing something right since 1960 in its efforts to help blacks overcome centuries of discrimination, oppression and poverty.

But something has also gone terribly wrong. Two enormous and increasing problems have almost totally overshadowed the effects of these gains for blacks as a whole. As a result, the median income for black families in 1981 was only 56 percent of that for whites—compared to a 55 percent disparity in 1960.

Unemployment among black males is sharply higher than among whites; 45 percent of black men older than 16 don't have jobs (more than 50 percent if an estimate of those who could not be located by the Census Bureau is included) compared to 30 percent of white men. The number of black men has almost doubled since 1960 and the unemployed among them have increased by 3.34 million.

Coupled with such widespread joblessness among black men is the steep and worrisome increase in black families headed by a female; 47 percent of all black families are now headed by a woman, up from 8 percent in 1950 and 21 percent in 1960. Because women's incomes still lag so far behind men's and because women often have family responsibilities that make it difficult for them to compete with men for jobs, families headed by women are twice as likely to be poor as those with a man present. Half of all the black families headed by women have incomes below the poverty level.

The absence of such a high percentage of men from black homes can't be completely attributed to historic discrimination; it has almost quadrupled since 1950. But there's no denying that government social programs have inadvertently contributed to family break-up; in many states, two-parent families aren't eligible for welfare and it is easy for an unemployed father to conclude that his family would be better off financially without him.

The social changes and relaxation in sexual mores in the last two decades have affected black families—as well as white—adversely. More than half of all black children are now born to single mothers, many of them teenagers who drop out of school and onto welfare rolls, often permanently.

Some single mothers do a heroic and successful job of rearing their children alone. In many families—especially blacks—close, loving relatives fill in for absent parents. But the new study underlines the obvious facts: raising children is a two-parent job, and without a father the odds are heavily stacked against youngsters caught in poverty and welfare dependency. Many of them grow up to repeat the same unhappy pattern.

There are no easy answers to these complicated problems. Government, which has been part of the problem, will have to be part of the solution. More and better job training programs would help. So would restructuring welfare programs to stop encouraging family breakup, although this is difficult, expensive and uncertain. More and better family life education in schools might be useful, although this is controversial. A further decrease in unemployment and continuing improvement in the economy would make a difference, although this remains difficult to achieve.

Most important, black men must be encouraged to realize how absolutely essential they are to their families and especially to their children. As this study makes clear, government can never be an adequate substitute for a father.

THE LOUISVILLE TIMES

Louisville, Ky., January 26, 1982

The latest effort by the Reagan administration to placate the small minority that believes it is possible to legislate morality won't work. And, as with many administration efforts, this one will strike hardest the "have-nots" in society.

The Department of Health and Human Services is gearing up to change a regulation to require that federally funded family planning clinics notify the parents of teen-agers who seek contraceptives at the clinics. This action flouts the will of Congress during the preparation of the legislation in 1978 that created the grants for counseling teen-agers.

While the goal of the rules change is to cut down on teen-age sexual activity, the result — in the view of many professionals familiar with adolescent sexual practices — is likely to be the opposite. As *The Courier-Journal* recently reported, most teens who engage in sexual activity do so for six months or more before seeking contraceptives.

If they know their parents will learn they are seeking contraceptives, they are likely to continue to take the risk of doing without. A recent study by the Urban Institute in Washington indicated the nature of adolescent sexual activity with statistics on teen-age pregnancies: Twenty-nine per cent of the births to white adolescents and 83 per cent of the births among black youths are illegitimate.

That racial discrepancy is apt to be aggravated if the suggested regulation change is made. Doris Schneider, executive director of Planned Parenthood of Louisville, correctly identified why: Youngsters who have money will obtain contraceptives either by paying for them at clinics — or by purchasing them elsewhere.

Such a policy, of course, is fully consistent with the attitude the President and his supporters have toward federally-funded abortions for poor women. And it is not a surprising turn for an administration that last year moved to limit funding for sex education and family planning centers for adults.

The trend is clear — and it's consistent. No doubt the next initiative will be to award a federal contract to a company that makes scarlet "S's" — for Sex — to be worn by offending teen-agers in penance.

ST. LOUIS POST-DISPATCH

St. Louis, Mo., June 26, 1982

According to the Census Bureau, the nation is experiencing a dramatic increase in the number of one-parent families. The number of such units has doubled, the bureau says, from 3.3 million in 1970 to 6.6 million in 1980, and that rise could well explain much of the nation's poverty.

In a recent article in the *New Republic*, Sen. Daniel P. Moyihan notes that in the change in famiy composition the absence of a father has worked the greatest hardship on minority groups and has led to to what he calls the "feminization of poverty." White female-headed families had a 1980 median income of $11,908; two-parent white families had a median income of $23,501. The comparable figures for black families are $7,425 and $18,593.

A 10-year study showed that the income of divorced men in Los Angeles County rose by 42 percent in the first year after the divorce, whereas the wives' income fell by 73 percent. One-third of fathers ordered to pay child support never make a single payment. Obviously, attempts to collect child support should be stepped up, but such efforts will not help many fatherless children.

They will be heavily dependent upon public assistance. Indeed, one-third of all children born during 1980 are likely to spend some time on welfare before they reach age 18. What kind of assistance will society provide for them? President Reagan has proposed that states — with their varying benefit levels — totally take over the Aid to Families with Dependent Children program. A better idea, as suggested by Sen. Moynihan, would be for Washington to assume full control of AFDC, guaranteeing uniform benefits. And the aid should be structured in a way that would not be an incentive to further child abandonment. The law cannot force fathers to be responsible to their children; but it can and should protect children abandoned by one parent from economic disaster.

THE ATLANTA CONSTITUTION
Atlanta, Ga., September 30, 1983

The NAACP has grabbed the nettle, to its great credit.

It will sponsor a conference of black organizations and individuals to address what it calls the "crisis of the black family." The description is sadly apt.

The breakdown of black-family structure over the last 20 years has been brushfire-fast and socially devastating — but a painful subject for blacks to address openly. Leaders have feared, not without reason as it has turned out, that the problem would be manipulated by opponents of racial justice to serve their own reactionary agendas.

In setting up a conference on the issue, the NAACP answers a call issued in the report published this spring as a result of the important Tarrytown and Wingspread conferences black scholars and leaders held over the last three years.

The conference report bluntly outlined the problem: In 1960 some 75 percent of black families included both husband and wife. Today 48 percent of black families with children under 18 are headed by women — and half of all black children under 18 live in female-headed homes. In 1979, the majority of black births occurred to single mothers.

As the conference report notes, female-headed homes are not inherently inappropriate for rearing children, but the absence of a male figure is a challenging situation at any economic level and especially debilitating when added to poverty. And the general feminization of poverty, which is nationwide and no respecter of race, falls with special harshness in the black community.

Income for black husband-wife families grew during the 1970s. Had it not been for the impoverishment of female-headed households, black family income would have shown an 11.3 percent gain rather than a 5 percent decrease.

Black-community silence on this problem has not warded off the tendentious politics which the silence hoped to avoid provoking. The Reagan administration has begun using the data, not to look for creative answers, but to hype its own often irrelevant and sometimes counterproductive agenda.

The problems of the black family, some in the administration are saying, have been caused by federal efforts to help the poor. The assertion ignores the rapid urbanization of the once largely rural black population, the cancerous effects of unrelenting unemployment at rates twice those of whites and the likelihood that the end of formal segregation has had, as its downside, the movement of the ablest, best educated black families, and their stabilizing influence, from black ghettos.

And for the problem of youth pregnancies, the administration bizarrely tries to restrict the access of teenage girls to birth-control methods.

Such grotesqueries make it impossible for the black community any longer to try to keep this problem to itself. And by raising the issue to the general engagement with it that is bound to follow the black summit, the NAACP opens the way for national understanding. The black community is likely to find that more Americans are prepared to help it look for solutions than are keen to mine the problem for putdowns.

THE COMMERCIAL APPEAL
Memphis, Tenn., August 15, 1983

IT GOES WITHOUT saying that the black family in America is in deep trouble. Half of all black children under 18 live in female-headed households. The majority of black births occur to single mothers. And the authority of the family and the church, long the strongest forces in the black community, has been eclipsed by antithetical forces of a destructive nature.

Two years ago, 30 prominent black scholars met in Tarrytown, N.Y., to examine that problem among others. Their conclusions, published recently under the title "A Policy Framework For Racial Justice," have created a stir among black leaders, because the conclusions point an accusatory finger at the black community itself. The truth often hurts.

The black scholars, noting that after "300 years of struggle and resiliency, black families need special attention," call upon the leaderships of churches, civil rights organizations and social clubs to take more responsibility in restoring black families to their former strength.

The black scholars are right, not only in their analysis of the problem, but in the solutions they offer. Twenty years ago, 75 percent of the black families in the United States included both a husband and a wife. Today only half can make that claim. And the future looks even more discouraging.

If the black family is to be restored to its former high status, it is essential that black leaders, who for the past two decades have been preoccupied with political gains, reassert their authority in the area of family unity. It is, of course, easier to say what needs to be done than to explain what happened.

Other minority groups in this country have been able to keep the family intact while pursuing social equality and legal justice. Hispanics, Chinese and Irish have done it. Why have blacks failed?

Writing 20 years ago in "The Family," sociologists Ernest Burgess and Harvey Locke noted that never before in history had a group of people been so completely stripped of its social heritage as were the blacks who were brought from Africa to America. They called it one of the best illustrations of the "disorganizing effects" a culture experiences when its members are widely dispersed.

Unlike other groups who have come to this country, blacks were forced to reorganize family structures without benefit of the common denominators of religion, language or social custom — and they were forced to do that under the yoke of slavery. Incredibly, they managed to put together a strong, tightly knit family unit similar to those they had known in Africa, but with one difference: While in Africa, households were headed by both male and female figures, the fact that male slaves in America were sold more regularly than female slaves made it necessary that females exert dominance in an effort to keep families intact.

Contrary to myth, black Americans have a heritage of family stability that has been unequalled in the white community. Family responsibility, sex education, religious instruction, all unifiers of the family, have been trademarks of the black culture over the years.

THROUGHOUT all the traumas of emancipation, industrialization and the civil rights movement, that pattern held — until recently, that is. Something has happened — no one seems to know for certain what — to unravel three centuries of remarkable adjustment.

Maybe it doesn't even matter why it happened. It has been blamed on urbanization, the migration of rural blacks to cities, unemployment, government subsidies, racism, any number of sociological factors. Whites, after nearly three centuries of unrelenting attacks on the black family, certainly must come to accept their role in the disintegration of what was once a strong, proud heritage. But the challenge is not so much to find out why — or to assess blame — as to take action where it can help.

Black leaders, particularly males, must find a way to reassert the necessity of maintaining strong family units. That is especially true here in Memphis, where crime and illegitimacy, the enemies within, pose greater threats to black social and economic gains than white resistance.

By turning their backs on their family heritage, blacks have become their own worst enemy. That, not white racism, may prove to be the real hindrance to black progress in the 1980s and beyond.

TULSA WORLD
Tulsa, Okla., September 28, 1984

IT HAS been no secret that in recent decades poverty in this country has been "feminized." Households headed by women account for a disproportionate share of the families living below the poverty line.

This is an awesome statistic for the 12 million children living in families headed by women. Overall, half of those children are classified as poor. For minority children, it's worse. More than 70 percent of black and Hispanic youngsters living in female-headed families are poor.

There is no magic cure for this ailment. But some useful things are being done. First, there is a major effort — backed by tough, new federal laws — to make absent fathers pay child support. According to the Ford Foundation, more than half the women raising children alone receive no support from the child's father.

But in most cases, the father can't pay because he, too, is poor. Much of the burden must ultimately fall on the public.

The chief welfare program for women with dependent children — Aid to Families with Dependent Children — is inadequate and uneven, according to the Foundation.

One suggestion worth exploring is the idea of reformulating AFDC in terms of child needs only and addressing parent needs in other ways.

The AFDC has always been controversial and subject to a lot of public mythology. Perhaps it is time to make a rational new appraisal to decide whether it is doing what it is intended to do, and, if not, how it can be improved.

The Detroit News
Detroit, Mich., September 4, 1983

A statistical portrait of black Americans recently released by the U.S. Census Bureau should have been a call to arms for black and white political leadership.

Instead, it has resulted in either silence or temporizing about a corrosive and worsening problem.

Those who want to put the best face on the evidence note that black life expectancy has increased since 1970, that the percentage of blacks who graduate from high school and enroll in college has risen, and that home ownership has climbed.

But any good news is far outweighed by the disturbing disintegration of the black family. In 1970, 28 percent of black households had a female head. In 1980, almost 41 percent of black households had a female head — compared to 12 percent for white families.

Trends in illegitimacy were also distressing. In 1980, more than half of all black babies were born out of wedlock compared to an 11 percent illegitimacy rate for white babies.

THE INDIANAPOLIS NEWS
Indianapolis, Ind., August 2, 1984

A milestone may have been missed in this year's election squawks about gender gaps and economic racism. Last year — for the first time — white males made up less than 50 percent of the American work force.

According to a study by the Federal Bureau of Labor Studies, white men made up 49.8 percent of the work force. By June of this year, their share of the labor had dropped to 49.3 percent.

It's not the drop, however, that is encouraging; the gains are the grounds for boasting. Women and minorities have made huge strides toward keeping pace in the work force.

The gains among women have been the greatest. In 1950, women were only 30.9 percent of the work force. Less than 25 years later, they make up 43.5 percent of the Americans at work — and the percentage continues to climb. More than 60 percent of America's women now have jobs.

The progress among minorities hasn't been quite as remarkable, but there have been some gains. In 1954, blacks and other minorities made up 10.7 percent of the work force. Now they constitute 13 percent of Americans with jobs.

These figures, of course, do not mean that the war against economic discrimination has been won. The jobs that both women and minorities hold tend to be lower-skilled and lower-paying positions, while the jobs white males have are closer to the top of the ladder in terms of both money and prestige. And women and minorities still claim disproportionate shares of the unemployment figures.

For those reasons, many Americans still remain dissatisfied — as they should be — with the roles women and minorities play in society. But that does not mean signs of progress should be ignored. Forward strides are being made, and that is something in which all Americans can take pride.

This is not a "black problem." The decline of the minority family has serious economic and political consequences for the entire society. And the numbers show that, despite all the state's efforts to promote parity between the races, the battle is being waged and lost on the family front.

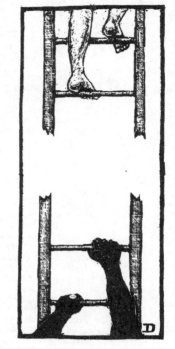

Female-headed families are, on average, poorer families. The median income of black female householders was only $7,510 in 1981, only about one-third of the median income of black married-couple families.

Indeed, the most encouraging piece of news in the Census study — news that should be trumpeted — is that black married couples are making some headway in closing the income gap with white married couples. This fact, more than any other, demonstrates the efficacy of encouraging stable family life.

Nevertheless, as a result of the large increase in female-headed households, black median income as a whole actually declined by 8 percent in real terms between 1971 and 1981. White median income also declined but at a lower rate, widening the income gap.

And, of the 9 million blacks below the poverty line in 1981, fully 70 percent were in families headed by women.

With almost one-half of all black children living in one-parent families in 1981, and 81 percent of white children living in married-couple families, the economic gap between today's black and white children is clear.

It is a gap likely to translate into missed opportunities, a gap that will undoubtedly limit the chances of the next generation of black children, a gap that is dividing and weakening the nation.

There are no easy solutions here. It won't be enough to simply denounce racism, as so much of the country's black political leadership appears content to do. It won't be enough to simply design another "program," as the liberals are inclined to do. And it won't be enough to simply ignore it and hope it goes away, as some conservatives tend to do.

We have to start talking about painful realities in a realistic way.

One place to begin is by frankly acknowledging that government cannot solve the problem. This was a myth perpetuated by people interested in votes rather than the community's welfare.

There are a couple of things government can do, however.

The design of current federal income supports may discourage family cohesion and encourage welfare dependency. A careful look at the incentives and disincentives of such programs is long overdue.

What sort of education system is needed for the growing number of American children with three strikes against them? Should it be an educational system designed by permissive sociologists and policed by civil libertarians? Or, should it be a highly structured and (dare we use the word?) disciplined environment that stresses rules and the fundamentals of learning?

Parents seem to favor the latter course, and so do we. Unfortunately, the attitudes of educators, lawyers, and judges are much less clear in this regard.

These are areas that may be amenable to government initiative. But are these the only initiatives a society can take to address a serious problem?

It wasn't all that long ago that political leaders spoke of the family as the fundamental unit of a free society. But, with the increased emphasis on the state's role in ordering society — the social contract — the importance of family ties — the family contract — has been steadily diminished.

The economic incentives for families to stay together are no longer as great as they once were. The risks of leaving a marriage, or never entering it to begin with, are greatly diminished.

A society can collectively decide that such incentives and risks are harmful and obsolete, and thus do away with them. But this should be a conscious decision. The penalties, as well as the rewards, should be understood by the society.

Instead of talking endlessly about what the government can do to solve problems created in large part by deteriorating family life, black and white political leaders might profitably address the problem at closer range.

What can be done to demonstrate the enduring value of stable family life?

One way to do it is to talk about the consequences that befall so many children who grow up in one-parent households. Yet we don't hear a single influential political leader, black or white, talking about these consequences.

Political leadership should not be confined to the art of explaining what the government should or should not "do" for this or that constituency. But, increasingly, it is.

America's black community, and Americans generally, are not well-served by this kind of political leadership.

THE CHRISTIAN SCIENCE MONITOR

Boston, Mass., May 14, 1984

RECOGNITION of the importance of the family in American life has come from yet another direction, a national conference on the black family, and on ways to strengthen it. The decision to hold the conference, as well as the ideas that emanated from it, is further evidence of the increasing attention being given the family in the United States.

Several recent studies have concluded that the American family in general is gaining support, after years in which it was widely said to be losing influence. Three months ago a study found that young Americans generally have a positive view of their families, and consider them an important center of support. More recently another study reported that three-fourths of American teens say they have "no serious problems getting along with any family members." Yet with the continued high rate of divorces and out-of-wedlock births, additional progress needs to be made.

The picture of the black family is similarly mixed. On the positive side, for many years black families have benefited from an informal support system provided by the extended families — grandparents, aunts and uncles, and so on. Under this system parents have been aided with everything from child care to financial aid to emotional support.

In a narrower sense the black family, now increasingly studied after years of little attention, is in need of strengthening. Slightly more than half of all black babies are born to unmarried mothers, and more than two-thirds of all black families headed by single mothers live below the poverty line.

The conference concluded that the responsibility for aiding black families was shared. Conferees said government should do more, such as providing full employment and sufficient wages. Between government and private industry, participants added, child care should be provided.

Then they took a further step: They said that blacks should increase the help they give to other blacks to strengthen the black family. This view symbolizes the importance of individual Americans, irrespective of race, aiding those who are less fortunate, an American tradition. Helping to build stronger families is a responsibility shared, in very different ways, by family members, the extended family and friends, other individuals, private employers, and government.

THE RICHMOND NEWS LEADER

Richmond, Va., May 14, 1984

Two events of recent days offer some encouraging signs that black leadership at last recognizes that it must act to reverse the one factor that threatens to undo much of black progress in recent years — teen-aged pregnancy:

— At Fisk University in Nashville a few days ago, some 200 black leaders met to discuss the deterioration of black family structure. It was the first of 43 meetings on the topic to be sponsored by Delta Sigma Theta, a national black sorority.

— Last week, Washington's Mayor Marion Barry announced a campaign designed to reduce teen-aged pregnancies in the District, which has the highest percentage of teen-aged pregnancies in the country.

Not long ago, either event would have been highly unlikely. When Daniel Patrick Moynihan — then a White House adviser — issued a report in 1965 suggesting that the black family structure was falling apart, he was assailed as a racist. Since that time, public notice of rising pregnancy and illegitimacy rates among black teenagers has been off-limits. Black leaders tended to blame a social calamity on poverty and racism, and white leaders dared not suggest that a high illegitimacy rate was an almost certain guarantee of continued poverty.

Black radicals called family planning efforts a white connivance for black genocide. Any study that condemned the welfare system for encouraging black teen-agers to become pregnant by providing the wherewithal for them to become independent was suspect. The "new morality" and a do-your-own-thing non-ethic contributed to the acceptance of illegitimacy. So today we have what is called the "feminization of poverty," largely a result of moral indifference and a failure to transmit cultural values to the young.

Blacks are not alone, of course, in suffering from an epidemic of illegitimate teen-aged pregnancies. In fact, the cumulative birthrate for white and Hispanic teen-agers stands at 221 per thousand, and the illegitimacy rate among those groups is rising. Among black teen-agers, the cumulative birthrate stands at 515 per thousand, a decline from 715 per thousand in 1971. (The cumulative birthrate measures the number of babies born to a certain group; some of the mothers may bear more than one child during their teen-aged years.) It is thought that the decline in the black teen-aged birthrate has resulted from legalized abortion. In contrast, the cumulative birthrate among Japanese teen-agers stands at 17 per thousand.

The pregnancy and illegitimacy rates among teen-agers is a national — not a racial — epidemic. Nonetheless, black leaders are properly concerned that 55 per cent of black babies are born to unwed mothers usually in their teens. When Moynihan released his report, the black illegitimacy rate stood at 26 per cent. When teen-agers have babies, and keep those babies instead of putting them up for adoption, they usually face the dead-end street of poverty. The problem is, about 90 per cent of all teen-aged mothers *do* elect to keep their babies, and it is not rare for those babies later to become teen-aged mothers, too.

There are no overnight cures for a pervasive problem that has been years in the making. There are, however, some possible remedies for the long run. Better education, of course, is a priority, as well as more accessible family planning help. Teen-agers need more motivation to plan their futures. And, as one social worker in New York advocates, stricter application of statutory rape statutes would be a big help in restraining careless young fathers who usually escape responsibility for their actions. Teen-aged mothers also need more persuasive counseling to convince them that the best answer for them and for their babies is adoption.

Quite likely, the only lasting solution lies in a sea change in public attitudes toward illegitimacy, especially among teen-agers themselves. It wasn't so long ago that society frowned on illegitimacy, and social disapproval was a strong force in teen-aged behavior. A teen-aged girl who "got into trouble" was dispatched to a distant relative, or to a home for unwed mothers, and her baby was adopted by a childless couple. Today, anything goes — and that is the attitude that has to be changed before teen-agers can be persuaded that unwed motherhood isn't cool. Such a change would not require a miracle: Just consider the recent change in public attitudes toward drunken driving.

Otherwise, as one black leader said, "I think we are going to have a lost generation of black youth that is ill equipped to enter the labor force or to form families." His fears should not be limited to black youths, but to all teen-agers who risk ruining their lives by having babies before they are psychologically, emotionally, or financially prepared to be good parents. Theirs is the tragedy of the moment, but it is a tragedy that will be compounded for the hapless and unfortunate infants they bear.

The Des Moines Register

Des Moines, Iowa, September 14, 1984

One of the biggest single problems facing black Americans is the startling number of divorces and separations that create single-parent households, with a growing number living below the poverty line.

According to a report to the National Urban League, there is a steady attrition in the number of black men who can support a wife and children and it is creating a crisis for the black family in America.

The report cited statistics from the Center for the Study of Social Policy, which found that 47 percent of black families were headed by women in 1982, and nearly 60 percent of those lived below the poverty level (median income of working black women was $7,802, as compared with $10,510 for black men; white men averaged $15,393).

The Urban League's research director, James McGhee, reported that since 1960 the divorce rate for blacks has jumped 400 percent, but even that understates the problem, as black couples separate at five times the rate for whites.

"The staggering rates of divorce and separation and the resulting financial drain contribute to the crisis which the black family now faces," McGhee said.

The league report put much of the blame on intense pressure on the black male in society, particularly by discrimination in education and employment. The toll of this discrimination emerges in self-destructive behavior such as drug- and alcohol-abuse.

The black male has a lower horizon because less is expected of him by society and he expects less of himself, McGhee said. Unemployment rates among black men between the ages of 20 and 60 reached nearly 30 percent in 1982, according to the report.

The message in this report is that discrimination is tearing apart the black family. Without the solid foundation of the family, future generations of impoverished blacks may never hope to break out of their circumstances. It is a trend all Americans should find intolerable.

The Philadelphia Inquirer

Philadelphia, Pa., June 20, 1984

There is a clear and present danger that the traditional family structure — the cohesion that enabled black Americans to endure and survive the indignities and brutality of slavery, Jim Crow and the struggle for equal rights — is deteriorating at an alarming rate.

This devastating trend detailed in a four-part series of articles in The Inquirer last week is made clear by the tremendous increase in fatherless homes during the last 20 years, an increase that has been accelerated even further by the proliferation of teenage pregnancies.

Female-headed households are estimated to be 42 percent of all black families, compared with only 21 percent in 1960. They are among the poorest in the nation and have been the single most significant contributor to the largest black-white family-income gap in nearly 20 years.

The data, compiled during a five-month investigation by staff writers Fawn Vrazo, Terry E. Johnson and Marc Kaufman, reflect the impact of changing mores and economic and political conditions that have locked a significant portion of a generation of blacks into a permanent underclass.

Poverty has had a more disparate and devastating effect on blacks, particularly women and children, than any other group. Racial discrimination, past and present, and lack of job opportunities have contributed greatly to the crisis of the black family. It also is true that changing values toward marriage, sex and divorce are involved. The solution must be found in examining all of these.

That will not be done easily. There are major political and ideological differences among social scientists and public officials about the cause and effect and what should be done to reverse the trend. Thus, the crisis is likely to deepen before it gets better, exacting enormous social and economic ramifications and posing a difficult but crucial challenge to the nation.

A key element if the trend is to be reversed must be concern followed by constructive leadership at the city, state and national level, but particularly from the White House. The Reagan administration has given scant evidence that it is prepared to confront the reality that The Inquirer articles detailed and that also was highlighted at a meeting of black leaders last month at Fisk University in Nashville, Tenn. The meeting, sponsored by the National Urban League and the NAACP, brought together representatives of more than 100 black organizations and schools and was attended by black social scientists, religious leaders and elected officials.

The group drafted a national agenda that urges a coordinated effort by black organizations to propose programs and solutions to the problem, with a major effort in establishing family planning and social agencies to deal with the problems of the black family. These agencies and programs, funded through private sources, would provide not only a support base but conduct social research and become advocates for the black family and for strengthening black culture.

Locally the effort has begun with initiatives by a number of groups and individuals such as the Urban League as well as state Sen. Hardy Williams, who has established Black Family Services Inc. But the effort to reverse the tide has to involve the public as well as the private sector. Cutting social programs and depending on volunteerism — the implied remedy of the Reagan administration — is not the way to go.

The answer, as with other deep-seated social problems, lies in coordinated efforts by all segments of government and society. The problem affects white as well as black America, the public sector as well as the private.

If the black family structure continues to erode, the ramifications will affect all America. Eventually all of America will bear not only the burden of that failure but the ultimate cost.

The TENNESSEAN

Nashville, Tenn., May 5, 1984

THE "Black Family Summit," sponsored by two prestigious black organizations and Fisk University, has taken a realistic view of the bleak status of black families in America.

The National Urban League, the National Association for the Advancement of Colored People, and Fisk University brought together this week a group of notable authorities on a broad range of issues which plague black families. Dr. Benjamin Hooks, executive director of the NAACP, and Mr. John E. Jacob, president of the National Urban League, issued the call for the summit.

The summit meeting held sessions devoted to virtually every aspect of human existence for black families — health care, economics, education, housing, nutrition, crime, the elderly, the young, male-female relationships.

But although the summit meeting touched on far-reaching issues, there was a common thread running through each session. Each and every session, regardless of the topic, repeated one unfavorable truth: The quality of life for blacks is drastically less than for whites. And it is decreasing.

The statistics are absolutely chilling. According to the most recent "State of Black America" report, the average income for black families is 58% of that of white families. Over 35% of black families live below the poverty level. One-third of black adults who want to work can't find jobs.

This disturbing dilemma is perpetuating itself through America's black children. Over 10% of black youths between the ages of 14-19 are not in school. And 83% of black teenage mothers are unwed.

Black female-headed households, which comprise 42% of all black families, have the lowest income of any family type. In fact, 70% of all black children living in poverty are in households headed by single females.

These formidable problems are easily defined, and will require massive efforts to solve. One thing is clear — America cannot continue to hold back this nation's black citizens. Neglecting the situation would add even more shame to what has become a national embarrassment. Every thinking, concerned person must recognize that many of this country's black families are in crisis.

It was appropriate that this historic national conference was held in conjunction with Fisk University. For 117 years, Fisk has dedicated itself to the mission of bettering the quality of life for black Americans. Yet this prestigious institution has been fraught with internal and financial problems that have cracked the schools's core and threatened its existence. Fisk University and many black American families share a common challenge — survival.

And it is also appropriate that the conference's opening session was held this week in a Nashville hotel literally yards away from the Tennessee Legislative Plaza, because state lawmakers are now considering legislation that would have a profound effect on the lives of thousands of Tennessee's needy children, many of whom are black.

Next week, the House will vote on a proposal that will increase the standard of need for the Aid for Families with Dependent Children — a federal-state assistance program for needy children of single parents. Tennessee currently has the lowest standard of need in the nation, and one of the lowest grant levels. Currently, the maximum that a parent and three children can receive is $154 per month.

This state's negligence of this vital assistance program is dumping thousands of black children into an endless poverty cycle. State lawmakers have before them legislation that will break that cycle. The passage of this momentous bill will restore dignity to this state, and renew hope to many black Tennessee families.

The problems of black families in Tennessee will not be totally erased with the passage of this single legislation. But it is without doubt a significant first step.

The participants in the Black Family Summit had the strength to look at an unsightly human problem through realistic eyes. The nation must muster the resolve to share that vision.

High Rates of Poverty, Unemployment Mask Social Stratification

The Census Bureau, in its data for 1983, reported that a record 12.1% poverty rate for whites in that year compared with a 35.7% rate for blacks and a 28.4% rate for Hispanic Americans. (The bureau's data were based on cash income only. The poverty line was drawn at an income of less than $10,178 for a family of four.) The National Urban League, in its ninth annual assessment of the "State of Black America", reported that black unemployment as of the end of 1983 was 17.6%, more than twice the rate for whites. "Hidden unemployment"—comprising workers so discouraged that they had ceased to seek work and part-time workers who could not find full-time jobs—was 33% among blacks, the report noted, also twice the comparable rate for whites. A study by the Joint Center for Political Studies, released in 1983, found that although black households made up 12% of all households in the United States, they held only 4% of total household wealth, and that the annual income of black families in 1979 was running about 60% that of white families.

These by now depressingly familiar statistics document the consistently lower economic status of blacks compared to whites in the United States. But they tend to obscure important advances that have been made, and to conceal equally important current trends. It is undeniable that black unemployment is disastrously high, and that employed blacks are overrepresented among service workers, laborers and equipment operators, and underrepresented in administration, sales and the professional and technical fields. It should also be noted, however, that the number of black doctors has tripled since 1960, and that the number of black lawyers has increased six times. The number of black-owned businesses increased between 1969 and 1977 to over 230,000, from 163,000. The proportion of black employees in craft, technical and professional fields increased from 11% to 21% between 1960 and 1980. What these figures and others indicate is that there is a growing black middle class—bankers, government employees, engineers, politicians, university professors, etc.—who have moved far beyond the level of simple economic survival. As many researchers have noted, however, the movement of successful young blacks up the economic scale has been accompanied by an increase in the number of blacks living below the poverty line, so that the statistics for black unemployment and median incomes have remained fairly consistent. The widening gap between poor blacks and middle class blacks is a phenomenon whose effects are difficult to predict. One salutary development is a movement by black community leaders to address the problems besetting black families, problems that appear to entrench them in poverty. (See pp. 70-75.)

The Washington Post
Washington, D.C., January 24, 1980

VIEWED FROM THE top of the ladder, economic progress by blacks has been continuous over the past decade. Rapidly increasing numbers of well-educated young black people have been moving into the professions, business and public administration. But viewed through the income statistics for the whole population, the pattern is much less promising. The gap between the average incomes of black and white families is not being closed. It is as wide now as it was a decade ago.

Vernon E. Jordan, the president of the National Urban League, does a service in calling attention to that second and less visible reality in the league's annual report on the state of black America. Twenty years ago the median income of black families was little better than half that of white families. Ten years ago it had improved significantly, to about 61 percent of the white level. But since then, there has been no further progress at all toward equality.

Similarly, 20 years ago more than half of all blacks had incomes below the federal definition of poverty. By 1970, the proportion had fallen to one-third. Since then, once again, there has been little progress. That proportion has fallen by several percentage points but, since the black population has grown, the number of black people living in poverty at the end of the decade was actually slightly larger than at its beginning. Unemployment among blacks, over the past year, has been more than twice as high as among whites. Over the last five years, the gap here has widened.

There is no mystery about this failure. In recent history there have been two periods when blacks moved rapidly closer to the national averages of prosperity. The first was World War II, with its tremendous labor shortages. The second was the 1960s, when vigorous federal social policy and tight labor markets reinforced each other. Blacks have gained most rapidly, and the cause of equality has flourished, in those times when everyone was doing well and the national economy was expanding strongly.

But the long boom of the 1960s ended in 1971. Since then, there have been two recessions and generally poor economic growth. You have heard much argument in the past few years over the desirability of economic growth. The comparison of incomes of blacks and whites contains one of the strongest arguments for continued growth. Without it, standards of living come to a standstill and the relative disparities and disadvantages are frozen.

A return to higher growth rates now probably depends first of all on this country's ability to bring down its inflation rate. The point is made by Bernard E. Anderson of the Rockefeller Foundation, who contributed the chapter on economic policy to the league's report. As long as high inflation rates persist, he observes, full employment is not likely to be sought very vigorously. The case for bringing down inflation, and speeding up economic growth, is essentially a moral one.

THE CHRISTIAN SCIENCE MONITOR
Boston, Mass., January 24, 1980

In the wake of the urban rioting of the 1960s, it was not uncommon to hear concerned and sympathetic whites remark that the frustrations of American blacks, while understandable, would not be resolved overnight. With hard-won civil-rights laws finally on the books, the even harder tasks of enforcing them and preparing the next generation to move into the economic mainstream would take time. So the reasoning went. Righting the wrongs of 200 years of discrimination and second-class citizenship would require patience and constant toil but, given time, gradual progress would be evident. Today, however, more than a decade later, two new reports on the status of black Americans seem to call such rationalizing into question. They paint a discouraging picture of little overall real progress.

In fact, instead of continuing to push ahead, as expected at the start of the 1970s, blacks actually lost ground to whites economically over the past 10 years, according to a new study by the National Urban League. For instance, a decade ago, black family income averaged about 61 percent that of whites. By 1978, it had dropped to 59 percent. In real purchasing power, the median family income of blacks rose only 3.1 percent to $10,879 between 1970 and 1978, whereas whites saw theirs increase by 6.8 percent to $18,368. Black unemployment (11.3 percent) remains more than twice as high as white joblessness (5.1 percent) and is actually higher than it was at the start of the 1970s (8.2 percent). Moreover, the poverty rate among blacks in 1978 was 30.6 percent as compared with 8.7 percent among whites.

And the gap shows up in other areas, too. A week ago a separate report by the US Civil Rights Commission labeled 1979 a year of "drift" in civil rights. It found nearly half of all minority-group school children still in "racially isolated schools," and it faulted Congress for using antibusing and other legislative riders for preventing federal action to speed up desegregation. The federal panel found that "housing discrimination remains widespread throughout the United States" with a "grim pattern" of minority families paying "disproportionately high costs for flawed, deteriorating, and overcrowded housing."

Both the Urban League and the Civil Rights Commission noted some signs of progress as well. However, the tenor of both reports was summed up in the commission's conclusion: ". . . the lack of enforcement by the executive branch of government, the weakening of good legislation by Congress, and the diminishing will and vision on the part of many Americans are discouraging."

The message from both is clear. In the rush to meet the nation's concerns about defense, inflation, and energy, Congress and the Carter administration must not completely lose sight of the sufferings of blacks and other minorities and of the long road still to be traveled before the last vestiges of discrimination can be said to have been wiped out, once and for all. Renewed dedication and a greater determination on the part of all Americans is needed to help more blacks achieve the economic and educational progress that continues to elude too many.

Chicago Defender

Chicago, Ill., February 4, 1980

It seems like the same story is repeated every two or three months: "Gap between black and white wage earners getting wider."

Actually, it's not the same story, but it is the same trend. Three or four times a year, some major economist or university or respected organization looks over the latest data to see if we're finally catching up — like everyone says we are. The latest study, reported last week by Vernon Jordan of the Urban League, revealed that blacks are still moving backwards relative to their white brothers. Over a 10-year period, average black income had dropped from 61 percent of average white income to 59 percent. Also, noted the Urban League, more blacks are in the poverty zone today than in 1970.

All of this contradicts the common view that blacks are going too far too fast and the belief that the old barriers to equal opportunity have been forever destroyed.

Reports like that of the Urban League are an indictment of the American system, and they also are a challenge to those blacks who have made it — who have escaped the poverty cycle and the ghetto.

There is no question that in the 1970s, thousands of our people have moved out of the storerooms and into the boardrooms of large corporations, into management positions and directorships and other well rewarded posts of responsibility. Obviously, their advancement has not led to the elevation of blacks in general. Quite the contrary, according to the grim figures. A few have soared ahead, and in most cases, they never looked back.

The kind of growing statistical lag reported by Jordan suggests successful blacks are just not using their new-found lofty positions as they might. For if they saw their success not so much as a personal conquest but the result of a whole people's struggle, they would see their paychecks and fringe benefits as carrying a heavy social responsibility.

ST. LOUIS POST-DISPATCH

St. Louis, Mo., January 25, 1980

The U.S. Commission on Civil Rights has issued its annual report, for 1979, and despite its attempts to be even-handed and to recognize progress, in fact there wasn't much. That might even be said for the whole decade, for the marked advances of the '60s toward equality of opportunity and equality before the law slowed to a crawl in the '70s.

A startling picture of the economic status of American blacks in the '70s has just been provided by the Urban League. The decade began with an expectation that blacks would make economic gains in relation to the white majority. Instead, the reverse was true. Ten years ago, black family income averaged about 61 percent of that of whites; in 1978, it had fallen to 59 percent. Black unemployment also rose to more than twice that of whites, while the number of blacks below the officially designated poverty level is greater than it was at the start of the '70s. So much for minorities' economic progress.

What about housing opportunities? The Civil Rights Commission is critical of the federal bureaucracy's efforts toward providing adequate housing for the poor and elderly, a disproportionate number of whom are minorities and women. The commission says the Department of Housing and Urban Development has not moved quickly to enforce fair housing regulations, and it views HUD's 1980 budget request as "a severe blow to the housing prospects of millions of families headed by minorities and women."

Then, what about educational segregation? While the commission commends Congress for not doing worse, it notes that Congress "aided and abetted" obstructionists by trying to make it more difficult to enforce desegregation policies. The chief instrument of this, once more, was the Eagleton-Biden amendment that forbids use of federal funds to bus students for desegregation purposes. It has been said that enforcement by fund-cutoff politically injures the agency responsible for it, in this case the Department of Health, Education and Welfare. But the other victims can be found somewhere among nearly half of the nation's minority school children, who remain in racially isolated schools.

So, as the 1980s begin, the nation can reflect that its largest minority has become relatively poorer and not much more integrated in the housing and educational fields. The Civil Rights Commission characterizes the government's performance during 1979 as largely one of drift. Vernon Jordan, president of the Urban League, says the international situation and the "spirit of Proposition 13" have diverted the nation's attention from civil rights. "The same people who charged that social problems couldn't be solved by throwing money at them," says Mr. Jordan, "are anxious to try to solve internatiional problems by throwing money at the Pentagon."

That is not an unfair description of President Carter's preliminary budget proposals. Mr. Carter, as we have noted, has hardly proved an activist on social programs. Yet, unless the president demonstrates a deeper commitment to civil rights, government and nation may proceed into the 1980s still floundering with divisive issues derived from centuries past.

Roanoke Times & World-News

Roanoke, Va., August 6, 1981

During the '50s, the migration routes went north — away from the cotton fields and cane brakes, into the industrial job centers. Black America was on the move toward a promised land of jobs, good pay and equal treatment.

For many, the promise was cruelly deceptive. But others found education, skills, and management experience at the end of the trek.

Now they're coming home. In the 11 states of the Confederacy, the number of blacks increased by almost two million from 1970 to 1980.

They are a different breed from the farm hands who made their way north three decades ago. Many are professionals and skilled workers joining an emerging black middle class.

And they are returning to a different South.

Thirty years ago, blacks weren't expected to vote in Mississippi. Today, 17 blacks sit in the Mississippi state legislature. All but three of them are men who left the state in their youth and returned.

They find a South that is vastly different from the land of their fathers. In 1950, blacks took the rear seats in public transportation. They rode on segregated railroad cars. They drank from black-only water fountains. They used black-only rest rooms, many of which served both males and females. They sent their children to black schools. Black women could not aspire to be secretaries, much less business executives. Black men could enter only those professions in which they could serve a black clientele. A black family traveling through the South could not stop at the handiest restaurant for a meal or take lodging at the first motel with a vacancy. Jim Crow was in charge.

Now, supported by federal laws and changing attitudes, the educated black has opportunities undreamed of by his grandparents.

This doesn't mean that the region is an unflawed Promised Land. Racism, though not the scourge it was, lingers in the back-waters and in some parts of the mainstream. Large Southern cities are battling urban decay, just as their Northern cousins are. And one middle-income Mississippi black — a lawyer who now sits in the state legislature — contends that the disparities between rich and poor are greater here than in the north.

But blacks now seem to feel free to follow the economic flow to the Sunbelt. That says positive things about racial progress here.

A healthy black middle class in the Deep South will be a benefit to the region. It will demonstrate to black youngsters that their horizons need not be limited to ghettoes or tenant shacks. It will demonstrate to skeptical whites that black people can be productive, constructive members of their communities.

Let us hope that in cooperating toward a new, more prosperous and more tolerant South, both races will submerge the bitterness of the past in a common vision for the future.

The Boston Globe
Boston, Mass., July 21, 1983

A new study comparing the economic status of blacks and whites in 1960 and now provides ample evidence of the fact that the task before those committed to ensuring genuine equality in the nation has become ever more complex.

The study, made by the Center for the Study of Social Policy, a private research organization, found that despite all the apparent racial progress of the last 20-plus years, despite substantial gains by blacks in education and literacy, despite the movement of blacks into managerial posts, the gap between the average income of whites and blacks remains as large today as it was in 1960.

What accounts for this, according to the study, is a widening income division within the black community and the fact that persistent discrimination results in blacks with comparable education earning considerably less than whites.

Perhaps the two most discouraging findings of the study are that 47 percent of black households are now headed by women, up from 21 percent in 1960, and that the number of black males who are unemployed has risen markedly.

Households headed by women are 1.7 times more likely to be poor than two-parent households.

According to the study, only 54 percent of black men over the age of 16 are employed today compared with 74 percent in 1960; if one considers that the Census data on which the study is based undoubtedly undercounts the number of adult black males, it is likely that over one-half of the black male adults in the country are, in fact, unemployed.

One might hope that increased educational attainment would close the income gap between whites and blacks, but, alas, it is not true. The study found that 47 percent of blacks with four years of college earned between $20,000 and $40,000, yet the same percentage of whites with no more than a high school education earned incomes within the same range. As the report noted, these figures suggest that job opportunities after schooling, rather than the level of schooling itself, may be more important in explaining the persistent white-black income gap.

The picture is indeed complex. It is also disheartening. Judged by the bottom line, by income, all the civil rights advances of the last two decades have failed to advance the relative standing of blacks as a group. So what does the nation do in the next 20 years if this economic measure of racial separation is to be substantially reduced by the 21st century?

Surely it will require more vigorous and more constant moral leadership from the White House than the nation has witnessed since the Reagan Administration took office. It will require more determined efforts by all segments of the society to take affirmative steps to reverse the inequitable treatment accorded blacks who are equally as edcuated and trained as their white counterparts.

It will require the nation once again to examine whether its own social policies encourage family instability. It will require vigorous targeted efforts to locate jobs in areas accessible to the black population and to provide the training necessary to make the jobs attainable.

It will require that in the short run of the next two decades the nation place a renewed emphasis on enhancing its social health as it strains to improve its economic health. In fact, increased participation by blacks in the economy as producers and wage earners is one of the keys to restoring the nation's economic health.

THE DENVER POST
Denver, Colo., January 15, 1982

THERE ARE now nearly 107 million people in our country's civilian labor force, nearly one out of every three Americans over the age of 16. Not all of them can find jobs.

The Labor Department calculates that 9.5 million members of the labor force were unemployed at the end of 1981. That's 8.9 percent of the total number of available workers.

The percentage is only a hairsbreadth away from the post-World War II record of 9 percent jobless, set in May 1975. Unless our economy does a remarkable turnabout within the next few weeks — an unlikely possibility, the rate seems certain to top 10 percent.

Nearly 2 million currently jobless Americans were forced out of the labor market by the recession that began last July when unemployment was only 7 percent (still high by historical standards). The recession shows few signs of ending. To a degree, this economic downturn was engineered by the government in an effort to wring double-digit inflation out of the system. And inflation is coming down.

In theory, rising unemployment is the short-term tradeoff for lower inflation. But try to explain this to a jobless head of household who's been pounding the streets looking for work, any work. Or to those younger Americans who cannot find their first jobs.

The stark statistics don't tell all of the story. They tell us simply that one of every 11 Americans who's currently searching for work can't find it. What's more, joblessness isn't distributed evenly within the labor force.

Unemployment rates for whites, for adult males and for adult females all were under the national average at 7.8 percent, 8 percent and 7.5 percent, respectively. But 16.1 percent of blacks and other minorities in the work force were jobless, as were 21.7 percent of teen-agers. Especially, perhaps critically, hard hit were black teen-agers, among whom the unemployment rate stood at 42.2 percent nationally.

In Detroit, the jobless rate for blacks between the ages of 16 and 19 hit 68 percent, an incredible proportion of deprivation.

We've been told repeatedly that unemployment will be cured when inflation is controlled, when the recession bottoms out and when the economy starts to hum once again. But will it?

Brighter days aren't far away for some jobless. They live in the West and the Sun Belt; they're predominantly white and generally adult. For the remainder, the economic prognosis is bleak indeed.

Our automobile and steel industries are crippled. Up to a million jobs have disappeared, or are about to disappear, in the Detroit and Pittsburgh regions alone. These were jobs where entry was easy, qualifications low and the pay relatively high. Countless other areas whose economic survival is in doubt dot the Midwest and Northeast.

Must the shadow of joblessness hang darkly over vast portions of our nation forever? We don't have an answer. Everything we've tried to cure the structural imbalance in the composition of our labor force has failed. And now we have an administration averse to trying to reduce unemployment through new job programs and projects such as government-subsidized training.

The American dream of a job for everyone who wants to work seems as unattainable now as it did 40 years ago. But the search for a solution to chronic joblessness — through renewed training programs, creation of new industries or whatever — must continue. To reject this premise would be to invite perpetual alienation from the least advantaged members of our population.

The Charlotte Observer
Charlotte, N.C., January 5, 1981

The U.S. Labor Department recently released statistics which tear away at a notion long held in this country, particularly in the South: that labor unions are at best racially callous, and at worst, anti-black. Blacks, the figures show, are now more likely to be represented by labor unions than whites.

Thirty-three percent of all black workers in agriculture and industry are represented by unions, compared to 26 percent of white workers. Black membership in unions has increased as much as threefold since 1960, and blacks are also emerging in union leadership positions.

The figures demonstrate a positive trend in race relations in the workplace. Earlier in this century, employers often imported black workers in an effort to break a strike or stop a union-organizing effort. For the most part, the practice of pitting one race against another in labor-management battles has ended.

Gone, also, is the time when unions closed their memberships to blacks. Unions have realized they need all the members they can get, particularly when support nationwide for unions seems to be declining.

The trend may have particular significance in the South, as northern industries continue their migration to the Sunbelt, and Southern blacks who once fled to the North for better jobs come home.

Because of that migration of industry, organized labor must make major gains in the South or become increasingly insignificant nationally. If unions make gains in the South, where social and economic progress too often have been handicapped by racial strife, the increasing racial integration of union membership and leadership could affect racial attitudes in Southern industrial towns.

"There is a growing respect among the blacks and whites for one another, a respect for workers as workers," says an assistant to Lane Kirkland, AFL-CIO president. Areas where large numbers of workers are represented by unions can only benefit from that kind of mutual respect.

The Hartford Courant

Hartford, Conn., August 7, 1983

Take a look at America today, President Reagan said in a speech last week. "Things are changing for the better."

He dismissed as "hogwash" the criticism that women and minorities are worse off, that he is insensitive to the needs of the poor. His administration has maintained that the issue of hunger is overdramatized by anecdotal evidence. Sure, there may be stories of families subsisting on chicken broth. But there is no study that shows that these are more than isolated occurrences, went the defense.

One day after Mr. Reagan's speech, the Census Bureau reported that the country in 1982 registered the highest poverty rate in 16 years. One in seven Americans — 34.4 million people — were consigned to life below the poverty level. Millions more had income slightly above the poverty line, and could be included in this nation within a nation.

Mr. Reagan said he was "perplexed." He quickly appointed a task force "to bring me a no-holds-barred study," to see if there is, indeed, hunger in America. He obviously isn't satisfied with reports from mayors and nutritionists that hunger is rising.

And, in a shameless defense of the indefensible, the White House deputy press secretary held that the rate of increase in the number of poor people was smaller last year than in the two preceding years. Is that supposed to be a consolation for the 34.4 million Americans who live in poverty?

Later in the week, the administration tried to bolster its case with the good news that the unemployment rate last month fell to a single-digit number, as if a 9.5 percent jobless rate were proof-positive of Mr. Reagan's concern for the poor.

One need not speculate about the legacy of the Reagan administration, if it continues cutting back on food stamps and on child nutrition programs; if it continues to oppose health care benefits for the unemployed; if it continues to emasculate public housing programs; if it continues to hedge about providing surplus food for the needy.

The president who wants to spend trillions of dollars for military defense should consider what his domestic policies are doing to national security. There cannot be strength when 35.6 percent of black Americans live below the poverty level, when one out of five children is destitute, when one-third of the Hispanic population lives from hand to mouth and when the income gap widens between men and women and black and white.

This other America has yet to be rediscovered by Mr. Reagan, whose policies are rooted in the belief that government should take minimal relief measures/to remove only the worst and most visible risks to domestic tranquility. To do more would, in his opinion, create unhealthy dependency.

Mr. Reagan and his ideological mates are engaged in what he describes as "intellectual housecleaning" in Washington. "In the name of growth, let's stop talking about billions for more dependency . . . In the name of America, let's stop spreading bondage, and start spreading freedom," he said. He chastised critics for worshiping "at the altar of forced busing and mandatory quotas."

Such an attitude at the center of government bodes ill for the nation.

A president who argues that affirmative action is a favor — a special break — for the disadvantaged, is a president who shows little interest in remedying the long-standing handicaps suffered by the disadvantaged. A president who says the smaller the government, the more the likelihood of opportunity and compassion, will not bring freedom to the 34.4 million Americans who live in the Third World.

A president who is "perplexed" by the latest poverty figures lives in a world far removed from reality.

the Charleston Gazette

Charleston, W. Va., September 25, 1984

FOR white and black Americans having a job is the cardinal issue, which puts the lie to those convinced that their society lacks the work ethic it once had.

A nationwide poll, conducted by Gallup for the Joint Center for Political Studies, learned that majorities of both races place unemployment first among all problems confronting government.

After agreeing on how critical is the failure to have a job, white and black Americans differ sharply respecting what are the next most crucial matters affecting their lives that government might be able to influence.

Blacks want the federal government to aid the poor and to guarantee their civil rights.

Whites want the nation's leaders to cut the federal deficit and to hold the line against inflation.

These divergent opinions reflect the status of the two races in their society.

Although in actual numbers more whites than blacks are mired in poverty, the percentage of whites better off vis-a-vis other whites and the whole population is considerably larger than the percentage of better-off blacks. Hence, a majority of whites worry about rising prices and a governmental debt, both of which ultimately could affect adversely their standard of living and societal status.

Big bad federal deficits and inflation don't pose awful problems to a family that is poor and has few of the conveniences, none of the goodies of life. Hence, blacks envision an entirely different set of priorities for their government.

The clashing viewpoints are understandable but also discouraging to men and women of good will in both races. If this nation is to forge the ideal state founders had in mind and political leaders and party platforms ever stress, all its citizens, regardless of sex, race and religion, should have similar opinions respecting what are their country's prime priorities and worst deficiencies.

The Washington Times

Washington, D.C., August 26, 1983

What are we to make of the latest Census figures on how things are going for blacks in this country? It's the old question of the glass that's either half empty or half full.

There's a lot in the new statistics to worry about and not just the unemployment figures — 18.9 percent in 1982 as compared with 8.6 percent for whites. The number of families headed by women with no husband present keeps going up. In 1970, it was 28 percent for blacks; now it's 41, next to 12 percent for whites. Real income for these black families has declined, as you might expect.

Although the causes of the huge jump in women-headed families are several (see Connaught Marshner's discussion of the subject elsewhere on this page today), the divorces that produce some single-parent homes are rising faster for blacks than for whites. Last year, for every 1,000 married blacks living together, there were 233 who had been divorced, more than double the white ratio and nearly three times what it was for blacks in 1970.

Egalitarian extremists will also pounce on the fact that only 13 percent of blacks hold professional or managerial jobs. For the work force as a whole, the figure is 22 percent.

But the optimists have at least something going their way too. The real income of blacks individually averaged a one-sixth increase over the decade since 1971, with a family headed by a married couple earning $1,250 a year more, in inflation-adjusted dollars, than the $18,370 it earned 10 years earlier. If it's a two-career family, it's close to, if not above, its counterpart among whites.

Best of all, home ownership, health, and education are on the rise for blacks, with significant differences in all categories from the way things little more than a decade ago. More black workers and their families are entering the middle class. In the face of great hopefulness implicit in that, questions of culture-biased tests and the like will eventually blow away, out of sheer inconsequence. Because people who work hard, go to school until they graduate and save their money have a way of making it through formal tests as well as through life's other challenges. They don't have to win by changing the rules of the game.

Granted there are traps hidden in these pleasing data. We know that to graduate from some schools is not as good as to graduate from others. It may be worth almost nothing as a credential for a job. But the sheer discipline of sticking with a project such as school is the beginning of responsibility, beyond which lie the prosperity and power that black Americans, like Americans of other races, want.

Anyway, you can't argue with the home-owning figures, which show that in the last decade, the number of blacks owning their own homes rose a remarkable 45 percent, from 2.6 million to 3.7 million. It doesn't matter that there was a 26 percent rise for whites in the same period. What counts is the stake in the system home-owning represents.

That's not only a fact to cheer for its merits; it's one that lights up the rest of the picture too.

The Miami Herald
Miami, Fla., December 7, 1983

THE SOCIAL revolution of the 1960s established the legal footing for blacks to achieve civil equality. But the more-critical struggle was yet to come. Blacks would have to attain economic parity before they fully could share the American dream.

Jesse Jackson and other black leaders have recognized that reality for at least a decade. From that realization has come Mr. Jackson's Operation PUSH and formal agreements with major corporations to recruit, train, hire, and promote blacks and to open doors for black services, franchises, and consultation.

Economic parity has been infinitely more elusive than social justice. The evasiveness of that struggle is reflected in the uneven progress of blacks in Dade toward employment and business equity. It is largely a story of failure, with shining examples of success. In *The Herald's* series on "The Isolation of Black Miami," a balance sheet is drawn that shows mostly deficits for blacks.

Blacks in Dade County lag the national average in proportion of professional managers and executives, and in the level of business activity. Although blacks compose 17 per cent of the county's population, blacks own only 2 per cent of the businesses. While the rest of black employers during the 1970s, the number of black employers in Dade County declined.

In Dade, as elsewhere, government has been a willing employer. This results in part from government's historic role as an ally. It also reflects the results of legal requirements for employment progress and open records.

In retail firms and hospitals, blacks here have found acceptance and employment. The record is dismal in other major industries, however, particularly in aviation, utilities, banking, and major law firms. Though Cuban entrepreneurs have become significant employers, they have hired blacks only sparingly. *The Herald* itself falls short too. Although it has a higher percentage of black news personnel than U.S. newspapers generally, *The Herald* acknowledges that it still does not have enough.

In short, private industry as a whole has fallen far short of its responsibility to open markets and jobs to all residents. The reasons are myriad, but none is so persuasive as to justify continued laxity. Finding quality black professionals *is* difficult, though not unduly so. Too many blacks fail to acquire necessary skills; but training, scholarships, and affirmative actions to develop skills must be implemented.

The success of firms such as Burger King, Southern Bell, Burdines, and the Ryder System in finding, training, and promoting blacks demonstrates that the goal is within reach. More than that, the resultant good will and economic boost makes a more-cohesive community.

Dade County's debit balance sheet of black economics can be reversed. But it will take the deliberate effort of all employers, not just a select few.

The San Diego Union
San Diego, Calif., August 2, 1983

The economic gap between blacks and whites is wider than commonly thought. So says a study by the Joint Center for Political Studies, which compares the personal property of blacks, $24,600 per household, to that of whites, $68,800 per household. That's a wide gap after two decades of dedicated government efforts to close it, and suggests that redistributing wealth may be more difficult than is understood even by redistributionists.

It appears that if government is to truly help blacks and other minorities to assume the economic place they deserve, a new approach is needed.

Most efforts to measure the black-white split use family earnings to measure financial well-being. Such studies find black income hovering at around 60 percent of white income for almost two decades. The study's authors are in a curious quandary to explain why the gap in actual wealth is so much wider than the gap in income — the gap between gaps, if you will.

They might start by realizing that wealth, properly understood, is profoundly different from physical riches such as houses, cars, or stocks. It springs from deep, metaphysical sources — not just last year's income.

Understanding this is central to understanding poverty, and hence to the failure of government spending to relieve it. Hand a man $10 million and you make him rich — but not any more able to generate wealth than he was before the dole. The wealthy man, or the man who is becoming wealthy, is somewhere down the street inventing a new production process, starting a Kentucky Fried Chicken franchise, or working overtime at the company plant.

Wealth, in other words, isn't easy to pass out, and this basic fact accounts for much of the failure of attempts to close the black-white gap.

This point is underlined by the study's findings on the composition of black wealth. Whites hold more than 40 percent of family equity in the form of financial assets and business or farm property, and only 12 percent in vehicles and household goods. Blacks, by contrast, hold only 11 percent of their wealth in financial assets, while devoting more than 22 percent to vehicles and household goods. The difference seems to suggest a stronger faith in the future, tighter family, and greater willingness to defer consumption on the part of whites.

Does this spring from any intrinsic difference between whites and blacks? Of course not. It's just that whites have been spared ensnarement in the welfare state web that has destroyed the black families, work incentives, and opportunities. Other racial groups — such as Asian Americans — have managed to quickly close the income and wealth gap precisely because they have not been on the receiving end of affirmative action and other special benefits.

The ultimate goal of social policy is not to provide a safety net, but to get people off the net altogether and onto the opportunity ladder — the private economy of real jobs and real production. How? Pass the President's urban enterprise zone legislation, which has languished in Congress for two years. Strip regulatory agencies of their ability to restrict black opportunities in industries from trucking to private health care. But above all, restructure and reduce the government programs that — as the latest figures prove all too painfully — have actually hurt the very people they're supposed to help.

The Oregonian
Portland, Ore., June 25, 1983

The Emergency Jobs Bill signed by President Reagan last March will provide $4.6 billion to help the unemployed get through the recession, but persons expecting it to be a panacea will be disappointed.

While the Jobs Bill is expected to provide approximately 400,000 jobs, there were 11.4 million persons unemployed the day Reagan signed the bill. Moreover, the segment of society hardest hit by unemployment — blacks — can expect no special relief and, in fact, may find the gap between white and black unemployment widened.

The unemployment rate for whites in 1982 was 8.6 percent; for blacks, it was 18.9 percent. As high as the rates were, they did not include what Focus magazine describes in its May issue as "discouraged workers." Unemployed people who have given up trying to find work would have increased the white jobless rate to 9.6 percent and the black jobless rate to 22.5 percent, according to the magazine produced by the Joint Center for Political Studies.

Nearly $3 billion of the $4.6 billion in the Jobs Bill is directed to public works construction. Black unemployment is not significantly reduced by creating construction jobs, because black workers are underrepresented in the craft areas that dominate construction. Given past employment patterns, black workers will fill 14,100 craft jobs and 13,500 laborer jobs, while white workers will get the remaining 224,400 jobs, according to Julianne Malveaux, professor of economics at San Francisco State University, who discussed the topic in Focus.

However, minority workers can expect to benefit from other provisions of the jobs bill: $150 million is proposed for weatherproofing of structures in low-income areas; summer youth employment programs have income standards; and $544 million is directed to social and community service program employment.

Any new jobs are to be welcomed in the recession, but persons responsible for hiring should understand the weaknesses as well as the opportunities in the Emergency Jobs Bill. Targeted hiring can help close the gap between black and white unemployment. In the long run, however, each community should look at and address the reasons for differences in the distribution of jobs for blacks and whites.

NDER
) PRIVATE

L

B

2

THE UNEMPLOYED

INFLATION FIGHTER

ST. LOUIS POST-DISPATCH
St. Louis, Mo., August 24, 1983

When President Reagan says that the best way to fight poverty among blacks and other minority groups is to take actions that strengthen the economy and curb inflation, he is criticized by liberals who contend that the best way to help these groups is to continually increase the amount of welfare they receive.

A just released Census Bureau study supports President Reagan's view. It found that blacks were hurt more than many other Americans over the last decade by a high rate of inflation and growing unemployment stemming from a stagnated economy. Economic setbacks of blacks tended to overshadow the substantial improvements over the last decade in blacks' educational attainment, the study reported.

For example, it was found that in 1981 the median-income of black families, adjusted for inflation, was down 8.3 percent from 1971, while the median-income for all U.S. families in 1981 was off 3 1 percent from 1971.

If the high rate of inflation and lack of growth in the economy in the years between 1971 and 1981 are deemed the principal reasons for blacks faring worse in economic and social terms, then it stands to reason that blacks and other minority groups are major beneficiaries of the strong economic recovery the nation is experiencing and an inflation rate now running at an annual rate of less than 4 percent.

Therefore, even though a great percentage of blacks still don't support President Reagan's policies, it is evident that in promoting the strong economic growth (9.2 percent growth in the second quarter of this year) and low-inflation rate, he is doing infinitely more for blacks than some liberal legislators in Washington.

The liberals' approval of big federal deficits during the 1971-81 decade brought on the double-digit inflation rate which in turn caused the economy to stagnate in that period.

San Francisco Chronicle
San Francisco, Calif., September 1, 1983

CIVIL RIGHTS LEADERS have, on the occasion of the 20th anniversary of the great March on Washington, turned the nation's attention once again on some unfinished business. Some reports which have also come to public notice almost simultaneously are, however, grounds for certain satisfaction. They also illustrate that emphasis in pursuit of the ideals of equality must now shift.

Lyle Jones, a researcher at the University of North Carolina at Chapel Hill, told the American Psychological Association the other day that the gap in achievement tests between white and black elementary and high school students has "appreciably narrowed over the 1970s." He believes that this encouraging trend will continue.

The Census Bureau has also reported that improvements in education, home ownership and health have been achieved by the nation's blacks in the 1970s. Unemployment has been a setback, it must be acknowledged, and this has severely affected young blacks far more than young whites.

CENSUS AND OTHER reports, it seems to us, clearly indicate where major emphasis must be placed in the years ahead. Income for black families in which both parents are present had reached an average of $19,620 by 1980, an impressive figure although still lagging by 15 percent behind the white average. But the income of families headed by one person, usually the mother, has dropped and the numbers of this type of family have rapidly increased. Today, almost half of all black children live in homes with no father present. The nation is experiencing the creation, sociologists tell us, of a permanent under-class as the black family disintegrates.

Children of these single-head families are prime drop-out candidates because of disillusionment and lack of motivation. A Labor Department study informs us that almost one-quarter of the nation's work force now holds college degrees and that the number of high school drop-out workers has sharply declined. If present trends continue — demand for higher education as an employment requirement and high drop-out rates of minority students — tragedy lies ahead.

BUFFALO EVENING NEWS
Buffalo, N.Y., July 27, 1983

Despite civil rights laws and despite gains by blacks in education, the economic disparities between blacks and whites remain unconscionably wide.

According to a study entitled, "A Dream Deferred: the Economic Status of Black Americans," blacks are no closer to economic equality than they were in 1960. In fact, the report says, "the economic gap between blacks and whites remains wide and is not diminishing."

Prepared by the Center for the Study of Social Policy, the report uses data from the 1980 Census and other government information. It blames the gap in average incomes between blacks and whites on the rise in the proportion of black families headed by women and the proportion of black men without jobs.

The system itself may be causing part of the problem. In some states, two-parent families are not eligible for social service assistance. Thus, if a man loses a job, he may feel that leaving his family is the only way to help it survive.

Between 1960 and 1980, the study says, the proportion of families headed by black women rose from one-fifth to about one-half. It pointed out that 14 percent of the white families with children under 18 are headed by women, while 47 percent of the black families are in that category.

Families headed by women are nearly twice as likely to be poor as two-parent families, the report said, and half of all black families headed by women had incomes below the poverty level.

The report says that only 55 percent of black males over the age of 16 are employed today, compared to 74 percent in 1960.

In addition, it pointed out that:

✔ The median income of black families was 55 percent of white families' median income in 1960 and 56 percent in 1981.

✔ Black unemployment is twice that of whites and has remained so for more than 20 years.

✔ Despite gains in education, blacks with comparable educations still earn less than whites. In white families whose head completed four or more years of college, 35.5 percent earn more than $40,000. The figure for blacks is 18.1 percent.

The study comes at a time when policy planners are debating how best to solve the problem of chronic poverty in this country. Clearly, new and more effective programs are needed to help people escape from numbing dependency.

The debate should not, however, overlook the continuing discrimination that has limited the chances of blacks. While the rudimentary right to enter the marketplace is often taken for granted, it is still too often denied to blacks.

Legislation and executive orders make up only part of the solution. A renewed national commitment to equality is needed to provide a new impetus toward solving what has already become a staggering national problem. To do anything else will leave the promise of America unfulfilled.

Detroit Free Press
Detroit, Mich., October 10, 1984

THE STATE of blacks in Michigan is pretty dismal — compared to that of whites, compared to that of blacks elsewhere, compared to black and white expectations of how life in America is supposed to be. The worst news, though, about the first annual statewide study of racial inequality is that it offers few certain prospects for improvement.

The study paints a startling picture of what it means to be a member of a racial minority in Michigan. Among blacks and other Michigan minorities, life expectancy is shorter, unemployment and infant mortality rates are higher, salaries are lower, two-parent or intact families scarcer and murder is the leading cause of death among the young. There has been a rise in the percentage of black students graduating from high school, but the gap between the percentage of whites and non-whites finishing college is widening.

The 190-page report, "The State of Black Michigan: 1984" was released by Michigan State University's Center for Urban Affairs and the Michigan Council of Urban League Executives. The first report of its kind in the country, it parallels in many respects the National Urban League's annual report, "The State of Black America." But in such areas as infant mortality, joblessness and crime, Michigan's blacks are worse off than blacks in other parts of the country.

The report does not try to tiptoe around problems or to make overly optimistic predictions about what blacks can expect in a country currently lukewarm in supporting equal opportunity policies. But that does not mean the state cannot do more to improve prospects for blacks — or that Michigan's blacks, who have managed many impressive gains over the years, cannot somehow rebound.

To some degree, black workers' needs are no different from those of white workers: more non-manufacturing jobs, more stable businesses. To the degree that Michigan's minorities are more concentrated in vulnerable blue-collar jobs, they have suffered more than other workers from a recession that has not yet ended here. Some 24.9 percent of non-white men and 17.9 percent of non-white women were unemployed in 1980, slightly more than double the rate for whites. Clearly, Michigan needs to do more specifically to encourage black business development and employment.

Blacks in Michigan and elsewhere can no longer count on strong federal support for job-training, but they can and should be given such opportunities by the state. Strengthening education and providing more training to upgrade skills remains the best single way to help minorities. The study, however, documents the need as well for continued affirmative action programs and for the freeing of more venture capital for minority business development. The black community itself — particularly the strong black middle class in Detroit and some other Michigan cities — should invest more of its earnings in community businesses, leveraging those investments with matching funds from foundations, Urban Development Action Grants, pension funds and other sources.

The report spells out clearly the consequences of inaction: continued erosion of black progress through job losses, losses in health insurance, family breakdowns, eroded community institutions, deepening social problems. These are consequences no group of people can long withstand without irremediable damage to the fabric of their communities and lives. The challenge facing Michigan is to transform a bleak report into a blueprint for change.

THE ATLANTA CONSTITUTION
Atlanta, Ga., October 11, 1984

Are you better off now than you were four years ago? If your answer to that question is yes, you are probably white. If it is no, chances are you are black. Forget the election-time economics lessons: A rising tide is no help at all if you're adrift in a leaky boat.

The Center on Budget and Public Priorities, a Washington research group, has assessed the impact of the Reagan years on blacks:

• Black family income (after inflation) dropped 5.3 percent from 1980; the economic gap between blacks and whites widened.

• Black unemployment rose from 14.4 percent in 1980 to 16 percent two months ago.

• Poverty among blacks is now near 36 percent, the highest proportion since 1966, when the Census Bureau first measured it.

These disparities are more than unfair. They threaten to polarize dangerously the attitudes of whites and blacks. They threaten to erode several decades of hard-fought progress toward racial reconciliation.

In 1968, the Kerner commission on civil disorders warned of "deepening racial division." It bluntly outlined the problem: "Our nation is moving toward two societies, one black, one white — separate and unequal."

It bluntly laid out the stakes: "To pursue our present course will involve the continuing polarization of the American community and, ultimately, the destruction of basic democratic values."

And it pointed to a safer course: "The alternative is not blind repression or capitulation to lawlessness. It is the realization of common opportunities for all within a single society. This alternative will require a commitment to national action — compassionate, massive and sustained, backed by the resources of the richest nation on this Earth."

It got *almost* that. The commitment was compassionate and massive. For 12 years — from the Johnson era through the Carter administration — a bipartisan consensus sponsored a broad effort to reconcile our racial and economic divisions.

But this commitment has not been sustained. Worse yet, the Reagan administration would have us believe that none is necessary. That miscalculation — if unamended — may someday exact a stiff social price.

The Detroit News
Detroit, Mich., February 2, 1984

Are the rich getting richer and the poor poorer? Is the middle class shrinking?

Those are certainly the underlying suspicions of those who are wailing about increasing numbers of hungry thanks to the Reagan administration. It will doubtless be the rallying cry of Democrats in 1984. Before the shouting gets any louder, it is time to note that the popular perception of increasing national economic inequality is just not founded in fact.

Consider income distribution. Since the end of World War II, the income distribution of American families has remained amazingly stable. In a recent National Journal article, economist Robert Samuelson stressed this point. For example, in 1979 the top fifth of U.S. families received 37 percent of after-tax income and 37.6 percent in 1984. The poorest fifth received 7.1 percent of after-tax income in 1979 and 6.6 percent in 1984. The income share of the middle three-fifths of families remained almost unchanged at 55.9 percent of after-tax income in 1979 and 55.8 percent in 1984.

Thus, there have been only slight shifts in income distribution during the years of Reaganomics and not a rapid increase in inequality. Of course, income distribution looks only at relative income positions. It does not mean that the poor did not suffer most from recession and tax policy over the last five years. After-tax income adjusted for inflation fell most for the poor because they were hardest hit by job loss in the recession and by higher Social Security taxes and local sales taxes. They were also hit by lower welfare benefits due mainly to state failure to increase welfare and food stamp benefits at the rate of inflation rather than federal cutbacks.

Blaming all this suffering on the Reagan administration is hard to justify. The recession resulted from attempts by Federal Reserve Chairman Paul Volcker to rein in the Carter-inspired inflation. Social Security tax increases are a Democratic preference. Sales tax boosts are state sins.

It is true, however, that two groups seem to be losing out. Black Americans are losing ground. The number of blacks living below the poverty line has increased since 1970 because of the increase in black families headed by women, from 28 percent of black families in 1970 to 40.6 percent in 1982. These female-headed households accounted for 70 percent of all poor black families by 1981. This trend cannot be blamed on Reagan policies.

Second, auto and steelworkers have suffered permanent job losses, but their experience is the exception. Their income losses must be seen in the light of previous exceptional income gains. In 1980, auto workers earned 48 percent more than the average of all nonsupervisory workers.

The rich aren't getting richer and the poor poorer. Democratic politicians are getting desperate.

THE MILWAUKEE JOURNAL

Milwaukee, Wisc., January 25, 1984

What is the "State of Black America?"

The National Urban League, in its annual report issued under that title, found grim conditions. The report described poor blacks as having an "out-of-sight, out-of-mind" place in the national consciousness.

Meanwhile, many blacks believe that the nation is in a "second post-Reconstruction era." They find disturbing parallels between contemporary political developments and those in the last century. Then, blacks, who had made gains in the years following the Civil War and emancipation, found a national government hostile to their interests and many white citizens complaining about "special favors" for the former slaves.

The analogy may be overdrawn. Nevertheless, many blacks are suffering in today's economic and political climate. "While white Americans celebrate a long-overdue economic recovery and a falling unemployment rate, black America is buried in a depression of crushing proportions," said John Jacob, the president of the National Urban League.

As evidence of blacks' distress, the report cited the high rate of black unemployment, particularly among teen-agers — 49% of whom lack jobs. Moreover, the report said, half of all black children live in households with incomes below the poverty level — that is, $9,862 for a family of four. The report also noted the troubling "feminization" of black poverty, reflected in the large number of female-headed households.

Meanwhile, the Reagan administration seems at best indifferent to blacks, and at worst hostile to their legitimate aspirations. A member of a presidential commission on hunger cavalierly cites blacks' athletic success to rebut reports of hunger. The Justice Department seeks to thwart use of affirmative action and busing to redress persistent discrimination against blacks in jobs and education.

Yet, there are bright spots. Blacks made significant political gains in 1983, as black mayoral candidates captured the city halls of Chicago and Philadelphia. Jesse Jackson's pursuit of the Democratic presidential nomination is expected to fail, but it already has heightened blacks' political awareness. The coronation of the first black Miss America and the flight of the first black astronaut may have made more forceful arguments for an open society than could have been made by lectures on civil rights.

So, the state of black America is mixed. Yes, there is progress, but there still are problems of poverty and prejudice. The urgent task of the nation's leaders — in business, labor and government — is to find solutions to those problems.

The Forum

Fargo, N.D., July 9, 1984

The news continues to be good for the nation's economy. On Friday came the best of news: The unemployment rate fell in June to 7.1 percent, the lowest percentage in four years.

This represents a dramatic increase in employment. It has come after a difficult time of recession brought on by the Reagan administration's war against inflation. When President Reagan took office some four years ago, the inflation rate was mired in the double digit range. It took a couple of years, but a tight money policy put the brakes on inflation.

The present inflation rate is about 5 percent, a rate that seemed almost unattainable before the present administration took over. This 5 percent rate has been constant for about two years.

All it not rosy, though. Interest rates have been rising slightly again, and the national deficit is a heavy burden. The two are tied together — the interest rate and the national deficit. The federal government must continue to borrow money to pay the interest on its borrowing for deficit financing. This demand drives the interest rates up.

Even so, there is a glimmer of hope on the horizon regarding the deficit. Some 10 days ago Congress passed and sent to the White House a combination of new taxes and federal program cutbacks which constitute a so-called downpayment on deficit reduction amounting to $13 billion through 1987. This will cut into an estimated $600 billion in federal deficits over three years. Not a big downpayment on deficit reduction, but a start.

The good news of a lowering unemployment rate is made better by the fact that the new jobs were spread across all population groups, with black Americans enjoying the strongest improvement. Unemployment of blacks has been severe for a long time.

Since November of 1982, when unemployment reached a post-Depression peak of 10.7 percent with more than 12 million out of work, the economic recovery has generated more than 6.5 million jobs, Friday's Bureau of Labor Statistics announcement revealed.

The decline in unemployment from May to June was concentrated among those who have been out of work from five to 26 weeks. The average duration of unemployment dropped from 8.7 to 7.2 weeks.

Unemployment in North Dakota, consistenly below the national average, was 5.3 percent as of May 1, the latest figure published. Minnesota's count as of June 1 was 6 percent.

The Birmingham News

Birmingham, Ala., June 4, 1984

The Labor Department issued its monthly unemployment report for May unusually early this year — on June 1, to be exact. There was good cause, however.

The good news was worth its early release, as unemployment dropped nationally by .3 percent to a new rate of 7.5 percent. Significantly, it also gave President Reagan the opportunity to comment on the decrease before leaving for Europe and the economic summit: The new figure, the president observed, equals the unemployment rate when he took office.

More important than its political value is the message of economic improvement for the nation as a whole. For, together with the decline in unemployment, the other side of the coin — total employment — reached a record of 105.3 million. In May alone, 890,000 new jobs were created, according to the monthly report.

The unemployment rate was the lowest since August of 1981, and represented a drop of 3.2 percent from the peak of 10.7 percent of Nobember 1982. Since that time, the number of jobless has been reduced by 3.4 million, with the reduced figure of 8.5 million workers now still without jobs.

Just as significant as the overall figure is the reduced unemployment among the various segments of the population. In every case the rate is down. Among adult men, the rate was down from 6.9 percent to 6.5 percent; among adult women, from 7.0 percent to 6.8 percent; among teenagers, from 19.4 percent to 19 percent; among whites, from 6.7 percent to 6.4-percent; among blacks, from 16.8 percent to 15.8 percent, and among hispanics, from 11.5 percent to 10.5 percent.

(Another significant finding of the report shows that, for the first time, more than half of all adult women in the nation are employed. The implications of that figure represent the fodder for considerably more analysis.)

The May figures are certainly good political news for President Reagan, but it is best of all for the Americans represented by the 0.3 percent statistical dip. The individual proof of self-worth and productivity is the real strength of the American economy, and every decrease in unemployment gives new life to that strength.

Black Teenage Unemployment; Subminimum Wage Proposals

Teenagers are, as a group, more afflicted by unemployment than any other, and the recent recession in the United States has taken a predictable toll. Even in 1983, as the economic cycle continued on an upswing, unemployment among 18 and 19 year olds remained at a critical level. As with unemployment figures in the population as a whole, the statistics for black teenagers are much higher than they are for whites of the same age. In October, 1983, the unemployment rate for black male teenagers was 42.7%, while that for white teenagers was 18.3%; the rate for black female teenagers was 56.1%, compared to 14.9% for whites. Many reasons have been cited for the high rates of black teenage unemployment, including the minority population explosion in urban areas in the 1960's and 1970's, but the gap between black and white unemployment rates is astonishingly wide, especially when it is remembered that black students made much greater strides in educational achievement during this period than did their white peers.

The Reagan Administration has consistently supported a decrease in the minimum wage during the summer months for teenagers as one way of combating the high unemployment rates for this age group. Administration officials contend that a decrease in the amount employers are required to pay teenagers would result in the creation of hundreds of thousands of new jobs and alleviate unemployment among minority teenagers. Opponents argue that instead, employers would merely replace older workers with lower-paid teenagers, and that in any case the most likely beneficiaries of such a measure would be white teenagers. Unions, of course, have consistently supported a higher minimum wage, which since 1981 has remained at $3.35 an hour, and have fiercely oppposed any decrease. In 1984, the Administration's latest proposal on a reduced teenage wage, which would have allowed employers to pay $2.50 an hour to youths under 20 years old from May 1 to Sept. 30, died in the face of opposition from organized labor, some senators, and the Democrat-controlled House. The proposal had been endorsed by the National Conference of Black Mayors, but denounced by members of the Congressional Black Caucus. (President Reagan has reintroduced this bill in 1985.)

Chicago Defender
Chicago, Ill., October 12, 1981

Nearly eight million persons were out of work last month. That is a rise of 300,000 from August. The increase was concentrated among men and women over 25 years old, usually the chief family breadwinners.

Those are the figures issued by the Labor Department. Meantime, the black jobless is higher than it ever was during the 1980 recession. One of the consequences of the great unemployment is that many "discouraged workers" do not look for work any more because they believe they will not find it. That goes for whites and Blacks both.

As usual, black teenagers had the highest jobless rate of any major category — 40 percent in September. While the White House and its intimates figure they can create several million jobs by going into unparalleled weapons manufacture, there is no indication in this general situation that the future of society, ours or anybody else's, is looking better.

The Courier-Journal
Louisville, Ky., July 6, 1980

THE CHRONIC problem of youth unemployment, which could reach crisis proportions during the current recession, is receiving fresh attention in Washington. And one of the most intriguing proposals comes from New York Congressman Jack Kemp, who has become almost a household word (and might become this year's GOP vice-presidential nominee) thanks to the controversial tax-cut measure that bears his name and that of Delaware's Senator William Roth.

As one would expect from such a staunch advocate of the free market and small-is-better government, Mr. Kemp believes the key to job creation is to get government — especially the tax-collector — off the back of business. But unlike the broad Kemp-Roth income-tax cut, his plan for generating inner-city jobs would be carefully targeted.

He proposes "enterprise zones" in neighborhoods with very high rates of unemployment and poverty. His bill would slash Social Security payroll taxes in these zones by 50 percent for workers 21 and older and by 90 percent for younger workers. Small companies that located or expanded in such zones would also receive investment tax breaks.

The cost of this program to the federal Treasury, and to the financially strained Social Security trust fund, is hard to guess. But Mr. Kemp proposes to minimize potential revenue losses by limiting the number of zones: the total number of people living in them could not exceed five percent of the national population. And, of course, the cost to the government would be offset to the extent that unemployed persons who now depend on welfare payments got jobs and started paying taxes, even at reduced rates.

A big attraction of the Kemp plan, compared with conventional job-creation and training programs, is that it would involve little administrative expense. The same is true of another, more widely discussed proposal for boosting teenage employment: a special "subminimum" wage for youths.

Though this idea isn't part of Mr. Kemp's enterprise-zones bill, it has long been a favorite of many of his fellow conservatives, including Ronald Reagan. But it's not at all popular with the leaders of organized labor. They fear that many employers would "fire fathers and hire sons," to take advantage of the lower wage.

Actually, federal law already permits a subminimum wage, equal to 85 percent of the minimum, for teen-agers who are full-time students and who work no more than 20 hours weekly during the school year or 40 hours in the summer. (With the minimum wage now at $3.10 an hour, the current subminimum is $2.63½.) Two disadvantages of the current law are that it doesn't apply to school drop-outs and is limited to certain kinds of employers.

The employment effects of the minimum wage have been debated for decades. Most economists agree, however, that at some point a minimum wage costs jobs. The higher the minimum, the less likely an employer is to expand his workforce, or at least to add jobs for those with few skills.

But the minimum wage alone can't explain one of the most disturbing elements of youth unemployment: the growing disparity between the jobless rate of black teen-age males and that of whites. According to the federal Bureau of Labor Statistics, unemployment rates for the two groups were almost the same in 1955. A decade later, the black jobless rate had jumped to almost twice the rate for whites. By 1978, unemployment among black teen-age males was 2½ times the white rate. (The disparity between jobless rates of black and white female young people grew less sharply during this period — but that's because young black females had a much higher jobless rate than whites to begin with.)

Improving the job prospects for young blacks will require a lot more than mere tinkering with the minimum wage. The Kemp approach presumably would help, if Congress passed it without yielding to the temptation to turn just about every congressional district into an "enterprise zone." But even targeting aid — and tax relief — to inner-city pockets of poverty might not work. Employment studies have shown that, even in the inner city, proportionately fewer black youths than whites can find jobs.

Special job-training programs will continue to be needed. And while the expenditure of more than $100 billion over the past 20 years on such programs seems to have done little good, there are notable exceptions. One experimental program with welfare recipients in Lowell, Massachusetts, has found jobs for more than 75 percent of the participants. Instead of emphasizing specific skills for specific jobs, it concentrates on motivation and on teaching the hard-core unemployed how to hunt for job openings, how to handle interviews and how to get along with employers and fellow employes once a job is found.

The lessons of the Lowell approach and other successful programs, plus special aid for inner-city schools, were to be incorporated in the Youth Employment Initiatives plan proposed by President Carter in January. But that $2 billion-a-year program fell victim to Mr. Carter's budget-cutting and didn't have widespread support on Capitol Hill, anyway.

There's no sign, at this point, that Jack Kemp's approach to creating inner-city jobs has broad support, either. But congressmen returning to their home districts for the summer will be exposed to plenty of warnings, especially from mayors and other urban officials, about the explosive danger of teen-age joblessness. It would be penny-wise and pound-foolish were these warnings to be ignored for the sake of a budget that clearly won't be close to balanced in 1981.

The Dallas Morning News
Dallas, Texas, June 20, 1981

Milton Friedman calls the minimum wage law "the most anti-black law on the books," because it deters employers from taking on untrained black youths. And darned if the perception isn't spreading — among blacks.

A national black polling firm says 37 percent of blacks favor a lower minimum wage as a means of reducing teen-age employment, against 36 percent opposed. The firm's chairman, who is the famous black sociologist, Kenneth Clark, says the results don't mean blacks are getting more conservative, just that "there is an overwhelming number of unemployed black teen-agers; respondents feel this (a special teen-age wage rate) might be a way of breaking that barrier."

Indeed it might be, if reflexive liberals in Congress would quit lambasting as "racist" every proposal to let employers pay teen-agers less money. Better a lower-paying job than no job at all, blacks are starting to say. "Racist" ideas seem to turn up in the oddest places these days.

St. Louis Globe-Democrat
St. Louis, Mo., February 2, 1981

One of the quickest ways to help millions of unemployed youths in this country would be to enact legislation that would create a lower minimum wage for workers under 21.

It has been evident for many years that a steadily rising minimum wage — it now is fixed at $3.35 an hour — has made it increasingly hard for young people lacking skills to find work. Teen-age unemployment has continued at unacceptably high rates as the minimum wage has moved up sharply in recent years. Among black and other minority youths, unemployment reached almost 37 percent last year.

A great deal of this alarmingly high jobless rate among youth is due to the fact that employers simply won't employ young people without skills at the federally-mandated minimum wage.

To many Americans who don't run a business, a minimum wage of $3.35 doesn't seem too high. They fail to recognize that a great many small businesses can't afford to pay any worker this amount when the latter must be taught how to perform their job and can't begin to justify a salary of this kind for many months.

So what happens is that owners of these businesses only hire those they know can perform effectively almost at once, leaving the jobless with no skills totally out in the cold.

If the minimum wage rate for workers under 21 were drastically reduced, to $2 an hour for example, many businesses could afford to employ unskilled workers in this age bracket and train them over a period of months. Millions of young people thus could get jobs that would allow them to acquire skills that in turn would enable them to continue improving their economic status.

This is preferable to maintaining a system that supposedly helps these millions of unemployed people but which, in reality, permanently freezes them out of the job market.

THE INDIANAPOLIS STAR
Indianapolis, Ind., November 15, 1981

Young blacks had the highest unemployment rate — 49 percent — among all groups listed in the U.S. Labor Department's latest jobless report.

A chief reason for this rate is the federal minimum wage law. The law is defended as a guarantee against worker exploitation. But in the case of young blacks it is a trap. It destroys opportunities. It wipes out freedom. It may even be making crime attractive as the only open economic outlet.

An eloquent critic of the minimum wage law as it applies to young blacks is a black educator, Dr. Walter E. Williams, who teaches economics at the George Mason University, Fairfax, Va.

Williams says that the unemployment rate for black youths was lower than that for whites in 1948, and that the minimum wage law is the main culprit behind the change. The law as revised by Congress in 1979 fixes the minimum wage at $3.35 an hour.

In an interview in Epic, publication of the Fiscal Policy Council, Williams said:

"The minimum wage tends to discriminate against anybody who can't produce $3.35 worth of goods and services per hour. Actually, the minimum wage understates the minimum hourly compensation an employer can make because he must pay Social Security taxes and unemployment insurance and other payments which really drive up the minimum worker compensation to about $4.10 per hour.

"The person in the labor force who has the lowest skills, who can only produce, say, $2 worth per hour, is most likely a teen-ager."

Under the guise of helping the poor the law actually is keeping poor families poorer by eliminating possible jobs for their teen-age members, Williams said.

If the law were changed to provide a youth differential, Williams believes, "there would be an increase in total employment. That is, there would be jobs born that would otherwise go unborn, and the rate of certain kinds of job destruction would diminish."

So if Williams is right, and his views are shared by many other economists and job market analysts, there is a specific cure for at least one major phase of current unemployment, and the medicine bottle is in the hands of Congress.

The Honolulu Advertiser
Honolulu, Ha., February 2, 1981

The idea of lowering the minimum wage for young people has been discussed for at least a decade, but with Ronald Reagan in the White House and the Republicans in control of the Senate it will get new and perhaps decisive attention.

Youth unemployment, especially for minorities, is among our severest social problems. The rate for disadvantaged young whites and non-whites is about 25 and 40 percent respectively. In the inner city, rates are higher since so many young blacks have simply given up looking for work.

OPPONENTS OF THE existing minimum wage argue that every boost decreases the number of jobs available to inexperienced young people.

Small businesses, which create most of this country's beginning jobs, simply cannot afford to pay young people for marginal work. Traditionalists bemoan the shortage of these idealized "first jobs," which are said to build character and aid maturity.

Opponents also argue that the minimum wage is inflationary because every increase adds pressure to raise higher-level wages all the way up the line.

The current proposal in Congress would provide for a youth minimum wage for those between 16 and 20 years old set at 75 percent of the federal minimum wage.

WHILE YOUTH unemployment is high compared to adult rates, a higher proportion of young people (46 percent) are working now than were working ten years ago (38 percent). And no one is sure how many actual new jobs the decreased minimum wage would create. It may not be that many.

If some employers decide to lay-off low-paid adults (who are often supporting families) to hire teen-agers at three-quarters of the minimum wage, opponents of the decreased minimum wage argue, the result could simply be more older people on the unemployment and welfare rolls.

Also, many feel that new jobs are less likely to go to disadvantaged black and minority youth than to middle-income white teenagers who look like better job prospects.

It is possible that ghetto kids will suffer in two ways if their parents are fired from minimum-wage jobs that are taken by young job-seekers whose main goal is extra money for recreation.

MOST EVERYONE agrees that the best way to create jobs for youth, white and non-white, is with an economic boom which offers opportunities for everyone.

That may be a long time coming. In the interim many Republicans want to tinker with the minimum wage, in part because it is the proud handiwork of Democrats and labor unionists dating from the New Deal.

If the two-tiered minimum wage is to be tried, and there seems to be a good chance it will be, one good suggestion is that it be tested carefully in selected kinds of businesses and carefully monitored by federal agencies.

Also, the trial should have a fixed termination after several years so that Congress will have to be shown the program's effectiveness before it becomes a permanent part of national life.

The Register
Santa Ana, Calif., August 2, 1982

All too rarely a public official suggests a direct and sensible approach to a social problem that involves less government control rather than new programs. When the official in question is one whose confirmation was surrounded by controversy, and when his suggestion is bound to stir yet more opposition, you begin to suspect you're dealing with a gutsy and independent guy.

Clarence W. Pendleton Jr., chairman of the U.S. Commission on Civil Rights, has called on business and organized labor to agree to a six-month trial program that would permit unemployed teen-agers to accept jobs at less than the minimum wage. Pendleton must have had an inkling of the kind of irrational response his suggestion would arouse, for he made it clear that he was speaking for himself as an individual rather than for the commission he heads.

Study after study has documented that increases in the minimum wage lead to increases in youth unemployment, especially among blacks. As Pendleton noted, "Black teen-age unemployment is at a crisis stage of 52 percent."

Another factor contributing to hard-core joblessness is also finally getting a modicum of recognition. One of the most important reasons for long-term unemployment is not so much a lack of skills as a lack of "job-readiness" — the mindset that leads to showing up every day on time and being willing to try and to learn. Most people acquire it from their parents, but others without a family work background have great difficulty developing it. Government training and welfare programs, far from fostering attitudes of job-readiness, tend to undermine them.

Permitting teen-agers to work for less than minimum wage might — though there's no guarantee — not only offer some immediate relief from unemployment, but help them, through experience, to develop reliability and feelings of self-worth that are the first steps to breaking a vicious cycle of dependency and hopelessness.

Pendleton's modest proposal may not get past the gates of organized labor, as he says it must to work. Too many union officials have invested too much psychic capital in convincing themselves that the minimum-wage law is the only thing that keeps poverty from being universal. The likelihood is that they will fight the idea tooth and nail.

And the children will continue to suffer.

The Commercial Appeal
Memphis, Tenn., February 10, 1982

IN 1950 half of the black teenagers in the nation had jobs. By 1970 that ratio had dropped to one in three. And by 1978 it had plummeted to one in four.

Clearly these are not the best of times for black youth.

Although the employment situation in Memphis today for black youth is considerably better than the national figures reflected for 1978 — and, in fact, exceeds the 1950 national average — black teenagers still are showing an unemployment rate of 40 per cent in the city.

Progress aside, that is an intolerable rate that inflicts serious hardships on those affected. Should the trend continue, it can only have a negative impact on the city's long-term economic and social goals.

As one of five test sites across the country, Memphis has attracted national attention for its Jobs For High School Graduates program. Initially financed by Gov. Lamar Alexander with $218,000 in federal funds, the year-old program was designed to function as a partnership between private enterprise and government.

To that end, the program's goals are admirable. Some success is reported by Don Sundquist, chairman of Jobs For High School Graduates, who says that 84 per cent of the 300 students enrolled in the program the first year found jobs, but that success is by definition limited to a select group of individuals and can only make a dent in the problem.

More to the point, perhaps, is how the situation ever became the economic albatross it is today, for not until the reasons for the current situation are understood will the economic movers of today's society — big government and private enterprise — be able to free society from the weight of that albatross.

Interestingly, John Cogan, a researcher for the National Bureau of Economic Research (a private study group based in Cambridge, Mass.), blames the high unemployment rate for black teenagers on two factors: technological progress in agriculture and increased coverage of the minimum wage.

During the economically critical period between 1950 and 1970, Cogan says, farm employment in the South declined by 65 per cent, thereby eliminating an important source of work for black teenagers. To make matters worse, he says, the teenagers displaced by mechanization on the farm were not absorbed by the nonagricultural sector because of economic restrictions imposed by the federal minimum wage law.

That analysis has been confirmed by other researchers, most notably Marvin Kosters and Finis Welch, who, in a study for the American Enterprise Institute, found that minimum wage requirements had doubled the employment instability of teenagers.

Donald Parsons, an economics professor at Ohio State University, reaches much the same conclusion: "Considerable evidence has accumulated over time that minimum wage laws seriously reduce the labor market prospects of teenagers." The only group that has benefited from minimum wage legislation, he says, has been older female workers — and he questions whether the overall effect of the legislation has been worth it.

What has happened is that the economic cycle begun with the passage of the minimum wage law in 1938, through action and counteraction, left unchanged older minority males with marketable skills, elevated the earnings of older women of all races and displaced black teenagers from the job market.

NOT MUCH IN the short run can be done about the loss of jobs in the agricultural sector. Mechanization has eliminated those jobs permanently. Neither should action be taken to lessen the gains made by minority females, since their victories were — and still are — instrumental in breaking the poverty cycle. In that context, we disagree with Parsons.

The only meaningful solution, of course, is for the government and private sector to work together in such a way as to create enough jobs for everyone. But with the federal government withdrawing more and more from that responsibility, it may become necessary to rethink the minimum wage law as it applies to teenagers, perhaps with a goal of lowering minimum wage requirements.

Should that happen, the burden will fall on the shoulders of private enterprise to push itself to the maximum, to experiment with new programs such as Jobs For High School Graduates — and last, but not least, to balance short-term profits with long-term economic and social gains.

Arkansas Democrat
Little Rock, Ark., February 27, 1981

Surprisingly, Gallup Poll finds a slight majority (20 to 21 per cent) of Americans opposed to a teenage minimum wage, one somewhat less than the standard $3.35 an hour applying to all jobs. The objections made to such a wage differential don't come to much — and, not surprisingly, the antis would rather have their objections than see a lesser wage reduce teenage joblessness, usually quoted at around 40 per cent for blacks.

Their silliest objection to a smaller wage is that a teenager can't live on a reduced wage. Can he or she live on the nothing that not having a job pays them now?

Then there's the objection that a teenage minimum is discriminatory. That's to confuse the marketplace with a social agency. Our system does make the social guarantee of a minimum wage, but only if you get the job — and nobody's guaranteed a job as a right. Even welfare isn't a right — so says the Supreme Court.

Another objection is that, under a differential wage, teenagers would grab off adult jobs. No doubt, they'd get some, but not many an employer would fire able, experienced adults under the illusion that maybe a dollar-an-hour's saving hiring raw help would end up profiting him.

Then we hear that employers would exploit a teenage minimum — meaning they'd make a rush to hire the teenagers at bargain rates. But surely it's not "exploiting" a boy to take him off the street and give him job experience and money in his pocket while preparing him for higher earnings now and later. It's how many an older man began — thankfully. And from a productivity viewpoint, early hiring of teenagers at a differential would be a better national "job training program" than all the expensive government job training laws ever enacted.

There's the social issue, too, in our need for a teenage differential. Idle teenagers, it's said, knock people in the head, rob and steal. Give them work and they'll turn into productive citizens. Even those who oppose the differential admit that. But it's no use asking an employer to solve society's problem by hiring raw teenagers at more than they're worth to him.

As the teenage jobless stats so clearly show, the teenager isn't worth a man's wage. So, the social consequences of teenage unemployment can be averted only by meeting the price the marketplace puts on unskilled teenager labor. That oughtn't to surprise — or pain — anybody, and it should delight all those (including teenagers) who believe that work at almost any wage beats idleness at any age.

The Idaho STATESMAN
Boise, Idaho, May 24, 1984

A reduced minimum wage for teen-agers, a proposal long popular among conservatives, is an idea whose time has come — at least for a trial run.

Youth unemployment in April, a month before 2 million youngsters will flood the job market, was 19.4 percent. Among black teens, the rate was 44.8 percent, and that figure regularly tops 50 percent in urban areas during the summer. A series of federal programs and subsidies in recent years has failed to put a significant dent in the statistics. Moreover, those programs do not put many young people to work in the private sector, where experience counts for the most.

President Reagan, who espoused the idea as a candidate, has renewed his push for a $2.50 hourly wage — 85 cents below the minimum wage. Mr. Reagan has gained an unexpected ally in his crusade: The National Conference of Black Mayors broke with other black groups recently in endorsing the plan. The mayors, while somewhat uneasy about their position, realize that some sort of relief is needed. They know that many teens who cannot find jobs grow up to join the hard core of the nation's adult unemployed.

The mayors opposed the measure before because they feared teen-agers would put adults who work at minimum-wage jobs in the unemployment line. The AFL-CIO is lobbying against the proposal for the same reason.

But the latest version of the bill would restrict employers to paying the wage only from May 1 to Sept. 30, and provides penalties if adult workers are replaced. Supporters have included adequate safeguards to ensure that adults aren't harmed and teens aren't exploited.

However, if the lower wage should fail to increase teen-age employment, it would be most unfair to leave it on the books. For that reason, Congress should provide for expiration of the proposal. If teen-age unemployment were to remain unchanged under the plan, the wage could expire, and the trial run could be written off as a noble effort that, like its public-financed predecessors, failed.

The News American
Baltimore, Md., May 18, 1984

Once again the Reagan administration is asking Congress to pass legislation permitting employers to pay youths looking for summer jobs less than the minimum wage. Specifically, the bill to be considered would permit a wage of $2.50 per hour, rather than the regular $3.35 per hour minimum wage. Employers could pay the lower wage for work between May 1 and Sept. 30 of each year, but they could not use it as a means of replacing older, higher-paid workers. Stiff penalties would be meted out to anyone caught using the lower wage for that purpose.

The president's bill went to Congress Thursday at the same time as he was honoring employers who last summer provided substantial employment for youngsters. Mr. Regan used the occasion to urge passage of the bill.

We commented here on this subject just a few days ago, but since then Labor Secretary Raymond Donovan has estimated that if the legislation goes into effect it could create 400,000 new jobs this summer alone. Additionally, the program has won the endorsement of the Conference of Black Mayors.

But once again there are critics of the legislation. They say the program would set a dangerous precedent in violation of the doctrine of equal pay for equal work. And they argue that the government could better tackle the problem of unemployment by using programs that provide youths with education, skills and work experience they need.

President Reagan has been pushing for the lower minimum wage program for three years. It would seem only logical to stop the bickering and give the idea a shot. The only way to find out whether it will create summer jobs and at the same time not hurt older workers is to try it. Otherwise we'll never know, will we?

AKRON BEACON JOURNAL
Akron, Ohio, June 4, 1984

PRESIDENT REAGAN'S proposal to lower the minimum wage for teen-agers is neither as promising a way to spark employment as he claims nor as sneakily anti-labor as some of his opponents charge. The debate is instructive, however, in showing how public policy can fail when it focuses on side issues rather than tackling the real problems.

The wage proposal itself would not do the harm organized labor claims and may well be beneficial in bringing into the workforce young people who would not otherwise be there. As a temporary measure, the lowered wage is probably worth a try.

The plan would lower the minimum wage from $3.35 an hour to $2.50 — only for workers 19 and younger, and only from May 1 to Sept. 30 each year. Teen-agers already at work before May 1 could not have their wages cut during the summer. Penalties for substituting young workers for old are heavy — six months in jail and a $10,000 fine — although enforcement would seem difficult.

The Reagan administration estimates the wage-reduction plan could create 400,000 summer jobs.

If those claims are anywhere near accurate, the lowered wage scale should have a positive effect. It would be a mistake, however, to assume that this measure is in itself a final solution to youth unemployment.

Labor Secretary Raymond Donovan promotes summer work as "an important first step on the career ladder," which it certainly can be. But the Reagan administration should realize that economic opportunities remain limited for teens and others.

According to Labor Department figures, last summer two-thirds of black teen-agers and more than 40 percent of white teen-agers failed to find jobs. For many of these young people, employment means survival more than a "step on the career ladder." Their wages would help support their families. Or summer work could mean a young person in a family with marginal income might save enough for college or other training.

Any work will help, but $2.50 an hour doesn't go very far toward meeting those kinds of needs. The Reagan administration will do young people a great disservice if it simply lowers the wage — locking young workers into a reduced salary structure — and assumes the increased employment figures have solved the problem. The wage plan must be combined with other jobs programs to allow young people — and others — to help themselves.

The Reagan administration has been lax in these types of initiatives. There is still room for federally sponsored work projects to restore roads, bridges, sewer systems; for extended tax credits to employers who hire disadvantaged youth, older workers and other hard-to-employ individuals; and for job-training initiatives. These programs need not be costly; infrastructure work needs to be done and more workers mean a larger tax base.

Economically, this nation is not yet into great times. Even with the recovery, there are more Americans out of work than when Mr. Reagan took office. The lower minimum wage can help, but it must be part of a comprehensive employment plan to make the recovery permanent. That still is missing from the Reagan administration's planning.

The San Diego Union

San Diego, Calif., May 13, 1984

Six years ago, Ronald Reagan said the minimum wage had "caused more misery and unemployment than anything since the Great Depression." His charge is especially true for black teenagers.

In 1948, the total teen-age unemployment rate was nearly 10 percent. Today, about 22 percent of white teens are unemployed, and the corresponding rate for blacks is almost 50 percent. This disparity is reason enough for the National Conference of Black Mayors to endorse the Reagan administration's proposal for a summer sub-minimum wage.

The measure would lower the minimum wage from $3.35 to $2.50 an hour for those 16 to 21 years of age with after-school or summer jobs from May 1 to Sept. 30 each year. A similar proposal was ambushed on Capitol Hill last year, but there is growing concern in Congress that something must be done soon to alleviate the unemployment rate among black youths.

The Reagan proposal would achieve that objective faster than most other federal jobs programs "at no cost to the government." That is the conclusion of U.S. Labor Secretary Raymond Donovan, who contends the sub-minimum wage would create 500,000 new jobs. This, coincidentally, is approximately the number of black teen-agers currently seeking work.

Many of these youngsters lack jobs because they lack rudimentary job skills. Yet they are caught in a vicious cycle because, whenever the minimum wage rises, employment opportunities are reduced for those with the fewest skills. This Catch-22 situation comes full circle by the time they reach their early 20s. Lacking either job experience or skills, many of these young adults turn to crime or become wards of the state.

The Reagan proposal would break this cycle by recognizing a basic law of economics — that the demand for labor is inversely related to wage rates.

Big Labor, which adamantly opposes the bill, argues that the sub-minimum wage would harm adult workers. Not likely. The Labor Department has promised to impose sanctions on any employer who sacrifices an older worker for a sub-minimum wage employee. Moreover, the unions' assumption coveniently forgets that lower wages would create service-related jobs, such as delivery boys, ushers, and elevator operators, that businesses cannot afford to offer at the prevailing wage rate.

The sub-minimum wage proposal is not a panacea that will solve the problems of black teen-age unemployment. Nor is it a Trojan Horse to displace adult workers with teens who are then consigned to sweatshops. Simply stated, the measure would give black youngsters an opportunity to get on a private payroll and gain job skills and experience instead of staying on the federal dole.

Those congressmen who constantly inveigh against social and economic injustice can do something about both by promptly approving the President's prudent proposal.

The Record

Hackensack, N.J., August 28, 1984

For some time now, the Reagan administration has been promoting legislation that would allow teen-agers to be paid a "subminimum wage" for summer jobs. This flawed notion has been beaten back in Congress, but Secretary of Labor Raymond Donovan is banging the drum again. He recently urged New Jersey's congressional delegation to get behind the Youth Employment Opportunity Wage Act, which the secretary calls by its all-too-accurate acronym, YEOW.

Mr. Donovan's timing seems odd at first blush. It's too late for the law — which its supporters claim would aid thousands of young people — to help any of them this year. But it isn't too late for the president's men to try to dispel the common criticism that they're unfair to those at the bottom rungs of the economic ladder. Election Day is still more than two months off.

YEOW may be a valuable political gesture, but as social policy it's a frivolous response to a serious problem. Teen-age unemployment is about 20 percent; among black youths, it's nearly 50 percent. These young people need work, and we all benefit when they become active participants in the economy. But the president's proposal would admit them to the mainstream only as second-class visitors, earning $2.50 an hour instead of the federal minimum wage of $3.35.

Some 5 million workers in this country earn the minimum wage; 70 percent of them are adults, most of them women. Theirs are high-turnover jobs, often seasonal in nature. Would an employer hire an adult to dish out hamburgers or haul crates for $3.35 an hour when he could get a kid to do the same work for $2.50? No. He'd hire the teen-ager and let him go at the end of the summer. In exchange for a small temporary benefit to the teen-ager — and a much larger cumulative benefit to the employer — serious harm would have been done to the market for unskilled adult labor.

Secretary Donovan says that the subminimum wage would "help put America's teen-agers to work and give them hope for the future." But it would cast some of America's adults further from the prosperous present for which the president and his party are taking self-satisfied credit. That's an unacceptable trade-off.

THE MILWAUKEE JOURNAL

Milwaukee, Wisc., April 26, 1984

The problem of unemployment among minority youth staggers the imagination. In that problem lie the seeds of social upheaval and the condemnation of millions of young people — largely black — to perpetual membership in America's social and economic underclass. Innovative weapons are required to attack the problem.

Thus, it is encouraging that the National Conference of Black Mayors has endorsed an idea that offers some hope of relief: pay teenagers less than the federally required minimum wage for summer jobs.

The mayors, who are well acquainted with the youth unemployment problem, are specifically backing a Reagan administration proposal to allow employers, from May through September, to pay workers between the ages of 16 and 21 an hourly wage of $2.50, or 75% of the minimum wage. Employers who used the young workers to displace other employes would be subject to fines and a jail term. That provision should be a shield against abuses.

The black mayors strongly support the concept of the minimum wage. However, they say they will support the Reagan experiment because of "the persistence of the tragedy of youth unemployment, particularly the problem of minority youth unemployment." As Mayor Johnny Ford of Tuskegee, Ala., puts it: "Our No. 1 concern is putting our people back to work."

Ford is right. The emphasis should be on putting young people to work, and not on cherished ideological concepts. If a carefully targeted sub-minimum wage can provide jobs for young people, it is well worth trying.

Mayor Maier, speaking of the city's emerging youth-gang problems, described many young people engaged in gang activity as "yearners, who can't be earners . . . dreamers who feel forced to become schemers." Job opportunities must be found if such young persons are to be diverted from gang activity, with its immense potential for a descent into more serious criminal conduct. Remember, too, that incarceration of a teenage offender is very expensive, costing about $30,000 per year in Wisconsin.

The sub-minimum wage is not the only answer to the problem. However, we believe it can prove useful in expanding job opportunities. That is why we have urged businesses in Milwaukee and elsewhere in Wisconsin to explore the concept. And that is why we welcome the responsible, politically mature statement of support from the National Conference of Black Mayors.

The Boston Herald
Boston, Mass., March 14, 1984

LIBERALS in Congress have gotten quite a bit of mileage these past few years in rapping President Reagan's efforts for the poor and disadvantaged — and they're doing it again with their criticism of his proposal for a summer sub-minimum wage for unemployed youth.

This time, though, they appear to have shot themselves in the foot.

The president's plan, while designed to aid all teenagers seeking work during the school vacation period, is aimed primarily at reducing unemployment among black teenagers.

If Mr. Reagan's foes in Congress thought they'd make a point with minorities by opposing the idea, they should be disabused of it by the reaction of the National Conference of Black Mayors.

That body has joined the president in exerting a "full court press" to persuade Congress to pass the proposal.

The jobless rate among young blacks is an appalling 50 percent. Some of that is due to the fact that they lack job skills.

They lack them precisely because the $3.25 an hour minimum wage has priced unskilled labor out of the job market. As a result, by the time they're in their early 20s they have no job experience, no references and no employment opportunities.

Reducing the minimum wage for those who are under 22 and who are hired between May and September will, the White House hopes, help reverse that discouraging condition by making it more economical and attractive for employers looking for summer help to hire unskilled young people.

Giving youth a crack at earning a paycheck during the vacation break at a salary scale of $2.50 an hour won't doom them to a life of sweatshop earnings.

The president's critics on Capitol Hill maintain that jobs filled by youths working for a sub-minimum wage will be at the expense of a higher-paid adults. That doesn't wash, for the history of American business has been that productive workers expand the economy and create more, not fewer, job opportunities.

If it is to do any immediate good, the sub-minimum wage should be in place before schools close in June. If it is not, the young people doomed to another summer of discouraging idleness will have only their false friends in Congress to blame.

Wisconsin State Journal
Madison, Wisc., May 16, 1984

The National Conference of Black Mayors — a group whose members are hardly enemies of liberalism or organized labor — has breathed new life into President Reagan's subminimum-wage proposal for teenagers.

Reagan proposed last year that businesses be allowed to pay young people between the ages of 16 and 21 a wage of $2.50 per hour, 25 percent below the federal minimum of $3.35. The lower wage would apply to after-school and summer jobs from May 1 to Sept. 30 each year.

Congress didn't act on the proposal. The administration is expected to introduce it again this month.

Its prospects may be helped by a resolution of support passed by the 254 black mayors. They argue, as we have, that a subminimum wage is worth trying as a way to reduce the staggering unemployment rate among minority teens (see the Christian Science Monitor column elsewhere on this page).

Adding substance to the proposal is a new study by the Center for the Study of Social Policy in Washington, D.C. which found that a chief reason for the explosive growth in the number of black families headed by women may be the unemployment problems of black men.

One solution, the study says, would be to get black male teenagers into the workforce and to keep them there. The subminimum-wage proposal could help by giving black teens work experience and an employment record.

Secretary of Labor Raymond Donovan believes the subminimum wage would create 500,000 new entry-level jobs in the labor force, approximately the number of black teens now looking for work.

Several black mayors join others in fearing that employers might replace adult workers with teenagers to save money. But the seasonal nature of the bill should help prevent that. If adults are supplanted anyway, the mayors' conference promises to protest.

"We want this program not to displace youth or adults currently employed at or above the minimum wage," said Sam Tucker, a director of the mayors' conference. "We will be the first to be out there raising hell if it doesn't work."

Congress should accept what the black mayors have acknowledged: The jobless rate among teens, especially minority teens, is so high and so persistent that the subminimum wage is worth a trial.

DESERET NEWS
Salt Lake City, Utah, February 6-7, 1984

Economic recovery doesn't mean much to a worker out of a job. For teenagers, the situation is especially tough; one in every four can't find work. For black teenagers, the situation is much worse; one in two needs a job.

To give young people work experience and the dignity of earning a paycheck, President Reagan again is urging Congress to pass a $2.50-an-hour youth wage. The present $3.35 minimum wage covers all workers. But few employers are going to hire unskilled youths when they can get older, experienced workers for the same wage.

While the unemployment index dropped to 8% in January for workers as a whole — the fifth consecutive month the jobless rate has declined — it has barely changed for young workers. For black teenagers, the out-of-work rate dropped from 49% to 47.9%. And for teenagers as a whole, the rate declined from 20.1% to 19.4%.

It's time to initiate a youth wage at least on an experimental basis to test its merits. The idea has been around for years, but has been vigorously opposed by labor unions. Among other arguments, some unions claim that hiring youth for a sub minimum wage would push out older workers. What nonsense. Few if any firms are going to replace experienced workers with unskilled, low-productivity workers.

If youth aren't employed, they frequently exact a cost from society in other ways: their idleness means increased crime, undeveloped skills, wasted talents. And unemployed youths tend to become unemployed adults, dependent on welfare. A teen wage is worth at least a two- or three-year experiment to see if it won't help solve these problems.

Minneapolis Star and Tribune
Minneapolis, Minn., May 27, 1984

To encourage youth employment, President Reagan has renewed his call for a sub-minimum wage for workers aged 16 to 19. Reagan proposes that employers be authorized to pay them $2.50 per hour, 85 cents below the legal minimum wage, for summer work. Reagan's intention is good, but the costs of his proposal would likely outweigh the benefits. Congress should again decline the president's request.

In April, teen-age unemployment stood at 19.4 percent. Among black youth, it was 44.8 percent. Similar rates for adult workers would classify as a depression. But among youth, such general figures do not adequately define the nature of the unemployment problem.

Unemployment is measured in two dimensions — by the number of people without jobs and by the length of time they are out of work. Young people are twice as likely to be unemployed during any year, and thus to have a consistently higher unemployment *rate*, than adult workers. That's because teen-agers are just entering the labor force and are ranked among the unemployed until they find a job, and because they are more likely to quit their jobs.

But the length-of-unemployment story is different. Teenagers tend to be unemployed for shorter periods than adult workers. Thus, over the course of a year teen-age workers are likely to be out of work more times, but not longer, than adults.

The truly worrisome youth-unemployment problem affects a small subgroup of young people. The Congressional Budget Office estimates that nearly two-thirds of the weeks of teen-age unemployment are concentrated in 10 percent of the youth labor force. Members of this 10 percent are disproportionately black, high-school dropouts from economically and educationally disadvantaged backgrounds. Given their employment handicaps, a sub-minimum wage alone is unlikely to entice employers to hire them.

But the sub-minimum wage would encourage employers to substitute young people earning $2.50 an hour for older workers who must be paid $3.35. The congressional Minimum Wage Study Commission estimated that one-third of the jobs created by the sub-minimum wage would come at the expense of displaced adult workers. The Congressional Budget Office concluded that the sub-minimum wage might cause jobs to be switched "from a population of adults with typically lower family income and more financial responsibilities to a population of teen-agers typically from families with higher income."

The United States does have a youth unemployment problem. But it is not the general problem suggested by high youth-unemployment rates. The most severe employment difficulty is concentrated among disadvantaged young people who are no more likely to be hired at $2.50 an hour than at $3.35. Rather than help those young people, a sub-minimum wage most likely would harm others: low-income adults whose jobs would be delivered to the sons and daughters of higher-income families.

Health Care: Mothers, Infants at High Risk

In comparison to whites, blacks have higher infant and mortality rates, a greater percentage of low birth weights among infants, and a shorter life expectancy. The rate of low birth weights among blacks has remained almost twice that of whites since 1960, as has the infant mortality rate. In 1979, four times as many black mothers died in childbirth, or as a result of complications, as did white mothers. Life expectancy figures announced by the National Center for Health Statistics in 1984 were 78.5 years for white women, 73 years for black women, 71.1 years for white men, and 64.4 years for black men.

Part of the explanation for these health statistics can be traced to low income levels, since families living near the poverty level are usually unable to afford routine, preventive health care. But even at income levels of under $5,000, according to 1980 data compiled by the U.S. National Center for Health Statistics, 25.6% of physician visits by blacks were to emergency rooms, rather than physician's offices or phone consultations, as compared to 11.2% of visits by whites. The particular vulnerability of black infants and pregnant women may be, in part, a reflection of the high black teenage birth rate, if one accepts the premise that teenagers are less likely than more mature women to seek adequate prenatal and postnatal care. (See pp. 70-75.)

In addition, blacks are at much greater risk than whites as the victims of crime. In 1979, black men were more than six times as likely as white men to be the victims of homicide. In 1983, the Department of Health and Human Services reported that homicide was the single largest cause of death for blacks aged 15 to 24. (For whites in the same age group, automobile accidents were the leading cause of death.) This would certainly affect life expectancy tables, especially since so many of the homicide victims are young.

These partial explanations do not account for the whole picture, however, and it remains something of a mystery why the life expectancy of blacks should remain so far below that of whites. One interesting finding in recent studies has been that the rates of hypertension and diabetes are much higher for all blacks than they are for whites.

The Boston Globe

Boston, Mass., January 21, 1984

Black Americans suffer disproportionate medical problems that, as Health Secretary Margaret Heckler put it, are "an affront to our ideals." Black babies have an infant mortality rate of 21.4 per 1000 live births, almost twice that of whites. Black adults have an average life expectancy six years younger than whites. Black men in parts of Georgia have a lower average life expectancy than black men in Kenya.

To address these problems, Secretary Heckler has created a Task Force on Black-Minority Health to review programs and make recommendations. Some remedies – such as no more budget cuts in health care programs – should be evident. Thirty-five percent of black Americans live in poverty, the highest percentage in 10 years. For them, health care provided by the government is the only resort. That aid has become even more critical because of the rising costs of medical care and because the high black unemployment rate – 17.8 percent – has resulted in the loss of health benefits for thousands of families.

Another prescription is more black doctors.

Black doctors have always been scarce. Segregated colleges and hospitals as well as poverty once barred many from the profession. Despite past efforts to address the scarcity, the percentage of black physicians has barely risen from 2.1 in 1950 to 2.6 percent in 1980. While one white doctor serves every 526 whites, one black doctor serves every 2040 blacks. Mississippi, which has the highest black percentage in the nation, has one black doctor for every 11,230 black residents.

The Reagan Administration can remedy this scarcity by restoring cuts in federal college loan programs – tuition at medical schools has doubled in five years – and by reversing its anti-affirmative action stances. Both steps are unlikely.

The private sector must also respond. Boston University has set an example with an Early Medical Selection Program designed to increase black medical students. Toward that end, BU has teamed up with the four black colleges that are part of Atlanta University and with Hampton Institute, also historically black, in Virginia.

Under the plan, black participants would spend three summers and their senior year at BU before medical school in a program similar to a pre-med curriculum in place since 1977. Funded by the Robert Wood Johnson Foundation in Princeton, the program would start with three students and expand to 10.

BU has also taken the lead in its medical school, with a minority enrollment of 13 percent, better than most. The national average peaked at 7.5 percent in 1975 and is now at six percent. Six medical schools have no minority students.

Duplication of the BU plan will lead to more black doctors. So will more federal or state government aid. Those new black physicians who are socially responsible will help produce healthier black Americans no matter who is in the White House.

Detroit Free Press

Detroit, Mich., January 14, 1984

THE STATE of Michigan and the city of Detroit have the unfortunate and embarrassing distinction of leading the nation in black infant mortality in 1982, and there are no indications that the situation is improving. But it must.

The spread between mortality rates for white and black infants in Michigan is shocking: 9.7 infant deaths out of 1,000 white births, and 24.6 for black births. In Detroit, the figures are even more deplorable: 11 deaths per 1,000 births for whites and 26.9 for blacks. That's too many dead black babies. And although the white infant death rate here is below the national infant mortality rate of 12.5 per 1,000, it's too many dead white babies, too.

Many factors contribute to the distressing situation, some easier to remedy than others. The federal government has cut back funding for the Pre-School, School and Adolescent Children (PRESCAD) program, although the program still is attempting to satisfy the need for pre-natal care. PRESCAD is operating with nearly $2 million less in federal and state funds than it did three years ago, however. Cutbacks in funding combined with poverty have been bringing an increased number of mothers to hospital maternity wards who have had no previous medical advice or care, no instruction on diet or the effects and demands of pregnancy.

Black women are more than twice as likely to bear babies with low birth weights, according to the Food Research and Action Center. Infants with low birth weights are three times as likely to have birth defects and 10 times as likely to be retarded.

Diet instruction for low-income black mothers doesn't help much if they don't get enough to eat. The recent conclusion of President Reagan's Task Force on Food Assistance that allegations of "rampant hunger" cannot be documented doesn't take into account the effects of hunger and malnutrition that may not be rampant but are nevertheless existent and pervasive.

There are a number of efforts aimed at getting mothers into pre-natal programs, but the figures indicate that not enough young mothers are participating, either because they have no money, don't know what facilities are available, or are too young and fearful to seek help. We must do better than that. The infant mortality rate in Michigan and Detroit is a scandal.

The Times-Picayune
The States-Item
New Orleans, La., August 24, 1984

Pittsburgh Post-Gazette
Pittsburgh, Pa., March 21, 1984

Among the best news in Louisiana this week is that the state is finally reducing an infant mortality rate that was one of the worst in the nation.

Thanks to a federally-funded, six-year program that teaches young mothers to care for themselves and their babies, the infant death rate dropped by about one-quarter since 1977 when 18.1 deaths per 1,000 live births were recorded to 13.5 deaths in 1983.

The new rate compares to 12.6 deaths per 1,000 live births nationally, said Sandra L. Robinson, secretary of the state Department of Health and Human Resources. While Louisiana obviously still has plenty of room for improvement, this state finally no longer has one of the highest infant mortality rates in the United States.

The problem that Louisiana faced is illustrated by a closer look at the 1977 figures that showed non-white infants had a 26.4 death rate while the rate for white infants was 12.6.

As Secretary Robinson explained, the main causes of infant mortality were low birth weight, poorly educated mothers who received no prenatal care and the fact that many of the mothers were under 18 years of age.

In 1977, the state used a $2.2 million federal grant to hire 8 nurses who are specialists in maternal and child health and family planning. These 8 became tutors who covered the state, teaching public health nurses in every parish how to deal with high-risk pregnancies.

Although the major goal of the program was to reduce infant mortality, it has had the interesting side effect of helping reduce the rate of births among young mothers.

In the New Orleans area, unmarried black females ages 11 through 19 make up a large number of the high-risk pregnancies seen here, said Secretary Robinson. Births in this group have declined from 27.8 percent of all live births in Louisiana in 1977 to 23.8 percent in 1983.

As the secretary noted, if society is to break the cycle of poverty — with children having children, thereby creating successive generations living solely off public assistance — it will take innovative educational and health care programs by government along with the support of the entire community.

Unfortunately, the federal grant that allowed the state to hire the 8 nursing specialists who got the educational and maternal health care program started is now about to expire. But Secretary Robinson said the state will continue to operate the program, retaining the same concepts that have helped reduce both the infant mortality rate as well as the number of adolescent and teenage children who give birth to children.

Although Louisiana is suffering through a period of pinched state budgets, this is a program that should be funded by the state. It would be a tragedy if the figures that have been improved were to return to their previous sorry state. The goal ought to be to improve them further.

Pittsburgh's shockingly high mortality rate for black infants one year old and younger is stimulating an effort to look beyond those statistics to the question of teen-age pregnancy and unwed mothers.

Although other factors are involved also, experts believe there is a definite connection between teen-age pregnancies out of wedlock and the fact that Pittsburgh has the highest black infant mortality rate in the nation. Statistics show that in 1982 (the latest year of complete record), for each 1,000 live black births in Pittsburgh, 29.7 died; the equivalent white figure was 10.1.

•

Various community institutions have begun to address the black infant mortality problem. Mayor Caliguiri has appointed a committee of physicians on the subject and on June 21 a conference on the subject will be held here, organized by the Pittsburgh chapter of the March of Dimes and the Urban League of Pittsburgh.

But the question of teen-age pregnancies may be less yielding to solutions, other than the traditional (but not very effective) admonition to chastity. There has been a staggering 500 percent increase in American illegitimate births to teen-agers since 1950.

Including adults as well as teen-agers, in Pennsylvania during 1979, for example, one of every six Pennsylvania babies was born out of wedlock. Among blacks, the percentage of babies born out of wedlock was 66.3 percent, and among whites 9.9 percent.

Two explanations are offered for the epidemic of out-of-wedlock pregnancies. One is that there is almost no stigma attached to having a baby out of wedlock. Fortunately, society is past the time when an unwed mother and her child were callously stigmatized by society, but contemporary permissiveness has created problems in the other direction.

Second, experts say many teen-agers *want* to give birth, if only so they can have someone to love. The catastrophic impact of early motherhood on education, job and marital opportunities — not to mention the ceaseless burdens of child care — are discovered too late.

So more than imparting information is needed; attitudes must also be changed.

Fortunately for Pittsburgh, in some ways this area is well-poised to begin addressing the related problems of teen-age pregnancy and infant mortality. For example, the city has a lower percentage of births from teen-age black mothers — one factor in the high infant-mortality rate — than other cities.

Pittsburgh also has a higher percentage of black women who have completed the eighth grade or high school than the average in other cities. But it falls behind in having a higher percentage of black families below the poverty level; a higher percentage of low-birthweight black births than elsewhere and a higher rate of premature births — as much as 23 percent higher than the national average in some black neighborhoods.

Some local agencies already are tackling the problem in various ways:

• The Pittsburgh public schools last fall inaugurated an updated sex education curriculum for grades six through 12 after considerable controversy. Not only is anatomy explained but, in the upper grades, information on birth control is provided, with the stress placed on abstinence. It is hoped that that theme will also figure in "rap sessions" at which middle-school youngsters will be able to meet and discuss problems they feel they can't broach at home.

• The Alma Illery Center in Homewood-Brushton has launched a set of peer discussion groups to grapple with the problem.

• The Health Education Center, a United Way agency affiliated with the Health and Welfare Planning Association, has commissioned a study on the subject in conjunction with an informal black women's network convened by Dr. Sandra Murray, an anatomist at the University of Pittsburgh Medical School, and Dr. Judith Davenport, a dentist.

• The Urban League of Pittsburgh has made the problem a top priority study project, as has the National Urban League. So far 19 agencies of the Urban League have established programs for unwed parents, five of them also involving fathers.

Local Urban League officials already have found some interesting models. One of the best is in St. Paul, Minn., where a family-planning clinic was placed right inside an inner-city school. Officials there were wise enough to broaden the clinic to include examinations for sports, college, as well as immunization programs so that students could visit the clinic without feeling conspicuous.

•

So there are partial remedies even if "the" solution remains elusive. To strengthen the effort further, perhaps ways can be found to involve churches and religious institutions in ways that don't discourage young people.

For experience is demonstrating that not just morality but the lives of babies are at stake.

THE MILWAUKEE JOURNAL
Milwaukee, Wisc., February 6, 1984

It's a disgraceful disparity. Overall, the health of Americans has improved significantly in the past decade. However, the health of black and minority Americans continues to lag far behind the health of white citizens. For example, the infant mortality rate for blacks is about twice as high as for whites; the 1982 life expectancy for blacks was 69.3 years, six years less than the record 75.1 years for whites.

Those statistics, delivered in the US Public Health Service's annual report on the nation's health, prove that this one nation has two distinct realities — and the reality of life for blacks and other minorities is considerably gloomier than for whites. "As long as this disparity exists, it remains an affront to our ideals and a serious challenge to those of us charged with maintaining and improving the public health," said Margaret Heckler, secretary of the Department of Health and Human Services.

She's correct, of course. But what's the solution? Heckler's immediate response was to create a task force to study the "disparity in the burden of death, illness and disability." The task force will investigate the health problems of blacks and other minority groups in an effort to assure that existing resources are being spent wisely.

The Reagan administration does not have a great track record on task forces looking into the woes of the underclass. Anticipating criticism, a Heckler spokesman said, "The work of the task force will prove that it's not just a cosmetic effort." We certainly hope so. The burden of proof is on the administration, which deservedly took its lumps for the narrow-minded approach of its hunger task force.

Some critics say — and they probably are quite right — that the administration already has enough data to justify immediate action to provide more health services to minorities. Still, the new task force could serve a useful purpose if it (1) evaluated existing data with the idea of better targeting resources and (2) took a broad approach and tried to pinpoint the impact of factors such as income, environment, workplace and lifestyle on the health of minorities.

Statistics show that the overall increase of cancers among blacks is twice that of whites and hypertension kills blacks 15 times more frequently than whites. In the workplace, blacks have a 37% higher risk of occupationally induced disease and a 20% higher death rate from occupationally related disease. Perhaps strict enforcement of health and safety rules on the job would have more impact on black health than would medical programs.

In any event, the task force should take a no-holds-barred approach — or it'll be seen as another dodge by the Reagan administration.

The Star-Ledger
Newark, N.J., July 26, 1984

Polluted air, toxic contamination and other killers on the contemporary American scene notwithstanding, life expectancy in the United States continues to register impressive increases.

Latest available data from the National Center for Health Statistics, in fact, indicate there is more life ahead for Americans than at any time in history.

Life expectancy reached a record high of 74.2 years in 1981, up from 73.7 a year earlier. And the age-adjusted death rate, which statisticians consider a better indicator of the chances of death over a period of time, dipped to an all-time low in that same year.

The age-adjusted rate is a calculation of how many deaths would have occurred if the 1981 population had the same age mix as that of 1940. For 1981, the figure was 568.2 deaths per 100,000, down an impressive 3 percent from the previous year.

Another encouraging development: Of the 15 leading causes of death studied, 12 declined in 1981.

And women once again showed they were the stronger sex. White women recorded a life expectancy of 77.9 years, black women 73 years, white males 71.1 years and black males 64.4 years.

These statistics, of course, have different relevancies for different people, from those who are concerned with health care and housing to the politicians learning to placate a growing group of older Americans.

For most of us, however, the expectancy projection is a fact of life we can all live with easily, as long as the trend is favorable.

THE TENNESSEAN
Nashville, Tenn., January 23, 1984

THE health of the majority of Americans is said to be better than ever before. But there is great disparity between the health of the majority and that of the minorities and the Reagan administration is launching another task force to find out why and what can be done about it.

Secretary of Health and Human Services Margaret M. Heckler, in announcing the task force, called the gap between blacks and whites "an affront to our ideals" and said it represents "a fundamental discrepancy in the quality of life of the American people."

There is plenty of reason for having such an opinion. Although black Americans' life expectancy increased 5.2 years from 1970 to 1982, compared with 3.4 years for whites, the life expectancy for blacks in 1982 was still only 69.3 years compared with 75.1 for whites.

The infant mortality rate, which is critical in determining average life expectancy, remains nearly twice as great for blacks as for whites.

A recent report by the non-profit Food Research and Action Center calls the high death rate of black babies an "Infant Mortality Belt" and says that if black and white infants had an equal chance of survival, 19,647 more black children would have lived in the last five years.

The Task Force on Black-Minority Health, which will be headed by Dr. Thomas E. Malone, deputy director of the National Institutes of Health, plans an extensive study of the problem, including an examination of genetic, environmental and lifestyle factors.

No doubt this kind of information will be helpful. But other studies already point to poverty, poor nutrition, a lack of health care, especially pre-natal care, and similar factors as the major causes of high infant mortality and lower life expectancy among minority groups.

The FRAC study showed that when blacks and whites of the same income were studied, the infant mortality rates were almost the same. "If we continue to have high rates of poverty, we're going to have to be prepared for high infant mortality rates, unless we are prepared to restore basic health care, basic nutrition programs and basic prenatal care to produce more healthy babies," said Ms. Nancy Amidei, FRAC's executive director.

Dr. Malone estimates that the task force's work will take at least a year to complete. It is good to have all the facts in hand, but it seems that if it was serious about the matter the administration would begin to attack the already identifiable problems of poverty, malnutrition and inadequate health care without waiting for the task force to complete its work.

Many of those who have been critical of the work done by the administration's task force on hunger don't have much confidence that the panel on minority life expectancy will do a lot better.

It seems the administration has a tendency to appoint a task force to study a problem when it doesn't want to deal with the problem, especially in the area of human services. It is hoped that will not be the case with the new task force. But considering the time the group expects to take to complete its investigation, the prospect for getting something done to lower the minority infant death rate soon is not bright.

The Pittsburgh
PRESS
Pittsburgh, Pa., March 18, 1984

In the category of good news and about time, include the announcement the other day that a study will be made to try to determine why Pittsburgh's black infant mortality rate is abnormally high.

The mortality rate of black babies born in Pittsburgh in 1982 was 29.7 per 1,000 births, nearly three times the white infant mortality rate of 10.1 per 1,000. The 29.7 deaths per 1,000 births was the highest in the nation that year.

The horrifying figures were reported last December by the Children's Defense Fund, a Washington-based group and released at Magee-Womens Hospital.

A committee of 17 physicians has been formed to study the problem and Mayor Richard Caliguiri tomorrow will ask City Council to allocate $10,000 to fund the study, which will center mainly on factors that might contribute to the abnormal figures.

We trust that City Council will have no problem with that allocation and the study team will be able to get on with its work without delay.

If the team can isolate possible causes by its July 1 deadline, the next step — corrective measures — can be taken.

In the meantime, as The Press suggested editorially last December, local foundations should take note of the research. They have the funds to underwrite that vitally important second step.

Richmond Times-Dispatch
Richmond, Va., August 13, 1984

A scan of the 1984 Democratic Party platform turns up this gem: "With the Reagan administration's cutbacks in prenatal care and supplemental food programs have come infant mortality rates in parts of our cities rivaling those of the poorest Latin American nations. Black infants are now twice as likely as white infants to die during the first year of life." Be assured the Democrats will have this precious stone on display during the coming campaign, the better to throw it at the president.

But recent news stories reveal an obvious flaw: Infant mortality rates in the United States have been falling for decades, and the past few years have been no exception. The rate was 12.6 per thousand in 1980, and provisional figures indicate it was 10.9 per thousand in 1983. According to findings published this month in the Journal of the American Medical Association, deaths among U.S. babies 4 weeks to 1 year old have dropped sharply during the past two decades. In line with that trend, Virginia's infant mortality rate apparently went down from 12.1 per thousand births in 1982 to 11.3 in 1983, though those figures are not final. And while it's true that the black infant mortality rate is twice that of whites, it's down considerably from 1962, when it was three times higher.

By no means is the problem solved. Infant mortality is of special concern to the Commonwealth because its rate is higher than the national average, and to Richmond in particular because one study found its rate among the worst of the nation's cities. Twelve communities in Virginia with high rates have received a total of more than $2 million in federal aid in 1984 to help bring them down.

The "Reagan cutbacks" of which the Democrats spoke are hard to find. During the period 1980 to 1983, spending by the U.S. Department of Agriculture's Food and Nutrition Service increased by $5.3 billion. Tightened eligibility requirements for food stamps meant a 45 percent hike in funding rather than the planned 75 percent hike; still food stamp funding increased by $3.7 billion. Funds for the Special Supplemental Program for Women, Infants and Children, which offers nutritional supplements for needy pregnant women and children, increased by $348 million. The Tax Reform Act of 1984, recently signed by President Reagan, designated $270 million for programs to provide health care to low-income pregnant women and to children up to 5 years old. Those figures don't include the distribution of more than $1 billion worth of surplus dairy goods in 1983 alone.

Critics rightly say that these numbers need to be adjusted for inflation. The American Enterprise Institute reports that funding for low-income benefit programs went up 8 percent in real terms from 1980-83.

Ideally such aid would reduce the number of low birthweight babies in the United States, a condition that hits blacks in this country twice as hard as whites. This imbalance "accounts for nearly all the difference in deaths between whites and blacks during the first month of life," says Washington health and nutrition consultant Carol Adelman in Policy Review magazine. All other things being equal among mothers — height, weight, socioeconomic status — black babies are still more likely to be born underweight.

Doctors aren't sure why. Despite all the health, welfare and education programs (including the provision of nutritional supplements to mothers and infants) during the '70s, the number of very low birthweight black babies actually increased 1 percent during that decade, says Ms. Adelman.

The reduction in the overall infant mortality rate during the past 20 years resulted primarily from medical advances. The high incidence of teen-age pregnancies, however, exerts upward pressure on the rate. "As a result of physiological immaturity, low birthweight is rather common among babies born to girls 16 and under," says Ms. Adelman, "and the problem is exacerbated when they fail to seek medical help until the last minute."

Fewer such pregnancies obviously would help. Baby talk from Democrats making goo-goo eyes at voters won't.

The Dispatch
Columbus, Ohio, July 10, 1984

The new government figures are out. Our life expectancy rate as Americans is a little higher.

If you're a white woman, you can expect to live 78.5 years and if you're a black woman, 73 years. White men can anticipate a life span of 71.1 years and black men, 64.4 years.

The rates reported by the National Center for Health Statistics are adjusted to the general age of the population, and, even with our higher percentage of older persons in 1981, the year reported, the annual age-adjusted death rate was the lowest in U.S. history.

We are getting so accustomed to this annual increase in life expectancy that it is hardly news and we yearn for the greater good news — when Americans are motivated and able to use those extra years in far greater numbers in happy, productive and satisfying ways.

However, each year's analysis has its special interests, and the 1981 report had some. In deaths reported per 100,000 population, heart disease remained far and away the greatest killer, with a rate of 328.7, although both it and second-ranked cancer, at 184, dropped slightly from 1980 rates.

Stroke, a distant third at 71.3 and accidents, fourth at 43.9, both increased slightly, and edging into the top 10 among disease fatalities are deaths we cause ourselves and others — suicides, ninth at 12 per 100,000, and homicides, 10th at 10.3. Both outranked post-natal deaths, birth defects and kidney disease.

The center figures held particularly good news for babies and blacks. The infant mortality rate of 11.9 per 1,000 live births was the lowest ever recorded in the United States. Although the life expectancy rate for blacks is still lower, it increased nearly twice as fast as the rate for whites between 1980 and 1981.

We can still work as a country at improving both those ratings while we await that ultimate sign of improvement — that we're all living both longer and better.

Fair Housing Laws: Inadequate Enforcement

The Civil Rights Commission reported in 1980 that the previous year had been characterized by a "drift" in civil rights. In housing, the commission said, discrimination against minorities remained "widespread" throughout the United States. Minority families and those headed by women, the report stated, were paying "disproportionately high costs for flawed, deteriorating and overcrowded housing." Later that year, a move in Congress to strengthen federal fair housing laws was abandoned, after a Senate motion to limit debate on the bill failed. At issue had been an authorization for the Department of Housing and Urban Development to bring suit against those charged with discriminating in the sale or rental of housing.

The nation's basic fair housing law, part of the 1968 Civil Rights Act, prohibits discrimination based on race, color, religion or national origin. But under current law, HUD is allowed only to mediate housing disputes between individuals and alleged violators, not to initiate legal action. The only other recourse for complainants of illegal housing discrimination is to bring a private lawsuit, an expensive course that is rarely undertaken. The attorney general can also sue alleged violators, but only on the basis of "a pattern or practice" of discrimination.

The issue that stymied the 1980 legislation has continued to undermine efforts to strengthen enforcement of fair housing laws. Civil rights groups favor legislative proposals that would, like the 1980 bill, allow HUD to refer housing complaints to administrative law judges, who would be empowered to award damages to victims and fine violators. Realtors and many members of the Senate prefer legislation that would shift the administration of the fair housing law to the Justice Department, giving the attorney general authority to intervene in cases brought by individuals, but only where "proof of intent to discriminate" had been found. In July, 1983, the Reagan Administration unveiled a proposal along these lines. The Administration proposal was widely portrayed as a symbolic gesture intended to deflect criticism about President Reagan's recent firing of three members of the Civil Rights Commission in order to replace them with his own nominees. (See pp. 122-135.)

The Providence Journal
Providence, R.I., December 15, 1980

No mistake about it: the political winds already are shifting on Capitol Hill. Some of the signs are positive and invigorating. But other omens of change in the political climate suggest something sour at work — a reactionary swing, even — and one such sign emerged last Tuesday with the demise in the Senate of an important fair-housing bill.

The scuttling of this legislation made a mark at once practical and symbolic. In practical terms, the death of the bill extinguishes efforts to plug a large hole in a historic law that was enacted in the interests of racial justice: the Fair Housing Act of 1968. This law made unlawful any discrimination on the basis of race or creed in the sale or rental of housing, but it lacked the teeth needed to be effective.

In an effort to provide enforcement powers, the House passed a strengthening amendment last June. This would have given the Department of Housing and Urban Development, which now can only mediate disputes involving alleged housing violations, the power to bring complaints on its own. For the first time, the law's assurance of fair access to housing would have been backed up by the kind of enforcement authority that any such law should have.

But the lame-duck Senate, with its liberals on the defensive and some of its conservatives feeling their oats, felt differently. It refused to end a filibuster against the bill, thereby killing the measure for this session — and perhaps for years to come, although Sen. Howard H. Baker Jr., the incoming Republican leader, says he will try for a "good" fair-housing bill next year.

The symbolism of this defeat may loom larger than its practical consequences, unhappy though these may be for any person unfortunate enough to be turned away from a house or apartment because of skin color. In a larger sense, what the fair-housing defeat suggests is a readiness, among a certain element in the Congress, to retreat from the gains won so arduously over the last two decades on behalf of racial justice. The fact that a filibuster could succeed against such a bill *in 1980* is dispiriting: it illuminates a recalcitrant mood on the part of some senators who still bridle at the idea of government's enforcing civil-rights laws. These are senators who would seize upon last month's election returns as a pretext for dismantling many of government's guarantees to protect the rights of minority Americans. (Senators Pell and Chafee, it is reassuring to note, both favored the fair-housing bill.)

This pliant outlook, this readiness to hedge on a national commitment enshrined in law, represents the less salutary side of what some already are calling a new conservative "era." If it does not hint at full-speed retreat from civil-rights advances, it suggests more trimming and temporizing, and this would do harm enough to the cause of racial fairness in America. There surely are ways of changing a political course in Washington without undermining fundamental legislative gains, and it is to be hoped that the 97th Congress can divine the distinction. .

St. Petersburg Times
St. Petersburg, Fla., December 11, 1980

Will history record Dec. 4, 1980, as the high-water mark of the civil rights movement? On that day, the Senate was able to break a Republican-led filibuster that was preventing debate on a fair-housing bill. But the filibuster resumed on the bill itself. By Tuesday, the cloture margin had evaporated, and the bill was lost. Such was the overture to Republican control of the Senate. Could Abraham Lincoln recognize this party?

Howard Baker, soon to be the majority leader, denies that what happened signifies that the civil rights movement is dead. He promises to try to pass a fair-housing bill early next year, "and a good bill, not just a bill in name only." On both counts, he faces a staggering burden of proof.

THE BILL that was defeated was mild and reasonable. It would have put some effective enforcement powers behind the 1968 Fair Housing Act, which allows the Justice Department to file suits only when a "pattern or practice" of racial, religious or sex discrimination exists. On account of that restriction, the department has filed only 350 cases in 12 years — winning nearly all of them, as it happens. Does anyone believe that 350 cases take the measure of housing discrimination in the United States?

The bill as written would have allowed the Department of Housing and Urban Development to charge violators before administrative law judges, who would have the power to impose fines of up to $10,000 and whose decisions could be appealed to federal courts. In a desperate attempt at compromise, Sen. Edward M. Kennedy, D-Mass., the floor manager, was willing to amend the bill to have federal magistrates hear the initial complaints. This was not enough for Orrin Hatch, R-Utah, the filibuster leader. His price was nothing less than two radical concessions that would have undercut the existing law as well as the pending bill. He wanted jury trials on all cases, even where the government is asking only for injunctions, not fines. And he wanted the standard of proof to be so difficult that, for all practical purposes, a landlord, broker or loan officer would have to be overheard boasting of an intent to discriminate.

BAKER MAY intend for the next Senate to do better, but has he looked at his own roster lately? The Judiciary Committee has jurisdiction over civil rights bills. Strom Thurmond of South Carolina will chair it. He was last heard proposing to repeal the 1965 Voting Rights Act. The Constitution subcommittee, which has initial jurisdiction, will be chaired by Orrin Hatch.

The Senate consists of people who have never felt the sting of racial prejudice, who have never had doors slammed in their faces for being black, who have never suffered the tears and rage of being penned in ghettos by the various silent, smug conspiracies of which the real estate world is capable. But throughout the mid-'60s and '70s, the Senate at least was able to think and to act in larger and nobler terms than the senators' privileged circumstances might suggest. What now?

Sen. Daniel Patrick Moynihan, D-N.Y., delivered the approriate challenge on the Senate floor Tuesday afternoon as the bill was declared dead. "In a month," he said, "it will be the responsibility of the gentlemen opposite who blocked it to come forward and give life to this principle. It will be their Senate, and there are many men and women on that side who know they are responsible. Let us hope they keep their promise."

THE RICHMOND NEWS LEADER
Richmond, Va., December 11, 1980

The refusal of the Senate to shut off a filibuster to permit a vote on a measure touted as a fair housing bill is being called a defeat for the most important civil rights bill of this session. The bill may have been many things, but a genuine civil rights bill it was not.

The measure, aimed at "putting teeth" in the 1968 Fair Housing Act, would have eroded further a basic concept of American law: An accused is innocent until proved guilty, and the state must prove that guilt. Under the defeated bill, however, any homeowner, landlord, or real estate agent could have been hauled before a federal accuser, found guilty of racial discrimination in housing transactions, and fined $10,000 on the spot.

The bill already approved by the House would have insulted the civil rights of homeowners, landlords, and real estate agents even more. That version would have placed the fate of the defendant in the hands of an administrative law judge appointed to his position in the executive branch. Even the Senate thought that delegation of judicial authority somewhat drastic, and a Senate amendment called for federal magistrates to act as trial judges.

Two questions remained murky about the Senate's compromise proposal. The first went to the issue of a defendant's constitutional right to a trial by jury. The second raised the issue of intent on the part of an accused violator. The bill was unclear on both points, and enough Senators proved reluctant to support such a threat against the rights of alleged offenders to jettison the bill. Too many judges already are confusing effect with intent to justify an expansion of their authority to undermine basic property rights.

"Fair housing" did not die in the Senate; it lives in the form of effective ordinances and laws in almost every community and state in the nation. These ordinances are tailored to fit the local and state circumstances as perceived by officials elected at local and state levels. But congressional Liberals, are not satisfied by the immense gains made recently in the elimination of bias in housing. They wanted to change the federal role from one of mediation to one of oppressive assumption of guilt against any hapless agent in a housing lease or sale.

Minority groups backed the measure on the theory that it would produce another symbolic federal commitment to their cause. The nation needs no more such symbolism to polarize race relations by intensifying racial hostility. Minorities already are learning the folly of symbolic policies that are beginning to work against them in cities where they now command majorities — as in race quotas, for instance, that now set forth certain percentages for whites in high school sports.

It is puzzling that supporters of this bill could not understand that it could have been turned against them, too. In some cities, white flight has reversed, and "regentrification" is occurring as urban housing is reclaimed from the minorities now living there. If this housing bill were in effect, a member of a minority group who might prefer to sell his house to his cousin or to his son could not refuse to sell it to the first buyer, on pain of suffering a $10,000 fine.

If the nation's voters said anything on November 4, it was that they are fed up with federal interference in every phase and aspect of their daily lives. This purported fair housing bill would have created yet another opening for federal assault on individual liberties. In rejecting it, the Senate merely took note of the election returns and spared the nation more symbolism that bureaucrats can turn into oppression.

The News American
Baltimore, Md., December 3, 1980

Before Ronald Reagan claimed the White House and ushered a host of conservative Republicans into a majority position in the Senate, a bill designed to put punch in the Fair Housing Act of 1968, and described as the most important civil rights legislation since the reforms of the 1960s, was expected to garner Senate approval with little difficulty. In fact, a compromise bill incorporating a more liberal House version of the Senate bill was expected.

Now, however, civil rights appear to be the last thing on the Senate's mind. On Monday, such well-known conservative senators as Orrin G. Hatch (R-Utah), Jesse Helms (R-N.C.) and Strom Thurmond (R-S.C.) moved in to deal the proposed amendments to the housing act a death blow by staging a filibuster when Senate Democrats tried once more to get the bill through the lame-duck session. As a result, and in view of the two-thirds majority the Senate needs to beat the filibuster, even the most optimistic among the bill's supporters are saying that at best they expect it to squeak by.

The amendments were proposed to allow the Department of Housing and Urban Development to file suits with administrative law judges on behalf of people charging landlords with discrimination, and chances are slim that the next Senate would pass such needed legislation.

The bill's opponents are saying the filibuster is not to be confused with being anti-civil rights. Instead, theirs is a fight to defeat a sloppy bill, they say, suggesting that fair housing would be better addressed in the next congressional session when there will be more time for debate and compromise.

The opponents — particularly Senator Thurmond — say the problem with the current bill is that it denies landlords the right to a jury trial — a basic civil right, they say — and that they prefer to see the courts retain control over such matters rather than have a federal agency bring suit before an administrative law judge and become prosecutor, judge and jury.

The argument sounds good, but a close examination of the record indicates otherwise. Under current law, people who believe they have been discriminated against must appear in court personally and file suit. The problem is that those most likely to face discrimination are the people who have neither the money, the knowledge nor the time to fight for their rights. Given the civil rights record of Senator Thurmond and many of the other opposition senators, the current fight to kill the bill appears suspect indeed. To argue, as they do, that the current bill should be defeated in the name of civil rights is ludicrous, but entirely likely nonetheless.

TULSA WORLD
Tulsa, Okla., October 16, 1981

PIONEERS of the modern civil rights movement had a great advantage over their present-day successors. Their enemy was plain and simple race discrimination. The issue was as clear as black and white.

But no more. The issues are foggy. Clear and specific goals are rarely defined. And a simple case of race discrimination — that is, an instance in which a person is denied some right or privilege solely because of skin color — is a rarity.

Consider two Court cases decided this week on the subject of housing discrimination.

In Connecticut, a Federal judge cleared the town of Manchester of U.S. Government charges that it intentionally excluded blacks and minorities from its population by withdrawing from a Federal housing program.

In Ohio, the 6th Circuit Court of Appeals held the opposite in a case against the Cleveland suburb of Parma. The community, the Court said, unlawfully discriminated against minorities by refusing to take part in a Federal housing program.

So the question of whether prosperous, mostly white neighborhoods must cooperate in building low-cost housing for the poor in the name of civil rights still awaits a clear answer by the U.S. Supreme Court.

The problem is that the public housing issue is not exclusively racial. Race is an oblique consideration. It is fair to assume that many residents of Parma and Manchester would welcome blacks and members of other minority groups who could buy homes in the neighborhood on the same basis as the present residents. Their discrimination, if you want to call it that, is not against black people, but against poor people.

The battle lines have changed beyond recognition. It is no longer a question of whether a black person can be denied the ballot, public education, housing or some other privilege solely because of skin color. The immediate question is whether well-to-do homeowners of all races must cooperate in bringing poor people into their neighborhoods under Federal programs.

Government-required integration of rich and poor may or may not be a worthwhile goal. (We believe not.) But those who advocate it would do well to state plainly what they are trying to do and quit pretending that the main issue is race discrimination.

The Virginian-Pilot

Norfolk, Va., April 5, 1982

The Supreme Court's unanimous decision in a fair housing case out of Richmond and a recent lower court decision in a Chicago housing case promise to advance the cause of eliminating lingering racial barriers that violate the law.

In the Richmond case, an equal housing group suspected Havens Realty of excluding blacks. So it sent a "tester" — a black woman — to try to rent an apartment. She was turned away by a claim of no vacancies, but a white tester who followed her on the same day was told he could be accommodated. The Supreme Court held that the black was entitled to sue for damages because her right to receive truthful housing information had been violated.

The case broke new ground when the court dismissed the argument that the 180-day statute of limitations had run. As Justice Brennan put it, "statutes of limitations such as that . . . are intended to keep stale claims out of the courts. Where the challenged violation is a continuing one, the staleness concern disappears." The continuing nature of the discrimination, he added, "undermines the broad remedial intent of Congress embodied in the (fair housing) act."

The decision means that complaints may be filed so long as the last asserted act of discrimination in a series of such incidents is within the 180-day period. That ruling serves to strengthen the hand of those seeking redress and reform.

In the Chicago case, an affluent black businessman sought to buy a $600,000 house in an exclusive neighborhood. Some residents of the community succeeded in excluding him by maneuvering to purchase the property for a white buyer. The black sued and won a record amount in punitive damages.

These may not be landmark legal cases, but each serves to help break up segregated housing. Since passage of the 1968 Fair Housing Act, considerable progress has been achieved. There has not, however, been a vast alteration of demographic patterns, and the effort to remove racial barriers necessarily continues.

Just how strong the effort will be under the Reagan administration is open to question. Columnist Colman McCarthy last week asserted that the Justice Department shows "little interest in enforcing the law." Assistant Attorney General William Bradford Reynolds retorted that Justice had been a litigant in four major housing cases last year, had filed an amicus brief (for the plaintiff) in the Richmond case and had recently filed two new suits alleging discrimination in apartment rentals in Boston and Detroit.

Other sources express doubt about Mr. Reynolds' enthusiasm for using the resources of the Justice Department to investigate fair housing complaints. Four of the six cases he cited were originated by the Carter administration. "The government has retired from the field," claims Martin Sloane, director of the National Committee Against Discrimination in Housing.

In his disappointment that reformist zeal no longer activates government policy-makers under President Reagan, Mr. Sloane may be guilty of hyperbole. Mr. Reynolds says "other housing discrimination complaints are under active investigation and will likely result in additional litigation." Let's hope he follows through. For the government to retire from enforcing the law — especially one so sensitive — would be a backward step ill serving the cause of equity for minorities or that of peaceful race relations.

Any slackening of enforcement would also tend to substantiate the impression that Mr. Reagan is less concerned than recent presidents of both parties about preventing a resurgence of Jim Crow practices. He — and the country — can't afford to make that mistake.

THE SACRAMENTO BEE

Sacramento, Calif., October 12, 1980

During the 1960s, the decade of civil rights and urban riots in America, a prestigious presidential commission shocked the country with its report on race and violence. "Our nation," it concluded, "is moving toward two societies, one black, one white — separate and unequal."

If it was meant as a call to action, this ominous declaration turned out to be more of a prophecy. It may have helped inspire the anti-discrimination laws, desegregation decisions and affirmative action plans that have been the touchstones of race relations in the past two decades. But for all this legal activity, the United States in 1980 is — on almost every score — more racially divided than it was in 1960. These years have been, to quote the National Committee Against Discrimination in Housing, a period of "resegregation, or the extension of previous segregation."

While the proportion of black professionals, managers and administrators has nearly doubled in the last 20 years, wider participation seems to have bred wider segregation. Nearly 75 percent of black lawyers work for the same employer: government. Among the 50 largest private law firms in the country, only 12 of the 3,700 partners are black.

The National Medical Association — an organization of black physicians that parallels the American Medical Association, like so many other separate black professional groups — reports that despite a doubling of the number of black doctors, there are only two private medical practices in the country in which blacks and whites are partners. Similarly, the fourfold increase in college enrollment by blacks in the last 20 years has been accompanied by increased social segregation — what the Wall Street Journal, in a recent report on integration, called "an edgy sort of voluntary racial separation."

At the lower level, segregation in the schools is more formal. Although there has been significant progress in school integration in the South, the U.S. Department of Education reports that in the Northeast and the West more black children were in segregated schools in 1978 than in 1960. Court-ordered desegregation seems to have done more to induce white flight than integration — as in Los Angeles, which dropped in three years from more than one-third white-Anglo enrollment to less than one-quarter; or Atlanta, where blacks comprised 45 percent of the school population when desegregation was first ordered in 1960 and now comprise more than 90 percent.

Like the 90 percent of American blacks who belong to all-black churches, the black school population is segregated in part by choice and in part in response to outright or subtle white racism. But, most compellingly, it is segregated as a result of housing segregation. In housing, a spate of anti-discrimination laws, a huge increase in the number of whites who tell pollsters they would be pleased to live next door to blacks, and the growing willingness and ability of black families to move to the suburbs have produced almost no integration anywhere in the country.

This pattern cannot be chalked up simply to personal preferences. When Harvard and the Massachusetts Institute of Technology recently made a joint study of housing practices in California and New York, states with some of the toughest anti-discrimination laws in the country, they found that nonetheless blacks were far more likely to be turned down for home loans than whites with the same income, and blacks were paying considerably higher interest rates on the mortgages they did get. As with the real estate agents who still steer black and white clients to different areas, it is apparent that many banks are operating on the edge of outright illegality.

Still, the problem does not seem to be centrally one of inadequate laws or enforcement. The legal scaffolding for integration is largely in place; it is personal and social indifference — or worse, sabotage — that prevents a structure being built around it. Among both blacks and whites, integration is not as fashionable a concern as it was when the presidential commission first made its report. But the prospect of a racially divided country is no less dangerous now than it was then — and no more inevitable. A different choice, as the commission said then, is still possible, and "there can be no higher claim on the nation's conscience."

THE COMMERCIAL APPEAL

Memphis, Tenn., July 14, 1983

A MESSAGE from President Reagan to Congress asserts there is a "consensus" that the mechanism to enforce the law against housing discrimination is too weak. The message accompanies his proposed legislation to remedy the situation. Shortly after sending the word to Congress, the President learned that a consensus was forming that his solution was also inadequate.

Currently, neither the Department of Housing and Urban Development nor the Justice Department can file suit unless a pattern or practice of discrimination exists. Otherwise, or where damages are sought, it's up to the individual victim of discrimination to bring suit. That's often an expensive proposition and a slow one, at that.

Reagan proposes judicial enforcement by the Justice Department when HUD cannot resolve the matter through conciliation. HUD has been fairly successful with conciliation. It was attempted in 697 cases last year and successful in 427. But that represents a small fraction of the 5,112 complaints of housing discrimination filed last year with the federal government or state and local agencies administering similar laws. Many cases cannot be conciliated.

The Reagan approach is still slow and of questionable effectiveness, depending as it does on the interest of the Justice Department

and already overcrowded court dockets. One reason time is important in these cases is that the law allows a third party to buy or rent the property in question before a temporary restraining order is granted. Another shortcoming of the Reagan plan is that a victim seeking monetary damages would still have to file his own lawsuit.

THE CONSENSUS growing in Congress is that a system of administrative law judges could better deal with unresolved complaints. The administration, predictably, opposes that on the grounds it would create a "whole new bureaucracy." As the 1984 election looms closer and his enemies among minorities and women increase, Reagan suddenly seems eager to show a greater sensitivity to their interests. But there are limits to how far he will go, apparently, and another layer of government is too distant.

Too bad. As Ralph Neas, executive director of the Leadership Conference on Civil Rights, a coalition of 165 national organizations, said, Reagan has again "missed a political opportunity and has gratuitously inflicted a political wound on himself."

The proposal to establish administrative law judges to hear discrimination cases is similar to a 1980 bill adopted by the House that

the Senate filibustered to death. President Carter had termed that measure "the most critical civil rights legislation before the Congress in years."

If anything, the need for an effective enforcement mechanism as increased since then, much as the discrimination complaints have risen from less than 3,000 in 1979. That number is rising, according to Bill West, director of the local Housing Opportunities Corp., because victims are becoming increasingly aware of the law and are encouraged by recent court decisions that are "really putting teeth in the laws, effectively, for the first time."

THE FILINGS are also attributable to help from centers like the three-year-old Housing Opportunities, a private, nonprofit corporation funded largely by city government that does counseling, fair housing investigations and referrals.

If the federal government means what it says in a law that is intolerant of discrimination, then justice shouldn't have to wait until a long pattern of abuses can be documented. Regardless of his political motivations or the other shortcomings of his proposal, Reagan deserves credit for going that far. But he shouldn't expect many kudos for a plan that still seems inadequate to reduce the odious practice of housing discrimination.

Newsday

Long Island, N.Y., July 21, 1983

Criticism of President Reagan's record on civil rights is finally penetrating the White House, it seems, and the administration is responding with a flurry of activity designed to mute it. These efforts, however belated or politically motivated, should be encouraged; at least they show a growing awareness of the extent of black disaffection.

First, Assistant Attorney General William Bradford Reynolds, who has done so

little as head of the Justice Department's civil rights division, took off on a tour of Mississippi with the Rev. Jesse Jackson as his guide. Reynolds found, not surprisingly, that voter discrimination still exists in that state, and he said he would do something about it. Then the Justice Department sued the State of Alabama, charging it with maintaining a segregated university system. And now Reagan says that he'll "put

real teeth" in the Fair Housing Act of 1968.

Teeth it certainly needs, but the administration's proposal would authorize little more than a bicuspid or two.

The biggest complaint against the existing law is that victims of racial discrimination in housing must seek relief in the busy federal courts, where final rulings often aren't made until long after the homes in question are sold or rented. The present law doesn't provide for any penalties, and the Justice Department may intervene only when there's a pattern of discrimination.

Under Reagan's proposal, the attorney general could much more frequently seek civil penalties against landlords, brokers and others involved in discriminatory real estate transactions. But victims of discrimination would still have to go to court on their own to recover monetary damages.

Fortunately for such victims of housing discrimination, a bill sponsored by Sen. Charles Mathias (R-Md.) and Rep. Hamilton Fish (D-N.Y.) offers a way around the glacial pace of the federal courts. It calls for administrative law judges to hear complaints under the Fair Housing Act. It also puts a 90-day limit on the required attempts at conciliation by the Department of Housing and Urban Development.

If the Reagan administration wants to show it's really serious about fighting discrimination in housing, it should get behind the Mathias-Fish bill.

The Oregonian

Portland, Ore., July 20, 1983

The Reagan administration's proposal to change the Fair Housing Act is little more than unadulterated image polishing, aimed at squaring itself with civil rights groups.

In contrast to the Reagan proposal, which would offer Justice Department help in prosecuting housing discriminators in court, a measure before Congress would set up a mediation board to decide disputes at much less cost to the litigants. More important, it could do it in a timely manner before the issue virtually becomes moot, as it often would if dragged though the crowded courts. Those discriminated against usually do not have the luxury of waiting out the clogged court calendar in order to keep their domiciles or find new places where they are welcome.

The civil rights groups, in opposing the administration's plan, say they have no confidence that the Justice Department would aggressively prosecute violators, considering its record in this field. Further, in the South, where most of the cases are to be found, the rights leaders have

pointed out that the practice of making political appointments to the federal district attorney offices has not encouraged belief that these prosecutors will move with much enthusiasm in housing discrimination cases.

Another point that might be raised against the scheme is that Justice has a tendency to seek out big, precedent-setting cases, passing over common cases, which make up the majority of problems in housing discrimination.

In the congressional measure, a special commission would be set up within the Department of Housing and Urban Development. It would have the power of the courts to order solutions to complaints. It could also impose penalties of up to $10,000 and assess compensatory damages.

Probably the best thing that can be said about the administration's proposal is that it has acknowledged that housing discrimination is a major problem and that the government must at least pay some attention to it.

THE LOUISVILLE TIMES

Louisville, Ky., July 18, 1983

Civil rights leaders and members of Congress who see blue smoke and mirrors in the Reagan administration's new "offensive" against housing discrimination are not hallucinating.

The initiative is seriously flawed — long on legal machinations but short on action. Unlike a bipartisan bill now before Congress, it seems unlikely to improve enforcement of the U.S. Fair Housing Act.

It does, however, reflect the administration's general nonchalance on equal opportunity issues. From the moment Mr. Reagan appointed William Bradford Reynolds, a corporate lawyer with no experience in civil rights law, to head that division of the Justice Department, it was clear that priorities were elsewhere.

The weak system now in place for enforcing fair-housing laws reflects the political compromises made to get the housing act passed. Current procedures require those who think they have been discriminated against to file complaints with HUD. Conciliation sessions with those accused of discriminating follow. Such sessions often are delayed or get nowhere. As the process creeps along, disputed property can be sold or rented, rendering the proceedings moot.

Mr. Reagan's approach would require another step beyond conciliation. If HUD determines that the parties are not getting anywhere, it could call in the Justice Department to investigate and, if necessary, prosecute individual complaints. Currently, prosecutions are made only where a pattern of discrimination can be ascertained.

In addition, the President would impose stiff penalties — $50,000 for the first offense and $100,000 for subsequent ones — upon landlords or real estate agents who are found to be discriminating.

While this sounds like a tough approach, it really is not. "Costly, lengthy and inefficient" is the way that the 165-member Leadership Conference on Civil Rights described the proposal in a letter to members of Congress.

For one thing, the 170 civil rights lawyers in the Justice Department already are overburdened. Having them handle housing discrimination cases would be non-productive. A far more effective, and ultimately speedier, system is offered in a bipartisan bill before both houses of Congress.

Conciliation would remain the first step in the process. The bill would assign administrative law judges to HUD who would be responsible for investigating and then adjudicating complaints if conciliation fails. While such rulings could be appealed to the federal courts, they would be far swifter and involve fewer federal officials than Mr. Reagan's plan.

Sen. Charles Mc.C. Mathias, R-Md., a co-sponsor of the housing enforcement measure, would limit the conciliation process to 90 days. A schedule of fines and provisions for compensatory damages would encourage real estate agents and landlords to settle prior to court proceedings.

Such an approach would give the drive against housing discrimination added teeth. Mr. Reagan's, on the other hand, is nothing more than an empty promise unlikely to move the nation closer to the goal of equal opportunity in housing.

The Miami Herald

Miami, Fla., December 1, 1983

SINCE the civil-rights revolution of the 1960s, Americans have repudiated the idea that quality of life decisively is controlled by one's skin color. Still racial discrimination thrives. It's more subtle and more sophisticated today than 20 years ago, but it's no less devastating.

In Dade County, racial discrimination in housing is rampant. The point was demonstrated convincingly in *The Herald's* series "The Isolation of Black Miami." Two *Herald* reporters, one black and the other white, found that renters routinely would reject a black applicant and minutes later accept a white applicant similarly situated.

The findings do not surprise so much as they stunningly lift the veil on racial hypocrisy. Laws against discrimination have been on the books for a generation, but it is the hearts and minds of individuals that must change.

Stronger enforcement of existing laws would help immeasurably toward that end. In the distorted psychology of biased rental managers, opening units to blacks becomes a self-fulfilling prophecy of decline. These managers refuse to accept well-qualified black apartment seekers in the illogic that property values will decline and other renters will turn away. Unflagging persistence in that attitude simply reinforces the notion.

Though anti-discrimination laws have been enacted, they have not been enforced vigorously. The Dade County Fair Housing and Appeals Board since 1969 has been charged with monitoring housing and employment discrimination in Dade. Yet the board wasn't empowered until 1980 to impose fines on those found guilty of discrimination, and it has exercised that power only once.

The board has been hampered severely in its anemic efforts because of a 75 per cent reduction in its budget. That resulted from widespread cuts in Federal funding for social programs. Metro commissioners wisely rejected a recommendation to eliminate the board altogether, relying instead on reports that the board's limited staff performed superlative work.

Commissioners must free the board to do more. Last year, the U.S. Supreme Court validated the use by equal-housing agencies of "testers" similar to *The Herald's* black and white reporting team. Budget cuts crimp the board's ability to conduct such tests, however.

Such testing is essential to build strong cases against those who flout anti-discrimination laws. Rental owners and managers will persist with impunity so long as enforcement of the laws remains lax.

Metro commissioners can put teeth in the laws by restoring the fair-housing board's budget. Only by putting the bite on bigoted rental owners can equality of housing ever be achieved.

The Boston Globe

Boston, Mass., July 15, 1983

Though the Reagan Administration should be praised for finally coming up with a fair-housing proposal, the hurrahs are short-lived when the merits are examined.

The need for a new and stronger measure to replace the 15-year-old fair-housing law is not at issue; how best to strengthen the government's enforcement powers is. Complaints, which have more than doubled in the past three years, can now only be negotiated to settlement by the Department of Housing and Urban Development. That method has worked in only 20 percent of the cases, according to Sen. Charles Mathias.

Mathias, a Republican from Maryland, and Sen. Kennedy have written a stronger fair housing bill, a measure with 40 cosponsors and the support of a civil rights coalition of more than 150 groups. It would allow HUD to refer complaints unresolved by arbitration to administrative judges who could award damages and levy fines. This procedure, also used by the National Labor Relations Board, would bypass an expensive and time-consuming effort in the federal courts.

Instead of supporting the Kennedy-Mathias proposal, the Administration has proposed resolution by referral to the Justice Department, which would then delegate the cases to the appropriate US attorney's office. Though that method would eliminate expensive legal costs for victims, it would put the housing bias cases into the backlogged federal courts in competition with major criminal cases and civil cases.

Even if discrimination suits did not get lost in that competition, by the time the cases proceed through the backlog it would be too late for the person who had faced discrimination to get the sought-after house or apartment.

Under the Mathias-Kennedy system, an administrative judge could hear the case within a week or a month after HUD negotiations failed. A speedy temporary injunction barring a rental or sale would at least preserve the option by those who had faced discrimination of living in the place under question. Administrative judges, who would be appointed by the President, would have housing expertise.

A stronger federal housing discrimination law is critical. Complaints are up nationally. In Boston, 80 percent of all minorities seeking housing face bias unless they limit their search to five neighborhoods or pay luxury rents. The city has approved a strong local fair housing ordinance, but only the state Legislature can provide the enforcement powers. The bill, which was rejected last year, is pending before the Legislature.

Some place to call home is an emotional and basic need. President Reagan deserves praise for efforts to guarantee that all Americans get the same chance at renting or owning a decent place in which to live. But the interests of all would be better served if the Administration supported the Mathias-Kennedy bill and the Senate approved the measure in this session.

THE SUN
Baltimore, Md., May 16, 1983

Senator Charles McC. Mathias has re-introduced the fair-housing bill, a measure that last gained public attention when it suffered death-by-filibuster in 1980. The bill has 37 co-sponsors in the Senate this time, which gets it off to an impressive start. But it faces all the obstacles of 1980, and then some.

For instance, Democrats controlled the Senate the last time this bill was debated. It died because of strong opposition from conservative senators such as Orrin Hatch (R, Utah) and Strom Thurmond (R, S.C.) In the present Congress, those two men chair, respectively, the Judiciary subcommittee on the Constitution and the full Judiciary Committee. These are the panels that must hold hearings and vote on the measure. That, and the fact the Reagan administration has shown no enthusiasm for a fair-housing bill, could make this an uphill battle for the sponsors.

Yet the proposal would not change the substance of civil rights law. It is a procedural measure designed to make the existing law more enforceable. The Mathias-Kennedy bill (named for its two prime sponsors) would establish an administrative hearing process to allow swifter action on complaints of housing discrimination. Administrative law judges would be empowered to impose civil penalties up to $10,000, to award damages, or to issue cease-and-desist orders.

Under the present system, enacted in 1968, the Department of Housing and Urban Development can try to mediate disputes that involve discrimination charges. Or, if the Justice Department finds a pattern of housing discrimination, it can file suit. Or, if an individual has the money, time and determination, he can himself take an individual suspected of housing discrimination to court. But none of these methods has proved satisfactory. In fact, Senator Mathias says the number of discrimination suits filed with HUD has risen from 2,931 in 1979 to 5,112 last year, while the department's success in conciliating those complains remains below 20 percent.

Most of the nation's past housing secretaries have advocated stronger authority to enforce the laws against housing discrimination. We hope the current administration will see the need, too. In addition to promoting fairness, the Mathias bill gives the Reagan administration a chance to refute in a substantive way the frequently leveled charge that it falls short when it comes to enforcing civil rights laws.

The Hartford Courant
Hartford, Conn., July 30, 1983

Housing discrimination will be eliminated not so much by passing new laws but by enforcing laws already on the books.

For 2½ years, the Reagan administration avoided carrying out the full mandate of the federal Fair Housing Act, which prohibits discrimination.

In Connecticut, a lawsuit filed against Glastonbury during the Carter administration was settled out of court by Mr. Reagan's Justice Department. Glastonbury agreed to file reports with the court showing that it is trying to comply with the law.

The administration decided not to appeal a federal court decision dismissing a suit against Manchester — the first housing discrimination case the Justice Department ever lost.

Now, there is a new game plan: Instead of confronting communities that exclude members of minority groups, the administration proposes to help individuals who have experienced discrimination collect damages.

Penalties for violating fair housing laws would be increased to $50,000 for the first offense and $100,000 for subsequent offenses. The Justice Department would be permitted to file charges on behalf of individuals, under the plan.

A far more effective way is for the federal government to pursue communities whose zoning laws, building codes or real estate practices have served as a barrier to persons from minority groups. Having individuals file complaints is costly and cumbersome, and can duplicate state anti-discrimination laws, such as Connecticut's.

The legislation proposed by the Reagan administration would replace a bill that has been supported by civil rights organizations. That bill, sponsored by Sen. Charles McC. Mathias Jr. of Maryland and Rep. Hamilton Fish of New York, both Republicans, would have the Department of Housing and Urban Development hear housing discrimination complaints. Cases would reach HUD administrative judges more quickly than they would the courts.

An administration intent upon eliminating housing discrimination should do more than help individuals file lawsuits against sellers and landlords who discriminate.

Racial prejudice remains embedded in many communities. It can be countered more effectively by withholding federal funds or forcing communities to change discriminatory zoning laws, as Mr. Reagan's predecessors attempted under the Fair Housing Act of 1968. Until the Reagan administration took office, the Justice Department won most of the fair housing suits it brought.

A White House interested in promoting fair housing would continue that 15-year-old crusade.

The Wichita Eagle-Beacon
Wichita, Kans., July 18, 1983

President Reagan sent a strong message to landlords who discriminate last week: Don't. Though some say his proposal to modify the Fair Housing Act is less workable than the Kennedy-Mathias approach under consideration by the Senate, and others question his sincerity, his entry into the issue is significant. A thorough debate is now assured. No other public figure can call attention to injustice as forcefully as a president.

Under Mr. Reagan's plan, the Justice Department would be empowered to sue discriminating landlords who refuse conciliation for up to $50,000 for first offenses, and up to $100,000 for repeat offenses. The present law in effect forces individuals claiming discrimination to fend for themselves by complaining to the U.S. Department of Housing and Urban Development, or to the federal courts. The Reagan plan still would require HUD to investigate complaints and attempt to resolve them by conciliation. But if conciliation failed, HUD would refer the complaints to Justice with a recommendation for court action.

The Kennedy-Mathias approach also emphasizes conciliation, but calls for HUD administrative law judges to hear cases that resist conciliation. The judges could extract penalties of up to $10,000, but their decisions would be subject to federal court review. Critics say this plan would be less time-consuming, but the administration says its plan, because of its stiffer potential penalties, would make conciliation more attractive to landlords accused of discriminating.

It scarely matters which argument is correct. The Congress now has two plans to work with; the bill that emerges well may be a compromise. In the meanwhile, the public's attention is focused on the weaknesses of the act, thanks to the president.

Nor does it matter whether the Reagan plan resulted from a desire to court minority voters, as some critics claim, or from a heartfelt desire to help victims of discrimination. Regardless of what has transpired before, the president now is committed to strengthening the act. Skillful politician that he is, he no doubt is well aware of the consequences of a less-than-enthusiastic effort to see his plan become law.

Fighting housing discrimination is what matters, and Mr. Reagan's proposal can't help but do that.

The Charlotte Observer
Charlotte, N.C., July 12, 1983

Although President Reagan's sudden passion for fair housing inspires some measure of cynicism, it's good to see attention focused on the problem. Even if the president's call for putting "real teeth" into the Fair Housing Act is politically motivated, it may aid congressional efforts to beef up enforcement of the law.

In his Saturday radio address, Mr. Reagan pledged to send Congress amendments to the Fair Housing Act of 1968. "We believe," he said, "in the bold promise that no person in the United States should be denied full freedom of choice in the selection of housing because of race, color, religion, sex or national origin."

Given this administration's record on civil rights enforcement, that rings a bit hollow, particularly considering the timing — just as the Senate prepares to open hearings on his three controversial nominees to the U.S. Civil Rights Commission.

Yet, whatever Mr. Reagan's motives, he may wind up helping members of Congress who've tried unsuccessfully for more than three years to make the law more than a largely empty promise.

The major problem with fair housing enforcement has always been that the law puts the burden on individual victims to press their case. Overworked investigators at the Department of Housing and Urban Development are able to handle only a fraction of the complaints they receive. And only in cases where a company is charged with a "pattern or practice" can HUD ask the Justice Department to investigate.

Although Mr. Reagan has outlined few details of his proposal, he did say it would allow HUD to request such legal action in individual cases of bias. That was precisely the plan pushed by the Carter administration in 1980 against heavy opposition from the housing industry — and defeated by congressional Republicans.

Perhaps the president's support will help win over some of those Republicans. Or perhaps another bill — to divert more bias complaints to state agencies and special administrative law judges — will indirectly benefit from the attention.

Despite the major gains this country has made in eliminating racial bias in employment, education and voting rights, discrimination in housing has been shown time and again to be rampant.

Fifteen years after the Fair Housing Act was passed, it's time to make it work.

Chicago Tribune
Chicago, Ill., March 5, 1983

Although the racial isolation of the suburbs is eroding as housing barriers to blacks crumble, old attitudes and habits die hard.

The pace of black movement to the suburbs has picked up dramatically since the federal Fair Housing Act of 1968 abolished any legal basis for housing discrimination, a ban reinforced by a growing body of court cases and pressure from the federal government.

In practice, few area communities continue to resist integration. Blacks have quietly moved into, scores of predominantly white suburbs without incident and now represent more than 10 percent of the population in 26 suburbs compared with only 14 suburbs 10 years ago. Since 1970, the black population in Chicago suburbs increased by 102,528—a hefty 80 percent.

But statistics tell only part of the story. Much remains to be done in altering old attitudes and fears on the part of black and white alike if the persistent vestiges of housing segregation are to tumble.

Unlike the scattered migration of most white ethnic groups who eventually were assimilated in suburban communities, most black population growth has been clustered in suburbs with long established black neighborhoods. More than 50 percent of all suburban blacks live in eight communities that comprise an expanding suburban "black belt." Working class blacks in particular have sought out communities where they feel safe and accepted—even though few blacks have encountered any serious hostility in their move to white suburbs. Such concentration, however, is quickly resegregating certain suburbs while 177 of the area's 258 suburbs continue to have less than 1 percent black populations.

The fact is that suburban resistance to integration has gradually diminished in the past decade. Fair housing ordinances have been adopted by 57 suburbs, and nearly all others adhere to state and federal housing guidelines. Several communities have successfully stabilized racial change and enhanced property values by vigorously combatting racial steering practices of realtors.

The few holdouts to integration are strongly ethnic blue-collar communities with older populations who resist assimilation and adjustment. The result is absolute opposition to integration, and this is rooted in a determination to preserve an old and isolated way of life.

The prime—and saddest—examples of this are the western suburbs of Cicero and Berwyn. Both have been embroiled in well-publicized discrimination controversies for nearly 30 years, and both now find themselves once again clashing with the federal government over local exclusionary practices.

Cicero has passed up $10 million in federal funds rather than risk having the money used as leverage to force integration and is now being sued by the U. S. Justice Department for discrimination in housing and municipal employment. The U. S. Department of Housing and Urban Development [HUD] recently turned down Berwyn's first request for $1.4 million in federal community development funds because the city wouldn't give adequate assurance it would comply with federal fair housing laws.

Such resistance ultimately will succumb to time, economics and the law. And it is costing both suburbs dearly, in social as well as economic terms with the loss of federal funds to help them cope with crumbling infrastructures and an aging housing stock.

Fair housing in the suburbs is at a crossroads. Whether it's the resegregation of black suburbs or the persistent isolation of ethnic white enclaves, the result is the same. It stifles the diversity that determines the health and vitality of a metropolitan area. Overcoming this demands a commitment from black and white alike. In the final analysis, the depth of their commitments will determine whether their communities prosper or die.

The Orlando Sentinel
Orlando, Fla., July 23, 1983

President Reagan has been called insensitive and even callous regarding civil rights issues, but even his severest critics don't brand him a bigot. Yet in the latest debate over the Fair Housing Act the administration is missing an opportunity to demonstrate its sincerity on civil rights.

The administration and most of Congress agree that the law is grossly inadequate. For example, it is administered by the Department of Housing and Urban Development, which can only investigate and mediate complaints. What is needed are strong deterrents and guarantees that housing complaints will be investigated quickly and that those caught discriminating will pay for their actions.

Such strong powers are proposed in bipartisan House and Senate measures. Both bills would ensure swift investigation of housing complaints by establishing a system of administrative law judges. And both would exact substantial penalties from those who deny others their housing rights.

But rather than back the bills, the administration is pushing for legislation that would be little better than the impotent and inadequate housing law. The administration's proposal would expand the powers of the attorney general, who now can file lawsuits only when he concludes there has been a pattern of discrimination. Under the Reagan plan, he would be able to sue on behalf of individuals. But housing discrimination is so widespread that the attorney general would be swamped with complaints. The White House says there were 5,112 complaints filed last year.

If the administration wants to help its civil rights image it should drop its paltry effort and back the bipartisan moves in Congress. The president can show that he believes the basic right to rent or purchase property is worth protecting.

The Atlanta Journal
THE ATLANTA CONSTITUTION
Atlanta, Ga., July 24, 1983

Freedom of access to housing is engraved in law. The Reagan administration has moved wisely to make fair housing laws enforceable.

More to the point, President Reagan has moved to preempt another fair housing initiative in Congress that sets no spending limits and creates another layer of bureaucracy.

The president's plan would allow the Department of Housing and Urban Development to forward individual cases of discrimination to the Justice Department for prosecution. Tough penalties are spelled out. Such a process leaves plenty of room for negotiation and keeps the law in the hands of professionals.

Under current law, the Justice Department can act only when it has reason to believe there is a pattern of discrimination.

Prosecutors at Justice have not been active in fair housing. Its civil rights division has 59 cases under review. Three have been tried, two are in court and eight have been settled. Housing officials received more than 5,000 discrimination complaints last year.

The Department of Housing and Urban Development receives the brunt of those complaints, but has no power beyond conciliation.

The Reagan plan is far preferable to the one introduced in the House and Senate. It would create a system of administrative law judges to hear complaints. That means to us another permanent layer of government, with a special-interest constituency to protect it.

Americans have a right to action on individual complaints, as opposed to the "pattern or practice" of discrimination required for action under today's law.

The president's plan would reaffirm that right. With civil penalties of up to $50,000 on first offense and $100,000 for subsequent offenses, the bill offers meaningful enforcement.

Minneapolis Star and Tribune
Minneapolis, Minn., July 16, 1983

If President Reagan hoped to improve his administration's civil-rights image by asking Congress for new powers to enforce anti-housing-discrimination laws, he has missed the mark. First, most civil rights groups favor a different approach. Second, while housing discrimination continues to be a national problem deserving congressional attention, racial minorities have a more basic need for jobs and education, without which they cannot hope to gain equal access to the housing market.

In the absence of a competing proposal, Reagan's bill to strengthen federal fair-housing enforcement might have won him some points. The president would have Congress authorize the attorney general to seek an injunction or up to $100,000 in civil penalties in cases where housing discrimination complaints can't be resolved through conciliation.

But there is another bill, broadly supported in Congress yet opposed by the administration, that many consider even stronger. It would create a system of administrative law judges to speed the handling of housing discrimination complaints, something civil rights groups consider essential to effective enforcement. This bill would also prohibit housing discrimination against families with children. The Reagan bill covers only racial minorities and persons with mental or physical handicaps.

Thus Reagan's competing proposal has been greeted not as an example of positive civil-rights leadership but as "gratuitous" interference with the effort already under way to make fair-housing laws more effective. Even some who welcomed the president's interest said he should never have offered a separate bill.

Nor can Reagan's fair-housing initiative erase his administration's negative record on such other civil-rights issues as affirmative action and school desegregation, or offset the disproportionate impact that his economic policies have had on blacks and other racial minorities. Little wonder that a recent Gallup Poll gave Reagan only a 10-percent approval rating among blacks.

Reagan has good reason to be concerned about the impact that a heavy turnout of black voters could have on the 1984 elections. But whether his fair-housing proposal was designed to soften their alienation or was simply a sincere attempt to win stronger enforcement of federal fair-housing laws, he has offered too little too late. His civil rights image, instead of being improved, has only been damaged further.

The Washington Post
Washington, D.C., June 15, 1983

IN A WELCOME announcement, the administration has now said it will address the high-priority civil rights issue of enforcing the 15-year-old law against discrimination in housing sales and rentals. Under that law, complaints are subject to conciliation by the Department of Housing and Urban Development. But if conciliation fails, private individuals must bring their own lawsuits in court to enforce their rights. The Justice Department can sue only violators who engage in a widespread pattern or practice of discrimination.

It has been clear for some time that this enforcement mechanism is ineffective. Congress has in the past considered but not enacted remedial legislation. Last month, Sen. Charles Mathias and 37 cosponsors introduced a bill with the backing of the Leadership Conference on Civil Rights. Now HUD Secretary Pierce has released details of a forthcoming administration bill.

Both proposals provide a new enforcement mechanism for individuals whose rights have been violated. Both would continue to refer cases to state agencies where appropriate. Both look to conciliation as a first step. Under either bill, a plaintiff could apply for a temporary restraining order to prevent the sale or rental of the housing in question during adjudication of the claim. Sen. Mathias proposes civil penalties of up to $10,000 on a first offense; the administration bill allows a $50,000 penalty in such circumstances.

The major difference between the two bills is the method of enforcement. The Mathias bill authorizes administrative law judges to receive complaints and issue orders. Their decisions would be reviewable first by a new Fair Housing Review Commission and eventually by federal courts of appeals. Civil rights groups believe that this kind of specialized administrative enforcement is faster than court suits. The administration disagrees: the bill Secretary Pierce describes would have the Justice Department bring suit in federal court on behalf of individuals when the HUD secretary so recommends. The essential element, though, is in both bills: the burden of enforcement is on the government rather than on the individual victim.

Administration action on fair housing is not only appropriate and right, it is politically smart. No less so is a recent announcement by Assistant Attorney General William Bradford Reynolds that he will tour Mississippi with black leaders to investigate possible violations of the Voting Rights Act. Steps like these counter the widely held belief that this administration has been at best indifferent to civil rights concerns that affect not only minorities but the general perception of American society as just and fair.

THE BLADE
Toledo, Ohio, July 19, 1983

HOUSING discrimination is not the emotionally charged matter it was in the 1960s. Nevertheless, modest improvements in enforcement procedures that President Reagan wants to add to the Fair Housing Act of 1968 appear to be reasonable, especially in light of more cumbersome changes that Senate liberals have in mind.

Mr. Reagan has offered a plan to strengthen enforcement provisions of the 15-year-old law. His legislation would allow the attorney general to seek an injunction or a civil penalty up to $50,000 if an individual can prove he has been discriminated against while trying to buy or rent property.

The Justice Department now can prosecute complaints only where there is evidence of widespread and systematic discrimination. When it enacted the law Congress did not provide administrative remedies for Americans who faced isolated housing problems. They had to file suits through the federal courts, a time-consuming and expensive process.

The liberal alternative, offered by Sens. Edward Kennedy and Charles Mathias, Republican of Maryland, justifiably has provoked William Bradford Reynolds, assistant U.S. attorney general for civil rights, to label it "a whole new layer of bureaucracy."

The Kennedy-Mathias bill would create a system of administrative judges within the Department of Housing and Urban Development. One can imagine how many more expensive patronage jobs would be created.

Segregated housing remains in most large cities, but it is not the all-pervasive problem it was a decade or so ago. Still, if the Administration can demonstrate that substantial numbers of Americans every year are denied relief because of the current law's limitations, then Mr. Reagan's proposal should become law.

The Dispatch

Columbus, Ohio, May 20, 1983

A RECENT survey of major American cities found that Columbus is among the least segregated in the nation.

The survey was conducted by the Washington-based Citizens' Committee on Civil Rights and focused on cities with black populations in excess of 100,000 people. The 1980 census puts Columbus' total population at 565,000 people, 124,000 of whom are black. The survey looked at block-by-block racial integation and an indexing system was used to rank cities. Zero would indicate total integration and 100 would indicate total segregation.

Columbus was given a ranking of 75, down from 86 in 1970. This city's present ranking ties it with New York City. Chicago had the highest ranking of 92; Cleveland was next with 91. Cincinnati had a 79, while Oakland, Calif., had the lowest rating — 59.

What do these numbers tell us about Columbus? They tell us, as City Development Director Ralph Smithers notes, that the city has made impressive strides during the last 10 years. They tell us that further improvement can be anticipated in the years ahead.

The numbers tell us, too, that there is a greater racial mix in this city than in most others in the nation, and where there is a healthy mix of housing opportunities, a healthy mix of educational, social and economic opportunities will also be available.

This is what is making Columbus great. Total integration — based on criteria established by the Citizens' Committee on Civil Rights or any other organization — should not be the city's goal, per se. What this community should continue to strive for is a climate in which any person, regardless of race, has the opportunity to live and work where he or she desires. If economic opportunities based on talent and ability are available, the monetary barriers that sometimes impede housing choice will tumble. Individuals and families will have the resources to change housing locations or to renovate existing residences, as is already the case in several sections of the city.

The national survey of housing patterns contains much to make all citizens of Columbus feel good about the city, and it suggests further progress. That progress should be encouraged.

Richmond Times-Dispatch

Richmond, Va., December 9, 1983

"If we were busing little kids, it would be a lot simpler," moaned an official of the Clarksville (Texas) Housing Authority. "But these are elderly people we're shuffling around. A lot of them are sick or disabled."

Busing "little kids" is old hat to federal judges who single-mindedly pursue racial quotas without regard to what this does to such values as parental freedom, a sense of community and support for public education. But in Clarksville, a federal judge with an ironic surname — William Wayne Justice — has carried this extreme tactic to perhaps its ultimate absurdity. He's ordering whole households to pack up and move, to swap apartments, and to do it pronto, by Dec. 15. In effect, he's busing (or trucking or whatever) entire families crosstown in the name of public-housing integration.

Even a commissar in Soviet Russia might shrink from uprooting families so abruptly from their homes.

Judge Justice's ukase results from his finding that Clarksville's two public housing projects are segregated. Thus, 25 black and 25 white families, chosen by lottery, must exchange residences so that the racial percentages of the two federally financed projects will please the eye of the court. People on both sides of this swap are upset. On 20 days' notice, they must give up neighbors and familiar surroundings. Some also face a net loss of rooms — for example, the woman who is being forced to move with her three children from a three-bedroom apartment to a one-bedroom one.

To a well-paid jurist with a lifetime job, complaints of low-income persons who will be giving up such things as a little rose garden or a place to pen animals no doubt seem like trifles. We wonder, though, how His Honor would like it if some authority decided that since he is paid out of the federal trough, he must immediately box his belongings and trade houses with another family — and just 10 days before Christmas at that!

There has been no official policy to keep the projects segregated, according to a local housing commissioner. Instead, "We just let people live where they wanted to live." That seems fair enough, given human nature. But if Judge Justice deemed that live-and-let-live violates federal law, he could have at least applied any racial criteria to future applicants for housing, rather than uprooting and upsetting so many families.

Justice in this case was not tempered by mercy. This ultimate extension of the busing doctrine is devoid of both common sense and compassion. But don't bet the family heirlooms against its becoming the latest rage in constitutional interpretation by the same judges who imposed busing on public schools while sending their own children to exclusive private schools.

THE PLAIN DEALER

Cleveland, Ohio, May 17, 1983

As if anyone needed to be told, there now is some kind of official confirmation of how segregated a city Cleveland actually is. According to the Citizens Commission on Civil Rights, Cleveland is the second most segregated large city in the nation, ranking only behind Chicago. A surprise? Not really, particularly to anyone familiar with the city's history. Before 1970 there had been deeply entrenched patterns of housing segregation in Cleveland, patterns that aren't likely to change in the years ahead without a conscious effort being undertaken to do so. But the conclusions of the study needn't be as discouraging as they might appear.

Research by the Cuyahoga Plan and other housing studies have shown that Cleveland's housing patterns do not reflect the positive changes that are occurring elsewhere in the county. In the past decade there has been an increase in the amount of racial diversity in the county. So, when looking at the metropolitan area as a whole, one can see favorable changes in housing patterns, particularly in the eastern suburbs.

But there are numerous factors contributing to this lack of change in housing patterns. The total population of the city has declined over the past decade. As a result, many of the residents who have remained are elderly and poor, those less likely to have the capability of exercising mobility in terms of making housing choices.

Public housing, too, has a been a contributor to the city's lack of racial diversity. Neither local nor federal government has made much progress toward providing new housing that would act to decrease housing segregation. In the 1970s, very little public housing for families was constructed on the West Side, while most such housing for families has remained on the East Side.

And what about education? Studies have shown that cities which experienced school desegregation have also witnessed some positive changes in housing patterns. But school desegregation in Cleveland did not occur until 1979, too late to have had any significance on data compiled in 1980 on which the Citizens Commission report was based.

Since 1980, however, there has been a greater emphasis placed on the importance of residential racial diversity in Cleveland, but its effects are difficult to measure. Many younger people are beginning to take another look at the city as an attractive place to live. Though statistically any inward migration may be presently insignificant, much of the city's future growth and housing changes will come from people desiring a move back into Cleveland from the suburbs. Such a desire was not present a decade ago.

Another encouraging aspect is the city's relatively good supply of lower-cost housing, particularly on the West Side. Though the housing market in Cleveland has been somewhat ignored in recent years, persons desiring to buy moderate-priced housing in the $30,000, $40,000 and $50,000 range can get much more for their money in the city than in any of the suburbs.

If city services and schools continue improving in the next few years, the interest and desire of more people to relocate in Cleveland will intensify. That provides reasons to believe that Cleveland will be a more racially diversified city in the future than it has been in the past.

THE MILWAUKEE JOURNAL
Milwaukee, Wisc., February 25, 1984

Racial integration is a desirable goal, but we have serious questions about a new plan to integrate Milwaukee's 4,625 public housing units for families and the elderly. The plan could result in numerous vacancies in many of the city's public housing projects while hundreds of eligible people remain on waiting lists — hardly a desirable situation from either a humanitarian or economic point of view.

Under the new compliance agreement between the Milwaukee Housing Authority and the US Department of Housing and Urban Development, people who qualify for public housing will not be placed in housing where their own race predominates until all the projects where the *opposite* race predominates are filled.

The agreement might work quite well if there were similar numbers of blacks and whites in the projects and on the waiting lists. However, that is not the case. To see how the agreement is likely to work, look at the statistics.

First, the 2,500 units for the elderly: They are occupied primarily by whites and the waiting list of 289 names includes 274 whites and only 15 blacks and other non-whites. Currently, there are 93 vacant units in four predominantly black projects — Highland Park, Hillside Terrace, Lapham Park and Cherry Court, all on the North Side. According to this new plan, those 93 units would have to be filled by whites *before* any whites would be offered any of the 96 vacancies in the 10 other elderly projects that are primarily white. Meanwhile, the 15 non-whites on the list could choose any of the 96 vacancies in the 10 primarily white projects.

Second, the 2,000 units for families: They are filled predominantly by blacks and the waiting list of 527 families includes 469 black and other non-white families and only 58 white families. Currently, blacks predominate in all five family housing projects and there are 58 vacancies in various sized units. Only after white families filled all the vacancies of a particular size and there were no white families on the list for that size, could a black family be offered a unit.

So much for the statistics. Now, consider a basic inequity. Black families who have been on waiting lists for years would not be offered housing, while white families would have a chance to move into public housing units almost immediately. Conversely, elderly whites would not be able to move into public housing until black elderly moved into all-white units.

In either case, will people accept the housing they are offered? We suspect many will not — and in the case of the elderly, we seriously question the desirability of forcing them to move from the neighborhood that has been their home, their informal support system.

HUD and the Housing Authority should go back to the drawing board. The focus of this compliance agreement is too narrow. Some of the public housing projects may be next to impossible to integrate without perverse side effect. Thus, rather than concentrate on public housing projects, housing officials should strive for a better way to racially integrate all kinds of federally subsidized housing in the city and, if possible, the metropolitan area. Then federal officials should be asked to consider the totality of the Milwaukee effort.

Los Angeles Times
Los Angeles, Calif., July 15, 1984

In a more perfect world William Bradford Reynolds, chief of the Justice Department's civil rights division, could correctly insist that "the natural consequences of peoples' choice of housing is not something the federal government ought" to regulate.

But discrimination denies too many Americans the housing of their choice. Without strong government regulation, the consequences of discrimination, rather than the natural consequences of choice, often result in neighborhoods that might as well have signs proclaiming For Whites Only.

The Fair Housing Act has prohibited discrimination in the rental or sale of housing since 1968. Yet 85% of black renters could encounter bias. Those in the market to buy a home have a 48% chance of experiencing discrimination, according to a 1978 Housing and Urban Development study.

Because of these persistent patterns, the Fair Housing Act needs tougher enforcement powers. Several such measures have been introduced during the past decade, with more success in the House than in the Senate. A bill that is pending, sponsored by Sens. Edward M. Kennedy (D-Mass.) and Charles McC. Mathias Jr. (R-Md.), would allow administrative judges to review complaints quickly—while the apartment or house was still available—and avoid the expense and delay of federal court.

Instead of backing that bill, the Reagan Administration would refer unresolved complaints to the Justice Department for prosecution in the backlogged federal courts. That tedious process would discourage many.

Although the Justice Department challenged alleged housing bias in Massachusetts, New Hampshire, Rhode Island and Delaware last month and in Illinois in April, only 17 suits have been filed since Ronald Reagan took office three years ago.

An average of 30 suits were filed per year during the Carter Administration.

Reynolds has zealously led the Reagan Administration's history-blind opposition to standard civil-rights remedies designed to address injustice—such as affirmative-action quotas, busing to achieve desegregation and construction contracts known as set-asides—specifically reserved for minorities. Last month he urged wide application of a narrow U.S. Supreme Court ruling that put seniority above racial considerations in layoffs.

His remarks have disturbed many, including some black Republicans. His policies "have been just about 100% wrong and despicable," William T. Coleman Jr. told the New York Times. "I don't think his positions are consistent with the law, with Republican Party philosophy or with the long-range interests of the country. It would be good if Mr. Reynolds were replaced."

Coleman, a highly respected corporate attorney and a Ford Administration Cabinet member, knows at first hand of Reynolds' misinterpretations of the law. Two years ago the Supreme Court, in an unusual but necessary step, appointed Coleman to defend a position abandoned by the Reagan Administration. The case involved federal tax exemptions for private schools that discriminate. In lower courts the government had argued that the Internal Revenue Code allowed the denial of tax-exempt status. The Reagan Justice Department changed that stance and lost to Coleman before the Supreme Court.

The majority of Americans want a colorblind society. Strong enforcement of tough laws can make that a reality. Until then, the civil-rights chief at the Justice Department should articulate an intolerance of wrongs and zealously enforce the laws that address those inequities rather than sanction the results of injustice.

The Miami Herald
Miami, Fla., March 24, 1984

THE SYMBOLS of bigotry used to be on open display. "Colored" and "White" signs adorned public edifices everywhere. The symbols fell, though, in the 1960s' social revolution, by order of Congress and the courts.

The symbols of bigotry today are invisible. They reside within the hearts and minds of men. They cannot so easily be felled by legal and judicial proclamation. But society must try. It must rid itself of the covert manifestations of bigotry in public accommodations as effectively as it eliminated racism's overt symbols.

The new program of Metro's Fair Housing and Employment Appeals Board to use "testers" to uncover discrimination in housing is a laudable, serious attempt to do just that. The board sends "testers" — some black, some white — to housing complexes to determine if there is evidence of racial bias. If bias is apparent, the board files a discrimination complaint. Proprietors stand to suffer fines and penalties and, worse, the public indignation following revelation of their unlawful practices.

This is the board's first use of "testers," a fact that says two things. It speaks to the widely held assumption, erroneous perhaps, that changing laws alone is sufficient to guarantee equal rights. It also attests to the difficulty that the board encounters as it competes with all other agencies seeking county budget funds. Dade no longer can afford laxity on either count.

Willful racial discrimination in housing exacts a heavy toll. It diminishes the quality of life for blacks, fosters cynicism, encourages racial intolerance, and perpetuates isolation — all problems that Greater Miami can do without.

The board's testers have begun modestly enough, by visiting housing locations from whence have come discrimination complaints. The effort is likely to remain modest, for there never will be enough "testers" to visit every housing rental or sales office in the county.

But the fact that selected units are tested and will continue to be examined puts everyone on notice to re-examine housing practices and ensure that bias is eradicated. Kudos to the housing-appeals board and to Metro commissioners for supporting the board's request for $75,000 in Federal funding assistance. It is a worthy project for a deserving cause.

Discrimination, whether overt or covert, is anathema to an open, pluralistic society. It must be fought on every front.

Part III: Civil Rights

Civil Rights Record of the Reagan Administration

President Reagan is constantly defending his record on civil rights against attacks from advocacy groups, members of Congress, political opponents and members of his own Administration. The attacks are in essence outraged objections to the implementation of a civil rights policy that differs fundamentally from those of previous administrations, both Democratic and Republican. In a 1981 speech to the NAACP, Reagan urged black leaders to look to "new ways of thinking" to achieve long-sought goals, saying that reliance on federal programs for assistance had created "a new kind of bondage" for blacks. Economic revitalization, he declared, was the best route to "black economic freedom, because it is aimed at lifting the entire country and not just parts of it." Acknowledging in July, 1983 that there was widespread public discontent with his Administration's civil rights policies, Reagan attributed this to a false "perception" of the record.

The criticism of that record ranges from accusations that the Reagan Administration has chronically underfunded and poorly staffed key enforcement agencies such as the U.S. Civil Rights Commission, the Equal Employment Opportunity Commission and the Justice Department's civil rights division, to charges of simple racism. Much of the disagreement centers around the Administration's stated opposition both to school busing as a method of desegregation, and to the use of quotas to enforce equal employment laws. Other complaints involve a diminished government role in enforcing fair housing laws, a drop in the number of high-level minority appointees in the Administration, a reduction in federal funding for the Legal Services Corp., and the dismissal of members of the Civil Rights Commission who disagreed with these actions or inactions. Certainly damaging politically was the Administration's failure to enthusiastically support extension of the Voting Rights Act in 1982, and what was widely interpreted as its support for racially discriminatory schools when it supported the granting of tax-exempt status to segregationist Bob Jones University.

When asked in 1981 if the Department of Justice in the Reagan Administration remained committed to the "general goals of affirmative action," Attorney General William French Smith replied: "What we're committed to is to eliminate segregation, and to provide equal rights for all citizens, and we intend to do what is necessary to accomplish that result." The carefully worded response indicates a radical change in thinking, a return to the early goals of the civil rights movement, before preferential treatment for minorities had become the norm. (See pp. 136-147.) As Thomas Sowell writes in his 1984 book, *Civil Rights: Rhetoric or Reality?*: "'Equal opportunity' laws and policies require that individuals be judged on their qualifications as individuals, without regard to race, sex, age, etc. 'Affirmative action' requires that they be judged with regard to such group membership, receiving preferential or compensatory treatment in some cases to achieve a more proportional 'representation' in various institutions and occupations." Sowell goes on to argue that the disadvantaged members of each minority group that affirmative action programs (as opposed to equal opportunity policies) are meant to help are precisely those who suffer the most from their implementation. The other side of this basic argument, that it is naive to assume that a policy of equal opportunity will be effective, is provided by John E. Jacob, president of the National Urban League, in the League's 1984 "State of Black America" report: "If this were truly a color blind and racially neutral society, and there were parity in the distribution of society's rewards and responsibilities, the [Reagan] Administration's approach would be reasonable. However, we are still afflicted by a racial spoils system that favors white males and excludes blacks, other minorities and women. We face not only the results of historic discrimination, but the effects of continuing discrimination...the Administration has sought to turn back the clock."

It would take a book in itself to explore the changes wrought in civil rights enforcement by the Reagan Administration, the reasons given for those changes, and their likely ramifications. The editorials reprinted in the following pages provide a lively debate on the cumulative effect of the Reagan Administration's most controversial civil rights policies, many of which are discussed individually in other sections of this book.

The Chattanooga Times

Chattanooga, Tenn., July 3, 1981

President Reagan got a mixed reception when he addressed the annual convention of the National Association for the Advancement of Colored People in Denver on Monday. The delegates weren't wildly enthusiastic, but they weren't hostile either. And the president's speech was a good one. He defended his policies vigorously, and came down hard on issues important to all people, especially blacks: racism, the Atlanta killings and the burden imposed by inflation and other economic woes. But the blacks, for good reason, are fearful that Mr. Reagan's domestic policies will impose a disproportionate burden on them, and may even erase some of the gains they've made over the past two decades.

Mr. Reagan's problem is that there is little he can do at this point, beyond making assurances, to persuade blacks that they have little to fear. The president has pushed through Congress budget cuts exceeding $40 billion, and come October, when the new fiscal year begins, the impact of those reductions will be starkly evident. Moreover, blacks still don't have a clear idea of the administration's civil rights policies; it has not, for instance, taken a stand on whether to support extension of the Voting Rights Act, portions of which expire next year.

Some of the blacks' concern is overstated. Mr. Reagan is correct in arguing that many government programs designed to help blacks have done the opposite by locking them even tighter into dependent status. Indeed, one valid criticism of liberals supporting such programs from the 1960s has been that they seemed unable to recognize that many of those efforts were abysmal failures. Moreover, there is merit in the president's argument that the stronger the economy, the better off all will be — including blacks.

But having said that, the fact remains that those arguments hardly justify the wholesale destruction of those programs, which is precisely the source of the blacks' apprehension about the Reagan efforts. And that apprehension is not relieved by Cabinet secretaries' pledges to come up with alternatives to achieving goals important to blacks (and other minority groups as well). Mr. Reagan used the line, attributed to President Kennedy, that "a rising tide lifts all boats" — meaning that as the economy improves, the fortunes of all, including blacks, will get better. The issue, of course, is how people dependent on the programs targeted for cutbacks will do while they wait for the tide.

The standard reply, as best we understand it, is that the Reagan administration apparently wants to replace the old way of doing things with what amounts to a new domestic economic order. In that way, so the scenario goes, blacks will be truly integrated into a better society that promises more and better jobs, higher pay, a better standard of living and all the rest. Maybe so. But the program, in effect, is asking blacks for a giant "leap of faith" in economic theories that have created doubt even among some white Republican conservatives.

What if it fails? If it does, Mr. Reagan will be criticized, the Republican Party will suffer at the polls and the middle and upper classes in this country will have to adjust to the consequences. But those risks pale in comparison to what poor people stand to lose if it turns out that all those neat economic theories are just that. That possibility, it seems to us, is exactly the reason why Mr. Reagan must offer the blacks something more tangible than he has so far if he expects their allegiance. We don't doubt for a minute that Mr. Reagan is totally committed to racial justice, and to improving the conditions in which too many blacks find themselves today despite all the federal programs from previous years. But the administration seems to be reversing the old John Mitchell line of "watch what we do, not what we say." That's not enough.

Detroit Free Press

Detroit, Mich., July 1, 1981

IF THE Reagan administration's economic program is indeed "a rising tide (that) lifts all boats," as the president said to a skeptical black audience Monday, then there will be time enough for applause.

To the members of the National Association for the Advancement of Colored People and to many of the rest of us, there is reason for skepticism about the prospect that rising general prosperity will take care of those who have lived on this society's crumbs. The black population represented in the NAACP turned to federal power not because of an innate love of central authority or of statism, but because the benefits simply had not trickled down.

And while it is certainly true, and fundamentally important, that inflation is a cruel tax, above all, on the poor, and it is true that the current unemployment falls hardest on the poor and the black, there is not much basis for faith that the supply-side economics will indeed lift the boats of America's blacks. There is, moreover, strong reason for believing that there is enough racism built into the American system that the problems of the black poor still do require both special federal authority and special support mechanisms.

The Voting Rights Act extension, which Mr. Reagan opposes in its present form, is but one example of what we see as a continuing special need. The Voting Rights Act is a piece of legislation that has worked; in those states where the right to vote was subject to historic tampering, it opened up the political process to blacks and chicanos. Is it no longer needed in its present form? Mr. Reagan asks us to take it on faith that it isn't. But blacks know one Reconstruction era ended in a tawdry sellout. Should they now accept another?

Beyond the straightforward matter of voting rights, there is the question of how to make urban school systems respond to the special needs of historically deprived people. Is federal support for remedial education a misuse of federal power or a welfare program? It is not, but it is being systematically dismembered.

Are the federal job training programs, the benefits for the working poor that are being hacked out of the federal budget now really a prescription for everlasting dependency? That was Mr. Reagan's message. But there is good reason to believe that the Reagan budget cuts will in fact in many instances perpetuate people on full dependence rather than providing them a gradual way out of that trap.

The fact that many specific programs have gotten in the way of general economic prosperity is a matter of serious concern. The case for moving quickly to a balanced budget, for cutting federal spending, for bringing some programs under control is undeniable.

What is debatable, and we think wrong, is the wholesale abandonment of important programs that have been working to break up much of the pattern of discrimination. Can industry really take up the slack for the least skilled members of society? In fact, the auto industry, for only one example, is moving out of its set of imperatives, to eliminate jobs for the long run, not to create them. The robotization of industry is needed to make the industry more competitive.

Mr. Reagan undoubtedly believes he can change the economy sufficiently to bring about the rising tide of which he speaks. Perhaps he can, for most of those who have not suffered the deprivations of poor education, poor childhood nutrition, the flight of industry and business from inner cities and from the so-called Frostbelt. But for many, those objective limitations continue locked in place. They have heard promises before, including promises of how the engine of private initiative could be made to work for them.

They, surely, can be forgiven for doubting the president's assurances. They know that too many times in American history, the rising tide has passed them by, or worse still, left them drowning in its backwash. The time may come when they will applaud the rising of the tide. But not now. Not on the basis of promises.

THE WALL STREET JOURNAL.

New York, N.Y., July 1, 1981

"Government is no longer the strong draft horse of minority progress," President Reagan told the NAACP in a major address Monday. "I ask you if it is not time to hitch up a fresh horse to finish the task." In one sense it was the least surprising of lines: Mr. Reagan has never given people the slightest reason to think he believed anything different. In another sense it was startling; it has been 20 years since it was thought politically possible for a President to stand before black listeners and not promise them major aid from the federal government. We are hearing a new language on the issue of race, and maybe a language with staying power.

From the time of the 1980 presidential campaign, various opponents have been trying to tag Mr. Reagan and his brand of conservatism with the label of racism or racial insensitivity. During the campaign the Democrats made a fairly frontal attack against candidate Reagan himself; it didn't work. Since the election, the argument has been different. The administration can't cut the social budget or the affirmative action machine or the apparatus of federal racial regulation, so the case goes, or it will be acquiescing in a national return to racial discrimination.

Just last week, for instance, the U.S. Commission on Civil Rights issued a lengthy statement on the Reagan budget. The report asserts that our present system of enforcement, social programs and categorical grants—the whole conglomeration—is the way we fulfill the constitutional promise of civil rights for all Americans. But there is "grave danger" that the drive to "balance the budget, cut taxes and expand the defenses of the nation" will harm the federal "responsibility to preserve, protect and defend" those rights.

In short, if you begin to hack away at some of these encrustations you not only harm minorities but hit at their constitutional rights; you are attacking the system's basic notions of fairness when you take the ax to CETA.

The same kinds of arguments and associations have already begun to plague public discussion of the voting rights act extension bill, which promises to be the first big civil rights debate of the Reagan administration. The current act, provisions of which will expire next year unless extended, not only guarantees the right to vote across the country but forces some areas with a history of discrimination to clear with the Justice Department any changes they may want to make in election laws and practices.

There have been some practical problems with the law as it stands: The Justice Department has too often spent its enforcement efforts not on protecting the all-important act of voting but on trying to set up local political arrangements that will get desired numbers of minority politicians elected to office. There are political problems with the act as well: Southern officials do not like to have to submit their election decisions for approval when most of the rest of the country does not. And the liberals and Democrats now trying to extend the act's supervisory powers for 10 more years are also trying to put in new "results-oriented" language that would only make these present difficulties worse.

Enforcement of the act should become more sensible. It would also be nice if in the extension process we could work out some less offensive form of supervision: The worst of the abuses that prompted the 1965 act are largely gone, voting bars are no longer the most significant block to minority progress, and you'd think it would be possible to take some public account of those facts.

It's not likely, though, that such temperateness is going to mark the debate. Instead, any attempt to ease up is going to be called a retreat from the most important promise the federal government has ever made to minority Americans. Because voting is indeed the central political right of a democracy, the charge is explosive—so much so that the administration might be well advised not to take it on. The worst problems can be corrected administratively, so that extension of the act becomes mostly a symbolic issue—"stigma" to the South vs. "retreat" on civil rights. A familiar debate and not an edifying one.

That is why it is something that Mr. Reagan's speech made a start at changing the categories. He asserted to the NAACP a hatred of racial discrimination; he said every bit as plainly that minority progress will now depend not mainly on often-failed special federal programs but on the progress of the economy as a whole. If over time his perception begins to sink in in more and more places, the change will be perhaps the most important contribution the President can have made to lifting us out of a decade of sterility in our discussion of minority welfare.

St. Petersburg Times

St. Petersburg, Fla., September 15, 1982

President Reagan's civil rights problem is how to appear to uphold the nation's ideals without alienating his own constituency. He has tried to manage it during the first two years of his presidency by denouncing racial discrimination while dismantling the machinery to do anything about it.

At best, that strategy can succeed for only a short time, and clearly it now is catching up with Mr. Reagan. Until recent months, charges that the administration was backing off civil rights issues seemed to have little impact on the public. Few people listened, for instance, last December when outgoing National Urban League President Vernon Jordan summed up his views: "The (decade of the) 1960s was about correcting a process that for so many years had been wrong, and that commitment was made by the nation. I see this administration encouraging the nation to renege on that commitment."

The President, torn between the ideals of his office and the fears of his hard-rock supporters, speaks one way and acts another on civil rights.

THIS WEEK the chairmen of 33 state agencies affiliated with the U.S. Civil Rights Commission said about the same. In a letter to the President, they wrote about the "dangerous deterioration" of civil rights enforcement and they criticized "the present dismantling of civil rights agencies." They also asked for a meeting with the President to discuss their concerns. A member of the White House staff responded that the President didn't have time for such a meeting. Clearly the President could only lose more at any meeting, so he was cutting his losses. But in race relations, failure to communicate usually is the first phase of trouble.

As if to add an exclamation point to that incident, the President's appointee to head the U.S. Civil Rights Commission, Clarence M. Pendleton Jr., described affirmative action as a "bankrupt policy." Minorities should not depend on "neo-reparations," which he said was government funding that does not produce goods or services. Instead, minorities should try new ideas, such as a sub-minimum wage for teen-agers and other forms of lower wages. What is left to suggest but a return to slavery?

In the usual political doubletalk, White House spokesman Larry Speakes denied any dismantling of civil rights programs. "The President has made it clear on many occasions that he will not permit a civil rights rollback, and he is proud of his record." Speakes said the administration's civil rights record was "stronger than any previous administration."

They are empty words when compared to the record. The administration has weakened the Civil Rights Commission, firing the distinguished Arthur S. Flemming and replacing him with Pendleton. The Justice Department no longer pushes school desegregation. The President waffled on renewal of the Voting Rights Act, seeking to weaken it until he saw he was about to suffer an embarrassing defeat. The administration granted tax-exempt status to private schools that discriminate against blacks, then asked Congress to outlaw such exemptions even though the law already prohibits them. The President's economic policies have hurt minorities, among whom unemployment is at record highs.

NONE OF THIS should have been a surprise. Mr. Reagan's performance on civil rights issues is like it was as governor of California. He is very much a product of his own time and place. Bill Boyarsky, Mr. Reagan's biographer, pointed out that the President enthusiastically accepts the values of the Midwest in the 1920s with his respect for all business and his mistrust of change. Mr. Reagan believes as he has quoted his father that "All men are created equal and (that) man's ambition determines what happens to him the rest of his life." Mr. Reagan opposed the landmark civil rights legislation of the 1960s on constitutional grounds. As governor he tried unsuccessfully to weaken California's open housing law. Mr. Reagan's election in 1980 at least in part represented a public reaction to the civil rights gains of the decades before.

So the President, torn between the ideals of his office and the fears of his hard-rock supporters, speaks one way and acts another. Many Americans will cheer that. But others, especially those who know that the promise of equal opportunity still is only a promise for many black Americans, will continue to hope.

THE SUN

Baltimore, Md., July 1, 1981

If warm hugs were all, President Reagan would be in solid with the National Association for the Advancement of Colored People. NAACP Chairman Margaret Bush Wilson, however, did not let Mr. Reagan's goodhearted embrace after his speech at the organization's Denver gathering blur her vision. She pointedly expressed the NAACP's deep-seated concerns about the adverse impact of Mr. Reagan's economic strategy and conservative social ideology on minorities.

The president's presence at this year's NAACP convention, with his wife Nancy, was a genuine gesture to repair the damage caused by his refusal to attend last year's meeting. Despite profound differences with the president, the NAACP, a 72-year veteran of political and civil rights battles, respects Mr. Reagan for the office he holds. It would have required excessive provocation, not typical of Mr. Reagan, for the organization to have been less than cordial in Denver. But the delegates who were prepared to listen to him politely, expect the president to give fair consideration to their concerns. As Mrs. Wilson said, "This is the beginning of a dialogue. We shall overcome."

The NAACP does not quarrel with Mr. Reagan's economic and social goals as much as with his methodology. On economics, for example, both Mr. Reagan and the NAACP are devout advocates of a growth-oriented economy and strongly support a bigger role for the private sector in creating jobs for everyone willing and able to work. Both have an equally strong distaste for welfare and other government handouts.

The NAACP, however, is concerned that the poor will bear the brunt of the Reagan budget cuts. As NAACP Executive Director Benjamin L. Hooks explained in Denver, the real problem will occur after domestic programs have been curtailed or eliminated —but the economic revival expected by the White House is not yet in place. What will happen to people who depend on food stamps, welfare and federally subsidized jobs during that period?

The NAACP has a point. The administration has failed to soften its economic game plan with some human soul. Compassion is lacking from the administration's budgeting approach. Mr. Reagan could find himself in hot water not only with the NAACP, but with a growing number of Americans if he does not rectify this situation soon.

THE LINCOLN STAR

Lincoln, Neb., July 1, 1981

America's poor have been held in bondage by government social programs, President Reagan said in Denver Monday, and they will be liberated by private enterprise.

His audience, the annual convention of the National Association for the Advancement of Colored People, was skeptical — and who could blame them? What in American experience suggests that poor blacks and other racial minorities can — if there are not fundamental changes in majority attitudes — ride the free enterprise system to economic independence and prosperity?

To benefit from the system you have to be part of the system, and those efforts undertaken in recent years to bring blacks and others into the system are part and parcel of the kind of social engineering that drives Reaganites crazy with resentment. Affirmative action, busing and other means to integrate schools to bring about equal opportunities in education, job training, minority loan programs, and so forth are the kinds of programs designed to give the disadvantaged the entry into the system denied them for so long. And this kind of government "interference" in private lives is as much hated by Reagan's philosophic brethren as the maintenance programs the president says has held the poor in bondage.

Those now in power would not only strip down the assistance programs — food stamps, unemployment, etc. — but would like to lay to rest all the other devices formulated to assure equality of opportunity — the opportunity to benefit from "free" enterprise.

The NAACP delegates were polite to the president, which was appropriate but perhaps difficult under the circumstances. He had just announced that the government ship was sinking and he was putting the poor out to sea in leaky lifeboats.

The Kansas City Times

Kansas City, Mo., September 21, 1982

Like fog at dawn, the devaluation of civil rights and equal opportunity is rolling across America.

The administration says the right words. But a pattern of actions contradicts them: Reversing Internal Revenue Service policy denying tax exemptions to racially discriminatory schools, then scrambling for legislation similar to the old IRS rule. Aloofness from the Voting Rights Act debate. Opposing busing for integration without offering alternative remedies. Recommending budget cuts for civil rights enforcement at major national agencies. Shaky appointments to commissions that monitor the nation's civil rights activities. A presidential announcement that the Great Society (including Head Start?) actually *harmed* minority children.

Periodically protests are made by organizations, predictably met by denial of retreat and presentation of this or that set of figures in rebuttal. An individual speaks out. But the lone voice and the group complaint are too soon and too easily washed away under powerful declarations from the office of the president. It's backed by the tide of conservative colleagues with other agendas and the pressure from avowed foes of equality for all citizens, regardless of race, sex or faith.

The country is getting used to seeing civil rights as a dispensable cause. Consider that it causes hardly a ripple when the head of the U.S. Commission on Civil Rights publicly disparages the concept of affirmative action. The long-sought remedy for exclusion from jobs and institutions, having finally gained recognition by the public and the blessing of the courts, according to Clarence M. Pendleton Jr., should be abandoned.

"Affirmative action is a bankrupt policy. We've used it up," he said, adding that "the door (to equality) is already open." Mr. Pendleton has some interesting ideas as to how those discriminated against can join the mainstream of the economy. Try new approaches, he suggests. A sub-minimum wage for teenagers. More wage concessions by employees.

It's hard to tell what wonderland Mr. Pendleton lives in. From his perception of how settled the issue of discrimination is, it's not the same streets most of us walk on. Doors like that don't stay open by themselves. The meek who relinquish rights might be rewarded hereafter but in this world, they usually get stepped on.

Unfortunately, he is doing his bit to shroud the face of civil rights as an issue.

Des Moines Tribune

Des Moines, Iowa, January 22, 1982

"For black Americans, 1981 was a year of economic depression, savage cuts in survival programs for the poor, and the betrayal of basic civil-rights protections."

This is how John Jacob, president of the National Urban League, summarized the suffering of minorities this week in the league's seventh annual "State of Black America" report.

The harsh words are supported by equally harsh facts.

Last month, unemployment among blacks hit 16 percent, twice as high as unemployment among whites. Last summer, the unemployment rate among black teen-agers reached 45.7 percent.

At President Reagan's insistence, Congress last year sharply cut spending on social programs. These cuts hurt the black community more than the white community, because a higher percentage of blacks need such help.

Jacob noted, too, the Reagan administration's negative civil-rights record: "From its backtracking on desegregating schools to its de-emphasis of civil-rights enforcement to its attacks on affirmative action, the administration created a feeling among many blacks that they were forgotten people," Jacob charged. He proposed that:

● Congressional leaders "inform the administration that further cuts in poor people's programs are unacceptable." These essential programs do not need to be cut further to balance the budget. The deficit can be closed "by scaling down the defense budget and by closing tax loopholes for special interests."

● Congress and the administration address the fear in black America that the nation's leaders are encouraging "a return to a past that denied basic human rights and tolerated racial discrimination."

The Senate could help alleviate that fear by following the House in approving extension of the Voting Rights Act. The administration should recognize that affirmative action still is needed.

No one wins when thousands of able blacks are blocked from giving their best to America because of short-sighted economic and civil-rights policies.

No one wins when a new generation of black Americans looking for their first jobs find the business community saying: "Get lost, kid."

No one wins when the president, by backtracking on civil rights, helps encourage the latent racism in the land.

The administration may be right in saying that mistakes were made by Democratic administrations and Congresses, but the drive to help black America achieve equality with white America was not a mistake. The president and this Congress have an obligation to do more than they have done to continue this mission. The state of black America is not good enough.

The San Diego Union

San Diego, Calif., October 24, 1982

Most of the political rhetoric directed at black Americans these days amounts to an undisguised attack upon the Reagan administration. Mr. Reagan, it is said, is guilty of backsliding on civil rights and of gutting the social programs that are particularly important to minorities.

So persistent has been this drumbeat that its message is believed not only by many blacks, but by no small number of whites as well.

We think the critics are selling President Reagan and his programs short. The America Ronald Reagan envisions would be one in which a disproportionately black underclass would be liberated from permanent dependence on government.

Equality of opportunity and an expanding economy would replace the dole as provider for those now poor or unemployed. In the process, the dignity and self-esteem that accompany economic independence would do more to promote equality than all the social programs of the past 20 years.

Hearing Mr. Reagan say all this hasn't persuaded many black Americans, in part because so many black leaders remain prisoners of the welfare-state mentality of the 1960s and 1970s. Thus, it is critically important

that prominent blacks who share Mr. Reagan's belief in the liberating potential of a meritocracy built on an expanding economy speak now in its defense.

Thomas Sowell and Walter Williams, two highly respected and outspoken black economists, have done just that. Both have shredded the myth of the welfare state and affirmative action as essential to black progress. Indeed, Mr. Sowell and Mr. Williams have demonstrated that dependency and quotas are barriers to the social and economic emancipation of minorities.

San Diego's Clarence Pendleton, now chairman of the U.S. Commission on Civil Rights, took a similar stand in a remarkable address recently to the National Association of Human Rights Workers.

The speech, excerpts of which are reprinted elsewhere in today's World Currents section, challenged black America and its traditional political leaders to abandon policies that have already failed.

Mr. Pendleton cited one study showing that "federal outlays for basic safety-net programs since 1950, in constant 1980 dollars, were $8 billion in 1950 and have swelled to $245 billion in 1980 ... (yet) every evaluation report indicates that the social programs

of the 1960s were a disappointing failure."

Exactly so. The cycle of dependency has not been broken nor has that disproportionately black underclass been moved much closer to self-sufficiency.

As for the civil rights movement, Mr. Pendleton noted that it had "transformed itself from being a civil rights watchdog to an economic redistribution movement — dispensing 'neo-reparations' from our tax dollars to their clients."

And what of affirmative action? Mr. Pendleton described it as a worthy concept but, in practice, a "bankrupt policy ... we must clearly understand that equality of opportunity does not mean equality of result."

Some black leaders will be tempted, no doubt, to react to such straight talk by accusing Clarence Pendleton of having "sold out" to the Reagan administration. But these accusations will have missed the point.

What Mr. Pendleton wants is "a revolution ... that reduces our dependence on government and prepares us and our children for the future." For the record, that is what President Reagan wants as well. It can only be achieved if Americans, of every race, have the courage and vision to look beyond the discredited policies of the past.

Mike Keefe THE DENVER POST '82 FIELD SYNDICATE

The Seattle Times

Seattle, Wash., January 14, 1982

DESPITE the Republican Party's efforts to reach out to minority citizens (a commitment to do that "has never been stronger," G.O.P. National Chairman Richard Richards said recently), the Reagan administration's race-relations record continues to suggest a disturbing retreat from anti-discrimination policies.

This week's flip-flop on tax breaks for private schools practicing discrimination was only the most recent example.

A White House statement said Mr. Reagan has been misunderstood on the tax question. The President is opposed, the statement said, to discrimination in any form. His decision to suspend an Internal Revenue Service rule disallowing tax exemptions for private schools where discrimination is sanctioned merely reflected his conviction that such policies ought not to be left to administrative fiat.

But nothing was said in the first announcement about Congress' enacting a law against such tax breaks. Only a heavy public protest caused a rethinking of the issue.

While the White House now supports legislation outlawing favored tax treatment for nonprofit groups that discriminate, the new policy announced last Friday will remain intact until Congress acts.

Taken by itself, the tax-break ruckus is not a large issue. Only about 100 private schools would be affected immediately. It takes on deeper meaning, though, in the context of earlier actions.

For example: The President's contradictory stands on extension of the Voting Rights Act. A backdown by the Departments of Labor and Education on enforcement of contracts and regulations designed to protect minorities and women. The appointment of an Equal Employment Opportunity Commission chairman with limited credentials. The dismissal of the chairman of the Commission on Civil Rights (at about the time of a commission report criticizing the laggard speed of school-desegregation efforts), and the appointment of a replacement who is an open critic of affirmative action.

Most Americans approve generally of Mr. Reagan's *laissez-faire* approach to the conduct of public affairs — in "getting government off the backs of the people."

But one place where the government should lead, not retreat, is in the attack against racial and ethnic discrimination.

THE LOUISVILLE TIMES

Louisville, Ky., September 14, 1982

Civil rights has never been a priority for the Reagan administration, a fact it did not take a stern letter from 33 state leaders in the field to prove.

Rather, the administration's record has been soiled repeatedly by efforts — great and small — to turn the clock back on a quarter-century of progressive change.

By drawing attention to that fact with their letter, however, the chairmen of state committees that advise the U. S. Commission on Civil Rights have performed a valuable service. Their letter exposes a record that destroys the myth, periodically advanced by the President and others, that the administration champions equal rights for all.

Some remember that the tone was set at the start of Mr. Reagan's 1980 fall campaign in Philadelphia, Miss., site of the 1964 slaying of three civil rights workers. There he declared that he believed in "states rights," long a code word for segregation, and he promised to reduce the role of the federal government in enforcing civil rights laws.

Since then, he has made good on his promise.

The new administration sought to extend tax exemptions for schools that practice discrimination — reversing a long-standing federal policy; the matter is now before the U. S. Supreme Court. And, of course, Mr. Reagan's massive budget cuts in social welfare areas hit the poor and the blacks hardest.

For months, the President threw roadblocks in front of extension of the Voting Rights Act of 1965. Early in his term, Mr. Reagan's Justice Department submitted a harebrained scheme for "voluntary" desegregation busing in St. Louis. Fortunately it was stillborn.

The man Mr. Reagan put in charge of Justice's civil rights division, William Bradford Reynolds, came to office igno-rant of that area of the law, having spent his career in the corporate world. That ignorance was illustrated by a plan for school desegregation that, in effect, resurrected the long-discredited notion of "separate-but-equal" schools.

But the Reynolds appointment was only one of several appalling ones that Mr. Reagan has made in the field. The 33 advisers to the civil rights commission noted that in their letter.

"With some exceptions," they told Mr. Reagan, "nominations and appointments to high positions in the leadership of the U. S. Commission on Civil Rights, the Equal Employment Opportunity Commission and the civil-rights division of the Department of Justice, as well as others, are distressing."

Remember William Bell, head of a one-man Detroit employment agency with no experience in the civil rights field, who was named to head the Equal Employment Opportunity Commission, which has 3,000 employees and a $10 million budget? Or B. Sam Hart, a Philadelphia, Pa., radio evangelist who opposed school desegregation busing, women's rights and equality for homosexuals but was appointed to the civil rights commission? The White House withdrew each nomination, but only after furor over the nominees' lack of qualifications for the jobs.

A glance at Mr. Reagan's schedule for the week is the best evidence of the low priority that civil rights has in this administration:

The better part of Wednesday will be devoted to Ferdinand Marcos, dictator of the Philippines. Much of Friday is slated for congressional campaigning in New Jersey. But, when the 33 angry civil rights leaders sought a brief audience with the President, the White House told them, sorry, there simply wasn't a moment to spare.

The Miami Herald
Miami, Fla., May 17, 1982

FEW PRESIDENTS in modern history have been so thoroughly viewed with distrust and misgiving by minorities and the poor as is Ronald Reagan. Finally, though, President Reagan has begun a campaign to improve his image among the disenchanted, especially among blacks.

To demonstrate his sensitivity, Mr. Reagan recently visited Mr. and Mrs. Phillip Butler of College Park, Md., blacks who were targets of a Ku Klux Klan cross-burning. The President held court with black students at a Catholic high school on Chicago's west side. He phoned to wish boxer Sugar Ray Leonard a full and speedy recovery from an eye injury. And Mr. Reagan, at the 11th

hour, softened his stand on extension of the Voting Rights Act, agreeing with a version endorsed by civil-rights groups.

Mr. Reagan's moves obviously are aimed for political gain. But he *is* a politician, one who knows the potential destructiveness of negative images and perceptions. Moreover, this is an election year. Republicans around the country need every vote they can get, from blacks, Hispanics, women, the elderly, the poor, the rich.

So the President is doing what any thinking politician would. He's trying to repair the damage to his political ship. Politicians throughout history have done no less.

Mr. Reagan's policies do hurt. His pol-

icies on the budget, taxes, housing, and education tend to hurt minorities and blacks most because those groups are proportionately poorer than other Americans. The 1981 Reagan tax cut increases the real income only of relatively high-income families, while cuts in social programs were largely harmful to poor families. So reports the Leadership Conference on Civil Rights, a Washington-based lobby group.

The Reagan recession brought unemployment to a post-World War II record of 9.4 per cent. Among blacks the rate is 18 to 19 per cent; among Hispanics it is 12 per cent. Housing subsidies that benefit the poor have been cut, but not tax benefits for private homeowners. Mr. Reagan supported tax exemptions for segregated private schools. He favors tuition tax credits. Both positions adversely affect the poor.

Worse, though, Mr. Reagan's public statements betray an archaic attitude about the status of race relations in America. The President said he was unaware that some schools that discriminate on the basis of race still function in America. "Maybe I should have [known], but I didn't," he said to the Chicago students.

In view of the harm inflicted by his policies, Mr. Reagan's efforts to rebound fall short. He has made only the first step; he still has a long journey to go.

Richmond Times-Dispatch
Richmond, Va., September 21, 1982

The truth hurts. Stung by President Reagan's recent assertion that the Great Society was more harmful than beneficial to poor black Americans, angry apologists for that bankrupt social experiment are denouncing the president as an unfeeling racist. To condemn LBJ's folly is, in the liberals' opinion, to favor perpetual poverty for millions of people who could not achieve a decent standard of living without the federal government's help.

But let us cite the following words in Mr. Reagan's defense:

"...Hundreds of billions of dollars have been spent to cure poverty. Yet, government officials tell us that more than one-in-three black Americans still lives below the poverty threshold. During the Great Society era the Model Cities program was born; today, one of its chief architects says the program was largely an expensive failure. During the Great Society era the food stamp program was born. The program cost $1.2 billion in 1970, and $9.1 billion in 1980; even though more than 6.7 million households received food stamps in 1980, the experts tell us there is still hunger in America...

"It is absolutely beyond dispute that the current panoply of social welfare programs — designed by politicians, social scientists, and the welfare bureaucracy — has fostered dependence, not independence. It is equally obvious that the American people, and especially the poor, can no longer afford, economically or morally, business as usual. To perpetuate a system that clearly isn't working is foolish, unfair, wasteful, and even racist."

Selections from a White House policy report? No, they are selections from a statement of purpose issued by The New Coalition for Economic and Social Change, a predominantly black organization

that advocates a drastic departure from the paternalism of the Great Society. The Coalition prefers approaches that "reject the notion that America's blacks need to be cared for" and afford blacks opportunities to use their own talents and abilities to advance.

The coalition and President Reagan are saying the same thing: By encouraging people to believe that the federal government would provide for them, the welfare programs of the Great Society undermined initiative and retarded black progress. Many poor blacks found themselves shackled into a "new kind of bondage" — to use Mr. Reagan's words — that made them wards of the government.

That blacks monolithically support the Great Society concept is a false impression that has been conveyed by liberals and especially by members of the civil rights establishment. These people derive political and economic benefits from the many programs that have been established to "fight" poverty, since such activities create jobs for bureaucrats and constituencies for liberal politicians interested in prolonging their careers. But many thoughtful blacks, like those in the coalition, recognize the insidious effects of doles, affirmative action and other government props and reject them. They prefer, instead, equality of opportunity in a non-discriminatory society, the right to participate in an economic system that would reward them on the basis of their abilities and accomplishments rather than because of their race.

By pursuing policies designed to achieve such objectives, President Reagan is showing that he is more interested in advancing the interests of blacks than are the liberals who still cling to the discredited notions of the Great Society era.

Des Moines Sunday Register
Des Moines, Iowa, July 25, 1982

For those who believe in civil rights, the Reagan administration's activities are worrisome not only for what they are doing today but for what they are undoing from yesterday. The hard-won civil-rights victories of the past two decades can be too easily lost — stolen under cover of a concern with excess regulations.

So it is reassuring to see formation of a group of 16 former top federal officials representing both parties to watch federal-government enforcement of anti-discrimination laws. It is no accident that the charge they have set for themselves is virtually identical to that given to the U.S. Civil Rights Commission.

The group includes two former chairmen of the commission and several former members, some of them ousted by Reagan in his unprecedented sweep-out of the commission. Its formation is a clear rebuke to the president, an indication of the strength of the feeling that this administration is trying to subvert the law by appointing enemies of the law to a commission intended to monitor enforcement.

Arthur Flemming, the distin-

guished (and moderate) Republican whom Reagan unseated as chairman, announced the new panel and said an early agenda item will be a report analyzing the implications of Senate-passed legislation barring federal courts in most instances from requiring busing to remedy illegal school segregation.

There is plenty more to look at, including:

● Restrictions on the Legal Services Corporation that will mean diminished access to the courts for minorities and the poor.

● The move by the Department of Labor to narrow the scope of affirmative-action regulations covering government contractors.

● Arguments in court by the Justice Department that private schools that discriminate on the basis of race should be permitted to keep their tax exemptions.

Such developments are distressing evidence of the mindset that produced a civil-rights commission dominated by people opposed to remedies for civil-rights violations. It is heartening to know that someone other than the foxes will have an eye on this chicken coop.

The Hartford Courant

Hartford, Conn., October 3, 1982

President Reagan admits to only one failure in civil rights. "(We) have failed to communicate what's in our hearts to the black community," he said.

Obviously, the president could have done better to communicate with civil rights groups in his first 20 months in office.

But Mr. Reagan's civil rights problem is not failure to relay what's in his heart. The problem is that he has communicated too well what's on his mind. He wants government to get off the backs of everyone, including traditionally oppressed groups in society.

This does not make Mr. Reagan a bigot. He probably is as offended by overt racism as most Americans. He must believe that without equal opportunity, a heterogeneous nation is doomed to mediocrity — morally, economically, socially, politically and militarily.

What's alarming, is how the administration promotes equal opportunity and respect for civil rights laws. These goals will be reached through voluntary action, through friendly persuasion and perhaps through incentives, argue White House strategists.

The effective way to combat discrimination is to stand up for "race neutrality," according to William Bradford Reynolds, head of the Justice Department's civil rights division. Thus, instead of insisting on affirmative action in the area of equal employment opportunity, the administration insists on "racially neutral employment decisions" and suggests that companies voluntarily expand efforts to hire minorities.

"In school desegregation cases," explains Mr. Reynolds, "our remedial formula emphasizes desegregation techniques that promote voluntary integrative student transfers and at the same time enhance the quality of public education." This bureaucratic gobbledygook translates into retrenchment.

And yet, President Reagan says critics "strike at my heart" when they suggest that "we are taking a less active approach to protecting the civil rights of all Americans." No matter how you slice it, that's just plain baloney.

Well, let's do some slicing:

● The administration fought hard to weaken the Voting Rights Act when the law was extended by Congress earlier this year. Only two voting rights cases have been filed since the president's inauguration.

● Hiring quotas are legal but wrong, even for government agencies, in Mr. Reagan's opinion. The federal government should not be in the business of suing employers who fail to meet their own goals in minority hirings.

● Only two cases of housing discrimination have been taken to court by the Justice Department since January 1981. The record is poor compared with the record of the Nixon, Ford and Carter administrations.

● Attorney General William French Smith, in departing from the policies of past GOP and Democratic administrations, says his department will not ask courts to order busing, even as a last resort. The administration might even ask courts to dismantle school busing plans already ordered by courts.

Using the number of civil rights suits filed may be an incomplete yardstick, but that is not the only measure of Mr. Reagan's civil record.

The record includes opposition to the Equal Rights Amendment, support for tax exemption to private schools which discriminate, refusal to enforce a law banning sex discrimination in federally funded education, suspension, or threatened suspension, of various regulations intended to benefit the handicapped and older people, and a dearth of blacks, Hispanics and women in the president's Cabinet, in federal court appointments and in regulatory agencies.

All this leaves little room for misreading the administration on civil rights. Mr. Reagan's goal of equal opportunity in education and employment cannot be achieved in the context of the fabled free marketplace, where voluntarism is king and where most people will act strictly according to constitutional ideals without ever being coerced by government to do so.

The door to equal opportunity will not be opened by good intentions. If there is a single most important reason for the existence of government, it is to make sure that disadvantaged citizens are actively helped by government.

Chicago Defender

Chicago, Ill., February 10, 1982

Is President Ronald Reagan a racist? Like most minority-owned publications, we have avoided casting so demeaning a label on our national leader. We have been content to call him a rigid conservative and the recipient of very bad advice on matters of economics and civil rights. Throughout his first year in office, hope remained that this personable, seemingly responsible man would come to understand the great inequality still gripping America.

Now we are into the second year, and if there has been any change in the President's posture toward minority concerns, it is in the direction of unfeigned hostility. Consider what has become of the Equal Employment Opportunity Commission: Castrated by the administration, leaving government and private employers free once more to hire, fire and promote on the basis of bigotry or any other whim.

Consider what has become of affirmative action programs: Attacked by the administration as wasteful, and allowed in business, education and labor to wither and die. Consider the fate of public school integration: Openly repudiated by high cabinet officials, with the Justice Department, in particular, ordered to halt busing efforts and stop prosecuting Jim Crow school districts.

Consider even the Voting Rights Act: Denied support from Washington and in serious jeopardy in many states. Can all these atrocities be the result of an honest, conservative stance? Or are we witnessing something else as we stand one-fourth into the Reagan term — something far more frightening? Once again, we pose the question which began this editorial.

The Sun Reporter

San Francisco, Calif., April 1, 1982

A Washington datelined story stated that President Reagan is troubled by fears among blacks about his administration, and that he has been wrongly portrayed as uncaring about the poor.

Reagan made this statement, among others, at a White House luncheon which he held for a group of black clergymen, carefully selected from different sections of the nation.

Whatever the image of the president among American blacks, it is one that he seems to have nurtured carefully, for ever since he made the change from the unadulterated fantasy of the world of films to the more pragmatic world of politics, blacks have regarded him as a man who has always sought top billings in old time vaudeville.

When serving as governor of California, the president revealed a profound lack of knowledge of state affairs, which he attempted to cover up by enunciating what he believed to be laugh-provoking one-liners, whenever he was being interviewed by members of the media.

His one-liners took one a more ominous tone when he started berating the poor. Most well-informed persons know that a large number of black poor in the nation are poor because of the prevailing racism which is especially designed to keep large number of blacks poor.

The Reagan vaudeville technique has not been altered one whit since his ascension to the presidency.

The Reagan attitude towards blacks has been one of appointing blacks who are more devoted to attaining the status of black anglo saxons than interested in devoting their time to providing worthwhile advice to the President about the plight of American blacks.

The black poor are very conspicuous because of their pigmentation, even though there are far more poor among other, non-black groups. Yet all the attacks on welfare mothers, food stamps, and other state assistance programs have been orchestrated against blacks. Both before Reagan's ascension to power, and since his administration took power, the assistance programs have seemed destined to end soon.

American blacks are uneasy about Reagan because he seems to lack knowledge both about domestic and foreign affairs, and because he seems to have surrounded himself with advisors who do not known any more than he does about domestic or foreign affairs.

Blacks, like other Americans, are concerned about the flippant one-liners, and about nuclear war, for they know that pigmentation will not protect them from a nuclear holocaust.

Yes, Mr. President, your image among blacks is that of an individual who cares ony for those who possess great wealth and power, and you, Mr. President, have done nothing to change the image which blacks hold of you.

Any change of that image will have to come from you, Mr. President, and there are few Americans who feel you are capable of making such a change of image.

OKLAHOMA CITY TIMES

Oklahoma City, Okla., July 14, 1983

NO matter what President Reagan does in the struggle to end unfair discrimination, it never seems to be enough to satisfy the professional civil rights advocates.

One wonders if their political mindset against the president renders them constitutionally unable to view objectively what he says or does and causes them automatically to reject any administration initiatives.

Such suspicions were aroused this week by the reaction to the filing of a suit by the U.S. Department of Justice against the state of Alabama seeking to dismantle its alleged "dual system" of higher education for whites and blacks.

The action was ridiculed by an official of the National Association for the Advancement of Colored People. He said it was compelled by a court order and that, anyway, it was timed for political advantage — to coincide with the NAACP's convention in New Orleans.

Similar scorn greeted Reagan's request for Congress to stiffen the Fair Housing Act, which prohibits discrimination in sale or rental housing because of race, color, religion, sex or national origin. The administration's bill would let the Justice Department sue fair-housing violators in federal court.

Civil penalties of as much as $50,000 for a first offense and $100,000 for a second offense could be imposed. The administration thinks this threat could persuade many violators to resolve complaints through mediation by the Department of Housing and Urban Development.

Under the present law, the Justice Department can initiate action only if it finds a "pattern or practice" of discrimination.

The civil-righteous crowd has relied traditionally on the use of bureaucratic clout to get what it wants, and this is the approach it prefers in housing discrimination cases. It is backing a bill in Congress that would set up a commission in HUD with administrative law judges to handle complaints. The commission would have the same powers as a court to order a solution and could impose civil penalties of $10,000.

Besides adding a "whole level of bureaucracy," as one Justice official objects, this bill would put HUD in the position of acting as prosecutor and judge. Administrative law judges are too much in evidence already and have attained a great deal of power. The device places a judicial function in the executive branch, where it doesn't belong.

Simply because the administration chooses a more orderly way of rooting out discrimination doesn't mean it isn't committed to the cause.

THE CHRISTIAN SCIENCE MONITOR

Boston, Mass., February 25, 1982

Recent events cry out for President Reagan to use his strong qualities of leadership in behalf of his long-stated commitment to strengthening civil rights. By doing so he could address the deep concern, expressed inside and outside his administration, that civil rights enforcement is now being undermined. And he could allow future historians to look back on this current Black History Month as one of progress as well as multiple protests:

• A 13-day civil rights march recalling Martin Luther King days in the South;

• An extraordinary uprising of Justice Department civil rights lawyers against what they see as internal failures to uphold the law;

• And this week a lengthy report in which the Leadership Conference on Civil Rights, representing many civil rights groups, details its conclusion that the Justice Department has become "the locus of efforts in the Reagan administration to narrow and weaken civil rights protection."

All this comes less than a month after Mr. Reagan assured Americans in his State of the Union message that the nation's long journey toward civil rights for all citizens "must continue with no backsliding or slowing down." Does he now agree with those who allege backsliding and slowing down by his own attorney general and assistant attorney general for civil rights? Or does he agree with these officials that they are not turning away from enforcement but from ineffective methods of enforcement? The President can display his leadership by ensuring that there is not a widening gap between his stance on civil rights and the practices of his administration.

Certainly the President was not well served by Justice Department advice to allow tax exemptions for private schools practicing racial discrimination. The same could be said of Justice's backing for a weaker extension of the Voting Rights Act than was enacted by the House of Representatives. Among other steps taken as signs of lessening commitment is the department's switch from the previous administration's support in the courts for a voluntary desegregation plan involving busing in Seattle.

Yet such impressions could be overridden by renewed evidence that the Justice Department is championing civil rights rather than forgoing means of enforcing them. It must not let opposition to busing for school desegregation appear to be reluctance about enforcing desegregation law itself. It must not let opposition to even voluntary affirmative action appear to be reluctance about enforcing equal employment opportunity laws. In such cases it ought to bring forcefully to public attention the alternative means of compliance it prefers — magnet schools, perhaps, or color-blind employment practices — and show them to be no less effective than the legally required or accepted means in the past.

President Reagan has much to think about in these days of budget turmoil. But nothing is more important to his country's future than the unity of its people under just laws, justly enforced. It deserves attention as wholehearted as that State of the Union pledge.

AKRON BEACON JOURNAL
Akron, Ohio, July 13, 1983

BY ANNOUNCING plans to "put real teeth" into the nation's fair housing laws, President Reagan seems to want to dispel the belief that he is lukewarm on civil rights.

That announcement is good to hear if it truly represents a substantive change, and not just a move to mend fences before the presidential campaign season officially begins.

Based on the record so far, blacks and other minorities have every reason to question Mr. Reagan's goals on fair housing and other civil rights issues.

Last year, the administration angered minorities by unsuccessfully defending tax-exempt status for private schools that practice racial discrimination.

More recently, Mr. Reagan announced plans to replace three outspoken members of the U. S. Civil Rights Commission who have repeatedly accused him of a lack of commitment to economic and social justice.

So far, his policy toward fair housing laws has concentrated on getting real estate companies to sign agreements that they will sell housing in a non-discriminatory way. The policy was weakened when the names of the signers were made confidential.

The Reagan administration has not shown much enthusiasm for going after those who violate the law. The Justice Department filed only five housing bias lawsuits in the last 2½ years.

But the President cannot be blamed for problems inherent in the existing law. Racial bias cases that wind up in court drag on for months — sometimes years — long after homes are sold and apartments are rented. And there are no real penalties in cases of proven discrimination.

The President wants substantial penalties: fines up to $50,000 for a first offense, up to $100,000 for repeated violations.

Another change would allow the Department of Housing and Urban Development to forward individual allegations of bias to the Justice Department. Under current law, the Justice Department can accept a case only if bias intent is proven.

It would be foolish to think that Mr. Reagan's timing on seeking these changes is an accident. This week, Congress begins hearings on the President's three new appointments to the Civil Rights Commission.

This is also the week that the NAACP is in New Orleans for its annual convention, a meeting in which Mr. Reagan's policies will be bitterly attacked by delegates and Democratic presidential candidates.

As a political pragmatist, the President cannot afford to ignore these issues, even if he has written off the black vote. Pollsters warn him that his administration's anti-poor and anti-minority image could threaten the entire Republican party.

Regardless of the political reasons, the fact remains that Mr. Reagan serves as President of all the people. His statement on fair housing — though overdue — is an encouraging departure from his dismal record on civil rights.

The Boston Globe

Boston, Mass., June 18, 1983

The dismissed members of the US Civil Rights Commission refuse to go quietly. The commission's latest criticisms of President Reagan substantiate a public perception that women and minorities have lost ground since he moved into the White House.

The numbers of presidential appointees reveal that there is little equal opportunity in the Reagan Administration.

President Reagan must do better as the commission has urged. Leaders must lead. Presidents must set the tone for the nation.

Why in 1983 is this issue important, 20 years after the passage of major civil rights legislation? Because in the job market, in housing and in other areas, women still face discrimination based on gender and minorities still encounter barriers based on race, ethnic heritage or religious beliefs.

To get the numbers, the commission had to threaten to issue subpoenas. For months, Reagan officials refused to comply with legitimate requests. Indeed, they had something to hide.

Both women and minorities have lost ground. During the Carter Administration, women accounted for 12 percent of the full-time appointees and blacks also accounted for 12 percent. Compare that to a dreadful 8 percent for women in the Reagan Administration and worse, a measly 4 percent for blacks.

President Reagan has defended his record. His is the first Cabinet to contain three women members and he did appoint the first woman to the Supreme Court. But his claims to more women than any other predecessor can only be true if the tabulation includes those appointed to part-time slots and advisory boards.

As for minorities, the Administration is trying, according to a spokesman. How hard? Less than a dozen black appointees serve in top policy-making positions according to news reports and no blacks serve in assistant secrtary positions or higher at the departments of Health and Human Services, Justice, Treasury, Labor, Agriculture, Energy, Defense and State.

Most critical are the judicial appointments, the federal bench and the federal prosecutors in the US attorney's office. In those areas, President Carter made significant inroads. Some 16 percent of the judges he appointed were black and 15 percent were women. Only 2.5 precent of President Reagan's judicial appointees have been black while 8.3 percent have been women.

This is not the first time that the commission has lashed out at the President. Perhaps that is why last month he fired three members, a black woman, a Latin woman and a Jewish man and appointed three white males considered more in line with Reagan policies. That attempt to stack the independent and bipartisan commission did not save Reagan from another blast. While his nominees are awaiting Senate approval, the current members including the Republicans continue to work.

The commission has no enforcement powers and only monitors the enforcement of civil rights laws. It does influence public policy with investigations, hearings and reports – including an attack on Reagan Administration interpretations on civil rights law and education that could hurt women, released this week.

Perhaps, presidential advisers justify the lack of minority and women appointments because most minorities cast their votes elsewhere and because of a growing gender gap indicating that more women are also supporting an alternative. Yet the President is president of all Americans not just those who voted for him. His appointments and policies must reflect that.

Pittsburgh Post-Gazette

Pittsburgh, Pa., July 20, 1983

President Reagan long has complained that his administration has been given a "bum rap" on its commitment to enforce laws against racial discrimination.

Bum or not — and on some issues, like Mr. Reagan's unsuccessful effort to restore tax-exempt status for racist private schools, the critics were dead right — the complaints seem finally to have had some effect. In recent days, the administration has undertaken a number of initiatives in the civil-rights field.

Last week the Reagan Justice Department filed its first school-desegregation suit, charging Alabama with maintaining a dual system of higher education. Recently the same department asked a federal court to enforce the Voting Rights Act in two Mississippi counties. Finally, and surprisingly, Mr. Reagan proposed strengthening the federal law against racial discrimination in housing, though his plan offered less protection than a bill already proposed in Congress.

Cynics argue that the flurry of civil-rights initiatives was prompted as much by the approaching 1984 presidential election as by any genuine change of heart on Mr. Reagan's part.

No one in or out of the Reagan camp thinks that the president has much chance of capturing black support should he choose to run again; the differences between Mr. Reagan and black opinion on affirmative action and spending priorities are simply too great.

Rather, the prevailing, and plausible, theory is that the president's image of insensitivity to civil rights — even as the term was understood in the pre-affirmative action days of the 1960s — jeopardizes his support from white liberals and moderates, including Republicans.

It is easy enough, for example, for Mr. Reagan to complain that critics of his three nominees to the U.S. Civil Rights Commission unfairly equate opposition to affirmative-action quotas with hostility to civil rights; thoughtful people do disagree about the extent to which race-conscious policies are necessary to compensate for past discrimination.

But that argument would get a much more respectful hearing if the administration had not sought to placate Bob Jones University and other racist private schools (a gesture withdrawn in the heat of public outrage) and if it had not been painfully slow to recognize the symbolic and practical importance of extending the Voting Rights Act.

So the appropriate verdict on Mr. Reagan's sudden interest in civil rights is "better late than never." But how much better — even for Mr. Reagan's re-election prospects — if he had been right from the start.

The TENNESSEAN

Nashville, Tenn., June 18, 1983

IT is fairly easy to understand why President Reagan wants new appointees on the U.S. Commission on Civil Rights, for it seems to be a burr under his saddle.

Last fall, chairmen of 33 state agencies affiliated with the commission bluntly stated that the President is to blame for a "dangerous deterioration in the federal enforcement of civil rights. The group complained that, "Persons without adequate background or commitment are routinely appointed to leadership positions on the commission and other agencies.

Last November, President Reagan dismissed Mr. Arthur Flemming as chairman of the commission, just at the time Mr. Flemming was about to publish a report blasting the administration on its policies on school desegregation. Mr. Flemming was replaced by Mr. Clarence Pendleton.

Just recently, Mr. Reagan decided to replace three of the six members on the panel who have been critical. But last week the commission had more criticism, and two Republican members endorsed the criticism.

The commission said the administration had made numerous "efforts to reduce federal civil rights enforcement in education,"and urged the President to halt such efforts. It said that the administration had interpreted the civil rights laws so narrowly that many colleges could be exempted from the federal ban even though students at the institutions received federal aid.

Mrs. Mary Louise Smith, a former chairman of the Republican National Committee, and a member of the commission, noted that the Supreme Court last month repudiated the administration's contention that it was legally required to grant tax exemptions to Bob Jones University of Greenville, S.C., and Goldsboro Christian Schools in Goldsboro, N.C., even though both practiced racial discrimination.

The statement came one day after the commission said it was "disappointed" that President Reagan had not appointed more blacks, women and Hispanic Americans to full-time, high-level positions in the federal government.

Clearly the administration is somewhat chagrined by such criticism, and would prefer a commission that not only does not rock the boat, but one that is blind to its failures in the area of civil rights.

Newsday
Long Island, N.Y., June 2, 1983

President Reagan contended in a news conference last month that his unpopularity among blacks stems from a "perception" problem fostered by the media, and that blacks wouldn't oppose him and his policies if the "truth" were known.

Let's look at the record:

● The President has just removed three members of the Civil Rights Commission while refusing to offer any reason for his action. Since two members had been fired earlier, that leaves only one pre-Reagan holdover, Jill Ruckelshaus, on the supposedly independent commission.

● The Reagan administration tried to grant federal tax exemptions to private segregated schools. The Supreme Court ruled such exemptions illegal last week.

● Reagan and the Justice Department remain opposed to affirmative action requirements and school busing to achieve integration.

● Reagan tried to weaken the Voting Rights Act — athough he subsequently sought to take credit for its extension.

● Reagan's overall economic policies have had a severe impact on low-income people, a disproportionate number of whom are black.

This is not a record to inspire faith and confidence among America's blacks and other minorities.

The only explanation given for the replacement of the three Civil Rights Commission members came from White House spokesman Larry Speakes: "The President did what he wanted to do," he said.

That's undoubtedly true; the question is why he wanted to do it. And the answer is not hard to divine: Reagan was uncomfortable with the commission, which frequently has been at odds with his administration over civil-rights policy and enforcement. But the commission is supposed to act as a watchdog and a protector of the rights of minorities, women, the aged and the handicapped, as spelled out in the Constitution and in civil-rights law.

To suggest, as Reagan has, that blacks are somehow being duped about his record by the media reflects a painful insensitivity to the effect of his administration's policies on the black community. If Reagan is serious, as he says he is, about attracting political support from blacks — who lately have been asserting themselves at ballot boxes in Chicago and Philadelphia — he needs to demonstrate in deeds that he has their welfare at heart. Given the weight of the evidence, claiming that they're misinterpreting the consequences of his policies because of a "hatchet job" by the press can only lessen Reagan's credibility with blacks.

Los Angeles Times
Los Angeles, Calif., June 17, 1983

The criticism that the U.S. Commission on Civil Rights has directed at the Reagan Administration's appointment record demonstrates again the need for commission members with unfaltering determination to break down bias.

A commission report this week faults President Reagan for appointing blacks to only 4.1% of the full-time, high-level Administration jobs; 12% of President Jimmy Carter's appointees to similar jobs were black. Latinos got 3.8% of the Reagan Administration's appointments, the report said, and women 8%. The Carter Administration appointed more of both. The commission especially scored the Reagan Administration for reversing a trend toward appointing more members of minority groups as federal judges, U.S. marshals and U.S. attorneys—

posts that it called "vital" to the interpretation of civil-rights laws.

It is the role of the Civil Rights Commission to oversee the nation's record in overcoming bias. For performing that function vigorously, Reagan wants to replace three commission members who have been most critical of his record. That is his prerogative, of course, because the members have no fixed terms.

But, in the current context, the move renders even more suspect his already weak commitment to civil-rights enforcement. His poor appointment record and his drive to replace people critical of it and other policies underscore his failure to grasp the role of government in opening full participation in American life to all its people.

THE SACRAMENTO BEE
Sacramento, Calif., July 26, 1983

William Bradford Reynolds, assistant U.S. attorney general for civil rights, denies that the flurry of civil rights actions initiated by the administration in the past couple of weeks has been politically orchestrated.

Yet after 2½ years of what, charitably, has to be called benign neglect and might more accurately be called hostility, and given the fact that one of those moves came under court order and another in an effort to head off more stringent legislation already pending in Congress, the government's moves had the unmistakable characteristics of a civil rights public relations offensive.

The list includes the filing of the Reagan administration's first school desegregation suit (against the state of Alabama and its state universities); the submission of legislation to beef up enforcement of the federal anti-discrimination law in housing; a move by the Justice Department asking a federal court to enforce the Voting Rights Act in Mississippi, and a well-publicized directive from the president ordering federal agencies to give greater attention to awarding contracts to minority businesses.

Not surprisingly, White House officials, confronting charges from civil rights groups that all this was too little and too late, went out of their way to emphasize what they called the president's longstanding commitment to civil rights.

But the record powerfully suggests something else. Ever since this administration came to office it has been under fire, even from its own attorneys, for lax enforcement of civil rights laws and practices that had been taken for granted by previous administrations, Democratic and Republican.

The Reagan administration tried to end what seemed a well-established Treasury Department rule (first adopted in the Nixon administration) against granting tax exemptions to segregated schools, arguing, despite court decisions upholding it, that there was no congressional authority for the rule: For the first time in years, the government in that case went to court on the side of segregation-

ists to support a segregationist argument.

The administration has also broken all precedent by removing three members of the U.S. Civil Rights Commission whom it apparently regarded as being too vocal in criticism of its own civil rights policies, even though the commission has no power but to investigate and make reports.

Some Republicans, trying to support the president, said the result of the new administration interest in civil rights should be regarded as more important than its apparently political motives. That interest, for example, is likely to make it easier to pass federal fair-housing law amendments even stronger than the administration wants, and one should be grateful for that. All the same, there remains that dismal record and the record leads to more than suspicion that the concern is not even skin-deep. Even the Alabama suit was undertaken only under the compulsion of a federal court order. Howard Metzenbaum, a liberal Ohio Democrat, calls it tokenism, and that's just about what so far it appears to be.

THE ATLANTA CONSTITUTION
Atlanta, Ga., June 20, 1983

Good timing is essential for success in comedy and other theatrical arts — such as politics. President Reagan has proven to be a master at the game.

Consider his protracted battle with the U.S. Civil Rights Commission. Last week, the commission released back-to-back reports criticizing the administration for deliberately reducing federal civil-rights enforcement in education and failing to appoint blacks, Hispanics and women to policy-making positions.

The panel echoed the sentiments of numerous critics when it said the administration had interpreted the civil-rights laws so narrowly that many colleges could be exempted from the federal ban on discrimination even though students enrolled at the schools received federal aid.

That indictment of civil-rights enforcement under Reagan was preceded by a study — using statistics furnished by the White House only under threat of subpoena — which showed that just 4.1 percent of Reagan's full-time appointees have been black, compared with 12 percent of President Carter's appointees.

The report, which gives the lie to the president's protestations that criticism of his civil-rights record is "baloney," also concluded that there has been a decline in the appointment of women, who accounted for 12.1 percent of President Carter's appointees but only 8 percent of Reagan's.

The report said the White House's own data showed there has been "an apparent reversal of recent progress in increasing minority representation" among federal judges and prosecutors, who often play key roles in interpreting and enforcing the civil-rights laws. Of the 298 judges appointed by Carter, 16.1 percent were black and 15.1 percent were women. Reagan has made 121 judicial appointments, only 2.5 percent black and only 8.3 percent women.

But as damning as the commission's finding would appear to be on the surface, Reagan has used his masterful sense of timing to neutralize much of the sting such a report would normally carry. The president has known for months the commission's report on his civil-rights record was in the works and that its conclusions were unlikely to be complimentary.

By moving several weeks ago to replace three members of the commission, he has succeeded in making the criticism, though the result of long study, sound like plain sour grapes. Now that's timing.

Chicago Defender
Chicago, Ill., June 25, 1983

The United States Commission on Civil Rights has correctly directed a criticism at the Reagan Administration's appointment record. The action demonstrates, once more, the need for commission members to continue their determination to break down bias.

The commission, reporting a few days ago, faulted the President for appointing Blacks to only 4.1 percent of the full-time, high-level Administration jobs. Twelve percent of President Carter's appointees to similar jobs were Black.

Latinos received 3.8 percent of the Reagan Administration's appointments, and women 8 percent, the report said. The Carter Administration appointed more of both.

The commission especially criticized the Reagan Administration for reversing a trend toward appointing more members of minority groups as federal judges, U.S. marshals and U.S. attorneys. It described these posts as "vital" to the interpretation of civil rights laws.

As is well known, it is the function of the Civil Rights Commission to oversee the nation's record in overcoming prejudice. But because commission members have been performing this function vigorously, Reagan wants to replace three commission members who have been most critical of his record. He has that right of course, but it is a rotten apple.

In the current context, that move renders his already weak commitment to civil rights more suspect.

The Washington Post
Washington, D.C., August 1, 1983

THE ATTORNEY general complained in a New York speech last week that he was not getting a fair break from the press when it comes to coverage of the administration's enforcement of the civil rights laws. The Justice Department is enforcing these laws "as vigorously as any administration ever has," said Mr. Smith, and he filled the speech with statistics to make his case.

Most civil rights groups that have criticized the Reagan Justice Department are less concerned with data on new suits brought. They object to what they see as a lack of commitment, a reversal of earlier gains and the administration's decision to oppose busing and hiring quotas. They also choose to define the issue in broader terms than the attorney general might, putting such issues as budget cuts, legal services and tuition tax credits into the civil rights category. This aside, the numbers used by the attorney general are worth examining.

He is proud of the fact that this administration has authorized the filing of three new school desegregation suits—only one of which has actually been filed—during the 30 months it has been in office. This, he says, is one more than the Carter administration undertook during the comparable time period. The last Democratic Justice Department did initiate nine school suits in four years, but four of these were filed within weeks of its leaving office. It may appear that not many suits were filed by either administration, but it should be remembered that most school systems in this country have been desegregated for some time. The attorney general did not discuss the fact that his department changed sides or altered earlier government positions in some school cases that had been filed before 1981.

In the area of criminal cases brought against civil rights violators, the administration's record is good. One hundred and nine of these cases have been initiated in 30 months, and four more have been authorized, which is better than any other administration. A comparable figure for the first 2½ years of the Carter administration would be 101. But while statistics on voting rights matters appear good—165 redistricting plans have been rejected and the department has "taken part in" 49 court cases protecting voters' rights—it is really impossible to compare this performance with that of any other administration for two reasons: 1) any administration in office when the decennial census data is released will have an unusually high number of cases—this administration had to review 21,000 election-law changes—simply because all political boundaries are redrawn at that time; and 2) in 1975 the Voting Rights Act was amended to cover four additional states and parts of six others. Of this group, the state of Texas alone accounted for a large proportion of the new cases.

It is true that 20 new public employment cases have been brought since 1981—the exact number brought in a comparable period in the Carter years—but it is the objective of these suits, individual relief and guaranteed access to an applicant pool rather than guaranteed jobs for minorities, that troubles civil rights groups. And while it is commendable that this administration has obtained the largest money settlement in history, in a Fairfax County discrimination case, where is the notation that this suit was brought by the previous administration? As for housing discrimination cases, one can only look at the attorney general's figures and ask "Compared to what?". Sure, the department initiated six new cases and participated in three more. But previous administrations had averaged 29 new cases brought each year.

Statistics are useful devices, but they must be evaluated carefully and in context. The attorney general has not distorted the figures he cited, but readers should keep in mind the comparisons he did not make, the changed circumstances that make comparison in education and voting rights cases difficult, and the policy changes that are the real bone of contention between the department and civil rights groups.

Roanoke Times & World-News

Roanoke, Va., July 18, 1983

WHEN THE final chapter on civil rights in America is written, Ronald Reagan will not be acclaimed as the second Abraham Lincoln. He came into office pledged to roll back federal powers, and in the minds of many supporters that meant ending federal meddling in racial matters.

Nevertheless, Ronald Reagan is not a racist, and he did not enter the White House with the intention of reversing the progress of black Americans toward equal rights and equal opportunities. The president probably is genuinely grieved at the public perception that he is not committed to the principle of racial equality. And so one should be cautious about imputing hypocrisy to the administration now that it is taking an active interest in voting rights in Mississippi, the pace of college desegregation in Alabama and the weakness of the enforcement powers in the Fair Housing Act.

The administration's recent emphasis on civil rights is politically wise. Though he will pick up few votes among black voters in the 1984 election, he does stand to hold the support of white citizens who would find it difficult to vote for a man perceived as racist.

Reagan's problem — and the problem of many of his advisers — is a reliance upon abstract principles without looking to their human effects.

Government should be colorblind, he believes. Therefore, it is wrong for government to require assignment of children to schools on the basis of race or to judge private employment practices by a color chart. But a total hands-off policy would almost certainly lead to blatant cases of discrimination in areas where good faith on racial matters still cannot be presumed.

Reagan believed that legal neatness and orderliness required that Congress, not the Internal Revenue Service, make the judgment as to whether racially discriminating private schools should be exempt from taxation. He thus reversed a long-standing policy denying such exemption and reaped a harvest of bad feeling on the part of blacks. He later backpedaled: He really *was* opposed to granting tax exemption, but he had to stick by his legal principle. His posture was unconvincing both to blacks and to the Supreme Court, which upheld the IRS' denial of tax exemption.

Reagan believed that the Legal Services Corp. was using taxpayers' money to pursue legal ends that were unpopular with most taxpayers. So he moved to cut federal support for the program. Blacks saw the corporation as the only means by which poor people could obtain needed legal advice and services.

Reagan wanted to free private enterprise from the burden of regulations that he felt were dragging it under. So he proposed a relaxation of anti-discrimination rules for federal contractors — reversing a 40-year trend. Blacks saw more social than economic significance in his move.

Early in his administration, the president appeared before the National Association for the Advancement of Colored People to stress the importance of helping blacks by helping the overall economy. But the cutbacks in services to the poor were felt long before the economic stimulus was felt, and the poor are preponderantly black.

And Reagan hemmed and hawed before finally taking a stand in favor of extending the Voting Rights Act.

Reagan and his advisers have been acting as one would expect objective observers to act if they came fresh to the United States, saw a racially diverse population and were asked to develop policies for that population — without receiving any background on the past discrimination that had handicapped a substantial minority of the people.

So when William Bradford Reynolds, head of the Justice Department's Civil Rights Division, went to Mississippi with Jesse Jackson and perceived the need to send federal registrars to the state, it was not a case of the leopard changing his spots. It was a case of scales falling from the eyes.

Reagan isn't backward about reassuring his right wing with symbolic stances: He favors a balanced-budget amendment while fostering record-shattering deficits; he favors public-school prayer. But until now he hasn't seen fit to make similar reassuring gestures toward the nation's largest minority.

So it's good, at last, to see Reagan belatedly recognizing that he has to offer black Americans more than abstract principles that sound good on paper but do nothing to reassure a segment of America that still feels itself largely shut off from the mainstream of national life. Maybe the motivation is politics. But one would like to think the president genuinely wants to establish his credentials as a non-racist sympathetic toward the plight of minorities.

the Charleston Gazette

Charleston, W. Va., November 23, 1984

DURING a campaign tour President Reagan was asked about his low standing with blacks. He replied that in his young days as radio announcer he "was fighting for civil rights before they called it civil rights."

"In fact," he said, "back in those days, broadcasting the Cubs and all, I was one of the handful of sports commentators throughout the country that was even then campaigning for the elimination of the rules that had kept minorities out of organized baseball."

Lou Cannon of *The Washington Post*, who has done extensive biographical research on Reagan, says he found no evidence of such militancy in Reagan's early career. Cannon said Reagan was a Roosevelt Democrat then, and at that time, President Roosevelt had not displayed any zeal for racial integration.

THE INDIANAPOLIS STAR

Indianapolis, Ind., July 16, 1984

President Reagan took a rhetorical pummelling in honor of the 20th anniversary of the Civil Rights Act. Most of the blows were routine — jabs at the president's alleged lack of compassion and the pursuit of policies supposedly inimical to the progress of minorities.

But he got one punch that he deserved. It came from Clarence Pendleton Jr., his own handpicked chairman of the U.S. Commission on Civil Rights.

Pendleton accused the president of stooping to the same kind of minority politicking as his opponents.

As evidence, Pendleton cited Mr. Reagan's convening of a special briefing restricted to blacks serving in the administration; the granting of "disadvantaged" status to Hasidic Jews, enabling them to qualify for certain federal business-related assistance, and the president's support for "set-aside" programs guaranteeing a share of construction contracts to minority own building firms.

In a letter to the president, Pendleton charged such actions "do mayhem to the Constitution and the civil rights laws." He is right. The president and Pendleton both contend that all law, all government programs must be color-blind. Yet in this election year here is the president apparently resorting to the old "numbers game" of ethnic politics.

The initial goal of the civil rights movement, Pendleton reminded the president, was "recognition and respect for all as individuals," a goal that must be adhered to. The chairman also refused to attend that briefing for blacks.

"Such meetings or briefings convened for groups by color, ethnicity or gender are divisive at best. This is what other administrations have done to show that government-designated minority groups are 'getting their fair share,' " he scolded. "Such meetings are contradictory to what you and I believe about working toward a race- and gender-neutral and colorblind society."

Since Pendleton's appointment he has consistently argued for an approach to civil rights law that neither favors nor discriminates against blacks and other minorities. He has stayed the course. The president, on the other hand, has strayed, lured by the expediencies of an upcoming campaign. Election year or not, he ought to get off the low road and back on the straight and narrow.

ST. LOUIS POST-DISPATCH

St. Louis, Mo., March 14, 1984

A report by the American Civil Liberties Union has charged that the Reagan administration's actions on civil rights "are at war with Congress and the courts," and that it has created "a dangerous crisis which could plunge the country back into historic patterns of race and sex discrimination."

Although that is a disturbing conclusion, the ACLU copiously documents how the administration has in effect repudiated a 30-year "bipartisan consensus reflected in scores of congressional statutes and thousands of court decisions." The report charges that the assault is "being led by President Reagan, directed by his White House advisers and carried out by the attorney general and top officials of the Department of Justice."

The report describes many instances in which the administration has reversed long-established government positions, thus curtailing civil rights protection for millions of Americans. It notes, for example, that Congress and the federal courts have repeatedly stated that a violation of the 1968 Fair Housing Act may be proven by showing that an intentional act of discrimination has been committed or that actions complained of have had a discriminatory effect. Although the "effects test" had been used by every prior administration and upheld on appeal, the Reagan Justice Department abandoned this concept in litigation and substituted the more difficult "intent" test.

On school desegregation, the report accuses the administration of "deliberately subverting congressional intent by undermining existing law instead of actively pursuing a policy of school desegregation." Although the 1964 Civil Rights Act gave the attorney general litigating authority to "materially further the orderly achievement of desegregation," the Reagan Justice Department opposed a voluntary desegregation plan in Seattle, which was later upheld by the Supreme Court. In St. Louis it objected to the voluntary desegregation plan agreed to by the city and many county school districts. In Bakersfield, Calif., it approved a voluntary magnet school desegregation plan that permits the continuation of segregated schools.

In applying the Voting Rights Act, the Reagan Justice Department cleared voting changes by jurisdictions with a history of discrimination, dropping the requirement that they prove the changes were not discriminatory. In a prisoners' rights case in Mississippi, a judge actually excluded the Justice Department from the litigation, saying its position was not consistent with the interests of the plaintiff inmates.

Responding to the ACLU charges, the Justice Department denied them and said they were politically motivated. Yet the non-partisan ACLU has issued many previous reports critical of Democrats as well as Republicans. What is alarming is the long-term effect the Reagan actions can have in undermining the Constitution and the rule of law.

St. Louis, Mo., December 10, 1984

The Reagan administration is making an extensive review of the guidelines used to detect patterns of employment discrimination against minorities and women, yet in view of its negative attitude toward affirmative action, civil rights groups are suspicious of the end results.

If the precise guidelines were all that were at stake, there might be a more general agreement that they could be modified. The last guidelines were issued in 1978, following earlier executive branch interpretations of the Civil Rights Act of 1964. In short, the rules have been followed by four previous administrations.

The present guidelines apply to employers of 15 or more workers and to all employment procedures, such as interviews and tests. The fundamental rule is that if the job selection rate for blacks or women, for example, is less than 80 percent of the rate for whites or males, that is taken as evidence of an adverse effect on the minority job applicants and may justify further investigation.

What are the objections to this rule? Some business leaders and Reagan officials contend that the 80 percent rule is too complicated, which it can be in application; that it burdens businesses with paper work, which it may well do; that it is applied too rigidly; and that statistics don't necessarily prove intent to discriminate.

An objective study might show that the 80 percent rule could be modified and the requirement for paper work reduced. It could hardly dismiss statistics as part of the evidence of discrimination, however, because a statistical pattern can illustrate the results of discrimination. Moreover, reducing every charge of alleged discrimination to a subjective test of intent would invite a multitude of court cases, without relieving business of legal burdens or reducing discrimination much.

Unfortunately, the civil rights retreats of the Reagan administration and the attitudes expressed by those involved in the study raise further questions. Clarence Thomas, chairman of the Equal Employment Opportunity Commission, which is charged with enforcing the employment law, is one of those who criticizes reliance on statistical patterns — but even he has been less opposed to affirmative action than the Justice Department, which is also a party to the new study.

Nor can civil rights proponents depend on help from the Civil Rights Commission as restructured to suit President Reagan. Staff director Linda Chavez says that "the guidelines actually handicap the employer searching for qualified individuals by forcing him to think in terms of race." Yet employers who discriminate obviously think in terms of race, and the civil rights law was expressly intended to make them think of race in a different way, to help remedy centuries of discrimination.

The Civil Rights Act would be meaningless without guidelines, and in view of continuing discrimination against women and minorities, the guidelines must not be made meaningless.

The Philadelphia Inquirer
Philadelphia, Pa., January 26, 1985

On Jan. 15, the day before the National Urban League released its annual report, "The State of Black America," President Reagan met with a group of blacks that included few traditional leaders.

Mr. Reagan spoke with a "grassroots" business organization on the anniversary of the Rev. Dr. Martin Luther King Jr.'s birth. Members of the fledgling group, called the Council for a Black Economic Agenda, characterized the meeting as symbolic but "progressive" because their ideas for black economic development represent "a new era" in which blacks can exploit the gains made during the civil rights movement.

"We've got ideas to contribute and I think that we can translate ideas into action. We need to move from slogans to specifics, from problems to solutions," said Robert Hill, a member of the group, which included conservative blacks as well as liberals.

Symbolic meetings are well and good but the nation's 28 million blacks are seeking a substantive response to the persistent problems of high unemployment, decreases in educational opportunities and growing disparities between the incomes of blacks and whites and other problems documented in the National Urban League report.

For the first time in nearly a decade the report contained an upbeat quality, along with a list of problems blacks face. Among the indicators of progress, the report said, was the elevation of Rep. William Gray 3d (D., Pa.) as head of the House Budget Committee; the Rev. Jesse Jackson's run for the White House; and a "revival of the interracial nonpartisan movement for racial justice," as evidenced by black and white cooperation to aid victims of famine in Ethiopia and to end apartheid in South Africa. The day after the report was released, Reuben V. Anderson was sworn in as the first black to sit on the Mississippi Supreme Court.

Despite progress, Mr. Reagan was criticized by many blacks for meeting with a "nontraditional" group. In itself, there is nothing wrong with listening to another voice. But the President has not fulfilled his responsibility by meeting with such a limited and unrepresentative gathering. Mr. Reagan should meet as well with the acknowledged black leaders. Most of their goals mirror those articulated by Dr. King. Using Dr. King's birthday to meet with a black group with limited interests and aspirations may be a perfectly good public relations tactic. But if the meeting fails to produce within the administration a new commitment to the concerns of blacks generally, it will stand as an ugly blemish on the memory of the martyred civil rights leader.

The Wichita Eagle-Beacon
Wichita, Kans., January 26, 1985

MANY blacks feel President Reagan's policies have left them behind in the past four years. The National Urban League's annual "State of Black America" report shows just how far they have been left behind, and how far Mr. Reagan has to go to improve his image with blacks.

The president claims his record on black issues has been distorted by the Urban League and other established black groups. But the statistics on blacks recently reported by the league speak clearly: At the start of President Reagan's first term, black joblessness was 12.9 percent; it is now 16 percent — more than double the rate for whites. Mr. Reagan says his economic recovery eventually will lift all boats, but that hasn't happened yet.

The extent to which the president has changed the fundamentals of political dialogue can be seen in the statement by Urban League President John Jacob that "We cannot place all our hopes on government." That is not only a political but a practical reality. There are serious problems within the black community that government alone can do little to solve. The deterioration of the black family over the past two decades is an example: 42 percent of all black families are headed by a single woman — and in more than half of these families, no one is employed. Mr. Jacob urges black private and community groups to pick up the slack left by the loss of federal funds to fight black teen-aged unemployment and pregnancy, high crime rates and poor education.

But Mr. Reagan also must do his part, by making new, vigorous efforts to reach out to the black community. His inaugural statements that all Americans, "white and black, rich and poor, young and old, will go forward together, arm in arm," was a good start, but the rhetoric must be backed up with action. The president needs to mend fences by meeting with black leaders, and not only those who agree with his economic views. He should speak out more strongly, as the National Urban League suggests, against South African apartheid. If he has alternative ideas to traditional social programs, he must explain more clearly to blacks why they are preferable. Enterprise zones are a good idea, but the president has yet forcefully to make his case directly to blacks.

Many black Americans remain skeptical about President Reagan at the beginning of this second term, and, given the record, they have every right to be. It's up to Mr. Reagan to put that skepticism to rest.

"CONTRARY TO A LOT OF DEMAGOGUERY THAT WE'RE HEARING, OUR ADMINISTRATION HAS MOVED WITH VIGOR AND VISION IN THE AREA OF CIVIL RIGHTS ENFORCEMENT!"

The Courier-Journal
Louisville, Ky., January 29, 1985

PRESIDENT REAGAN'S apparent effort to drive a wedge between black Americans and some of the more prominent black leaders might have easier going if he had more facts to support his visions. It's reminiscent of his wishful attempts, when Interior Secretary James Watt was trying to sell or lease virtually all the nation's resources, except maybe the national parks, to convince people that the Reagan administration was the best friend the environment ever had.

Now the topic is economic progress for blacks, and the President, twice in recent days, has undercut their traditional leaders. On Martin Luther King's birthday, January 14, he met with a group of black business executives, educators and others who share his view that economic development in depressed areas is better than the traditional ways of fighting poverty. No one from such organizations as the NAACP and Urban League was invited. Then, in a newspaper interview three days later, Mr. Reagan criticized some black leaders for distorting his record in order to keep their constituencies voting Democratic and ignoring their very real gains.

The tide lifts all boats

Fair enough: The President got only 10 percent of the black vote in November, but his popularity rating among blacks has been growing. He wouldn't be much of a politician if he didn't harken to advisers who say he could help his party if he'd spend more time urging these people to register and vote Republican.

The only trouble with this tidy script is that the main actor, characteristically, is out to lunch. He has his broad and mostly laudable visions, including one about a color-blind America in which everyone has an equal opportunity and in which a rising tide of economic good fortune "lifts all boats." But down in the homes and streets where everyone else lives, things tend to be drastically different.

Shoot, they're even different at the White House, as *The Washington Post* reported yesterday about a meeting of black Republican leaders last week with Vice President Bush. People who attended that meeting were quoted as saying that their access to Mr. Reagan is limited, their suggestions are ignored and that few of them have received jobs, contracts or other tangible rewards for their loyalty to the party and the President.

It would be grounds for a chuckle or two if the subject weren't so serious and the complaint so common. Almost *everybody's* access to President Reagan is limited, including the public's. The other day, he held his first press conference in six months. He pops up constantly in carefully planned snippets on TV or in the newspapers, and like any super politician he's always on the telephone congratulating an astronaut, a winning team or someone who just pulled a drowning child from a pond. But he doesn't have much of a head for details, except the ones he memorizes just before his sessions with journalists, and he has this odd habit of saying one thing while letting the people who work for him do another.

That's where the meetings with black leaders come in. The Reagan administration has done some good things in the field of civil rights, and some that are terrible. Its critics and supporters don't all agree on what programs are in the best interest of black citizens who are struggling, not only for an equal chance, but in many cases for a chance even to get to the starting line before the contest is over. The President, by choosing to meet only with supporters, and then only with supporters who aren't expecting political favors in return, simplifies everything. The real world grinds on. Mr. Reagan, having solved another grave problem, turns to the next chapter.

THE MILWAUKEE JOURNAL
Milwukee, Wisc., January 24, 1985

Once again, the National Urban League has irked President Reagan by reviewing the "State of Black America" and finding it grim. The president's rejoinder is that black leaders are misleading their people about the policies and achievements of his administration.

It certainly would be unfair to lay all of the blame for blacks' troubles at the White House door (and no responsible black leaders have done so). Still, some administration policies have distressed ordinary black citizens, not just their leaders.

On issues such as school desegregation and affirmative action, this administration has abandoned the stances of earlier administrations (including Republican administrations) that strongly championed civil rights. The president has effectively converted the once-independent Civil Rights Commission from an independent monitor of civil rights enforcement into a mouthpiece for administration policies.

Moreover, many poor blacks have suffered as the safety net has been weakened through severe budget cuts in social programs. According to the league's report, unemployment among blacks — 16% — is more than double the 6.5% unemployment rate for whites. The unemployment rate among black teenagers staggers the imagination.

The New York Times recently reported on studies showing that the income of one in four New Yorkers was below the poverty line, and that income disparities between blacks and whites had widened.

In his defense, the president talks about his proposals for enterprise zones and his efforts to expand opportunities for black entrepreneurs. He says black leaders ignore his efforts in order to preserve their own positions.

Undoubtedly, the administration hopes that its economic programs will spur prosperity for all. However, established black leaders would be derelict if they refrained from legitimate criticism.

If the administration wants to improve its standing with blacks, it should be sensitive to the problems of deteriorating cities, where millions of blacks live. And it should seek to improve public education, a sure path out of the ghetto pathology.

Indeed, a drive to better the education of poor, urban young people, through such programs as the laudable Head Start effort, could pay rich dividends. A broad constituency for such efforts well may exist, including even supporters of the administration's lukewarm civil-rights enforcement and its reductions in social spending.

Minneapolis Star and Tribune
Minneapolis, Minn., January 9, 1985

President Reagan's support for a new civil-rights bill in Congress is at once encouraging and disappointing. His endorsement reflects a willingness to revive the government's fight against discrimination. But it also betrays a misunderstanding of the challenges of that fight. Shoring up federal civil-rights enforcement requires a stronger measure than the bill he favors.

Congress and the president have been quarreling over the best way to enforce civil-rights laws ever since the Supreme Court ruling last February in the Grove City College case. That ruling sharply limited the government's authority to punish schools that violate the federal ban on sex discrimination. The court ruled that the government could not cut off all federal financial aid to a school if discrimination was found in only one of its programs. The ruling left most schools free to discriminate in admissions, athletics, hiring, courses, housing — any program not receiving direct federal help.

The president nevertheless welcomed the decision as a repudiation of needless government intrusion. But many lawmakers felt that the court's narrow interpretation contradicted the intent of the antidiscrimination law, and worried as well that the court's reasoning could be applied to other civil-rights statutes. A bipartisan group of lawmakers quickly wrote a bill meant to restore the enforcement authority the high court had removed.

The measure was straightforward: It would have forbidden any recipient of federal money to discriminate on the basis of sex, age, race, national origin or handicap. It passed the House overwhelmingly, but faltered in the Senate's preadjournment rush. Supporters understandably blamed the White House for its failure. If the president had embraced the bill, they argued, it would have passed without trouble.

Such arguments spurred Senate Majority Leader Robert Dole, R-Kan., to prepare a new version of last year's bill, which Reagan now pledges to support. That promise marks a refreshing turnabout for a president who has often seemed insensitive to the civil-rights struggle. Dole's bill would restore civil-rights enforcement for schools, but would do nothing to assure enforcement for the many other institutions — hospitals, social-service programs, transportation and housing agencies — that also receive federal funds.

If President Reagan objects to discrimination in schools, he should find it equally worrisome elsewhere. That is why the president would be wise to look closely at last year's bill, or at a similar measure soon to be offered by Sens. Edward Kennedy, D-Mass., and Lowell Weicker, R-Conn. (and supported by Minnesota Sen. Dave Durenberger). Both proposals would flatly prohibit discrimination in all federally funded institutions. Both would turn the president's proclaimed allegiance to civil rights into action. He should embrace the broader bills.

THE INDIANAPOLIS NEWS

Indianapolis, Ind., January 21, 1985

As reports go, the National Urban League's annual survey, "The State of Black America, 1985," was not too encouraging. It said, among other things, "that racial polarization and black alienation from the majority society increased in 1984."

Even given its partisan source, the Urban League's report is not to be ignored. The message it conveys is one of extreme frustration.

In an overview chapter, John Jacob, president and chief executive officer of the Urban League, wrote:

"In virtually every area of life that counts, black people made strong progress in the 1960s, peaked in the '70s, and have been sliding back ever since."

Jacob leaned heavily upon economic numbers to make his case, particularly those numbers dealing with jobs. Black unemployment stood at 16 percent at the end of last year, more than twice the 6.5 percent recorded for whites. The gap is widening.

In addition to — and probably connected with — the economic hardships blacks face, there are other frustrations. Nearly a quarter century after the first civil rights demonstrations to end segregation, many of the nation's blacks are living in segregated areas.

In those areas, a system of cultural values exists that is foreign to what the report called "the majority society." One out of four black babies born today is a child of a woman 19 years old or younger. Nearly 90 percent of the young mothers are not married.

These are statistics of moral breakdown, suffering and perpetual welfare. Clearly, they merit more innovative remedies than have been suggested in the report. Using the numbers as a club, "The State of Black America, 1985" attacks President Reagan, asserting that his "record is deplorable and includes continuing attacks against affirmative action, the unwarranted entry of the Justice Department into civil rights cases in an effort to turn back the clock."

Not surprisingly, the report suggests the solutions to many black problems lie in restoring policies of the past: more social spending, cutting defense spending and imposing federal authority on the private sector to end unfair hiring practices.

These "solutions" have to be considered part of the problem. After 20 years of civil rights legislation and massive government spending designed to eliminate poverty, the average black male earns 59.7 percent of what the average white male does. In 1960, the figure was 59.6 percent. Unless climbing one-tenth of one percentage point in two decades can be considered a victory, the policy of having government spend black poverty away would seem to have failed.

What it has done, however, is perpetuate and institutionalize the suffering and segregation. In some areas, perhaps even more than in the 1960s, there are still two Americas, one white and one black, and the distance between them is widening.

At the conclusion of its report, the Urban League cites its own self-help programs as an encouraging sign. They are encouraging, but many more such programs must be initiated by blacks themselves.

The problems confronting black Americans call for new solutions. Both politicians and civil rights activists should devote their energies to finding these new answers. They should represent more than just tinkering with past policies; the situation calls for an overhaul. And it ought to be done soon.

BUFFALO EVENING NEWS

Buffalo, N.Y., January 28, 1985

THE NATIONAL Urban League's 10th annual report on the state of black America contains a plea for President Reagan to begin to "heal the breach between his administration and black people."

The league candidly acknowledges that government cannot solve all minority problems. It "admits there are some things we ought to be doing, and we're prepared to do them." But the league specifies a "handful of small steps" that could address the differences constructively.

It urges administration support, for example, of civil rights legislation that would strengthen federal anti-discrimination rules weakened by an adverse Supreme Court decision last year. The administration has pledged to support such remedial legislation, a pledge that should be vigorously followed up. The report also urges a halt to cuts in social programs that hurt the poor, and exhorts the administration to persist in its initiative — blocked in the past by House Democrats — for urban enterprise zones. In addition, the league wants intensified pressures, beyond the administration's quiet diplomacy of "constructive engagement," against South Africa's abhorrent apartheid system.

Honest differences over specifics can exist, but the Urban League speaks realistically about minority problems. Many budget reductions under the Reagan administration have fallen on low-income people. The economic recovery of which the president boasts has been under way for more than two years, with millions of jobs created. Still, black unemployment averaged 16 percent last year, more than twice that of whites. Thus the recovery has been uneven, and the persistence of black joblessness poses exacting challenges that must be addressed.

Perhaps most importantly, the Urban League asks for meaningful dialogue between black leaders and the administration to discuss differences, bridge the gulf and replace polarization and rhetoric "with substance."

The league's report describes the Reagan administration attitude toward blacks as "deplorable." That alone, even if the administration considers this a gross misperception, must alert President Reagan to the need for a positive response as his second term as chief executive of all the people begins.

Chicago Tribune

Chicago, Ill., January 20, 1985

The National Urban League's condemnation of the Reagan administration's civil rights record used the wrong measurements and overstated the case, but it had a point.

The administration's basic response to the American dilemma of race and the promise of equal opportunity has been indifference to both. And the Urban League certainly read the election returns right. Blacks overwhelmingly voted against President Reagan because he gave them nothing to replace played-out programs, such as affirmative action and school busing, which his administration has worked to reverse.

But President Reagan understands the electorate, too, and he sees that those old approaches to equality of opportunity have a small and shrinking constituency. He has persisted in dismantling the civil rights policies of his predecessors because he knows that a majority either agrees with him or acquiesces.

The Urban League's complaint suffers for its insistence upon these old programs as the proper measure of commitment to the goal of equality. But that does not mean the league was wrong to say the administration's program is simply one of retreat. President Reagan's program is vulnerable to criticism because it offers no alternative.

And while the political energy has gone out of the old civil rights movement, President Reagan still cannot afford to remain indifferent. A diverse society suffers when it becomes as deeply split along any fault line as ours has on race. It is the President's responsibility to make an appeal across the accidental categories of birth and unite the country in a common understanding.

There are other, less abstract reasons for President Reagan to concern himself about the question of opportunity in this country. One of them is crime. Another is the deterioration of cities. Another is the horrible state of urban public education.

These social blights affect everyone, even those who applaud President Reagan's efforts to curtail old civil rights programs and cut back on social spending. And there is something President Reagan can do about it.

He can take the lead in establishing a renewed and increased national commitment to early education for the children of the growing urban underclass. They are the people who now seem doomed to slip more deeply into poverty. They are the ones who grow up dispirited and unprepared to seize opportunity even when it comes within their reach.

There is a considerable body of research to show that a program of early education could make a significant difference in the level of achievement these children attain. It is not a new idea. It is one that has proven effective in the past. It does not conflict with the basic principle of equality the way many of the old racial preference schemes did. It improves opportunity and strikes at one of the causes of this country's most intractable social problems.

President Reagan may prefer to disregard what the Urban League said about his administration, and the Urban League may prefer to resist the thought that some of its old approaches have gone out of date. But both are shortsighted if they fail to see the value in striking out on an innovative course.

If President Reagan wants to go down as a leader who made a contribution to solving the most troubling domestic issues of his time, he will launch a bold new program of early education of the children of the urban underclass and show the skeptics that the old civil rights agenda is not the only way to enhance equality of opportunity. And if he does, the Urban League ought to be the first to support him in the effort.

Reconstitution of the U.S. Civil Rights Commission

President Reagan dismissed the chairman of the U.S. Civil Rights Commission, Arthur Flemming, and Vice Chairman Stephen Horn, in November, 1981. Flemming, 76, a former secretary of health, education and welfare, was an outspoken Republican supporter of affirmative action and school busing programs, and had served on the commission since 1974. He was replaced by Clarence Pendleton Jr., 51, president of the Urban League of San Diego; Horn's replacement, Mary Louise Smith, had served as chairman of the Republican National Committee from 1974-1977. The changes, Administration officials explained, were made out of a desire to have people on the panel whose views "closely mirror the President's."

The White House announced in May, 1983 that three members of the commission who were critics of Administration policies would be replaced by Democrats who agreed with President Reagan's opposition to racial quotas and school busing. The President's intended course of action met with a stalemate in the Senate, which refused to confirm his nominees. The House, when it voted to extend the authorization of the Civil Rights Commission for five years, also passed an amendment stipulating that members of the panel could be removed only for "neglect of duty or malfeasance in office." To "break the deadlock," according to a White House statement, President Reagan dismissed the three Democratic members he wanted to replace Oct. 25, 1983. The White House statement said the President acted because the Senate Judiciary Committee had been considering reauthorization of the panel "specifically as constituted, with its incumbent members. Such a move, the statement declared, threatened the President's "constitutional power of appointment."

Reagan's dismissal of the three commission members—Mary Frances Berry, a professor of history and law at Howard University; Blandina Cardenas Ramirez, an educator in San Antonio, and Rabbi Murray Saltzman of Baltimore—provoked a flurry of protests in Congress; there was talk of turning the Civil Rights Commission into a congressional advisory body with members appointed by the House and Senate. The commission, bipartisan by law, had been established under President Eisenhower in 1957 as an independent advisory body, differing from cabinet departments in that it was not meant as an instrument of presidential policy. Its members served at the pleasure of the President, whose nominees were subject to Senate confirmation. No other President had attempted to so drastically alter the membership of the commission. Critics of the Reagan Administration's removal of holdover members stressed that such action undermined the independence and integrity of the commission and politicized its function. They charged that the move to dismiss three panel members, all critics of the Reagan Administration's civil rights record and of its opposition to racial quotas and school busing, was nothing less than an attempt to silence all opposition. (The replacement of all three members would give the commission a five-member majority appointed by President Reagan, and, presumably, sympathetic to his viewpoints on civil rights issues.) Administration officials countered that the civil rights groups were not really concerned about the independence of the panel but only wanted to protect their own favored policies. President Reagan said he had merely selected nominees who "don't worship at the altar of forced busing and mandatory quotas" and who "don't believe you can remedy past discrimination by mandating new discrimination." (See pp. 24-38, 136-147.)

In November, 1983, Congress passed legislation to reconstitute the commission as a creature of Congress and the Administration. The composition of the new commission, which was authorized for six years, represented a compromise between Reagan and the Congress. It would have eight members, four appointed by the president and four by Congress; the commissioners could be dismissed only for cause. Pendleton remained as the panel's chairman, and Linda Chavez Gersten as its staff director. Reagan's new appointees were: Morris B. Abram, former president of Brandeis University; John H. Bunzel, a senior research fellow at Stanford University's Hoover Institute, and Esther Gonzalez-Arroyo Buckley, a Texas high school science teacher. The congressional appointments were: Francis F. Guess, the labor commissioner of Tennessee; Robert A. Destro, an assistant professor of law at Catholic University, and a reinstated member, Blandina Ramirez. The new U.S. Commission on Civil Rights in January, 1984 officially renounced the use of racial quotas for promotion of black and other minorities, and said it would reassess busing as a means of desegregating schools.

FORT WORTH STAR-TELEGRAM
Fort Worth, Texas, November 25, 1981

While there is some question concerning the amount of influence wielded by the U.S. Civil Rights Commission these days, there can be no question that that influence will be wielded in a far different manner under Clarence Pendleton, President Reagan's choice to head the agency, than it has been in the past.

Pendleton, who will become the commission's first black chairman if he is confirmed by the Senate, has already made it clear that he will steer the agency on a radically different course than that chosen by his predecessors.

The chairman-designate, in his first public statement since being named to replace the ousted Arthur S. Flemming, said his goal would not be to eliminate poverty, which has been one of the cornerstones of the commission since its formation.

Instead, Pendleton said, he will concentrate on the necessity to create wealth. "The best social program I know is a job," Pendleton said. "That is the way we must go."

In other words, supply-side philosophy has come to the Civil Rights Commission.

Many black leaders throughout the country regard Pendleton's appointment with suspicion, if not downright hostility. Flemming, who was appointed by then-President Richard Nixon and who continued to serve through the terms of Gerald Ford and Jimmy Carter, was a strong advocate of affirmative action programs, busing to achieve racial balance in the schools and other aggressive measures not embraced by the Reagan administration and he had broad support throughout the black community.

From an ideological standpoint, Reagan's dismissal of Flemming and appointment of Pendleton are understandable, but they widen even greater the chasm between the president and the nation's black population.

The Chattanooga Times
Chattanooga, Tenn., November 27, 1981

When it comes to ensuring that one's subordinates will toe the official line, nothing is more effective than firing an official given to speaking his mind. That's the signal Preident Reagan transmitted last week when he removed two members of the Civil Rights Commission — supposedly an independent body.

In recent months the CRC has been quite critical of the administration's civil rights policies, especially those involving affirmative action, budget cuts and voting rights. In response, Mr. Reagan removed the body's chairman, Arthur S. Flemming, and member Stephen Horn, president of California State University at Long Beach. It's worth remembering that Mr. Flemming, himself a Republican and a member of the Eisenhower cabinet, was named to the CRC in 1972 when then-President Nixon forced the resignation of the previous chairman, the Rev. Theodore Hesburg of Notre Dame University.

Mr. Flemming's replacement will be Clarence Pendleton, a conservative black Republican who is president of the San Diego Urban League; he shares the administration's opposition to affirmative action hiring programs and busing to achieve school desegregation. Mr. Horn will be succeeded by Mary Louise Smith, former chairman of the Republican National Committee.

Mr. Reagan, of course, has the legal right to change the commission's make-up anytime he chooses, and the White House asserted the changes were made simply to allow the president to put his own people on the body. But there is merit in Mr. Flemming's contention that he was in effect fired because the commission did not shrink from criticizing the administration's civil rights policies.

The president's action was unusual but more than that, it could have the effect of discouraging honest, constructive criticism. That is the only power the commission had in trying to ensure proper respective for the civil rights of Americans. Now, apparently, even that is likely to be muted.

The Evening Bulletin
Philadelphia, Pa., November 23, 1981

Many blacks, expecting little from a conservative administration, now fear the worst in their continuing fight for racial equality. Perhaps they are overreacting. But these two developments last week should concern all of us:

☐ William Bradford Reynolds, the assistant attorney general for civil rights, announced a major policy change. From here on, the Justice Department will not seek integration of an entire school district simply because one portion is racially segregated.

Reynolds maintains this means the department would focus on specific schools where the evidence indicates state-enforced segregation was intentional. Civil rights attorneys, however, argue that you can't prove violations against school authorities except on a district-wide basis.

The Justice Department and the White House need to demonstrate that this policy will not prove a retreat to the days of separate and unequal public education.

☐ The White House abruptly fired Arthur Flemming, respected member of President Reagan's own party, as chairman of the U.S. Civil Rights Commission.

Flemming, 76, received no advance notice. According to rumor, he was fired over a commission report critical of police brutality against minorities.

Clarence M. Pendleton, picked to succeed him, would become the commission's first black chairman. But, some say, Pendleton is out of step with black rights leaders.

Pendleton, 51, is in step with Reagan, favoring jobs and economic opportunity to employment quotas.

He was born and educated in the District of Columbia, a city with one of the highest minority concentrations in the country. He has been president of San Diego's Urban League for six years.

Pendleton will have an opportunity to expound on this at Senate confirmation hearings. The senators should probe Pendleton's civil rights philosophy and plans for running the Civil Rights Commission.

The law that created the commission during the tumultuous civil rights protest of the '60s made clear that presidents have the choice of chairmen. There's no quarrel about that. But the mission of the Civil Rights Commission under Flemming and, before him under Notre Dame's Father Theodore M. Hesburgh, has been to serve as the nation's prodding conscience on civil rights.

We wish we could say we no longer needed laws to guarantee civil rights. But racial bigotry and discrimination still exist in America. If the economy worsens, there's apt to be more.

There's much to be done. It's up to President Reagan , with the help of the Senate, to assure that the Civil Rights Commission is able to do its part of the job.

OKLAHOMA CITY TIMES
Oklahoma City, Okla., November 18, 1981

PRESIDENT REAGAN has made a couple of interesting and politically astute appointments to key positions in his administration.

Clarence M. Pendleton, a black, was named to replace Arthur S. Flemming, a liberal Republican, as head of the U.S. Civil Rights Commission. Dr. C. Everett Koop, a skilled pediatric surgeon, has just been confirmed by the Senate as surgeon general of the United States.

In one case the president has effectively disarmed potential opponents of the Civil Rights Commission choice before the battle lines could form. In the other, he has reassured the conservative wing of his political base that he remains committed to the pro-family and pro-life concept.

Pendleton happens to be a Republican, but he is also president of the Urban League of San Diego. It would be hard for civil rights activists to criticize his appointment to the Civil Rights Commission chairmanship, except perhaps on an "Uncle Tom" basis, a ploy that could backfire on them.

At the same time, the White House said another commission member, Stephen Horn, is to be replaced by Mary Louise Smith, former national chairman of the Republican Party. Her selection may have been intended to answer feminists' complaints about Reagan's purported lack of commitment to women's rights, although she is not known as an activist in this respect but rather as a long-time laborer in the GOP vineyard.

Flemming, who often gives the impression of a liberal Democrat masquerading as a Republican, was understandably upset about being replaced. But he should have been fired long ago. He opposes virtually everything Reagan stands for and has no business in this administration. Indeed, just as the change was announced, Flemming issued a report criticizing the Reagan administration policies on school desegregation.

He claimed they are "in conflict with the Constitution." He said the Constitution "requires desegregation" but that the administration has opposed desegregation plans in Houston, Seattle and Chicago. That distorts the issue, however. Just because the administration might dislike a specific plan worked out under jurisdiction of some federal district judge, it doesn't follow that the administration favors a return to classroom segregation.

The opposition to Koop has been led by labor and feminist organizations and the American Public Health Association. They allege he is "insensitive" to issues dealing with women — a charge that doesn't hold water, inasmuch as a substantial number of women agree with his anti-abortion stand.

Those against Dr. Koop seem to fear that he will use the position to push anti-abortion views and his advocacy of traditional roles for women. The truth is that advocacy in such a key administration post was never a problem, as long as the official held views favored by liberals.

THE MILWAUKEE JOURNAL
Milwaukee, Wisc., November 16, 1981

President Reagan's graceless dismissal of Arthur Flemming as chairman of the US Civil Rights Commission adds fuel to the raging perception that the administration is hostile to civil rights enforcement.

Because the commission's chairman serves at the pleasure of the president, Reagan's move was within the president's rights, as Flemming conceded. Nonetheless, the timing of the announcement of Flemming's removal — virtually at the same time the commission released a report critical of the administration's school desegregation stance — makes irresistible the conclusion that the dismissal was in retaliation for Flemming's unyielding insistence on strong enforcement of civil rights laws and desegregation orders.

Augmenting the impression of White House petulance and punitiveness was the pointed failure of the president's spokesman to mention Flemming by name in announcing that Clarence Pendleton, a conservative black Republican from California, had been appointed as the new chairman of the commission.

The Reagan move against Flemming matched the lack of grace shown by President Richard Nixon in ousting Father Theodore Hesburgh as commission chairman nine years ago. As did Nixon, the Reagan administration denied any connection between the removal and the critical statements of the commission or its chairman. That explanation didn't wash in 1972 and it doesn't wash now.

In both instances, the White House mistook the role of the commission, which is an independent agency established by Congress to advise on enactment of civil rights laws and to monitor enforcement. The commission is not an instrument of administration policy. Indeed, the Civil Rights Commission would be unworthy of its name were it to become an apologist for and an abettor of the retreat from strong enforcement of the laws.

As for Flemming, he is a justly respected and committed citizen, whose integrity has led him to serve principles, not politicians. That he leaves office with Reagan's enmity adds luster to Flemming's already brilliant accomplishments in a variety of government posts.

The Hartford Courant

Hartford, Conn., November 20, 1981

In the last few weeks, Secretary of State Alexander M. Haig Jr. and National Security Adviser Richard V. Allen have undermined the Reagan presidency with in-fighting, loose talk of a nuclear warning shot and Mr. Allen's acceptance of a magazine gratuity.

Budget director David A. Stockman's "ramblings" to an editor have challenged and undercut the effectiveness of the administration's entire economic policy.

Yet, not one has lost his job.

The only person President Reagan has fired in the last week is Arthur S. Flemming, chairman of the U.S. Commission on Civil Rights for the last eight years and a Nixon appointee. He is also the first person in the commission's 24-year history to be involuntarily removed from office.

Mr. Flemming owes his downfall, not to intemperate remarks or a threat to the national security, but to his support of busing to end school desegregation and affirmative action to improve the employment of minorities and women. School desegregation and equal employment are two goals central to the federal agency charged with overseeing the equal rights of all Americans.

He has been replaced by Clarence M. Pendleton, a black conservative from Mr. Reagan's home state of California. He was chosen in part because his civil rights views "would closely mirror the president's," according to one White House aide.

The administration has defended Mr. Pendleton's hiring and Mr. Flemming's firing as part of its effort to fill all posts with Reagan loyalists.

The chairmanship of the commission on civil rights, however, has not been a political position that has changed from administration to administration. Since his appointment in 1974, Mr. Flemming has headed the commission under four administrations — three Republican and one Democratic. His Republican loyalties harken back to his service as secretary of health, education, and welfare in the Eisenhower administration.

The White House apparently finds effective enforcement of the civil rights laws more threatening than aides who may have accepted bribes, alarmed the European allies or destroyed White House credibility on Capitol Hill.

That is a message which should disturb black and white Americans alike.

Minneapolis Star and Tribune

Minneapolis, Minn., December 18, 1981

If there was any doubt about the validity of Arthur Flemming's criticisms of the Reagan administration's commitment to equal rights, it was dispelled last month. On the same mid-November day, two events occurred: First, the U.S. Commission on Civil Rights, which Flemming has headed since 1974, issued a report noting that the goal of desegregated schools had not yet been achieved for many black Americans — and that the administration has "tended to support" sentiments against busing as a means to that goal. Second, President Reagan removed Flemming from his post.

Flemming, a former president of Macalester College in St. Paul, responded to his dismissal by repeating his concerns. Members of the commission, he said, feel an obligation "to call the shots as we see them. We feel it would be wrong to attempt to temper our findings and recommendations to what we understand to be the views of an administration that happens to be in power at a particular time.

"We feel [that administration officials] are headed in the wrong direction. We feel they're headed in the direction of either eliminating or weakening affirmative action as a method of achieving equal employment opportunity."

There has been ample evidence that Flemming is right about the administration's direction. In recent months, Vice President Bush said the administration wants to relax or drop guidelines forbidding discriminatory hiring practices, setting out employers' responsibilities to prevent sexual harassment, banning sex discrimination in school athletics and requiring schools not to discriminate against the handicapped. Earlier, the Education Department proposed an end to rules designed to protect school employees against sex bias. The Labor Department decided that handicapped people shouldn't be able to sue employers for job discrimination. The Transportation Department dropped its requirement that mass-transit systems be accessible to the handicapped.

"All of us, including minorities and women, have something to fear if people succeed in either eliminating or weakening methods we need to use in order to take the Constitution of the United States and make it a living document," Flemming warned as he left office. It is meaningless, in other words, to claim commitment to a goal, but to reject effective means of achieving that goal. But that is what is happening in Washington today. The result could be the halt, or reversal, of the nation's long, slow progress toward equality of opportunity for all its citizens.

The Register

Santa Ana, Calif., November 27, 1981

Arthur S. Flemming has been informed that his services will no longer be required as chairman of the United States Commission on Civil Rights. Flemming is to be replaced by Clarence Pendleton who, if confirmed, would be the commission's first black chairman. The Reagan administration doubtless felt that Pendleton's appointment would make a nice statement. They would have made a better statement by abolishing the commission and finding another job for Pendleton, if he really needs one.

The U.S. Commission on Civil Rights is a classic example of how "temporary" agencies assume permanent status in government, a textbook illustration of how government gets out of control.

The commission was established in 1957, with a two-year life span, a budget of $200,000 and 15 employees. Its mandate was to investigate violations of the 15th Amendment's guarantee of the right to vote, to collect information on violations of the 14th Amendment (guaranteeing equal protection of the law), and to review the laws and policies of the federal government to detect inadvertant or purposeful violations of the two amendments. It was supposed to focus attention on the subject of civil rights, get the government moving in the arena, and fade out of the picture, after congratulating itself on a job well done.

We would be the last to contend that the federal government is now doing a perfect job in ensuring civil rights for all, but the government's consciousness has certainly been raised. The Voting Rights Act was passed 16 years ago. Over 130 statutes and executive orders regarding civil rights are now on the books. The government allocates about two-thirds of a billion dollars a year to civil rights enforcement.

A naive person might suppose that, having seen this flurry of activity, the Civil Rights Commission would have concluded that its function, essentially an advisory one, had been fulfilled long ago, and quietly gone out of business.

Like most bureaucracies, however, the commission looked around for other things to do. It became the nation's most dogged advocate of forced busing as the only acceptable solution to discrimination.

In recent years the Commission has ranged far afield, becoming something of an institutional gadfly. In 1977 it was publicizing photographic essays on migrant workers and learned studies on "The Working and Living Conditions of Mushroom Workers." It has criticized stereotyping of women on commercial television, and called for laws requiring that all guns be kept locked and unloaded. It has issued reports calling for the elimination of spanking as a child-rearing tool. One is hard put to understand the relationship of such recommendations to voting rights and discriminatory laws.

The issues the commission has, in its eccentric later years, chosen to address may well be important. But we don't see why the taxpayers should be paying people to explore and publicize them. Most of the issues do not lack for advocates who are willing to promote their ideas without taxpayer subsidies. Last year the U.S. Commission on Civil Rights had a budget of $14 million (28 times its original allocation) and a staff of 285.

$14 million won't balance the federal budget, but it would make a little bitty dent. Closing down the commission would also establish a healthy precedent. It would send a signal that this administration was not afraid to bite the bullet and close down agencies that have long outlived their usefulness. It might even constitute a suggestion that the federal government should not be in the business of taking taxpayers' money and using it to promote a political or social agenda.

If government is ever to be brought under control, dozens of government agencies that have either outlived their usefulness or proven their uselessness will have to be abolished outright. Never mind the knee-jerk reaction that would follow because of its sensitive subject field: the Civil Rights Commission would have been a good place to make a stand.

Rocky Mountain News

Denver, Colo., February 15, 1982

SAM Hart is hardly the kind of guy most civil rights champions would want to go to the well with. He's against the Equal Rights Amendment for women, against abortion, against busing to integrate schools and against the government's protecting civil rights for homosexuals.

Hart's positions aren't all that unusual, of course. What makes them significant is that he has been nominated by President Reagan to serve on the U.S. Civil Rights Commission, which is supposed to look out for the civil rights of all Americans.

In one fell swoop during an interview the other day, Hart, a black radio preacher from Philadelphia, alienated various women's groups, black civil rights groups and the gay community. His hostility to homosexuals was especially pronounced, declaring that "God made Adam and Eve, not Ada and Eve or Adam and Steve."

Sen. John Heinz of Pennsylvania has asked the Senate Judiciary Committee to put a "hold" on the nomination until he can look into Hart's qualifications.

Better yet, the White House ought to consider withdrawing the nomination. Hart obviously is out of sync with the purpose of the Civil Rights Commission.

The News American

Baltimore, Md., March 4, 1982

We think the Rev. B. Sam Hart did a favor to President Reagan, himself and the rest of us by removing himself from consideration for a post on the U.S. Civil Rights Commission.

President Reagan nominated the Philadelphia radio evangelist last month. The selection stirred considerable criticism because of Rev. Hart's opposition to school busing and to women's and homosexuals' rights; in addition, the reverend's civil rights credentials were seen as weak, his moral posturing a bit overblown.

When he realized he had was no chance of landing the commission post, he charged that "many, many" communists and homosexuals have "infiltrated" the top level of the government and the media. According to Rev. Hart, it is because such people have so much power and influence that he had to withdraw his nomination.

We suspect that the Rev. Hart, bitter and disappointed because he lost a job, simply said the first thing that came to mind. We give him the benefit of the doubt. But if he calculatedly made his accusations without any intention of furnishing proof, he was irresponsible to an extreme. Shades of late Senator Joseph McCarthy, who not once proved any of his 1950s charges that the Department of State was riddled with reds. McCarthy was a United States senator; Mr. Hart is a rather obscure radio preacher. But the potential for mischief still remains. Unless the churchman can back up his charges, we say he has the responsibility to tell the public he misspoke out of frustration.

The News and Courier

Charleston, S.C., March 15, 1982

According to some conservatives, two surefire qualifications for success in this United States are to be black and female. The proposition is dubious, to say the least. There are simply not enough black females sitting on top of the world, outside show business, to support the argument.

What might be called "reverse racism," in fact, may make it more difficult for members of minority groups, unless they are stereotypes, to reach positions of prominence in society.

Take the case of the Rev. B. Samuel Hart. Now it is not impossible that his nomination as a U.S. Civil Rights Commissioner owed something to the fact that he is black. It is also not impossible that the bitter opposition to him had something to do with the fact that he is a conservative. For some strange reason, blacks are not expected to be conservative and the Rev. Mr. Hart's political views appeared downright provocative to many people. At a press conference he called, but now regrets, he expressed his opposition to trendy tolerance of homosexuality, expressed his doubts about the equal rights amendment and said that he opposed busing to integrate public schools.

The Rev. Mr. Hart, who has been described as "a radio evangelist," says that he felt constrained to withdraw his name from consideration for the post because of the opposition to his appointment. He attributed this hostility to his conservative views although he insists that his opinions are shared by the majority of Americans and that, far from being an ultra rightist, he is a moderate.

The Rev. Mr. Hart felt that he would be able to give the commission "balance" and it is, certainly, a pity that his views will not now be reflected on the commission. However, as with a number of other controversial nominations for delicate posts in the field of human rights, the reason that the Rev. Mr. Hart seemed unlikely to receive the blessing of the Senate may have nothing to do with his political views.

The withdrawal of the Rev. Mr. Hart came after press allegations that he owed the Pennsyvania Minority Business Authority $23,542 in penalties and delinquent principal payments on a loan.

Would that a concern for principles could always triumph over racial or political bias.

Chicago Defender

Chicago, Ill., March 25, 1982

Completely disregarding substantive objections to the selection of Clarence M. Pendleton, Jr. as chairman of the United States Commission on Civil Rights, the Senate Judiciary Committee, last week, approved his nomination. Pendleton was President Reagan's choice.

The President could not have picked a greater foe of Civil Rights even if he had nominated the Grand Keagle of the Invisible Empire of the Ku Klux Klan. Pendleton is against busing whether for racial mix or pupil numerical balance. He is against Affirmative Action however just the contention. He is against the 1966 Voting Rights Act in its present fool-proof form.

These are the three components of Civil Rights that hold up the framework of an important racial advance in a divided society. Mr. Pendleton is a disciple of Reagan. Together they will turn the Civil Rights movement into a Seventh-Day Adventist forum. The new chairman of the Commission will not forego his plantation etiquette; he answers his master's beck and call faithfully.

The Philadelphia Inquirer

Philadelphia, Pa., February 21, 1982

In his press conference Thursday, President Reagan rose to the defense of his appointment of the Rev. B. Samuel Hart to the U.S. Civil Rights Commission. Every bit of information to emerge in the two weeks since Mr. Hart's selection became known dramatizes that confirmation of the appointment would be grossly offensive.

It would have the effect of declaring that the position of the government of the United States on the rights of American citizens is that of Sen. Strom Thurmond (R., S.C.), Sen. Jesse Helms (R., N.C.), Rep. Trent Lott (R., Miss.), the Rev. Jerry Falwell and others of their view of life and human justice who, like them, facilitated and now are aggressively supporting Mr. Hart's appointment.

Mr. Hart, a Philadelphia minister with broadcasting interests, was virtually unknown by anyone sensitive to civil rights until Mr. Reagan's interest in him became known. Since then, his statements and examination of his previous articulations have revealed him as virulently opposed to human dignity and rights of full citizenship for women (about whom he condescends), for blacks (about whom, though black himself, he takes the position of the unreconstructed Southern racists who support him), for Americans concerned with government subsidization of racially segregated institutions (for which he supports tax exemptions) and for homosexuals (whom he vitriolically insists are "sinners" unentitled to the rights of citizenship).

Mr. Hart's home-state senators — John Heinz and Arlen Specter — have an inescapable responsibility in this situation. Both have raised questions about the appropriateness of his appointment, but neither has yet set forth the only morally acceptable position. That is a flat, public commitment that Mr. Hart is unfit to serve and that his confirmation will be opposed with all their energies.

Mr. Hart was an unknown when Sens. Specter and Heinz expressed skepticism. Two weeks have passed. How long will it take them to recognize the reality of the appointment — and to take positions on it?

THE COMMERCIAL APPEAL
Memphis, Tenn., February 18, 1982

THE U.S. Civil Rights Commission has accused the Department of Agriculture of discriminating against black landowners. By offering more favorable loans to white farmers, by not providing adequate information to black farmers and by stacking county loan committees with white farmers, says the commission, the Department of Agriculture is sounding a death knell for black farmers.

As a result of that discrimination, concludes the commission, the "survival and operation of blacks in agriculture is at stake."

While there can be little doubt that black landowners are in trouble (in 1969 they numbered 133,973, compared with 57,271 in 1978), there is no convincing evidence that the dwindling number of black landowners is a direct result of racial discrimination by the Department of Agriculture.

On the contrary, it seems to be a problem faced by small farmers everywhere, black and white. Lured by the ready cash of large corporations and stifled by the lack of money available for loans, small farmers are finding it increasingly difficult to stay on the farm.

Jerry Pennick, the executive director of the Emergency Land Fund, a Southern-based nonprofit organization dedicated to stopping the decline of black land ownership, says if the current trend continues blacks will disappear from the ranks of American landowners within a mere four years.

The statistics speak for themselves. In 1969, for example, Tennessee blacks owned 285,000 acres of land. By 1978, that number had dropped to 177,000. Neighboring states report an identical trend. In 1969, blacks in Mississippi owned 1.3 million acres of land; by 1978 it had fallen to 677,000 acres. In 1969, blacks in Arkansas owned 286,000 acres; by 1978 it had gone down to 194,000 acres.

If black ownership is declining as rapidly as the statistics indicate, it is a discouraging sign for those who advocate economic independence for blacks. To a great extent, the Mid-South's future is dependent on the speed with which black residents get into the mainstream of a free enterprise economy. Black land ownership can help achieve that goal.

"We feel once that is lost," says Pennick, whose studies were quoted in the commission report, "we've lost any hope of economic independence."

TO REVERSE the trend. Pennick is organizing a campaign to educate black landowners about the importance of staying on their land and using it to earn a livelihood. He agrees with the commission that black farmers have been denied equal access to low-interest loans, but he also sees other causes for the decline in black land ownership, the same type of social and economic factors that have discouraged white landowners from pursuing a farming career.

Although the commission's charges that the black decline is "rooted in racism" seems a bit off the mark, some of the commission's findings do indicate a need for a greater sensitivity by the Department of Agriculture to the needs of black farmers.

One of the things that especially rankled commission members was the fact that the racial composition of the three-member FmHA committees that approve loans has changed drastically in recent years. In 1979, says a spokesman for the commission, there were 33 blacks on the loan boards in Tennessee. One year later, that number had fallen to two. There is a similar situation in Mississippi, with the number of black board members falling from 48 to 21.

That's not necessarily a sign that blacks are being discriminated against. It simply may reflect the fact that there are fewer black farmers and that those remaining are showing less interest in continuing. But the above figures on loan committee memberships, along with the statistics on the overall trend, are an indication that the Department of Agriculture does need to make a greater effort to involve blacks in the process.

The Charlotte Observer
Charlotte, N.C., February 16, 1982

Where, you have to wonder, does President Reagan keep finding these people? After last year's debacle surrounding his nomination of Ernest Le-Fevre to be the administration's human rights watchdog, you'd think the president would be a little more sensitive.

Now Mr. Reagan is trying to figure out what to do about his choice of the Rev. B. Sam Hart to serve on the U.S. Civil Rights Commission.

Mr. Hart, the choice of such reliable civil rights champions as Sen. Strom Thurmond, R-S.C., and the Moral Majority, recently held what the administration viewed as an "ill-timed" press conference.

Mr. Hart announced, among other things, that he opposes the Equal Rights Amendment and school integration achieved through busing. That may be consistent with the administration's policy. But it is not reassuring to those national leaders — and there still are some — who are actually concerned about civil rights.

The Dallas Morning News
Dallas, Texas, February 24, 1982

CAN you believe it? The Rev. B. Sam Hart, Ronald Reagan's recent nominee to the U.S. Civil Rights Commission, is against *busing*.

It is the clincher, the rock-bottom affront to the civil rights community, which is currently after him with hammer and tongs. Hart, though black, is against the panacea now being pushed as the answer to our racial problems.

Can a man of such — how to put it? — asymmetrical views protect civil rights in America? It depends perhaps on how you define protection. Hart's opponents don't define it so much as they inflict it, busing being the supreme example.

Busing is good for you: Such is the fashionable orthodoxy. Never mind how many people, including black people, detest it; never mind all the school systems it's helping destroy. If you're against busing, you're probably a racist.

This isn't caricature. The charge has been made explicitly and often and will be leveled again, as Hart's nomination wends through the Senate. Being black, Hart may be difficult to label as a racist; so the approved line will probably be that he's "insensitive."

It's a word that Hart's critics should use sparingly, because, doubled back, it can be used to flay them. Who's "insensitive," indeed, when the vast bulk of the people reject social experiments that the experimenters nevertheless insist on pursuing to their bitter conclusions?

Hart's critics strike us as remorselessly elitist — contemptuous of differing opinions, determined to make of the U.S. Constitution a forcing-bed, after the manner of Procrustes, the legendary inn-keeper who stretched or compressed his guests according as they were too long or too short for the mattress.

Forcing-beds evidently aren't for B. Sam Hart, a man who doesn't swallow as absolute gospel the doctrines of professional spokesmen for civil rights. If nothing worse than this can be said of the gentleman, let's confirm him.

Sam Hart won't make it to meetings of the U.S. Civil Rights Commission, and that's probably as it should be. But the Hart story seems ultimately less about Sam Hart than about the personnel procedures at the White House.

Mr. Hart, you'll remember, is the black evangelist the administration decided three weeks ago to name to the Civil Rights Commission. The appointment created immediate controversy when in a newspaper interview Mr. Hart opposed busing, the ERA and the concept of "gay rights,"

Richmond Times-Dispatch
Richmond, Va., February 28, 1982

Understandably, President Reagan wishes to lay to rest accusations that his administration is insensitive to black Americans. Just as understandably, he wishes to appease the Religious Right, a key GOP constituency that feels the administration has tossed too few plums its way. So the Rev. B. Sam Hart, who is black and an evangelical, looked like an ideal choice to nominate to the U.S. Civil Rights Commission — a man who could do political double-duty. In fact, Mr. Hart was a terrible pick, a fact a thorough background check of the gentleman would have revealed. Unfortunately, somebody on the president's staff was napping. Again.

Late last year, the president nominated William M. Bell of Detroit to become chairman of the Equal Employment Opportunity Commission. Mr. Bell represented himself as a bigwig in the job-placement business and received Mr. Reagan's blessing on that basis. After the administration had committed itself to Mr. Bell, it was learned that, in fact, he was the sole employee of his firm, had never in his career supervised more than four workers and had helped no one get a job in all of 1981.

Just as the administration was wiping the last of the Bell egg from its face — splat! — along comes an omelet a la Hart. While Mr. Reagan was stoutly defending the Philadelphia minister from attacks by liberal groups incensed by his views on busing, homosexual rights and the like, a dismal series of embarrassing facts surfaced about Mr. Hart's finances. First, he owes $4,400 in back taxes to Pennsylvania. Second, a broadcast company that he owns defaulted last fall on a $100,000 loan guaranteed by the Small Business Administration. Third, he is $23,541 behind in payments to a Pennsylvania minority loan pro-

gram. Given Mr. Reagan's record of rebuking those who irresponsibly fail to repay public loans, the president had no choice Friday but to "accept" Mr. Hart's request that his name be withdrawn from consideration for the civil rights post.

This kind of shoddy spadework is intolerable. In the first place, it costs the Reagan administration incalculably in public confidence. (We can hear the detractors now: "These are the guys who are going to restore the economy, save us from the Russians and stabilize the Western Hemisphere? When they're ignorant of liabilities in their appointees that even an Inspector Clouseau would trip over?") Mr. Hart evidently was picked for the post last October. Yet four months later Mr. Reagan could tell the world in a press conference, "I am quite confident in his quality and his ability for that job." Is the president's appointments staff composed of bears in hibernation for the winter?

And what does this sort of spectacle do to the morale of American blacks, who for the second time now under this administration have seen one of their own propped up only to be knocked down in disrepute — all because of amateurish record checks? When some are only too ready too seize on the foibles of high-status minorities as "typical," this administration bears a special responsibility to avoid touting men like Mr. Bell and Mr. Hart. There are too many qualified blacks around to excuse such negligence.

Nobody at the White House is exactly jumping up and down to take responsibility for the Hart snafu. Evasiveness is a character flaw that, coupled with incompetence, adds up to the same deficiency that cost Mr. Hart his job. Should the same standard not apply to people who habitually hand the president half-baked dossiers?

The Virginian-Pilot
Norfolk, Va., March 4, 1982

among other things. Civil rights leaders and Washington politicians predictably jumped all over the Philadelphia preacher.

At the time, we thought Mr. Hart was unfairly criticized. After all, he favored integration and also equal rights for women. Since Mr. Hart's views were the White House's, we thought the administration should have been rushing to the evangelist's defense. As it happened, though, the White House inexcusably stood by as Mr. Hart twisted slowly in adverse political winds.

Perhaps one reason for this was the story of Mr. Hart's finances, reported after his interview on civil rights. Mr. Hart defaulted on a Small Business Administration loan. He is in arrears on repaying a minority loan program in Pennsylvania. He

owes $4,400 in back state taxes. Yet if these facts led the White House to forsake Mr. Hart, they are also facts that should have been known inside the White House when his appointment was being contemplated.

A well-informed personnel office wouldn't have selected such an imperfect vessel as Mr. Hart to carry its views on civil rights to the commission. As with a couple of other Reagan appointments, one gets the feeling that the personnel people might have relaxed their investigations of Mr. Hart as soon as they learned he was black. This administration, commendably pledged to the principle of merit and opposed to judging people by their skin color, obviously has a good way to go.

The Birmingham News
Birmingham, Ala., September 15, 1982

Has the U.S. welfare system become a racist crutch for blacks?

Should it be replaced by private programs that encourage individual initiative?

A newly formed group of black conservatives which met this week in Arlington, Va., answers both questions in the affirmative.

The organization — the New Coalition for Economic and Social Change — was formed by a group of successful black businessmen, political activists and academicians in 1981 as an alternative voice to the traditional civil rights coalition. Its first president is Clarence M. Pendleton Jr., who is also chairman of the U.S. Civil Rights Commission.

The organization will conduct public policy analysis and research and make its findings available to the public to assist in public debate over government policies and issues.

Pendleton opened the two-day conference stating the organization's intention to draft a new black agenda. "We must stop blaming every failure, we must stop blaming every closed door on racism," he told the 200 conferees, and "foster self-help and individual initiative."

He declared that the Great Society programs have failed in their mission of fostering economic opportunity and ending poverty, especially among black people. He told the conference that blacks must stop looking to government for solutions to their problems.

One should welcome the formation of the new coalition. While it will no doubt take time for it to establish its credibility with the black people it wishes to serve primarily, it will fill a void in national debate over welfare issues and provide a philosophical base for blacks who have become disillusioned with traditional civil rights groups.

From a historical perspective, the organization may be viewed as part of the nationwide swing to conservative principles which has resulted in determined challenges to the conventional liberal wisdom of the past 50 years. If it does no more than change the monolithic image of blacks, shared by perhaps both whites and blacks, it will have accomplished a worthwhile task.

But one can expect more from the new coalition. Armed with facts other civil rights groups have tended to ignore, it can offer hope and new avenues for young black people to explore in their quest for achievement in the nation's political and economic life.

Few would question the need for such an organization — black or white — which is dedicated to measures which will inevitably lessen government's repressive and misguided efforts to effect social and economic change.

THE LOUISVILLE TIMES

Louisville, Ky., May 27, 1983

The Reagan administration keeps insisting its intentions toward the U. S. Commission on Civil Rights are honorable. Yet its approaches are as subtle as those of the Sioux toward George Armstrong Custer at Little Bighorn.

The three members of the commission fired by President Reagan this week voted on April 12 to subpoena documents on civil-rights law enforcement by the departments of Education and Labor. The White House can deny all it wants that the firings were not in retaliation for the subpoena vote and were part of an effort to curb the commission's independence. Anyone who believes the White House can be persuaded that there was no Holocaust.

There was even a preliminary decision to dump the outspoken Jill Ruckelshaus along with the other three. But, as noted here on Wednesday, someone belatedly realized how very gauche that would be. So instead of trotting out four new members of the commission, three white males were brought before the TV cameras.

For appearance's sake — and appearances, after all, are everything with the Reagan administration — Linda Chavez was seated with them for the formal introductions. She is being nominated to be the commission's staff director. That is not the same as being a policy-making commissioner.

For the record, if Morris Abram, John Bunzel and Robert Destro are confirmed by the Senate, the membership of the Commission on Civil Rights will consist of one black male, two white females and three white males with distinctly conservative views. It's a ratio that accurately reflects the concerns of the Reagan administration.

THE CHRISTIAN SCIENCE MONITOR

Boston, Mass., May 27, 1983

President Reagan's three new nominees to guard Americans' civil rights have records of involvement with the subject. By acting in office with the concern and independence they cited this week, they could ease negative impressions left by the circumstances of their appointment to the Civil Rights Commission.

This is the six-member, bipartisan body whose last report before Mr. Reagan's election concluded that "the lack of enforcement by the executive branch of government, the weakening of good legislation by Congress, and the diminished will and vision on the part of many Americans is discouraging."

It is one federal agency that has been relied upon to call things as it sees them. It has tried to do so amid controversy over Mr. Reagan's efforts to fill it with appointees sharing his civil rights views.

The panel criticized the administration for opposing affirmative action in two major cases. It added that such "active opposition to all but the most limited and ineffectual forms of affirmative action ignores the entrenched nature and pervasive extent of race, sex, and national origin discrimination."

There was a dissent by Reagan-appointed chairman Clarence Pendleton. But more recently he joined the commission in unanimously voting the extraordinary step of subpoenaing federal information on government hiring practices. Only then did the commission get assurances of cooperation.

Such appearances of reluctance on civil rights enforcement, like Mr. Reagan's foot-dragging on a strong Voting Rights Act extension, have threatened to overshadow his statements against bigotry and violence — which the commission itself has praised.

Now the credentials of the new Reagan appointees threaten to be overshadowed by other matters in Senate confirmation hearings. These include further controversy over purging the panel and substituting supporters of Reagan opposition to such civil rights remedies as affirmative action in hiring and court-ordered busing in school desegregation.

As for credentials, nominee Morris Abram is a former president of Brandeis University who has served on the Lawyers' Committee for Civil Rights Under Law. Robert Destro, an assistant law professor at Catholic University, has been general counsel for the Catholic League for Religious and Civil Rights in Milwaukee. John Bunzel, a senior research fellow at Stanford's Hoover Institution, has made a study of civil rights law.

But the nominees, whatever their qualifications, have been put on the defensive. They assured skeptics that they really were committed to civil rights and would be independent in their judgment. One even said he disagreed with Mr. Reagan on the Equal Rights Amendment. Presidential aides only contributed to skepticism by at first limiting press access to the nominees and then opening it up under pressure.

In such needless ways Mr. Reagan's own declared commitment to civil rights gets put under a bushel. He has the leadership ability to restore the civil rights "will and vision" whose loss discouraged the commission in 1980. A commission that hangs onto its independence can help him do so if he chooses.

The Washington Times

Washington, D.C., March 22, 1983

Ronald Reagan is no racist. Or sexist. We know him and we know that's true. Otherwise we'd have worked for his defeat rather than election to the White House. The President's top adviser also hate bigotry as much as we. But somebody over there has fouled up royally. And given the rabid Reagan haters a handy excuse to smear Reagan and his administration on so-called civil rights.

"So-called" because we know what civil rights once meant and still should mean if the republic is to survive and prosper. It means if others may walk in someplace and buy a sandwich, you may not be barred because of some external characteristic like complexion, gender or religion. Not that because of color, sex, or national origin you're entitled to the sandwich at half-price or gratis.

Congress established the U.S. Commission on Civil Rights in 1957 (yes, back then) to get and spread information about who's denying whom equal protection under the law. Who's stopping whom from buying the sandwich, renting the hotel room, using the rest room, or getting the job the applicant is qualified for.

This needed function became bastardized by the welfarist statists into reporting who's allegedly denying someone the "right" to the sandwich hasn't the money to buy or the job he hasn't the qualifications to hold.

Stacked with pre-Reagan members who know the president is itching to replace them with true civil rightists, the commission has regarded every day as an opportunity to take a last stab at Reagan and at its own chairman, Reagan-appointee Clarence Pendleton Jr., a man greater than who in intellectual clarity, acuity and independence none exists. He's also black.

The commission garners from the federal bureaucracy information it's entitled to under the law — and indeed needs in order to function properly as a civil rights watchdog — and then proceeds to misuse it outrageously. Recently it took Education Department budget figures and released a report accusing the administration of total retreat on civil rights — the new kind, that is. No increase in Title I funds for special classes for poor and minority children; ergo racism.

Another report reaffirmed support for mandatory school busing that the administration, a majority of black citizens and other anti-racists like us oppose. (We think forced busing *is* racist, of the worst, condescending variety.) Anther line in a commission report said administration budget trims cause unemployment and underemployment, again implying racism, sexism and ageism.

This sort of ism guilt the commission has been accusing the administration of from day one. We might note that Congress has abetted this corruption of civil rights meaning by expanding the original commission mandate. It used to be citizenship rights of blacks, Hispanics and native Americans (Indians). It now comprises 16 "protected classes," including Southern and Eastern Europeans of native descent (people who can trace their origins back to Spain, Greece, Italy, Czecheslovakia and so on), women, and the handicapped. Excluded, for the moment, are baby seals.

Understandably, the White House and executive departments and agencies may be somewhat piqued. Some, including the White House and the federal Office of Contract Compliance haven't been forthcoming with the information the commission wants. Can you blame them? Yes.

First, because whether used, misused or shamelessly abused, the information is what the law entitles the commission to have; and one does not choose the statutes he wishes to obey. The democratic citizen labors instead to get Congress to change them. Any dim-eyed desk man in the vicinity of the Oval Office who doesn't understand this should get to be an unemployment statistic. Second, as we said, such recalcitrance only gives the truth-twisters a club to bloody the administration.

President Reagan has said he wants to move this from a color-conscious to a color-blind society. This goal isn't in the interest of the commission as presently constituted or the client groups it has come to serve. For them, the civil right to buy the sandwich has turned into a social right to have someone else pay for the sandwich. An entitlement, much as the indisputable civil right to be hired on merit alone has turned into the disputable right to get the job *because* of race, gender, national origin or bad eyesight. Which is why the Civil Rights Commission has lost its intellectual and moral authority. And why the president will need congressional help, for a change, in putting appointees of Clarence Pendleton's persuasion on the commission.

BUFFALO EVENING NEWS
Buffalo, N.Y., June 4, 1983

In making a wholesale change in the composition of the U.S. Civil Rights Commission, President Reagan went too far last week in acting to re-shape the commission to his liking.

If the Senate confirms the three new members named by Mr. Reagan, five of the six panel members would be his appointees. While members serve at the pleasure of the president, there has been no comparable shakeup of the commission since it was established in 1957 to investigate complaints and make recommendations regarding civil rights.

By avoiding such a large-scale replacement of incumbent commission members, Mr. Reagan would have displayed greater sensitivity to the impact on the nation's minority groups and to the need to maintain a diversity of viewpoints on this advisory agency. Whatever the president's intention, many civil rights leaders have interpreted the change as an effort to weaken civil rights enforcement.

Nevertheless, the appointees — Morris B. Abram, former president of Brandeis University; John H. Bunzel, former president of San Jose Universi-

ty, and Robert A. Destro, assistant law professor at Catholic University — all appear to be persons of experience and substance, and they have pledged their independence of the White House. Although Mr. Destro once suggested that there was no need for the commission, he said after his appointment that he views civil rights as "the top constitutional priority for all Americans."

Much of the criticism of the three nominees apparently springs from the fact that they share Mr. Reagan's opposition to racial quotas and school busing as means of combatting discrimination and its effects.

Whether one agrees or disagrees with their stand on these particular issues, it does not provide a valid basis in itself for judging their qualifications to serve on the commission.

The more fundamental tests of the nominees are their individual backgrounds and records of past service, their character and competence and their dedication to advancing the civil rights of their fellow citizens. Those are the matters the Senate should explore in its coming hearings on the fitness of the nominees to serve on the commission.

The Union Leader
Manchester, N.H., June 13, 1983

Columnist William F. Buckley Jr., commenting on certain reactions to President Reagan's nominees to the Civil Rights Commission, cites the fact that the three men — New York lawyer Morris Abram, political scientist John Bunzel and Washington law professor Robert Destro — have much in common. In his column in last Thursday's edition of The Union Leader, Buckley pointed out:

"They are all three political liberals, and they are all three Jewish."

To be sure, there are other similarities: the three long-time civil rights activists share President Reagan's opposition to affirmative action quotas in hiring and placement and court-ordered busing to desegregate schools. They believe, as does the Reagan administration, that government has a legal and moral mandate to remove discrimination from this country root and branch and that it is sheer hypocrisy to tolerate a society where we condemn discrimination on the one hand while condoning it on the other.

However, it is Buckley's point about the religious affiliation of the President's nominees that we believe requires more open discussion in the news media and the halls of Congress. He finds that the Anti-Defamation League is justified in lashing out at critics of the President's nominees, explaining:

" . . . What it comes down to is that Jewish opposition to the quota system has not only the obvious moral base, but is also self-interested. You do not need to go any further than to a student directory

at Harvard or Berkeley to ratify what you intuited, namely that Jewish students are unusually well-qualified as a class, compared to any other group of students. And you need not travel far to confirm what you also intuit, namely that black students tend to be behind the average in educational attainment."

However, Buckley is quick to point out, "this is not an inquiry into why this should be so. It is merely a recognition that it is so, and that the fight between the Morris Abrams and the Jesse Jacksons is only at the rhetorical level a fight about minority 'rights.' It is also a fight, in the case of Morris Abram, by someone who has fought throughout his lifetime for civil rights for blacks, and for their advancement, but is not about to endorse public policies whose effect is to deprive well-qualified Jewish students of their leverage on higher education."

Buckley's point is well taken. Moreover, although he didn't raise the consideration in his column, the blunt truth of the matter is that there is more than a little overt and covert anti-Semitism involved in the opposition to Abram, Bunzel and Destro. And it is to that anti-Semitism, which, as ADL literature has pointed out with great regret over the years, is rampant in the nation's black communities, that much of the appeal of black demagogues such as Jesse Jackson is being directed.

That's the truth. Why not talk about it openly?

—Jim Finnegan

The Boston Globe
Boston, Mass., May 30, 1983

President Reagan's tampering with the US Civil Rights Commission reinforces his reputation of not caring about equal opportunity for all.

His action in replacing three critics is the latest in a series of moves that have persuaded many minorities and a growing number of women that almost any other candidate will do should Reagan seek re-election.

Repeatedly, he has dismissed charges that Republicans have written off blacks. "I'd have perfect confidence in our chances with black voters," he has said, "if we could get the truth to them."

The truth is that none of his new appointees, whatever their views on civil rights questions, is a minority or a woman. Only one, Morris Abram, should be entrusted with monitoring the enforcement of federal civil rights laws and policies.

Another appointee, Robert Destro, a law professor, has questioned the need for the commission. "If it were to go out of existence today, it would not be missed," Destro testified five years ago at a Senate subcommittee. Let private groups such as the NAACP and the National Organization for Women perform the commission's duties, he said. One of his past employers, the Catholic League for Religious and Civil Rights, has accused the commission of fostering anti-Catholic prejudice and ignoring discrimination against white ethnics.

Another appointee, John Bunzel, testified against extending voting rights protections. He has also attacked affirmative action as a policy that "encouraged racially preferential treatment and fostered a 'numbers definition' of discrimination that redefined equality of opportunity not as 'equal rights for all' but as some form of group proportional equality."

Even Abrams, who has a laudatory history of civil rights advocacy, has questioned affirmative action.

Affirmative action is one of the methods that has helped to correct historical inequalities. Groups that have suffered most because of those injustices – black Americans, other minorities and women – embrace the concept. Those same groups have been hardest hit by Reagan Administration policies – as documented in several scathing reports from the federal Civil Rights Commission.

Perhaps that criticism motivated the President to silence his critics. However, the critics at times have included Clarence Pendleton and Mary Louise Smith, who are the incumbent chairman and vice chairman of the commission and are both Reagan appointees.

Commissioners serve indefinitely at the pleasure of the President. Replacing the chairman is not without precedent, but no chief executive has previously made wholesale changes as Reagan has done.

Though the commission can only monitor enforcement of civil rights laws, the independent and bipartisan agency has influenced national public policy through reports, investigations and hearings during its 26-year history.

Reagan's tampering will politicize and weaken a once strong and independent voice. Stacking the commission will reinforce the impression that the Reagan Administration is lax on civil rights.

Newsday

Long Island, N.Y., November 19, 1983

Uniquely among federal agencies, the U.S. Civil Rights Commission relies on persuasion and scolding to fulfill its mission; it has no enforcement power. To be effective in safeguarding civil rights, the commission must be as independent as laws and people can contrive to make it.

That independence, which has made the commission a thorn in the side of every administration since its creation 25 years ago, has come under severe attack by the Reagan administration. Until last week, in fact, the commission's very existence was in jeopardy.

But now the administration has reluctantly agreed to a compromise that will make the commission a joint legislative-executive undertaking. Its membership will be increased from six to eight, with Congress and the president entitled to appoint four members each. Instead of serving indefinite terms as they do now, members will be appointed for six years. And they may not be removed except for abuse or neglect of office.

The practical effect of the compromise, which was overwhelmingly approved by the Senate on Monday, is that two of the members recently fired by President Reagan will keep their seats and two of his nominees will be seated without the confirmation the Senate had refused to provide. The commission will continue to have an equal number of Democrats and Republicans. The president will appoint the chairman, the vice chairman and the staff director, but only with the concurrence of a majority of the commissioners.

We only hope the new arrangement will maintain the commission's independence. Without that, it becomes a meaningless body no matter who does the hiring and firing.

THE DAILY OKLAHOMAN

Oklahoma City, Okla., August 6, 1983

CONGRESS appears bent on making President Reagan an offer he shouldn't refuse.

The House has voted to extend the life of the U.S. Civil Rights Commission — but with a political booby trap attached. They would give the commission another five years beyond its scheduled Sept. 30 expiration, but at the expense of blocking Reagan's attempt to replace three of the six members.

Reagan's offer to extend the commission for 20 years if the terms of its members were staggered was rejected.

His desire to replace half of the commission with appointees who share his views against enforced busing and affirmative action "quotas" is understandable. But under the House-approved bill, commissioners could be removed only for neglect of duty or malfeasance.

By attempting to prevent Reagan from replacing half of the commission with nominees of his own choice, Congress is inviting a veto. And if the Senate goes along, that opens up the possibility of getting rid of this useless and contentious commission.

Sacrificing three nominees to get rid of a commission the country never needed in the first place would be a small price to pay, and Reagan should take Congress up on the offer. The commission could pass into oblivion Sept. 30, and few would mourn its passing.

The Morning News

Wilmington, Del., July 18, 1983

THE U.S. CIVIL Rights Commission is an independent, advisory body. Since 1957, the six-member commission has been monitoring the impact of federal laws and policies on discrimination. Though the commission has no enforcement powers, it exerts influence as the nation's conscience.

The independence of that conscience, some say, was put in jeopardy by President Reagan when, in May, he asked for the resignation of three commissioners. Earlier in his administration he had replaced two other commissioners, thus leaving Jill Ruckelshaus as the lone long-term holdover.

Civil rights commissioners serve no specific terms, so there was no need to make any changes this spring. But ever mindful of catering to those of his supporters who can best be characterized as having the Strom Thurmond mentality on civil rights, the president asked a black woman, a Hispanic woman and a rabbi to resign from the commission. His three new appointees, awaiting Senate confirmation, are white and male. Their credentials are excellent, especially in the case of Morris Abram, a leader of long standing in the civil rights movement. But the appearance is unfortunate when women and racial minorities are displaced in this manner.

And that is what the uproar is about. Delaware's Sen. Biden, who serves on the Senate Judiciary Committee, told the nominees bluntly: "You're not the issue. . . . The perception, the signal, being sent out is horrible."

Why did an administration that by recent actions on fair housing and segregated university education in Alabama showed that it is trying desperately to establish its civil rights credentials, fumble so clumsily on ordering changes in the civil rights commission?

The Honolulu Advertiser

Honolulu, Ha., November 1, 1983

When last we discussed the U.S. Commission on Civil Rights, efforts were underway to find a compromise to save the 26-year-old watchdog panel.

On one side was President Reagan who wanted to fire and replace three of six commissioners. On the other were several senators and civil rights leaders who hoped, if the commission could not be saved as is, to gain some permanency in return for expanding the body to include two new Reagan appointees.

WITH negotiations deadlocked, Reagan last week moved to fire the three most liberal "holdover" members. If he succeeds in replacing them, he will have appointed two-thirds of the commission. He has already named a new staff director who does not need congressional approval.

The commission is now in limbo. Its legal authority expired at the beginning of October and a required 60-day phase-out is underway. If Congress does not act by November 29, the commission could actually go out of business, something no politician wants to be blamed for. The firings leave it without a quorum.

The commission has no enforcement powers, but its role as a public conscience for the president and the Congress on civil rights matters makes its pronouncements powerful, especially before an election.

The commission has often rubbed presidents the wrong way, but the Reagan administration has been especially criticized. One report labelled White House school desegregation policies unconstitutional and another denounced current affirmative action policies.

The most recent report says that two years of austerity have eroded federal civil rights enforcement, particularly in the Departments of Justice, Education, Labor, Health and Human Services, Housing and Urban Development, and the Equal Employment Opportunity Commission. Administration officials, using the same data, disputed the charge, saying that civil rights enforcement, including spending, has increased.

AS IN THE past, Congress will almost certainly reauthorize the civil rights commission before it goes out of business. But there may be a move to end the president's appointing authority, something sure to be opposed by the administration and Republicans in the Senate.

Without political independence, the commission will lose much of its stature and influence, both with government agencies and with the minority groups whose civil rights are most often in jeopardy. There is bound to be continuing opposition to the "Reaganization" of the body.

Thus the effort to defuse the political liability of commission criticism is backfiring and only further confirming for many the judgment that civil rights have a very low standing in this administration's priorities.

THE TENNESSEAN
Nashville, Tenn., October 28, 1983

THE decision by President Reagan to fire three members of the Civil Rights Commission is in keeping with his intent either to control the body or to destroy it.

The dispute over the commission began last May when the President attempted to replace Ms. Mary Berry, Ms. Blandina Ramirez and Rabbi Murray Saltzman, whom he fired Tuesday, with Messrs. Morris Abram, John Bunzel and Robert Destro, all of whom share Mr. Reagan's civil rights policies.

The firings were unexpected because members of the Judiciary Committee had worked out a compromise that would expand the commission to eight members, but would permit present commissioners to remain and give the White House two new nominations.

The White House had balked at this, saying the compromise legislation would thwart "the President's ability to exercise his power of appointment." The firing of the three holdovers leaves the commission without a required quorum. It cannot even meet until at least one more member is confirmed by the Senate.

Technically, the commission went out of business Sept. 30, however there is a 60-day wind-down period before it ceases to exist.

The Civil Rights Commission was created by the Congress as an independent body charged with making findings of fact and to advise both the legislative and executive branches on the progress or shortcomings of civil rights efforts and the administration of justice.

The commission has done so and it has been critical, not only of this administration but others. However, Mr. Reagan seems to regard it as a nagging busybody. In part that view may have been shared by former President Nixon. It was he who dismissed the Rev. Theodore Hesburgh, the president of Notre Dame as chairman. The replacement was Mr. Arthur Flemming, a Republican moderate.

But Mr. Reagan then dismissed Mr. Flemming and appointed Mr. Clarence Pendleton, who has been somewhat less than critical of the Reagan administration. Now he has fired three others.

The obvious reason for all this is that the rights commission has criticized the administration for naming few women and minority members to important posts, for cutting the budget to aid school desegregation, and for slicing education funds which, the panel said, would harm programs for minority and handicapped students.

It is evident the President does not respect the independence of the commission and would not even if the numbers were expanded. The only alternative now seems to be that suggested by Sen. Joseph Biden, D-Del., who wants to establish an eight-member, bipartisan commission in the legislative branch which would be independent of the White House and beyond the reach of the President.

Such a commission is needed for there is no similar group to play "watchdog" over civil rights matter and Justice Department enforcement. But it must have independence and the ability to criticize, if necessary, any administration which is indifferent to or opposed to carrying civil rights programs forward.

"YOU SHOULDN'T STAND FOR IT — IT'S A BLATANT ATTEMPT TO INTERFERE WITH YOUR INDEPENDENCE!"

The Detroit News
Detroit, Mich., October 28, 1983

WHEN the president of the United States cannot appoint members of an agency of the executive branch who support his policies, something is wrong.

If a president is to be required to maintain opponents of his policies within his administration as a kind of permanent opposition, why do we have two major political parties? Why do we need Congress?

These questions arise from the furor over President Reagan's firing of three members of the U.S. Civil Rights Commission so that he may replace them with appointees more congenial to his anti-quota and anti-busing views. The questions can be put another way: If an obligation exists for the Civil Rights Commission to act as some sort of permanent internal critic of an administration, will the same people who are denouncing the president's action demand that anti-quota civil rights commissioners be appointed if a president who favors quotas takes office?

Somehow, we doubt it.

Quotas carry no intrinsic moral weight. Indeed, they are morally suspect. At best, quotas are a tool for achieving a policy goal. People who favor the use of this means have occupied positions at the Civil Rights Commission. Now, the voters have elected a president who made no secret of his opposition to the use of quotas during his campaign. But the ousted civil rights commissioners don't want to lose positions from which they can advance their own agendas. That's all there is to it. It's understandable that people who favor one civil rights enforcement policy don't want to make way for people who favor a different approach, but it's hardly a great moral issue.

There would be some justification for the outcry if Mr. Reagan had nominated a klavern of ku kluxers as replacements for the ousted civil rights commissioners. But former Brandeis University President Morris Abram, Catholic University Law Professor Robert Destro, and Hoover Institution Research Fellow John H. Bunzel don't exactly fit that description. As a matter of fact, they are all Democrats. Their chief sin, in the eyes of those whom they would replace, is that they have a different view of the nature of civil rights. That view was best summed up by another liberal, the late U.S. Supreme Court Justice William O. Douglas, who said, "There is no constitutional right to be preferred."

That this view, and appointees of the quality of Mr. Abram, should arouse such antipathy in the civil rights establishment is a measure of how distorted civil rights policy had become.

The Idaho STATESMAN

Boise, Idaho, October 24, 1983

A Justice Department attorney's parting shots and a disclosure that his boss back-dated a memo give new indications that the Reagan administration's civil-rights enforcement effort is not what it should be.

The attorney, Timothy Cook, quit Monday, becoming the 17th of 21 attorneys in the special litigation section to leave since William Bradford Reynolds became civil rights division chief a little more than two years ago.

Cook charged that Reynolds ignored career staff attorneys' recommendations on litigation and, without notifying lawyers who had been working on lawsuits for years, instructed trusted aides to file briefs in the suits.

Reynolds brought in five special assistants "to keep the career attorneys in line" and disallowed midlevel supervisors and section chiefs from approving the filing of even minor court papers or discrimination suits, Cook said.

Cook also claimed Reynolds turned the Justice Department publication *Civil Rights Forum* into "a propaganda rag" and ordered a staff member to kill a *Forum* article on the celebrated Bob Jones University tax case. After the Reagan administration came into office, the Justice Department changed sides in the Bob Jones case only to suffer an embarrassing loss at the U.S. Supreme Court.

The back-dated memo explained Reynolds' rationale for approving a redistricting plan submitted to the Justice Department by Louisiana Gov. David Treen. Because the memo was filed a month after it was written, it allowed Reynolds to ignore a deadline by which Treen was to have submitted the plan.

Eventually, a three-judge federal panel threw out the plan, which split the black vote in Jefferson Parish. The court said the plan was "an electoral scheme" that "minimized the black citizenry's electoral participation." The ruling marked the first time the courts invalidated a redistricting plan drawn up under the Voting Rights Act and approved by the Justice Department.

Reynolds and Attorney General William French Smith refused to be interviewed about Cook's allegations, and a Reynolds spokesman denied that the civil rights division chief made any political deals in approving the Louisiana redistricting plan.

That denial wasn't 24 hours old before it was reported that Reynolds referred to blacks seeking participation in a South Carolina school-segregation case as "those bastards."

Reynolds' problems add credence to the view that the administration has not combatted segregation in the schools and discrimination in employment and housing. The disclosures have stripped Reynolds of his credibility. If the administration is to make any credible claim to an adequate enforcement effort, Reynolds must resign and the Justice Department must get on the ball.

DAYTON DAILY NEWS

Dayton, Ohio, October 29,1983

Almost drowned out by the sounds of the U.S. invasion of Grenada was President Reagan's artillery blast at the U.S. Civil Rights Commission, knocking it out of business for now.

The Civil Rights Commission has criticized the administration's policies and performances, so five months ago the president asked to replace the three members most critical of his record.

Congress balked. Negotiations ensued, with some promising compromises, but President Reagan tired of talking with the Republican-dominated Senate Judiciary Committee. The president fired the three most vocal commissioners. Now the commission can't conduct any official business since it has no quorum.

While a president is expected to guard prerogatives, and while all presidents have

---

The president fired three members of the Civil Rights Commission, whose opinions he hasn't been happy with.

---

been goaded by the Civil Rights Commission, this is the first president to stoop to a purge and knockout of the commission, which has only the power to probe and persuade.

Since Congress doesn't feel it can reach any new agreement with President Reagan about maintaining the commission as an "independent" executive agency, it is considering a bill to put the commission under legislative control. That may be the best alternative for the next year or so. Mr. Reagan's actions were a clearer statement of his administration's civil rights attitudes than anything the commission could have said.

Reno Gazette-Journal

Reno, Nev., May 24, 1983

As President Reagan gears up for an apparent re-election bid, he reportedly is concerned about his standing among minorities.

That is the reason one senior White House aide gives for Reagan's decision to replace several members of the Civil Rights Commission. The president fears the present commission will continue to criticize his civil rights record, so he wants to load the board with conservatives who will not hinder his campaign.

Yet this purge of the commission will further alienate minorities. They will see their suspicions of Reagan confirmed. And if the commission is silenced, minority leaders will not be. They will fire steadily at Reagan, and some of their most powerful ammunition has just been handed to them by the president.

They will point out that the president has given whites majority control of a commission designed in large part to help non-whites.

They will point out that the only Hispanic member of the commission is being removed — at a time when Hispanics are likely to become America's largest minority.

They will point out that some of the president's prospective appointees oppose affirmative action — when the struggle continues for equal rights in the work place.

They will point out that one prospective appointee wants to eliminate the commission — when the commission's work is far from done.

They will point out that the president originally planned to replace four members of the seven-member commision when the Senate was in recess, so the changes could not be discussed by that body. That plan has now changed because of criticism, but minority spokesmen will not forget that Reagan originally chose the back door instead of the front.

They also will point out that the president's original plan was to remove two women and add just one, lessening the influence of women on the commission. Commission member Jill Ruckelshaus was written off the purge list at the last moment, probably because her husband has just become head of the Environmental Protection Agency; in other words, her job was saved not by civil rights convictions but by political consideration. This will not reassure women, many of whom think Reagan does not understand their problems.

Of course, the president has the right to replace commission members at any time; they serve at his pleasure. He also has a right to appoint persons whose philosophy resembles his.

Yet the proposed changes must be questioned on three grounds:

☐ The majority of Americans favor attempts to guarantee civil rights for minorities and for women, so the move appears questionable politically.

☐ Minorities should be strongly represented on the commission, because they understand the problems and are adamant about attacking them. A commission with a white majority, without a Hispanic and with less feminine representation will be a weaker, less effective commission.

☐ Affirmative action is vital to women and minorities. Federal support remains extremely important. The idea is not to disenfranchise men and whites through rigid quota systems, but to actively encourage the hiring and promotion of women and minorities who can do the job, and to give them equal pay for doing that job.

The president's actions do not speak well for his political acumen or his civil rights program.

Detroit Free Press

Detroit, Mich., January 22, 1984

TO NO ONE'S surprise, the National Urban League's annual report on the state of blacks in America is bleak reading. There may be an economic recovery going on out there, but half of all black children still live in households below the poverty level, the unemployment rate for blacks is more than twice the rate for whites, and half of all black teenagers and a third of blacks aged 20 to 24 are out of work. It's a white recovery and a black depression. The obvious question is what we're going to do about it. The answer from Washington is very little.

The current laissez-faire social policy and deficit-burdened economic policy are not calculated to produce jobs when and where black Americans need them, or to prepare the unemployed for the jobs that will be available. It isn't merely a matter of dollars, although the cutbacks in public assistance hit black families hard.

In diverse pecksniffian ways, the federal government now undermines the very goals it professes to want to achieve. Congress will vote funds for the propagation of chastity, but not for day care centers that would permit single mothers to work. Some federal programs will pay the cost of job training, but not a penny of support for the trainee's family, reducing the choice to either preparing for a new job or eating, but not both. The president prescribes prayer and discipline for the public schools, but brushes off the suggestion that the federal government might have an interest in remedial reading as well.

Teenage pregnancy is probably the No. 1 cause of family poverty in the United States. It isn't only black teenagers who get pregnant; in fact, the statistics show pregnancies among unwed white teenagers increasing at a faster rate than among blacks. But because of the special circumstances of minorities in America, black teens and their children are more likely to suffer from poverty, malnutrition and lack of education. The administration's answer to that problem was the squeal rule.

Last week the new, Reaganite Civil Rights Commission issued a statement deploring the affirmative action promotion policy of the Detroit Police Department and, by inference, chiding the Supreme Court for not striking it down. It would be nice to think that the simple exhortation not to discriminate would be enough to solve the nation's racial problems, and erase the economic discrimination against minorities, but a hundred years of history says it is not. It is doubtful that qualified blacks would be moving up even at the rate they are in public and private employment, if there had not been the spur of equal-opportunity programs to prod employers into significant action. Affirmative action is a constitutional minefield, all right, but the courts and the rest of the country are cautiously picking their way through it, with some success, while the administration merely blunders about on the sidelines, trying to call the whole thing off.

As for the black Americans at the very bottom of the income ladder, from the 14-year-old daughter of a welfare mother who herself becomes pregnant, to the unemployed and unskilled young men hanging out on the corner, too many of them are merely responding to what they perceive their limited choices to be. If there aren't any jobs, if school is incomprehensible, if government offers you a stipend barely adequate for survival but throws up roadblocks to every attempt you make to get off the dole, it takes a very strong countervailing influence to keep people from simply giving up. A sensible public policy would do everything possible to widen those choices and provide that countervailing influence; another administration in Washington might have taken it as a special mission to alter the appalling statistics contained in the Urban League's report. It's a good bet this one will simply ignore them.

CIVIL RITES COMMISSION

Los Angeles Times

Los Angeles, Calif., January 18, 1984

The reconstituted U.S. Commission on Civil Rights is sending mixed messages. One, to the White House, proclaims independence "of all outside wishes or pressures, whether they come from the White House or any other group." Another, to minorities and women, says that the commission is backtracking on its historic commitment to affirmative action to overcome discrimination.

After a protracted fight last year, Congress and the White House agreed to keep the commission alive by changing procedures under which its members were appointed. To no one's surprise, the new commission has an ideological tilt that resembles that of the Reagan Administration far more than did the old commission.

The commission went on record as opposing the plan under which the Detroit Police Department is trying to increase the number of black lieutenants and generally disavowing "the use of racially preferential employment techniques, such as quotas." It also voted to drop a study of the effects of cuts in financial aid on colleges where most of the students are black or Latino.

The commission has no enforcement powers, and never has had. But in the past its reports and advisory opinions have focused on areas in which society needs to do better in combating discrimination. It provided moral leadership in that direction. In short, it symbolized a commitment to progress. It's not off to a good start. Its words have an empty ring when viewed in the context of its first actions.

The Wichita
Eagle-Beacon
Wichita, Kans., January 9, 1984

Considering some of the changes that seem to be in the making, continued operation of the U.S. Commission on Civil Rights under that name soon may be as marvelous an example of newspeak as renaming the multiple warhead MX a Peacekeeper.

If the restructured commission's new staff director, Linda Chavez, has her way, that body no longer will concern itself with such matters as how cutbacks in student financial aid may affect colleges whose student bodies are predominantly black or Hispanic. "Unless the commission wishes to establish that federal student financial aid is a civil right guaranteed to minority students, this project would appear to be clearly beyond our jurisdiction," she says.

The commission's new general legal counsel is to be Mark R. Disler, whose previous duties in the Justice Department's civil rights division often involved preparation of briefs to undercut previous civil rights policy. The new emphasis, it seems likely, will be to accentuate the negative in regard to effects of such policies as affirmative action, use of court-ordered busing for school integration purposes, and bilingual education.

There have been some excesses in the zeal with which some of those remedies have been carried out, and there have been some abuses. But that doesn't negate the fact the real goal of civil rights legislation is to make it possible — by mandating equal opportunities for all — for members of minority groups to escape the poverty level in which they long were mired by prejudice.

THE ATLANTA CONSTITUTION
Atlanta, Ga., March 3, 1984

The U.S. Commission on Civil Rights took another step backward recently with its new staff director's gratuitous swipe at the policymakers of the past.

Having already disavowed quotas, the commission is now preparing to repudiate court-ordered busing for school desegregation — tools, Reagan appointee Linda Chavez implied, that had the support of liberals only.

"Much of the tragedy of civil rights in recent years," she said, "is that it has become the purview of liberals."

Nothing could be further from the truth.

Court-ordered busing, numerical goals and timetables have been weapons in the battle to end racial discrimination for more than 20 years — weapons that former Presidents Nixon and Ford, who could hardly be classified as "liberals," wielded with little less enthusiasm than Lyndon Johnson and Jimmy Carter.

The bipartisan but increasingly conservative Supreme Court has vigorously supported their use — and so, until its overhaul by President Reagan in a blatant bid for ideological control of the historically independent watchdog agency — did the bipartisan Commission on Civil Rights.

The White House has made no secret of its disdain for what it calls "liberal" thinking, and which it has mistakenly attributed to some of the staunchest Republicans and moderates of the past two decades. But there may have been hope that such narrow-mindedness had not yet filtered down into the ranks of the civil-rights commission and its staff, despite the policy changes.

That hope has been dashed by Ms. Chavez's divisive remarks, suggesting once again that the once fiercely nonpartisan commission, now a mouthpiece for the administration, not only has lost its independence but has bought into the Reaganite political distortion that defines and denounces every position left of the far right — conservative, moderate, merely pragmatic — as "liberal."

The San Diego Union
San Diego, Calif., August 14, 1984

During the Democratic presidential primaries, Walter Mondale boasted that, if elected, he would dismiss President Reagan's appointees to the U.S. Commission on Civil Rights.

But last Monday, after Commission Chairman Clarence Pendleton Jr. criticized Mr. Mondale for using the panel as a political football, Mondale aides explained that their boss had not meant what he said. What he said was: "First, I'm going to fire everybody they've hired. And then I'm going to hire everybody they've fired." The next day, the Democratic nominee contradicted his staff and repeated his intention to "restructure" the commission.

The campaign is barely three weeks old and already Mr. Mondale has been characterized by several editorial cartoonists as a man impaled upon a weather vane, shifting his position in response to the slightest political wind. The characterization was particularly appropriate, given his flip-flop over the Bert Lance affair. And Mr. Mondale's latest statement about civil rights is even more pertinent because it suggests he cannot decide whether to continue playing the demagogue or risk appearing indecisive by backing away from his hollow boast to fire the commissioners.

Mr. Mondale's demagoguery notwithstanding, it should be recalled that a 1983 law reconstituting the commission specified that members could be removed by the president "only for neglect of duty or malfeasance in office." In fact, the law was designed to prevent the very politicization of the commission that the Democratic nominee is proposing.

AKRON BEACON JOURNAL
Akron, Ohio, May 5, 1984

THERE IS something unsettling about the U. S. Civil Rights Commission plunging into presidential politics. But it is doing exactly that, by demanding that the Rev. Jesse Jackson reject the support of Black Muslim leader Louis Farrakhan.

We feel no love for Mr. Farrakhan. His threats and hateful statements during this presidential campaign serve as a vivid example of how racism and extremism can take many destructive forms.

And Mr. Jackson's refusal to reject this inflammatory follower continues to disturb all those who take the candidate's speeches about equality and justice seriously.

But the Civil Rights Commission has just emerged from a sometimes bitter, highly partisan struggle between the White House and Congress over its very survival.

Its image as an independent, bipartisan panel has been badly damaged as a result of those chaotic months. The public must be convinced anew of the integrity of the commission if it is to resume its former role as a moral leader for the nation.

Instead the panel seems to be continuing on a questionable path. Its latest action, a memo requesting that Mr. Jackson disavow Mr. Farrakhan's support, was initiated by two appointees of President Reagan. Such a memo carries an uncomfortable hint of politics more than principle.

The commission decided to take on Mr. Jackson on the same day that one of those appointees, Morris Abram, received a letter from Mr. Reagan repudiating the Ku Klux Klan's endorsement of his re-election.

As he did in 1980, Mr. Reagan had the good sense to reject this year's endorsement by this loathsome group. However, the President's repudiation came two weeks after the Klan endorsement and just before Mary Frances Berry, a Democrat and one of his most vocal critics on the commission, was to bring up the issue before her colleagues.

Thus neither party is blameless as presidential politics seeps into this supposedly independent commission. The Civil Rights Commission has an important role to play in pointing out where bigotry and violence exist. But in this election year, partisanship threatens to drown out its voice as the nation's conscience.

The Pittsburgh
PRESS
Pittsburg, Pa., August 15, 1984

For months, Walter Mondale has been saying that President Reagan has "trashed" the federal Civil Rights Commission and that he (Mr. Mondale) has a plan to set things right: "First, I'm going to fire everybody they've hired. And then I'm going to hire everybody they've fired."

Morris Abram, a Democrat who is one of Mr. Reagan's hirees on the commission, pointed out to Mr. Mondale that his threat runs contrary to a new law that prevents presidents from firing members of the commission.

Mondale aides began backing off, saying that their candidate didn't intend to try anything illegal.

Then the former vice president returned to the fray and said he would seek changes in the law so that he could fire Reagan appointees and "restructure the commission so that it speaks independently again."

Now there's a bit of irony. The new law, which Mr. Mondale wants to change, was fashioned by Democrats in Congress for the precise purpose of making the commission independent.

The measure came about because Mr. Reagan had fired three commissioners and nominated three of his own choosing. Congressional opponents stymied the appointments and passed a law reconstituting the commission to keep commissioners out of White House clutches.

Under the existing system, Congress and the president each appoint half the commissioners. They serve for specified terms and a president can't remove any of them except for neglect of duty or malfeasance in office.

A majority of the present commission may not agree with Mr. Mondale's approach to civil rights issues, but the body has never been more "independent" from a structural standpoint.

Mr. Mondale seems not so much interested in having an independent panel as in having one that will agree with him.

THE ⬛ SUN
Baltimore, Md., August 17, 1984

It was bad enough when Walter Mondale, in frenzied debate during the primaries, used as an occasional applause line a promise to fire all the Reagan appointees to the Civil Rights Commission and rehire all the members President Reagan had fired. It's even worse to keep repeating the line now when he, his staff, his interviewers and audiences all know that he probably can't and certainly shouldn't do that.

The law governing the CRC, as rewritten last year, provides that members serve fixed terms and may not be removed except for "neglect of duty or malfeasance in office." The terms of only two of the six pro-Reagan commissioners expire in the next presidential term, and while all six hold views that are anathema to the liberal civil rights establishment, that is a far cry from "neglect" and "malfeasance." If presidents routinely fired commissioners for their views, the commission would no longer amount to anything.

It doesn't amount to much now. The president not only fired members for no cause last year; then he reneged on a deal with Congress and stacked the present commission. We called it a rubber stamp when it was reconstituted last year, and it pretty much has been just that on important issues. Worse, after years of aloofness from political campaigns, three members have seen nothing wrong with taking formal, open roles in the current election race — two for the Reagan-Bush ticket, one for Mondale-Ferraro. That's just unacceptable. One, a Tennessee Reaganite, has just quit. The others should, immediately.

Mr. Mondale knows all this. Unlike Mr. Reagan, he sympathizes with the original objectives of the Civil Rights Commission. He therefore should be doubly circumspect in avoiding rhetoric and promises that would serve only to politicize and degrade it further. He would perform a great service in this campaign if he would drop the fire-and-hire applause lines and plainly spell out for the public how the agency can recapture its old independence and unflinching integrity. A good starting point would be freedom from White House interference and dismissal, no matter who sits in the Oval Office.

Baltimore, Md., April 23, 1984

The call by some members of Congress for a cutoff of funding for the Civil Rights Commission raises an interesting question about the 27-year-old panel: Should it be dismantled when lawmakers disagree with its work or when a majority of the commission members holds unpopular views?

The chairmen of the Congressional Black Caucus, the Congressional Hispanic Caucus and the Congressional Caucus on Women's Issues say "yes." They have asked a House Appropriations subcommittee to end funds for the panel on October 1. They say the commission is no longer independent, and thus it should not survive.

Those lawmakers are correct when they say the commission is not independent. The majority were chosen by President Reagan because they agree with his opposition to quotas and busing. The commission also has said it's not empowered to assess the effect of Reagan budget cuts on social programs, which is convenient for Mr. Reagan in this election year. The old commission thought it was empowered to assess Reagan proposals, and its assessments were not favorable to the president.

That's why we have a new commission.

But the membership of the new commission is not permanent. By law it is empowered "to investigate allegations that U.S. citizens were being deprived of the right to vote and have that vote counted by reason of color, race, religion or national origin; to study and collect information concerning legal developments constituting a denial of equal protection of the laws under the Constitution; [and] to appraise the laws and policies of the federal government with respect to equal protection of the laws." And that law will be on the books long after the current members are history.

The commission serves as the conscience of the government. It doesn't make laws; it only collects information. The question is should it be shut down if it fails to collect that information for a period, or if it chooses to collect radically different information under one administration.

We think not. The composition of the panel can be changed significantly by the next president. It can survive this period of adversity and resume its traditional role in the years to come.

THE WALL STREET JOURNAL
New York, N.Y., May 4, 1984

This week the U.S. Civil Rights Commission managed to put pressure on both Ronald Reagan and Jesse Jackson to separate themselves from purveyors of racial hatred. The dual action came about after some frantic politicking by commission members who belong to rival factions of the body. No matter. After years in which our civil-rights institutions were the exclusive property of the left, this new evenhandedness is a pleasure to see.

When the Ku Klux Klan endorsed Ronald Reagan back in the 1980 presidential campaign, he repudiated its support unequivocally. Two weeks ago, spokesmen for the president were asked about reports that a Klan leader had once again urged his members to vote for Mr. Reagan in November. This time the Reagan people were more noncommittal. Mary Berry, a Democratic appointee on the Civil Rights Commission, wrote a memo saying that unless Mr. Reagan came up with something better on the subject of the Klan, he should be put on the next meeting's agenda for commission action.

But when the Reaganites learned of these doings, they produced a more explicit repudiation of the Klan. Ms. Berry still did not fully approve of it, but her initiative was dead.

Then the Reagan appointees turned the tables on her. They wrote a memo similar to her own, this one saying that if presidential candidate Jesse Jackson would not repudiate the support of Nation of Islam leader Louis Farrakhan, Mr. Jackson's name should go into the dock at the next commission meeting. The commission should also ask whether other presidential candidates were unequivocally repudiating the support of hatemongers, the Reagan appointees added.

The commissioners approved this second proposal unanimously, though Ms. Berry later complained that the whole transaction was politics.

The substance of what the commission did is highly refreshing. Not so long ago, this body was of one political view. Its actions were predictable and almost always on one side of the day's partisan battles. Now the members are arguing with one another, struggling for not only tactical but also moral advantage. The sight is not graceful, but the phenomenon is healthy. And, as we can now begin to see, the results are likely to be a far sight better than they were in the commission's days of uniformly biased and smugly self-satisfied piety.

The substance of what the commission did this week is also procedurally refreshing. The Klan not only has a history of obnoxious acts behind it, but is based on a whole doctrine of racial distinctions that is abhorrent to our most central political principles. Mr. Farrakhan, too, has been committing some obnoxious acts: talking about the greatness of Adolf Hitler, threatening the life of a reporter. But, like the Klan, this Jackson supporter is even more dangerous than these overt acts let on. His whole doctrine is one of separation of the races and fomenting racial resentment. Both parties richly deserve to be drummed out of our political arena.

What the commission did this week is also procedurally refreshing.

Affirmative Action Quotas: End of Equal Opportunity?

The Reagan Administration proposed new regulations in August, 1981 to ease antidiscrimination rules currently imposed on federal contractors. The proposed regulations would exempt employers with fewer than 250 workers and a federal contract worth less than $1 million from a requirement to submit written plans for hiring and promoting women and minorities. (The current rules applied to companies with 50 or more workers and a $50,000 contract.) Among other changes proposed, the Labor Department would not require remedial action from contractors unless their employment of women and members of minority groups fell below 80% of their availability in the work force, instead of requiring that women and minorities be hired in proportions equal to their availability. The department would also eliminate a requirement that employers furnish a written summary of their affirmative action programs. The proposals were announced by Labor Secretary Raymond J. Donovan, who said the revisions would retain "the necessary safeguards for protected groups, while cutting down on the paperwork burden for employers." They would relieve nearly three-quarters of companies doing business with the government from the "burden" of affirmative action paperwork, he said. (Similar proposals were submitted by the Labor Department in 1983, but with their application expanded to contractors with 100 employees and a $100,000 federal contract.)

President Reagan has been clear about his position on affirmative action programs from the first news conference of his presidency, when he said that although he thought great progress had been made in civil rights, "there are some things...that may not be as useful as they once were, or that may even be distorted in the practice, such as some affirmative action programs becoming quota systems." The Administration's unprecedented move to limit the scope of federal antidiscrimination laws, shifting the regulatory emphasis from past infractions to future compliance, nevertheless caused an upheaval and revived a long-standing debate about the purpose and effectiveness of all affirmative action programs as they have evolved.

The guidelines that Reagan wants to change were established in 1964 by President Johnson. Executive Order 11246 used the phrase "affirmative action" to describe hiring and promotion programs to be undertaken by federal contractors, and stipulated that these programs must be monitored by the Department of Labor's Office of Federal Contract Compliance Programs (OFFCP). The impetus behind the order was the dawning realization that the Civil Rights Act, passed earlier the same year, though it insisted on equal treatment of the races, could easily be side-stepped through apparently race-neutral policies that actually perpetuated past discrimination. Under President Nixon, the order took on a further dimension when it was revised to state that the affirmative action taken by companies to recruit and promote minorities must be "results oriented," forcing contractors in violation of the order to meet numeric goals by specified deadlines.

It is this characteristic of affirmative action programs that has met with the greatest opposition. Critics of results-oriented quotas maintain that such numeric goals have in fact established a system of 'reverse discrimination,' depriving unprotected employees of opportunities for hiring and promotion (and unprotected students of places at universities and colleges) that would otherwise fall to them. In many cases, it is argued, the minority employee or student who benefits is less qualified than his unprotected competitors; because of the pressure placed upon personnel or admissions offices to meet their required percentages, standards of acceptance for applicants in the protected groups are often lowered. In the end, critics point out, such programs frequently have the opposite of the intended effect, since a pattern develops in which employers or professors come to assume that the black student or worker will not perform as well as his white counterparts, largely as a result of the lesser qualifications with which he or she started. This school of thought is not limited in its adherents to members of the Reagan Administration; many liberal thinkers, and black conservative economists Walter E. Williams and Thomas Sowell, among others, share the view that the end product of affirmative action is a lessened regard for the achievements of blacks, and that race-neutral policies are both more equitable and of greater value to the groups they are meant to benefit. Such a view replaces the relatively recent determination to make amends for historical discrimination of blacks and other minorities with a belief that each individual should be judged on his or her own merits, without regard to race, religion, or gender. (See pp. 106-121.)

Roanoke Times & World-News
Roanoke, Va., August 2, 1980

Midge Decter, senior editor of Basic Books, Inc., and a former associate editor of *Harper's,* accurately assesses the impact of affirmative action programs favoring race and sex. The recipients of preferential treatment, she writes, "tend to suffer from a serious decline in self-respect." How could it be otherwise? Writing in the summer issue of *Policy Review,* she notes: "At the heart of affirmative action, no matter how the policy is defined, lies the simple proposition that the individuals being hired or admitted or promoted would not in their own individual right. No matter how passionately affirmative action is sought and defended by its client groups, this underlying proposition is one that must breed painful resentment."

The author finds it "incongrous" that blacks and women are linked "under the common heading of disadvantaged minorities" and hopes that history can explain it someday. Current events suggest that the female activists discovered the blacks had a technique that worked in the 1960s and adopted it for themselves. Political opportunity, not logic, dictated that a majority — women — pretend it is a minority. Aside from that side issue and considering the effects of affirmative action on society as a whole, Ms. Decter writes:

The assault on the old idea that in America equality means equal opportunity has an impact far wider than merely those toward race and sex. The message being hammered home is, to put it bluntly, that society is a racket. There are no such things as standards of performance. There is no such thing as achievement. Above all, there is no such thing as justice. To live in accordance with the belief that standards of achievement or juustice have a reality, that they matter, is to be a sucker.

A society cannot long remain vigorous and productive when so much massive cynicism about its principal beliefs is permitted to spread through the underground consciousness.

● The key word above is |how| "long." There may be a kind of rough, mystical justice in one generation of "affirmative action," the sugar-coated word, the liar's word, for discrimination based on race and sex. The generation that could not see the difference in principle, that tolerated or welcomed reverse discrimination as a confession of guilt, perhaps earned the burden it is carrying. But if there is to be more than another generation, another 25 years, of discrimination based on race and sex, this country will not be what it was. It may even lose the memory of the principles that kept American society from being a racket.

The Hartford Courant

Hartford, Conn., May 7, 1981

Republican Sen. Orrin G. Hatch of Utah admits that his proposed constitutional amendment to ban affirmative action programs will not pass Congress, let alone be ratified by the states.

But he wants to proceed with hearings on Capitol Hill so that the issue will be debated. Many opponents of affirmative action are afraid to speak up for fear of being labeled as racist, he says.

The senator does not seem to have a shortage of experts willing to testify against government programs giving minorities and women preference in jobs and education. Lawyers professors, businessmen and politicians have lined up to claim at the hearings that affirmative action denies some people constitutional rights, that preferential treatment puts a badge of inferiority on minorities, that a constitutional amendment makes sense.

In our society, courts decide on the constitutionality of laws. The courts have upheld affirmative action legislation approved by Congress, as well as presidential orders reserving 10 percent of government contracts for minority-owned businesses and requiring contractors to prove that they do not discriminate by race or sex in hiring.

To defend affirmative action programs is not to say they are without fault. There have been excesses and outright wrongdoing. Preferential treatment does put a stigma on black professionals, as Harvard University political scientist Martin Kilson concedes. But the burden is not intolerable. And where there is wrongdoing, it can and should be corrected.

Affirmative action never was offered as the ideal solution. After nearly two centuries of racial inequality, it would have been unrealistic to suddenly declare a national policy of racial neutrality and expect it to bring blacks into the American mainstream. The same goes for women in society.

Remedial action was, and still is, necessary. No one would argue that the remedies should stay forever. The hope is that America will mature sufficiently in the next 10 or 15 years so that affirmative action programs will become unnecessary. But they are necessary now and they have brought more blacks, Hispanics and women into the professions, businesses and schools than ever before.

Our suspicion is that Sen. Hatch and other opponents do not really want to debate the issue, which has been debated at length.

They simply want to encourage the Reagan administration to be passive on this civil rights matter. If the White House goes easy on enforcement, Congress will not holler, Sen. Hatch seems to be saying.

Surely there are enough members of Congress concerned about equal opportunity to holler. If they don't, it will be up to civil rights groups to take the executive branch to court to make sure that affirmative action laws are being enforced.

St. Petersburg Times

St. Petersburg, Fla., August 26, 1981

Americans are not fools. They know what is going on when the Reagan administration Labor Department, piously claiming it is "cutting down the paperwork burden for employers," relaxes the federal government's enforcement of anti-discrimination rules.

FOR 100 YEARS, minorities have suffered discrimination from employers and from unions when they tried to get jobs. The construction industry and smaller companies were particularly hard for black workers to enter. The civil rights laws of the 1960s legally prohibited some forms of discrimination, but resistance to minorities remained strong in the job market. For black teen-agers, little has changed since the 1950s. Many of them cannot find jobs. Their unemployment rate is much higher than other groups.

Using powers granted by law, former President Lyndon Johnson in 1966 issued an executive order requiring all companies doing $50,000 worth of business with the federal government to take steps to stop discriminating against women and minorities. The government cannot enforce such rules unless it knows what's happening. Thus, there were forms to be filled out.

Even with the executive order, discrimination has continued. Some employers still resist the American promise of equal opportunity in the job market.

On Tuesday, the Reagan administration officially proposed an easing of Johnson's rules. At present, firms employing 50 or more workers and getting $50,000 or more in taxpayers' contracts must write affirmative action plans. President Reagan is exempting all companies up to 250 workers and $1-million in tax funds. Labor Secretary Raymond J. Donovan says enforcement will be voluntary, which means there won't be much enforcement at all.

For women and blacks, the changes will mean that fair treatment in the job market will be harder to get. Discrimination will increase.

Several national polls show that black Americans are fully aware what is happening to them. The polls show that at a time when white Americans are more optimistic about the future, blacks are increasingly gloomy and pessimistic.

TWO BLACK spokesmen quoted by *The New York Times* summarized the mood. Samuel DuBois Cook, president of Dillard University in New Orleans, said: "Blacks are in a bag of serious pessimism. A sense of hopelessness is there." Carl Holman, president of the National Urban Coalition, said: "Blacks feel themselves in a kind of Dunkirk position."

Americans are not fools. When citizens read that the administration is cutting down paperwork for small firms doing business with the taxpayers, they assume that will be good for those businesses. They also will ask whether permitting more discrimination against minorities is good for the country. If they are not prejudiced, they will answer that it's not good for America when any group feels it is in a "Dunkirk position."

The News American

Baltimore, Md., September 29, 1981

Watching the Reagan administration dismantle two decades of affirmative action efforts in nine months has been a lot like seeing a patchwork quilt being slowly ripped apart at the seams. The Department of Justice decision last week to go back to dealing with discrimination cases on a case by case basis is perhaps the most serious setback of all.

If the policy is executed as recommended by the department's civil rights division, affirmative action as a way of achieving equal opportunities for minorities will be just another lump on the growing scrap heap of civil rights gains tossed out by the Reagan administration.

Already major retrenchment has been initiated in the area of federal contracts, school hiring, and school admissions. And such conservative stalwarts as Rep. Robert S. Walker of Pennsylvania and Sen. Orrin G. Hatch of Utah are dreaming up dozens of other destructive legislative measures.

The administration's stance has resulted in a sad moral and constitutional retreat for the nation. For all the legal and emotional fury individual affirmative action programs have stirred at times over the years, there has been little doubt that the objectives have been sound. Assuring every American, regardless of race or sex, equal opportunity in the workplace is the very essence of what America is supposed to mean.

Unquestionably some programs that seemed fair and workable in concept have proven flawed in application. The solution is review and compromise, even though they have the potential to breed conflict and confrontation. But with the constitution as its compass, this nation usually can absorb healthy differences and remain true to itself.

Unfortunately, the Reagan policy is no such attempt at accommodation. It is a abandonment of the ideal of equality and an abdication of the federal government's duty to guarantee it. The case by case approach, for example, is a transparent impediment to achieving equality because it is unbelieveably costly and time consuming.

The Reagan administration's decision to close its eyes to this can only be viewed as a deliberate attempt to blunt the effects of tools that work. Therein lies, apparently, the real complaint of affirmative action foes — the process works too well.

The Boston Globe

Boston, Mass., August 27, 1981

President Reagan has proven himself a master of political symbols, so he should understand clearly the message sent by the Labor Department's proposal to ease antidiscrimination rules for businesses having contracts with the federal government. It is likely to be perceived, and understandably so, as a lessening of the federal commitment to ensure that minorities get a solid foothold in the American economy.

Minorities have never been considered a part of the President's political constituency. Yet they are part of his presidential constituency and he ought to be working to enhance their confidence in him, not to erode it. A President has a duty to seek to unite the country, not divide it, and should strive particularly to avoid divisions along racial lines.

Granted, easing federal regulations is a major Reagan goal, but even within this wide-ranging agenda, an early attack on affirmative action guidelines was hardly essential. There are plenty of other areas where regulations could be withdrawn or watered down with considerably more promise of actually achieving economic efficiencies.

The Labor Department plan would be disquieting at any time, but it is particularly troubling now. Public opinion surveys show that blacks are substantially less sanguine about their prospects in the years ahead than whites; blacks give Reagan markedly lower grades for presidential performance than whites. Samuel DuBoise Cook, president of Dillard University in New Orleans, told the New York Times recently: "Blacks are in a bag of serious pessimism. A sense of hopelessness is there."

Analyses of the poll results show this is true regardless of income and does not reflect the particularly harsh effect on minorities of the Reagan cuts in social programs.

The Reagan Administration argues that reducing paperwork requirements on smaller federal contractors and lessening government policing of adherence to hiring guidelines will induce more voluntary compliance. That simply flies in the face of history. No reasonable observer can doubt that in construction work particularly, minorities have been the victims of systematic discrimination. Further, any firm that finds the affirmative action guidelines too burdensome is free to avoid doing business with the federal government.

Affirmative action policies seek to reverse the history of discrimination and to use public money, raised from taxpayers of all colors, as a tool in that effort. The legality of the approach has been upheld repeatedly. It is a particularly important instrument for "leveraging" permanent job opportunities for minorities now when federally sponsored job-training and employment programs are being sharply reduced.

To lessen the federal government's affirmative action efforts is an ill-considered decision, both as substance and as symbol.

The Honolulu Advertiser

Honolulu, Ha., September 3, 1981

For nearly 20 years, affirmative action has been a firm policy of the federal government. Through laws executive orders and rulings by the courts, efforts to end racial and sexual discrimination in the work place have been pursued.

For the most part, it has been a success. That more minority groups and women are in the work force, and often in better paying positions they previously were denied, is evidence of the effectiveness of federally-enforced programs.

BUT NOW the Reagan administration, citing regulatory reform, wants to reduce the number of businesses directly affected. It wants to eliminate or reduce paperwork involved in reporting compliance with affirmative action guidelines.

In essence, the administration would exempt firms which do business with the government which have fewer than 250 employees and a federal contract worth less than $1 million from preparing a written plan for the hiring and promoting of women and minorities. Present rules apply to companies with 50 or more workers and a contract worth $50,-000.

One safeguard which would continue requires federal contractors doing at least $10,000 worth of business to hire and promote women and minorities regardless of whether a written plan is prepared.

Yet this carry-over requirement would be weakened by other changes which lessen federal pressure on firms to comply with guidelines. The administration is in effect saying to businesses: we now trust you to carry on in the same spirit.

IS SUCH TRUST justified? Certainly in many cases the private sector has done extremely well in hiring and advancing women and minorities. But it must be remembered that most of the progress of the past two decades has come only because of federal pressure.

Indeed, the forces which led to the institution of national guidelines have not been removed. A U.S. Commission on Civil Rights report issued earlier this year found evidence of "continued inequalities (that) compel the conclusion that our history of racism and sexism continues to affect the present."

It went on to say that its review "shows unmistakably that most of the historic victims of discrimination are still being victimized and that more-recently-arrived groups have also become victims of ongoing discriminatory attitudes and processes. Social indicators reveal persistent and widespread gaps throughout our society between the status of white males and the rest of the population."

The administration will find some support for its position because, as many involved in affirmative action implementation will agree, the paperwork load has become great. But the solution is not to cut back on those regulated; the better answer is to reform the administrative process while maintaining necessary protection for those victimized.

Ironically, there is the possibility the Reagan approach may result in just as much if not more paperwork.

A state official here says the only recourse someone may now have would be through the courts rather than administrative review. Reducing guidelines could lead to an increase in litigation.

IDEALLY, of course, it would be best if there were no need for affirmative action. But that is not the reality.

We are only now beginning to right historic inequities. To begin to reduce government efforts in this area would be an unfortunate step backwards. That is what the Reagan administration is proposing.

ST. LOUIS POST-DISPATCH

St. Louis, Mo., August 31, 1981

The Reagan administration is wasting little time in retreating from efforts to remove race and sex discrimination in employment. The latest move, announced by Secretary of Labor Raymond Donovan, would relax job discrimination rules for employers who do government business.

Mr. Donovan wants to require written affirmative action programs from contractors having 250 or more employees and government contracts in excess of $1 million. Written programs are now required of companies with 50 or more employees and $50,000 contracts. The secretary contends that his plan would free 75 percent of employers from the written requirement and still protect 77 percent of the workers now affected by the rules.

Those figures are being challenged by minority and women's rights groups, and by former Secretary of Labor Ray Marshall. The latter, who served in the Carter administration, says he does not believe "in a lot of paperwork," but thinks it a mistake to lower the threshold for compliance. "Most of the employment in the country is in small firms," he says. Civil rights spokesmen say the proposal would send the wrong signal to public and private employers.

As to private employers, the Justice Department said a few days ago it would abandon a policy adopted during the Nixon administration. The abandoned policy requires employers to accept temporary minority hiring goals in settling job discrimination cases. Without specific goals, compliance with fair employment law would be hard to measure. And without written assurance of minority hiring under government contract work, compliance could be meaningless. The wrong signals already have been sent.

The Boston Herald American
Boston, Mass., September 7, 1981

The Reagan administration has proposed sweeping changes to cut back — but not abolish — the federal affirmative action program.

The proposal would limit the size, extent, and force of equal employment regulations for 200,000 firms holding federal contracts. The new regulations would keep anti-discrimination protection in place for 77 percent of the 30 million workers currently protected, according to Labor Secretary Raymond J. Donovan.

We support the easing of the "stick" of burdensome affirmative action regulations, but ask Mr. Reagan to propose a "carrot" of tax breaks or other economic incentives to induce companies to work against job discrimination.

Ronald Reagan was elected on a Republican platform that declared "war on government overregulation." Affirmative action, although not singled out in the platform, is considered by many Americans to have been guilty of overregulating private hiring procedures. By voting for Reagan, a majority of Americans showed their desire to cut back regulations such as affirmative action.

Reverse discrimination and quota systems are repugnant. Employment must be based on merit.

But the Republican platform also calls for "total integration of the work force (not separate but equal)."

Job discrimination by race, creed, color or sex is abhorrent. An America where women and minorities are denied jobs in a country which squanders its human resources, and turns its back on its values.

How can the war on overregulation be reconciled with the goal of total integration of the work force?

We believe that the Reagan proposals are a good start, but only address half the problem. By cutting regulations, the government will allow businesses to streamline hiring procedures, and put back merit in the hiring equation. This is necessary.

But the goal of total integration must not be discarded because of the abuses of affirmative action. Rather, a positive program of inducements for bringing women and minorities into the work force should also be developed by the federal government. By giving employers tax breaks for hiring women and minorities, the government could spur voluntary improvement, and stimulate the profit motive.

America's economic recovery is dependent on the removal of government from the back of business. It is also dependent on the harnessing of the work and creativity of all Americans.

Positive inducements would add balance to the president's program. Affirmative action must not be allowed to become affirmative reaction.

Nevada State Journal
Reno, Nev., August 31, 1981

The maze of regulations engulfing businessmen needs to be reduced, as President Reagan intends.

Yet there are certain areas in which reduction of regulations can seriously threaten the social strides that this nation has made in the past few years. One of these areas most certainly is equal opportunity employment.

Until a very short time ago, great discrimination existed in the hiring of blacks, Hispanics and other racial minorities and, of course, women of all races. They found it harder to get a job; when they got one, they found it harder to be promoted; and they found it harder to receive equal pay for equal work.

The civil rights movement of the 60s began to change that, and the women's movement added significant impetus. But without the active aid of the federal government, the movement would not have made nearly as much headway as it has; nor will it make as much headway as it should in the future, if the government now retreats at this crucial time.

And yet that is just what the Reagan administration wants to do. In plans announced last week, it would significantly ease antidiscrimination rules for federal contractors. Only contractors having 250 or more employees would have to file formal documents saying they are taking steps toward affirmative action. And contractors with 250 to 499 employees would be permitted to file abbreviated affirmative action programs.

In addition, the government would redefine affirmative action goals. The current numbers defining underutilization of women and minorities would remain in effect, but contractors would not have to correct deficiencies unless minority employment fell below 80 percent of this figure.

This is no small matter. Some 200,000 contractors and 30 million workers would be affected.

But more than this, the entire tone of affirmative action in all areas of employment would be affected. And affected for the worse.

Ellen M. Shong, director of the Labor Department's Office of Federal Contract Compliance Programs, claims that because of lessened regulations, employers will be more willing to work with the government and there will be more job opportunities for minorities.

This is wishful thinking. A great deal of prejudice still exists in this country, and it will not go away without persistent attack. General education of the public helps, of course; but only the federal government has the persuasive power to assure that we remain on the right course toward equal jobs and equal pay for all.

The Reagan administration must reconsider its policy, and continue to pursue affirmative action with energy and enthusiasm.

Los Angeles Times

Los Angeles, Calif., August 26, 1981

Instinct leads those who have supported affirmative-action programs, as we have, to question any apparent relaxation of federal government requirements for the hiring and promotion policies of companies seeking to do business with the government. But do such suspicions hold up in cold analysis of the Reagan Administration's new proposals? Is it possible to reduce the paperwork about which so many complain, with some justification, and yet not reduce the commitment to equal employment?

The answer to both questions is yes. Unfortunately, the Reagan Administration has not really performed the latter service. Reducing so-called burdensome paperwork by reducing the companies covered is like cutting off your arm because it pains you; you're left with a reduced capacity to do the job.

Both the nature of the Labor Department proposals and other actions within the department confirm the suspicion that more is at stake here than just filling out forms. For example, the Administration would eliminate the requirement that companies having 50 to 250 employees file written plans examining any potential discrimination problems and detailing recruitment and promotion procedures for women and minorities. The proposals also would allow contractors with 250 to 499 employees to file much more general reports than are now required.

In reducing reporting requirements, the Reagan Administration would rob the government and outside groups of information needed to monitor the progress of the kind of small companies that provide 80% of the nation's new jobs. These are also the size firms that provide the experience that allows minorities and women to move then into more responsible, higher-paying jobs with larger companies.

If Administration intent isn't clear from these proposals, it should be from its call in July for public comment on whether the government should continue to seek back pay in settling cases in which job discrimination is proved. Back-pay awards have been the backbone of anti-discrimination efforts. Even though no policy revisions have been proposed yet, the Administration is already holding up settlement of at least one major case in which back pay has been recommended.

There is no question that government investigators frequently demand much more information than they will ever need, and that providing it can be particularly onerous to small companies that lack the computers or the personnel to compile it. However, the Carter Administration was on record before it left office with proposals that would have simplified affirmative-action reporting requirements while not reducing the quality of the information reported. All government contractors would have been affected; many had been consulted in developing the regulations, and approved of them. They never took effect.

The Labor Department's action reaches beyond government contractors, of course. Such policies set the national tone for efforts to treat fairly the groups that have been discriminated against in employment. The tone is no longer quite so clear.

The Dallas Morning News

Dallas, Texas, August 28, 1981

"AFFIRMATIVE action" is humbuggery. True, the motive — elevating minority-group members, socially and economically — is laudable enough.

But the means — conscious, government-enforced discrimination against "privileged" groups, in behalf of supposedly unprivileged ones — flout the traditional understanding of equal opportunity, which is that you rise because of what you do, not because of regulations devised in your behalf. What good is it, demolishing one form of discrimination, if in its place the government rears another form?

The government is going to do less rearing in the future, which represents a gain for common sense and human liberty. The Labor Department has announced new regulations that would free all but the largest construction companies from some of affirmative action's more suffocating impositions.

Whereas the government's standards for hiring and promoting women and minority-group members now affect contractors with 50 employees and government contracts of only $50,000, the bench marks are being raised to 250 employees and contracts of $1 million.

Companies with up to 499 employees must still affirm their commitment to equal-opportunity employment, but they may file less detailed affirmative-action programs. Nine affirmative-action steps will henceforth be enough; it has up to now been 16.

Not even a conservative administration is going to abolish reverse discrimination outright, as plainly it deserves to be abolished. Over the past dozen years, "affirmative action" has developed a large and bellicose fan club, composed of virtually all spokesmen for women's and civil rights organizations. The administration does not need such grief as abolition, at least instant abolition, would bring it.

Maybe the best that can be hoped, for the present, is that the rough edges of affirmative action can be planed down, to leave as few splinters as possible in the hands of those forced to grasp it.

There still will be some splinters. "Equal opportunity" is after all a hazy goal. What is "equal"? And what is an "opportunity"? The Reagan administration thinks the government too often has given forced and unnatural answers to the questions. The administration would rely less on naked force, putting an end, as one Labor Department spokesman says, to "mindless confrontations with employers who have been acting in good faith."

This is sensible. So also would be an admission by society-at-large: that, while discrimination has in times past helped keep minority-group members down, the worst way now of spurring them on is setting up government programs that encourage feelings of inferiority and dependence. Programs, to cite an egregious example, like "affirmative action."

Tulsa World

Tulsa, Okla., August 16, 1981

AMONG the many initiatives of the Reagan Administration to aid business and industry is a reconsideration of the much-maligned affirmative action program.

The program admittedly has been administered ineptly and in many cases overzealously to the point that skin color became a determining factor in employment.

Too many claims have been filed alleging discrimination and too many Government bureaucrats have had a stake in maintaining a large file of pending discrimination cases. Too often, employers have been pressured to "settle" discrimination cases to rid themselves of the nuisance and expense of defense.

Reagan and his lieutenants have suggested a shift in the zeal with which affirmative action has been pursued. Some Republicans in Congress are pursuing Constitutional Amendments to make "quotas" illegal in hiring.

But there is a real danger that the pendulum will swing too far. It can hardly be argued that some form of affirmative action was needed, if for no other reason, to focus employers' attention on the problems of minority employees.

Certainly a re-evaluation of the manner in which affirmative action has been administered is in order; perhaps some changes in the laws are necessary.

Let's not kill what essentially is a fair and necessary program, however.

The ultimate solution to racial strife in the U. S. is economic and the sooner that all Americans, whatever their ethnicity are able to compete for jobs on an equal basis, the sooner the racial problems will ease.

Here's a program that has been injured by zealots pushing too hard and too fast to right the wrongs of the past. Let's don't compound the problems by turning them over to zealots on the other side of the issue.

THE RICHMOND NEWS LEADER
Richmond, Va., June 9, 1981

If regulatory changes now contemplated by the Department of Labor take effect, small contractors may hope for some relief from the incessant demands of the Office of Contract Compliance. These demands impose heavy paperwork burdens and impossible hiring practices on many contractors who must comply or lose their federal contracts.

The Reagan administration wants to reduce the regulatory burden that brings so much grief to small businesses. An outline of proposed changes, not yet approved by Labor Secretary Ray Donovan, would exempt all contractors with fewer than 250 employees. There would be a reduction of paperwork and an end to requirements for fixed hiring goals for women and minorities in the trades.

Employers no longer would be socked with stiff back-pay penalties for women and minorities, nor would the hiring of construction workers have to be based on the percentages of women and minorities in the overall work force. Contractors with outstanding records in meeting past requirements could expect to be spared from review for as long as five years.

These changes make sense. Ever since Washington assumed the task of forcing contractors to hire 1.4 women plumbers and 2.7 minority electricians on each job, small contractors have been under the gun. Many of them have gone out of business, because they have found it impossible to spare the time to deal with the federal requirements themselves or to find the extra money to hire someone else to do it. These former contractors find some irony in the strident drive for affirmative action to create jobs — a drive that has diminished the total number of jobs available to everyone.

The Department of Labor is on the right track, although its proposed changes do not go far enough. The mood of the public signals an impatience with all federal efforts to pervert equal opportunity by reverse discrimination, regardless of its fancy euphemisms. It is encouraging that the Labor Department recognizes that affirmative action, and all of its unattractive offspring, may be the wave of the past.

Chicago Defender
Chicago, Ill., October 19, 1981

The Justice Department's Civil Rights Division has called for an end to Affirmative Action as generally understood. "We no longer will insist upon, or in any respect, support the use of quotas or any other numerical statistical formulae designed to provide to non-victims of discrimination preferential treatment based on sex or race, or national origin."

The meaning of this stand is crystal clear. It is consistent with the Reagan administration's anti-social, anti-black commitments. There is no logical reasoning in defense of this glaring retreat from justice and equity. Victims of bias in employment and promotion in the industries have no recourse to the federal government for lodging their complaints — for the government is now in tune with those who want to demolish civil rights.

It was President Johnson who initiated "Affirmative Action" to reduce to a minimum the chances for denial of opportunities to racial minorities and leaving them no slice of the cake. The Justice Department re-institutes the practice of racism in industrial and commercial establishments which had begun to veer their practices towards justice and fair play.

Detroit Free Press
Detroit, Mich., August 27, 1981

THE PROPOSED easing of affirmative action rules for federal contractors may eliminate some excess paperwork, but it could also wipe out the progress of minorities in the job market. At present, affirmative action requirements apply to any firm having more than 50 employes and a federal contract of $50,000 or more. The Reagan administration proposes to excuse from compliance any employer with less than 250 workers and a contract smaller than $1 million. Despite the disclaimers that easing the rules won't hurt women and blacks, that proposed new threshhold sounds unrealistically high.

The affirmative action program has helped to break the pattern of discrimination and indifference that has held back women, blacks and Hispanics in the work force. Without some such extraordinary effort, it could take generations more before minority workers have truly equal access to jobs and promotions.

Minority workers have suffered from decades of systematic exclusion, of course, but they are also confronted with more subtle barriers to employment. Most minority workers live in the city; most new jobs are created in the suburbs.

Surveys show that from a third to 40 percent of all blue-collar workers and a lesser number of white-collar and professional workers get their jobs through information or referrals by family and friends — that is, through an informal network to which minority or women applicants may have little access. It is not necessary for an employer to be a bigot in order for job opportunities to be closed off to blacks or women or Hispanics — only that the employer be indifferent, unaware or unwilling to make the extra effort required to broaden the makeup of a work force.

The federal affirmative action program helped to crack the indifference (or sometimes willful ignorance) of many employers. There are blacks, women and Hispanics in skilled trades and offices and professional positions today who would not be where they are except for the goad of affirmative action. Now that goad will be removed for a substantial number of employers. The easing of the rules will be particularly unfortunate in the construction industry, which has a large number of small contractors and subcontractors and has been notoriously slow to improve its minority hiring.

Affirmative action made federal contractors conscious of the need to search out and accept minority applicants. Without it, we risk a perpetuation of the cruel and arbitrary discrimination of the past. The affirmative action program may need to be streamlined or adjusted, but it must not be dismantled.

FORT WORTH STAR-TELEGRAM
Fort Worth, Texas, December 24, 1981

It is encouraging to find that President Reagan takes a more positive position on affirmative action plans than do Attorney General William French Smith and Bradford Williams, head of the Justice Department's civil rights division.

At his most recent news conference, the president said he doesn't "see any fault" with voluntary affirmative action plans established by companies and unions that are designed to give hiring preferences to minorities.

"This is something that simply allows the training and the bringing up (of minorities) so that more opportunities are there for them in voluntary agreement between the union and management — I can't see any fault with that. I am for that," the president said.

Reynolds has said that he would like the Supreme Court to reverse its 1979 Weber ruling that stated that federal civil rights laws don't prohibit affirmative action programs established jointly between unions and employers. Smith said the Justice Department would have taken a different approach to arguing the Weber case if he had been in control.

Smith has stated his opposition to the use of racial quotas in hiring and school desegregation. Reynolds has taken the position that the Constitution and Title VII of the 1964 Civil Rights Act prohibit discrimination based on race against whites as well as blacks.

The effect of the Smith and Reynolds position would be to make it illegal for companies and unions, which determine that it is in their own interests to hire and promote more minorities, to do so. That amounts to more of an intrusion into the affairs of private concerns than federal regulations requiring affirmative plans.

The president's position, despite its lack of teeth, is certainly more reasonable. He is being consistent. He is saying, if effect, that he is against the excessive regulation that accompanies federal affirmative action requirements and not advancement opportunities for minorities.

The Chattanooga Times
Chattanooga, Tenn., January 21, 1982

Unemployment among blacks now stands at about 17 percent, a five percent increase since last January, but at his press conference on Tuesday, President Reagan denied he is ignoring blacks' concerns. Later, however, he asserted that while he supports "affirmative action" (on jobs), he is opposed to "quotas." That is a distinction without a difference since it is difficult to see how Mr. Reagan can reject numerical requirements while professing support for affirmative action, since both to a certain extent favor one group of people over another. Mr. Reagan's comments Tuesday are especially interesting in light of his past statements on the matter.

In a previous press conference, Mr. Reagan seemed to endorse the Supreme Court's *Weber* ruling in a 1979 affirmative action case. In that case, Brian Weber, a white worker, alleged he had been discriminated against because his employer, Kaiser Aluminum and Chemical Corp., had agreed to a voluntary plan with the United Steelworkers Union that created an on-the-job training program. One feature of the plan was that it reserved half the job openings for blacks. The Supreme Court upheld the plan.

Although Mr. Reagan conceded his ignorance of the ruling, he said — after a reporter accurately outlined the case — "I am for that" (the voluntary aspect of the plan). But a few days later, the White House retracted the president's approval by saying that while "the president favors voluntary affirmative action programs," he opposes any that contain numerical requirements, whether or not the program is voluntary.

The White House's "clarification" of the president's position ignores the most important aspect of the *Weber* decision — the fact that it gives businesses the ability to fashion voluntary affirmative action programs. Such programs obviously are valuable in overcoming the long-standing inequality of opportunity that have plagued blacks for years. Besides, it seems odd that the administration would favor imposing federal regulations that prohibit management and labor to agree on programs that work to their mutual benefit.

Voluntary affirmative action plans are valuable for both employers and employees, but more than that, they constitute a just social policy.

●

Of course, with more than 9 million people now out of work, the real issue is jobs — for blacks *and* whites. Mr. Reagan, having checked the Sunday edition of *The Washington Post* and discovered 24 pages of advertisements for workers, said Tuesday that "what we need is to make more people qualified to go and apply for those jobs, and we're going to do everything we can in that regard."

The question is, how? Under Mr. Reagan, the administration has slashed job training programs, reducing the Comprehensive Employment and Training Act by a third and eliminating a program to retrain unemployed automobile workers. Unless he is planning a dramatic reversal for the 1983 budget to be submitted soon, Mr. Reagan's comments about training men and women for available jobs must be regarded as useless rhetoric — and a cruel exercise in raising the hopes of the unemployed.

THE PLAIN DEALER
Cleveland, Ohio, January 21, 1982

The federal government ought not get involved with voluntary affirmative action programs negotiated between employers and unions to remedy job discrimination. And we think the Justice Department is wrong to be looking for a case to challenge previous Supreme Court decisions that voluntary affirmative action programs are a lawful means for eliminating discriminatory practices in employment.

Specifically, members of the Reagan administration have said they want to find an appropriate case to try to reverse the Supreme Court's famous Weber decision. In the Weber case the court held that an affirmative action program negotiated between Kaiser Aluminum & Chemical Corp. and the United Steelworkers of America was a proper tool to correct obvious racial imbalances in Kaiser's craft jobs.

The plan set aside a percentage of slots for blacks in a job training program with the intent of increasing job opportunities for blacks. Brian Weber, a white Kaiser employe, challenged the plan, claiming discrimination because he was excluded from the job training program.

The Supreme Court could have interpreted Title VII of the 1964 Civil Rights Act to side with Weber, saying he was discriminated against because of his race. The court, however, determined that the intent of Title VII was to increase job opportunities for minorities and to open doors to blacks in occupations historically shut to them.

The Reagan administration seems to oppose voluntary affirmative action programs which unavoidably set quotas or tend to lend preferential treatment. But the Supreme Court has addressed this troubling issue of quotas and has applied proper standards in affirmative action cases where blacks clearly have been victims of discrimination. Here is a case of voluntary agreement between management and labor which has been upheld by the court. It makes no sense for the federal government to pick another fight to start the battle all over again.

DAYTON DAILY NEWS
Dayton, Ohio, January 5, 1982

It has been more than two weeks, but the White House is still mopping up after President Reagan's most recent press conference. The latest clean-up: Mr. Reagan does not — repeat: not — support affirmative actions programs for black employment even if they are voluntary.

This from White House press spokesman Larry Speakes. He says the President believes, after all, that the case in question was "wrongly decided" by the U.S. Supreme Court. The court, in a landmark ruling, upheld an affirmative action plan that had been negotiated by the Kaiser Aluminum Corp. and the United Steelworkers Union.

Asked at his Dec. 17 press conference if his administration's opposition to affirmative action would include such voluntary plans, Mr. Reagan, clearly unfamiliar with the idea, hemmed and hawed and finally talked himself around to thinking, aloud, that affirmative action is okay if it is voluntary, what with him being for volunteerism and all.

This seemed a not-unreasonable position, but William Bradford Reynolds, the Justice Department's assistant attorney general for (for?) civil rights, feels otherwise, and now Mr. Reagan's handlers have put the President officially on record as agreeing with Mr. Reynolds.

Mr. Reagan's obvious ignorance of many administration's policies, which supposedly are his own, is disturbing in its own right. In this instance, it is even more distrubing that a President who has opposed nearly every national effort to achieve racial equity America is so dug in against that goal that he opposes even the efforts that are freely agreed to by companies and their workers.

THE LOUISVILLE TIMES
Louisville, Ky., January 5, 1982

Affirmative action is not all that complicated: It's a program of hiring, pay and promotion practices designed to rectify the effects of past racial or sexual discrimination. Some politicians, however, have trouble figuring it out.

Take Gov. John Y. Brown. On the campaign trail in 1979, he was confused when asked what he thought of affirmative action. To his credit, his administration has given significant responsibilities to both women and blacks.

The prospects for President Reagan are less encouraging. In a press conference last month, he confessed ignorance about the U.S. Supreme Court's ruling on private industry affirmative action policies. After hearing a reporter's description of a system upheld by the high court, the President said he liked the sound of it. That ruling approved quotas established under a plan voluntarily negotiated by the Kaiser Aluminum and Chemical Corp. and the United Steelworkers of America.

Perhaps the President should have claimed ignorance as Mr. Brown did. If so, he would have been spared the embarrassment that resulted when his No. 1 civil-rights aide, Assistant Attorney General William Bradford Reynolds, explained last weekend that Mr. Reagan didn't really know what he was talking about.

Actually, the administration *opposes* affirmative action, and the President thinks the U.S. Supreme Court erred in 1979 when it gave the Constitution's blessing to quota systems freely negotiated by labor and management.

No matter what one thinks about affirmative action — and this newspaper has expressed doubts about whether the federal government should enforce rigid racial or sexual quotas — the President's snafu is disturbing.

It indicates that Mr. Reagan has not bothered to learn about an important civil-rights issue, and it confirms the suspicion of those who fear that he is not really concerned about using the powers of his office to support racial and sexual equality.

The appointment of Mr. Reynolds, a corporate lawyer who confessed that he, too, was ignorant of civil rights law and would have to take a crash course in it, was another sign of the Reagan administration's *laissez faire* approach to equal opportunity.

Both Congress and the Supreme Court have endorsed affirmative action as a remedy for past discrimination and, until Ronald Reagan moved to Washington, so did the executive branch. The President's claim of ignorance is just one more sign that those seeking equal opportunity in this country have no ally in the Oval Office.

THE CHRISTIAN SCIENCE MONITOR
Boston, Mass., January 7, 1982

White House aides have now clarified President Reagan's position on affirmative action programs. The clarification unfortunately invites disturbing questions about the administration's commitment to voluntary jobs programs in general as well as its willingness to come to the support of minorities and women long locked out of many manufacturing and professional positions in the US.

In a press conference Dec. 17, it should be recalled, Mr. Reagan said that he favors "the training and bringing up" of minorities so "there are more opportunities for them, in voluntary agreement between the union and management." The President was answering a question from a reporter about the Weber case of 1979 in which the US Supreme Court upheld a voluntary agreement between Kaiser Aluminum and Chemical Corporation and the United Steelworkers Union that set numerical goals for hiring blacks in a job training program. Now, according to a spokesman, Mr. Reagan is said to believe that the Weber decision was wrong, and that while the President "does favor voluntary affirmative action programs," he finds the "racial quota unacceptable."

The underlying concern about Mr. Reagan's position is the matter of how to go about ensuring access to jobs in the first place. Unfortunately, Mr. Reagan's assumption that the market economy will absorb all those persons willing to work irrespective of race or gender has not proven to be true. The whole rationale for quotas was to help alleviate years of imbalance in the workplace so that the labor force more closely reflected the composition of society as a whole.

Granted, there are legitimate claims to be met on all sides. Management and labor surely would not want quota programs in place that could so lower job and professional standards as to endanger certain operations, such as aviation. But such situations — in highly technical fields — are rare.

The administration is basing its entire recovery plan on the need for new investment and slashing federal programs geared to the poor, minorities, and the disadvantaged. But it is forgetting that there must be investment in "human formation," such as job training, education, and working conditions, as well as in new plants and equipment. American businesses, moreover, have a proper stake in ensuring that those persons who live near a plant have as much access to jobs within that facility as persons from outside the community, or just parts of the community.

The administration recently proposed a sweeping revision of the Labor Department's entire affirmative action program, exempting 75 percent of all firms that had been covered, although still retaining controls on the majority of all workers now covered. That earlier revision, coupled with Mr. Reagan's criticism of even voluntary jobs agreements that contain quotas, adds up to a major departure in discrimination policies in effect for a generation now. Congress, and the American people, should refuse to retreat from the nation's worthy objective of ensuring equal access to jobs by every person.

THE MILWAUKEE JOURNAL
Milwaukee, Wisc., January 19, 1982

Apparently we praised President Reagan too soon for his offhand answer to a reporter's question about voluntary affirmative action agreements between unions and employers.

The president was asked Dec. 17 whether he agreed with a Justice Department official who had said the government should try to get the Supreme Court to abandon the principle it established in the Weber case. The court ruled that it was permissible for a union and a company to agree to temporarily favor blacks in recruitment for a job training program if the purpose was to remedy the effects of past discrimination.

Reagan said he had not heard of the Weber case, but he added: "If this is something that simply allows the training and bringing up (of minorities) so that there are more opportunities for them, in voluntary agreement between the union and management, I can't find any fault with that. I am for that."

A presidential aide now says Reagan was misled by the question. According to the aide, the president thinks the Weber decision was wrong.

That's a pity. Left to his instincts, Reagan said the decent thing when confronted with an unfamiliar question. We're sorry some underling overruled him.

The Cleveland Press
Cleveland, Ohio, January 5, 1982

There's a good deal of confusion about where the Reagan administration stands on voluntary affirmative action programs involving private employers. And for good reason.

The Department of Justice is saying one thing about the celebrated Weber case, the president seemed to say another at his Dec. 17 press conference, and now the White House press office has put some different words in Reagan's mouth.

The Weber case resulted in a landmark Supreme Court decision in 1979 which approved an agreement between a private employer and a union — Kaiser Aluminum and the United Steel Workers — to conduct an affirmative action program for training minorities and moving them into skilled jobs.

Under the agreement, 50% of the openings in the training program at a Kaiser plant in Louisiana were reserved for black employees until the percentage of black skilled workers in the plant equaled the percentage of blacks in the local labor force.

William Bradford Reynolds, assistant attorney general for civil rights, claims that the Weber case was "wrongfully decided" and says the Justice Department is looking for an appropriate case in which to seek a different Supreme Court ruling. Reynolds objects to numerical goals and quotas even though they may be in affirmative action agreements that involve private firms, are voluntary and carry no government compulsion.

When asked about the Weber case at his press conference, President Reagan acknowledged an unfamiliarity with the details of it but said he didn't see anything wrong with voluntary agreements between management and unions to bring up minority workers.

White House press spokesman Larry Speakes said the other day, however, that Reagan does object to "a rigid racial quota" and therefore is in agreement with the Justice Department on the Weber case.

The administration's position is, to say the least, confusing at this point. The last word probably hasn't been heard.

Frankly, we think the Justice Department and the White House ought to leave the Weber decision alone. The case was correctly decided in 1979, in our opinion.

The decision hasn't created chaos or even consternation in the workplace, as far as we can tell, nor is there any great groundswell among private employers to overturn it.

Richmond Times-Dispatch
Richmond, Va., August 4, 1983

Forget it, Mr. President. Unless you are prepared to become totally submissive to their wishes and embrace their philosophies, you are not likely to satisfy feminists and black civil rights activists. They concluded long before you were elected that you were a prejudiced Neanderthal, and a prejudiced Neanderthal you will remain, in their eyes, until and unless you renounce some of your most cherished principles and grovel in repentance.

In one of the most dramatic and significant moves a president ever made to strengthen the role of women in governmental affairs, you appointed the first female Supreme Court justice. To stress your commitment to the principle of political fairness for black Americans, you strayed from a campaign position and dismayed many of your friends by supporting extension of the federal Voting Rights Act. In many instances, this law, as you yourself once acknowledged, unfairly punishes sections of the country that are not guilty of discriminating against black voters. You withdrew, under criticism from liberals, your support for tax exemptions for Bob Jones University, a private college that prohibits interracial dating and marriage.

Have these and other pro-women, pro-black moves earned you the gratitude and admiration of feminists and civil rights activists? Of course not. They castigate you for not doing more. Yes, you appointed the first woman to the Supreme Court and you do have two women in your Cabinet. But, the extremists' calculators show, you have appointed a smaller total number of women to federal jobs than Jimmy Carter did. And didn't you hesitate, for goodness sake, before you endorsed the Voting Rights Act? Moreover, everyone knows that you are opposed to forced busing as a tactic to attempt to achieve racial balance in public schools.

Exactly what would it take for you to please these people, Mr. President? It would take your complete conversion to their demented doctrine that the only way to dispense social justice is to dole it out in quotas. So many women here, so many blacks there. Forget about quality and ability. Numbers, Mr. President! Your liberal critics want numbers!

In your speech to the American Bar Association early this week, you made this statement:

"We aim for a cross-section of appointments that fully reflects the rich diversity and talent of our people. But we do not, and will never, select individuals just because they are men or women, whites or blacks, Jews, Catholics, or whatever. I don't look at people as members of groups; I look at them as individuals and as Americans. I believe you rob people of their dignity and confidence when you impose quotas. The implicit, but false, message of quotas is that some people can't make it under the same rules that apply to everyone else."

This is a sound and just view, and most Americans surely share it. Most people know that you do not achieve social justice by, to quote you again, "mandating new discrimination" in an attempt to "remedy past discrimination." Most people know that in a fair and just society people are hired and promoted because of their skills, talents and knowledge — not because of their race, religion or gender.

Forget about trying to appease the feminist and civil-rights extremists, Mr. President. It is futile. Instead, cleave to your principles and continue to advocate fairness and true equality for all Americans. Such a philosophy will result inevitably in the recognition of individual merit, a concept that is far more just and honorable than the doctrine of the quotamongers.

The Philadelphia Inquirer
Philadelphia, Pa., April 5, 1983

The word is out that the Reagan administration is intent on revising regulations under which the Department of Labor enforces affirmative-action employment requirements on companies that do business with the federal government. The final draft has not been released, and thus there can be hope for improvement, but on the face of what has been said the changes are distressing.

There can be no question in reasonable Americans' minds that any number of racial and ethnic minorities, and women in general, fall far short of equitable inclusion in the labor force, in terms of numbers, positions and pay. There can be no question either that however bitter the realities of the present and past there is no moral basis on which the democracy that is America can abide such systematic denial of access to its mainstream.

How to use the powers of government to work toward achieving equality is a confounding question. There are no easy devices, and no guarantees that any can fulfill their highest aspirations — whether in housing, education, access to public facilities or marketplaces, or in hiring. The moral imperative, however, is that every practical device be used, and used in aggressive good faith.

Affirmative action, the practice of hiring and promoting on the basis of proportional representation by race, sex or ethnic origin, is difficult, genuinely controversial, administratively burdensome and slow, since much of its most effective impact may take decades, or generations. That it is both potentially effective and morally imperative is beyond reasonable dispute.

Responding to criticisms, and perhaps to pressures internal to the administration, the Labor Department is about to revise the rules under which companies that contract to do work for the federal government must practice affirmative action. Reportedly, those revisions include lowering the threshhold for those that must prepare affirmative action plans from contracts of $50,000 and 50 or more employees to $100,000 and 100 employees. They would require that complaints be filed only in the names of specific victims — thus subjecting them to retaliation — rather than by class-action, as is now permitted. They would weaken both enforcement and penalty provisions.

Some or all of that would be welcomed by companies that feel burdened by the red tape of it all — and understandably so. Bureaucracies have a natural tendency to expand function and paperwork to fill the time, space and budget available. Especially for small firms in competitive atmospheres, the weight of paperwork can be staggering. But surely, if that is the main argument for amending the affirmative-action program, administrative efficiencies can be achieved in another, more positive manner.

Whether for good or bad, the specifics of the revisions are less important than the general message. If revisions that are widely and properly perceived to be a turning backward are put through it will be a clear, if implicit, declaration that the government of the United States, from the top, has changed direction, turning from a course of extending democratic principles to one of indifference.

That message, more significantly than the numbers, would be a tragic error — socially, politically and economically. It would say to millions of Americans that there is less hope and less justice — and a lesser commitment to righting that — than before the rules were watered down. Mr. Reagan is entitled to set his political course, and if that is to alienate the Americans who look to affirmative action for relief, so be it. But the country as a whole, its democratic tradition and its dignity, deserve better.

THE ATLANTA CONSTITUTION
Atlanta, Ga., June 22, 1983

The U.S. Labor Department, ready to relax affirmative-action requirements for federal contractors, would have us believe that the program has been nothing but a pain in the in-basket.

As opponents tell it, the program has created blizzards of paperwork that have all but frozen the flexibility of private industry. The derisive catch-phrases have been etched indelibly in the public mind: "drowning in red tape . . . social engineering . . . burdensome . . . ."

Throughout this assault, solid evaluations of the program's effectiveness have been in precious short supply. So two years ago, the Labor Department set forth to find out: Has affirmative action worked, or hasn't it?

The results are in now — contained in a report that the Labor Department has not seen fit to publish. And guess what? Affirmative action has worked. What's more — by the Labor Department's own reckoning — it has worked remarkably well.

From 1974 to 1980, the rate of minority employment among federal contractors grew 20 percent. Among companies not covered by affirmative-action rules, it rose only 12 percent. Women made even bigger gains. Their employment grew 15.2 percent in affirmative-action firms, but just 2.2 percent in other companies.

Nevertheless, the Labor Department is pressing ahead with its plans to reduce sharply the number of firms which must comply with affirmative-action rules. It would restrict the number of workers eligible for relief as a result of violations. And it would discontinue its policy of reviewing a firm's compliance before awarding a contract.

Paperwork? Red tape? Sure, there is room for improvement. The federal bureaucracy could stand some tightening, and perhaps it could be made more efficient.

But that isn't what the Labor Department has in mind. It would *dismantle* much of the affirmative-action program. Its cries of government-bloat ring hollow in the face of its own compelling evidence that affirmative action works.

OKLAHOMA CITY TIMES
Oklahoma City, Okla., December 23, 1983

THE most flagrant bias in this country in the civil rights area is that displayed against Reagan administration efforts to promote equal treatment without regard to sex, race or national origin but without use of coercive quotas.

The professional civil rights lobby has succeeded in putting across the idea that the administration is hostile to the hopes and aspirations of blacks, ethnic minorities and women. Because the lobby has enjoyed long-time access to the electronic and print media, it has planted this perception deep in the public's mind.

Efforts by President Reagan or his administration to portray his true objectives haven't erased the image. At the president's news conference the other night, Reagan was asked a highly opinionated question about his prospects for winning re-election in 1984 (assuming he does run).

He should have challenged more forcefully the way the question was phrased. The reporter asked the president if he thought he had enough support from white males to win in 1984, considering that, according to the questioner, "the administration has completely alienated blacks, is ignoring the needs and wishes of Hispanics, has cut programs that benefit the poor and is against equal rights for women."

That, in the terminology of the Washington pundits, is the conventional wisdom. But it is a distortion of what the administration approach constitutes in attacking illegal and illogical discrimination.

In the area of racial discrimination it opposes the use of race to reach a desired objective. William Bradford Reynolds, assistant attorney general for civil rights, explained why in a September meeting of chairmen of state advisory committees to the U.S. Commission on Civil Rights:

"Remedial goals, quotas or set-asides based on race perpetuate the very evil that the 14th Amendment seeks to remove. They erect artificial barriers that let some in and keep others out, not on the basis of ability but on the basis of the most irrelevant of characteristics under law — race."

In the area of sexual discrimination, the administration gets a bum rap because it opposes the Equal Rights Amendment, a position favored by many women but which earns it the opprobrium of the radical feminists. Yet the administration has agreed to support changes in 112 federal laws that are considered discriminatory toward women, while opposing 12 other changes and agreeing to study another six.

Thus, it is hard not to think the civil rights lobby's hostility to Reagan is based primarily on his refusal to go down the line with it on its political agenda.

The Washington Post
Washington, D.C., June 9, 1983

NO VERBAL finesse will close the gap between those who generally support racial quotas and those who don't. No sleight of hand will unite the people who believe that affirmative action should require "best efforts" only and those who insist that it must include both a numerical measure of progress and a reformulation of standards if that is necessary. And no soothing dialogue will reconcile the passions of the patient with those whose patience is exhausted. Waiting is hard. Changing is hard. So the increasingly acrimonious argument about means, even among those with a shared ultimate goal, will be hard to resolve.

Many supporters of numerical targets and affirmative action are unimpressed with the discomfort others feel about such matters. They are unimpressed as a moral matter, and perhaps unshaken as a political matter with the depth and pervasiveness of the misgivings in many quarters. Some blacks unfairly dismiss the objections as racist or insensitive. But that broad indictment is inaccurate, if racism means racially motivated prejudice and animus. The more common motivation is a sense that quotas are unfair and violate principles of merit to which the objectors are devoted. True, this agressive notion of fairness was sorely lacking for many generations when the victims were black, not white. And true, principles of merit are sometimes overstated and often poorly practiced, through biased measurements and unchecked discretion. But the fact remains that motives and sensibilities in this area are complicated beyond simple moral labels.

There is a similar story on the other side. Critics of numerical measures and aggressive affirmative action are largely deaf to impatient cries, and unpersuaded by arguments that progress and its pace must be measured. But over three decades, racial progress was energized by formal, often legal, requirements invoked because personal good will had been wanting for centuries. Someone whose political consciousness was shaped by that experience may well think that trusting the good faith of white employers as a class is foolish. So the supporters, while in important respects insensitive to the costs of actions they favor, have an important message about history and practicality.

The sharpness of the public and private discussions will abate only if each side listens for the merit embedded in the arguments of the other, and resists the urge to characterize differences in stark and unforgiving moral terms. And each must recognize the need to accommodate. Those who oppose hiring quotas should acknowledge that a system of best efforts has to be subject to monitoring, and that could mean accepting burdensome paper work and public scrutiny in order to demonstrate that the effort is serious. Those who favor more stringent measures must agree that so-called "remedies" which create a class of identifiable new victims are as wrong as no "remedies" at all.

THE INDIANAPOLIS STAR
Indianapolis, Ind., July 27, 1983

Perhaps the most controversial and emotion-laden proposal for overcoming discrimination in hiring is the "quota" system. It's a policy, to be followed either by court order or federal agency edict, insuring the hiring or promotion of people of specified ethnic groups, even if they are less qualified than other job applicants who by accident of birth are of other ethnic groups.

It differs from "affirmative action" programs, designed to seek out *qualified* members of certain ethnic groups to fill jobs.

A persuasive point on the subject has been made by Morris B. Abram, former president of Brandeis University and former president of the American Jewish Congress, and one of three Democrats President Reagan has nominated to the United States Commission on Civil Rights.

Why, Abrams asked, does no one insist on quotas for brain surgeons? It is a point well taken. Who, facing vital surgery of any kind would, if he had a choice, not select a doctor who reached his post through competence over one chosen to fill a quota?

The late Roy Wilkins, who headed the National Association for the Advancement of Colored People, was a formidible foe of the quota system. He assailed it in an article "The Case Against Quotas"

Howard I. Friedman, current president of the American Jewish Congress, maintains that quotas, ostensibly aimed at curbing discrimination, actually foster it by "requiring preferential treatment for individuals who have not themselves been discriminated against at the expense of other applicants, some with superior qualifications, who do not belong to the particular groups that are being compensated for past discrimination."

Friedman adds that quotas "demean and stigmatize the very people thay are intended to benefit by convincing many of those they work and study with that they are incapable of measuring up on their own."

Abram summed up his credo to the Senate Judiciary Committee as "equal opportunity for all with no guaranteed results for any."

Abram's long history of fighting for civil rights and equal opportunities for all people led Rev. Martin Luther King Sr. to urge his confirmation to the commission.

Certainly Abram's arguments against quotas cannot be summarily dismissed as the views of a bigot or a racist. His arguments will have to be faced on their merits. And those arguments appear to have plenty of solid, unbiased support.

The ⚘ State

Columbia, S.C., April 27, 1984

DR. MARY Frances Berry, a member of the U.S. Civil Rights Commission, was in Columbia last week to speak to a group of black law students at the University of South Carolina.

Dr. Berry, a black educator who now teaches at Howard University in Washington, D.C., was typically outspoken and blunt in her views about what blacks want, the need for affirmative action to improve job opportunities for minorities, and other civil rights topics. She blasted the Reagan administration's social programs and urged blacks to return to the militancy of the early 1960s if the President is re-elected.

Mr. Reagan tried to replace Dr. Berry and two other commissioners last year with three persons whose civil rights views were closer to his own. He disliked the positions of the members he attempted to fire on such things as racial quotas and school busing.

The upshot was that the Senate at first refused to confirm Mr. Reagan's appointees, although they had distinguished records in the field of civil rights. Instead it restructured the commission, increasing its membership from six to eight and giving the majority and minority leaders of Congress the right to name four of the members. Dr. Berry returned to the commission as an appointee of House Majority Leader Jim Wright of Texas.

At its first meeting, the commission, bipartisan by law, set out to establish a new agenda, one generally less activist than the previous commission's. Dr. Berry predictably objected to some of the shifts in emphasis.

First, the commission declared it is not bound by previous policies. Then is said it would distinguish between civil rights policy and social and economic policies, adding that it considered its jurisdiction limited to civil rights policy.

The commission decided, for example, that its concern is with discrimination in a federal program, not its funding level. In keeping with this, it voted 5-3 to cancel a study of the effects of reductions in student aid to predominantly minority institutions. To proceed, the commission majority said, would have meant that it viewed federal student financial aid as a civil right guaranteed to minorities rather than social policy.

Finally, the commission tackled the thorny problem of affirmative action and racial quotas, which some activists have come to consider synonymous. It distinguished between "affirmative action programs designed to increase the pool of blacks who are able to compete on an equal or color-blind basis with non-blacks and a quota system under which blacks and whites are treated unequally."

It argued affirmative action is inconsistent with quotas which gives preference to members of a racial group. The statement said racial preference constitutes another form of "unjustified discrimination" and creates "a new class of victims," namely whites denied a job or promotion because the black quota isn't filled.

The new policy endorses affirmative action programs that include minority recruiting, training, education and counseling that enhance the opportunities for minorities and females to compete for jobs and promotions on the basis of merit.

New Vice Chairman Morris Abram said he would like to "re-establish the pristine purity and simple justice of the concept of affirmative action when it first developed — before it became vested with all kinds of reverse discrimination and meaning."

Dr. Berry dissented and urged further study. But Mr. Abram said he didn't need more study of a principle that rests on constitutional bedrock: Equal means equal.

It's hard to argue with that, although activists will. The commission, it seems to us, has set the correct course and properly defined its mission.

The Des Moines Register

Des Moines, Iowa, August 16, 1984

An interesting Catch-22 has evolved as a result of conflicts between efforts to eliminate discriminatory hiring practices and efforts to overcome past discrimination.

Many employers are striving to raise the numbers of women and minorities on their payrolls; indeed, the federal government mandates that public employers and private companies that do business with the government have "affirmative-action" plans for hiring more minorities.

But employers who don't want to be charged with age, sex or race discrimination are advised not to ask applicants to give their age, sex or race on an application. Federal Equal Employment Opportunity rules forbid government employers from asking for such information from applicants for most jobs, and good sense dictates that other employers do likewise.

Short of interviewing every job applicant, how's an employer to know which candidates are minorities? In the case of applicants with first names that are interchangeable for men and women, how does one guess the sex?

It's also a dilemma for the minority or female applicant: Do you delete details about sex or race for fear a racist or sexist employer will automatically pigeon-hole your application, or do you volunteer the information in hopes you'll get a better shot at the job from an employer with an aggressive affirmative-action plan?

Where's Joseph Heller now that we need him?

Rocky Mountain News

Denver, Colo., March 31, 1984

IF only other federal officials had the backbone of William J. Bennett, chairman of the National Endowment for the Humanities.

For two months now, Bennett has defied the Equal Employment Opportunities Commission — a misnamed agency is ever there was one. What the commission demanded of the endowment was not so much hiring opportunities as numerical hiring "goals." The difference is the chasm between affirmative action as originally construed and quotas.

Bennett rejects quotas.

"We cannot comply with any inquiry that has as its premise the idea that there is a proper and improper mixing of races, creeds, colors, or sexes in the workplaces of this country," he says.

If that sounds like a commonplace plug for the value of individuals, it is nevertheless the stuff of controversy in today's civil rights climate.

No longer do individual rights guide the imagination of many government officials and activists. For them, group "rights" are paramount.

Thus the EEOC, without a shred of discriminatory evidence, goes about prodding employers into turning colorblind hiring policies into policies whose very essence, ironically, is the consideration of factors irrelevant to the job.

Bennett will have none of it. Happily, neither will the endowment's 26-member National Council on the Humanities, which has come to his support. Said one member in explaining the council's position: "We are bound by the Bill of Rights."

So is the EEOC, for that matter.

THE DAILY OKLAHOMAN
OKLAHOMA CITY TIMES
Oklahoma City, Okla., June 4, 1984

A MEASURE of the change in direction of the U.S. Commission on Civil Rights is revealed in the latest issue of its periodical, "Civil Rights Update."

The commission became the battleground last year in the struggle between the Reagan administration and civil rights activists over the most effective way to end racial discrimination. President Reagan sought to replace three holdover commissioners with appointees of his own choice.

Senate liberals managed to block his appointments and threatened to create a new commission beholden to Congress. A compromise expanded the commission to eight members serving staggered six-year terms — four named by the president and four by Congress.

The commission is still split, but Reagan appointees are in the majority. They are committed to a new course that upholds affirmative action but rejects quotas as "another form of unjustified discrimination."

Linda Chavez, commission staff director, explained the distinction in a speech earlier this year to the Anti-Defamation League of B'nai B'rith when she said:

"The dispute over quotas boils down to the question of whether rights inhere in individuals (the position of the current majority) or in groups (the position of its opponents). For, when you set up a quota which will benefit those who have not been personally discriminated against, what you are doing is benefitting individuals solely because they belong to a group whose economic and social interests you want to promote."

The nation has come to the point, she continued, where — counting women and minorities — 70 percent of the population of the country is entitled to some preference.

"And the end is not in sight," she said. "It seems to me that we are faced with only two choices. We can continue to go down the quota route, exacerbating group tensions all the way. Or, as the commission believes, we can retrace our steps and start fresh with a renewed dedication to the value of individual rights."

The commission still faces trouble. The heads of the black, Hispanic and women's congressional caucuses are trying to derail the panel by getting its funding eliminated at the end of this fiscal year Sept. 30. If the civil righteous people can't control the game, they want to pick up the marbles and go home.

WORCESTER TELEGRAM
Worcester, Mass., May 25, 1984

According to Linda Chavez, staff director of the U.S. Commission on Civil Rights, the United States has reached the point where "70 percent of the population of the country is entitled to some preference. And the end is not yet in sight."

In other words, 70 percent of all Americans belong to minorities and groups that are entitled to special treatment under various civil rights rules and regulations.

This is the legacy of the philosophy that moved directly from affirmative action to quotas. Affirmative action requires employers to make special efforts to provide jobs for qualified people who belong to various minority groups. It is an effort to get more justice and fairness into the system.

Quotas, on the other hand, undermine justice. As Ms. Chavez put it recently in a speech to the Anti-Defamation League of B'nai B'rith, "The dispute over quotas boils down to whether rights inhere in individuals or in groups. When you set up a quota that will benefit those who have not been personally discriminated against, what you are doing is benefiting individuals solely because they belong to a group whose economic and social interests you want to promote . . . We can continue to go down the quota route, exacerbating group tensions all the way. Or, as the commission believes, we can retrace our steps and start fresh with a renewed dedication to the value of individual rights."

That, of course, is what the big Civil Rights Commission row was all about a few weeks ago. The Reagan administration was dead set against the idea of quotas and set about changing the membership on the commission. Liberals screamed bloody murder, but the new approach reflects the views of most Americans. After all, practically all of us are members of some minority group. But most of us don't expect special privileges and preference. As Ms. Chavez pointed out, the quota route was the road to nowhere but bad feeling, hostility and injustice.

The News and Courier
Charleston, S.C., August 19, 1984

An annoying thing about "affirmative action," the equal rights philosophy to which Gov. Richard W. Riley is, at a very late date, dedicating his administration, is that it is subject to some very loose definitions. The result is that you can hear three speakers discussing affirmative action and come up with very widely separated ideas about what it really means to those who are going to be affected by it for better or worse.

That was exactly the case when Gov. Riley took the podium at a state sponsored workshop this week. He defined affirmative action in terms of equal job opportunities, which is what most people would like it to be — and what politicians pushing it always pretend it is.

At the same forum, however, another speaker, Dr. Jacquelyn A. Mattfeld of the College of Charleston, noted that affirmative action means giving the opportunity to the individual whose group is least represented. That, if we take it correctly, implies preferential treatment, just the opposite in other words to the equity to which Gov. Riley subscribes.

Finally there is the opinion — vague and nonspecific, sidestepping the issues of equity addressed by the other two speakers — that was expressed by James E. Clyburn, the state commissioner for Human Affairs. To Mr. Clyburn, if what was written about what he said was correct, affirmative action is merely a matter of education, of overcoming some long-standing attitudes.

Putting all those thoughts together, the result is confusion. What is "affirmative action" really, if all those experts differ so widely in their interpretations of it?

The truth is that how you stand on affirmative action depends on where you sit. From his chair in the political arena, Gov. Riley sees affirmative action as a good way to get votes. Apart from what she may think about the idea personally, Dr. Mattfeld must see it as something to which she has be in official accord because she works for a state institution. And Mr. Clyburn, of course, is the state's principal affirmative action officer.

If all the named above, all of them biased in one way or another to the proposition that affirmative action is a good idea, can't get together on a working definition of what it is they are talking about, then nobody can.

Our impression is that affirmative action experts like it that way. As long as people don't understand what's going on they won't complain.

Putting aside all the bumf about how it compensates for past injustices, affirmative action boils down to withholding jobs from one group of people in order to give them to another. It's as simple as that. And as unfair as that. No wonder politicians prefer to keep the public confused about what it really is.

Minority Business Contract Quotas Debated

The Supreme Court ruled in July, 1980 that Congress had the authority to redress past racial discrimination through the use of quotas in government contract awards. The ruling in *Fullilove v. Klutznick* joined the *Bakke* decision (1978) and the *Weber* judgment (1979) as the high court's third major consideration of the constitutionality of affirmative action programs. (See pp. 164-171.)

The *Fullilove* case concerned a challenge to a provision of the Public Works Employment Act of 1977 that required the Department of Commerce to set aside 10% of federal public works contracts for construction companies owned by minorities. Two lower federal courts had also upheld the law, in the face of arguments that it constituted "reverse discrimination" against whites.

The majority opinion in the *Fullilove* case stated that "Congress had abundant evidence from which it could conclude that minority business had been denied effective participation in public contracting opportunities...We reject the contention that in the remedial context the Congress must act in a wholly 'color-blind' fashion." It was the first time that the high court had expressly backed the awarding of federal funds based on the race of the recipients. Legal experts noted, however, that the decision specifically involved congressional power. It appeared to leave open the question of whether federal agencies or departments could on their own mandate contract quotas.

In recent years, many local governments have established programs to ensure that a certain percentage of contracts are awarded to minority-owned businesses, and to businesses owned by women. The Reagan Administration has consistently opposed these voluntary efforts, along with all affirmative action programs based on 'numbers.' The Republican platform for 1984 explicitly rejects the use of quotas to remedy discrimination in employment, education or housing, because they "are the most insidious form of discrimination against the innocent." (See pp. 136-147.) In 1984, the Justice Department entered a Florida case concerning such a program, instituted in Dade County after the Miami riots of 1982. (See pp. 172-177.) The Justice Department, siding with a predominantly white contractors' association, maintains that the contract compliance ordinance adopted by the county is unconstitutional, because there is no proof that the black contractors who would receive business as a result of its provisions had been discriminated against in the past.

The Kansas City Times

Kansas City, Mo., July 8, 1980

The major Supreme Court ruling mandating affirmative action in federal public works grants etches another opening of the market arena to minorities. Welcomed by civil rights leaders as a giant step in correcting past racial inequalities, the decision sanctions as constitutional the use of race to grant benefits in light of historical exclusion of minority segments of the population.

The justices, in Fullilove vs. Klutznick, affirmed congressional authority to set quotas that guarantee minority-owned businesses a 10 percent share of public works grants. Seen as an endorsement of the federal government's affirmative action efforts, the justices said Congress acted within its constitutional and legal authority in 1977 when it reserved 10 percent of $4 billion in federal public work grants as "minority set-asides."

While the most recent high court action leaves many aspects of the question unanswered, it laudably continues in the direction of supporting the principle of affirmative action that began with some confusion in the Bakke decision in 1978. In that case the court ordered admission of Allan Bakke to a California state medical school, saying that specific numerical quotas were not permissible although affirmative action guidelines were.

Last year, the court upheld voluntary affirmative action in the private sector in the Brian Weber case. Numerical guidelines have been set in some court-ordered school desegregation plans. All involve different parties as well as somewhat different aspects of a similar issue, yet the continuous thread of the federal judiciary has been to strengthen mechanisms for remedying past injustices by approving blueprints for minorities to catch up with the rest of society.

Opponents of the principle of affirmative action point to such practices as examples of reverse discrimination. The phrase is a contradiction. Assuming the fact of simple, endemic discrimination against minorities, the court has moved on to mandate remedies that may or may not be painful to previously favored majorities. That is as it should be in a society proclaiming justice for all.

The court is expected to refine the scope of constitutionally consistent affirmative action in two new cases accepted for review in the fall term. Relying on past decisions, minorities can be encouraged to expect further positive statements that will widen the doors to economic and educational opportunities historically locked from the inside.

THE WALL STREET JOURNAL.
New York, N.Y., July 7, 1980

Few constitutional principles have received more attention in the courts this last decade than the promises, implied and specific, of "equal protection of the laws." Certainly none has been shaped into more legalistic contortions, all in the name of racial and social justice.

The Supreme Court last week plunged deeper into the morass that has been created out of this simple, straightforward and noble concept in its decision in *Fullilove v. Klutznick.* It upheld a 1977 federal law requiring that 10% of federal public works contracts be set aside for business firms operated by racial minorities.

Now it takes a lot of wit to prove that, in the narrowest sense, all bidders on a contract are being treated equally under the law when one class of bidders has 10% of the business reserved for them. The court drifted around this issue, as it has in the past, by offering a broader definition of "equal protection." In essence, the majority held it to be constitutional for Congress to discriminate in favor of some racially defined class if that class has been discriminated against in the past.

The class the legislation was specifically designed to favor was, of course, blacks, or people who are sufficiently black to justify that racial classification. A true legalist would say that we now need racial classification laws, South Africa-style, to guide the letting of federal contracts.

It is of course a sad fact of American history that in the past black people have been so classified, even officially, and denied rights that the Constitution supposedly guaranteed them. It can even be argued that such things still happen in a society that still is trying to eradicate the lingering vestiges of a hateful racial discrimination, although examples of official discrimination are becoming increasingly rare.

It can be expected, and even desired, in our society that courts sometimes will extemporize, adapting the basic guiding principles of constitutional and common law to the need to adjust political and social conflicts. But it is equally true that the courts risk a breakdown of law and legal processes when they stray too far from these principles in their search for adjustment.

The endorsement of an explicit quota based on race strays a long way, in our view, from the equal protection principle. And, in this particular case, unlike some school desegregation cases, even the evidence of past discrimination in the award of contracts falls somewhat short of persuasive.

Some day, we suspect, the courts will have to try to back away from what they have entered here. The deeper they go, the harder it will be.

The Sun Reporter

San Francisco, Calif., June 26, 1980

When the U.S. Supreme Court made its historic ruling in the Bakke case some years ago, many proponents of affirmative action expressed fears that the ambiguities of the decision left the doors wide open to increased attacks on minority aspirations by the enemies of affirmative action who had backed Bakke's successful attempt to get himself inserted into the UC-Davis medical school at the expense of minority applicants whom the school said it would rather admit. Indeed, the years since Bakke have seen an alarming escalation of efforts to undermine the legal basis for affirmative action, as groups have tried to take advantage of the numerous loopholes in the high court's Bakke decision.

Happily, the Supreme Court has given little further solace to the enemies of affirmative action since the Bakke decision. The first, and most significant victory for minority groups in this regard came shortly after Bakke, when the court refused to dismantle the affirmative action apparatus in a job training program with the Kaiser company to enable Brian Weber, a white worker at Kaiser, to squeeze his way in among the numerous qualified minority applicants, who had been passed over for years in favor of whites. Another victory came when the courts rejected an attempt by Sears Roebuck

and Co. to dismantle its affirmative action because it was too complicated and allegedly self-contradictory.

Now the U.S. Supreme Court has dealt another, equally welcome blow to the enemies of affirmative action, in the form of a decision last week rejecting an attack on affirmative action brought by the U.S. Chamber of Commerce on behalf of the hundreds of thousands of businesses who are required to hire minorities because they do business with the federal government.

The Chamber had argued that the order, signed by President Lyndon Johnson in 1965, imposed illegal racial quotas on private industry, but the high court rejected that claim without comment. The case started when the Chamber objected to a federal court ruling that affirmative action programs in some Alameda county facilities were not up to legal standards. We are pleased to see, by this recent action, further evidence that the U.S. Supreme Court intended its potentially devastating decision in the Bakke case to be interpreted strictly, and not as a broad cudgel with which to beat affirmative action to death all over the country. We would be even more pleased if the enemies of affirmative action would get the message too, and stop clogging up the courts with harassing lawsuits.

The Philadelphia Inquirer

Philadelphia, Pa., July 6, 1980

Opportunities for minority-owned businesses to obtain a fair share of federally funded public works contracts have been advanced in commendable fashion by a 6-3 decision of the U.S. Supreme Court upholding the Public Works Employment Act of 1977. The decision should spur Congress to use its powers more vigorously to improve economic opportunities for racial minorities on a broad front through affirmative action legislation.

The 1977 law required that 10 percent of federal grants totaling $4.2 billion for public works projects go to businesses with at least 50 percent ownership by blacks, Hispanics, Orientals, Indians, Eskimos or Aleuts. The statute was challenged on grounds of "reverse discrimination" with the plaintiffs alleging that businesses not minority owned were denied equal protection of the law.

The act had been upheld by federal district and appellate courts in New York. In affirming their decisions the Supreme Court declared, in an opinion by Chief Justice Warren E. Burger, that the objectives of the 1977 law "are within the power of Congress to enforce by appropriate legislation the equal protection guarantees of the 14th Amendment."

Mr. Burger, citing abundant evidence of prior discrimination against minority-owned businesses, went on to say that "Congress has necessary lati-

tude to try new techniques such as the limited use of racial and ethnic criteria to accomplish remedial objectives." He rejected "the contention that in the remedial context the Congress must act in a wholly color-blind fashion."

Unlike previous affirmative action cases that have come before the Supreme Court, this one dealt with minority-owned businesses rather than minority employes or other minority individuals, and it addressed questions about the authority of Congress rather than private institutions to prescribe affirmative-action remedies for racial discrimination, when expenditure of federal funds is involved.

Although the decision does not deal specifically with problems of racial discrimination against persons seeking union membership and employment with firms holding government contracts — discrimination that has been especially blatant in the hiring of equipment operators for construction projects in the Philadelphia area — the result should be more aggressive enforcement of minority rights to fair economic opportunity wherever they are violated.

The Congress should reappraise its own responsibilities in light of the Supreme Court decision. Affirmative action is a power the Congress should use effectively in the enactment of future legislation involving expenditure of federal funds.

THE COMMERCIAL APPEAL

Memphis, Tenn., July 7, 1980

THE U.S. Supreme Court's ruling Wednesday on racial quotas still leaves unanswered questions, but it was particularly significant because for the first time the court endorsed the award of federal benefits on the basis of the race of the recipients.

The ruling, therefore, went beyond the famous Bakke case, in which the court said two years ago that a university could consider race in its admission policies but failed to set forth when quotas could be used constitutionally. It also went beyond a case last year in which the court approved voluntary racial quotas in the hiring and promotion practices of private companies.

In its next term, the court said, it would rule on when a state may use racial or sex preferences in public jobs and also on whether racial quotas may be used in public school systems if the quotas limit the number of blacks who can enroll in a neighborhood school.

The case decided Wednesday involved a public works program that reserves 10 per cent of its contracts for minority firms.

Congress, the ruling said, has the power both to induce voluntary programs of equality through its spending authority and to outlaw directly discriminatory actions. "In no organ of government, state or federal," wrote Chief Justice Warren Burger, "does there repose a more comprehensive remedial power than in Congress."

However, the court produced no majority rationale for upholding the constitutionality of the federal program. The opinion signed by Burger and two other justices was based primarily on Congress' special powers. Three justices who voted with them reasoned separately that the question of the constitutionality of the set-aside for minority contractors "is not even a close one." The three dissenters argued that any racial preference violates the Constitution's "colorblindness."

CONGRESS' POWERS aside, it seems not only logical but also necessary to take race into consideration when devising remedies to past racial discrimination. As in the Bakke case, it's clear that guidelines can be designed to improve opportunities for minorities without creating undue hardships for whites. But quotas, themselves, have to have limits lest they promote the same kind of discrimination, in reverse, that they're supposed to eliminate. If used, they need to be carefully tailored to a specific situation. The Supreme Court has a long way to go before it defines the whole problem of quotas and provides the guidance that the nation must have to resolve the issue.

The Cleveland Press

Cleveland, Ohio, July 7, 1980

In an important decision, the Supreme Court for the first time has clearly upheld racial quotas, ruling that Congress could set aside 10% of federal public-works contracts for firms controlled by minority groups.

The court's 6-3 decision stems from a correct reading of the Constitution. Congress was given broad powers to remedy wrongs, including the effects of past and present racial discrimination.

Also, when Congress passed the law in question in 1977, a case could be made that minorities were not getting a fair share of federal construction work. Blacks, comprising 11% of the population, received less than 1% of the contracts.

Even though Congress had the right to legislate as it did, it is hard not to sympathize with the white contractors from New York who brought the unsuccessful lawsuit. By excluding them from bidding on $400 million of contracts, they argued, the law was subjecting them to reverse discrimination.

In addition, as Justice Paul Stevens pointed out in a dissenting opinion, the law gave a monopoly over certain government work to blacks, Hispanics, Orientals, Indians, Es-

kimos and Aleuts. History teaches, he said, that monopolies lead not only to "high prices and shoddy workmanship" but also to "animosity and discontent" by those left out.

Moving from the constitutional to the practical, one sees that trouble can flow from the court's ruling. It is so broad that minority groups will seek to apply it to jobs, housing, education and any other area where they can persuade Congress to give them preference status.

Meanwhile racial and ethnic groups not mentioned in the 1977 law are sure to lobby for minority status for themselves now that it carries advantages.

The result could well be a fragmented, quarrelling society made up of clans zealously guarding their separateness. But to be successful, America must encourage racial and ethnic minorities to enter the mainstream and pull together with the rest.

Congress, therefore, should be most cautious in handing out the privileges that will be demanded. And all of us must work toward the time when merit, and neither quotas nor discrimination, will determine a person's reward.

The Dallas Morning News
Dallas, Texas, December 1, 1980

A FEW minority-rights spokesmen, as they style themselves, have been fretting publicly over what happens after next Jan. 20, when Ronald Reagan becomes president. Will the United States go marching backward to the pre-civil rights Dark Ages?

"Spokesmen" presumably have to talk this way, but that does not oblige others to shoulder their concerns. It seems safe to assert that the civil rights policies of the new administration are not going to disadvantage any racial group — which should be quite a contrast with the policies of past administrations.

The reigning idea in civil rights is that you help minorities mainly by leaning on the majority. Herewith one of numerous possible examples.

The bureaucracy tries to secure work for minority businessmen by requiring grant recipients to set up quota systems. Last spring, for instance, the Transportation Department issued rules requiring state highway and transportation departments either to funnel specific percentages of contract jobs to minority- and female-owned enterprises — or face the loss of federal funds.

Texas, through Atty. Gen. Mark White, protested that the requirement violates the state's competitive bid laws.

The meaning of the federal requirement, of course, is that the state (read: the taxpayers) must reject lower bids if the bidders have fewer minority contractors lined up than do higher bidders.

Other federal departments have evolved and implemented similar guidelines. For example, the Environmental Protection Agency. It stipulates, for jobs so limited as sewer system improvement, that bidders come up with minority subcontractors. Nor is the minority subcontractor even obliged to offer his services. The bidder must go out and find him.

How much does this help minorities? Not all that much. A subcontractor with many minority employees might lose the job because he is white. How does this help his workers?

For too long the government has been hung up on the question of who's black and who's white — a nobler kind of discrimination, you might say. But is not discrimination discrimination regardless of who peforms it? And doesn't it ultimately hurt more people than it supposedly helps?

We trust the Reagan administration will stop the fooling around with foolish guidelines and do the things that genuinely will help minorities — stop inflation, create more jobs. modify the minimum wage law to bring employment costs in line with the value of the job performed. The government's present civil rights approach is bankrupt. and it is time for all to recognize that fact.

St. Petersburg Times
St. Petersburg, Fla., January 21, 1982

In the last 25 years, black citizens have made major advances toward equal opportunities in education, jobs, housing and voting rights. But only a few have been able to establish businesses that can compete in America's free enterprise system for a fair slice of the economic pie.

Most blacks are employees, not employers; most are buyers, not sellers.

That disparity is sharply drawn in a three-year survey of supply purchases by the City of St. Petersburg.

In 1978, 1979 and 1980, only 10 of 25,000 city purchases orders went to minority businesses. Total purchases cost $90-million, but only $14,032 went to minority vendors.

THE CITY'S 41,000 blacks and other minorities compose about 20 percent of the total population, but their access to city purchases was less than half of 1 percent.

To help close that gap and stimulate the organization of minority businesses in St. Petersburg, City Manager Alan Harvey today will ask the City Council to pass an ordinance that would relax bidding requirements and earmark a small portion of city purchases for minority businesses, even if they do not submit the low bid.

The proposal would increase the city manager's authority to make discretionary purchases up to $5,000 without seeking competitive bids. The current limit is $2,500. It also would give the city manager flexibility to bypass a low bid and award purchase contracts to minority businesses when the the extra cost is within "reasonable" bounds.

Such purchases would have to conform to a schedule of "reasonable" variances. On purchases up to $20,000, the minority bid could exceed the low bid by no more than 10 percent; up to $40,000, 9 percent; declining to a 1 percent overrun on contracts of $1-million or more.

DURING THE first year, the expected cost would be less than $25,000 — merely a token advantage for minority businesses. But the token would send a strong signal to the black community that the city government wants to help minority businesses succeed and is willing to help them get started with a share of city business.

Quarterly goals would be set for purchases from minority firms. When the goals were reached, purchases would revert to straight competition.

Although the measure may be challenged as reverse discrimination, interim City Attorney Michael S. Davis thinks it can be sustained if the city documents the effects of past discrimination which has hindered minority access to city business. Davis also recommends that the ordinance include a provision to assure that the minority business advantage will end when parity is achieved and the effects of traditional discrimination have been overcome.

Why do white-owned businesses have a monopoly on city purchases of supplies and services for the public?

SIMPLY because there are virtually no black competitors for a fair share of that business. Generations of prejudice, deeply ingrained into every aspect of American life, have made it difficult for blacks to break economic barriers and qualify for business loans.

The few who do get businesses started have been hit hard by current economic conditions. Many are failing. In 1972, 319 minority-owned businesses operated in St. Petersburg; now only about 200 survive and only one of those, a black-owned office and janitorial supply business, provides products that the city needs to buy.

Harvey's attempt to stimulate minority business enterprises is strongly supported by the St. Petersburg Area Chamber of Commerce, the Community Alliance and the NAACP.

The St. Petersburg Times also recommends adoption of the ordinance.

By encouraging the formation of minority-owned business, the manager's proposal would create new jobs, helping minority workers to become self sufficient. The entire community would benefit from reduced costs for welfare and other social programs.

BEST OF ALL, it's a good start at giving minority businesses a chance to become equal competitors in the marketplace. That is right and fair.

To make the process work, Harvey will need to monitor the program carefully to guard against fraud or other abuses. The program should not become an institutionalized way to squeeze more money out of the taxpayers.

The News and Courier
Charleston, S.C., July 17, 1980

The U.S. Supreme Court gave its blessing again to what has come to be known as "affirmative action" when it ruled that Congress was within its rights in guaranteeing minority businesses 10 percent of federal public works grants. The ruling put the court's stamp of approval on quotas in yet another area of minority interest. Consequently, it created one more contradiction in remedies prescribed for discrimination because of race or ethnic background.

Public works programs are paid for with tax money. Grants and contracts should, therefore, be awarded to contracting firms or other businesses that bid low and have the best performance records. To say that 10 percent—or any set percentage—of public works jobs must go to "minority" businesses is simply to promote the practice of racial discrimination in reverse.

Where it should be mandating color blindness in public works funding and hiring, in accordance with espoused national principles, the court is trying to make a right from two wrongs. Just as a business or an employee should not be denied a job opportunity because of color or national origin, so should they not be given such an opportunity solely on the basis of color or national origin.

In its minority jobs decision, the court seems to be saying that equitable ends can be achieved through inequitable means.

THE INDIANAPOLIS NEWS
Indianapolis, Ind., October 3, 1984

People who say they want to promote minority businesses should listen to James Jimerson. He could tell them how to do it.

Jimerson is the president of Housekeepers Maintenance Service and Supply Inc., a company that markets cleaning supplies and offers lawn maintenance and custodial services. Early this week, Jimerson's company was named Indiana minority small business of the year. Next week, it could become the national minority small business of the year.

Jimerson started the business in 1978 with bank loans. In the six years since then, the company's gross revenues have grown from $5,000 to seven figures. The names on the payroll have jumped from two in 1978 to a current 215. And the company is now doing business in four states, including Indiana.

So Jimerson should know something about beginning and running a successful minority business. What does he say is the secret?

"It's the way you present yourself to your potential customers. Now if you present yourself as a minority, then they will treat you as a minority. . . . We do not treat our company as a minority firm. We treat our company as a firm, a majority firm.

"When we talk to an individual about a contract or buying supplies and equipment from them, we don't say, 'Hey, we are a minority firm' or that we're a disadvantaged business or what have you. We compete at the local market at the level everybody else is competing on."

In other words, the key to beginning and running a successful minority business is the same key to beginning and running any successful business.

It's not hard to understand why Jimerson's company won the minority small business award. We congratulate both him and his company.

The Providence Journal
Providence, R.I., February 9, 1984

Minority owned business enterprises will get a welcome helping hand in Rhode Island in the next few years. An executive order signed by Governor Garrahy sets goals for awarding at least 10 percent of the state's contracts and purchase orders to minority firms by fiscal 1988.

The order notes that "a long history of legal, social, cultural and economic barriers have prevented blacks and other racial minorities from enjoying an equal share in America's opportunities." To overcome such obstacles, too often raised as a consequence of prejudicial and discriminatory attitudes, the state purchasing agent is directed to take affirmative action to promote opportunities for qualified minority firms.

Such a public commitment is as welcome as it is overdue. Those who argue that few minority-owned companies have been available in the past should ask themselves why that was true. The answer involves centuries of white dominance and belief in the myth that some groups are inferior to others, that they do not possess the talent or ability to succeed as entrepreneurs, and so on.

Those who have experienced rejection on the basis of race, color or national origin often suffer from low morale and injured self-esteem. Starting a business is difficult enough without the imposition of unfair and illegal handicaps. Lack of confidence destroys initiative. The individual with 10 strikes against him from the start is not likely to welcome the heat of competition when others play by different rules.

The state's position as an equal-opportunity purchaser of goods and services, striving to overcome past inequality, sends a positive message. It tells victims of past discrimination that their chances of becoming a state supplier are not only even with others but perhaps a shade better, all other considerations being equal.

The governor did well to point to goals — as opposed to mandatory quotas. Flexibility must be maintained in the spending of taxpayers' money. Experience, reputation, and price still must govern the bidding process — along with minority considerations.

The executive order speaks of Rhode Island Minority Business Enterprises (MBE's), but surely out-of-state MBE's would also qualify in meeting the goals.

The governor's action launching this program is commendable. It parallels federal procurement requirements and at long last recognizes not only social injustice but injustice in the marketplace. With proper monitoring and enforcement by a 15-member commission yet to be named, it should mark a proud advance toward open competition free from artificial and unlawful barriers.

THE PLAIN DEALER
Cleveland, Ohio, July 18, 1983

Throughout the civil rights struggle, the cry has gone up from protectors of the status quo that the doors opened to minorities by federal courts were somehow special favors that took away the "rights" of the majority. We heard it about buses, lunchrooms, schools, employment, housing. And in recent days we heard the cry again after the U.S. Court of Appeals (6th Circuit) upheld Ohio's guarantee that minority firms must get a minimum percentage of state contracts.

"Reverse discrimination," complained an executive in the construction industry. "It takes away the open bidding process." Balderdash. If anyone should know about discrimination, it is a contractor, for the construction industry has been one of the toughest to crack for both minority tradesmen and minority businessmen.

But Ohio's law goes beyond construction, embracing all contracts. Minority firms must get 5% of construction work, 7% of construction subcontracts and 15% of all other contracts. This means minority firms can supply the state with anything from paper clips to word processors to insurance. While the percentages are not high, they help minority firms get into the marketplace and grow. In construction alone, minorities could get at least $25 million worth of business a year. The remaining $475 million in expected work leaves plenty of contracts for other firms.

A traditional complaint regarding both public and private contracts has been that minority firms are too small to provide a certain service or expertise. But, of course, if they don't get contracts, they don't grow or develop the needed skills. This vicious circle has limited many companies for years. In overruling a federal judge who threw out the minority set-aside law last year, the appellate court held that the General Assembly had "identified the discriminatory practices in state contracting and noted the economic disadvantages these practices had visited upon minorities."

The ruling was indeed a vindication of affirmative action, which is firmly established on the national agenda. Ideally, strong performances on government contracts will enable minority firms to compete better in the private sector and ultimately enhance the economic health of minority businessmen and employes.

After years of vigorous lobbying against the set-aside and then suits against the law itself, it is time Ohio's contractors accept reality and racial fairness instead of trying to restrict competition and access to the industry. We hope the case is not appealed; if it is, the Supreme Court should refuse to hear it.

The Orlando Sentinel

Orlando, Fla., October 19, 1984

Let's hear it for theft, government-style. Last week Orange County commissioners stole a page right out of the city of Orlando's playbook when they set a goal of giving 18 percent of the county's work to minority-owned businesses and 6 percent to businesses controlled by women.

This kind of action, far more than inflated rhetoric, will help minorities and women achieve the kind of equality that counts in the long run — economic equality. Despite some reservations from the county's public works staff, the plan also could save taxpayers money. A spokesman for Walt Disney World estimates that its minority set-aside program has saved that corporation $600,000 by fostering greater competition.

Take note: These are goals, not quotas. Commission Chairman Lou Treadway pointedly said he expected the public works staff to reject any bids that were too high, even if they would help fill in the percentages.

The commission, in short, is directing county government to seek out and encourage companies owned by minorities and women to enter the competition for county business, but it is not writing a blank check that would allow good intentions to be abused.

Just as important, the county's action takes official recognition of the fact that most businesses owned by minorities and women are, relatively speaking, the new kids on the block.

The 1964 Civil Rights Act and subsequent legislation and court rulings helped break the bonds of discrimination, but equality on the books does not automatically translate into real-life equality. Entrepreneurial efforts by minorities and women, together with actions such as that taken by the Orange County Commission, help to bring theory far closer to practice.

THE ATLANTA CONSTITUTION

Atlanta, Ga., April 18, 1984

Atlanta's minority-participation program, which supposedly guaranteed minority businessmen a share of lucrative city contracts and big-bucks construction projects, was a bold and innovative move when it was introduced in the 1970s.

It was looked on as *the* model by cities across the country trying to decide how to deal blacks and other minorities, who traditionally had been excluded from participation, an equitable share of the public-sector pie.

But even as it was being heralded as the way to go in the 1970s and '80s, the Atlanta program proved to be seriously flawed by a weakness that threatened to subvert the very intent of the program: Some white contractors used minority fronts in order to qualify for lucrative contracts.

Further eroding the impact of the program was the city's overly generous attitude in allowing major contractors — caught in bogus joint ventures — a second chance to find a legitimate minority subcontractor and keep their contract.

That indulgence had the effect of penalizing businesses that complied with city regulations and actually encouraged contractors to try to circumvent those regulations; the penalty for doing so was, incredibly, another chance to do it right.

That made a mockery of the intent of the program and, in many instances, caused lengthy and costly delays in major projects. Now, that weakness may have been fixed.

The City Council voted Monday to penalize contractors who try to circumvent city regulations on minority participation by setting up sham corporations headed by minorities. It's about time.

Under a new ordinance, if the winning bidder turns out to include a bogus minority partner, the contractor will automatically lose the contract. That is as it should be.

The whole idea behind the minority-participation program was to create the kind of climate in which businesses headed by women, blacks and other minorities could gain a footing and flourish, eventually becoming able to compete in both the public and private sector.

Even with its flaws, the program has produced important successes. Several promising new firms have been hatched. Fledglings have grown strong and able to fly on their own. The economy of the whole city benefits from spreading the work, and the income from it, around. The program should have an even better chance of reaching its full potential now that its Achilles' heel has been patched.

Atlanta, Ga., March 12, 1984

The Reagan administration has found still another target for its antagonism to efforts geared to overcoming the effects on America and Americans of three centuries of slavery, segregation and racism. It has attacked the way in which many local governments are encouraging the development of black free enterprise in their communities.

The administration has turned against local governments, such as Atlanta, that set aside some portion of their business for black-owned companies. That practice is unconstitutional, according to the Reagan Justice Department, which has entered a Dade County,

Fla., dispute on the side of a predominantly white contractors' association.

There is no evidence, Assistant Attorney General William Bradford Reynolds asserts, that the black contractors who would benefit from the law had been victims of discrimination.

Maybe so. But how is our society then to recover from the consequences of a time when a tire dealer, say, went bankrupt because discrimination aced him out of city-hall contracts? When the black entrepreneurial impulse was frustrated by bank prejudice against loans for black business start-ups?

How would the administration otherwise get business going in a black community that is grievously undercapitalized? Not by welfare, it says. Not, in fact, by any means.

Dade County adopted its contract compliance ordinance in 1982 after race riots — fueled by complaints that blacks were virtually excluded from the county's economic life — rocked Miami. The decision was sound. As recently as 1980, the Supreme Court upheld a federal law requiring 10 percent of the amount of every federal public-works grant to be earmarked for minority-owned businesses.

Now, however, the issue will have to be litigated out again, against the Justice Department's attempts to limit "racial selection devices" to "identifiable victims of unlawful racial discrimination."

Meanwhile, to maintain that it is misunderstood by its critics, as the administration does while chipping away at decades of progress, is no longer merely insulting; it's impossible.

THE SUN

Baltimore, Md., October 7, 1984

Minority Business Enterprise Legal Defense and Education Fund, Inc. owes its being and operating strategy to an older parallel organization with the similar goal of breaking down restrictive racial barriers through the judicial system. The NAACP and its Legal Defense Fund successfully spurred the nation's courts and, ultimately, the society itself to concede important civil rights to black Americans during the 1950s and 1960s with landmark class-action suits. Now, this minority business-oriented legal defense organization hopes to do the same thing.

Recently, the organization, founded in 1980 by Representative Parren J. Mitchell (D, Md., 7th), took giant strides in that direction. The group opened its national headquarters near Captiol Hill in northeast Washington and announced that 40 attorneys have agreed to provide pro bono services to the organization. The organization's directors will screen its cases to avoid representing individual businesses or legal concerns, unless they feel the situation will result in a landmark settlement or affect the major business community.

At the housewarming party for the organization's new headquarters, Mr. Mitchell took great pride in announcing the legal defense fund is totally supported by minority businesses and its supporters, not the federal government, private foundations or giant corporations. "It is owned and belongs to you," he said.

It is terribly unfortunate that this organization ever had to come into existence. Its new structure is a sad monument to the fact that the nation's 600,000 minority firms are isolated within the nation's larger business community. Despite Mr. Mitchell efforts at passing legislation aimed at strengthening minority and small businesses, those laws often have gone unenforced by the Reagan administration. In fact, considering the current administration's attitude of aggressively reversing and deliberately overlooking existing civil rights and affirmative action laws, this latter-day legal defense fund will have more than enough work to justify its establishment.

The Houston Post

Houston, Texas, August 28, 1984

Some confusion arose last week over the Houston City Council's passage of an ordinance setting minimum goals of hiring minority contractors for city business. Although the set percentage goals appear to fall far short of the 20 percent called for by some black leaders, the ordinance may be a giant step in the right direction for minority enterprises, which in the past have received a pitifully low 3 percent of the city's overall business.

The ordinance establishes these goals for minority businesses: 16 percent of the money spent for professional services, 10 percent spent on construction jobs and 7 percent on purchasing contracts. Overall, this means minority businesses — controlled and managed by women or minority persons — will get 11 percent of the total expenditures in those categories. When this 11 percent is applied to the estimated $296 million to be spent next year, as opposed to about 3 percent in the past year, minority businesses will receive a fairer share of city projects. And the new ordinance not only calls for increased percentages in future years, but also requires bimonthly updates on how close the city is to its target.

The process used to develop the ordinance was not flawless and will continue to be cussed and discussed as the Sept. 11 bond election approaches. But the ordinance itself represents a commitment to minority businesses the city has never had before.

St. Petersburg Times

St. Petersburg, Fla., September 28, 1984

St. Petersburg's plan to help minority-owned businesses get more contracts with the city has not given them nearly as big a boost as anticipated. It is disappointing that the plan has not been more successful. City Manager Alan Harvey's commitment to find other ways to help minority-owned companies should get full support from the council, the Chamber of Commerce and the community.

Two years ago, the City Council approved a special ordinance that allows the city to award contracts to minority businesses even if they do not come in with the lowest bids. Council members also set a goal. They decided that minority-owned companies should receive at least 5 percent of the money spent by the city for goods and services.

SO FAR, the city has not even come close to meeting that goal. During the last 12 months, the 193 minority businesses registered with the city received only 1.1 percent of the money spent by the city. Harvey cites two reasons for the lack of progress: There are relatively few minority businesses in St. Petersburg that provide the goods and services the city needs. And many of those businesses cannot meet expensive bonding and insurance requirements that accompany most city contracts.

Generations of prejudice, deeply ingrained into every aspect of American life, have made it difficult for blacks and other minorities to break economic barriers and qualify for business loans. That is why there are so few black competitors for city contracts.

Government programs alone cannot solve that problem. Attitudes have to change. All the people in the community, not just city government, have to give some of their business to minority-owned companies to increase their chances of success. The St. Petersburg Chamber of Commerce should step up its efforts to encourage white-owned, large, established businesses to help minority business enterprises get started.

THE COUNCIL also should support Harvey's efforts to make the city's plan more successful. He has suggested breaking projects put out for bid into smaller increments so that minority businesses have a better chance to compete against large firms; eliminating some of the city's bonding and insurance coverage requirements for smaller contracts; and speeding up the city's payments to vendors to lessen the financial burden on minority businesses.

Harvey is to be commended for sending a strong signal to minorities that the city government wants to help minority businesses succeed and is willing to help them get started with a share of city contracts. It is right and fair to give minority-owned companies a chance to become equal competitors in the marketplace. But that will not happen until the entire community supports minority enterprises.

Buffalo Evening News

Buffalo, N.Y., July 11, 1984

NEW YORK State's minority business enterprise programs, requiring generally a 10 percent minority business representation in government construction projects, serve the worthy purpose of increasing opportunities for minority contractors.

In a disturbing report based on a year-long inquiry, however, the State Commission of Investigation charges that the effort to expand opportunities for minority-controlled construction companies needs a "total re-evaluation and a radical overhaul."

The commission said that instead of expanding business opportunities for legitimate companies, the programs have resulted mainly in the creation of sham organizations that masqueraded as minority-run subcontractors.

State regulations require that prime contractors with major contracts employ subcontracting companies controlled by minority investors and executives. According to the commission, however, contractors have often complied with the regulations by setting up phony minority companies to take advantage of funds set aside for minority contractors.

Two of the business ventures criticized by the report involved Buffalo firms, and both have disputed the commission's report as inaccurate and unfair, contending that they followed the spirit of minority business enterprise regulations in pursuing construction contracts.

We can't judge the merits of the commission's allegations concerning particular programs, but there is enough evidence in separate findings in other areas of the state to suggest a statewide problem needing corrective action.

It seems clear enough that current supervision of minority programs is all too flabby and susceptible to abuses. The commission found that the absence of a single statewide program has led to "regulations which are unrealistic and unwieldy, multiplicitous yet easy to circumvent." The report recommended that the state create uniform regulations under the centralized control of a single office to monitor compliance.

With the state moving into a major $1.25 billion bond-financed transportation program, it is particularly important that Gov. Cuomo and the Legislature follow up on the commission's findings to ensure that efforts to advance minority opportunities are not undermined by costly abuses.

Minneapolis Star and Tribune

Minneapolis, Minn., October 5, 1984

In theory, government programs that earmark public-construction money for companies owned by minorities and women create opportunities for disadvantaged citizens. But this week's Star and Tribune series, by reporters Joe Rigert and Tom Hamburger, showed that Minnesota's understaffed minority-contract programs are hobbled by abuse. The abuse could readily be stopped — if the agencies involved complied with rules that are supposed to govern them.

An array of state and local programs exist to help women- and minority-owned contracting companies break into the economic mainstream. But the programs don't work well. Much of the minority-contract money ends up in "front" companies controlled by white, male contractors. Such contractors have created "disadvantaged" firms of their own by shifting ownership or spinning off new firms to wives, daughters or minority acquaintances with little contracting experience. That tactic has deprived truly disadvantaged companies of contracts they might otherwise have won.

Of $179 million granted to disadvantaged Minnesota businesses during the last four years, at least $49 million — one fourth of the total — has gone to firms closely tied to well-established white, male contractors. Meanwhile, other minority- and women-owned companies without such ties are struggling to compete. They, too, benefit from the programs. But a special survey by the Minnesota Poll, published with this week's series, ranked competition from front companies No. 1 among problems facing women- and minority-owned firms.

Their troubles could be eased if the Minnesota agencies that administer minority-contract programs enforced their own rules, which prohibit awarding contracts to fronts. But the agencies are understaffed and underfunded. They do not closely examine minority-owned firms before awarding contracts, and they do not visit job sites unannounced to ensure that minority contractors are on the job. Violators are rarely punished.

The problems are surmountable; Seattle's minority-contract program provides one model for reform. There, minority-contract applicants are carefully checked and regularly audited; minority firms are barred from subcontracting more than 25 percent of a contract amount; job sites are regularly inspected; violators are penalized with the loss of contracts. Minnesota can reduce minority-contract abuse in the same way. The state should provide the money and the determination to tighten eligibility rules, scrutinize minority contractors and firmly enforce the law.

Supreme Court Rules Seniority Supersedes Affirmative Action

The Supreme Court ruled in June, 1984, that courts could not upset valid seniority systems in an effort to protect the jobs of minority workers hired under affirmative action. The case stemmed from a 1980 consent decree between Memphis and the Justice Department, under which the city agreed to raise the percentage of its black firefighters to 11.5% from 4%. A federal judge, citing the agreement, had ordered the city to preserve the jobs of newly hired blacks during a 1981 fiscal crisis in the city. The order meant that white firefighters with many years' seniority were laid off when the city reduced its public employee payroll.

The city and the predominantly white firefighters union had unsuccessfully challenged the judge's order to preserve the jobs of blacks during the layoffs, in the U.S. 6th Circuit Court of Appeals. But the Supreme Court majority reversed the appeals court in a ruling which turned on Title VII of the 1964 Civil Rights Act. (Title VII prohibited employment discrimination based on race or sex but exempted from interference "bona fide" seniority systems that had not been set up for the purpose of discrimination.) The court's majority opinion stated: "Title VII protects bona fide seniority systems, and it is inappropriate to deny an innocent employee the benefits of his seniority in order to provide a remedy in a pattern suit such as this...Even when an [minority] individual shows that the discriminatory practice has had an impact on him, he is not automatically entitled to have a nonminority employee laid off to make room for him. He may have to wait until a vacancy occurs, and if there are nonminority employees on layoff, the court must balance equities in determining who is entitled to the job."

The Supreme Court decision in *Firefighters v. Stotts* was the most significant victory for the Reagan Administration to date in a civil rights case. Predictably, most proponents of affirmative action viewed the ruling as a major setback for minorities and women, while union leaders regarded it as a victory for objectivity in firing and hiring. Benjamin L. Hooks, executive director of the NAACP, assailed the ruling. "To uphold the 'last-hired, first-fired' doctrine in a nation that has a history of excluding classes of people because of race, creed or sex is to turn our backs on the reality that such discriminatory practices have had and continue to have upon excluded groups."

The Chattanooga Times

Chattanooga, Tenn., June 16, 1984

In ruling Tuesday that courts cannot order employers to modify valid seniority systems to protect recently hired black workers, the U.S. Supreme Court was attempting to preserve some fairness for both sides in a divisive issue. The dimensions of the problem were acknowledged in the dissenting opinion, which remarked on "the difficulty of reconciling competing claims of innocent employes who themselves are neither the perpetrators of discrimination nor the victims of it." The court's ruling was sensible.

The case arose in Memphis where, under a consent decree that ended a hiring discrimination lawsuit, the city agreed to an affirmative action program to hire minority firefighters. Since those hired under this plan were the last to be given jobs, they would have been the first to be laid off under normal seniority principles. When Memphis experienced financial problems, it temporarily laid off or demoted 40 junior firefighters, 15 of whom are black. One of those hired filed a motion in federal court to enjoin the city from such layoffs. The city soon found the money to rehire the men, so they were only briefly off their jobs.

Affirmative action programs can be helpful in redressing past practices of discrimination in hiring, but they are most valuable in ensuring that minorities have opportunities for jobs equal to those of whites. Had the court upheld the injunction, thus imperiling the jobs of white firefighters with greater seniority, it would have had to invalidate a section of the Civil Rights Act of 1964. That section outlaws employment discrimination on the basis of race or sex, but it also explicitly protects valid seniority systems that were not set up to circumvent the prohibition against discrimination. A lower appellate court had recognized the validity of the city's seniority system but ruled nevertheless that it had to be modified to accomodate the consent decree's provisions.

Nothing doing, the Supreme Court majority said: "[I]t is inappropriate to deny an innocent employee the benefits of his seniority in order to provide a remedy in a pattern or practice suit such as this." It's important to remember that the principle upheld by the court will benefit minorities as well as whites. The farther up the seniority ladder that minorities advance, the greater the protection they will enjoy. The court's Memphis ruling was an attempt to prevent a mutually beneficial system from being destroyed.

THE LOUISVILLE TIMES

Louisville, Ky., June 15, 1984

The Supreme Court's decision in a Memphis affirmative action case has the Reagan administration all charged up, and understandably so. The ruling seems to uphold the Reagan view that the seniority rights of white fire fighters must be protected at the expense of jobs won by blacks under a minority hiring and promotion program.

The day after the decision was announced, William Bradford Reynolds, head of the Justice Department's civil rights division, crowed that many court-ordered preferential hiring programs are now open to challenge, and that his staff would reassess them.

He also repeated the administration theory that only individuals who can prove they are victims of discrimination or were deterred from applying for a job have a right to special treatment. This approach would rule out plans that attempt to increase the representation of women or minorities in public and private employment.

This position, Mr. Reynolds claims, is one of "racial neutrality." In the absence of provable discrimination, he says, government shouldn't intervene.

In the first place, he has probably set his hopes too high. The Memphis case had to do only with the troubling issue of whether affirmative action goals give recently hired blacks some protection from layoffs in bad times.

The outcome admittedly bodes ill for other programs that may be reviewed later. It's too soon, however, to order up a dirge for hiring goals. The Supreme Court has given its blessing to affirmative action in some situations and has refused to meddle, for example, with the Detroit police department's hiring and promotion program.

Moreover, Mr. Reynolds's ranting about "racial neutrality" is preposterous. Hiring policies in the past have been outrageously biased, and a neutral solution has yet to be found. In cities with large black populations, blacks even today often hold a small percentage of the jobs in public safety and other agencies. Sad to say, a lot of employers actively searched for qualified women, blacks and other minority workers only when pressed by the federal government.

Mr. Reynolds must of course remedy discrimination against individuals. But that is hardly the answer to the exclusion of groups of people from the economic mainstream. He is oblivious

to the larger, and urgent, goals of affirmative action — to integrate the work force and banish the specter of a divided and unequal society.

Instead of chipping away at the legal underpinnings of affirmative action, government officials and labor union leaders should be looking for ways to make it work. The Memphis case, for instance, needn't have gone as far as it did. A strong case has been made that the court shouldn't have reviewed it, since the complaining white firemen went back to work in a month.

Seniority might not even have become a hangup if the city had tried through early retirement of older firemen and other arrangements common in the private sector to advance the goal of racial balance. While experience counts in fighting fires, seniority is not necessarily the most important attribute in a physically taxing job.

In getting the decision it wanted, the adminisration introduced new uncertainties in a program crucial in the long run to all citizens. That's all the more reason why communities should try to avoid court tests of potentially crippling conflicts.

Rocky Mountain News
Denver, Colo., June 15, 1984

THE U.S. Supreme Court's ruling that job seniority rights take priority over racial quota hiring agreements when a city is forced to lay off workers is indeed a far-reaching decision.

But it is not necessarily the setback to blacks or other minorities or women that some civil rights spokesmen have claimed.

The case involved firefighters in Memphis where, after years of being excluded, blacks had finally begun winning jobs on the force.

A lower court had told the city that it couldn't use the "last-hired, first-fired" formula when it faced a budget crunch a few years ago. Instead, the judge said, it had to retain a certain percentage of blacks, even if they had fewer years of service than some whites who were laid off.

Not so, the high court has said in a 6-3 decision. Title VII of the 1964 Civil Rights Act specifically protects "bona fide" seniority systems.

"It is inappropriate to deny an innocent employee the benefits of his seniority to provide a remedy" to a previous pattern of discrimination, Justice Byron White wrote for the majority.

In the long run the decision should be of benefit to those who have been discriminated against in the past, as they win wider entry into jobs they were once excluded from and as they themselves gain seniority.

It is true that the United States, despite efforts to the contrary, is still far from being a colorblind society. But movement in that direction is not speeded by making race, whether white or black, the qualification for exceptions.

Although the court also held more broadly that the antidiscrimination laws apply only to individuals who are "actual victims" of discrimination rather than to disadvantaged groups as a whole, this is by no means a signal to abandon affirmative action hiring programs.

On the contrary, there should be even greater efforts to recruit members of groups who for too long have been denied even the chance to start earning their own seniority rights.

The Birmingham News
Birmingham, Ala., June 14, 1984

Trying to eliminate the effects of sexism and racism practiced in years past will be a thorn in the side of this country for years to come. As important as it is for those issues to be dealt with as quickly as possible, there may be times when they conflict with even more pressing, but equally legitimate, public concerns.

At least that seemed to be what the U.S. Supreme Court was saying this week when it ruled that "last hired, first fired" lay-off plans should not be scrapped to protect affirmative action plans.

The crux of the matter was this: The city of Memphis a few years ago adopted an affirmative action plan designed to help reach an employment goal of 50 percent blacks and promised to try to promote qualified blacks to 20 percent of department vacancies.

Three years later, however, the city found itself in what one judge described as an "unanticipated economic crisis," and proposed citywide layoffs of employees. Lawyers for the National Organization for Women argued that seniority should not be the sole basis on which employees would be laid off.

Such a standard would mean that women and blacks hired since the affirmative action plan went into effect would bear the brunt of the layoffs, thus negating efforts to reduce the past effects of job discrimination.

The court ruled otherwise. Ironically, in an opinion penned by Justice Byron White, the justices said that any court order protecting blacks from the layoffs would violate the Civil Rights Act of 1964 by unfairly discriminating against white workers.

Both the court, whose ruling is now the law, and the NOW lawyers made compelling arguments. But it seems to us that a third side of the question ought to mentioned — the interests of the general public.

In a time of "economic crisis," the foremost concern of public officials should be how best to provide the best services for citizens — black and white, male and female — under limited financial constraints. It seems to us the best way to do that, if layoffs are required, is to keep the most experienced people possible — black or white, male or female — on the job.

The Idaho STATESMAN
Boise, Idaho, June 18, 1984

In the most important affirmative-action ruling in years, the U.S. Supreme Court last week nudged back the clock on attempts by women and blacks to secure their rightful position in the workplace. Unfortunately, the court had no choice.

By a 6-3 decision, the court said white workers with seniority cannot be fired to protect less-experienced employees hired under affirmative action plans.

During a period when many governments and corporations have been trimming or freezing employment, the ruling bodes ill for blacks and women.

The problem is that many white male employees with seniority got their jobs because of discriminatory practices that slowly are being eliminated with the help of affirmative action programs. Still, it is not any given employee's fault, and the Supreme Court recognized that. It's hard not to be sympathetic to longtime workers threatened with losing jobs when employers lay off workers.

The Civil Rights Act of 1964, the basis for affirmative action programs, specifically said that it was not designed to give preference to any person on account of race or sex, even to correct imbalances. Putting affirmative action ahead of seniority would have amounted to exactly that.

The decision came in a Memphis, Tenn., case in which lower courts had banned layoffs of newly hired black city firefighters during a financial crunch in 1981. Only the year before the city had settled a lawsuit by agreeing to upgrade the promotion and hiring of blacks.

While the Ford administration's Justice Department in 1974 successfully had sued Memphis to obtain a consent decree to hire more black firefighters, this time around the Reagan Justice Department sided with the whites in opposition to "reverse discrimination."

The ruling does not end affirmative action programs seeking to correct longstanding patterns of race and sex discrimination that bite at the core of a just society. Unions and interest groups still can seek agreements and contracts that provide for hiring and promoting of qualified women and blacks so they achieve a duly proportional representation in numbers, wages and power on the job.

CHARLESTON EVENING POST
Charleston, S.C., June 20, 1984

Whether affirmative action was dealt a setback or a mortal blow when the Supreme Court upheld the last-hired, first-fired concept in layoffs in the Memphis Fire Department will be debated widely in the months to come. There is less room for debate, however, on two effects of the court's ruling.

Writing for the majority, Justice Byron White said the fire department's seniority system was consistent with provisions of the Civil Rights Act of 1964. Lower courts were wrong, the majority found, when they ordered Memphis to put racial considerations ahead of seniority by laying off white firemen with more seniority than blacks. Sued under the rights action in 1977, Memphis had agreed to take affirmative action by hiring more black firemen. Then Memphis was hit with money woes and had to lay off, rather than hire, firemen. That's when the seniority question was raised.

The high court did more than affirm rights of seniority. It looked back at the language and intent of the Rights Act. It determined that Title VII of the act does not permit the ordering of racial quotas in business or in unions.

If it means anything, the decision in the Memphis case means that reverse racial discrimination is no fairer than initial racial discrimination. Two wrongs never make a right.

St. Paul Pioneer Press
St. Paul, Minn., June 15, 1984

The Supreme Court's ruling Tuesday upholding the primacy of seniority rights has two things in common with virtually all affirmative action cases. One is that the decision should fail to lend itself to unqualified satisfaction on the part of victors. The fact that disproportionate numbers of minorities may wind up losing their jobs is very troubling. The second common point is that those disappointed by the judgment should not assume terrible consequences resulting automatically from it.

The high court ruled that other courts could not order employers, in the interest of affirmative action, to lay off white employees instead of more recently hired minority workers. By a 6-3 margin, the court agreed with white firefighters in Memphis that their seniority rights had been illegally breached when two lower courts said that the city was obliged to dismiss them during a fiscal crisis in 1981.

Writing for the majority, Associate Justice Byron White argued that Title VII of the 1964 Civil Rights Act protects bona fide seniority systems as long as they were not designed to discriminate. This is a proper reading of the statute, regardless of what one may think of the opinion as social policy. The dissent, written by Associate Justice Harry Blackmun, focused on questions of procedure rather than merit.

The city of Memphis had previously entered into a consent decree aimed at increasing the number of blacks in the fire department; two lower courts had interpreted the agreement's aims as taking precedence over existing seniority provisions.

Dilemmas raised by affirmative action are routinely excruciating because valued principles compete with each other. In this instance, conflict between the goal of firmly observed, racially neutral seniority rights, and that of expanded racial diversity in the work place, is impossible to eliminate, at least in the immediate future. But it's a clash that can be softened.

Leaders in organized labor profess strong devotion to affirmative action. Affirmative action activists, on the other hand, are determined that those last hired will no longer be the first fired.

Nothing in the Supreme Court's ruling would seem to prohibit unions from bargaining for layoff policies that might accommodate, however partially, these two precepts. It is difficult but not impossible to conceive of contract language that would defend the practice of seniority rights but at the same time safeguard, if only somewhat, the relatively recent gains of minority employees. It is the kind of solution bound to satisfy no one and perhaps unrealistic to expect. But more than any alternative, it would spread economic burdens around.

While some people are quite disturbed by the court's decision, others of like interest have described it as "by no means a disaster" and "important but limited." If past cases are an indication, these latter evaluations will prove correct.

After just about every civil rights ruling, there are predictions the sky will fall on racial progress. The fear has been understandable, but nothing has crashed yet. For example, the half-a-loaf Bakke ruling on higher education admissions in 1978 diminished in no discernible way the commitment of most colleges and universities to racially eclectic student bodies.

Nor is anything likely to crash because of the Supreme Court's opinion this week, especially if the next major recession can be delayed a few years until a more significant number of minorities accrue a more substantial amount of seniority.

This measured confidence also takes into account possible plans by the Reagan administration, as suggested by Assistant Attorney General William Bradford Reynolds on Wednesday, to use the Memphis ruling as a wedge against virtually all court-imposed affirmative action plans. At best, the decision offers tangential support for this tack. It should not be pursued, as doing so would be unhelpful, unwise and unsupportable.

The Des Moines Register
Des Moines, Iowa, June 16, 1984

Affirmative action — the policy of hiring minority workers in ratio to their numbers in society — would cause little controversy if the economy were constantly expanding and creating new jobs. But since the economy tends to expand and contract, the only practical way to expand minority employment, short of displacing whites, is to hire members of minority groups only as jobs become available.

What then in periods of economic decline, when employers must reduce their workforce? Should workers with seniority be laid off to preserve the gains so slowly achieved by affirmative action? Or should the newly hired minority workers be sacrificed to in favor of workers protected by seniority agreements?

The Supreme Court ruled this week that laying off white firefighters with seniority in an effort to preserve gains by black firefighters would be the very sort of discrimination the Civil Rights Act of 1964 sought to eliminate.

If the union seniority agreement is legal, the court said, "it is inappropriate to deny an innocent employee the benefits of his seniority . . ." for the purpose of saving the job of a black.

This could be interpreted as the court's saying employers should strive to hire more blacks and Hispanics so long as the economy is healthy, but when recession hits, they're the first to go so whitey keeps his job.

In fact, the court relied on reasoning in an earlier case involving the Teamsters union in which the court ruled that affirmative-action goals could be achieved without displacing workers:

"Even when an individual shows that the discriminatory practice has had an impact on him, he is not automatically entitled to have a non-minority employee laid off to make room for him. He may have to wait until a vacancy occurs . . . ," the court said then.

●

There may be better ways of choosing candidates for layoff than tenure alone, but length of service certainly should be taken into account. And, just as it would be unfair to replace white workers with blacks to correct past sins, it would be unfair to protect all newly hired members of minority groups by laying off whites when the workforce shrinks.

Both ways are painful; neither is entirely fair. But keeping a new worker at the expense of a long-time worker is more painful and more unfair than what the court commanded.

The Salt Lake Tribune
Salt Lake City, Utah, June 19, 1984

The Justice Department's gleeful reaction to a Supreme Court ruling last week reeks with ultra-conservative myopia. It bodes ill for civil rights in this country.

At first, the court's decision regarding the layoff of Memphis firefighters seemed fairly innocuous. From most accounts, it apparently meant that minorities and women could not count on job security, at the expense of white males with seniority, when it came time to reduce the workforce. That sounded fair enough.

However, the day after the court rendered its decision, U.S. Assistant Attorney General William Bradford Reynolds, grinning broadly, announced plans to review hundreds of federal court orders to remove racial quotas and other job preferences for groups of public employees.

He and other Reagan appointees in the Justice Department smugly proclaimed vindication in their opposition to quotas as a remedy for past job injustices. Their contention is that the Civil Rights Act of 1964 allows job preferences for individual victims of discrimination, not for commonly victimized groups.

We take this to mean that aggressive affirmative action plans — those with specific goals for hiring and promoting women and minorities — will no longer be ordered by the court or even encouraged by the feds.

In the absence of employment guidelines, it will be up to employers and employees to figure out what's fair. Only blatant miscarriages of justice will lead to outside adjudication. And even then, only the individuals filing the action will benefit from the outcome, although the discriminatory practices might be the result of biases against a whole class of people.

It would be nice if employers voluntarily eradicated discrimination from the workplace. More likely, however, fewer employers will bother balancing their staffs with minorities and women under the lenient, flexible policy being pronounced by the Reagan administration.

Consequently, what started as a test case in one city could impede the urgent removal of all cultural barriers against better job opportunities for women and minorities nationwide.

The Houston Post

Houston, Texas, June 17, 1984

Early last week, the U.S. Supreme Court handed down a decision that showed good judgment, a sense of fair play and a commendable ability to read the language of the Civil Rights Act of 1964. What the justices said was that when job layoffs become necessary, affirmative action quotas do not override bona fide seniority systems — ones that clearly were not put in place for the purpose of discrimination.

And that's really all the ruling answered. The majority opinion was careful to a fault to avoid extending the decision beyond the question of who must be taken off a payroll first.

The very next day, William Bradford Reynolds, an assistant U.S. attorney general who is the nation's chief civil rights enforcer, started crowing that the ruling called into question "more than hundreds and less than thousands" of court orders which are already in effect — orders that affect questions of hiring and promotions, and are in no wise related to the high court's decision. But Reynolds nonetheless wants to exhume those long-decided cases and re-examine them.

The question of whether affirmative action is a good idea can be argued back and forth all day long, but the irreducible fact is that it is the properly enacted law of the land. Legal niceties aside, what Reynolds proposes would cost millions of taxpayers' dollars and thousands of hours in preparation and trial time on the part of his staff and the already overburdened legal system. This comes from an appointee of a regime supposedly committed to cutting costs and simplifying federal government.

Assistant attorneys general do not undertake such sweeping action except at the behest of someone higher up. This action smacks of a cynical and heavy-handed attempt on the part of the administration to accomplish in the courts what it knows it could never achieve in the legislative arena: the piecemeal dismantling of the Civil Rights Act.

SYRACUSE
HERALD-JOURNAL

Syracuse, N.Y., June 18, 1984

There is fear last Tuesday's Supreme Court ruling on seniority will hurt affirmative action and other civil rights programs aimed at remedying past racial discrimination.

The Reagan administration hasn't done much to assuage the fear.

Within days of the decision, the Justice Department made clear its intent to review, with an eye toward modification, hundreds of court orders requiring employers to use race or sex quotas for hiring, promotions or layoffs.

That's a regrettably hard line for a dilemma that demands sensitivity.

The case involved Memphis firefighters. The city had an affirmative action program to integrate the fire department. When city budget problems forced cutbacks, Memphis said it would lay off strictly according to seniority. That meant recently hired blacks would lose their jobs first.

Black firefighters sued and won a federal court injunction protecting the affirmative action program — and their jobs. The lower court ruled that the seniority system had to be modified to preserve gains by blacks. Three white firemen, each with several years seniority, were laid off instead.

The Supreme Court disagreed with the lower court. It ruled that while the 1964 Civil Rights Act outlawed employment discrimination on the basis of sex or race, it explicitly protects "bona fide" seniority systems that were not put in place to further discrimination.

In order to displace a valid seniority system, the court's majority said, it has to be shown persons were "actual victims" of discrimination. In such cases, it said, "they may be awarded competitive seniority and given their rightful place on the seniority roster." The court found no such direct discrimination in Memphis's system.

Protection of valid worker seniority is protection of a valid civil right. An individual who has worked for one company for years is entitled to some assurances his job won't be snatched away because of economic uncertainties.

But that doesn't solve the thorny problem of protecting minority jobs.

In time, the seniority system will help minorities. Seniority rules are objective — a whole lot safer than subjective considerations employers have used for decades to deprive minorities and women of jobs.

In the meantime, employers — and, if necessary, courts — should avoid direct showdowns between affirmative action programs and seniority rights. Each is too important to be subjugated to the other.

▽ ▽

Rather, the focus should be on finding alternatives to layoffs so that everyone gets maximum economic protection. Options might include job sharing or shorter hours for all workers. California and Arizona have laws allowing imposition of a four-day work week and the use of unemployment insurance to cover the fifth day.

The court's action was considerably less than the full frontal assault on minority protection that some portray it. It leaves intact remedies available to discrimination victims. But its message is firm and clear: Don't mess with jobs.

It's hard to argue with that logic. But it's also hard to argue with the logic — and fairness — behind affirmative action. If the administration uses the court ruling as a lever to weaken civil rights laws, it may get precisely the opposite result.

Several recent Supreme Court rulings have tended to legitimize the concept of "reverse discrimination." They've modified the impact on whites displaced by affirmative action programs. But the rulings have tinkered, not overturned.

The court remains solidly behind the Civil Rights Act, and can be expected to resist vigorously any effort to permit a preference for one racial group at the expense of another.

The Star-Ledger

Newark, N.J., June 19, 1984

In the early civil rights battles, the issues were quite clear and the sides were quite clearly divided. On the one hand were the discriminators, usually motivated by racial enmity. On the other were the victims of discrimination, usually blacks or other minorities. While the battle to end discrimination was not an easy one, in these matters, anyone with even a partly developed social conscience was able to distinguish right from wrong.

In more recent cases involving racial and other minorities, the issues are often more complex. It is frequently not so much a battle between right and wrong as between competing claims, each with a degree of merit.

One of the thornier questions has involved municipal job policy at a time, which has occurred with some frequency in recent years, when layoffs of workers were required because of fiscal constraint. Many of the affected municipalities had, comparatively recently, added minority workers. The question has been: Who is to go, the senior white workers or the newer minority workers?

Those stressing civil rights issues have argued that society's debt to underprivileged minorities must take precedence and the minority workers must be retained. Other groups, particularly the Justice Department lawyers of the Reagan Administration, have argued that it is unfair to protect minorities' jobs at the cost of the jobs of senior white workers.

The Supreme Court has now adjudicated this matter and has concurred with the Administration's point of view. By a 6-3 vote, it has ruled that seniority plans cannot be scrapped when hard times hit in order to protect racial minorities or women.

Its ruling upset a lower federal court decision in Memphis, Tenn., later upheld by a federal appeals court, that banned the firing of black workers during austerity-dictated layoffs. In the majority opinion, Justice Byron White cited both Title VII of the Civil Rights Act of 1964 and a 1977 Supreme Court decision interpreting the 1964 law.

The issue is an emotionally charged one, and will continue to be so, no matter how the courts ruled. The high court's ruling will have an impact in New Jersey, where a lower federal court has directed New Jersey municipalities to protect newly hired minority employes from the impact of layoffs. This lower court ruling is likely to be overturned as a result of the Supreme Court action.

Too often, the courts have been forced to rule in matters such as this one because Congress has evaded its responsibility to impose a legislative solution. The Supreme Court ruling is the law of the land— but only because Congress has failed to update its 1964 statute to cover a problem that was not a matter of contention at the time.

The high court has taken a pragmatic stand in upholding seniority. It properly addresses the fundamental issue of employment in terms of length of service. There are, of course, arguments that can be be made on both sides of this highly sensitive question. Congress still has the final decisive voice.

THE CHRISTIAN SCIENCE MONITOR
Boston, Mass., June 14, 1984

SOME of the most challenging times are those when rights, legislated or perceived, of different segments of society appear to be in conflict. This is such a time in the United States, particularly in the workplace. Blacks, women, and young workers are all demanding entry into the economic system. Older workers seek to remain in it. Minorities and women seek special assistance to make up for past discrimination; white males, especially the unionized, push back — also on grounds of fairness.

Yet out of today's challenges, as with those of any other time, can come an adjustment that brings greater equity to all segments of society. The perspectives and leadership of minorities and women make distinctive contributions to a nation with unmet needs plentiful enough to employ all.

A major American requirement now is to gear national policy so as to create jobs in sufficient numbers to reduce unemployment and end the perception of conflict. Results over the past 12 months are encouraging: Buoyed by recovery, American industry created more than 4 million new jobs. The challenges to continuing this rate of increase are formidable, however, and should not be minimized.

The US must also improve substantially its public educational system, so that today's students are adequately educated to hold tomorrow's jobs. Most positions will require people adept at reading, thinking, and dealing with technology. Blue-collar jobs that the undereducated can fill will continue to decline.

For today, the area of contention is affirmative action vs. the seniority system. The US Supreme Court has now ruled that when economic hard times force layoffs in public agencies, the seniority system takes precedence. The last hired are to be the first fired, even though those may be minorities or women who have obtained their jobs through affirmative action. The decision does not deal directly with affirmative action in any other form, such as hiring or promotion.

Ironically, this ruling comes as both minorities and women are making significant advances in the workplace. And when they, and older Americans, are becoming stronger politically. Yet given the high unemployment rates of blacks, and the continued disparities in salary between men and women, enormous progress remains to be made in society — whatever the court's decision — to see that both groups attain their rightful place.

Distressing as it is to see jobs taken from people who have been historically disadvantaged, many Americans would approve of the Supreme Court's decision in this case, on grounds it is inequitable to penalize blameless people who have been in the job longer. We concur.

THE COMMERCIAL APPEAL
Memphis, Tenn., June 13, 1984

IN A DECISION with wide ramifications, the U.S. Supreme Court yesterday ruled that the Memphis Fire Department was wrong to lay off veteran white workers to keep newly hired blacks on the payroll.

The ruling is a victory for supporters of the seniority system and a defeat for supporters of affirmative action. The two issues — seniority and affirmative action — are not mutually exclusive by definition, but practical and legal applications in recent years have put them on a collision course. In essence, the Supreme Court ruled that affirmative action must give way to seniority in cases in which the minorities involved are not actual victims of discrimination.

Philosophically, there was no way for the court to reach an equitable decision. How is it possible to fairly choose between two innocent victims? In this case, both the white firefighters with seniority who were laid off and the newly hired black firefighters had legitimate claims. The white firefighters who were laid off were never charged with discrimination and the newly hired black firefighters kept on the payroll were never proved to be victims of discrimination.

If anything, the 6-3 decision points out the difficulties of assisting minorities in getting to where they ought to be.

There is no question that the Memphis Fire Department over the years discriminated against black job applicants. When Carl Stotts, the black firefighter whose discrimination lawsuit instigated the personnel policies overturned by the Supreme Court in yesterday's decision, joined the department in 1955, he found himself fighting fires from a station house where all the firemen were black. Treated as a second-class fireman by his white supervisors, he recalls once being told to step away from a fire where white hotel guests were partly undressed.

For nine years Stotts watched new firemen hired, none of whom were black. During the 1960s more than 500 recruits were hired and only 29 of them were black. Finally, after waiting for two decades for a promotion, Stotts sued, charging the department with discrimination. He won and the City of Memphis was ordered to take affirmative action to hire minority firefighters.

While under a court order for affirmative action, the city announced in 1981 that dwindling revenues made it necessary for a certain number of firemen to be laid off. Seniority, said the city, would be the yardstick.

Since those hired under the affirmative action plan were the last hired, they would have been the first fired under the city's layoff plan. To protect their jobs, the black firefighters obtained a federal court order prohibiting the city from using seniority as a guide for its layoff policy. It was that court order that was overturned yesterday.

Writing for the majority, Justice Byron White said that "bona fide seniority systems" were protected by federal discrimination laws. Said White: "It is inappropriate to deny an innocent employee the benefits of his seniority in order to provide a remedy . . . (for discrimination)."

The Reagan administration, along with the AFL-CIO, the Anti-Defamation League of B'nai Brith and the Memphis Fire Department, argued that seniority rights should take precedence over minority rights when the minorities affected were not actual victims of discrimination.

In opposition, the National Organization for Women, the American Civil Liberties Union and the American Jewish Congress argued that affirmative action is being frustrated by layoffs according to seniority.

WITH SENIORITY rights ruled superior to minority rights in cases in which no actual discrimination has occurred, where does that leave proponents of affirmative action? How secure can any job obtained under affirmative action be now that the Supreme Court has ruled so firmly in favor of seniority rights?

Obviously, new solutions will have to be found. It will be more difficult now to help minorities realize the opportunities that have so long been denied them, but that should in no way reduce the nation's commitment to finding equitable means of correcting past wrongs and eliminating present and future discrimination.

The battle for civil rights clearly has entered a new era. No longer is it possible to paint the issue in stark black and white terms, as it was in the days when Jim Crow laws were there for everyone to see. The discrimination of today is more subtle, less visible, and often resistant to legal remedy.

Choosing between seniority rights and affirmative action was a no-win situation. Either way, the innocent were bound to be hurt. Somehow those who believe in equal rights must find innovative ways of fighting the age-old problem of discrimination. As long as the innocent are pitted against the innocent, there can be no victors.

The Seattle Times
Seattle, Wash., June 13, 1984

CIVIL libertarians are understandably worried about a U.S. Supreme Court ruling affecting job security because of its implications for a wider effort to dismantle the affirmative-action concept, long a key weapon in the nation's anti-discrimination arsenal.

In a 6-3 decision, the court ruled that job-seniority plans may not be set aside in favor of programs that treat minorities and women preferentially. The question was raised in a suit against the Memphis Fire Department.

The department was faced with the prospect of having to lay off employees during a budget crunch. Blacks, who were often the last hired, were exempted from layoffs and demotions. The firefighters union called it discrimination against whites and a majority of the nation's highest court now has agreed.

This turnabout is not fair play. The fundamental principle underlying affirmative action is that equality is a hollow word until access and opportunity are equal for all citizens without regard to race, creed, or sex. Affirmative-action programs have increased the participation of minorities and women in almost all elements of the American labor force.

Those advances could not have been made without the legal clout of affirmative-action laws. Meantime, conditions have not improved to an extent warranting a retreat from special efforts to integrate the workplace.

Finding remedies to offset the effects of centuries of racial deprivation and abuse requires the striking of delicate and complex balances in a country with a "color blind" Constitution. Steps taken to date have caused some dislocations of their own, along with a lot of protests, but have been accepted as a matter of public policy on grounds that the whole nation stands to benefit from the bringing of disadvantaged minorities into the economic mainstream.

The court's decision this week cannot erase all of the gains of the past two decades, but it likely will make further victories in the battle against discrimination harder to achieve.

THE SAGINAW NEWS

Saginaw, Mich., June 17, 1984

The Supreme Court is supposed to settle great constitutional issues. Its decision that black firefighters in Memphis did not enjoy special protection against layoffs settled only a small one.

Relying mostly on the basic 1964 Civil Rights Act and the court's own precedents, it breaks no new constitutional ground.

It does not involve workers where there is no seniority system. It applies only when there are layoffs. It seems further limited to cases where there is a seniority system, layoffs — and a prior legal order to remedy past discrimination, as in Memphis.

But it is important just the same, in its implications for much broader questions of civil rights — those that go to the heart of settling grievances involving discrimination according to race or sex.

That is undoubtedly why many — but, significantly, not all — civil-rights and similar groups denounced the ruling.

With the law and precedent against them, attorneys for the black firefighters pleaded, in fact, for no decision at all. They pointed out that the whites who claimed they unfairly lost their jobs had quickly been rehired. Three dissenting justices agreed there was no real issue to rule on.

The majority did, however, use the case to assert a key principle. It said color-blind seniority systems take precedence over color-conscious affirmative action plans. So the court took the side of individual rights — seniority can adhere only to a person — over those of a class or group, since race or sex is a group characteristic.

In that connection, it's important to note that Justice William Rehnquist repeated that individuals who have suffered discrimination qualify for legal relief.

Courts can even order seniority systems modified to make up for such bias, he said. But in Memphis, none of the black firefighters had been so victimized.

If civil rights, then, belong to persons, not groups, the whole concept of affirmative action and "goals," if not quotas, comes into question. No wonder many black and women's leaders are disturbed. Much of their effort has been devoted to redress for historic discrimination against entire classes of citizens.

That this has been a shameful part of our past is undeniable. In that context, it's fair to argue, too, that some persons may enjoy undeserved "seniority" at the expense of others. But should persons who have violated no one's rights lose their own to make up for what happened in the past?

It is a classic conflict, a worthy issue for the Supreme Court that must, eventually, settle it. The reactions to the limited Memphis decision suggest how difficult that will be.

Benjamin Hooks of the NAACP said he fears its import "in a nation that has a history of excluding classes of people because of race, creed or sex."

Justin J. Finger, head of the civil rights division of the "Anti-Defamation League of B'Nai B'rith, speaking for a group which has historically suffered from quotas, called the ruling a "great victory."

If the court is wise enough, it will somehow uphold the rights of individuals, as it did this time, while preserving justice for those who, because of their group membership, have not had a reasonable chance in our society. That will take a fair quota of wisdom, for sure.

Pittsburgh Post-Gazette

Pittsburgh, Pa., June 14, 1984

In ruling this week that seniority may take precedence over affirmative action when employees must be laid off, the U.S. Supreme Court undoubtedly set back the cause of integrating the American workplace. By definition, a "last hired, first fired" (or first furloughed) policy penalizes black Americans and other groups shut out of employment in the past.

But the 6-3 decision, in a case involving temporary layoffs of black firefighters in Memphis, leaves most of the legal edifice of affirmative action intact. Equally important, the court's deference to the seniority system acknowledges a conscious decision by Congress that the cause of an integrated society would be harmed, not helped, by a perception that progress for minorities requires breaking promises made to workers at the time they were hired.

In the Memphis case, the city had entered into a consent decree to settle complaints of racial discrimination in hiring and promotion. While the agreement established numerical goals for hiring black firefighters, it did not address the question of layoffs. In 1981, a fiscal crisis required the city to lay off some of its firefighters, and in doing so it followed a seniority procedure contained in its contract with the firefighters' union.

A federal judge then ruled that the seniority system had to be modified to preserve the gains made by blacks in the consent agreement. It was this decision that the U.S. Supreme Court has reversed, despite the fact that the case is arguably moot since the laid-off black firefighters were rehired after a month.

The court's decision is as important for what it did not say as for what it did.

The ruling does not in any way jeopardize affirmative-action hiring programs. Indeed, earlier this year the high court refused to review an appeals-court decision upholding the city of Detroit's use of racial quotas in the promotion of police officers. Moreover, unions and companies remain free to enter into agreements reserving places in training programs for minority workers. Such an agreement was upheld in a landmark 1979 Supreme Court ruling.

Nor does this week's decision prevent individual blacks — or women or Hispanics — from challenging seniority-based layoffs on the grounds that they were personally discriminated against in the past and thus deserve to receive compensatory seniority. It is even possible that changes in seniority systems could be included in consent decrees involving employers and aggrieved members of minority groups.

All that having been said, it is still a fact that this week's decision compromises the objective of remedying past discrimination against blacks and other disadvantaged groups. Allowing a black worker to challenge a seniority-based layoff on the grounds that he personally was denied employment in the past doesn't reckon with the plight of another black worker who never even considered applying at that time — because it was common knowledge that blacks would not be hired. Affirmative-action hiring plans have succeeded in integrating the work force as much as they have precisely because they go beyond proven cases of discrimination against individuals to rectify a pattern of discrimination against an entire group.

So this week's decision does create a loophole in the national effort to redress the evils of racism. But it is a loophole not of the court's making: Title VII of the Civil Rights Act, the law that provided the framework for the original Memphis consent agreement, contains an explicit guarantee that civil-rights enforcement would not threaten "bona fide" seniority systems that were not put in place with discriminatory intent.

The politics of that reservation are obvious. Organized labor, which played an admirable part in lobbying for the enactment of a whole sequence of civil-rights laws, regards seniority as close to sacred.

It is easy to conceive of objections to laying workers off according to the accident of when they were first hired: For one thing, length of service is obviously no guarantee of productivity or enthusiasm. For another, there seems to be something unjust about a system that requires laying off a young worker with a family before an older colleague with no dependents and the early prospect of retirement with Social Security or pension benefits.

But seniority achieved its pre-eminent status for a reason. Fearful of capriciousness or favoritism on the part of employers, unions sought an objective standard for deciding who must forfeit his job in the event of a reduction in the work force. However inflexible it might seem, especially when the competing interest is overcoming past racial bias, a layoff procedure based on seniority is perceived by many Americans as the essence of fair play.

In reflecting that consensus, Congress sought to prevent a situation in which civil rights would be viewed as the enemy of keeping faith with employees. This week's Supreme Court decision, for all of its troubling implications, merely ratifies that political judgment.

Newsday

Long Island, N.Y., June 26, 1984

The U.S. Supreme Court did *not* issue a ruling two weeks ago attacking broad affirmative action programs — although you might think it had from what the Justice Department has been saying.

William Bradford Reynolds, head of the department's civil rights division, has been depicting a narrow court decision involving the Memphis fire department as a sweeping vindication of the administration's distaste for affirmative action. With that broad interpretation in mind, Reynolds has ordered his division to review many existing or pending settlements of job discrimination cases — reportedly including those involving the Nassau and Suffolk Police Departments. But Reynolds is overreaching the court's ruling.

In the Memphis case, several fire fighters were laid off from their jobs when the city's budget got tight. Because blacks who had been hired recently under an affirmative action agreement had least seniority, they were the ones furloughed. A federal court subsequently ruled that the city should preserve gains in minority hiring by laying off whites, despite their greater seniority.

In overturning the lower court, Justice Byron White wrote for the Supreme Court's majority that the seniority system could be set aside only if the newly hired blacks had themselves been the victims of prior hiring discrimination by the department. Short of that, he wrote, neither the city's affirmative action agreement nor civil rights law called for abrogating the seniority system.

But Reynolds is trying to stretch the court's reasoning to embrace many affirmative action programs aimed broadly at redressing past hiring bias — not just those that conflict with seniority. That's justified neither by the Memphis decision nor by any standard of fairness or decency. Reynolds' campaign mustn't deflect the nation from its commitment to remedy the workplace injustices that minorities have suffered.

The Wichita Eagle-Beacon

Wichita, Kans., June 15, 1984

Ideally, a U.S. Supreme Court decision is analogous to a well-focused beam of light: It illuminates and clarifies a specific area of law. The Justice Department, which argues that this week's "last-hired-first fired" job layoff decision also illuminates adjacent areas of anti-discrimination law — promotion and hiring — appears not to understand that.

The Justice Department's apparently willful confusion, however, should come as no surprise. Justice hopes the decision — which said only that valid job seniority plans take precedence over affirmative action plans when layoff decisions must be made — will be a useful tool in its continuing assault on hiring quotas. William Bradford Reynolds, Justice's chief civil rights attorney, made this clear Wednesday, in announcing the department would "take a hard look" at hundreds of court-ordered affirmative action programs dealing with promotion and hiring, as well as layoffs.

Mr. Reynolds insists earlier Supreme Court decisions, which upheld affirmative action programs in higher education and hiring, still are valid. He didn't see fit to explain — because he can't, one suspects — the disparity between that assertion and his assertion that this week's decision also applies to promotion and hiring.

Justice's confusion notwithstanding, affirmative action is the law of the land in promotion and hiring — and in layoffs not governed by valid seniority-based labor contracts. That's good, for the constitutional imperative that all Americans be given equal opportunity in the workplace often is meaningless without affirmative action. The practice has worked effectively — and usually fairly — in correcting historical patterns of discrimination against minorities and women. If Justice's "hard looks" result in court action against promotion and hiring plans, judges should interpret this week's decision in the narrow sense the Supreme Court obviously intended.

THE KANSAS CITY STAR

Kansas City, Mo., June 14, 1984

Fortunately, it will take more than one court decision on one program to end affirmative action in this country. The Supreme Court's ruling that when layoffs are required seniority may not be scrapped to protect affirmative action plans is a setback for the concept. But it is not mortal. Some legal experts question its broad applicability although there is general agreement it will affect situations in other cities where disputes over hiring and firing are similar to those in the Memphis firefighters case.

Most civil rights groups consider the decision a negative. While it must be emphasized that the practice and shape of affirmative action is immensely more varied and extensive than the disputed Memphis version, any official action chipping away at rightful attempts to correct historical routines of discrimination is distressing. It is especially sad to watch this resolution held up as a victory for the federal government which, until Mr. Reagan, has been considered a last resort for minority justice. Mr. Reagan has never tried to hide his antipathy for affirmative action schemes. But if the time has come when a blow to civil rights is a mark of accomplishment for this country's leadership, our troubles are much deeper than even budget and deficit figures indicate.

No one of maturity expected that eliminating discrimination on the job, for women or minorities, would be quick or painless. Affirmative action—in which a numerical quota is only sometimes one element, incidentally—is a remedy when neutral standards for hiring and promotion are not enough to reroute long-and widely practiced ways of slamming doors. The recession that forced layoffs was a crucial element in the case the court decided. Perhaps as the court indicated, that is a unique circumstance excusing a retreat. There will always be some kind of excuse, however, for individuals and institutions resistant to a society of equal rights and opportunities.

Legitimate questions about the practice of affirmative action are posed by two competing ideals: a vision of equal treatment and a passion for self-wrought personal progress. It must be remembered, however, that the latter can be made impossible if cultural structures and government itself deny the former. Then extraordinary strategies are justified. As Eleanor Holmes Norton, former Equal Employment Opportunity Commission head, has said, it is often assumed "that affirmative action is a gratuity, the functional equivalent of welfare, for the purpose of awarding jobs and other benefits to the historically unfit or undeserving rather than a legal remedy developed in thousands of cases by federal courts after minorities and women established discrimination by the preponderance of the evidence."

The remedies will self-destruct, once the task is accomplished. So far, it's a very incomplete job.

The San Diego Union

San Diego, Calif., June 18, 1984

The Supreme Court ruling in the case of the Memphis fire-fighters is an overdue step toward eliminating some of the affirmative-action injustices committed in the name of racial equity.

In last Tuesday's 6-3 decision, the justices held that a court may not compel an employer to protect the jobs of recently hired black employees at the expense of whites who have more seniority. In other words, justice is properly colorblind in such matters.

The case began in 1980 when a black Memphis fireman charged in court that the municipal fire department hired and promoted employees upon the basis of race. A subsequent consent decree established an affirmative action policy within the department. Soon thereafter, the city was forced to lay off firemen because of financial problems, and because blacks were generally the last hired, they were informed they would be the first to go. Whereupon the courts intervened again and directed the department to abandon its seniority system in order to provide preferential treatment to minority employees.

The U.S. Supreme Court ruled that, in trying to protect these workers from layoffs, the Memphis Fire Department had violated Title VII of the 1964 Civil Rights Act, which explicitly protects "*bona fide*" seniority systems that were not in themselves designed for the purpose of discriminating against workers on the basis of race or sex.

What the high court did was to rule against the abuse of one group's civil rights solely for the benefit of another group. This, of course, sustained the original congressional intent.

When the U.S. Senate debated the proposed civil rights legislation 20 years ago, its supporters insisted that their bill was designed merely to give minorities a fair chance in the job market. Indeed, the late Sen. Hubert Humphrey promised that the statute would never be used to discriminate against anyone, much less establish employment quotas. Once the bill became law, however, a series of court interpretations spawned an endless succession of lawsuits concerning minority and majority access to the workplace.

Although last week's Supreme Court ruling avoided a more sweeping decision about the va-

lidity of affirmative action goals and quotas in hiring and promotion, it left the door ajar for a closer look at court-mandated preferential employment practices.

Indeed, the U.S. Justice Department is acting already to implement the court's decision. William Bradford Reynolds, who directs the department's civil rights division, has ordered a review of specific affirmative action programs to determine whether they are legally justified. He clearly hopes to restrict preferential treatment to those employees who can prove they were denied work or promotion because of their race or sex. Moreover, Mr. Reynolds is "taking a hard look" at the hundreds of affirmative action decrees in which the federal government is involved.

If quotas are wrong when they are used to deny employment to a black or a woman, they cannot be justified when they prevent a white male from working. The Supreme Court ruling on seniority implied as much, and we are encouraged to expect that future court decisions will enhance that enlightened interpretation.

The Boston Herald

Boston, Mass., June 14, 1984

THERE was a distinction, in the Supreme Court's decision on seniority rights that, in Boston, should not be overlooked or ignored.

It said that seniority does rule in layoffs made necessary by budget emergencies. But it also said it does not apply in desegregation situations.

In this city, then, it would appear that white police and firemen laid off during the economic crunch of 1981, while minority members with less seniority were kept on might — and that word is emphasized — might have cause for action. But the several hundred white teachers furloughed because of a racial-balancing order by Federal Judge W. Arthur Garrity Jr. might not.

Admittedly, the decision does put a dent in affirmative action programs which opened the doors to employment in public safety jobs to women, blacks, and others who, prior to their enactment, didn't have a prayer of getting that kind of work.

But it need not destroy them, nor should it be used as a weapon to sabotage them. Even Allen Blair, one of the lawyers representing the Memphis, Tenn., Firefighters Association which brought the case to the Supreme Court, said: "We were coming from the standpoint of protecting seniority. By no means were we in favor of doing away with affirmative action."

That must be remembered, and guarded against, in Boston where the layoffs of '81 bore some similarity to the circumstances of those which impelled the high court to rule in favor of the plaintiffs.

In one sense the issue might well be moot, since most, if not all, of the public safety personnel furloughed here have by now been rehired or have chosen other employment. But there is talk by union officials of filing suit to recover salaries lost by what the court might also decide were illegal layoffs.

It is easy, of course, to be generous when one's own situation is not at issue. But it is obvious that such a suit, if won, could prove ruinous to the fiscal stability of a city administration struggling to keep an inherited deficit from getting any worse.

If the Memphis ruling is found to apply here, the police and fire unions will win an important point. We hope they'll be content with that, without exacting the pounds of flesh — in the form of payments or possibly new layoffs — which might result from it.

"I HAVE TO LAY YOU OFF—THE OTHER GUY'S GOT SENIORITY."

The Cincinnati Post
Cincinnati, Ohio, June 15, 1984

The U.S. Supreme Court's decision that job seniority rights take priority over racial quota hiring agreements when a city is forced to lay off workers is an important one for Cincinnati.

Forty two police officers were laid off last month under an affirmative action plan after voters rejected an earnings tax increase in the May 8 primary. The plan was required by federal Judge Carl Rubin who held the city to a consent decree which protects minority city employees from layoffs in order to achieve racial balance.

The U.S. Justice Department said that it will appeal Judge Rubin's order. Judge Rubin has indicated that he wants to rehear the police layoff case in which he made his ruling. And the city has said it will take no action but will abide by whatever ruling is made.

The Supreme Court decision itself should not be viewed as the setback to blacks or other minorities or women that some civil rights spokesmen have claimed.

The case involved firefighters in Memphis where, after years of being excluded, blacks had finally begun winning jobs on the force.

A lower court had told the city that it couldn't use the "last-hired, first-fired" formula when it faced a budget crisis a few years ago. Instead, the judge said, it had to retain a certain percentage of blacks. This meant it had to lay off some whites with more years of service than blacks who were retained.

Not so, the high court has said in the 6-3 decision this week. Title VII of the 1964 Civil Rights Act specifically protects "bona fide" seniority systems. "It is inappropriate to deny an innocent employee the benefits of his seniority to provide a remedy" to a previous pattern of discrimination, Justice Byron White wrote for the majority.

In the long run the Supreme Court decision should be of benefit to those who have been discriminated against in the past, as they win wider entry into jobs they were once excluded from and as they themselves gain seniority.

Memphis says its cadet firefighter classes are now 50 percent white and 50 percent black. Thus if that city ever has to make seniority-based layoffs in the future, they will affect both races equally.

Although the court also held more broadly that the antidiscrimination laws apply only to individuals who are "actual victims" of discrimination rather than to disadvantaged groups as a whole, this is by no means a signal that affirmative action hiring programs may now be abandoned.

On the contrary, there should be even greater efforts in Cincinnati and elsewhere to recruit members of groups who for too long have been denied even the chance to start earning their own seniority rights.

Richmond Times-Dispatch
Richmond, Va., June 14, 1984

Most court pundits thought the Supreme Court would dodge on grounds of "mootness" the thorny issue of seniority systems vs. affirmative action raised in the Memphis firefighters case. After all, the three white firefighters who were laid off during a 1981 budget crisis, in order to protect the jobs of more recently employed blacks, were rehired less than a month later. But the experts were wrong. Six of the nine justices said the question of back-pay claims sufficed to keep the issue alive.

And by confronting the issue squarely, the six gave vitality to an important principle: Social progress for minorities ought not be achieved at the expense of hard-won rights of the innocent majority of workers. Creating a whole new class of victims is not the fair way to combat the effects of past discrimination.

"Last hired, first fired" may seem a cruel guideline for those who find themselves jobless again so soon. But the plight of the veteran employee forced out of work despite seniority protections guaranteed him under a union contract is no less compelling. Both deserve sympathy, but if only one job slot is available, both cannot have it, absent some innovative time-sharing arrangement, which is not always feasible.

Even though Memphis and the firefighters union have a legitimate seniority system that is not racially discriminatory, lower courts held that it must be modified because of a consent decree under which the city agreed to a goal of increasing the black proportion of the fire department to 11.5 percent, from 4 percent. Writing for the majority, Justice Byron White pointed out that Section 703(h) of Title VII of the 1964 Civil Rights Act explicitly protects *bona fide* seniority systems from being overridden when there has been no intent to discriminate.

"It is inappropriate," he added, "to deny an innocent employee the benefits of his seniority in order to provide a remedy in a pattern or practice suit such as this."

The lower courts had violated the so-called "four corners" rule by going beyond the bounds of the 1980 consent decree to insert points the city had never agreed to. In effect, they had awarded the protections of seniority to the newly hired black firefighters even though there was no evidence they had been victimized by racial discrimination.

"Even when an individual shows that the discriminatory practice has had an impact on him," Justice White added, "he is not automatically entitled to have a non-minority employee laid off to make room for him. He may have to wait until a vacancy occurs, and if there are non-minority employees on layoff, the court must balance the equities in determining who is entitled to the job. Here, there was no finding that any of the blacks protected from layoff had been victim of discrimination and no award of competitive seniority to any of them."

White

The Memphis case is far from being the final word on quota systems in all their harmful forms. But it is an important decision that eventually (since legitimate seniority systems are color-blind and objective) may be seen as protecting the civil rights of whites and blacks alike.

Los Angeles Times
Los Angeles, Calif., June 15, 1984

Asst. Atty. Gen. William Bradford Reynolds has seized on the U.S. Supreme Court's narrowly focused decision placing seniority above racial considerations in layoffs, and seeks to use it to rein in broader affirmative-action plans that he has long opposed. Reynolds has announced that the Justice Department will review all court-ordered affirmative-action plans involving the federal government to rid them of "race-conscious" provisions. The court's decision in the case of furloughed Memphis firefighters simply won't support Reynolds' broad attack on affirmative action, which is by definition race-conscious.

The Supreme Court's decision this week concerned senior white firefighters who had been laid off because of a fiscal crisis in Memphis. Some more junior black employees kept their jobs as the result of a court-ordered plan designed to try to mitigate the "last hired, first fired" rule that so often works against minorities and women. Much of the discussion in both the majority opinion and the dissent centered on two points: whether the case was moot because the firefighters had been rehired within a month, and whether seniority was in effect absolute. There was little discussion about broader affirmative-action questions, and what there was revolved around memoranda and speeches when the Civil Rights Act of 1964 was being passed, not around the act's language itself.

Reynolds fails to acknowledge the specificity of the court decision, preferring to take a wide ideological swipe at affirmative action in general. Until the nation is truly colorblind, employers must make special efforts to open opportunities for minorities to get jobs, win promotions and hold onto their jobs when times are tough. If the employers refuse to make such efforts on their own, courts may have to help them to guarantee civil rights. Reynolds' approach can only undo the progress that has been made.

TULSA WORLD
Tulsa, Okla., June 18, 1984

PERHAPS the most significant fact about the U.S. Supreme Court's decision on affirmative action programs and seniority systems in the Memphis Fire Department is that it was even issued.

In a 6-3 decision, the court held that "last hired, first fired" seniority plans cannot be scrapped to protect affirmative action programs.

The central question: What are cities to do when layoffs must be made and seniority rules seem to conflict with affirmative action programs.?

The suit arose when a federal judge ordered Memphis to disregard its seniority system when laying off fire fighters. As a result, three white firemen, eligible to keep their jobs under the seniority system, were laid off to avoid firing minority workers. The workers were rehired a few weeks later.

The Court refused to rule in a similar lawsuit 13 months ago on grounds that the workers had been re- hired, and the question was moot. But this time, the justices did not duck, even though they had a precedent for doing so.

That the court went ahead decided the case suggests some fundamental rethinking of the court's position on race and affirmative action.

In the past, the court has defended affirmative action on the grounds that it was justified to correct prior illegal discrimination. One problem with this policy is that it punishes people for actions they had nothing to do with. A white male whose family came to America this century is asked to atone for wrongs he and his ancestors were never guilty of.

In short, the Court is now saying that rights, including those guaranteed by the 14th Amendment, are conferred on individuals, not on racial or ethnic groups. In other words, the decision is a wise step toward a truly color-blind legal system.

THE LINCOLN STAR
Lincoln, Neb., July 23, 1984

The Justice Department, inspired by its victory in the Supreme Court ruling favoring seniority plans over affirmative action goals, has now carried through on its pledge to use the Memphis firefighters' case to overturn other affirmative action programs involving hiring and promotion quotas.

It has asked the 11th Circuit Court of Appeals in Atlanta to strike down the promotion policies of the Alabama state patrol. Ironically, it was the Justice Department, under then-President Nixon, which entered the case in 1972 on the side of black state troopers. In 1983, a federal judge ordered that for every white officer promoted a black officer also must be promoted until every rank from corporal to major was 25 percent black or until the department came up with an equally acceptable plan. The Justice Department now has switched sides.

If the Justice Department seems schizophrenic, it may only be reflecting society, or, more accurately, reflecting a society that is unsure how to achieve its goals. At best, we can only achieve them imperfectly.

WE WANT blacks and other minorities to be able to move into the mainstream, but we are sometimes indifferent to the subtle and often not-so-subtle forces that prevent their doing so.

Many Americans find the idea of a strict quota system repugnant. It goes against the grain of the work ethic and the idea that one can and should achieve on individual merit. Others feel quotas are the only means to effectively achieve equal minority participation. Discrimination is so pervasive one must use extraordinary means to eradicate it.

It's hard to call a middle ground when talking of people's livelihoods, their ability to draw a paycheck and support their families.

There is, perhaps, no ultimate solution, since prejudice cannot be wiped off the chalkboard like a bad word. If government has gone too far in trumpeting minorities, it can be argued that for too long it turned a blind eye to their needs.

WHAT WILL be most interesting to follow as the Justice Department systematically goes about righting these alleged excesses is the tact it takes, if in the wake of its policies, it discovers black gains halted and the ranks filled with whites while blacks seek unemployment benefits. Will it then take its case of unfairness to the courts or to Congress?

If the Justice Department knows of better ways to achieve equality it should pursue them. But it must recognize that affirmative action policies were instituted with full Justice Department support to right the discrimination wrongs. Have we now come so far that their removal need nothing in its place to assure compliance with the Civil Rights Act of 1964?

Strict racial quotas may not be the answer, but laissez faire did not work either.

The Record
Hackensack, N.J., June 22, 1984

The ink was barely dry on the Supreme Court's recent anti-affirmative-action ruling when Assistant Attorney-General William Bradford Reynolds announced his latest crusade. He said that the Justice Department would now try to undo other federally engineered hiring plans that called for hiring women and members of minority groups.

The attack is unwarranted. Last month, the court decided that white firefighters in Memphis cannot be made the only scapegoats for a budget crisis that required layoffs. Members of minorities and women — though hired under affirmative-action rulings — can be fired as well. Mr. Reynolds has long fought the notion of setting aside slots for nontraditional workers for any reason. Now, he's found his excuse in this ruling to get the federal government out of the business of enforcing racial justice.

The government trained its resources first on a New Jersey case. Mr. Reynolds asked U.S. District Judge H. Lee Sarokin to reverse one of the most progressive and thoughtful hiring rulings in this category. In May, Judge Sarokin ruled that fire departments in 12 New Jersey cities, including Newark, could not fire newly hired blacks because it would upset gains made under the cities' minority-hiring plans. That meant white workers, even though they had seniority rights, would have to be let go. Judge Sarokin also ruled that furloughed whites should be compensated for up to a year by the federal government.

Mr. Reynolds, who called the decision "the most bizarre" he'd ever seen, wants to unravel it. In doing so, he must overturn a longstanding, complicated resolution worked out over many years. These municipalities agreed to hire blacks in 1980, only after it was established that the cities had refused to hire them in the past. When city budget cuts and layoffs became necessary, last-hired black workers were the first to be let go. After Judge Sarokin's ruling, the state legislature found the money to make sure no one lost his or her job and the case became moot.

Overturning it now, as Mr. Reynolds wants to do, won't result in any hiring changes. It will simply stir fears in these newly integrated fire departments about who might get fired in the future.

Mr. Reynolds's war on affirmative-action plans in New Jersey and elsewhere ignores the benefits such agreements have had for everyone. Employers have found that hiring qualified blacks, Hispanics, and women did not undermine efficiency and productivity; it's been a boon to employers. For one thing, affirmative action increases the talent pool from which employers choose workers. Hiring minorities has also eased racial tensions in communities where black authorities — such as policemen and firefighters — have been all but absent in the past.

In his ruling last May, Judge Sarokin observed, "This country owes a debt to its minority citizens to compensate them for generations of degradation and deprivation." Society has repaid that debt in part by using affirmative action, but Mr. Reynolds seems determined to keep that debt outstanding.

Review of Detroit Police Dept. Affirmative Action Plan Refused

The Supreme Court in Jan., 1984 refused to review, thus letting stand, a decision upholding the legality of a voluntary race-based quota in the Detroit police department. The Detroit affirmative action plan had been instituted in 1974 after a federal court found discrimination against blacks in the city's police department. Under the pact, the city agreed to hire and promote equal numbers of black and white police officers. The Lieutenants and Sergeants Association, a Detroit police union, had sued to have the plan overturned.

The high court action in *Bratton et al v. Detroit* was a rebuff to the Reagan Administration, which had filed a brief in the case in December, 1983, asking the Supreme Court to rule that race-based affirmative action plans were inherently unconstitutional if they included quotas. The Justice Department brief argued that the Detroit plan violated the 14th Amendment's guarantee of "equal protection of the laws" for all citizens.

The Justice Department's argument attempted to secure the uncertain middle ground left open in two landmark Supreme Court rulings: *University of California Regents v. Bakke* (1978) and *Weber v. U.S.* (1979). In the *Bakke* case, the court had struck down a race-based admissions program at a California medical school, narrowly ruling that the school must admit a 38-year-old white engineer who had claimed that the school's minority-admissions plan had made him a victim of "reverse discrimination." In the *Weber* case, the court had ruled that employers and unions could establish voluntary programs, including the use of quotas, to aid minorities and women in employment. The decision turned back a challenge by a white worker who had been denied a place in a special training program at a La. plant of Kaiser Aluminum & Chemical Corp., although two black workers with less seniority than he had been admitted to the program. The court rejected the argument that the training program violated Title VII of the 1964 Civil Rights Act, which bars discrimination in employment on the basis of race. The majority opinion stated: "It would be ironic indeed if a law triggered by a nation's concern over centuries of racial injustice...constituted the first legislative prohibition of all voluntary, private race-conscious efforts to abolish traditional segregation and hierarchy."

The majority opinion in the *Weber* case stressed the "narrowness" of its ruling, since it applied only to voluntary plans by private employers: "Since the Kaiser-USWA plan does not involve state action, this case does not present an alleged violation of the Equal Protection Clause of the Constitution...The only question before us is the narrow statutory issue of whether Title VII forbids private employers and unions from voluntarily agreeing upon bona fide affirmative action plans that accord racial preferences." In effect, the Justice Department in 1984 had attempted to establish that the Detroit plan was unconstitutional because it was instituted by a public employer.

DAYTON DAILY NEWS
Dayton, Ohio, January 13, 1984

It's an old tactic. When you don't like the message, kill the messenger. President Reagan didn't like the messages he was getting from the U.S. Civil Rights Commission so he fought to get a new one. Now the new commission is working up a new message.

Linda Chavez, the new staff director to the commission, is recommending changes in the program to emphasize possible adverse effects of affirmative action, racial quotas and court-ordered busing.

In her memo to the eight commission members, Ms. Chavez recommended a study of affirmative action in college hiring and admissions. "A general decline in academic standards coincided with the advent of affirmative action in higher education." Empirical proof for her statement? None. It is a theory in search of proof.

The Reagan administration has its mind made up; all it wants now is good PR material from the commission. For example, the

The new commissioner of the Civil Rights Commission wants to study the evils of integration techniques. Yes, Massah Pres'dent.

U.S. Justice Department has fought the affirmative action program for the Detroit police department; having lost in a recent Supreme Court decision on the matter, the administration vows to fight on.

Twelve years ago, Detroit was 44 percent black; its police force, only 18 percent black. Detroit then selected equal numbers of blacks and whites for the police force, each from merits lists. Now the department is 32 percent black (the city, 63 percent black) and police brutality complaints have dropped 75 percent since 1972. If Ms. Chavez works hard enough, though, she surely will be able to see something terrible about this.

ST. LOUIS POST-DISPATCH
St. Louis, Mo., January 18, 1984

Having officially declared its "independence" from the White House, the new Civil Rights Commission largely named by President Reagan has lost no time in preparing to do his bidding.

Mr. Reagan violated an understanding with Congress in creating a new commission in his own image, and his image is one of opposition to fundamental past practices as to school busing for desegregation and use of numerical targets for affirmative action in employment. The commission hasn't reached the busing issue but it quickly took on affirmative action. It voted 6-2, with only holdovers from the previous body dissenting, for a resolution saying that employment quotas themselves amount to discrimination.

To illustrate, the majority chose a case that the administration has attacked in court. It involves the Detroit police desegregation program for hiring and promoting an equal number of whites and blacks. Blacks now constitute about one-third of the police department. The alternative was to leave law enforcement in a predominantly black city to a department that was 82 percent white. Brutality complaints have dropped since then.

The basic reason for this voluntary program, though, was to provide for specific goals — call them quotas or whatever — to remedy past discrimination against blacks by placing them in positions which they had been denied. Without specific goals, the idea of affirmative action is nebulous. It is the sort of thing that the Reagan administration can praise and obstruct at the same time. That is the course its "independent" commission is taking.

THE MILWAUKEE JOURNAL
Milwaukee, Wisc., January 17, 1984

It isn't fully clear why the Supreme Court rejected the Reagan administration's attack on affirmative action in the Detroit Police Department. The Justices simply refused to hear the case, giving no reasons for the action.

Even so, the result is commendable. It means that Detroit can continue a program that is bringing more blacks into supervisory positions in the Police Department. That is an important objective, not just to provide employment opportunities that unfairly were denied to blacks in the past but also to improve relations between the department and a large black citizenry.

Although the high court's refusal to accept an appeal does not set a national precedent (in the sense that an actual ruling on a case does), the action implicitly sends a signal to the Reagan administration that it is heading down the wrong track with its broad attack on affirmative action.

The administration hoped to prove that the affirmative action plan, by using race as a criterion for promotion of black police officers, unconstitutionally discriminated against whites. We acknowledge that affirmative action can work to the disadvantage of some white applicants. There is no perfectly neutral way to eliminate the dreadful legacy of racial discrimination. However, the legacy must not be allowed to remain.

As the Supreme Court properly found in the landmark Bakke case, affirmative action plans are sometimes too crudely drawn. Sometimes they need to be revised so they will not rely too heavily on rigid quotas. The Reagan administration was wrong, however, when it contended that the police department should give no preference to blacks on the basis of their race. Some preference is necessary until the effects of historic discrimination are overcome.

The San Diego Union

San Diego, Calif., January 19, 1984

The U.S. Civil Rights Commission has taken a sharp change of direction with its condemnation of preferential quotas in hiring and promotion. The liberals are reacting as though the commission had come out for the repeal of all the Civil Rights legislation enacted during the last 20 years.

What the commission is doing is urging government agencies to pay more attention to what those civil rights laws really say. They say that discrimination is wrong, period.

Affirmative Action programs that established quota systems for hiring and promoting minorities have been oblivious to that point. In particular, the commission appealed to the U.S. Supreme Court to rethink its recent rejection of an appeal on behalf of white policemen in Detroit who have been the victims of racial discrimination in their jobs.

The court is allowing Detroit to keep separate promotion lists of white officers and black officers, promoting one black officer for every white officer promoted, regardless of merit or seniority. The aim is laudable enough: To create a police force in which the number of black officers in higher ranks is in line with the number of blacks in Detroit's population, as it presumably would be if there had been no racial discrimination on the Detroit police force in the past.

The Civil Rights Commission is now giving formal recognition to what anyone with a sense of simple justice can see: That Detroit is squeezing white officers out of promotions for which they are otherwise qualified, and for no reason except their race. And that, according to any reasonable concept of civil rights, makes them victims of racial discrimination.

The recognition of this "reverse discrimination" has been a long time in coming at high levels of government. Indeed, the courts have been ambiguous at best in defining how far an Affirmative Action program can go in redressing the effects of past discrimination of minorities before it becomes guilty of discrimination against the majority in the here and now. The Civil Rights Commission cannot dictate to the courts or to the Congress, but it can bring its moral suasion to bear on those institutions and others that deal with issues of discrimination and Affirmative Action.

The commission today is more qualified to speak out on the issue as a representative body than it was before the row between Congress and the White House that nearly ended its existence last fall. When Congress balked at President Reagan's attempt to replace members of the commission who disagreed with his views, a compromise was struck. What was formerly a six-member commission appointed by the President has been reconstituted as an eight-member body with four members appointed by the President and four by the two parties in Congress.

Democratic candidates for president who sniff an election issue in the commission's denunciation of quotas should keep this in mind. Walter Mondale, it turns out, was talking through his hat when he said he would fire the commissioners appointed by Mr. Reagan if he were elected president. Under the new legislation, neither the commissioners appointed by a president nor those appointed by Congress can be fired for political reasons.

The commission followed up its 6-2 vote against racial quotas by scolding an anonymous White House official who was quoted as saying the commission is "on our side." Not so, said a message directed to 1600 Pennsylvania Avenue. "The commission will remain independent of all outside wishes or pressures, whether they come from the White House or any other group."

President Reagan, long a critic of the reverse discrimination evident in quota hiring and promotions, obviously has sympathizers on the commission but he can expect to be rebuffed if he tries to control it. The liberal activists who dominated the commission for many years — and led it to the embrace of quotas, mandatory school busing, and other doubtful remedies for discrimination — also have been pushed out of the driver's seat.

What does that leave us? It leaves us with a Civil Rights Commission composed of members chosen in equal numbers by the administration and Congress and who are independent-minded enough to resist political pressures from whatever direction. The commission, after all these years, may finally be ready to justify its existence.

Los Angeles Times

Los Angeles, Calif., January 11, 1984

The U.S. Supreme Court has once again sent an unmistakable signal to the Reagan Administration that it is not going to alter the basic thrust of affirmative action programs that seek to erase the legacy of discrimination. The court did not say that in so many words, but it implied as much in declining to hear a challenge to the promotion plan of the Detroit Police Department. None of the nine justices voted to hear the case.

The Detroit plan calls for alternating promotions to lieutenant, choosing one white candidate, then one black, until half the lieutenants are black. The names are drawn from lists that rank the candidates in order of their ratings on the same numerical system. The plan is achieving its goal: Ten years ago, only 18% of the department's officers were black; now the figure is 32%. Detroit officials had defended their plan as necessary because of "massive, intentional past discrimination" within the department. That discrimination was also harming police relations with the community.

But the Detroit Police Officers Assn. sued to block the policy, picking up U.S. Justice Department support late last year even though the officers had lost similar challenges at both the district and appeals court levels. Indeed, U.S. District Judge Damon J. Keith had ruled that the city had acted reasonably, and the U.S. 6th Circuit Court of Appeals added that the Detroit policy "is a valid, legitimate response to . . . identifiable discrimination."

The decision not to hear the Detroit case has no negative implications for affirmative action programs established by public agencies. It is a silent endorsement of lower court rulings that uphold those programs and is in line with the Supreme Court's own decisions on the general concept of affirmative action, on specific programs agreed upon by private employers and labor unions, and on plans mandated by Congress.

Until the day that everyone can look beyond race or sex in deciding who to hire and promote, it is the business of the public and private sectors to take positive actions to assure equal opportunity. Perhaps now the Administration will understand that the courts are serious about that responsibility.

The Des Moines Register

Des Moines, Iowa, January 11, 1984

Welcome to the newly constituted U.S. Civil Rights Commission, which is going to study all the things that are wrong with the efforts to guarantee civil rights for all Americans.

The primary qualification, either for commission members or for staffers, appears to be opposition to mandatory busing and quotas. General Counsel Mark Disler having dutifully sworn his allegiance to these principles, the commission can get on with the program outlined by its new staff director.

And what a program it is: 10 projects dear to the old commission to be altered or canceled, a study of how affirmative action has harmed ethnic Americans of eastern and southern European descent and and a look at what the director called "the fundamentally radical" principle that women should receive the same pay as men for comparable jobs.

Director Linda Chavez also proposes an examination of how affirmative-action programs to bring more minority students into colleges are connected with the "general decline in academic standards," and what factors besides discrimination may account for "disparities in income, education and status indicators" for women and minorities.

There's nothing wrong with training a keen eye on possible negative side effects of civil-rights remedies; doing so can improve their efficacy. But Chavez's proposals go far beyond that: tearing down the remedies, looking for ways to pin the blame on them for other ills — where in such plans is the unjustly treated human being on whose behalf the commission exists?

There were danger signals aplenty when President Reagan succeeded in dismantling the old commission, but the resulting congressional compromise had offered the brief hope that anything as cynical as this agenda could be avoided.

It almost sounds like the kind of Civil Rights Commission George Orwell might have written into "Nineteen Eighty-Four."

Detroit Free Press
Detroit, Mich., January 22, 1984

TO NO ONE'S surprise, the National Urban League's annual report on the state of blacks in America is bleak reading. There may be an economic recovery going on out there, but half of all black children still live in households below the poverty level, the unemployment rate for blacks is more than twice the rate for whites, and half of all black teenagers and a third of blacks aged 20 to 24 are out of work. It's a white recovery and a black depression. The obvious question is what we're going to do about it. The answer from Washington is very little.

The current laissez-faire social policy and deficit-burdened economic policy are not calculated to produce jobs when and where black Americans need them, or to prepare the unemployed for the jobs that will be available. It isn't merely a matter of dollars, although the cutbacks in public assistance hit black families hard.

In diverse pecksniffian ways, the federal government now undermines the very goals it professes to want to achieve. Congress will vote funds for the propagation of chastity, but not for day care centers that would permit single mothers to work. Some federal programs will pay the cost of job training, but not a penny of support for the trainee's family, reducing the choice to either preparing for a new job or eating, but not both. The president prescribes prayer and discipline for the public schools, but brushes off the suggestion that the federal government might have an interest in remedial reading as well.

Teenage pregnancy is probably the No. 1 cause of family poverty in the United States. It isn't only black teenagers who get pregnant; in fact, the statistics show pregnancies among unwed white teenagers increasing at a faster rate than among blacks. But because of the special circumstances of minorities in America, black teens and their children are more likely to suffer from poverty, malnutrition and lack of education. The administration's answer to that problem was the squeal rule.

Last week the new, Reaganite Civil Rights Commission issued a statement deploring the affirmative action promotion policy of the Detroit Police Department and, by inference, chiding the Supreme Court for not striking it down. It would be nice to think that the simple exhortation not to discriminate would be enough to solve the nation's racial problems, and erase the economic discrimination against minorities, but a hundred years of history says it is not. It is doubtful that qualified blacks would be moving up even at the rate they are in public and private employment, if there had not been the spur of equal-opportunity programs to prod employers into significant action. Affirmative action is a constitutional minefield, all right, but the courts and the rest of the country are cautiously picking their way through it, with some success, while the administration merely blunders about on the sidelines, trying to call the whole thing off.

As for the black Americans at the very bottom of the income ladder, from the 14-year-old daughter of a welfare mother who herself becomes pregnant, to the unemployed and unskilled young men hanging out on the corner, too many of them are merely responding to what they perceive their limited choices to be. If there aren't any jobs, if school is incomprehensible, if government offers you a stipend barely adequate for survival but throws up roadblocks to every attempt you make to get off the dole, it takes a very strong countervailing influence to keep people from simply giving up. A sensible public policy would do everything possible to widen those choices and provide that countervailing influence; another administration in Washington might have taken it as a special mission to alter the appalling statistics contained in the Urban League's report. It's a good bet this one will simply ignore them.

The Birmingham News
Birmingham, Ala., January 22, 1984

The U.S. Civil Rights Commission has been reconstituted, and for the better. No longer will it be a sanctuary for an ideology which posits that some Americans are more equal than others or that a higher justice supersedes the the U.S. Constitution.

In its first meeting, the new commission — made up of four Reagan appointees and four appointed by Congress — voiced the concept that will guide its policies and studies: The white majority has rights as well as members of minority groups.

That view accords with the U.S. Constitution which forbids discrimination for reasons of race, creed or national origin. It also is consistent with civil rights legislation which forbids discrimination on the basis of race, sex or age.

So what is causing all the hysteria among liberal Democrats? Three majority viewpoints: (1) That quotas in affirmative action programs violate the civil rights of whites and perhaps others; (2) that forced busing of school children to achieve racial quotas in schools violates the civil rights of all children forced to participate and is counterproductive, and (3) that the U.S. Constitution is color-blind.

It should be acknowledged that the old commission had lost its usefulness. Granted that it exerted an important influence, much of it a necessary part of the nation's movement toward justice in earlier days of civil rights reform, in later years, its claim that it was a non-partisan agency convinced few.

One trusts the damage done the social and political fabric of the nation by quotas and other questionable affirmative action devices are transient. Even granting the validity of efforts to ensure that economic and other opportunities are equally open to all in America, it remains true that if the powers of government continue to be used past any reasonable necessity to suspend the constitutional guarantees of one group and to grant special rights to others, the Constitution may eventually lose its authority in every area.

TULSA WORLD
Tulsa, Okla., January 19, 1984

THE U.S. Commission on Civil Rights reversed past policy Tuesday and denounced affirmative action quotas as "unjustified discrimination."

The Commission's action, coming after President Reagan reorganized the panel, will surely be the target of political attack. But the Commission is right. Affirmative action quotas are a direct affront to the principle that the nation's laws should be color blind.

The Commission's criticism of affirmative action quotas concerned a plan in Detroit in which promotions from police sergeant to lieutenant are made alternately from separate lists of black and white candidates. In a resolution, the Commission said such plans "create a new class of victims and, when used in public employment, offend the constitutional principles of equal protection of the law for all citizens."

It is important to recognize that one can criticize affirmative action quotas while believing whole-heartedly in equal rights and racial integration. Affirmative action quotas were developed as a mechanism for fostering equality. One can criticize this mechanism while espousing the principle of racial equality. Indeed, it is hard to see how one can believe in racial quotas and oppose racial discrimination.

Affirmative action quotas have probably set back the cause of racial harmony more than they have aided it. They foster the idea that different races should be treated differently — the very thing civil rights advocates originally opposed.

In its landmark desegregation case, Brown v. Board of Education, the Supreme Court noted the harm done in treating people differently just because of skin color. "To separate (black schoolchildren) from others of similar age and qualifications solely because of their race generates a feeling of inferiority as to their status in the community that may affect their hearts and minds in a way unlikely ever to be undone."

The same logic applies to affirmative action quotas, for they treat people differently solely on the basis of race.

As a practical matter, job quotas ignore the causes of minority employment problems. A major reason why minorities do not hold public jobs in proportion to their percentage of the population at large is that minorities suffer from poor schools and training. Those social and educational shortcomings prevent may minority members from earning those jobs.

Affirmative action quotas "solve" the problem by papering over it. The place to solve the problem is in the public schools. If minority group members — indeed, all deprived people — had access to quality education, there would be little need for affirmative action quotas.

Newsday

Long Island, N.Y., January 23, 1984

The reconstituted U.S. Civil Rights Commission began last week by declaring its independence from the President and criticizing Walter Mondale for his threats to fire several of its members if he's elected. The whole purpose of staggered terms on the commission was to prevent presidents from dismissing members whose views on civil rights don't match their own — as Ronald Reagan tried to do last year. So Mondale had it coming.

But from there on the commission's performance went rapidly downhill. For all its self-proclaimed independence, it announced a series of decisions that essentially parroted the views of the Reagan White House.

First the commission voted to cancel a study of the way the administration's cuts in student aid have affected predominantly black and Hispanic colleges. Then it reversed its 1981 endorsement of hiring and promotion quotas in affirmative-action programs to rectify past discrimination against minorities and women. It even announced its intention to reconsider its longstanding position that busing is an acceptable technique for achieve school desegregation. Shades of the Reagan Justice Department.

After the commission had done its week's work, the National Urban League released a report on the "State of Black America." It said that while the unemployment rate was 8.3 per cent nationwide in November, it was 17.3 per cent among blacks. And last week the Census Bureau reported that the wages of white women entering the job market in 1980 were farther behind white men's starting pay than they had been 10 years earlier.

Evidently job bias isn't licked yet. Until it is, the Civil Rights Commission shouldn't be suggesting that discrimination is preferable to specific affirmative-action goals and busing is a greater evil than segregation. With so much still to be done, it's premature to relinquish these remedies of last resort. If the commission advocates doing so, a dissenting member was right last week to describe it as "no longer the conscience of America on civil rights."

THE ARIZONA REPUBLIC

Phoenix, Ariz., January 21, 1984

THERE probably are more useless federal commissions functioning in Washington, but the U.S. Commission on Civil Rights surely qualifies as being one of the most useless.

For proof, one need only consider the decision of the commission and its newly impaneled members that condemns the use of racial quotas.

The commission calls them "unjustified discrimination" in affirmative action programs.

The vote to condemn quotas was 6-2, and reflected the conservative makeup of the panel.

Just three years ago, however, when the panel was liberal, the commission endorsed racial quotas as desirable tools in affirmative action.

With the new decision, liberals are howling for an oversight investigation from Congress.

To what end?

The commission has utterly no power to impose its ideas on anyone. It is advisory in nature, and self-serving groups are free to use its decisions for whatever propaganda suits their purposes.

And the howls for an oversight investigation by liberals and others who claim the new panel is racist merely proves the silliness of the panel's existence.

Presumably, the critics would be happy if the panel endorsed quotas. But then conservatives could demand an oversight investigation.

The reason that Congress recently forced President Reagan to reorganize the commission was so Congress would have control over appointing half of the eight members.

That in itself makes the commission political in character, and its decisions and votes unquestionably will continue to reflect ideological biases — conservative or liberal — of its members.

The vote to condemn quotas presumably grew out of essentially the same information as the 1981 vote endorsing racial quotas.

The commission cannot alter civil rights laws. It cannot enforce civil rights laws. And it obviously cannot make up its mind from one term to another on what makes good civil rights practices.

Inescapably, the commission is a waste of time and, unquestionably, a waste of taxpayers' funds.

The State

Columbia, S.C., January 30, 1984

THE U.S. Civil Rights Commission has reversed a guiding principle adopted in 1971 to break down racial or sexual discrimination in employment — the use of quotas.

The about-face by a 6-2 vote came at the first meeting of the newly reorganized advocacy agency and was regarded by civil rights proponents as a philosophical shift engineered by President Reagan.

Mr. Reagan tried to fire several commissioners last year to replace them with his own appointees. The resulting controversy was settled by allowing the President to name four commissioners and congressional Democrats to name four. Previously, the President appointed the entire commission.

The commission was created as an independent, bipartisan civil rights monitoring agency, but it has no enforcement or policy-setting powers. It has served more or less as the civil rights conscience of the government.

So, whatever the philosphical shift, there isn't going to be any change in federal programs of affirmative action. The affirmative action rules of the Equal Economic Opportunity Commission are part of enforcement of the Civil Rights Act. Those who contract with the federal government will still be bound by affirmative action rules under the Office of Federal Contract Compliance Programs.

Furthermore, federal courts have upheld workplace quotas, and there is no indication the U.S. Supreme Court is changing its attitude.

The State has opposed the use of numerical goals and timetables to end employment discrimination because they are counterproductive in producing another class of persons discriminated against.

We agree, then, with the changed outlook of the commission, but we are not at all sure that it will make any difference. It will take an act of Congress to abolish quotas and that isn't forthcoming.

The Orlando Sentinel

Orlando, Fla., January 19, 1984

With a new majority at its helm, the new U.S. Commission on Civil Rights is taking a sharp turn to the right of its predecessor. The commission denounces the use of racial quotas in employment and the use of school buses for racial integration.

At this point it matters little whether the commission is right or wrong. The politics that engulfed the commission last year has destroyed its credibility.

That's not the way it always was, and that's not the way it should be now. The commission was established in 1957 to be a non-partisan watchdog of the government's efforts on civil rights. But President Reagan tried last year to replace three commissioners with three who were more suited to his own go-slow point of view. Political independence got pushed aside. The result was a compromise that dissolved the old commission and gave Mr. Reagan a majority on the new one.

No doubt there will be more pronouncements against past policies. Already the new commission has dropped a study to determine whether cuts in student aid have hurt black students. What we haven't heard are constructive alternatives — just the sound of the dismantling of incentives for civil rights progress.

The Evening Gazette

Worcester, Mass., January 19, 1984

Of all the mechanisms society has used to achieve civil rights for minorities, numerical quotas were always the most unsettling. Many thoughtful people could not believe that hiring based on race was the way to achieve justice.

Nevertheless, many well-meaning people have urged quota systems as the way to redress ancient wrongs. Government regulations, as devised by the Civil Rights Commission and enforced by the courts, have required public and private employers to choose employees on the basis of "minority" status, such as black, female, Hispanic and the like. Nathan Glazer, the Harvard professor, wrote a book, "Affirmative Discrimination," that raised big questions about this approach.

Quotas are now out of favor. Experience has shown that quotas sometimes result in the hiring of less qualified people at the expense of more qualified individuals. Quotas — even when applied for all the right reasons — undercut the idea of equal protection. Quotas have actually increased racial suspicions rather than the other way around. The existence of separate lists for white and black hiring does not help foster racial togetherness and equality.

The new Civil Rights Commission, in its recent statement against quotas, is certainly reflecting the view of the Reagan administration. More important, it is, we believe, echoing the deep feelings of most people.

A dissenting member of the commission, Mary Frances Berry, said the "Civil Rights Commission is no longer the conscience of America on civil rights." Whatever the commission is or isn't in the way of conscience, its repudiation of quotas brings it into the mainstream of American thinking.

Many will agree with Morris B. Abram, a Democrat on the newly reconstituted Civil Rights Commission, when he says that "Equal does not mean you have separate lists of blacks and whites for promotion, any more than you have separate accommodations for blacks and whites for eating. Nothing will ultimately divide a society more than this kind of preference and this kind of reverse discrimination."

The commission's new stand on quotas is welcome. It should prompt some renewed hard thinking about the issue. Best of all, it may help renew the struggle by all to remove barriers to equal opportunity.

Minneapolis Star and Tribune

Minneapolis, Minn., January 20, 1984

The U.S. Civil Rights Commission's condemnation of quotas as one remedy for race discrimination isn't surprising. With White House allies in the majority, the commission predictably supported administration views. Tuesday's vote is discouraging because it shows that the commission has lost its independence and that Americans have lost a powerful nonpartisan voice against discrimination.

The vote represents a reversal of commission policy followed by four administrations. Racial quotas — court-ordered hiring goals and timetables — have long been accepted as a last-resort remedy to proved discrimination. Such strong measures, said the old commission, are sometimes the only way to overcome the legacy of slavery and achieve a climate of equality.

On the surface, the new commission's position seems reasonable. The panel argues that remedies against discrimination should be color blind. It says that members of minority groups who are not the proven, personal victims of discrimination should not be rewarded by quotas. And it contends that court-ordered quotas "merely constitute another form of unjustified discrimination (and) create a new class of victims." In short, says the commission, hiring preferences for minorities are wrong;

race-blind hiring is the only fair system.

But those arguments fail to take into account the pervasiveness of prejudice. Generations of segregation have created discriminatory patterns that can be removed only by conscious, sustained effort. As Minnesotans learned in the 1960s and regularly relearn in the 1980s, seemingly color-blind hiring is sometimes inherently prejudicial. When discrimination persists and other tactics fail, society needs a force of last resort to change an employer's hiring practices. Quotas are one such force.

To discard quotas would be to undercut a basic premise of affirmative action: that fair employment, far from being color blind, requires explicit recognition of race. The courts have consistently endorsed color-conscious remedies to discrimination. As Supreme Court Justice Harry Blackmun wrote in a 1978 opinion, "Government may take race into account when it acts not to demean or insult any racial group, but to remedy disadvantages cast on minorities by past racial prejudice."

Used carefully and sparingly, the quota is a useful tool in the quest to right the wrongs of America's past. Why abandon a well-tempered tool?

THE RICHMOND NEWS LEADER

Richmond, Va., January 23, 1984

Last Tuesday many American rivers reversed their courses. Temperatures rose into the low 90s in International Falls, Minnesota. Smog miraculously vanished from the Los Angeles area. Nary a breeze stirred in Chicago. And in Washington the cherry blossoms impetuously burst into bloom.

None of those phenomena occurred, of course, but a phenomenon on as grand a scale did: After a two-day meeting, the U.S. Civil Rights Commission issued some findings that, for the first time in its 26-year history, made some sense. It said several harsh things about racial quotas that create a new class of victims, disengaged itself from the policies of previous Civil Rights Commissions, and refused to endorse a report by its predecessor on blacks in Alabama. It was as if a major shift had repositioned the San Andreas fault from California to the south of France.

Reaction from the commission's customary cheerleaders was swift and bitter. Critics charged that the commission was a puppet of the White House. A black Congressman and a black minister called for abolition of the commission for its "irrelevance." A hold-over member of the commission charged that it had changed its watchdog role to a lapdog role. In that regard, it might be noted that the commission is composed of eight members, four appointed by President Reagan and four appointed by Congress. The commission's votes ranged from unanimous to 6-2 on the issues it decided last week — hardly an indication that the commission majority took its orders from the White House any more than it took them from Congress.

It may be inferred from the commission's actions that a majority is committed to a change in course that might restore some credibility to a largely discredited mouthpiece for the racist Left. The agenda of former commissions emphasized quotas in hiring, forced busing for school integration, racial preferences and color consciousness in every phase of society, and instant upheavals to accommodate those commissions' strange ideas of "equality," in which — in Orwell's words — all were equal, but some were more equal than others. Former commissions ventured well beyond their narrow authority to study discrimination and violation of civil rights. They made sweeping pronouncements on social and economic policies, undertook studies into situations far outside their purview, and extended their support of radical remedies well beyond the limits of common sense.

The new commission has reaffirmed its commitment to civil rights — for all Americans, not just for a favored few. It sets a worthy goal of achieving a color-blind society, in full recognition that the government has an obligation to guarantee equality of opportunity, but no duty to guarantee equality of results. It acknowledges that legal remedies must be made available to individual victims of discrimination, but opposes policies that victimize innocent parties on the basis of a supposed bias against an entire group. A case in point is Detroit, where promotion quotas hold back qualified white policemen to increase the number of black lieutenants, in the absence of any proof of discrimination against individual blacks having been denied promotions on the basis of their race. That is an important distinction: Civil rights belong to individuals, not to classes of individuals; in Detroit, the civil rights of whites denied promotions are being trampled.

In the past, members of the Civil Rights Commission marched in lockstep — parroting a divisive, radical line that countenanced no dissent. Its rigid adherence to theories disproved in practice and disavowed by majorities of both races shaped its role as a gadfly, not as a serious means for achieving racial harmony. In the past couple of years, the former commission spent most of its time denouncing the effects of the Reagan administration's social and economic policies on minorities, although those effects (if they were, in fact, consequences of administration policy) were unintentional and were not caused by deliberate discrimination. That commission's partisan stance almost put it out of business last fall, and it would have been good riddance.

The new commission apparently understands its purpose better: It is not there to divide America along racial lines, but to help heal racial differences by protecting everyone's civil rights. It will operate as an independent body beholden neither to party nor to civil rights radicals who formerly considered it "their" commission. Perhaps now there can be — as one new commission-member hopes — "free and honest debate" that can better define how far the nation has come, and how far it has to go, to guarantee everyone's civil rights, regardless of race. If so, the new commission will embark on a worthwhile course that no longer will dictate blind adherence to blatant civil wrongs in the name of civil rights.

THE CHRISTIAN SCIENCE MONITOR

Boston, Mass., January 18, 1984

It is disappointing to see the new direction of the reconstituted US Commission on Civil Rights. Certainly there is validity in scrutinizing effects of past actions aimed at ending discrimination, which is the commission's new focus.

But this should only be one part — and a small one, at that — of the commission's whole task. The larger segment should be addressing the nation's current and future civil rights needs; there is no evidence that the commission plans to do this.

For the past three decades, since the 1954 US Supreme Court decision overturning racial segregation in public schools, the focus of the nation's civil rights effort properly has been on relations between blacks and whites. Enormous progress has been made: Change has been produced in the laws and customs which for three centuries had restricted black Americans to positions of economic and social inequality.

But the nature of the nation's civil rights struggle now has changed. Today it essentially is in two parts — protecting the gains of the past by blacks and addressing new civil rights needs not envisioned a few years ago.

Blacks are particularly concerned that — in difficult economic times and as the national pressure for equality lessens — black workers will be the first fired when jobs are scarce. Just this month black workers won a court suit on this issue. A federal judge ordered the city of Newark, N.J., to restore 46 black and Hispanic firefighters to the city payrolls. They had been hired four years earlier in a move to end discrimination, only to be fired last month in a budget squeeze.

Blacks have similar concerns about housing and educational equality, especially with the recent decline in federal funds available as loans to college students.

The Civil Rights Commission ought to be looking at these questions. Beyond them, it also should be examining the nation's new civil rights issues. Hispanics and Asians are the new immigrants, the newest minorities. In some cases both have reported wide-ranging discrimination, from housing to employment. Their situations need examining, and Americans should know the facts.

A major national requirement, which broadly falls into the civil rights category, is to pay women on the same scale as men for doing similar jobs. Numerous studies have shown inequities, and many lawsuits are in process. Last month a federal judge ordered the State of Washington to pay at least $800 million in current and past wages to its female employees, on grounds the state had evidenced "direct, overt, and institutionalized" discrimination against them.

Just this week a census department study reported that in the decade from 1970 to 1980, the wages of women taking jobs for the first time fell further behind the salaries of men in their first jobs, despite the educational gains women had recorded in that time. Such evidence of an unequal employment footing for Americans should arouse the Civil Rights Commission to inquire into its causes and potential for redress.

One thing it should *not* do is get enmeshed in a political tit for tat and it is dangerously close to that now. In its initial meeting this Monday the commission fired back at Democratic presidential front-runner Walter Mondale for his comments the previous day that, if elected, he would replace the commission's Reagan appointees. The commission ought now to be, as in past years, able to operate independent of politics. Its welcome assertion Monday of independence from the White House should be matched by independence from this year's broader political skirmishing, which already has begun to focus in part on inequality of opportunity and treatment of minorities under the current administration.

It appears inevitable that the newly-constituted commission's first statement of purpose will be taken as a political signal. Some will see it as a retrenchment in civil rights by an agency that heretofore has been in the forefront of examining and voicing the nation's civil rights needs. Some will see it as a statement that the nation has gone far enough in providing civil rights to its minority citizens. And some will feel it is additional evidence that President Reagan, who appointed four of the commissioners, is not interested in the needs of the have-nots, or the disenfranchised in American society.

These are impressions the commission needs to correct. The way to do so is by broadening its agenda to include the nation's current civil rights needs.

The Philadelphia Inquirer

Philadelphia, Pa., January 16, 1984

Linda Chavez has a busy agenda. The new staff director of the U.S. Commission on Civil Rights, recently appointed by President Reagan, aims to redirect the panel's work totally. She has set a new conservative course that, among other changes, opposes affirmative action to reverse job discrimination against women and minorities. Instead, she would have the commission examine the "adverse consequences" of such programs in the past on ethnic whites.

No sane person would claim to have a perfect or painless remedy for discrimination. But the change of course Ms. Chavez has proposed smacks more of revising the questions to suit partisan political interests than it does of searching for new answers.

The commission was established by Congress in 1957 as an independent bipartisan agency to investigate discrimination and monitor equal rights progress in voting, housing and education. Its mandate broadened over the years to include sex, age and handicap discrimination. It often criticized sitting administrations but none sought to bring it under White House control. But the commission was anathema to conservative supporters of President Reagan, and he appeared to take much of its criticism personally.

During this past year, a dispute erupted between Congress and the President over Mr. Reagan's attempt to replace all six commission members. The result: a new commission of eight members, half appointed by Congress and half by the President. However, charges were leveled that the President reneged on reappointing two Republicans whose absolute loyalty to the White House on rights issues was suspect. The result — six of eight members reflect White House views.

One of the ousted members, former national Republican chairwoman and lifetime Republican Mary Louise Smith, said she doubted that the administration understood "the role of an independent commission. I believe an administration does have a right to expect loyalty, but I also believe there are some independent commissions that must remain independent to retain their integrity and usefulness."

Ideological purity also seems to underlie the Chavez agenda, which calls for cancelling or altering 10 projects approved by the old commission. Her proposals for new commission studies reflect her attitude toward past goals. She would examine the link she sees between declining academic standards and affirmative action in higher education, review the "radical" idea of equal pay for men and women for equal work and cancel a study of the effects on minorities of cuts in student aid.

Few Americans of good will of any race would question the usefulness of hard and honest analyses of the many programs opposed by Ms. Chavez and by conservatives, including court-ordered busing and bilingual education. But there is little good will apparent in Ms. Chavez's approach. Its tone and thrust prejudge the issues in advance. The new staff director has decided, in her words, that blacks' major problems are no longer civil rights problems and neither the commission nor the government can solve them.

Instead, says Ms. Chavez, the commission should aim for a "colorblind nation." Perhaps that will come true one day, but it hasn't yet. The need still exists for an independent commission — with open-minded members and staff — to monitor progress in keeping with its original mandate. Better no commission at all than one that simply pursues preconceived results.

Roanoke Times & World-News

Roanoke, Va., January 15, 1984

'C ONSERVATIVE" attitudes toward civil rights can be strikingly unconservative.

Case in point: The recent memorandum to the U.S. Civil Rights Commission from its new staff director, Linda Chavez. The memo outlines a radically revised agenda for the reconstituted commission, which — stacked now with Reagan supporters — is expected to go along.

Arguing that education, housing and income gaps between the races aren't proof of discrimination, Chavez wants to block release of a study of such differences between the white and black citizens of Alabama.

Arguing that the government has no responsibility for making higher education affordable to minorities, Chavez wants to cancel a proposed examination of the effects on minorities of Reagan cuts in student aid.

Arguing that affirmative-action programs discriminate against whites, Chavez wants to conduct a study of their impact on Americans of eastern and southern European descent.

Her proposals depart sharply from the civil-rights concerns of previous commissions, but that alone is not what makes them so unconservative. In a more fundamental sense, they are unconservative because they are based on abstract principles that take no account of historical context and the concrete world.

As an abstract proposition, for example, it's true that economic and social disadvantage among minorities isn't proof of discrimination. Neither do we have proof that the sun will rise in the east tomorrow morning.

But the historical context — on past mornings, the sun always has risen in the east — suggests strongly it will do so tomorrow. And the long history of white supremacy suggests strongly that marked differences of whites and blacks in Alabama are a legacy of discrimination.

As an abstract proposition, for another example, a colorblind society should have no use for affirmative-action programs that give preferences to special groups. But those like Chavez who seem to think such a society sprang into being merely upon the formal nullification of the old segregation laws are blind to history and naively — and most unconservatively — confident in the goodness of human nature.

Chavez' concern for Americans of eastern and southern Europe descent would be touching, except for its absurdity. Blacks (and, in lesser numbers, American Indians) occupy a unique place in the quest for a colorblind society. It's not of their making, but is the consequence of centuries of officially sanctioned injustices at the hand of the white majority.

To be sure, ethnic discrimination in America occasionally has touched other groups. But never so pervasively for so long. The beast was named Jim, not Giuseppe or Stanislaus, Crow.

THE SUN

Baltimore, Md., January 11, 1984

We like the idea of a colorblind society, advanced by the new staff director of the Civil Rights Commission. But we know our society has not been one, and that's why courts have ordered special remedies to correct constitutional violations against certain minority groups. Now that some of those remedies have been in place for 20 years, it is legitimate to ask whether they have had adverse effects on other citizens.

Linda Chavez, the commission's staff director, has proposed a study to answer that question. It is a fair proposal that reflects the view that no group should damage others in its effort to protect itself. What's wrong with that?

Well, in Mrs. Chavez's case, the idea is stretched beyond reasonable limits. She not only wants to study the effects of affirmative action on white ethnic groups, she apparently wants to stop studying the plight of minorities and stop monitoring the effect of government actions on those people who have been the traditional targets of discrimination.

Mrs. Chavez wants to cancel ongoing studies dealing with student aid and the economic condition of blacks in Alabama because those things, in her opinion, are not civil-rights issues. What she is saying is the concept of civil rights should be changed now that Mr. Reagan's hand-picked commission and staff director have taken over. She represents the segment that has had enough of protecting minorities, and that segment won the battle over the Civil Rights Commission.

The trouble is the commission neither wrote the laws nor ordered remedies such as busing. Congress and the courts took those actions in response to violations of the Constitution. The commission's job has been to comment on the enforcement of the laws, and Mrs. Chavez clearly wants to give those comments a different tone, a radically conservative tone that reflects the Reagan administration point of view.

But the fact that the commission may now take a different view of civil rights statutes does not diminish the responsibility of government to enforce them. Unless Congress and the courts do an about-face, too, they are still the laws of the land.

The Washington Post
Times Herald
Washington, D.C., January 20, 1984

THE DUST was just settling from the contentious reconstruction of the civil rights commission when first its staff director and then its new majority made plain that they intend to alter dramatically the commission's way of doing business. Both seem to be generally sympathetic to the president's idea of what today's civil rights efforts should entail. Our sense of it is that the issues the commission has seized on are serious and legitimate ones, but that it is far from clear yet whether they are attacking them in serious and legitimate ways.

At the heart of the argument on and over the commission lies a large, politically unresolved question. It is whether civil rights activity on the part of the government should be viewed quite strictly as a matter of providing and guaranteeing equal opportunity to all citizens or of providing and guaranteeing them not just equal opportunity but in fact equal results—that is a definite share of society's monetary and other rewards.

This question has been with us for a while. It was bound to arise when the fact became plain that the enactment and enforcement of much equal opportunity legislation had left millions of its prospective beneficiaries no better off materially than they had been before. Merely declaring them free to do many things did not make it possible for them to do so, did not in any way deal with or diminish the disadvantage they had incurred from years of past discrimination which continued to inhibit and restrict them. "Go be a concert pianist or a brain surgeon or a multimillionaire," the society would tell them; "we have eliminated the legal barriers to your doing so —aren't we nice?"

In the mid- to late 1960s steps began to be taken to address this very delicate, complicated, important issue. So-called guidelines and de facto cases and busing and quotas and goals and the enlargement of the civil rights mandate to include more people and more kinds of deprivation were the stuff of argument and action. But precision and care didn't last. By the mid- to late 1970s all distinctions seemed to have been blurred: policies and programs affecting racial minorities were uniformly seen as being racial in nature and as reflecting a pro- or anti-civil rights position. Civil rights had come to be regarded by many as rights uniquely owing to racial minorities, and conflicts between the civil rights of groups were seen as something else—as white racist efforts at repression usually.

Good and necessary and justifiable efforts to make the civil rights mandate more complex, to help ensure that it would be more than a policy declaring and providing "rights" that could not be exercised, got overwhelmed by sloppy thinking and misguided arguments and programs. And it was this that provided the opening for Ronald Reagan. His new civil rights commissioners, like his new Justice Department, pledged to restore the issue to its pristine clarity and virtue. The government would go back to real civil rights issues and principles, to the original thing. Thus, the new staff director at the commission, Linda Chavez, and the new majority variously speak of such things as the need to stop viewing economic programs as civil rights imperatives, the anti-civil rights implications of numerical quotas, the fact that all disadvantage is not a function of discrimination.

Intellectually—in theory—much of what they say is right. And, in our judgment, there has been for some time and continues to be a need to make some reasonable distinctions concerning what is a civil right and what is a socially desirable result. But the haste with which the newly re-formed commission has been issuing its pronouncements; its debating-team-type insistence that it is right in all things and the losers discredited and wrong; its failure to try to send any message of reassurance to a large and apprehensive constituency of blacks and other racial minorities who had come to see the commission as a champion and a friend—all this is truly disturbing.

There is a useful reform to be achieved. It cannot be made vindictively or as punishment. It most assuredly does not consist of undoing genuine civil rights progress in a blanket attack on some of the errors of recent years. The commission itself will have to choose whether its accomplishments are to be political and transitory or moral and enduring.

The Detroit News
Detroit, Mich., January 11, 1984

Linda Chavez, new staff director of the U.S. Commission on Civil Rights, has fired the first shot in what will doubtless be a heated debate over redirection of the commission and national civil rights policy. She noted, among other things, that many social problems like high unemployment, low educational attainment, and a high rate of out-of-wedlock births are problems that "are not amenable to solution by civil rights laws or the Civil Rights Commission.

Predictably this will stir up a hornet's nest. Critics will argue that Ms. Chavez and President Reagan, who appointed her, are throwing civil rights out the window.

But Ms. Chavez and other Reagan appointees on the commission are hardly a bunch of right-wing maniacs. They are moderate Democrats or Republicans and a number were civil rights activists in the days when securing the basic rights of all Americans was worth your life. They and a growing number of other fair-minded observers fear civil rights could be undermined if not protected from the excesses of recent years.

Ms. Chavez's comments really don't seem so startling, except to those whose vested interests are being threatened. It seems obvious, for example, that minorities, and blacks in particular, face social problems that are beyond the scope of civil rights laws' ability to enforce equal treatment. Indeed, the best evidence is that the last 10 years of increased civil rights enforcement in voting, employment, and housing, as well as affirmative action programs (which translate into hiring and educational quotas), has not closed the economic and social gap between blacks and whites.

In many ways, some elements of the black community have actually fallen further behind. Between 1971 and 1981, median income dropped by 8 percent as the number of poor, female-headed, black families rose, and out-of-wedlock births increased to more than half of all black births.

Ms. Chavez also questioned the ways the commission has measured discrimination in the past. For example, is statistical underrepresentation or overrepresentation of a racial group in a particular job area or university class evidence of discrimination even if unintentional? Not necessarily. There are disproportionately greater numbers of Asian-Americans in mathematics and engineering fields and a significant underrepresentation in law and humanities. But nobody calls this evidence of discrimination.

If disproportion denotes discrimination, then every ethnic and racial group can claim to be underrepresented somewhere. Taken to its extreme, statistical representation alone leads to absurdities such as the recent suit against the University of Detroit, in which students complained that the grading curve flunked disproportionately large numbers of blacks and was thus discriminatory. And despite the U.S. Supreme Court's refusal this week to hear the Detroit police officers' "reverse discrimination" case, we suspect that sooner or later the high court will find itself unable to resist striking down such quota systems.

Quotas conflict with basic American notions of justice and democracy because they mean preferential treatment. The law should not be rigid, and perhaps affirmative action made some sense as a gesture of good faith toward those who had been systematically deprived of the fruits of citizenship. But how long should affirmative action continue? At what point does it become a protective device for special interests rather than a tool for providing equality of opportunity? How do you enshrine quotas in the law without risking that one day they will be used against the groups they are supposed to aid? And how do you avoid debasing standards in schools and the work place if you reserve a fixed percentage of positions for certain groups?

These strike us as honest and real questions. For too long they have gone unasked out of a sense of social guilt, desire to do right, and — let it be said — fear of the reaction of civil rights groups seeking to perpetuate their claims to leadership among minority groups.

We hope Ms. Chavez and the Commission on Civil Rights will pursue their arguments. It will be a healthy thing for the body politic, and not least for minority groups. We suspect they know, even if their self-appointed leaders won't admit it, that civil rights risks getting a bad name if it's distorted in favor of bad ideas that aren't even producing the desired results. Ms. Chavez is seeking to protect, not attack, civil rights.

Acquittal in Beating Death of Black Executive Unleashes Riots

Miami, Fla. was declared a disaster area by the federal government May 22, 1980, in the wake of violent rioting in the city's black neighborhoods. The rioting erupted May 17 just a few hours after an all-white jury in Tampa had acquitted four former Dade County police officers who were charged in the fatal beating of Arthur McDuffie, 33, a black insurance executive from Miami. (The officers had been dismissed from the force following the incident.) McDuffie had died in December of the preceding year, four days after having been chased down for a traffic violation.

Isolated incidents of rock throwing and bottle throwing gained momentum soon after the McDuffie verdict and spread rapidly into looting, arson, beatings and shootings. Three whites were dragged from an automobile and beaten to death. A black was killed by police after allegedly firing a pistol at a patrol car. Two others were shot and killed, reportedly while looting. National Guardsmen were rushed into the area by Gov. Bob Graham as the turmoil continued; a dawn-to-dusk curfew was imposed. By the end of the month, the disorders in Miami had resulted in 16 deaths, injury to more than 300 persons, nearly 1,000 arrests and an estimated $100 million in damage to property. Large areas of the city lay in smoldering ruins, with buildings burned out and businesses gutted. It was the worst racial rioting to hit an American city in more than a decade.

The U.S. Civil Rights Commission reported in July, 1982 that the 1980 Miami race riots had stemmed from the anger and frustration felt by blacks because of their "pervasive and institutionalized exclusion from full participation in the economic and social life of the city." The report stated that blacks in Dade County were systematically isolated from the mainstream in housing, jobs, business, politics, education and the justice system.

Miami remained a tinderbox for several years after the riots, experiencing sporadic uprisings caused by racial friction. Major riots broke out again in December, 1982, after a police officer shot a black youth in a game arcade. The Hispanic policeman charged with manslaughter in the death of the black youth was acquitted in March, 1984. The defendant had been the fourth Miami policeman to be tried for the manslaughter of a black in a 12-month period. Each policeman had been tried by an all-white jury. One officer had been convicted.

The Miami Herald
Miami, Fla., June 25, 1980

THE ROOTS of black Miamians' discontent run so deep, and spread so wide, that it would take years to dig them out even if every white back in Dade County were to bend to the task.

Not every white back will bend to help blacks, of course. In the body politic, prejudice is arthritis.

But more white backs are bent now than ever have been before. So far, it's difficult to tell how effective the digging will be. There's too much dust, and it has barely begun to settle.

The McDuffie Riots destroyed more than the lives of 17 people, the property of hundreds more, the jobs of still more. They destroyed the delusion that blacks will remain content to be shut out of the prosperity that is almost exclusively the domain of whites in Greater Miami.

Nor is economic prosperity the only domain from which Miami blacks feel excluded. As a survey taken after the McDuffie Riots reveals, black Miamians feel excluded from the equally fundamental domain of justice itself.

The survey, reported at length in Sunday's Herald, was conducted by this newspaper and the Behavioral Science Research Institute of Coral Gables. It showed that nine out of 10 blacks here think they cannot get a fair trial before a white jury. Indeed, as many believe they can't get a fair trial in Dade County, period.

Most blacks feel their lives are too much under whites' control. Four out of five think there aren't enough black leaders. Three out of four think the state attorney's office is biased against blacks. And nine out of 10 think the arrival of the Sealift '80 Cubans will hurt their own chances for economic progress.

Whether those perceptions are true is almost beside the point. What's important is that blacks perceive them to be true. It's therefore just as crucial to create a perception of fairness and justice as it is to create them in fact.

Blacks' belief in Dade's justice system will be difficult to re-establish. It will require unrelenting efforts to increase the number of black police officers. It will require the appointment of more blacks as prosecutors and judges.

Economic justice may be easier to achieve, although "easier" is a relative term. A starting point would be for Dade's business community, which is overwhelmingly white-controlled, to try as it never has tried to work with the public schools to train blacks for jobs for which there are continual local openings.

The jobs exist. The blacks who could be trained to fill them also exist. What does not exist is an effective mechanism to match the local job market with the local schools' capabilities in vocational education. Building that mechanism should be at the top of the business community's riot-recovery agenda.

Los Angeles Times
Los Angeles, Calif., May 20, 1980

The black experience began in America as tragedy, and continues as tragedy. After the black uprising in Miami, the governor of Florida, Robert Graham, said, "Black Americans, as well as white Americans, have worked long and hard since the days of the first civil-rights marches to secure a fair portion of the American dream for all our citizens . . . . We have come too far, worked too hard to see that everything is lost in one more night of needless violence and rage."

On one level the governor is correct. Dramatic gains have been made in the legal status of blacks since the 1960s, but the mass of blacks remain on the lowest rung of the economic ladder.

In Dade County, whose borders are the same as the metropolitan area of Miami, the unemployment rate of blacks is more than twice that of whites. It is estimated at 8% for whites, including Latins, and 17% for blacks, who make up about 15% of the county's population.

The comparative figures on the number of Dade County residents living below the poverty line are equally ominous. The state figures for non-Latin whites is 10%, for Latins 18% and for blacks 38%.

Leaders in Miami, white and black, agree that the black community is seething with a sense of frustration and hopelessness, and that the recent influx of refugees has increased their anxiety and bitterness. American blacks have been forced into job competition not only with Cubans but also with thousands of black immigrants from the West Indies. They see the new arrivals as one more barrier placed between them and their opportunity to earn a living.

The acquittals of four white policemen in the beating death of a black Miami insurance executive was perceived by the black community as the latest in a series of injustices committed by the police against blacks.

In 1979, the police raided the home of a black schoolteacher in the mistaken belief that he was a cocaine dealer. The teacher said that he and his son were beaten, but no action was taken by the police.

Six months ago, an off-duty white policeman shot and killed a black, 22, whom the officer suspected of being a burglar. A grand jury voted not to indict the officer, who said that his gun went off accidentally.

Also last year, a white highway patrolman was accused of sexually molesting an 11-year-old black girl. The original judge, refusing probation, recommended that the officer be sent to an institution for sex offenders. A second judge, who later entered the case, granted probation.

In the seven-week trial of the four police officers, the jurors heard testimony from three former Miami policemen that the insurance executive had been fatally beaten and that records were falsified to make it appear that he died in a traffic accident. The six-man, all-white jury deliberated for two hours and 40 minutes, acquitting the policemen on all counts.

The perception in the black community was that the system of justice had failed, and the U.S. attorney in Miami tacitly agreed. He will go to a grand jury Wednesday to bring federal charges of civil-rights violations against the four officers.

But, even though the jurors believed that they had returned a fair verdict based on the evidence, the system failed in a much larger sense by not dealing adequately with the unrest among the black population in Miami. The Community Relations Service of the U.S. Justice Department said, "It was a situation that was allowed to fester too long without something positive being done about it to the satisfaction of the black community."

And beyond that is the economic reality confronted by masses of American blacks. The historic dilemma of race in America will not be resolved until blacks have an equal opportunity to claim their "fair portion of the American dream." □

Boston Herald American

Boston, Mass., June 3, 1980

For millions of Americans, the televised scenes of the recent rioting in Miami together with the tragic toll of dead and injured can only have evoked painful memories of the fires that seared so many of this country's cities during the 1960s. Now, as then, we are left to ask why it happened.

By all accounts, the immediate provocation was the acquittal of four former Dade County police officers charged with the beating death of an insurance agent apprehended for a traffic violation. The insurance agent was black. The four policemen charged with killing him were white, as were the members of the jury that acquitted them.

But however outrageous these circumstances, and especially the jury's decision, this case alone seems unlikely to have incited the worst rioting in the United States in more than a decade.

In fact, the death of the insurance agent and the acquittal of those charged with his murder were but the latest in a series of incidents perceived in Miami's black community as evidence of a racially motivated double standard of justice and law enforcement.

These corrosive suspicions, and the simmering discontent they bred, were surely compounded by the economic distress of much of Miami's black population.

Nearly 40 percent of Dade County's 225,000 black residents have incomes that fall below the poverty level. Unemployment in the black community there stands at 17 percent, a full 10 percentage points higher than the national unemployment rate. And, unless Miami's black community has somehow escaped a national phenomenon, unemployment among black youths in Miami probably runs to 40 percent or more.

Thus, it is not terribly difficult to understand how some of those living in Miami's Liberty City ghetto could imagine that the statistical gains registered by black Americans in the aggregate since the early 1960s had no relevance for them.

It is a lamentable fact of American political life that voter registration among poor blacks is abysmally low. For whatever complex mix of reasons, all too many ghetto dwellers see no point in the conventional forms of political participation.

There can be no doubt, then, that some portion of the motivation for the mayhem in Miami should be attributed to rage on the part of people who saw themselves as dispossessed and, worse yet, powerless.

None of this, of course, can be permitted to justify murder, assault, arson and looting — all integral components of the rioting in Miami. The casualties, some shot by snipers and others dragged from their cars and kicked to death, include blacks as well as whites.

Property damage ran into the hundreds of millions of dollars. Some of the businesses looted and torched will not reopen, and this will mean fewer jobs for black citizens who need them desperately.

Nor will the rioting do anything, for the moment at least, to improve race relations in a city, like so many others, where racial harmony is a fragile commodity requiring constant care.

Still, there are constructive lessons that can be learned. One is that the quest for maximum economic opportunity for all citizens must be pursued lest we condemn an underclass of poor — not all black by any means — to permanent dependence, despair and frustration-spawned violence. Another is that while this larger challenge is being met, public officials must ensure that law enforcement and administration of justice are color-blind, and that this is so perceived by every citizen.

THE DAILY OKLAHOMAN

Oklahoma City, Okla., May 23, 1980

AS Miami slowly returns to normal, after days and nights of uncontrolled violence, most Americans will agree with the black civic leader who told reporters he was unable to explain what had happened because he could never understand mob psychology.

"It has taken us 12 years to attract business back into this community after the 1968 riot disaster," he said, "and now all our assurances are proved worthless. Their investment is gone, their employees are out of jobs and their customers must go elsewhere to shop. I doubt they will ever come back. And why did this happen? There is no real explanation."

In the riots of the past two decades, the pattern has been much the same. Some trigger, often a rumor or false assumption, started mobs raging into the streets. But a mob must do something destructive. So cars are overturned and set afire, sometimes before the occupants can escape. Then storefronts are attacked, windows shattered and easy access assured.

The looting follows almost immediately. What is looted is not what the looters need. But in every case so far documented, there have been buyers for the loot on the scene within hours. In Detroit, they backed vans up to intersections and loaded their purchases on the spot. It was reported that color TV sets went for $20 that day.

It is a complete breakdown of respect for the law, and those who set buildings and cars afire or shoot aimlessly into crowds deserve no sympathy. Yet they always get it, from the bubble-heads who blame "society" for their "long-suppressed anger." Such apologies make a travesty of justice.

The Miami riot started ostensibly because four former policemen were acquitted by a jury of beating a black man to death. Washington reacted by promising new federal charges against those found innocent of murder.

If we are to have jury trials, as assured by the U.S. Constitution, we cannot permit government officials to order new trials for those the jurors find innocent, simply because they may already have been convicted in the minds of some authorities and a sector of the public. That is lynch law at best and tyranny in the end.

No matter how badly President Carter needs minority votes, he should condemn what happened in Miami and those who perpetrated the crimes.

St. Petersburg Times

St. Petersburg, Fla., May 27, 1980

Miami's burned-out, bloodied ghettoes look like a war zone. The fires are out. The dead have been buried. The streets are sane.

As quiet returns and the long, hot summer begins, Florida's largest and richest city is searching its soul — analyzing why three days of black rage erupted and asking how the scars can be healed.

If the McDuffie riots had any positive effect, it is that Miami's white power structure is painfully aware of the human despair in Liberty City.

"It's like the old story about hitting the mule with the two-by-four," said a leader of the Greater Miami Chamber of Commerce. "You've got my attention."

AT THE COST of 16 lives and property damage in the billions, that is a dubious achievement. The saddest, most ominous aspect of Miami's agony is that the May 17 explosion of fire and death was a replay of the past — and not much has changed for Miami's black minority since the race riots of 1968.

That outburst of violence spurred a Model Cities renewal program, in which more than $200-million in federal funds were poured into Liberty City, much of it in concrete. But it did not erase the historic social and economic deprivation that fueled black despair.

Miami's rate of unemployed blacks is almost twice that of all unemployed. Worse, among black teenagers the unemployment rate is so high that for almost every youth employed, one is looking in vain for work. More than half the population in Miami's ghettoes is under the age of 19.

While blacks make up 15 per cent of Miami's population, they own only one percent of the businesses with paid employees.

Miami's record of unequal opportunity, unemployment, poor housing, poverty and double standard of justice is typical of other urban centers.

UNDER THE mounting pressures of inflation, it is the poor who suffer most. Not only in Miami, but in St. Petersburg and every other American city, most of the poor are black.

Miami's three days in May got everybody's attention. The question now is whether the nation's attention will be translated into action for human equality.

Onetime black activist Bernie Dyer, who helped quell the 1968 riots in Liberty City, has almost lost hope.

"There has to be an institutional change," he said. "We have got to open up the system so more folks can get a piece of the action. If that is not done, nothing will change. Too much of the power is held by a select few people who really don't care about black folks."

From the war zone of Liberty City, that is the nation's foreboding for the summer of 1980.

St. Louis Globe-Democrat

St. Louis, Mo., May 23, 1980

The U.S. Justice Department's belated intervention in the fatal beating of a black man by white Florida policemen provides more questions than answers.

If the Justice Department felt that it had a civil rights complaint in the death of Arthur McDuffie, why didn't it pursue a parallel case with the state of Florida?

By waiting until deadly and destructive violence afflicted Miami before seeking civil rights indictments against the four ex-officers acquitted by a jury, the Justice Department shows an unsteady hand.

There is strong reason to suspect that the accused men used excessive force in subduing McDuffie and that the state organized its case poorly. Four trained police officers should not find it necessary to batter an unarmed man's skull to bits in order to place him under arrest. The defense testified that McDuffie, a karate expert, fought fiercely and struggled for an officer's gun after a high-speed chase.

The violence triggered by the Florida jury's acquittal erupted because the victim was black and the accused are white. It seems fair to conclude that there would have been no rioting had the victim been white. And it might well be that the Justice Department would not be interested if the victim were not black.

It's been suggested by some that the accused are put in double jeopardy by the Justice Department action, but this is not so. The state of Florida had a right and duty to prosecute the murder case and the federal government has a right and duty to act in civil rights violations.

A question remains whether the Justice Department will be diligent in pressing civil rights complaints against the rioters who killed, burned and looted. The innocent victims of the racial violence and their families are entitled to the same degree of concern by the federal government.

As usual there are those who attempt to justify the rioters' behavior because of social and economic conditions in the black community. Such shallow reaction is insulting to the intelligence of rational people.

Newsday

Long Island, N.Y., May 21, 1980

Miami's violent landscape has been imprinted this week with horrifying images—images that many Americans thought a decade ago they would never see again: A black child killed near his home by white gunmen driving past in a pickup truck; three white youths dragged from their car by a black mob and beaten to death; people burning their own neighborhoods in an orgy of self-destructive rage.

No matter what provokes it, such behavior simply breeds more violence, more ugliness and more hatred. It is a classic vicious circle in which perceived injustice—in this case a white jury's exoneration of four white former policemen charged, while they were officers, in the fatal beating of a black businessman—triggers retaliatory violence that in turn generates still more bloodshed and destruction.

As President Carter said, "Violence can contribute nothing to the resolution of problems or alleviation of grievances."

Yet violence does demand official response, and Carter's decision to dispatch Attorney General Benjamin Civiletti to Miami was a good one. Civiletti quickly demonstrated a degree of sensitivity by pointing out that "there is a great perception of injustice, which has brought a sense of frustration and rage" to Miami's black community.

"A great perception of injustice" is what lies behind much of the Miami violence. It is a perception among black people that many police are racist, that the white society doesn't regard this racism as a serious problem, that a white policeman who kills a black person without cause is likely to get away with it because the justice system tacitly condones such conduct.

As Newsday columnist Les Payne pointed out last month, a study of homicides committed by police between 1959 and 1968 indicated that the number of black victims was disproportionately large in relation to the number of blacks in the general population.

What's more, many black people perceive the American justice system as stacked against them in a variety of other ways: They not only see white policemen escaping punishment for killing or brutalizing blacks, but they see such exonerations dispensed by all-white juries or predominantly white bureaucracies. And they are convinced that blacks get harsher treatment than whites in the courts.

There are other problems that contributed to the rioting, of course. Foremost among them is the declining state of the economy. The unemployment rate for blacks in Miami is two and a half times the rate for whites and Hispanics; unemployment among young blacks is estimated at 40 per cent. On top of that, there has been a huge influx of Cuban immigrants, exacerbating the already tense relationship between the area's black and Hispanic communities.

These conditions all form a litany that recalls Watts, Detroit and Harlem in the '60s and the outcries then about jobs, housing and a society that was seemingly incapable of redressing racial wrongs.

So the smoke rising from Liberty City should carry a message to people throughout this country: The American society is still not close to purging itself of discrimination and racial injustice. Certainly some progress has been made, but we Americans should not delude ourselves into believing that the conditions that produced the Miami riot do not exist in other places.

If violence can serve any positive purpose, Miami can remind Americans that the problems of the ghetto and the inner city, of injustice and discrimination, of racism, mindless hatred and pent-up rage, still haunt this country.

The News and Courier

Charleston, S.C., May 20, 1980

While the volcanic eruption of Mount St. Helens signalled that nature was on the rampage in Washington, men were on the rampage in the streets of Miami, far across the country.

A race riot, said to have been touched off by the acquittal in Tampa of four white former policemen tried in the death of a black businessman, left at least 13 dead, 200 injured and more than 250 arrested. It left smoke curling from three dozen buildings, stores looted, schools closed and streets patrolled by National Guardsmen called in to beef up police ranks.

That what started as a protest to perceived injustice in the courts could so rapidly degenerate into a wave of shooting, burning and looting is testimony to the mindlessness of rioters. How is breaking a store window and walking away with clothes or a TV set related to what went on in a courtroom 220 miles away? What has setting fire to a police car in Miami to do with a jury's verdict in Tampa?

The answers are, of course, nothing. Obviously the Miami rioters were looking for an excuse to go on a rampage. There are legal ways to protest court decisions seen as miscarriages of justice. Those ways were ignored in favor of violence. Violence in the streets takes innocent lives, costs taxpayers and businesses money, and — in the case of Miami — puts added strains on race relations. It accomplishes nothing else.

The Wichita Eagle

Wichita, Kans., May 20, 1980

The stunning verdict of innocent in the case of four white police officers accused of beating a black Miami resident to death understandably sent shock waves through southern Florida's black community. The bestial nature of the alleged crime, set against a backdrop of repeated incidents of white police-black resident confrontations, created the tinderbox into which the spark of mob violence was dropped over the weekend.

While it is difficult to second-guess a jury, particularly given the constitutional guarantee of every accused person being regarded as innocent until proven guilty, some very serious questions must be asked about the administration of justice in Dade County, which includes the Greater Miami area. It also is important that federal indictments charging the officers with violation of Arthur McDuffie's civil rights be sought swiftly, if indeed the evidence supports such action.

The prosecution in the McDuffie case should have been aware that if an innocent verdict came down from an all-white jury, as eventually did happen, a violent reaction from the black community was almost predictable. This isn't to say white juries can't be as impartial as any other jury, but the long string of racial incidents in Dade County over the past couple of years should have made the selection of some black jurors to hear this particular case almost a requirement.

Beyond that, the state attorney's office had a record of dealing leniently with alleged civil rights violations within the Metro Public Safety Department, including at least two cases in which the wrong person was apprehended — one having been shot to death, the other severely beaten. In both cases, the offending officers were found to have acted negligently, but without criminal intent.

The perception of the Metro police by the black community, then, aligns one "side" against the other in a situation that only can mean future racial trouble for the beleaguered southern metropolis, unless the Miami area political leadership seizes the opportunity to restore not only order but a climate of equity among the population.

It is the creation of such a climate that provides the necessary margin of "protection" in a situation such as the acquittal of the accused in the McDuffie case. If the black residents of Dade County had been able to feel the police and the prosecutor's office were on "their side" as well as the side of the white community, the policemen's acquittal undoubtedly would have raised little protest.

There is a lesson here for cities such as Wichita, as well. Unless the political leadership anywhere nurtures the kind of climate that lets all people know their concerns are being equally considered, there is a chance of a violent response to perceived inequities.

Miami residents of all colors and creeds should work together now to see that the violence stops, and that reason is restored. The killings and atrocities that have occurred obviously solve nothing, but only contribute to the atmosphere of fear and racial hatred that has poisoned the hearts of too many too long.

THE STATES-ITEM

New Orleans, La., May 21, 1980

Almost as shocking as the explosive racial violence in Miami, which has wrecked much of that city's business district and left 16 persons dead and hundreds injured, was the apparent insensitivity of local officials to the smoldering grievances of black residents.

A deep sense of ill treatment by local law enforcement officials and the local criminal justice system among blacks has come to the fore as the causes of the Miami eruption are sifted.

Numerous other factors doubtless are involved: A 17 percent unemployment rate among Miami blacks, as compared to an 8 percent rate among whites and Hispanics, had aggravated tensions. The latest influx of Cuban refugees and the further competition for jobs they represented did not help matters.

Then, too, the intensity of the violence suggested the presence of a substantial criminal element, the sort who are only too eager to loot and burn under the cover of any disaster.

The spark that lit the fuse was the acquittal of four white policemen by an all-white jury in the beating death of Arthur McDuffie, a black insurance man. The seating of an all-white jury in such a sensitive case will impress many outsiders as something that should have been avoided. Miami blacks complain of other injustices at the hands of all-white juries.

In a throwback to what we had hoped was a bygone era, it apparently will remain for the U.S. Justice Department to restore a sense of balance to the justice system in Miami. U.S. Attorney General Benjamin R. Civiletti, dispatched to the scene by President Carter, promises a federal investigation in which "all will get a fair shake and fair play."

The Miami eruption is disquieting because it questions the widely held presumption that the nation had moved beyond most of the circumstances that gave rise to the "long hot summer" of 1967. Whether the conditions in Miami today are peculiar to that city alone is a question for the leaders of other urban centers to ponder.

THE SUN

Baltimore, Md., May 20, 1980

The really threatening American volcano is the urban, social, racial one whose awesome terror and power we glimpsed in Miami over the weekend. Twelve years after the widespread urban rioting that followed Dr. Martin Luther King's murder, we are still living on the slopes overlying forces of despair, discrimination and mutual hatred that can, if not relieved, do enormous damage to our nation.

This volcano has been dormant (more or less) since the late 1960s. But the same forces that caused those riots have not been alleviated. In 1968 a special commission concluded that one of the basic causes of the rioting was widespread black poverty. Subsequent to the riot commission report, the Bureau of Labor Statistics began keeping records on central cities. White unemployment there climbed from 4.9 to 5.5 percent, 1973-79. In the same period black big city unemployment rose from 9.5 to 12.6. The percentage of urban blacks living below the poverty line at the time of the riot commission study was 24.7 percent. A Census study of last year put it at 31.5 percent. Those statistics are getting worse as the recession takes hold.

As bad as discrimination in jobs and income is, the basic causes of black fury then and now are insensitivity and brutality by white police. The 1968 commission study found that blacks placed police practices at the top of their grievance list. The commission concluded that "police are not merely a 'spark' factor. To some Negroes police have come to symbolize white power, white racism and white repression. And the fact is that many police do reflect and express these white attitudes." The Miami riots erupted after a jury acquitted four white former police officers accused of using fatal force in subduing a black man they had arrested on a traffic charge. We are pleased that the Department of Justice is going to begin presenting evidence to a grand jury of alleged violations of federal laws by the four ex-cops. Dual prosecution of incidents such as this one is not the best way to proceed. But when local prosecutors, judges and juries do not do their job, as they appear not to have done in this case, the federal government has an obligation to move in.

This will be the sixth time since 1977 that the Justice Department has so acted. Does that signal a rise in excessive use of force by police in white-black cases? Does it signal a rise in white tolerance of excessive use of police force against blacks? It may well signal one or the other, if not both. In the first half of fiscal 1980 the Community Relations Service received 142 percent more complaints of excessive police force than in the first half of 1979. Statistics in this field aren't completely reliable, but some students of race relations believe that the trend is definitely up. They postulate that in the aftermath of the 1960s riots, many urban police departments were made more concerned about the sensibilities of ghetto communities, but the passage of time has dulled that sensitivity.

More unemployment, more poverty, more police-community tension: We are living on the slope of a volcano more threatening that Mount St. Helens.

THE DENVER POST

Denver, Colo., June 12, 1980

A MOTORCADE carrying the president of the United States was stoned by members of an angry crowd Monday. The incident did not take place in Tehran or some other city in a hostile foreign land. It happened in Miami, Fla.

All concerned are trying to make light of what occurred. President Carter says he really didn't notice, although that explanation is difficult to accept in view of the fact that he was booed and jeered and, according to the Associated Press, he "ducked into his car and sped off" when the rocks and bottles started to fly. A Miami police officer blamed "a few kids at the back of the crowd."

We must question the wisdom of permitting the president to visit a section of Miami where 16 persons were killed in a bitter racial riot only a few weeks ago. What is perceived as a Carter-induced recession — to halt the course of ruinous inflation — has stirred deep anger and frustration among the black poor who are most immediately affected.

Jimmy Carter was swept into the presidency in 1976 by overwhelming black support. No doubt it was his desire to show the blacks that he cares about their problems, and shares their concerns — which he certainly does — that led him to Miami's devastated districts.

But aside from the political implications of this particular occurrence, there is reason for alarm about the anger that threatens the nation's unity. When it is unsafe for the president to visit any particular part of the land, we are in trouble.

Anger in the streets, already fierce enough to provoke a rock-throwing incident targeting the president, must be cooled by responsible leadership. Further violence is bound to trigger an equally deplorable reaction. The shameful violence of the Sixties must not be repeated.

The Birmingham News

Birmingham, Ala., May 20, 1980

There is absolutely no way to justify the 16 deaths, scores of injuries and millions of dollars worth of property damage that resulted from the needless terrorism set loose in Miami over this weekend. To think that some of those who instigated the violence did so in the name of "justice" only makes a twisted mockery of the word.

Looting and violence began in the city Saturday night shortly after an all-white jury trying a Miami case in Tampa found four ex-Miami policemen not guilty in the fatal beating of Arthur McDuffie, a black insurance salesman. Doubtless the verdict was only a trigger that set off a bomb which must have been ticking for some time. Whatever racial problems might have been boiling under Miami's surface, however, they certainly weren't cured by the wanton street violence that ensued.

McDuffie was slain under questionable circumstances to be sure and prosecutors were right to take the evidence against the policemen involved before a jury. On the other hand, however, the four police officers accused of his death were tried in the same manner that anyone else accused of a crime would have been tried. To say that an injustice was done because the jury was all-white and did not return a guilty verdict—that is to say, apparently, that justice *couldn't* be done because no blacks were on the jury—is a very dubious theory indeed upon which to waste 16 lives.

The melee in Miami will serve no end in the long run save that of promoting senseless suffering and an atmosphere of racial distrust that may fester in the city for years to come. That is especially tragic considering that there apparently were racial problems in the city needing serious attention before the riots broke out: Now they will only be all the more difficult to grapple with. It takes a perverse logic to hold up such results in the name of "justice."

The Dallas Morning News

Dallas, Texas, June 1, 1980

When that Miami mob gathered to throw rocks, bottles and insults at President Carter the other day, among the signs shaken at him was one saying:

"Tax the rich, rebuild black Miami."

Taxing the rich was indeed a Jimmy Carter campaign promise four years ago. He defined "rich" as meaning having higher income than the median. That means that the family now making $20,000 or so a year is officially rich. No doubt that family will agree that this is one promise Carter kept, full up and brimming over.

But his riotous hosts in Miami don't seem to have noticed. Another thing they don't seem to have noticed is that the taxpaying "rich" aren't the ones who took to the streets and tore down black Miami a few weeks ago.

Times~Colonist

Victoria, B.C., May 21, 1980

Two eruptions shook the United States this past weekend; one was natural, the other man-made.

Kitty-corner across the continent from Mount St. Helens' sky-high plume of ash and gas, racial rioting broke out in the predominently black Miami suburb of Liberty City.

Both eruptions were violent, both brought death and destruction, and both were uncontrollable. Sunday night, after widespread looting, scores of fires and 15 people dead, a police officer in Miami said: "We've almost given up trying to protect property. It's totally out of control, it's survival out there."

Mount St. Helens had lain dormant for 123 years before unleashing the awesome forces stored within its depths.

Rioting in the magnitude that struck the streets of Miami was last seen during the Detroit riots in 1968 and the Los Angeles Watts riot in August 1965.

Nature held her tongue for over a century. But the release of pent-up hostilities within men are more frequent. Although mountains offer few examples of volcanic eruptions, it seems probable that their secrets will be explored, controlled and perhaps harnessed before solutions are found to human eruptions.

Arkansas Gazette.

Little Rock, Ark., May 20, 1980

It has been a year of bad news and worse luck for the country. The reports of inflation and recession, of frustration in recovering our hostages in Iran, of strain in resettling Cuban refugees, have been followed now by word of terrible race riots in Miami, at least 14 persons having been killed over the weekend following an acquittal in the trial at Tampa of four white police officers.

The scenes at Miami have been frightful, with wanton killing and mutilation in and around the city's ghetto area. The casualties include hundreds of injured. Such an explosion of violence attests to a seething unrest in Miami that must surprise most Americans, who think of life in South Florida as a subtropical idyll but are aware now that Miami suffers the same tensions as New York or Los Angeles.

The scenes, in any case, are a flashback to the turbulent sixties, when hundreds died in race rioting in large cities across the country. Most of us thought this kind of disorder had been consigned to the past, that blacks had recognized its utter futility and that the white establishments in the cities had learned, at the least, to guard against inflammatory situations involving police practices.

The chain of events in this riot began with the death at Miami December 17 of a black businessman named Arthur McDuffie, who was allegedly beaten to death by four white Miami policemen. There had been so much media attention to the case that the trial was moved to Tampa, where all the defendants were acquitted Saturday of various felony charges by an all-white jury.

It is difficult at this distance to form hard conclusions about the trial but it seems inconceivable that a case of this nature would be brought to trial before a jury formed without a single black member. The federal government, properly, is moving now to indict the defendants on charges of violating the civil rights of the man they are accused of killing. It is a recourse all too familiar in the Deep South, as memories of the infamous civil rights murders at Philadelphia, Miss., will attest.

The blundering mismanagement of justice in the Florida courts evokes both the riotous sixties and the maxim that to disregard the mistakes of the past condemns us to go on repeating them. The lessons written in the blood and smoke of the sixties have not, alas, been universally learned.

THE CHRISTIAN SCIENCE MONITOR

Boston, Mass., May 19, 1981

The anniversary of Miami's Liberty City race riot calls for the spirit of those enduring words from James Thurber's last book: "Let's not look back in anger, or forward in fear, but around in awareness." The anger and the fear may be tempting, as the death and destruction are remembered and the causes of black frustration are found largely unresolved. But to look around in awareness is to see the beginnings of attitudes and actions that could foster community peace and justice in the future.

According to a new Ford Foundation study, there were probably as many blacks involved in saving whites from harm as in harming whites. But the riot was unusual as a spontaneous uprising against white people — not touched off, by an immediate violent incident or involving primarily criminal elements. It came after blacks had apparently waited months for justice to run its course; then they were convinced of continuing injustice when police officers were acquitted of the fatal beating of a black insurance man.

The sense of injustice may have been overriding, but it was added to a pervasive sense of deprivation in economic, social, and political ways as well. A concern now is that the Reagan administration's cutbacks on CETA jobs and other economic programs will make it more difficult to reduce the deprivation. Thus conditions for unrest would remain.

But this is where some of the less publicized aspects of the Liberty City aftermath have to be considered. It seems to have taken Miami a year to wake up, as it was put to us

by an editor at the Miami Herald, which has provided such notably thorough coverage of the situation. In some other cities, the business community has been quicker to move toward listening to the needs of the black community and responding to them. Now, however, a board has been set up with business representation. It has the potentiality to move constructively on proposals for economic revitalization plans. .

Part of the good news is that individuals have not waited to go ahead with assistance in their own ways. Minority employees of one company, for example, use their own off hours to work with children on how to prepare themselves for job opportunities.

At the same time, there has been progress on some of the recommendations of a governor's panel on the riot. A civilian review board was set up to check on complaints of police brutality, and it has had some effect. There has been a concerted effort to include blacks on jury panels. Strides have been made in minority recruitment for the police force.

And here is one of the unexpected signs of hope in the situation. Has police morale been destroyed? Are the police hated? No. There seems to be a fresh community sense of the importance of the police. Perhaps the lower-than-expected turnout for a march marking the riot anniversary was another indication that Liberty City wants to turn away from such tragedy. If enough officials and others continue to look around in awareness, the 1980 riot will be the last.

DESERET NEWS

Salt Lake City, Utah, May 20-21, 1980

The curse of racial violence still besets America.

In Miami over the weekend, rioters, both black and white, killed at least 19 people, and wounded 350 others. Burning and looting in the mostly black Liberty City section caused hundreds-of-millions of dollars worth of property damage.

The riot — the first of the 1980s — seems out of season. Race riots erupted in many American cities during the late 1960s. First, 34 persons were killed in Watts, a section of Los Angeles, in 1965. During the next few years, racial violence claimed scores of lives in Newark, Harlem, Cleveland, Baltimore, Washington, and other American cities.

Rioting reached a bloody crescendo in Detroit in 1967 when 40 persons were killed.

During the late 1970s, the black ghettoes of the nation were relatively calm. Americans could hope that large race riots had been put behind them.

Miami shows that hope was false.

Though the Miami riot comes after a time of relative peace, its immediate cause was similar to the triggering incident in other earlier race riots: in Watts, Harlem, Newark, Cleveland, Detroit, and other cities, riots began after incidents involving police and black people.

In Miami, the riot started after an all-white jury acquitted four white policemen of charges stemming from

the death of black insurance agent Arthur McDuffie. The black youths shouted "McDuffie, McDuffie," as they took to the streets.

As tragic as the Miami riot is by itself, Americans must now fear that it will herald a new wave of senseless violence.

In retrospect, it seems clear that the news of rioting in Watts sparked violence in other cities, and they in turn helped further spread the conflagration. News of riots in Miami could provoke outbursts from a new generation of young blacks.

Since the years of urban strife, America has striven hard to overcome the effects of racism. The nation has achieved only partial success. Though many doors are open to blacks that were previously closed to them, blacks still suffer from unemployment, poverty, and broken families in disproportionate numbers.

The current recession is likely to worsen the unemployment of black youth, and the coming summer could match the long hot summers of times America would rather not repeat.

Rioting and violence will not solve any of the problems that beset America or its black minority. The Miami riot is deeply discouraging, for it brings back to the land the senseless actions and foolish hatreds that should have been left behind.

ALBUQUERQUE JOURNAL

Albuquerque, N.M., May 21, 1980

In the realm of human knowledge and theory, there is little that could have been done to forestall or remedy the disastrous eruption of Mount St. Helens in the state of Washington. Yet it would be self-defeating to entertain the thought nothing more could have been done to prevent, or to respond to the human eruption that took place simultaneously in the opposite corner of the continent.

The senseless killing and maiming of fellow humans and the destruction of millions of dollars worth of property in and around Miami shock the American people into a grim realization: The nation, collectively, still has not dealt adequately with the inequities, tensions and frustrations that cause any combination of people to strike out suddenly, violently and blindly against other members of their species.

It would be easy, but it would achieve nothing, to attribute the tragic Miami riots to the tantrums of spoiled children who have learned through experience that abnormal behavior can win attention, lead to desired rewards and carry little risk of recrimination.

It would be another form of evasive rationalization to dismiss individual and collective acts of violence as the logical outgrowth of prolonged suppression, historic patterns of exploitation or widespread indifference to the plight of the disadvantaged.

The greatest danger inherent in the Miami eruption is the threat to the delicate balance, achieved through ages of trial and error, in the time-tested judicial system that has served American society so well. The greatest protection for minorities as well as majorities lies in its demonstrated capacity to promulgate verdicts that may prove unpopular with any or all segments of society. To abridge, or to even attempt the abridgement, of the constitutional protections afforded to all criminal defendants would be a blunder for which unborn generations of Americans would pay dearly.

But the discretionary processes whereby issues are brought before the nation's courts for litigation and ultimate trial are subject to concern, discussion and searching examination. If there is a dual system of criminal justice, as alleged, in any of the 50 states, the susceptibility at the prosecutorial level is the highest. It is there where any search for complicity should begin, and it is there where efforts to reform the criminal justice system should be concentrated.

Chicago Defender

Chicago, Ill., May 23, 1981

The riot that erupted in Miami over the fatal beating of a black insurance executive, had a different motivation and perception from the racial disorders in the 1960s. So concludes a preliminary report of a study of the Florida disturbances that left 18 dead and destroyed some $80 million in property a year ago.

The study reminds us that the rioters themselves came from a more law-abiding and representative group of residents than those who participated in the Watts riot in 1965 and the Newark disorders in 1967. The report added that not since the slave uprisings before the Civil War had Blacks risen spontaneously with the sole purpose of beating and killing whites. "It was not within the bounds of our study," the report said, "to speculate whether the Miami riots will become the national norm."

We can answer that. The pattern will be repeated elsewhere giving similar set of insufferable circumstances.

Criminal Justice System; Weighted Against Blacks?

Black Americans are not only far more likely than their white counterparts to be the victims of crime, they are much more likely when charged with crimes to end up in jail or prison, and when convicted of crimes for which the death penalty is the severest sentence, to be executed. Several studies by private corporations and academic researchers have found also that sentences imposed on blacks tend to be consistently longer than those imposed on whites convicted of similar crimes and with similar criminal records—and that blacks are more likely to serve their whole sentence, without being paroled.

Another aspect of the criminal justice system, the procedure by which juries are selected, has long been the target of criticism by civil rights advocates. The issue revolves around the peremptory challenges used by both defense and prosecution lawyers to screen prospective jurors before a trial, giving the lawyers the power to reject a certain number of jurors without citing cause. Civil rights groups have long complained that some prosecutors regularly use these challenges to eliminate black would-be jurors in order to enhance the possibility of convicting black defendants. In a decision in 1965 *(Swain v. Alabama)*, the Supreme Court had ruled that individual incidents of such exclusion could not be considered in violation of a defendant's guarantee of equal protection, unless it could be proved that the prosecutor had a history of excluding black jurors. The high court refused to decide a similar case in 1983 *(McCray v. New York)*, although Justice Thurgood Marshall opined that the court should accept the case because of the "almost universal and often scathing criticism" of the Swain ruling. Most recently, a federal appeals panel in New York City ruled in Dec., 1984, in the first decision of its kind, that prosecutors could not exclude prospective jurors solely on the basis of race. The case involved a black defendant who had been convicted of robbery by an all-white jury; the prosecution had rejected one Hispanic and seven black prospective jurors.

Chicago Defender
Chicago, Ill., March 16, 1981

There's little consolation in the latest Gallup Poll figures which show that 66 per cent of the American public now endorses the death penalty for the most serious crimes including murder. That's up 4 points since 1978 and 24 points since 1966!

And while we can sympathize with the frustration many people feel about the relative ineffectiveness of most rehabilitation programs, the early release of dangerous criminals and the likelihood of repeat offenses, we do no believe killing others is the answer to anything. The criminal justice system is badly run in most cities and states, and stupid mistakes are made almost routinely. But that, we submit, is a solid reason for not pushing the death penalty. The mistakes go both ways, and for every vicious maniac who beats the rap, there may well be several innocent and undeserving convicts sitting on death row.

The answer, as always, is to tighten up the system, not revert to barbarism. Despite the massive and growing trend, it is noteworthy that the Gallup Poll shows only 44 percent of non-whites favoring the death penalty. That is a smaller percentage than any other category in the poll results. Since Blacks and other non-whites are disproportionately victims of murders, rapes and other horrors of the streets, an outsider might wonder why there is not more minority support for capital punishment.

The reason is that minorities understand far better than most whites how easily they can become the unwitting victims of our flawed criminal justice system. Arbitrariness, racism, ignorance and arrogance are traits which can be found in judges, juries and prosecutors as well as in the identifiable criminal element.

Pittsburgh Post-Gazette
Pittsburgh, Pa., August 31, 1981

There is probably no subject of greater interest to whites and blacks than crime and the administration of justice. And while crime transcends race because all Pittsburghers are its victims, the community ignores its racial aspects at its peril.

Three recent, if disparate events help illustrate the point:

• Western Penitentiary, bursting at the seams with 1,160 men, experiences an ugly confrontation between inmates and guards. Correctional personnel defuse what is described as the tensest situation in the last five years.

• The University of Pittsburgh Center for Social and Urban Research releases a study that finds that the race of a juror is not significant in determining how he or she may react at a trial, regardless of the race of the defendant. But those familiar with Common Pleas Court insist that some criminal lawyers consistently behave as if race does matter — and challenge prospective jurors accordingly.

• The General Assembly, by a wide margin, refuses to permit implementation of sentencing guidelines, the result of a major study by a blue-ribbon panel of judges, prosecutors, lawyers and academics from around the state. The recommendations, designed to bring more consistency in sentences, are condemned as not tough enough.

The seeds for future trouble are to be found here — trouble with clear racial overtones. Consider just these two facts:

From 60 to 65 percent of Pennsylvanians in prison are black, both in state institutions and Allegheny County's jail.

Asked if they believe the justice system discriminates against them, just under 50 percent of Pittsburgh blacks answer yes.

Obviously, this is not a subject that lends itself to a quick fix. Rising crime rates, particularly violent crime rates, have troubled this community and confounded the best minds of the nation for three decades. And the complex mix of environmental and ethnic history that is the legacy of every black (and white) Pittsburgher is not really understood, let alone susceptible to change.

Prejudice, economic inequality and social disparities are going to be a part of the community — and nation — for the indefinite future. But this is no excuse for what is going on (or, to be more precise, what isn't going on) in a number of areas, as the Post-Gazette reported in its recent reports on black life in Pittsburgh.

Prisons are case No. 1. If the Commonwealth is determined to detain more citizens in jail for longer periods, it ought at least to accompany this effort with building programs; the current flirtation with two-prisoners-to-a-cell solutions is a prescription for disaster. There also needs to be an increase in the number of blacks working in corrections. Approximately 10 percent of the guards at the county jail are black, while at Western Penitentiary the figure is closer to 5 percent. These numbers are way too low, given the fact that a disproportionate number of crimes are being committed by and against blacks.

Similarly, sentencing standardization is also a necessity, in terms of both simple justice and the immediate need to do something about prison overcrowding. Guidelines — mistakenly rigid though the Legislature may make them — at least would make it easier for courts effectively to use scarce prison space for those best kept off the streets. The present system finds rural judges jailing people for property crimes, while judges in Pittsburgh are forced to give the benefit of the doubt to people found guilty of much more serious offenses.

Consistency in sentencing would also help deal with the perception among black Pittsburghers that the system discriminates against them — though this is a posture that will be changed in a general way only after years of experience.

And that experience has to include participation by blacks in all aspects of the criminal justice system.

Fortunately, progress has been made in this regard in the Pittsburgh police department, where a court-ordered affirmative action program has brought black employment up to 12 percent, one of the better records in the nation among urban police departments. The Pennsylvania Poll also has found that there has been concurrent progress in police-community relations, with more Pittsburgh blacks (26 percent) thinking things have improved than believing they've gotten worse (16 percent). But both of these advances are relative, with a bad situation merely being less bad.

And in other key areas there is disturbing evidence of backsliding, most particularly in the legal profession which is a key to both access to the judiciary and attitudes about the courts and justice. There are only 110 blacks among Greater Pittsburgh's 5,000 lawyers, and black enrollment in District law schools, which has hovered between 3 to 5 percent for the past 12 years, appears to be declining, as it is nationally.

This record is among the worst of the professions locally and an embarrassment (and challenge) to the county bar which should be taking the lead in affirmative action. A racially-integrated bar is no guarantee against prejudice in courtrooms nor a promise of heightened confidence among blacks in the justice system, but it would be a significant help in bringing about change in both areas.

Matters of race are an integral part of the local crime problem. To pretend they are not is blindness, just as it is foolish to hold that relief from this scourge is to be found solely with the clank of a closing prison door. If there is one area where the community's current sympathy for benign neglect on black/white relations won't work, it is here.

THE KANSAS CITY STAR
Kansas City, Mo., August 31, 1981

Many people are hard put to believe that justice prevailed in the death of Stephen Harvey, the 27-year-old black jazz musician who was brutally slain in November near Liberty Memorial. An all-white Jackson County Circuit Court jury acquitted a white defendant in a trial presided over by a white judge. The county prosecutor and the assistant prosecutor who tried the case are white, as are two other men whose first-degree murder charges were reduced in return for their testimony on behalf of the prosecution. Now further action against them is tenuous. The judge has refused to accept their guilty pleas to a lesser charge because he considers the evidence against them to be weak.

Those connected with the prosecution were stunned by the jury verdict. Yet no one can ever know precisely what factors influence a jury, in this case or any other. Each juror must be persuaded beyond reasonable doubt that a defendant is guilty. Any trace of uncertainty, no matter how subtle the source of it, can be decisive in the final outcome.

In this case two witnesses stood to gain by helping the prosecution. They testified they were present but did not participate in the killing. Something about the arrangement made between the prosecution and those two witnesses, though accepted procedure in criminal cases, could have hurt the credibility of the state's case. No one knows for sure. The defendant claimed he was innocent, a contention upheld by the jury. Thus the acquittal could have been prompted by a number of elements, none racial.

No defense of the system in this instance is likely to wash with many blacks, however. From their viewpoint the perceived injustice is not an isolated instance but another episode in a long string of inequities in a white-dominated society. They know the history of lynchings, railroadings, false arrests and denial of rights. Their suspicions that minorities cannot get justice are based on things that have happened to them and their forebears.

Without question advances have been made. The number of blacks in government has increased appreciably, including appointment of minority members to the Jackson County Circuit Court and other judicial positions. But not enough.

Minority representation is extremely important in all endeavors of a pluralistic society—voting in elections, holding public office and myriad other activities in and out of government. It is a clear signal that the system is open to and serves all. Sometimes it doesn't seem to work very well. There are failures. And when these failures seem to have racial connotations, the dismay is going to be felt, whether justified or not.

It is too much to ask for patience, please—that is the song of centuries. It is not too much to expect that the chance for all to participate will be accelerated by the institutions and professions involved—law, the political parties, the courts and general government.

St. Petersburg Times
St. Petersburg, Fla., August 17, 1983

Florida courts deal sternly with young offenders — especially if they are black. Black youths are far more likely than whites to be transferred from juvenile to adult courts for trial. If convicted, they are far more likely to be sentenced to adult prisons or jails.

The sharp disparity in black and white justice in the Florida courts was clearly drawn this week in two provocative reports by St. Petersburg Times writer Helen Huntley, who detailed the findings of two recent studies — one statewide, the other focused on Pinellas County.

The state study, conducted by the Florida Juvenile Justice Institute director and other researchers, showed that the number of youths sent to adult court for trial has skyrocketed in the last five years since Florida toughened its stance toward juvenile crime.

Although most youths who face judgment as adults are whites, black youths stand trial in adult courts and are sent to adult prisons or jails in numbers far exceeding their proportion in the population.

BLACKS MAKE UP about 21 percent of Florida's under-18 population and account for about 30 percent of juvenile arrests. But in 1981, black youths made up 47 percent of those transferred to adult courts and 51 percent of those sentenced to adult prisons and jails.

A study of the juvenile justice system in Pinellas County during an 18-month period in 1979 and 1980 showed similar trends. Disproportionate numbers of black youths were tried as adults and sentenced to prison or jail terms.

White or black, many Florida juveniles who commit serious crimes will face judgment in adult courts and be committed to adult prisons. This hard-line justice is not limited to crimes of violence. It also is meted out to many children 17 or younger who are accused of less serious crimes.

The sharp increase in children being transferred from juvenile to adult courts is the result of a 1978 law which gave state attorneys the power to take 16- and 17-year-olds directly to adult court without asking a judge for approval.

Previously, that decision was made by a circuit judge under specific guidelines designed to protect children and afford them a better chance for rehabilitation. Now, state attorneys arbitrarily can file adult charges against children, even on the first felony offense.

The change has produced proof of the state government's mistreatment of children. The average youth sent to adult court is not a violent criminal but a 17-year-old white male arrested for burglary, with a previous record of juvenile offenses. More than three-fourths are transferred for nonviolent crimes. Most are sentenced to adult prison or jail.

Youths who have private lawyers are more likely to get probation and less likely to get prison terms than those who don't. That is one reason that black youths, most from homes of deep poverty, get the harsher punishment.

Pinellas-Pasco State Attorney James T. Russell apparently has used more discretion than other Florida prosecutors in sending children to adult court. The direct-file rate for Pinellas juveniles is below the state average and has declined as the juvenile crime rate has decreased. Statewide, the number of children sent to adult courts has increased while the crime rate was going down.

EVERY STATE has some provision for trying juveniles in adult court, but Florida treats children in adult court more harshly than many other states. It is a system where vengeance and punishment far outweigh compassion and attempts at rehabilitation.

We think Florida's children should be salvaged, rather than discarded in prisons that are schools for crime.

The findings of the way Florida's juvenile justice system is working call for repeal of the 1978 law and the return of all youthful offenders to juvenile court jurisdiction. The judge, not the prosecutor, should decide whether they are transferred to adult court. The findings also point out the critical need for the expansion and improvement of youth rehabilitation programs.

And the unequal justice for black youths calls for fairness. In Pinellas, the scales might be more balanced if the St. Petersburg Community Alliance monitored the treatment of blacks on a long-range basis.

Although juvenile records by law are confidential, the researcher who conducted the Pinellas survey obtained a court order to examine the files. The Community Alliance could do the same.

Continuing scrutiny by such a respected organization could do much to close the broad disparity in black and white justice.

Roanoke Times & World-News

Roanoke, Va., May 20, 1983

THE final few pages have been written in the story that unfolded when an off-duty Roanoke police officer shot a shoplifting suspect last August.

The officer, C.E. Wicks, was found innnocent of any criminal charges; but Police Chief M. David Hooper, to his credit, decided that the officer overreacted in the incident and fired him.

Now the Justice Department has closed an investigation of the incident and has cleared the police department and Wicks of violating the black suspect's civil rights.

The investigation was undertaken at the request of the then-head of the local NAACP chapter, who charged that the shooting was only one part of a pattern of discrimination against blacks, manifested in the use of excessive force.

The NAACP has a watchdog function, and was right to ask for an investigation. The Justice Department action does not close the book on the broader NAACP charge, only on the question of Wicks' violation of any federal criminal civil rights laws.

That broader charge is hard to prove or disprove: It boils down to a matter of perception. The police chief has publicly reviewed several cases in which the NAACP claimed excessive force, and in those cases the claim appears to be unfounded.

The NAACP isn't going to give up its adversary function, and it shouldn't. The running battle is likely to continue, and it serves to keep the police aware of the importance of relationships with minorities. But the Wicks case is closed; and, though their were no heroes in the story, there were apparently no official villains either.

THE ATLANTA CONSTITUTION

Atlanta, Ga., June 6, 1983

The U.S. Supreme Court has only put off the inevitable: It recently refused to take up a case that would have compelled it to reconsider a 1965 ruling which implicitly permits the exclusion of prospective jurors on racial grounds.

That ruling has tied the hands of appellate courts in several states, in which black defendants — convicted by all-white juries — claimed they were denied the right to fair trials. In New York, a prosecutor had used peremptory challenges to remove all seven blacks from a group of prospective jurors.

By refusing to hear the arguments for reconsideration, the court forces the states to, in the words of three justices, "serve as laboratories" a while longer — an approach that has led to gross disparities in the dispensing of justice: A Brooklyn, N.Y., prosecutor has prohibited her staff from using peremptory challenges on the basis of race, religion, sex or national origin, and the Supreme Courts of two other states — California and Massachusetts — have barred the practice on state constitutional grounds. But in New York, Illinois and New Orleans, other prosecutors have used peremptory challenges to remove all blacks from groups of prospective jurors, in cases against blacks.

The Supreme Court's 1965 finding — that the use of peremptory challenges to exclude blacks was not, in and of itself, a violation of a defendant's rights — "has been the subject of almost universal and often scathing criticism," as Justice Thurgood Marshall noted in an opinion favoring reconsideration. Few defendants have the resources to establish a pattern of racially motivated jury challenges by a prosecutor's office, as required under that ruling.

Four of the nine justices agreed with Marshall, but three were loath to intervene at this time — stemming perhaps from what some of them have described as an excessive workload. The court is, by most accounts, overburdened; and the peremptory-challenge issue is a complex one, not likely to be dispatched with ease.

But the court has for 18 years at least implicitly condoned the exclusion of jurors on racial grounds — a situation long overripe for review. It was a dangerous precedent, and the court has set another in allowing it to stand.

THE PLAIN DEALER

Cleveland, Ohio, December 17, 1983

Thousands of volts of electricity killed Robert Wayne Williams and John Eldon Smith this week, and it wasn't lightning. Given the lottery-like characteristics of our judicial system, however, the two murderers killed in Southern electric chairs might just as well have been struck by something every bit as random.

That, indeed, was a point made by the U.S. Supreme Court 11 years ago when it judged the imposition and implementation of the death penalty to be unconstitutional. Said Justice Potter Stewart, "The death sentences are cruel and unusual in the same way that being struck by lightning is cruel and unusual."

Since that ruling, 37 states wanting to impose capital punishment have revised their laws in an attempt to meet Supreme Court guidelines. Figures compiled by the American Civil Liberties Union, defense lawyers and university researchers indicate that the states have not done the job very well. If rationality and certainty are among the standards by which we judge our legal system, the games of chance applied in capital cases come nowhere close to passing muster.

The most significant figures are provided by researchers at the University of Iowa, who spent months analyzing the application of capital punishment in Georgia. The researchers plugged hundreds of variables into their computers to ensure accuracy.

They found that, among those convicted of murder, blacks were four times more likely to be sentenced to death than whites. They found that killers of black victims were far less likely to be sentenced to death than were killers of white victims. In that light, how can we believe that capital punishment provides justice for the families of victims? It is not justice when society tells many black families that their murdered sons and daughters do not deserve the same retribution provided to families of white victims.

The figures vary from state to state. Nationally, only a small number of murderers, about 3%, have been sentenced to death since 1973. Those who were sentenced to pay the ultimate penalty often could not afford the best legal counsel, or lacked the pedigree to attract sympathetic juries, or had the bad luck of facing particularly bright prosecutors and/or tough judges.

Eighteen men and two women are currently on death row under the new death penalty statute enacted by the Ohio Legislature in 1981. The law is one of the tightest in the country; the legislature took great effort to protect the right of defendants. Yet even the Ohio system may be subject to inconsistent application—county prosecutors must decide whether to file capital charges, and prosecutors don't always think alike.

Sentencing inconsistencies can be tolerated when the sentences are reversible, when mistakes can be corrected. But there is no turning back after the executioner throws the switch.

There is another alternative—mandatory life imprisonment without parole, which is not, relatively, as expensive as many suspect. Writing in a recent issue of the New Republic, defense lawyer David Bruck pointed out that New York state spends $1.8 million just to take a capital case through the initial trial and the first stage of appeal. That, says Bruck, is twice the cost of a life term.

It is hard, if not impossible, to be sympathetic with a murderer. But it is equally difficult to respect a legal system as imperfect as the one we use to carry out society's desire for vengeance in the wake of murder. The sooner the executioner is retired, the sooner we can concentrate on punishments that are swift, certain and fair.

THE TENNESSEAN
Nashville, Tenn., July 8, 1983

A private research group has discovered what was already widely suspected but seldom confirmed by formal study· non-white persons convicted of crimes in America are punished more severely than white persons.

A Rand Corporation criminologist found that courts in California, Michigan and Texas typically impose longer sentences on Hispanics and blacks than on whites convicted of comparable felonies and who have similar criminal records.

In California the average sentence for Hispanics is six months longer than for whites and almost a month and a half longer for blacks.

In Michigan, blacks have to serve seven months longer than whites, and in Texas the sentences are three and a half months longer for blacks and two months longer for Hispanics.

Not only do these minorities receive longer minimum sentences but once imprisoned some serve a greater proportion of their original sentences than whites do, the Rand report said. The researcher added that the differences could not be explained by differences of the prisoners' behavior in prison.

The two-year study, which was sponsored by the National Institute of Corrections, U.S. Department of Justice, makes comparisons between whites and minority groups in more than 30 categories of offenders' behavior and the criminal justice system's responses to that behavior.

The study did not find any widespread, conscious prejudice against certain racial groups on the part of judges.

In fact, in 80% of the cases, judges follow the sentencing recommendation made in the probation officer's report.

"These reports are usually very comprehensive 'portraits' of offenders, containing personal and socioeconomic information, as well as any details the probation officer can get on their criminal habits and attitudes," the report said. It added that such information "distinguishes between races better than it predicts which offender will again commit crimes when he returns to society."

Somewhat surprisingly, most of the comparisons of the arrest, prosecution and conviction process showed little or no difference in the way the races were treated. Only at the sentencing stage did a definite bias against non-white convicts show up.

There is some progress in the fact that the races are being treated more equally in arrests, prosecutions and convictions. But it is a shame on the judiciary that many judges — who should be upholding racial justice — are, perhaps unwittingly in many cases, perpetuating racial injustice.

The study covered only the three states mentioned, but there is no reason to believe the situation would be any better in other states. In fact, the chances are good that racial inequality in sentencing is more pronounced in some other states than in those studied.

The report should cause judges throughout the nation to re-examine their sentencing procedures to make sure their courts are not perpetuating a type of racial discrimination that should have been eliminated from the criminal justice system.

ST. LOUIS POST-DISPATCH
St. Louis, Mo., July 12, 1983

If you are a black or Hispanic defendant, the system puts its thumb on the scales of justice in confining you to prison. That in essence is the finding of a study done by the Rand Corp. on the treatment of criminals in California, Texas and Michigan. The study concluded that black and Hispanic criminals in those states were sentenced to prison more often and served longer terms than whites with similar criminal records who were convicted of comparable felonies. Rand — a private, nonprofit organization — did the study for the U.S. Department of Justice.

In California, the average prison sentence was 6 ½ months longer for Hispanics and almost 1 ½ months longer for blacks; in Michigan, it was almost seven months longer for blacks; and in Texas the average term was more than 3 ½ months longer for blacks and two months longer for Hispanics. Not only did minorities in those states receive longer minimum sentences but, once in prison, they served a greater proportion of their original sentences than whites did — a disparity that could not be explained by differences in their prison behavior.

One explanation offered by the study for the difference in treatment was that blacks, because of their distrust of the system, are less likely to participate in the plea bargain process, under which they might get lighter sentences. And although the study showed that blacks commit disproportionately more crimes than whites (because they are more subject to "economic distress"), it also showed that the system makes the situation worse by imprisoning them unjustly for longer terms. In the end, therefore, the criminal justice system — by treating minorities more severely — is labeling them unfairly as more serious criminals, is reinforcing their feelings of alienation and thus is helping to perpetuate a vicious cycle of crime and harsher treatment.

The Washington Post
Washington, D.C., June 1, 1983

SUPPOSE YOU are a black man charged with murdering a white man. Before your trial begins, a group of prospective jurors is ushered into the courtroom and, one by one, they are questioned by the prosecutor and by your lawyer. At the completion of this examination, the prosecutor announces that he will use his peremptory challenges —he is entitled to reject up to 20 jurors without stating his reasons—and excuse jurors B, C, J and M, all of whom are black. This procedure leaves you with an all-white jury. Is this fair?

In 1964, in the landmark case of Swain v. Alabama, the Supreme Court decided such a case. There is no violation of the equal protection clause, wrote Justice White for the majority, if in an individual case the use of peremptory challenges results in the selection of an all-white jury. There might be such a violation if "the prosecutor in a county, in case after case, whatever the circumstances, whatever the crime and whoever the defendant or victim may be, is responsible for the removal of Negroes," but this was not the case before the court.

Since 1964, federal courts have adhered to the Swain decision; in some state courts, however, judges have ruled that such a racially motivated use of peremptory challenges violates the state constitution. In California, challenges may not be used to exclude jurors because of race, religion or ethnic origin. Massachusetts and New Mexico have also adopted variations on this rule. What we have, therefore, is a federal rule allowing broad discretion in jury selection to lawyers on both sides of a case, and a much stricter standard limiting discretion in a few states based on judicial interpretation of state law.

The Supreme Court accepts this diversity and this week declined an opportunity to revise the Swain standard and apply the stricter rule to everyone. A majority of the court declined to review three cases, one each from New York, Illinois and Louisiana, where the use of peremptory challenges by the prosecutor resulted in all-white juries and convictions were upheld by state appellate courts. Because this issue is of great and recurring interest, however, two separate opinions were written on the matter. Justices Marshall and Brennan believe Swain was wrongly decided and wanted to take these cases in order to overrule that decision. Justices Stevens, Blackmun and Powell write that they too would like to take another look at Swain, but not right now. They'd like to look at the experience in California, Massachusetts and New Mexico before considering whether to impose similar restrictions on all courts.

There are important questions at stake here. Does the California rule in practice, for example, require a prosecutor to assemble a jury that is racially and ethnically balanced? Is it necessary, in order to try a defendant of Albanian descent, to have someone with the same ethnic heritage on the jury panel? Have we gone too far in allowing lawyers to reject jurors for no reason, or should any citizen without bias or conflict of interest be given a chance to serve?

It is an unusually frank admission that some justices want "to allow the various states to serve as laboratories in which the issue receives further study" before they reconsider the Swain rule. But when they do reach the question, their review will have the benefit of what has been learned in California, Massachusetts and New Mexico, which should serve to make their decision practical and workable as well as constitutionally sound.

TULSA WORLD
Tulsa, Okla February 4, 1984

A FEDERAL judge in Atlanta Friday rejected a statistical study of Georgia death penalty cases which showed that murderers of white victims are far more likely to get a death sentence than murderers of blacks. Judge J. Owen Forrester said the study, conducted by Professor David Baldus of the University of Iowa, did not prove intentional racial discrimination by prosecutors or juries.

(The judge overturned on other grounds the death penalty of Warren McCleskey, convicted of murdering an Atlanta policeman.)

Professor Baldus' findings were considered the most serious challenge to Georgia's death penalty law — and capital punishment generally — since it was enacted in 1973. After examining nearly 1,000 Georgia cases and 250 variables, Baldus concluded that, on average, the odds of getting the death penalty were three times greater if a killer's victim was white rather than black. Baldus offered no explanation of what was behind this disparity.

The issue is of great importance to Oklahoma because of a similar study by a Stanford University professor. As reported in the World's Opinion section last week, that study examined capital punishment in Oklahoma and found that the death sentence was given in 7 percent of cases with white victims but in only 1 percent of cases with black victims.

Stanford University Law Professor Samuel Gross said his study indicated that in death penalty cases juries still discriminate, although perhaps unconsciously, along racial lines.

The studies do not indicate that anyone has been sentenced to death solely because of his race. And they can be used to support the argument that more murderers, not fewer, should be sentenced to death.

The Baldus study in Georgia and the Gross study of Oklahoma indicate that, for whatever reasons, juries are far more severe in their treatment of killers when the victims are white.

They raise perplexing questions. Is the proper response to this evidence to vacate the death sentences of those accused of killing white victims or assure that more murderers of blacks get the death sentence? Can any system or law ever eliminate unconscious discrimination by juries which are given discretion to decide who should be executed?

The Providence Journal
Providence, R.I., January 3, 1984

It is odd that while racial discrimination is banned by law in the United States, it is practiced freely in the nation's courtrooms. There is nothing extraordinary about trial lawyers using their peremptory challenges of potential jurors to eliminate those who apparently conform to a group stereotype.

It is possible, for example, to keep all blacks, Hispanics, women or Catholics off a jury if a prosecutor or defense attorney believes it is in his or her client's interest to do so.

To what extent a recent ruling in U.S. District Court in Brooklyn, N.Y., will affect this practice is not certain. Judge Eugene H. Nickerson in *McCray v. Abrams* held that the systematic exclusion of blacks and Hispanics from juries is unconstitutional. He said that such abuse would have to be determined at a court hearing. In the original *McCray* case, the prosecutor had 15 challenges. She used 11 and dismissed all seven blacks and one Hispanic in the jury pool. The defendant, Michael McCray, is black.

"The Constitution prohibits a strategy of keeping blacks off juries entirely, but is indifferent to a situation in which no blacks ever sit on juries in cases in which the defendant is black," the judge wrote. "The equal-protection clause prohibits racial discrimination not only because race is almost always irrelevant, but also because distinctions based on race are invidious."

The significance of Judge Nickerson's admirable ruling is not that an age-old practice will be eliminated. That hardly seems likely, because the 1965 U.S. Supreme Court case *Swain v. Alabama* authorizes the practice unless a pattern of prosecutorial abuse is established. Until that decision is altered or overturned, it remains law. However, in *Swain* five justices invited federal and state courts to reexamine the concept and Judge Nickerson responded.

The latest decision could be a forerunner of change at the highest level. It also doubtless will put trial lawyers on notice that blanket exclusion of minority group members will no longer be ignored by the presiding judge. To the extent that added restraint strengthens respect for the law and the judicial process, Judge Nickerson's decision will be a positive development. Former U.S. Supreme Court Justice Arthur J. Goldberg, who dissented in the 1965 *Swain* decision, said, "*Swain v. Alabama* has been thoroughly discredited."

If it helps to persuade the highest court on the right course of jurisprudence, so much the better.

The Orlando Sentinel
Orlando, Fla., May 22, 1984

For a lawyer, picking a jury is based in large part on old-fashioned gut instinct. Whether you serve on a jury may depend on everything from your age to your occupation to what you wear into the courtroom. Lawyers pick people that they think are likely to side with their cases. But the color of your skin shouldn't be a factor.

Yet race often is a factor, and for several months state legislators, prosecutors and defense attorneys have been trying to figure out how to prevent that. The debate grows out of two tense Miami trials where all-white juries cleared police officers in the deaths of two blacks. Some Miami lawmakers say blacks feel victimized and alienated by what they see as an all-white criminal justice system.

The anger and distrust won't be erased any time soon, but solving the problem is worth the effort. The potential is also there to produce a cure that is worse than the problem. The jury selection process shouldn't be made so restrictive that justice itself is the victim.

The best proposal is a bill in the House to let judges be the judge on whether attorneys are excluding people solely because of race. The judge would have the power to act, possibly even to declare a mistrial and start jury selection over with a new group of potential jurors.

The Senate — under pressure from prosecutors who don't want any change — has a different idea. It would limit the number of times an attorney can dismiss a potential juror without saying why. Instead of a maximum of 10 automatic challenges, each side would have only four. That plan doesn't solve the problem, though, and it ties the hands of attorneys.

Certainly, the defense attorney for a nuclear war protester doesn't want a jury of ex-military police on his hands. And he should be allowed to exclude those jurors without giving a reason. Cutting the number of challenges isn't the answer. Setting up a way to combat racially motivated jury selection is.

The problem is by no means restricted to Miami's courts. It is not unusual for blacks to be bumped from juries solely because the defendant or the victim is black too. In Orange County, blacks were excluded from juries in a highly publicized rape case and several murder trials because attorneys said they feared black jurors would be too easy on the accused. The same argument wasn't made about whites or women.

The House bill says that attorneys can still act on instinct in excluding potential jurors. The only restriction is that the reaction can't be to skin color. That's just. And justice is what the courts should be seeking.

The Oregonian

Portland, Ore., May 12, 1984

Have you noticed that the states have been executing more of their citizens lately? The U.S. Supreme Court, impatient with appeals, has a majority that wants to get on with executions. It is as if it believes life itself can be a cruel and unusual punishment if prolonged.

Capital punishment is "in" in America. More persons have been executed by the states in America this year than at any time since 1965. And the toll will grow, topping perhaps all modern records if the 1,350 inmates now on death row are executed at the current rate.

The only thing slowing the rate may be that the court's effort to speed up the system has confused it. Cutting out second and third postconviction appeals has made the outcome of emergency appeals more chaotic and less predictable, some defense lawyers have said. Supreme Court justices, The Wall Street Journal reported, still find themselves deliberating in the middle of the night while the executioner waits to pull the switch or push in the needle.

A minority on the court believes the state should not be allowed to execute its citizens. Justices William Brennan and Thurgood Marshall believe all executions are unconstitutional. "The court is deluding itself and the American people when it insists that those who have already been executed or are today condemned to death have been selected on a basis that is neither arbitrary nor capricious," the minority wrote recently.

Those who oppose generous appeals policies must accept the legal fiction that all defendants get strong court representation, that the poverty-stricken receive the same careful defense afforded by the wealthy, and that a rich man is as likely to be executed for murder as a person without means or friends.

A recent study shows that a person in Georgia is 10 times more likely to receive a death sentence for killing a white than for killing a black person. And in Florida, where the governor has signed 77 death warrants since 1979, the ratio is 8-1.

The U.S. Supreme Court, famous for reading election returns, must ask itself whether it is fair to track the pollsters where human life is the issue. The current sentiment found in polls makes the majority's job easier, because it reflects a strong revival of support for the death penalty. But should popular passion rule over law and equity?

Also, the court must ask itself whether human life should not have the same fair treatment in a civilized nation as property, or whether there ever can be enough equality in the courts to warrant giving the state the capricious power of life and death over those it governs.

The Dispatch

Columbus, Ohio, July 16, 1984

Death row is less the place it once was: a depository of men and a few women who languished in prison cells for years while interminable appeals were exhausted. Still, five death row inmates died last year of natural causes. Ironically, this matches the number executed during the year.

But the pendulum is swinging back and — good or bad — more inmates are making their date with the executioner. Even the methods by which they die are changing.

With five executions last year and 10 so far this year, the death sentence is becoming less a ritual of endless legal maneuvers and more a grim reality. The courts — including the U.S. Supreme Court, which during its just-completed term held that judges, in sentencing, could overrule juries that recommended leniency in capital cases — appear to be less sympathetic and more inclined to shorten the appeals process.

According to Justice Department statistics, a record 1,202 inmates were awaiting execution at the end of 1983, an increase of 13 percent from the previous year. Last year 113 left death row. Beyond the five who were executed, most others had sentences and convictions overturned.

The death row population typically consists of a male subject who has spent two years and four months there, is 31 years old and was convicted of another felony before being charged with a capital crime.

Racially, death row last year included 620 white inmates, 500 blacks, 72 Hispanics, 7 American Indians and 5 Asians.

There were only 13 women.

Forty-one percent of these inmates had completed high school, 44 percent never married, 20 percent were divorced or separated and 2 percent were widowed.

Geographically, 65 percent were from the South. Those executed were one each from Alabama, Florida, Georgia, Louisiana and Mississippi. Another 21 percent were from the West, 11 percent from the North Central States and 3 percent from the Northeast. In all, 38 states have capital punishment.

The largest death row populations were Florida (193), Texas (163), California (149) and Georgia (102). Ohio had 24 death row inmates as of May 1.

Electrocution, used in 18 states including Ohio, remains the most common method of execution. But four other states have added lethal injection as an option; two others converted from other means to injection; while eight other states use gas; four, hanging; and two, the firing squad.

The last person executed in Ohio was Donald L. Reinbolt of Columbus, who died in the electric chair on March 15, 1963, after conviction of first degree murder and armed robbery.

Without getting into the merits of capital punishment, all these numbers add up to one thing: Staying alive on death row is a lot harder than it used to be.

The Miami Herald

Miami, Fla., March 31, 1984

IN A pluralistic and dynamic society, it is no longer sufficient for Justice merely to be blind to an individual's color. Now she must also appear to be impartial. That more-difficult standard requires a careful re-examination of the practice of excluding some jurors from service in some trials on account of their race, sex, or ethnic origin.

Dade County Bar President Neal Sonnett commendably has taken on the difficult task of studying discrimination in jury selection. The fact that no blacks were accepted as jurors in any of the four recent trials in which white police officers were tried for killing black men has made obvious the need for such a study.

In one of those trials, Officer Robert Koenig was convicted of manslaughter in the death of Donald Harp. Thus it cannot reasonably be assumed that the race of the jurors necessarily determines their verdict in any particular case.

Nevertheless, it is common knowledge that lawyers use their right arbitrarily to exclude a certain number of jurors to influence the racial composition of a jury. That right, called the "peremptory" challenge to distinguish it from the challenge for cause, in which a reason must be given, is used by both sides. When the defendant is black, his lawyer might use the challenge simply to get rid of a white juror in order to make room for a black one. When the victim is black, the prosecutor might use it to try to eliminate a black juror.

The issue thus is complex though hardly new. Mr. Sonnett and his fellow trial lawyers already know well the intricacies of the jury-challenge technique. They know, too, the damage that is inflicted on the criminal-justice system's credibility when that technique is abused in a way that inflames public opinion and mocks the Constitution's guarantee of a fair trial.

It should not take three months for Mr. Sonnett's task force of lawyers and lay observers to study the issue and report on possible remedies. The Legislature opens its 1984 session on Tuesday and is scheduled to adjourn in June. If reform is to come this year, then, the task force must move quickly.

Outright abolition of the peremptory challenge certainly is a possibility, but other, less-drastic steps may prove equally satisfactory. A greater role for the judge in questioning or selecting jurors, for example, might suffice. Other states have grappled with the issue; their experience might hold a key that would serve Florida's needs.

Time is important, however. In the absence of a carefully considered report from the Sonnett task force, the Legislature might overreact and impose a draconian solution. Equally likely, the lawmakers could adjourn without taking any action on the jury proposals before them, thus reinforcing the impression of many black Floridians that the jury system is weighted against them.

The task force thus should move quickly to take advantage of the momentum of public opinion while deflecting any hasty overreaction.

Part IV: Politics

Municipal Politics: Black Leaders Gain Ground

1983 could be called the year of the black mayor. In municipal elections across the country, beginning with the Chicago mayoral race in April, black candidates were voted into office in a dramatic string of victories that many black leaders hoped would have important repercussions for the 1984 presidential election. Twenty black candidates became the mayors of cities with populations of more than 100,000; among the largest cities to elect blacks to their highest office were Chicago, Los Angeles, Philadelphia, Detroit, Washington, New Orleans and Atlanta. By the end of 1983, there were 248 black mayors nationwide, compared to 86 a decade earlier.

The widely publicized Chicago campaign was bitterly divisive, with race overshadowing all other issues and largely determining the breakdown of votes. But it was the exception. The race in Philadelphia, where W. Wilson Goode, a Democrat, defeated two white rivals, is often adduced as a contrast. Goode, 45, received about 25% of the white vote in a campaign that was conspicuously free of the racial slurs and unpleasant incidents that had marked the Chicago race. In Hartford and Birmingham, the incumbent black mayors easily won reelection; in other cities, the successful black candidates were city or state officials who also had a track record in office to rely upon, and the respective races of the candidates did not become an issue.

In many of the cities where black mayors were elected, the successful candidates benefited from large minority populations united by their aversion to the Reagan Administration. In addition, voter registration drives increased the registration of black and Hispanic voters in some cities by up to 25%. Often, the votes that elected a black candidate evinced a burgeoning coalition of blacks, Hispanics, and white, mostly young, liberals. Many black leaders expressed the hope that this new coalition, particularly if its turnout was high, could swing the nation's vote in 1984 to a Democratic presidential candidate.

As it turned out, that hope was not fulfilled, but the growing influence of black politicians in positions of power should not be underestimated. Blacks have headed major American cities for only about 15 years, and many of them took office during a period of urban economic decline; the mayors elected in 1983 must now cope with the great reduction in federal support channeled to city and state programs under the Reagan Administration. Nonetheless, many black mayors have made great progress in the hiring of minority municipal workers and allocation of funds for minority neighborhoods and businesses. Some of the hardest fights have occurred with labor unions over affirmative action plans for city police and fire departments. (See pp. 154-171.) Perhaps most importantly, the black leaders in America's cities are increasingly aligning themselves with the "mainstream" corporate community, and the political leaders of other cities, in order to achieve their goals.

Chicago Tribune
Chicago, Ill., April 14, 1983

Now if we can just get the gaper's block cleared, Chicago can get its show back on the road.

Eyed as a potential debacle, the mayoral election was instead a spectacular show of democracy. After weeks of brutal, sometimes shameful campaign warfare, 8 out of 10 Chicago voters surged to the polls and voted their minds in perhaps the most independent exercise of political freedom in the history of the city.

Those who saw it witnessed a revolution. What has been the most tightly controlled and bullied big city electorate in the country engaged in a free-for-all involving a woman incumbent, a black, an Irishman and a Republican Jew, then emerged intact with its head held high.

T . freedom to vote tamed the passions, just as freedom is supposed to do, and today Chicago's future rests on the cornerstones of an unlikely new coalition that, if nothing else, reflects this city's greatest traditions of diversity.

The optimism is mixed with equal measures of fear and skepticism, a natural consequence for the losers of any hard-fought battle. All the more so when the outcome means change so profound. Calming and comforting is the burden of the victors in a democracy. And that is Mayor-elect Harold Washington's greatest challenge.

Sure, the racial lines cut sharply with many voters. But in other places they blurred significantly, melding blacks, whites and Hispanics to give the first black mayor of Chicago his margin of victory. Two of 10 Chicagoans who did not share Harold Washington's race still shared in his election. And while that may not make this the world's capital of brotherly love, it is at least a good beginning.

Still, the mandate is a fragile one, and the tolerance for error will be small. The problem of race will not miraculously evaporate in the sunshine of the new dawn Mr. Washington proclaimed so eloquently when the vote was finally in Wednesday morning. His election did not prove race was irrelevant, only that it was not decisive. He will have to find further gracious words and gestures to soothe this city's raw spots. The record of past errors that nagged at Mr. Washington during the campaign undoubtedly cut away at his measure of support, but he can overcome it now by putting together a new record of achievement.

By then the eyes of the nation and the world will be turned elsewhere. They will have found new roads where men and women seem hell-bent on a collision course with history. Despite all of its political careening and the uncertain curves ahead, Chicago can be proud today of being the place where the accident did not happen.

The Philadelphia Inquirer
Philadelphia, Pa., April 15, 1983

The ifs and could-have-beens and maybes of Chicago's mayoral election will be hashed over for days, but one sturdy bit of evidence emerged Wednesday that the voters made the right decision in choosing Harold Washington over Bernard J. Epton. That came when Mr. Epton did not appear at the city's "unity luncheon" that was attended by Mr. Washington, the two politicians he defeated in the Democratic primary in February — outgoing Mayor Jane Byrne and Cook County State's Attorney Richard M. Daley — as well as about 30 religious, civic and political leaders. It was a gathering to symbolize the need for Chicagoans to come together in the wake of a particularly divisive election.

By every bit of reckoning but one, Mr. Epton should have made it to the luncheon. With race having been the principal issue, Chicago has been through the most polarizing election in its colorful, tumultuous political history, tearing the social fabric of the city in ways that will not be repaired easily or quickly. But a show of unity and acceptance of the voters' decision is a time-honored American political tradition, and thus Mr. Epton owed it to the 617,000 men and women who voted for him — 48.3 percent of the electorate — as well as to the city at large to have appeared at the luncheon. His stated reason for being absent and sending his brother in his stead — that the invitation came too late — has a very hollow ring.

The one valid excuse that Mr. Epton might have had for skipping the luncheon was that the strain of the campaign and disappointment of losing a real chance to be Chicago's first Republican mayor in more than half a century simply overwhelmed him. There is evidence of that in his bitter, ill-mannered post-election comments about his "black friends," Mr. Washington and the news media and his refusal to concede or congratulate the mayor-elect. So, if those statements reflected his state of mind, as they apparently did, it may be that Mr. Epton only would have made matters worse if he had attended.

In either case, whether Mr. Epton is simply a bad loser or a man pushed by events beyond the pale, there can be little doubt now that Mr. Washington is better fitted by experience and temperament to govern Chicago. And that, in the final analysis, not the fact that Mr. Washington will be Chicago's first black mayor, will be of lasting importance to the people of the city. By not making the effort to attend the unity luncheon, Mr. Epton revealed himself as either a man incapable of standing up to the political heat or a man whose self-interest left him without the faintest concept of what will be required to make the best of Chicago's political polarization and make the "city that works" start working again.

The Idaho STATESMAN

Boise, Idaho, April 15, 1983

For Chicago Mayor-elect Harold Washington, it was a night to be optimistic: "Chicago has seen the bright daybreak for this city and perhaps the whole country," he proclaimed. "Blacks, whites, Hispanics, Jews, Gentiles, Protestants and Catholics of all stripes have joined hands to form a new Democratic coalition."

Perhaps, but we doubt many Chicagoans bubbled over with such sentiments after enduring a campaign riddled by racism and charges of corruption. Neither Washington nor Bernard Epton, the Republican candidate, conducted the sort of campaign that could be confused with a "bright daybreak."

In fact, this campaign — like the erratic "reform" tenure of Jane Byrne, Washington's predecessor — was an all-too-clear reminder that some of our country's biggest cities are floundering without leadership and effective governments. Chicago, for years known as "the city that works," began to lose that reputation after the death of Mayor Richard Daley, the strongman who headed the last of the great urban political machines.

Cleveland suffered through more than a decade of fiscal and racial discord after a similarly divisive election that was heralded as a vote to break the power of a machine and lead to a brighter future.

We shed no tears at the demise of Boss Daley's machine. But it is ironic — and troubling — to realize that democracy failed to produce an effective successor to Hizzoner when it gave Chicago the caustic Byrne. In the racist, vitriolic campaign of 1983, it may have failed again.

The Washington Post
Times Herald

Washington, D.C., April 12, 1983

MERCIFULLY, Chicago's mayoral campaign has ended. The accounts of that campaign were ample cause for despair. But many lessons one might be inclined to draw from tonight's election results have more to do with one huge, complicated city than with national patterns of race relations or party politics. As Hamilton Jordan observes on the opposite page, the Chicago election is not a microcosm of black/white political relations nationally.

Both candidates, Republican Bernard Epton and Democrat Harold Washington, indulged in villainy: Mr. Epton with his ambiguously race-baiting slogan, "Before it's too late," and Rep. Washington with his narrowly racial "We want it all." Mr. Epton's record on race, however, has been outstanding as a liberal state legislator. And Rep. Washington has followed earlier divisive statements that emphasized disdain for deals with white power brokers with less visible efforts to garner white support and build an inclusive transition team. On balance, the two candidates aren't villains, but they did precious little to resist the mounting ugliness. Each sought to gain from it, and in the process proved himself no nobler than the grimy process.

A more attractive black candidate with a more conciliatory campaign style would obviously have done a better job of holding white Democratic voters. It may be true that most whites just aren't "ready," as they say. But the events in Chicago are not a good indicator of broad backlash. There are too many special circumstances: from Jane Byrne to Jesse Jackson, from the decaying Daley machine to the politicized police force.

Beyond Chicago, there are more and more signs of effective black political participation across the nation. Growing numbers of black candidates not only claim a solid base among black voters, but reach out to address a broad range of issues and compete with some success for white votes. *That* is the dominant pattern. The lesson from Chicago is that the impressive political strength blacks now can wield in many places should be nurtured, not squandered by flawed candidates and reckless campaign tactics.

It is already a cliché to say that everyone has lost in Chicago, whatever the outcome of the vote. Only a miracle of successful leadership on the part of the new mayor can bind the wounds and make Chicago a winner. That would provide the most important lesson of all.

TULSA WORLD

Tulsa, Okla., April 7, 1983

THE RACE for mayor of Chicago has taken a dismal turn. It now appears the election might be decided by the color of the candidates' skin rather than any legitimate campaign issue.

Harold Washington, the Democratic candidate, is black. Bernard Epton, the Republican, is white.

Washington won the Democratic primary in an upset, garnering only slightly more than one-third of the votes in a three-way contest. Despite that vulnerability, the Democratic party was expected to close ranks behind the nominee and continue Chicago's tradition of Democratic mayors.

That has not happened. Instead, the race issue has monopolized the public's attention and some Democratic ward leaders are defecting to Epton.

There are legitimate questions about Washington's past. He served a prison sentence for failing to file federal income tax returns and was suspended from the practice of law in 1970 for failing to provide paid-for legal services. But there is a widely-publicized perception in Chicago, right or wrong, that Washington's record has become merely an excuse for opposing him because he is black. Washington's critics say he raised the racial spectre himself by repeatedly telling black voters, "Now, it's our turn."

One cannot sit in Tulsa and accurately judge the motives of voters in Chicago. But this much is certain: It is a shame that skin color is even mentioned as a decisive issue in an American election in 1983.

It says that America is a long way from the Promised Land of true racial brotherhood and equality.

Los Angeles Times

Los Angeles, Calif., April 15, 1983

Even if he had not been elected in the most divisive and racist campaign in Chicago history, Harold Washington would still face daunting challenges as he prepares to move into City Hall.

The nation's second largest city is in deep financial trouble. It will be almost impossible for the schools to balance their next budget. The two transit districts serving the city are broke. And Illinois state government is in no position to come to the rescue as it has in the past.

But of equal urgency is the manner in which Chicago's first black mayor moves to heal the wounds from his brawling encounter with Republican Bernard Epton. Washington will take office with the knowledge that only 18% of the city's whites support him, and he will head a police department that was openly pro-Epton.

The mayor-elect must persuade his political opponents that he will treat them fairly; at the same time, he must try to satisfy the expectations of his black supporters, who were promised a more important role in the governing of Chicago. It must be said of Epton that he was a poor loser and left it to Washington to appeal for unity and tolerance.

The test now is whether Washington will have a chance to prove, as other black mayors have proved—certainly in Los Angeles—that race is irrelevant to honest and effective government. But that will depend as much on his willingness to forgo vindictiveness as it will on the acceptance by white citizens of the fact that the city has a black mayor, whether they like it or not.

Washington's acceptance by the white majority could banish once and for all the divisive legacy of the late Mayor Richard Daley. Daley held absolute control over the city for two decades by playing off one ethnic bloc against another, but granting enough patronage to all to keep them in line.

It may be a forlorn hope, given the bitter contest preceding his election, but the new mayor has an opportunity to do more than govern the city wisely. A successful administration would be the first step toward bringing Chicago together.

The Seattle Times

Seattle, Wash., April 14, 1983

THE choices — Republican Bernard Epton and Democrat Harold Washington — weren't all that great. And the campaigns of each scarcely were models of the political process at its best.

Mediocrity, in fact, long has marked politics in a city where joblessness is among the nation's highest and the budget deficit exceeds a staggering $1 billion.

The heavy problems afflicting Chicago got far less attention in the Washington-Epton contest than the racist appeals of both sides: Epton campaigning on TV for election of a white mayor "Before It's Too Late," and Washington exhorting his fellow blacks to support him because "It's Our Turn."

Given the agitated state of race relations in the nation's third-largest city, it is good that Washington was able to eke out his narrow (less than 3 percent) margin of victory, although the results are likely to mean that the nation will see more, rather than less, of race as an electoral issue in the months ahead. The Rev. Frank Watkins, press secretary for the Rev. Jesse Jackson's Operation PUSH, said yesterday: "The nationalization of the Chicago election has inspired and galvanized black voters around the country and around the world. It gives greater emphasis and momentum to the idea of a black presidential candidacy."

All in all, it was a tawdry, lackluster affair that got widespread notice because of the race issue and because of its litmus-test implications for Republican and Democratic fortunes nationally.

"The whole nation is watching," Washington said in an acceptance speech pledging an effort to heal the city's wounds. But most Americans doubtless disliked much of what they saw in the weeks leading up to Tuesday's vote.

The Salt Lake Tribune

Salt Lake City, Utah, April 14, 1983

Since he's a Democrat, there shouldn't be much surprise that Harold Washington was elected Chicago's new mayor. It's because he's the city's first black mayor that creates special attention and speculation.

Had Mr. Washington's opponent, Bernard Epton, won, that he is white might not have been as important as the first victory by a Republican in a citywide Chicago election in 52 years. Democrats have for five decades controlled Chicago politics. They still do. But that situation is now fatefully entangled with racial issues.

The Chicago campaign, as exhaustively reported, brought out all the city's race-based undercurrents. The black-white divisions were pitted against each other as never before, in appeals for support or rejection of either Mr. Washington or Mr. Epton. The candidates themselves tried to downplay that aspect, but neither was successful.

Now Mr. Washington has won. Will racial differences dredged to the surface recede as the city returns to day-to-day living? Or has too much been said--and heard--to allow return of pre-campaign normalcy?

The answers could depend substantially on how Mr. Washington mayors, to a lesser but pertinent extent on how Mr. Epton soothes his partisans. As candidate, Mayor-elect Washington described himself as leader of a reform movement, determined to give everyone a fair shake in Chicago. Some analysts claim it was this theme which attracted "liberal" non-black city voters to his side.

If Mr. Washington can make the changes that effectively distribute the "spoils," if his programs and policies do heal the wounds and defuse bitterness, if the wait-and-see period is used to demonstrate that Harold Washington is a mayor for all of Chicago, not selected parts, the city, one of the nation's mightiest, will persevere, no worse off than for the fact that another Democrat has won 'another term in the mayor's office.

ALBUQUERQUE JOURNAL

Albuquerque, N.M., April 14, 1983

After all the hot air of a particularly vituperative campaign, the Windy City has elected its first black mayor by giving the nod to Democrat Harold Washington.

Chicago voters turned out in record numbers to give Washington a narrow margin of victory.

And rarely has one election seemingly offered grist for so many pet theory mills.

The choice for Chicagoans was between electing the first black in history or the first Republican in a half century. Perhaps the result shows residents of Illinois' largest city fear Republicans more than blacks?

The choice for Chicagoans was between a candidate offering a thinly veneered appeal to racial fear and a candidate with a history of financial and legal difficulties. Perhaps the results show Chicagoans are more tolerant of financial peccadillos than of racism?

We doubt both of the above and, in advance, most of the finely cast analysis sure to be offered by national commentators of print and tube.

The results in fact probably include hefty minority doses of racial pride and racial prejudice. But the primary deciding factors most likely were the candidates' stands on local Chicago issues such as services and parks and taxes and all the other little issues that are the preoccupations of municipal government.

That part of the race is not national news, of course, so we in the hinterlands haven't been exposed to much of it.

The pending job for Mayor-elect Washington — and the Chicago electorate — is to turn their backs on all of the national publicity the racial aspect of their election has engendered, and get on with the job of running their dynamic city.

Politics in the Windy City have come a long way since the days of the Daley machine, the last of the urban political dinosaurs left from the era of city hall "bosses."

THE ATLANTA CONSTITUTION
Atlanta, Ga., March 29, 1983

"I have never seen such hate — not in Mississippi or Alabama — as I see here in Chicago." — Dr. Martin Luther King Jr., Aug. 6, 1966.

There is no question that both Chicago and the nation have changed for the better since those tortured days 17 years ago, when a violent white mob attacked King and his followers while they demonstrated for open housing. The raw hatred of those times — in the North and South — has long since faded into an obligatory lip service, at least, to racial equality and toleration.

But there are aberrations. One of those unfolded Sunday as Harold Washington — a black man, a Democrat and a candidate for mayor of Chicago — encountered an ugly group of jeering white demonstrators outside a church on the city's northwest side. The crowd (numbering around 150) prevented Washington and former Vice President Walter Mondale from worshiping.

In a matter of minutes, the Chicago demonstrators managed to rip the mask from the code words and symbolism that usually disguise racial issues in American politics. They illuminated an important if not terribly surprising point: While we have made much progress as a nation of blacks and whites working together, we have a long way to go. The old dragon of visceral racism isn't dead yet.

But there is an irony here, too. Sunday's demonstrators, from Chicago's old Polish, Italian and Irish neighborhoods, believe that blacks already have uprooted them from their homes. "To them, Harold Washington's presence represents the beginning of blacks uprooting them again," said the Rev. Francis Ciezadlo, pastor of the church.

The irony is this: That whites feel politically threatened at all is a sign of progress. It indicates that blacks — in the tradition of the Irish and other ethnic groups — are slowly making their way into the mainstream of American life through the doors of city hall.

With each new push, of course, there has been resistance. But at the same time, the politics of racial inclusion are chalking up some impressive gains — from Atlanta to Los Angeles to Detroit to Richmond to Augusta to Birmingham to New Orleans.

The Chicago demonstrators represent only a pocket of protest against the much larger trend of black inclusion. Ultimately, their angry sentiments will melt into oblivion — where they belong.

As the Irish discovered in the 19th century, urban political control does not mean instant economic gain. But it's a start. The first step toward progress, after all, is simply playing the game. In Chicago, blacks are finally making their move. The assorted white ethnic groups of that great city shouldn't have too much trouble understanding that.

The Morning News
Wilmington, Del., April 14, 1983

THE JOKES HAVE BEGUN. "Chicago, the city where many voter registrations are carved in stone." "With 100 percent of the vote in, Harold Washington narrowly won the race for mayor of Chicago. Supporters of Bernard Epton are waiting, however, until 110 percent of the vote is in before they will consider conceding defeat."

The Windy City has always been the butt of political jokes, but it drew new attention to itself with Tuesday's close election of Mr. Washington as the city's first black mayor. What happened in Chicago during this vicious campaign was no joke. It made race the overriding issue of an election in which both candidates glibly insisted it was no issue at all.

It is conceivable that many Chicagoans voted against Harold Washington not because he is black but truly because he served 36 days in jail for failing to file income tax returns for four years. They may indeed have voted against him because he was suspended from practicing law for five years for failing to perform legal services for which he had been paid.

Many white Chicagoans who traditionally vote Democratic contend that those were the reasons. It would be easier to accept that claim if Chicago voters were not traditionally less than fastidious about the political cleanliness of white Democratic candidates for office.

It is conceivable that many registered Democrats voted for Bernard Epton because they truly found him qualified to be the city's first Republican mayor in half a century. That would be easier to accept if Mr. Epton were not so obviously a cipher in Chicago's ranks of formidable political candidates.

What is apparent in this election is that the reasons voters give for supporting whom they do are not necessarily the real reasons. Even clearer is that the polarization of Chicago by the Epton-Washington contest cannot simply be transferred to every metropolitan mayoralty where white and black candidates oppose each other. Nor can it simply be translated into a floodtide of black influence in national politics, particularly presidential politics.

Had Harold Washington's background been impeccably virtuous and had Bernard Epton's administrative qualifications been overwhelming, it might be possible to make a persuasive case that race was the only factor in Chicago.

That is not the case. Harold Washington is now in the position of a man whose partisans want desperately for him to succeed and whose opponents are equally eager for him to fail.

At the moment, he is being watched simply as the first black man to be mayor of Chicago. Other U.S. cities have black mayors. Some are outstanding, others are not. Four years from now, Harold Washington will still be black but he will also have had the opportunity to assure that he is judged then for his performance as a Chicago mayor, not as a Chicago black.

Roanoke Times & World-News
Roanoke, Va., April 3, 1983

CHICAGO is not noted for blending grace, chivalry, or even standard decency into its political life. So the nation shouldn't have been surprised to see the "Abomination of Desolation," — political bile mixed with racism, if you will — standing in the holy place in the Windy City. And Palm Sunday was an appropriately inappropriate time for it to appear.

Nobody should have expected the Chicago partisans to greet former Vice President Walter F Mondale as if he were entering the city on the colt of an ass. But they didn't have to act like braying donkeys when he appeared.

Mondale chose Palm Sunday to make a symbolic appearance at a Palm Sunday church service with Rep. Harold Washington, the Democratic Party's candidate for Chicago's mayorship. Mondale was there to heal the wound created by his endorsement of one of Washington's opponents, Richard M. Daley, in the Democratic primary.

As they entered St. Pascal Catholic Church on the northwest side of Chicago, demonstrators swarmed onto the church steps, booing loudly and chanting the name of Washington's white Republican opponent, Bernard E. Epton. They also chanted "carpetbagger Mondale," using an epithet employed by white Southerners to deride Yankee opportunists who came South during Reconstruction.

The two Democrats chose to leave the church rather than subject the congregation to that kind of agitation. That, at least, was a graceful thing to do.

Neither Mondale nor Washington is above criticism. Choosing a place of worship on a sacred occasion to make a symbolic political statement isn't the height of good taste. Washington is a man who — whether intentionally or through inexcusable negligence — broke the federal tax laws and spent time in jail for it; that makes him vulnerable to attack from angles other than racism.

But the clowns who swarmed over the church steps to hurl their political insults overstepped the limits of good taste. Their actions were so reprehensible that even Epton disavowed them. Let us hope the candidate continues to rise above the level of some of the people who support him.

THE COMMERCIAL APPEAL
Memphis, Tenn., April 14, 1983

THE BROAD SHOULDERS that have come to symbolize Chicago will soon belong to a black mayor.

Between those shoulders is a mind that has marked Harold Washington as intense, hard-working and politically astute. It helped him parlay the hopes of black Chicagoans into a historic political victory that has caught the attention of the entire nation. It gave him confidence to pledge to destroy a machine that rewards political allegiance at the expense of job performance.

THE OTHER SIDE of Harold Washington is his conviction for not filing federal income tax returns, his law license suspension for accepting fees for legal work he never performed and his curious history of not paying bills. He did a masterful job of bringing neophytes into the political process, but he hurt his own cause immediately after the Democratic primary by not alleviating the concerns of traditional white Democrats. They were rightfully puzzled by his election-night remarks and those by Jesse Jackson that, "It's our turn" and "We want it all."

What does he want now? Washington may have been hinting at it during his early morning acceptance speech when he told supporters, "I will initiate your reforms. But I challenge you, I charge each and every one of you, to rededicate your efforts to heal the divisions that have plagued us."

The power of Chicago's mayor may be limited in these post-Daley years. But if there's something he can do, it is to instill a feeling throughout the city that he really will be the mayor for *all* of Chicago.

PLAYING PEACEMAKER should not deter Washington from keeping his main campaign promise, though, which is following through on federal court decisions to abolish a patronage system that benefits the pols more than the taxpayers. Eight years ago, he told a newspaper columnist that while he wanted changes in the patronage system, he did not want it abolished. "It helped other ethnic groups," he said at the time. "Why should it be denied use by my people?"

Much has happened since then, including the disappointing administration of Jane Byrne, who had promised to eliminate patronage and ended up using it for her own purposes. Washington will be similarly tempted to use the system to reward his friends. But his campaign pledge was clear. Even in a city where patronage has been refined to an art form, Chicago should be able to survive its passing much as other cities across the country have.

The worldwide spotlight will soon shift from Chicago, leaving the analysis of that city's interesting politics where it belongs —to Chicagoans. Before that attention is diverted, though, Memphians and others across the country would do well to remember Washington's name. As mayor of the nation's second-largest city, as a black leader with the largest constituency, as an outspoken opponent of Reaganomics, Washington will doubtless wield influence in national party politics.

UNTIL A MORE dramatic victory is achieved, Washington will symbolize a demonstration of black political power of a different sort from those that filled the '60s. The battleground this time is the ballot box. It was made possible only after large voter-registration drives that Washington considered a prerequisite for his campaign. Washington received nearly all the votes cast by blacks, a majority of votes registered by Hispanics, but slightly less than 20 per cent of votes cast by whites, election day polls indicate. Voting returns show that many neighborhoods went solidly for Washington or for his Republican opponent, Bernard Epton.

That does not show a cross section of support that most leaders like to have when they begin an administration. As dramatic a victory as Tuesday's election was, a greater one may be achieved over time if Washington's broad shoulders represent a renaissance for Chicago on this, its 150th birthday.

St. Petersburg Times
St. Petersburg, Fla., April 14, 1983

The racist campaign that threatened to tear Chicago apart will pose difficult challenges for Rep. Harold Washington as the city's first black mayor. Deep hatreds will not be dispelled easily, and only good government for all the people will begin to heal the bitter divisions that afflict the nation's second largest city.

If the Congress needs evidence that the U.S. Civil Rights Commission should be renewed for 20 years when it expires in September, the Chicago campaign offered urgent proof that the commission has plenty of unfinished business in dealing with the pervasive problems of discrimination and prejudice.

PRESIDENT REAGAN has proposed reauthorization of the commission, whose work during the past 25 years has contributed much to the nation's civil rights progress by monitoring all levels of government for their compliance with and enforcement of the civil rights laws. The Congress should act promptly to assure that the commission's work goes on.

The Chicago campaign, one of the most vicious in history, exposed the ugliest sores of hatred and fear that fester not only in that troubled city, but across the nation. With the campaign's end, the healing can begin.

If Chicago's ordeal raises the nation's consciousness of the racism so deeply ingrained in our society and inspires the public conscience to deal with it, all Americans will benefit.

As a nation, the past 25 years have taught us that much of the prejudice and fear that fire racial tension can be dispelled by communication, understanding and simple human fairness. That lesson can be extended to Chicago.

The Kansas City Times
Kansas City, Mo., April 14, 1983

That black power affirmed by radicals more than a decade ago has been transformed into ballot power in the nation's second largest city, Chicago. The undercurrents of race and racism in the Chicago election — as exploited by both candidates, their advisers, political workers and the public — will remain deplorable. They are hostile to the stability of the American political system, which repeatedly has shown it can adjust as previously disenfranchised voters discover their power and flex their muscles.

Racism in Chicago will be a very tough nut to crack; however, putting cynicism aside for the moment, the mayor-elect has a great opportunity to demonstrate magnanimity toward those who opposed him so hatefully. That will be but the first step if Chicago is to evolve as a city that can look beyond the color of a candidate's skin to find leadership. How the city handles this fateful issue undoubtedly will influence the shape of national politics for some time to come.

The election of Rep. Harold Washington, a Democrat who ran mostly against the power of the white-dominated Democratic machine, is proof that political power comes from voter registration, organizing, identification with a candidate and marching to the polls on election day. Around the core of black voter support for Mr. Washington, however, were a sufficient number of white — Democratic? — votes to make his victory possible.

Mr. Washington's race against the Republican candidate, Bernard Epton, is a national political story because race almost always is high on the agenda of national politics. The Washington victory cannot be seen as an end in itself, but as a step in the evolving American system. Already there is talk, however hasty, of 1984 being the year that one or more blacks will make serious bids for president or vice president. That is a welcome development.

Beyond that, though, what happens in Chicago during Mr. Washington's four-year term will be watched by people of all races and political persuasions for clues to the shape of politics in this decade and beyond. But first, his task is to preside over what has become an ever harder city to govern. He should be judged by how he accomplishes that. The rest is secondary.

Mr. Washington has promised to dismantle the remnants of the Daley Democratic machine, which already has fallen into disrepair. Many surely assume that he will signal to blacks that it's now their day to feast at the table of spoils politics. Nothing could please white racists more. The tone of Mr. Washington's campaign, however, leaves one with the hope that he will resist pressures to do that — that he will strive for a city government that rises from the decaying frame of the old machine and gradually adapts to less divisive ways of running one of the nation's most important cities. We wish him luck, courage and success.

The San Diego Union
San Diego, Calif., April 10, 1983

Racism undoubtedly will be the reason for some votes in the Chicago mayoral election Tuesday. But it is highly unfair to categorize as racist all voters who eschew black Democrat Harold Washington for white Republican Bernard E. Epton.

Indeed, the Democratic Party may lose the Chicago mayorship for the first time since 1927, but not entirely for reasons of race. Rather, because of Mr. Washington's questionable background and his pledge to abolish political patronage.

In the context of Chicago politics, Mr. Washington's promise has profound implications. For years, under the late Mayor Richard Daley, the city's Democratic machine dispensed patronage appointments and other largesse through the party's ward organizations. It was a system accepted with few reservations in the white ethnic neighborhoods that strongly supported the late mayor. But blacks, who now comprise 40 percent of the city's population, were permitted only limited access to political rewards.

Mr. Washington's plan to fill city jobs on the basis of merit, therefore, has particular appeal to blacks. It is unlikely, however, that so many of the city's Democratic ward leaders would turn their backs on their own party's nominee, if Mr. Washington had not threatened their turf by promising to take away their patronage power and fill city jobs on the basis of merit.

Actually, Mr. Epton's own pledge to be fair as a Republican mayor in filling city jobs offers the Democratic regulars far more hope for retaining power. It is Mr. Washington's record that is deservedly a dominant issue with many, and perhaps a majority, of Chicago voters. He has served time in jail for federal income tax evasion. He failed to file his federal tax returns for 19 consecutive years. He was suspended from the Illinois bar for bilking his clients. And, he has been sued a number of times for failing his creditors.

Many voters, especially in the white ethnic neighborhoods where the work ethic remains powerful, find Mr. Washington's sins of omission and commission sufficient reason to vote Republican.

Although Mr. Washington castigates his opponents as racist, it was he who stooped to a blatantly racial appeal in the Democratic primary, which he won with about a third of the vote.

His slogan, "It's Our Turn," helped him win an unusually large black vote. His two primary opponents' incumbent Jane Byrne amd Richard Daley, son of the late mayor, split the white vote and, thereby, made possible Mr. Washington's minority victory for the Democratic nomination

An appeal for blacks to support one of their own differs little from ethnic politics practiced, for example, by Jewish and Italian candidates in New York, and Irish candidates in Boston.

After Mr. Washington won the nomination, however, he did little to assure white voters that he would look after their interests. To the contrary, he threatened them with possible violence in the streets, if blacks "get the feeling that this campaign is going to turn into a race war."

Mr. Washington also rejected an offer from Mr. Epton, who has a strong civil rights record, to agree jointly that racism has no place in the campaign.

Although Mr. Washington has been leading in the polls, he is said to be slipping and could lose Tuesday's election. If this happens, Mr. Washington will not be a victim of racism so much as a victim of his own scandalous record, his insensitivity to whites, and his threat to other Democratic politicians.

The News American
Baltimore, Md., April, 12, 1983

Thank heavens the Chicago election ends today. A nastier, dirtier campaign we cannot remember. And the unfortunate part about it is that, no matter who wins — Harold Washington, a black Democratic congressman, or Bernard Epton, a white Jewish Republican — a major American city has been polarized passionately between black and white.

Even in the closing moments of the campaign the racial rhetoric continued. When Epton refused to appear on the same television show with Washington, Washington said, "He won't even sit in the same room with me. He thinks he's in South Africa." Epton responded by deploring Washington's tactic of using race as an issue, but did not back away from using a thinly-veiled racial slogan.

Chicago's problems — like any major city she has plenty — have been playing second fiddle to the mud-slinging and the charges and counter charges on the part of both candidates. The hatred this all has engendered will be a long time dying in the Windy City. The only hope is that other cities will take note and try to avoid a duplication.

THE CHRISTIAN SCIENCE MONITOR
Boston, Mass., May 19, 1983

Voters in Philadelphia have shown that a mayoral campaign between a black candidate and a white candidate need not degenerate into a nasty, no-holds-barred contest where race becomes the dominant issue. Exit polls in Tuesday's Democratic primary — where former City Manager W. Wilson Goode defeated former Mayor Frank Rizzo — indicated that large numbers of voters perceived the contest in terms of substantive issues, i.e., who would do the best job regarding city finances, transportation, housing.

That is not to deny that race was a factor. It was. But, as Mr. Goode observed after his victory, it was not "the" issue, as it largely was in Chicago last month where Congressman Harold Washington barely squeaked past a white Republican opponent in that city's general election. In the Chicago primary contest, it might be recalled, Mr. Washington won very few white votes. In Tuesday's Philadelphia primary, by contrast, Mr. Goode won in part by appealing to white voters, although, as expected, he snapped up black wards by large percentages.

Mr. Goode carried impressive credentials from 17 years of public service to the nation's fourth-largest city. A sharecropper's son, he is a graduate of the prestigious Wharton School and knows as much about Philadelphia's financial situation as anyone in that city. And, unlike Mr. Washington in Chicago, he has no clouded history of disbarment and unpaid income taxes.

Philadelphia has not had a Republican mayor since 1947. Will the race issue become more of a factor in the general election in November? One trusts that will not be the case. Mr. Goode's GOP opponent, financier John Egan, has indicated that he wants to wage a campaign based solely on issues.

The Philadelphia primary vote, like the Chicago election last month, underscores just how unpredictable the racial element is in the larger national political process. If Mr. Goode becomes mayor there will be blacks at the helm in four of the nation's six largest cities — including Tom Bradley in Los Angeles and Coleman Young in Detroit.

The national political parties will undoubtedly take careful note of the fact that blacks now are registering in unprecedented numbers in many communities. The political landscape is changing.

The Miami Herald
Miami, Fla., May 21, 1983

PHILADELPHIA offers a most refreshing contrast to Chicago in the comparative conduct of the two cities' mayoral campaigns. It offers valuable lessons that political leaders elsewhere, including Miami, ought not overlook.

A black man, Harold Washington, became Chicago's new mayor only after an ugly campaign in which both he and his white opponents shamelessly exploited the issue of race. That was irresponsible political leadership. It inflamed racial division in Chicago. It already hampers Mayor Washington's ability to govern.

Another black man, W. Wilson Goode, won the Democratic nomination for mayor of Philadelphia on Tuesday. He defeated former Philadelphia mayor Frank L. Rizzo. They avoided Chicago-style racial mud-slinging, and thereby served their city well.

That is not to say that the question of race was unimportant in Philadelphia Blacks voted overwhelmingly for Mr. Goode, whites disproportionately for Mr. Rizzo. Ethnic loyalty is always a factor in American politics. Recognition of that gave rise to party ticket-balancing, such as when party slates include perhaps one Italian, one Jewish, and one Irish candidate. When black-white competition enters American politics, ethnic consciousness intensifies, as anyone even dimly aware of U.S. history knows.

"Race is always a factor," Mr. Goode acknowledged upon winning. "The thing you try to work through in all [campaigns] like this is to make sure that it does not become the issue. I'm convinced it was not the issue in this campaign."

To the extent that it was not, it is because Mr. Goode and Mr. Rizzo, to their enormous credit, pledged early on to refrain from remarks that might inflame racial division. Both stood by their pledges. The racial issue was an unavoidable undercurrent, but it was never made into demagogery by either candidate.

That's responsible political leadership. Philadelphia is better off for it. May it continue to characterize the campaign in the City of Brotherly Love on through to the general election in November.

And may the political candidates in other American cities with ethnically diverse voting blocs — such as Miami — emulate the example set in Philadelphia.

THE MILWAUKEE JOURNAL
Milwaukee, Wisc., May 19, 1983

W. Wilson Goode's defeat of redoubtable former Mayor Frank Rizzo in Philadelphia's Democratic mayoral primary sets the stage for a November contest with Republican John Egan in which Goode is likely to become the first black mayor of the City of Brotherly Love. Goode's primary victory, like Chicago Mayor Harold Washington's earlier triumph, further demonstrates blacks' new strength in American politics.

Unlike Chicago's election, Philadelphia's contest did not have strong racial overtones. Goode asked less directly for black votes than had Washington. And even Rizzo, strongly identified with Philadelphia's white ethnics, largely eschewed racial rhetoric. Moreover, while Washington got only 6% of the white vote in his primary race, Goode captured about 25% of the votes of Philadelphia's white Democrats.

Does this mean that racial feelings are less strong in Philadelphia than in Chicago? Perhaps not. However, to its credit, Philadelphia managed to have an election in which race did not become the campaign's dominant element. The city's task is to maintain that low-key approach to race through the November election.

As for the emergence of black political strength, the new element appears to be the fervent conviction among black voters that black candidates can win. That new-found faith has made the difference between apathy and activism. Admittedly, blacks take some heat for exerting their power as a voting bloc, but that has been the path to political power of every other group in America.

If Goode wins in November, four of the nation's six largest cities will have black mayors; already in office are Washington in Chicago, Tom Bradley in Los Angeles and Coleman Young in Detroit. These elections are changing the nature of leadership in the black community. Non-elected black leaders drawn from the church or the civil rights movement or community action groups should not be disparaged. They still have a vital role, including that of keeping black politicians accountable.

Yet the sometimes rough-tongued Young of Detroit once said that there was a difference between a leader who "runs his mouth" and one who, like Young, "runs a city." The election of more black mayors places blacks at the levers of real political power and helps make political participation a valid option for black citizens. That's solid progress.

The Times-Picayune
The States-Item
New Orleans, La., May 19, 1983

W. Wilson Goode's defeat of former Mayor Frank L. Rizzo in Philadelphia's Democratic primary is tantamount to his election as that city's first black mayor. He already is the first black Democratic nominee for mayor of Philadelphia. Mr. Goode, the son of a sharecropper, must defeat Republican John Egan in November's general election, but in a city where Democrats hold a 5-to-1 margin, he should surmount the opposition with ease.

If elected, Mr. Goode will take his place on the growing list of "firsts" for black candidates nationwide. In fact, the election of black mayors is becoming so commonplace that it may soon draw no more attention than the launching of yet another satellite. Among the larger cities with black mayors are Los Angeles, Chicago, Detroit, Newark, New Orleans and Atlanta. Many smaller cities and towns have black mayors and other top elected officials.

The election of Democrat Harold Washington as mayor of Chicago drew concentrated national attention because of the dramatic nature of the contest — the dying gasp of the machine politics that had ruled the city for generations and a campaign with unbridled racial overtones. But if racism was a major factor in the Philadelphia primary, it was more subtle.

As a former chairman of the Pennsylvania Public Utility Commission and for three years managing director of Philadelphia's city government under retiring Mayor William Green, Mr. Goode already was a familiar face to Philadelphians. He also appears to be professionally qualified to be mayor.

While the voting divided largely along racial lines, Mr. Goode, recognizing, as do other modern mayors, the need for unity, declined to call his nomination a triumph for blacks exclusively. Still, there is no denying that his victory is one more sign of the maturation of black politics in America. And that is all to the good, for pluralism is what American society, politics and government are supposed to be all about.

The steady increase of blacks in politics presages the maturing of American society and government. We will have arrived when the election of yet another black mayor is no longer cause for special comment.

THE PLAIN DEALER
Cleveland, Ohio, May 19, 1983

In rejecting the politics of bluster and bigotry, Philadelphia's Democratic voters this week wisely returned former Mayor Frank L. Rizzo to the retirement he deserved. His two terms in office during the 1970s were marked by tumultuous relations with anyone who disagreed with him and blunt remarks that many blacks and others considered racist. Thus it was a sweet primary victory for W. Wilson Goode, a former city managing director, who is expected to become Philadelphia's first black mayor with a victory in November.

Goode, a sharecropper's son with 17 years of government experience, had been expected to win from the start of the campaign. He carried most of the black vote and also about 25% of the white vote. Despite a 5-1 Democratic margin in voter registration, biracial backing will be important to defeat Republican John J. Egan Jr. and independent Thomas A. Leonard, both white, in the general election.

The race issue, which had disrupted last month's election in Chicago, did not dominate the Philadelphia campaign in spite of Rizzo's history of divide-and-conquer tactics. The low-key Goode and the flamboyant Rizzo concentrated mostly on jobs, the economy and crime — the public concerns of the '80s. Rizzo, an ex-police chief, could no longer pander to prejudice and fear as easily by appealing for law-and-order, a theme of the '60s and '70s. The primary results were as much a rejection of Rizzo as an endorsement of Goode.

Nevertheless, unlike Chicago's Harold Washington, whose troubled career and black-oriented campaign invited political attacks, Goode offered impressive credentials and a broader appeal to voters. Goode, 44, is to be congratulated for blocking the comeback attempt of a man who never should have been mayor in the first place. And Philadelphia can be welcomed to the ranks of cities, beginning with Cleveland 16 years ago, in which pigmentation is not a complete bar to someone of personal and political ability.

Pittsburgh Post-Gazette
Pittsburgh, Pa., May 19, 1983

Though they anchor the state of Pennsylvania on either side, Pittsburgh and Philadelphia are miles apart politically as well as geographically. There are few Western Pennsylvania politicians who, on returning from the supposed City of Brotherly Love, have not been moved to remark on how ugly and fratricidal politics "over there" can be.

All the more reason to acknowledge the civility of the campaign for the Democratic nomination for mayor of Philadelphia, which ended Tuesday with a victory for former city official W. Wilson Goode and a defeat for former Mayor Frank Rizzo.

Mr. Goode is black and Mr. Rizzo is white. Those distinctions would not have attracted so much attention were it not for two bits of history: Mr. Rizzo's long-time image as the standard-bearer of white reaction and, more recently, the racially polarized campaign earlier this year for mayor of Chicago.

But neither recent nor ancient history shaped the Philadelphia campaign. Mr. Rizzo did make an early and ill-advised foray into commenting on the Chicago race. (He compared Harold Washington, the Democratic candidate who had served a short prison term for tax violations, to Al Capone.) But his appeal was for the most part statesmanlike and free of racial appeals.

For his part, Mr. Goode, a less flamboyant candidate than Harold Washington, also strove to de-emphasize the racial issue, a posture that should serve him well in his fall campaign against Republican nominee John Egan, the chairman of the Philadelphia Stock Exchange. In that contest, as in the primary, brotherly love may be too much to hope for, but not civility and fairness.

THE ARIZONA REPUBLIC
Phoenix, Ariz., May 19, 1983

PHILADELPHIA may not be quite the "City of Brotherly Love" that William Penn envisaged, but Philadelphia has demonstrated that a black and a white can run against each other for mayor without unleashing the ugly forces of racism.

Chicago papers, please copy.

In last month's mayoral race in Chicago, race was the only issue.

Neither candidate had any visible qualifications for the office, and neither pretended to.

Harold Washington, the Democratic candidate, appealed to blacks to vote for him because he, too, is black.

Republican candidate Bernard Epton attempted to frighten whites into voting for him simply to keep a black from getting control of city hall.

Washington won because the blacks voted almost solidly for him. His margin of victory came from affluent white liberals with feelings of guilt about blacks.

There was almost none of this Tuesday in Philadelphia's Democratic mayoral primary.

Both Frank Rizzo, a white, and W. Wilson Goode, a black, agreed early in the campaign not to make racism an issue. Except for a few minor lapses, they didn't.

They stuck to issues — jobs, the economy and crime.

Voters were not asked to buy a pig in a poke.

Rizzo, a former policeman, had served two previous terms as mayor, making a record for himself as a law-and-order man.

Goode, a graduate of the Wharton School, had served as state public utilities chairman until current Mayor William J. Green made him manager of the city.

Much of Goode's financing came from whites. His staff was thoroughly integrated.

No one feared that he would make city hall a black fiefdom.

Blacks voted almost solidly for Goode, but a significant number of whites did, too, primarily because of a widespread belief that Rizzo as mayor had enforced "nightstick law."

Rizzo has said that he will support Goode in the election against Republican candidate John Egan. This should make Goode a shoo-in in a city where Democrats outnumber Republicans 5 to 1.

On the basis of his record, Goode should make a good mayor.

Not a good black mayor. A good mayor, period.

Detroit Free Press
Detroit, Mich., May 19, 1983

PHILADELPHIA and the country were the real winners in that city's mayoral primary. And for that, both the winner, W. Wilson Goode, and the loser, Frank Rizzo, deserve a great deal of credit.

In the aftermath of last month's Chicago mayoral election, in which race became the most important campaign issue between Bernard Epton and Harold Washington, it was feared Philadelphia would also become divided along racial lines.

But Philadelphia proved that a mayoral election in a large, racially mixed U.S. city can pit black man against white and be decided only on the basis of who is better qualified. Without stirring up the race issue, Philadelphia made Mr. Goode the first black candidate to win a major party endorsement in the city's history.

Mr. Rizzo, the former mayor of Philadelphia during the '70s, should be given special commendation for keeping the race issue from the forefront. His eight-year tenure as mayor was marred with charges of racism, but he campaigned with restraint this year.

Mr. Goode, the city's former managing director, will face Republican John Egan and independent Thomas Leonard in the November election. With Democrats outnumbering Republicans five to one, Goode should easily become Philadelphia's next mayor.

The Philadelphia primary is a step toward erasing the consciousness of the black-white issue in elections. What we might hope for, ultimately, is a day when black can run against white and the thought of it as a campaign issue will never cross anyone's mind.

The Dispatch

Columbus, Ohio, May 19, 1983

THE PEOPLE of Philadelphia are well on their way to demonstrating to the nation and the world that the contest between black and white candidates for the office of mayor need not be the type of vicious, bitter and denigrating experience witnessed recently in Chicago. The candidates for the Philadelphia post should be praised for their decency and restraint thus far, and encouraged to continue their efforts to make the campaign a substantive one.

Democrats in the City of Brotherly Love have selected W. Wilson Goode as their candidate for mayor. Goode defeated former mayor Frank Rizzo in a primary Tuesday by about 53 percent to 46 percent. Goode, a black, now faces Republican John Egan in the November election. Democrats in Philadelphia outnumber Republicans 5-to-1 and the GOP hasn't elected a mayor there since 1947.

The situation resembles the one that existed in Chicago earlier this year when U.S. Rep. Harold Washington, a black, secured the Democratic nomination in a three-way primary and then went on to victory — but only after a dirty campaign filled with racial undertones and gutter tactics by both the Democrats and the Republicans.

Philadelphia is not without racial problems. A recent survey of American cities with large black populations concluded that Philadelphia is one of the most racially segregated cities in the country. The Citizens' Committee for Civil Rights, which conducted the survey, gave Philadelphia a rating of 88 on a scale of one to 100 in which a low score indicated substantial housing integration and a high score indicated substantial segregation. Chicago received the most-segregated city distinction with a rating of 92. Philadelphia's rating positioned it as the nation's fourth most-segregated city.

Thus, the potential for a Chicago-like campaign apparently exists in Philadelphia and it is incumbent upon the candidates to ensure that their campaigns reflect the honor of the office they seek to obtain.

People of different races can live and work together for the overall good of the community. Philadelphia has a grand opportunity now to demonstrate this fact. The people of the city where the U.S. Constitution was drafted should show through their actions that the principles of freedom and dignity which are embodied in that document endure in Philadelphia.

SYRACUSE
HERALD-JOURNAL

Syracuse, N.Y., May 19, 1983

W. Wilson Goode's victory in Philadelphia's Democratic mayoral primary is a pleasant contrast to last month's bitter mayoral election in Chicago.

Potential similarities were present. Each showdown pitted a black candidate against a white candidate in a racially-uncomfortable city. In both cases, the black candidates won.

But that's where the similarities ended, thankfully.

The Chicago election was a bitter affair, marred by blatant racial strategies on both sides. Republican Bernard Epton's campaign slogan — "Epton. Before it's too late" — was a clear appeal to white voters not to let a black gain control. Epton's campaign jingle even had as its tune "Bye-Bye, Blackbird." Nothing subtle there.

Congressman Harold Washington squeeked in by getting out a heavy black vote. However, constant battles with the old guard, white-controlled city council have stymied his efforts to govern.

▽   ▽

Many people looked for a repeat in the Philadelphia primary. Former mayor Frank Rizzo, one of the nation's premier rednecks, went one-on-one with Goode, the sharecropper's son who became a top aide to retiring Mayor William Green.

Rizzo, who was barred by law from seeking a third term four years ago, deserves credit for generally keeping the contest clean. He cooled his familiar rhetoric and combativeness, and kept a lid on his temper.

Goode also conducted an issue-oriented campaign, stressing economic issues rather than race. But he still isn't home free. Goode must face Philadelphia Stock Exchange chairman John Egan, considered a strong Republican opponent in a city that usually votes Democratic.

And lest too much is made of the potential for racial antagonism as the key issue in both Chicago and Philadelphia, it's worth noting there was a big difference in the caliber of black candidates.

▽   ▽

Although Goode has never held elective office, he has a distinguished record of service in Philadelphia government, including three years as managing director, the city's No. 2 job responsible for running the police, fire, streets and other operating departments. Goode tried to appeal to whites as well as blacks, and early indications are he got at least one-third of the white vote. In short, he was not an ideal *black* candidate; he was an ideal candidate, period.

Washington could make no such claim. Although he's won plenty of elections, including a seat in Congress, his cavalier approach to filing — more precisely, *not* filing — income tax returns won him a short jail term in 1972 and made his civic service pose questionable at best.

A victory for Goode in November would put black mayors at the helm of four of the nation's six largest cities — Chicago, Los Angeles, Detroit and Philadelphia.

That's strong evidence that blacks can do well in the electoral process. It should be a sign of further advances in the 1980s.

FORT WORTH STAR-TELEGRAM

Fort Worth, Texas, May 15, 1983

A whole week has elapsed since W. Wilson Goode, a black man, defeated former Mayor Frank Rizzo in Philadelphia's Democratic mayoral primary, and there have been no news reports of racial incidents or rhetoric in connection with the upcoming general election.

That is not surprising, since the primary was remarkably clean in that respect. It is reasonable to suppose, therefore, that a different kind of political dynamics regarding race operates in Philadelphia than in Chicago, where race became the dominant factor in the contest between recently elected Mayor Harold Washington and his Republican opponent, Bernard Epton.

Of course, both Rizzo and Goode had the benefit of Chicago's ugly example as an object lesson against such folly. Goode had staked out the high ground as the candidate of unity. Rizzo was effectively precluded from playing up race as a campaign issue because he had to combat a reputation for having promoted division in the City of Brotherly Love while he was mayor.

The lack of race-tinged campaigning in Philadelphia does not mean that race will not be a significant factor in the final mayoral shootout. Goode received more than 95 percent of the black vote in the primary. And it must be presumed that he will do equally well among black voters in the general election.

But Goode faces a more attractive Republican opponent in John J. Egan Jr., president of the Philadelphia Stock Exchange, than Washington faced in Chicago. And there could be a strong independent candidate in the race — Thomas A. Leonard, a former city controller who dropped out of the Democratic primary. Goode, who received 30 percent of the white vote in the primary, could have a problem holding on to enough of the white vote for victory.

The main strategy of the Democratic nominee appears to be to make the Philadelphia mayoral election a referendum on the economic policies of the Reagan administration. The idea is to rally Democrats of all hues around Goode. If that can be accomplished, he is virtually assured of victory, since no Republican has been elected mayor of Philadelphia since 1947.

Goode's ability to command the support of the majority of Philadelphia's Democrats will depend in large measure on whether or not Rizzo supports him. And Rizzo has not yet committed himself to doing so. Even so, given the caliber of his opposition, Goode could be in trouble. Had Washington faced such quality opposition, he might not have received enough white votes to win.

Whoever wins the general election, it is unlikely that Philadelphia's city government will experience the kind of political aftershock from the election that has rocked Chicago. This is especially true if the candidates continue to refrain from focusing upon race as a campaign issue.

The Honolulu Advertiser
Honolulu, Ha., May 19, 1983

The contrast between mayoral elections in Chicago and Philadelphia is worth noting again. Both cities saw contests between black and white candidates, but the way in which that circumstance was handled was dramatically different.

In Chicago, campaign advertising quite unsubtly played upon the racial fears and tension to be found in any large American city.

In Philadelphia, campaigning in the Democratic mayoral primary was kept on a much higher level. As one observer wrote, "In the privacy of the voting booth, skin color may indeed turn out to be precisely what the campaign was about. But the public dialogue of the campaign, on the streets and on the air, has been about something else."

That something was the character and performance of Frank Rizzo, the "supercop" who was a controversial mayor for eight years in the 1970s. He was unable to shake his image as a racial polarizer and troublemaker.

The winner was W. Wilson Goode, the son of a sharecropper with a masters in business from the Wharton School of Finance who had been city managing director. He still faces a general election battle, but is considered the favorite since Democrats outnumber Republicans in Philadelphia by five-to-one.

One lesson from this election, then, is that while race may be a factor in the voting of many individuals, racism should not be openly and purposefully used as a campaign tactic.

One result of the candidacy of Goode, Harold Washington in Chicago, the unsuccessful former Los Angeles mayor Tom Bradley in his bid to be governor of California, 226 other black mayors, 21 black members of Congress and many other blacks in politics, has been a dramatic upsurge in black voting power.

It comes at a time when many blacks in this country believe that political operatives in the Reagan White House have written off their votes as unwinnable and unneeded. Unless more than just routine denials are used to refute that perception, it could become quite costly not only to Reagan but to other Republican politicians as well.

Chicago Tribune
Chicago, Ill., May 19, 1983

W. Wilson Goode, a black, has won the Democratic mayoral primary in Philadelphia by a substantial margin over former "tough cop" Mayor Frank Rizzo. It is a victory that invites comparisons with Chicago's recent mayoral election, but such comparisons are not appropriate.

Although Mr. Rizzo was viewed as a hero of white racists, it was neither a racist nor a rancorous campaign. As Mr. Goode put it, race was a factor, not an issue. He disdained the "it's our turn," us-against-them approach and instead appealed to the full spectrum of the Philadelphia electorate. Mr. Rizzo at one brief point tried sporting a Bernard Epton button, but when that quickly proved a losing gambit he backed away and spent most of the campaign attempting to erase his old "tough cop" image.

Also, Mr. Goode was not running as an anti-establishment outsider but as a leader of the establishment with 17 years in public life, culminating in his service as Philadelphia's city managing director.

And, his primary victory came with a substantial 54 percent majority [which included a solid 25 percent of the white vote] in a two-way race, not with a mere plurality eked out in a three-way split.

All this is far from saying that politics in "the city of brotherly love" is without racist strains. The history of Mr. Rizzo's two terms as mayor is evidence enough of that. But Philadelphia experienced its catharsis on the race question at the end of Mr. Rizzo's last term four years ago, when, employing a "vote white" campaign, he attempted unsuccessfully to pass a referendum removing a constitutional restriction against his serving a third term.

Mr. Goode is not yet mayor. He faces a particularly strong Republican challenge from stockbroker John Egan, the easy winner in the GOP primary. Former city controller Thomas Leonard, who almost ran as a third spoiler candidate in the Democratic primary, may run as an independent in the general election in November.

But, win or lose, Philadelphia and the nation have already been well served by this election. If the noisy belligerents in Chicago's City Hall would cease their fractious combat long enough to learn at least some small lesson from Philadelphia's decorous example, every Chicagoan would have reason to be thankful.

THE ☐ SUN
Baltimore, Md., May 19, 1983

"The clear lesson to itself and other cities and states large and small is that racist politics Chicago-style is not inevitable, is not a wave of the future. It is not a necessary or inescapable dynamic of the integration of sound political leaders from minorities into the mainstream of the American process of power." So says the *Philadelphia Inquirer* this morning. And it is correct.

The City of Brotherly Love has provided a welcome corrective to the worldwide view that Chicago might, indeed, be the wave of the future. W. Wilson Goode and former Mayor Frank Rizzo ran very hard for the Democratic mayoral nomination. Mr. Goode is black (and a Morgan graduate) and Mr. Rizzo is white — and a white who in the 1960s and 1970s welcomed the reputation of being a tough cop and a tough mayor undeterred by black cries of racism as he worked for "law and order." But both candidates avoided racist rhetoric and both made genuine appeals to all racial and ethnic voting groups in the city. In the end, the candidate who could win both black and white votes, was nominated.

This truly is the wave of the urban future. It has been for some time. Kurt Schmoke was elected state's attorney here last year by appealing successfully to white and black voters. So did the three men — two white and one black — elected to circuit court judgeships in the city last year. And before that in Atlanta, Cleveland, Los Angeles and other cities, black candidates were elected mayor by white-black coalitions. One Philadelphian described the Goode-Rizzo contest as "a-racial." It was and so have been many elections in America in recent years. Not all, but many. In fact, for all the racist atmospherics in Chicago's general election, Harold Washington almost surely won because he, not his opponent, muted race-related themes and appealed to all voters.

Even as Philadelphians were nominating Mr. Goode Tuesday, Denver voters were ousting a mayor of 14 years' standing. That race involved the mayor, one other serious white candidate, a Hispanic and a black. The campaigning and voting there, too, was a-racial. The veteran mayor, who had been perceived as a friend by the blacks, got a large part of the black vote; the Hispanic got support from voters of all hues, and predictions are that the Hispanic and white candidate left in the runoff will now run color-blind, ethnic-blind campaigns. That is the way it should be, in Denver and everywhere else.

St. Louis Globe-Democrat
St. Louis, Mo., May 19, 1983

Mayoral election returns in Philadelphia and Denver prove the growing power of black and Hispanic voters. More importantly the results show that substantial numbers of white voters will support qualified candidates regardless of race.

Philadelphia Democrats nominated W. Wilson Goode, a black sharecropper's son, to be their candidate for mayor in the November election. Goode defeated former Mayor Frank L. Rizzo's bid for a comeback in a campaign that was steamy but not marred by appeals to racial prejudice as was the case in Chicago last month.

Democrats outnumber Republicans 5 to 1 in Philadelphia. This means that Goode, managing director in the cabinet of retiring Mayor William Green, is heavily favored to defeat Republican John Egan.

In Denver's nonpartisan election, Mayor William McNichols was knocked out of office after 14 years. The top vote getter was Federico Pena, a former state legislator, who will face former district attorney Dale Tooley in a runoff on June 21.

A howling spring blizzard on Election Day was no help to McNichols, reminding voters of the Christmas Eve storm that the mayor's administration bungled, leaving streets blocked for days.

Pena ran with the support of the Rocky Mountain News, Denver's leading newspaper, while the Denver Post endorsed Tooley.

If Pena succeeds in June, he will join Henry Cisneros of San Antonio as a Latin mayor of a major U.S. city. If Goode is elected in Philadelphia, he will join Chicago's Harold Washington, Los Angeles' Thomas Bradley, Detroit's Coleman A. Young and Atlanta's Andrew Young on the list of prominent black mayors.

Jesse Jackson's 1984 Candidacy: Measuring the Results

The Rev. Jesse Jackson's candidacy came at a time when the participation of black voters in the electoral process had increased significantly, and when dissatisfaction with the Reagan Administration was strong among minority and low-income groups. His bid for the presidency, outlasting that of a handful of white Democratic contenders, was undoubtedly important simply as a symbol of black political power on the federal, rather than local, level. Jackson sought as his constituency not only blacks but "locked-out people" in the United States, those who felt their concerns were ignored by the Reagan Administration and their economic fortunes untouched by the recent recovery. In announcing his candidacy, the civil rights leader said he was entering the presidential race to "help restore a moral tone, a redemptive spirit and a sensitivity to the poor and the dispossessed of this nation."

Jackson's candidacy received a boost just over a month later, in January, 1984, when he returned from a successful "pilgrimage" to Syria to secure the release of captured U.S. flier Navy Lt. Robert O. Goodman Jr. The White House, uncomfortable with this intervention, stressed beforehand that Jackson was going "as a private citizen, not as a representative of the U.S. government"; but after his return, President Reagan met with Jackson and Goodman, saying that Jackson's "mission of mercy" had "earned our gratitude and our admiration." Six months later, when Jackson secured the release of 22 Americans and 26 Cubans from Cuban prisons during a tour of Central America, his actions were decried by Administration officials as unlawful personal diplomacy.

The Syrian trip focused attention on Jackson's positions on Middle East issues, and particularly his controversial advocacy of a Palestinian homeland. In February, when Jackson's use of the ethnic slur "Hymies" to refer to Jews while talking to a black reporter became public, the incident aggravated an atmosphere of tension between American Jews and blacks. Although Jackson publicly apologized for the remark, the situation was later made worse by the involvement of black Muslim leader Louis Farrakhan, who had supplied Jackson's campaign with bodyguards and political support. In a radio broadcast, Farrakhan called Milton Coleman, the black reporter who had disclosed Jackson's reference, a "no-good, filthy traitor" and warned: "One day soon we will punish you with death." Despite the offensive nature of Farrakhan's remarks, however, Jackson refused to repudiate his political support, saying that while the apparent death threat was "distasteful," the pressures to disavow Farrakhan were "a form of harassment" by the white media. (In a later broadcast, Farrakhan called Judaism a "gutter religion" and the existence of Israel as a state "an outlaw act." Jackson disavowed these comments.)

Despite these setbacks, Jackson's campaign garnered more support among voters and delegates than was generally predicted. His portion of the delegate count numbered over 370, out of a total of 3,931, by the end of the primary season in June—a tally, the candidate claimed, that failed to reflect his much larger share of the popular vote. In mid-May, Jackson calculated that he had won 21% of the popular vote in primaries, but was represented by only 9% of the delegates. (See pp. 236-241.) Where Jackson did win a sizable percentage of the total vote, the overwhelming majority of his supporters were black voters; the "rainbow coalition" he sought never became a significant force.

It is difficult to assess the overall impact of Jesse Jackson's presidential campaign. To many observers, it appeared that Jackson's primary goal in the 1984 race was to reawaken the flagging civil rights movement by bringing its priorities into the political sphere, and to demonstrate the power of a mobilized black electorate. One of the surest ways to demonstrate influence—to stress that black voters could no longer be counted on to automatically support the Democratic presidential nominee—involved the danger of alienating the Democratic Party and thus losing leverage within it. Other black politicians viewed Jackson with wariness, afraid that his vocal demands, his sometimes flamboyant style and his gospel-tinged rhetoric would alienate other segments of the Democratic Party. In the end, Jackson managed to perform the ticklish feat of both forcing some concessions from the party, reflected in the platform approved by the Democratic convention, and delivering to it most of the black vote in the 1984 election. (See pp. 114-125, 236-241.) But Jackson's major contributions may simply have been to awaken the American electorate to the considerable power of black voters, and to accustom all voters to the idea of a serious black contender for the nation's highest office.

Chicago Tribune

Chicago, Ill., August 22, 1983

The Rev. Jesse Jackson is on the cover of Time magazine and the subject of media attention worldwide. He is planning a trip to Europe to visit the GIs in Germany and meet with the monarchy in the Netherlands. He has spurred black voter registration and manned the polls in the South. A trip several months ago to symbolic New Hampshire, the first state to hold a presidential primary, brought forth a remarkable show of public interest and support. And the national convention of Operation PUSH in Atlanta rang with choruses of "Run, Jesse, run."

While Rev. Jackson has not officially declared his candidacy, his special brand of dynamism is a welcome addition to the most prestigious game in American politics. Any and all black candidates have the right to run. And why not Rev. Jackson? Even his adversaries, of which there are multitudes, must concede he is charismatic, fears no issue and has a forcefulness that makes people listen and think.

His maneuvering will make for a fast-paced political season, as the other Democrats jog this way and that to keep up with his nonstop schedule and his nonstop preaching. But, as with all things, there are cautions. A Jackson candidacy, any black candidacy, will make for good politics. But some people say it could swing the Democratic nomination to someone less sensitive to black interests. Opinion is divided on that, of course, and it just might be that with Rev. Jackson in, everybody in the field is going to have to court Rev. Jackson's ultimate support.

The effect on the Democratic convention outcome may be debatable, but there are some certainties.

Already Rev. Jackson's flirtations with the presidency have split black leaders three ways. Some, of course, favor his candidacy. Some do not think any black should interfere in 1984 with a strong white Democrat's chance to defeat President Reagan; others are enthralled by the idea of a black running, but not necessarily Rev. Jackson.

If Rev. Jackson runs, he will do so without the backing of some black powerhouses, particularly Mayors Coleman Young of Detroit and Andrew Young of Atlanta and NAACP Director Benjamin Hooks. Gary Mayor Richard Hatcher is in his corner and doing groundwork to see whether Rev. Jackson should go for it. Chicago's Harold Washington, noting the lessons of his own election, has no problem with a black running, but he is unlikely to back Rev. Jackson. In the end, then, Rev. Jackson could find himself deeply dividing the movement he is running in order to solidify.

What's more, he is going to have to consider the grave dangers a candidacy would cause for Operation PUSH. If Rev. Jackson runs, Operation PUSH will automatically become his political organization, imperiling its status as a social agency and its federal and private donations. Will his successor in PUSH be able to maintain the excitement about voting or schools or a boycott that Rev. Jackson's mere presence elicits among everyday people? Will his successor inherit Rev. Jackson's knack for reaching the common man? PUSH's role in serving basic human needs, in simply giving hope to those who are downtrodden, carries on the tradition of Martin Luther King Jr. and ought not be jeopardized without the most serious consideration.

Rev. Jackson is going to guarantee that the presidential season will be an exciting one, whether he finally declares his candidacy or decides to help deliver it to another candidate of his choice.

ALBUQUERQUE JOURNAL
Albuquerque, N.M., November 2, 1983

He is articulate, experienced in the public sector, consistent in supporting the principles he espouses, has worked for constructive change in society and has charisma. He also meets all the legal requirements for becoming his political party's presidential nominee.

Primarily because of his color, however, the Rev. Jesse Jackson is unlikely to win the Democratic Party's nomination. Many Democrats would prefer that Jackson not even seek the nomination since he might take black votes away from former Vice President Walter Mondale.

Nowhere in the U.S. Constitution is it written that the president must be a white male. Yet neither the Democrats nor Republicans have seriously considered, much less nominated, a black as their presidential standard bearer. Jackson's decision to enter the race might be seen by many as a futile, hopeless gesture. Perhaps it is, but his candidacy might force the other Democratic candidates to discuss campaign issues more thoroughly and to clarify their positions.

No matter what the achievements or expertise of Jackson, his candidacy raises a specter of racism. It's a specter that haunts the United States in spite of the accomplishments of blacks in nearly all facets of the society.

All Americans should welcome Jackson's candidacy for the Democratic Party's presidential nomination.

The Sun Reporter
San Francisco, Calif., July 27, 1983

In a limited way, we support Rev. Jesse Jackson's efforts.

There is too much talk and confusion in the air generated by alleged Black leaders, many of whose present political actions demonstrate how little or nothing they know about the political process.

Some 250 Black leaders who met in East St. Louis two weeks ago, led by Bishop H.H. Brookins, have been precipitous in endorsing Jackson for President.

This is discussion and asking time in which candidates are discussing crucial national issues and pleading for support in the national 1984 Presidential primary.

By going whole hog and endorsing Jackson for President, the Black leaders have discouraged the possibilty that Jackson's campaign can gain leverage by forcing the more prominent Presidential candidates to come to Blacks and seek their support by moving toward the new America which Jackson envisions: an America with jobs for everyone; an America in which all children are adequately educated; an America in which those who presently suffer from racism, sexism and classism are no longer outsiders, and will be included democratically in the decision making process.

We have always encouraged Black candidates to seek public office, from dog catcher, if he's elected, to the presidency of the United States. It's a right of all citizens to seek public office. Moreover, some Black person has to begin the journey to the White House.

Blacks who criticize Jackson demonstrate ignorance on one hand and maybe prejudice on the other; both make them vulnerable. We've had some experience in criticizm by alleged Black leaders. In 1966 a Black publisher dared to become the second Black man iun the history of the country to seek the governorship of a sovereign state: the first was an unknown Black candidate who sought the governorship of Arkansas in 1868. Eight years after the 1966 Black gubernatorial candidate in the California primaries, in 1974, two Black Lieutenant governors were elected - Dymally in California and Brown in Colorado. The 1966 Black gubernatorial candidate in California discussed the important issues and today eight of his platform programs have been enacted into law.

So, with these reservations, we say Right On, Jesse Jackson.

With Blacks active on the campaign trail in 1984 for the Presidency of the United States, a new day will begin in the nation's political process.

We support Jackson's efforts, but we say his efforts to influence the final selection of the Democratic nominee are foolish.

One hundred years after Lincoln's Emancipation Proclamation, the whole system of democrato-capitalist government has failed. Blacks in this nation gave blind support to the Republican party for 60 years [1872-1932], and 50 years of unwavering Black support to the Democratic party [1936-1982]. The most dramatic demonstration of Black political power in the 120 year history of Black political participation came in 1976. The world recognizes that Black political power elected James Earl Carter in 1976, as 55 percent of the solid white south voted for Gerald Ford and 92 percent of the solid Black south voted for Carter. If 10 thousand Blacks had switched votes or stayed home in two or three states [Ohio, Pennsylvania or Mississippi], Ford would have been President.

Black Democratic politicians are critical of Jackson's ruining their game by encouraging a Black candidate in the 1984 Democratic primary election. However, we criticize Jackson for his failure to recognize that the present political system will never satisfy the needs of Blacks who suffer from racism, women who suffer from sexism, or those citizens who suffer from classism in this country.

Therefore, we cannot endorse Jackson's efforts in the Democratic party. We've urged him to strike a new blow for freedom for Blacks by joining those courageous young Blacks who in 1981 organized a National Black Political Party. These young Blacks have been warned that such a course of basic political action, based solely on race or Blackness, is doomed, just as the five previous attempts to build a National Black political party also failed.

America needs a social democratic political party which offers hope and promise for using government to change the evils that dominate the present military-industrial political complex which rules Fortress America.

Whether or not there's a Democrat or Republican victory, the long history of exploitation of the people by the laissez-faire, capitalist-democratic system continues slowly to degenerate into Constitutional fascism, American style.

Prophetically, Jackson has an opportunity to sound the clarion call for the founding of a new political force in America: The Socialist Democratic Party.

We are sure that Black "preachers-turned-politicians" and the Black Anglo-Saxons will not agree with this analysis. But history itself will prove the correctness of our analysis. So we say, get straight in your political ideology, Jesse. Get straight, young Black activists who will build a national Black Political Party. Lead America toward a new day. Then we can say, Right On! All those outsiders in America who suffer from racism, classism, and sexism can organize behind a prophetic new beginning by the most despised and rejected Black Americans. To such a combination, we can truthfully say Right On.

THE INDIANAPOLIS STAR
Indianapolis, Ind., August 28, 1983

Federal auditors say two organizations headed by the Rev. Jesse Jackson misused more than $1.7 million in government grants and contracts. They suggest that the money be returned.

The two units are Operation PUSH Inc. and its subsidiary, PUSH for Excellence Inc., which received taxpayers' money for projects aimed at training young blacks and encouraging them to stay in school and learn as much as possible.

Auditors from the Education Department's inspector general's office reported that funds had been spent contrary to federal regulation and that expenses and claims were not properly documented. In some instances, they said, federal money was used for fund raising.

Education Secretary T.H. Bell stressed that the findings were preliminary and that PUSH officials possibly could provide the missing documentation and satisfactorily explain the disbursements under question. We hope they can and do as we don't like seeing taxpayers' money misused.

Bell said audits were routine and that the only reason these received "all this publicity is that the Rev. Jesse Jackson is running for president." That's probably true.

Whether or not the PUSH groups can justify the expenditure of the $1.7 million, the case draws public attention to the money taxpayers are forced to shower on an array of private groups, some of which promote activities many taxpayers oppose.

Just to name a few and the tax money they received, there's National Council of La Raza, $600,000; George Meany Center for Labor Studies, Inc., $99,008; National Conference of State Legislatures, $538,389; Natural Organization for Women Legal Defense Fund, $156,345, and Planned Parenthood Federation of America, $3,490,807.

In the last instance, taxpayers fund pro-abortion propaganda. One Planned Parenthood booklet outlined a three-year plan which calls for eliminating "where necessary and possible, restrictive legislation at the local, state or national levels which impedes access to abortion," and supporting abortion and other services abroad which cannot be directly financed by the U.S. government.

Sen. Jeremiah Denton, R-Ala., said recently, "When an effort is made to cut these programs, the groups that benefit from them organize marches amd mobilize their public relations departments to attack such efforts. They shout that Mr. Reagan is trying to hurt the needy. By 'needy' they mean themselves."

It's time for the people who pay the freight, the long-suffering taxpayers, to mobilize a campaign to make Congress offload such organizations from the gravy train they have ridden for so long.

TULSA WORLD
Tulsa, Okla., November 2, 1983

THE Rev. Jesse Jackson, to the dismay of many Democrats, has decided to seek the party's nomination for the presidency.

The Chicago civil rights leader's presence in the race, according to the pundits, is expected to hurt former Vice President Walter Mondale, perceived to be the candidate of labor unions and minority groups, in his race against Sen. John Glenn of Ohio, the moderate.

What Jackson seeks, at least on the surface, is not to win but to encourage more black citizens to register to vote and become involved in the nomination process.

Beyond that, however, Jackson could become a decisive factor at the Democratic convention if he goes in with a good bloc of delegates and if Mondale and Glenn are running close.

Mondale would no doubt get Jackson's support. But at what price?

Could Jackson be aiming just a bit lower than president? Say vice president?

St. Louis Globe-Democrat
St. Louis, Mo., June 24, 1983

In considering the prospect of a black candidate for president, it is fair to ask whether a white, activist preacher would be a likely nominee of either the Republicans or Democrats in 1984. The answer clearly is no.

If the present mayors of Chicago, Los Angeles, Detroit and Atlanta were white, would any one of them be nominated for president by either the Republicans or Democrats? Not likely.

Since many blacks feel that the Rev. Jesse Jackson is the most viable black presidential candidate at this time, it is obvious that Jackson's color is the main thing he has going for him.

Jackson is unattractive to many voters, black and white, because of his militancy. His unfair pressure tactics against Anheuser-Busch, Inc. have made him unpopular in St. Louis and elsewhere.

In the best of worlds there could come a day when both major political parties may nominate blacks or females for president, thus eliminating prejudice based on race or sex as a consideration of the voters.

Jackson's clout lies mainly in his ability to register black voters. Unquestionably rising numbers of black and Hispanic voters have influenced the outcome of recent big city elections and will continue to do so.

Harold Washington catapulted into national prominence by being the first black elected as mayor of Chicago, joining Thomas Bradley of Los Angeles, Coleman A. Young of Detroit and Andrew Young of Atlanta on the list of big city black mayors. Wilson Goode is favored to be elected Philadelphia's first black mayor in November.

Denver, with a large Spanish-speaking population, has just elected Federico Pena as its first Hispanic mayor. Henry Cisneros, San Antonio's first Hispanic mayor, was re-elected recently. These results can be taken as welcome signs that prejudice toward minority candidates is eroding significantly.

A presidential preference poll that showed Jackson running third among Democrats, trailing only former Vice President Walter F. Mondale and Ohio's Sen. John Glenn, has put other Democratic hopefuls in something of a sweat.

Ultimately Jackson is in a position to harm Mondale more than the others by drawing big blocs of blacks. In a sense the Democrats and black voters deserve the political mischief Jackson is capable of causing. While grumbling that Republicans don't do enough for them, blacks have slavishly voted for Democrats since the days of Franklin D. Roosevelt.

Ideally there will come a day when there will be a choice of attractive black candidates for president, based on experience in holding important public office.

Blacks deserve better than the likes of Jesse Jackson to be their trail blazer in aspiring to the presidency.

THE ARIZONA REPUBLIC
Phoenix, Ariz., November 1, 1983

JESSE JACKSON has talked himself into running for the Democratic nomination for president.

Now the question is: How far can Jesse go?

The tentative answer must be: Not very. He suffers from too many handicaps.

From Mayor Tom Bradley of Los Angeles to Mayor Julian Bond of Atlanta, there is almost no support for Jackson among black political officeholders. The same is true of black civil rights leaders, including Coretta King, widow of Martin Luther King Jr.

At the very least, this means Jackson will have to start from scratch in building a campaign organization.

Raising money also will be a problem for Jackson. He says he expects to get it from the congregations of black churches. It's questionable that he will get enough. Several black Baptist bishops already have come out against the idea of mixing religion and politics.

Jackson's biggest problem is that he's never been identified with any issue except civil rights, and civil rights is not a major issue today.

So where can Jackson look for votes? Mostly among young blacks. Jackson thinks millions of them, and some Hispanics, will pour out to vote for him simply because he is black.

This, he says, will enable him to arrive in San Francisco with a sizable bloc of votes, enough to hold the balance of power at the convention.

He may be disappointed. The polls show that former Vice President Walter F. Mondale has as much support among blacks as Jackson, and a great deal more among Hispanics. Mondale's support is likely to grow as the primaries and caucuses grow nearer, because blacks will have to consider a fact even Jackson admits: He can't possibly win the nomination.

Jackson, smart as well as glib, is taking a gamble. He may, in spite of all the barriers, run well enough to become a factor at the convention.

On the other hand, he could stumble right at the opening gun. That will come on March 13 with the primaries in Georgia and Alabama.

The Chattanooga Times
Chattanooga, Tenn., December 5, 1983

Since the announcement of his presidential candidacy several weeks ago, the Rev. Jesse Jackson has been crisscrossing the country, speaking wherever he can find an audience, and preaching the message that 1984 will be a year in which black voters can have a greater political impact than ever before. There's an element of truth at work here.

There is also a lot of "conventional wisdom" at work as well. As in: Mr. Jackson will (a) get virtually no white votes but will (b) instead function more as a catalyst for increased black voter registration, thus increasing blacks' influence, especially in the primaries. His candidacy will (c) take votes away from Walter Mondale, presumably the most logical candidate of the minorities, and that in turn will (d) toss the nomination to a more conservative Democrat, Sen. John Glenn. Finally, Mr. Glenn will (e) stand a better chance of winning the presidency in 1984 because he will pick up support from a majority of blacks and other minorities because he is not Reagan.

The problem with conventional wisdom, though, is twofold: It's usually too conventional and it's usually not wisdom. How about a different scenario?

We suggest Mr. Jackson will (2) receive a lot of primary votes from blacks and whites for the simple reason that many Democrats, ourselves included, are weary of the continuous recycling of the same old ideas and programs — not to mention candidates — that turn up every four years. This year, front-runner Mondale is doing the same thing, trying to stake out a position distinct from Ronald Reagan, whom he terms "radical," while applying the adjectives "sensible" and "responsible" to his own proposals. The primaries this year could be a rerun of 1968, when voters rallied around alternative candidates — George Wallace and Eugene McCarthy come to mind — as a means of protest.

Besides, it is more logical to argue (b) that the growing black political power created the Jackson candidacy, not the other way round. As Paul Delaney noted in last Sunday's New York Times Magazine, black registration has been increasing over the past year and shows no sign of slowing down. Mr. Jackson is merely giving voice to the not-so-subtle sounds of discontent that are increasingly being heard not only among blacks but among whites as well. Most of them, blacks and whites, have been affected most adversely by recent economic conditions and by the Reagan administration's upside-down priorities. Anyway, many blacks will (c) still vote for Mr. Mondale and other candidates.

It is pointless at this stage to predict whether (d) and (e) are even remotely possible. One thing is for sure, however. Mr. Jackson is certain to force Mondale, Glenn et al to be a lot more specific on key economic issues than they have been so far. When that happens, so much the better.

Chicago Defender

Chicago, Ill., March 22, 1983

The movement to put up a Black candidate for the 1984 presidential election is not a futile gesture, nor is it a case of self-hypnosis in a moment of hysteria. If the six million unregistered Black voters, mostly in the South, can be driven to the polls by arguments laced with race pride, and if the major big cities with Black mayors can be made to realize the multiple advantage of backing a Black candidate for President, the threat will outclass the illusion of shadow-boxing and become close enough to reality to yield substantive power.

The mathematics of the experiment would remove it from the misadventure of a midnight dream into a bargaining-table deal invested with irremovable power and recognition. That means that one of the two existing major parties — Democrat or Republican — which gets the support of the Black party would be assured of victory.

This is the propitious time to challenge with vim, logic and voting might the monopoly of a two-party system which has far too long ignored the economic plight of the masses and their basic social needs. Mind you, this Black party in time would draw dissatisfied, disappointed whites into its camp.

The political operation of this Caesarian operation staggers the imagination. We may not be able to elect a Black president, but we will have a hell of a voice in determining what Democrat or Republican goes into the big house on Pennsylvania Avenue.

Detroit Free Press

Detroit, Mich., March 22, 1983

THE FALLACY in Jesse Jackson's threat to run as a black candidate for president is so readily apparent that the effort will probably fizzle. As a warning to those who hope to gain the Democratic nomination, though, and as an invitation for Republican change, it is a useful exercise.

An independent black candidate in the 1984 general election would probably assure the defeat of the Democratic candidate for president. The practical effect would be to pull the politics of the country sharply to the right. Most black politicians recognize that fact. Jesse Jackson is, moreover, not the anointed spokesmen for black politicians in this country; the threat would have more credibility if it were coming from Andrew Young or Coleman Young. Such a candidacy would have a self-destructive quality about it, and many black politicians will disdain it for that reason.

Even coming from Jesse Jackson, though, and certainly coming from Julian Bond, such a threat does say to Democratic candidates that they had better not presume too much about the black vote in 1984. There is a lot of anger and frustration among blacks and among black politicians. The Chicago mayoral election, with Jane Byrne's write-in campaign and the seeming ambivalence of parts of the Democratic organization, has added to that sense of alienation.

If that anger and frustration become serious enough — or so Messrs. Jackson and Bond are attempting to say — then the black voters in this country just might, in effect, sit out the '84 presidential election. Their threat is a cry for those who would be president to speak out on issues that blacks consider to be important. It is a way of keeping pressure on candidates, as they put together their coalitions for '84, to make sure that they don't slight the interests of blacks. Whatever leverage it provides has to be exercised now, well before the primaries and caucuses start next winter.

In fact, the Democratic candidates ought to give high priority to reversing the pattern of neglect of the interests of blacks and other minorities. They should do so not only because it is good electoral politics, but because it is right. The alienation of blacks and black voters is something that ought to get a lot of attention not just from the Democrats but from the Republicans as well. It remains a major issue for the American society, even at a moment when economic issues in general have to be regarded as more politically compelling.

Lincoln Journal

Lincoln, Neb., December 13, 1983

Jesse Jackson says he was "totally surprised" that Alabama's largest black political group decided, 118 to 36, to endorse the presidential candidacy of Walter Mondale, and not him.

He blamed unreliable leadership in Alabama Democratic Conference, saying the black Southerners were far removed from the people they supposedly represent.

Rather presumptuous, that analysis.

Rather pragmatic, the conference's endorsment.

The central theme of the black delegates was not that they love Jesse less but that they despise Ronald Reagan more, and the evaluation was that Mondale stands a better chance than Jackson in 1984 of whipping the incumbent Republican.

Seems reasonable.

That black Americans who have struggled for years strengthening the political process should make such an assessment is a powerful statement, hard as it may be for the flamboyant Jackson to accept.

The Wichita Eagle-Beacon

Wichita, Kans., May 17, 1983

The Rev. Jesse Jackson, speaking to the American Society of Newspaper Editors in Denver last week, gave some new perspective to the idea of a black person being a serious candidate for president in the 1984 election. Whether such a candidate were to win or lose isn't really as important, he said, as the impact he or she might have on national political policy.

A black candidacy would "give white America a chance to hear some fresh ideas. When running, we may lose — just as most white people do when they run. But the byproduct of running is. .getting ideas on the front burner."

The argument against a black person making a concerted campaign for the presidency is that it could backfire by siphoning off votes from mainline candidates who have expressed sympathy with black concerns. That could result in the election of candidates not particularly sympathetic — and blacks could be even worse off than they are now.

But there is an attractive element to the Rev. Jackson's reasoning. That is that a serious black candidacy could do more than perhaps anything else to disavow the stereotype of black political figures as "picketeers and protestors," as the Rev. Jackson put it. Rightly or wrongly, the perception among many blacks, at least, is that those figures currently are ignored when they speak out about defense, foreign policy or economic concerns — subjects that don't relate directly to black concerns.

The question that immediately follows is whether Jesse Jackson is the one to carry the black banner, then, in the 1984 election. Though he told the editors he had not decided to run, he gave every indication he was entertaining the idea, at least. Even as he did, he implored the editors not to lock him "in a box" by referring to him as a "black leader." When that happens, he said, "they are not describing me, they are circumscribing me."

Blacks could prove to be an even more potent force at the polls through a campaign announced by the Rev. Jackson to register 10 to 15 million Southern black voters before 1984. Such an effort could bring the creation of "a new progressive Southern coalition" that could alter the make-up of American politics radically.

And that could put more "ideas on the front burner" than even a black presidential bid that had little real chance of success.

Roanoke Times & World-News

Roanoke, Va., March 27, 1984

IT WAS a beautiful Saturday afternoon this past weekend, with further opportunity for diversion provided by the University of Virginia's basketball game against Indiana in the NCAA Eastern Regionals.

So why were 289 Roanoke Democrats willing to spend the afternoon at a mass meeting to begin the process of choosing Virginia delegates to the party's presidential-nominating convention in San Francisco? And why did so many (113, to be precise) of those willing to forgo the customary weekend pleasures turn out to be backers of Jesse Jackson, a man with virtually no chance of winning the nomination?

It didn't happen everywhere. But it happened in enough places in Virginia — not only in Roanoke, but also in rural places such as Franklin County and in big cities such as Richmond and Norfolk — for Jackson to finish about even with Mondale, at least for the time being, in the quest for national-convention votes from the Virginia delegation.

If Mondale and Hart were boll-weevil Democrats with bleak records on civil rights, black enthusiasm for the Jackson campaign might be explicable as the only way to register

discontent with the conservative drift of the times. That, however, is manifestly not the case. (Interestingly, Mondale has done best among black voters when he has needed their votes the most; without black defections from Jackson, Mondale would have lost the Alabama and Georgia primaries and might well have had to abandon the campaign.)

On the other hand, the extreme improbability of the Democrats' nominating a candidate unsympathetic to black aspirations actually may be working to Jackson's advantage. If the threat to those aspirations is perceived as coming from Rea-

ganite Republicans rather than from any of the mainstream Democrats, then there's no great harm in "wasting" a vote on Jackson in a Democratic primary or caucus.

Besides, a Jackson vote might not be wasted even by the standards of traditional hardball politics. If the Mondale-Hart contest stays close all the way to San Francisco, then the Jackson delegates — plus the uncommitted delegates getting elected here and there — could be pivotal in deciding the outcome. Meanwhile, officials for the Jackson campaign note the campaign's value in inspiring blacks, especially previously unregis-

tered members of the younger generation, to get into the habit of voting.

Such answers, though, beg the basic question. Political pros inside and outside the Jackson camp may be weighing the scenarios, sizing up the potential impact of Jackson's candidacy on first the Democratic convention and then the general election. But rank-and-file citizens don't give up their Saturdays just to fulfill a politician's strategic designs.

Clearly, Jackson's message and its manner of delivery strike a responsive chord in many Virginia hearts.

THE CHRISTIAN SCIENCE MONITOR

Boston, Mass., November 1, 1983

Once you've said the Rev. Jesse Jackson's entry tomorrow into the Democratic presidential race expands the field to eight, it's hard to know what to say next. The Jackson candidacy admits many unknowns into the American political equation.

In the annals of black political progress, his presidential bid marks the second such serious effort for blacks, the first in more than a decade. Such milestones are worth noting. Yet even within the black community, whether the Jackson candidacy is the best strategy for achieving minority political aims is sharply debated.

Black voters themselves will have to decide whether a black candidacy in the Democratic Party best serves their interests — or whether they should invest their votes among white candidates who have a better chance of election. This is always the critical decision of voting blocs — whether the bigger potential prize from going it alone is worth abandoning the security of coalition.

And by taking the very step of announcing for a White House run, as a candidate in a party that is predominantly non-minority, Mr. Jackson is inviting whites to judge his candidacy on its wider merits — on his personal qualifications for the office, his character, experience, and judgment, without regard to color.

Mr. Jackson's lack of a specific political record makes it hard to judge his impact on the Democratic race. He has not held elective office. His background was in civil rights and in self-help education programs. He has been more a man of the pulpit as a preacher, more a social worker in civic life, than a politician. His credentials are chiefly those of an articulate speaker at public rallies, largely in minority communities, not those of a proven professional in legislative or executive chambers.

Few figures step confidently into the presidential arena without having held a major public office. Shirley Chisholm, the first prominent black to have run for the presidency, had served in Congress as a representative from Brooklyn before entering the party nomination fight in 1972 — a year, with Alabama's George Wallace running too, when race was more of a divisive issue than it is now.

Jackson's claim to credibility is the likelihood that he can benefit from, and in turn give shape to, the renascent black political movement in the United States. That movement was already under way independently of Mr. Jackson. Rep. Harold Washington's recent success in the Chicago mayoralty was one manifestation of the faster return to the voting booth among blacks than among whites since 1980. Still, the symbolic promise of a Jackson candidacy — that it might motivate substantially more blacks to register, and hence sweep into office blacks running at lower levels next November — has strong appeal. So does the contention that blacks would have more leverage on the Democratic Party through the primaries and at the convention next summer on issues of jobs and benefits and other matters vital to blacks.

The risks from an embarrassing voter reception for the Rev. Mr. Jackson should be taken into account, too. Mr. Jackson has been pulling less than half of potential black votes. In mayoralties, blacks successfully running for the first time typically win 9 out of 10 black votes, and 1 in 5 white votes. There is no way to know what to expect of black candidacies on the national level, however.

The conventional wisdom is that Mr. Jackson hurts Walter Mondale more than John Glenn. If Mr. Mondale wins the first tests in Iowa and New Hampshire, the horse-race analysts might discount the Mondale edge somewhat more by saying: Wait until next week in the South, where Senator Glenn is already stronger and the Rev. Mr. Jackson will cut into Mondale's base.

But the fact is, the Jackson candidacy will constitute a major experiment in American voting life. How much a factor race will be among blacks' and whites' decisions we will have to wait to see.

The Hartford Courant

Hartford, Conn., November 2, 1983

The fascinating part of Jesse Jackson's presidential candidacy is that even if he loses, he — and the political process — wins.

Mr. Jackson, the popular black minister and social activist who is expected to announce Thursday that he will seek the Democratic nomination, probably will lose his bid. He will not likely have the money, the organization and the broad base of support to conduct the kind of national campaign that would give him a strong chance of success. Walter F. Mondale and John H. Glenn Jr., to name two, do have those advantages.

But his goal seems to be as much to introduce an element of diversity into national politics and to invigorate minority voters as it is to claim a nomination. Mr. Jackson observes that minorities, "because of race, religion and sex, have been discouraged from seeking to serve at the highest in this nation. Part of our mission is to break down that barrier so as to open up the options for everybody."

And he exults at the enthusiasm he believes his potential candidacy has generated among those he calls "the locked-out people." The Jackson camp estimates that a black presidential candidacy could result in up to 3 million new black voters. The results of such a boost in the number of registered blacks would outlive Mr. Jackson's candidacy to have an impact on other elections.

That is the real promise of such a candidacy, and the anticipation of it has caused discomfort across the spectrum. President Reagan's advisers are said to fear a Jackson candidacy because it will inspire blacks to vote. Many black leaders fear that Mr. Jackson will sap strength from Mr. Mondale, who they feel is in a better position to help minorities.

Politics remains a restricted process, however, until a pioneer comes along. Mr. Jackson may fail to reach his destination, but he's charting the course for others who one day will face an easier journey.

THE COMMERCIAL APPEAL
Memphis, Tenn., April 11, 1983

SOME PROMINENT black political leaders are seriously discussing whether a black should run for president in 1984. They have little or no hope, apparently, that a black could win. The candidacy would instead be a symbolic gesture to the Democratic Party that they will not tolerate being taken for granted.

They are unsure yet whether this drive would ultimately increase black political influence. But they are miffed at the national party officials. As their feelings intensify, these black leaders are finding differences even among themselves.

The "black leadership family," as they call themselves, centers on Mayor Andrew Young of Atlanta, congressional delegate Walter Fauntroy of the District of Columbia, Rep. Mickey Leland of Texas, Mayor Richard Hatcher of Gary,

Jesse Jackson

Ind., and Jesse Jackson of Chicago, founder of People United to Save Humanity (PUSH).

Young, a supporter of former Vice President Walter Mondale, cautions that a black candidacy would hurt both Mondale's bid and chances of defeating President Reagan. Most of the others counter that a black protest candidacy may be warranted anyway, but they don't want any black to run unless "the family" approves. And since the group's last meeting

in Atlanta on March 11, Jackson has threatened to bolt "the family" if it decides not to support a black candidacy.

THEIR DISILLUSIONMENT with the Democratic Party stems from several factors. They think the party was insensitive on issues like jobs and aid to the poor until the economy was so bad that it became clear that these problems were not confined mainly to blacks. Many black officials felt betrayed when Mondale and Sen. Edward Kennedy of Massachusetts endorsed white candidates in the Chicago mayoral primary that Rep. Harold Washington, a black, won.

Some blacks say they are frustrated that while they have been one of the Democrats' most loyal constituencies, whites have not returned the favor — not in setting the party's priorities and not at election time. A record 21 blacks are now in Congress, all Democrats, including one who represents a Kansas City district that is 80 per cent white. But the elections that stand out are the ones in which white defections from the party cost blacks unexpected losses in the campaign for governor of California and a U.S. House seat from Mississippi.

Those disappointments aside, blacks are becoming more adept at flexing their political muscle. Spurred by the harshness of Reaganomics and wary that other minorities, especially Hispanics, are gaining power, blacks are conducting impressive registration drives and working toward increasing their representation in local offices — most notably in the mayor's offices of Chicago and Philadelphia. "It's pivotal what white Democrats in Chicago will do," says Rev. Joseph Lowery, president of the Southern Christian Leadership Conference. "If they don't support Washington, that might be some indication of what white Democrats are like in the country."

THE BITTERNESS blacks would feel if Washington lost or if W. Wilson Goode lost in Philadelphia to former Mayor Frank Rizzo — who has been particularly adept at baiting blacks during his political career — should not be underestimated. More unhappiness would result if "the family" drew up an "agenda" of black concerns and its members felt their interests were ignored.

A symbolic black candidacy could influence candidate and party positions, elect more black delegates to the convention and increase black voter turnout. But might a weak candidacy backfire, diminishing the political influence blacks have gained in many cities and set blacks and whites against one another in a way that would hurt the party and the country?

Although the group of black leaders may consider this bid to be strictly symbolic, a black presidential candidacy next year could have a major impact on the outcome of the race and on black political power. They should consider the practical implications before plunging forward.

THE SACRAMENTO BEE
Sacramento, Calif., April 13, 1984

With his strong recent showings, Jesse Jackson has moved into the political big leagues — in his phrase, he has gone "from the Harlem Globetrotters to the NBA" — and he should be judged by big-league rules. That still hasn't happened. Even in the wake of blunders that probably would have sunk any other presidential candidate, Jackson is still getting deferential treatment from the two Democratic front-runners and nearly a free ride from most of the media.

It's patronizing to apply a double standard which turns the Hartpence-to-Hart episode into a front-page story, suggesting that Hart is as evanescent as the Great Gatsby, while giving Jackson's past and present a once-over-lightly. Jackson's a good show, the implicit message reads, but shouldn't be taken seriously. That's not only unfair to the other candidates, it is also condescending to Jackson.

For millions of black Americans, the Jackson campaign realizes a dream: a black man running hard for president. His support in the black community has steadily grown, from 50-plus percent in Birmingham to margins of 75 percent to nearly 90 percent in Chicago, New York and Philadelphia.

Much of that support comes from blacks who haven't been involved in politics — Jackson's candidacy has vastly increased the proportion of blacks voting in the Democratic primaries — and that growing black political participation is a welcome and important development. It is appropriate, however, to distinguish between the cause — a fairer deal for black Americans — which is just, and the candidate, who often seems careless and uninformed about matters of state, and divisive in stirring up racial and ethnic tensions.

There has been little effort to probe deeply Jackson's agenda on education and jobs and welfare, issues about which he might be presumed to have thought carefully, little willingness to ask how his grandiose and loosely sketched social welfare agenda is going to be paid for. How, after all, does one interrupt a sermon to press for details? On foreign policy, Jackson has combined grandstanding — the trip to Syria, the forthcoming mission to Nicaragua — with simple sloganeering, as if jingles could produce peace.

Sometimes, Jackson's misstatements are simply stunning, as when he tells the New York Times that the "B-1 missile" — not the bomber — should be scrapped, or claims that the entire budget deficit could be balanced out of Pentagon cost overruns — overruns that, substantial though they may be, hardly add up to $200 billion. And what is one to make of the claim, pressed at his Rose Garden press conference, that the Syrians had the "right" to kill Lt. Robert O. Goodman Jr.?

What is most frightening, though, is the legacy of divisiveness that Jackson is creating. His equivocation over the "Hymie" remark — reiterated just last week in a Newsweek interview in which he mused about "Jewtown" — has churned up hostilities between longtime allies, blacks and Jews. His continuing loyalty to Louis Farrakhan, leader of the Nation of Islam, who threatened with death the reporter who disclosed Jackson's slur, embraces thuggery. "A bit inciteful and intemperate" is how Jackson described the threat; and, while Jackson disassociated himself from Farrakhan's statement, he also offered to "mediate" between Farrakhan and the reporter as if there were something to negotiate about. Even that stance was more forceful than Jackson had been when, a month earlier, Farrakhan had threatened all Jews in the wake of the "Hymie" story.

Jesse Jackson has blamed his troubles on everyone else — on the *Meet the Press* interviewers last Sunday for "harassment" in repeatedly questioning him about Farrakhan, on the racism of whites who don't vote for him, on the media for the "caricatures" they paint. But just imagine what fate would befall Walter Mondale or Gary Hart had either failed promptly to condemn a supporter who threatened a critic with death.

DAYTON DAILY NEWS
Dayton, Ohio, April 16, 1984

More than most election years, 1984 has seen — and will see more —real discussion of important ideas. All major segments of American political opinion are being aggressively and well represented by presidential candidates.

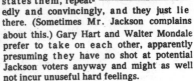

But the ideas of one candidate — the Rev. Jesse Jackson — are not being debated. He states them, repeatedly and convincingly, and they just lie there. (Sometimes Mr. Jackson complains about this.) Gary Hart and Walter Mondale prefer to take on each other, apparently presuming they have no shot at potential Jackson voters anyway and might as well not incur unuseful hard feelings.

There is danger in this. If ideas are repeated often enough, they take on a legitimacy they may not deserve. President Reagan has said so often that the United States undertook unilateral disarmament in the 1970s that it has become a fact, even though it never happened.

Mr. Jackson deserves to have his ideas taken seriously enough to be publicly addressed. He does not, however, deserve to have them swallowed whole.

SYRACUSE
HERALD-JOURNAL
Syracuse, N.Y., February 2, 1984

What's all the fuss about Jesse Jackson's PUSH organizations accepting donations from the Arab League?

At this point, we're not endorsing Jackson — or anybody else — for the presidency, and we really don't have all the facts about how the PUSH network handles its finances, but we have difficulty indicting the candidate because two organizations he was associated with, before he was a candidate, accepted large sums of money from the Arab community.

The reasons for the implied criticism — although nobody yet has said the contributions were illegal — are political. The implication is that since PUSH has been heavily endowed by an Arab entity, Jackson is somehow anti-Israel.

We don't believe anyone can make a political judgment on Jackson's leanings based on such circumstantial evidence. And we don't buy the underlying tone that there is something immoral, if not illegal, about the grants.

Of course, there can be no dodging the political implication of the appearance that Jackson had "done business" with the world Arab community. But, in fact, there is no reason to doubt the claims of the general counsel to the PUSH Foundation that Jackson may not have known about the contributions.

Now, if the Arab League, or any other world organization with special interests, should contribute big bucks to his presidential campaign, that's another matter. Then, of course, his financial connections become fair game for the critics.

But not until then.

The Miami Herald
Miami, Fla., March 31, 1984

TENSION hung like smoke in the air as the three survivors entered the small ring under the white lights for the big fight. For one hour they went at it. Each man fought hard and skillfully, each showed that he belonged there, each showed that he was a professional at the top of his form. And when it was over, all the judges agreed it was a split decision, and everyone who watched filled out his own scorecard.

Walter Mondale, Gary Hart, and Jesse Jackson stood toe to toe and slugged it out in a magnificent debate on Wednesday night. Their ring was a small table on the stage at Columbia University's Low Memorial Library in New York City. Dan Rather of CBS News was the referee. A nationwide television audience shared the excitement with the few hundred spectators present. What they saw was a classic bout.

The prize at stake was, of course, next Tuesday's Democratic Party primary in New York state, followed by Pennsylvania's one week later, and ultimately the party's Presidential nomination. This debate potentially was a make-or-break test. With the title on the line, all three finalists came out swinging. Mondale and Hart repeatedly exchanged heavy blows in sharp, close in-fighting, while Jackson deftly alternated between mixing it up with them and circling just out of reach, above the fray.

It was marvelous theater, filled with drama, aggression, and enlightening exchanges. Each man demonstrated both toughness and composure under heavy pressure, each displayed his strengths for the crowd's consideration, and each thus delivered an ultimate reassurance that if he should go all the way, he would be up to the challenge.

So who won? Dan Rather and CBS surely did, for his direction of this title match was as superb as his network's production of it. The American public surely did, for the voters got a good, long look at just what these three would-be champions are made of, which means this debate was a triumph for the process and the public. Yes, but who won?

Split decision. Mondale, Hart, and Jackson fans each give their man the nod. The winner, on points, will be known only when the final scorecards are tallied — starting Tuesday in New York.

WALTER MONDALE IS AMBITIOUS

JOHN GLENN IS AMBITIOUS

GARY HART IS AMBITIOUS

JESSE JACKSON, ON THE OTHER HAND IS AN UPPITY OPPORTUNIST

The Philadelphia Inquirer

Philadelphia, Pa.. July 12, 1984

"The Democrats will tell you," the Rev. Jesse Jackson said Saturday night, "if you don't vote [for them] Reagan will get you, if you don't vote, the Democratic Party will leave you. They aren't going nowhere. Stand still."

For what?

"Stand still, don't make any panicky decisions. Just stand still and take your signal. If you voted for me in January, February, March, April, May and June, just wait for my signal in July, August, September and October."

Thus the week before the Democratic National Convention became charged with the anxiety, among Democrats, and the hope, among Republicans, that Mr. Jackson intends to fulfill the threat, long lingering beneath the surface, to lead a boycott of the November election.

Why would he?

Time and again, Mr. Jackson has said black Americans have been taken for granted by the Democratic Party — while being humiliated by Republicans. In a recent interview with Washington Post staff writer Juan Williams, he was reported to have said he is "prepared to advise blacks to stay home and risk 'four more years of humiliation rather than stand for four more days of being taken for granted by the Democratic Party.'"

Mr. Jackson has grounds. In the past, he has worked hard with white Democratic candidates, has received promises, direct or implied, and has been left empty-handed. Like it or not, like Mr. Jackson or not, it is not hard to believe that *he* believes the time has come to stop accepting IOUs.

Is his present strategy one of hardball political maneuvering, quite orthodox among political players with regional or ethnic constituencies? Or is abstentionism, to prove a longer-term point, the core of Mr. Jackson's personal political objective?

The answer must come in his "signal" or signals. Mr. Jackson is far too canny to tip his hand prematurely.

Black Americans and any number of others long have had enough power to be wooed during campaigns but not enough to ensure support of their aspirations when policy decisions come. They *have* been taken for granted — by Democrats and Republicans.

No more than 1 percent of all elected officials in America are black, while 11.9 percent of Americans are. Consciousness of that disproportion leads many American blacks to protest that they are victims of political deprivation. In any system, people who feel deprived of any effective share of power face a fundamental question: to participate or to abstain? To work within, by persuasion, or to withhold support in a dramatically exemplary fashion?

By and large, it has been the history of American politics that the mainstream will broaden itself to incorporate the deprived — slowly perhaps, but soon enough to avoid radicalization of the political system.

Nothing short of actual revolution could more fundamentally change U.S. political structure than the emergence of radical factionalism. Multiparty legislatures, government by alliances of factional interests brokering power — the sort of coalition bargaining that long has dominated many European democracies — could be the product of such an evolution.

Arguably, and this is the heart of Mr. Jackson's tactic, it would be a good thing — better than being taken for granted — for Americans so far outside the real power of government, public process and private privilege that they have no effective share of America's dynamics.

From the opposite vantage point, it would be disastrous to the institutional stability of America. It would beget greater and greater factionalism, isolation, erosion of the foundations of the system of democracy that has been the unique, self-renewing genius of U.S. political evolution.

Mr. Jackson's demands, the price the Democratic Party must pay to forfend his threat, are far from specific — which is evidence of his canniness as a political bargainer. But the threat is one of great force.

Immediately, a Jackson-led boycott of the general election would be taken by most observers virtually to guarantee re-election of President Reagan, and possibly very significant increases of Republican power in Congress and local offices. Overhanging Mr. Jackson's strategic considerations, and those of the more centrist elements of the Democratic Party, of course, is the question: Would a boycott work, what percentage of his followers could he deliver — or keep at home?

More distantly, if it were effective it could put Mr. Jackson in a position of exercising vast power in future local and state elections. That could give him a substantial personal political influence seldom before exercised in local dynamics by an outsider.

Or, if Mr. Jackson plays his hand to the limit, just short of standing still in November, he very well might awaken politicians in both parties to the realities of alienation of those who feel — and are — taken for granted. Or, quite possibly, he may be playing his potent hand for more obscure motives.

Whatever Mr. Jackson's motives may be, increasingly now he is making public statements that are irresponsible, inflammatory, divisive — to the point of amplifying the impression of bigotry toward Jews and arrogant scapegoating of other elements of the American political process that have been, and will continue to be, valuably supportive of black aspirations.

That has one inevitable effect, among many: To put extraordinary pressure on mainstream Democrats to reject him. That, in turn, has all the earmarks of Mr. Jackson's contriving a situation in which he could lead an abstentionist movement while blaming his, and his followers', alienation on the Democratic Party.

Watch for the signal. Or signals. At the very least, the Jackson game will be to provide the most interesting show in San Francisco next week.

THE MILWAUKEE JOURNAL

Milwaukee, Wisc., April 15, 1984

Jesse Jackson won't win the Democratic presidential nomination, but he has won a significant share of power for himself and his constituency. He fully deserves his heightened influence in the party councils.

Jackson has started a forest fire of black political involvement. Yet, he has not been the divisive force that some people had expected of him. Rather, he has contributed to a broadening of the party's base by bringing previously uninvolved blacks into the Democratic fold. That could prove crucial to the party's eventual nominee.

Charisma partly explains Jackson's success. With his commanding presence and peerless oratorical skills, Jackson affects the stance of a born leader. Some speakers stir audiences. Jackson ignites them. Yet, he also has shrewd political instincts, as he has shown in his trip to Syria to free Navy Lt. Robert Goodman, and in his behavior in the debates among presidential candidates.

However, Jackson's political acumen has seemed to desert him in the continuing flap over his slur of Jews as "Hymies" and New York City as "Hymietown." Jackson, who would have demanded the head of any white candidate who made similarly derogatory references to blacks and to Washington, D. C., was unconscionably slow to admit his remarks. He also has failed to repudiate statements by supporter Louis Farrakhan, the leader of the Nation of Islam, who appears to have threatened Milton Coleman, the newspaper reporter who revealed Jackson's slurs. Thus, Jackson has undercut the moral basis of his candidacy.

Nonetheless, Jackson has managed to retain much of the moral force of his campaign. His specific views on defense matters and foreign policy questions are debatable. Yet, who can debate the appeal of his saying, "We must end the nuclear arms race and save the human race"?

Most importantly, Jackson is the forceful, fervent spokesman for those he calls "the left out and the locked out." Surely, Walter Mondale and Gary Hart also care about people at the bottom of the economic pyramid. Yet, they haven't demonstrated the feeling of Jackson's passionate discussion of "young people in the dawn of life, poor people in the pit of life, old people in the sunset of life." In Shakespearean terms, Jackson is Banquo's ghost, haunting the political feast with reminders of "the least of these."

Having won significant political influence with his approach, Jackson can be expected to drive a hard bargain for his constituency at the Democratic National Convention. For example, he threatens to withhold his support from any candidate who does not promise an end to the South's traditional second primaries, which have the effect of diminishing black political power.

Perhaps Jackson's terms are too harsh. Yet, his stance exemplifies the message of his campaign: Blacks intend to be heard and respected.

However, Jackson's most important message perhaps is addressed to people who may be too young to vote in 1984. He has aimed at the highest rung of the political ladder. His quest tells every black boy and every black girl in America that they need no longer place any ceiling on their aspirations.

The Providence Journal

Providence, R.I., May 10, 1984

The 1984 Democratic presidential race stays hot. Surprise has followed surprise — and the latest came on Tuesday, when Sen. Gary Hart managed to best Walter Mondale in the Indiana and Ohio primaries. By thus staying alive, the Coloradoan has increased the chances that the Democrats' July convention will shake San Francisco to its roots.

The ups and downs have confounded political experts across the country. At first, Gary Hart was just another outsider. Then came those early New England primaries, where he thrashed Walter Mondale, forged ahead and shook up Democratic presidential predictions. Thereupon the Mondale machine gasped, sputtered, got itself together and took off in high gear. Senator Hart looked to be fading fast. The Rev. Jesse Jackson was scoring more impressively in some states, and until this week the Mondale locomotive was beginning to look unstoppable.

But in winning Ohio and Indiana on Tuesday (however narrowly), Senator Hart showed that he has stamina and, to certain kinds of Democrats, an appeal that Walter Mondale can't match. Mr. Jackson did impressively, as well: he scored a second in Maryland (where Mr. Mondale won easily) and drew a solid 25 percent of the vote in North Carolina. These results may not have scrambled the nomination race anew. But they should enliven what had been a dispirited Hart campaign, add luster to Mr. Jackson's achievement — and keep pressure on Mr. Mondale.

The former vice president, who by now has corraled more than 1,500 of the 1,967 delegates needed for nomination, remains a heavy favorite. But Senator Hart has shown himself to be resilient and resourceful, and his bloc of 890 or so delegates is likely to climb to well over 1,000 by the end of the primary trail. Unless Mr. Mondale has managed by then to nail down an unshakeable majority, Democrats can look forward to a wide-open convention with still more surprises in store.

Gary Hart's appeal to Democrats remains definable more by what he is not than by what he might, as president, be. Unlike Mr. Mondale, he is closely linked neither with organized labor nor the nostalgic liberalism of Great Society days. He fancies that he is not wedded to old ideas, but can't convince many Democrats that he has many original new ones. On some issues he is refreshingly independent; on others, he seems wedded to warmed-over party platitudes. He remains something of a curious fig-ure, and this novelty (or ambiguity) remains part of his political appeal.

Mr. Jackson, now with over 300 delegates, may prove to be the historic figure of the entire political year. With more verve and style than the other Democratic contenders combined, he is forcing a reshaping of the political dialogue in ways that seem certain to last. Striving chiefly on behalf of blacks, he has pushed his presidential quest nearer the mainstream of American politics than any black politician before him.

Whatever happens in remaining primaries, neither Mr. Hart nor Mr. Jackson will let San Francisco get dull. The combat yet could bring on a deadlocked convention and a surprise nominee. It could spill enough Democratic blood to give President Reagan a fairly easy re-election victory. By contrast, it could galvanize Democratic efforts to sign up unregistered voters. Even if his challenger and the sort of challenge remain unclear, President Reagan had better prepare for a tough battle.

THE DAILY OKLAHOMAN

Oklahoma City, Okla., September 5, 1984

ALMOST overnight, the Rev. Jesse Jackson has become the most prominent and quoted spokesman for black Americans, as well as a polarizing force to be reckoned with on the national political scene.

Jackson didn't really expect to win the Democratic presidential nomination, but his showing with black voters in some of the primaries was impressive enough to force an accommodation with Walter Mondale. Jackson's price for lending his active support to the Mondale-Ferraro ticket was a chunk of campaign funds and staff, plus assurance of his input on issues and policies.

Already it's become part of the conventional wisdom of some elements in the national media that Jackson is the equivalent of a modern political pied piper who will lead an overwhelming majority of black voters into the Mondale-Ferraro fold come November.

What disappoints is the national media's disregard or down-playing of those black voices raised in opposition to Jackson's shrill diatribe against President Reagan and his administration.

Jackson's revivalist "Amen, brother" style of rhetoric notwithstanding, the fact is that he does not speak for all black Americans. In particular, he does not speak for increasing numbers of minorities who, by virtue of their own dedication and achievement, resent being pegged automatically as camp followers of the mercurial Jackson.

For example, the stirring pro-Reagan speech at the GOP convention by the pastor of one of the largest black congregations in Los Angeles received little notice.

Likewise, while a national TV interview show over the Labor Day weekend afforded Jackson more exposure, the endorsement of President Reagan's re-election by a prestigious black clergyman was paid scant attention by the national media.

From Dr. Joseph Harrison Jackson, pastor of a large Chicago church and president of the 7-million-member National Baptist Convention, came an endorsement of President Reagan's re-election because of his belief that Jackson's candidacy was divisive. This from a black Democrat.

Now from a young black publisher and consultant, William A. Keyes, comes another plea that the liberal big-spending policies advocated by Jackson are not in the best interests of black Americans. In a lecture at The Heritage Foundation in Washington, Keyes urged conservatives to expose the "truth that forty years of liberal policy-making in Washington has been a disaster for most black Americans."

Keyes noted that when the liberal "Great Society" programs began, "only one of every 20 black families was on welfare. But today, after 20 years of federal programs and billions of dollars, one in five black families are on welfare."

The assumption that all black Americans agree with Jesse Jackson does a disservice to those who comprise an expanding black middle class. Those who think Jesse has all the black votes in his pocket could be in for a rude surprise.

The State

Columbia, S.C., February 6, 1984

THE REV. Jesse Jackson's attempt to blame corporate America for the problems of the poor opens new possibilities for his quest for the Democratic Presidential nomination.

In scheduling public hearings for those left jobless by plant closings to vent their anger, the S.C. native also stepped up his attack on President Reagan's economic policies. His appeal to class prejudice is a move to put his candidacy on more substantial grounds than race.

Indeed, the voices of the structurally unemployed should be heard and constructive answers sought to their problems. But such emotional shows as Mr. Jackson projects to let people "personally" tell political leaders and corporate executives about the effect of plant closings promise little more than good media copy and a few votes. It is a case of trying to capitalize on problems rather than solve them.

Of course, nobody likes to see a plant closed. To a corporate executive, a closed plant stands as a stark business failure. The effect is tragic to all concerned — employees, businesses in the community and every caring person.

But if Mr. Jackson looks more closely, he will see that forcing a plant to operate at a loss indefinitely also has its cruel consequences. It diverts resources, capital and labor from more productive pursuits. And while it may not easily be apprehended by those hardest hit — those without jobs — pursuing unprofitable economic ventures deprives other people of jobs — people who would benefit from more productive use of labor and capital. Indeed, keeping a sick plant open might well force a company into bankruptcy.

The people whom the Rev. Mr. Jackson talks about being victimized are more visible than those who fail to get the jobs that are never created. Still, the latter are very, very real.

Thus, the Rev. Mr. Jackson's road show promises more heat than light, more hype than results, more confrontation than deliberation.

The Honolulu Advertiser

Honolulu, Ha., March 20, 1984

Another Tuesday, another Democratic presidential primary.

But this one is Illinois, the biggest and most hotly contested state to date. It is also Chicago, the nation's third largest city with a heartland symbolism all its own and some dangerous local political shoals for the candidates.

IN THIS two-level contest with three candidates, it's conceivable that all three could win something important.

Walter Mondale, with a superior organization and strong support among the Democratic establishment, appears virtually certain to take the most delegates. His backers say that is what will count at the San Francisco convention in July.

But there is a separate popular vote of increased importance, and there Gary Hart is given a good chance. A strong showing seems essential to give his now-slowed momentum another boost.

HART WILL benefit by Jesse Jackson's appeal to black voters, votes that might otherwise go to Mondale. But Jackson is also being seen as more than just a Chicago boy picking up the hometown vote, a subject discussed in an adjoining column.

In recent weeks, the black civil rights leader has managed to save his federal matching funds with a strong showing in the South and minimize the damage with an apology for his unfortunate, anti-Semitic comment about New York as "Hymietown".

In the eyes of some political experts Jackson has emerged as a pivotal force between Mondale and Hart, and potentially a key power broker in San Francisco.

Of course, Tuesday's truism can be Wednesday's outdated theory in this kind of hectic horserace campaign.

But, if Jackson won't be up front when a Democrat finally gets the nod as party nominee, he has made a point as the first major black candidate for president, and he will be a factor in the choice and what happens next.

AND, ONCE again, a big question, for this year at least, will be whether his candidacy will have helped the Democrats to victory or defeat.

The Boston Globe

Boston, Mass., February 3, 1984

The surprise — and delight — of the 1984 campaign is the emergence of Jesse Jackson as a serious and credible presidential candidate. In the all-candidate debates and in his individual appearances, Jackson has proved himself to be not just a curiosity, but a political leader who compels the same kind of serious attention as do the other seven principal Democratic contenders.

When Jackson first made it known that he was considering making a run for the Democratic nomination, the image most Americans had was that he was as an ambitious black preacher from Chicago with a colorful style of speaking but with no particular record of accomplishment and with no political philosophy beyond that of any other veteran of the black civil rights movement.

The dramatic mission to Syria, during which he obtained the release of Lt. Robert Goodman, proved that Jackson had a flair for the dramatic and the instincts of a successful gambler. Although the mission did not define Jackson's foreign policy, it put him on the scene of the major foreign policy issues of the campaign — and caught the nation's attention.

The nationally televised debate from Dartmouth provided a look at Jackson in the full context of the campaign. Up on the stage with the other seven Democratic contenders — a former vice president, four US senators, a former senator and presidential nominee, and a former governor — Jackson showed himself to be as knowledgeable and articulate as any of the others on a wide range of issues.

The past few days which Jackson has spent in the Boston area have provided the opportunity to evaluate the impact of his candidacy on the Democratic campaign.

To many observers, Tuesday night's foreign policy debate at the Kennedy School suggested that the Democratic field has developed a clear alternative to the Reagan foreign policy. This alternative is based on recognition of the needs of the Third World and on the necessity to negotiate with the Soviet Union rather than engage in confrontation with it.

Credit for this progressive movement must go also to George McGovern, who has emerged as the party's conscience. Both McGovern and Jackson have articulated — and Jackson has dramatized — the need for America to become involved in the struggle for social change in the Third World, as an ally, not as an opponent.

The Third World connection has become particularly sharp with the disclosures that Jackson's Operation PUSH has received sizable donations from the Arab League. Jackson has characterized the controversy as "an attempt to vulgarize Arabs," similar to historic attempts to destroy sympathy and support for Jews, blacks and other minorities.

It is more than coincidence that at the Harvard debate the Democratic field began to articulate a broader version of Jackson's personal message: that there must be an end to the Reagan Administration's attempts to "vulgarize" any racial or ethnic group, demonize the Soviet Union or trivialize the Third World.

Roanoke Times & World-News

Roanoke, Va., July 19, 1984

ON MONDAY night, New York Gov. Mario Cuomo delivered a powerful speech to the Democratic convention that established his credentials as a major-league politician. On the next night, the Rev. Jesse Jackson followed with a powerful speech that established his credentials as a major-league crusader.

While an effective politician must have a bit of the crusader in him, and an effective crusader a bit of the politician, the two are not the same. Can Jackson make the transition? Does he want to?

There's a time to compete, Jackson said, and a time to cooperate. In deciding to cooperate, in using his considerable oratorical powers to urge the election of the Democratic ticket in November, though his own name won't be on it, Jackson chose the politically wise course.

A majority even of those who voted for him in the Democratic primaries, according to at least one poll, in fact prefer Walter Mondale for the presidency. Mondale and Jackson may disagree on some issues, but those differences are small compared with the gulf that separates Jackson and his constituency from the policies of the Reagan administration. Never in his life has Jackson held public office; more than rivalry lay behind the reluctance of veteran black politicians to embrace Jackson's bid for the presidential nomination.

In short, had Jackson withheld his support, he would have run the serious risk of looking silly. For a prophet, such risk is acceptable; indeed, it may come with the territory. But for a politician, looking silly can be fatal.

Jackson earned respect within the party, not to mention 10 percent of the convention's delegate votes for president. His speech, containing substantive argument as well as rhetorical flourish and personal confession, enhanced that respect.

Moreover, Jackson has set up a situation in which he can demonstrate another mark of the effective politician: the ability to deliver votes. Whatever the fate of the Mondale-Ferraro ticket, it appears almost certain that Jackson's constituency (heavily, but not exclusively, black) will support it overwhelmingly. If that happens, it may stem from hostility to Reagan rather than from loyalty to Jackson; who, though, can know for sure?

Despite all the political implications, however, the tone of Jackson's speech remained as much prophetic as political.

A prophet can proclaim that "God is not finished with me yet," and can assume the mantle of vicar of a nation's dispossessed; no politician can be so audacious. A prophet can apologize for a mistake of the head that was not of the heart, and be believed; a politician, though he need not be so pure of heart, learns to avoid such mistakes. A prophet can "energize" the soil, then leave it for others to plow; a politician must see the work through to harvest.

Near the end of his speech, Jackson returned to a theme that has been a hallmark of his career from long before he became a presidential candidate. He called on America's young people to turn disadvantage into opportunity, and opportunity into productive service.

It is a call that Jackson might well ponder for himself. What use will he make of the opportunity created by his crusader's foray into politics? Is his productive future as the crusader, or as a politician?

THE PLAIN DEALER

Cleveland, Ohio, March 23, 1984

Hear now Democratic presidential candidate the Rev. Jesse Jackson coming to grips with political reality: "White support is coming slow," says he, because of "historical [racial] polarization" and the media's penchant for portraying blacks as "less intelligent ... less hardworking ... less universal ... less patriotic ... and more violent than we [whites] are."

Jackson is indeed having trouble gathering whites to his "rainbow coalition," and he is indeed frequently identified as the "black candidate." Hence Jackson generally is right to be critical of institutionalized political segregation and discrimination. The title "black candidate" is racially active, immediately characterizing his support and his candidacy in racial terms rather than political ones.

There are other reasons, however, for Jackson's inability to attract broader support. Many voters—black and white—clearly are dissuaded by his evangelical style. And many others distrust the quixotic nature of his campaign, which cannot win the nomination and therefore does not have the potential to dethrone President Reagan. Such pragmatists are diametrically opposed to campaigns of whimsy and futurism, and may be Jackson's greatest nemesis.

Jackson's campaign is whimsical and futuristic. It was clear from the outset that its triumph would be the legitimacy it conferred on black politics and future black candidacies. In that regard, it would be a resounding success even if it halted today. For the first time, a black leader has been established both as a national political figure and a convention power, achievements that seemed impossible last summer. But it also is whimsical because Jackson professes to desire a candidacy he cannot win, and because much of his support has resulted from the media coverage he now castigates.

Jackson's remarks are inappropriate for two reasons. First, his "rainbow coalition" is rhetorical fiction—the voter registration drives that founded his candidacy were not aimed at the poor and disenfranchised, but at blacks who are poor and disenfranchised. Jackson's campaign has been a fundamentally black one. Second, what did he expect? He's the one who targeted black voters; he's the one who decided to chart new political waters; he's the one who decided to risk the slings and arrows of political pioneerism. Such courage and vision is diluted by naivete.

THE SUN

Baltimore, Md., July 6, 1984

Now that President Reagan has spoken out, ever so softly, against Jesse Jackson's tendency to trash his own country while traveling abroad, another politician is still to be heard from. His name: Walter F. Mondale.

The prospective Democratic presidential nominee probably is loath to echo Mr. Reagan's suggestion that Mr. Jackson has violated the Logan Act, which prohibits private citizens from negotiating with foreign governments. In this, Mr. Mondale has our sympathy. The Logan issue is pure baloney, as White House praise last winter for Mr. Jackson's success in obtaining the release of Navy Lt. Robert Goodman from a Syrian prison amply confirms. But Mr. Mondale's opinion of the foreign policy views Mr. Jackson expounds abroad and, more particularly, the propriety of his comments, is a legitimate area for public inquiry.

During his trip to Central America last week, Mr. Jackson described the Panama Canal (an economic asset of incalculable value to Panama) as a "badge of disgrace" for this country. He told the Sandinista regime in Nicaragua that U.S.-backed "contras" should lay down their arms while, in dealing with El Salvador, he treated its leftist rebels as a legitimate force. And he professed feeling "good vibes" for Cuba's Fidel Castro, who responded by releasing 49 prisoners — some Americans held on drug charges, the majority Cubans jailed for political reasons. (One of the latter, Andres Vargas Gomez, who spent 22 years behind bars for opposing Communism, dismissed Mr. Jackson's "moral offensive for peace" by saying it was "a moral offense" to deal with an oppressor.)

On the page opposite, emotions stirred by Mr. Jackson's travels are ventilated in two contrasting columns by George Will and Carl Rowan. Contrary to Mr. Will, we do not believe Mr. Jackson is deliberately helping leftist dictators; contrary to Mr. Rowan, we do not consider him qualified by ideology or instinct to be secretary of state.

What we do believe is that Mr. Jackson considers himself a "Third World American" entitled to articulate views that are wholly at variance with the foreign policy concepts of the Washington Establishment. "There was a lot of understanding," he said after his eight hours with Fidel Castro. "He's in the Third World and I have a Third World experience growing up in America.... We identify with a lot of the same people in Africa and Central America."

As a private citizen, Mr. Jackson would have every right to say anything he wants. But as a candidate for president, a politician with special status at home and abroad, Mr. Jackson is way out of bounds. Does Mr. Mondale agree?

Post-Tribune

Guarding Your Interests Daily

Gary, Ind., January 5, 1984

It is a remarkable story. The Rev. Jesse Jackson goes to Damascus, asks Syria's president to release an American officer held prisoner for almost a month, and it is done.

In its simplest, restricted context, the freeing of Lt. Robert Goodman is a happy story. Perhaps it really is an uncomplicated story of personal persuasion and humanitarianism; it will not be left in that context, because it is undeniably entwined in politics and diplomacy.

Our opinions

Jackson has disclaimed personal political motives in the Damascus mission. Some believe him, many will not; but no matter — his political stature has been enhanced. He is still a presidential candidate whose chances of winning the nomination are remote, but he also is a candidate whose influence cannot be denied. It must be dealt with.

It does no good to speculate about what Jackson would have done if the American officer were white, or about what Syrian President Hafez Assad would have done if Jackson were white. And it is foolish to now regard Assad as a nice guy. This decent act, whatever its motives, does not change the man.

The deeply important issue now is what the Syrian decision means. It is quite possible that the Syrians had a prisoner they did not want and were glad to get rid of a political burden while looking like humanitarians. Even that does not downgrade the Jackson effort. He cut through the red tape and the trepidation about demanding the lieutenant's release and proved that one-on-one talks, devoid of dicussions about deals and tradeoffs, can work in the right situations. Maybe, just maybe, there's a lesson in that.

Syria could be willing to talk instead of fighting, and the Reagan administration should be exploring that possibility. Whether the freeing of Lt. Goodman is a big step toward peace is speculative, but it is a dramatic change in the solemn, apprehensive, suspicious script that has been followed for so long.

Jesse Jackson's credibility has been helped. Syria's credibility has been helped. Even the Reagan administration looked relatively good, despite its earlier worries about the Jackson trip. It did not put undue pressure on him to call it off and the president was quick to give him the credit for a remarkable accomplishment.

How candidate Jackson handles this triumph is important, too. We hope he does not now consider himself an official diplomat, or a spokesman on American foreign policy. Reagan is still supposed to be in charge. As for Jackson's candidacy, he proved again that he is a master of timing, unafraid to try the unusual. Nothing that he does publicly, of course, can be separated from the political campaign. And even when he may not really be campaigning, Jesse Jackson puts verve into a campaign that features more dullness than enlightenment.

The San Diego Union

San Diego, Calif., May 23, 1984

The Rev. Jesse Jackson's frequent references to the Third World have generated renewed interest in the phrase. Although many voters have a vague understanding that this geopolitical classification encompasses the underdeveloped countries, there is general confusion about its origin and the nations that belong to the First and Second Worlds.

The phrase Third World first emerged during the late 1950s, following the Bandung Conference of non-aligned nations in Indonesia. It gained general acceptance during the next two decades to describe poorer African, Asian, and Latin American countries with high illiteracy rates and burgeoning populations.

By contrast, the First World consists of highly-developed countries including the United States, Western European nations, and Japan. The Second World is made up of communist states.

These world designations are sometimes inexact and confusing. Where, for example, does one place Yugoslavia, which distances itself from Moscow and is neither highly-developed nor economically depressed? Then there is Communist China, which fits into the Second or Third World categories, but considers itself a Fourth World country, a phrase generally reserved for impoverished nations such as Bangladesh and Senegal.

As though this were not enough, several years ago there was even talk of a *Fifth World* consisting of South Africa, Taiwan, Israel, and those nations that are increasingly isolated in the world community.

Suffice it to say that the geopolitical-phrase game is similar to a sporting event; you can't keep the contestants straight without consulting your program.

JACKSON GAINS RELEASE OF PILOT FROM SYRIANS

JACKSON TALKS WITH NICARAGUANS AND CUBANS

JACKSON MOVES UP IN POLLS!

HELLO, JESSE? HEY-WHAT'S HAPPEN'EN? SAY, HOW'D YOU LIKE TO BE MY NEXT SECRETARY OF STATE?

San Francisco Chronicle

San Francisco, Calif., July 19, 1984

THAT MOST majestic of quadrennial rituals, the roll call of the states, had not been completed last night before the word was out that Senator Gary Hart was on his way to the Moscone Center to concede that his candidacy was ended. As if by magic, the blue and white signs of Walter Mondale were predominant and the calls for unity were being heard.

And, within minutes, the three foes, Mondale, Hart and the Rev. Jesse Jackson, who were involved in such ardent, even angry, opposition during the long primary campaign, had begun the process of reconciliation and unity. They had finished the playoffs, said the Rev. Mr. Jackson, and now they were on the way to the Super Bowl and the White House.

There are those who may dispute this. There are great issues still dividing a party having difficulty finding its way. The first gesture toward finding common goals came emotionally from the party's most unpredictable candidate the night before.

THE REV. MR. JACKSON met one major issue head-on early in his address: the split between Jewish Democrats and the Jackson campaign caused by Jackson's own indiscretion and by his delay in repudiating some outrageous remarks of Muslim Louis Farrakhan. He appealed for a restoration of the alliance between Jewish social idealism and blacks suffering injustice which was such a major factor in the civil rights struggle of the mid-1960s.

"If there were occasions when my grapes turned into raisins and my joy bell lost its resonance, please forgive me," he said. "Charge it to my head and not to my heart. My head is so limited in its finitude, my heart is boundless in its love for the human family. I am not a perfect servant. I am a public servant. As I develop and serve, be patient. God is not finished with me yet."

There was great poignancy for many in the huge convention audience as the Rev. Mr. Jackson recited the names of the voting drive martyrs of those days when a great wave of the idealistic young went to the South to challenge a racist establishment. He reminded his audience of the very great sacrifices made seeking elemental justice. The presence of an articulate, comparatively young black man appearing before the nation as a presidential candidate is, perhaps, a monument to all who sat-in, boycotted, registered and risked. Some of the people from Selma, Birmingham, Biloxi and Little Rock, those who dared to try, are convention delegates today.

The Birmingham News

Birmingham, Ala., July 20, 1984

The Rev. Jesse Jackson's address to the Democratic National Convention Tuesday night was remarkable on several counts.

It was perhaps less exciting than was expected by many, although this can be attributed to the essential fact that he — at least in his speech — made his peace with the Mondale forces and adopted a call for party unity. Unity, for good or ill, is simply not as exciting as division, as the Rev. Jackson's career is witness.

Even so, the speech remains an historic one by any account. It was the first time that a black spoke to a national political convention as a serious presidential candidate. The significance of such an event can hardly be overstated. Whether one approves of Jesse Jackson's political views or not, the fact that he summoned the will and drive to bring himself to such a point in history must be applauded.

At the same time, it remains important to distinguish Jesse Jackson as symbol from Jesse Jackson as political operative. Much was made of the fact, for instance, that Jackson's speech left many of his supporters in tears of joy on the convention floor. Yet the question must be asked whether those tears were for the substance of what Jackson said, or simply for the fact that he, a black candidate, was saying it before the convention on national television at prime time.

As a speech, Jackson's rhetoric suffered from the same excess that marked much of his campaign. Contrasted with New York Gov. Mario Cuomo's cool, yet highly effective, oratory of the night before, Jackson's speech came off as rather self-centered sermonizing.

The real test of Jackson's legitimacy as a national political figure will be in the months to come. If he follows the theme of his rhetoric and works for a conciliation of interests — if, in essence, he becomes a party man — then his standing will be immeasurably strengthened as a political figure.

If, however, his principal aim continues to be the personal elevation of Jesse Jackson, it is likely that the enthusiasm he is capable of rousing will be increasingly restricted to his hard-core supporters.

It will be interesting to see how the answer to that question develops in the coming months. For the Democratic Party and the candidacy of Walter Mondale, it will be more than merely interesting, however; it could be the difference between debacle and a respectable campaign.

The Morning News

Wilmington, Del., July 19, 1984

THE REV. Jesse Jackson's extraordinary address to the Democratic National Convention fused the dreams of the past with the hopes of the future — not only for black Americans but for all Americans.

His presence on the podium in San Francisco was a triumph. He was there at no one's sufferance. He was there because he demonstrated to his party and to the nation that he and those he represents constitute a powerful political force.

On Tuesday night, Jesse Jackson concluded his race for the presidency with a concession speech that gave no quarter on principle. He would not, he said, abandon those whose support had fueled his campaign: ". . . the disinherited and despised."

The full political impact of Jesse Jackson's quest for the presidency will not be known until Election Day. His declaration that he would be proud to support the nominee of the Democratic Party was an open acknowledgment that he had lost. It was also a potent political statement: The support of the Rainbow Coalition he leads is essential if the Democrats are to win in November.

Twenty years ago black Americans and other minorities were struggling for basic civil rights. In 1984, a black American stood before the Democratic National Convention as a major power broker. The tireless efforts of all those who labored in the civil rights movement were crystallized Tuesday night when Jesse Jackson mounted the podium. He is a symbol, of course. But only a fool could dismiss the political power which is the essence of the symbol.

It was a measure of Jesse Jackson, the man and the politician, that in his speech he tried to repair the wound he inflicted on himself and the Democratic Party. With grace and style, he apologized for remarks about Jews that offended Jews and non-Jews alike.

Given political realities of the times, it was obvious from the start that the Rev. Jesse Jackson could not hope to be the Democratic Party's nominee in 1984. Yet there was no hollowness to his ringing contention Tuesday night that "Our time has come." He has altered the way power is sought and brokered. The political and symbolic repercussions of his candidacy have already begun.

Newsday

Long Island, N.Y., July 19, 1984

In a performance that was part stump speech and part sermon, part pride and part contrition, Jesse Jackson held the Democratic convention and a nationwide television audience under his spell Tuesday night.

It was a moment of glory he had earned the hard way, against odds that seemed insurmountably high at times — and surely would have been only a few years ago.

Jackson's task at the convention was about as difficult as a political balancing act can be. If he hadn't endorsed the Democratic ticket, his political career might well have ended in San Francisco. But by embracing it, he risked appearing to abandon the goals of his most devoted followers. He met the challenge head on by acknowledging the Democratic Party's imperfections and calling on it to send "a signal that we care" to "the damned, disinherited, disrespected, despised."

And then he made a forthright attempt to close the rifts that his campaign had opened — especially between blacks and Jews — and to prevent new ones from forming. "If in my low moments . . . I have caused anyone discomfort, created pain or revived someone's fears," he said, "that was not my truest self . . . Please forgive me."

For his overwhelmingly black "Rainbow Coalition," Jackson pointed to accomplishments that are real indeed. Even though his forces lost some fights on the floor, the Democratic platform bears his imprint and the party cannot ignore the concerns he has raised.

The political problem for America's blacks is how to translate their voting power into real leverage, given their traditionally low turnout and historic adherence to the Democratic Party. Jackson demonstrated through his candidacy that blacks and other minorities constitute a formidable voting bloc — when they're motivated to vote.

How to motivate them is the political problem the Democratic Party must face. One way might be to give Jackson an important and visible role in the campaign, with emphasis on registering and turning out new voters. Making a place for Jackson — while retaining the loyalties of those who disagree with him — will be a major test for Walter Mondale. His campaign's success will depend heavily on his ability to translate into reality the unified effort that all the party's leading figures now claim to seek.

THE ATLANTA CONSTITUTION
Atlanta, Ga., April 5, 1984

Even as Walter Mondale was luxuriating in his big win in the New York Democratic presidential primary, Jesse Jackson, coming off an impressive showing himself, pressed a rhetorical maneuver that could put the former vice president in a no-win bind: "I would be a good president," Jackson said. "I would be a good vice president. I am qualified for the job."

He is not qualified. Jackson has no public-office experience. His role as the head of an organization, PUSH, that he created himself, hardly measures up. Geographical ticket-balancing is an old political tactic, and the balancing would be no more untoward if it were by race or gender.

But ticket-balancing alone is no longer enough. Vice presidents have had to step in during two recent presidencies — John Kennedy's and Richard Nixon's. Voters have become uneasy with vice presidential nominees who have nothing better to recommend them than political credentials.

Yet Jackson shows signs of beginning to run for the vice presidency. The proposition could kill the Democratic nominee in the general election, if he were forced into accepting it, or kill him in the general election, if he resisted and alienated the new voters whom Jackson, to his credit, is exciting about the political process.

Jackson has begun to develop strong political credentials. He ran virtually even in New York with slumping Gary Hart, who was able to hold only half of the "Yuppies," his core constituency of young urban professionals. Jackson turned the trick he said he could pull off: black participation was up almost 100 percent over four years ago. It has increased wherever Jackson has run.

The most important question raised by the New York primary is neither whether Mondale has recaptured Big Mo nor whether Hart has lost it, but how Jackson intends to use his developing political position.

If it is to press an enlivened social conscience on the Democratic Party and its nominee, well and good. If it is to harry the nominee and party with personal claims, then Jackson will trivialize his accomplishment and abandon to disappointment or disillusionment the very voters he has brought into the process.

CHARLESTON EVENING POST
Charleston, S.C., July 19, 1984

SAN FRANCISCO — The word most often used to describe Jesse Jackson's performance before the Democratic Convention this week was "electric." That's no overstatement. While not everyone will agree with former California Gov. Jerry Brown that Mr. Jackson's emotion-packed appearance produced the best speech he ever heard, it doubtless will be remembered. Jesse Jackson brought the delegates roaring to their feet, tears to eyes all over the hall and, finally, hands entwined. It should have been enough to make watching Republicans very nervous.

Mr. Jackson, in fact, made a conscious effort to alleviate concerns about his Rainbow Coalition effort that have been expressed by members of his own party. While his phrasing may have been awkward and his timing bad, South Carolina Sen. Ernest F. Hollings had some pithy criticisms this week of the direction in which Mr. Jackson has been going.

In effect, what Sen. Hollings told South Carolina delegates is that regardless of what it's called, the Rainbow Coalition is being perceived as just a device for getting more for blacks. The campaign, in the senator's view, has taken on more of a racial hue. Rather than saying "I am somebody," the senator complained, the new theme song seems to be, "I am some race." Further, the senator believes Mr. Jackson's dabbling in foreign affairs has been an unwise course and suggested he get back to doing what he does best, motivating the youth of this country with his own success story.

Understandably, the senator's message didn't play well with many Jackson supporters. Still, there were black leaders willing to agree with his message if not his presentation. Mr. Jack-son sought to prove some of those criticisms of the Rainbow Coalition wrong. As a preliminary to his address, supporters of all hues appeared before the convention to attest to their belief in the cause. The theme was that he had given the disadvantaged and the disenchanted, those on the outside looking in, a vehicle for working within, and, perhaps even taking over, the system.

Further, his speech was one of the peacemaker who was willing to bring his talents to work for the party in November. And there was that dramatic, emotional apology for any past mistakes that even his harshest critics had to concede was masterful.

The Jackson speech was not, however, the address of a political moderate, one of the group to whom the Democrats are trying so desperately to appeal. While his remarks may have been embraced by most delegates, the big question is how he was perceived in living rooms across the country.

But while there clearly is a big push among party strategists to appeal to Middle America this November, they aren't fooling themselves about their constituency. They also need all those extra votes it now is hoped Jesse Jackson can help deliver. No question, the day after the Jackson address a Democratic victory seemed more possible than the day before.

St. Petersburg Times
St. Petersburg, Fla., July 19, 1984

Editorial correspondence

SAN FRANCISCO — For nearly an hour Tuesday night, a black man commanded the podium of the Democratic Party and the attention of the entire nation. American politics can never be the same in the aftermath of Jesse Jackson's heartfelt and moving speech.

People will not soon forget what he said, but the larger significance lies in why he was there. Jackson has given a political voice to millions of people who didn't think they had one — and has enhanced their political influence as well. As former Florida Gov. Reubin Askew observed, the 1984 Democratic convention will be "historic . . . it gave more than lip service to expanding the party."

Jackson wasn't the first black to run for president. That footnote belongs to Shirley Chisholm, the former congresswoman who seconded his nomination Wednesday night. But Jackson *was* the first to campaign as if he thought he could win and he made his supporters believe their votes would matter.

THE POINT, of course, is that you don't have to have *all* the votes to succeed in politics — just enough to make the difference. That explains the vast wave of relief that swept the convention hall when Jackson declared he would be "proud to support" the party's nominee. The *quid pro quo*, quite obviously, is that Jackson will have the nominee's ear.

What will he do with his new found influence? Jackson tried hard Tuesday night — and, we think, sincerely — to heal the dangerous breach that has developed between black and Jewish voters. It is important to remember that while certain incidents in Jackson's campaign exacerbated those differences, they did not originate there. Black anti-Semitism existed long before Jackson's candidacy called attention to it. The tragedy of that is as Jackson himself expressed it: "We are bound by shared blood and shared sacrifices . . . by our Judeo-Christian heritage . . . much too threat-ened as historical scapegoats to go on divided one from another."

Yet the gulf is there, and it is much to be hoped that Jackson's eloquent apology will begin to close it. Earlier, a *Los Angeles Times* survey of convention delegates found that Jackson's delegates are still favorably impressed, by a 3-1 ratio, with the Nation of Islam leader Louis Farrakhan even though Jackson himself had finally repudiated Farrakhan's anti-Semitism. In the same poll, 78 percent of Jewish delegates answered yes to the question. "Do you think Jesse Jackson can be accused of anti-Semitism?" But it was also significant that 53 percent of the Jewish delegates thought Jackson had been treated unfairly in the apportionment of delegates. What better evidence could there be of the "shared passion for social justice" of which Jackson himself spoke?

JEWS AND BLACKS indeed have a common interest in most of what Jackson's Rainbow Coalition stands for — including peace in the Middle East. But the coalition's agenda can be stretched only so far without snapping. Support for the Palestine Liberation Organization, which remains devoted to the destruction of Israel, would plainly stretch it much too far.

✔ ✔ ✔

Atlanta Mayor Andrew Young deserved better than to be booed when he spoke in opposition to Jackson's minority plank that called for the abolition of runoff primaries. There are fairer ways to elect blacks to Congress and other offices than by saying they should be able to win with less than a majority of the vote. Plurality election could be a dangerous two-edged sword. There are legislative districts in Florida, for example, now represented by blacks, where whites might be nominated instead. The campaigns of blacks, women and Hispanics will be better served by enthusiastic voter registration campaigns and strict enforcement of the voting rights laws.

THE BLADE
Toledo, Ohio, August 6, 1984

IT IS true that Jesse Jackson is a somewhat controversial figure, who has, as he says, received threats against his life. But Mr. Jackson now is a private citizen again, and the Administration acted properly in withdrawing the Secret Service protection that he was granted as a potential presidential candidate.

In denying Mr. Jackson's request that the protection be continued indefinitely, a Treasury Department spokesman noted that this service normally ends when an individual is no longer a major presidential contender. Protection also is not as a rule provided private citizens other than former presidents and for a limited time, former vice presidents.

Mr. Jackson obviously is no longer a candidate now that the Democratic convention has ended with the formal nomination of Walter Mondale. Whatever motivation might exist for threats against Mr. Jackson could not be based on any perception that he remains a candidate, even though he may well still have a political role to play during the remainder of the campaign.

One certainly hopes that Jesse Jackson, or any other prominent figure in American life for that matter, does not become the target of an attack. But if the U.S. Government provided Secret Service protection for every prominent person who might be the subject of threats, it would be impossible to perform that task.

To extend such protection for Mr. Jackson at this point would set an undesirable precedent in the treatment of other political figures in the future.

The Courier-Journal
Louisville, Ky., July 19, 1984

DIALOGUE, if not peace, seems to be breaking out all over. U.S. and Soviet negotiators have agreed to improve the hotline between Washington and Moscow, and Jesse Jackson wants to set one up between American blacks and Jews. Judging from the rhetoric in San Francisco, some Democrats are even more ambitious: they would establish a direct, two-way link between the federal government and every individual American with a grievance about domestic and foreign policy.

All this talk about talk can get downright bewildering. But it could be a sign of health for the Democrats if it means that the party's factions are ready to talk away their differences and work together to beat Ronald Reagan in November.

Mr. Jackson's emotional speech Tuesday night, only hours after his forces had lost three of four party platform battles, was especially important in that regard. He defended his historic crusade for the presidency and called on delegates to support him on the first ballot as "a vote for conscience and conviction." But he also apologized for whatever offense he may have given to any groups, and he promised to back the Democratic ticket in the general election.

The apology and the pledge of support should go a long way toward healing wounds that Mr. Jackson himself inflicted on the party — and on his candidacy. His slurs against Jews and his long reluctance to disavow Louis Farrakhan, a preacher of racial separatism and religious hatred, had undercut his claim to the moral high ground during the primaries.

Admittedly, a single speech — even one as prominent as Tuesday night's — won't dispel all suspicions about Mr. Jackson's motives and beliefs. And his ideological position — to the left of the mainstream of an already liberal party — could send some independent voters scurrying into the Reagan camp.

On balance, though, Mr. Jackson probably remains more an asset than a liability to the party. His success in persuading blacks to register as voters during the primary season may already have strengthened the Democrats' chances for the fall. And his talent and energy, when they aren't self-deflected by silly or even hurtful remarks, are needed in a party that frequently seems content to rest on the accomplishments of years gone by.

WORCESTER TELEGRAM
Worcester, Mass., July 19, 1984

Anyone who watched the Rev. Jesse Jackson's moving speech to the Democratic Convention Tuesday evening could hardly fail to be struck by the drama of the event. Here was a man who, 20 years ago, might have been turned away from a lunch counter or a hotel because of the color of his skin. Today he is a national figure with enough political power to sway the national political convention of a major party.

Despite everything, black Americans — and minority Americans in general — have come a long way. They are moving beyond tokenism. They are at last being heard. Their demands are becoming part of the national agenda. They are moving toward full citizenship.

Yes, it has taken a long time — an appallingly long time. But progress has been made. Discrimination still exists, but at least some kinds of discrimination are against the law. Victims of discrimination have some hope of redress. Even more important, more and more Americans are seeing discrimination as unworthy of our national traditions, as un-American.

America still has a long way to go, but let's note that it has come a long way. It is moving in the right direction, and that is what counts.

Birmingham Post-Herald
Birmingham, Ala., July 11, 1984

Jesse Jackson has warned that if he and black issues are not treated fairly at the Democratic National Convention he may urge blacks to sit out the presidential election.

At this time it is unclear if Jackson is maneuvering for more power at the convention or is seriously considering leading a boycott. However, if he calls on blacks not to vote it would be extremely bad advice, which they would be wise to discard.

In a remarkable interview with The Washington Post, Jackson spoke as though he were the unquestioned leader of black Americans, who would do as he said on election day.

Jackson said the Democrats need his "voluntary, enthusiastic support" to bring out a large black vote for the party's nominee if President Reagan is to be defeated. He added that he expects blacks to await his "signal" about voting and follow it.

The candidate hinted he would withhold his support unless the party changed its rules on the allocation of delegates and outlawed runoff primaries, which he contends discriminate against minorities and women.

Jackson's words had a patronizing ring, as if blacks were children who needed his "direction" — his own word — on whether it would be in their interest to vote or abstain.

In addition, the thought is bizarre that people who struggled for decades for the right to vote would shun the polls in an important national election because it suited the needs of a self-proclaimed leader.

Blacks know, and Jackson should keep in mind, that political power and often economic advancement come from turning out and voting in large numbers, while nothing good comes from wasting one's franchise.

In the interview and in recent pronouncements Jackson has evidenced a swelled head over his success in drawing many blacks into the primaries and winning about 85 percent of their votes. He ought to understand that, in a race with two whites, other black candidates, such as Mayors Andrew Young of Atlanta or Tom Bradley of Los Angeles, probably would have done as well.

Arkansas Gazette.
Little Rock, Ark., October 11, 1984

Rev. Jesse Jackson returned to Arkansas Tuesday, on his 43rd birthday, doing his full duty for the Democratic ticket in rousing speeches urging support for Walter Mondale, Geraldine Ferraro, and other Democratic candidates for office. It was good to have him back in the state, demonstrating that his differences with Mr. Mondale had been settled and the wounds of the Democratic presidential contest healed.

Mr. Jackson ran a strong second to Mondale in the Arkansas Democratic caucuses last spring. If the presidential race is close in Arkansas, a strong turnout by the black voters who have been Jackson's principal constituency could make the difference in this state. Mondale should get 90 per cent of the black vote for reasons that Jackson stated anew on his latest Arkansas visit. Like other supporters of Mondale, Jackson was excited over the Democratic nominee's performance in the first presidential debate Sunday night.

After speaking earlier in Magnolia and Forrest City, Jackson arrived in Little Rock two hours late for a press conference and rally that drew some 300 partisans, including Hillary Rodham Clinton, the governor's wife, to the East Little Rock Community Center. She thanked Jackson for the inspiration he provided several years ago "for us to improve the quality of education" in Arkansas.

Jackson told reporters that Mr. Reagan, without cue cards, is a "reading machine," that he "cannot cope with coherent thought" and that the impact of the debate was such that "we are beginning to realize it is possible to change administrations." He told the crowd later that Mondale had "set up Reagan in Louisville" and will "knock him out in Kansas City" — in the second debate scheduled October 21.

Jackson is a formidable speaker and leader, one who motivates his followers to action. His trip to Arkansas will surely help reinvigorate the Democratic organization and the Mondale-Ferraro forces generally in this state. In the case of black voters, Jackson's visit must remind them, if any reminder is needed, of the enormous disservice done by the Reagan administration to the interests of disadvantaged people in general and black people in particular. In the post-war era no one has done so much damage to the cause of civil rights, the cause of equality, as the incumbent President who is now seeking re-election.

THE TENNESSEAN
Nashville, Tenn., September 3, 1984

MR. Walter Mondale has spent the past week building a coalition which includes several diverse elements. including his former opponent, the Rev. Mr. Jesse Jackson.

After meeting with Mr. Mondale, Mr. Jackson declared that he would embrace and campaign for the Mondale-Ferraro ticket. He also vowed he would continue to register voters and stress the importance of President Ronald Reagan's defeat.

Mr. Jackson was not Mr. Mondale's only former rival who has thrown support to the Mondale-Ferraro ticket. Former Republican Congressman John Anderson, who ran for president as an independent in 1980, also endorsed the Mondale-Ferraro ticket last week. Mr. Anderson received 5.8 million votes, over 7%, in 1980 primarily from liberal Republicans and young professionals.

In addition, Mr. Mondale was endorsed by the League of Conservation Voters. This will be this first time in that group's 14-year history that the League will actively campaign against an incumbent president.

Endorsements are important — but they do not necessarily translate into votes. It remains to be seen if Messrs. Jackson and Anderson can inspire their supporters to actively work for the Democratic ticket. But, in a very short time, Mr. Mondale seems to be on the way to molding a coalition as interesting and diverse as any seen in a national election in some years.

ARKANSAS DEMOCRAT
Little Rock, Ark., August 2, 1984

Nominal Democrat Jesse Jackson has been acting like a third-party candidate all during his nominal spring and summer chase for the party's presidential nomination. Now, he's talking about running as an Independent candidate for U.S. Senator on the South Carolina ballot – against incumbent Republican Strom Thurmond.

Jackson is supposed to be working up the black South for Mondale-Ferraro. How much good can he do the Democratic presidential ticket haring off like that on his own?

We wouldn't begin to guess whether he will carry through with it, but it seems fairly certain that his South Carolina organization has been caught napping on what was to have been a petition drive to ballot him as an Independent. The deadline for that has already passed – and the only possible way Jackson could run now is as a write-in candidate.

We wouldn't discount his chances of pulling a big, if not a winning, vote through write-ins, but that would surely kill off what hope his party's senatorial nominee, Melvin Purvis, has of pulling off an upset against Thurmond, who is heavily favored for reelection. But the effect on the national ticket could be worse.

The Democrats have been long-suffering about Jackson because he's the key figure in the Southern strategy on which Mondale-Ferraro's hopes depend. If he flunks his assignment to rouse the black South, the party won't have much use for him.

THE DENVER POST
Denver, Colo., July 9, 1984

JESSE Jackson hasn't reached the level of Louis XIV, who flatly declared "I am the state." But Jackson does seem to assume that he somehow embodies at least the black citizenry of this country.

In Kansas City Saturday night, Jackson urged black Democrats to await his "signal" after the party convention in San Francisco and not automatically line up with the Democratic nominee. Sunday he added he expects black voters to follow his guidance and not vote in the presidential election if he determines that the Democratic Party has not treated him fairly and ignores issues affecting blacks.

Of course, if the Democratic Party were so suicidal as to actually ignore black concerns, it could expect blacks to extract vengeance at the polls. But the Democratic convention is no more likely to ignore blacks than it is to nominate Ronald Reagan. What Jackson is really trying to do is to set himself up as somehow the only legitimate representative of black America — and its sole power broker.

That's a slight to thousands of able black leaders such as Tom Bradley, Barbara Jordan and Julian Bond on the national scene and skillful local figures such as Wellington Webb and Regis Groff. There is no one black leader in a country with millions of involved and sophisticated black voters, each quite capable of weighing events independently and making their own decisions.

The thought of black Americans waiting mutely for a "signal" from Jackson and transferring their loyalties blindly wherever he directs them has no relationship to reality. But it does illustrate the arrogance and self-interest that increasingly mar the Jackson campaign.

THE INDIANAPOLIS NEWS
Indianapolis, Ind., August 3, 1984

The Rev. Jesse Jackson has decided not to run for a U. S. Senate seat in South Carolina. For that we are thankful, because Jackson has become tiresome.

When Jackson first announced that he was running for president last fall, we said that he had the opportunity to do great good or great harm. He is now in danger of taking the latter option.

Granted, Jesse Jackson has made some positive steps toward integrating the American political system still further. Doubtless, his campaign politicized many previously unregistered and apathetic blacks. Without question, he gave American blacks a feeling that their voices and their statements could be heard from a political podium.

Still, his campaign has also done a good deal of harm.

The tension between many blacks and Jews has grown, largely because of Jackson's own comments and his tardy and hesitant condemnation of Louis Farrakhan's anti-Semitic statements. Jackson made an effort to decrease this tension with his speech at the Democratic National Convention, but he has undercut that message of conciliation since then by saying that the Democrats are pandering to the Jews.

His adventures in foreign policy deserve a long and critical look in their own right. While he has had some success in achieving the release of political prisoners in Syria and Cuba, Jackson also has helped to send confusing signals to both the United States' allies and enemies. Thus, he has helped to create further confusion abroad.

And now, Jackson has taken to pummeling both the Republican and Democratic parties for their "racist" attitudes. He has blasted President Reagan consistently for his opposition to affirmative action and many social programs Jackson favors. Jackson also has attacked both Walter Mondale and Geraldine Ferraro for not including more blacks in their campaign staffs.

Some of his criticisms are valid ones, but his response is not. Even while denying it, Jackson issues thinly veiled threats that he will ask America's blacks to boycott the November election.

He says he will help to elect the Mondale-Ferraro ticket, but that he will maintain his independence. "There are," he says, "two campaigns, the Democratic campaign and the freedom campaign. And there are times when the freedom campaign has to march to the time of a different drummer."

Perhaps this is true in a very idealistic sense, but it is also dangerous. Jackson essentially is saying that black Americans should remain separate from America's two great political institutions, the Republican and Democratic parties.

This approach runs counter to Jackson's avowed goal: a fully integrated society — a "rainbow coalition" — blind to questions of race. That is a laudable goal, but it is one that he is now undermining rather than furthering.

The best thing Jesse Jackson could do from now until November would be to use his influence to get blacks to vote — for either party or candidate. His campaign's greatest success was that it gave blacks hope that the political system would speak for them, too. It would be a shame if Jesse Jackson destroyed that hope now.

The Dallas Morning News

Dallas, Texas, August 16, 1984

If Walter Mondale is annoyed, in a minor way, at Jesse Jackson these days, it is not hard to see why. Jackson pledged help for the Democratic ticket, but the kind of help he's been giving lately Mondale would probably rather see go to Reagan.

Apparently miffed by Geraldine Ferraro's joking about blueberry muffins in Mississippi, Jackson responded by taking his thoughts to the press. He told the media that the "Mondale campaign has no media strategy, no coherent regional or national strategy and no themes to attract black voters."

Jackson clearly has his own media strategy, which is to get ink and TV footage at every opportunity. But it is hard to see how he expects this kind of public sniping at the party's chosen ticket to help Mondale's cause or his own. The Democrats have a tradition of closing ranks and muting their differences, once the campaign against the GOP begins. Jackson is defying that practical custom, a fact that many Democrats are not likely to forget.

If he continues, he'd be wise to frame his future political plans in terms of a third party. The Democratic Party has few strict requirements for those it supports, but one of them is the ability to distinguish friend from foe and to act accordingly.

The Virginian-Pilot

Norfolk, Va., September 5, 1984

Walter Mondale and the Rev. Jesse Jackson agreed last week that Mr. Jackson would be of greatest help to the Democratic Party in the South. Mr. Jackson's job is to get out the black vote. In many Southern states, it is conceivable that a large turnout of blacks on Election Day would provide enough votes to ease Mr. Mondale past President Reagan — in states such as Alabama, Arkansas, Georgia, South Carolina, North Carolina, Tennessee and Mississippi. And if Mr. Mondale cuts into Mr. Reagan's strength in the South, well, the Democrat's chances to gain the presidency improve from "improbable" to "maybe." That's Mr. Jackson's role in this campaign.

Given that, what was Mr. Jackson doing in Norfolk on Labor Day? Of all the Southern states, Virginia is the least likely to go for Mr. Mondale. In most Southern states, Mr. Reagan beat Jimmy Carter in 1980 by just a few thousand votes; in Virginia, Mr. Reagan won by 237,000. Strictly in efficient use of campaign time, Mr. Jackson would have been better off someplace else.

So why was Mr. Jackson in Norfolk? One reason, of course, is that he's well-received in Hampton Roads. He draws large crowds when he speaks, and he has the support of many politically active blacks. But the second reason — the most important, by far — is that Jesse Jackson has two roles in the campaign of 1984: (a) to help Mr. Mondale and (b) to help local and state black politicians keep up the pressure for greater black participation in politics.

Regardless of who wins the presidency, the role of blacks on the national level will diminish as soon as the votes are counted. There are no blacks of national reputation in the House of Representatives; there are no blacks in the Senate; there are no black governors. The strength of black politics is at the local level, with mayors and city council members. That is where black voters, who tend to concentrate in urban areas, make the most difference.

Despite the misgivings voiced by some blacks about his role (see Carl T. Rowan's column on this page today), Mr. Jackson is in an enviable position. By encouraging blacks to vote for Mr. Mondale, he will get at least partial credit if Mr. Mondale beats Mr. Reagan in any Southern state. By encouraging blacks to register and participate in local politics, he is strengthening local black politicians and, not incidentally, building a grass-roots network for the future.

Pittsburgh Post-Gazette

Pittsburgh, Pa., August 7, 1984

The Rev. Jesse Jackson has decided not to compete for a South Carolina U.S. Senate seat. The fact that he even contemplated such a race so late in the political year indicates that the black civil-rights leader is moving away from the disdain for pragmatism that marked his recently terminated quest for the White House.

A state, rather than a national, campaign would have offered Mr. Jackson two advantages over his recent presidential candidacy. First, it would have given him status as a politician working his way up the political ladder rather than sweeping down from above with a self-appointed mission. Second, it would have helped build up contacts, funding and supporters on a manageable scale, resources that could be deployed in the future for a tangible cause such as another contest for either the House or the Senate.

During his presidential campaign, Mr. Jackson helped his party by increasing registration and making the campaign a lot more interesting to an often bored public. But for all his magnetic qualities, he was hindered by a disorganized campaign, a foreign-policy agenda tilted to Third World concerns and super-ambassadorial exploits that may have alienated as many voters as they impressed. Through it all, he never quite convinced the nation that he was a politician with his feet on the ground.

That is partly why his campaign came to an unsatisfactory end in San Francisco, where, despite the brave speeches, Mr. Jackson and his supporters had little specific to show for all their hard work.

Mr. Jackson now has announced that he will not, after all, challenge South Carolina's incumbent Sen. Strom Thurmond, but even his consideration of such a race shows a shift in his perceptions. By even mulling over a bid, Mr. Jackson was thinking conventionally. He was turning over in his mind the best way for him and other black Americans to make an impact on the political establishment. That course, he seems to have decided, is to involve himself in accepted apprenticeships such as regional elections.

If and when he prevails in one of those contests, he will have succeeded in harmonizing two equally valuable worlds: one of symbolism and inspiration, the other of hard-nosed political reality.

The Washington Post

Washington, D.C., September 6, 1984

THE OLD DREAM of southern populists—a coalition of blacks and poor whites—has been a will o' the wisp for most of southern history. For years most southern blacks were denied the right to vote; then, when they could vote, for several years almost all whites voted reflexively against the candidates blacks favored. Now the vision of a biracial populist coalition is being invoked again, this time by the national Democratic Party. Only in the event that such a coalition can be assembled does the Mondale-Ferraro ticket have a chance of winning electoral votes this year in the South.

The signs are not auspicious. It's something of a landmark when 14 southern Democratic state chairmen meet with Jesse Jackson and representatives of the national party, as they did here last week. But Mr. Jackson, for reasons which cannot be explained away as simple racial prejudice, is unpopular with southern white voters. A recent poll by the Joint Center for Political Studies shows that a Jackson endorsement makes white southerners less rather than more likely to support the Mondale-Ferraro ticket by a 19 to 8 percent margin.

The Democrats' strategy is to turn this around by, in Mr. Jackson's words, "an economic agenda that can meet human needs." The same idea, in different words, was the hope of the populist strategists of the 1890s. They, like Mr. Jackson, pointed out that most southern whites were clustered near the lower end of the national income scale. But American voting habits have never been a simple function of economic status. It was when southern whites had incomes far below the national average that they balked at voting for candidates supported by blacks. Only in the 1970s, when southern income levels approached and in some cases exceeded national averages, were they more willing to do so.

And of course economic issues are not the only basis for voters' decisions. It's true that Jimmy Carter's winning coalitions in Georgia in 1970 and in the South in 1976 resembled the blacks-plus-(relatively)-poor-white model. But he lost many of those votes in 1980. White southern voters tend to support an assertive, even aggressive foreign policy and to favor increased defense spending; Jesse Jackson's praise of Fidel Castro, and Walter Mondale's emphasis on arms control, are not vote-winners in Dixie. White southern voters also tend to oppose the Democrats' positions on many cultural issues.

The Democrats, by daring to feature Jesse Jackson in their southern effort, are gambling that by inspiring a large black turnout and emphasizing economic issues, they can overcome the deficit they face on foreign and cultural issues. It's a long shot.

The Power of the "Black Vote"

At first glance, it would seem that black voters can have only a limited impact in national elections, since the number of black Americans of voting age is only about 10% of the total. But in fact, there are other factors that combine to give the black electorate greater power than its percentage of the population alone would indicate. In regard to presidential elections, blacks are strategically located, with high concentrations living in four of the five northeastern and midwestern states with the most electoral votes: California (47), New York (36), Texas (29), and Illinois (24). (A presidential candidate must garner at least 267 of 535 votes in the electoral college in order to win the election.) Black voters can also wield considerable influence in the South, in the past a Republican stronghold but increasingly recognized as a fertile ground for Democratic persuasion; in six states, blacks comprise more than 20% of the voting age population. According to some estimates, the number of unregistered blacks in these southern states is greater than the margin of votes received by Ronald Reagan over President Carter in 1980.

Recognizing this latent power, black leaders and politicans have long emphasized the importance of voter registration and participation. A massive surge in national turnout for the 1982 congressional elections, after near-stasis for almost a decade, was particularly strong among blacks and blue-collar workers. These segments of the voting population, historically "lost," were evidently spurred by dissatisfaction with the policies of the Reagan Administration. Jesse Jackson's 1984 presidential campaign was able to capitalize on the dissatisfaction and mobilization of the black electorate, benefiting from previous voter registration campaigns and building upon the momentum created in local and state elections. (See pp. 186-195.) In fact, Jackson's signal success in registering voters in the South, using the pulpit as a forum, spurred a counter-campaign headed by Sen. Jesse Helms (R, N.C.) and the Moral Majority's Rev. Jerry Falwell to register conservative Christians.

St. Petersburg Times

St. Petersburg, Fla., August 8, 1980

For a long time, both major political parties have taken black votes too much for granted — the Democrats assuming they couldn't lose them and the Republicans acting as if there were no point in trying to win them over. So, for the sake of the two-party system as well as the future of the black minority, it is good that Republican nominee Ronald Reagan is actively courting their votes.

Reagan went to New York this week to speak at the Urban League's convention and to make what has become the obligatory inspection tour of the depressed, devastated south Bronx. He promised economic solutions of the sort that would depend on private initiative responding to government incentives. Meanwhile, aides were saying that Reagan as president would uphold existing anti-discrimination laws although he does not favor specific quotas for minority hiring.

BEFORE LEAPING on the Reagan bandwagon, however, blacks would do well to ask for some more explicit guarantees of his commitment to them. While he is no bigot, his early career was hardly characterized by belief in the federal government as the guarantor of minority rights.

He opposed the landmark federal laws that have done the most for blacks — the Civil Rights Act of 1964 and the Voting Rights Act of 1965. In campaigning for governor of California in 1964, he said he favored repeal of the state's open housing law, an event that did not come to pass. In a Washington speech in 1966, he attacked the Johnson administration's civil rights propos-

als as "grandstand stunts" to attract black votes.

Asked about that early record, in a *Los Angeles Times* interview this year, Reagan said he opposed the 1964 act, which guaranteed equal access to public accommodations, because of his belief in a person's "right to do with his property what he wants to do." Reagan said he no longer opposes the act, "because I recognize now that it is institutionalized and it has, let's say, hastened the solution of a lot of problems."

WHAT REAGAN never seemed able to perceive as governor, and which he will have to convince blacks and other minorities that he now understands, is that state action alone is insufficient to assure equal justice and equal opportunities under law. Some states are well-motivated, but others are not.

One serious flaw in Reagan's economic solutions, as he describes them to blacks, is his advocacy of a youth differential in the minimum wage, which he contends would encourage employers to hire unskilled black teen-agers. This, of course, would be a windfall to those industries which already hire mostly teen-aged help, such as the fast-food industry.

Secondly, it would cause great hardship to millions of older workers. If an employer is to choose between an older unskilled worker who is entitled to the minimum wage, and a teen-age worker who can be paid a subminimum wage, which is the employer likely to hire?

These are the kinds of questions black voters should consider in deciding which candidate for president will be best for them and for the country.

THE PLAIN DEALER

Cleveland, Ohio, July 17, 1980

This was to be the year that the Republican party — the party of Abraham Lincoln and emancipation — constructed some bridges to America's black community. The selection of Detroit as the GOP convention site, a city with a black Democrat as mayor, was to be a symbol of efforts to reach out for the support that was so significant in electing Jimmy Carter in 1976.

This bridge building, of course, has again failed. Of the 1,994 GOP delegates in Detroit, only 2.8% are black. That is the smallest black representation within the GOP delegate ranks since the 1968 convention that nominated Richard Nixon.

Even so, the 56 black delegates won a victory of sorts in forcing Ronald Reagan and his convention controllers to allow Benjamin L. Hooks, executive director of the NAACP, to address the convention. A refusal by Reagan would have risked a walkout by the tiny band of black Republicans.

In an effort to placate minorities Reagan met with the black delegates. But his words and the tone of GOP planks on the economy and on social issues were hardly soothing. Reagan relies too much on oversimplified economics. He needs to develop, if he genuinely wants black support, a better understanding of the problems of blacks. This is especially true at a time when economic disparities between blacks and whites are widening again.

To be sure, Reagan is now a supporter of some civil rights laws. That is an enlightening conversion, even though it is tardy. But he still opposes affirmative action and other programs intended to try to guarantee equal opportunities for blacks. His views are mired in contradictions for 27 million American blacks.

It was Bill Brock, the GOP national chairman, who a few years ago laid out a challenge for Republicans to lure more black voter support. His efforts were naturally politically motivated, but they were admirable in intent.

Reagan was certainly correct in declaring that it takes courage for black Americans to be Republicans. Hooks, who gave a passionate speech to the GOP delegates and won only polite applause, was equally right in feeling that Reagan and other leaders of the Grand Old Party of Lincoln do not understand the problems of black America.

THE CHRISTIAN SCIENCE MONITOR

Boston, Mass., March 4, 1980

To identify voters by race is to risk lapsing into the very racism which hampers solution of the world's other problems. The continued identification of voters by race suggests the sad limitations of the present phase of social and political evolution. It obviously has to be done in South Africa, where race benightedly remains the criterion by which voting is confined to the white 20 percent of the population. It can hardly be avoided in Rhodesia, where the good news is that more than 90 percent of eligible black voters went to the polls in the first internationally recognized elections giving the vote to the black majority.

Alas, the color coding of voters hangs on even in a country with America's long history of seeking to spread freedom and equality ever wider among its citizens. Yet "the black vote" seemed anything but monolithic as represented by the more than a thousand delegates at the recent National Conference on a Black Agenda for the '80s held in Richmond. A basic challenge that emerged was the need for black leaders and black voters, like the rest of the country, to be prepared for full individual participation in an increasingly sophisticated political scene — and to undertake that participation.

Indeed, why should there not be more than 90 percent of America's black minority turning out if this proportion of Rhodesia's black majority can turn out? Yet, as of last year, fewer than a third of some 15 million eligible black voters in the United States were estimated to be registered, and fewer than a third of the registered have tended to go on and vote. No wonder more than 50 black organizations are joining in a voter registration drive.

Not that nonblack Americans have been exemplary voter participants in recent years. But the turnout in 1980's primaries and caucuses has been unexpectedly high. This is the kind of "big mo" — to use a candidate's phrase for momentum — that ought to be fostered in all segments of the voting population. We like the idea of the Rev. Jesse Jackson, a major voice at the Richmond conference, that registering to vote ought to be as much a part of the growing-up ritual for American young people as high school commencement.

But besides getting out the vote there must be information on the political process, on the domestic issues such as unemployment and equal rights that particularly affect black Americans, and on the foreign issues such as the Middle East in which black leaders are displaying a growing healthy interest. It was easier when they were dealing with racism at lunch counters, said one of the conference delegates: "Now we have to deal with budgets and international problems. To do that, you need to have a broad information base. We've got to transmit that down to the level where the average person can understand."

Cynics, noting the divisions at the conference, contrast with those participants who found it successful in setting up an agenda against which candidates can be tested. Besides the economic issues there was the Equal Rights Amendment, for example, and the severing of US ties with South Africa. The latter is one of those issues on whose dimensions black Americans have disagreed. Some, like Andrew Young when he was United Nations ambassador, argue that US business should stay in, while strengthening its stand on rights for black South Africans, in order to help the economic situation for blacks. Mr. Jackson argues that US business's benefits to perhaps 100,000 employees in South Africa are outweighed by the injustice to millions of disenfranchised blacks that is condoned by continuing to do business there.

But it will do black Americans no good to test candidates according to the black agenda if they do not then go out and vote. The cynics again say that black conferences have been held before — and there has not been enough follow-up to sustain their brave words. Things can be different this time, if both black and other Americans decide not to leave their political decisions up to someone else.

The Sun Reporter

San Francisco, Calif., November 6, 1980

The Grand Old Party is enjoying the bubbling, heady champagne of victory and Ronald Reagan moves toward the establishment of a transitional task force. The Democratic Party is attempting to discover the far-reaching causes as well as the unknown effects of the blood-letting which resulted from Reagan's landslide victory over Jimmy Carter. Apparently in 1980 the electorate held the Democratic Party—the Congress and the White House—responsible for the legacy of broken promises wrought over four years by the man who inquired: "Why not the best?," who said: "I will never lie to you," and "I promise to develop a government as good as the American People."

The 39th President of the United States, Jimmy Carter, was beholden to the Trilateral Commission, the National Business Roundtable and the Foreign Policy Association; his loyalty to these three entities made of Candidate Jimmy Carter, who mouthed populism, a lying and conniving politician. A Carter victory would have completely dismembered and destroyed the Democratic Party. All segments of the old Roosevelt Coalition, with the exception of Black voters, deserted the Democratic Party.

Blacks in the USA are at the same crossroads as they were in 1932, when Blacks were the last to desert the sinking ship of Hoover Republicanism, as they went down to defeat supporting Herbert Hoover and the party of Abraham Lincoln. It was not until 1936 that Blacks joined Roosevelt's coalition, and Blacks have remained loyal to the Democratic Party for lo 44 years.

The voters have held not only Jimmy Carter responsible for four years of ineptness, but the Democratic majorities in the House of Representatives and Senate as well, majorities for the Democrats not exceeded since the '36 and '38 Roosevelt Congresses.

The Carter administration and the '76-'78 Congresses failed to provide leadership or solutions to the grave problems of '76-'80. Democratic liberals of the U.S. Senate were knocked off as sitting ducks on a pond by the electorate. The loss of Magnusson, Cluver, Church, Bayh and McGovern in the U.S. Senate is the price which liberals must pay when they procrastinate and move around in circles, shadow boxing with the grave problems which beset the body politic. While the Democrats do not lose control of the House, many important committee chairmanships will be held by conservative Democrats. The victory of the Republican Party, led by Ronald Reagan, the oldest president-elect in history, must serve as a warning to all liberals who spent too much time in verbalizing the need for social change while doing very little to structure a legislative program for government action in the crises of inflation, unemployment, inadequate housing, poor education of our children, and inadequate medical care, in a time in fact of grave economic crisis.

The defeat of Jimmy Carter was also a defeat of Black bourgeois Democratic leadership. Never have so many words been uttered by the Black religious and political leaders such as Jesse Jackson, the Congressional Black Caucus and Black liberals who have feasted at the federal trough for many years. If physical punishment for their crimes against the Black electorate were meted out, each of these Black leaders-without-portfolio should be given fifty lashes in the village square. Since such is not possible, we would hope that the Black masses, especially the Black under-class, who gave so much to Jimmy Carter's first victory yet received so little, will repudiate these false pharoahs who preached the nonsense of Blacks rescuing Carter from defeat while both Carter and the preachers were singing "Amazing Grace".

Having lived for eight years under Governor Reagan in California, we are not disposed to commit suicide because Reagan has now been shared with the 49 other states of the Union. Reagan will undoubtedly have a more broadly diversified administration in the Executive Branch. As California's former Governor, Reagan recognizes the dangers involved when a political newcomer becomes chief executive of the state or a nation, promising to drive the scoundrels out. The conservative reactionaries in the infrastructure of the US federal government will only laugh: Reagan, at best, will last only eight years; the Civil Service and the old establishment boys will last forever. They have seen administrations come and go.

The fact that Ninety percent of Black voters followed their self-appointed leaders from the churches and the upper economic levels into the Red Sea of Carter's defeat should indicate to the Black masses that they must develop Black leadership for the '80's and '90's. Political power is too important to Black survival and liberation for the Black masses to continue to swoon under the sweet, sonorous words of political chameleons who have led them into the wasteland of the Reagan landslide.

The Black masses are at the crossroads. The next four years are programmed for more bleakness. The Democratic Party is in a shambles.

The differences between Blacks and Jews, Blacks and organized labor, Black females and the feminist movement, the Black underclass and the Black Anglo-Saxons, are much greater than their common interests and destinies.

Black America faces four alternatives:

1) to stay with the Democratic Party; 2) to unite with a new broad-based coalition and form a viable Citizens Party; 3) the complete alienation of the Black underclass from the Black middle-class, with Black middle-class, free enterprise advocates moving toward the Republican Party; or 4) the establishment of a national Black political party, destined to organize the masses into a formidable grass-roots political instrument from the ground up, challenging White liberals and Black-Anglo-Saxons who up until now have demonstrated little or no concern for using political power as an instrument to change the sordid lives of the Black under-class.

Irrespective of Republican victory in the hard-fought '80 campaign, US citizens are warned that neither the Republican Party nor any other party in power will respond to the people's needs without organized demands and without persistent pressure from the masses for effective programs developed to serve the needs of 225 million people.

Only eternal vigilance is the guardian of the people's rights.

Post-Tribune

Guarding Your Interests Daily

Gary, Ind., August 20, 1981

Black America is at a fork in the road. And there are no simple answers to the theme of a recent Post-Tribune series posing the question, "Which way black America?"

Some would suggest movement to the left, following "civil rights" tactics that have been effective in the past, with many of those who were leaders in years gone by taking the lead again.

But clearly there are others who seek a new road, new blood, new ideas, opting for a shift to the right, a more conservative approach. That group believes black Americans must rely on using mainstream strategy to find a niche in mainstream society.

What is good for the country as a whole will automatically benefit black America, these new zealots insist. Not so, argue their counterparts, because America remains divided into two societies as distinct as black and white.

The sentiments of both deserve attention. Because we consider both sides to have some merit, we find ourselves somewhere in the middle on how the problems of black America may most effectively be tackled.

The so-called traditional black leaders may over-emphasize time-worn rhetoric that falls on deaf ears after a point. And some of them may be more self-oriented than people-oriented.

And the so-called alternative leadership may be writing off a vital segment of the black community with the insensitive "I got mine, you get yours" inference of some of their ideologies.

It is clear that racial discrimination and bigotry still exist in overt and covert forms in American society. The "promised land" that the Rev. Martin Luther King Jr. spoke of is still somewhere in the distance and his dream of racial harmony — and equally important racial parity — has yet to materialize.

The ultimate solution will rely on some blend of the protest and agitation necessary to draw attention to a problem and the negotiation and cooperation needed for two opposing entities to sit at the same table and work out solutions.

The movement for equality for all Americans in the 1980s will necessitate some cohesiveness in the black community. It isn't necessary to agree on all or even most things. But the aim of disagreement should be to explore the most feasible position, not merely to air differences.

Finally, the struggle for black America is not a battle that other Americans can allow them to fight alone. It is intolerable that any people in a land of freedom and opportunity should be relegated to second-class citizenship economically, politically, socially or mentally.

It won't be a fight easily won — that of continuing change toward social progress. But it is a battle that everyone, without exception, must know the joy of winning or everyone, without exception, stands to wind up losers.

"LOOK, WHEN WE SUGGESTED YOU PEOPLE SHOULD WORK THROUGH THE POLITICAL SYSTEM WE HAD NO IDEA YOU'D BE GOOD AT IT!"

Winnipeg Free Press

Winnipeg, Man., July 16, 1980

The shape of the Republican campaign for the presidency this fall is indicated by the party platform that was drawn up for the nominating convention by the platform committee and by the kind of delegate who showed up:

Once through the formality of nomination, Ronald Reagan is going to reach out for the white, silent majority of which Richard Nixon spoke so fondly. He hopes to attract the skilled blue-collar workers whose jobs are at risk, the white-collar workers who are angry about the decline of their purchasing power, the elderly who worry about the erosion of their retirement income, urban dwellers who fear that their communities will go bankrupt, farmers angry about lost sales and reduced earnings because of the grain boycott. Conspicuously absent from his list of desired voters are blacks in general and those women who believe that they should have greater rights, including that of abortion.

Black America has been written off by Mr. Reagan. He recently made the deliberate political gesture of rejecting an offer to address the National Association for the Advancement of Colored Peoples. This was in harmony with the composition of the state delegations to the convention, whose selection processes were tightly controlled by Reagan operatives. The 1,994 delegates and 1,994 alternates are 98 per cent white, 72 per cent of them with family incomes over $30,000 annually and 43 per cent with family incomes over $50,000

annually. Not one is known to be unemployed, effectively shutting out poor, jobless, black citizens.

The delegate selection was also skewed against women, who form 50 per cent of the voters but only 30 per cent of the delegates. Women voters with even a minimal commitment to feminism were shown that their support is not wanted when the Reagan operatives guided the party platform committee to a repudiation of a 40-year-old platform commitment to equal rights for women. Support for the Equal Rights Amendment has been virtually eliminated. Furthermore, the platform now advocates a constitutional amendment to outlaw abortion and contains the unconstitutional suggestion that a Reagan administration would pack the judiciary with judges who oppose abortion.

Party platforms tend to be as little regarded in office as campaign promises. They do, however, give an indication of the way a candidate hopes to gain his support. Mr. Reagan's signal to the electorate is clear and current opinion polls suggest that he could beat Mr. Carter today with his mix of can-do optimism, anti-welfarism, support for big defence spending, tax cuts and backing for the traditional no-divorce, no-abortion family. Whether he can do so in November depends on how well he can continue to sell himself — and the bizarre policy baggage he is picking up in Detroit — to those voters who did not attend perhaps the most unrepresentative gathering since the 1964 convention that sent Barry Goldwater off to a landslide defeat.

THE KANSAS CITY STAR
Kansas City, Mo., July 6, 1982

It's no secret GOP leaders are making an effort to woo black voters in this year's election campaign. Neither is it a secret that many black activists and ordinary citizens are dissatisfied with administration performance on everything from budget policies that hit hard at the poor to civil rights. Even at the celebratory signing of the historic extension of the Voting Rights Act, invited guests were reserved if not caustic in their comments.

Such a season of discontent could produce bitter withdrawal and little else. But the National Association for the Advancement of Colored People proposes a better response: an intensive assault from within the system.

At the NAACP annual convention, strategy was laid to increase political action among blacks using as a centerpiece the largest voter education and registration drive that the 73-year-old organization has undertaken. The goal: 1.5 million new black voters by November.

Delegates were urged to return to their 1,800 branches, train volunteers to recruit block captains who would have the responsibility for finding potential voters, getting out information about candidates and issues as well as reminding neighbors to vote on election day. In the 105 congressional districts where elections are considered particularly crucial to minority interests, for example, the organization hopes to have a minimum of 250,000 block captains in the field.

If the campaign is overwhelmingly successful, it could hardly be expected to dramatically change the makeup of Congress or reverse noxious administration policies. It could persuade elected officials at all levels to listen, confer and be more sensitive to legitimate concerns of American minorities. They can hardly ignore this bit of information from the Commerce Department's Bureau of the Census: In the 1980 presidential election, black voters were the only major demographic group to increase their participation.

The Providence Journal
Providence, R.I., July 3, 1982

No American can claim to be a full citizen if he fails to register to vote — nor should he feel entitled to criticize a system in which he won't participate. The current drive of the National Association for the Advancement of Colored People to obtain 1.5 million additional black voters by November is an appeal to good citizenship.

The NAACP's announcement at its annual convention in Boston was followed by one in Providence at the offices of the Urban League of Rhode Island, where the executive secretary, the Rev. Errol E. Hunt, said "Each of us has the opportunity and obligation to express preference through the electoral process."

One of the state's most prominent black leaders since the hectic days of the 1960s civil rights protests, Mr. Hunt recognizes that there *are* ways to fight City Hall (or the State House or the U.S. Capitol) and that the most powerful is the ballot. Political leaders can ignore appeals to reason and compassion, while giving lip service to noble ideals. They cannot ignore election-night figures that remove them from office.

As of the elections in November, 1980, 9.8 million blacks were registered to vote. The NAACP's goal amounts to a 15 percent increase. That is not impossible. The group's Tampa, Fla. unit, starting in March, has already achieved an 11.5 percent increase in black voters of that area.

It is unfortunate that the NAACP, which does not officially endorse any candidates or parties (as was made clear to the Providence branch when its president, Antone Cruz, sought to change that policy), coupled its voter registration kickoff with hopes that President Reagan might be sent "back to the purple mountains of California." Individual NAACP officers or members are certainly free to criticize Mr. Reagan, but he does have the support of some blacks and it would be better if the voter registration drive could be nonpartisan.

In Rhode Island, the registration of minority-group members has the backing of 25 civil rights, religious and social organizations. Mr. Hunt said non-voters must get the message "that voting in the American system is one right that has mellowed, matured and become more important as our constitution has aged." That is a truly patriotic emphasis placed squarely where it belongs — on the civic consciences of all Americans, minority or otherwise.

Nevada State Journal
Reno, Nev., April 29, 1982

Washoe County's black leaders say they will be working hard this year to get more of their numbers involved in the political process. And indeed they should.

The struggle against prejudice has not been won, in Nevada or anywhere else. And the victories that have been won must be rewon again and again — because prejudice never fully goes away. It is part of the human psyche.

So fragile is the psyche that it must constantly be reassured that it has value. It finds this reassurance partly through the belief that its group is better than other groups — because if its group is superior, it is superior, if not to the people in its group, at least to the "others" over there. So people often find it psychologically necessary to demean others — other races, other religions, other nations.

This is not the only reason for prejudice, of course. Prejudice arises also out of the simple fact that people are different, and we do not always trust those differences. We are uncomfortable with the things we do not understand, and it is often easier to degrade them than to tolerate them.

Unfavorable economic times also increase prejudice. Financial problems make people angry, and this anger moves easily along racial and religious lines.

So in this uncertain political and economic climate, we see a resurgence of prejudice nationwide. We see the Ku Klux Klan growing stronger; we see anti-Semitism sprouting with renewed vigor.

And where we do not find direct prejudice, we often find a lessening of interest in equality. People are busy with their own lives now; they lack the time and the interest for righting the wrongs of the world.

Into this vacuum dangerous movements are sweeping, which could lessen the equal rights victories won with such effort during the 1960s and early 1970s.

At the national level, especially, we see determined efforts to weaken such landmark achievements as affirmative action and the Voting Rights Act. Obviously some who wish to weaken these safeguards are not actively prejudiced; they sincerely believe that government has intervened too much in personal matters, or that regions where civil rights was once a problem will not renew their persecutions if the federal hand withdraws. But they are wrong; and their actions, if successful, will surely lead to increased discrimination.

In this climate, Bertha Woodard, president of the Reno-Sparks chapter of the NCAA, rightly wonders if Nevada will again be called the "Mississippi of the West." Nevada as a whole has a record of considerable prejudice. One can still hear the familiar tones reverberating in the streets, the bars, the neighborhoods. The Klan seems to be undergoing a revival in this area. And as Mrs. Woodard notes, discrimination continues on a general level. It is not as blatant as it was 20 years ago, but it is there.

It is also noteworthy that a black candidate has never been elected to office in Northern Nevada. Blacks are not that numerous of course; nevertheless, some black candidates have been qualified for elective office and have been overlooked. Local governments, also, have been slow to bring blacks and certain other minorities into the governmental process.

So the local NAACP is surely in staging a voter registration drive. And so is the Northern Nevada Community Political Action Committee in trying to get a qualified black elected.

Other minorities, such as Hispanics, should also become more involved in the political process. This process offers minorities their best opportunity to hold the gains already made, and to wage new battles against discrimination. On occasion, of course, the political system listens to its conscience on its own; but it listens to numbers much more often.

Therefore the minorities must make their voices heard — and they can do this best by voting and by becoming actively involved in politics and government.

The Washington Post
Times Herald
Washington, D.C., August 25, 1983

THIS SUMMER, efforts have been launched to register more black and more Hispanic voters. Leaders of these efforts, such as Jesse Jackson, point out that if only a small percentage of black non-voters in, say, Alabama had voted, the 1980 election there would have come out the other way. That's true in dozens of cases, and not just because blacks cast about 90 percent of their votes for Democrats in most general elections. There is a very large pool of non-voters of every race, ethnic origin and description—enough to change the result of almost any election. In the 1982 congressional and state elections, about 63 percent of those eligible to vote did not do so. In the 1980 presidential election, 46 percent of those eligible didn't vote.

What is striking is that, while voter turnout as a percentage of those eligible was in continuous decline from 1960 to 1980, barriers to voting fell during those years. The Voting Rights Act of 1965 enfranchised millions of blacks in the South. In dozens of states laws were changed to make it easier to register and to vote. The period during which you had to live in a state before you could vote was reduced, by court decision, from as much as two years to 30 days. Yet for years fewer and fewer Americans bothered to vote.

Why? The baby boom generation is one answer (as it is to so many questions): young people who don't have roots in a community aren't very likely to vote, and the baby boom supplied a large number of young people who delayed putting down roots for an unusually long time. Charged attitudes are another reason: people are more cynical about government and politics and, it is hypothesized, less likely to vote. Another, more benign possibility: in a time of widespread prosperity and no general war, issues simply weren't so pressing for many people; so however much they grumbled to pollsters, they didn't bother to vote.

That may be changing. The 1982 elections saw a rising turnout, as compared with 1978—the first in 20 years. The baby boomers are aging, attitudes are a little more positive, and issues (the recession, for instance) may impinge more on people's lives. But keep in mind that the higher turnout doesn't necessarily mean more minority or Democratic voters. Blacks turned out in larger numbers in many states in 1981 and 1982. But in California higher turnout came mainly from opponents of a gun control ballot initiative; if it hadn't been for these new voters, Thomas Bradley would have become the nation's first black governor. Conservative activists now are urging their followers to register and vote. It's not clear that they have a motivating issue; but if they do, higher turnout may end up helping Reagan Republicans as much as liberal Democrats in 1984.

Low turnout has been called a danger to democracy. But it is more a symptom than a disease, and to the extent that it indicates that people don't feel much affected by government, it is not even that. Higher turnout may be evidence of health, but some of those who are calling for more turnout may not be pleased with the choices of those who vote for the first time in 1984.

OKLAHOMA CITY TIMES
Oklahoma City, Okla., September 23, 1983

VIEWS expressed here this week by a black government official throw further doubt on how much so-called "black spokesmen" actually are speaking for their race.

National news organizations and networks have a tendency to seek out the same small group of black leaders whenever a race issue arises that seems to require comment. Invariably, the reaction is political. That is, it is critical of President Reagan and his administration.

Because they and like-minded black personalities in politics and entertainment are so widely quoted, the public gets the impression all black people are opposed to Reagan.

Not so, said Henry T. Wilfong Jr., a recently appointed black official with the Small Business Administration. He is the SBA's associate administrator for minority small business and capital ownership development. Black businessmen, Wilfong said, tell him they do better during a Republican administration than when Democrats are in power.

Furthermore, he said it is a misconception that blacks in general think Reagan is anti-black.

Wilfong noted the blacks' traditional adherence to the Democratic Party. Some blacks have suggested such blind allegiance actually works against their best interests because the party takes their loyalty for granted. Wilfong had a more applicable reason: economics.

The Reagan philosophy of reducing government involvement in private industry and letting the free market determine a business's success or failure works better for black as well as white businessmen, Wilfong said. Instead of guaranteeing black business contracts, the SBA is now providing the necessary management services that will render such businesses price-competitive and thus able to make it on their own.

THE INDIANAPOLIS NEWS
Indianapolis, Ind., September 14, 1983

The story can be told in numbers and events.

Recently more than 250,000 persons gathered in Washington to mark the 20th anniversary of Martin Luther King's "I have a dream" speech and the first March on Washington. Not coincidentally, the event's organizers also used the event to protest the economic hardships minorities endure.

Jesse Jackson, one of the featured speakers at the Washington rally, has been unofficially running for president all summer. In the states in which he has been traveling and speaking, black voter registration has jumped as much as 25 percent.

Jackson's pitch to register those new voters is that black voters and a black president can effect change in Washington. The message is simple — "from the outhouse to the White House" — and it meets with applause. Whenever he speaks, Jackson is distracted by chants of "run, Jesse, run."

Not all these rumblings are distant ones. Indianapolis recently hosted a rally in honor of the Overground Railroad. The city is also one of seven participating in an ambitious new program to combat crime in black communities. And Jackson will soon be touring the state of Indiana — testing the waters for votes and support.

These activities add up to a new spirit of black activism.

One local black leader said, "The voter registrations, the black candidacy and black activism show that blacks care about the way they're treated again. They're not asking for action, they're demanding it."

Many black leaders predict another civil rights "golden age" like the one that produced the Civil Rights Act of 1964 and the Voting Rights Act of 1965. The old methods of cultivation, they say, will once again bear fruit.

Others aren't so optimistic. Another local black leader said, "I don't think the people who want a black to run for president understand how difficult it will be to change things. These problems aren't as simple as they say they are."

That last statement bears consideration. One of the themes of the recent march on Washington and one of the frequent themes of Jackson's speeches is the shabby status blacks have in the American economy.

It's an injustice no one denies. Blacks earn only a little more than half as much as whites and they're twice as likely to be unemployed.

Unfortunately, it's an injustice that's unlikely to be cured by legislation. The problems black leaders and black activists confront in the 1980s are not as clearcut as the ones that confronted their predecessors. Denying a black person the right to vote was clearly unjust; not hiring him because he's not well-qualified isn't. The muddiness of the issue and the slow pace of black progress to economic parity have been frustrating.

Such frustration supports much of the new black activism and the support for a Jackson candidacy.

It's an understandable frustration, but it shouldn't be allowed to obscure reality. The federal government is not to blame for the economic plight of blacks and legislation won't end economic discrimination.

This should not discourage black leaders and activists from attacking the problems that confront them, but it should discourage them from promising easy legislative solutions and raising unrealistic expectations.

The Orlando Sentinel

Orlando, Fla., May 23, 1983

A black presidential candidate has "a real chance of winning," says the Rev. Jesse Jackson, who last week launched a major voter registration drive in the South. While that may be Mr. Jackson's typical bombast — he wants to be that presidential candidate — you have only to look to Chicago to realize the power that a voter registration campaign can bring.

Though progress has been made since the 1965 Voting Rights Act was passed, the South remains a largely untapped source of black political strength. In 1980, more than half of America's 26.5 million blacks lived in the South, according to the Bureau of the Census. Blacks made up only 11.7 percent of the U.S. population, but in the South it was 21.9 percent.

The percentage of voting-age Southern blacks registered in 1980 was 60.3, a bit higher than for blacks nationwide. But that still was short of the percentage of Southern whites who were registered — and, when white voters already are reluctant to vote for black candidates, that difference means a lot.

The impact is seen in Congress where, of 20 black congressmen, Rep. Harold Ford of Memphis is the only Southern member. Mickey Leland represents a Houston district. But the Census Bureau counts Texas as being in the West.

There's another reason why a voter registration drive can be significant: Black populations in the South generally are not concentrated and their clout is diminished. For instance, Mississippi's population is about 35 percent black and, in 1980, 72.3 percent of voting-age blacks there were registered. Yet all five of Mississippi's congressmen are white.

By comparison, New York has a far smaller percentage of blacks, but they are more concentrated. That makes electing blacks to Congress far easier than in mostly rural Mississippi. Thus New York has three black congressional members.

Though the energy behind this campaign may come from one man's personal ambition, the South is fertile turf for plowing. Mr. Jackson may have his problems leading this effort but he has latched on to a fundamental principle of politics: The road to power at the voting booth begins with voter registration.

Richmond Times-Dispatch

Richmond, Va., June 4, 1983

Anybody who pooh-poohs the simmering political importance of the "black vote" should consider this: Virginia Republican Paul Trible last year defeated Democrat Dick Davis for a U.S. Senate seat by about 34,000 votes. In that election, some 44.5 percent of the state's 330,000 black registered voters cast ballots. But only half of Virginia's black voting-age population is registered to vote. If 70 percent of all voting-age Virginia blacks had been registered, and 70 percent of that group had voted, what would have been the election's outcome (other factors constant)? Since 85 percent of black citizens normally vote Democratic, Mr. Trible would have lost the election by ... 116,000 votes.

The Joint Center for Political Studies, a black research organization, has found that in six of the 11 Southern states, including Virginia, the number of unregistered blacks exceeds the Republican presidential victory margin in 1980. As for the North, columnist George Will writes: "No candidate since Dwight Eisenhower in 1952 has won the presidency without carrying at least three of these six Northern industrial states: Illinois, Michigan, New Jersey, New York, Ohio, Pennsylvania. In these states there are approximately 5.5 million blacks of voting age — a lot of them hitherto unregistered."

Several high-powered black groups are trying hard to sign up these non-voting millions. The Atlanta-based Voter Education Project, for example, last year registered 200,000 Southern blacks in four months. The group hopes to add another 1.5 million black voters to the electorate before 1984. That would be a stupendous feat, but determined people have accomplished more difficult tasks.

●

The registration drive is ominous for Republicans, because black antipathy for Ronald Reagan may send extraordinarily large numbers of blacks to the polls in 1984. But does it make sense that the Republican Party and Black America should be at political war? A Republican president abolished slavery, and, as late as 1956, a Republican presidential candidate, Eisenhower, got about four of every 10 black votes cast. President Reagan alluded to this odd polarization at his last press conference, when he said that blacks would support him "if we could get the truth to them."

The president's assertion contains some merit. It has become a veritable convention of the major media to portray Mr. Reagan as a scourge of the poor, while most black leaders berate him as an undoer of black gains. Evidently they prefer liberal Democratic policies, which, while bettering the lots of some blacks, have helped create an underclass of black citizens sentenced not only individually, but generationally, to the tenement and the public-housing project — hothouses of social pathologies.

Moreover, Mr. Reagan is given little or no credit for actions that, were they performed by a Democrat, undoubtedly would draw warm praise. After some waffling, the president supported extension of the Voting Rights Act — a stand, by the way, that angered most conservatives. He refused to seriously challenge phaseout of the federal PACE exams in favor of tests ensuring "equality of results" among all racial-group applicants. The Reagan Justice Department has opposed 134 proposed changes in voting procedures, including some in Virginia. Apparently unimpressed, most black leaders dwell on Mr. Reagan's opposition to unfair and non-statutory "quota" systems that often penalize people solely because their skin is white.

But Republicans need to recognize that blacks are no more likely than anyone else to vote against their economic interest. The Joint Center for Political Studies correctly notes: "[N]ot only are the black poor dependent on government transfer programs; the black middle class is also heavily reliant on the public sector for employment opportunities and contracting arrangements." Conservative Republicans like Mr. Reagan seek to shrink the state. This is good, but it nonetheless alienates them from most black Americans, who see Big Government not as threat but benefactor.

●

So what should the Republican Party do? Abandon its limited-government credo in order to prove itself non-racist? Enter the black-vote auction, "outbidding" the Democrats with more, and more costly, programs for blacks? While perhaps creating some black Republicans, these tactics not only would flout the party's defining principles (thus producing a net political deficit). They also would perpetuate the evils of paternalism that beset many blacks. No, what the Republicans must do is to promote policies that draw more blacks, confident and competitive, into the private sector.

President Reagan already has taken some steps in this direction: His "urban-enterprise zones," for example, aim to punch roads of hope through the inner-city dead ends. While no one supposes that this program, which grants firms tax breaks if they locate in the slums, will singlehandedly erase black-white economic differentials, it represents the kind of experimentation that Republicans need to undertake to diversify black employment. Mr. Reagan's push for private-school tuition tax credits seeks to increase blacks' educational opportunites: Studies have found that urban blacks enrolled in private schools do remarkably better as a group than their public-school peers.

At the same time, Republicans should intensify their efforts to combat the propaganda of the civil-rights junta. If the administration isn't "getting the truth" to blacks, it should encourage more black conservatives to speak out in black communities against the baneful welfare mentality. Such spokesmen are sorely needed. During most of the history of their struggle for equality, blacks benefited from an ideologically variegated leadership. From current civil-rights figures comes a distressingly unanimous cry: more government intervention.

Black Republicans might talk about Miami's Little Haiti, where West Indian immigrants, many arriving here with little but sacks on their backs, are fast ascending the economic ladder. Not every Haitian is ready to buy controlling stock in IBM, but Washington Post writer Edward Cody describes Little Haiti as a place of "economic scrambling" and "self-reliance" where seven out of 10 people reject food stamps and where more than 100 small restaurants and shops leave "an impression of vitality." Incredibly, some local American blacks say the Haitians are "undermining the job market by accepting misery wages." But the immigrants are determined: Their children won't grow up in a rat nest.

●

A hundred years ago the Republican Party was the party of black liberation. Will it also be known as the party that finally channeled Black America into the national mainstream? Only a conservative president can accomplish that, because liberalism is a deception. Only a courageous president can accomplish that, because powerful elites champion stale orthodoxies. History does not give us many such men, but at this moment history is kind.

The Oregonian

Portland, Ore., August 21, 1983

Instead of hurting Democratic presidential candidates, the entry of a black candidate, such as Jesse Jackson, the 41-year-old civil rights leader, into primary races can only stimulate registration and provide a larger base for the party candidate nominated at the convention next year in San Francisco.

Efforts to cool interests of black presidential candidates, particularly Jackson, on the grounds that their efforts would prove divisive ignore the fact that lively primaries have wide appeal and stimulate registration, adding to the potential numbers voting in the fall race. Republican strategists believe Jackson is the only Democrat who can fire up any black voter excitement, and that this enthusiasm could hurt Republicans in November.

Benjamin Hooks, executive director of the National Association for the Advancement of Colored People, said he resents having a symbolic black candidate. However, if it generates a large turnout in the primaries, a candidacy like Jackson's need not prove symbolic.

And, it might be asked, what is wrong with symbolism? It can be a beginning, a start, a foot on the ladder, a place for candidates to learn how to build organizations and to cope with the multitude of election laws across the nation.

Jackson is hardly just symbolic. If he runs, he would command a far greater following than did Shirley Chisholm, the New York congresswoman and the last serious black presidential candidate, who ran in 14 primaries in 1972.

In black registration efforts, such as PUSH, or People United to Serve Humanity, which is a part of the Southern Crusade, there is a drive to add 2 million black voters to the registration rolls in 11 Southern states where there is a potential of 3.4 million unregistered blacks. There also are 13.8 million unregistered whites in the South.

A dynamic speaker like Jackson pulls in crowds and fires up local registration workers.

As a candidate, he would have greater resources, more extensive media coverage and wider platforms.

As for fear that Jackson would prove divisive, there is nothing new in that among Democrats, particularly in the primaries. The test of party unity will come not in the campaigns of ethnic challengers, but in how well the party can pull itself together after all its major candidates get through strapping each other.

CHARLESTON EVENING POST

Charleston, S.C., August 8, 1983

In a recent news dispatch having to do with voter registration efforts, The Associated Press noted that some Columbia blacks contend that registration of black voters could be increased significantly if the state permitted door-to-door registration — a practice the attorney general declared unlawful several years ago. Among those sharing that belief, the AP said, is a lawyer who is a spokesman for Jesse Jackson's PUSH organization, which is conducting a national registration drive. "You have to go where the people are to register blacks," the AP quoted the lawyer as saying. "You have to go to the churches and the basketball courts." Perhaps. Yet there are indications that going to the people might not provide the ultimate answer, either.

The relaxation of residency requirements, the ready availability of transportation and the outreach programs of many county boards which send vans here and there as a citizen convenience have combined to make registration easier than ever before. Despite such changes and accommodations, however, the number of registered black voters in South Carolina decreased this year by more than 30,000 when the rolls were purged. The number of white voters declined by more than 68,000. Voter lists are purged for several reasons, including death and relocation to other states, but the majority of names are removed in the summers of odd-numbered years, in compliance with a state law requiring the automatic removal of the names of all persons who have not voted in the previous two years.

The total number of names dropped from the registration rolls this summer says plainly that thousands and thousands of citizens are not interested in exercising their rights to vote — that they do not care enough about their lives, their communities and their state to go to the polls and cast their ballots.

Such manifestations of widespread voter apathy raise the obvious question of whether more effort should be directed toward stimulating the registered voters and less toward registering prospective voters. Obviously it is easier to lead people to the registration books than it is to get them out on election day.

THE WALL STREET JOURNAL.

New York, N.Y., July 13, 1983

The Democratic Party is now commonly referred to as a party of special interests. Last weekend, for instance, the Democrats' traveling caravan of presidential aspirants appeared before the National Women's Political Caucus. This week, we're reading about their presentations to the NAACP convention. We take it, then, that this means we are to regard black Americans, all 27 million of them, as we do any of the other groups in the special-interest galaxy —that is, we can't really know for sure what calculations of self-interest every black person in America might make on a given issue, so to get a handle on what the group thinks about anything, we simply assume its opinions are identical to those of its officially designated leadership.

Thus, kicking off the NAACP convention this week, Executive Director Benjamin Hooks said the organization would not endorse a presidential candidate but that it opposes Ronald Reagan. Under the rules of the political-opinion game, one may now reduce Mr. Hooks' remark to its generic form: Blacks are anti-Reagan.

Maybe by and large they are anti-Reagan. But does this also mean that black Americans wholeheartedly embrace the programs of the Democratic alternative? Should one feel safe in saying that at the very least, black America looks to the federal government's substantial presence as its best bet for getting a window seat on the American gravy train? We wonder.

In yesterday's Journal, reporter Erik Calonius recorded the reflections of the poor and unemployed in Memphis. "What I'd like to tell Reagan," Robert Taylor told Mr. Calonius, "is get me five a week. That's what I want, five days of work a week." Five a week is the issue.

If you're a young black man or woman who wants to get out of school, find a job, get married, have a family and do the sort of things families and husbands and wives do for 30 or 40 years, the key questions are: Is the American economy going to create enough jobs to accommodate you? And are you going to have the job skills and social skills needed to win one of those jobs and hold onto it? Evidence is emerging that some of the newer leaders in the minority community are beginning to think of their longer interests in terms of solid achievement.

For instance, the place where Americans have traditionally acquired most of these skills is in

school. Measuring up academically is now a national priority, and a new, achievement-oriented breed of nonwhite school superintendents in cities like Washington, Chicago and New York is working hard to see that the many black kids in those school systems succeed. These administrators need all the political support they can get in their efforts to raise standards and restore order in their classrooms. But what remains the one, school-related litmus test of pro-black sentiment among the current civil-rights community? Busing. For years, improving the atmosphere for learning inside city schools has been an afterthought, not a priority. Whose priorities best represent blacks on the education issue?

The quick answer is, no one who opposes huge transfusions of federal aid for education or any other black need. Support for beneficent federal spending is regarded as the sine qua non of a proper pro-black attitude. Is it?

In 1969, the percentage of blacks below the poverty level was 32.2%; in 1980, it was 32.5%. One reply to those figures is that the federal anti-poverty effort obviously needs to be expanded. But maybe the figures are saying that the programs actually don't or can't do all that their sponsors promised. If the latter explanation carries any validity—and we think it does—then might it not make sense for someone among the black leadership to do some hard thinking about committing another generation of blacks to this strategy? Congress recently passed a $4.6 billion jobs program; it has created few jobs, and is bogged down in a bureaucratic morass.

Whatever one's feelings about issues such as these, we're certain that the notion that black Americans now constitute a "special interest" is pernicious. It implies that an awful lot of people who well understand the complexity of their own problems can always be counted on to cast their vote in a lump, and that the lump will go to whoever can concoct a "safety net" or some other airy promise.

This sort of reductionist view of black America's interests may have gotten a lot of people elected in the past, but we're not so certain it will best serve blacks in the future. Perhaps it's time for blacks as individuals to start asking black leaders and white politicians how they propose to get them *out* of the safety net and into Robert Taylor's "five a week."

THE COMMERCIAL APPEAL

Memphis, Tenn., July 28, 1983

"THERE'S A MAN coming around taking names," went a popular litany of the civil rights movement in the 1960s. But the man taking names was not the local voter registrar. Nor was his list what could be called an exercise in good government.

Today, 20 years later, there's a different man going around taking names. And if he's not the voter registrar, he's as likely as not to be looking for the registrar in an effort to get his name and others put on the voter registration list.

As a recent series of articles by reporters with The Commercial Appeal demonstrated, there is a stirring across the Mid-South among voting-age blacks, who, perhaps for the first time since the Voting Rights Act of 1965 was enacted, have discovered the worth of their combined voting strength.

There are probably any number of reasons blacks have rediscovered the ballot box. A president viewed as insensitive to their wants and needs. A feeling of abandonment by white, liberal politicians. A sense of excitement over the recent election of black mayors in Northern cities such as Chicago and small towns in Arkansas and Mississippi. Or simply a realization of what political power is all about.

The reasons that it is happening are of less consequence than the fact that it is happening. As turning points in history go, the present phenomenon must be put in the same historical category as the legislation that made it possible. Just as the Voting Rights Act forever changed politics in the Mid-South, so will the current voter registration drives.

In the beginning, it was the right to participate, not the opportunity to make a difference in individual elections, that excited black voters. It has taken time for black office-seekers both to overcome the legal hurdles put before them and to learn the intricacies of the political process. What we see happening today is the inevitable result of the democratic process.

BLACKS STILL have a long way to go before they have political parity with whites in the Mid-South, but the progress that has been made is both encouraging and indicative of changes to come.

Mississippi now has more black elected officials than any other state. Black political activists there are dissatisfied, as could be expected; but if you consider that blacks, who make up 8 percent of the elected officials in the state, are in the majority in 29 percent of the states 82 counties, then it becomes apparent that black voters are nearly one-third along the road to achieving political parity. That's no small achievement considering the obstacles that have been put before them.

Tennessee, where 1.6 percent of the elected officials are black, and Arkansas, with 2 percent, have a long way to go before blacks achieve political parity with whites, but as a recent voter registration drive in West Memphis and current drives in Memphis indicate, the changes are likely to be accelerated in the years ahead.

Thirty-six years ago, President Truman's Committee on Civil Rights concluded that changes were needed in the federal law to give blacks equal access to the political process. "In recent years the situation in the deep South has changed to the point where it can be said that Negroes are beginning to exercise the political rights of free Americans," said the committee. "In the light of history, this represents progress, limited and precarious, but nevertheless progress."

Much has happened since Truman's committee envisioned a brave new world of black political equality. Of course, by today's standards, the progress acknowledged by the committee seems meager indeed. That's how far we've come. And it's a good reminder of how far we have yet to go.

THE ARIZONA REPUBLIC

Phoenix, Ariz., June 5, 1983

ALTHOUGH Jesse Jackson is sounding like a candidate for the Democratic nomination for president, the flamboyant black civil rights leader isn't under the illusion he could win, of course.

That's not his objective.

He thinks black votes in the primaries could give him enough delegates to make him the power broker of the Democratic national convention. He also believes his candidacy would cause millions of blacks who never had voted to register to vote for him.

There are 3 million unregistered blacks in the South alone.

Since they would vote Democratic, they could make the South Democratic again.

That would give all black leaders, including Jackson, real clout in the party.

It was the election of Harold Washington as the first black mayor of Chicago that gave Jackson this vision.

Black registration skyrocketed when Washington announced his candidacy.

Jackson is sure that a black candidate for president would have the same effect.

Black leaders who originally dismissed Jackson's idea are having second thoughts.

They're beginning to agree that a black candidate for the Democratic nomination could make blacks a power in the party.

However, few of them believe the candidate should be Jackson.

Jackson is not especially popular among other black leaders. One reason is envy of his ability to publicize himself.

Another is that he's "all mouth."

He loves to orate, but he avoids the drudgery of running a movement or campaign.

White Democratic leaders are of two minds about the idea of a black running for the nomination.

They agree that it would increase black registration, and thus enable the Democratic nominee to capture at least part of the South.

On the other hand, the prospect of the party becoming hostage to a minority makes them uneasy.

That could in the long run cost them countless white votes.

Sooner or later, however, there will be a black candidate for the Democratic nomination. When that happens, the whole shape of presidential politics will be changed.

THE SUN

Baltimore, Md., March 26, 1984

When Rev. Jesse Jackson entered the Democratic race for president last fall, he said his campaign could expand the base of the party by tapping people who did not feel they previously had a real stake in it. On that subject, he has been quite right.

With his charismatic presence, riveting oratory and message for the "dispossessed," he has sparked increased voter participation among blacks around the country. His campaign and the voting drives that accompany it have caused large jumps in registration and have resulted in impressive showings for Mr. Jackson in states with sizable black populations. He captured 19 percent of the total vote in the Georgia primary, 21 percent in Alabama and 20 percent in Illinois.

In the three southern states that held primaries this month, there were 86,000 more black voters on the rolls than two years ago — 35,366 in Alabama, 34,642 in Georgia and 16,277 in Florida. There was also a massive black outpouring for Mr. Jackson in Illinois, particularly Chicago, where he helped bring out the vote last year that allowed Harold Washington to become that city's first black mayor.

This surge in black voter participation did not begin with Jesse Jackson's campaign. It's more accurate to say the campaign came in response to the trend that was already developing, a trend that started after the election of Ronald Reagan four years ago. Mr. Jackson's presence has given it a boost.

The increase has historic significance. Until this year, blacks have had lower voter participation rates than whites for reasons that reach back into the nation's history. Beginning in the late 1800s, they were kept from voting in the South by poll taxes, literacy tests and a variety of other obstructions designed to prevent them from exercising the citizenship granted after the Civil War. When legal obstructions were finally overturned by federal courts, blacks were kept from voting by a system of intimidation that lasted until at least the mid-Sixties when the Voting Rights Act was passed.

Now, the black vote will carry more weight than ever in the Democratic Party. It could give Mr. Jackson a major role at the party's convention this summer and it will be vitally important to the Democrat who faces Mr. Reagan in November. If the new voters attracted by Mr. Jackson go to the polls this fall, they will be a windfall for whomever the Democrats nominate in July.

ARKANSAS DEMOCRAT
Little Rock, Ark., July 24, 1984

Sen. Dale Bumpers says it's demeaning to the South for Republican strategists to say there'll be a "white backlash" against Jesse Jackson's efforts this fall to register Southern blacks to vote Democratic. The South, Bumpers says, is no more racist than other regions.

No it isn't. The right term for what he's talking about is "conservative political reaction" to Jackson's registration of new Democrats, who just happen to be black.

Jackson's Atlanta center says 650,000 new black voters have registered in 11 Southern states this year – and, of course, the figure will rise as Jackson hits the trail for Mondale there. Is it "white backlash" for the region's pro-Reagan white conservatives to register and defend themselves against Jackson's efforts to use black Democratic registration to recover Southern states narrowly lost to Ronald Reagan in 1980? Of course not.

The talk all comes from a *Washington Post* reporter's quoting certain unidentified GOP figures as saying privately that Jackson's registration efforts to date have "alienated" white Southerners, led to increased white registration, and created a "racial polarization."

All the Republicans can cite for that proposition is an increase in Southern white registration – something normal in an election year. But while nobody would say that Jackson's efforts aren't responsible for some of it, maybe a lot of it, it's more sensible to take a political rather than a racist view of such "polarization" as there is.

The racist reading arises, we suppose, from the fact that a black is registering blacks – and that Southern whites are automatically supposed to react to that with counter-registrations of their own.

But Jackson isn't a candidate for anything. Earlier, he did register blacks in his own interest – to swell his primary totals – but he never had a chance, and everybody knew his followers would go for Walter Mondale when it was all over. That's the case now as Jackson continues his registration efforts. If Southern whites are indeed reacting to Jackson with a counter-registration of their own, it's not because they're "anti-Jackson" but because they're pro-Reagan.

To call that a white backlash or racial polarization is not only politically inexact but also gratuitously racist in itself – and it would be wise not to attribute these sentiments to the *Post* reporter's Republican strategists. He didn't name them, he paraphrased most of what they said, and the only backlash he quoted them as mentioning was one against the efforts of black leaders to "polarize" blacks against Ronald Reagan.

The Evening Gazette
Worcester, Mass., May 19, 1984

Blacks and Hispanics are getting special attention in this 1984 presidential election campaign. To call attention to that fact seems at first to be insensitive, if not racially biased; to ignore it is foolish.

This week Walter Mondale was in an East Los Angeles school asking kids why they hadn't seen much of Gary Hart lately; Jesse Jackson crossed the border into Mexico to say illegal aliens looking for work were not hurting the U.S. economy, but helping it; and Ronald Reagan was honoring Michael Jackson at the White House.

In Texas alone, Hispanic organizers hope to add more than a million new Mexican-American voters to the rolls by fall. In 1982, as many Hispanics as whites voted in Texas state elections, and turnout among registered Hispanics was as high as 86 percent.

Like every major ethnic group before them, blacks and Hispanics are coming of age politically in the United States. Black mayors in large cities have become commonplace. The mayors of Denver, Miami and San Antonio and the governor of New Mexico are Hispanic.

Candidates court this emerging ethnic vote with various pledges and promises. But the issues that interest blacks and Hispanics are not much different from the things other Americans care about. Mondale was leaning hard on his record for supporting poverty programs. That may be part of his appeal to black and Hispanic voters, but he should not neglect the issues of inflation, balanced budgets and national defense. These affect all Americans.

The Miami Herald
Miami, Fla., October 9, 1984

THE DEMOCRATS' strategy to win the White House by registering two million previously inactive women, blacks, and other minorities is being swamped by an army — perhaps three million strong — of heretofore-unregistered white conservatives. "One of the lessons we learned," says Rex Harris, campaign manager for the Rev. Jesse Jackson in North Carolina, "is the quickest way to register white conservatives is to hold a black registration drive."

The intensity of the registration effort in North Carolina is unmatched. More than 77,000 new black voters were enrolled, compared with 100,000 white conservatives who are expected to vote for President Reagan and other conservative politicians. "We may have created a monster," Mr. Harris says.

Nonsense. Every person eligible to vote has a right and civic obligation to register. That's the American way. If the right to vote has been turned into a partisan weapon this year, so be it. Let every point of view find expression in the ballot box. Better there than in the streets.

According to the Washington-based Center for the Study of the American Electorate, white Christians were the one group of nonvoters unaffiliated with any political organization in 1980. This year much of the Republicans' support, especially in the South, will come from this group. The Moral Majority's voter-registration drive is rolling along, targeted at the estimated 45 million fundamentalists in this country.

Ironically, black preachers wrote the book on grass-roots registration drives. "God bless them for it," gloats an organizer for white-fundamentalist churches.

The enrollment this year of unregistered segments of society is a healthy development. In this Presidential election in particular, where the alternatives are so clear, the people — all the people — should be heard.

This, in a very real sense, is the Reverend Jackson's legacy. Yet his supporters and other Democrats wring their hands. Let them instead redouble their efforts to register more voters who share their views. That, as it should be, is how elections are won.

The Hartford Courant
Hartford, Conn., January 14, 1984

When the Voting Rights Act of 1965 was passed, fewer than 300 blacks held elective public office, according to the Joint Center for Political Studies, a non-profit research group.

Considerable progress has occurred since then; in July 1983, there were more than 5,600 black elected officials. Gains in the South have been particularly noteworthy.

Behind this trend is one equally important: Blacks are becoming more politically active. Black voter registration increased by 600,000 between 1980 and 1982, the center reported, and almost 6 percent more blacks voted in 1982 congressional elections than in 1978.

Despite the progress in black political participation, however, much remains to be done. Even with the growth in the number of black officials, only about 1 percent of elective offices are held by blacks, and many blacks still are not registered to vote.

Were he alive today, Martin Luther King Jr. surely would call attention to the length of the path ahead. But we think he would be greatly pleased to look back at the distance traveled. It is fitting that this news comes just before his birthday, which is Sunday.

THE TENNESSEAN
Nashville, Tenn., August 30, 1984

TENNESSEE Sen. Howard Baker and Gov. Lamar Alexander agreed last week that the Republican party should be doing more to attract black members.

Senator Baker credited Governor Alexander with doing "an extraordinarily good job in his outreach to minorities," but said that nationally, the party was doing a "miserable job" attracting blacks.

The senator is right — only 3% of the delegates to the Republican convention were black, and that is indeed a poor showing. But what could be expected with a party whose record on minorities has gotten so miserable?

Why should blacks be attracted into a political party that had no minority plank in its 94-page platform? Why should black Americans be attracted to an administration that prefers missile systems and defense contracts to public housing and job training programs. And why should blacks support a President that replaced members of the U.S. Civil Rights Commission for criticizing his policies toward minorities?

Recent national reports indicate that the poverty gap has widened during the Reagan administration. There are more homeless people now in America than at any time since the Depression. Lines at food banks, rescue shelters and social service agencies have lengthened since 1980 — and most of the people standing in those lines are black.

Virtually all power in this nation stems from politics. Minorities realize that, and are running for office and registering to vote in record numbers. But they will undoubtably vote for candidates who listen to them, and they will surely select a party that invites them into the mainstream. Currently, that is not the Republican party.

THE ATLANTA CONSTITUTION
Atlanta, Ga., April 26, 1984

Jesse Jackson may never become president of the United States, but his symbolic march along the trail that leads — in his words — "from the outhouse to the White House," has already begun to pay important dividends.

Jackson has been a lightning rod for black aspirations. He has raised the political efficacy of those — the young, the poor — who had previously stayed away from the polls, figuring their ballots would make little or no difference in the quality of their lives.

Jesse Jackson

He has raised the political ambitions and the confidence of his black brethren, who — bolstered by increased black voter registration, particularly in the South — are declaring and running for public office on the city, county, state and national levels apparently in greater numbers than ever before.

Since 1982, more than 500,000 blacks in 11 Southern states have signed up to vote, boosting the black percentage of registered voters in the region from 13 to 16 percent, according to the Voter Education Project.

And black candidates from Alabama to Mississippi to Georgia have decided to enter the political arena — many for the first time — because of the enthusiasm and interest Jackson has stirred in black communities across the country.

Much attention has been focused on Jackson and what price he will exact from the Democratic Party for his support for the party's nominee in November. But preoccupation with that narrow point overshadows his broader accomplishments, and overlooks the important movement he merely represents. That is a shame.

He has shown the Democratic Party and the nation that there is a large body of black voters out there who are interested in the political process and who are willing to support candidates who genuinely address their needs. In a round-about way, he has brought us a step — a small one, to be sure — closer to having a political system that at least attempts to be inclusive, responding to the needs of whites, blacks, women, the rich, the poor and other minorities.

He is showing us that blacks have not written off the system; that they are willing to work to make it better for all of us. But they don't want to continue to be forgotten between elections. The question is: Is anybody listening?

DAYTON DAILY NEWS
Dayton, Ohio, April 26, 1984

Just a couple of years ago, when voting turnout had been dropping for 20 years, public discourse turned to the possibility of mechnical solutions: How could we make it easier to register or vote?

Today that whole debate may be obviated. Registration and voter turnout are unmistakably on the rise across the nation, even though public bodies never really got around to doing much about the problem. The latest good news comes from Dayton, where registration is up 8.8 percent from 1980, even though population is down more than 2 percent.

Why? The words "Jesse Jackson" come to mind. His role is undeniable. In heavily black sections of Dayton, one-fourth of the 8.8-percent increase has come just in the last month. There can be no mistaking what's going on.

But there is more. Could the Rev. Jackson have had the the same kind of impact in, say,

> *For Jesse Jackson to mobilize blacks, the basic anger had to be there.*

1976 or 1980? Probably not. The basic anger had to be there.

Ronald Reagan may be playing a bigger role in the new phenomenon than Mr. Jackson. Black voting soared in Chicago and rose in Philadelphia in mayoral races before the Jackson campaign started. Although President Reagan was not on the ballot in those races, there is every reason to believe that the political awareness his unusual presidency has generated among blacks was at work.

The black community has not been alone in its new activism. In 1982 elections across the country turnout was up. And in 1984 primaries several turnout records have been set.

Lincoln Journal

Lincoln, Neb., November 15, 1984

President Reagan should be concerned about the apparent black and white voter split. In fact, we all should.

As a country that has painfully grown from slavery and segregation and as a country whose cities only a decade ago burned with racial anger and hatred, we should seek to understand and then eliminate the discord growing along racial lines.

Although Reagan's winning margin borrowed heavily from the traditional Democratic voters including the working class and ethnic voters, some 90 percent of the black vote went to Mondale. A lot of hand-wringing went into the discussion over the gender gap, but estimates of this so-called gap between the sexes was never more than 16 percent.

The Republican Party has never attracted large numbers of black voters. But that support has never been less than in the past presidential election. The massive Jesse Jackson-inspired registration of black voters highlighted the nearly unanimous tilt of black Americans to the Democratic Party.

The National Urban League in its ninth annual "State of Black America" report issued last January said the Reagan administration is "almost universally regarded by blacks as the most hostile administration in the last 50 years."

Clearly, there's a problem.

AS THE MOST popular president in recent times, Reagan has the power to do many good things. Among them would be bridging the racial chasm.

Reagan can do this at the start of his second term by calling black leaders to Washington for discussions. He did this at the start of his first term. Although one could argue it was to little avail, such a move could not be considered a bad one.

If Reagan and the black leaders could achieve an on-going dialogue, perhaps Reagan could see some of the deleterious effects his programs have had not only on poor blacks but on all poor Americans.

Some of the concerns may be beyond a Reagan solution. Listening, however, is the first step to understanding. And no problem is solved without its being understood.

MANY OF the concerns of black Americans are economic. The recession has not ended for many of them. Although the September jobless rate for black Americans fell nearly 1 percentage point, it still stood at an astounding 15.1 percent compared to 6.4 percent for white Americans. The unemployment rate for black teens was much higher, as was the number of blacks who held part-time jobs but sought full-time work or who had given up looking for work.

The difference between black and white median family income was nearly $11,000 at the start of the decade

and it has not appreciably closed. And the number of black families living in poverty continues to grow.

MANY ALSO view this administration as applying brakes to the gains made in equal employment opportunities. In case after case, in Detroit, Memphis and New Orleans, the Justice Department has reversed itself on affirmative action plans for minority workers, rejecting plans to hire and promote black employees. Some of those plans originally were formulated by the Justice Department under

previous administrations going back to Richard Nixon.

If there has been "no discrimination of any kind in this administration," as Reagan asserted in a June news conference, then a face-to-face meeting with these black leaders certainly would drive that point home. If the misunderstanding is of perception only, then let Reagan clarify his support. If discrimination in this administration is a reality, a meeting with black leaders is needed more than ever.

THE MILWAUKEE JOURNAL

Milwaukee, Wisc., November 14, 1984

Once again, black voters proved the most loyal of all the Democratic Party's constituencies in the recent presidential election. Once again, that fact poses a problem for blacks and for the Democrats.

With the exception of Jewish voters, no constituency came close to matching the 90% vote that blacks gave the Mondale-Ferraro ticket. Meanwhile, as has been the case in the past several elections, the Democrats again drew only about 38% of the white vote across the nation.

Political observers differ on whether these results truly bespeak racial polarization. They certainly bespeak trouble — let alone the prospect of a long electoral dry spell — for the Democrats.

How does the party meet its problem? The Democrats must make themselves attractive to the broad electorate. However, the party must not abandon its most loyal constituent group. At least one of the major parties must be an advocate for those who, in large part because of past discrimination, still bring up the rear of the American parade. Indeed, it would be tragic if future Democratic presidential candidates never saw anything blacker than a bowling ball as they campaigned.

We believe that Democrats can retain the deserved loyalty of black voters and attract other segments of the electorate by sounding the theme of economic growth. This need not be incompatible with a more equitable distribution of resources. In fact, much of the bitterness of the discussion of affirmative action, for example, may stem from the effort to slice a shrinking economic pie. Blacks, no less than other Americans, would welcome an expanding economy.

However, Republican notions about expansion seem unlikely to appeal to blacks if these notions are seen as part of an approach that involves repealing the civil-rights gains of earlier times. True, Republicans lost a majority of the black vote in the era of President Franklin Roosevelt. Yet, at least until the election of 1960, many blacks found it possible to vote for GOP candidates. The task of the Republican Party is to recapture that level of confidence.

For their part, blacks should continue their steadfast course of improving their turnouts at the polls, thus enabling them to voice their legitimate demands authoritatively — upon both major parties.

SYRACUSE
HERALD·JOURNAL
Syracuse, N.Y., November 9, 1984

Black voters went heavily for Democratic candidate Walter Mondale. No surprise there. It has happened in every recent presidential election. The Democrats can count on overwhelming support from the black community.

Sometimes it works; Jimmy Carter owed his election in 1976 to black votes in strategic states. More often, it's a wash; black votes for the Democratic candidate are offset by white Democrats fleeing to Republican nominees.

In 1984, it was a disaster for the Democrats.

Pundits even came up with a catchy phrase to describe what the solid black voting bloc caused among Southern white voters: "White flight."

In state after Southern state, white voters jettisoned traditional Democratic loyalties to vote for Ronald Reagan. Many were turned off by the campaign of the Rev. Jesse Jackson, and worried about the huge successes of Jackson's voter registration drive.

The flight was overbooked. In a few Southern states, upwards of 80 percent of the whites voted for Reagan.

That statistic has Democratic strategists panicky. Enough so, one political scientist warns, that black voters may be overlooked in future presidential elections.

"Leading Democrats are already focusing on how to recapture the white middle class," says Lucius Barker, chairman of the political science department at Washington University in St. Louis. Barker, a Jesse Jackson delegate at last summer's Democratic convention, predicts such a change of focus will work against blacks' interests.

Part of the problem rests with black voters themselves. Democrats can take them for granted because so many routinely vote Democratic. In this election, an estimated 90 percent cast ballots for Walter Mondale.

Philosophically, Mondale was a lot closer to their concerns than Ronald Reagan, but that doesn't help practically.

Black voters will never account for more than 10 percent of the electorate, making them an important but not overwhelming bloc. Currently their influence is confined to one party and since they've shown exceptional electoral loyalty over the past 20 years, they risk being taken for granted by that party.

Black voters might be better off, in the long run, by making their way into Republican, as well as Democratic, ranks.

It's happening here and there in some Northern cities, including Syracuse. Republicans have nominated some blacks and are consequently attracting more black voters.

Nationally, though, there is no strong incentive for the Republican Party to stress black concerns. But blacks have it within their power to change that by providing the best political incentive of all — votes for candidates *of either party* who understand their concerns.

They might be surprised at how much more actively both Republicans and Democrats court them when their vote can't be taken for granted.

Minneapolis Star and Tribune

Minneapolis, Minn., November 23, 1984

President Reagan did not need, seek or get much support from black voters in his easy reelection campaign. But the Republican preelection political analysis, Reagan's campaign indifference to wooing black voters and the 90-to-10 black-vote margin for Walter Mondale are dangers for the nation. They reflect and reinforce a racial split in political behavior that would be unacceptable in other realms. The split is inconsistent with national ideals of racial integration. It narrows the appeal of both political parties, fuels black accusations that whites are bigoted and strengthens white notions that all blacks think alike. Those are wrong directions in U.S. public opinion.

As a shaper of opinion and the president for all citizens, Reagan should point a better direction. If he hears advice to write off blacks — or any other ethnic group — as unnecessary to Republican electoral successes, he should reject it. If pollsters or tacticians cynically tell him that ignoring blacks will strengthen his standing among certain whites, Reagan's rejection should be more emphatic still. And if he believes that his policies will benefit blacks more than traditional Democratic programs, he should argue that point, not just assert it.

In particular, Reagan needs to make his case in black communities and with black supporters to back him up. There are such supporters, though relatively few; there are such arguments, though politically prominent blacks usually dismiss them. Paradoxically, the Reagan administration could strike a blow for better race relations by forcefully challenging those black leaders. It should explain repeatedly, for example, why it supports a teenage subminimum wage as a weapon against high black youth unemployment. It should justify its cuts in public-housing construction on the grounds that housing vouchers can serve the black poor better. It should rally black parents around its resistance to court-ordered school busing. It should promote its proposed urban enterprise zones as a way to bring jobs to inner-city ghettos.

The point is not that Reagan's policies should be adopted. The point is for Reagan to take black issues seriously by advocating his preferred ways to address them. Reagan will not meet that need unless he argues out his policy disagreements with dominant black leaders and acknowledges alternative black leaders in their place. The task requires administration meetings with black spokesmen who denounce it — the Congressional Black Caucus, for example, black mayors, black leaders of civil-rights groups. Reagan should say out loud why Republicans think that they know better than Democrats how to offer black citizens a fairer shake.

No matter how eloquent, Reagan would not convert implacable foes; he might indeed discover that some of his race-related policies are dead wrong. But he has an obligation to speak directly with black Americans about his agenda for moving the nation closer to true racial integration. And by speaking with blacks, Reagan would speak volumes to whites and others too. He would affirm that he is black Americans' president as well as everyone else's. He would demonstrate that while politicians may disagree on the policies needed now for further racial progress, neither party imagines that race has yet become a matter of indifference.

The nation needs to hear such a message from its president.

The Des Moines Register
*Des Moines, Iowa,
October 29, 1984*

What happened to civil rights and the presidential campaign?

It's sort of understood, isn't it, that Walter Mondale knows all there is to know about the old civil-rights fight and is committed to it? And that Ronald Reagan thinks it should all have been handled differently but wishes women and minorities realized that that doesn't mean he doesn't care about them, right?

Moreover, when Mondale talks about the poor, you can assume he is thinking of the civil-rights question; same thing goes when Reagan picks up on that theme, disputing everyone's figures that show the poor have gotten poorer under his administration.

Has it become unfashionable to talk about things that matter a great deal to poorer women and minority members? How much have you heard about the higher rates of unemployment among blacks than whites? About how the birth rate among black, unwed teen-agers has shot up astronomically? About the impact of the federal budget cuts on single-parent households, or about those families' difficulties in getting good child care?

How long since someone brought up Reagan's intrusions into the independence of the Civil Rights Commission? Since someone made an impassioned plea for the Equal Rights Amendment?

Come to think of it, when you do hear about civil rights, the dispute is not on advances, but on whether areas where some improvement has been made will even be held. Will women's athletics lose the standing they finally achieved? Are those states that have already approved a comparable-worth pay program pursuing "a truly crazy proposal"?

When it comes to civil rights, what you don't hear says more than what you do; and what you don't hear says a topic vital to the family of America is looking more and more like an orphan.

Voting Rights Act Extension Raises Quota Question

Senate hearings began in January, 1982 on extending the 1965 Voting Rights Act for another 10 years. The legislation, considered the cornerstone of civil rights policy, had two parts, one permanent, the other scheduled to expire in August of that year. The permanent provision banned literacy tests and other electoral practices formerly used to prevent minorities from voting. The temporary section required some states and local jurisdictions—those with a history of discrimination or of low minority election turnout—to obtain approval from the Justice Department before making any changes in election laws. In October, 1981, the House had voted to make the temporary section, affecting six southern states, permanent. The Reagan Administration favored a 10-year extension of the whole act, with the proviso that any violations found under the permanent part of the act would have to be proved on the basis of an intent to discriminate, rather than by electoral results. If the standard for violations focused on results, Attorney General William French Smith testified, "quotas would be the end result." In addition, Smith said, the Administration supported provisions that would allow jurisdictions covered under the temporary section to be exempted.

The standard-of-proof issue became the pivotal point in a heated partisan debate in the Senate. The "intent to discriminate" standard adopted by the Administration had come from a Supreme Court decision in 1980 regarding elections to the City Commission in Mobile, Ala. The court found that the fact that no black had been elected to the commission, even though blacks constituted a third of the city's population, was not enough to prove discrimination. The challengers, the court ruled, had to show that the election procedure had been adopted with an intent to discriminate. A complication was added to the Senate debate on the Voting Rights Act when an Alabama federal judge ruled in April, 1982, in the same case, that Mobile's city election system was indeed discriminatory and had been adopted, a century before, with the intent to discriminate against blacks. Supporters of the "intent to discriminate" standard said this showed that it was not as difficult to prove intent as its opponents maintained. Foes of the Administration bill, on the other hand, pointed out that the Alabama decision had taken over 10,000 hours of lawyers', witnesses' and paralegals' time, plus a year of the judge's time, to reach, and that it did not reflect current circumstances but those of a hundred years earlier.

A compromise bill was drafted in the Senate Judiciary Committee and eventually passed by Congress in June, after filibuster attempts in the Senate were quashed. The final language stated that violations of the Voting Rights Act could be proved "if, based on the totality of circumstances, it is shown that the political processes leading to nomination or election...are not equally open to participation" by minority groups. The compromise bill also stated that "nothing in this section establishes a right to have members of a protected class [minority groups] elected in numbers equal to their proportion in the population."

St. Petersburg Times
St. Petersburg, Fla., May 6, 1982

An aide to Sen. Bob Dole, R-Kan., said that the senator's objective in gaining the bipartisan compromise Tuesday on extension of the 1965 Voting Rights Act was "to save the Republican Party."

More accurately, he might have said "to save Ronald Reagan," whose programs of prejudice have alienated blacks, Hispanic-Americans and millions of the jobless poor, along with some loyal Republican leaders who now seem less inclined to follow him blindly.

Against rising currents of dissent, Reagan abandoned an attempt to gut the nation's most effective civil rights law and bestowed a White House blessing on the Dole compromise. He even expressed a hope for its swift passage by the entire Congress.

THE BILL, approved by the Senate Judiciary Committee and sent to the full Senate, is a fair, constructive resolution of a controversy that should have ended long ago. The voting rights extension might have passed the Congress last year, had Reagan not played to the battalion of Senate bigots in trying to make the law unenforceable.

Dole's compromise drew the full, if somewhat reluctant, support of civil rights groups eager to get the act extended before Congress is embroiled in the summer battle on the Reagan budget.

Dole said he has assurances that House leaders will go along with the compromise language in two key clauses of the act.

The first relates to how a court should judge whether minority voters have been victims of discrimination. Under the current Voting Rights Act, the Supreme Court has ruled that plaintiffs must prove the discrimination was intentional. The House version sought to reverse the high court rulings by directing the courts to judge discrimination only by the results of election procedures, not by the motives behind them.

THE DOLE amendment goes beyond the "results" standard by requiring the courts also to examine the "totality of circumstances" surrounding discrimination charges. To mollify Senate opponents, who claimed that the House version would lead to racial quotas in elective representation, the amendment explicitly states that minority groups have no right to proportional representation based on race.

The House bill also made permanent a clause in the law, scheduled to expire in August, that requires districts with a history of discrimination to get Justice Department clearance for any changes in election laws. The Dole compromise extends this clause for 25 years and provides for a mandatory review after 15 years.

Both the House and Dole versions provide that states or districts that have complied with the letter and spirit of the law for 10 years may be exempted from the "preclearance" requirement.

The compromise assures minority voters equal access to the ballot box. Any attempt to delay its passage, such as the threatened filibuster by Sen. John P. East, R-N.C., should be immediately squelched.

TULSA WORLD
Tulsa, Okla., February 14, 1982

ON AUGUST 6, 1965, President Lyndon Johnson signed the Voting Rights Act, guaranteeing black Americans' right to participate fully in the political life of this country.

The law was hotly contested and long debated. And the final Senate vote fell largely along regional lines. To this state's credit, both of its U.S. senators, Mike Monroney and Fred Harris, voted in favor of the act.

Ronald Reagan, then governor of California, said he supported the goals of the act, but opposed the act itself.

Much has changed since 1965. Or has it?

The Voting Rights Act is now up for renewal and debate on the bill will again be heated.

Ronald Reagan, opponent of the bill 17 years ago, is now a supporter of the law. The president declared in his State of the Union address that he "strongly supports" the proposed 10-year extension of the bill.

Strom Thurmond, the lone Republican to vote against the bill in 1965, is now the chairman of the Senate Judiciary Committee. In that position, he is trying hard to scuttle renewal of an effective act.

The 1965 act focused on voting rights violations in the southern states, because that is where problem of ballot box discrimina-

tion was most acute. One provision required southern states to get "pre-clearance" from the Justice Department before altering their local election systems. The object was to make sure blacks' voting rights were not stymied through legal subterfuge.

Thurmond now wants pre-clearance to apply to all states. On its face, this seems to be a push for equal treatment, but, in fact, it is a bid to gut the act by over-burdening the Justice Department's enforcement capabilities.

The Voting Rights Act should be extended, and Thurmond's gimmickry rejected.

Pittsburgh Post-Gazette

Pittsburgh, Pa., February 22, 1982

Not long ago, there were fears that major obstacles would be placed in the way of extending the landmark 1965 Voting Rights Act, which has changed the face of politics in the South by dramatically increasing black political participation.

Thanks to a sustained campaign by civil-rights groups — backed up with voluminous evidence of the persistence of discriminatory practices — extending the Voting Rights Act is now a foregone conclusion. Even President Reagan, who used to muse ignorantly about the supposed injustice of the act, has been educated in the importance of "pre-clearance" of changes in voting procedures in the South.

But the unexpected and gratifying consensus on the value of the Voting Rights Act itself has not prevented a major confrontation between the president and civil-rights groups on a corollary but controversial issue — that of "intent."

In addition to requiring "pre-clearance" of election changes in states with a history of voting discrimination, the 1965 law also prohibits — and allows court challenges to — procedures anywhere in the nation, however longstanding, that deny voting rights "on account of race or color." It is this part of the law, Section 2, that has become the lightning rod for controversy.

In 1980, in a case involving a challenge to the at-large city commission of Mobile, Ala., the U.S. Supreme Court held that the Constitution's guarantee of equality in voting, the 15th Amendment, does not prohibit election procedures that simply have the *effect* of diluting black political power. What is required, the court held, is a showing of discriminatory *intent*. That decision also dismissed a challenge to the Mobile system under Section 2 of the Voting Rights Act, which the court treated as a restatement by Congress of the constitutional amendment.

Fearful that the Mobile decision would make it harder to challenge election procedures that discriminate against minorities, the authors of the Voting Rights extension passed by the House last fall voted in effect to overrule the decision, pursuant to Congress' right to interpret the 15th Amendment.

Under the House-passed bill, which also has been introduced in the Senate, a challenge to an election procedure need not prove discriminatory "intent," only discriminatory "effect." But there is a proviso in the bill that statistical under-representation of a minority group in government will not "in and of itself" constitute a violation of Section 2.

For the Reagan administration, Senate conservatives and many of the same groups who have opposed affirmative-action programs in employment and education, that disclaimer is a fig leaf for what they predict would become a guarantee of racial quotas. The House bill, they warn darkly, would allow challenges to any system of election in which blacks, for example, were not elected in proportion to their numbers in the population. Finally, they argue, members of racial minorities would be encouraged by the law to believe that only members of their own race could represent their interests.

Those are not ridiculous arguments, but they ignore some important realities.

As with many affirmative-action programs, there is some tension in the voting-rights controversy between the goal of a color-blind society and short-term color-conscious measures to deal with patterns of racism and discrimination.

In an ideal world, no eyebrows would be raised if, at a given point in time, black and white voters in a given area, weighing a whole range of considerations, chose to elect a council or commission that happened to be all-white — or all-black. In the real world, a governmental body that has no black members is almost certainly less likely to take the concerns of black citizens seriously.

In that same real world, the courts, the Justice Department and the Congress have good reason to conclude that black voters are being harmed when their power at the ballot box is consistently diluted over a long period of time.

President Reagan's allies in the Senate admit as much when they argue that under their "discriminatory intent" standard, it would still be possible to challenge systems — like all-at-large city councils — that consistently exclude blacks. And to prove "intent," as the Senate conservatives also point out, one need not "read the minds" of election officials living or dead, as some liberals have argued. A judge can *infer* discriminatory intent from a variety of factors.

What, then, is the core of the controversy over "intent" vs. "effects"? To a great extent, the dispute is ideological, even theological. Conservatives and neo-conservatives have a visceral fear that activist federal courts will stretch the discriminatory "effects" test to make proportional representation the norm nationwide, even though the House bill explicitly says that statistical under-representation is not to be equated with bias.

For their part, liberals believe that racism is so pervasive in American politics that the "intent" test, however fair it might be in the abstract, would provide judges inclined to wink at discrimination with a convenient loophole. Better, they believe, to err on the side of protection for racial minorities.

That is also the Post-Gazette's considered view. It should be kept in mind that the Voting Rights Act owes its very existence to a bold decision by Congress to cut through the Gordian Knot of provable "intent" by simply *presuming* discrimination in states where voter turnout was low and otherwise acceptable "devices" like literacy tests were in use.

Critics of the House bill are right in saying that its "effects" test represents a further leap. But who, seriously considering the disadvantages that blacks continue to suffer in and out of the political process, can say with certainty that it is an impermissible one?

The Kansas City Times

Kansas City, Mo., April 19, 1982

In spite of economic woes and other pressing budget matters, the question that now rises above all others for many Americans is the future of the Voting Rights Act, centerpiece of minority progress and unquestionably the most important piece of civil rights legislation of the year, probably the decade.

Immediately, the question is whether the Senate Judiciary Committee now studying the issue will support the House version of extension backed by civil rights activists and passed by a vote of 389-24 or the Senate version favored by the Reagan administration.

Standing in a pivotal position is Sen. Bob Dole, seen by many as the key vote on the 18-member Judiciary where nine members are co-sponsoring the House bill. Mr. Dole has not yet taken a position on either version though he does support extension of the act.

In what has become one vehicle for legislators and others who do not want to see the the law extended, the Senate version would have alleged victims prove that local or state officials *intended* to discriminate in order to seek relief under the Voting Rights Act. The House measure requires only that the result of state or local action be discriminatory. That wrangle over intent vs. effect now overshadows other controversial elements of the extension proposal.

Mr. Dole reportedly is working on a compromise of the two positions that would be substituted for the explosive section. With understanding for his delicate position — voting for the House version would place him squarely in opposition to his administration and the powerful head of the Judiciary Committee, Sen. Strom Thurmond — we would urge extreme caution in any kind of compromise wording.

Ensuring the effectiveness of this signal law must be the prime consideration of Congress. Any tinkering that would weaken it is not only a cruel rebuff to minorities but dangerous to all of society. In House debate, considerable compromise already has occurred in the areas of the pre-clearance provisions, a bail-out clause and on the question of the results test. Further conciliatory "adjustments" could well topple the entire structure; at the least, they threaten to drag debate on dangerously close to the late summer deadline for extension.

By taking a firm and courageous stand behind the strong, bipartisan House measure, Mr. Dole can assume a positive leadership role for the right to vote and for law and order. He would be doing the country a patriotic service. And incidentally, a favor to the Republican Party, too.

THE SACRAMENTO BEE
Sacramento, Calif., February 14, 1982

Debate over two words jeopardizes the Voting Rights Act extension bill in the Senate. Those words are "intent" and "effect." They mean the difference between a law that has teeth and one that is virtually unenforceable.

The law currently permits prosecution only when a victim can prove that public officials intended their voting practices — such as racial gerrymandering or switching from district elections to at-large races — to discriminate against minorities. A proposed amendment in the extension bill would strengthen the law by making it necessary for victims to prove only that the voting procedures had the effect of discriminating against them. The Reagan administration opposes the change, however, calling it a sweeping amendment that will lead to upheaval in the electoral process. The fears are unfounded.

The change merely clarifies Congress' original intention, which was to outlaw any state or local voting regulation that has "the effect of discriminating against minority-group members." The clarification is necessary because the U.S. Supreme Court ruled in 1980 that Congress had meant to outlaw only those voting practices that discriminated purposely.

Until the court's ruling, cases had been based on the effects of discrimination. Thus the amendment, contrary to the administration's fears, would add no new or unknown element to the law but would simply maintain a longstanding test of discrimination.

Without the amendment, it will be all but impossible to get inside the heads of public officials and identify specific intent for specific discriminatory acts. In the case of laws that have been on the books for years and where the public officials who adopted them are no longer available or alive, the burden of proof becomes insurmountable.

The question of intent, moreover, misses the fundamental point. We cannot afford the time and energy required to explore why the votes of blacks, Hispanics and other minorities have been diluted: One reason is just as bad as the other. Unless the amendment is adopted, victims of discrimination will be left with no effective mechanism to change unfair voting practices. And the Voting Rights Act, which came into being in 1965 to secure the civil rights of minority citizens, will be left toothless.

Richmond Times-Dispatch
Richmond, Va., April 8, 1982

Ronald Reagan's triumph in the 1980 presidential election encouraged hopes that the Federal Voting Rights Act would be purged of its inequities when it came up for renewal in 1982. Well, it is 1982, and critics of this monstrosity will consider it a victory if they can persuade Congress to extend the act in its present form. This shows how successful supporters of the act have been in convincing the nation that it is one of the most noble civil rights statutes ever put on the books.

During the presidential campaign, Mr. Reagan criticized the act primarily because of the harshly discriminatory features of its pre-clearance section, which applies to nine states, most of them in the South, and to portions of 13 others. No covered state or community may adopt any law, make any decision or take any action that might affect the voting rights of racial minorities without the federal government's approval. Ostensibly, the purpose of this provision is to guarantee blacks the right to participate in the electoral process — a worthy objective — but as it has been enforced it has gone far beyond this. Richmond was forced to adopt a ward system of councilmanic representation favorable to blacks because federal officials concluded that the city's annexation of a predominantly white suburban area sever-

al years ago unfairly diluted black voting strength. It was Mr. Reagan's view in the campaign, and it is our view today, that if the pre-clearance provisions are fair they should apply to the entire nation. Merely because some areas of the South erected barriers to black voters in the past is no reason that Southern states should be singled out for punishment in perpetuity.

But since the law does not apply throughout the country, most Americans have not felt its impact and are not aware of its inequities. To them, the act is exactly what its title implies — a measure to protect voting rights — and who could be against that? The constituents of most congressmen are therefore either indifferent about the fate of the law or in favor of its retention, attitudes that strengthen and embolden extreme supporters of the statute. They demonstrated their power in the House of Representatives by pushing through legislation that not only would retain the odious anti-Southern features of the preclearance provision but would make them even more oppressive. Under the House bill, the necessity to prove that a particular law was intended to be discriminatory in order to nullify it would be replaced by the necessity simply to prove that the results of the law would be discriminatory.

At this point, most members of the Senate, incredibly, have indicated their support for the House bill. White House sensitivity to charges that the Reagan administration is anti-black has undermined the president's resolve to seek alterations to the present law that would make it fairer. As a result, congressional critics of the act, including South Carolina Sen. J. Strom Thurmond, would settle for extension of the law in its present form. And there is a strong possibility that the atrocious House version will prevail.

It is all very distressing. Protecting citizens, and especially minorities, against discriminatory voting laws and practices is a legitimate function of the federal government. But the unacknowledged objective of the Voting Rights Act is to promote proportional representation. Federal enforcers push for governmental systems and legislative district boundaries that would virtually guarantee the election of some blacks, a goal that is inconsistent with traditional American principles of representative government. If the newly extended act substitutes "results" for "intent" as the standard for determining whether a particular state law or action is discriminatory, a quota system of representation will be almost inevitable. Some court eventually would conclude that

any electoral system which failed to give minorities legislative representation in proportion to their population was discriminatory on its face.

Writing recently in The Washington Post, Attorney General William French Smith made this observation:

"There is of course nothing wrong with the situation in which freely cast votes happen to elect minorities in proportion to the number of minorities in the electorate. What is disturbing, however, is a legislative effort to compel reorganization of electoral systems to guarantee such a result on the basis of the abhorrent notions that blacks vote only for blacks and whites only for whites. As a society, we have moved well beyond that."

Have we? A congressional decision to extend the Voting Rights Act in its present form would confirm the attorney general's opinion that racially motivated proportional representation is unacceptable to American society. It also would leave Virginia and other areas covered by the preclearance provision exactly where they are now: under the thumb of the federal government. That would be a victory? Only in the sense that it is always a victory when you can prevent a situation from going from bad to worse.

The San Diego Union

San Diego, Calif., April 21, 1982

The Voting Rights Act of 1965 has been so important in overcoming barriers of discrimination in election practices that President Reagan and both political parties are committed to extending it for another 10 years.

There is a serious danger, however, that this successful law will become the victim of over-enthusiasm for the concept of civil rights which it attempts to support. The Senate is balking and for good reason, at new language written into the act by the House. At stake is a profound change in how the federal government would view evidence of discrimination in our political system.

Since 1965, the Voting Rights Act has broken down most of the provisions in state and local election laws that had been designed to keep blacks or other minorities from voting or to dilute their effectiveness at the polls. For all this success, civil rights advocates have been disappointed that more minorities have not been elected to public office as a result.

Complaints that an imbalance of whites vs. minorities in elected office was evidence of continued discrimination in election laws were rebuffed by the U.S. Supreme Court in 1980. The court ruled that the Voting Rights Act could be used only to challenge election practices which were adopted with the intent to discriminate against minorities. It could not be used to demand that minorities be represented in elective office in proportion to their numbers in the population.

It is that court decision which the House version of the extension bill seeks to overturn, providing that election practices can be challenged if they have discriminatory results. The issue of intent vs. results is the essence of the debate now shifting to the Senate.

Clearly, the House bill would take a giant leap in redefining what amounts to discrimination in the political process. It would lead to a "quota" system for the proportional representation of minorities in elected bodies. It would open the gates for suits in federal court seeing "discrimination" where none actually exists.

A Senate Judiciary subcommittee has reported, for instance, that the system for electing a city council in San Diego would be a likely candidate for a civil rights complaint in federal court, at least as the council is now composed. The reason: Only one of the eight members of our present council can be identified as a "minority." The House bill would see this as evidence of discrimination inasmuch as the number of blacks, Hispanics, Asians and other minorities in our city population would demand that there be two "minority seats" on the council. It would be immaterial that San Diego has not tried to discriminate against minorities in the way it elects a council.

Injecting such racial or ethnic tests into the political process is exactly what the Voting Rights Act should be preventing, not encouraging. It is no wonder that the Senate subcommittee concluded that the House bill would "move this nation in the direction of increasingly overt policies of race-consciousness" and would result in "a total retreat from the original objective of the Voting Rights Act."

The pattern of intentional discrimination in state and local election laws, which developed in some parts of this country in the 19th Century, demanded the federal intervention made possible by passage of the original Voting Rights Act 17 years ago. The act has brought enormous gains in securing the rights of minorities to participate in the political process.

The act needs to remain on the books — but not as an instrument for introducing the mischief of racial quotas into the election of state legislatures, county boards of supervisors, city councils, and school boards. The Senate should prevent such a perversion of the purpose of the act by insisting that intent be the test of discrimination in election procedures. It is the only test that makes sense.

THE DAILY HERALD

Biloxi, Miss., April 26, 1982

While Congress is considering a 10-year extension to the Voting Rights Act, the lawmakers should give serious consideration to amending it to require expedient decisions by the Justice Department in exercising review powers over affected states.

Mississippi's current dilemma is in large measure due to the dilatory attitude of the Justice Department which is required to review even the minutest change in voting procedures in the nine states completely covered by the 1965 act and the 14 other states partially affected.

Item: The Mississippi Legislature in special session last August approved a congressional redistricting plan which was submitted promptly to the Justice Department for review.

Item: The Justice Department dilly-dallied until March 30, only three days before the legal deadline for party candidates to qualify for one Senate and five congressional races, before informing state officials of the plan's rejection on grounds it diluted black voting strength by dividing heavy concentrations of black voters among the 1st, 2nd and 3rd congressional districts.

This inexplicable delay, more than any other factor, has created political pain and public confusion. The state, with considerable merit, is petitioning a three-judge federal panel for a postponement of the June 1 primaries since it appears doubtful an appeal of the plan rejection to a District of Columbia court can be brought to a decision with the necessary time frame.

If Justice had acted prior to the convening of the 1982 session of the Mississippi Legislature, the appeal process conceivably could have been completed and adjustments to the redistricting plan made, if required, prior to the qualifying deadline.

This, in turn, might have negated the filing in federal district court in Greenville of a suit by blacks seeking approval of their own plan proposing creation of a black majority 2nd Congressional District.

Unfortunately, no simple courses of action can now be taken to clear the muddy Mississippi political waters. Predictably, the confusion has given rise to charges of behind-the-scenes political maneuvering by Republicans and Democrats to achieve special advantages for their candidates.

True or not, the situation which made such confusion possible also may affect the conduct of state judgeship and local school board elections totally unconnected with the congressional redistricting. Costs of campaigning and conducting elections may escalate.

The Justice Department cannot escape its share of the blame and should not be permitted to avoid its responsibility to those states which, alone of the sovereign 50, must submit their electoral processes for the approbation of a federal agency.

The apparent perception in Washington, D. C., that Voting Rights states are vassal political subdivisions needs to be corrected.

If the Justice Department cannot perform more responsibly, the Congress might do well to prescribe a remedy. We still like Sen. Thad Cochran's proposal to extend the Voting Rights Act to all 50 states and to give federal district courts the power to review and clear proposed election law changes to insure civil rights of all citizens are protected.

the Charleston Gazette

Charleston, W. Va., April 27, 1982

THE REAGAN administration talks a good civil rights game but plays a weak one. It favors tax exemption for religious schools that discriminate, its Justice Department has been less than enthusiastic in civil rights enforcement, and now the administration is impeding passage of an adequate voting rights act.

A voting rights bill was passed 389-24 by the House. It has 65 co-sponsors in the Senate. Spokesmen for Reagan have been playing a bad game. While crying that they favor voting rights legislation, they have been working hard to dilute the bill.

The argument is over a section that says that voters do not have to prove that exclusion from the political process was deliberate. The approach is an attempt to offset a 1980 Supreme Court decision which required voters to prove intent before they could prove discrimination.

Attorney General William French Smith argues that the law would result in election of minority candidates proportional to the number of minority voters participating. The idea has been denounced by civil rights leaders, and by such organizations as the American Bar Association and the League of Women Voters.

The proposed act returns the law to where it was before 1980. Between 1965 and 1980, no court opinion called for proportional representation. In fact, in every case decided before 1980 in which proportional representation might have been a remedy, the courts specifically rejected it.

The House bill, and the Mathias-Kennedy bill in the Senate, would let courts consider all factors in deciding whether an election is discriminatory — the nominating process, responsiveness of those conducting the elections, history of discrimination and so on. The House bill establishes those standards and it specifically excludes election results alone as proof of discrimination.

The Senate Judiciary Committee is scheduled to vote on the bill this week. We urge Sen. Robert C. Byrd, D-W.Va., a member of the committee, to vote on the bill as introduced as a visible demonstration that the American Congress is dedicated to protecting the rights of minority members, even if the American president is lukewarm about it.

Detroit Free Press

Detroit, Mich., February 18, 1982

IT IS a march to bring tears to the eyes of those who remember its predecessors. Once again, it is black and white together, singing "We Shall Overcome," and dedicating themselves to the goals of justice and equal rights. But the air of hope that made the marches of the '60s so stirring has been replaced by grim desperation.

"Not in vain," murmured one of the demonstrators retracing the steps of the famous 1965 Selma-to-Montgomery march that led to enactment of the Voting Rights Act. But the struggles of the past must surely seem in vain, sometimes, to the survivors of that march and all those who benefited from it. The Voting Rights Act will expire this year unless Congress renews it. And though there is support for its renewal, the Reagan administration is pushing changes that civil rights leaders believe would seriously weaken the law.

More to the point, many of the country's blacks feel abandoned and even betrayed by the Reagan administration. And no wonder. This administration is pursuing economic policies that worsen the plight of the poor, has supported a Senate bill barring federal courts from ordering busing to desegregate schools and has proclaimed that the denial of tax exemptions for segregated private schools — a policy pursued by three administrations — has "no basis in law."

In cities such as Detroit, people make doomsday jokes about the president's expensive china, Nancy's elaborate gowns and the nation's mounting unemployment rate. It is a far cry from the days when the swelling oratory of Martin Luther King and the commitment to change of Lyndon Johnson created a climate in which blacks and other disadvantaged people felt justified in looking to Washington for relief.

Tony Liuzzo, of Southfield, whose mother, Viola Liuzzo, was gunned down after the end of the Selma march, is participating in the re-enactment. He said he feels the struggle for justice is as important today as in the '60s. In fact, it is even more so. Progress toward equal rights has not only slowed, it has been reversed. Rights and protections bought with sweat and blood are being eroded, tossed aside, lost.

We may never again see the sort of massive marches that flourished in the '60s, those marches of hope and triumph. But it is useful and necessary to renew our commitment to the ideals of all those who marched and struggled and worked for social justice. Should we ever let their spirit die, it will mean the death of their dreams — and of the American dream as well.

The Boston Globe

Boston, Mass., April 17, 1982

The Reagan Administration, though a latecomer to the cause, supports a simple 10-year extension of an important piece of civil rights legislation, the 1965 Voting Rights Act. "That act must be extended," the Attorney General has said, articulating the President's position.

That sounds like strong backing. It is not.

The Administration successfully opposed a tougher version, which called for permanent extension, during a Judiciary subcommittee vote. That House-approved bill, introduced in the Senate by Sens. Edward Kennedy and Charles Mathias (R-Md), and cosponsored by 65 others, would have also provided an easier standard – effect versus intent – for proving violations.

That test, effect or intent, fuels a portion of the debate.

Effect, a standard part of the initial act, was modified in 1980. The US Supreme Court ruled that a 1911 law mandating at-large rather than single-member municipal districts in Mobile, Ala. could not be considered discriminatory – despite the effect of diluting the black vote – unless the lawmakers had intended to discriminate.

Intent, Reagan's Attorney General William French Smith argues, is a better standard. An effects test, he says, would focus on election results, leading to a quota system for electoral politics and triggering litigation directed at every level of elections across the nation.

"Scare tactics," respond supporters of the stronger measure.

An effects test, they argue, would allow courts to examine a history of discrimination, nominating procedures, election results – an aggregate of factors that result in black or Hispanic citizens having little or no chance of election. Intent, they argue, is almost impossible to prove. Who will admit they intended to discriminate? What of the now-dead originators of old laws still on the books? Can they confess racial motives from the grave?

Another provision of the revised version remains at issue.

The new "bailout" system would allow individual counties, found in compliance for 10 years, freedom from the federal review known as preclearance and required before changes in voting systems. Opponents want a weaker "bailout" method. Sen. Strom Thurmond (D-S.C.) found unacceptable the permanent extension of that provision, which he said would raise more questions. A longtime foe of the entire act, Thurmond now favors a simple extension, as does the Reagan Administration.

Why all this debate 17 years after the act took effect?

Despite progress, blacks remain a disproportionately low number of southern officeholders. In 30-percent-black South Carolina, no blacks hold state senate seats. In 20 majority-black counties of Georgia, no blacks hold office. In parts of the South, voting discrimination remains widespread and persistent, according to a 10-year report on the impact of the act, compiled by the American Civil Liberties Union.

As the debate intensifies, civil rights groups gear up with tactics more familiar during past eras. On Monday, the Southern Christian Leadership Conference will hold a rally in Tuskegee, Ala., to kick off a march to Washington.

Progressing on foot and in cars through 825 miles of Alabama, Georgia, South Carolina, North Carolina and Virgina, they will urge people to lobby for extension of the bill, register black voters and hold several hearings on alleged voting rights violations. During two months on the road, they will focus too on the need for jobs and peace.

Meanwhile, the bill to extend the act is scheduled to go before the Senate Judiciary Committee on April 27. A fight can be expected.

Federal surveillance must continue. Standards, provable in courts, must be adopted. The Kennedy version must be passed to ensure the right of every American to participate fully and fairly in the electoral process. It is not too late for the Reagan Administration to join the right side of the battle.

FORT WORTH STAR-TELEGRAM
Fort Worth, Texas, May 11, 1982

Seldom has the art of the possible been practiced to better effect than in the compromise agreement that was crafted by the Senate Judiciary Committee extending the Voting Rights Act of 1965. The bill, which has the support of President Reagan, civil rights leaders and prominent Democrats, should have no trouble winning approval in the House, although it softens somewhat one of the main provisions of the House bill passed last October.

The House bill included language designed to offset a 1980 U.S. Supreme Court ruling that required proof of intent to discriminate as the test for a violation of the Voting Rights Act. Civil rights advocates argued that intent is impossible to prove. The House sought to remedy the problem by spelling out in its bill that the effects of discrimination are sufficient to constitute a violation.

Attorney General William French Smith and some members of the Senate Judiciary Committee argued, however, that the effects test would have the effect of mandating proportional representation and of automatically outlawing all at-large voting systems for municipal, county and state legislature elections.

The committee kept the essentials of the effects tests, thereby making it possible for civil rights attorneys to file voter discrimination lawsuits with some expectations of success. Its version of the extension of the act would allow a judge to use a broad spectrum of evidence — such as inconvenient polling hours, suspect election results, allegations of insensitivity of officeholders to their minority constituents and the makeup of voting districts — to determine if voter discrimination has occurred.

However, the compromise spells out clearly that racial quotas on city councils, school boards and in state legislatures are not required under the provisions of the act.

The compromise is a decided improvement upon the original act, which has been instrumental in promoting the participation of millions of minorities in the political process since it was enacted 17 years ago.

ARKANSAS DEMOCRAT
Little Rock, Ark., May 6, 1982

Well, glory be! Thanks to Bob Dole of Kansas, constitutional fairness has triumphed in the Senate Judiciary Committee's approach to extension of the Voting Rights Act. Who'd have thought it? The Judiciary Committee has voted 16-1 for the new approach.

Liberals agreed to drop the goal of "color quotas" for minorities and to limit the revision's aim to averting the gerrymandering down of the full effect of the individual vote. The compromise – which has President Reagan's "heartfelt" support, should have everybody else's, too.

Major civil rights organizations, including the NAACP, went along only reluctantly with the compromise. They wanted the act to guarantee proportional racial representation at every level of government – something that federal court here rejected for Little Rock city government.

In compromising the issue, the committeemen reasoned as the court did. Under the revision, proportional racial representation can come about in only one way – when a judge finds that a new districting law in any district of the states affected by the act produces a *pattern of discrimination* against a minority and that the drafters deliberately intended to diminish the minority's overall political voice in that district.

The key word is deliberate, and it makes all the difference. The old language of the Voting Rights extension didn't provide for any trial of intent. It addressed itself to making sure all new laws would provide minorities proportional political voices according to their numbers. The only required proof of denial of that right would have been that sole showing in court. If the ratio between a minority's political voice and its numbers had been less than exact, there would have been an automatic finding of discrimination.

That's put now. Minorities will get no such statutory guarantee. But each voter, whether of a minority or not, is assured that the full weight of his vote won't be downgraded by racial gerrymandering. The test of discriminatory districting will not be a finding (as such) that the law will result in less than exact proportional representation by race. Such deviations are often the product not of prejudice but of an effort to make districts contiguous and compact. The test would be whether the variation can be reasonable defended as resulting from problem racial-geography. In deciding whether it can or can't be, judges are to take into account the "totality of circumstances."

Nobody could ask for more – or less. The only thing properly at stake in any voting legislation is enforcement of the *individual's* constitutional right to vote. Uner the Constitution, bloc voting rights don't exist, let alone black bloc voting rights – only a color-blind guarantee to each individual voter.

The way to ensure that guarantee is to make as certain as possible that drafters of new election laws do their districting without thought of race – negative or affirmative. That means not diluting black residential concentrations by arbitrary splits – or gerrymandering "affirmatively" to unite separated black concentrations.

As near as possible, the revised Voting Rights Act addresses itself to maintenance of this color-blindness via court tests of discriminatory intent. That restores due process for states and localities – while guaranteeing the individual member of a minority the full weight of his vote. Anyone can back the act's passage now in good conscience.

Post-Tribune
Gary, Ind., May 10, 1982

It looks like an extension of the Voting Rights Act is going to make it through Congress. It's about time; the current law expires in August.

There should never have been a question about extending the law; it is needed to assure the voting rights of all Americans. But the conservatives in Congress have been fighting to weaken the act.

Given the split in opinion, the Senate Judiciary Committee did the appropriate thing. A coalition of liberals and conservatives on the committee drew up a compromise that the committee approved Tuesday 17-1. The compromise has been endorsed by both President Reagan and civil rights organizations. With that backing, the legislation should pass the Senate floor vote, although there will be some protests from conservatives led by Sen. Jesse Helms, R-N.C. The only "no" vote on the committee came from Sen. John East, R-N.C.

A similar version of the bill was approved 389-24 by the House last October.

The compromise extension bill outlaws any voting procedure or jurisdictional boundaries which would discriminate against blacks, Hispanics or Indians. It allows a judge to use a wide range of evidence in deciding whether voter discrimination has occured. It also says that nothing in the renewed measure requires racial quotas; however a judge who finds discrimination could redraw voting districts to guarantee minimum representation for minorities.

It is a compromise that both sides, except for the far extremes, can live with. Congress should move now to pass it quickly, not letting those extremes stall things, so the president can sign it into law before the enforcement provisions of the current law expire.

There should be no lapse in guaranteeing voting rights.

The Des Moines Register
Des Moines, Iowa, May 7, 1982

In a season dominated by bad news, the compromise agreement on extension of the Voting Rights Act is a development to be happy about. Iowans can take satisfaction in the role played by Senator Charles Grassley (Rep., Ia.) in working for the compromise.

The Voting Rights Act of 1965 is the basic civil-rights legislation. It has come before Congress again this year because key sections will expire in August. There is broad agreement that the act should be extended, but there has been sharp disagreement as to how strong the extension should be.

The major dispute centered on the standard required to prove that an election law or practice is discriminatory. Last fall, the House of Representatives approved an extension that would permit redress upon proof that an election procedure "results in the denial or abridgement of the right to vote." A similar bill was endorsed by 65 senators.

The Reagan administration and its conservative backers in the Senate then resorted to scare tactics. They claimed that, under such a "results test," if the results of an election did not reflect the racial makeup of a community, the election laws of that community could be struck down as discriminatory. This could lead to a system of proportional representation based on race, the argument went.

That was nonsense. The House bill specified that election results need not reflect the racial makeup of a community. Nevertheless, the scare tactics persuaded the Constitution subcommittee to replace the House's "results test" with an "intent" standard, under which it would be necessary to prove that a challenged election procedure was adopted with the intent to discriminate, This would have made it nearly impossible to strike down most discriminatory election practices.

Grassley provided the deciding vote in committee in favor of the "intent" standard, but he pledged to work for a "middle ground" between "intent" and "results." He lived up to that promise this week, when he backed the compromise.

This consists basically of the House bill's "results" test, plus additional reassurances that no right of proportional representation by race will be created.

The compromise was approved 14-4 by the full Judiciary Committee, and there is every indication that the Senate will give its overwhelming approval. All Americans should be glad for this outcome.

Chicago Tribune
Chicago, Ill., May 9, 1982

There is no better example of how badly the Reagan administration has faltered in its civil rights policy than the compromise bill to extend the Voting Rights Act that just passed the Senate Judiciary Committee. The administration has been on the defensive on civil rights issues ever since the fiasco involving tax exemptions for racially discriminatory private schools, and its weakness showed in its acceptance of a bill in the Senate whose language is muddy enough that it could be interpreted to require racial quotas in elections.

On the face of it, the administration should have been in good political position on the Voting Rights Act, which was first passed in 1965 to put an end to poll taxes and literacy tests and other devices that kept blacks and other minorities from voting. The law has been galling to the South ever since it was passed, since it includes provisions that require a number of mostly Southern electoral units to clear any changes in their election laws with the U.S. attorney general or the federal court in the District of Columbia before they are put into effect. The law was originally to lapse in five years, but it has twice been extended. Despite some initial consideration in Congress about whether to let the Act simply go out of existence, the Reagan administration supported another ten year extension.

But that was not enough for some civil rights groups. They wanted a fundamental change in the law. A 1980 Supreme Court decision had held that federal statutes and the Constitution only prohibit election laws that can be proven to be intentionally discriminatory. The civil rights groups wanted to overturn this decision by amending the Voting Rights Act, and the Reagan administration properly objected.

The civil rights groups wanted the law to forbid any election system that would result in the election of a disproportionately small number of blacks and certain other minorities. And this could lead to racial quotas in elections.

Racial quotas are unfortunate in any context. They insult the principle of equality of opportunity by dividing up society's spoils on the basis of the accident of birth. They breed resentment and sap morale and the incentive to achieve. Too often civil rights advocates have endorsed quotas as short term methods to show quick results, then later insisted upon them as a kind of moral right.

In politics, racial quotas would be especially obnoxious. It is one thing to forbid election arrangements gerrymandered to reduce the power of minorities. It is quite another to require that, no matter how the electorate feels about the candidates before it, they have to elect a given number of minorities or face suit by the Justice Department.

Racial quotas in elections conflict with the very idea of self-government. They substitute a stiff, automatic rule of law for the messy, organic procedures of politics. They put the political process in a straitjacket.

You might have thought that the Reagan administration had the high ground in the battle against quotas. Disenchantment with quotas in other contexts has been growing, and the time hardly seemed right for extending their application to the sacred institutions of self-government.

But the administration squandered any good will it had in civil rights during the debacle over whether racially discriminatory private schools should qualify for tax exemptions. The on-again, off-again support the administration gave to Bob Jones University thoroughly discredited it and opened it to the charge that it was pandering to special, benighted constituencies and had little interest in racial equality of opportunity.

So when the Voting Rights Act extension came up in the House, the statistical approach prevailed over administration objection. And in the Senate, the administration felt compelled by the weakness of its political position to join a compromise bill that, while it does not go as far as the House measure, muddies up the law in such a way that any federal court that is so inclined can find that it was intended to overturn the 1980 Supreme Court ruling.

The administration has been boxed into supporting the very kind of muddled legislation that allowed courts and regulatory agencies to introduce racial quotas in other contexts. It has lost the opportunity to keep intact and simple the Voting Rights Act, which has been extraordinarily effective in making the right to vote a reality for minority groups once unconscionably excluded. It has lent its name to the kind of unprincipled confusion that a lot of people once hoped it would be able, carefully and sensitively, to reform.

THE SUN
Baltimore, Md., May 5, 1982

President Reagan did the right thing in coming out for the Senate version of the Voting Rights Act extension written primarily by Senator Charles Mathias (R, Md.), then amended by Senator Bob Dole (R, Kan.) with Mr. Mathias's approval. Messrs. Mathias and Dole represent just about the opposite and outer limits of mainstream Republicanism. Their joint backing of a Voting Rights Act extension indicates how broad the support is in the Congress for this measure.

For the president to have sided with the few Southern and Southwestern extremists who opposed the extension would have been folly. It is disturbing to see evidence that there are senior presidential advisers who prefer the extreme position on this matter politically and philosophically.

There is really only one issue as far as the extension of this act is concerned—whether local voting laws can be challenged on the basis of discriminatory *results* or only discriminatory *intent*. The House passed (and Senator Mathias proposed) an extension of the original 1965 act that says that where local voting laws *result* in discrimination against black voters, federal relief may be sought. Civil rights advocates had assumed that the old law implied that. But in 1980, the Supreme Court issued a confusing ruling in a Mobile (Ala.) case that seemed to say the old law only covered voting laws whose *intent* was to discriminate. Since it is extremely difficult and time-consuming to prove intent in cases of this kind—and usually a misuse of judicial time and resources—the House wrote into the extension a *results* standard on proof of discrimination.

The administration and Senate allies Strom Thurmond, Jesse Helms and a few others kept insisting that this change would lead courts to order proportional representation: for example, if a city were 50 percent black, the election of a council two-thirds white would be illegal. That was an absurd, phony argument. All the House principals who spoke for the *results* test made a clear legislative history for judges to follow to the effect that proportional representation was not sought nor called for.

At any rate, Senator Dole's amendment makes it even more explicit that a *results* test may not just take into account numbers of voters and winning candidates. It must be based on the *totality* of the circumstances in each case. Discrimination must exist and must be proved. Proportional representation is explicitly ruled out as a requirement. This "compromise language" allowed the president to get out of the corner with some grace, and for that alone Mr. Dole deserves thanks. The Republican Party has got to demonstrate to blacks and other minorities that it is not and will not become just the party of the country club set.

Chicago Defender
Chicago, Ill., June 30, 1982

The Voting Rights Act has been extended for another 25 years. That's good.

What's interesting about all that action in the U. S. Congress, was the racism of Senator Jesse Helmns, North Carolina Republican, in the course of the debate, to filibuster against the act "until the cows come home," as he put it.

It is an unhappy recollection of the past — that of a senator so opposed to the Black right to vote. All this has taken place in 1982. Voting rights violations in the South are still common, despite the law granting Blacks the right to vote.

Any notion that the battle is over for the right to vote is a mistake. People of good will need to be vigilant against any upsurge of reaction, such as that of Helms and quite a few others in high places.

CHARLESTON EVENING POST
Charleston, S.C., June 22, 1982

Although they rarely tangle in public, it's no secret that South Carolina's senior senator, Republican Strom Thurmond, and South Carolina's junior senator, Democrat Ernest F. Hollings, don't always see eye to eye.

Sen. Thurmond was openly angry last week, however, when Sen. Hollings cited South Carolina in general and Thurmond's home county of Edgefield in particular, as reason enough to extend the 1965 Voting Rights Act.

While Sen. Thurmond voted for the extension (in part, he says, to make it easier to seek modifications later), he couldn't let the Hollings comments pass unchallenged. Unlike Sen. Thurmond, we don't find it outrageous that Sen. Hollings "ran down his own state." We neither expect nor want U.S. senators to function in Washington as mere extensions of state chambers of commerce.

Neither can we applaud the misuse of one's own state, as Sen. Thurmond has charged, for personal political advantage. The Thurmond charge referred to Sen. Hollings' contention that South Carolina's history of voting rights violations was enough justification to extend the act for another 25 years.

Sen. Hollings noted that South Carolina still has a literacy test on the books and that certain counties, specifically Edgefield, have been found to have engaged in illegal voting activities as recently as 1980.

What Sen. Hollings didn't say is that other states like New York have literacy tests. Unlike some of those other states, South Carolina has not applied the test in at least 20 years. Neither has the Edgefield matter finally been resolved in the courts. Regardless of the outcome, that county's problems don't justify the implication that there are widespread problems in the state. To the contrary, of the more than 1,300 proposed voting process changes submitted to the Justice Department from South Carolina since 1965, only 24 have been rejected outright.

Extension of the Voting Rights Act is all but an accomplished fact. Some needed modifications of that act have not been made primarily, as Sen. Thurmond noted, because objections to the act unfortunately are incorrectly perceived as opposition to those protected by the law. Few realize, however, that not even the names of voting precincts can be changed in those states covered by the act without approval from Washington.

If Sen. Hollings has knowledge of voting rights violations he, of course, has a duty to focus the spotlight back home. But, if all the senator can cite is a law no longer enforced and a case already pending in the courts, then we have to agree with Sen. Thurmond. The Hollings statement sounds like presidential campaign rhetoric designed to prove to the rest of the country that the silver-haired senator from Charleston doesn't fit the old Southern stereotype.

EVENING EXPRESS
Portland, Maine, June 22, 1982

The U.S. Senate's swift, decisive move to extend the Voting Rights Act for 25 years is clear reaffirmation of this nation's dedication to the constitutional right of all Americans to participate in the democratic process.

The 85-8 vote last week was the largest margin of passage for civil rights legislation in modern history. Passage took just 10 days.

The House, which overwhelmingly approved a different version of the measure, will likely vote this week to accept the Senate version, and President Reagan is expected to quickly sign it into law.

The Voting Rights Act was first adopted in 1965, extended in 1970 and again in 1975. It prohibits state and local officials from using any voting practice or procedure that results in discrimination against blacks, hispanics or other minority citizens. Nine states and parts of 13 others with a history of voting discrimination must get advance approval from the Justice Department before changing election procedures.

Portions of the act expire in August unless the House and the president follow the Senate in approving the extension. Fortunately, it's not likely any delay will be encountered. House leaders say they'll recommend approval of the Senate bill, and a White House spokesman says the president will sign it.

The extension should have a clear, speedy path into the federal law books. Racial discrimination has no place in the voting booth—or anywhere else—in the United States.

The Atlanta Journal
AND
THE ATLANTA CONSTITUTION
Atlanta, Ga., June 19, 1982

Sen. Jesse Helms, R-N.C., vowed to filibuster the 25-year extension of the 1965 Voting Rights Act "until the cows come home." His bovines keep late hours, apparently, because as near as can be determined they filed in about 2 a.m. Friday. Perhaps there was a party in the back 40. That's appropriate, because the passage of the extension is worthy of a celebration for those who cherish justice.

There is no denying that progress has been made since 1965 toward seeing that every citizen is afforded the right to register and vote. The act is generally considered the most successful of the civil-rights laws of the 1960s. It is credited with encouraging the registration of more than 1 million blacks and other minority voters.

However, while there have been dramatic increases in the numbers of black and other minority voters and elected officials, there is still widespread discrimination in election practices around the country.

The act will retain federal supervision in 22 states with poor minority-voting records, but spells out new rules under which those states can bail out from scrutiny by the Justice Department and federal courts.

After a year of sending ambiguous signals, President Reagan said last month he will sign the measure into law when it reaches his desk. With this important piece of legislation behind it, the Congress can turn to other pressing issues.

"BACKA THE BUS"

THE MILWAUKEE JOURNAL
Milwaukee, Wisc., June 30, 1982

A national commitment to fairness has been renewed with final approval of the extension of the Voting Rights Act of 1965.

"The right to vote is the crown jewel of American liberties, and we will not see its luster diminished," President Reagan properly said as he signed the bill at a White House ceremony. The president will add substance to his eloquent words if his administration demonstrates a sturdy resolve to enforce the Voting Rights Act and other important civil rights legislation.

Meanwhile, members of Congress deserve credit for overwhelming approval of the bill. In both houses and in both parties, members recognized the truth pronounced 17 years ago when President Lyndon Johnson asked Congress to enact the legislation:

"Rarely are we met with a challenge, not to our growth or abundance, our welfare or our security, but rather to the values and the purposes and the meaning of our beloved nation.

"The issue of equal rights for American Negroes is such an issue. And should we defeat every enemy, should we double our wealth and conquer the stars, and still be unequal to this issue, then we will have failed as a people and as a nation."

In that speech, Johnson acknowledged the complex nature of many civil rights issues. One issue, though, was not complex. The denial of the ballot on the basis of race was wrong. Prodded by the president, the nation fashioned a remedy.

Now, the nation has resoundingly said again that the old wrong — sometimes in a new guise — will not be tolerated.

THE TENNESSEAN
Nashville, Tenn., June 22, 1982

THE Senate has finally approved by an 85 to 8 vote a quarter-century renewal of the enforcement provisions of the landmark Voting Rights Act of 1965 in a victory that is satisfying and encouraging for millions of minority voters in this country.

Although the House passed a similar measure 389 to 24 last October, the fate of the extension in the Senate was in doubt early. Not only was there strong opposition from some Southern senators, but President Reagan initially opposed some of the provisions.

But ultimately some of the opposition faded, and even Mr. Reagan came around and said he will sign it into law. But Sen. Jesse Helms, R-N.C., vowed to fight it until "the cows come home."

Mr. Helms and a small group of filibustering senators set out either to talk the measure to death or, failing in that, to overwhelm it with amendments. Neither worked. The filibuster was cut off. And the Senate beat back easily the amendments that the opposition offered.

The 10-day battle on the Senate floor was reminiscent of the civil rights battles of the 1960s, but had neither the duration or intensity. Senator Helms finally gave up under pressure from fellow Republicans frustrated with the delay and afraid that the continuing fight might have repercussions this fall.

And, Senate Majority Leader Howard Baker added his pressure, agreeing to schedule votes on other issues even dearer to Mr. Helms' heart by summer. The North Carolina senator knew the votes were against him, and the best that he could do would be to delay the inevitable.

Since there are only minor differences between the Senate and House versions, these are likely to be worked out swiftly and without controversy.

Under its most important provision, the voting rights measure extends indefinitely a system under which states which have poor minority voting records must come to the Justice Department for pre-clearance on changes of local or state voting procedures.

There is a new set of rules covering the next 25 years for voter jurisdictions to bail out, or escape Justice Department or court approval over voting law changes. For the first time a county would be able to escape continued scrutiny, even if the rest of the state is still under supervision. But the bailout procedures are fairly tough.

Because of an earlier Supreme Court ruling, there is a new standard under which a federal judge can find that a city, county or state has discriminated against black or other minority voters if the effect of governmental action is racial discrimination. Opponents had wanted an "intent" standard, in which it would have had to be proved that discrimination was intentional on the part of local officials. But assessing motives is difficult and often impossible.

The Senate has spoken clearly on the landmark legislation and it is hoped that the extension quickly becomes law.

The Honolulu Advertiser

Honolulu, Ha., July 5, 1982

President Reagan has ensured continuing and needed federal involvement in the civil rights field by approving extension of key enforcement provisions of the historic Voting Rights Act.

The landmark bill, passed in 1965 and extended in 1970 and 1975, has been the cornerstone for improved minority civil rights over the past two decades.

Notes Congressional Quarterly: "The law is widely considered the most effective civil rights measure ever enacted."

HAD THE enforcement sections been allowed to lapse, as some southern senators in particular wanted, the muscle would have been taken out of the law.

This country has not developed to the point where it can afford to trust the advancement of civil rights for all citizens to goodwill alone.

Essentially, the congressional measure that President Reagan signed does the following:

● Extends for 25 years Section Five enforcement regulations which apply to 25 states in whole or in part (including Hawaii).

● Beginning in 1984 the Voting Rights Act will allow these states to "bail out" from federal scrutiny if they can prove to federal judges they have had no voting rights violations for the previous decade.

● Establishes a "results" test to determine such abuses. The administration wanted an "intent" test, that is, authorities would have to show local lawmakers intended to discriminate when developing new voting laws. Obviously that would be difficult to prove. Instead, the test is whether that discrimination has resulted from election guidelines.

● Extends for 10 years bilingual requirements for some jurisdictions, including Hawaii.

These were to have expired in 1985. This provision calls for the availability of bilingual ballots and other election material if a community has a certain percentage of minority members.

We have opposed Hawaii's inclusion under this regulation, since in practice it primarily results in expensive and unnecessary bureaucratic headaches. Relatively few people here have used the material.

But considering that there are other areas of the country where the bilingual requirement is valuable, continuation of the regulation is for the better. Hawaii's problems in this instance are secondary to the greater good.

APPROVAL OF the voting rights extension is one of the few civil rights advances the Reagan administration can claim.

Indeed, in this area, its record has not been exemplary.

The president and his advisers have acted either too slowly or with great insensitivity on race-related issues.

It took some time for the president to come out in favor of an extension, and no administration official testified before Congress on this subject last year.

The number and visibility of high-level minority appointees (or women for that matter) are the exception.

The effect of deep budget cuts in social programs has a disproportionate impact on minority groups. And administration economic policies have pushed unemployment to record highs, again affecting blacks and others more severely.

There was also the president's ill-advised attempt to give white-only private schools tax-exempt status. That the administration tried to change this 12-year-old policy was bad enough. That Reagan and his close advisers were surprised at the harshness of the opposition only confirms in some minds insensitivity toward racism.

AT HIS RECENT news conference, Reagan with considerable emotion defended himself: "I was raised in a household in which the only intolerance I was taught was intolerance of bigotry."

No one should doubt Reagan's sincerity. But when racial prejudice can still deny to an American his or her rights, the country requires more of a president that good intentions. It demands forceful and uncompromising advocacy of civil rights.

This administration can do better in meeting that vital test.

THE SAGINAW NEWS

Saginaw, Mich., June 22, 1982

The U.S. Senate has extended the Voting Rights Act of 1965 another 25 years — by the largest margin of any civil rights law in federal history, 85-8.

The action ends more than a year of legislative warfare, in the best possible way: By assuring millions of Americans continued access to the "right that makes all other rights possible," as the franchise has often been described.

The Voting Rights Act has also been described as the most successful civil rights legislation in history. It would be difficult to quarrel with that.

The numbers tell the story. Black registration has increased 11-fold in Mississippi. The number of black elected officials in the South has increased from 100 to more than 2,400. Politicians now court the minority vote.

That does not mean minorities can dictate the national agenda. It does mean their concerns can no longer be ignored, as they were for so long when artificial barriers were erected to their participation in democracy's most basic exercise.

But the Voting Rights Act does not apply to the South alone. That is one reason the Senate, and House before it, had a tough time with this latest extension (previous ones came in 1970 and 1975). Michigan, in fact, comes under its provisions. So do such states as New York, California, Massachusetts, Colorado and Hawaii. It applies anywhere minorities have historically suffered loss of representation.

Sometimes that deprivation has been deliberate, other times not. Judging the difference has not been easy. One major obstacle to extension was fear that the courts would assume power to order purely proportional representation. The bill, as adopted by the Senate, will bar such rulings.

That seems fair. The goal is to make sure minorities have a voice, not a guarantee, in representation. The means is to require federal review of any changes in election law that might have an impact on the ability to vote.

The new law is not ideal. We would have preferred, for instance, to allow local option on bilingual ballots. In some areas, including Saginaw, their use has not always justified taxpayer cost to prepare them.

But the importance of this legislation overcame such localized objections. Sen. Donald W. Riegle Jr. of Michigan put it in terms of "the ultimate measure of our freedom." Sen. Carl Levin called it "of monumental importance to all Americans."

The decision, as Congress finally saw it, came down to the basic question of assuring all Americans the right to go to the polls and help pick the people who will represent them, from the most local unit of government all the way to the presidency. Congress saw it right, regardless of conservative — and White House complaints.

After the Senate acted, White House aide Larry Speakes called the Voting Rights Act extension "something we have sought and worked with the Congress on in some detail."

Is the law still needed? Unfortunately, yes. Since it was passed 17 years ago, the Justice Department has counted more than 800 alleged violations of minority voting rights, through redistricting or other means — half of them since the latest extension in 1975.

The compromise took into account some of the objections which gave President Reagan some pause. But as approved by Congress, the chief protections are maintained. The new Voting Rights Act includes nothing that America cannot live with — and confirms a principle that must be part of a truly democratic nation.

Jackson Challenges Primary Runoffs, Delegate Selection Rules

In the party platform approved by the Democratic convention July 17, 1984, two provisions proposed by candidate Jesse Jackson were adopted, in amended form. One, a compromise provision, strengthened an affirmative action plank. The other called for "an in-depth study" of the primary runoffs that are a part of local and congressional elections in the South, and for the abolition of these "second primaries" where they could be proved to "discriminate or act to dilute the votes of minority citizens." Jackson had advocated the complete elimination of primary runoffs throughout his campaign, making the issue a "litmus test" for his eventual support of the Democratic presidential nominee.

Under the runoff-primary system, when a clear majority is not won by any candidate in the initial primary, the two leaders compete in a second primary, in order to ensure majority support for the victor. Jackson argued that this system, used in 10 southern states, had the effect of eliminating black candidates who might win the first primary with a plurality of votes in a multicandidate field, but were unlikely to win the subsequent runoff in a contest against a white candidate. Election experts maintained that the primary runoffs did not necessarily discriminate against blacks, and some black politicians disagreed with Jackson's vehement demand for their elimination. The compromise reached at the Democratic convention reflects Democratic nominee Walter Mondale's stance of opposition to the runoff primaries only where they can be shown to discriminate against minority candidates.

Another set of rules that Jackson challenged were the complex guidelines governing individual states' selection of delegates for the 1984 party convention. Currently, a candidate must win about 20% of a primary vote in order to qualify for any share of the delegates at stake. Jackson felt this "threshold"—in some states as high as 25%—should either be lowered, or replaced with straight proportional representation, since it severely limited convention representation for candidates with a smaller constituency. Jackson also proposed that caucuses, in which delegates are elected by registered party members in discreet political districts, be eradicated or altered. Delegates are usually assigned under the caucus system to congressional districts in proportion to the size of the Democratic vote in that district, regardless of actual voter participation. Jackson argued that the high turnout of voters who supported him in some districts was unmatched by delegate representation because of these rules. In addition, Jackson objected to a rule, adopted in 1982, that designated a certain number of state elected officials as unpledged delegates who could vote independent of their state's primary or caucus results. These procedural questions, many of them explored also by candidate Gary Hart, are among the items on an agenda, drawn up by the Rules Committee of the Democratic Convention, to be addressed by a special "Fairness Commission" in 1985. (Jackson's effort to have the Democratic Party award him with uncommitted delegates in 1984 in order to even the perceived disparity between his share of the popular vote and of delegates, was unsuccessful.)

THE SUN

Baltimore, Md., April 19, 1984

Rev. Jesse Jackson is campaigning against the Southern practice of holding runoff elections in primaries. He wants the Democratic convention and presidential nominee to denounce the practice. Mr. Jackson says runoffs discriminate against blacks. He's not the only one who thinks so.

Critics often cite as proof the case of H. M. Micheaux of North Carolina's Second District. In the Democratic primary in 1982, Mr. Micheaux, a black legislator from Durham, came in first with 44 percent of the vote. Two candidates trailed. Because no one got 50 percent of the vote, there was a runoff. I. T. Valentine, Jr., a white former state party official, who got 33 percent of the first primary vote, beat Mr. Micheaux 54-46.

But here's another example of the runoff at work: In 1982, Bo Ginn led a 10-candidate field in the Georgia Democratic gubernatorial primary. He won 35 percent of the vote. Runnerup Joe Frank Harris got 25 percent. Mr. Harris won the runoff 55-45. Both candidates were white.

Racism really has nothing to do with this issue. The runoff developed during the one-party rule days in the South. General elections, which in other states worked to ensure that majority-backed candidates were elected to office, meant nothing. The primary *was* the election. Without a runoff, it would have been possible for candidates opposed by 60-70 percent of the electorate to win office. That's hardly a formula for good government.

But that was then, this is now, say critics of the runoff. Southern black Democrats, who once were denied the right to vote in the primaries, vote in very large numbers. If there were no runoff, says Mr. Jackson, an additional 10 to 15 blacks "and other progressives" would be elected to Congress from the South. Really? In the North Carolina race mentioned above, old Bullet star Jack Marin, a Reagan Republican, would have probably have beaten Mr. Micheaux in the 1982 general election. As it is, he lost to Representative Valentine, who is conservative, but a lot less so than Mr. Marin.

Do away with runoffs and there would be more results of that kind. One Southern representative estimates that without run-off primary elections, only "a couple or three" blacks would be elected — not the 15 to 20 mentioned by Mr. Jackson. The bigger fallout, in his view, would be general election victories for "15 to 25" conservative white Republicans. Who would be hurt most by that? The very constituency Mr. Jackson is trying to lift up black Southern voters.

ST. LOUIS POST-DISPATCH

St. Louis, Mo., December 7, 1983

The Rev. Jesse Jackson has put the Democratic Party on notice that he intends to fight for rule changes that would enhance his chances of being selected at the party convention next year. That, no doubt, comes as a shock to the Democratic establishment and to any of the other seven candidates for the presidential nomination who thought Mr. Jackson would be content to devote himself to registering black voters for the greater glory of the party.

Mr. Jackson says that the present rules, which the party endorsed last year, discriminate against the selection of black convention delegates. There is little question but that they do just that — in addition to working against the selection of women and other minority delegates as well as against the interests of what the Democrats in headier days saw as the salvation of their party, the grass roots. The Democrats now think that success next year will depend most on the involvement of the regulars, and, hence, 568 elected public officials and party leaders are already assured positions as convention delegates.

Specifically, Mr. Jackson says he will ask the Democratic National Committee to abolish the winner-take-all rules that will make it more difficult for him to pick up delegates in congressional districts with large black populations. He intends to challenge the so-called threshold rules in districts with proportional representation. These require candidates to obtain a certain level of votes before they qualify for delegates on a proportional basis. Finally, Mr. Jackson wants changes in the rules setting aside delegate positions for party regulars and he wants the so-called census undercount to be considered in calculating minority representation.

Party officials and campaign advisers to former Vice President Walter Mondale had hoped to persuade Mr. Jackson to concentrate his campaign on voter registration, *The New York Times* reports. The enormous benefits to the party, were he to confine his efforts to that task, are obvious. In 11 Southern states that would be important to the re-election of President Reagan there are some 3.4 million unregistered blacks of voting age. Nationally, the Louis Harris organization estimates that if blacks improved their voting participation in 1984 to slightly more than 55 percent, Mr. Reagan would have to carry the white vote by 55-45 percent. That would be a popular vote landslide, which he did not achieve in 1980.

But why should Mr. Jackson consent to function as an errand boy for his party? As a practical matter, the more he discusses the issues, the more he engages the other candidates, the greater interest there will be in his campaign. That, in turn, cannot help but result in increases in black voter registration, which is the key not only to greater black political power but the fortunes of the Democrats next year.

THE CHRISTIAN SCIENCE MONITOR

Boston, Mass., April 19, 1983

JESSE Jackson's presidential candidacy is presenting the Democrats with dilemma after dilemma. Out of this could come creative ferment for the party. On the downside, it's at least deeply nettling.

The Rev. Mr. Jackson's foreign policy positions, on South Africa and the Middle East particularly, lie outside the party's activist consensus. The preacherly way Mr. Jackson formulates things and, to be candid, his color, have made his opponents and Democratic professionals self-conscious in dealing with him.

All this comes to bear on Jackson's list of complaints about his party's current political system. Jackson wants to end the double or runoff primary for state and federal offices in some 10 Southern states. He wants a change in national-convention delegate rules — ending winner-take-all or winner-take-most provisions, and replacing caucuses with straight proportional primaries for apportioning delegates to the national convention.

Jackson has been leaning heavily on Walter Mondale to endorse a lawsuit in Mississippi federal court that would banish the runoff primary under the Voting Rights Act. Gary Hart has joined Jackson, who has made such support a nonnegotiable condition for his backing of an eventual Democratic nominee.

The trouble with Jackson's case about the double primary is that there is little empirical evidence of its impact on black candidacies. In some elections, it apparently does discriminate against blacks. In a field of several whites and a black, whites will divide their votes among whites; in a runoff with a white against a black, whites vote for the white. Says Washington political scientist Austin Ranney: Ending the runoff primary would likely mean many more black candidates, and a handful more

blacks elected, but the largest gain would be in Republican victories.

The Voting Rights Act considers the discriminatory consequences of election practices, not just the intent of those who set up the practices. Hence the argument that the Southern runoffs were set up early in the 1900s before blacks became a political force, and thus were not intended to discriminate against blacks, may be beside the point. In the one-party South, a primary runoff was meant to bring order to an often chaotic process and stage a meaningful election, since the final against a Republican was a mere formality.

Some black candidates in the South — an Andrew Young or Julian Bond in Atlanta — have managed to do well under the current system by mobilizing the black constituency and appealing to the moderate white community.

The Reagan administration has joined the Jackson lawsuit to challenge the runoff primary. This highlights the issue this election year for the GOP's benefit.

Nonetheless, Mondale and the Democratic leadership should support the suit, at least to find out whether it is applicable in all jurisdictions. As in school desegregation decisions, the review of evidence by courts has been the only way through the walls of resistance and argument about motives and facts. If the ruling goes against any jurisdictions, they should pledge enforcement. And the party should review the issue on its own.

But primary runoffs are not in themselves discriminatory. Runoffs can whittle down a large field to the broader-appealing candidates. They lessen the chance of an extremist candidate sneaking in. A blanket ban on runoffs does not seem necessary or wise.

The Chattanooga Times

Chattanooga, Tenn., December 10, 1983

The Rev. Jesse Jackson's effort to strengthen his quest for the Democratic presidential nomination is leading him toward a fight with his own party that could be disastrous, for him and the Democrats' 1984 nominee, which assuredly will not be Mr. Jackson. There is hardly a better guarantee of GOP victory in 1984 than a searing intra-party fight among Democrats.

In interviews last week, Mr. Jackson said he intended to challenge and, he hopes, to change Democratic party rules governing the selection of convention delegates. As one of eight candidates for the nomination and the only black, he considers the rules unfair to blacks. If the party does not change rules he says are unfair to blacks, Mr. Jackson, says he will challenge the seating of delegates at the convention.

The implicit charge of racism has Democratic party officials upset, and justifiably so. Mr. Jackson charged on *Meet the Press* that a "majority of the [party] leadership happens to be locked out." The rules, drawn largely by a commission headed by North Carolina Gov. James B. Hunt Jr., do make sweeping changes in the selection of a nominee. The hope is they will enable the party to retreat from guidelines written by an earlier commission after the 1968 election that plunged the Democrats into intra-party chaos — and, some say, led to its problems at the polls.

But it is wrong for Mr. Jackson to charge that the new rules are racist. Of the 70 members of the Hunt Commission, 10 were black. (Two of them, Walter Fauntroy, the District of Columbia delegate to Congress, and Gary, Ind., Mayor Gary Hatcher, are now leaders in the Jackson campaign.) Moreover, the rules contain safeguards aiming at ensuring a fair though proportionate representation of women and minorities at the convention.

Mr. Jackson particularly objects to two rules. One permits "winner-take-all" victories by congressional district in some state primaries; the other requires that before candidates are included in the division of primary votes in states where delegates are distributed proportionately, they must get 20 percent of the vote. Mr. Jackson says those rules work for front-runners and against candidates whose support is derived chiefly from blacks. That's true as far as it goes, but the same rules will work to his advantage if he assembles his "rainbow coalition" of blacks, Hispanics and others.

Almost any system of rules imaginable helps a candidate with widespread support — Walter Mondale, for example -- to come up with a majority. But Mr. Jackson seems to want the rules changed so that a candidate with minority support can prevent a leading candidate from assembling a majority.

Two other objections: Mr. Jackson is displeased that the Hunt Commission allotted 568 convention votes to elected officials and party leaders. But it's common sense to give added influence to men and women who have actually won elective office and are responsible for party affairs year round. Also, he says the rules should be adjusted to compensate for alleged "census undercounts" of blacks and other minorities. Trouble is, no one has ever proved such undercounts. Besides, the party already apportions delegate strength by Democratic vote, which actually gives blacks more representation.

The Democrats' efforts for 1984, which stand to be aided in no small way by Mr. Jackson's success in registering thousands of new black voters, could be upset by his destructive attacks on the rules. That would be unfortunate, both for Mr. Jackson and for the party.

Houston Chronicle
Houston, Texas, May 24, 1984

There is no doubt that Texas voters want a presidential primary. But there is considerable doubt they will get one unless everybody keeps the pressure on.

The Democratic Party's county and senatorial district conventions last weekend were full of resolutions asking a direct vote on presidential nominees instead of the confusing, go-to-the-polls-twice caucus system. Public opinion has shown overwhelmingly in favor. The governor is foursquare for a pri-mary. The state Democratic chairman has allowed as how "some changes are necessary."

But the State Democratic Executive Committee has refused to go on record as favoring scrapping the caucus and conducting a binding primary. It is going to undertake a "study" later this year.

Whatever the merits of the contention that Democrats shouldn't be arguing among themselves now, but concentrating on defeating the Republicans, the executive committee's reluctance to even favor a primary points up that it isn't going to be easy to get one. And time, and "studies," are not on the side of a primary.

Whether to have a primary isn't going to be the most exciting issue in the world come late this year, or next year. That alone could be enough to scuttle chances of a change. If Texans are going to have a direct, simple vote to nominate presidential candidates, as they should, they are going to have to hold some feet to the fire.

THE INDIANAPOLIS STAR
Indianapolis, Ind., July 30, 1984

Mondale forces at the Democratic Convention may have defeated a move to eliminate primary run-offs but that doesn't mean that the effort is dead. The Rev. Jesse Jackson and many of his supporters still maintain the run-offs are a political shill game designed to keep blacks out of office.

The run-offs, a staple of the voting system in 10 Southern states, require that if no candidate receives a majority of votes in the primary, then the two top finishers compete in a second primary to determine the party nominee.

Jackson contends run-offs hurt blacks because whites tend to "vote race." Defenders contend run-offs help produce nominees with broad party supporters still maintain the run-offs are a political shell game designed to keep blacks out of office.

If Jackson is correct in saying whites will vote for whites against blacks in a runoff, those same whites, in the absence of a runoff, would coalesce around one white candidate in the first primary anyway. Eliminating runoffs won't stop bigotry; it will merely shift to the first primary.

Even had the convention adopted Jackson's view in its platform, states could continue to hold run-off election. Only state legislatures, or in some cases the state parties, have power to abolish runoffs. They are not apt to do so at the request of a national convention.

Run-offs, in reality, can benefit blacks. In Georgia's 1974 gubernatorial race, segregationist Lester Maddox finished first in a 12-man primary while anti-segregationist George Busbee ran a poor second. Without a runoff, Maddox would have been governor. But in the runoff, Maddox's base of segregationists was too narrow. Busbee was elected by winning almost all the votes of the supporters of the other 10 candidates.

Further, in this year's congressional race in Georgia's 5th District, Rev. Hosea Williams, a black candidate, said he expects to be defeated in the primary but is pinning his hopes on the runoff.

The one-primary system Jackson advocates doesn't assure that the person nominated represents the majority of a party. Run-offs do. Opposing them is tantamount to opposing rule by the majority — the numerical majority, that is, not the racial majority.

There may be practical rather than ideological reasons why the convention didn't oppose run-offs. Many Democrats obviously were reluctant to alienate conservative white Southerners, who were likely to interpret a rejection of run-offs as a surrender to liberal blacks.

The Democratic ticket, the convention may have concluded, is going to have a tough enough time in the South without driving many party members into the ranks of Republicans.

Even granting that, the foundation of democracy, from which the Democrats derive their name, is the principle of majority rule. The convention ruled correctly.

THE INDIANAPOLIS NEWS
Indianapolis, Ind., April 28, 1984

Politics is littered with irony, and one of the supreme ironies of the current political season may be the Rev. Jesse Jackson's opposition to dual primary systems which require runoffs when no candidate gets a majority of votes in the initial election.

Jackson contends such dual primary systems discriminate against black candidates who may receive a plurality in an initial primary election but lose in a runoff when it becomes a two-candidate race.

The concept which Jackson criticizes is the very concept which is giving him leverage and may make him an even larger presence in July when Democrats convene in San Fransisco to select a presidential nominee.

Jackson is one of three surviving candidates in the Democratic presidential primary. Recent delegate totals show Walter Mondale leading with 1,129 delegates, Gary Hart in second place with 626 delegates and Jackson trailing with 167 delegates.

In all probabilty, Jackson will arrive at the convention with fewer than one-tenth of the delegates committed to voting for him. By all accounts he should be a minor factor in the contest — a footnote at the convention.

But, because the rules of the Democratic party require that the eventual nominee win a majority of the delegates to the convention — not a mere plurality — Jackson enjoys a presence in the race and a leverage far in excess of his delegate support.

Both Mondale and Hart know that Jackson's bloc of votes may be critical to capturing the party's nomination. Even if the nomination is not decided by Jackson's delegates, Jackson's endorsement of the eventual winner will take on symbolic importance in the ensuing general election campaign. Thus, Jackson is being treated deferentially by Mondale and Hart and will undoubtedly exact some concessions on the road to San Francisco.

It is unlikely that Jackson would be in quite the same position but for the requirement that the party's nominee emerge with a majority of the delegates. Thus, Jackson's own candidacy emerges as exhibit number one in defense of an election system he seeks to abolish.

Yielding to some pressure, however, Jackson made reference in his recent appearance in Indianapolis, to a "compromise" with Gary Hart; namely, that there would be no runoff primary when the leading candidate receives a significant plurality. The number used loosely was 40 percent.

Associated Press writer Dick Pettys recently wrote about a study by two University of Georgia political scientists who analyzed 215 runoff primaries in Georgia between 1965 and 1982. They noted that black candidates who emerged with a plurality in the initial primary election contest won 70 percent of the runoff elections they engaged in. That was identical to the success rate for white candidates with a plurality in the initial election and a win in the ensuing runoff.

Georgia state Sen. Julian Bond, a veteran of Southern politics where runoff primaries prevail, told Pettys, "I don't think changing the system will achieve the results he (Jackson) wants. Changing the second primary . . . will mean more blacks will win Democratic primaries . . . (but) you may cause the election of more (white) Republicans (in general elections)."

Runoff primaries did not come into vogue in the South to blunt the emerging strength of black voters. The runoff emerged in the post-Reconstruction days when blacks were already disenfranchised by poll taxes, literacy requirements and other discriminatory voting obstacles. It reflected the political reality that in most of the South there was a one-party system — the Democratic party — where whoever won the party's nomination automatically won the general election.

There is nothing inherently racist about the structure of runoff primaries. It is merely a logical system of ensuring that the winning candidate emerge with a majority of support from the voters.

Any political structure is vulnerable to racial exploitation as long as voters use race as a criterion in the voting booth. Evidence indicates that both black and white voters are about equally inclined to vote on the basis of racial considerations.

That Jackson, a beneficiary of the coalition politics inherent in the runoff concept, is playing a trump card to abolish that concept is ironic indeed.

The Times-Picayune
The States-Item
New Orleans, La., May 5, 1984

We are indebted to the Rev. Jesse Jackson for bringing into the current political debate a flaw in the electoral process we had not really paid much attention to. It is not, however, the flaw Rev. Jackson perceives, but the reverse of it.

Rev. Jackson insists that party primaries — for elective office, not for presidential preference — should be won by plurality rather than by majority. The Southern states and Oklahoma require a majority to win a primary, which means a runoff when necessary. Our view is that if the procedure is to be changed, the other states should be made to require a majority rather than the other way around.

Rev. Jackson sees in the majority requirement a deliberate impediment to black victories at the polls. Suppose: Three candidates, two whites and one black, contend in a primary and the black gets, say, 45 percent of the vote. If only a plurality is required, the black wins; if a majority is required, there is a runoff and the combined white vote can defeat the front-running black. It doesn't always work that way — a combined black vote split between two black candidates in a primary can defeat a front-running white — but it undeniably can.

Party primaries are nominating elections — their winners meet in a general election for the final decision. As such, they developed from party rules, even if the practices were later adopted as public law. The South's divergent practice reflected its divergent political situation. It cannot be considered a device to exclude blacks, for blacks in years past were excluded from any kind of election, but a reflection of the fact that the South was a one-party region in which the party primary was tantamount to a general election. Thus a majority vote was required for victory.

Majority rule is designed to do two things: to field candidates with the broadest support among their constituencies and to create a government with the broadest support among the total constituency. The United States has been spared — by fortune more than by conscious design — the deleterious effects of plurality "rule," which, with its frequent accompaniment, proportional representation, has saddled many other nations with government by coalitions of squabbling minority parties.

Today's minority can be tomorrow's majority, and minorities are hardly helpless in the American political system. Their chief weapons are organization and persuasion, and the benefit to the total body politic of majority rule is the force it exerts on groups with special interests to broaden their appeal to the whole community.

The Washington Post
Washington, D.C., May 2, 1984

JESSE JACKSON charges that Democratic Party rules have cost him 221 delegates he has earned in primaries and caucuses. Is that so? If it is so, is it unfair?

Begin with primaries. Mr. Jackson has won 17 percent of the votes, but only 11 percent of the delegates in primaries. The main reason is that party rules give a candidate no delegates unless he gets a minimum share of the vote—a threshold—in a state or district, usually 20 percent. In states where Mr. Jackson has met or come within 1 percent of the 20 percent threshold, he has gotten 22 percent of the votes and 20 percent of the delegates; the arithmetic of the rules has cost him about 11 delegates (of a total of 3,933 at the convention). In other primaries, he won 12 percent of the votes and 3 percent of the delegates. The threshold rule has cost him about 50 delegates in primaries.

Is that fair? Democrats want thresholds to discourage splinter candidates. We think a 20 percent threshold is too high, and the Democratic Party several weeks ago encouraged state parties to lower their thresholds. But we don't agree with Mr. Jackson if he's saying that any threshold level, however low, is inherently unfair.

It's harder to measure exactly how many delegates the rules have cost Mr. Jackson in caucuses against what he would have won by proportional representation. In many states, delegates are elected by congressional district; in some of these, notably Virginia, large turnouts in a few districts netted Mr. Jackson most of his delegates, but gave him no help in winning delegates in other districts where caucuses were more sparsely attended and Mr. Jackson had practically no support. So he ended up with a lower percentage of delegates than of caucus attenders. But it doesn't seem intrinsically unfair to apportion delegates to districts in proportion to Democratic vote, which is what produces such results. In some cases, such rules have worked for, as well as against, Mr. Jackson. Any caucus system will produce such results, and Mr. Jackson says caucuses are "inherently undemocratic." But how many are ready to accept the consequence of this view: primaries in all 50 states?

The overall impression Mr. Jackson makes, by charging that the rules have cheated him of 221 delegates, is that the system is unfairly biased. But when you look at the details, you find good-faith bases for each rule that Mr. Jackson complains of. You could construct a set of fair rules that would give Mr. Jackson a larger number of delegates, and it might well be prudent politically for party leaders, in filling at-large delegate seats, to choose Jackson supporters. But it's also possible to construct a fair set of rules, as the Democrats tried to do, which enables winning candidates to accumulate a majority and denies candidates representation in states and districts where they have only splinter support. The Democrats' current system —except for the unduly high threshold—tends to do that. If Mr. Jackson were winning in most states the kind of impressive victories he won in the South Carolina caucuses and the District of Columbia primary, he would have the delegates he would need to put him on the road to the nomination.

THE LINCOLN STAR
Lincoln, Neb., May 19, 1984

In all fairness, and to truly reflect the stated wishes of Nebraska's Democratic primary voters, the state party ought to send at least two, and maybe even three, delegates to the national convention pledged to support the Rev. Jesse Jackson.

Because of national party rules, which provide for a minimum "threshold" vote for presidential candidates to automatically be assigned pledged delegate slots, Jackson could end up with no Nebraska delegates despite winning 9 percent of the popular vote in the primary election.

Nebraska will send a delegation of 30 members to the Democratic national convention in San Francisco in July. National party rules aside, fairness demands that Jackson should receive 9 percent of those delegates. And that's at least two.

The Democratic state convention can provide those slots if it wants to when it meets in Omaha next month.

Or it can deny Jackson those delegates — and, in effect, disenfranchise more than 13,000 Nebraska Democratic primary voters.

IF JACKSON'S final vote total in the 2nd Congressional District rises by at least 60 after the official count is completed, he automatically would receive one of the 24 delegate positions apportioned in proportion to the results of the primary vote. The second Jackson delegate could be provided within the six positions reserved for "uncommitted" party and elected officials.

At least two elected officials who support Jackson — Sen. Ernest Chambers of Omaha and Omaha City Councilman Fred Conley — have filed as candidates for those slots.

If Jackson is not automatically accorded one of the seats among the 24, it would be difficult to provide him with two seats among the six, but it could be done. Four slots, in effect, already have been claimed. Under party rules, two must go to the new state party chairman and vice chairman elected at the state convention in June, and two essentially have been reserved for Gov. Bob Kerrey and Omaha Mayor Mike Boyle.

BUT, IN SPITE of the clamor among other party and elected officials for the last two remaining "uncommitted" seats, both, in that event, should go to Jackson delegates.

If Nebraska Democrats are to be faithful to their voters and fair with their candidates, if they are to be truly "democratic," and if they are to listen to the voice of a minority viewpoint within their party, then they should apportion all of their delegates in a manner that reflects — and respects — the wishes of all of the members of their party.

Nebraska Democrats have an opportunity to set an example for the nation, and for their party, by going that extra step beyond national party rules to assure equity and justice.

That means a 30-member delegation which, based on the primary vote, would include at least 17 votes for Gary Hart, at least eight for Walter Mondale and at least two for Jesse Jackson.

That is the only fair way to do it.

The Orlando Sentinel
Orlando, Fla., April 30, 1984

Is it racist for Florida and other Southern states to hold two-stage primaries, including a runoff between the top two finishers if no one wins a majority? The Rev. Jesse Jackson says so, but his cure won't work. Overall, the runoff system is fairer than the one-shot process that most states use.

The case Mr. Jackson makes is practical and anecdotal. He cites examples in Mississippi, North Carolina and elsewhere when a black candidate ran first in round one, then lost the runoff when white voters united behind the white runner-up. Scrap the runoff, he says, and blacks will get more representatives in office.

But there's a basic problem: democracy. A one-step primary is particularly undemocratic where one party dominates, as the Democratic Party does in much of the South. It's bad in principle but also in practice. A candidate of whatever color who slips by with 20 percent of the votes in a primary will have a hard time representing both the party and the public.

And don't forget: A party runoff isn't a voter's last chance to express racial bias. A bigot can vote for the other party's candidate. That's why many Democrats say Mr. Jackson's reform would help Republicans most. He pushes the change, in effect, as a gimmick to bypass racial bias. It won't work.

A runoff system isn't rigged against blacks, though it has been used that way in some cases. It ensures that a party nominee is the choice of a majority of the party members voting. Thus in districts with a black majority, a runoff can do the opposite of what Mr. Jackson objects to. It can keep a single white candidate from winning a nomination against several black contenders.

Perhaps Mr. Jackson can be consoled by recalling the Georgia race 10 years ago when segregationist Lester Maddox tried to retake the governor's mansion. He led the field with 36 percent, then got stomped in round two as most Georgia Democrats rejected him as a relic. And in Florida it has let progressive Democrats such as Lawton Chiles, Reubin Askew and Bob Graham win statewide races despite runner-up status in the first primary.

While Democrats should reject Mr. Jackson's attack on runoffs, they also can promote fairness by conceding his case against the rules for awarding convention delegates.

Many states require a candidate to get 20 percent of the vote to win any delegates. That's meant to screen out frivolous candidates but has shortchanged Mr. Jackson by giving him just 7 percent of the delegates even though he was getting 17 percent of the votes. Party chairman Charles Manatt is right to urge state parties to try to close the gap when appointing their at-large delegates.

As far as the runoff elections go, some day a candidate's color won't matter. Voters of both races will stop tilting so heavily toward the candidate whose skin looks like theirs. That pattern is a shame that time and effort — not an end to runoffs — will change.

Wisconsin ⚑ State Journal
Madison, Wisc., April 9, 1984

Rules of the Democratic National Committee were changed for this election at the urging of Walter Mondale and others to make it more difficult for lesser candidates to succeed.

One such rule says that a candidate cannot have national-convention delegates pledged to him unless he wins at least 20 percent of the vote in at least one congressional district in each state.

Jesse Jackson, who is fighting the rule, easily qualified by winning more than 20 percent of the vote in the 2nd and 5th Congressional Districts.

Those two districts represented the bulk of Jackson support, though he had backing in Racine and Rock Counties in the 1st District. At the other extreme, he didn't get a single vote in the 4th District and only two votes in the 9th District.

THE ARIZONA REPUBLIC
Phoenix, Ariz., May 14, 1984

JESSE JACKSON has reiterated his warning that he will not support any candidate for president who does not join him in demanding the abolition of runoffs in primary elections.

Without Jackson's support, the Democratic nomination might not be worth a lead penny.

In several states, mostly in the South, if a candidate does not get a majority of the votes, a second primary, known as a runoff, is held, pitting candidates who finished first and second against each other.

Jackson says the system discriminates against blacks. When there are three or four contenders in a primary — one black, the others white — the black may finish first only to find those who supported the whites ganging up against him in the runoff, he says.

He's right about that.

What he overlooks is this: When there are three or four contenders, one white, the others black, the same thing may happen in reverse.

The problem is racial prejudice, not the runoff. The Democratic Party can eliminate the runoff but the prejudice may remain.

If the Democrats nominate a black with less than a majority of the votes, the disgruntled white majority might shift its support to a white Republican.

And what would Jackson have achieved except to weaken his own party?

The runoff wasn't invented to discriminate against black candidates in the South. It was invented at a time when there were no black candidates — or black voters, for that matter.

And there's a very good reason for it. Look what happened in the recent Texas primary.

There were three candidates for the Democratic nomination for the Senate. Race was not involved. All three are white.

Rep. Kent Hance came in first with 455,583 votes, State Sen. Lloyd Doggett second with 454,610 votes, and former Rep. Robert Kreuger third with 453,559 votes.

If that were that, Hance would be the Democratic candidate for the Senate even though 66 percent of the voters in his own district preferred his opponents.

Fortunately, there will be a Hance-Doggett runoff, and whoever wins will go into the campaign with the support of a majority of the party rank-and-file.

That's the way it should be, Jackson notwithstanding.

The Pittsburgh PRESS
Pittsburgh, Pa., April 19, 1984

The Rev. Jesse Jackson has handed the Democratic Party a monumental headache by demanding that, as a price for his support, the party platform and presidential nominee oppose runoff primaries.

Rev. Jackson contends that a second primary, when no candidate gets a majority in the first round, violates the Voting Rights Act and discriminates against blacks in the 10 southern states where the practice exists.

Most legal experts disagree. The consensus is that the Voting Rights Act does not outlaw all runoff primaries, only those whose effect is to discriminate on the basis of race.

Though cases can be found where a black led in a multi-candidate primary and then lost to a single white opponent in a runoff, double primaries should not be automatically barred in a society based on majority rule.

There are still one-party areas in the South where winning the Democratic primary is tantamount to election. Crowded races are common. In an eight-person contest it is possible for a candidate to "win" with 15 percent of the vote. Such a candidate lacks both a mandate and broad party support.

On the other hand, forcing the top two finishers into a runoff leads them to reach out to a wide electorate and guarantees that the eventual nominee is the choice of a majority of party voters.

Rev. Jackson argues that eliminating runoffs would lead to the election to Congress of 10 to 15 more "blacks, other minorities and white progressives." Perhaps. But is it the purpose of election laws to produce predetermined results?

In any event, Rev. Jackson probably is mistaken. A number of shrewd southern Democrats say his changes would produce more black nominees, but many of them would lose in the general election as white voters went Republican.

Reagan administration strategists seem to agree. Rev. Jackson has sued in Mississippi to strike down runoff primaries and the Justice Department, of all people, has said it might enter the case on his side. Hmmm.

The Seattle Times
Seattle, Wash., April 2, 1984

COMPLAINTS made by Jesse Jackson supporters over procedures used in the recent Democratic precinct caucuses here raise questions about integrity and ethics that can neither be ignored nor obscured with debate over how the dispute should have been handled.

They also offer one more compelling reason why this state should replace the caucus system with a presidential-preference primary.

The Jackson people have filed a lawsuit against the Democratic State Central Committee charging that minorities and women were discriminated against during the neighborhood meetings. As redress, they are asking that the disputed caucuses be held again.

Some of the charges should be investigated. Accusations that delegates were incorrectly or unfairly assigned should either be proved or put to rest. If rules were ignored to show favoritism to Walter Mondale and Gary Hart, the committee should want to know that.

The central committee says the grievances should have been made to the party's credentials committee. Obviously, the Jackson people had little faith in the impartiality of that group. They also know that they will gain a little political mileage out of a public airing of the complaints.

Jeff Smith, communications director for the central committee, is probably right in believing that a lawsuit will prove fruitless. Repeating some of the caucuses is not a reasonable remedy. For that procedure to be valid, the same people would have to participate and vote in precisely the same way. It isn't possible to ensure that this would occur in each contested precinct.

But that does not excuse the state committee from its responsibility to the people who participated in the caucuses and expected a fair process. The charges should be examined carefully and steps taken to protect the integrity of future caucuses and the party's credibility.

The Dallas Morning News
Dallas, Texas, April 13, 1984

High on Jesse Jackson's political agenda is abolition of Southern runoff primaries — Texas' among them. Jackson constructs the following syllogism: Black candidates deserve election; runoffs deprive black candidates of office because even when blacks get pluralities, they commonly fail in runoffs with white candidates; therefore, runoffs are racist. To end this condition Jackson is suing in federal court under the Voting Rights Act of 1965.

But the matter is more complicated than Jackson makes it out. Runoffs have a robustly democratic purpose — to guarantee majority rule; a plurality winner is ipso facto the candidate of a numerical minority. Hence Jackson comes off sounding undemocratic.

Nor would abolition of runoffs necessarily guarantee the election of blacks. Say, for argument's sake, that abolition gave the Democrats a string of mostly liberal black nominees, victorious because of splits in the white conservative-moderate vote. In that event, conservative-moderates, for ideological much more than racial reasons, would defect in droves to the Republicans. Jackson's own failure to attract white votes suggests precisely this outcome.

A savvy and adroit politician, Jesse Jackson. But one can't help wondering whether he's thought this particular issue all the way through.

THE MILWAUKEE JOURNAL
Milwaukee, Wisc., December 12, 1984

Jesse Jackson may be right when he says the Democratic Party's rules for selecting its 1984 presidential nominee "threaten my quest for the nomination," but that is not a sufficient reason for altering the rules at the 11th hour.

The rules, adopted almost two years ago, weren't designed to be a roadblock to Jackson. He wasn't a candidate at the time — or even one of the oft-mentioned "hopefuls."

Jackson is simply wrong when he says the rules lock out women and minorities. The party requires that national convention delegate seats be divided equally among males and females. The rules also require active efforts to include members of racial minorities and poor people in each state delegation to the convention.

Jackson may be correct when he says the present rules, had they been in effect in 1972 and 1976, would have kept George McGovern and Jimmy Carter from being nominated. One set of rules may improve the chances of long-shot candidates such as McGovern or Carter, while another set enhances the advantage of an insider such as Walter Mondale or John Glenn. That doesn't necessarily mean that one set of rules is good and the other set evil.

For example, in the early 1970s, the party liberalized its rules in order to ensure greater participation by rank-and-file citizens and to eliminate bossism.

Later, the party decided that it had carried a good idea too far. It had excluded many major Democratic officeholders, people whose knowledge and counsel were needed at national conventions. To remedy the problem, the new rules provide that a substantial share of the delegate seats will be set aside for elected officials.

The party undoubtedly will continue to make periodic changes in its rules, in response to various needs and pressures. But it should make the changes in a systematic way, with ample time and opportunity for various factions to gather information, marshal their supporters and argue their cases. Once the rules are adopted under such a procedure, the party has a duty to make them stick at the nominating convention.

If party leaders start making exceptions to please individual candidates, there will be little hope of avoiding chaos.

THE ATLANTA CONSTITUTION
Atlanta, Ga., July 15, 1983

If not for the reasons cited by the Rev. Jesse Jackson *et al.*, it may be time anyway to review the electoral system which requires runoff elections when no candidate receives a majority in a primary. Does this system serve the electorate as well as a one-shot primary would do, with nomination by plurality if that's the way the cookie crumbles?

The primary runoff is a uniquely Southern offering to the nation's political evolution, and, interestingly, the rest of the nation has begged off. Only nine states have it, all either Southern or nearly so (Oklahoma).

Jackson, joined by other black leaders, including Atlanta Mayor Andrew Young, suspects the system of working against — and of being intended to work against — black voters. They point out that a black candidate who might win a plurality, when white votes split among several candidates in a busy primary field, can then be ganged up on by white voters in the runoff.

True, but the system sometimes works *for* black candidates, too. Without it, in some jurisdictions black candidates might never even get into a runoff, a platform from which black-community concerns can be placed into political play. Jesse Jackson has grabbed a double-edged blade.

The argument for the runoff has been that in *de facto* one-party states — you will recall the Solid South — the requirement for a majority vote in the primary or its runoff compels consensus-building and prevents rule by cliques. Reserving majority decisions just for the general election was meaningless. Republicans never won.

But if only tentatively so far, two-party politics are coming to the region with their blessings — the opportunity to trade scoundrels periodically before either party gets elbow-deep in the till. There are now sometimes real bipartisan elections for state and local offices. By focusing a vastly greater amount of public attention on Democratic candidates — Republicans, both less numerous and more ruly, rarely have runoffs — the system retards development of the full two-party system which the region needs.

The system is expensive, increasing election costs to the public by 50 percent (and to candidates' contributors by maybe as much as 100 percent) — and it incites the very problem that it is designed to manage: A plethora of candidates. Longshot candidates angle for the second spot in the runoff, hoping lightning will strike down the leader; even sure losers run, hoping to parlay their primary loss into political power by horse-trading their followers, or trying to, to one of the runoff battlers.

Maybe the primary runoff is still the thing to do. But however questionable his claims against the system may be, Jesse Jackson at least reminds us that the system is only familiar, not sacrosanct. If it is sound, it will survive the review it deserves in the light of contemporary politics.

Selected Bibliography

Books

Sowell, Thomas, *Civil Rights: Rhetoric or Reality?*, William Morrow and Company, Inc., 1984.
Williams, Walter E., *America A Minority Viewpoint*, Hoover Institution Press, 1982.

Articles

Eastland, Terry, "Redefining Civil Rights," *The Wilson Quarterly*, Spring 1984.
Hagstrom, Jerry and Guskind, Robert, "This is the Year of the Black Mayor, But Next Year Will Test Black Power," *National Journal*, Nov. 19, 1983.
Kamarck, Elaine Ciulla, "Fight Over Delegate Rules for '88," *The Nation*, March 2, 1985.
Loury, Glenn C., "A New American Dilemma," *The New Republic*, Dec. 31, 1984.
Puckrein, Gary, "Moving Up," *The Wilson Quarterly*, Spring 1984.
Sitkoff, Harvard, "The Second Reconstruction," *The Wilson Quarterly*, Spring 1984.
Stanfield, Rochelle L., "Reagan Courting Women, Minorities, But It May Be Too Late to Win Them," *National Journal*, May 28, 1983.
Wilson, William Julius, "The Black Underclass," *The Wilson Quarterly*, Spring 1984.

Reports and Studies

Center for the Study of Social Policy, "A Dream Deferred: The Economic Status of Black Americans," July 1983.
Editorial Research Reports: "Affirmative Action Reconsidered," July 31, 1981, p. 555; "Black Leadership Question," January 18, 1980, p. 43; "Black Political Power," August 12, 1983, p. 591.
Institute for Urban Affairs and Research, "Stable Black Families Final Report," December 1983.
National Center for Education Statistics, "Participation of Black Students in Higher Education: A Statistical Profile from 1970–71 to 1980–81," November 1983.
National Urban League, Inc., "The State of Black America 1984," Jan. 19, 1984.

Index

THE SOUL OF A TREE

THE SOUL OF A TREE
A Woodworker's Reflections

GEORGE NAKASHIMA

introduction by Dr. George Wald

KODANSHA INTERNATIONAL LTD.
Tokyo, New York and San Francisco

Detail of English walnut bench. The tree that produced this beautifully grained wood was probably planted during the reign of Elizabeth I, who ordered the reforestation of great tracts.

Distributed in the United States by Kodansha International/USA Ltd., through Harper & Row, Publishers, Inc., 10 East 53rd Street, New York, New York 10022.

Published by Kodansha International Ltd., 12-21 Otowa 2-chome, Bunkyo-ku, Tokyo 112 and Kodansha International/USA Ltd., 10 East 53rd Street, New York, New York 10022 and 44 Montgomery Street, San Francisco, California 94104. Copyright in Japan 1981 by Kodansha International Ltd. All rights reserved. Printed in Japan.

Designed by Dana Levy

First edition, 1981

JBN 1072-789688-2361

Library of Congress Cataloging in Publication Data
Nakashima, George, 1905—
    The soul of a tree.
    Bibliography: p.
    1. Furniture making. 2. Trees. I. Title.
TT200.N3   684.1'04   81-80655
ISBN 0-87011-482-4   AACR2

Contents

To Marion,
   Suzu,
   and The Mother

Acknowledgments

My gratitude to Marion, who—even if not completely convinced—has labored so long to back my stubborn efforts, efforts to create beauty and truth in objects and environment. She understands the idea of the Karma Yogin, who follows the yoga of action.

To Herb Gordon, whose proposal that I do this book at first seemed far-fetched.

To Quentin Fiore, who over the years has advised me with warmth on so many facets of writing.

To Tad Akaishi for his continued interest in producing a worthy book.

To Anneke Orr, who so skillfully typed my manuscript.

And, lastly, to my two children, Mira and Kevin, who seem to be interested in carrying on my "mad" project.

The cedars of Lebanon contributed greatly to the development of
Near Eastern civilization, just as the *hinoki* cypress did in Japan.
Huge branches spread out from a massive bole. Today, these cedars
are kept from loggers; places where ancient groves remain have been
designated protected areas.

Foreword

There are two birds, two sweet friends, who dwell on the selfsame tree. One eats the fruits thereof, and the other looks on in silence.

Mundaka Upanishad, III, 1.

For humankind the trees—their roots in the ground, their heads reaching into the sky—have seemed always to bind together the universe. Almost all mythologies look to the Earth as Mother, bringing forth and nursing life, and to the Sky with its sun as Father, the fructifying principle; though in one very early Egyptian cosmology, perhaps in deference to the rains that swelled the Nile, these roles were reversed: the sky-goddess, her body spangled with stars, arching over the prone earth-god Keb, who bore upon his back all vegetation. Either way, life emerges from the coupling of such deities of earth and sky. And as is so frequently true, the myths foreshadow our present science. We now know that all life on Earth runs ultimately on sunlight, working through the intermediation of plants. Using the energy of sunlight, plants react carbon dioxide from the air with water from the ground to form sugars and the by-product oxygen, which is returned to the air. From the sugars, together with salts from the ground, plants synthesize all the manifold stuff of life.

But throughout the ages, humankind has looked to the trees to feed not only the flesh, but the spirit. It was beneath a tree, said to have been a fig, that Gautama Buddha had his Night of Illumination. Then he meditated for seven days under the sacred Bodhi tree, then another seven days under a great banyan, and a third seven days under the Tree of the Serpent King who dwelt among its roots, before setting out on his glorious mission. It was to Jonah that God sent a tree, first to give him shade and then to teach him compassion. And closer to our own time, though perhaps still in the realm of myth, we are told that Isaac Newton, driven from Cambridge into the countryside by the Plague, was inspired by the fall of an apple to formulate the law of universal gravitation. What is almost surely not a myth is that two years of enforced rustication among the fields and woods of Woolsthorpe, coming just after four years of study at Trinity College, seem to have produced in Newton a strange sense of intimacy with the universe, so that thereafter he seemed to know just what to expect of it, by intuition rather than analysis.

And then there was the episode in the Garden of Eden. Of the trees in the garden only two were forbidden, but God had mentioned only one. Otherwise there would have been no story, or a vastly different one; for the tree not mentioned was that of Eternal Life, and Adam need only have eaten of it first to be immune to God's threat that if he ate of the other tree he would die. If it had been a Greek story, the other tree would have been the Tree of Knowledge. But this was a Jewish story, and so that other tree, in concord with the Jewish obsession with justice, became the Tree of Knowledge of Good and Evil.

Eating of its fruit, that first human pair lost their innocence. I rather think that in reality the tree was in no way remarkable; but it was the means through which they were persuaded into the first act of self-assertion that made them human. Outside the garden as within, there were the trees, offering food and shelter; and for the quiet times, also knowledge, and the knowledge of good and evil.

Mythologies the world over hark back to a primeval state of perfection. It is curious that both the ancient Hindu and Greek traditions agree in dividing human history into four stages, always deteriorating, each worse than the one before. It is perhaps a primitive perception of the workings of our second law of thermodynamics, the law that expresses the apparent running down of our universe.

The ancient Greeks began history with the Golden Age, then Silver, Bronze, and finally our own, harsh Iron Age. The Hindus began with the perfect Krita Yuga, something over four million years ago, having achieved somehow a chronology that Western science is just catching up with, since it is only now that we are coming to accept some such figure for the age of man. Then humanity began to deteriorate: from the Krita Yuga to Treta (still three-quarters intact); to Dvapara (half-gone); to the present Kali Yuga, named for Kali, the goddess of destruction and dissolution. By Hindu reckoning, the Kali Yuga began about 3,000 B.C., hence close to the founding of the earliest cities. As Nakashima tells us here, the oldest trees go back that far, silent witnesses to virtually the whole of civilization, indeed active participants, for much of civilization has been a struggle between the trees and the cities, the trees nurturing life, the cities ultimately destructive, coming in our own time to a crescendo of destruction that now threatens the continuance, surely of civilization, and perhaps of the human race and much of the rest of life on the Earth.

Yet Kali is not all despair. She is an ambiguous goddess, for her work of destruction prepares for and promises rebirth. In India, in recognition of that promise, she is worshiped as Mother Kali. And in the Mosaic tradition, God's curse on Eve (i.e., Life) was that "in pain shall ye bring forth young." It is the pain of creation.

One can gain knowledge from words, but wisdom only from things. I have spent my life in schools, permeated with knowledge, but short on wisdom. I have taught and been taught knowledge; but one cannot teach wisdom.

Nakashima has wisdom. He is probably the wisest person I know. He tries to tell us here how he came by that wisdom. It is in giving rather than taking, in listening rather than telling, in doing rather than exhortation. He has words, as we see here; but they are measured; they come out of living with trees, and wood, and tools for the working of wood.

Already in the living tree, the wood has died. Once it lived, and made the new ring of growth. Then the living parts of the cells died, leaving the cell walls as wood. When the whole tree dies, its usual fate is to rot, disintegrate, eventually to go back into soil. Nakashima makes the wood that he has rescued live again in new ways. He is at once artist and craftsman, as are all artists. His vocation is both to discover and create: to reveal the forms and patterns that he sees potential in the wood. As he himself says, he must wait, sometimes for years, until he sees those patterns and forms in the tree, the log, the raw timber; and then evokes them.

It is a quiet enterprise, and Nakashima is an extraordinarily quiet man. He is one of the quietest and most serene persons I have ever known. So-called quietism is something else, meaning passivity. But Nakashima's is the Karma Yoga, the yoga of action. He is the creator, the builder, the comrade of hills and streams and woods. They speak only to the silent, the attentive listener. Nakashima's silence goes with his wisdom of things. Even among persons, the most important communications are wordless. When Nakashima talks, it is quietly, spaced with silences, translated out of a greater, endless, wordless conversation.

As he says, he makes the dead wood live again in new ways. I am reminded of a story told me by my Northern Cheyenne friend, Hyemeyohsts Storm, who wrote the great "Seven Arrows." He said that once, when he was a boy of twelve, his uncle let him drive the tractor, pulling a mower. He was going along, feeling proud and grown-up, when suddenly he realized that he had run over a nest of rabbits. The older rabbits had been spry enough to get away; but when he got down to see what had happened he found that the mower had cut off the legs of a baby rabbit. As he held the little corpse, feeling a bit sick, his uncle came up and said, "Ah! I see you have cut off *your legs!* Now you must eat that little rabbit, *so that it can run again!*"

In this century it has become commonplace to declare that everything is relative. Not so, either in science or in art. The important thing is to know which things are relative, which universal. In all this Universe there are no further chemical elements than those we know or can prepare synthetically here. In the same sense, I think that good art is universal. It knows no barriers of space, time or culture. We recognize it at once in cave paintings of 12,000 B.C., in the tribal sculptures of Africa, New Guinea or the American Northwest Coast; in the pottery of ancient Peru, Mexico, China, Crete and Persia. We, as undoubtedly our forebears, have produced, along with the good, much bad art. In the long run, we recognize that too.

Nakashima says that we have not made a great building for two hundred years That is just the age of the Industrial Revolution. For a time, the Industrial Revolution promised humanity endless leisure and abundance; but in one massive convolution which has been gathering momentum throughout the past century, it is spreading a pervasive ugliness wherever it reaches, is devastating the planet, and now, in the suicidal preparation for nuclear war, is threatening the human species with self-extinction.

If that ultimate disaster should come—and it may, as Nakashima knows and we are both in the struggle to prevent—and some human beings survive, they will find again in time the beautiful and meaningful things their forebears fashioned, and will be proud again of what it most means to be human, to be on this planet the singular animal that knows and creates, *Homo sapiens* and *faber*, man the scientist and artist.

It is people like Nakashima who in every age realize that human promise, who construct our abiding human heritage. For things made of stone, and clay and wood endure, even as the generations come and go and cities and civilizations rise and fall. And the trees will be there as always, watching in silent witness as they have done throughout the ages.

George Wald
Cambridge, Mass.

The European walnut is called variously English, French, Italian,
Circassian, Persian, and Kashmiri walnut, depending on where it is
found growing. The bark is usually gray. The wood is also a shade of
gray but varies considerably from tree to tree. Some walnut wood
has areas that are almost black. The grain, in general, is extremely
well figured, sometimes burled. The sapwood from a healthy tree is
almost white, maturing to a warm gray when properly cured. Seen in
profile, the European walnut, like its American cousin, is easily
recognizable because of its rich, heavy branching.

Introduction

A tree provides perhaps our most intimate contact with nature. A tree sits like an avatar, an embodiment of the immutable, far beyond the pains of man. There are specimens, like the Yaku *sugi*, a type of Japanese cedar, which in their single lives have spanned the entire history of civilized man. These specimens were already substantial trees when Mohenjo–Daro was in flower and Europe lived in caves. Hundreds of generations have marched past. Civilizations much greater than ours have risen and turned to dust.

We woodworkers have the audacity to shape timber from these noble trees. In a sense it is our Karma Yoga, the path of action we must take to lead to our union with the Divine. Each tree, each part of each tree, has its own particular destiny and its own special relationship to be fulfilled. We roam the world to find our relationships with these trees.

There was a cedar from the Island of Yaku with a rotted-out core as large as a small cottage. Hundreds of years before it had been cut down for timber, some thirty feet above ground level. Now, its remains stood, surrounded by a crown of small trees which sprang from its living cambium, or outside layer.

There are also examples of such cuttings in the Ho River rain forest in the Pacific Northwest, with fantastic burls and figures, slowly crumbling to dust.

It is sad that some of these noble trees, awesome cathedrals of the forests, are debauched by the greed, insensitivity and gracelessness of man.

We work with boards from these trees, to fulfill their yearning for a second life, to release their richness and beauty. From these planks we fashion objects useful to man, and if nature wills, things of beauty. In any case, these objects harmonize the rhythms of nature to fulfill the tree's destiny and ours.

Each flitch, each board, each plank can have only one ideal use. The woodworker, applying a thousand skills, must find that ideal use and then shape the wood to realize its true potential. The result is our ultimate object, plain and simple.

THE SOUL OF A TREE

This white oak stands about a mile down the road from our New Hope workshop. It was about a decade old when Columbus discovered America in 1492, but it's long been called a "Penn's woods tree" because it stands on land that was part of the grant from the English crown to William Penn in 1682

There are three lumber sheds on our New Hope property where I store hundreds and hundreds of boards and slabs—about a third of my inventory. These I say I'm "ready to use" at any moment. *Opposite:* We try to keep all the boards from one log together, in *boule* order, that is, in the order sawn. Long boards are best stored on end so that we can leaf through them more easily. Before boards come here, they are air-dried for a year or two after sawing and are treated to kiln heat (no steam) for a maximum of ten days to two weeks.

I use chalk to make initial indications about where cutting is to be done, but once I make a final decision, I make the lines in pencil. *Above*: Every board must be carefully examined because there is almost always some kind of defect or imperfection, for example checks, or cracks, which must either simply be filled up or made an issue in the design. *Below*: The desk in the Conoid Studio where I do most of my designing. For this, I use few special instruments—no T-square— but simply sketch very accurately to scale. All the designs I develop here we have dubbed "Conoid."

I am quite at home here, in my environment among the boards.

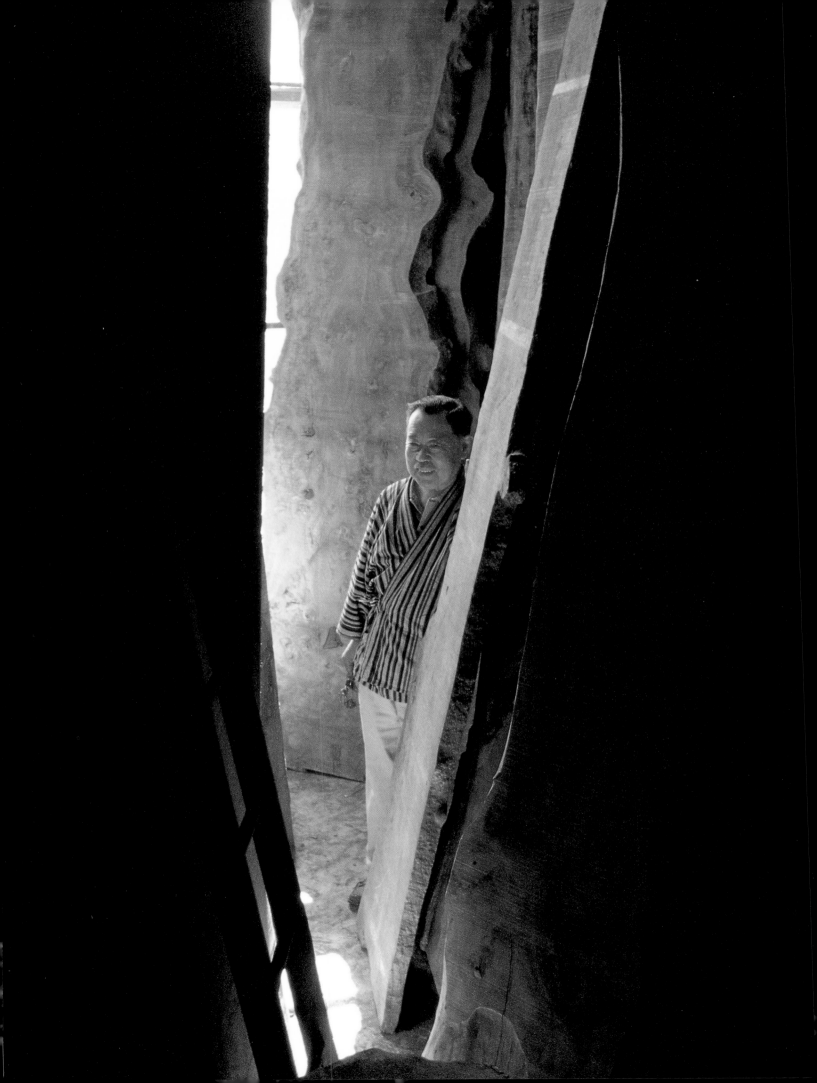

My son Kevin carved these signs after my brushwork; he is interested in concentrating on the business side of our shop. My daughter Mira, with whom I'm shown here, is a trained architect and is actively involved in designing and making furniture.

This iron chrysanthemum must have been a door pull in Japan, but I installed it as a knocker on the walnut-and-teak door of the Conoid Studio.

Above, left: These boards, mostly Persian walnut, are relatively short—only about eight feet in length—and they are most conveniently kept in the lumber shed in *boule* form in racks, horizontally. *Right*: For making chairs, templates and variety of Japanese, European and American tools. The heat lamp is for temporarily shrinking the wood of spindles for a tight fit.

Below, left: An exterior view of our Minguren Museum, built in the mid-1960s, where we display unique specimens of wood from the four corners of the world, many of my original designs, and other artifacts and objects which have inspired me. Literally translated, *minguren* means "people's tool association" and refers to a crafts movement in Japan with which I became involved about fifteen or twenty years ago. *Right*: My wife Marion, son Kevin and I prepare to share our evening meal in the house we built over three decades ago.

I hadn't planned on having a mosaic on the west side of the Minguren Museum, but Ben Shahn was visiting us a few years after it was built, and when he saw that this great expanse of wall was sheltered, he said, "Here is where we should have a mosaic," and promptly drew the cartoon. Gabriel Loire interpreted the cartoon and made the mosaic in Chartres in three-by-seven-foot panels which he shipped to us and we installed about a dozen years ago.

Authentic in every detail, this tea room (*above, left*) is in our so-called Mountain Villa, about two dozen yards above our house. *Right*: Adjustable pothooks, called *jizai-kagi,* hang over the central hearth in many Japanese farmhouses. The motif of the adjusting weight of this one, which is in our Minguren Museum, is typical—a fish. *Below, left*: A work depicting a dove by Ben Shahn hangs against a panel of walnut in our Minguren Museum. *Right*: The Japanese word *sansō* means "mountain villa," in other words, a retreat, exactly what we consider the last building we erected in New Hope. It was completed in 1978.

Building the Conoid Studio was a true adventure. The arching roof—a double reverse conoid—was a complete experiment. It took ten yards of concrete (each yard weighing about three tons) to pour the roof, which is only a thin shell two-and-a-half inches thick. The engineering was done by Mario Salvadori. The span is forty-by-forty feet, but no beams or poles support the roof. The entire weight rests on the concrete arch on the south side of the building, shown here, and the back wall which is about eight feet high.

Overleaf: This *tatami*-matted area is a projection that gives the line of the building some interest. Windows are covered with *shōji* screens that gently diffuse the southern light. The coffee table is of weathered redwood root, almost black.

Two book-matched boards of English walnut make up the dining table in our Mountain Villa. Free-shaped, but roughly hexagonal, it measures about six-by-six feet. This is one of my favorites because the wood is so richly grained—the heartwood almost black. The free edge is appealing too for it makes the table less formal than a perfect rectangle, square or circle. The Conoid chairs, in walnut, have figured single-board seats. Directly behind the *shōji* screens is a full kitchen. *Below:* For a time, I had this walnut Lounge chair with a single free-shaped arm in the entryway of the Conoid Studio which, as shown here, must be approached by a small arched bridge. *Right:* Our Mountain Villa has a traditional Japanese *genkan*, or vestibule. The sliding doors on the *getabako*, literally ''shoe box,'' where doffed street shoes are put, are of walnut. The polished black stones come from Japan.

In the large entry hall of our Minguren Museum stands a great slab of English oak burl, cut "through and through."
The low cabinet is all French walnut, including the vertical grilles and the back. Here it is used like a credenza, but because
the back is so beautifully finished, it was originally conceived of as a room divider—to be appreciated from all angles.

Overleaf: Detail showing the dovetail joint on a
cabinet made of East Indian rosewood.

PART ONE

The Making of a Woodworker

The long vistas of the Pacific Northwest, the west slopes of the
Cascade Mountains, where I used to hike as a boy.

1

Timberline

As a boy, I enjoyed roaming the mountains of the Pacific Northwest. Higher and higher I climbed, passing the great Douglas firs which punctured the heavens. Exploring along the way, I would follow the river beds or the railway tracks until the trees ended—at the timberline.

Above this line, simple vegetation grows, such as lichen, but most leafy plants are no more. Just below are the stunted evergreens fighting for survival in difficult conditions. The lean mountain goat, with his short horns, picks his way among the stones. A bit farther down there are dog's-tooth violets, the "Jeffrey's" shooting star, the Indian paintbrushes and a kind of fir tree called the Noble. It is a land where a young heart may search out the meaning of existence.

My memory pictures a small pond out of which springs a great wall of granite joined at its top by a seeming ocean of rock and stone that reaches upwards into the snow and beyond. There are bits of ice floating on the pond's surface. It is absolutely clear, but its bottom cannot be seen. To bathe in its water is a personal rite.

Along the edge of the rock wall runs a small, worn trail a finger and a half wide. A tiny mountain mouse scurries along, stops. We look at each other. This is our universe; we embrace it. I try to imagine how the mouse survives when the snow comes, for it falls early and remains late. The mouse must somehow make a life for itself under the white blanket. Nearby, there is a thick bed of mountain heather, fragrant, the finest sleeping place imaginable.

It is a lonely land with long vistas, just this side of *samadhi*, the eternal trance. Below are the Straits of Juan de Fuca, where the evening sun blazes red as it sets in the moist air of the rain forests of the Olympic Mountains.

There is an awesome feeling in the immensity, the absolute serenity of these rude lands of passionless silence. No birds sing. A bald eagle glides noiselessly in the thin air above. Occasionally, the wail of a coyote far below can be heard.

While climbing a minor peak where the vegetation thins out, I would run up the

Near the timberline in the Pacific Northwest. Small crystalline ponds
set like jewels in the wilderness.

In the rain forest long festoons of moss hang from the trees' lower limbs.

slopes silently. Crossing a shoulder of the mountain, I would often see herds of deer grazing. At such times I would lie motionless watching them for hours.

These solitary trips had a profound meaning for me. I had a sense of viewing creativity at its source. These trips dramatized for me the joy of living simply, close to nature, of fishing in small lakes nestled like jewels in the crease of a mountain, lakes probably never fished before, lakes where even the world's worst fishermen could make a catch.

On these climbs, I had an irresistible yearning to explore the next pass, to see what lay on the other side of the mountain, to gaze at new vistas. Crossing meadows of mountain flowers, I would stop to talk to the stunted bonsai-like evergreens which clung to life in the harsh environment, sometimes rooted only to a crevice in a rock.

On other occasions, I would hike with a group of scouts through the magnificent forests of the Olympic Peninsula. We would make trips from Hoods Canal to the Pacific Ocean, crossing several passes over three thousand feet high, hiking dozens of miles up river valleys along headwaters to the great rain forests and then on to the ocean. Although none of us weighed much more than a hundred pounds, we all carried full packs weighing about thirty-five pounds. Covering thirty-five miles was a good day's effort. I remember one trip when, my feet covered with blisters, I wore completely through a pair of shoes. Still, I pushed on across the mountain meadows, redolent of flowers.

Near the timberline grows a species of blueberry, the bush perhaps no taller than the width of two hands. On these plants grow huge, dark berries, juicy and delicious. To me these were *prasad*, the Sanskrit word for the food of the gods. Strangely, when exhausted from a day's climb and unable to go one step further, I would always seem to find this friendly berry just under my elbow, ready to restore body and soul.

At the western end of the tunnel that goes through the Cascades there was a real frontier town, Tyee, consisting of a few houses, a general store and a saloon to serve

The suns sets blood red in the rain forest of the Olympic Peninsula,
across Puget Sound and the Straits of Juan de Fuca.

those who maintained the railway beds. Tyee, in the State of Washington, was about
six miles from the site where a young friend of mine and I had camped while working
on the railroad. After our evening meal, we often made the trip there. At times we
would look in on the saloon and hear the crash of a handful of silver dollars on the bar.
About half the length of the railway bed leading to Tyee was covered by snowsheds.
One side of these sheds was cut into the mountain. The other side and the slanted
roof were built of fir timbers, about a foot and a half square. These timbers were laid
square side by side over supports to form a roof that would keep snowslides off the
right-of-way. We would walk on top of the snowsheds or on the railroad beds.

My friend, younger than I, could stride only the distance between one tie and the
next, so his fast-moving legs became practically a blur. We played a game which called
for walking the rails for a mile without falling off. Sometimes we would catch a freight
train moving slowly up the Cascade slope. We'd run like fury alongside and grab the
handle that formed part of the boxcar ladder. Then we'd swing aboard. If the trains
consisted entirely of boxcars, it was even possible, on level stretches, to jump from a
train going one way to one going in the opposite direction. We would start from the
locomotive, running as fast as possible towards the caboose, and leap to the other train
at just the right moment.

In my early teens I worked as a "gandy dancer" on a maintenance crew. A gandy
dancer was so called because of the rhythm he kept when shoveling gravel and poking
it under loose railroad ties. It was hard and rough work, earning a man's pay, which
helped to finance my education. At times rails had to be replaced. Rails are extremely
heavy, especially those set around curves. About twelve men in pairs, each at the end
of a huge "tong" would lift the steel rail in unison, barely clearing the ground, and
carry it only a short distance at a time. Then the rail would be attached to the wood ties
with huge square spikes. The roadbed had to be sturdy and solid, since quarter-mile-
long freight trains were pulled or pushed by three or four locomotives of great size and
weight.

A view of a vast forest on the long hike down from the mountains.

In spite of the backbreaking work, the railroads of the Old West held great charm for me.

One night, darkness caught me by surprise as I headed down from the timberline. Far below, a long line of flares filed up the slope. A search party—for me! Rushing down the steep incline toward them, I moved faster than was prudent, steadily gaining momentum. Suddenly, my heels dug into the scree to check my headlong flight. In the half-light I saw a log lying horizontally across my path. I skidded to a stop, my legs just grazing the log. Another foot and I would have broken one or both knees as I crashed into the log.

Those were great days on the slopes. It was my joy to sleep exhausted in a railroad car or to nestle in a bed of fragrant mountain heather after a day's climb.

During the long hikes down, I never failed to be struck by nature's many moods—the harsh reality of the stunted trees at the timberline hanging by threads of roots to small crevices; then the moss hanging from deep in the tops of trees in the rain forest of the Ho Valley, where only the slenderest shafts of light reached the ground; finally the great cathedral of magnificent trees, straight and taut, fully ten feet in diameter. These were my personal relationships—ones that I would cherish through the years.

Paris. Sacré-Coeur.

2

Paris

Eventually, I studied architecture at the University of Washington. During the summers, I continued to work on railway gangs and later in the salmon canneries of Alaska. These jobs gave me the opportunity to indulge my passion for hiking through miles of wilderness and taught me to enjoy the solitude and quiet of lonely places. Once I led a party of four men across a narrow inlet near Ketchikan. Thanks to my experience on far-ranging hikes, I was able to beach our rowboat, walk twenty miles through deep forest, climb a peak and return to our beached boat without so much as a trail to follow.

After postgraduate architectural studies at the Massachusetts Institute of Technology, I worked for several years in the New York area. Much of this work was with the Long Island State Park Commission on projects of architectural design at Jones Beach, Sunken Meadow Park and Montauk Point. Eventually, this work gave out, and I left on a long trip around the world, which stretched into a vagabondage of over seven years.

In my 1929 Ford touring car, with its beautiful heart-shaped hood, I drove from New York to the West Coast to take leave of my parents. When I told my mother that I was leaving on a trip around the world, she said nothing. However, since I was still young and barely started on my career, she hid her apprehensions with some effort. Although he said little, my father understood well my frame of mind. He too had wandered for years, around China, before settling down in the United States.

Upon returning to New York, I sold my lovely car and bought a second-class, around-the-world steamship ticket. Because the English pound had dropped by almost half in relationship to the dollar, I was able to book passage on British ships at a very favorable rate. I stopped off in London for some dental work, since rates were lower there, and after a few weeks left for Paris.

Just what drew me to Paris, I don't quite remember, although in 1928 during my college days I had studied architecture in Fontainebleau and had spent some time in Paris. Probably, I felt a need to round out my French experience.

I found a tiny room for eight dollars a month in Alésia on the outskirts of Montparnasse, over a shop that sold ornamental ironwork. It had no heat, as was usual in Paris then, no inside plumbing and just one light socket. At the cafés, we would joke about the toilet, which consisted of two raised places for the feet, located over a drain in the concrete floor.

Having decided to stay in Paris for a year, I divided my resources, which amounted to $200, into twelve parts. This meant I could spend $16 per month, half for rent, half for other expenses.

At the time—the early thirties—Paris was the seat of a great creative movement in art and literature, centered in Montparnasse. It was a time vibrant with excitement. Old forms were breaking down along with many middle-class prejudices then prevalent. Polite starvation was a way of life, especially for the artists at the center of the creative movement. I was happy to be living in this electric atmosphere, to be part of the international creativity evident on all sides.

I became interested in Nietzsche, intrigued by his wonderful sense of freedom. I read *Thus Spake Zarathustra* in French, because secondhand French books were so cheap. This book was, in a sense, a springboard for my departure from the ordinary sources of inspiration. I no longer felt any particular attachment to technology or to the rootless concepts of art popular at the time.

Feeling as I did, it was perhaps inevitable that I should become disenchanted with the strictures and limitations of architecture, the profession I had prepared for.

As it happened, the Pavillon Suisse, a very early Le Corbusier building, was under construction within walking distance of my room. Unlike many buildings of that period, this one did have an aura of excitement because of its use of new forms and a fresh use of concrete. I faithfully visited the site of this new expression of architecture almost every week. The forms used had an interesting suggestion of creativity, which, to my mind, was encouraged by the open spirit of Paris.

Cathedral of St. Stephen at Bourges. Thirteenth-century France in all its glory. The peak of Western culture. What the spirit of the Divine makes possible for man to do! It impressed me greatly. If only we could achieve a tiny portion of such soaring beauty, catch its aura. . . .

There was always a fine congeniality in the Parisian cafés. One could sit all afternoon over a *demi* of beer. The talk, centering mostly on the new movements in art, had a strong undercurrent of exhilaration, a fervid conviction that new concepts were being born, old forms torn asunder. No one worried whether the new movements were great or not, but certainly they were vivid and alive. For me, though, there was a persistent nagging that this was not the whole truth.

I became friendly with Ivan, a Russian composer, and his American wife, Lucille. Ivan was a tall man, with a fine, ascetic, craggy face. He said that his father had been minister of finance under Nicholas II, the last Russian czar. The whole family was deeply involved with music. Ivan's uncle had been director of the Leningrad Conservatory. The family had escaped from Russia during the Revolution and had settled in Paris.

Ivan and I became close friends. We spent long evenings together reading *The Brothers Karamazov* aloud. We lived each chapter. I felt I could reach the Russian soul, its depth and tragedies, through Ivan. The contrasts between Ivan Karamazov and Alyosha seemed to me particularly Russian. I seemed to remind Ivan of Alyosha, and at times he would call me by that name. He began teaching me Russian, and I taught him some simple Japanese.

It was through Ivan that I got what I considered very fine employment in a small music publishing firm. In order to work full time in France, one needs a worker's card, issued only to French citizens; we were able to bypass this because I did piecework. I earned about sixty dollars a month, a sum I considered bordering on luxury.

The owner of the firm was a Frenchman who had lost an arm in World War I, and who continued to fight the war in his head. He was the only Frenchman in the publishing house. The staff was made up of Ivan, an English woman, a Danish woman and me.

It was a strange business. Ivan would go to see a foreign film and copy down the

Impression of Paris. There was always a feeling of lightness and a certain richness with an insistence on tradition. I could not help feeling that Paris lived in the past in spite of the powerful inspiration of modern art and architecture.

musical score as he heard it. We would then publish the score. Initial publication in France entitled us to receive royalties, and this was the mainstay of our business.

One of my principal tasks was to trace the music staff lines on a sheet of special paper. I used a five-pointed pen with a particular kind of ink. Ivan would write the music on this, and then we would print it. The process we employed for printing was similar to lithography, but we used a ground glass surface instead of stone.

Among other tasks, I especially enjoyed making deliveries backstage at the music halls. Even though I seldom got a chance to talk to them, I was able to get close to such stars as the Spanish singer Raquel Miller, Josephine Baker, Mistinguette, and others who were the toasts of Paris.

At one point, I was finally able to buy a bicycle, something I had been wanting. I delighted in taking long trips. Occasionally, I stayed in hotels, but often I slept in haystacks in order to economize. Toward the end of a trip through Normandy and Brittany my money ran out, so I covered the final 120 miles from Alençon to Paris in one day. It was beautiful weather. The rolling hills and villages were a delight. I met almost no one, not even a fellow cyclist. An exception was one motorist who had just become engaged and was so happy that he piled me with my bicycle into his car and took me to the next town.

Northern France and especially Normandy appealed strongly to me. I was influenced by more than my love for trees and wood at that point. The architecture of thirteenth-century France always impressed me as a demonstration of the peak of human spirit. I visited Chartres many times, always reveling in its construction and beauty, and marveling at the delicacy of its design and the glory of its glass. That so much greatness could have been achieved by the citizenry of the small town of Chartres staggers the imagination. Here was a testament to the deep yearning of the human spirit. Mont-Saint-Michel, built and rebuilt from the thirteenth through the fifteenth centuries, also represented for me a glory that our present age with all its vast

technology cannot equal. I can imagine a community joined by faith building these grand monuments. I can visualize the butcher and the baker working side by side with the stonecutter, while the duchess would be helping push the stone cart.

I loved France and the French people. Like most of the French workmen, I'd wear a pair of widewale corduroy trousers that tied at the bottom to keep the dirt out of one's shoes. At times French people would stop me in Paris to ask for directions. However, although I spoke French quite well and could almost joke like a native, I always felt a bit like an outsider.

At the time I had a strong feeling that an era in Paris was dying. I cannot explain this feeling, but it shocked me deeply. One day, rounding a corner in Montparnasse, I had an eerie sensation that I was gazing on death. To my mind, the hectic activity in the arts, literature, music and architecture represented not truth, but a game—one to be played out, but one which, rootless, eventually would die. This impression was intensely personal and I dared not speak of it to others.

I had always regarded Paris as a stopping-off place, a place where I would be able to fill out my acquaintance with the culture of the West at a time when there was a surging energy in art and architecture and a creative spirit bent on changing the world.

In every sense, when I left France, I would be putting it behind me for good. I had received there what was necessary for me. It was time to move on, and I would leave the whole modern art movement with its egotism and lack of beauty. Now, I felt, it was my destiny to make the long sea voyage to Japan, home of my ancestors.

Particular details seem to embody the whole spirit of a culture. In ancient Greece the Doric capital and Dipylon vase; in northern France the cluster of delicate columns in a cathedral; in Japan the simple but eloquent sweep of a thatched roof.

3

Tokyo

I was deeply drawn to Japan, the land of my forebears. I had visited relatives there some years earlier, but only for a short period. I longed to find and touch the creative roots of tradition, to trace my fingers through the white sand and feel its essence, to focus on a tree and experience its meaning, to join its karma, its destiny, with mine in order to search out the reason why my people look on nature with reverence as they do. All these were facets of experience that I must savor.

After a year in France and six weeks at sea, I found Japan a dramatic change. I stayed at my mother's ancestral home in Kamata on the outskirts of Tokyo. Landowning farmers, the Thoma family often spoke of how it had once been possible to walk all the way to the next railroad station without crossing anyone else's fields. This was a distance of about a *ri,* or two miles. Theirs was a typical farmhouse, substantially built, centered around the *oyabashira,* the mother post. This and some of the other columns and beams were hewn out of *keyaki,* or zelkova, an oriental elm, a very fine native hardwood. The house had originally had a thatched roof, but was now covered with metal, perhaps for fire resistance. There were a number of rooms, all fitted with *tatami,* the Japanese grass mats. These rooms were multipurpose. The *futon,* or bedding, was folded up in the morning and put into large wall closets so that the room could be used for other activities. The guest room, which served as my room, was in the southwest corner of the house, considered a most auspicious location. The rooms of a Japanese house are located according to their relationship to the cardinal points on the compass; the entryway, guest room, and toilets all should be most propitiously placed according to this superstitious rule.

The property was not far from Tokyo Bay. I often walked across our land toward the area which is now Haneda, one of Tokyo's airports. Along the shores of the bay were long racks of drying seaweed which turned almost black in the sun. My mother had spoken of catching shrimp in a creek that no longer existed, but which had once run behind the house. My uncles would from time to time stroll gaily along the banks of the Tama River, playing their bamboo flutes, the *shakuhachi*, becoming quite happy and carefree and forgetting their problems. My grandmother's ancestral home, similar in construction and architecture to the one in which I was staying, was located in Kawasaki, across the Tama River from Kamata. Hers was also a landowning farm family, and I often went with my grandmother to visit her relatives. She was tiny and considerably stooped like most elderly Japanese women of her generation. She walked slowly, but I managed to adjust my pace to hers. We had a warm relationship. Elderly Japanese women are not especially expressive, but she always had a dear smile for me.

It seemed to me that the life and customs in Kamata were of a former age. The house was completely Japanese, with a wooden veranda running around the whole structure. Every morning, winter and summer, this veranda was wiped off with a damp cloth using scattered tea leaves from the day before to pick up the dust and dirt and for finish. There was no heating in the house, except for a charcoal brazier set in the middle of the room which was used to warm the hands and the lower part of the body. When it became extremely cold, a box-shaped frame would be placed over the brazier and a heavy quilt laid on top. This was called a *kotatsu*. Since the brazier was set in a pit in the floor, it was possible to put one's feet and legs under the quilt to keep them warm. In this way, we could stay reasonably comfortable while burning a minimum of fuel. Often it was colder inside the house than outside, so we would put on extra clothing when coming inside.

The nature of the *kotatsu* meant that activities were seriously curtailed in cold weather. Obviously, one couldn't move around very well sitting in that position. My uncle would smoke his pipe, which had a long wooden stem and a small metal bowl that held just enough tobacco to allow him to take a few draws, or he would poke around in the ashes for a dying ember which he would turn over to obtain its last bit of warmth.

Even in midwinter, when there was snow on the ground, the sliding doors would be opened completely so that the winter sun poured into my room. I would sit there and practice *o-shuji*, calligraphy, with brush and ink. Since I didn't have a brazier in the room, my fingers would become so cold that I had difficulty holding the brush. It is almost impossible to do calligraphy wearing gloves. *O-shuji* is a true art form, with a deep meaning for both the Chinese and the Japanese. Important calligraphic writings are often displayed on scrolls and in frames. I greatly enjoyed practicing this art.

My grandfather, whom I never met, was a man of considerable vision but, unfortunately, ahead of his time. He had invested heavily in municipal water and in the electric railroad. Perhaps it was too early for this kind of business venture to succeed. At any rate, he lost a large part of the family property.

My mother left this ancient property in Kamata at an early age to take up a position in the imperial palace in Tokyo. Probably one of the youngest members of the court at that time, she was made an attendant to the court taster, Takeko Horikawa. In those days the court taster was very important and, in a sense, one of the first ministers of the realm. Takeko Horikawa came from a very good Kyoto family, and as court taster she was directly responsible for the lives of the emperor and empress, ensuring that their food would not be poisoned. She had a number of other attendants in addition to my mother.

My mother had often talked at great length about the small details and intimacies of living in the imperial palace. She seemed to be especially impressed with the kitchen and serving staff, which numbered about thirty young men who were evidently selected for their size and handsomeness. I found my mother's stories enthralling and was surprised that her memories remained so vivid after such a long time.

Mother was in attendance during the reign of the Emperor Meiji (1868-1912) and was so taken by it all that at one time she wanted to spend her life in the court. The routine of the palace was extremely disciplined and seems in many ways to have resembled life in a convent. Mother had very little contact with the outside world, but

My mother's family lived in this house in Kamata. The Thoma's
house was rather typical of a large Japanese farmhouse. Originally it
was outside of Tokyo, but now the city has grown to encircle it.

once a year she was allowed to visit her family and was transported home in a court
palanquin carried by four men.

The emperor led an especially secluded life. If, for instance, the members of the
court went out to amuse themselves in a rare snowfall, he could not look at them
directly, but had to sit hidden by a bamboo curtain and enjoy their games from a
distance. There were also stories about how much he liked the scorched rice that stuck
to the bottom of the cooking kettle. Since this was considered rather plebian food, it
had to be brought to him on the sly.

Through Takeko Horikawa, my mother became friendly with the emperor's
consort, a woman from Kyoto, who gave birth to the future Emperor Taishō (r. 1912-26).
Mother was also close to Murakumo Nikkō, the youngest sister of the Emperor Meiji,
who had taken Buddhist vows to become a nun. When Murakumo, who was greatly
loved by the Japanese people, was unable to attend public functions, my mother would
sometimes go in her place.

After some six years in the palace, my mother left Japan to go to the United States
and marry my father. She probably did this for a combination of personal and familial
reasons. She was in a sense a picture bride, but the two families were well acquainted,
and it is likely that she had met my father at some earlier point when he was still in
Japan.

My father was of samurai ancestry, a member of a family from Tottori Prefecture
on the coast of the Japan Sea. His father had been a warrior, fighting with his sword
throughout the length and breadth of Japan in the cause of the imperial house at the
time of the Meiji Restoration (1868). As a result of his loyalty, he was given a
ceremonial family sword by Arisugawa no Miya, a younger brother of the Emperor
Meiji. My grandfather was a commanding officer at the battle of Ueno in Tokyo, one of
the decisive engagements in the Restoration wars. At that time he and his men were
stationed at a restaurant which specialized in duck. Once, under attack, they took up

the *tatami* from the floor of the establishment and used these to shield themselves from missiles. Many years later, the surviving warriors had a reunion and formed the *Gannabe Kai*, or "Duck Stew Club."

My wife's family too was of samurai ancestry—from Satsuma, in central Kyushu. At one time the Satsuma people revolted against the imperial forces, of which my grandfather was a part. It is possible that in the great battle that ensued, our forebears fought against each other.

One of the most extraordinary things about Japanese history is that in the short span of two generations the country was transformed from a feudal society, based on the way of the sword, to a modern industrial state.

*   *   *

In 1934, a friend of my father arranged for me to work in the architectural offices of Antonin Raymond. Raymond was an American of Czech birth who had arrived in Japan to work with Frank Lloyd Wright on the old Imperial Hotel (completed in 1922), and then stayed on and set up his own practice. Raymond's office created buildings that were a synthesis of modern architecture and traditional Japanese design, the two having many similar characteristics. The simple unornamental forms and the exposed structural elements are typical of both.

Junzō, one of the architects in the office, and I became quite friendly. He taught me many of the wonderful traditional customs of Japan. Together we would read ancient classical literature such as *The Ten-Foot-Square Hut* or the *Hōjōki*, the musings of a priest in the beautiful language of the twelfth century. In the early spring, we would go off into the mountains to see the plum blossoms, barely visible through the falling snow. In warmer weather we would visit his family's handsome house on the seashore at Hayama. Lying on our backs in the delicately made tea house there, we would empathize with the beautiful graining of the carefully selected cedar boards that had been used for the ceiling.

We traveled a good deal. We took trips to Kyoto, the ancient capital, to enjoy the shrines and temples, fabulously built wooden structures expressing the beauty and eternal quality of the island people of Japan, and the deep reverence these people have for nature, the sweet sadness of never breaking the bonds of Nirvana. We also traveled to Nara, where I found more architectural expressions of the innate spirit of the Japanese, and to Hakone to rest our bodies and our spirits in the relaxing hot springs. In Ise, once again, in the appreciation of its Grand Shrines, we experienced the indwelling of the Japanese spirit.

I owe so much to Junzō and his deep understanding of the Japanese psyche and culture. He felt, too, my yearning to understand it, and took me in hand. He knew so well the elegance and power of simplicity, the beauty of proper materials in building, the delicacy of unfinished wood, the traditional and modern creative proportions, where the error of a fraction of an inch can make the design fail absolutely. He knew these things well in both the time-honored Japanese design and in the free, modern concepts, and he passed them on to me.

Japan was in a state of flux when I was there, and this was particularly visible in architecture, which strove to merge tradition with the requirements of a modern nation. There was a tendency to throw out the old for the new, while attempting to retain the core of the past. The discipline, the creativity, the innate spirit of Zen were to be kept; the forms could change. The concentrated intensity of skills, the drive for perfection and truth, were all disciplines of the past but could be used as steps into the future.

I had many relatives whom I would often visit. Since there is a great closeness among kin in Japan, visits would become eventful occasions. The salutations became quite elaborate, the ladies bowing until their heads touched the floor, uttering formal, polite phrases between bows. Traditional foods of high quality and great quantity were brought out to load the low tables.

Gardens and garden houses seem to embody the core of the Japanese spirit in relation to nature. So different from European gardens! The gardens of Saihō-ji and Ryūan-ji, temples which I visited on my first trip to Kyoto, impressed me greatly and I realized they represented a high peak. Sketched here is the Shōkin-tei (Pine-Lute Pavilion) in the garden of the Katsura Detached Palace, near Kyoto, which was built in the early decades of the seventeenth century.

All would sit on *tatami*. More and more relatives would come in, and more and more *sake* would be consumed. There would be long conversations on the health of individual family members and stories of the exploits of our warrior ancestors. The battles my grandfather fought, their places and times, the precise details of each encounter were related. It was a time of special warmth and family talk.

I spent five years in prewar Japan, and it was different from the intensely modernized country that Japan has since become. It was a great experience to savor the life of my forebears after having spent my youth in America. The sensitive environment, the expressive language, the excellence of the architecture and crafts, the traditions and the personal relationships—all touched me to the depths of my being. What seemed necessary to me was to synthesize these traditions with the demands of the contemporary world. But, once again, it was time to move on.

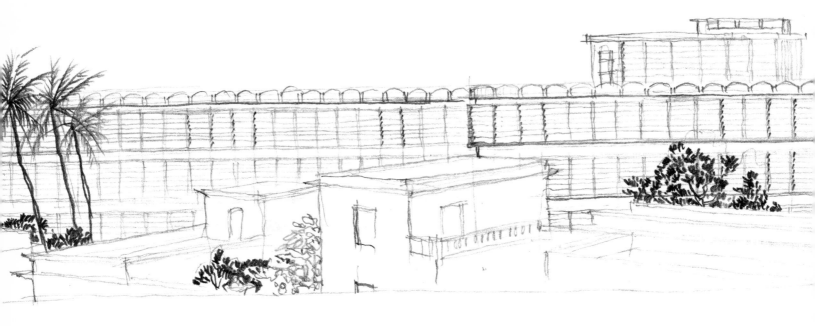

Golconda, the primary residence at the Sri Aurobindo Ashram, Pondicherry, India. The plans were drawn up in 1937. Under the Mother's guidance, and in spite of the rather primitive conditions the work was remarkably executed. This was one of the first high-test reinforced concrete buildings in India and even to this day remains beautifully maintained.

4
Pondicherry

It was the mid-thirties. The Raymond office in Tokyo, which had a design and construction project for the main building in the Sri Aurobindo Ashram in Pondicherry, India, asked for a volunteer to undertake the work. No one else seemed interested, and since I had always been fascinated by India, I offered to go. In the Japanese tradition, friends and colleagues saw me off on my journey. From Tokyo I traveled by boat to Colombo, Ceylon, and then by train up the east coast of India, going via Trichinopoly to Pondicherry.

I arrived at the ashram quite early in the morning. Here I was received warmly by the Mother, Mira, and members of the ashram. It was not long before I slipped into the routine of the simple life led there. I made friends almost immediately, joined them at meals, participated in the few set occasions, like evening meditations, and began my task of designing and constructing the ashram's major building.

This was some ten years after the ashram community had been organized. When I arrived, there were about two hundred men and women from all over the world living there. The monklike life was beautiful and unadorned. The day had not yet come when the ashram would have a more direct relationship with the outside world. Since I felt I was receiving more than I was able to give—the answer to all my searches, finally conferring meaning on my life—I refused a salary and joined the community. Sri Aurobindo gave me the name of Sundarananda, which translates from Sanskrit into English as "One who delights in beauty," the suffix -ananda meaning "delight."

The saga of Sri Aurobindo is a colorful one. He was the father of Indian independence, one of the early activists. He had been placed in prison in Alipore, Bengal, for forcefully advocating India's complete separation from Britain. Some of his followers were sent to Europe to learn how to make bombs. After a year, Sri Aurobindo was released, but during this time in prison an inner voice had told him to leave activism behind and devote his life entirely to things spiritual. Once released, he went to Pondicherry, a French settlement in India, which had a better political atmosphere for him than did British-held areas of India. Sri Aurobindo was accompanied there by a few of his followers. Later, the leadership of the activist movement in India was assumed by Gandhi.

Sri Aurobindo was a man of prodigious personality. He had the scope and psychic sweep needed to encompass and enlighten the small, dark crannies of the human psyche and give a sense of profound hope to all. A highborn Bengali, *kshatriya* by caste, he had been educated in England at Cambridge and King's College and had mastered Latin and Greek long before learning Sanskrit. Mira, the "Mother" of the ashram, was a French citizen of Egyptian and Turkish parentage, and a woman of deep spiritual nature. She had met Aurobindo early in the century but had later gone to Japan, only to return permanently to Pondicherry in the early twenties. Theirs was a meeting of two extraordinary psychic spirits, the most perfect in our age.

The practical affairs of the ashram were in the Mother's care. Among other things, she was in direct charge of the current building project. All important spiritual problems and questions of a psychic nature, as well as less important matters, were sent to her in writing for decision and advice. Most of us kept notebooks containing the questions we sent her along with the answers we received. Some of these notebooks, which grew to be quite thick, were published in book form.

Five times a year, on the birthdays and anniversaries of the Mother and Sri Aurobindo, festivals known as the Darshan days were held. At these times, the two would receive their followers. Thousands of people would come from all over India and the world to receive their blessings. These pilgrims were from all walks of life, high and low, but they came without distinctions of caste or creed. Some traveled great distances on foot to attend the celebrations.

The weather was always perfect on the Darshan days. There was great anticipation those mornings. In our freshly washed *dhotis* or saris, we would wait patiently in the brilliant sunshine. When we were received on these occasions, we would present the Mother with a flower, usually a lotus, and place our heads on her lap to receive her blessing. She would give us each a flower in return. Next we would place our heads on Sri Aurobindo's lap and receive his blessing. A state of bliss and light would pervade our bodies. These were the most wonderful of days, the only times that the Mother and Sri Aurobindo would directly receive their followers.

The yoga of Sri Aurobindo was a great light along the shores of the Bay of Bengal. His followers all felt it. From all over the world they came, all devoted, sincere and searching; all surrendering to this divine concept. His spiritual presence, his teaching and example provided his followers with the basis for a unique existence.

The daily routine was extremely simple. There was no early morning saying of the offices, no dogma or ritual, no mantras, no ablutions under a waterfall, no counting of beads—only a complete freedom, as long as one's aspirations were sincere. The search for pure illumination took precedence over a spirituality-stifling dogma.

Meals were generally taken in the dining room, a handsome place with great, high ceilings and French doors, in a building constructed by the French colonials. Men and women ate separately. In the main dining room the *sadhaks*, or disciples, all sat facing the same way, eating off small traylike tables. Some ate with spoons, but most used just their hands, in the native fashion. It was fairly easy to be adept with the hands, especially as the food was extremely simple. For breakfast: hot milk, several slices of whole-wheat bread, and a banana. At noon: yogurt, a vegetable curry, bread and a banana. Evening: the same as at noon, but with rice.

There was no undue preoccupation with food and its enticements. The simple food tasted good, but we didn't have cravings for it. It was, of course, vegetarian, with no fish and not even so much as an egg. Meals were taken in complete silence—long rows of fine faces, most of the men with full beards and hair to their shoulders. They wore *dhoti*, the simple, white cloth wrapped around the lower part of the body, with another cloth thrown over one or both shoulders. Sometimes a saffron-colored *punjabi*, the long shirt, would also be seen.

Detail of louvered windows of Golconda. There were no sash windows. Instead, horizontal louvers (made of asbestos cement) permitted the maximum movement of air, important in the tropics.

The only fixed event of the day was the evening meditation, conducted by the Mother. At about seven o'clock, she would come part way down the staircase and stay there for about thirty minutes before returning upstairs. Not a word was said. Many people were present, sitting at random on the polished red lime floor of a room that opened onto the courtyard. Most sat in the cross-legged Indian fashion, but some in the lotus position, and a few on chairs. The object of the meditation was first to quiet and control the mind and then, in silence, to aspire to unity with the higher divine forces. I am sure that many achieved this. The silence would be intense. In season, the strong, sweet odor of oleander would float into the room. Even this small formality of the evening meditation was not obligatory, and many did not attend. At any given time there would be only about fifty of the group present, but this would be quite enough to fill the available space.

Once a month there was a semirite, call "Prosperity," at which disciples received their simple needs: a *dhoti*, a bar of soap and two rupees. Often a disciple would refuse the rupees. These gifts were presented directly by the Mother, so we felt doubly blessed.

My room at the ashram, in a building put up by the French colonials, was extremely simple. It held a cot with a thin pad and the ubiquitous mosquito netting, a desk and chair, and an extraordinarily comfortable lounging chair with a canvas seat and long arms, over which I could throw both legs. In addition, there was a rack for clothes and a small, netted food container. This remarkable item sat on four legs in a small receptacle of water. The purpose of this island-moat arrangement was to keep ants out of the food. Unfortunately, this did not always work because the ants devised a method of crossing the moat. They would run down the side of the container and ride on the surface tension of the water to the forbidden delights awaiting them.

My particular task was to design and help construct Golconda, a multistory dormitory for the disciples. This project was financed by Sir Akbar Hydari, then prime minister of the State of Hyderabad. The ashram spirit had helped his son, and the building was donated in gratitude. The name Golconda comes from that of an ancient Muslim city, at one time the capital of Hyderabad.

This was to be the major structure in the ashram. It was to be one of the first high-strength, reinforced concrete buildings in India. Since the design was to be completely open, the task was to build a straightforward structure that would solve the problems peculiar to this type of architecture in a tropical country. Since ventilation was important, large horizontal louvers were installed. These could be closed during the rains, which at times would come in horizontally. All of our architectural problems had to be solved within the spirit of Sri Aurobindo's teachings.

Golconda was something of a "do-it-yourself" project. I found myself not only the designer, but something of a general contractor. Besides providing the usual architectural drawings and details, and arranging for construction equipment from Japan, I designed the shuttering (formwork) and also the steel, which came from France.

Since Pondicherry didn't have a wharf, the steel was brought in from a freighter anchored in the Bay of Bengal on boats made of palm trunks lashed together. By the time they were unloaded on the beach, the steel rods had been bent so that they looked like a mass of spaghetti. From the shore they were dragged by bullock carts to the building site, where long lines of laborers hammered them straight.

Gradually our building rose. With the devotion and concentration of the ashram spirit, we were able to achieve a workmanship of extraordinary quality, extremely difficult in any other society. We tolerated only one-eighth inch off plumb in our verticals, and even at the butt joints there was little cement leakage.

There were many innovations such as the large, thin, bowed concrete roof tiles, approximately three and a half feet by five feet, and one inch thick. These were made at the building site with a double thickness, the lower being a concrete slab. The double thickness was important because of the almost continual intense heat of the tropics. The concrete work had almost a metallic ring when struck, rather than the usual thud.

The furniture which I designed tested our technical skills. The chairs, benches and tables were fashioned from great teak timber squares, sometimes two feet by two feet. These were sawn by hand with a pit saw, which requires two men—one on the timber and one in the pit. It would often take half a day to a whole day to cut one board. Our method of sharpening tools was as elementary as one could imagine. We simply spread hard, coarse sand on a board and began our rough sharpening. As we worked, the sand grew finer and finer, and our tools sharper and sharper. Furniture making at Pondicherry was an elemental baptism in the craft of woodworking.

Our undertaking, I felt, in some small way helped further the process of eliminating the caste system, still pervasive in India then as now, for we were all laborers and craftsmen together in a common cause. When a group of people concentrate with absolute sincerity and devotion on the common objective of a divine life, a creative spirit permeates the group's whole existence. There is a never a harsh word, never an egotistical argument. The group members are beyond pride. Of dualities there are none—no success or failure, no right or wrong, no just or unjust, not even good or evil. Everything becomes the handmaiden of a deeper search for consciousness; all fades into an awesome light. Movements are slow and measured, smiles heartwarming. There is none of the frenzy of the outside world. Conversations revolve around a simple, unique theme of search for divine union, for all are believers or near-believers.

One cannot construct a highly sophisticated building or run a large-scale ashram by being inactive, negative or pessimistic. Thus, there is an intensely active side to many aspects of Karma Yoga, the path of action. The ashram itself carried on various practical activities: a book printing and binding shop, a blacksmith and machine shop, a bakery and kitchen, a farm and a dairy. In addition, there were unskilled laborers performing the many ordinary tasks necessary to bind a community together.

There were evenings of great beauty, with music and dance, usually held in the

My room in the Sri Aurobindo Ashram. While engaged in building
Golconda, which was to be a residence for disciples, I lived in a
house built by the French when Pondicherry was a French colony.
The colonial houses were mostly of brick, with teak and palm rafters
supporting the flat roof, which consisted of bricks laid on edge at a
forty-five degree angle, an ingenious method of support. Covering
the brick was a very fine lime stucco.

quarters of Dilip Kumar Roy, who had a large room and terrace overlooking the Bay of
Bengal. Dilip was an accomplished instrumentalist, and he was often joined by
Sahana, who had one of the loveliest voices in all of Bengal. Sahana's room was on my
street, and her voice, raised in devotional songs, would often fill the still, soft air of the
evening. There was a great variety of instrumentalists and dancers. It was pure delight,
and the "*Atcha!*" of approval would ripple through the room.

The ashram was not an institutionalized religious organization, actually not a
religion at all. There was no structure or dogma of any kind. It was a collection of men
and women of all ages from all parts of the world, which was quite an unusual thing in
India at that time. Tamil was the language of the Pondicherry area, but Bengali was
also largely spoken at the ashram, since many *sadhaks* were Bengali. French and
English were the most common European languages. Whatever one's nationality, the
salutation in the ashram was made by placing the hands together as if in prayer;
sometimes one would touch these to the forehead and bow slightly, or say "*Namaste*,"
or "*Namaskar*." We were of many races, nationalities, creeds and religions, but all were
united in a driving quest for an ultimate truth. There was absolute equality and, in a
sense, freedom. There were no impositions on what one could do, as long as it was
done with the spirit of sincerity. To an extent, the lives in the outside world from
which we had come were recognized, and our quarters varied accordingly.

My helper Shiguru, his name a corruption of Shiva Guru, was a very devoted and
useful man. He was so intent on pleasing that, on the occasions when I had my meal
brought to my room, he would butter my bread on both sides.

About a year after I had come to the ashram, Margaret Wilson, the forty-year-old
daughter of Woodrow Wilson, arrived. Although she was scheduled to stay for only a
short visit, she fell more and more under the spell of the sincere environment.
Eventually she took the name Nishta and stayed at the ashram for the rest of her life.
Jotindra, a young engineer, and I spent many delightful evenings listening to Nishta's

The terrace off my room in Pondicherry. My room was at the left and the structure at the right was my bath, which had a faucet and non-flushing toilet. The trees stretching over the walls were papayas, which grew to the height shown and bore fruit in about a year. On this terrace, a friend who was quite an expert taught me Hatha Yoga.

stories of the White House and her travels with her father in Europe. She had one of the few refrigerators in the ashram, so we had the treat of a glass of cold water as we passed the time.

I had another very dear friend in Mridu, a roly-poly Bengali woman who was Sri Aurobindo's cook. Often she would call to me in Bengali, "Sundarananda-*ji, kamon achen* (come for some) *prasad*." The food that she spoke of was that returned to the kitchen by Sri Aurobindo, who ate sparingly; it was blessed by his having touched it. Her kitchen was just a small woklike pan placed on an alcohol burner that sat in the middle of the rough floor in her simple room; there was also a small closet covered with insect netting to store the food. She was a sweet woman with a wonderful disposition.

Even while Sri Aurobindo was alive, legends spread throughout India that he ate only banana flowers and floated ten feet above the ground. These were at least partially true, for flower fritters cooked in ghee, or clarified butter, were often a part of his diet, and he never left his quarters on the second floor of his house until he died.

Most of the problems that seem to bother the outside world were not problems at the ashram. It was an extremely "low energy," non-consumer-oriented society; there was no wasting of resources. People even went so far as to straighten out old nails so they could be reused. There was a certain amount of technology employed, but this was of an intermediate nature at the most. In a cenobitic society, problems such as the population explosion seemed far removed from us. Perhaps someday all the world will be able to move in this fashion.

After two years, the time came for me to decide whether to stay on for life at the ashram or return to the outside world. The way of life in this haven was perhaps as close to heaven on earth as is possible. As with all major questions, the Mother had the final say as to what my future was to be. When I finally decided that I wanted to leave, I asked her for permission. She wrote her answer in the center of a sheet of paper: "yes," in letters so small that I could barely read them.

In a sense, I participated in life at the Sri Aurobindo Ashram during its golden age, when all of the disciples were in close touch with both the Mother and Sri Aurobindo. It was, in a way, an ideal existence on earth, without a trace of rancor or harsh words, arguments, egotism, but with all in concert in search of a divine consciousness.

But outside the ashram there was difficulty in the air. Japan had already invaded China by 1939, and a larger war seemed imminent.

It became for me a question of living a life of great beauty in isolation, or of going out again into the world. I think there was within me an instinctive resistance to withdrawing from life as I'd known it. I concluded I would have to fight for truth outside the ashram's protective environment. It was a most difficult decision.

Thompson-Nealy House, dating to the Revolutionary period, stands about a mile down the road from the workshop. Seemingly built to last forever, houses like these had walls of local fieldstone from twenty inches to two feet thick. They were heated by great "walk-in" fireplaces. Whole logs were dragged in by horse; this is why the design calls for doors on opposite sides of the room—so the horse could be led through one and out the other.

5

New Hope

When I left India in 1939, international tension was already building. I finally made it back to Tokyo on a Japanese refugee ship from Shanghai to Nagasaki. It was in Tokyo that Marion, my wife-to-be, and I met at the apartment of a mutual friend. Jokingly, I showed her a photograph taken in India of me wearing a turban. When prospective marriage couples are first introduced in Japan, it is the custom to exchange photographs, and I was performing a variation on this. Later, when I called her, she had difficulty remembering who I was. Despite this inauspicious beginning the relationship developed, and soon afterward we were engaged.

I stayed on in Tokyo for six months helping Kunio, a friend with whom I had worked in the Antonin Raymond architectural office, with a project and then left for the United States. Marion joined me in Seattle, where we were married in 1941.

After having spent seven years in Asia, with its tradition of fine craftsmanship, I felt I should take a survey trip from Seattle to California to see firsthand what was considered the best of modern American architecture. The work of Frank Lloyd Wright was especially disappointing to me, although the forms used were interesting and the results were causing a certain excitement in the architectural world. I found the structure and the bones of the building somehow inadequate, however, and the workmanship shoddy. I felt that I must find a new vocation, something that I could coordinate from beginning to end. I decided to follow woodworking as my life's work.

Then Pearl Harbor broke, and all of us of Japanese descent were put in concentration camps. My wife and I and our newly born daughter were sent to a camp in Idaho. This I felt at the time was a stupid, insensitive act, one by which my country could only hurt itself. It was a policy of unthinking racism. Even Eskimos with only a small percentage of Japanese blood were sent to the Western desert to die.

Luckily, in Idaho I met a fine Japanese carpenter trained in Japan along traditional lines, and we joined forces. He had the discipline resulting from long years of experience in which each step was learned with consummate perfection. I was his designer, but also his apprentice. We worked well together, scrounging in scrap woodpiles for bits of lumber. Sometimes we received permission to go out into the desert of central Idaho to find bits of bitterbrush, a brave shrub of great character which grows only a few feet in a hundred years. I learned a great deal from this man, through his hundreds of small acts of perfection. He helped me with many of the basic woodworking skills—for instance the correct sharpening of a chisel. We used a traditional Japanese waterstone, which if handled well can produce the finest of edges. If used improperly, the expensive stone can be ruined by gouging it out or putting a "belly" on it. He also taught me to sharpen a Japanese handsaw with its very deep gullet. The Japanese saw not only has saw teeth, but below each tooth, a further deep recess which takes away the sawdust without clogging. Working with him was a rewarding experience and one that I greatly appreciated.

Later, it was announced that if we were willing to move from the West Coast area, we could leave the camp. Fortunately, Antonin Raymond, for whom I had worked in Tokyo, owned a farm in Pennsylvania. He invited my family to join him there. I was to work on his farm.

This was our start in New Hope.

After a year of doing general farm work, it was quite clear to me that chickens and I were not compatible. Their delight in flying into the trees only meant that I would have to climb after them. We decided to start out on our own. It was midwinter. We rented a small house with a two-car garage. The three walls of this outbuilding were constructed of boards and battens—but without the battens. The fourth side was open. This became my first woodworking shop in Bucks County. We lived and worked in the small house with its gradually improved workshop for three years. The house had a wood-coal stove and well-pump in the kitchen; the only other heat was provided by a stove in another room. Frost would form on the inside walls, but we survived. Our earnings were meager.

At first I worked only with hand tools, building chairs, tables and benches. Gradually, I added a few machines. We received some help in the beginning from an organization just starting in the field of modern interior furnishings, which hired me to do design work. The income from this helped me to pioneer a craft concept in a world that was growing accustomed to mass-produced goods. I was perhaps one of the first of the woodworkers of the early forties, a time when craftsmanship was not regarded as an important concept.

My daughter was now about three years old. When the weather was good, she would play on my workbench and drive long rows of nails into a soft board.

Through a great act of generosity, a landowner whom we hardly knew offered us three acres of land to be worked off on barter, exchanging construction work for the deed. This was true American goodness of heart. With no collateral whatsoever, he offered us the title to our property. His construction plans changed, so we finished paying for the land in money.

To settle on a piece of virgin land was for me the culmination of a long quest, beginning at the timberline of the Pacific Northwest and passing through that feeling of decay in Paris during the early thirties, the rich warmth of spirit in my ancestral home near Tokyo, and the search for "something else" in Pondicherry. Our land in Bucks County surrounded by rolling hills, hardwood forests, and farms interspersed with fine stone houses built by the English Quakers have become the core of our existence.

Our property enabled us to test my concepts of decentralization, intermediate technology and living off the land. Like the early American pioneers, we would exist close to the soil and trees. Our purpose as a family was to integrate work and life, first with Marion and daughter Mira, and later also with Kevin, my son. For a time, too, my wife's father lived with us. He was most kind and gave us a sum of money for Mira's education, which we borrowed and later returned. She finally received a good education at Harvard University and Tokyo's Waseda University.

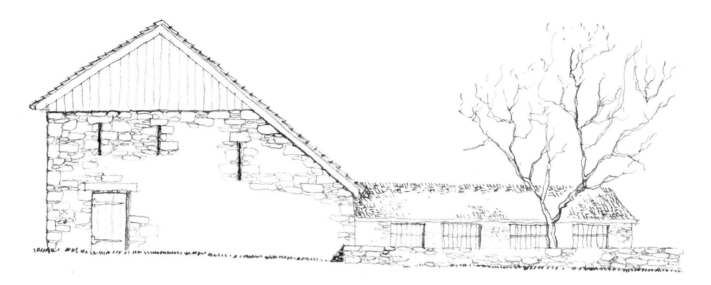

The barn behind the Thompson-Nealy House is a fine example of sturdy Bucks County construction. Barns like this one, some built in the eighteenth century, represent early American architecture at its best. The stonework of the English Quakers was outstanding, the walls still straight and true, free of cracks, after roughly three centuries. The roof rafters of hemlock were often tapered. The timbers of oak, chestnut and even at times of walnut, display the same joinery as seen in furniture.

Like the farmer who first builds his barn, we built our workshop first. Andy, a teenager who had great faith in my future, helped me build it—a simple structure of cement block and wood framing. A part of it still remains.

I started work commuting from our rented house, a distance of about three miles. During the winters, snow often blocked the roads, which were not plowed as they are now. I would walk both ways in snows almost waist deep. When conditions permitted, I went back and forth in my small jalopy.

The following spring I started building a house for my family. Through a curious circumstance we acquired a tent to live in during the early phase of our home-building. A young helper who lived across the road was having trouble with his wife and asked if he could pitch a tent on our property. I agreed. When it was in place he made up with his wife, and with his permission we moved into his tent. It worked out quite well, and although the only utility we had was electricity in the workshop, we survived.

At no time did we have more than fifty dollars in cash, but by scrounging materials, gathering stones off the property, digging foundation by hand, and working evenings and weekends, I was able to build a rough structure by Thanksgiving. At one point we gave a party for friends to help me dig a pit for the septic tank. Our first winter in the house was bitterly cold, and the faucet froze in the kitchen.

We built, quite literally, on the principle of laying stone upon stone. We had considerable stone on our land, and it was simply a question of hauling it by wheelbarrow to the building site.

There is a wonderful feeling to be had in erecting a stone wall. There is a sense of order and permanence. A good wall will last for generations and even millennia. We had a small automobile, a coupe with the back trunk cover torn out for hauling. At

I call our reception house a *sansō*, or "mountain villa," in Japanese. I built it in the finest manner possible and worked entirely with materials cast off from my workshop. Castoff though the building materials were, they were quite unique since the rich and rare woods that I normally use are not generally obtainable. The floor, for example, is made of red birch and walnut boards with extraordinary figuring. Most of the outside construction was done with a single dead elm. This elm, about five feet in diameter, could not be lifted by one huge forklift, but required two. The elm had been cut into two-and-a-half-inch-thick boards. Once cut, there seemed to be no client demand since the wood was light in color and not unusually grained. So, we happily used it in the reception house.

every opportunity we would pick up stones along the road after the spring thaw, or from the creek beds of friends. Towards the completion we did buy a small quantity of stones. Thirty years later we are still enjoying our small house.

With the assistance of a helper, we did all of the electrical work and plumbing in addition to the general construction. The first section of the house was built for $3,500, but we later added on to it when our son was born. The addition included another bedroom, a remodeled bath, and a new heating system. By the time the house was finished, it was paid for. There was no thought of a mortgage or loans.

Contrary to the usual current living patterns, we act as a producing family, and in a broader sense a community of workers. Now we have grandchildren and hope that they will join us. Andy, my young, imaginative friend, has passed away, but our group is devoted to producing, with concentration and devotion, the finest objects from a splendid collection of woods from all over the world.

For over thirty years we have worked the land, clearing large sections of heavy undergrowth, at first by hand and later with machines. There were times when my small family and I dug out matted roots by hand, fifty square feet at a time, to prepare a lawn. As our affairs improved, we added buildings when needed. We even built, by whimsy, an arts building inspired by a biomorphic stone, nestled in the woods, so alive-looking that we dug around it, making a pond. The building was roofed with plywood, a "warped shell" of an experimental nature, in the form of a hyperbolic paraboloid.

To satisfy my original interest in architecture, I have designed and built six roofs of different warped forms on our property: three hyperbolic paraboloids, and three conoidal forms of different materials and shapes.

Our approach is to realize a synthesis between the hand and the machine working as a small unit. It is a return to the business methods of the early American craftsman

who made chairs, tables and cabinets, and put them in carts for transporting and selling directly to the customers who wanted them.

There is no need for mass marketing, since our production is small and enough people are interested in buying. The usual intermediate costs can be put into finer quality materials and workmanship. This craft-rooted business, operated on a basis somewhat analogous to the rules of work of St. Benedict, now ships from our acres in New Hope to many parts of the world, and has also working relationships with producing units in Takamatsu, Japan and Ahmedabad, India.

Over the years our three-acre plot has grown and grown. Our integrated environment has expanded to include family home and workshop facilities, showrooms for furniture and lumber samples, storage space for raw lumber, and a small Japanese-style "mountain villa" with a small room for the tea ceremony. Meanwhile, we have created a congenial atmosphere for a combined family and business life which even takes into account our grandchildren.

Even in a "money" system our integrated approach seems to make sense. For construction we used, as much as possible, locally cut timber, quite green but inexpensive. Also, other materials such as local fieldstone, which at that time required only the labor of placing it. My wife and daughter often helped me arrange and select the stones.

The milling was done in my workshop with mostly locally sawn hardwoods used for flooring, paneling, windows, doors and special timberwork, including several forty-foot long beams tapering from six inches by fourteen inches to six inches by six. Controlling every step in the process has been a great adventure. In the beginning I did most of the work by myself, later with considerable outside help, but always under my supervision.

When we first came to New Hope, it was still a sleepy, little, picturesque town,

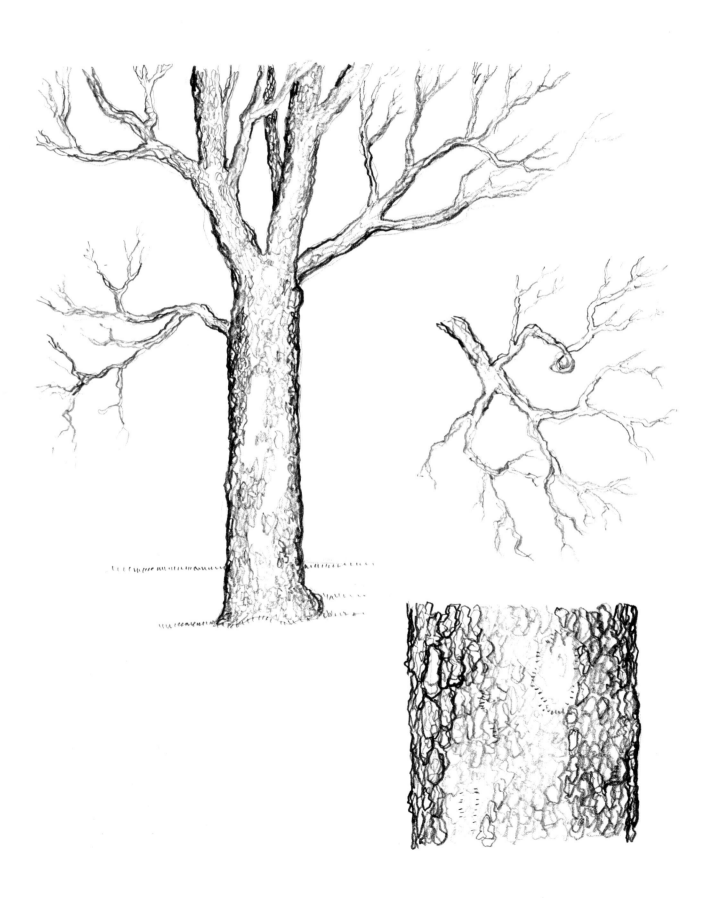

An American black walnut growing in Bucks County. About three-and-a-half feet in diameter. Magnificent specimens grow over a large part of the United States and produce a fine and esteemed lumber for furniture. Related to the European and Asiatic walnuts, sometimes called the gray walnut, this species is propagated largely by squirrels that hide nuts for the winter and cannot keep track of them.

The trees that are best for furniture usually come from a woods and have long, straight trunks, sometimes stretching thirty feet from the base to the first branch. Reaching for the sun, these trees drop their lower branches quickly. The bark of the walnut tree is scaly, but this characteristic varies from tree to tree. Occasionally a "cat face" is seen on the surface of the trunk, a scar from an injury. The small branches of this tree are relatively thick and rich with heavy buds.

Since the profile and texture of the branching is unique, a walnut tree can be spotted a half mile or more away and with field glasses from three miles away. Professional lumber spotters can locate them from helicopters and small planes.

Because of overcutting, this precious species has become quite scarce. The main trunk is cut into a single log and, destined for sliced veneer, can command an extraordinary price today. But the lumber most interesting to me is the next log, with the crotch attached, because here is where unusual figuring is to be found.

enjoyed and appreciated by artists and writers. It is still something of that, but tourists and housing developments are changing its character. New Hope has been our redoubt, our last stand against mediocrity in our system. It was nice to go it alone, to forge a life in the wilderness, to fight against commercialism and bigness.

By good fortune, or perhaps by some sort of divine guidance, this area has proven ideal. It is roughly in the middle of the eastern megalopolis, between Boston and Washington. Many areas are still quite wild, including our own and nearby woods, through which it is possible to walk a mile surrounded by big trees without seeing a house. Deer graze in open areas and make trails through the forest.

We have managed to bypass the whole money system, having never had a mortgage and practically nothing in the way of loans, perhaps like the early English Quakers who built so splendidly on this land.

It seems to work.

PART TWO

The Tree

PITH CENTER

The bitterbrush, similar in general appearance to the sagebrush but very slow-growing, is found in the Idaho Desert and other harsh Western environments. The bush shown here is about two hundred and fifty years old; it is four inches wide at the base and two and a half feet high.

6

The Pith Center

Ⓜy kinship with the tree dates from the day I first stood among the great forest giants in the rain forest of Washington's Ho River valley. Later, in Japan, my meeting with the twelve-hundred-year-old *keyaki,* an oriental elm, in a temple garden in Takamatsu—with only one living branch left—heightened my sense of wonder and spurred me in my search for the origin of the noble tree.

Trees spring from tiny seedlings only two hands tall. From such small beginnings, great trees can develop. Consider the Yaku *sugi* which may attain a diameter of forty feet and an age of five thousand years. The pith may still be there, although often it has rotted away. Should the center still remain, it still has the same diameter and height that it had in the beginning of its life. It experiences an existence unknown in the animal world. The seedling of this ancient tree germinated many millennia ago during the age of the Vedic spiritual poets. The seedling then started the process of life and growth which continues to this day. It is hard to perceive the destiny of the genes in this small bit of life. There must have been some relationship with a greater spirit.

The pith could easily have been reduced to dust during this long period of life, since the core of a tree, botanically dead, has a tendency to deteriorate. But the tree lives on, producing an infinity of new cells year after year.

Over the millennia the continuous living juices have risen on the inner side of the cambium layer, the xylem, to the peak of its leafing, returning on the outer side of the cambium, the phloem, with its sugars to produce the body, the structure of the tree.

The cambium layer houses the tree's living tissue. Each cell carries on its task of transporting vital fluids until new growth takes over its duties. The cell passes into the core, the heartwood. The staggering total of fluids rising and falling in the trees around the world constitutes a veritable Niagara.

The roots of a tree, too, have vital functions to perform. They anchor the tree. They search for water, without which the tree cannot survive. In dry areas, roots range far and wide, hunting water. Many hardy trees like the oak have a main root, called a

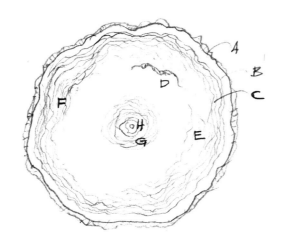

A - BARK

B - CAMBIUM LAYER

C HEART WOOD BEGINS

D WIND SHAKE
(year of the storms)

E WET YEARS
(open fast growth)

F DRY YEARS
(tight slow growth)

G EARLY FAST GROWTH

H. PITH

This cross section of a tree shows how much trees develop around the pith. Each concentric layer of wood indicates a year's growth in temperate climates. Trees of the tropics don't always have such annual rings, but where they do appear they represent extreme contrasts between wet and dry.

The older, inactive, central wood of a tree, called the heartwood, is usually darker and harder than the newer growth, the light, sometimes even white, sapwood that lies just inside the cambium layer of a tree.

taproot, which plunges deep into the earth. Others like the beeches and willows have instead many smaller roots which reach in all directions, fairly close to the surface.

In the leaves of a tree, that marvel called photosynthesis takes place. Water and minerals from the soil, carbon dioxide from the air and light from the sun combine in mysterious ways to produce the very substance of a tree's life. Without this miraculous process there would be no flora, no fauna, no man.

In each growing season in temperate zones, a tree adds on a layer of wood—a growth ring. If you examine the cross section of a tree trunk, you will see a number of these rings circling the pith. These annual rings vary in width, reflecting changes in rainfall and climatic conditions. In tropical areas, where growth is continuous, trees sometimes don't form discernible rings.

The record of all that the average tree has witnessed and endured is written in its growth rings. They tell by their number how old the tree is. They help to pinpoint when droughts, floods, fire and insects ravaged the land and when life-giving rain fell in abundance. During difficult growth periods, the rings of some trees are so narrow and close together that it is almost impossible to count them.

The cells in the pith center do not grow appreciably. Even after the formidable spread around the center, the center itself has not become taller. With the patience of God, the cells have developed, billions of them, on all sides of the pith center, producing the body of the tree.

If this seemingly eternal life, as eternal as any life can be, were ultimately to drop, it should be the hand of man which gives the tree a new existence, shaping its body for use and beauty. The ultimate form the trees may assume is unknown. Bit by bit, as the sculptor creates, the revelation continues.

If, by the greed or needs of man the tree is felled, decay sets in, and the pith rots away. But there remains an urge to live. A circle of offspring can grow from the

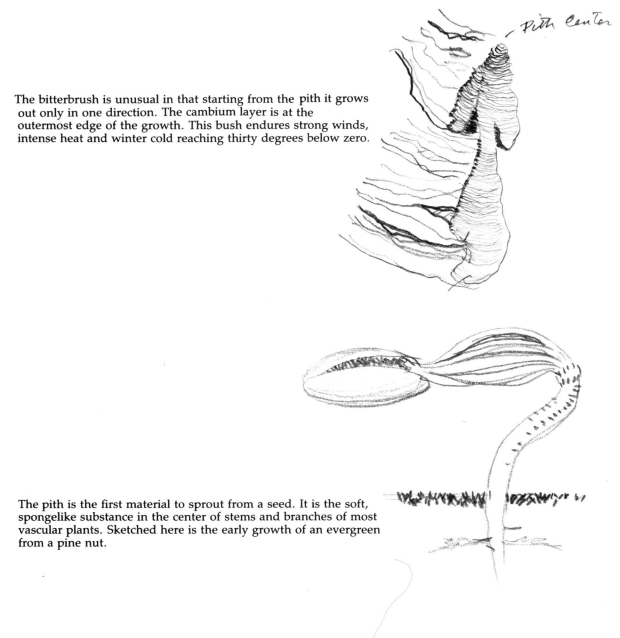

The bitterbrush is unusual in that starting from the pith it grows out only in one direction. The cambium layer is at the outermost edge of the growth. This bush endures strong winds, intense heat and winter cold reaching thirty degrees below zero.

The pith is the first material to sprout from a seed. It is the soft, spongelike substance in the center of stems and branches of most vascular plants. Sketched here is the early growth of an evergreen from a pine nut.

cambium layer, forming what are sometimes called "crown trees." The pith is gone, but a new generation springs up in its place.

In trees that resist decay, large sections can die, leaving small areas still living, hanging on to life. The dead parts of trees like the bristlecone pine can become weather-beaten over centuries of harsh climate. The desert bitterbrush can grow out horizontally from the center, dying as it grows, while the cambium layer, a half circle, remains the only living tissue. This small, brave bush can grow this way for hundreds of years. The manzanita and the sagebrush grow in a similar way. This is a type of life adapted to the harshness of the western desert where climate ranges from extreme cold to great heat with very little rainfall.

We are left in awe by the nobility of a tree, its eternal patience, its suffering caused by man and sometimes nature, its witness to thousands of years of earth's history, its creations of fabulous beauty. It does nothing but good, with its prodigious ability to serve, it gives off its bounty of oxygen while absorbing gases harmful to other living things. The tree and its pith live on. Its fruits feed us. Its branches shade and protect us. And, finally, when time and weather bring it down, its body offers timber for our houses and boards for our furniture. The tree lives on.

The Yaku *sugi*. This noble tree has grown for millennia on Yaku Island, off the south coast of Japan's southernmost major island, Kyushu.

7

The Yaku Sugi and Other Trees

On the mountainous island of Yaku, off the coast of Kyushu, grow old *sugi* trees, or cedars, that seem eternal. They are among the grandest gifts of nature, and have spanned perhaps the whole history of civilized man.

They are great trees, their bodies the cathedral of all time. Specimens stand over many millennia, the wood resistant to decay, the nemesis of most trees.

There are Yaku *sugis* that are over forty feet in diameter at the base, their gnarled trunks reaching a hundred and thirty feet into the air. While not as tall as the California sequoia, they are larger in diameter. It is the diameter that indicates their age. These cedars, like most old evergreens, rise from a single stalk, but branch at random. Some are said to be over five thousand years old. Others were cut down hundreds of years ago for timber. Out of their stumps, which rise about thirty feet above the ground, have grown new trees which are the crown trees. The center of the stump has rotted out, leaving a huge cavity, large enough to hold a small house. How the original tree was cut without modern equipment is a mystery.

Some Yaku *sugis* less than a thousand years old are not honored with the title, but must humbly accept the name of *ko sugi*, or "small cedar." The cedars of Yaku normally produce annual rings about 1/32-inch wide, many times the growth of the bristlecone pines of California, which may grow only a few inches in a thousand years.

It is strange that on this small, typhoon-swept island, where the natives speak of thirty-five days of rainfall a month, there should grow one of the oldest residents on earth. Actually, there are over four hundred inches of rainfall per year, or almost double the rainfall of the Ho River rain forest in the state of Washington. As with people, adversities in nature often produce great character. Yaku is located in the Ginza belt of typhoons, making life there hazardous for flora and fauna as well as people. While heavy rainfall is favorable to the growth of cedars, the high winds of Yaku would be fatal to the trees, if it were not for their root structure with a great

Looking heavenward through the center cavity of a Yaku *sugi* felled centuries ago. The outline of a figure in the lower right indicates the scale. Along the rim grow crown trees.

spread at ground level. Without that support the wind would topple the Yaku cedars, as it does so often most giants of the forest. Nature is a great engineer.

The island of Yaku is quite small, about seventy miles in circumference. It consists of numerous peaks, the highest rising 6,300 feet. Because of its terrain, the island has three climatic zones: subtropic, temperate and fairly cold. These cedars grow in the temperate zone. How this tree has managed to exist for so long in this unfriendly land—fighting typhoons that can throw a twenty-thousand-ton ship onto the beach—remains a mystery.

It is possible these very trials that have produced the "grape" burls, fantastic patterns, striations following the growth rings, an esteemed quality of grain. All of these characteristics are evident in the Yaku *sugis* along with the venerable quality of having lived long and witnessed much. The wood and the tree are now classified as national treasures, guarded closely by government control, difficult to buy and extremely expensive.

The Yaku *sugi* is awesome indeed, as perhaps every piece of wood is awesome, for it contains the majesty of all the divine forces that exist on the plane of nature's own objects. The Japanese have a reverence for this tree, for its eternal quality, for the wood itself, for its karma. Its wood was used in the new palace in Tokyo.

The wood is quite distinctive and can be recognized at once. The grain is more pronounced than in most cedars. One can muse on what became of the wood cut from the Yaku cedars centuries ago. Perhaps precious boards cut from it by hand still grace temples or shrines in parts of Japan, especially on the island of Yaku, or in Kyushu.

The Yaku cedars have spent their lifetime witnessing the long and awesome march of generation after generation of the human race, the march of nation after nation. They have seen cultures, civilizations, one after another rise and fall. By human inspiration, or by sheer egotism, great cities were constructed, finally to return to dust. Some are no longer remembered even as names. Pataliputra flowered, the Chou

Tule cypress. The figure in the outline shows the enormous scale of
"El Tule," a Mexican swamp cypress, perhaps the largest in girth of
all the great trees. The oldest may never be definitively known. This
tree is also known as *sabino* or *arhue huete*.

became great; and Sanskrit, the greatest of all human tongues, recorded the Vedas, the
Upanishads and the Bhagavad Gita.

Conquerors conquered, vast armies trudged across endless lands with the goal of
domination. Men in unbelievable numbers died to impose their egos, while masses of
humanity perished to defend themselves. Heroic monuments were built commemorating these events. Architecture, art, music and poetry flourished. Epic literature was
written to describe these happenings. In the end, it all dies. Some thoughts, ideas and
inspirations from earlier cultures are still with us, but there are few continuous threads
throughout the history of man.

The cedar of Yaku stands, and man's petty turmoils wash about its feet.
Throughout the millennia its life juices have flowed and will continue to flow, while
our civilization goes to dust.

In other parts of the world there are similar trees which have witnessed these
movements of history. In Taiwan there is a specimen five or six thousand years old,
which is similar to the Yaku cedar. The red-barked cedar of the Ussuri Taiga in Siberia
is said to be about the same age. "El Tule," also called "El Gigante," in Oaxaca, which
inspired the building of the church of Santa Maria del Tule, is also about that age and
may possibly be the largest in diameter. How the tule cypress, a tree that requires
considerable rainfall, took root and survived in the dry climate of that area of Mexico is
one of nature's wonders. Perhaps its roots have reached some underground wellspring. The life span of the bristlecone pine of the High Sierras in the Inyo National
Forest is on a par with the others. It, too, lives in a hostile environment: its rate of
growth over the centuries has been minute. It survives near the timberline where most
leafy plant life ends and the snows begin.

The baobabs stand apart. Although they are huge, sometimes reaching almost a
hundred feet in girth, their ages are obscure, for they do not have annual rings like
most trees which grow in temperate climates. What sometimes pass for annual rings in

Sugi, or Japanese cedar, or cryptomeria. Long, straight, taut trunks. Very resistant to rot and decay. Temples and shrines, some comparable in scale to the European cathedrals, often had cryptomeria pillars which were dressed to perfect cylinders. Since the *sugi* grows in tight stands, each tree shares nourishment with its neighbors.

I am reminded of a great *keyaki,* or oriental elm, which I saw in a temple garden outside Takamatsu City, the capital of Kagawa Prefecture. It measured about ten feet in diameter. On it hung a plaque saying that the tree was twelve hundred years old. My friends and I were interested in buying the tree when the proper moment came, but, unfortunately, the tree was felled and went to somebody in Osaka. I feel sure its full potential, its resurrection as wooden objects useful and beautiful to man, was never realized.

There is great excitement in opening a great tree, especially when the burls and the intense figuring of the log converge as they meet the root system. The roots themselves are usually much richer in graining than the trunk, and if one has the patience to dig out the dirt and rocks from the roots, the effort is usually well rewarded.

Sometimes old trees are almost a total loss, however, making one feel that younger, more vigorous trees offer better possibilities for producing extraordinary lumber. These are chances one takes in buying logs. Over the years of buying, though, one gains astuteness in judgment, and good wood from older trees far surpasses losses from them.

The *hinoki*, or Japanese cypress. This particular specimen grew in the open, hence the heavy branching and short butt. Usually, the *hinoki* grows in woods where it develops a long, cylindrical trunk with very little taper. The wood is highly esteemed in construction and for interiors. It works well and polishes to a high sheen if dressed with a sharp plane. It is highly resistant to decay. For this reason, it is used in the construction of the Ise Grand Shrine, the primary place of Shinto worship in all Japan. The *hinoki* is usually considered the source of the best cypress wood. The Taiwan cypress is second and the American cypress, third.

A redwood tree. The sequoia and the redwood are related to each other, but are, strictly speaking, entirely different species. The redwood grows along the coast of California while the sequoia is an upland tree that grows on the western slopes of the Sierra Nevada range, also in California. Another relative, the metasequoia, once thought to be extinct, has been discovered in the interior of China. Roots from these trees, left from logging operations over a century ago, can be dug out today; they produce extraordinary slabs of wood with spectacular figuring and great interest.

Baobab

the baobab are hard growths caused by unusual weather conditions or severe storms. The wood of the tree is quite pulpy. In some of the trees, room-sized openings, large enough to sleep a number of men, have been carved out. One specimen is said to be over four thousand years old. The rate of growth varies and the tree can actually reduce in girth during periods of drought. The wood, which is as much as 60 or 70 percent moisture, can be sucked like a cactus to quench a thirst. The trunk is extraordinarily large in relation to the limbs, making it appear that the tree has been turned upside down so that its roots stick up into the air. Although a native of Africa, it has been known to grow in Australia, India and England.

Trees contribute much to the development of areas where they grow. Lumber from the cedars of Lebanon undoubtedly helped to shape the ancient cities of the Middle East. The Japanese cedar, *sugi*, and the Japanese cypress, *hinoki*, supplied beauty and needed strength to the great wooden temples and shrines of Japan, where round columns, two to three feet in diameter and great in length, were used to support these magnificent Japanese structures. The evergreens of the American West Coast helped make possible the rapid growth of that area and of America as a whole.

All of these trees started life somewhere near the dawn of civilized man. It matters not which is the oldest or the largest. The wonder is in their being.

The bristlecone pine, claimed by some to be the oldest living tree on
earth. It is certainly one of the slowest growing. With many examples
of this species, large sections of the tree die while a lesser part with
its cambium layer, a mere fragment really, continues to live. This is a
remarkable example of nature's tenacious fortitude. The bristlecone
pine grows principally at an altitude ranging from seven to ten
thousand feet.

In America called "oak burl" and in England called "burry oak," this species should be cut when the last of its life juices are ebbing, when its only future is decay. The wood is usually burled, but the extent varies from tree to tree. Sawing this "treasure" calls for the precision of a diamond cutter. We have sawn boards from these burls as large as five feet in width by twelve feet in length. Each of these oak burls can occur only once, in a never-to-be-repeated design. The burry oak's root structure can be every bit as spectacular as what is above ground.

The great Douglas fir which covers a large part of the western slopes of the United States is not a fir at all, but a false hemlock. Its fibers are long, straight and strong. Its heavy, scaly bark is a natural protection against forest fires. This venerable tree has been much used and has contributed greatly to the development of American civilization, just as the *hinoki* did in Japan, and the Lebanon cedar did in the Near East.

91

This venerable English oak in Sherwood Forest, Nottinghamshire, England, is at least four hundred years old and has a diameter of about ten feet. This oak seems to have started life in the open. A forest tree has a longer butt since, when young, it must stretch for sunlight. Many nations designate trees like this one as special natural monuments, but perhaps they should go further and call them "National Living Treasures." These treasures should be cut with reverence when their life span has been fulfilled. Their aged beauty and great character must be preserved in objects built of their wood to provide a record of their heritage and history.

8
Timber

When trees mature, it is fair and moral that they are cut for man's use, as they would soon decay and return to the earth. Trees have a yearning to live again, perhaps to provide the beauty, strength and utility to serve man, even to become an object of great artistic worth.

Each tree, every part of each tree, has only one perfect use. The long, taut grains of the true cypress, so well adapted to the making of elegant thin grilles, the joyous dance of the figuring in certain species, the richness of graining where two large branches reach out–these can all be released and fulfilled in a worthy object for man's use.

How to acquire logs and what to do with them calls for creative skill. There is so much that is wasted and unrealized. Consider the great timbers, some ten feet in diameter, piled across slopes and gulleys to make railroad beds in the early days of this country. Or the magnificent zebrawood log, from which boards fully four feet wide and eight feet long could be cut, but which instead is cut into pieces three-eighths inch thick, six inches wide! What a waste of a majestic opportunity! This is the psychology of match-stick manufacture. And the tragedy of once-in-a-lifetime timbers cut into veneers so thin the light can shine through. What a waste, simply for money!

Logs from all over the world make their way to my storehouse. Some are of great value, some quite inexpensive but with interesting possibilities. There is need always to select and to search, even to look underground where the most fantastic grains can often be found.

Each species of tree has its own characteristics. Extremely long fibers and resistance to rot are characteristics of the cedar, the cypress, and, in a way, the spruces and hemlocks, the firs, and the other evergreen trees. These characteristics are important where tautness and resistance to weather are necessary. The woods from these trees often have beautiful, very straight graining and are useful in architecture for grilles like the starburst *asa-no-ha*, and even musical instruments. One of the finest

Deciding how to cut this great walnut log—with a crotch at one
end—about nine feet long and four feet in diameter (note the scale)—
was quite a challenge. Seven limbs had been cut from it and the
general configuration, contour and characteristics gave promise of
spectacular, "once-in-a-lifetime" graining.

The judgments in sawing must be swift and exact. Thickness,
trimming and direction of the cut are vital considerations that
ultimately determine whether you produce magnificent lumber or
firewood.

perhaps is the Japanese cypress, and not far behind are the Port Orford cedar and the
Alaska cedar, neither of which, incidentally, is a true cedar at all, but a cypress.

The European walnut, whether from Kashmir, the area around the Caspian Sea,
southern Russia, northern Iran or eastern Turkey, or from western Europe, is among
the finest of furniture woods, and one I use with frequency. American walnut, a
different species, is also greatly admired, especially by Europeans at this time.

Cherry and other fruitwoods produce material of great quality. Black persimmon,
often considered the finest of Japanese woods, is now extremely rare.

All woods have graining—patterns created by the trunk fibers. However, the grain
of many woods, pine and maple for instance, is regular and comparatively uninteresting, while that of walnut, cherry and other fruitwoods is intricate and exciting.

Quite often the finest of grains exist underground in the root structure of many
fine trees that are condemned to rot. The roots are difficult to pull out, and often are
deeply imbedded with stones which can be the nemesis of a sawyer. Some roots
preserve their great beauty even if left underground for a hundred years, for example,
those of the California redwood.

Burls, growths on the trunks of many trees, in the shape of flattened hemispheres,
are also very much esteemed. Sometimes they grow in a single clump, but at other
times they may cover most of a tree. They do not seem to be particularly harmful to the
health of the tree, and seem to have a joy and exuberance that greatly enhances the
tree's charm.

The sawing of logs is of prime importance. Each cut requires judgments and
decisions on what the log should become. As in cutting a diamond, the judgments
must be precise and exact concerning thickness and direction of cut, especially through
"figures," the complicated designs resulting from the tree's grain. If a figure is cut
properly, the beauty locked in the tree will gradually emerge. If cut improperly, most is
lost. Gradations in color, owing to the chemical composition of the soil in which a tree

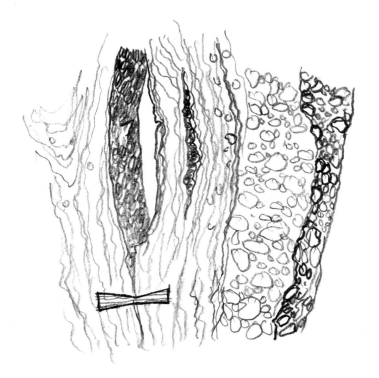

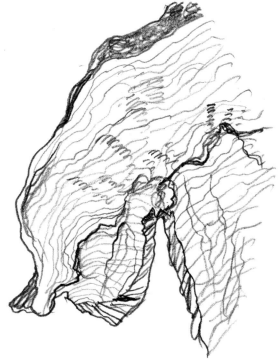

Butterfly-shaped inlay of rosewood reinforces the area below an opening, most likely a "wind-shake" in highly figured English walnut. The separated fibers have weathered as they heal.

Some of the finest, most interesting grains are found underground, in the massive roots of trees. Here the richness of the soil seems to have been absorbed. This sketch shows a detail of an English walnut root end that has been sawed into a slab; I used it for an end table.

grows, as well as the sharp contrast between dark heartwood and light sapwood, will add their charm.

There is drama in the opening of a log–to uncover for the first time the beauty in the bole, or trunk, of a tree hidden for centuries, waiting to be given this second life. There are fine surprises, but also disappointments.

A great walnut, about five and a half feet in diameter, was once given to me. It seemed to have great character. A small limb pocket was filled with concrete at the top but neither a tree expert nor I imagined that the whole center had rotted out and was filled with concrete! There was only about a foot and a half of wood around the circumference. The tree had not fallen because it was a concrete column! We were finally able, with great effort, to take it down. The wood was interesting, but like many aged logs it had a tendency to be soft and weak.

I recall another instance when two logs were on the platform ready for sawing. They were English walnut. At first, there was only a suspicion that we were in the presence of a great natural wonder. The saw was a large, commercial band saw. The logs were close to six feet in diameter. They were too large! The only recourse was to hack off protrusions and excess width with a chain saw and an ax. It was devastating to see this magnificent wood handled in such a fashion, but there was no other way. Even before the log was opened up, the experienced eye could see the incredibly lovely grain, figuring and color where a bit of bark had been knocked off. Here indeed was precious timber.

The revelation in the opening of the log with the first cut or two was amazing. Sensitivity, instinct and long experience came to the fore at this point. The graining and the quality of the slabs made them an English treasure. One wonders why the English timber merchants allowed these logs to leave the country. Not being able to cut the full width of the prime boards was a disappointment. I even considered calling several hand sawyers from Asia to execute the sawing.

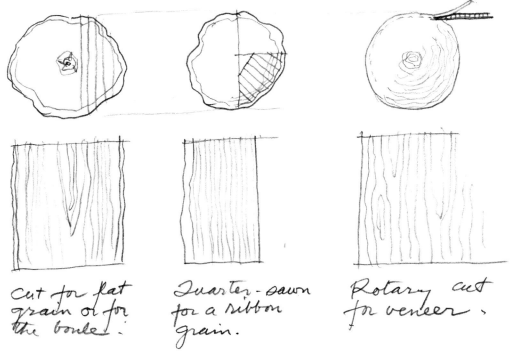

cut for flat grain or for the boule.

Quarter-sawn for a ribbon grain.

Rotary cut for veneer.

These simple sketches show ways logs are commonly cut into lumber, and the effect the sawing method has on the grain. I prefer sawing "through and through"; with this method the cut is tangential to the annual rings and lets us see the fullest range of graining and figuring that the log offers. Quartersawing does produce solid lumber, but since only a quarter of the log is used for each series of passes through the saw, the boards are not as wide as they might be. Since the cut is made at ninety degrees to the growth rings, the grain seen on the board is parallel—what we call "ribbon grain."

With rotary veneering, the entire log is "peeled" into a single thin sheet of veneer. Thin plies or veneers are glued together with the grains at right angles to make plywood. Beautiful hardwoods are often wasted this way to make thin surface veneers.

Although we could not realize the full potential of these logs, they were of amazing quality, with a graining that would never happen again. We were able to cut boards about four feet wide and seven feet long, each board unique, each board magnificent.

The key man in the process of cutting logs is the sawyer, one of the great craftsmen of our age with steady nerves and experienced judgment. It is necessary to have an almost silent dialogue with this sawyer. Few words are spoken, but thickness, the direction of the cut, the positioning of the log—all must be decided with precision.

During a day we saw perhaps thirty logs, some giant in size, each different from the others. Each must be analyzed to produce its full potential. As the hours pass, a silent symphony of visual tones unfolds, the beautiful expressions of nature's treasures, an occasional crescendo where the beauty touches one's heart. There is nothing like it. The workday finally ends. I am exhausted, but happy to have witnessed this unfolding spectacle.

How thick a plank should be depends chiefly on the diameter of the log. To avoid splitting, wide planks are cut relatively thick. Trees usually grow vertically without twisting, but sometimes they grow in a spiral. Some trees change direction, twisting a few years clockwise and then counterclockwise, making a natural plywood. A tree that grows in a spiral must be cut extra thick to prevent warping. Sometimes outside cuts are thicker still to prevent cupping.

Cutting logs entails a great responsibility, for we are dealing with a fallen majesty. There are no formulas, no guidelines, but only experience, instinct and a contact with the divine.

Commercial "grade" sawing by "rolling the log," the method used with almost all hardwoods in this country, is one of the most barbaric of practices. No attempt is made

Whichever name it goes by—plainsawing,"sawing for the *boule*", or sawing "through and through"—this method is by far the best way of realizing the full potential of a log in terms of graining and figuring. If the timber is fairly even and round, lumber may be sawed from the log consecutively, without any interruptions. Top and bottom "dogs," as seen in "A" , bite into the log after it has been mounted on the saw and guide it through the saw blade or band.

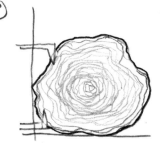

If the log is uneven, with many knots, as in "B", it is usually better to saw lumber only to the middle of the log, as shown, and then swing the remaining half-log 180 degrees and "re-dog" it, with the flat side flush against the saw guide.

For the best figuring, the log should pass through the saw with the crotch upright as in "C." This produces rich graining at the intersection of the trunk and branches. Large knots should be placed at the top, however, so that most of the boards can be cut "clear," that is, without having the knot appear in the center of the plank.

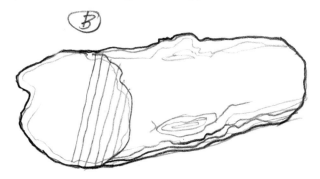

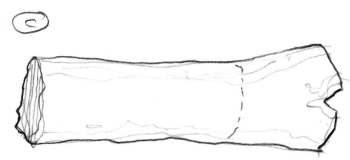

to bring out the log's inherent beauty. No slice is wide enough to do justice to the tree's figures and graining. The potential of the log is lost, and it ends up only as expensive yet uninteresting lumber. Quartersawing—sawing parallel to the rays which radiate from the log's center—is also popular. And it too is undesirable since it is wasteful and also fails to make full use of the log's width with its great potential for spectacular figuring.

The proper way to treat fine timber is to cut for the *boule,* starting from one side of the log and cutting through it without slabbing or squaring the log. This method of sawing is also known as "sawing through and through." If the log is a proper shape, with no unusual branching, and the equipment appropriate, this can readily be done.

Some trees in particular should be cut at the precise moment of maturity. Then the curing and drying should begin. The sapwood of American walnut is quite white when freshly sawn. A gradual process of graying takes place in the weathering until only a thin strip of white is left next to the heartwood. This is the moment for the most gracious of grains. A short while later the white is gone, and all becomes gray and less interesting. For some woods, like cherry and ash, the air drying should last only a few months, as after that an unattractive blue stain sets in. Other species are almost indestructible. I recently cut a magnificent rosewood which must have been left out to weather for about a dozen years.

The best lumber should be air-dried for one or two years, the rate of drying depending on factors such as the species, the season and the climate. In India, where it is dry and hot, the drying time can be short.

The best time to log and saw is during the fall and winter, when the weather is cool and the sap is not rising. The final process is to kiln dry, which removes the excess

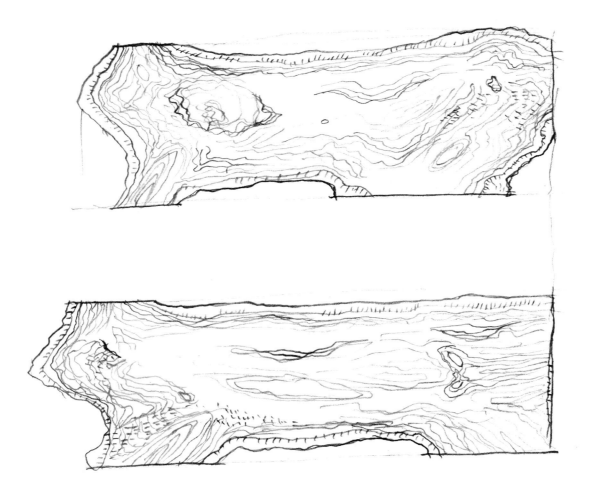

These sketches show two pieces of lumber sawn from one of our "once-in-a-lifetime" logs, American black walnut, about two hundred years of age. The tree was well past its prime when it was cut since we could see much dead wood in the log; the sap had been flowing only in a restricted part of the bole; it had only patches of living sapwood. This sapwood was almost stark white, a nice contrast with the warm gray of the rest. The log was roughly five feet in diameter and eleven feet long. The estimated weight was over ten tons. The lumber I've sketched here, though taken from near the outside of the tree, is still quite wide.

Our problem was how to saw the log. Most band-saw mills in this country do not have the capacity to handle this wood. To cut a full-width flitch would require an "Alaska mill," a long two-motor chain saw riding on a frame. Using this kind of saw would have been a tedious operation, time-consuming and expensive. The saw kerf loss would be close to one-half inch for each cut and, including the hand inaccuracy, the loss could be close to an inch. If we were to use a precision band saw, the saw kerf would be only a one-eighth inch per cut, and the alignment would be almost perfect.

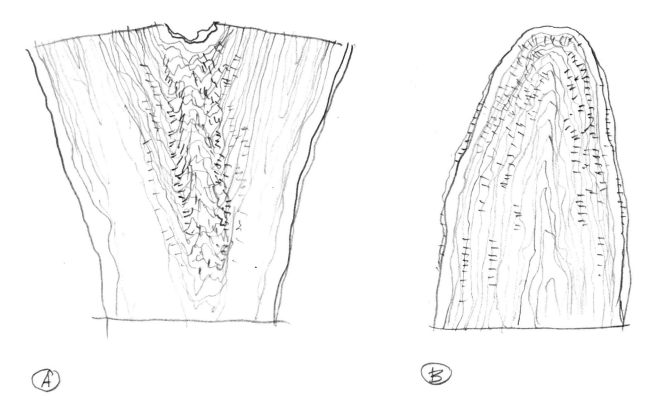

(A)   (B)

Methods of cutting when there is a crotch in a log. Usually, cutting across the crotch produces the finest figuring as in "A." This cut also provides the greatest usable width. Cutting along the crotch, as in "B," results in a somewhat triangular piece of lumber with less surface area to work with. The figuring is less intense too. At the point where a tree branches freely, three or more crotches may be found. The result in the lumber can be truly extravagant figuring.

moisture and "sets" the grain. Kiln drying of raw lumber produces unnatural-looking lumber. To rectify the "raw" look of kiln-dried lumber, it is often steamed with sawdust to produce a "mature" appearance. More often than not this process "kills" the grain and produces a dead-looking wood.

Planks and boards are the stock of the woodworker's trade. We store them in sheds in *boule* form, all the planks cut from a log grouped together. We memorize the qualities and potential uses of all of them. Planks are best stored upright, since it is easier to leaf through them. Selections are made as required and taken to the shop.

These rough but majestic "bodies" go on to be made into objects to enhance the lives of men.

I walk through our woods almost daily to catch its moods but also to locate dead trees for firewood and to clear out the heavy undergrowth. It is a never-ending process. The oak sketched here is one of the largest trees on our property, about three feet in diameter. Nearby is a walnut distinguishable by its thick, crooked branching and its scaly bark. In the background is an ash with its straight trunk and thin branching, a tree that seems in great haste to reach the sunlight. A beech with its smooth gray bark is easy to spot. The beech is the only tree I know of that can grow without having its bark rupture—the bark seems always smooth.

9
The Woods

I go back often to the land from which the timber has come, the woods and forests around the world. It is like visiting relatives, like my son's trip with his Irish godfather to Ireland. I share the joy of the forest and all of its moods.

Whether it be the few remaining virgin deciduous areas in the eastern United States, the great stands of the sequoia in California, the rain forest in the lower Ho River valley in Washington, the Circassian forests of the Caspian Sea area, the timber reserves for the construction of the Ise Shrine, or the timberline along the upper reaches of the mountainous regions of the world, there is an aura of maturity, a sense of conflict ended.

In younger areas of vegetation, however, an unseen battle is being fought as species and individual members of the plant world struggle to survive. Deep in the woods there is a reaching out for sunlight so that the cycle that transforms life-giving moisture into sugars can be completed. The competition continues. Some species have learned to survive with less sunlight than others, and many trees have died, returning to the soil from which they came.

Other battles have been won. In many cases the strongest have endured against great odds, overcoming intense cold, gales, and meager soil, hanging precariously between splits in rocks, growing despite a lack of nourishment. Plants battle against nature's forces, and against each other. The weakest die. But their death allows other trees to grow with the straight trunks that are so useful and necessary to man.

The struggle continues, silently mirroring the conflicts of men. There is the same will to live. Many woods are filled with vines, some parasitic, others using trees for support as they reach for the sun. In the process the host tree can be strangled or toppled over. Poison ivy as thick as a man's leg coils serpentlike up a trunk, destroying the tree in its own effort to survive.

The undergrowth varies. Certain species need only a little sunlight, and are able to live beneath their host trees without killing them. Others reach up toward the skies in

Our woods in New Hope are on the edge of a moraine. Huge boulders, deposited long ago by glaciers, lie strewn about. Most of these boulders are heavily weathered, some are covered with gray lichens. Areas of the land were once cleared for farming, but most of the land, too rocky for tilling, was left as forest. Small creeks run through the woods.

their search for maximum sunlight. Some grow faster than others, leaving the slower species to seek their own destinies.

Brush growths such as the spice bush and the black haws in our area seem to have no other purpose than to make life difficult for man and beast. The long, sharp thorns of the black haws can make an almost impenetrable thicket. Their berries might give nourishment to a few birds, but the problems they provide in a forest hardly make this seem worth it.

As the woods rise from the lowlands to the timberline, there is a gradual weeding out of species, for many can only survive in the gentler climates. In the ascent, long stretches of meadows, flowers peering out from under the snow, become more frequent, then the Noble fir, shaped like a bonsai and sometimes made into one, and finally the noblest of all, the bristlecone pine. Along the route are the casualties—large stands of trunks, bleached by the sun, rain and snows, of those that did not survive. These are the ghost forests.

Man can participate in this world of silent nature. To take part is to join in a creative process. A jungle can be made into an area of beauty with a certain amount of work. To care for the woods is to witness all: nature unfolds, the seasons pass, creatures make their lives, the footprints of nature's great variety appear on the newfallen snow. The spring and the sun are eagerly anticipated, leaves and blossoms showing themselves through the late snow. The pulse of life quickens as the sun grows warmer. The pale green of early leaves appears, and the sparkling walnut shoots seem to explode like green fireworks. Then midsummer. In the forest the sun sends long shafts of light to the ground, as if through the rose window of a cathedral. Fall comes, and the leaves of the walnut, which produces such extraordinary wood in its short growing season, are the first to fall. Finally the trees stand naked, their limbs etched against the autumn sky.

Our woods cover about twenty-five acres and have several small brooks running through them. Caring for this space is a lifetime project. We clean out the dead brush

and unpleasant undergrowth from one section, only to have it grow back again. But it is necessary to do this. The dead wood is a perpetual source of heat and energy, the most logical use for the castoffs of nature.

It is a great pleasure to spend several hours in the woods, putting nature's house in order. The brush is piled up to be used as fuel or to disintegrate, ultimately returning to the humus that gave it birth. It is a creative undertaking to bring order and beauty out of a tangle of confusion. Even the deer seem to enjoy the open spaces we make. Whether they like it because of the increased visibility or the ease with which they can move, they seem happier and are much more in evidence.

For some reason, the animals do not seem to feel that a small tractor is their enemy, although they may run if a man walks through the woods. Once when I was on my small tractor pulling a weedcutter, I came upon a doe and several fawns in a clearing. The mother was not at all frightened, eventually leaving the fawns and going off to take care of other tasks. In half an hour she returned. Having used me as a babysitter, she hadn't been the least concerned for the safety of her children!

Winter is quite destructive to our woods. The winds and heavy snows will tear off branches. A high wind will uproot a tree from the moist ground.

In the deep woods the constant struggle for sunlight continues. The lower limbs wither, die, and fall off, for the healthiest trees send their best branches skyward.

When large branches split or break off, they make the woods unsightly and create dangerous situations. Over the years I've pulled many of these dead, split branches off the trunks. Once I was pulling a fairly large branch and it suddenly gave way, knocking me breathless to the ground. As it fell, two long shards of wood broke off, each fifteen to twenty inches long and as sharp as a spear. I was wearing heavy rubber boots with leather tops. One of the shards pierced one boot's heel, while the other slashed through it. Lying on the ground, I waited for the pain to start, for it seemed as if I'd been crucified. But as my senses returned, I realized the wood had gone through

Spring is always a happy season in our woods. The May apple, jack-in-the-pulpit, and skunk cabbage are all poking through the wintry earth, and there is a blush of pale green in the trees. Small animals leave tracks on the banks of our brook. Watching over all is the great oak.

the boot, but not my foot: all I had were scrapes on my sole and heel. Nature is compassionate.

To be intimate with nature in its multifaceted moods is one of the greatest experiences of life. A squirrel plants a walnut for its winter nourishment but loses track of it. In the spring this forgotten walnut sprouts. In three hundred years it will reach maturity. It will be a majestic tree. Ultimately, its life juices will leave its body and the tree will become useful to man. All species of trees have their usefulness: some for the beauty of their grain, some for their strength, others for their durability and longevity and still others for various and sundry reasons. Most offer their bodies to man, offer lumber for his shelters and contribute to some of the noblest structures ever conceived.

A mature tree has witnessed much. In complete silence it stands immobile, a god consciousness. It is a moving experience to walk through the forest alone, to recognize each tree as a divine body, to pass in its presence day after day with a growing understanding.

At times it becomes necessary to cut a trail through the woods to facilitate working there and to haul out dead trunks for firewood. The trail is only wide enough for a tractor, and my son and grandchildren ride over it on their cycles. It seems so easy to cut a path through the thick underbrush, but to find the proper route in relation to the major trees and the contour of the land, to protect the brooks, stay clear of swampy areas, dodge the large outcroppings of rocks put down long ago by glaciers—all this has taken eight years to plan. There is now about a quarter of a mile of trail, less than half of what we need.

The forest must continue to exist. Otherwise there will be no life. Each year much timberland is cut down, some never to grow back. Consider the British cuttings on the east coast of India. Eventually the land became a desert. Without the forests, it is hardly likely that man would continue to exist. My small contribution is an attempt to help preserve it.

PART THREE

The Making of an Object

Conoid chair. The seat is cantilevered from the uprights. The
joint requires precise craftsmanship and skill. The two
horizontal "feet" slide easily, even over carpets.

10

New Life for the Noble Tree

We have selected and amassed our materials. From the world over have come timbers, many of fine quality, others the rejects of man and nature, all to be realized in one form or another, all to be made useful to man and possibly objects of beauty. We must make things with great hope and faith, for there is joy and fulfillment in creation. We must try to recapture a close relationship with nature.

I go back often into the wilderness, to find kinship beside a rock, behind a tree or under a leaf. I meditate and listen for answers. Since I am alone, the answers must be personal and inspired by movements I can feel intensely but cannot perceive or see. It is a lonely but satisfying quest.

There are so few who listen to the inner voice. In ages past, it would have been easy to join a crusade, to become a member of a community dedicated to building a great cathedral, to hew the great timbered doors, to carve a spirit in stone to grace the glorious facade.

But one must work alone, building objects of wood. With a mendicant's eye, a *sadhu*'s perception, a ragpicker's sense, I poke my way through the valley of the fallen giants, finding here and there fragments which will be given a second life. I roam through the rain forests where light barely filters through. . . .

Years ago, a parcel of logs was available in London. Ragged but huge, they were laid out in neat rows in a log yard on the edge of the Thames. These were of English walnut and other species—majestic trees, now lying dead and held for commerce. Their future, their karma was in limbo. They could be used creatively or they could be degraded by forces of the marketplace, ending up at best as paper-thin wood sheets decorating the dashboards of fine automobiles.

Such proud bodies can appear in any part of the world. In most cases, they return to the earth whence they came after releasing the great energy stored within them. At other times, they are realized as things of beauty, to the delight of the spirited imps playing about with light heart within them. Every fiber of the tree's being, each group

Here I am walking through a part of our woods that is mostly ash, maple and poplar. Our property must have once been logged for walnut, but not in the last five decades or so. I cut this trail myself—clearing the area of poison ivy, honeysuckle vines and wild grape. In parts of our woods, there are maples and walnut; the oldest tree is an oak with a diameter of about three feet.

of fibers, all join together to form an ecstatic whole to be released by a divine concept.

These hulks from all over the world are gathered together at the sawmill to be made into lumber. As the flitches drop off, we glimpse a spectacle never before seen, a truly breathtaking experience.

Here are hundreds of these silent trunks, many with the hint of greatness, some grim and ungainly, with unknown potential and possibilities. From the far corners of the world they have come. From the reforestation of the first Elizabeth (who was far-sighted enough to restore her forests after they had been cut down for her fleet); from Carpathia, the extraordinary burled trees. From the rich rain forests where eastern Turkey, northern Iran and southern Russia meet, the noble old trees. From Kerala in southwest India, the rosewood and laurel. From Shikoku the deep, rich graining of the *keyaki*, also known as zelkova or oriental elm. From the American West the cypresses, so taut and resistant to rot. The cedars and cypresses can last thousands of years, if properly used. From near our home, the majestic American walnut, with its rich, heavy branching and beautiful graining, to be treasured and loved.

A large truckload of lumber comes in after several years of curing, wood purchased perhaps five years ago and cut into lumber with some foresight of how it would one day be used. I often find that timber with the most character is from trees past their prime, sometimes even from trees dead a short while, before decay has set in. Sometimes the planks are banded in the original log form, called the *boule*, the planks sawn straight across from one side of the trunk to the other without interruption. Sometimes, although the lumber is not in *boule* order because of much handling, timbers from the same log are readily identifiable because of their deep and consistent graining. The planks, of many lengths, may range in thickness from approximately one inch to perhaps four inches. We have varied requirements.

As I look over the incoming truckload of lumber, I see the boards from a tree which was mature during the American Revolution, having embedded in its bole bullets fired in battle. Next I notice boards from the "Moon Tree," in Pennsylvania, dating from the William Penn grant. Then, huge slabs from the "Big Oak" in lower Bucks County, and finally venerable slabs from the Yaku *sugi*.

The lumber is taken off the truck by hand, each board quickly studied for its ultimate use. Sometimes an immediate role is assigned: a coffee table, a dining table, an end table. Other planks are separated into general categories according to probable future use and stored. Size, shape, thickness, figuring and unusual graining, even defects, all contribute to the decision as to what the future life of each board will be.

Study and assessment begin to uncover the perfect use for each part of each board. The lumber in some *boules* are obviously suited to panel work of various types, from a table top for a home, consisting of a single board three to eight feet wide, to one for a corporate board room, consisting of several "book-matched" boards of extraordinary width and length.

The attractive side-by-side arrangement of a number of boards, known as *book-matching*, is the product of a keen eye, and experience and instinct. Finding the proper alignment for other panels might take several hours, but eventually an order and harmonious pattern take shape.

Some slabs are selected for their uniqueness. There may be a large hole where decay has started and the tree has healed itself, a positive statement of life which makes an extraordinary design expression. Still other slabs dramatize the effects of great storm damage, where the fibers separated and the healthy parts joined together, making a new design pattern. These are called *wind-shakes*. Then there are planks from the tree the grain of which dances with abandon, and roots with figures as subtle and sublime as a Chinese ink painting.

This mound of lumber we have unloaded, taller than a man, three times as long and twice as wide, is a challenge. The meeting of tree with man is filled with drama. The tree started life in an earlier period of history; mature and fulfilled, it has finally

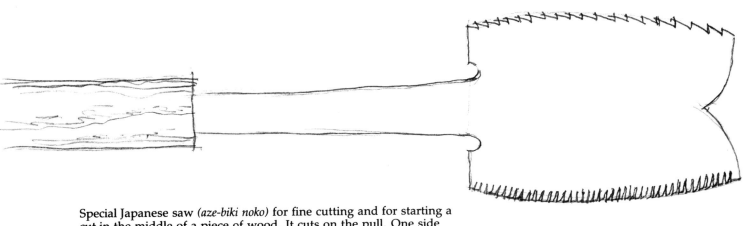

Special Japanese saw (*aze-biki noko*) for fine cutting and for starting a cut in the middle of a piece of wood. It cuts on the pull. One side cross-cuts, the other rips. The handle is of paulownia wood (*kiri*) for lightness and appearance.

succumbed to the woodsman's ax and saw. This could be the end. Or the tree could live again. . . .

The tree's fate rests with the woodworker. In hundreds of years its lively juices have nurtured its unique substance. A graining, a subtle coloring, an aura, a presence will exist this once, never to reappear. It is to catch this moment, to identify with this presence, to find this fleeting relationship, to capture its spirit, which challenges the woodworker.

There is a story in Japan of a young man from the country who went to the city and apprenticed himself to a woodworker. He was convinced that this was to be his life's work, and his parents agreed. A simple fellow, he had great determination and capacity in his craft. Back in his village his parents awaited word of his progress. First a year, then another, and finally a third passed, but still no word. The city was not so far, they thought. Why can't he at least visit us? Then, after five years, an envelope arrived. Hastily opening it, they found no letter; all it contained was a long wood shaving, ten feet long, neatly folded and perfect in every way, not a skip anywhere. The simplest of statements, it told all, like broad simple ink strokes in fine calligraphy. The father, immediately understanding, exclaimed: "Ah, my son has made it." There was great joy in the household that evening.

Like all true craftsmen, a woodworker is completely dedicated, with a strong sense of vocation. Often his craft has been handed down from generation to generation. A woodworker's hands develop in a special way with intense and concentrated use. The flesh becomes stronger and heavier in certain areas, better fitted to grasp and use the tools.

He has a special intensity, a striving for perfection, a conviction that any task must be executed with all his skill. Basically the woodworker is not driven by commerce, but by a need to create the best object he is capable of creating. Even if the object were to be destroyed when finished, the craftsman would still give the task his all.

A basic decision faced by the woodworker is whether to work with solid wood or veneer. Good veneer is sturdy, light, attractive and will not warp. Solid wood is heavy. It tends to split, shrink and swell. And it can warp.

It may take half a working day to saw a log the size of the one shown above. We are just about ready to paint the cut ends—with whatever paint that's handy—to keep the exposed area from end-checking, that is, from cracking as it dries. We also paint over areas where the bark is gone to keep the wood from drying and cracking. *Left*: This log loader has a clamshell-like grip and can lift a log that weighs four tons. *Right*: Inspecting the logs for sawing. *Opposite*: Detail of white oak bark.

Even so, I use only solid wood, plainsawn. Why? Because for me solid wood is honest and real. The grain on the surface you see runs all the way through the wood. It isn't just glued on. Solid wood mellows with age. It weathers well. Scratches and scars can be sanded out. Indeed, marring often adds charm to a piece. Good solid wood has a permanent surface, not just a protective skin.

Problems of splitting and shrinking can be solved by good design. Furniture, though heavy, need not look bulky if proper proportions are used.

My choice must be solid wood over veneer, for the sake of honesty.

The primary consideration in the working of wood is the wood itself and what it is to be used for. Coniferous, or cone-bearing, trees generally produce what is called softwood. Deciduous trees, that is, trees that lose their leaves during certain seasons, are usually classified as hardwoods. The terms *hardwood* and *softwood* refer to types of trees. Many hardwoods do indeed have surfaces that are very hard—like hickory, mahogany, walnut, cherry—but some hardwoods have soft wood surfaces, such as butternut and yellow poplar. If you dug your fingernail into these two hardwoods, the dents would be just as conspicuous as one made on lumber of softwoods like Douglas fir, white fir or redwood.

Any wood that has a "soft" surface should never be sanded, because sanding tends to collapse the wood cells, creating grooves. Wetting, on the other hand, tends to expand the cells, and this produces a "grain rise." Wood with a soft surface should be finished by hand with a hand plane, preferably a wooden block. With a hand plane, a mirror finish, clearly seen across the light, is possible. Finishing paper, no matter how fine, cannot produce the same effect or quality.

With woods that have a hard surface, the problem is quite different, especially with woods that have figures or burls. Extremely gifted men are able to hand-finish figured walnut with a wood block plane, but it is almost impossible to eliminate the small "digs" when planing ripples, figures or burls. A brilliantly sharp edge on the plane always helps. But, it is a question of a craftsman's pride to achieve as perfect a surface as possible, and quite often it becomes necessary to use a fine finishing paper to acquire this perfection.

The selection of material becomes important, since a piece of furniture is basically an engineering problem. Strong woods such as hickory are used for special purposes such as spindles. They can be made quite thin and present a delicate, balanced appearance. A board can have a cross-grain which, though handsome, makes it unusable where strength and solidity are called for, since this type of grain is susceptible to breakage. Old stock, even from dead trees, often has extraordinary character which young, upstart trees seldom have. Unfortunately, as trees age the fibers become weaker. Young hickory, for instance, is stronger than old hickory. The woodworker must continually weigh advantages and disadvantages to determine the best use for each part of each timber.

In the making of things, there are always questions of balance, proportion and scale. In a traditional Japanese house, the proportions used have been perfected over many generations. A variation of as little as half an inch in the horizontal can mean a devastating failure. In the same way, one mismatched board in a cabinet can be a disaster.

The final test of a piece of furniture is the finish. It is not only the mirror surface, but the depth of a penetrated oil finish with a final light protective coat that counts. The woodworker must look deeply into the heart of a board. Conversely the finest finish of all can sometimes result simply from aging, like the finish of the timbers in Japanese wood temples, some of which are over a thousand years old.

To make a box is an act of creation, for one is producing an object that never existed before. One is also making something that is useful. A box leads to a chair, a chair to a house, a house to a shrine. To create a cathedral one must only search for the divine truth, to look for the hand of the charioteer in the Battle of Kurukshetra to point the way.

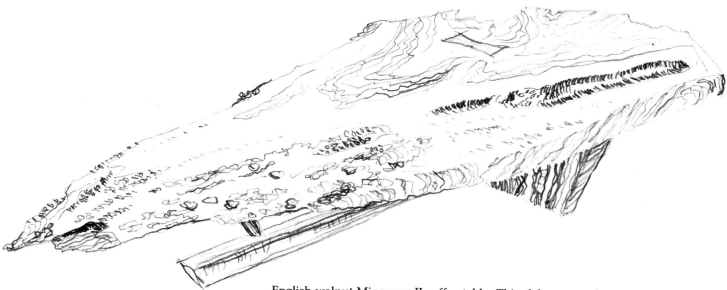

English walnut Minguren II coffee table. This slab was cut from one of the great trees of England. An irregularly shaped tree to begin with, the irregularities became accentuated as it grew. A deep furrow remains, giving its surface a sculptured look. The usual market for fine timber would not find much use for such a slab, practically a reject of nature. I have sometimes rescued these great slabs from the dump heap and sometimes, with luck, seem to give them a second chance at life as good furniture. The natural forms with all their bumps and "warts" survive. To fashion such a piece of wood into fine furniture is almost an act of resurrection.

The necessity of matching each piece of wood with its ultimate use concerns us. We treasure the cypress which becomes the *asa-no-ha*, the most gracious of grilles, the hickory which becomes spindles to support the back of a chair, hand-shaved for grace and beauty, delicate and strong, and, most precious of all, the *ten ita*, the "heavenly plank," which becomes the surface of a useful object where nature can be seen rejoicing in all its glory. We revel in the marvel of nature's design in a piece of wood, so complicated and yet so simple.

Of course, fine devoted people are involved.

There is Minato-san, whose body is somewhat crippled but who does some of the finest work I have ever seen. He can make the *trompe d'oeil* corner where the end grain appears on both sides, made by hand with absolute precision.

There is Mario, who left his native Calabria to work in this country and became a fine craftsman.

There is Jim, who entered the shop during his secondary school years and with long experience has developed great skills.

There is Adam, who served his apprenticeship in Austria, completely trained in the German manner, accomplished to the fine degree that can result only from years of apprenticeship.

There is Bob, whose skills are diversified. Besides being most adept at making furniture, he can build structures superlatively and is accomplished at the art of laying stone; he can plaster, make fine frames and grilles for paper-covered *shōji*, and do all aspects of construction work.

There is Jerry, a young man who possesses extraordinary native skills, and who employs them well.

There is Jon, sensitive and fine, who works well, with intense concentration.

There is Frank, who can spot a walnut on the far horizon, and then take it down without any splitting.

The sawmill in operation. The saw "dogs" bite in on the right, top and bottom, of this American walnut log. About ten pieces of lumber have already been taken off. This commercial band saw can accommodate a log forty-three inches wide and can cut veneers one-eighth-inch thick and three feet wide the entire length of the log. *Below*: With American walnut, there is generally a great color distinction between heartwood and sapwood, as this freshly sawn board shows. The grain of this species, however, is fairly regular throughout.

American walnut lumber in *boule* form, ready to air-dry for about two years. Wood strips prop the boards apart to allow the free circulation of air.

Book-matching. Sketch "A" shows two book-matched boards of
Persian walnut. This method of matching is usually the most
satisfactory. A balance is achieved even when up to an inch of wood
is removed in the working. A book-match does not have the dull
regularity of thin veneer "matching." A natural opening in the wood
(between the top and second "butterflies") adds visual interest and
also provides for greater useful width. Sometimes, boards with "free-
shaped" openings about a foot long can be used, creating interesting
table tops out of almost hopeless lumber.

There are Mira and Kevin, my offspring, who have a definite interest in continuing
this work as a family tradition.

To unify all of the activity, there is Marion. Without her to manage our business,
to keep the books, to advise and console, to press the hundreds of practical decisions,
the work would come to naught. My wife is a true partner.

Woodworking requires many skills. Acquiring them provides an apprenticeship
for the thousand judgments that must be made to shape a good wood object. Even in
an industrial age there are benefits to be derived from a tenacious drive to do perfect
work.

A simple process like sharpening a chisel can go wrong too easily. The barbarism
of using a power grinder indicates that the sharpening has been left undone too long.
The woodworker must recognize the fine feel of a "feather" which indicates that the
blade is still not sharp. He must know the type of whetstone needed to draw a perfect
edge. He knows that a fine waterstone cannot be surpassed.

The thousand skills the fine furniture maker needs include: the ability to make the
proper selection of material for a fitting design conceived with grace, utility and beauty;
the marking and cutting; the instinctive selection of the proper tool among many; the
use of a fine marking gauge, or the setting of the machine to execute a joint; the feeling
for proper tolerances for fit; the final assembly and check for square and selection of
correct glues for each operation; and finally the finishing to bring out the depth and
beauty of the grain. And, last but not least, he needs the dedication, devotion,
concentration and love to build as perfect an object as possible.

Running a small hand industry requires the wearing of many hats to compete with
mass production. It calls for the following:

1. Advanced hand craftsmanship in wood.
2. A good knowledge both of traditional tools and advanced machines.
3. An instinctive feeling for design, based on knowledge of materials and
   woodworking techniques.

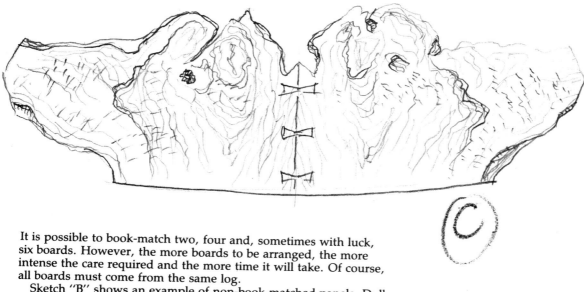

It is possible to book-match two, four and, sometimes with luck, six boards. However, the more boards to be arranged, the more intense the care required and the more time it will take. Of course, all boards must come from the same log.

Sketch "B" shows an example of non-book-matched panels. Dull and uninteresting. Almost always a mistake.

Sketch "C" shows two-board book-match of English walnut root planks. Roots are difficult to book-match because they often become warped in drying and much wood is lost in leveling. But, results can be extraordinary.

4. The experience of a good log buyer, who can size up a log whether fallen or standing—who can "feel" the excellence of grain and of the figuring or burls without cutting into the timber.
5. The hard skills of economy and bookkeeping.
6. An understanding of the problems of the sawyer and the willingness to stand beside him and make quick decisions as to how to turn the log to get the most interesting boards, the best figuring, the precise thickness of each log—the thousand decisions that can't wait.
7. Competent draftsmanship, to transliterate ideas into drawings.
8. Knowledge of *dendrology*, the science of trees.
9. Familiarity with interiors and forms of structures so that objects can relate properly to their environment.
10. Some knowledge of engineering and stresses, to feel the "moment" in a joint and watch for the possibilities of failure.
11. Familiarity with the processes of curing, both natural and with applied heat.
12. An artist's sense of color and texture, since wood has many tones and textures which must be related.

The hats are many and few can wear them. True craftsmen are devoted to their craft. I remember a house I designed in Tokyo many years back. It was built by men of great skill who rode many miles on bicycles to come to work and ate simple lunches of rice balls containing pickled plums. Their devotion to the work was all-consuming. When a man executed an extraordinary joint, it was cause for minor celebration, and we would all stand back and admire the work.

Craftsmanship is a silent skill. People who talk excessively cannot take part.

In New Hope, we work with wood, in a sense an eternal material, for without a tree there would be no human life. And we work with solid wood, not veneer, the better to search for its soul. We meditate with a board sometimes for years. We search for the essence, to share its joys and tragedies. A thousand experiences and skills spring into action. We are making something!

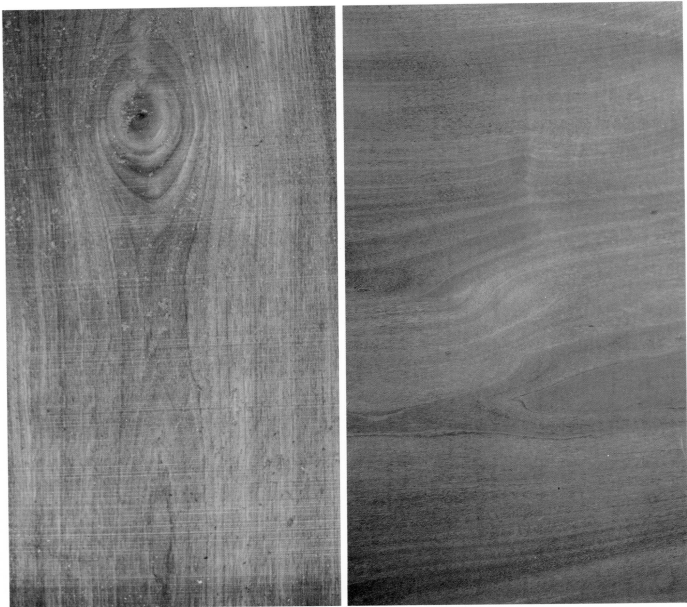

Walnut directly off the saw, uncured and with a greenish cast.

Dressed American walnut on a chair with a single-board seat.

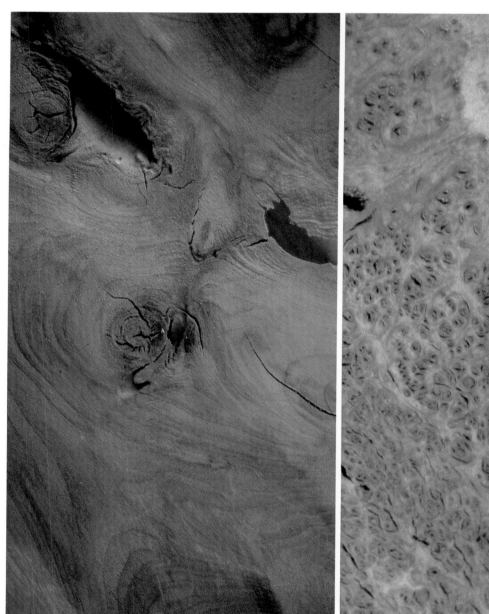

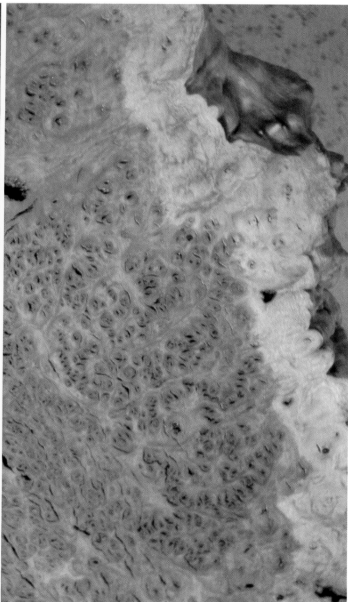

English walnut with figuring that seems to make a mysterious mask or face.

English oak burl coffee table. Note the light band of sapwod and the burling through the entire slab. Of all species, this tree is the one most likely to be burled throughout, but some specimens have none of it, and others have it only in patches. Nothing is entirely predictable.

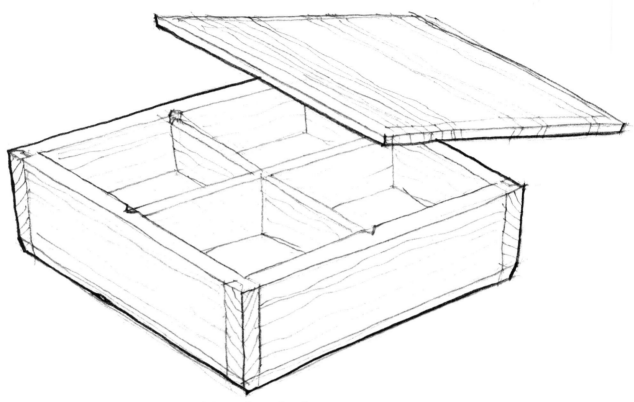

Difficult box joinery. All four corners of this walnut piece have double-end grains. The top is made of quartersawn wood to reduce warping.

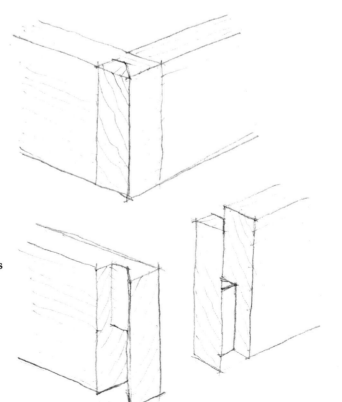

Corner joint for box. Note that the end grain of each board shows at the corner joints. This joinery requires great skill, since forcing can snap the end grain off.

11

A Thousand Skills, A Thousand Voices

Our skills have been sharpened, the designs made. The shed has been adequately stocked, the decision of solid wood versus veneers has been settled in favor of solid. The inventory of experience has been accumulated. The work commences.

The object is to make as fine a piece of furniture as is humanly possible. The purpose is usefulness, but with a lyric quality—this is the basis of all my designs.

The selection of timber is made in the shed, brought into the workshop and marked out for cutting. As far as possible, all elements are from the same tree. However, for some purposes, such as the need for strength, a different material may be used—for instance, hickory for spindles in a chair.

It is a stirring moment when out of an inert mass drawn from nature we set out to produce an object never before seen, an object to enhance man's world; above all, a tree will live again. . . .

For millennia, the working of wood was almost entirely a hand operation. The lathe was often powered by the craftsman's assistants. It could also be activated by waterpower, and sometimes simply by feet.

The reality of the age, however, brings up the question of machinery. As much as man controls the end product, there is no disadvantage in the use of modern machinery and there is no need for embarrassment. Gandhi and his spinning wheel were more quixotic than realistic. A power plane can do in a few minutes what might require a day or more by hand. In a creative craft, it becomes a question of responsibility, whether it is man or the machine that controls the work's progress.

Woodworkers follow a long tradition dating certainly from the beginning of civilized man. The first wheel must have been wood. Possibly, man moved heavy objects on wood rollers. Woodworkers of quality must have existed in the Vedic age in India and, of course, among the Egyptians and the Greeks. Joseph and Jesus of Nazareth, as well as the shrine and temple carpenters of Japan, followed an honored craft. These skilled artisans from the far-gone past speak with urgency and insistence. They are lighting the lamp for us to follow.

Japanese tools. A standard chisel with a very hard cutting edge of steel, backed with a type of softer steel to make it easier to sharpen on a stone. It is hollow ground on the flat side. It is used quite often for carving out mortices. Opposite are two views of a wood block plane. For quality work, this sort of wood block plane of hard *kashi* (a type of oak) is unsurpassed. Even though most woodworkers have to use power tools, the serious woodworker should practice dressing lumber with a hand plane like this. There is a certain psychic lesson in learning how to feel wood. There is something wrong with metal against wood.

The selection of furniture parts is always most important. Of the roughly ten thousand boards available in my warehouse, the perfect choice must be made for each part of each board. Sometimes five or ten years pass before a board is selected for use. There must be a union between the spirit in wood and the spirit in man. The grain of the wood must relate closely to its function. The abutment of the edge of one board to an adjoining board can mean the success or failure of a piece. There must be harmony, grace and rhythm. It is so easy to place the wrong board, out of the ten thousand available, next to the wrong one, resulting in a mismatch. Sometimes a number of boards are shifted about until the right combination is found to make the happy whole.

There is so much individuality in these boards. Some are of great distinction and nobility, others plain and common, still others of such poor aspect that they must be relegated to the scrap pile. Each species of wood too has its own strong personality. The long fibers of the cypress contrast with the exuberance and beauty of its fine burls. The strong figuring vibrates with joy, at times through the whole bole, at other times only at the junction of several main limbs branching out. Roots, too, have strong personalities, especially where they meet the tree's trunk, producing fantastic richness of graining. Roots must be used in a precise and exact way. They may be cut round or square or oval. Or they may be left entirely natural, or "free."

Quite often the shape, size, texture and the extravagances of graining dictate the design and function of an object. Here the relationship of man to timber prevails as the two live comfortably together day after day, without tiring of each other.

Gradually a form evolves, much as nature produced the tree in the first place. The object created can live forever. The tree lives on in its new form. The object cannot follow a transitory "style," here for a moment, discarded the next. Its appeal must be universal. Cordial and receptive, it should invite a meeting with man.

The rough dressing down of a plank, the study of the contours, sizes, shapes, thicknesses; the rough chalk markings, the fine marking, the final cutting; the joinery and assembly, the finishing to bring out the depth of grain—all these steps follow one after the other, each with its own responsibility.

We must make as perfect an object as we know how. The final but essential requirement is to finish the top surface by hand. A good workman can achieve perfect surface work with a hand plane alone. To achieve a fine result, a carpenter may spend days surfacing the faces of a post in a Japanese house. For the best work, the bit is sharpened after each stroke, not because it is dull, but because the finest finish demands it.

What a wonder fine furniture can be—a chair to rest a human body, a table at which to work or to partake of food. A cabinet to organize and store the things for daily use. The parts are assembled, the joints designed and made ready to be put together. Solid wood moves, breathes and lives. The joints must be designed with this in mind.

It is in the making of the joints that skills count. The joints should not be too loose or so tight as to split a member. The shoulders of the joint should fit tightly and slightly compress the wood of the receiving member. In a house the joints should be a drive fit, that is, pounded in. A slop fit, even if held with a wedge, is not adequate. Compound tenons and mortices, shoulders for cinching and drawing up, compound shoulders for wedging, the thousand methods of joining several pieces of timber together—all of this joinery is designed so that a certain distension due to drying need not be serious and indeed often helps by tightening a bond.

The decline in quality of modern furniture is probably due in part to the use of the quick, easy and cheap dowel joint. The decline of modern domestic architecture can be traced to the popularity of the stud wall put together with hammer and nails, a type of construction calling for no joinery at all. By contrast, the early American house and barn with their excellent joinery still represent the best we have produced and will greatly outlast contemporary buildings.

Good joinery, whether in buildings or for furniture, is difficult to design and even more difficult to execute. It should be thought of as an investment, an unseen morality.

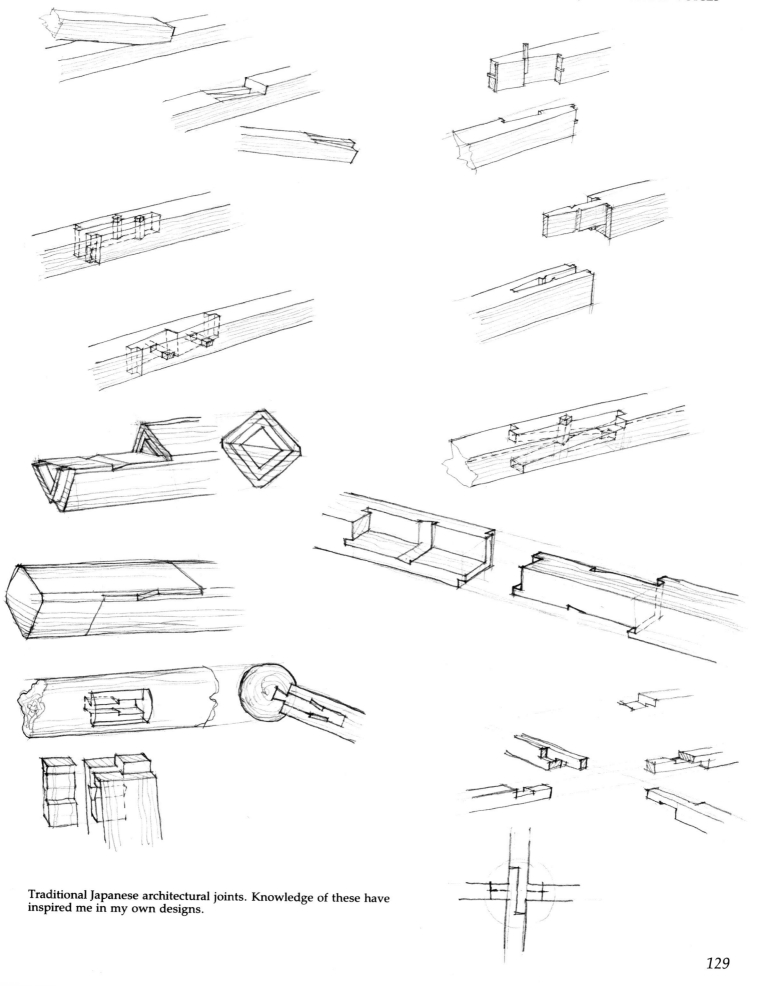

Traditional Japanese architectural joints. Knowledge of these have inspired me in my own designs.

A complete set of standard Japanese chisels. The handles are of a tough and hard type of oak, *kashi*.

The dovetail chisel is a tool the Japanese use for making mortices for butterfly inlays and for getting into tight corners. I had this one made for me in Japan a few years ago, but I still use some of the tools that I picked up on my first trip to Japan in the thirties—hammer, plane and marking gauge.

This small saw crosscuts on one edge and rips on the other. Like all Japanese saws, it cuts on the pull. With it, I can start work in the middle of the board or clean out a depression. *Below*: Sharpening a standard chisel. This photograph shows the hollow ground on the flat side. I use only a waterstone.

The precision, intricacy and sophistication of the *asa-no-ha* grille, illustrated on page 139, in which twelve members come together, are indeed staggering.

Joinery was highly developed in Japan, originally the land of great evergreen forests where the fervor of the people drove them to construct great shrines and temples, some on the grand scale of the European churches and cathedrals. The work was done by carpenters, the *daiku*, master builders, without comparison any place.

Japanese joinery is a highly developed technique, formalized and exact. Each type of joint has a name and the procedures for each follow precisely in the proper order. The work was and still is done by hand with tools of an excellence that the West has not known, tools to meet every joinery requirement. The work goes extremely fast, the chips fly.

The greatest of these master builders who traditionally were also the designers and architects in wood were the *miya daiku*, the "shrine builders." These were the princes of construction, versed not only in building but also in structural proportions. Theirs was a skill acquired only by creative doing for generations. They were masters of the mystery of how four beams and two posts meet, the perfect pitch of a roof, the subtle relationship of one material to another.

Preserving the techniques of fine joinery can help save us from the onslaught of mediocrity in our furniture and housing. The great cypresses and cedars of the Orient are fast being depleted, the Lebanon cedar is almost extinct and even the fine American cypresses, the Port Orford cedar and the Alaska cedar, are in short supply. But new trees grow and the wood that can still be joined is luckily still adequate, though limited. We can still make joints to our hearts' content, joints that are honest, sound and enduring.

Hardwoods with beauty of grain and texture, even when accompanied by twisting, warping and other irregularities, can often be used for furniture. Joints for furniture are normally simpler than those used in buildings, since the structural demands are not so great. The craftsmanship, however, must be precise, since the stability of the entire piece of furniture depends on it.

In Japanese, *kodama*, the "spirit of a tree," refers to an experience known to almost all people of this island nation. It involves a feeling of special kinship with the heart of a tree. It is our deepest respect for the tree which impels us to master the difficult art of joinery, so that we may offer the tree a second life of dignity and strength.

Any joint can be made by hand, but where the machine can do the work more efficiently, I use the machine. Yet, there are many areas where only hand tools can be used. At such times the finely developed Japanese tools are effective and in many cases the only answer to tight problems.

The Japanese hand tools include the offset chisels, fan-shaped chisels, chisels ground hollow in the back with a slightly tempered carbon steel cutting edge and a soft steel backing; saws that can start cutting in the middle of a board (saws that cut on the pull), marking gauges with a knife for a point, an ax like nothing seen in the West. After using the Japanese wood block plane, there seems to be something sacrilegious about a plane with a steel block!

Toolmaking is still a great art, even in power machinery. The research on tools can be a study in itself. Familiarizing oneself with the many different types, the various toolmakers, the care and sharpening of tools and, of course, the techniques of using them—all this could alone fill a lifetime.

Tables

We are faced with the problem of making a working surface, a table top. This surface can be composed of glued-together smaller parts, a book-matched pair, or a single slab. Often the characteristics of a single slab dictate the size and design of the piece. In book-matching the butterfly inlay is invaluable. It adds strength to the joinery and, just as important, it adds a creative design element. Where it is placed, its size, color and texture are all vital considerations. The butterflies should contrast with the boards,

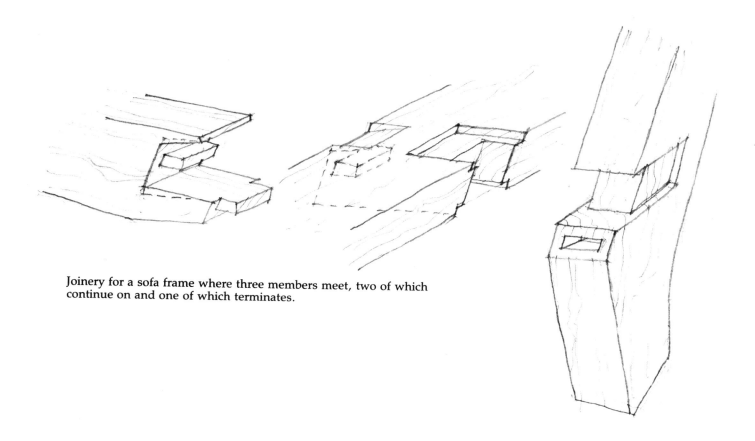

Joinery for a sofa frame where three members meet, two of which continue on and one of which terminates.

matched for attractiveness. Their grains should be perpendicular to each other for strength.

Originally the entire process was done with hand tools. Today we use a power tool for the preliminary work. First we hollow out the areas to be fitted with the butterfly-shaped piece with a router. Then we fit the joint with a flat chisel and clean out the corners with a fan-shaped Japanese chisel. Finally, the butterfly is placed in the area prepared to receive it and glued securely. The top, made to protrude a bit, is planed smooth and sanded before final finishing.

Some of the happiest table forms are accidental or realized through imagination. Triangular pieces are extremely beautiful and useful in furniture making. The flairs at the base of a tree usually produce the richest graining, nature's fantasies. These are unique and must be designed for one specific object, and that alone.

Then there are rectangular tables of various dimensions and woods—great long tables for conference and dining, all of solid wood. Contemporary international treaties might benefit from being written on a good honest table. How can one expect a sincere treaty signed on veneer, green felt, or on wood grained to look like marble?

Finally, to meticulous care, proper proportions, sound structure and honest creative design all working together, we add a fine finish. The finish stands for our faith, our integrity.

Chairs

What a personality a chair has! Chairs rest and restore the body, and should evolve from the material selected and the predetermined personal requirements which impose their restrictions on form, rather than the other way around. Some parts, such as spindles, are used primarily for strength, and aesthetics becomes a secondary consideration. These can be beautiful, however, and the error of just a sixteenth of an inch in the thickness of a spindle can mean the difference between an artistically pleasing chair and a failure.

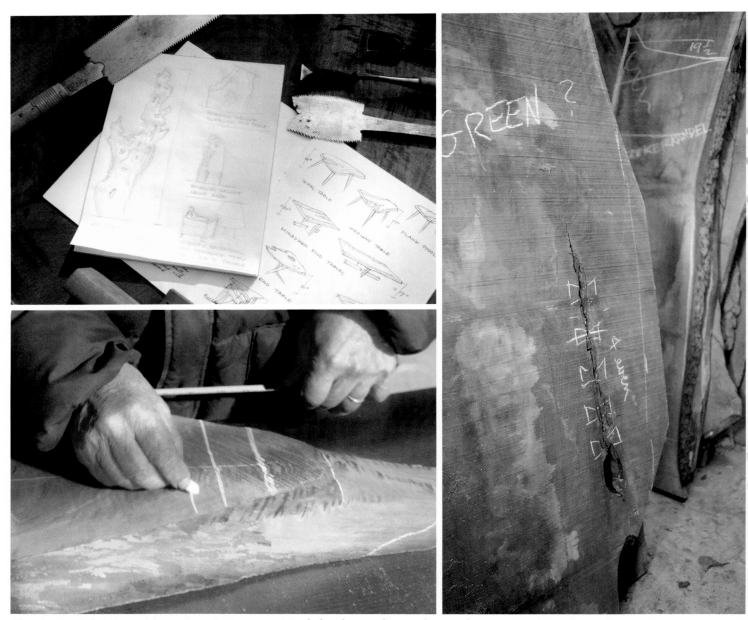

Sketches and drawings. Many times I give my original sketches to the purchaser who requests them. Some designs that become standard items are named after the customer for whom they were originally made. *Below*: I make any number of preliminary drawings in chalk to get a feeling for the proportion of the object we are creating. It's easier to make a final decision where to cut if there is something to see on the board. I make final markings in pencil. *Right*: A rough plank shows where butterfly keys will be made, along with the name of the customer.

Single-board tops for desks and tables in the lumber shed are marked with dimensions, special work and customer name.

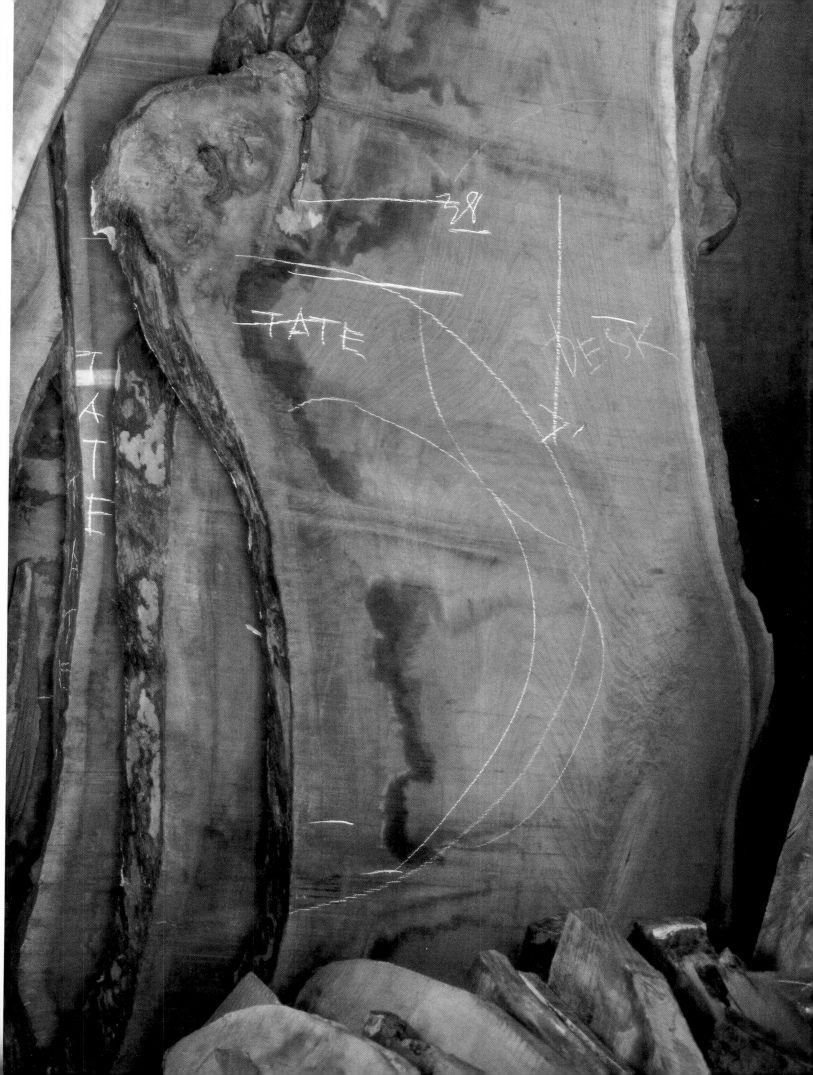

The post is very important in traditional Japanese architecture. Here are examples of how wood is prepared for posts. The *menkawa,* at right, is a post with four planed sides; the four unplaned surfaces are left with natural contours. Large stands of *sugi* and cyptomeria are grown as materials for these posts. The trees are planted close together so that, as they grow, the lower limbs drop off and the trunks are almost perfect cylinders.

The *shi-ho-masa,* or "four-sides straight-grain," post is perhaps known only in Japan. It is best for stability and elegant appearance.

The *shibori* takes it name after the art of tie-dying because the mottled underbark looks like a dyed-fabric pattern. Trees actually grow this way, but they can also be cultivated to achieve this unusual feature.

The sketches of the *menkawa* and *shibori* posts show V-shaped cuts which run lengthwise down the back of the post. These result from a saw cut made in the green timber. During the curing process, the cut opens up to a "V," eliminating the possibility of other cracks and the danger of splitting. The *shi-ho-masa* is cut into proper shape only after curing, so there is no "V" opening.

SHIBORI

SHI-HO-MASA

MEN KAWA

Function, and beauty and simplicity of line are the main goals in the construction of a chair. If a chair's purpose is only to impress people or to show rank, then it becomes ostentatious and carved to death.

Cabinets

Cabinets are useful for the organization and storing of things; they may also be objects of beauty. Fine woodworkers are often called cabinetmakers. Making a fine cabinet for storing the warrier's armor, sweets for the child or any other purpose can be a truly rewarding accomplishment.

A large vertical storage piece in the grand tradition of Chinese cabinets or European armoires, chests of drawers, small bedside units, small chests of drawers for organizing small things, ladies' dressing boxes, filing cabinets, wall-hung pieces—all these help to make life orderly.

Traditionally in a Japanese family, a *kiri* (paulownia) tree is planted at the birth of a daughter. This tree is fast growing, beautiful of grain, light in weight and easy to work. When the daughter marries, the boards from this tree are made into a chest for her trousseau. The lightness of the wood makes it easy to transport. *Kiri* wood is never finished; in time, if it becomes soiled, it is resurfaced simply with a plane.

Desks, Beds and Lamps

Some of the most creative moments of the poet and prophet must have taken place at a desk, so the desk must be sincere. One must start with a great or modest slab of wood of rich or simple graining. Nothing much more is actually needed, except possibly a small cabinet to store writing necessities.

Roughly dressed walnut. Because of the check, or crack, a butterfly key will have to be made; the proportions are marked in chalk.

Beds and reclining pieces are important objects of furniture, and too often they become ostentatious. But they can be so simple as to be put away during the day so that the room may be used for other purposes.

Screens and room dividers are useful to break space into a number of areas, and they can be most decorative. They have been used throughout history.

Lamps, also used through the ages, can add a good deal to the decor of a home. The *andon* (paper-covered lamp) lighted by a candle or a wick is a lyric and useful device. It must be the most economic type of light source.

Furniture should be lived with and not treated as something overly precious. A certain amount of scratching and denting adds character to a piece. (In the trade, surface marring is called *distressing;* in our family it's "Kevinizing," after our son who could, when young, "antique" furniture in record time.) To me, there is nothing quite so uninteresting as a shining, perfectly smooth surface that looks as though it has never been used.

People have been indoctrinated with the idea that fine wood is fragile. Of course, this is true of veneers when the surface is only $\frac{1}{28}$ to $\frac{1}{40}$ of an inch thick, sometimes even less. If these veneers are not treated with great care, their surfaces can easily be destroyed. Because of this fragility, a highly polished protective coating must be applied. When the surface deteriorates, no remedy is available to refinish it. Good, solid wood, on the other hand, treated with a penetrating oil finish, has a permanent surface and not merely a protective skin.

Small dents and scratches, if objectionable, can be removed by applying a wet paper napkin to the damaged area. Leave the napkin on the area overnight or until it dries out. This will cause the wood fibers to swell to more or less their original stage. The resulting spot can be rubbed with steel wool and finished with a light oil.

The key to fine workmanship lies in the drive for perfection and the development of skills to achieve it. Perhaps as a backlash to industrialism and commercialism, a new concept seems to be taking hold. The large number of young people, many of them college graduates, who want to do truly fine work is astonishing. Even in my shop, where many questioned at first whether our work made sense, the reactions are now enthusiastic. There is a pride evident today in work well done. Many strive to create and to create well.

In my shop, each woodworker is an individual craftsman, free to work out his own *sadhana,* spiritual training to attain deep concentration resulting in union with the ultimate reality. Each person can do what he finds most suitable within certain guidelines. Our relationship and attitudes are based on the teachings of Sri Aurobindo and the ashram of Pondicherry. The will must aspire to produce as fine an object as is humanly possible. Each man must find his own personal truth. The endeavor must be to bring out the beauty and proportion, the textures and depth of the material used, to produce something that may last forever.

This may seem an anachronism in our age. But there is a battle to be won. For many years I have struggled to make my dream a functioning enterprise. At times, I felt it unjust that all the wild birds in my woods could sing all day long while I sweated in a craft the world didn't seem ready for. Now the points of light appear in the wilderness more frequently and afford additional opportunities for creativity.

To the advantage of craftsmen, the modern commercial system has produced its own built-in difficulties. The costs to a large manufacturer of mass-selling small objects are now so high, involving so many middlemen, that it is possible for craftsmen to build a better product and sell it for less by direct contact with the buyer. This helps in some measure to explain the resurgence of the craft movement.

The maker of fine wood furniture reaches out into hundreds of lives, listens to voices and shares in the lives of so many people, giving and receiving.

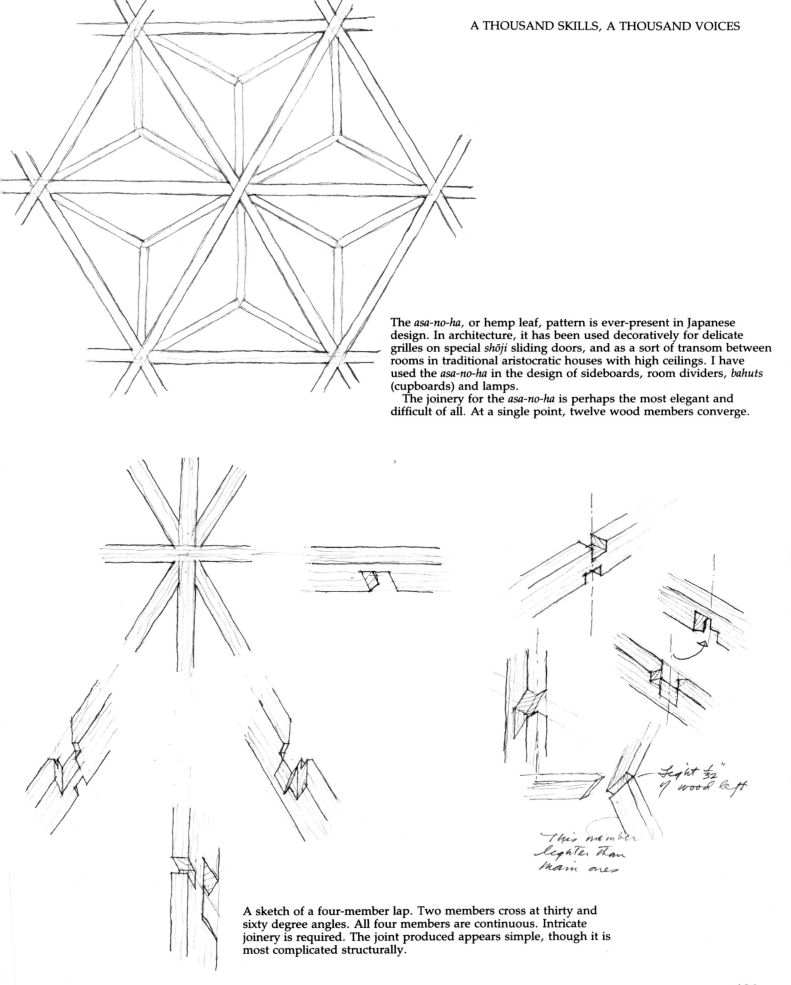

The *asa-no-ha*, or hemp leaf, pattern is ever-present in Japanese design. In architecture, it has been used decoratively for delicate grilles on special *shōji* sliding doors, and as a sort of transom between rooms in traditional aristocratic houses with high ceilings. I have used the *asa-no-ha* in the design of sideboards, room dividers, *bahuts* (cupboards) and lamps.

The joinery for the *asa-no-ha* is perhaps the most elegant and difficult of all. At a single point, twelve wood members converge.

light ± 1/32"
of wood left

This member
lighter than
main ones

A sketch of a four-member lap. Two members cross at thirty and sixty degree angles. All four members are continuous. Intricate joinery is required. The joint produced appears simple, though it is most complicated structurally.

Stack of walnut seats for Conoid chairs. In general, seats are made from knotty pieces of wood that do not have adequate length for table or desk tops. The knots are cut out and the boards are matched and glued. "Matched" seats, like those shown here, are less costly than single-board seats, another possibility.

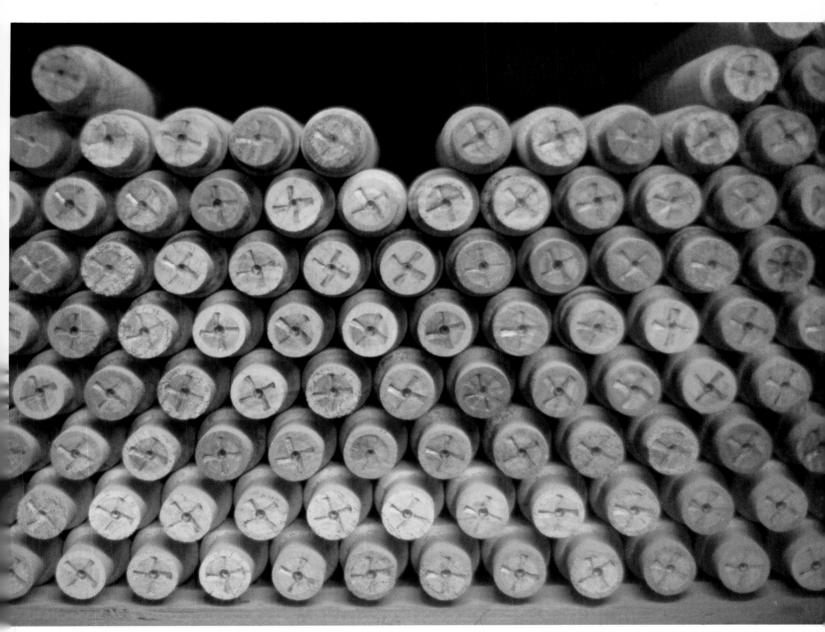

Our chair legs are a concession to mass production. These we turn out seven hundred at a time on an automatic lathe.

NEW

NEW PLUS ARMS

GRASS SEATED

ARM

CHILD'S

4 LEGGED HIGH

HIGH MIRA

MIRA

LOUNGE

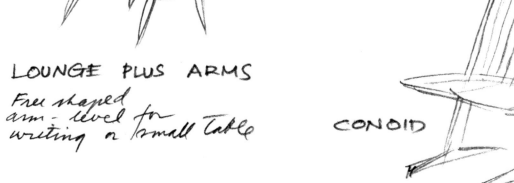

LOUNGE PLUS ARMS

Free shaped
arm- level for
writing or small table

CONOID

Here and on the following pages is a step-by-step illustration of the making of our Conoid chair. Seats ready for hand assembly. *Below*: Backrests are cut to shape. *Opposite*: Heat lamps temporarily reduce the diameter of the spindle just before assembly. When shrunk, it is glued and fixed firmly into the seat; in time, the spindle will expand to its former diameter. The result is a non-loosening joint. Early American chairs were made in a similar way with well-seasoned spindles inserted into green-wood seats, which would tighten up around the spindles.

Chiseling the foot member of a Conoid chair for a tight fit into the upright.

The upright (or leg) is put into a vice to receive the completed foot, but once the foot is glued and fitted, the joint is clamped and held under pressure for a minimum of two to three hours.

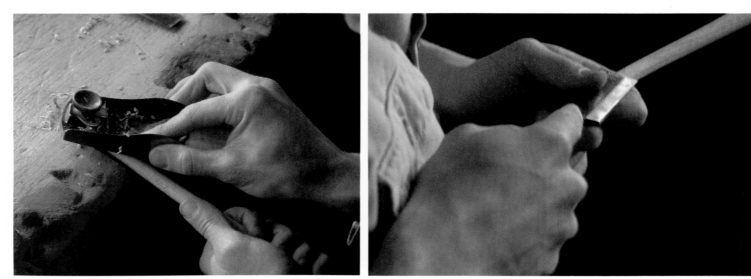

Spindle shaving is done mostly with a hand plane, but we also use a chisel for hand-shaving details.

Clamps are used to help fix feet to legs, then the legs are attached to the seat.

Next, spokes are inserted. After the backrest is added, the chair is completely assembled. The usual finish is five coats of tung oil, each allowed to penetrate the wood and then wiped off by hand; the final coat is polished with steel wool. The chairs are wiped with a cloth with finishing oil just before packing and crating.

NEW CHAIR
plus arms

LOUNGE CHAIR plus
free shaped arm or
without - left or right

Free
edge

BENCH + BACK

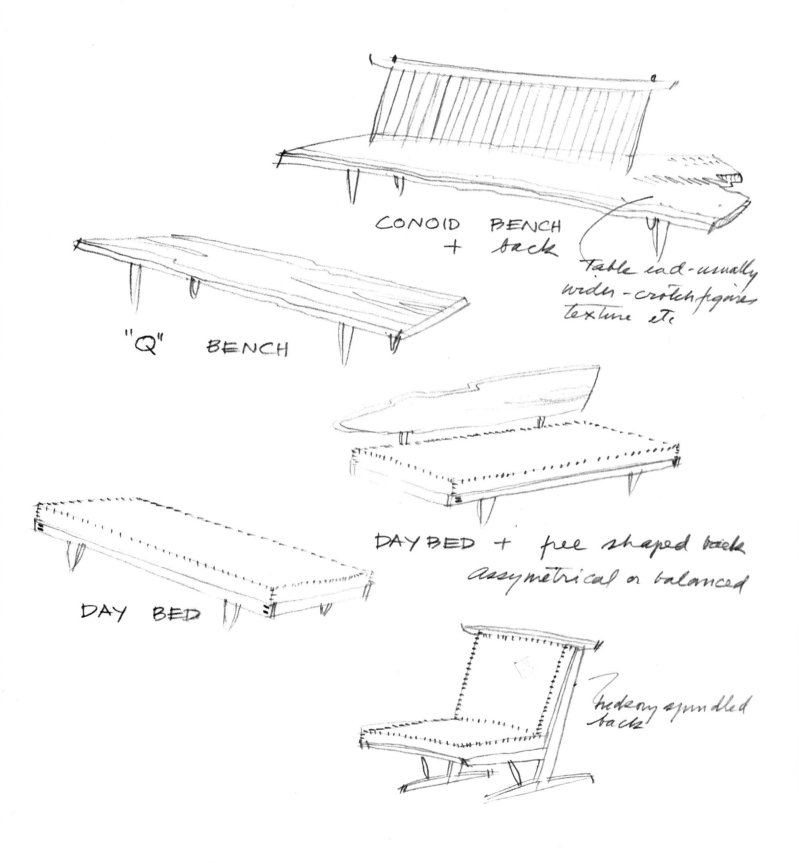

CONOID BENCH + back

Table end - usually wider - crotch figures texture etc

"Q" BENCH

DAY BED + free shaped back
assymetrical or balanced

DAY BED

Hickory spindled back

The Conoid chair. I designed and made the first chair in 1969 and since then there has been a steady demand.

East Indian rosewood table top. A rotted out area has been cleaned and spanned with a butterfly key, also of rosewood.

Surface of English walnut and
butterfly inlay of rosewood.

Minguren I coffee table made of book-matched
English walnut root. At right, detail of the free
edge. Boards made from roots are difficult to
book-match both because roots tend to dry
irregularly and because the grain can—and
does—run every which way.

Joinery details. These dovetail joints are typical of what we do on cabinets and benches.

Dovetail joinery on a walnut cabinet. Some of the initial cuts are made with a precision saw, but the handwork that goes into a joint like this is considerable.

Greenrock stools. Bases are walnut. Here the
cushions are made from antique Japanese cloth:
indigo-dyed cotton with stenciled patterns,
woven and colored over a century ago.

Greenrock coffee table in American walnut. This
table looks deceptively light despite a top that is
a two-and-a-half-inch thick slab, measuring
thirty-one-and-a-half inches square. It stands
sixteen inches high.

Even the fusebox of the Minguren Museum (*above, left*) enjoys the woodworker's touch; here a mortice and tenon, with the tenon projecting.

Seat of walnut and spindles of hickory.

Single-slab walnut bench with back.

I first conceived of the Mira chair as a highchair so that our baby daughter Mira could sit with us at the table. I eventually added a foot support, which made it very convenient as a bar or potter's stool.

Sometimes described as a Windsor derivative, the New chair is a basic design with several variations; the one shown here has both arms and rockers; we make the chair in walnut or cherry with hickory spindles.

I began to work on the Conoid chair with the idea of designing a chair that had only two legs; I put on the bladelike feet to support the chair. The design has worked well. A conventional four-legged chair is hard to move over a carpet, but the Conoid chair can be slipped over carpeted surfaces with ease.

This redwood-root coffee table has great sculptural qualities because the graining is so convoluted. The table top seems to have emerged directly from the material.

Two walnut Conoid chairs in the Minguren Museum stand like sentinels before an extraordinary piece of buckeye burl root, cut crosswise in a great slab that will someday make a superb table or desk.

Persian walnut room divider. Even the back is finished with solid wood. The vertically grilled sliding doors are backed with pandanus cloth, made from a Southeast Asian palm.

The top of this room divider is made of a single board of Persian walnut. It also has a solid-wood back. On it is displayed a "stele" of English walnut, a single slab of beautiful sculptural wood. *Below*: A cabinet of East Indian rosewood with doors faced with *asa-no-ha* grille work. Called the Odakyu cabinet after the Japanese department store where it was first exhibited. In Japan, major department stores not only function as retailers but also play an important cultural role. They support many art exhibitions, seminars on cultural topics, and the like.

The Minguren Museum has a roof that is a hyperbolic parabaloid. The inverted U-shape line of the roof seen in this picture shows the parabola. The span of the room is thirty-six-by-thirty-six feet, but note that there are no trusses or beams. *Below*: The Minguren I coffee table was first shown in Tokyo around 1972. This one, of English oak burl, is on display in our Minguren Museum and is flanked by two Lounge chairs with single arms.

This table was originally designed in the mid-1960s for Frenchman's Cove, an out-of-the-way resort in Port Antonio, Jamaica. The first tables, in walnut, were made for the dining room of the resort's "Great House," or main lodge, but the one shown here is made of East Indian laurel, a rich hardwood from Kerala.

Umbrellas and *zōri,* or sandals, are left outside the door of the Mountain Villa. Once inside, guests relax in one large room that combines living and dining areas. The posts are red cedar and the purlins white oak. The floor is a combination of American walnut and red birch. The fireplace is local Pennsylvania fieldstone, and there is an apparatus behind the fireplace designed to heat the entire building with circulating hot air. The coffee table is buckeye burl root, and the Greenrock stools are covered with indigo-dyed cotton from Japan's Meiji period, around 1870. The wall hanging, calligraphy done by Ben Shahn, says *tomi,* or "good fortune."

This hanging wall case of East Indian laurel (temporarily supported by a wood upright) has an unusual top. The board was used without much trimming so the top has a free-edge front and an extreme overhang at one end. Above hangs a serigraph of Ben Shahn's *Cat's Cradle* and at left stands a piece of Bizen pottery.

The Conoid Studio. Floors are shaded from all walnut (and a few planks of rosewood) to solid cherry. All are set in with screws and plugs. *Tatami* mats, imported from Japan, have been placed on a raised platform near the south windows, making a good display area.

The Minguren Museum. Both the double-glazed glass and the paper-covered *shōji* are effective insulators. The stairway is made of three-inch thick oak planks cantilevered twelve inches into a fieldstone wall.

MINGUREN I

MINGUREN II

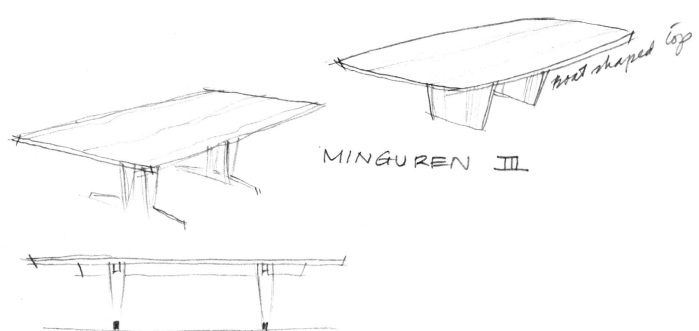

nut shaped top

MINGUREN III

MINGUREN IV

The small dining table I built into our house echoes the design of my Minguren tables, sketched above. Note the similarity of the bases. Both the top and the base of this small table have been taken from a single piece of figured English walnut. The Conoid chairs have single-board seats of figured Persian walnut.

CONOID TABLE

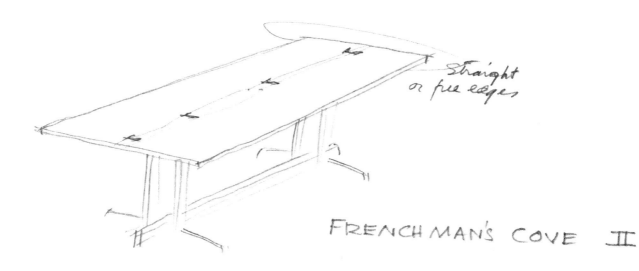

FRENCHMAN'S COVE II

straight or free edges

The Rockefeller table is similar in design to these sketched here.

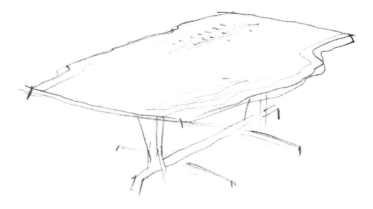

SINGLE BOARD CONOID

The dining table made for Governor and Mrs. Nelson A. Rockefeller in 1974 for their home at Pocantico Hills. Here set with Imari ware, the Rockefeller table is two book-matched boards of East Indian laurel. The Conoid chairs are walnut. We also designed the cabinet, to the left; it is a design I call *bahut*, after the French word for this sort of living and dining room furniture.

The family room of the home of Governor and Mrs. Nelson A. Rockefeller built in Pocantico Hills, near Tarrytown, New York, in 1974. The table is solid walnut and has quite an unusual design. The top consists of a basic square, but each side of this square is the base of a triangular addition—these additions make the table quite large in surface area. Behind the table on the wall hangs a large calligraphic work by Shiryū Morita.

SLAB #1

ROUND MINGUREN

Round coffee Tables can often be
made in a 2 board book match
of unusual graining — sometimes
with natural forms around the perimeter

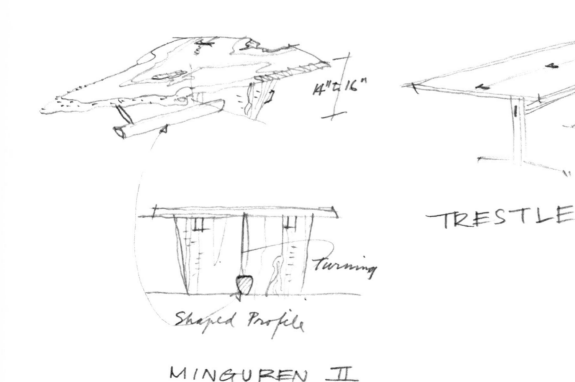

TRESTLE

MINGUREN II

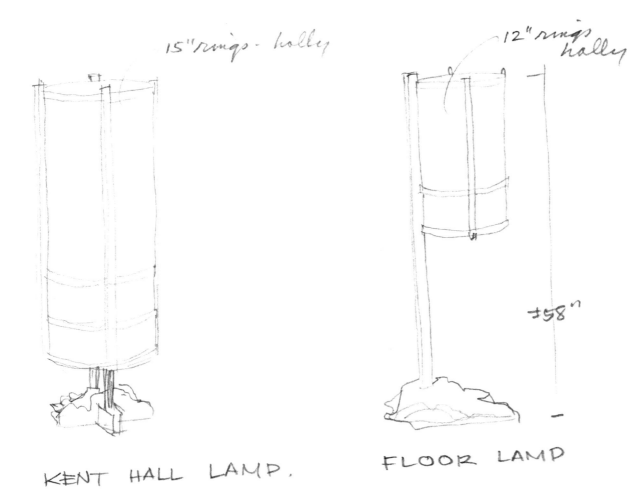

15" rings - holly

12" rings holly

≠58"

KENT HALL LAMP.

FLOOR LAMP

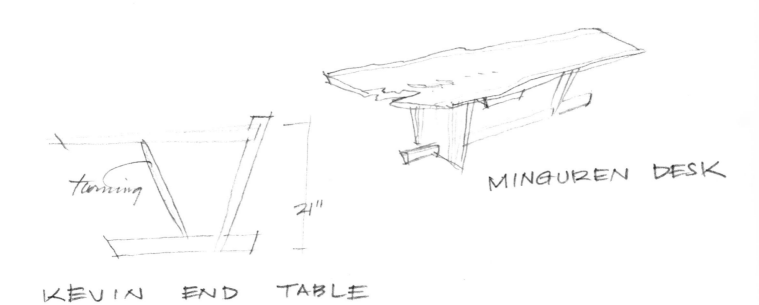

turning

21"

KEVIN END TABLE

MINGUREN DESK

Architect Junzō Yoshimura designed a Japanese-style home for
Governor and Mrs. Nelson A. Rockefeller in Pocantico Hills, near
Tarrytown, in 1974. From the living room is a panoramic view of the
Hudson River Valley. I provided about two hundred pieces of furniture
in all—from small lamps and occasional tables, like the pieces sketched
on the two preceding pages, to dining tables and chairs. All the
furniture shown in these color photographs were designed and
produced in our New Hope workshop—except the loveseats in front of
the fireplace, and even then we made their wood bases.

Epilogue: Transformation

My life has been a long search across the tumbling screes on mountain slopes around the world to find small points of glowing truth.

Backed into a soulless steel and glass jungle which threatens the disintegration of our systems and institutions, we face an unknown future. With a prodigious drive we have built the first true megalopolis, but we have produced so little of any intrinsic value. There is not a single monument in recent centuries to express any sort of transcending human will or soul. Taken as a whole, we have the poorest assemblage of architecture in the history of man, without a single building of greatness.

There are few to listen or to see, but a small nucleus of truth resides in the crannies of the world waiting for a receptive ear. The Karma Yogin, he who follows the path of action, understands the road that must be taken. We are on the verge of a great and heroic revolution, a revolution of the soul—a revolution so vast and influential that the revolutions of the West, the French, the American and the Russian, will appear childish and impotent. The transformations stretch out into endless vistas before us.

The transformation calls for the joining together of those who seek "something else," who aspire to new lives free from material desire, who can throw open their arms in charity and create purer forms than we have ever known.

With so many people of good will searching for bits of light, a great movement will one day arrive based on the union of total freedom with a creativity that we cannot see or even conceive of.

It is a difficult movement, a pioneering movement, similar in a way to that experienced by the early English settlers. The movement involves not only beating back the wilderness but also beating back the soulless urban jungles throughout the world.

It is sad that when some movements arrive their time is already past. Such is the case with "modern" art. "Modern" architecture was interesting and exciting in the thirties, but by the eighties structures have become filled with dead forms. The new buildings do not have the staying power and catholicity of architecture during the truly great periods.

The deep, rich movements, which produced the Dipylon vase, the Doric column, the Chartres cathedral, the Katsura Detached Palace, all were significant in their youthful vigor and simple creativity. May we return to that spirit. It is not man's prerogative to destroy himself. We can only believe in the warm golden light in the darkness.

Since I am a woodworker, the practical aspects interest me primarily. The materials used, the utility of an object, the forms developed are vital. The necessary skills and the resultant beauty must be there. Arts and crafts should be based on pure truth, taking materials and techniques from the past to synthesize with the present. We should be content to work on a small scale and integrally with nature and not violate it.

In a personal way my family and I have gone underground, since we have little relationship to contemporary mores, institutions, economy or systems. Ours is a search for pure truth in the most realistic of ways—the making of things.

There was no other way for me but to go alone, secure with my family, placing stone upon stone, seeking kinship with each piece of wood, eventually creating an inward mood of space, then bit by bit finding peace and joy in shaping timber into objects of utility and perhaps, when nature smiles, beauty.

Chronology

1905   Born in Spokane, Washington, eldest child of Katsuharu Nakashima, of samurai lineage, and Suzu Thoma Nakashima, who, as a young woman, served under Takeko Horikawa, official court taster for the Emperor Meiji (r. 1868-1912).

1917-23   A member of the Boy Scouts of America, attaining the rank of "Eagle." Scouting activities provide opportunities for close contact with the natural world with long hikes through the Cascade and Olympic mountains.

1925   First visit to Japan, meeting many relatives.

1929   Graduates from the University of Washington, Seattle, with the degree of B.Arch. In 1928, awarded scholarship for undergraduate year abroad; takes Diploma at the École Américaine des Beaux Arts, Fontainebleau, France, and wins Prix Fontainebleau for his architectural studies.

1930   Graduates from Massachusetts Institute of Technology, Cambridge, with the degree of M.Arch.

1930-31   Paints murals for the Pennsylvania capitol in the studio of Richard Brooks, New York.

1931-33   Architectural designer, greater New York area, with the Long Island State Park Commission and the New York State government.

1933-34   Lives in Paris, employed part of the time by music publisher, Yves de la Casinière. Continues to Tokyo by steamer through the Suez Canal, with short stops in India and China.

George Nakashima at age two. Spokane, Washington.

Posed in her court robes, Takeko Horikawa, under whose direction my mother served in the court of Emperor Meiji in the 1880s.

1934-36   Joins Antonin Raymond's architectural firm in Tokyo. Young colleagues include Kunio Maekawa and Junzō Yoshimura.

1937-39   Arrives at ashram of Sri Aurobindo in Pondicherry, Tamil Nadu, India, as architectural representative of Raymond's office to design and supervise construction of major building, Golconda, a dormitory. Becomes disciple of Sri Aurobindo, and is honored by being given the Sanskrit name Sundarananda ("One who delights in beauty") by the great Hindu spiritual leader himself.

1939   Returns to Japan via China on one of the last Japanese refugee ships after the outbreak of war in China. For six months helps friend Kunio Maekawa, who has just established his own firm, with architectural projects. Kenzō Tange, a recent college graduate, is also an employee.

1940   Engaged to Marion Okajima, born in America and of samurai lineage, a teacher of English at a private school in Tokyo. Each returns to Seattle, Washington, as political situation in the Pacific deteriorates.

1941   Marries Marion. A daughter and son, Mira and Kevin, are born in 1942 and 1954.

1941-42   Establishes a furniture workshop in Seattle, an integrated operation foreshadowing the method of operation in New Hope; development interrupted by the Pacific War and the internment of all those of Japanese ancestry.

Sri Aurobindo, founder of the ashram in Pondicherry, personally autographed this picture and presented it to me for my architectural work for the community.

Mira Richard, the Mother of the ashram.

1942-43	Interned with family at Minidoka, Idaho.
1943	Resettled in New Hope area, Pennsylvania.
1944-46	Starts making furniture in a shop in Bucks County, Pennsylvania, just outside New Hope.
1946	Moves to Aquetong Road in New Hope and establishes craft-furniture business. Through the years, receives numerous commissions for furniture and some architectural design from various parts of the world.
1952	Receives Craftsmanship Medal from the American Institute of Architects.
1960	Begins to teach his own integrated woodworking methods by designing and consulting for two native shops—one in Ahmedabad, in India's Gujarat region; the other in Takamatsu, Kagawa prefecture, Japan.
1965	Daughter Mira marries Tetsu Amagasu in Tokyo. They have four children—Satoru, Maria, Shanti and Misha.
1979	Named Fellow of the American Crafts Council, New York.
1981	Recipient of the Hazlett Award for the Crafts, given by the State of Pennsylvania.

Accomplishments

Awards

Gold Craftmanship Medal, American Institute of Architects, 84th Annual Convention, New York

June 1952

> "George Nakashima, inheritor of great traditions, conscientious pupil of cunning and skillful masters, the American Institute of Architects is honored to confer upon you its Craftsmanship Medal. You have perpetuated in your work in the design and making of furniture the highest standards of past ages of handicrafts, and that respect for good materials and honest labor, that recognition of human use by rich or poor, that will in any age distinguish great craftsmanship; we salute your original and distinguished effort to employ the machine and its resources sincerely, to give our own day beautiful furniture and other objects, by whose standard we will not be ashamed to measure architecture."

Award for Craftsmanship, Miami Chapter, American Institute of Architects

November 1959

Silver Medal of Honor in Design and Craftsmanship, The Architectural League of New York

April 1960

> "In Recognition of the Excellence of Design, Appropriateness of Concept and Materials Expressed in His Furniture and Showroom in New Hope, Pennsylvania."

Catholic Art Association Medal   August 1969

> *"He holds that normal work combines truth to form with goodness for use, and in this combination achieves a holiness. George Nakashima clearly practices such craftsmanship. We ask him to accept this token as an expression of our gratitude for his example and admiration for his work."*

Award and Title of Fellow, The American Crafts Council, New York November 1979

Silver Plaque Award for the Arts, Central Bucks Chamber of Commerce, Bucks County, Pennsylvania May 1980

Gold Medal and Title of "Japanese-American of the Biennium in the Field of the Arts," Japanese-American Citizens League, San Francisco August 1980

Honor Award for Inspired Creativity and Outstanding Sensitivity in Design, The Pennsylvania Society of Architects of the American Institute of Architecture September 1980

Hazlett Award for Outstanding Achievement in the Crafts, the State of Pennsylvania, Philadelphia May 1981

My furniture was shown at the Museum of Modern Art in 1951, and this small "module" was sent on an international exhibition that toured Europe.

Exhibitions

Asterisks indicate major exhibitions and one-man shows.

America House, New York, NY   September 1950

Museum of Modern Art, New York, NY   January   1951
    "Design for Use, U.S.A."
    (Later shown abroad as part of a cultural exchange program.)

*Philadelphia Art Alliance, Philadelphia, PA   October   1951
    "Contemporary Furniture by Nakashima"

U.S. State Department, at the U.S. Embassy, Tokyo   January   1952
    "Artists of Japanese Ancestry Who Have Received Recognition in the
    United States"

*Knoll Associates, New York, NY   June   1952
    "Exhibition of A.I.A. Craftsmanship Medal Winner"

Museum of Contemporary Crafts, New York, NY   February- 1957
    "Furniture by Craftsmen"   April

The Kikkoman display in the concourse of Grand Central Station, 1962.

*Kikkoman Shoyu International, a promotional exhibition for Kikkoman products designed and built by George Nakashima in the concourse of Grand Central Station, New York, NY   April   1962

Akron Art Institute, OH
  "Why Is an Object?"   September 1962

*Parry Barn, New Hope, PA
  "A Comprehensive Exhibit," a show consisting of over 100 pieces, sponsored by the New Hope Historical Society   July   1963

Carderock Springs, MD
  "Model Home Exhibit"
  (A four-bedroom model home completely furnished with eighty-five pieces.)   November 1963

Museum of Contemporary Crafts, New York, NY
  "Designed for Production: The Craftsman's Approach," sponsored by the American Federation of Arts and circulated throughout the United States for two years.   April-May   1964

*Wallace Laboratory, Cranbury, NJ
  "Tea and Tranquility," a replica of a Japanese teahouse, shown at the American Medical Association Convention in San Francisco, and also at meetings in Chicago, Miami, and New York City.   June   1964

My first large exhibition in Japan was in 1968 at the Odakyu Department Store.

Hunterdon County Art Center, Clinton, NJ "First Hunterdon Craft Exhibition"	July- August	1967
Nelson Gallery-Atkins Museum, Kansas City, MO "Friends of Art"	February	1967
*Odakyu HALC, Tokyo, Japan First Exhibition	March	1968
*Odakyu HALC, Tokyo, Japan Second Exhibition	September	1970
*Renwick Gallery, The Smithsonian Institution, Washington, D.C. "Woodenworks," co-sponsored by the Minnesota Museum of Art, Saint Paul, where the exhibition opened in January, 1972.	February	1972
*Odakyu HALC, Tokyo, Japan Third Exhibition	September	1973
Cincinnati Art Museum, Cincinnati, OH "Change of Pace"	October	1975

La Soledad, San Miguel de Allende in Mexico, 1975.

*Odakyu HALC, Tokyo, Japan Fourth Exhibition	September 1978
*Museum of Fine Arts, Boston, MA "Please Be Seated"	June 1979
*The Hand and the Spirit, Crafts Gallery, Inc. Scottsdale, AZ	October 1979
*Full Circle, Alexandria, VA "The Enduring Craftsmanship of George Nakashima"	November 1980

Selected Commissions

Major Commercial Projects

Commercial display design for Kikkoman International   1962
    Exhibition in Grand Central Station Concourse
    Produced by Lennen & Newell, New York, NY.

Designed garden for the American Federation of Arts   1962
    Headquarters at 41 East 65th Street, New York, NY

Frenchman's Cove, Port Antonio, Jamaica, West Indies   1951-61
    Furnished the "Great House" and the "Katsura House," two lodges
    of this resort hotel. The manufacturing for the "Katsura House" was
    done in High Gate, Jamaica, with native workmen.

Major Interior Work: Churches and Temples

St. John's Church, Huntingdon Valley, PA	1958
Temple Sinai, Washington, D.C.	1961
Mt. Saviour, Elmira, NY	1961-63
Greensburg Cathedral, Greensburg, PA	1962
Portsmouth Priory, Portsmouth, RI	1962-71
Sisters of the Immaculate Heart of Mary, Morrisville, PA	1962
Westminster Methodist Church, Westminster, MD	1962
Novitiate for the Sisters of Charity, Greensburg, PA	1963
Sisters of Charity, McKeesport, PA (complete interior)	1963
St. Denis Convent of Mercy Academy, Monroeville, PA	1964-67
Princeton Jewish Center, Princeton, NJ	1966
Assumption of the Blessed Virgin Mary, Feasterville, PA	
Private Chapel in the residence of the Bishop of Savannah, GA	

The Church of Christ the King in Katsura, on the outskirts of Kyoto, 1964.

Major Interior Work: Colleges

Duquesne University, Pittsburgh, PA	1951
Columbia University, Kent Hall Lounge, New York, NY	1964
Carnegie Institute of Technology, Pittsburgh, PA	1966
Mount Mercy College, Pittsburgh, PA	1968
University of Pittsburgh, PA	1968

Integated Design Projects: Architecture and Furnishings

St. Paul's Church, Karuizawa, Japan   1935
Golconda, Sri Aurobindo Ashram, Pondicherry, India   1939
  A large disciples' residence, Golconda, presented Nakashima with
  his first great opportunity to combine original architectural design
  with complete furniture design.
Church of Christ the King, Katsura, Japan   1965
  Nakashima's daughter, Mira, trained as an architect, assisted in the
  design and supervised the construction.
Monastery of Christ in the Desert, Abiquiu, NM   1972
La Soledad, San Miguel de Allende, Guanajuato, Mexico (including
  design of altar)   1975

Bibliography

All items comprising this bibliography are magazine articles about George Nakashima, his design and his work. This list has been arranged chronologically (as well as according to language) primarily in order to show the continuous interest in Nakashima since the mid-1940s when he established his craft workshop in New Hope, Pennsylvania.

English-language Publications

INTERIORS "Modern Doesn't Pay or Does It?" Bernard Rudofsky	March	1946	pp. 66-75
FORTUNE "Furniture Industry, the Handicraftsman in Wood" George Nelson	January	1947	p. 63
SCIENCE ILLUSTRATED "A Designer Who Works by Hand" John Corcoran	July	1948	pp. 80-83
CRAFT HORIZONS "Nakashima" Mary Lyon	Autumn	1949	pp. 16-19
ARTS AND ARCHITECTURE "House of George Nakashima, Woodworker"	January	1950	
SCENE "Designed for Living" Eddie Shimano	May	1950	pp. 30-37
INTERIORS "The Year's Work: Residential"	August	1950	p. 77
HOUSE AND HOME "George Nakashima, His Furniture, His House, His Way of Life"	March	1952	Cover and pp. 80-89

ARCHITECTURAL RECORD "Knoll Exhibits Work of A.I.A. Craftsmanship Medal Winner"	July	1952	p. 13
LOOK "A Chair for Mira"	September 23	1952	p. 98
HOUSE BEAUTIFUL "Fireplaces"	October	1952	
JUBILEE "George Nakashima, Woodworker"	July	1953	pp. 20-27
LIFE "Oriental Fireplace"	December 7	1953	
HOUSE BEAUTIFUL "A Hand Crafted Object Needn't Cost More"	October	1954	
ARCHITECTURAL FORUM "Romantic Realism"	May	1955	pp. 150-153
HARPER'S MAGAZINE "After Hours: Majority of One"	July	1955	pp. 82-84
ART IN AMERICA "Nakashima, American Craftsman" Edgar Kaufmann, Jr.	December	1955	pp. 30-33
CRAFT HORIZONS "Craftsmanship in Architecture"	May-June	1956	pp. 26-31
INDUSTRIAL DESIGN "The Craftsman as Designer-Producer" Don Wallance	August	1956	p. 81
CRAFT HORIZONS "Furniture by Craftsmen"	March- April	1957	p. 36
ARCHITECTURAL RECORD "Sea Shell Roof, Adventure in Structure"	November	1957	pp. 183-188
ENGINEERING NEWS RECORD "Conoid with Corrugations Makes an Unusual Roof" Matthys P. Levy and Paul Weidlinger	December	1957	pp. 46-48
HOUSE BEAUTIFUL "Redwood Shelter"	May	1958	p. 223
HOUSE BEAUTIFUL "The Glorification of Wood" Group designed for Widdicomb Mueller	October	1958	Cover and pp. 172-177
ARCHITECTURAL RECORD "Nakashima Designed Furniture: Tomorrow's Traditional?"	November	1958	p. 244
LOOK "Nakashima and Son" J. Peter	April 28	1959	pp. 67-69

ARCHITECTURAL RECORD "A Lumber Storage House, New Hope, PA"	July	1959	p. 217
MARYKNOLL MAGAZINE "Artist Who Works With Wood" Joseph M. Michenfelder	March	1960	pp. 4-10
PROGRESSIVE ARCHITECTURE "A Craftsman's Philosophy"	October	1962	p. 74
HOUSE BEAUTIFUL "When a Cabinet Maker Builds He Makes Wood Sing"	April	1963	pp. 154-155
ARCHITECTURAL AND ENGINEERING NEWS "Names"	September	1963	p. 119
MEDICAL WORLD NEWS "Tea and Tranquility"	June 5	1964	
LITURGICAL ARTS "Church of Christ the King, Katsura, Kyoto, Japan"	February	1965	p. 49
LITURGICAL ARTS "Monastery of Christ in the Desert, Abiquiu, New Mexico"	August	1965	pp. 132-133
JUBILEE "Return to St. Benedict, New Mexico"	September	1965	
LITURGICAL ARTS "Church of Christ the King, Katsura, Kyoto, Japan"	November	1966	
SUNDAY BULLETIN MAGAZINE "Woodworking and a Search for Wisdom"	January 28	1968	pp. 8-10
LIFE "Fulfilling our Need and Nostalgia for Wood—The Craftsman"	June	1970	pp. 75-79
SMITHSONIAN "A Way to be Free: Nakashima's Life" Miriam Plotnicov	September	1972	pp. 62-67
TODAY (Philadelphia Inquirer Magazine) "Nakashima's Secret for Riches and Happiness"	February 17	1974	Cover and pp. 16-29
MIAMI HERALD MAGAZINE "Nakashima's Art"	March 14	1976	
H. AND S. DECORATING GUIDE "An Artist Who Makes Tables and Chairs" Robert Perron	Fall	1976	pp. 130-133
HOUSE BEAUTIFUL Nelson Rockefeller House "A Place of Silent Beauty"	October	1978	pp. 93-99

| FINE WOODWORKING
"George Nakashima, For Each Plank
There's One Perfect Use"
John Kelsey | January/
February | 1979 | Cover and
pp. 40-46 |
| TOWN AND CONTRY
"The Spirit of George Nakashima"
Hugh Best | February | 1981 | pp. 167-171 |

Japanese-language Publications

GEIJUTSU SHINCHŌ "George Nakashima"	March	1956	p. 198
KOKUSAI KENCHIKU "George Nakashima's Showroom"	May	1956	pp. 38-39
JAPAN ARCHITECT "George Nakashima, Woodworker"	February	1963	pp. 59-68
KOKUSAI KENCHIKU "Minguren Nakashima Chair" Hiroshi Ogawa	May	1965	p. 69
JAPAN ARCHITECT "The Katsura Catholic Church, Kyoto"	September	1967	pp. 89-92
GEIJUTSU SHINCHŌ "George Nakashima Returns to His Ancestral Home"	May	1968	pp. 89-94
FUJIN NO TOMO "George Nakashima's Furniture" Tsutomu Watanabe	July	1968	pp. 132-135
SPACE DESIGN	May	1968	pp. 83-84
DESIGN "George Nakashima, Woodworker"	June	1968	pp. 65-71
FUJIN KŌRON "A Walk with Beauty—George Nakashima's Furniture Exhibition"	June	1968	pp. 197-199
SHIN FUJIN "The Magic of Wood Grain" Yūichirō Kōjiro	October	1968	pp. 98-107
SHŪKAN ASAHI "George Nakashima, the Woodworker Who Thinks of Trees' Second Life"	August 18	1970	pp. 137-140
SHIN JŪTAKU "Father's House" (with furniture by George Nakashima)	September	1970	pp. 1-8
MAINICHI GRAPH "Taking Hold of the Soul of a Tree"	October 4	1970	pp. 16-23
SPACE DESIGN "I Will Make a Tree Live Again" George Nakashima	January	1974	pp. 40-43

JAPAN ARCHITECT "The House at Pocantico Hills"	September	1976	pp. 143-160
SHŪKAN GENDAI "World-Famous Woodworker Returns to Japan"	June 1	1978	pp. 3-11
KATEI GAHŌ "A Visit with a World Famous Woodworker, George Nakashima" Yūichirō Kōjiro	September	1978	pp. 119-130

Publications in Other Languages

AMERIKA (Russian) "Poetry in Wood"	April	1973	pp. 23-27
AMERYKA (Polish) "Poetry in Wood"	April	1973	
AMERIKA (Russian) "Nakashima's Fireplace"	November	1973	

Unpublished Works

Hepler, Paul Howard. "A Study of the Work Training and Craft Processes of a Contemporary American Wood Craftsman." Doctoral Dissertation, Teacher's College, Columbia University, New York, 1969.

Glossary of Terms

In a completely unselfconscious way, George Nakashima uses Japanese, French and Sanskrit words when he writes and talks, and this is simply evidence of the influences of having lived in several different cultures. He also makes frequent use of terms special to architecture and woodworking. Indeed, he has developed his own personal, subjective usage, which is understandable in view of his four decades of operating and directing his New Hope workshop. Thus, the brief explanatory notes to the terms that follow, by the author himself, should make clear his occasional idiosyncratic usages.

ANDON	A paper-covered, vertical lantern; a traditional Japanese lamp.
ASA-NO-HA	Literally, "hemp leaf." This decorative pattern, a stylized rendering of the hemp leaf, is ubiquitous in Japanese design—it appears on fabrics, decorative papers, and lacquer and inlay work among other decorative arts. The *asa-no-ha* wood grille is perhaps the most sophisticated design made. See page 139 for a sketch.
ASHRAM	A monastic community in India, usually with a living guru.
AVATAR	A god-man. In Hindu mythology, the incarnation of a diety in human or animal form is known as an *avatar*.
BAHUT	The French term for a chest or cabinet, especially one having a rounded top, and used as furniture.
BATTEN	A narrow but long strip of wood used to cover the small gap between two vertical boards in building construction.
BOARD	A flat slab of sawn wood, usually not too large, that is relatively thin in relation to its width. Often used interchangeably with the term lumber.
BOLE	The trunk of a tree.
BONSAI	Literally, "potted plant." The Japanese art of cultivating dwarfed trees or shrubs; even if only a foot or so high, the specimens have a mature appearance. Some prized *bonsai* trees are several hundred years old.
BOOK-MATCH	"Matching" lumber to show the wood grain to best advantage is an important concern for the woodworker. Two successive boards from the same log, laid side by side like the double-spread pages of an open book, are said to be *book-matched*. See the illustration on page 121. Boards taken off a log with an especially fine saw lend themselves to an almost perfect match because of the minimum kerf loss.

BOULE	French for "ball, sphere or globe." In lumbering, the expression is "cutting for the *boule*." It means to cut a log from one side to the other, without turning it and without first trimming it square, so that the boards can be grouped in the order that they were cut to resemble the rounded, *boule*-like form of the log. For an illustration see page 32. The expressions "plain-sawing" and "sawing through and through" may also be applied to this sawing method.
BURL	An abnormal, rounded outgrowth or enlargement on the trunk or branch of a tree. Causes of burls are not yet perfectly understood, but burls appear not to affect the health of the tree. On close examination, a burl may seem to be comprised of a mass of buds or "eyes." These make the alignment of the wood fiber very irregular so that the grain of burled wood forms clusters of round curls. Sometimes burling may be concentrated in one area, but with some species, like the English oak burl, it may even occupy the whole tree. See page 123 for an illustrated example.
	Clusters of burls in the wood forming the shape of a bunch of grapes are known as *grape burls*. A literal translation of this expression is also often used in Japanese.
BUTTERFLY INLAY	In woodworker's parlance, a small wood member shaped somewhat like a butterfly to hold two boards together or to reinforce a weak spot. The grain of the butterfly member must run at right angles to the boards. The butterfly inlay is both functional and decorative, as the photograph on page 154 shows.
	The bottom of the butterfly is tapered slightly. Glued, it is forced into the place which has been prepared for it. A screw is driven into each wing, from below, for extra strength. The butterfly is made to stand about $\frac{1}{16}$-inch above the surface so it can be finished flush after the glue has dried.
CAMBIUM	Near the bark of a tree, between the phloem and the sapwood, is a thin layer of cells known as the *cambium*. These cells, through which the vital fluids of the tree rise and descend, produce the new wood and bark cells of each year's growth.
CHECK	A split in the wood, usually radial—that is, across the rings of annual growth—sometimes seen in the standing tree but most often after felling. *Checking* is the result of stress or shrinkage in the wood during drying.
CONOID	A three-dimensional geometric form with a base that is a square or rectangle. One side rises in an arch, or parabola; the opposite side is a low rectangle. Between the arched and rectangular sides extends a rounded plane.
	We call one of our buildings, which I designed after this geometric form, the Conoid Studio. The roof is experimental—a thin shell of concrete two-and-a-half-inches thick, spanning feet forty square. See page 35.
	Designs developed in this building are called *Conoid* pieces.
CROSS-GRAIN	Cutting or marking wood at a ninety degree angle to the direction of the fibers in the wood. This term also refers to wood that is cut so that the grain runs parallel to the width of the board.
CROWN TREES	After a large tree is cut, smaller trees may sprout from the cambium layer of the exposed cross section of the trunk, forming a circlet of new growth. These are called *crown trees*, and often grow to considerable size.
CUPPING	During curing, boards often become distorted, and the edges and ends rise slightly to form a depression or "cup" in the center of the board.

DAIKU | The Japanese expression for carpenter—or better, a master builder. *Dai* means "great," and *ku* is "construction."

DARSHAN | A Sanskrit term used to denote the periods when a spiritual or religious leader receives his disciples and followers.

DENDROLOGY | The science and study of trees.

DOWEL | A wood member, cylindrical in shape, that fits tightly into a corresponding hole and is used to fasten or align adjacent wood pieces.

DRESS DOWN | To smooth the surface of a roughly sawn board or plank with a hand or machine plane.

FEATHER | One "feels" a feather in sharpening a blade. It is a microscopic rough edge that develops during the first stages of sharpening and becomes limp like a feather as sharpening progresses. It must be removed by honing on a very fine stone as a final step.

FIGURE | The pattern produced in a wood surface by coloration irregularities and annual growth rings. Deviations from the regular grain lines such as knots and burls contribute to the design of the figure. The most extravagant figuring is usually found in boards cut from the crotch of a tree, where two large limbs or the trunk and a limb intersect. Sometimes the whole trunk may produce figured wood, as with heavily burled trees.

FIT, DRIVE | In wood joinery, the word *fit* refers to the accuracy with which one member is joined to another. A thirty-secondth of an inch becomes important; this can be the difference between a tight-fitting joint or a loose, ill-made joint. When a joint is so tight that one member must be pounded into the other, it is called a *drive fit.*

Traditionally, Japanese houses were built with drive-fit joints. Carpenters worked to create the joints, and then another group of workers, called *tobi,* were put to work assembling all the joints.

FIT, SLOP | A joint where one member slips into the other with no friction is called a *slop fit.*

FLITCH | A board cut longitudinally from the trunk of a tree with the outer bark left on.

FREE EDGE | This is a phrase we coined in our New Hope workshop to describe a board or plank that has been debarked but otherwise left with a natural edge.

FUTON | Japanese bedding, consisting of a light mattress and quilt, which are folded up daily and kept in large built-in cupboards. From the same word, comes *za-buton,* which are flat pillows used as cushions for sitting on the floor in *tatami*-matted rooms.

GRADE SAWING | Commercially, logs are sawn in a number of ways to produce different "grades" of lumber, and the term *grade sawing* refers to this practice. For example, hardwoods are obtainable at most retail lumberyards in the following grades:
"FAS," or "Firsts and Seconds"
No. 1 Common
No. 2 Common
No. 3 Common
"FAS" is the most expensive because this lumber, cut from the outer portions of the log is clear of knots and perfect. No. 3 Common, taken from nearer the center of the log, is least expensive because it is knotty and is more liable to be defective.

GRAIN	Strictly speaking, grain refers simply to the direction or orientation of wood cells, particularly the fibrous elements. In different lumber one sees a number of grain types—straight, wavy, coarse, fine, etc.—but even in the same piece of lumber, different grain patterns are produced by winter wood and summer wood, the winter wood being slow-growing and hard, usually of a darker color. The type of grain that is seen in a piece of lumber is dictated in part by the method used to saw the log. See sketches on pages 96 and 99.
GRAIN RISE	Some woodworking techniques, especially heavy sanding to finish wood, tend to collapse the cells in the wood. But, wood cells are resilient, and this compression is only temporary. When the wood is wetted, the cells will resume—more or less—their original shape and stand up again. This produces roughness in the finish of the wood, otherwise known as *grain rise*.
HARDWOOD	Botanically, the group of trees that are broad-leaved, bear flowers, and shed their leaves annually. The term does not refer necessarily to the actual hardness of the wood. In general, hardwoods make good furniture because of their interesting grain and figures. See page 116 for further discussion of *hardwood* and *softwood*.
HEARTWOOD	The aged core of a tree, extending from the pith to the sapwood, which has ceased to contain living cells. Heartwood, which may be penetrated with gums and resins, is usually darker and harder than sapwood.
HINOKI	Japanese cypress.
HYPERBOLIC PARABALOID	This geometric form lends itself to extremely rigid building construction, and inspired my design for the roof of our Minguren Museum. See page 173. The hyperbolic parabaloid is derived from a mathematical formula that combines hyperbola and parabola.
JOINERY	The art and science of joining wooden parts together. Each of the hundreds of methods of joining two wood members may legitimately be called a *joint*. Some joints are made at right angles, others with wood members extending in the same direction. If the latter, the joint is called a "splice."
KARMA	Sanskrit, "destiny."
KERF	The cut or channel made by a saw.
KEYAKI	Oriental elm; see entry on zelkova.
KOTATSU	A traditional Japanese foot-warmer. A small charcoal brazier, sometimes set into a special recess in the floor, over which is placed a low table, draped with a quilt. The quilt keeps the warm air beneath the table and one stays cozily seated and quilt-swathed at the table. Even today, when more and more new homes in Japan are designed with central heating, an electric version of the *kotatsu* remains popular because it saves energy.
KODAMA	"Tree spirit" in Japan's animistic Shinto lore.
KSHATRIYA	A major Hindu caste, literally "warriors," including the military and governing occupations. Sri Aurobindo was of the Kshatriya caste.
LUMBER	Any wood cut out of a log into usable pieces. In our New Hope workshop, we use not only the word *lumber*, but also *board* and *slab*. Scale is the distinguishing factor; while "lumber" and "boards" mean about the same thing, "slabs" are much thicker. (In England, the term *timber* is used for what we in America call *lumber*.)

MANTRA — Sanskrit word used to define mystically charged words or phrases, recited repetitively to achieve spiritual development.

MIYA — In Japan, a Shinto shrine.

MORTICE — A term used in joinery to refer to the square or rectangular hole made in a piece of wood to receive the male member, or *tenon*.

NIRVANA — A Sanksrit term meaning "extinction of individual existence." A state of absolute bliss, characterized by release from the cycle of reincarnation, this is the supreme object to which all Buddhists aspire.

OYABASHIRA — Literally, "mother post." In Japanese farmhouses the most important structural member, usually a quality timber, is popularly called the *oyabashira*. My mother remembered using the perfectly planed and age-burnished *oyabashira* in her ancestral home as a mirror.

PARABOLA — The plane curve formed by the intersection of a cone and a plane parallel to one of its sides.

PHOTOSYNTHESIS — The process by which nature converts water and carbon dioxide into carbohydrates, using sunlight as the source of energy through the chlorophyll-containing cells in green plants.

PHLOEM — The thin layer of living tissue between the bark and the cambium layer that conducts food from the leaves to the rest of the tree. It eventually becomes part of the tree's bark.

PITH — The elementary growth of the infant tree from the seed. The *pith center* (as we call it in our workshop) never grows any wider than at its start, but it remains until the tree is destroyed or decayed, usually becoming a thin hollow. The plainsawn plank in which the pith appears is generally considered defective because it is usually surrounded by poor wood, often checked, or split.

PLANK — In the terminology which we've developed in our New Hope workshop, the smallest or relatively small pieces of wood are called *boards* (or *lumber*); larger ones are called *planks*; the largest (and thickest) are called *slabs*.

PLYWOOD — Made of thin layers (plies) of wood glued tightly together. Usually, grains of adjoining plies are laid at right angles. An odd number of plies is generally used in order to achieve balanced construction and strength. This means that the grain pattern on both front and back runs in the same direction. Precious hardwoods are often sliced into thin veneers for the front layer of plywood.

PRASAD — Sanskrit, "the food of the gods." In an ashram, the food sent to the guru; any food that is returned is considered blessed and is highly esteemed, somewhat like a sacrament.

PUNJABI — A long, shirt-like garment originating in the Punjab, in the northwest part of the Indian subcontinent; it is loose-fitting and popular throughout India and Pakistan.

QUARTERSAWN — This term describes a log, cut longitudinally into quarters, each of which is then sawn into lumber by cutting at right angles to the annual growth rings. This produces a stable wood product, not liable to warping; the grain has a ribbonlike character. See page 96 for a sketch.

ROLLING THE LOG	In commercial sawing, rolling the log refers to the way logs are rotated on the saw carriage to facilitate the cutting of various "grades" of lumber. First, four longitudinal cuts are made to eliminate the rounded sides (this is called *slabbing*), which transforms the log from a long cylinder to a postlike square. Then, after each successive cut, the log is turned ninety degrees, or "rolled." This method is well suited to sawing grade lumber. The outermost cuts produce lumber that is almost exclusively sapwood (not too highly prized) and innermost cuts, near the core, make knotty and defective boards. These become the lowest grades. Heartwood boards, or intermediate boards, are prime pieces.
SADHANA	Sanskrit. A methodology for reaching an inner truth in a spiritual consciousness.
SADHAK	Sanskrit. A disciple or seeker.
SAKE	Japanese rice wine.
SAMADHI	Sanskrit. A trance.
SAMURAI	A member of the warrior class in premodern Japan. After the imperial restoration in 1869, the days of this military aristocracy were numbered as feudal ways were replaced by the establishment of a modern state. The class as a whole was abolished in 1871, but the ethic of the samurai, including the following characteristics, has remained an important thread in Japanese culture: uncompromising loyalty, single-mindedness, preparedness, decorum, compassion, and readiness to die, whatever one's cause.
SAPWOOD	The layers of wood next to the cambium, phloem and bark, containing living cells, which move water from roots to leaves. Sapwood is usually lighter in color than heartwood. When the cells closest to the core of the tree lose their vitality and cease their active involvement in the life support of the tree, they turn into heartwood. Also called *xylem*.
SHAKUHACHI	A Japanese flute made of bamboo.
SHŌJI	In Japan, a sliding screen made of thin wood strips and covered with hand-laid paper. *Shōji* are used both for partitioning rooms and to cover windows. They insulate well against heat and cold and also act to diffuse light.
SHOULDER	In wood joinery, the flat surface of a wood member beyond which the tenon projects, or in which a cavity (mortice) has been made. The flat shoulders "bear the weight" of the joining of two wood members.
SHŪJI	Japanese, "calligraphy." The practice of writing characters in ink and brush is such an art that it is usually referred to with an honorific modifier as *o-shūji*.
SLAB	In our New Hope workshop, the term *slab* means a large, heavy plank. In sawyer's parlance, though, a *slab* is a semiround cut taken off a log when sawing it into a long square, in preparing for *rolling the log* and producing grade lumber.
SLABBING	Sawing a log into a long square form by making four longitudinal cuts; the four semirounds are called *slabs*.
SOFTWOOD	Botanically, the group of trees that are needle-bearing or cone-bearing, for example, the Douglas fir, white fir, or redwood. The term does not refer to the actual hardness of the wood. See page 116 for further discussion of *hardwood* and *softwood*.

SQUARING A LOG	Making a log square by *slabbing*.
STRIATION	Stripelike pattern in the wood of some types of trees which is formed by alternating dark and light grain.
STUD	Pre-cut wood, usually two by four inches, chiefly used in American building construction as upright posts in a framework for a wall covered with sheets of wallboard. This sort of wall is called a *stud wall*.
SUGI	Japanese cedar; cryptomeria.
TAPROOT	The main root of a plant, growing straight downward from the stem. In large trees, the taproot can produce interesting wood, full of character.
TATAMI	A two-inch-thick mat, covered with fine-woven straw, measuring about three by six feet. The floors of the main living rooms in Japanese-style houses are covered with *tatami*. So widespread is the use of *tatami* that it has long been the practice to use multiples of this module to measure the areas of both floor space and real estate.
TEN ITA	Japanese, literally "heavenly board." The term is used to describe a piece of lumber, outstanding because of its graining, figuring or color, that is to be used for a top of a piece of furniture—a table top, desk top or the like.
TENON	In wood joinery, the square or rectangular projection on a wood member that is to be inserted into a receiving cavity of matching size (mortice).
TIMBERLINE	That altitude on a mountain slope where timber and other flora end and the naked stones take over.
TUNG OIL	A hardening resinous oil extracted from the seeds of the tung tree, used for finishing furniture. It seems to have been first used by the Chinese, but today tung oil is a widely used product and available in most hardware stores.
VENEER	Thin sheets of wood, from $\frac{1}{100}$ to one-fourth inch thick. Veneers are usually sliced off the log with a large knife, but they may be sawn. Veneers of hardwood are used as a finish, or top layer, on plywood or another stable material for furniture and paneling.
WOODWORKER	One who makes things in wood, adopting an approach that seeks to integrate both art and craft. This is how the term is largely used today, and I believe that my pioneering efforts in this area since the forties have contributed to the acceptance of the new and deeper meaning of the word. In the earlier decades of this century, the primary inspiration to art and design was the machine and mass production; one only need turn to such groups as the Bauhaus in Germany for an example. By the mid-1940s, at least in furniture design, there were only "styles," executed by designers and put out by mass production. But, today the trend has reversed somewhat, with the limitations of mass selling and mass production now being recognized. The woodworker has a new place, actively participating both in the design and the production of unique items made of wood.
XYLEM	Sapwood.
YOGA	Sanskrit, "yoking" or "union." A Hindu discipline aimed at training one's consciousness for a state of perfect spiritual insight and peace, "a union with the Divine."
YOGIN	One who practices yoga.

ZELKOVA   An oriental elm, highly esteemed in Japan, where it is called *keyaki*. In earlier days, it was used both for buildings and for furniture, but now, having become relatively scarce and expensive, it is used mostly for furniture.

ZEN   A major form of Buddhism that arose in China and that developed in a unique way in Japan in the thirteenth century. Zen stressed self-discipline through meditation and appealed greatly to the samurai class. Zen inspired many Japanese art forms.

As a common noun, the word *zen* (*o-zen* with the honorific) refers to a small, low table for eating.

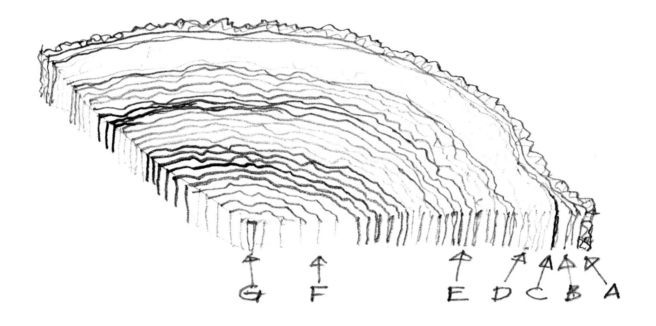

The growth of a tree

A. OUTER BARK The protective skin of a tree. The way bark expands characterizes the species of the tree: some scale off, some create fissures, and some seem almost elastic in their smoothness.

B. PHLOEM The sugars produced by the leaves are conducted to the roots and the trunk through this layer.

C. CAMBIUM LAYER Produces new wood and bark by the creation of cells.

D. XYLEM, OR SAPWOOD Through this layer moisture runs from the roots through the leaves and evaporates. This is the tree's "living" tissue. The sapwood is almost always lighter in color than the heartwood, producing delightful contrasts, but it is conventionally regarded as undesirable for fine woodworking. It is usually slightly softer than the heartwood.

E. HEARTWOOD The bulk of the tree, composed of cells no longer carrying vital juices—essentially dead. In some instances, the heartwood decays, leaving the tree a living shell.

F. EARLY GROWTH Fast growth of the tree in its youth. This heartwood is often knotty and therefore inferior.

G. PITH Where it all started.

Photo Credits

定価10,000円
in Japan

WRITTEN & DESIGNED BY KIT HINRICHS

TYPE
WISE

WITH DELPHINE HIRASUNA

NORTH LIGHT BOOKS

CREDITS

Authors:
Kit Hinrichs
Delphine Hirasuna

Designer:
Kit Hinrichs

Illustrator:
Regan Dunnick

Project Coordinator:
Gayle Marsh

Editorial Assistant:
Mary Lou Edmondson

Editor:
Diana Martin

TYPEWISE

Published by North Light Books, an imprint of F&W Publications, Inc., 1507 Dana Avenue, Cincinnati, Ohio, 45207. First Edition.

94 93 92 91 90 5 4 3 2 1

LIBRARY OF CONGRESS

Library of Congress Cataloging-in-Publication Data

Hinrichs, Kit.
Typewise / Kit Hinrichs and Delphine Hirasuna.
p. cm.
Includes Index.
ISBN 0-89134-356-3 (hrdcvr)
1. Printing, Practical–Layout. 2. Type and type-founding.
I. Hirasuna, Delphine, 1946- . II. Title.
Z246.H55 1990 90-7460
686.2'24–dc20 CIP

This book is dedicated to Diana Martin with heartfelt thanks for her infinite patience and perseverance.

TABLE OF CONTENTS

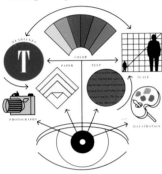

❺ Approachable Type

Invite readership by making type
friendly and accessible

❻ Type As Identification

Create logotype that conveys the
corporate personality

❼ Type With Panache

Build an image with distinctive style
and sophistication

❽ Evocative Type

Recreate the moment with type that
captures a time and place

❾ Environmental Type

Stand out from the crowd with high
visibility signs

❿ Type as Information

Enhance readability, credibility and
comprehension

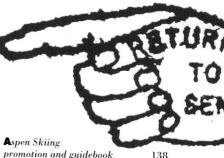

⓫ Energetic Type

Set the trend with a look that's young
and provocative

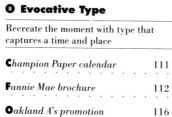

Design, the act of putting constructs in an order or disorder, seems to be my... It is the ... responsibility... our species has... and constitutes the only chance of the thinking, foreseeing and constructing animal that we are, to preserve life

The mechanics of typography — points, picas, didot, leading, kerning, em quad, en quad, and so on — have often been dissected in a textbook manner. Of course, these elements are not what gives typography its life, eloquence, and personality. The technique, if it can be rightly called that, is in the designer's judgment process, in gathering the right data to make informed intuitive decisions — or as Kit Hinrichs says, to "unlock the doors to ideas."

In preparation for writing this book, Kit and I taped several hours of conversation on typography. Although TypeWise was originally intended to be a less personal presentation, it became clear that readers would benefit most from hearing Kit talk about typography in his own words, not filtered through the voice of another writer. Hence, the book begins with a question-and-answer interview in which Kit discusses his philosophy of typographic design and how he works to make type itself talk. The remainder of the book is devoted to the methodology of working with type and to typographically focused case studies of projects completed by Kit and his partners at Pentagram.

DELPHINE HIRASUNA

Q. Why a book on typography, Kit?

What do you hope this book will give the reader?

A. I hope it will provide an understanding of how typography is used as a communications tool. From a graphic design perspective, type is more than grey matter on either side of a photograph or an image; it is a vehicle for presenting information and ideas. More than that, the visual form and shape of individual typefaces convey different impressions that can be used to capture the author's/client's tone of voice. Typography itself can persuade and reinforce the ideas presented in words.

I might add that this is not a history book. I am not an authority on the history of typography. My view is that of a practitioner, of someone who uses typography as one of a range of tools available to communicators.

Q. Graphic designers seem to focus more attention on images than on type. Is typography the least understood element of design?

A. I wouldn't say it's the least understood, but maybe the most underrated in terms of effectiveness. I believe many people don't realize how important typography is to total print communications — how it enhances an image, how it can become the image, how it influences a reader's understanding of ideas or the way in which those ideas are communicated. Typography is as important as the imagery used.

Q. Is legibility the most important gauge of typographic effectiveness?

A. Good typography involves more than legibility. Type is one of the strongest emotional tools available to designers. Everyone, no matter what his age — sixty, thirty-five, or fifteen — has absorbed and continues to absorb a whole series of visual and typographic impressions that have a personal meaning. The Century Schoolbook typeface used in children's primers, for instance, conjures up images in our collective memories, just as the organic letterforms used on

Police badge

Red letter edition of the Bible

No Parking sign

United States currency

World War I poster

I WANT YOU
FOR U.S. ARMY
NEAREST RECRUITING STATION

Every culture has its own design vernacular that comes from shared experiences and values. For Americans, the images shown here have inherent meaning, even if we don't read the words. Designers familiar with a culture's symbols can make visual assumptions without "defining" each element and can work with common images to convey unspoken messages. As designers communicate more and more with international audiences, the need to be conscious of cultural vernacular becomes even greater.

Tattoo Art

Manhole cover

Return mail stamp

Vegetable sign

License plate

psychedelic posters of the 1960s impart a different message. Typography used in World War II propaganda posters or in newspapers, street signage, Bibles, scientific journals, wanted posters, postage stamps, and novels conveys emotional as well as informational messages.

On a daily basis, we are exposed to the typographic vernacular of various businesses, services, and cultures. By that I mean the vast array of written and typographic messages that are everywhere in our lives.

Q. Can you give some examples of what you call "typographic vernacular"?

A. These fall into two categories. The first and most interesting group is the "one-of-a-kind" message — hand-lettered "For Sale," "Fresh Produce," or "No Parking" signs. These naive, nondesigned "typographic" images are a vital, ever-changing part of our common culture.

Before "Sesame Street," children learned the basics of reading from "Dick and Jane" story books. For that generation, Century Schoolbook typeface evokes memories of early education.

The second group is designed or at least professionally engineered. It includes everything from license plates and money to neon signs to computer display type, tattoos, crate stencils, and bus transfers. The often funky typographic "look" of these items may transcend its original use, becoming a symbol for a whole industry or cultural expression.

We as graphic designers need to be aware of typographic vernacular on a conscious level and understand the common visual language of certain typefaces. This awareness allows us to use given typefaces at appropriate times and in the most effective ways.

Q. How does someone learn about the emotional value of different typefaces?

A. It's all there within us. It's a part of our common culture, both national and international. It's a matter of just asking yourself the correct questions, of drawing on your own memories.

Helvetica

I'm not talking about absolutes here. A single typeface may be used 150 different ways, in different contexts, bringing a different meaning to a poem or a business article, for instance. Every use of the phrase "See Spot run" does not have to be in Century Schoolbook — which conveys images of primary education, of legibility and accessibility. But the combination of the phrase and typeface recalls a much broader emotional meaning of childhood comfort and stability, of a more simple and less stressful time.

Q. If certain typefaces bring specific feelings to mind, doesn't their use always create cliches?

A. Cliches may be the most undervalued tools of our profession, as they represent our culture's commonly accepted ideas and images of itself. For the designer, it is crucial to understand cliches and know when to twist them in fresh and interesting ways. Often by simply contrasting the cliche you enhance the message being communicated. Jack Summerford, a Dallas designer, did that with a poster. He typeset the word "Helvetica" in Garamond No. 3. It's elegant in its simplicity. From the word you expect one image but get something completely different. Designers who understand the typographic cliches, the historical context of the typeface, gain control of their craft. They know when to specify which typeface to create the appropriate response.

Size, weight, and scale of type are also part of the appropriateness. A frilly Spencerian script blown up across a page suddenly conveys a surprisingly new impression, a much stronger image. Think of typography as imagery. It isn't just a set of letters. It's words and ideas. Typography is the vehicle to express those ideas most effectively.

Q. Do you have a process to develop your typographic ideas?

A. I tend to think of the total — be it a poster or an entire book — as an environment, as a graphic ecological system in which type, color, scale, paper, illustration, and photography all work together in harmony. They cannot be examined individually because it is the balance, the totality of the system that makes it work or not work.

Q. How do you develop your "graphic ecological system"? How do you start the process of generating ideas?

A. I begin by gathering information through client briefings, written outlines of the client's objectives, identification of the intended audience,

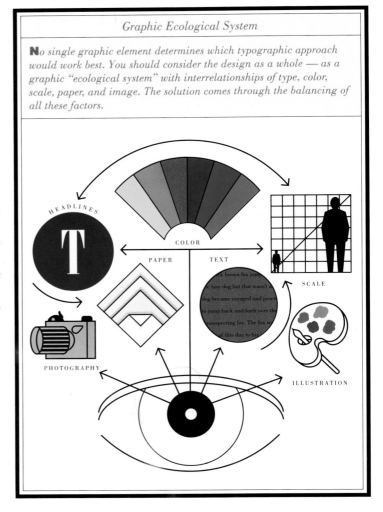

Graphic Ecological System

No single graphic element determines which typographic approach would work best. You should consider the design as a whole — as a graphic "ecological system" with interrelationships of type, color, scale, paper, and image. The solution comes through the balancing of all these factors.

HEADLINES

COLOR

PAPER   TEXT

SCALE

PHOTOGRAPHY

ILLUSTRATION

the budget, and possibly the medium. I also keep a lot of visual stimuli around — reference books, typebooks, magazines that I'm continually sifting through. One thing that works for me is the ability to draw. The connection between hand and eye — putting random sketchy ideas on paper and contemplating them — helps me expand those ideas. For me the approach to the solution often lies in free association. It's a matter of stepping back and leaving myself open to the possibility that all ideas are relevant — not locking any doors to ideas. Once the doors are open, the most unusual things begin to be generated. What gets the ideas flowing is the information gathered beforehand. Within that information, the solution always exists.

Once you've gathered essential information, the solution often lies in free association, considering the possibility of any and all ideas.

Q. How do you recognize the best solution?

A. A creative solution always seems to be one that, when seen, appears obvious, but completely unexpected. Anyone seeing it understands it immediately. It does not require explanation. Everything fits. There are no holes, no rough edges, it feels complete. You understand it more from an intuitive than from a logical thought process.

Once the idea is there, once it has been stated, I'm able to make the appropriate decisions. It seems extremely clear. I may say, "The best way to express that idea will be with a photograph." I'll probably have an idea of who the photographer should be and even a feel for the light and mood of the photograph, how complex or simple it needs to be, how large it should be on the page. Same with typography. The idea will suggest the appropriate typeface, the scale, weight, leading, and spacing.

Q. Are you influenced by other designers?

A. Certainly. As a young designer I was very influenced by people like Milton Glaser, Willie Fleckhaus, Seymour Chwast, Don Trousdale, Paul Rand, Henry Wolf, Chermayeff and Geismar, Herb Lubalin, Lou Dorfsman, Saul Bass, along with such pioneers in the field as William Morris and Alexey Brodovitch.

As my career developed, the influence of my peers became stronger with people like Massimo Vignelli, Dick Hess, and Takenobu Igarashi. But the strongest influence has come from my Pentagram partners and previous partners Tony Russell, Marty Pedersen, and Vance Jonson.

Film poster by Saul Bass

Magazine cover by Herb Lubalin

Wall mural for CBS cafeteria by Lou Dorfsman

Record poster by Milton Glaser

Poster by Seymour Chwast

Book plate by William Morris

Poster by Dick Hess

Environmental number by Takenobu Igarashi

Bus poster by Alan Fletcher

At some point, you become influenced not only by your peers and your own culture, but by peers in other cultures. I feel it's part of a designer's responsibility to draw from as many experiences as possible in order to keep ideas fresh in the way they are presented. When you look at other cultures that literally have different alphabets, different social attitudes toward color, different ways of reading, all those things influence you and force you to look at your work in new ways.

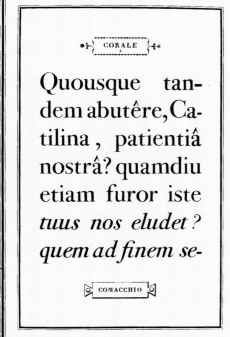

Classic typefaces remain vital and fresh even over the centuries. The letters cut by Giambattista Bodoni in the eighteenth century, for example, are still in frequent use. Visually attractive, Bodoni type is easy to read, beautiful as individual letters, and harmonious as a unit.

Q. Your method sounds straightforward, but some may argue that is not always the case. What's the biggest pitfall? A lack of adequate information?

A. No. I think that is rarely the problem. Without being too metaphysical, I think the problem lies in being unable to unlock the doors to ideas. The pitfall comes when someone assumes there are always logical solutions to things, that there are "seven rules" to follow, that design is a science and not an art. The designer must pursue a solution that contains logic but is not necessarily a logical solution.

Q. You have said a particular typeface will occur to you as part of the design solution. Doesn't that mean you must be familiar with hundreds of typefaces? If so, how did you learn?

A. I'm still learning. I can't tell you the number of times I've looked through typebooks. Part of the process when I'm developing a project is to review typefaces — familiar ones and new ones — to see if I have a visual connection between the character of that face and the story I want to communicate. The associations I'm trying to make are often multi-tiered, multi-informational. So, as I review typefaces I ask myself a number of questions to help make these associations. What will the headline type be? What is supposed to happen at each level of information? How should the text relate to the headlines and images? Will there be sidebars, pull quotes, footnotes, or captions? Should the type complement or contrast the images? Do I let the type lie back quietly behind the image and have the image tell 90 percent of the story? Or is the type going to be the story, the strongest element?

Q. Obviously, designers need to stay current. Is it important to have a historical sense of typography as well?

A. Mankind doesn't progress without being influenced by its predecessors. Speaking specifically about type, it's important to look back to understand the times in which a typeface was created, what was going on politically and sociologically, the technology available then, what has happened to the face over time. It's quite fascinating. It gives you a deeper understanding of the character of the typeface, why it was designed the way it was and how it has been used and perhaps abused throughout its history.

Q. Can you give examples of evolving typefaces?

A. Bodoni. He was an eighteenth-century Italian master printer and type founder. Bodoni's characters are considered modern as his serifs are unbracketed. His letters are beautifully proportioned and very elegant. His work was heavily influenced by early Roman letterforms. The invention of metal type allowed him to create characters with strong contrasts — thick and thin strokes in each letter. Bodoni's type was designed for handsetting, the technology of his day. Over the centuries several interpretations of his typeface have come along, adapted for the latest technology. The best examples remain faithful to Bodoni's original proportions and idiosyncrasies.

This A.M. Cassandre poster from the thirties captured the mood of the Machine Age. Both the sans serif type and image conveyed the hard-edged, streamlined impression of efficiency.

Sans-serif type became prominent during the twentieth century's Machine Age. Its streamlined, hard-edged look implied efficiency, and serifs were viewed as superfluous and unnecessary. It helps to understand that changes in society and technology are often associated with the emotional character of a typeface.

Currently there are about a half-dozen broad groupings of type — sans-serif and serif, and within these, Old Style, Transitional, Modern, Wedge Serif, and Slab Serif, as well as Scripts and Ornamentals. Computer type may eventually evolve into another category.

Q. Are variations of classic typefaces as good as the originals? What do you look for in the cut of a face?

A. I like to go back and use cuts of faces that are as close to the original drawings as possible. Many of the modern variations of metal cuts have a kind of synthetic look. The original faces had a certain character — in many cases a little funky and irregular, but the modern updated faces seem to smooth out all the edges and remove the personality.

Q. Do you see computer-generated typography playing a larger role?

A. Yes. It's a question of to what degree. Many young designers have made computers their tool of choice. Technological improvements are occurring at an amazingly accelerated pace. While drawbacks still exist, it has advanced far enough so that we are using this technology extensively.

Q. What are the advantages of computer-generated typography?

A. The advantage is that it allows the designer to become the typographer, which goes back to how things were four hundred years ago. Historically, the

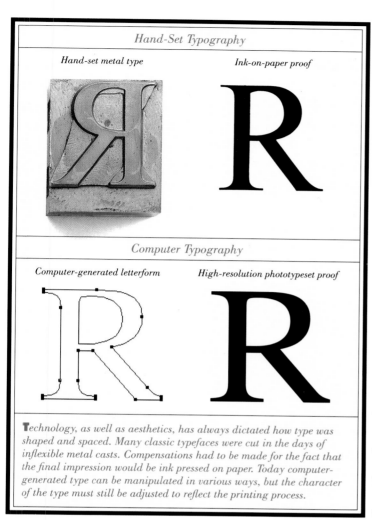

Technology, as well as aesthetics, has always dictated how type was shaped and spaced. Many classic typefaces were cut in the days of inflexible metal casts. Compensations had to be made for the fact that the final impression would be ink pressed on paper. Today computer-generated type can be manipulated in various ways, but the character of the type must still be adjusted to reflect the printing process.

designer/typographer set and often created the type and designed the page. With computers we can do that again. The flexibility of this medium gives designers the opportunity to explore more options with greater speed before making a final choice.

Some very good new typefaces are being designed primarily for computers, with an understanding of a computer's capabilities and limitations, on screen and in printout. Faces designed by Matthew Carter of Bitstream, for instance, are excellent. He designs *with* a computer *for* a computer. Yet, his design embodies the same aesthetic and artistic sensibilities found in typographers of a century or two ago.

Q. How about the negatives?

A. I think there are several aspects of computer-generated typography that need to be approached with special care. For example, while the democratization of typography — giving everyone access to the tools — has resulted in an upgrade of low-end, inhouse publications such as reports and newsletters, it has also led to a lot of ugly stuff — artificially distorting faces, making them too bold, too italicized, instead of redrawing them.

This was especially true when computer type first appeared. Engineers, not designers, developed the earliest type for the sole purpose of functioning efficiently with the computer. Aesthetics were not considered at the time.

Typefaces were often blown up from 6 points to 72 points without regard to kerning, proportion, or balance.

Over time, this problem has been alleviated as design considerations have become incorporated into computer-generated faces. But today the economic advantages offered to computer users sometimes obscure the fact that publishing in whatever medium still requires the same design judgments it has always demanded over the centuries.

Q. How important is it for a designer to understand all typographic technologies? Do you go to your typographer to observe new processes?

A. I think it is valuable to be aware of all typographic processes. It's especially important for new designers to see hand-set and hot-metal type because this historical development gives you a richer understanding of typography in general.

It's also important to be aware of the numerous variations in the redrawing of the same typeface within different contemporary typesetting systems. The most important point to remember, however, is not the technology but the *character* of the type that best communicates your ideas.

Q. Doesn't typography go through trends? Aren't certain faces in vogue?

A. No doubt about it. Each generation creates new typography or reinterprets existing typography, often based on earlier typographic styling or historical art periods — Victorian, Arts and Crafts, Art Nouveau, Art Deco, Classical Modernism, Russian Constructivist, and so on. Each face is altered and enhanced by its new "creator" to reflect or become the style of the day.

Emigre, the magazine and typographic design firm, founded by designers Rudy VanderLans and Zuzana Licko, is producing a wide range of exciting ultra-contemporary typefaces generated on and for computers. Years hence, we are likely to identify Emigre as the typographic style for the 1990s, in the same way we connect Art Nouveau typography with the start of the twentieth century.

While a core of ten to fifteen classic typefaces makes up about 90 percent of my work, I am continually trying to learn about and experiment with a number of fringe, period, and trendy type fonts. This 10 percent provides the accent, the surprise, the twist that adds special energy or evokes feelings that the classics never will. Here are a few of my favorites.

Circus posters, Wild West shows, and sundry advertising bills from the late 1800s employed headlines set in dramatic, oversized wooden type. These complex, highly crafted, and ostentatious faces capture the emerging personality of America.

Moore Computer became an instant period piece of the late 1960s and early 1970s, attempting to emulate the look of computer programs. Like the technology of the era, the face dated itself immediately.

Non-geometric curved letterforms epitomize the sensuous style of the Art Nouveau movement of the early twentieth century.

Stencil, with all its derivations, is a perfect example of vernacular growing from typography. The strictly functional stenciling of crates for shipping became validated as an import/export symbol in the 1920s and was elevated to art by Georges Braque and the Cubists.

Cloister initials and other "illuminated" letters were hand painted by monks in the fourteenth century. A more modern, cast metal version was developed during the Arts and Crafts period of William Morris in the late nineteenth and early twentieth centuries.

Fraktur conjures up many interesting images: Medieval Europe, Teutonic castles, the Gutenberg Bible, old English pubs. Although rarely used anymore for full headlines, this face offers intriguing initial caps.

The ornamental Romans date from the late 1700s, and they experienced a revival in the 1920s and 1930s. These faces are making a comeback mostly in contemporary magazines.

The Roaring Twenties may be represented as graphically by Broadway, Parisian, Modernistic, and Chic as by flappers and jazz. These extremes of thick and thin, with and without serif, capture a glimpse of the era.

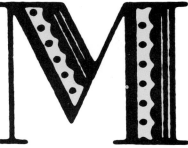

Even with word processors, typewriter type still signifies messages with immediacy and basic, honest information. Avoid the modern "cleaned up" versions, however. They lose the tooth and grittiness of the original.

The 1990s may be remembered for a flood of newly generated computer faces from Emigre, a magazine/ type design firm in California founded by two immigrants. The diversity, range, and quality of these "Mac" faces demonstrate a youthful exuberance and have influenced new directions in typography.

Less-than-beautiful Brush scripts of all persuasions may be one of the quickest ways to call up the 1950s with its drive-in movies, hula hoops, and car fins.

Q. Do you use "vogue" typefaces often?

A. Although I use maybe fifteen classic typefaces most of the time, when I have a project that requires a very contemporary look, I expand my typographic vocabulary accordingly.

Q. How would you categorize the faces you use most often?

A. I think in terms of three categories of typography: Classics, which transcend all periods of design; Period, which represent former and future eras; and Vogue, which exhibit the most extreme (the best and often the worst) in current typography. I also have typographic styling categories: leading, letter spacing, paragraph indents, initial caps, caps and small caps, dingbats, and all those kinds of tricky, voguish things that designers tend to do.

Q. Do you talk to the writer while the design is in progress?

A. I like to get together with the writer from the beginning of the project because it's useful in developing a design solution. We can bounce ideas off each other, often strengthening the content of each other's work. Together we can arrive at a sense of the appropriate length for the copy, the pacing of the project, the style and tone of voice, what can best be communicated through images or text. It's a back-and-forth process, a collaboration.

Q. How influenced are you by the content of the copy? Some designs out there are eye-catching but appear to have little to do with the text. Why do you think this happens?

A. I feel it's imperative for the design to reflect the content of the text. Inappropriate images juxtaposed to copy and incongruent typographic choices can confuse the message, making it unintelligible. This often occurs because the designer is looking at the page and asking, "How does it look?" not "What does it say?" Designers can get so involved in other parts of their craft that they forget the basics — like reading the copy.

Q. Isn't it also true that we tend to think in terms of division of labor — the writer communicates; the designer illustrates and adds style. Do designers forget that they too are communicators?

A. That's often the case. Because we are in a visual business and there's so much style intertwined with the communications we're involved with, sometimes a designer will substitute style for content. It's the curse of the profession. Many design "stylists" can become very "hot," do very exciting images, but they aren't communicating anything except their own style. Ideas drive communications. When ideas determine the right style to be presented, a work will never be flat; it will always be fresh.

Communication isn't the sole responsibility of the writer. Good design can't be separated from good communications. Design without content is just decorative style.

Q. How can readers use this book to develop their own design decision process?

A. I think the case studies will illustrate how elements are pulled together, what the thought processes were in arriving at a particular choice. What I hope this book will accomplish is to share several years' worth of my experiences so people can unlock more doors sooner than they might have otherwise.

In considering any creative work, the question arises: What part of the creative process can you quantify? Why did Milton Glaser choose those colors for Dylan's hair in his poster? Why did Paul Rand use a square serif instead of sans serif type in the IBM logo? Sometimes the answer is a shrug and a reply, "It felt right." But the choice surely was not a random toss-of-the-coin decision. Some method of deduction — conscious or otherwise — was applied to arrive at each particular solution.

On every assignment, designers make hundreds, often thousands, of individual judgments. The interplay of each one ultimately determines the fabric of the design.

While it's impossible to pinpoint where creative ideas are found, it is possible to identify the steps in the creative process: defining the problem, gathering information, and checking ideas for appropriateness. The answers to certain universal questions provide information on which to base creative judgments. The very act of posing the questions helps define and refine the solution. The solutions will be as unique and individual as the designers who create them.

Asking the right questions

As communicators, we've all heard the three principles of problem definition: audience, message, vehicle. Some communicators go after these answers very superficially — name, rank, and serial number. Others probe almost in a psychoanalytical way to understand the subtleties.

You don't have to be both designer and "shrink." But sometimes designers play an essential role in helping clients articulate who they are, what they are trying to achieve. The quality of information gathered before a project begins can lead to better, more focused design and ultimately to more effective communications. In a real sense, information is an essential tool for making subjective judgments and channeling your creativity to appropriate design solutions.

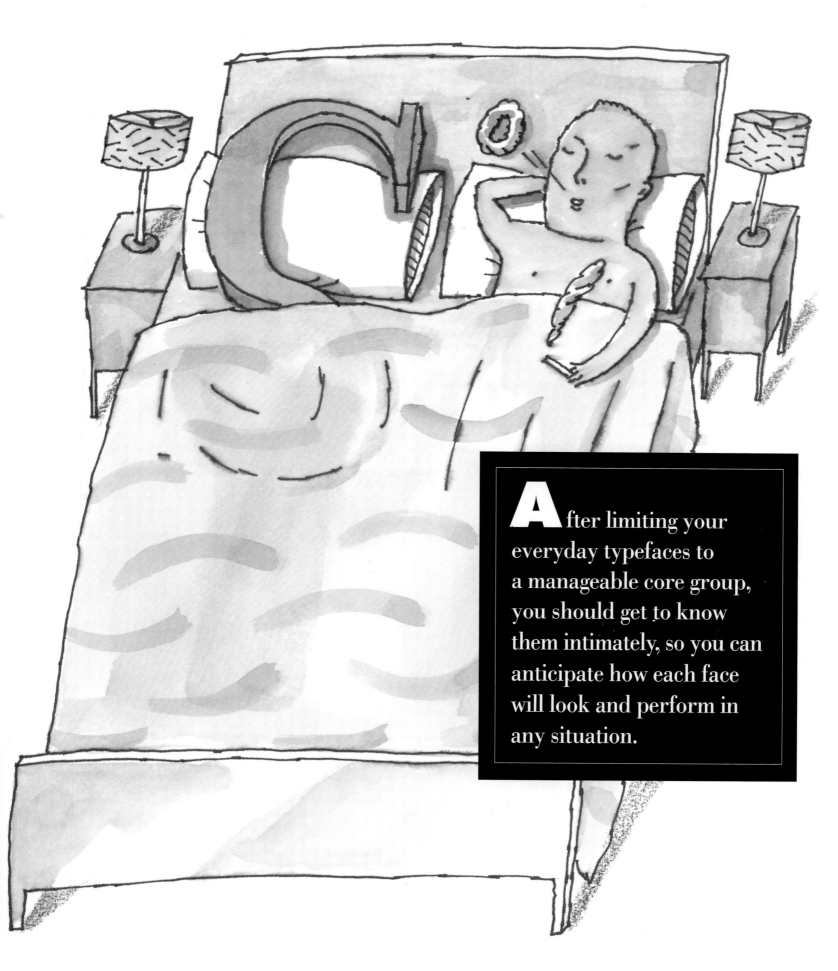

After limiting your everyday typefaces to a manageable core group, you should get to know them intimately, so you can anticipate how each face will look and perform in any situation.

Who is the client?

Literal identification gives you only a cardboard image of who the client is. Try to identify their operating philosophy and style, distinction from competitors, vision for the future. Are they established leaders or number two and trying harder? Are they considered conservative or progressive? A New England financial institution established prior to the American Revolution evokes an identity different from that of a California bank founded by six Stanford MBAs. That doesn't necessarily mean the New England bank should be presented as staid and traditional or that the California bank should automatically appear in the latest flash-and-trash style. To dispel stereotypical conceptions, the client may want to project the opposite of the expected.

Who is the audience?

Profession, age, sex, geographic location, income level all may be decisive factors in the design approach. Aeronautical engineers...Southwestern cattle ranchers...high school students...factory workers. Who are the readers, what are their interests? A Medicare brochure targeted to senior

THIS DATED TYPEFACE WAS CHASING ME. I WAS RUNNING, BUT STAYING IN ONE PLACE...

citizens would rule out the use of grey 6-point Copperplate Gothic type on a blue background. A skateboard promotion directed at teenagers obviously demands a different approach than does a mortgage lending brochure aimed at first-time home buyers. But try not to assume the obvious. For instance, toy catalogs pitch to grandmothers, not to eight-year-olds.

What's the message?

What are we trying to communicate here? Is the piece purely informational, or is the goal to sell, entertain, persuade, call to action? How do we want the audience to react? What impression do we want to create? An annual report may be required to disclose only the straight facts and figures, but the visual message can communicate far more about the company's personality, philosophy, and vision.

The choice of the correct typeface can help your corporate clients come to grips with the visual identity crisis they sometimes experience.

It's important to consider the environment in which the message will be viewed. Elements that limit the reader's attention — time, space, weather, lighting conditions — may influence your typographic choice.

What's the medium for communication?

A poster. Brochure. Direct mail catalog. Electronic media. Three-dimensional exhibit. The answer forms the parameters of the project. If the chosen medium is complex — a 148-page catalog with multiple messages and levels of information, for instance — the typography, to sustain interest, probably requires complexity too. A book intended to have a long shelf life will also influence typographic choices. Posters, on the other hand, are intrinsically ephemeral, leaving greater latitude for typographic experiments.

What's the environment?

The term "environmental graphics" is typically associated with indoor/outdoor signage, but it includes much more. The dairy case in a supermarket, for example, is the environment in which the typographic impact of a milk carton must be evaluated. A darkened theater becomes the environment for a film title. Consideration of surroundings must include all the elements that compete with or limit the reader's attention — time, space, weather, speed, and lighting conditions. A billboard must be read from a car speeding by at fifty-five miles per hour, narrowing the choice of typefaces and sizes considerably — as does the candlelight when you read a menu card in your favorite restaurant.

What are the available resources?

Budget is not a deterrent to creativity, but it does affect how you implement that creativity. A realistic evaluation of the budget will help determine whether a piece is printed in one or four colors, as a postcard or as a monolith the size of Mount Rushmore. Awareness of the total budget will also aid you and your client in using available resources most effectively.

Building a typographic vocabulary

Okay, you're confronted with a mind-boggling number of typefaces to choose from, not to mention the different typehouses who produce variations of the same face and dozens of newly created faces for computers too. How do you whittle this down for practical use?

Looking at one of those ten-pound type specimen books for the first time can be intimidating. The average tome contains about 750 individual typefaces, along with multiple drop shadow, backslant, and outline variations — most of which are either ugly, illegible, or both. A colleague once called these fonts "faces only a mother could love." Then, of course, there are pages of dingbats, rules, and other typographic ornamentation that heap layers of complexity onto an already bewildering array.

The Desert Island approach

Making sense of this confusion and picking out the essential typefaces you'd want along if you were stranded on a desert island is the first step in building a personal typographic vocabulary.

Keep in mind that most seasoned designers typically work with only a limited number of typefaces. They generally build their typographic vocabulary from a combination of classic faces, type that represents their own highly personal style, and specialty faces proven to be effective in unique situations.

These they subconsciously arrange in tiers, from everyday, all-purpose typefaces, to reliable secondary choices, to assorted specialty faces that can be brought out for specific occasions.

Start with favorites

Probably no two designers will agree on exactly which ten or fifteen faces to include in their own basic vocabularies, but they will almost always include a balanced selection of three or four faces from each broad type grouping — serif, sans serif, and slab serif — that they are likely to use 80 percent of the time for

The typographic "forest" can present an intimidating number of choices to new designers. The challenge is to narrow this selection to a core group of typefaces that reflects individual style and practical needs.

both headlines and body text. For example, my basic typographic vocabulary, built and refined over several years (and still evolving), includes Bodoni, Garamond, Century Old Style, Janson, Times Roman, Memphis, Cheltenham Old Style, Franklin Gothic, Futura, Helvetica, News Gothic, and Univers.

Augment with variations

Most designers usually augment their core group with another fifteen to twenty-five faces that are often subtle variations — Baskerville as a variation of Caslon; Memphis for Rockwell; Helvetica for Univers. This second tier of typefaces is used with varying frequency, sometimes making the "A" list and sometimes dropping back to second place.

Eclectic typefaces

There's a third tier of specialty faces that includes a grab bag of eclectic typestyles earmarked because they may best represent the most contemporary look or a specific period of history, a culture, an art style, or maybe just a unique style that appeals to the idiosyncratic nature of the designer. This last list ebbs and flows in number and variety depending on current trends in type, recent discoveries of old, less familiar faces, and newly designed faces.

Getting to know a family of typefaces — capital letters, lower case, italics — involves learning its strengths, shortcomings, and idiosyncrasies.

Know your faces

No matter what your choice, it's important to become intimately familiar with the faces in your core group. Every curve and angle of a face should be studied; the way a face changes with different leading and spacing; how it looks in all caps, small caps, and upper and lower case. Know what happens with a change in size and color, reverse or positive. Your core faces should work in combination with each other and be versatile enough to be appropriate in nearly all situations.

Typography can speak in a roar or a whisper. Through its tone of voice, type projects how the text "sounds" visually. It can enhance a message, contrast it, or detract from it.

May I have a banana?

Topographic typography

Typographic styling can be compared to a good road map. It tells you where you are and where you're going. It points out the routes available to your destination and emphasizes the most efficient ways. It also highlights and explains points of interest. And all this is communicated with symbols that are consistent and easy to read.

Although comparing type to a map is accurate, the analogy is incomplete. Along with showing the route, designers must convince readers that the trip is worthwhile, and entertain and retain the attention of travelers who have varying degrees of interest in the subject.

Be enticing

One way is by presenting information in the order in which people tend to read: headlines first, then pull quotes and blurbs, followed by captions, and finally the body text. Providing levels of information ensures that even uninterested readers will glean some knowledge of the subject, while others may be drawn into the comprehensive body text.

Tone of voice

Great storytellers have always understood the importance of tone of voice. Knowing when to whisper or to shout adds a richness and color to their story. The same is true of visual communicators, and type is often the best means of affecting that tone of voice. How should the text "sound" visually? Conversational or authoritative? Boldly assertive or gently persuasive? Urgent or relaxed? Factual or poetic? Typography can capture these moods. Through style, scale, color, and position on a page, type can tease or demand. It can even speak with an accent. The "tones" are as different as the audiences and as individual as the designer. Consider the typographic images that come to mind for a Grateful Dead poster compared to an invitation to the Boston Symphony's opening night.

More often than not I rely on classics because trendy typefaces are often so stylish that they overpower the message by calling too much attention to themselves.

Like clothing, however, type goes through fashion fads. When hot pink with just a hint of chartreuse appears in leading fashion magazines, these colors become the rage everywhere. When Univers 59 italic with wide letter spacing is hot…ditto. That's not to say that voguish typefaces should be avoided. They often represent the most current "edge" graphics.

Of course, there are situations where trendy typefaces are appropriate and desirable, even when the look isn't contemporary. The best and most representative typeface modes are closely identified with a period, and no re-creation of the era would be accurate without using them to set the typographic mood.

These typefaces experience revivals — like the psychedelic 1960s type reminiscent of Art Nouveau or the De Stijl or Constructivist faces from the early twentieth century resurrected in the 1980s.

When you analyze the typography of a particular decade, you recognize two major points of identification: first, the specific groups of typefaces that were "in"; and second, the style in which they were set (leading, letter spacing, combinations of typefaces, etc.). I use both to reflect a period but not to mimic it.

There is a need for continual experimentation in typography, but be confident in your knowledge of the basics before heading off into every new typographic direction. Trendy typefaces should be used sparingly, with common sense and with awareness of the message — not the superficial style — you want to communicate.

Not just a pretty face

The classics, or at least my classics — Bodoni, Caslon, Century, Helvetica, Futura, Franklin Gothic, Garamond, Memphis, for example — are typefaces for all seasons, for all occasions. They transcend any single period of time.

Like a basic black dress, some typefaces are tastefully appropriate for a number of occasions. Trendy typefaces can set the mood for special situations.

Like a basic black dress or a pair of Levi's, they can be dressed up or down and fit in nearly anywhere.

No single designer or school of design can predict which typeface will become a classic.

People read on a number of levels. Some stop at the headlines and captions; others read the entire text. Typographic styling organizes information to increase readership and understanding.

Classics emerge from repeated use by thousands of designers, in thousands of situations worldwide. Their versatility is expressed through their range of weights, the "color" of the typeface when set in body text, the intrinsic quality and aesthetic integrity of the drawing of each letter, and the way these characters look when combined into words, paragraphs, pages, and books. Although there have been a few instant classics (Helvetica, to name one), most are proven over time and set the standards for others to meet.

Even if you primarily use classic faces, your designs don't need to become predictable. I've always found that true creative freedom was derived from working with numerous constraints — time, money, size, color, whatever. Restrictions force you to review the options available. A limited number of typefaces allows you the opportunity to explore the variety within the character of each face, to ask yourself how it works at different sizes, mixed with other faces, in all caps,

Build a hierarchy

To handle complex material — be it primarily image, a mix of images and text, or exclusively text — you must establish a hierarchy of information and the order in which you want that information to be read. This ordering of information can take many forms. Ordering by size and importance is perhaps the most obvious but very effective hierarchy. Creating a pattern of even-sized images and either positioning them in a normal reading sequence or interrupting the pattern to signify importance is another approach. Or take advantage of contrast — different weights of type, Roman vs. italic, color against a background, complex vs. simple, for example. Certainly position of type and image — centered, top right-hand corner (at least in the Western culture), balanced on a page — aids in directing the reading sequence.

Initial caps, subheads, and sidebars are other typographic techniques that act as signposts and a means to break down information into more digestible bits.

All printed pieces have typographic pacing whether the designer intends it or not. The pacing may be boring or static. Or it can move readers along, offer delightful pauses and visual relief, provide continuity, and establish reading guideposts.

You could compare pacing and design to the same quality in literature or music. Most finished pieces, whether visual, written, or composed, have not only a beginning, middle, and end, but also a momentum with swells and lulls, crescendos and diminuendos, leading to a climax and denouement.

Typographic pacing plays a role similar to that of a musical motif — an underlying theme developed in various colorations throughout a composition. The cohesiveness and familiarity provided by this melody establish reference points and carry the music forward. In printed pieces, readers expect the same thematic unity, counterbalanced with elements of surprise.

Typography is the way we "dress" our ideas for presentation. Individual styles may vary, but the look must be appropriate to the occasion and environment.

Color

The even or irregular pattern created by the combination of the letters in each font defines its individual "color." A page gains color several ways — through word and letter spacing, the contrast of Roman to italic, bold to light, and the line leading between copy. Used correctly, the texture created by the typographic variety of faces, column widths and copy settings (flush left, right justified) contributes to making a page's color reflect the emotion and content of the message.

Appropriateness

The final measure of typographic design (and design in general) is its appropriateness to the client, the target audience, and the conditions in which this message is presented. In other words, is the typographic tone of voice appropriate to the message?

It's like knowing what to wear to a business meeting or a beach party or a formal museum opening or a camping trip. All have appropriate gear estab-

lished by tradition and practicality, which are reinforced daily through individual use and cultural media. Typography is the way we "dress" our ideas, and we communicate the credibility of those ideas effectively by "dressing" them for the occasion.

This shouldn't be confused with uniformity. Using the apparel analogy again, let's imagine a Wall Street "power breakfast" at the '21' Club. All of the brokers are wearing business suits, but the cut of each suit is quite different. One may be wearing a vest, a Brooks Brothers' shirt, and wing-tip shoes. Another may have on suspenders or a bow tie. Each person is distinctive, dressed in a style appropriate to his or her individual personality, yet appropriately outfitted for the occasion.

Be consistent with the message

The typographic design should be consistent with the message you are trying to deliver. Be aware that every time you choose a typeface it communicates something. It enhances the message or detracts from it. It makes a statement; therefore, the choice should not be made arbitrarily or independently of the message. If leadership is the subliminal message, don't use a wimpy typeface.

Also, be aware of what your audience expects and consciously choose to provide that or not. For example, a classically conservative typeface for a Johnny Walker ad may be right for the *Wall Street Journal* but inappropriate if the ad is to appear in *L.A. Style* or *Interview* magazine.

Your typographic judgment will become more refined with every piece of information you gather about your client and audience. Sometimes by contrasting the anticipated image, you can draw more attention to the message. There are times when you want to stand out from the crowd, make a statement, challenge convention, be irreverent, jar readers into seeing you differently. Choosing an unexpected typeface may then be the appropriate means.

The wrong typeface can be perceived as pretentious or incongruous with the message. The choice of typeface must not only complement the total design but accurately reflect who the client is.

Twice a year all the Pentagram partners converge for four days somewhere in the world to review our experiences of the past six months and to plan (or guess) where we'd like to be or what we'd like to be doing in the future. Although some time is directed to the "housekeeping" of our collective, by far the most important and involving discussions center around the design "case studies." These studies give us an insider's look at the successes, shortcomings, political problems, and creative challenges encountered in each other's projects. The following pages are a typographically focused series of selected case studies presented by the graphic design partners of Pentagram.

Founded in 1971, Pentagram is organized around fourteen design partners based in offices in London, New York, and San Francisco. Each designer came to Pentagram with extensive experience and an established reputation in his or her design field.

1 Woody Pirtle / New York

2 Peter Harrison / New York

3 Etan Manasse / New York

4 Kenneth Grange / London

5 Alan Fletcher / London

6 Theo Crosby / London

7 John McConnell / London

8 John Rushworth / London

9 Kit Hinrichs / San Francisco

10 Mervyn Kurlansky / London

11 Colin Forbes / New York

12 David Hillman / London

13 Neil Shakery / San Francisco

14 Linda Hinrichs / San Francisco

Type as art — either whole words, individual letterforms, or the physical shape of the text — can be used to amplify the meaning of the words, create a mood or metaphor, form a decorative pattern, or become a visual pun. Typically such imagery is a one-of-a-kind experience, illustrating book titles, headlines of magazine articles, advertisements, invitations, or posters. The image dictates the choice of typeface. Part of the fun is to be able to step away from classic typefaces so essential for readability and consider all the eccentric, funky, clumsy, sometimes illegible or downright ugly faces you may otherwise never use. Applied sparingly and appropriately, typography can turn words into art.

FOUND ALPHABET

Letterforms don't always come from typographers or designers, but can be found among everyday items around the office, at home, or in nature. From paper clips to scissors, this "found alphabet" of twenty-six "lettergrams" was collected in the London office and is a simple exercise in typographic observation.

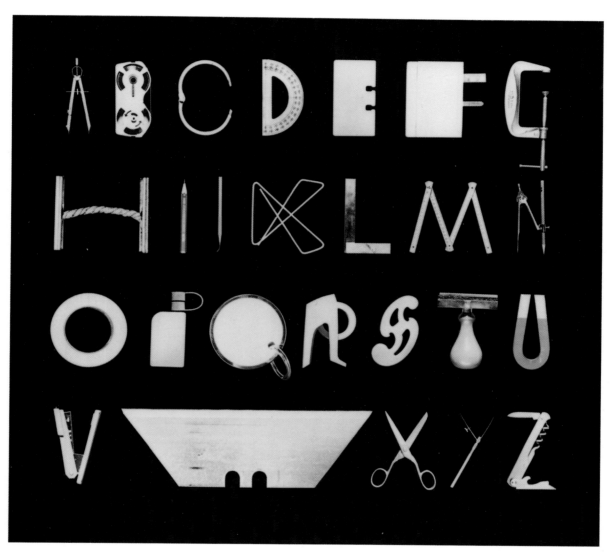

This alphabet was gathered for an article on creativity for Preston Polytechnic School of Art's magazine. The practice of viewing images as possible letters (initial caps, distinctive artwork, etc.) is an important approach to maintain within your vernacular typography file.

McCall's Magazine

McCall's magazine asked us to illustrate an article on Christmas decorating from A to Z — and needed it within ten days, start to finish. In the heat of August, we worked on finding Christmas nutcrackers (causing a few sleepless nights). Although most of the imagery was a literal illustration of the copy, a few typographic images lent a different dimension to the story and also served to reinforce the A–Z aspect.

*O*ur gumdrop G allowed us to photographically produce a colorful letterform and present a familiar Christmas item in a nontraditional way. The letter G was roughly based on Windsor Bold Condensed.

CHRISTMAS FROM A TO Z

A compendium of marvelous ideas to help you celebrate the joy, wonder and glory of the season

ADVENT, *the season beginning with the fourth Sunday before Christmas (November 30th this year), traditionally spent in prayer and fasting in preparation for the Feast of the Nativity. Endless to a child, but no time at all for grown-up preparations like shopping, cooking, baking. Speed up this seemingly endless period for small children with an Advent calendar, handmade or bought, to ceremoniously reveal a new surprise each day.*

DESIGN JONSON PEDERSEN HINRICHS & SHAKERY

T*he initial cap A, for Advent calendar, served as a strong graphic introduction to the article. The hand adds a rather surreal touch to the two-dimensional A. The D sidebar, with its centered Roman text, provides a change of pace from the rigid columns of flush-left italic copy. Half-line paragraph spacing throughout gives the material a little more room to breathe.*

ALMONDS, spiced and roasted; buried in brittle, studding a torte; snowbound by fondant; knotted in small kerchiefs for stocking stuffers.

ANGEL wings snipped from tracing paper to decorate packages with heavenly originality.

APRONS for everyone on your list, from baby pinafores to roomy, no-nonsense versions for the boys and men.

B

BOWS, even for the most tailored souls at Christmas — shining satins, luxurious velvets, taffeta to wrap a package. Tie up a whole tree or beribbon a wreath or garland.

BREADS in infinite variety, the epitome of homemaking, in crusty loaves, presented on a rough-grained breadboard and tied with a gingham dish towel.

C

CANDLES, to gleam and glow and flatter every face: a battery of lights on a table or top of a chest, brightening a mantel, or set up at different heights in stemmed goblets. Plant colored votive lights in garlands down the center of a buffet table, or at every setting of a formal dinner table.

CENTERPIECES of every sort and surprise. Try a paper one of pleated shiny paper fans in the brightest colors; cutouts of birds and butterflies; streamers of crepe paper instead of ribbons; small unfolding honeycomb bells.

COOKIES—as presents for each name on your list, and plenty more for around the house. Calories are for forgetting.

CRANBERRIES strung like rubies, to wind around a tree, to ring napkins, to wrap in garlands. Fill little baskets with cranberries to hold place cards.

CRÈCHE, the manger where Christmas began. The figures of Mary, Joseph and the Christ Child, surrounded by angels, shepherds and animals, may range from 18th-century Neapolitan versions, dressed in fine fabrics, to naive Mexican folk art to Ecuadorian dough sculptures, to simple plaster or wooden figures found close to home. Nestle yours under the tree, on a table, in a bay or picture window, with straw and greens to set the scene.

D

BASKETS, perennially popular for decoration, utility and collecting. Pack tiny ones with wrapped candies for open-house presents. Line and pad a medium-size basket with a pretty print, add lace edgings and bows and fill with aromatic soaps. Arrange a bunch of cocktail napkins like flowers in a small basket, or pack a larger one, like Red Riding Hood's, with home-made goodies.

BAUBLES AND BEADS for sparkle—circling a tree, winding around a length of greenery, filling a crystal bowl with glitter, arranged like ripened fruits in an epergne.

DELLA ROBBIA
wreaths and garlands, after the Renaissance sculptors. Make one for the center of the table with fresh fruits studding the greenery—use apples, oranges, lemons. Wrap with rich cords.

DOLLS,
strings of them, cut from paper for the tree. Miniature plastic dolls from the five-and-dime, with angel wings attached for added delight.

DOORWAYS
adorned with damp-proof decorations: oilcloth stockings, filled with greens and ornaments; branches of greens wrapped and bowed with outdoorsy ribbon; a front door covered in midnight blue, starred like a night sky with many tiny lights.

DOVES,
flocks of them, on your tree. Two-dimensional doves cut from plain white paper, with wings attached separately to alight on any package. Ensnare them with silver cord or ribbon.

DRUMS,
made from coffee tins or oatmeal boxes cut down to size and covered with white paper. Band with red and blue ribbons, crisscross with colored tapes or yarn.

In addition to the opening letter A, the initial cap typography was of great importance to the article's style. Century Old Style was chosen for headlines, initial caps, and body text. The subheads are all Futura Extra Bold, all caps. Century was an obvious choice. Not only is it a very outgoing, friendly face, but the initial caps (especially when shadowboxed) conjured up all those warm Christmas feelings from children's alphabet blocks.

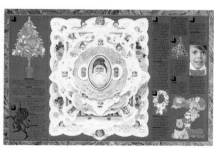

Our early sketches included many typographic letter illustrations, including a fruitcake slice of F and a baked bread B, plus an idea that was ultimately used in the final design — a candleholder C.

When using cap subheads within body text, especially in a bold face like Futura, you should drop the point size at least one point to maintain proper balance between subhead and text.

The 3-D letterforms were photographed and used in several different configurations, lending an element of surprise to each of the promotional print pieces.

DESIGNER'S SATURDAY

Designer's Saturday is a three-day annual event hosted by the furniture manufacturers of America at the IDC (Industrial Design Center) in New York. The contract design show attracts a large number of interior and industrial designers. Promotion for the event includes a poster, invitations, trade ads, and other print pieces. Drawing on the three-dimensional nature of this show, Colin had letterforms built in the Bodoni typestyle. These eight-inch, lacquered wooden letters were treated as imagery in the promotional campaign.

The design solution grew out of Colin's observation that it would be interesting to treat type as a piece of furniture for this event.

As physical objects, the letterforms became sculpture, revealing the intrinsic grace and beauty of the Bodoni typeface. The varied shapes and weights in each Bodoni letter sustain visual interest, something that a sans-serif face probably wouldn't do.

PARTY INVITATION

Not all projects have "global" impact; some are just plain fun. Alan designed a twenty-first birthday party invitation for the daughter of his client and old friend Bob Gross, chairman of the Geers Gross advertising agency.

Alan turned the invitation into a full-color poster, which seemed a more inventive solution for a party and ultimately a longer lasting memento of the event. A playful collage, created with bright colors and hand-cut letters from wood type specimens, set a festive mood. The handwritten invitation reinforces the casual mood of the party.

JOHN ELLIOTT CELLARS

John Elliott Cellars is a London-based spirits wholesaler who imports fine French wines. When Alan was asked to develop the company's identification, the image of early nineteenth-century French drinking songs set as ideograms seemed to capture both the product and a mood of conviviality.

A couple of nuances to note in the preparation of the final typographic art: First, the choice of a hand-set type gives a historic, crafted quality; second, the subtle shift in type weights calls attention to the company name and creates the illusion of wine in the glass.

John Elliott Cellars Ltd, 11 Dover Street, Mayfair, London. Telephone: 01 493 5135
Wholesalers of Fine Wines & Champagne
Buvons, amis, et buvons à plein verre.
Enivrons-nous de ce nectar divin!
Après les Belles, sur la terre,
Rien n'est aimable que le vin;
Cette liqueur est de tout âge:
Buvons-en! Nargue du sage
Qui, le verre en main,
Le haussant soudain,
Craint, se ménage,
Et dit : holà!
Trop cela!
Holà!
La!
La!
La!
Car
Panard
A pour refrain:
Tout plein!
Plein!
Plein!
Plein!
Fêtons,
Célébrons
Sa mémoire;
Et, pour sa gloire,
Rions, chantons, aimons, buvons.

Scouring the office library soon unearthed examples of wine glasses to work with. Although the origins of the "wine glass" are based on early ideograms, Alan extended the height of the original glass by including the company's name and message.

CORPORATE IDENTIFICATION

Corporate identification often includes typography as an integral if not primary element in its imagery. This group of diverse symbols illustrates the use of type manipulation in the creation of corporate images.

A promotion piece for Simpson Paper Co., this track-like logo was created by Woody for a fictitious railroad company.

John Rushworth combined elements of architecture and craft in the symbol for Art and Architecture, a society promoting collaboration between artists, craftspeople and architects.

Two related ligatures, one Roman and one italic, were adopted as the colophons for Faber and Faber, a British book and music publishing house. John created this italic ligature, signifying "fortissimo" to musicians, which proved a perfect symbol for Faber Music publications.

Digitized O's form the logo designed by David for Orchid, a software manufacturer in the U.K.

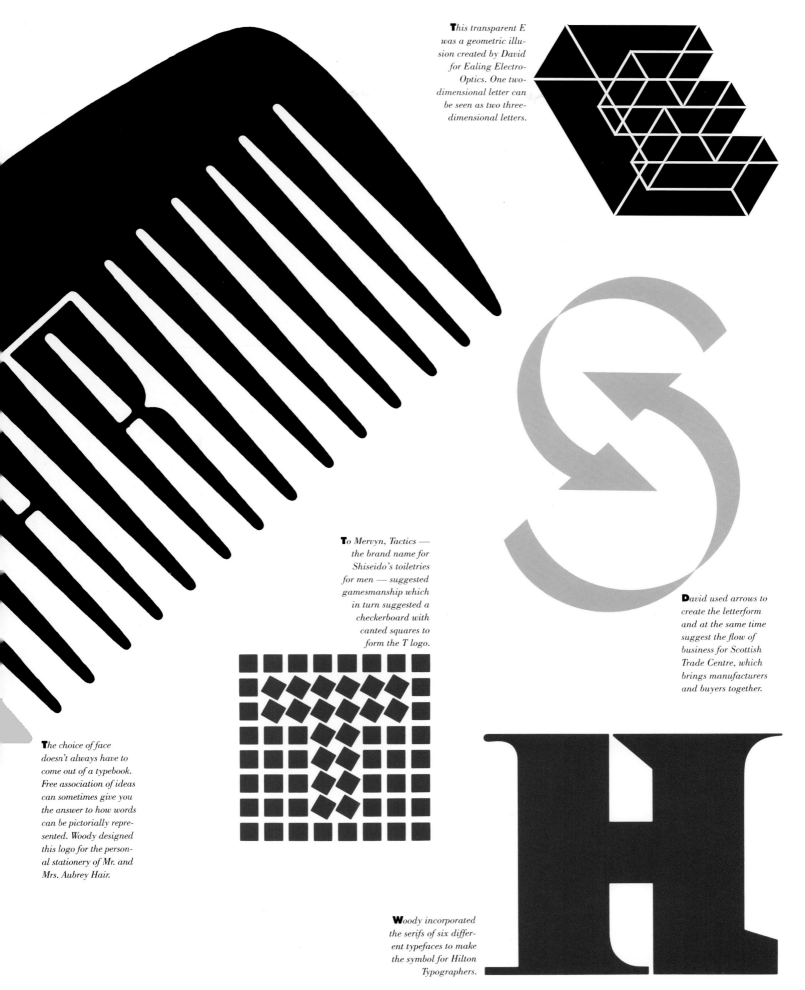

This transparent E was a geometric illusion created by David for Ealing Electro-Optics. One two-dimensional letter can be seen as two three-dimensional letters.

To Mervyn, Tactics — the brand name for Shiseido's toiletries for men — suggested gamesmanship which in turn suggested a checkerboard with canted squares to form the T logo.

David used arrows to create the letterform and at the same time suggest the flow of business for Scottish Trade Centre, which brings manufacturers and buyers together.

The choice of face doesn't always have to come out of a typebook. Free association of ideas can sometimes give you the answer to how words can be pictorially represented. Woody designed this logo for the personal stationery of Mr. and Mrs. Aubrey Hair.

Woody incorporated the serifs of six different typefaces to make the symbol for Hilton Typographers.

EXHIBITION POSTER

Pentagram partners meet semiannually in selected cities around the world to discuss business, works in progress, and finished projects. Our spring 1989 meeting in San Francisco was scheduled to coincide with the opening of an exhibition of Pentagram work. The partners hosted a gala reception for the design community, local clients, and friends.

For the poster, Neil wanted to represent the work of all three offices and give a hint of the more than one thousand images created for international clients, while still giving a strong identification to Pentagram and the exhibition. He came up with a push-pinned typographic composite spelling Pentagram, created from logotypes designed by the partners.

THE ART DIRECTORS CLUB

For more than sixty years, The Art Directors Club (New York) has sponsored the largest, most prestigious exhibition of advertising and design in the United States. When asked to design the Call for Entries, our first thought was to create a series of images that described the competitive categories in the exhibition together with well-known landmarks. Jack Unruh, who illustrated Manhattan's skyline for the cover, was one of ten nationally prominent artists and designers contributing their interpretation of New York scenes.

NAPOLI '99 FOUNDATION

The Napoli '99 Foundation, a society formed to create an awareness of the city's physical problems, enlisted the help of thirty designers from around the world to graphically demonstrate the level of decay in the city's cultural monuments and architectural masterpieces. All the Pentagram partners' contributions focused on interpreting the theme through the single word "NAPOLI" to communicate the idea.

Showing the classical typeface Perpetua falling to pieces was John's way of demonstrating the broken architecture and environmental decay of the city.

A STATEMENT AGAINST POLLUTION. A poster commissioned by NAPOLI '99 Foundation as a contribution towards the cultural image of the city.

Alan used wood type specimens for the word Napoli. He presented them in bright tutti frutti colors to symbolize the cheerful Neapolitan attitude, and then dampened the mood by throwing ink at the letterforms to represent pollution.

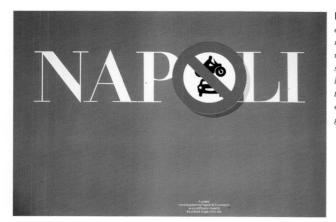

David's approach was directed more toward noise pollution than visual pollution. The simple substitution of a letter with an international road sign created a powerful iconographic symbol.

Mervyn constructed three-dimensional cardboard letters to suggest concrete structures and projected a photograph of graffiti onto them. The graffiti letters were then photographed to illustrate the problems of vandalism.

Some typefaces simply feel comfortable, like a favorite pair of tennis shoes or Sunday supper at Grandma's house. These unpretentious typefaces don't suggest any particular bias but invite leisurely reading. Often we associate them with familiar, everyday objects such as our first reading books, bus tickets, and old Sears Roebuck catalogs. Common to all approachable typography is easy legibility — simple serifs and letterforms that aren't hard-edged or florid. That isn't to say a typeface must be plain or dull to be approachable. The letterforms of Century Schoolbook, for instance, are beautifully proportioned and visually interesting, which explains why it has traditionally been used in children's books. The friendliness of this typeface comes from its accessibility, without an attempt to be clever, contrived, or more eye-catching than readable.

SLUMBERDOWN

Slumberdown, one of Britain's largest makers of continental quilts and duvets, wanted to increase its presence in stores and retail outlets by creating a "shop within a shop." John developed a flexible display system using graphic quilted panels that could be hung on a frame. The medium used to display our client's story — a full-sized quilt — made a positive connection between the cozy quilt and the storybook theme.

John chose Garamond, often used in children's nursery books. Even with the period illustrations, the look is still fresh and contemporary, and from a production standpoint, the face is easy to reproduce in silkscreen on cloth.

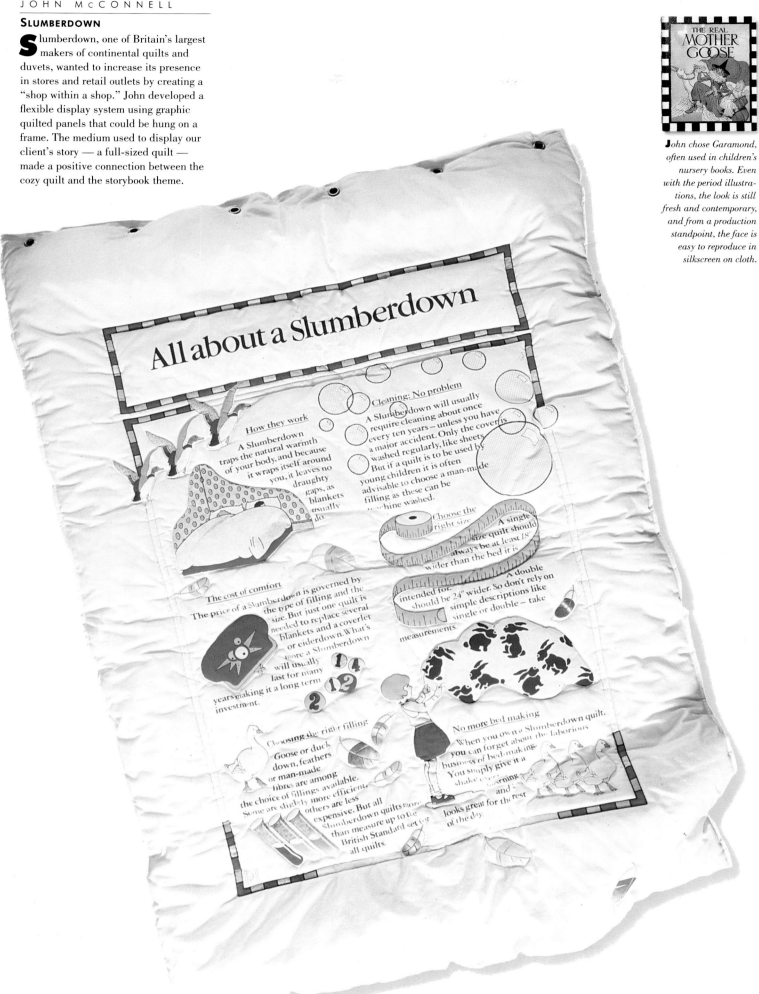

All about a Slumberdown

How they work

A Slumberdown traps the natural warmth of your body, and because it wraps itself around you, it leaves no draughty gaps, as blankets usually do.

Cleaning: No problem

A Slumberdown will usually require cleaning about once every ten years – unless you have a major accident. Only the cover is washed regularly, like sheets. But if a quilt is to be used by young children it is often advisable to choose a man-made filling as these can be machine washed.

The cost of comfort

The price of a Slumberdown is governed by the type of filling and the size. But just one quilt is needed to replace several blankets and a coverlet or eiderdown. What's more a Slumberdown will usually last for many years making it a long term investment.

Choose the right size

A single size quilt should always be at least 18" wider than the bed it is intended for. A double should be 24" wider. So don't rely on simple descriptions like single or double – take measurements.

Choosing the right filling

Goose or duck down, feathers or man-made fibres are among the choice of fillings available. Some are slightly more efficient, others are less expensive. But all Slumberdown quilts more than measure up to the British Standard set for all quilts.

No more bed making

When you own a Slumberdown quilt, you can forget about the laborious business of bed-making. You simply give it a shake every morning, and it looks great for the rest of the day.

VEGETABLES BOOK

Published by Chronicle Books, *Vegetables* was intended to get readers to take a fresh look at these common foods they eat every day. The subject was presented in four sections: a history of vegetable agriculture in California; an A–Z compendium of fascinating facts and folklore, along with buying hints and nutritional information; a glossy section of full-color vegetable photographs and illustrations; and finally, recipes.

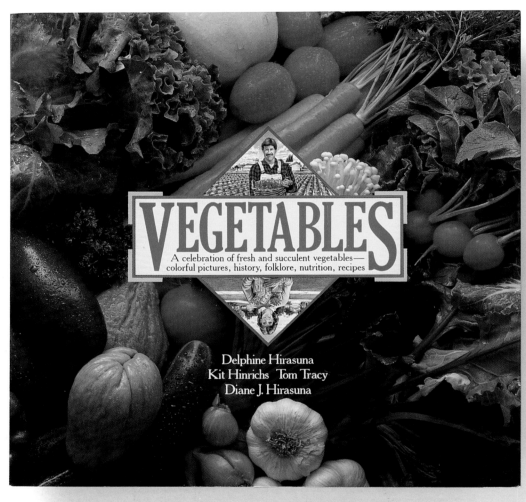

For a subject like vegetables, the typographic tone of voice had to be unpretentious, accessible, and vaguely nostalgic. Cheltenham Old Style created that effect. The cover design, reflective of crate art of the 1940s, was treated symmetrically, with brighter tones in the center. The first and last letters of "vegetables" were used to bracket the subtitle.

Originally the authors picked the playful title Veggies, but were overruled by the publisher's East Coast reps who thought it evoked a "California airhead" image. Like the original title, the choice of typeface for Veggies was slightly funky and rough-edged.

Seed packet artwork lent visual interest to the numbers in the table of contents and also created a turn-of-the-century feeling that was friendly and wholesome.

VEGETABLES

CONTENTS

VEGETABLES:
THE EARLY YEARS

Sunny California's famed farmlands were parched plains until irrigation turned the state green.
Pages 5–35

VEGETABLES:
A TO Z

Vegetables have been the source of legends, myths, wars, and miracle cures.
Pages 37–71

VISUAL
VEGETABLES

Strange and beautiful, vegetables have personalities all their own.
Pages 73–119

VEGETABLE
RECIPES

Most versatile of foods, vegetables can be served as soups, salads, side dishes, entrées, and desserts.
Pages 121–137

Entwining vegetable imagery around the type helped to meld the two elements and reflected the book's theme.

***B**udget limitations dictated that the same illustration style and matched colors be used throughout two sections of the book. Images for the A-Z text were made by inking silhouettes from old engravings, and the initial caps for the alphabet added color accents. The recipe section presented the type of ethnic cuisine and number of serving portions in plate circles at the top of each recipe. The typographic treatment enhanced visibility of this important information while creating an interesting graphic detail.*

Everything grows there. You can drive for hours past green acres. Fresno County, located in the center of the state, leads the nation's counties in agricultural production.

FIRST SETTLERS

It's hard to believe that when the first settlers arrived during the gold rush of 1849, they couldn't envision the valley as the agricultural "Eden" it has become. In the summer, all they saw was a barren plain, the ground cracked for lack of moisture and temperatures hovering above one hundred degrees. Newcomers from the Midwest and East didn't know what to make of the region, which was wet and lush from about November through May and dry and forbidding from May through October. There were no sudden summer thunderstorms, nor was there ever any winter snow. The land defied familiar farming practices.

The would-be gold miners did not, however, come to farm, though many had previously been farmers. Their goal was to stake their claim, get rich, and go home.

Soon many found that mining was frustrating and unprofitable, while recognizing that farming offered a more assured route to riches. "Plant your lands; these be your best gold fields, for all must eat while they live," one new Californian advised his sons.

Food was extremely costly in the early years after gold was discovered on the American River in Sacramento. The burst in population happened too quickly for the Spanish rancheros to supply the demand. Much of the food came in by ship around Cape Horn.

Luther Burbank was a pioneer in developing new varieties of vegetables. Today, researchers with the United States Department of Agriculture and at various universities work on breeding vegetables that grow faster, taste better, keep longer, and contain more nutrients.

Those who turned to agriculture applied methods practiced back home beyond the Rockies, and grew the crops they knew best, such as wheat, oats, and barley. Dry-land farming, which relies on whatever moisture nature provides on a seasonal basis, was the common practice in the Midwest, but in the Far West it produced uneven results, since some crops didn't come into full maturity before the annual heat wave hit.

Beans were the first important vegetable crop grown in California. Until the gold rush, they played an insignificant role in the West. Enterprising farmers, however, quickly noted that miners were buying imported beans by the bushel to cook over the campfire by their claims. Soon bean vines were sprawling all over the state. By 1859, California had the highest return of beans in the nation. At the start of World War I, farmers were exhorted to grow even more beans for our soldiers overseas. In 1918, California produced more than eight and a half million bushels. Even after the war, beans remained the state's most important vegetable crop. Lima beans, native to Peru, were particularly well suited to California's climate and soil and made up about a third of the bean production.

IRRIGATING THE CENTRAL VALLEY

Still, California didn't realize its agricultural potential until irrigation practices became widespread. Without a pipeline of water, the fertile Central Valley was only suitable for farming half the year. Average annual rainfall ranges from seventeen inches in Sacramento to

12

In a bit of early packaging psychology, this company appealed to the consumer's ceaseless demand for homemade goodness by wrapping its tin cans with a Glass Jar label.

13

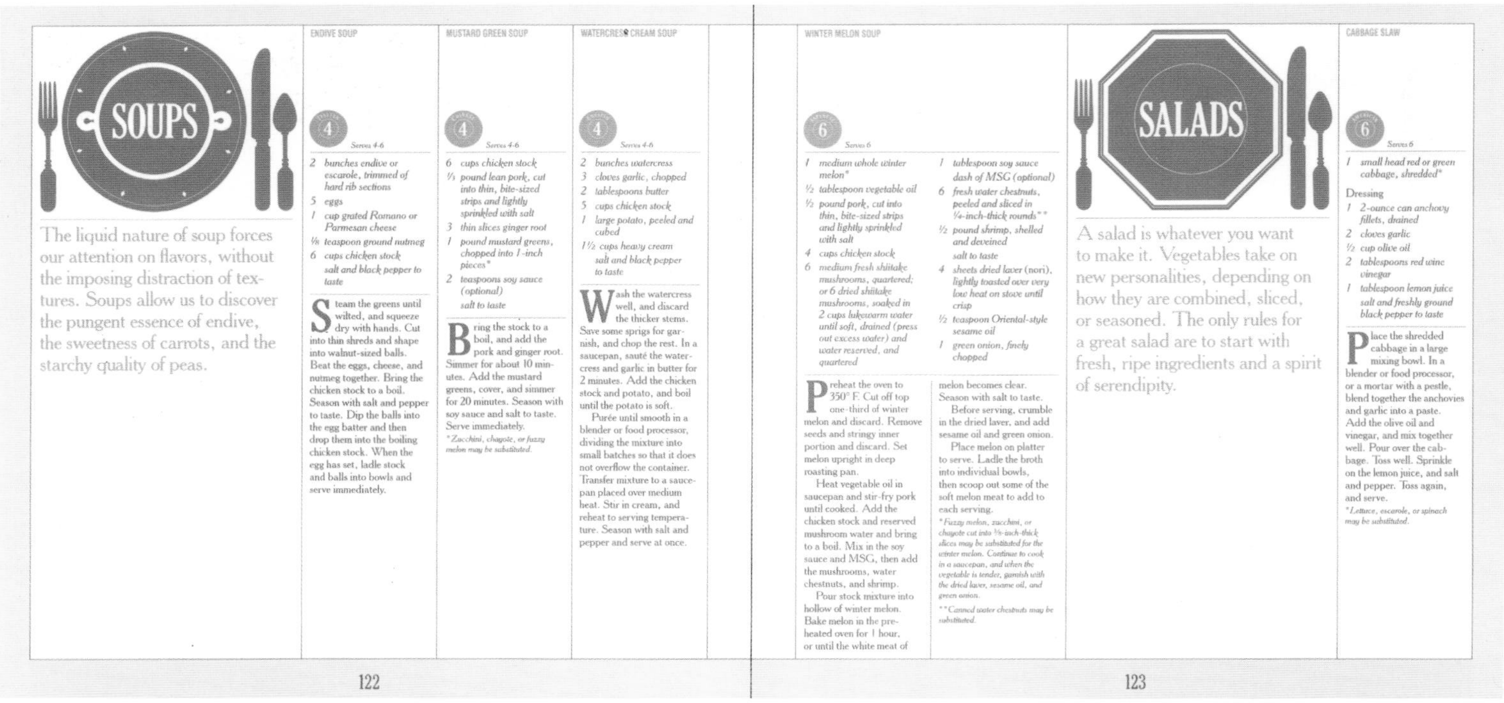

SOUPS

The liquid nature of soup forces our attention on flavors, without the imposing distraction of textures. Soups allow us to discover the pungent essence of endive, the sweetness of carrots, and the starchy quality of peas.

ENDIVE SOUP

4 Serves 4-6

- 2 bunches endive or escarole, trimmed of hard rib sections
- 5 eggs
- 1 cup grated Romano or Parmesan cheese
- ⅛ teaspoon ground nutmeg
- 6 cups chicken stock
- salt and black pepper to taste

Steam the greens until wilted, and squeeze dry with hands. Cut into thin shreds and shape into walnut-sized balls. Beat the eggs, cheese, and nutmeg together. Bring the chicken stock to a boil. Season with salt and pepper to taste. Dip the balls into the egg batter and then drop them into the boiling chicken stock. When the egg has set, ladle stock and balls into bowls and serve immediately.

MUSTARD GREEN SOUP

4 Serves 4-6

- 6 cups chicken stock
- ⅓ pound lean pork, cut into thin, bite-sized strips and lightly sprinkled with salt
- 3 thin slices ginger root
- 1 pound mustard greens, chopped into 1-inch pieces*
- 2 teaspoons soy sauce (optional)
- salt to taste

Bring the stock to a boil, and add the pork and ginger root. Simmer for about 10 minutes. Add the mustard greens, cover, and simmer for 20 minutes. Season with soy sauce and salt to taste. Serve immediately.

*Zucchini, chayote, or fuzzy melon may be substituted.

WATERCRESS CREAM SOUP

4 Serves 4-6

- 2 bunches watercress
- 3 cloves garlic, chopped
- 2 tablespoons butter
- 5 cups chicken stock
- 1 large potato, peeled and cubed
- 1½ cups heavy cream
- salt and black pepper to taste

Wash the watercress well, and discard the thicker stems. Save some sprigs for garnish, and chop the rest. In a saucepan, sauté the watercress and garlic in butter for 2 minutes. Add the chicken stock and potato, and boil until the potato is soft.

Purée until smooth in a blender or food processor, dividing the mixture into small batches so that it does not overflow the container. Transfer mixture to a saucepan placed over medium heat. Stir in cream, and reheat to serving temperature. Season with salt and pepper and serve at once.

122

WINTER MELON SOUP

6 Serves 6

- 1 medium whole winter melon*
- ½ tablespoon vegetable oil
- ½ pound pork, cut into thin, bite-sized strips and lightly sprinkled with salt
- 4 cups chicken stock
- 6 medium fresh shiitake mushrooms, quartered; or 6 dried shiitake mushrooms, soaked in 2 cups lukewarm water until soft, drained (press out excess water) and water reserved, and quartered
- 1 tablespoon soy sauce
- dash of MSG (optional)
- 6 fresh water chestnuts, peeled and sliced in ¼-inch-thick rounds**
- ½ pound shrimp, shelled and deveined
- salt to taste
- 4 sheets dried laver (nori), lightly toasted over very low heat on stove until crisp
- ½ teaspoon Oriental-style sesame oil
- 1 green onion, finely chopped

Preheat the oven to 350° F. Cut off top one-third of winter melon and discard. Remove seeds and stringy inner portion and discard. Set melon upright in deep roasting pan.

Heat vegetable oil in saucepan and stir-fry pork until cooked. Add the chicken stock and reserved mushroom water and bring to a boil. Mix in the soy sauce and MSG, then add the mushrooms, water chestnuts, and shrimp.

Pour stock mixture into hollow of winter melon. Bake melon in the preheated oven for 1 hour, or until the white meat of melon becomes clear. Season with salt to taste.

Before serving, crumble in the dried laver, and add sesame oil and green onion.

Place melon on platter to serve. Ladle the broth into individual bowls, then scoop out some of the soft melon meat to add to each serving.

*Fuzzy melon, zucchini, or chayote cut into ⅛-inch-thick slices may be substituted for the winter melon. Continue to cook in a saucepan, and when the vegetable is tender, garnish with the dried laver, sesame oil, and green onion.

**Canned water chestnuts may be substituted.

SALADS

A salad is whatever you want to make it. Vegetables take on new personalities, depending on how they are combined, sliced, or seasoned. The only rules for a great salad are to start with fresh, ripe ingredients and a spirit of serendipity.

CABBAGE SLAW

6 Serves 6

- 1 small head red or green cabbage, shredded*

Dressing

- 1 2-ounce can anchovy fillets, drained
- 2 cloves garlic
- ½ cup olive oil
- 2 tablespoons red wine vinegar
- 1 tablespoon lemon juice
- salt and freshly ground black pepper to taste

Place the shredded cabbage in a large mixing bowl. In a blender or food processor, or a mortar with a pestle, blend together the anchovies and garlic into a paste. Add the olive oil and vinegar, and mix together well. Pour over the cabbage. Toss well. Sprinkle on the lemon juice, and salt and pepper. Toss again, and serve.

*Lettuce, escarole, or spinach may be substituted.

123

Section dividers were designed to call to mind the character and feel of crate labels commonly used for shipping vegetables and fruit in every farming community until a few decades ago.

Although Cheltenham Old Style was used throughout *Vegetables*, changes in type size, color, and measure and the integration of imagery allowed each section to have its own character without breaking the continuity of the book.

D

Do not peel or slice a cucumber until you are ready to use it. The skin holds in the moisture. Refrigerated in plastic wrap, it should keep well for about a week.

DAIKON
dīe'-kone

OTHER NAMES: Raphanus sativus longipinnatus.

NUTRITION: Vitamins A, B₁, B₂ and C, calcium, and iron.

PEAK SEASON: Year-round.

If you're going to eat lots of rice, you have to eat daikon, the Japanese say. Daikon, which translates as "large root," contains diastase, an enzyme that aids in the digestion of starches. Being a rice-loving people, the Japanese make this white radish a part of their daily diet.

Daikon grows to about eighteen inches long and has a juicy, slightly peppery flavor.

The Japanese have at least a hundred ways to cook with daikon. Raw, it can be grated and eaten with fish or meat. It's added to miso (fermented bean paste) soup. It's used to make flowers for a garnish, and is that stringy white stuff that's put with sashimi (raw fish) in Japanese restaurants. It can be shredded with carrots and dressed with a sweet vinaigrette for a salad. Or it can be cut into chunks and put in stews. A nice characteristic of daikon is that while it will get soft when cooked, it won't dissolve.

Takuan, pickled daikon, is as popular in Japan as pickled cucumbers are in America. In the seventeenth century, Priest Takuan invented a method of drying daikon in the sun and then preserving it in rice bran and salt by pressing the mixture with a heavy stone. Some say that Takuan's tombstone is shaped just like the pickling stone.

Until a few years ago, daikon was sold only in bunches, because it was assumed only Asians were buying it. Today it can be bought by the single root or even a half root.

When buying, look for firm radishes with smooth white skin. Remember, the summer crop is usually a bit spicier than the winter crop because it gets less water.

To store, refrigerate in a plastic bag. It should keep crisp for more than a week.

E

EDIBLE CHRYSANTHEMUM

OTHER NAMES: Chrysanthemum coronarium, garland chrysanthemum, shungiku, tong ho.

NUTRITION: Vitamins B and C and minerals.

PEAK SEASON: Late August to early March.

Chrysanthemum is not only Japan's national flower; one variety is a very popular vegetable.

The edible chrysanthemum is called shungiku by the Japanese or chop suey greens and is harvested for its aromatic leaves and flower buds. Since the buds are sold unopened, it's not an attractive plant. The Japanese treat it as a leafy vegetable, serving it alone as a side dish like spinach or combining it with meats and other vegetables. The flavor is quite strong, so cook it before eating.

If shungiku isn't available, you can substitute ordinary garden chrysanthemum leaves. The leaves can be dipped in batter to make tempura. Flower petals can also be blanched and added to salads. Actually, the petals don't have much flavor, but they do have great color.

Shungiku is sold in bunches in Asian markets. To buy, pick the ones with firm leaves and tightly closed buds. Avoid any bunches that look wilted or yellow.

Refrigerate in a plastic bag. Use within about four days.

EGGPLANT

OTHER NAMES: Solanum melongena, aubergine, nasubi.

NUTRITION: Small amounts of vitamins and minerals.

PEAK SEASON: July through August.

This native of India is part of the so-called deadly nightshade family, which includes potatoes and tomatoes. It was introduced to Europe in the thirteenth century, brought in via the Middle East along the silk route from China.

The Arabs, who received this "egg fruit" from China around the fourth century, probably have the greatest number of ways of preparing it. In fact, it's considered part of the "bride price" to have a repertoire of dozens of eggplant recipes. In Turkey there's a dish called imam bayeldi, which is stuffed eggplant simmered in olive oil. Translated as "swooning imam," it is said that when the religious leader's wives served this dish, he swooned in ecstasy.

The French, who call eggplants aubergine, are famous for their ratatouille, a tasty vegetable stew consisting heavily of eggplant.

Most people in the United States are familiar with the large, purple globe eggplant. There are several other varieties, including long, oval ones that the Japanese call nasubi.

There are also small egg-shaped white varieties, which may explain how the vegetable got its name.

Eggplant was part of the cargo that came into Europe via the Middle Eastern silk route. At first it was greeted with distrust. The Italians called it a mad apple, and herbalist John Gerard claimed it had "mischievous qualities."

Eggplants are sort of spongy and bland, which make them exceptionally versatile. They absorb the flavor of whatever they are cooked with, while supplying a certain bulkiness that acts as a meat "extender."

To buy, look for eggplant with taut, shiny skin. Old eggplants develop bitter skins and tough seeds.

Refrigerated in a plastic bag, eggplants will keep for about five days.

ENDIVE AND ESCAROLE

OTHER NAMES: Cichorium endivia crispa, curly-leaf endive; Cichorium endivia latifolia.

NUTRITION: Vitamin A and iron.

PEAK SEASON: Year-round.

Escarole and endive are like fraternal twins, which creates some confusion.

Although they look like they belong to the lettuce family, botanically they are chicories. And, being chicories, both are slightly pungent.

Endive grows in a loose head and has crisp, curly, ragged-edged, narrow leaves. The outer ones are green, becoming progressively yellower toward the heart.

Escarole is a broad-leaved endive. Its leaves curl a bit and its heart is a pale yellow, too.

The two are related to the Belgian endive, also called witloof, which is a blanched broad-leaved chicory sprout, but their relationship is very distant.

Produce stores sometimes mark endive as escarole and both as chicory, and it all gets very confusing, especially if you have sent someone else to do the shopping and he or she doesn't know which one you meant.

Endive and escarole date back to ancient times. In France, however, they weren't considered a food until about the fourteenth century.

Europeans often add these leaves to soups and other cooked dishes, but in the United States, they are mostly used raw in salads.

To buy, look for tender, crisp leaves with no sign of wilting.

Refrigerated in plastic bags, they will keep for about three days.

ENOKITAKE MUSHROOM
ē'-no·kēy·tah·kay'

OTHER NAMES: Flammulina velutipes, snow puff, golden needle.

NUTRITION: Vitamins B and C, potassium, iron, and phosphorus.

PEAK SEASON: Year-round.

I was first introduced to this delicate white mushroom in Kyoto, Japan, several years ago. A friend brought out a huge bowlful of enokitake, which she added to sukiyaki. These mushrooms had such a wonderful silky texture that, much to the astonishment of my host, I proceeded to eat about a pound of them, ignoring everything else on the table.

50 51

MUSHROOMS

Once available only at the whim of nature, mushrooms today can be cultivated as a commercial crop. New Asian varieties of fungi are coming on the market each year. Two of the most popular Asian mushrooms are shiitake, a pungent-flavored fungus that tastes like it grew wild in the forest, and enokitake, a delicate threadlike mushroom with a velvety texture.

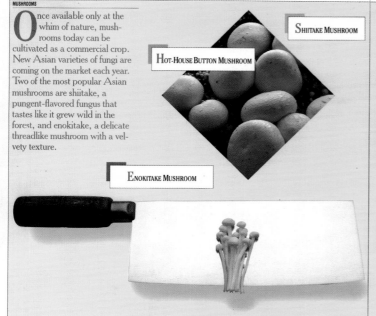

HOT-HOUSE BUTTON MUSHROOM

SHIITAKE MUSHROOM

ENOKITAKE MUSHROOM

80 81

THE NATURE COMPANY

The Nature Company is founded on the premise of "increasing our sense of wonder in the natural world." Through mail-order catalogs and retail stores, the Nature Company offers products that range from inflatable dinosaurs to malachite earrings and animal print T-shirts to fossils. Its stores, located in shopping malls, museums, and at historical sites around the country, create a tranquil shopping environment often enhanced by falling water, wind chimes, lush green plants, and the music of natural sounds.

The Nature Company first asked us to translate its corporate philosophy into a visual identity. Selecting the correct typeface was a key. The company had adopted an educational approach for most of its products and wanted to convey the atmosphere found in the store as a place where families could come to shop in a nonintimidating environment — something between the British Museum of Natural History and The Gap. We chose Century Old Style to capture that feeling.

Notepad cubes have become popular in The Nature Company's graphics line, covering subjects from minerals to flowers to butterflies and fish. The use of Century Old Style caps provides for strong name recognition and also harmonizes with the subject matter. Note: The Nature Company logo (top) in corporate uses always includes the "bunny." But we've designed the system to allow for the substitution of other natural images such as leaves, elephants, birds, etc. This adds interest and subtly expands the identification of the company without blatantly stamping its logo on every item.

PAPERS OF STONE

THE NATURE COMPANY

THE NATURE COMPANY

· AFRICAN EL...

THE NATURE COMPANY CATALOG

Soapstone
little bunny 3 ...
to The Nature Compa...
soapstone as a delightfu...
the gentler side of nature.
$8.00

Look at
the World as
if Through the
Eyes of a Dragonfly!
...e Brimfield lens to your eye
...ene before you divided in...
...., much as dragonflies and
...tric sectors revolve while
...n upright and in place!
...field Lens is housed in
...turned wood housing
...at and hold in itself
...ted, and vary from
...hink this is one of
...tical devices to be
...... (the entire first
......t to our staff)
... Lens $10.95

A Gentle Duck That's at Home Indoors or Out.
The gentle charm and realism of our preening mallard captivates
all who see it (the first to reach us became an office mascot).
...ade by 7 lbs. of durable bonded marble for use outdoors under all
...weather conditions, or indoors as a natural sculpture. With
gently weathered, hand-finished patinas, these handsome
...sculptures are as delightful as center-
...pieces on dining tables as they are
...by garden walkways. 11" x 9"
#2510 $65.00

A Stylish Set of
Mallard Tie and
Suspenders.
Outrageous, fun, and
urbanely stylish, these
mallard ties and sus-
penders are as attracti...
as they a...

...s a pair
...temporary
...displaying single,
...ens of polished
...ne Brazilian sodalite
...on sterling silver
...wires. 2⅝" long.
#2101 $23.00

For one spring catalog, we developed a tabloid-sized publication to highlight the year's top fifty products. Numbering of the items gave a unique aspect to the content. The complex, "knitted" look of the page required a highly flexible format for the type, from flush left to flush right to centered to irregular rag-arounds. This would normally be a typographic nightmare, but within the context of these high-energy layouts, it works.

The correspondence of caption to product is important in catalogs. We've found that placing type adjacent to the product gives an immediacy of identification and improves the buying climate.

Many products sold by The Nature Company, from bird seed to cedar chips, are marked with simple labels and tags.

A basic style guide explaining correct type, spacing, and visual relationships has allowed the company's inhouse design group to implement its own limited packaging program.

There's always a surprise in store at the Nature Company—a special magic that mixes dinosaurs and dolphins, crystal kits and telescopes, fine art prints and discovery tools that kids can use. There are maps to hang on your walls, and maps to put in your pocket; intriguing objects to display as well as experiments to do. At the Nature Company, there's always more to discover!

Call Toll Free 800 227-1114 in California: 800-782-0033

11 Who's Who in The World of Animals.
Without a doubt the most readable, best illustrated survey of the world of animals available today, The new Macmillan Illustrated Animal Encyclopedia contains more than 1900 full color illustrations by renowned wildlife artists and concise biographies of the animals by leading authorities. All major families of birds, fish, reptiles and mammals covered. An invaluable reference tool and beautiful artwork in its own right. 9¼" × 11½", hardbound. #3121A $35.00

12 Inflatable Globes Great for Any Age.
These brightly colored and fully detailed vinyl Earth globes are just as accurate as any formal table model, but they can also be dropped, squeezed, kicked or carried in a pocket to school. Just blow them up and they'll stay full for months! 10½" diameter. Sold as a set of two. #1151A Pair of Globes $10.00

13 "Flying Puffins" for Jugglers or Puffin Lovers.
This happy set of bean-bag puffins is actually designed for juggling. Their great popularity makes us feel, however, that lots of people are taking them home for personal puffin pets. 3¾" high. #1115A Set of three $10.75

18 Dolphin Trifold Notecards From The California Academy of Sciences.
The playful, popular Pacific White-Sided Dolphins from the California Academy of Sciences Museum are the subject of The Nature Company's newest note cards. Each trifold card is packaged with a blank sheet of fine notepaper to provide additional writing space. You'll have trouble deciding whether to send these off in the mail or to keep them as desktop sculptures for yourself! 4½" × 7½." Set of eight cards and envelopes. #4343A $8.95

AUDUBON ZOOLOGICAL GAR

20 This Monkey Climbs Up The Back and Over!
Each of these shoulder-clinging monkeys is an original airbrush T-shirt design by Ken Holly (creator of our last season's hit Venus Flytrap shirt), and features printing both on the back and over the shoulder onto the front. They're highly unusual and original, and a lot of fun to wear. 100% cotton, in adult sizes S (34–6), M (38–40), L (42–44) and ExL (46). Be sure to specify size. #5133A $16.95

21 Our Favorite Sea-Otter Poster.
One of the finest contemporary animal photographers, Jeff Foott always captures the spirit of his subject perfectly. His California Sea Otter—the latest in the Nature Company's Wildlife Series—is a fine example, with its irresistably lifelike detail. Available unframed or framed (as shown) in metal sectional frames with acrylic pane. 25" × 27". #9165A Unframed $20.00 #9166A Framed $90.00

14 Patricia Hunter Paints The Grevy's Zebra.
From an exhibition of her original works at the Nature Company, Patricia Hunter's extraordinary painting of the Grevy's Zebra captures in both scale and composition the beauty of an exquisite African animal. Our poster reproduction is available unframed or framed in metal sectional frames with acrylic pane. 25" × 36".
#9121A Unframed $20.00
#9122A Framed $105.00

16 Our Cuddly Bunny.
Ready to jump into spring, but plenty warm enough to cuddle this winter, our new bunnies are furry, soft and virtually irresistable. 12" × 9", of all-acrylic fiber.
#1116A $25.00

15 A Poster Celebration of Animals.
Tigers watch, lizards lurk, monkeys wait and a good many of the rest of the New Orleans' Audubon Zoological Gardens join in this terrific new poster that will delight nearly everyone and every age. 14" × 38". Available unframed, or framed in black metal sectional frames with acrylic pane.
#9281A Unframed $15.00
#9282A Framed $82.00

17 Grow Your Own Crystals!
Each of these spectacular crystal growing kits yields a crystal about five inches long and several smaller ones. Though not the real minerals they resemble, they display the same structural qualities and beauty. Each kit contains a packet of pre-mixed chemicals which dissolve in water and form their crystals in about five days. For ages 12 and up.
#1131A "Amethyst" purple $9.95
#1132A "Emerald" green $9.95
#1133A "Quartz" white $9.95
#1134A Set of Three Mineral Kits $27.75

19 Dino Mugs Are Mealtime Hits.
The clever people at Plum Designs have put their wonderful dinosaur designs on four brightly colored, heavy-plastic stacking mugs that will bring many lunchtimes of delight for all the neighborhood kids.
#1104A Set of 4 Dino Mugs $11.25

24 Our Best Discovery Kit Ever!
This special assemblage of three of our most popular discovery tools includes a solid metal gyroscope, a 4¾" radiometer whose photo-sensitive blades spin under the influence of light, and a 3" acrylic prism for casting full-color rainbows in the sun. Equipment for hours of fun.
#1191A Science Discovery Kit $14.50

23 World Wall Map Can't Rip or Tear.
One of the graphically finest large-scale wall maps we've ever seen— bright, bold and contemporary, usable anywhere from an executive boardroom to a children's playroom. Made of a unique, virtually indestructible and non-tearable paper, Tyvek®, from Du Pont. Measures 53¼" × 30½".
#8260A $20.00

22 Dinosaur Models From Originals in the British Museum.
Our fine set of lifelike dinosaurs in extra-heavy molded plastic are modeled after full-size originals in the British Museum. They'll satisfy the most ardent dinosaur collector. Set of four includes Diplodocus (19½"), Woolly Mammoth (4½"), Triceratops (5½") and Megalosaurus (7").
#1102A Set of Four $14.00

---

dding finesse and impact to the ubiquitous 800 telephone number is another important detail in the development of a catalog. We originally chose Onyx because its compressed letterforms allowed us to have a large size without losing much product space, and it contrasted well with Century Text. The only drawback was its thin "thins." Unfortunately, when screened to create a colored seal, we found that many buyers misread a 4 for a 1 and were calling a very irate company twenty-four hours a day. We rectified the problem by photographically compressing Century Bold Condensed.

Original Onyx.

Revised Century Bold Condensed.

he best proof of a type's effectiveness is in multiple, varied uses. Specialty products like this kid's Tyrannosaurus rex T-shirt exemplify the continuity of image allowed by a consistent but flexible typographic approach.

THE NATURE COMPANY

PTERANODON
36" x 96" GIANT INFLATABLE

when dinosaurs ... sea. The great-
...r and ...t 27' wingspan. Yet
...s ago, ...e as 20 pounds and had a
...more a glider than a flier,
...ngs.) Pteranodon soared
...d without breaking its fragile
...jaws, but scientists still aren't
...e Nature Company's inflatable
...with a wingspan nearly 8' wide.
...hanging, Pteranodon comes with a
...res.

©1987 The Nature Company, P.O.
Box 2310, Berkeley, CA 94702

THE NATURE COMPANY

IGUANA
14" x 74" GIANT INFLATABLE

Giant among today's lizards, the Iguana is harmless to other a...
lives in areas between southern Canada and the tip of South...
habits and form of Iguanas vary greatly: some live in tr...
are ground-dwelling, and one is marine. Although th...
North, Central, and South America, a few species...
the Tonga and Fiji Islands and some smaller s...
of the U.S./Mexican border. The Nature C...
is accurately detailed and measures 14" x...
allow for easy attachment to walls or ceilin...
for repairing accidental punctures.

CAUTION: THIS PRODUCT IS NOT TO
BE USED AS A FLOTATION DEVICE.   Made in Taiwan.

THE NATURE COMPANY

COMMON KINGSNAKE
40" x 26" INFLATABLE

Snakes are among the ... most beautiful reptiles, with color and
scale patterns equaling some ... of nature's finest designs. The Common
Kingsnake of Western America is patterned with alternating bands of plain black and
yellow. The Common Kingsnake lives in many habitats, from forests to deserts and
marshes and is found in the United States from coast to coast. It is non-poisonous, and
lives on other snakes, frogs, birds, eggs and small mammals. This 40" X 26" inflatable
model details every surface of the snake, and is as perfect as a sculpture as it is in its
functional role in warding off unwanted garden pests. Patch kit included.

©1987 The Nature Company, P.O. Box 2310, Berkeley, CA 94702   Made in Taiwan.

CAUTION: THIS PRODUCT IS NOT TO BE USED AS A FLOTATION DEVICE

MULTITUDES

A CRASH OF RHINOCEROSES. A SCHOOL OF FISH. A LITTER OF PUPS. A FLOCK OF SHEEP. A STRING OF PONIES. A COVEY OF PARTRIDGES. A PRIDE OF LIONS. A HERD OF ELEPHANTS. A PLAGUE OF LOCUSTS. A COLONY OF ANTS. A COVEY OF QUAIL. A KINDLE OF KITTENS. A LEAP OF LEOPARDS. A POD OF SEALS. A SLOTH OF BEARS. A RAFTER OF TURKEYS. A PACE OF ASSES. A WALK OF SNIPE. A GAM OF WHALES. A NEST OF RABBITS. A GANG OF ELK. A FALL OF WOODCOCKS. A DULE OF DOVES. A SKULK OF FOXES. A DISSIMULATION OF BIRDS. A SPRING OF TEAL. A PEEP OF CHICKENS. A BEVY OF ROEBUCKS. A BUSINESS OF FERRETS. A BALE OF TURTLES. A PITYING OF TURTLEDOVES. A DRIFT OF HOGS. A PADDLING OF DUCKS. A SIEGE OF HERONS. A TRIP OF GOATS. A CHARM OF FINCHES. A CETE OF BADGERS. A DECEIT OF LAPWINGS. A SHOAL OF BASS. AN EXALTATION OF LARKS. A DROVE OF CATTLE. A SINGULAR OF BOARS. A TIDINGS OF MAGPIES. A GAGGLE OF GEESE. A CONGREGATION OF PLOVERS. A HUSK OF HARES. AN UNKINDNESS OF RAVENS. A LABOR OF MOLES. A RICHNESS OF MARTENS. A CAST OF HAWKS. A KNOT OF TOADS. A DESCENT OF WOODPECKERS. A SOUNDER OF SWINE. A MUSTERING OF STORKS. A CLUTCH OF EGGS. A BOUQUET OF PHEASANTS. AN ARMY OF CATERPILLARS. A HOVER OF TROUT. A FLIGHT OF SWALLOWS. A TROOP OF KANGAROOS. A CLOWDER OF CATS. A WATCH OF NIGHTINGALES. A BARREN OF MULES. A SHREWDNESS OF APES. A RAG OF COLTS. A MURMURATION OF STARLINGS. A BUILDING OF ROOKS. A SMACK OF JELLYFISH. A HARRAS OF HORSES. A PARLIAMENT OF OWLS. A ROUTE OF WOLVES. A HOST OF SPARROWS. AN OSTENTATION OF PEACOCKS.

THE NATURE COMPANY

Poster: © 1999 The Nature Company · Copy and Compilation: © 1988 Michael Wein · ANIMAL WISDOM ENTERPRISES · Design: Pentagram · Printing: Paper N Inc.

"**M**ultitudes" started as a collection of animal group names brought to The Nature Company as a potential product. The piece had been set in Helvetica and carried no emotional impact. This kind of product lives or dies on the choice, size, style, and color of type. Cheltenham Old Style in caps and small caps was chosen as the new type for several reasons: Its character was compatible with Century Old Style and put in mind English alphabet books; the condensed drawing of the face allowed large point size; the caps/small caps gave consistent color to the text and set off the colored animal engravings. The box rule was part of the overall graphic vocabulary we created for The Nature Company.

STARS & STRIPES

Stars & Stripes began as a modest fund-raiser for the San Francisco Chapter of the American Institute of Graphic Artists (AIGA) and mushroomed into a major auction of original work by ninety-six leading graphic designers and illustrators. Contributors were asked to design a contemporary interpretation of the American flag and keep the artwork to a 12x18-inch size. An editor from Chronicle Books was invited to attend the auction and the following day asked to publish the works.

Chris Hill's pencil flag defined the book's theme on the cover. Composed of 2,400 colored pencils, the artwork graphically combined the flag and a design tool in a single image. The textured background provided a complex area for the book title so strong, clean type was essential. "Stars & Stripes" was set as a single word title, using a change in type weight to optically achieve the word spacing.

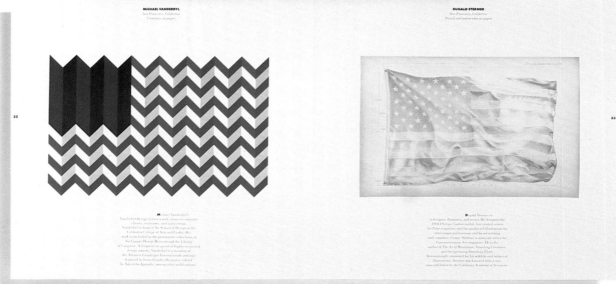

The typography was kept simple and unobtrusive to avoid detracting from the art on each page. Futura Extra Bold was used for the designers' names and initial caps. The text was in Bodoni Book. Because we wanted to give this presentation a museum catalog feel, we maintained a symmetrical format with all type and images centered. Along with accommodating the various styles of the artists, the typography had to complement Americana featured in the introductory chapter.

STARS&STRIPES

By Kit Hinrichs

A Celebration of the American Flag by 96 International Designers and Artists

THE BLIMP BOOK

Baron Wolman, a photographer/publisher friend fascinated with images of flying, approached Neil about designing a book on the Goodyear blimp. The book, two years in the making, contains some of the best aerial photography ever taken from a blimp, as well as of one. The project's challenge was to develop a format and typographic design that captured the spirit of the blimp without overpowering the photographs.

Sometimes you discover a face that says, "Use me," for a specific piece. Frankfurter is one of those faces. Its shape and genre were perfect for the title, and its numbers gave a special stamp to chapter heads. Neil contrasted the "blimpish" Frankfurter type with Helvetica Light, using caps for the chapter heads and upper and lower case for the text.

BEHOLD
THE
BLIMP!

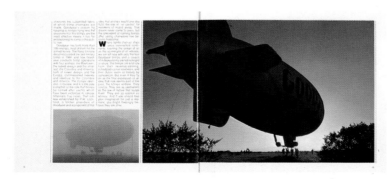

The documentary tone of the photography seemed to demand a fundamental, no-nonsense journalistic approach. Justified columns and vertical rules gave a newspaper-like formality to the typography. As a foil to these Falstaffian dirigibles, I can't imagine a better styling.

NEIMAN MARCUS

In addition to carrying a vast array of nationally branded merchandise, Neiman Marcus develops and markets a considerable range of proprietary items, from suits and dresses, chili and popcorn, to baby products. Woody was asked to design a line of packages for Neiman Marcus baby lotions, oils, and shampoos.

Since the "NM Baby" project required the design of individual items and a complete product line, establishment of a uniform typographic style and graphic format was a must. Bodoni was ultimately selected because of its classic, upmarket demeanor and its compatibility with the line's illustrative image and delicate pastel color range.

In the initial stages of design development, many concepts, formats and typestyles were explored, from script to Futura Extra Bold. But once the "cow jumped over the moon" graphic was accepted, Bodoni emerged as the right route to follow.

Typography often serves as a corporate icon. Used in this manner, the chosen typestyle does more than present an impression of the company; in effect, it visually becomes the company. Because its recognition value is built up through repeated association of the corporate name and typeface, the look should not easily grow tiresome. As such, typography used for identity must appear contemporary yet classic, distinctive yet extremely flexible. The "alphabet" must have enough depth and breadth in weights, sizes, and italics to accommodate a variety of uses — from stationery, brochures, and product identification to outdoor signage — and be adaptable enough to work in combination with other typefaces and design styles. Plus the typeface must be able to evolve with the company as it grows and shifts in direction over the years.

MANDARIN ORIENTAL

The Mandarin Oriental operates a group of prestigious hotels in the Far East and western United States. They asked us to create a corporate identity system that conveys an impression of luxury and class with an oriental flair. Alan made a folding fan the corporate emblem and set the name of the hotel group or individual hotel in Garamond between two rules below the fan. The identity system used a separate color for each hotel — for example, red for Hong Kong, saffron for Bangkok, and so on — plus grey for the Hotel Group.

MANDARIN ORIENTAL
THE HOTEL GROUP

THE MANDARIN
MANILA

THE ORIENTAL
SINGAPORE

THE MANDARIN
HONG KONG

THE MANDARIN
VANCOUVER

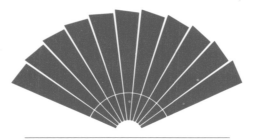

THE ORIENTAL
MACAU

THE ORIENTAL
BANGKOK

Plantin captured the deluxe personality of the Mandarin Oriental and fulfilled a very practical need. Since the application of the identity had to be done locally in countries throughout the Pacific Rim, Alan had to select a typeface that was readily available all over the Far East. Research indicated that Plantin was available in metal typesetting and photo-setting systems.

ART CENTER

Art Center College of Design, with campuses in Pasadena, California, and Vevey, Switzerland, is one of the world's most prominent design schools. Art Center students are educated in such diverse disciplines as transportation design, illustration, photography, advertising design, graphic design, film, and environmental design. When we were asked to aid them in developing an identification program, it was a rather daunting assignment, not only because of the school's international standing but because every member of my graduating class of 1963 would be watching.

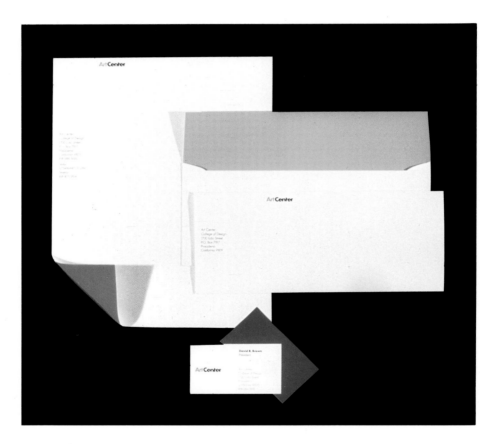

The basics of the stationery program obviously key off the logotype. We had two messages to deliver here: the strong, professional, well-managed organization; and the bold, creative designer leadership position of the school. The "corporate" side we managed with a restrained use of color (grey and warm red) and a distinctive, not artsy, stationery format. The creative aspect was handled with solid primary colors on the back of the letterhead and business card and inside the envelope.

Within the profession, the name of the school has never been the formal Art Center College of Design, just the punchy Art Center. We fel the main identification of the school s oul. use that as the official wordmark. Al ough one might be inclined to choose the ost contemporary typeface to show the scho as a cutting-edge design institution, we purposely chose a more restrained approach for two reasons: First, the audience was broad, including design professionals, students, businesses, government, and nonprofits; and second, the logo was only a small part of a complete communications program. It was crucial that the logo not compete with hat complement the posters, catalogs, magazines, invitations, newsletters, and sundry other items that should be more contemporary.

The logo is based on Futura Extra Bold with many subtle variations, like T's with one-sided crossbars. We connected "ArtCenter" and let color or value difference separate the words.

These spreads from Art Center Review, a tabloid magazine sent to alumni, affiliates, and students, show the flexibility of the design format. The narrow, newspaper-like setting of Bodoni works equally well in setting off the trademark pencil (a regular feature), student work, or a conglomeration of different typefaces. The composition of the word "magazine" below demonstrates the variety of typographic tones, styles, and periods appropriate to the article on magazine design. Bodoni captions were set vertically to simulate Japanese characters on the fourth spread.

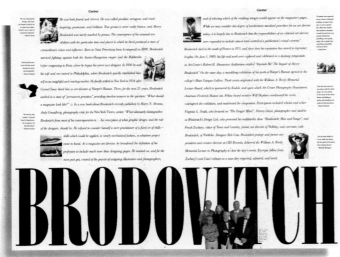

Art Center's discrete logo allows each of the school's publications to maintain a distinct identity. Review's front cover features a custom-designed alphabet by Photo Lettering for its masthead, befitting the unique standing of the college in the design field. The striking cover also includes a table of contents strip using images and Bodoni numerals and text.

Published by
Art Center College of Design

ArtCenter

Summer Issue, August 1987
Volume 1, Number 4

REVIEW 4

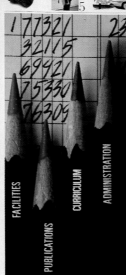

1 7 7 3 2 1   2 3
3 2 1 1 5
6 9 9 2 1
7 5 3 3 0
7 6 3 0 9

FACILITIES
PUBLICATIONS
CURRICULUM
ADMINISTRATION

Published by
Art Center College of Design

ArtCenter

Spring (Reprint) Issue, April 1988
Volume 2, Number 3

REVIEW 3

1987

ArtCenter

Summer Issue, September 1987
Volume 2, Number 2

REVIEW 2

Published by
Art Center College of Design

ArtCenter

Spring Issue, May 1987
Volume 1, Number 1

REVIEW 1

MOMA OXFORD

The Museum of Modern Art Oxford — a small, distinguished museum housed in a converted Victorian brewery — approached us to design its graphics program, which included hanging banners, a signage and stationery system, shopping bags, and a complete poster campaign for numerous gallery exhibitions. The architecture of the building, with its columns and structured layout, inspired the linear pattern of the new identity, while an extra bold modern typeface for the name provided dramatic contrast to the vertical rules.

Signage for Café MOMA and elsewhere is a combination of Futura Light and the Extra Bold used for the logo. This grouping makes a handsome, adaptable, yet consistent format for the museum.

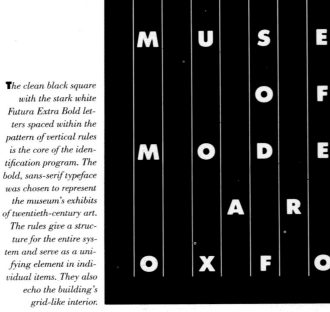

Mervyn developed a poster series to publicize upcoming exhibitions. The distinctive rule of the museum's identity system quickly associated the event with MOMA without prominent mention in the headline.

The clean black square with the stark white Futura Extra Bold letters spaced within the pattern of vertical rules is the core of the identification program. The bold, sans-serif typeface was chosen to represent the museum's exhibits of twentieth-century art. The rules give a structure for the entire system and serve as a unifying element in individual items. They also echo the building's grid-like interior.

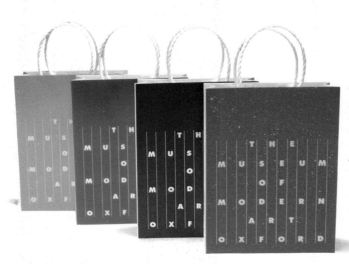

The museum ID system had to be flexible enough to work in several colors without losing its integrity. The purity of the black-and-white, "umbrella" identity served to enhance and emphasize colorful individual items like bags and banners.

SOUL BURNING FLASHES

YAYOI KUSAMA: SCULPTURE

5 NOVEMBER 1989 – 7 JANUARY 1990

THE MUSEUM OF MODERN ART OXFORD

With financial assistance from The Japan Foundation. The Museum of Modern Art receives financial assistance from The Arts Council of Great Britain, Oxford City Council, Oxfordshire County Council, Visiting Arts, and Southern Arts

30 Pembroke St. Oxford OX1 1BP

Recorded Information: 0865 728608

Admission £1.00 Concessions 50p Friends Free

Tuesdays – Saturdays 10am – 6pm Sundays 2am – 6pm Mondays Closed

EDITIONS PAYOT

Editions Payot publishes fiction and nonfiction books in French. John was commissioned to develop a program for both lines. He knew that confidence in the quality of the publisher is key in giving the public the confidence to buy authors who are lesser known or up-and-coming. A tasteful, consistent cover program establishing identity for the line and bringing individuality to the authors was the goal. The ongoing program includes the design of more than 150 titles per year.

 This initial cap P, using a traditional book publishing symbol as the counter, was developed as the company trademark to aid in identifying books at a glance on the front and spine of each edition.

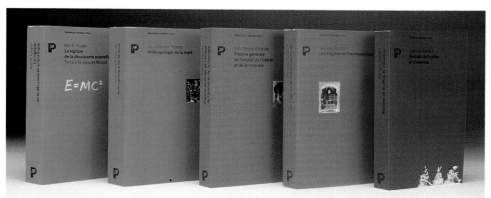

The nonfiction line is distinguished by its bleed, spectrum backgrounds with uncomplicated graphic or photographic images and Helvetica typography. The bleed black background with a broad range of illustrations is used for fiction. Typography is Caslon upper and lower case for this series.

InfoWorks

nfoWorks, a contract furniture market held in Dallas, creates a new theme for each year's show. Woody was asked to symbolize information that works along with design, technology, and productivity. The entire promotional program was built around cropped segments of the mark and InfoWorks wordmark. The fractured sections found their way onto shopping bags, posters, badges, and promotional brochures.

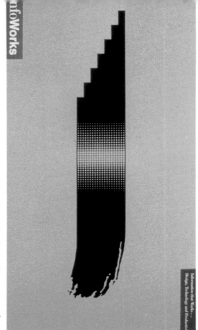

A bold central graphic element was fashioned to be international in feel and visually striking in a large interior space. The concept was a black mark that began as a brush stroke and grew through various stages of digitized sections. The mark symbolized culmination of the productivity theme.

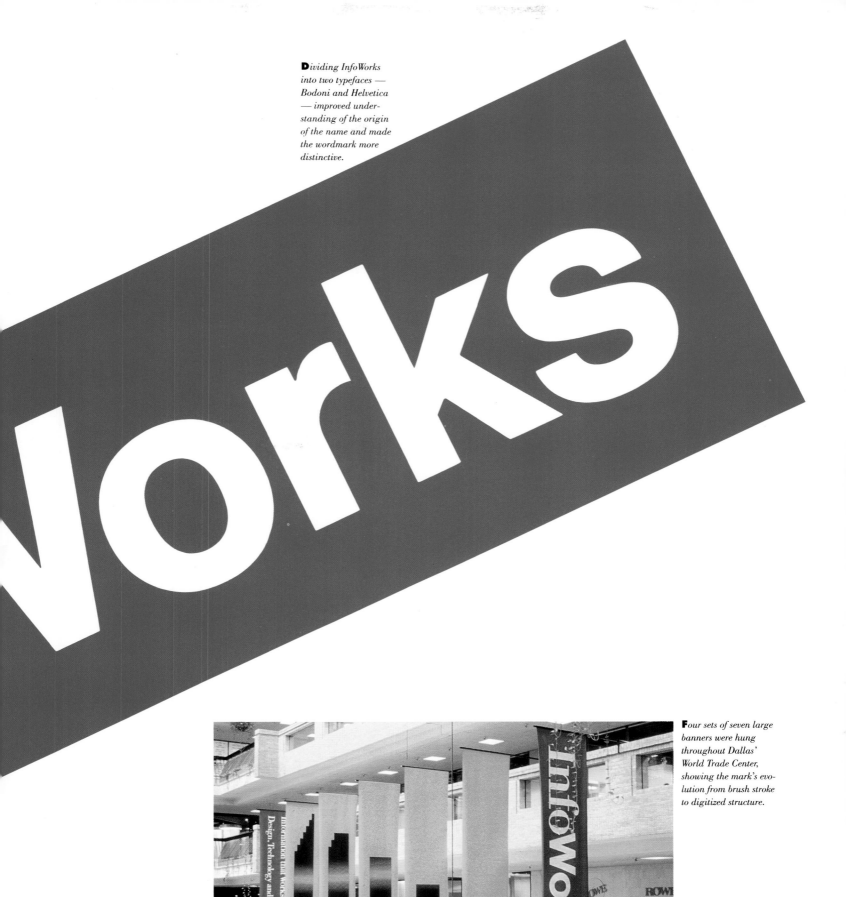

Dividing InfoWorks into two typefaces — Bodoni and Helvetica — improved understanding of the origin of the name and made the wordmark more distinctive.

Four sets of seven large banners were hung throughout Dallas' World Trade Center, showing the mark's evolution from brush stroke to digitized structure.

NATIONAL GRID

The British government has operated nationalized utility companies for more than fifty years. The National Grid Company was created in 1989 in a move to privatize many government monopolies. As the nation's major carrier of electricity, the National Grid sought two identification solutions: to create an identity separate from the government and to raise awareness and reassure its constituents that the job is well in hand.

The National Grid needed an extensive sign system for its equipment and properties, along with safety, no trespassing, and other informational signs. Helvetica, set flush left and aligned with the symbol's center, created clear, informative signage. All "danger" information was called out in red.

John created a stylized high-tension tower as the corporate symbol, with the name in Helvetica Light. This typeface was selected because its clean, well-drawn letters communicated a no-nonsense, no frills, let's-get-to-work attitude, while visually reinforcing the structure of the symbol.

National Grid symbols have been produced for executives and customers on such diverse items as ties, paperweights and lapel pins.

REUTERS

Reuters is an international news agency and communications network headquartered in London. In addition to supplying press information, the company provides a high-speed data service to businesses and financial institutions. When Alan began the project over fifteen years ago, the brief was to create a distinctive, memorable logotype that could be used in any scale and reproduced in virtually any material and that would be recognizable when reproduced by different techniques. Design excellence is particularly important to Reuters as its clients are sophisticated experts in communications.

The Reuters van is one of the dozens of applications for the logo, ranging from annual report to the desktop monitor.

Punched tape machines once used for information transmission provided the idea for the corporate logo. The uncomplicated line-only styling allows it to be reproduced in fine engraving or flexography with no discernible loss in image.

Helvetica was used as the corporate face for the stationery program because it is readily obtainable on photosetting equipment around the world. It also serves as a neutral typeface.

Many corporations present a corporate logo as a gift to clients, employees, and customers — thoughtful but not useful. Alan's solution was to turn it into a game puzzle. Given much patience and a steady hand, the stainless steel ball bearings can be juggled to reveal the company logotype.

Sometimes, as in the case of fashion, it is not what you say but the way you say it visually that counts most. Typographic style can communicate quality, elegance, good breeding, exclusivity. A letterform of classic beauty makes a statement of its own. It speaks volumes about the subject, implying by association that this is a person or product of sophistication, taste, and uncompromising high standards. Type with panache isn't staid. It's distinctive and sometimes irreverent without being outrageous, current without appearing trendy. Inherently, panache is transitory, redefined with the changing times — and always the epitome of self-confident style.

ALBERINI WINE

Alberini, a Texas vintner that imports Italian wines, asked Woody to develop a distinguished, "Eurostyle" bottle label. With the current flood of wines from all over the world, Alberini was interested in taking some risk in producing the label. The main challenge was that it had to have style.

The distinctiveness of the label has many elements, starting with the use of Univers 39 as the typeface. It's extremely contemporary in appearance (spaced type) but grounded in classic typographic traditions. Turning the type sideways gives the label its edge — not only because of the angle, but because the formal, almost rigid, typographic organization is so contradictory to wine label convention that you can't avoid paying attention to it. The simple, clean typography plays against the colorful background of a waving Italian flag.

SKALD MAGAZINE

Skald is a quarterly travel magazine designed for Royal Viking Lines — the premier worldwide cruise line. Past Viking passengers (who represent over 50 percent of the line's current passengers) are the audience. This is a highly sophisticated group of travelers who look for the unusual and unique in travel, along with the most luxurious accommodations and superior service.

The editorial focus is on destinations and the means to get there. The writing tone and design are decidedly soft-sell.

The magazine's thematic identity is the exclusive use of exotic faces on each cover. Polar bears and Tutankhamen, animal totems and Japanese children all serve to represent the personalities of regions of the world to visit.

The title overprinting the gold Chinese character reinforces the message of China quite effectively, while giving the word visual depth. Two contrasting measures of type provide an opportunity to tell a secondary story in conjunction with the main text and add visual texture to the page. The centered caption text in the timeline separates the main text and adds a museum-like symmetry to the objects.

Bodoni, chosen for its timeless quality and elegance, is the primary and standard headline face for the magazine. The body text is Century Old Style, with Helvetica Italic for captions. The contrast of the two text faces gives quick and easy identification to each element. A drop initial Bodoni cap beginning each caption is a simple segue between the faces.

Rdraw Wider

shorten the "L" for better #

overlap serif

SKALD

Condense 10%

The Skald masthead is a modified Bodoni. Letter spacings between the K and A and the L and D were too extreme in their normal configurations, so the foot of the L was shortened and the entire A redrawn. The word was then condensed 10 percent to achieve greater size and strength on the cover.

SKALD

Every issue has a "Day-in" center spread. The role of this section is to involve the reader in an insider's look at that edition's special city. The spread always includes a map, an overall numbered guide to the map, and a visual reference to each location.

Typographically, there are several levels to these spreads. A combination of Helvetica and Bodoni type gives a hierarchy to the information, as do the numbers reversed from red circles to identify key points. These same identification points are cross-referenced for easy comparison with the main text and serve to break up a rather dense block of copy. The main text is set in Century Old Style Italic, signifying a subtle difference from major articles and softening the entire look of the page.

The table of contents is intended not only to inform, but to pique interest about the stories in each issue. The images, of course, carry most of that burden, but the oversized page numbers add a strong informational and graphic impact to the page.

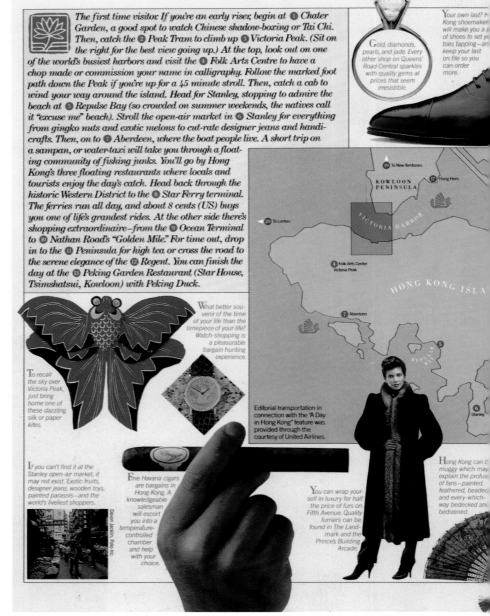

The first time visitor: If you're an early riser, begin at ❶ Chater Garden, a good spot to watch Chinese shadow-boxing or Tai Chi. Then, catch the ❷ Peak Tram to climb up ❸ Victoria Peak. (Sit on the right for the best view going up.) At the top, look out on one of the world's busiest harbors and visit the ❹ Folk Arts Centre to have a chop made or commission your name in calligraphy. Follow the marked foot path down the Peak if you're up for a 45 minute stroll. Then, catch a cab to wind your way around the island. Head for Stanley, stopping to admire the beach at ❺ Repulse Bay (so crowded on summer weekends, the natives call it "excuse me" beach). Stroll the open-air market in ❻ Stanley for everything from gingko nuts and exotic melons to cut-rate designer jeans and handicrafts. Then, on to ❼ Aberdeen, where the boat people live. A short trip on a sampan, or water-taxi will take you through a floating community of fishing junks. You'll go by Hong Kong's three floating restaurants where locals and tourists enjoy the day's catch. Head back through the historic Western District to the ❽ Star Ferry terminal. The ferries run all day, and about 8 cents (US) buys you one of life's grandest rides. At the other side there's shopping extraordinaire—from the ❾ Ocean Terminal to ❿ Nathan Road's "Golden Mile." For time out, drop in to the ⓫ Peninsula for high tea or cross the road to the serene elegance of the ⓬ Regent. You can finish the day at the ⓭ Peking Garden Restaurant (Star House, Tsimshatsui, Kowloon) with Peking Duck.

What better souvenir of the time of your life than the timepiece of your life? Watch-shopping is a pleasurable bargain hunting experience.

To recall the sky over Victoria Peak, just bring home one of these dazzling silk or paper kites.

If you can't find it at the Stanley open-air market, it may not exist. Exotic fruits, designer jeans, wooden toys, painted parasols—and the world's liveliest shoppers.

Fine Havana cigars are bargains in Hong Kong. A knowledgeable salesman will escort you into a temperature-controlled chamber and help with your choice.

Editorial transportation in connection with the "A Day in Hong Kong" feature was provided through the courtesy of United Airlines.

You can wrap yourself in luxury for half the price of furs on Fifth Avenue. Quality furriers can be found in The Landmark and the Prince's Building Arcade.

Hong Kong can be muggy which may explain the profusion of fans—painted, feathered, beaded and every-which-way bedecked and bedizened.

Gold, diamonds, pearls, and jade. Every other shop on Queens' Road Central sparkles with quality gems at prices that seem irresistible.

Your own last? Hong Kong shoemakers will make you a pair of shoes to set your toes tapping—and keep your last on file so you can order more.

KOWLOON PENINSULA

VICTORIA HARBOR

HONG KONG ISLAND

❶❾ To New Territories
⓲ Hung Hom
❹ Folk Arts Center Victoria Peak
❼ Aberdeen
❺ Repulse Bay
⓴ To Lantau

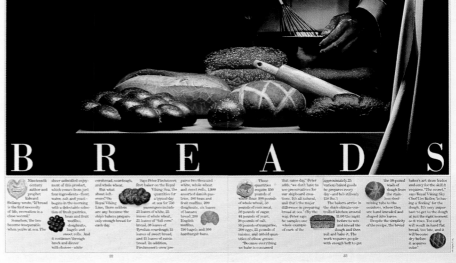

B R E A D S

A typeface can take on a completely different look purely by its spacing. The isolated letterforms echo the isolated loaves of bread that illustrate the story.

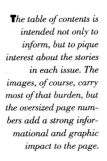

SKALD

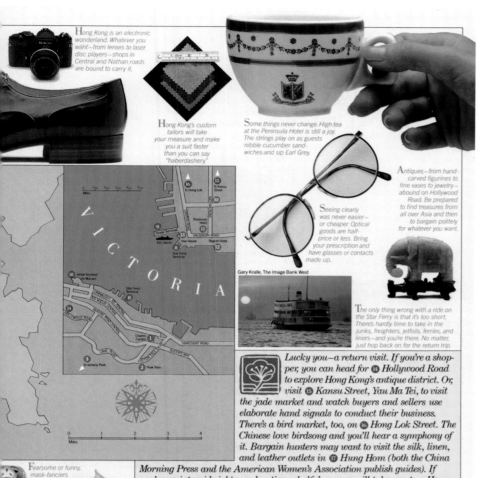

Hong Kong is an electronic wonderland. Whatever you want—from lenses to laser disc players—shops in Central and Nathan roads are bound to carry it.

Hong Kong's custom tailors will take your measure and make you a suit faster than you can say "haberdashery."

Some things never change. High tea at the Peninsula Hotel is still a joy. The strings play on as guests nibble cucumber sandwiches and sip Earl Grey.

Antiques—from hand-carved figurines to fine vases to jewelry—abound on Hollywood Road. Be prepared to find treasures from all over Asia and then to bargain politely for whatever you want.

Seeing clearly was never easier—or cheaper. Optical goods are half-price or less. Bring your prescription and have glasses or contacts made up.

Gary Kralle, The Image Bank West

The only thing wrong with a ride on the Star Ferry is that it's too short. There's hardly time to take in the junks, freighters, jetfoils, ferries, and liners—and you're there. No matter, just hop back on for the return trip.

Lucky you—a return visit. If you're a shopper, you can head for 14 Hollywood Road to explore Hong Kong's antique district. Or, visit 15 Kansu Street, Yau Ma Tei, to visit the jade market and watch buyers and sellers use elaborate hand signals to conduct their business. There's a bird market, too, on 16 Hong Lok Street. The Chinese love birdsong and you'll hear a symphony of it. Bargain hunters may want to visit the silk, linen, and leather outlets in 17 Hung Hom (both the China Morning Press and the American Women's Association publish guides). If you're an intrepid sightseer, devoting a half day or so will take you to a Hong Kong you've never seen. Forty-five minutes by 18 jetfoil will take you to the Portuguese colony of Macau with its Mediterranean avenues and non-stop casinos. A half-day bus ride will take you into the 19 New Territories, through small farms tended by black-clad Hakka women and parkland where monkeys play in the trees and lotus dot the duck ponds. At the trip's end you'll come to Lok Ma Chau, and look across the Shum Chun River to the Bamboo Curtain which serves as China's border. Another half-day alternative is a trip to 20 Lantau on a junk to see unspoiled beaches and enjoy a vegetarian lunch at a Buddhist monastery. For repeat visitors, Hong Kong's adventures never end.

Fearsome or funny, mask-fanciers will find whatever they seek in Hong Kong.

Whether it's an antique vase or a dinner set painted to your design, Hong Kong is a bazaar of fine shopping for porcelain.

Major Photography: Henrick Kam

First IMPRESSIONS
European explorers came home from the South Seas with sea-stung cargo—journals rich with their adventures, memories and first impressions.

The occasional typographic wild card gives an added style to the publication. The loose script is not only a fresh flourish, but a meaningful piece of historical calligraphy of the kind found on early sailing maps.

The captions are set in the normal styling of the rest of the magazine but often rag around the image. The reason for not keeping a uniform measure and style is twofold. First, a complex spread like this needs to have the copy relate to the individual subject for easy identification. Second, since the images fit together like a jigsaw puzzle, why not enhance this with integrated type?

The integration of cherub with title adds a richness to the words and content to the message. It's important to note that the cherub is not just placed on top of the words or overprinted but is truly entwined. You could describe it as the difference between an off-the-rack and a custom-fitted suit.

The rather formal, bookish structure of the spreads created by box rules, centered folios, and traditional typography allows for a greater freedom in use of extremely varied art and photography.

AN INTRUDER IN THE JUNGLE

FISH

FISH

Some of life's spoil-sports grump, if it's fun, it must be illegal, immoral or fattening.

But there's an exception to that tiresome rule. The exception is fish, glorious, delicious, non-fattening, good-for-you fish. From the delicate pink of poached salmon to the shimmer of rainbow trout to the succulent quiver of a Bluepoint oyster—the creatures that inhabit the sea are one of life's pleasures that are good for the body as well as the spirit.

On Royal Viking Line, the acquisition, delivery, preparation and presentation of fresh fish and shellfish preoccupy the talents and energies of a small, but fiercely dedicated, cadre of food people. It all begins with Bob Koven, Purchasing Agent and self-confessed lover of halibut, shark, and almost anything else that comes equipped with gill or shell. Koven's job is to find, purchase, and arrange delivery of enough fish to feed some of the world's most demanding and discriminating diners—Royal Viking Line passengers. As a small example

Lobster

of the magnitude of Koven's job, "On an average we fly 700 pounds of live lobster every 21 days to each ship." Accomplishing that job finds him on the tele-

phone chasing Australian lobster tails and Hawaiian mahi-mahi, it finds him arbitrating tastes in smoked salmon (the Norwegian officers and crew claim Norway's is best, some European chefs argue for the Scottish variety, the Americans advocate the smoked Pacific delicacy), and it finds him investigating

Pink Alaska Salmon

possible substitutes for the extravagantly expensive Alaska King and Dungeness crab. (There aren't any acceptable substitutes, he says, at least not on Royal Viking Line.) But Koven, demanding procurer though he is, pales next to the toughest critics of all—the Royal Viking Line chefs. "Each chef

must approve each shipment of fresh fish," explains Koven. That approval process can be nerve-wracking for the suppliers. "The delivery meets us at port, and the chef makes his personal inspection and taste tests. If he's not happy, he can reject the whole shipment."

What does the chef

look for? "He looks for freshness, for color in the gills, for bright eyes, for firm, non-flabby flesh. He'll pop open a few oysters and taste."

Getting the fish to shipside is no small task. At many ports, local suppliers and distributors bring the fish in. There's salmon,

Swordfish

halibut and rockfish in Alaska; salmon, shrimp, haddock, lobster and smoked fish in Scandinavia; beautiful rainbow trout, just one hour out of the water, in Greece;

delicate crab legs and sea bass in Chile; live lobster, orange ruffy and John Dory in Australia; and Pacific specialties like mahi-mahi, ono-skipjack tuna, and ahi-yellowfin in Hawaii. In other ports, Koven maintains quality control by air freighting everything

22

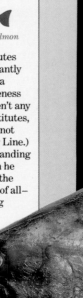

Although fish are not officially stamped to indicate freshness, we borrowed the typographic vernacular from prime, "Grade A" beef and transferred it to the title — adding information, visual interest, and color.

Our idea of combining type and image seemed simple until we saw how much the salmon would obscure the word. Since we wanted to shoot the fish with ice and water literally on top of the type (thus preserving the refraction of the type through water and ice), we cut an already quite condensed typeface (Onyx) in half and filled in the letterforms where the fish would overlap.

from oysters and top neck clams to salmon, swordfish, and snapper to ships in the Orient and the Mediterranean.

"We give the chefs a long, long list of what's

Red Snapper

available, and they order from that."

That list varies according to the weather, food fashions, and the creativity of local suppliers. Part of the challenge of Koven's job comes from the dazzling variety Mother Nature herself supplies. We live in a watery

world, with the world's oceans covering more than two-thirds of the planet's surface. Inhabiting those oceans are nearly 25,000 species of fish and shellfish. From the cold, seemingly inhospitable waters of the North Atlantic come herring and cod, haddock and halibut,

John Dory Fish

skate and witing; from the Mediterranean, sardines and anchovies, red mullet, anglerfish, bass, swordfish, and some varieties of tuna; from warmer tropical waters, sweet red snapper, croaker and shrimp.

Serious fish enthusiasts claim almost everything is edible in the sea, and will wax euphoric over the joys of pickled whelks and sea urchins on toast. Though these may never show up on Royal Viking Line menus, the variety is boundless—and best of all, surprisingly, reassuringly, good for you.

What's special nutritionally about fish is that it marries the complete protein of the animal kingdom with the low fats of the vegetable kingdom. What fat there is in fish is the best variety—unsaturated,

Norway Haddock

easily digested, and eagerly used by the body's tissues. The protein is high quality, rich in amino acids, and, except for shellfish, remarkably low in cholesterol.

Legend has long maintained that eating seafood has a salutary effect on one's love life. That belief, as luck would have it, is grounded in some fact. Seafood is rich in the elements—Vitamins

Ahi-Yellowfin Tuna

A and D, phosphorus, iron, copper, and iodine —that nutritionists believe contribute to both libido and performance. Little wonder then, that Lord Byron and Casanova were great lovers of both seafood and ladies. Madame Pompadour, no minor light in affairs of the heart, was reported to have cooked up filet of sole a la Pompadour before her liaisons. Claims scientist Dr. Nicholas Vinette, "Those who live almost entirely on shellfish and fish are more ardent in love than all others."

Living entirely on seafood seems like a blessing rather than a deprivation when you travel. There's salmon to enjoy off Sitka's coast, smoked eel at the fjords, and delicious sea bass from the waters near Puerto Montt. For those who love to travel, to eat, and to love, fish is a triple delight.

The narrow columns of type visually contrast the word "FISH" and allow for numerous fish silhouettes to punctuate the copy.

Terry Heffernan

23

AMERICAN PRESIDENT LINES

American President Lines — a Pacific Rim intermodal cargo carrier — requested a long-term format for its wall calendars (a mainstay of that industry). Competition for wall space is fierce in worldwide shipping offices, and a graphically compelling, informative calendar was crucial. The solution, viewed in hindsight after several years, has proved to be an effective, flexible format that has subtly evolved without losing its original strengths.

One hundred and forty years ago, the Pacific Ocean was a quieter place. Gold had not yet been discovered. California was a collection of cattle ranches and sleepy towns, and little trade existed between the Pacific Coast and Asia. But in 1848 events took place in California that changed the United States, the Pacific Ocean and the world. American President Lines and its predecessors participated in these events. In 1988 we celebrate our 140th anniversary. To recognize such a landmark, this calendar salutes the events and ideas that shaped our company and your marketplace. By using photographs that reflect the spirit and the style of each period, this year's calendar covers 140 years of service on land and sea. We take pride that APL and affiliates in the American President Companies group have grown and prospered through serving the Pacific, the Indian Ocean and North America–the world's most dynamic trading regions. Today, we look to the future with confidence. We anticipate continued good fortune for all of us blessed with ___ __ _____ in these vital markets.

Times Roman provided many attributes in a single face: style… classic in character, elegant in its drawing, with a family of weights and variations; strength… a businesslike, unfussy character that complemented APL's corporate identity; legibility… when you need to read them from across the room, the clean, clear numerical configurations are outstanding.

rican
Pres nt Lines
1988 C lendar

The overall concepts from year to year have covered such diverse subjects as international interdependency, art of the seas, puzzles, a 140-year view of APL, and so on, yet the strong typographic structure and consistently arresting photographic images by Terry Heffernan have accommodated these thematic changes comfortably.

Silk fever reached its peak in the 1920s, and raw silk dominated cargoes from Asia. The value of some cargoes approached $10 million, and getting them to port on time was of the essence. The regular schedules of passenger ships made them a reliable transport, so while passengers swarmed the upper decks, stevedores packed the cargo area with bundles of raw silk. Then captains and crews raced across the sea, cutting crossing time from 19 to 10 days. The President Jackson (1), outrunning all the others, made the voyage from Yokohama to the port of Seattle in just nine days and 50 minutes.

The moment the silk-laden ships touched dock, hatches flew open and the silk was unloaded into waiting trains. Unloading took as little as eight minutes per railcar; the whole process was finished before passengers disembarked. Threatened by high insurance costs, hijackers, and trade speculators, these locked and sealed "silk trains" traveled nonstop across the continent with every light and flag set in their favor to make the best time possible. The fastest trip—from Yokohama to Seattle by ship, then on to New York by train—took just 12 days, one hour, and 15 minutes.

July

Sunday	Monday	Tuesday	Wednesday	Thursday	Friday	Saturday
					1	2
3	4 Independence Day/ GUAM, PRICO, USA Phil-Am Friendship Day/ PHIL	5	6	7	8	9 Dominion Day/CAN
10	11	12	13	14	15	
17 Constitution Day/ROK	18 Rivera's Birthday?/PRICO	19	20	21 Liberation Day/GUAM	22	
24 Hari Raya Haji/ SPORE, MAL**	25 Hari Raya Haji/SPORE Constitution Day/PRICO Eid-Ul-Azha*/BAN	26 Eid-Ul-Azha*/BAN	27 Eid-Ul-Azha*/BAN Barbosa's Birthday?/ PRICO	28	29 Buddhist Lent/THAI	
31						

*Subject to the Moon †Half Day **Idul Adha/INDO

June

S						
			1	2	3	4
5	6	7	8	9	10	11
12	13	14	15	16	17	18
19	20	21	22	23	24	25
26	27	28	29	30		

AMERICAN PRESIDENT LINES

The desire to present not only handsome photography and calendar dates but international holidays and detailed editorial comments required this multitiered typographic design format. The relationship of color, size, and positioning brings a visual and informational hierarchy to the copy.

'21' CLUB

New York's elite '21' Club sought to establish a new identity system when its ownership changed. The new management wanted to signal a vital, contemporary direction but preserve the traditions for which the restaurant was famous. The identity system designed by Peter had three core elements: a logotype around '21'; marbleized paper that changed color palette for individual pieces in the program; and graphic reference to the Club's well-known iron jockey hitching posts, done through a specially commissioned Paul Davis painting of jockey and horse.

Torino numerals created a distinctive image for '21.'

Bodoni in wide letter spacing resembled hand-set type and suited the mood of the Davis painting.

THE BREAKFAST CLUB

Ancillary identity pieces for '21' were set in Torino all caps.

The typography for '21' had to suggest elegance, style, and refined taste. The choice of two classic typefaces — combined with marbleized paper and traditional oval and square shapes to frame imagery — made the statement that this is an enduring institution. In its final form, the '21' identity program encompassed more than a hundred items, ranging from cigar boxes, menus, and matchbooks to wine labels.

NEIL
SHAKERY

MERCURY TYPOGRAPHY

To promote its services, Mercury Typography asked six San Francisco Bay Area designers to create a poster featuring their favorite typeface. Neil chose Times Roman, setting off each character in the alphabet so that the beauty of individual letterforms could be fully appreciated.

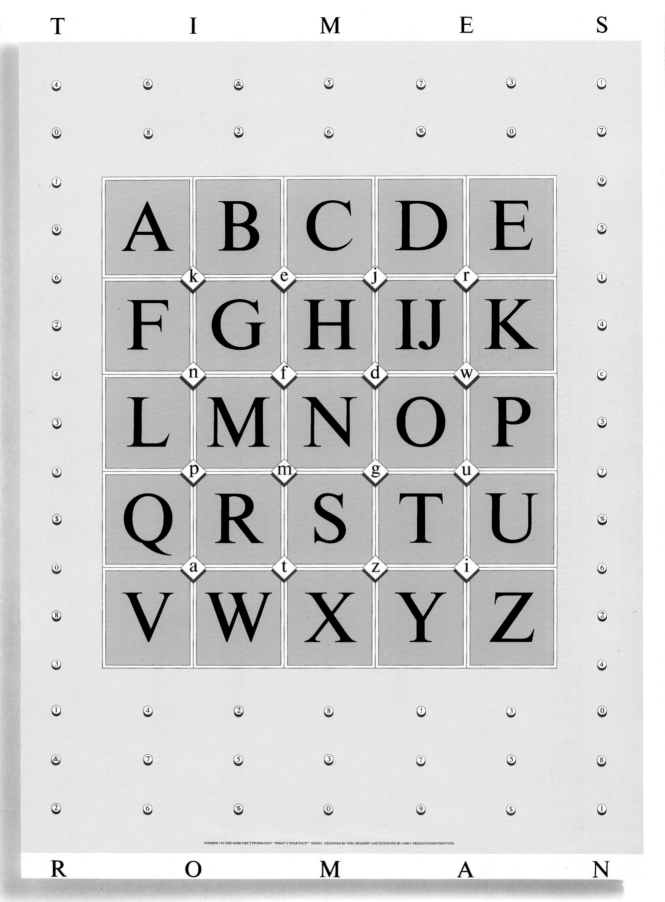

NUMBER 2 IN THE MERCURY TYPOGRAPHY "WHAT'S YOUR FACE" SERIES. DESIGNED BY NEIL SHAKERY AND SCREENED BY HERO PRESENTATION PRINTING.

BEAUX ARTS BALL

The Beaux Arts Ball is the major fund-raiser for the design and architectural wing of San Francisco's Museum of Modern Art. Each year a different design firm is asked to create theme graphics for the ball, including posters, invitations, tickets, and program. Traditionally it is a masked ball, so we incorporated masks symbolizing San Francisco's food, ethnic groups, architecture, and unique climate in a single poster.

When developing the poster and bus shelter cards, we felt the masks carried so much style and mood that the typography should play a more supportive role. The headline copy is Copperplate Gothic with Futura Light Text. Please note the flush left or right copy on each corner of the sheet. Justifying copy against the edge helps define the poster's proportions. Futura Extra Bold initial caps give a visual accent to text copy.

Saturday, November 18
9:00 PM – 2:00 AM
San Francisco Marriott
777 Market Street

Ball Tickets: $75
Dinner and Ball: $300

Tickets Available at:
City Box Office: 392-4400
Bass Ticket Outlets:
762-BASS

For further BALL information call: 362-7397

COSTUME PARADE

AWARD CATEGORIES:
Tremendously Titillating Teams
Dynamic Duos
Sensational Single
Triumphantly Tasteless
Best of Ball

JUDGES:
Andrew Belschner
Michael Casey
Orlando Diaz-Azcuy
Charles Pfister
Bill Thompson

WITH ENTERTAINMENT BY:

Peter Mintun
Viva Brazil
Timmie Hesla and the
Converse All-Stars
The Solid Senders
The Ultras
Pastiche
E.C. Scott

Plus a MIDNIGHT SURPRISE not to be missed!

TO benefit the Department of Architecture and Design of the San Francisco Museum of Modern Art. Presented by the American Institute of Architects, San Francisco Chapter and the Modern Art Council of the San Francisco Museum of Modern Art. Sponsored by the San Francisco Marriott.

B E A U X

A R T S

1 9

8 9

B A L L

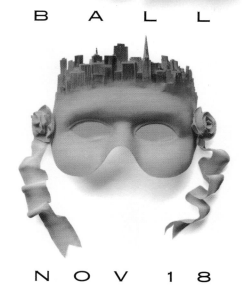

N O V 1 8

US WEST

As one of America's "Baby Bells," US WEST provides telecommunications services to more than ten million customers in fourteen western states. In all its annual reports, US WEST has sought to establish its regional identity through the use of a western motif, such as Navajo Indian designs. The primary photographs, however, featured its state-of-the-art technology and worldwide scope.

Garamond, a classic serif face, was selected to enhance the western flavor of the report. The large point size makes the text more inviting to read.

NO MATTER HOW SOPHISTI-
CATED OR SIMPLE THE
APPLICATION, THE TELE-
PHONE STILL HAS ONE
BASIC FUNCTION: HELPING
PEOPLE AND COMPANIES
MAKE THE MOST OF
THEIR TIME.

‹ U S WEST OVERVIEW ›

They call us a "Baby" Bell. But we've grown so much in our first six years, we're not sure the description still fits. ♦ Since 1984, our annual revenues have grown 33 percent, to $9.7 billion; net income 25 percent, to $1.1 billion; assets 63 percent, to $25.4 billion; and your quarterly dividend 48 percent, to $1.00. ♦ We've grown in scope, focusing on four areas: communications, data solutions, marketing services, and financial services. ♦ And we've grown from a regional phone company and directory publisher to also become a leader in the American financial services and marketing services industries and a rapidly growing international communications company with active or proposed projects in Hong Kong, the United Kingdom, France, Hungary and the Soviet Union.

Strategic Focus: COMMUNICATIONS/DATA SOLUTIONS

U S WEST Communications (formerly Mountain Bell, Northwestern Bell and Pacific Northwest Bell) provides

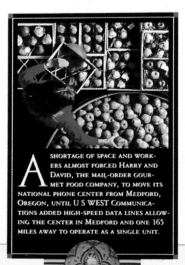

A SHORTAGE OF SPACE AND WORK-ERS ALMOST FORCED HARRY AND DAVID, THE MAIL-ORDER GOUR-MET FOOD COMPANY, TO MOVE ITS NATIONAL PHONE CENTER FROM MEDFORD, OREGON, UNTIL U S WEST COMMUNICA-TIONS ADDED HIGH-SPEED DATA LINES ALLOW-ING THE CENTER IN MEDFORD AND ONE 165 MILES AWAY TO OPERATE AS A SINGLE UNIT.

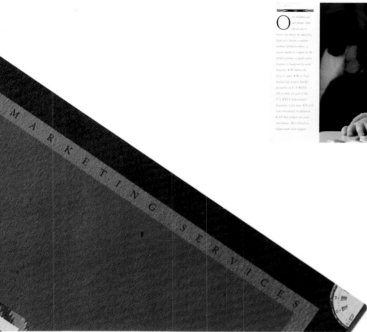

The six-page educational insert maintained typographic continuity by using the same body text and caption style as the operations section, and by breaking from the large, wide measure of the body text, it graphically announced a change of subject.

Reversing captions out of black would have been inappropriate for longer copy, but at this length, it serves as a sidebar story and adds a strong design element to the western character of the spread.

TELECOMMUTING CAN BE A GREAT WAY TO SKIP RUSH-HOUR TRAFFIC, AND MAKE THE MOST OF YOUR TIME. COMBINE A PERSONAL COMPUTER, FAX MACHINE, AND A PHONE—ADD VOICE MESSAGING AND CUSTOM CALLING FEATURES LIKE CALL WAITING AND SPEED CALLING—AND YOU'VE GOT THE INGREDIENTS FOR THE PERFECT OFFICE-IN-THE-HOME.

MEAD CORPORATION

Mead, the parent company that produces Mead and Gilbert papers,
has sponsored a major annual report show
in the United States for more than twenty
years. Mead asked Peter to prepare a promotion for release in the month of
September, which is traditionally the time
when companies get serious about the
design and paper selection for annual
reports. Peter created a piece that was not
only for, but about, September and all the
unique events — from Chairman Mao's
death to Buddy Holly's birthday — that
occurred in that month.

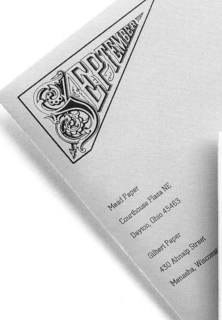

Mead Paper
Courthouse Plaza NE
Dayton, Ohio 45463

Gilbert Paper
430 Ahnaip Street
Menasha, Wisconsin

A Month of Days from Mead and Gilbert Papers

City Light with its crisp
serifs and mechanical
letterforms offered a
nontraditional, slightly
quirky, typographic
complement to the irrev-
erent, tongue-in-cheek
images. The centered
date on each diary page
serves as a signal differ-
entiating it from the
"National Cat Health
Care Month" and
"Opportune Time to
Begin Logging"
spreads that punctuate
the promotion.

September may be the ninth month of the year, but all the same it is a time for beginnings. The school year starts; so does the football season, the fall TV schedule, the eating of oysters and the Jewish New Year. Indeed, the origins of eight percent of everything on earth can be traced to the month of September: chop suey (1896), the city of Los Angeles (1781), General Motors (1908), The New York Times (1851), Mickey Mouse (1928), the 'Star-Spangled Banner' (1814), the nickname 'Uncle Sam' (1813), and carpet sweepers (1876). They were all concocted, established, founded, published, born, composed, thought up or patented in the month of September. September isn't the end of the year, but even so it is a time for endings – the lease on the cottage by the lake, for example, the regular baseball season, reruns on TV, the eating of fresh corn, summer and the slathering-on of sunscreen. In years past, September has been the end of the line for George Washington (1799),

William McKinley (1901), Nathan Hale (1775), Huey Long (1935), John L. Sullivan (1892), child labor (1916), the old city of London (1666) and the Japanese in World War II (1945). George Washington gave his Farewell Address in September; the others were assassinated, hanged, shot, KO'd, prohibited, burned and defeated, in that order. September is a time for putting certain things into the ground and for taking others out. We plant spinach, lettuce, radishes, winter wheat and celery. We harvest squash, pumpkins, apples, grapes, brussel sprouts, kale, peppers, cranberries and collards. In September, birds begin their southward migration, following the sun as it slips below the equator and brings summer to the southern hemisphere. Meanwhile, up in our neck of the woods, deciduous trees turn brilliant autumn colors, mornings and evenings become chilly, and once again the nights grow longer than the days.

September 1966: First clown training [1] school established in Venice, Florida

September 1930: First non-stop flight, Europe [2] to the US, completed in 37 hours, 18.5 minutes

September 1976: [9] Death of Mao Tse Tung

September 1966: 'Bald is Beautiful' [10] Convention, Morehead, North Carolina

September is National Cat Health Month

September 1966: [5] National Rifle Contest, Wisconsin

September 1901: President William [6] McKinley shot in Buffalo, New York

September 1892: First [27] book matches patented

September 551 B.C.: [28] Confucius' birthday

"Great Man reaches complete understanding of the main issues. Petty Man reaches complete understanding of the minute details."
– Confucius, c. 500 B.C.

September 21 Birthdays

1415: Frederick III, Holy Roman Emperor & King of Germany (1452-1486) 1452: Girolamo Savonarola, Italian religious reformer 1645: Louis Jolliet, French priest, explored the Great Lakes 1737: Francis Hopkinson, composer, designed first American flag, 1777 1756: John Loudon McAdam, invented macadam road surface 1789: Margaret Smith Taylor, former First Lady, Zachary's wife 1832: Louis Paul Cailletet, French physicist, pioneer in liquefying gases 1840: Marcel V. Goud Ottoman sultan, went nuts after brief reign 1855: Sara Delano Roosevelt, mother of Franklin Roosevelt 1866: Charles Nicolle, Nobel bacteriologist, typhus transmission 1866: H. G. Wells, English writer 1867: Henry L. Stimson, Truman's atomic policy adviser, said "Drop the bomb" 1894: Ethel Percy Andrus, founded American Assoc. of Retired Persons 1895: H. T. Webster, cartoonist, creator of Caspar Milquetoast 1900: Aristotle Onassis, Greek shipping magnate 1902: Sir Allen Lane, paperback publisher, founded Penguin Books 1904: Hans Hotzing, painter 1927: Edward Bullard, proved continental drift 1908: Kwame Nkrumah, President of Ghana (1957-1966) 1912: Chuck Jones, cartoonist, created Roadrunner & Coyote 1914: John W. Mauchly, co-inventor of ENIAC computer 1934: Leonard Cohen, singer, songwriter and poet 1934: Siam Stewart, jazz bassist, hummed along with his solos 1915: Roy O. Chapin, Jr., Chairman of American Motors (1967-1970) 1926: Donald A. Glaser, Nobel Prize in physics, invented bubble chamber 1931: Larry Hagman, actor 1932: Melvin Van Peebles, playwright 1933: Clifford L. Alexander, Jr., first black Secretary of the Army (1977-1980) 1934: Leonard Cohen, singer, songwriter and poet 1944: Hamilton Jordan, Jimmy Carter's Chief-of-Staff 1947: Stephen King, best-selling horror writer (Carrie) 1948: Michael Faraleus, first to score perfect 10 in platform diving 1949: Ellen V. Futter, President of Barnard College 1949: Artis Gilmore, NBA center for San Antonio Spurs

September 1692: Last persons hanged [22] in the American colonies for witchcraft

According to the Farmer's Almanac: early September is the optimum time to begin logging

September 1936: [7] Buddy Holly born

September 1916: Emergency Revenue [8] Act doubles the rate of income tax

Some typefaces evoke the mood or impression of a period of time, an exotic place, a distinct culture, an art movement, a sport, an industry, or a specific influence in ways nothing else can. Evocative type should not attempt to mimic a time or place, but to echo and reflect its character. While the design itself might be contemporary, the type can bring an element of nostalgia or a time-dated quality as desired. Type can also be used to set a subliminal tone and actually tie several different periods, styles, or looks together with a common thread. To do this effectively, designers should not only have a sense of history but be as familiar as possible with the typographic vernacular of their own and foreign cultures.

CHAMPION PAPER

Champion's laid papers were viewed primarily as stationery stock, and the company wanted to show other uses. For the promotional program, Champion wanted to feature six individual and unrelated places. To tie these locations together, Neil designed a uniform look by creating separate fold-down posters, each highlighting a specific place.

Times Roman was selected because it appropriately expressed a character common to the diverse locations featured. An extremely readable typeface, Times Roman makes what might normally be a daunting amount of copy inviting to read. Names of the locations and paper are printed in soft colors to provide product identification without overpowering the images or text.

FANNIE MAE

For the fiftieth anniversary of Fannie Mae — the Federal National Mortgage Association — Peter was asked to prepare a commemorative book that explains the activities of this quasi-governmental nonprofit organization. The basic idea was to discuss the "American Dream" of owning your own home and Fannie Mae's role in helping people achieve that goal. The book is organized into depictions of American life over the past half century and told by decade.

Since we were trying to evoke a sense of five distinct periods of time while still maintaining a consistent typographic look, we selected Garamond for its universal, classic character that felt comfortable in each decade.

The Dream of Home

Yes, we Americans want a home of our own. Probably not the one we grew up in, or even the one we live in now, much as we love it. The fact is, we want a succession of homes. We are a nation of movers, not homesteaders. Nearly fifty million of us — one out of five Americans — will move this year. ¶ Our mobility is a trait that distinguishes us from our Old World forebears. They inhabited the same ancestral homes — and the same social strata — for generations. In America, we move as easily from home to home as we do along the social and economic ladder. Sometimes we even take our home with us, as an astonished Charles Dickens discovered while on a tour of New England in 1840. "I walked into the village," Dickens wrote, "and met a *dwelling house* coming down hill at a good round trot, drawn by some twenty oxen!" ¶ We Americans are a nation of immigrants — for the most part poor immigrants — some even unwilling immigrants. It has been the greatest dream of these immigrants to work and save and own their own homes. It's a dream that burns just as brightly today in the minds of new immigrants and those who have not been able to afford this dream — the poor and homeless. ¶ For those of us who can afford a home, we don't want just any home, we want a better home, a home more suited to our rising station in life and to the size

of our growing family. For us Americans, a home is rather like a suit of clothes. Starting out, we inhabit hand-me-downs, perhaps a bit frayed in places and in need of repair. Later, if we make enough money, we hope to pick out brand new homes, right off the rack so to speak. Eventually, upon achieving a measure of success, our ultimate dream is to have a home tailor-made to our specifications — to reflect the importance of our

accomplishments and the uniqueness of our needs and tastes. ¶ The typical American home is, of course, a detached single-family house. And what does it look like? As the social and cultural historian Russell Lynes once  observed, "If you were to ask almost anyone, even a child, to make a picture of a typical [American] house, the chances are that he would draw a more or less square, two-story house, with a front door in the center flanked by a couple of windows on either side, and with a steeply pitched roof and a chimney at one end, or possibly with one in the middle. He would, in other words, draw something like a Cape Cod cottage." Mr. Lynes went on to add, "But the American house is not this....it is a confusion of styles, of romantic notions, of avenues of escape, and of hopes for utopia." ¶ Whatever effect living in such houses may have had on the American psyche, the business of *building* the houses has certainly been a driving force in the American economy. The materials used in the typical American house — of which some 1,200,000 were built in 1987— include 9,726 board feet of lumber, 55 gallons of paint, 302 pounds of nails, 750 feet of copper wire, 55 cubic yards of concrete, 12 windows, 10 interior doors, four exterior doors, two toilets, three sinks, 15 kitchen cabinets, a refrigerator, and a dishwasher. The $150 billion spent on residential construction in America each year in the mid-1980s accounts for something over four percent of the gross national product. In addition, home building triggers over $50 billion in other expenditures for such items as labor, utilities, sales taxes, and real estate taxes. Not surprisingly, residential construction

The introduction was set off from the rest of the book by the use of a wide-measure, heavily leaded copy. As is often the case in wide-measure settings, the use of paragraph symbols allows the page to maintain a continuity of color and not be hampered by bad paragraph breaks and dreadful widows. Note that most of the images with copy ragged around them are at the beginning or end of the measure, thus reducing the amount of copy interruption.

HOME

FANNIE MAE: FIFTY YEARS OF OPENING DOORS
FOR AMERICAN HOME BUYERS

1948
1958

1938
1948

A *series of section openers was designed to identify the decades, each with a pattern reflective of the art or graphic style of the period but faithful to the same typographic styling.*

FANNIE MAE'S FIRST DECADE BEGAN IN THE HOUSING SLUMP OF THE GREAT DEPRESSION AND ENDED IN THE UPSWING OF THE POST-WAR BUILDING BOOM. IN 1938 YOU COULDN'T BUILD A HOUSE. IN 1948, YOU COULDN'T BUILD ONE FAST ENOUGH.

TEN MILLION RETURNING WAR VETERANS CREATED THE GREATEST DEMAND FOR HOUSING IN U.S. HISTORY — AND STARTED A BABY BOOM AS WELL.

The all-caps copy with its wide leading helps to set the captions off from the major body text, which was set in upper and lower case with normal leading.

AMERICAN HOME BUILDERS MOBILIZED IN A MASSIVE EFFORT TO BUILD TWO MILLION HOUSES FOR DEFENSE WORKERS DURING WORLD

WAR II. THE HOUSES WERE TEMPORARY, BUT THE NEW MASS-PRODUCTION METHODS OF CONSTRUCTION WERE HERE TO STAY.

LIVING IN QUONSET HUTS, POST-WAR, JEWARD'S BAY, NEW YORK

THIS QUONSET HUT WAS ONE OF MANY SOLUTIONS TO THE POST-WAR HOUSING SHORTAGE.

THE PREFABRICATED HOUSE MAY LOOK NEW, BUT IT ISN'T. ANOTHER, IT MAY HAVE LOOKED NEW-ENGLAND, BUT ITS ANTECEDENTS ACTUALLY TRACED BACK TO THE SIXTEENTH CENTURY.

WORLD WAR II, DEFENSE WORKERS' HOUSING, RADFORD, VIRGINIA

EXTERIOR PREFABRICATED HOUSE

The advances achieved in building technology in the doldrums of the Thirties produced a variety of inexpensive materials, such as composition board, cinder block, and asphalt tile. Handcrafting gave way to mass production, which led to the most far-reaching advance of all: prefabrication. Back in 1936, passersby had gawked at the prefab house that home builder Foster Gunnison had erected in Grand Central Station. But undeniably, the use of factory-built doors, windows, and walls cut construction time and costs substantially. During World War II, some 200,000 prefab units were built in the rush to build houses for defense workers. After the war, however, no amount of building could keep up with the demand. More than ten million returning war veterans again took up residence, many wherever they could find it — in trailers, quonset huts, surplus grain silos, or with relatives. ¶ The end of the war brought about one of the greatest housing booms in American history. Housing starts shot up from 116,000 in 1941 to one million in 1946, then 1.2 million in 1947. A good part of the increase was fueled by the 1944 G.I. Bill of Rights, which offered returning veterans long-term VA-guaranteed mortgages with no money down.

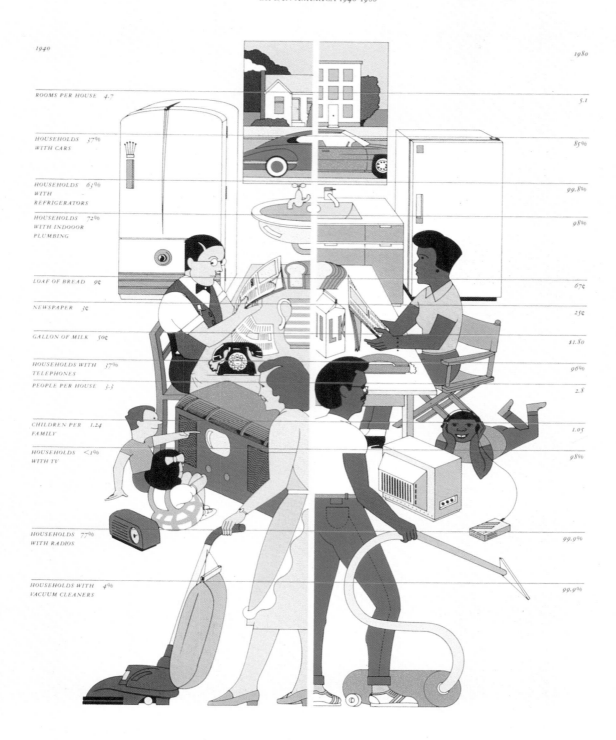

LIFE IN AMERICA 1940-1980

1940   1980

ROOMS PER HOUSE   4.7   5.1

HOUSEHOLDS   37%
WITH CARS   85%

HOUSEHOLDS   63%
WITH
REFRIGERATORS   99.8%

HOUSEHOLDS   72%
WITH INDOOR
PLUMBING   98%

LOAF OF BREAD   9¢   67¢

NEWSPAPER   3¢   25¢

GALLON OF MILK   50¢ $1.80

HOUSEHOLDS WITH   37%
TELEPHONES
PEOPLE PER HOUSE   3.3   96%
                                                                                                                          2.8

CHILDREN PER   1.24
FAMILY   1.05
HOUSEHOLDS   <1%
WITH TV   98%

HOUSEHOLDS   77%
WITH RADIOS   99.9%

HOUSEHOLDS WITH   4%
VACUUM CLEANERS   99.9%

59

The inventive design of
this chart by Nigel
Holmes lets the reader
make swift graphic
comparisons between
time periods. The sin-
gle hairline rule across
both sections makes for
easy reading of the
statistical data.

Graphs in the form of
pictograms vividly con-
veyed other data with a
minimal use of text.

OAKLAND A'S

The Oakland A's baseball organization (like most big league ball teams) promotes the team and its varied activities to corporations in hopes of financial support through the sale of box and season tickets, advertising sales, and product promotions. This promotion was developed in conjunction with ad agency Hal Riney & Partners and had been predetermined to evoke the feeling of pinball games in the 1940s and 1950s. The tone of the copy was decidedly tongue-in-cheek, intended to take a humorous view of baseball and its rituals.

Setting text to conform to shapes is a wonderful device to identify special information and highlight important areas of interest, but be warned that you must work closely with the writer to achieve quality results. The subtle use of letter and word spacing also aids in fitting copy to specific line lengths.

The funky, cozy character of Cheltenham was perfect for both the copy's tone of voice and the down-home, 1940s look of the illustrations. It worked well for straight text, sidebars and heads but was also easy to set in curves and boxes when needed to call up the traditional baseball typography found on scoreboards, uniforms, and banners.

The vernacular typography inherent in the illustrations themselves dictated that only one typeface be used in an involving but secondary fashion. Where appropriate, we pulled type and images from the illustration to enhance the message.

SIMPSON PAPER

When Simpson introduced a new line of recycled papers, the company wanted a concept that suggested the outdoors and a concern for nature — something between L.L. Bean and the National Park Service. We suggested "The Naturalist" as the overall theme in its broadest interpretation — from botanist to poet to composer. The artwork was gathered and commissioned to recall a simpler time — not over-produced, but with honest, traditional values.

The choice of type for the cover and the naturalists' names gives a typographic preview of the individual essays found behind each stepped page. The source of the cover type was an old Bernhardt Brothers type specification book from the 1920s. As the type was unavailable from any typographer, we photostatted the face and cut it together. Printing the cover in letterpress added credibility to the simple, low-tech character of the promotion.

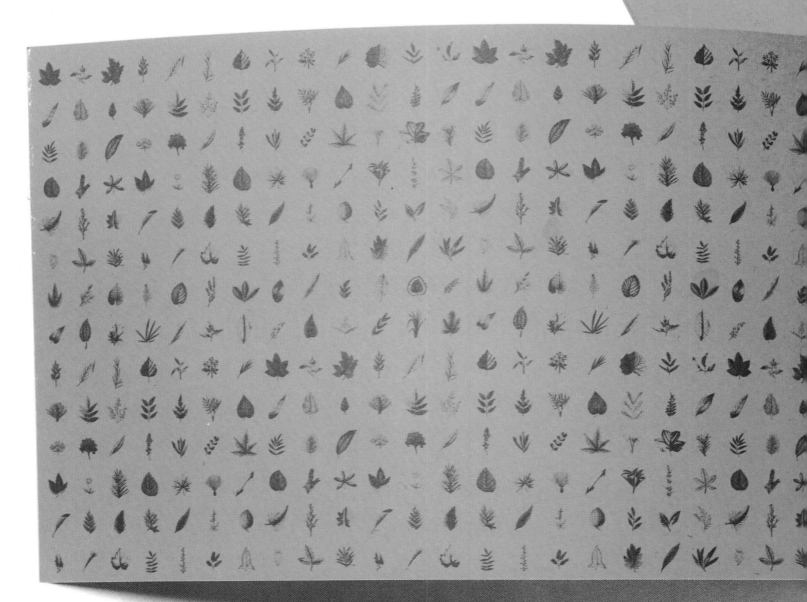

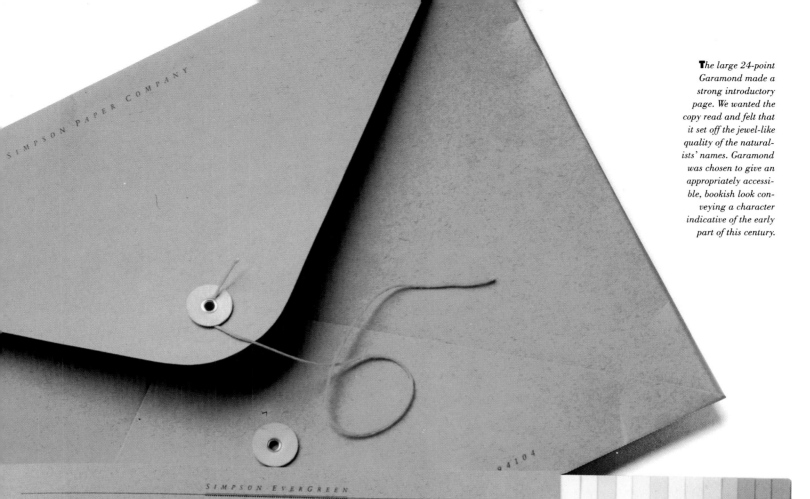

SIMPSON PAPER COMPANY

The large 24-point Garamond made a strong introductory page. We wanted the copy read and felt that it set off the jewel-like quality of the naturalists' names. Garamond was chosen to give an appropriately accessible, bookish look conveying a character indicative of the early part of this century.

SIMPSON EVERGREEN

Naturalists come in many types. There are those who engage in scientific studies, write nature essays, paint or photograph landscapes and creatures, or simply reflect on man's place as a participant in the larger world. Whatever their medium of expression, they bring to their subject a sensitivity to the marvels of nature. Through their eyes, our attention is turned outward to a blade of grass, to the land as it once existed, to the order of evolution, to the song of a robin. All inspire an appreciation of the natural world. In this same spirit, Simpson has developed EverGreen Text and Cover with respect and consciousness of our natural resources. This completely new recycled paper is part of Simpson's effort to use the gifts of the forest wisely and efficiently. With this introduction of EverGreen, Simpson celebrates the role of naturalists in America.

SPRUCE TEXT 70 LB

Jack London

MERIWETHER LEWIS

IGOR STRAVINSKY

Theodore Roosevelt

Henry David Thoreau

Johnny Appleseed

Carleton E. Watkins

John Burroughs

Dugald Stermer

Walt Whitman

ANNE MORROW LINDBERGH

Aldo Leopold

JOHN JAMES AUDUBON

Typographic echoes are important in a book that has so much variety in it. Our choice of Engravers Regular and Bold was an echo of the front cover type. It also captured the feeling of Audubon's period. Note: As you can imagine, initial caps can be awkward with quotation marks when used at their normal size. We find the use of the quotation marks sized to the body text is a satisfactory solution.

The type, like the quote, has a rugged elegance to it. Memphis Bold was also a face in common use during Jack London's era. Please note the rags around the wolf. We normally avoid ragging around centered images because of the difficulty in legibility. However, we decided to continue with a single measure as the interruption of only a few lines was manageable, and the look of a bookplate would have been adversely affected if we had changed to two columns.

THE SONG OF THE WOOD THRUSH, ALTHOUGH COMPOSED OF BUT A FEW NOTES, IS SO POWERFUL, DISTINCT, CLEAR AND MELLOW...LIKE THE EMOTIONS OF THE LOVER, WHO AT ONE MOMENT EXULTS IN THE HOPE OF POSSESSING THE OBJECT OF HIS AFFECTIONS, AND THE NEXT FALLS IN SUSPENSE, DOUBTFUL OF THE RESULTS OF ALL HIS EFFORTS TO PLEASE.
— JOHN JAMES AUDUBON

AN ORNITHOLOGIST AND ARTIST, JOHN JAMES AUDUBON (1785-1851) PAINTED THE BIRDS THAT INHABITED THE SWAMPS AND FORESTS ALONG THE OHIO RIVER. HIS FULL-COLOR, FOLIO-SIZE PAINTINGS OF MORE THAN 1,000 BIRDS WERE PUBLISHED AS A SET IN "THE BIRDS OF AMERICA." EVEN IN 1835, EAGER ART COLLECTORS PAID $1,000 FOR THE EDITION.

WHITE COVER 80 LB.

"Nature has many tricks wherewith she convinces man of his finity—the ceaseless flow of the tides, the fury of the storm, the shock of the earthquake, the long roll of heaven's artillery—but the most tremendous, the most stupefying of all, is the passive phase of the White Silence. All movement ceases, the sky clears, the heavens are as brass; the slightest whisper seems sacrilege, and man becomes timid, afrighted at the sound of his own voice." ❧ Author Jack London, from "The White Silence."

Best known for his novel, "The Call of the Wild," Jack London (1876-1916) made the awesome power of nature the protagonist in many of his adventure tales about the rugged Northwest and Klondike territory.

KRAFT COVER 80 LB.

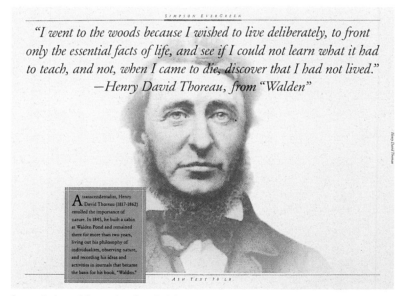

"I went to the woods because I wished to live deliberately, to front only the essential facts of life, and see if I could not learn what it had to teach, and not, when I came to die, discover that I had not lived."
—Henry David Thoreau, from "Walden"

A transcendentalist, Henry David Thoreau (1817-1862) extolled the importance of nature. In 1845, he built a cabin at Walden Pond and remained there for more than two years, living out his philosophy of individualism, observing nature, and recording his ideas and activities in journals that became the basis for his book, "Walden."

ASH TEXT 70 LB.

Janson Italic and Roman best described the classic nature of Thoreau the philosopher/writer/naturalist. In a practical vein, the type needed to be strong enough to print over his photograph without losing its character.

"ACTS OF CREATION ARE ORDINARILY RESERVED FOR GODS AND POETS, BUT HUMBLER FOLK MAY CIRCUMVENT THIS RESTRICTION IF THEY KNOW HOW. TO PLANT A PINE, FOR EXAMPLE, ONE NEED BE NEITHER GOD NOR POET; ONE NEED ONLY OWN A SHOVEL."
—Aldo Leopold, from "A Sand County Almanac"

Aldo Leopold (1887-1948), who once worked for the U.S. Forest Service, was an early advocate of wildlife management in America and instrumental in defining contemporary land ethics. His book, "A Sand County Almanac" is considered a classic in environmental literature.

IVORY COVER 80 LB.

Candide, not your everyday book face, was selected to reflect the overall 1920s-1930s feel of the piece and to resemble the etched look of the pine cone and bough. The large, line-spaced quote allowed the biography to run gracefully between lines. Note: All-caps settings pose a legibility problem in long text.

The choice of Boston Script came after finding these wonderful shell prints. We noted that the numbers and Latin titles on the print were etched in script, and we felt that script would not only be historically correct but also appropriate to the lyrical nature of the author's quote.

One of America's heroes, Meriwether Lewis, demanded a ceremonial, almost plaque-like look for the typography. In keeping with the formality of this approach, Bembo caps and small caps in a justified measure were chosen. Size and leading were changed to separate his quote from his biography.

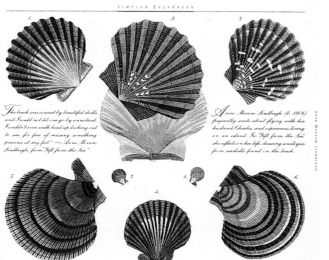

The chiseled look of Memphis Bold Condensed serifs enhanced David Stevenson's wood cut illustration. The all-caps name J. Burroughs cut in the log gave us the idea to use the same initial caps in the body text.

Cheltenham Bold Condensed was outgoing, down-to-earth, and when set within the box rule, made an interesting contrast to Ward Schumaker's bright, loose apple illustrations and handwritten names.

Environmental typography is directed primarily by the conditions in which it will be viewed, although it does not preclude consideration of the emotional value inherent in a typeface. The external setting can alter visual impact and convey a different message from that same face used on a printed page. Physical constraints — such as lighting conditions, weather variations, and normal viewing distance — as well as manufacturing costs may narrow the choice of typeface and determine whether it is executed in three-dimensional letterform or silkscreened on a wall. Typically, environmental signs are permanent installations that convey public information — safety warnings, establishment names, freeway directions — and, as such, the type style must appeal to a broad-based audience of passersby.

London Docklands Development Corporation

JOHN McCONNELL

DOCKLANDS

London Docklands Development is responsible for developing industrial space on docks in the east end of London. The company wanted to show that a transformation was underway and to provide urgently needed directional signs. John designed huge sculptural arrows that added color and interest to the desolate landscape. The shape of the sign communicates as much as the words.

The freestanding arrows, each eighteen feet high and weighing two tons, were made from sheet steel and coated with the same salt-air resistant paint used on North Sea oil rigs. Special fixing points allow the signs to be moved using cranes and forklift trucks. Helvetica Medium provides the name efficiently and leaves the character and style to the arrow.

ALAN FLETCHER

LLOYD'S OF LONDON

Established in 1698, today Lloyd's of London is the center of the international insurance market. Lloyd's moved into its sophisticated new headquarters, designed by Richard Rogers Associates, in 1986, and Pentagram was commissioned to design signage for the high-tech building. Alan's approach was to create signs that would complement and emphasize the innovative architecture while providing an effective system of orientation.

Signs were precision engineered, like the architecture itself, and set forward from the surface by insertion between the modular wall panels of the building. Each sign was designed and engineered by hand, and letters and numbers were cut out of aluminum panels by computer laser. The panels were stove-enamelled in primary colors to enliven and code the areas in the building's interior. The signs were designed, manufactured, and installed over eighteen months.

In addition to the standard direction, information, identification, and statuary signs, a number of special signage projects were undertaken, including a numbering system for underwriters' desks, a plaque commemorating the opening of the building by the Queen, and a large granite cylinder in the street to identify the building, embellished with a compass rose to point you in the right direction.

ABCDEFGHIJ
KLMNOPQRS
TUVWXYZ12
34567890

Once the concept of cut stenciled letters was established, the question of which of the many stencils to choose arose. Corbusier Stencil, designed by architect Le Corbusier, seemed the ideal choice. Not only was he an architect of monumental stature, his alphabet is the most distinguished and handsomely designed.

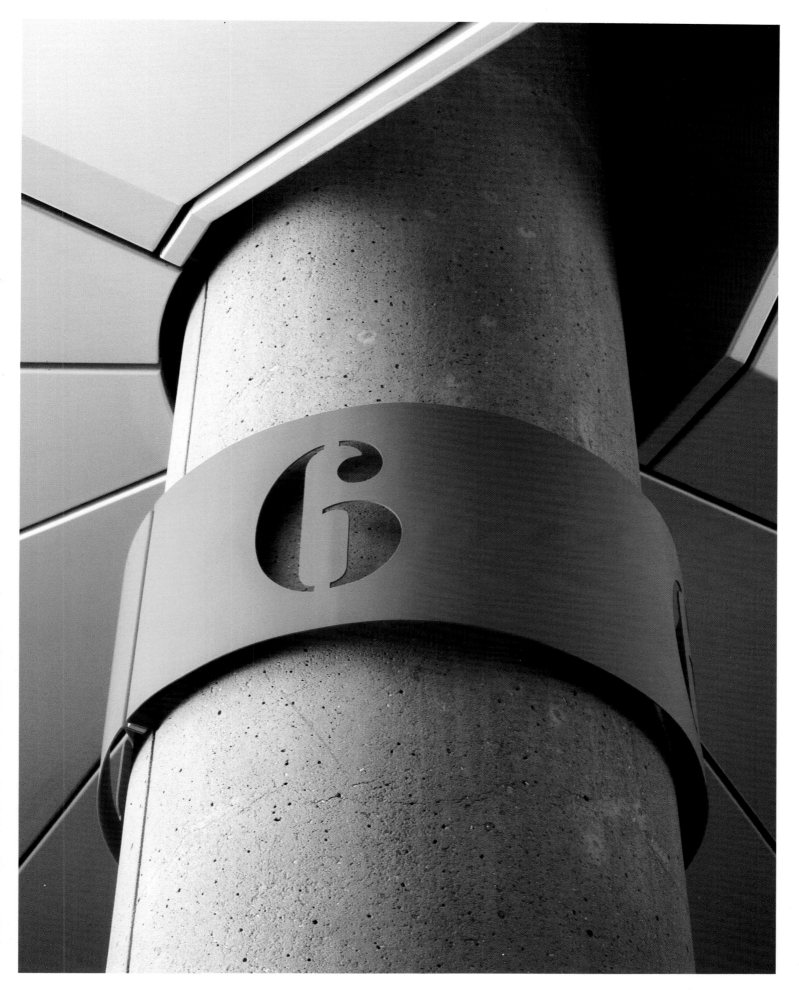

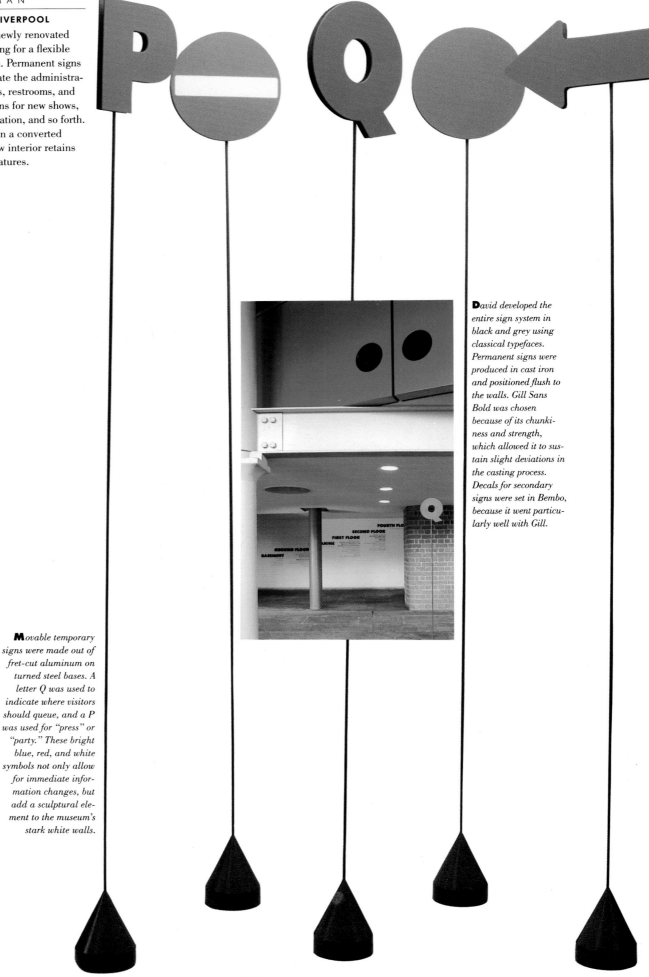

TATE GALLERY OF LIVERPOOL

The Tate Gallery's newly renovated museum was looking for a flexible interior signage system. Permanent signs were needed to designate the administrative offices, cloakrooms, restrooms, and movable temporary signs for new shows, closed exhibits, information, and so forth. The gallery is located in a converted warehouse, and the new interior retains many of the original features.

David developed the entire sign system in black and grey using classical typefaces. Permanent signs were produced in cast iron and positioned flush to the walls. Gill Sans Bold was chosen because of its chunkiness and strength, which allowed it to sustain slight deviations in the casting process. Decals for secondary signs were set in Bembo, because it went particularly well with Gill.

Movable temporary signs were made out of fret-cut aluminum on turned steel bases. A letter Q was used to indicate where visitors should queue, and a P was used for "press" or "party." These bright blue, red, and white symbols not only allow for immediate information changes, but add a sculptural element to the museum's stark white walls.

NORWEST CENTER

Architect Cesar Pelli commissioned Pentagram and Calori + Vanden-Eynden to produce the interior and exterior signage for the Norwest Center, a major new building in downtown Minneapolis. The edifice replaced a classic 1930s Art Deco building that had burned down, and part of Peter's brief was to retain a continuity of style.

The deeply beveled brass capital letters add a degree of finish and architectural quality rarely seen in contemporary signage. The brass rules running behind the letters bring a Deco look to the type and fit comfortably with the Deco image on each side of the entrance.

Elevator floor signs are illuminated glass with etched rules behind the brass letters, typographically linking the exterior and interior of the building.

LEO'S

Leo's new management team decided to change the image of this cooperative food store chain in England from its original low-end, marginal service tradition to a more efficient, modern, and upscale market. A new building was designed as the prototype for the upgrade, and Pentagram was commissioned to develop an appropriate identification and complete signage program for the new stores.

The comprehensive program included parking and bus signs, employee aprons, departmental and directional signs, as well as supermarket basket handles. The blue type with red diamonds became a well-defined hallmark throughout the store.

The checkout counters' prominent red diamonds (echoing the logo) and handsome Bodoni numbers support the sense of order and efficiency.

The major sign is a white cube erected above the store for 360-degree visibility. Mervyn selected Bodoni because of its classic quality. That typographic characteristic aids significantly in countering the previous low-end, low-service stigma of the stores.

When we pick up a newspaper or instructional manual, we look for information — clear, simple, succinct. We expect the material to be presented in a style that will not strain our eyes or our patience but will promote quick comprehension. In some instances, immediate, no-nonsense facts are all the reader seeks. Text intended to educate, however, elicits different emotional expectations. When a book or financial report is selected, for example, readers are prepared to receive lengthier, more detailed data that they hope will be interesting and even entertaining. Tradition has made serif faces the preferred style for books, newspapers, and educational texts. Frequent exposure to certain typefaces has even preconditioned us to expect a scholarly or authoritative account when they are used. Awareness of these distinctions can sharpen the impressions we make.

THE NATURE CONSERVANCY

The Nature Company and the Nature Conservancy, a nonprofit environmental organization, collaborated on producing a calendar describing little-known facts about unusual, endangered, or extinct plants and animals. Entitled "The Daily Planet," it took the form of a note cube containing 365 ecological facts. Gary Overacre ingeniously illustrated a panoramic landscape that ran around the entire cube.

Information was intended to be brief but encyclopedic. We chose the bookish Garamond for the text, while calling out the names of the flora or fauna in Franklin Gothic. The date, which needed to be "first reading," was made the largest element and was further set off by being placed outside the boxed rule.

POTLATCH CORPORATION

Potlatch is a diversified forest products company that manufactures fine printing papers, paperboard, tissue, and wood products. In an annual report theme series that ran over six years, the company presented an encyclopedic look at a single aspect of its business from both a historical and a contemporary perspective. Photographs, illustrations, and charts were combined with vignette-style captions that allowed readers to glean information without necessarily reading an entire essay.

The large copy block, set in Times Roman, presented the subject overview, with captions conveying detailed information. Recognizing that readers typically look at images first, then read captions, and finally, maybe, read the longer text, we made the text invitingly large. Scale, position, and color gave the text prominence, even with many competing images.

An all-text story caption — in this case the Logger Titles glossary — could throw off the balance of a spread. The solution was to treat it as a single visual element by boxing and coloring the text. The use of initial caps and a mix of italic and Roman faces created a lively visual effect and set the copy apart from the captions. The subdued grey kept the copy from overpowering the impact of the primary text.

Potlatch

1983 Annual Report

1987 Annual Report

Logger Titles:
More Color than Pomp

Bull-of-the-Woods
On-site boss of a logging operation. Now called "bullbuck."

Chokersetter
Person who attaches short cables, called chokers, to logs for skidding. Also known as a "hooker."

Donkey Puncher
Yarding equipment operator. In the old days, portable steam engines were called "donkeys."

Hook Tender
Boss of the rigging crew.

Road Monkey
Road maintenance man. Also called "swamper."

Sky Pilot
A religious logger.

Swivelhips
A fast rigging man.

Tally Whacker
Person who recorded log measurements called by the scaler.

Timber beast
Any logger. Also called "brush ape."

Whistle Punk
Person who passed signals from the rigging slinger or chokersetter to the donkey puncher when yarding logs.

Woodpecker
A poor hand with an ax.

Jon Biebl, an independent contractor for Potlatch in Minnesota, is among a new breed of loggers. A century ago the profession attracted many adventurers. Today loggers are often well-educated businessmen who look upon timber harvesting as a silvicultural science.

Pine

High in the Sierra Nevada mountains stands a gnarled bristlecone pine with only a few tufts of green needles protruding from its grey limbs. The 4,600-year-old tree, named Methuselah, is the oldest living thing on earth.

Like Methuselah, pine is a survivor. The hundred or so pine species have a natural range from the Equator to the Arctic Circle. The genus has evolved to survive in nearly every climate. Sometimes this means that seeds lie dormant in the ground for years, waiting until the right conditions allow them to germinate.

No wonder primitive man worshipped pine. Its evergreen needles that flourished even in winter convinced him pine was eternal. Ancient Greeks and Romans, too, regarded pines as sacred. And Mayan Indians believed pines were not only living but animate beings.

Western Europeans held no such mystical beliefs, but they greatly respected pine for its practical value. Tall, straight and durable, pine timber was ideal for construction, furniture and shipmasts. More uniform and supple than most hardwoods, pine could be easily worked with simple tools. Other parts of the tree were useful, too. Nut-like seeds of some species were deliciously edible. Pine resin made pitch products important to shipbuilding, which later created the naval stores industry.

The broad applications for pine served as an important force in the development of Western man and gave impetus to settlement in North America.

Pine, fortunately, is not only the most prevalent tree genus on earth, it's also the most versatile. In the United States, 36 pine species play a major role in the forest products industry.

For Potlatch, pine is vital in each of our three land-based operating regions. In Idaho, Potlatch grows ponderosa, western white and lodgepole pines. In Arkansas, loblolly and shortleaf are the key pine species. In Minnesota, jack and red (Norway) pines dominate our softwood management program.

Pine is used in virtually all of Potlatch's manufactured products—lumber, particleboard, specialty products, fine printing and business papers, bleached pulp and paperboard, and household tissue.

Certainly, if ever a tree deserved to be revered, pine would be the popular choice. For centuries it has inspired man spiritually and offered him shelter and livelihood. And with responsible forest management, pine will continue to serve man for centuries to come.

On some Potlatch lands in Idaho, harvest time might come only once a century, since it can take nearly an average person's lifetime for a tree to reach sawlog-size maturity.

Rotation periods can be equally long in northern Minnesota, while lands in southern Arkansas produce sawlogs as often as every 35 years.

Growing and harvesting raw material is a complex task. Even before one tree is cut, woodlands experts devote many hours to studying the ramifications of a harvesting plan on overall forest management. They sometimes need to act as trustees for young stands of trees that will be bequeathed to another generation to harvest. At the same time, supplying sufficient raw materials to meet current demand is essential.

At Potlatch, each mill specifies how much wood fiber it will need to run its

logs to give better spacing to young stands. Selective harvesting and overstory removal take out designated trees which block light and rob nutrients and moisture from younger, faster-growing trees. Other areas may call for a clearcut—complete removal of a tract of timber, for economic or environmental reasons.

By implementing varied silvicultural, or "farming" methods, it is possible to achieve specific management objectives, while pulling together the sizes and species required by the mills.

Keeping all these factors in mind, logging managers

Harvesting Timber

manufacturing operations for the year. Specialists trained in logging and forestry analyze these budgets to determine how much wood to cut and in what sizes and species. With this information, they determine harvest sites, equipment mix, and a delivery schedule.

A key consideration in their calculations is the concept of sustained yield/allowable cut. This means that in establishing a harvest plan, managers must balance wood fiber needs, both current and future, with the rate of forest regeneration.

In Arkansas, Idaho and Minnesota—Potlatch's three wood basket regions—the woodlands departments satisfy volume requirements through a combination of logging on company land, buying contracts to log on other ownerships, both public and private, and log purchases.

Economic considerations are basic to any harvest scheme, which also must consider terrain, timber size and conditions, stream and drainage patterns, soil types and wildlife protection.

Incorporated into the plan are a number of forest management options. For instance, some raw material can be secured from commercial thinning—the removal of small diameter

plot boundaries for stream buffer zones, skidding trails, yarding sites, and road construction that will protect the forest floor and prevent soil erosion.

From there, loggers determine the complement of equipment needed to carry out the operation efficiently and economically.

After the entire harvesting plan has been laid out, the logging crew is ready to move in. As part of the evolution of forest management into a science, logging has become less an occupation of brawn and daring, and more of an exacting skill. Over the years integrated forest products companies have learned to utilize parts and grades of logs that at one time had no market value. As a result, the logger's skill is more critical because it affects total wood fiber recovery and the products that can be made from the log.

In many ways, timber harvesting must be viewed as the essential preparatory step to a new growth cycle, as well as the culmination of the old. After all, timber management involves much more than cutting down trees and moving them out of the woods. The care that we take in managing our timber supply is our legacy to future generations.

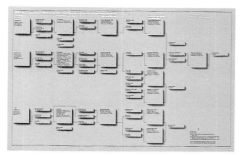

Charts and graphs can either help readers visualize complex information or bore them to death. Color codes for this flow chart are based on the cast shadows used on many of the silhouetted photos in the report. The necessity of using 7-point type mandated Helvetica as the type choice because of its readability.

Hand-lettered branch type is an essential element in communicating a Wild West tone and integrating headings into the image.

History

The invention of paper in China in 105 A.D. created a force that transformed the world. In every culture it reached, paper provided a convenient means of disseminating knowledge and accelerated the development of civilization.

Before paper was introduced to the West in 1150, the written language was largely reserved for priests, scholars and aristocrats. The common man could neither read nor write. Writing materials were rare and expensive, and the task of writing itself was laborious. Parchment to make a single Gutenberg bible, for example, required the skins of 300 sheep.

The spreads shown on this page come from different annual reports, but we maintained a continuity of design and typography from issue to issue while varying details. This theme on paper-making featured a timeline that ran along the bottom of each page. The timeline was set in Helvetica to set it apart from the captions.

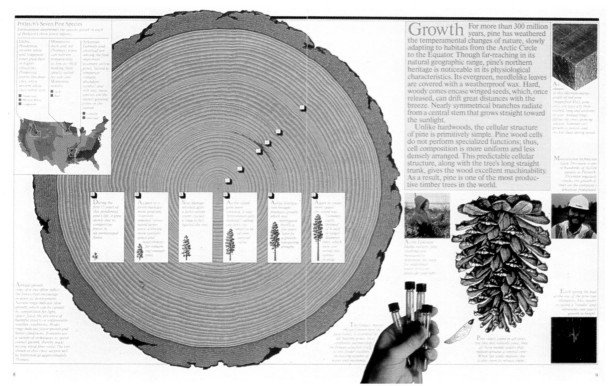

Growth

For more than 300 million years, pine has weathered the temperamental changes of nature, slowly adapting to habitats from the Arctic Circle to the Equator. Though far-reaching in its natural geographic range, pine's northern heritage is noticeable in its physiological characteristics. Its evergreen, needlelike leaves are covered with a weatherproof wax. Hard, woody cones encase winged seeds, which, once released, can drift great distances with the breeze. Nearly symmetrical branches radiate from a central stem that grows straight toward the sunlight.

Unlike hardwoods, the cellular structure of pine is primitively simple. Pine wood cells do not perform specialized functions; thus, cell composition is more uniform and less densely arranged. This predictable cellular structure, along with the tree's long straight trunk, gives the wood excellent machinability. As a result, pine is one of the most productive timber trees in the world.

A cross section of a log illustrated events that affected the life of the tree. Boxed numbers were keyed to inset information. Note that the initial caps for all italic captions are in Roman to add subtle interest.

Distorting the "load ticket" type created a 3-D effect for the graph illustration below.

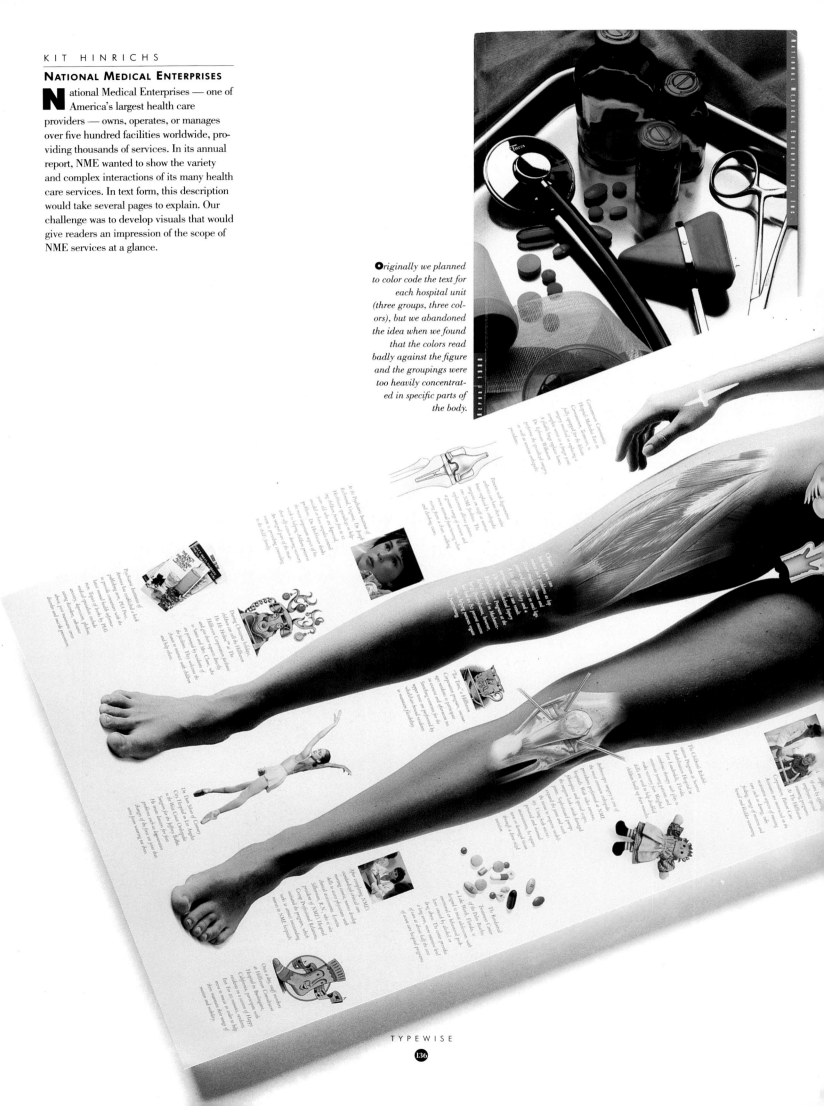

NATIONAL MEDICAL ENTERPRISES

National Medical Enterprises — one of America's largest health care providers — owns, operates, or manages over five hundred facilities worldwide, providing thousands of services. In its annual report, NME wanted to show the variety and complex interactions of its many health care services. In text form, this description would take several pages to explain. Our challenge was to develop visuals that would give readers an impression of the scope of NME services at a glance.

Originally we planned to color code the text for each hospital unit (three groups, three colors), but we abandoned the idea when we found that the colors read badly against the figure and the groupings were too heavily concentrated in specific parts of the body.

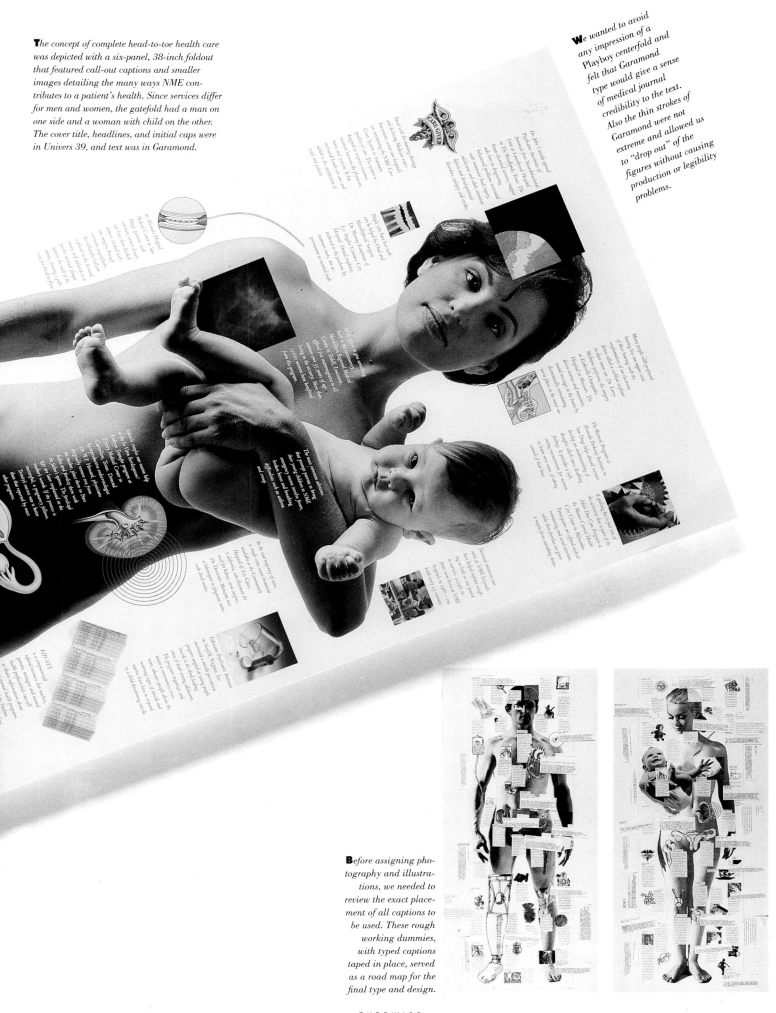

The concept of complete head-to-toe health care was depicted with a six-panel, 38-inch foldout that featured call-out captions and smaller images detailing the many ways NME contributes to a patient's health. Since services differ for men and women, the gatefold had a man on one side and a woman with child on the other. The cover title, headlines, and initial caps were in Univers 39, and text was in Garamond.

We wanted to avoid any impression of a Playboy centerfold and felt that Garamond type would give a sense of medical journal credibility to the text. Also the thin strokes of Garamond were not extreme and allowed us to "drop out" of the figures without causing production or legibility problems.

Before assigning photography and illustrations, we needed to review the exact placement of all captions to be used. These rough working dummies, with typed captions taped in place, served as a road map for the final type and design.

ASPEN SKIING COMPANY

Aspen Skiing Company, with major resorts in Aspen Mountain, Buttermilk, and Snowmass, operates the lift areas, ski schools, and other programs as well as two luxury hotels at famous Aspen, Colorado. A reorganized management asked ad agency Hal Riney & Partners along with Pentagram to prepare an advertising and promotional program highlighting Aspen's year-round attractions.

A *highly visible but understated campaign pitched the upscale skiing crowd through advertisements placed in sophisticated periodicals such as* Travel & Leisure, Esquire, *and* Vanity Fair.

L*inda created an uncomplicated format, using caps/small caps styling, for all cover art. This gave a unified identity to the program collateral and allowed for changing images and color coding materials to match individual needs, for example, ski maps for each resort area, ticket folders, and so on.*

B*embo — elegant and distinctive — was chosen as the typeface for all advertising and promotional materials. At first, however, the ad agency and Pentagram were using two different typographers, which resulted in completely different settings and a different look.*

SUMMER 1989

FROM THE BASE OF ASPEN MOUNTAIN, THE SILVER QUEEN—THE WORLD'S LONGEST, SINGLE-STAGE, VERTICAL RISE GONDOLA—TRAVELS TO THE 11,212-FOOT SUMMIT IN 13 MINUTES, REVEALING A MAGNIFICENT, 360-DEGREE VIEW. DAILY DURING THE SUMMER, YOU MAY GAZE UPON THE PEAKS OF SOME OF COLORADO'S LOFTIEST "FOURTEENERS," DISCOVER AN ABANDONED MINER'S SHACK, LEARN TO DIFFERENTIATE BETWEEN A YELLOW-RUMPED WARBLER AND BLACK-CAPPED CHICKADEE OR TREAT YOURSELF TO A LEISURELY OUTDOOR LUNCH AT THE SUNDECK.

THE ASPENS
SNOWMASS · ASPEN

Aspen Skiing wanted to promote the fact that the area was a great place to visit even after the prime ski season. It did this with a calendar of cultural events that included everything from the famed Aspen Design Conference to balloon races.

The amount of information required to explain the comprehensive range of summer activities could have been a nightmare if not organized correctly. The informational difference was achieved by the typographical texture created with contrasting all caps, upper and lower case, justified and ragged copy.

The cornerstone of the collateral program was the 160-page Aspen Guide, which included colorful accounts of the area's natural history and early settlements, along with directories of shops, tours, lodging, and ski areas and restaurant critiques.

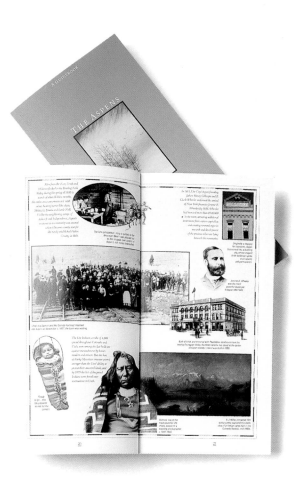

"When I am skiing at European ski resorts, I have always a dream of real deep powder, perfect groomed slopes, friendly people at the lift stations and excellent service in hotels and restaurants. When I came to Aspen, my dream became reality."

—*Günter Reimann*
Travel Editor/Abendzeitung
Munich, West Germany

30

The adjoining map, one of several throughout the guide, indicates historical buildings by number. Helvetica was chosen to convey the map information clearly, but Bembo continues as the major textface. The colored triangles are used to indicate the direction of the entrance.

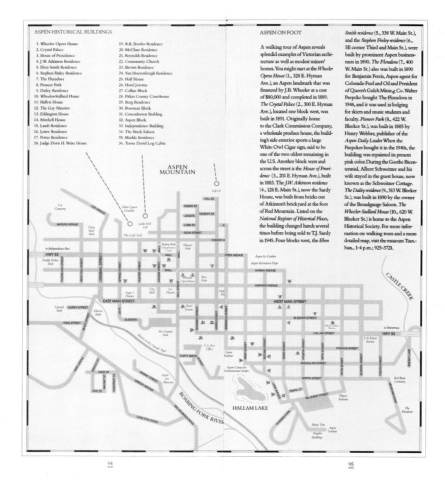

94   95

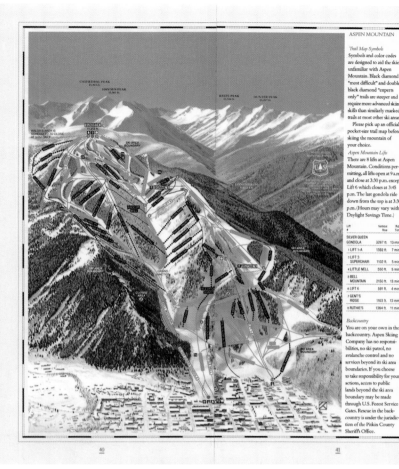

Trail Map Symbols
Symbols and color codes are designed to aid the skier unfamiliar with Aspen Mountain. Black diamond "most difficult" and double black diamond "experts only" trails are steeper and require more advanced skiing skills than similarly marked trails at most other ski areas.

Please pick up an official pocket-size trail map before skiing the mountain of your choice.

Aspen Mountain Lifts
There are 8 lifts at Aspen Mountain. Conditions permitting, all lifts open at 9 a.m. and close at 3:30 p.m. except Lift 6 which closes at 3:45 p.m. The last gondola ride down from the top is at 3:30 p.m. (Hours may vary with Daylight Savings Time.)

Lift #		Vertical Rise	Ride Time
SILVER QUEEN GONDOLA		3267 ft.	13 min.
1	LIFT 1-A	1302 ft.	7 min.
3	LIFT 3 SUPERCHAIR	1102 ft.	5 min.
4	LITTLE NELL	550 ft.	5 min.
5	BELL MOUNTAIN	2150 ft.	13 min.
6	LIFT 6	591 ft.	4 min.
7	GENT'S RIDGE	1103 ft.	13 min.
8	RUTHIE'S	1364 ft.	11 min.

Backcountry
You are on your own in the backcountry. Aspen Skiing Company has no responsibilities, no ski patrol, no avalanche control and no services beyond its ski area boundaries. If you choose to take responsibility for your actions, access to public lands beyond the ski area boundary may be made through U.S. Forest Service Gates. Rescue in the backcountry is under the jurisdiction of the Pitkin County Sheriff's Office.

40   41

Ski maps are amazingly complex because of the variety of information they must communicate: the direction and names of the runs, degrees of difficulty, relative proximity to lifts, and restaurants, first aid stations, etc. To facilitate readability against a busy background, trail names were set in Helvetica caps and reversed out of colored panels. Major landmarks were set in Bembo caps.

It's important to maintain a family look in a communications program, even for leaflets that change frequently. This illustrated series of single-leaf flyers used the same typographic styling as the balance of the group.

LODGING IN THE ASPENS
by Elizabeth Fanon

Lodging accommodations in The Aspens range from slopeside luxury hotels and small country inns to condominiums with fully-equipped kitchens and renovated Victorian homes.

Most lodges included in *A Guidebook to The Aspens* offer a complimentary continental or full breakfast and après-ski refreshments. Many condominiums include daily maid service in their rates.

In the listing following are members of either the Aspen Chamber or Snowmass Resort Associations, many of which have been assigned Quality Ratings by the Aspen-based Premier Lodge Rating System. These ratings represent a composite of overall quality, maintenance, care, ambience, amenities, facilities, services and extras provided. Members not choosing to be rated by Premier are listed with a brief description. All properties are listed in alphabetical order by property type. For information on renting private homes, contact property management companies or the Aspen or Snowmass Central Reservations.

RATINGS AND CODES
The guidebook's rated properties have designations of 1-5 Mountain Peaks, with 5 being reserved only for those considered exceptional—both in terms of The Aspens and nationwide. Some properties have been recognized as a [Special Lodging Experience] or [Exceptional Value].

▲▲▲▲▲ *Exceptional lodging; usually full-service.*

▲▲▲▲ *Superior accommodations; above-average services and facilities, but may not be extensive.*

▲▲▲ *Very good value and pleasant accommodations; fewer but fine services and facilities.*

▲▲ *Good lodging value with fewer services and facilities. Often well-priced, desirable lodging.*

▲ *Meets most basic lodging needs; economical and unpretentious. Few or no facilities, and limited service.*

△ *Represents a "plus" in services, facilities or comfort.*

LEGEND KEY
P—*outdoor or indoor heated pool.*
HT/S—*hot tub/sauna.* C—*cocktail lounge on premises.* M—*meeting facilities.* F—*fireplace in some or all rooms.* T—*courtesy airport transportation.* R—*restaurant on premises.* (AE, V, MC, etc.)—*credit cards.*

$$-$$$ — *indicates regular season rates charged for the smallest to largest available room or condominium unit. Prices during value and holiday season fluctuate dramatically; please ask for details when booking your reservation.*

ASPEN AND SNOWMASS PROPERTY MANAGEMENT COMPANIES
(These listings include companies and their rentals that are not wholly managed by the company listed.)

Aspen Central Properties
Specializing in individually owned properties throughout Aspen. 415 E. Hyman Ave., Suite 105, Aspen; 303-925-7301.

Aspen Chateaux Company
Located one block from the Silver Queen Gondola. Amenities vary depending on property. 731 E. Durant Ave., Aspen; 303-925-1100.

Aspen Choice Properties
Specializing in condominiums in the Aspen/Snowmass area. Many different locations and amenities to choose among. 630 E. Hyman Ave., Suite 1, Aspen; 303-925-1328.

Aspen Club Management
Guests at all managed properties have complimentary privileges at the Aspen Club health and fitness center. The company manages several condominiums at Chateau Chaumont, Chateau Dumont, Southpoint, and private homes. 520 E. Durant Ave., Aspen; 303-925-6760.

Aspen Gondola Management
Full-service company with properties ranging from economy to luxury. 617 W. Main St., Suite B, Aspen; 303-925-4517.

Aspen Resort Accommodations
A small company representing a variety of properties in the Aspen area. A duplex on E. Hopkins and a duplex and cottage at 518 West Francis were quality rated, but other condominiums and homes were not. 100 S. Spring St., Aspen; 303-925-4772.

Aspen/Snowmass Care
A wide variety of condominiums and homes in Aspen and Snowmass, ranging from economy to luxury. P. O. Box 6026, Snowmass Village; 303-923-4488.

Aspenwood Condominium Management Company
Offering studios to two bedrooms with loft units in the vil-

133

Because of the diversity of services offered at each lodge, Linda devised a series of symbols ranging from "five mountain" (exceptional) to "one mountain" (basic) for easy identification. By hanging the lodges' names in the left margin, a quick alphabetical search can be made.

THE GUARDIAN

After nearly twenty years of the same design format, The Guardian sought a more contemporary style that applied the benefits of new technology. Any change, however, was tampering with tradition and the way people perceived and read their newspapers. Part of David's challenge was to keep these traditions in mind along with the fact that daily newspapers must be hastily put together by a team of journalists who are usually not trained designers.

A goal was to use the speed and flexibility of new technology to bring back the craft of newspaper design. Once the format was developed, about fifty journalists and subeditors had to be trained to carry it through. David presented layouts in a foreign language because he felt it helped journalists focus on the look rather than the written treatment of the story.

The Guardian
before its redesign.

The feature sections are set in flush left and rag right columns.

The hard news section is set in justified columns.

The computer allowed David to invent his own point system so that all text could be aligned on a page. A separate program was written for dropped caps. The section heads are all combinations of Garamond Italic with a Franklin Gothic "Guardian," giving a visual reprise to the masthead styling. The body text is Nimrod, a computer-generated typestyle.

CHAMPION PAPER

As do all fine printing paper companies, Champion regularly produces promotional material that shows the range of their papers and demonstrates their ability to handle a variety of printing techniques. For this assignment, we were asked to create a calendar that visually described time. Our solution was to design a calendar illustrating twelve periods of time, from eons to seconds, by progressively reducing the size of the image as you reduced the amount of time and the length of each page. By perforating the leaves just below the calendar dates, we also created a paper swatch book.

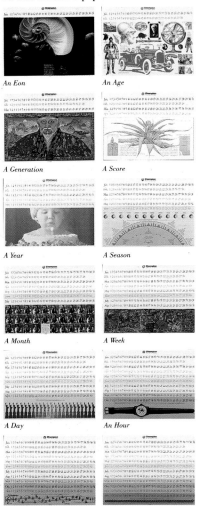

An Eon *An Age*

A Generation *A Score*

A Year *A Season*

A Month *A Week*

A Day *An Hour*

A Minute *A Second*

We reviewed several typefaces — Times Roman, Goudy, Palatino — before settling on Garamond, which had handsomely drawn, old style numbers that had sufficient style to maintain interest over a long period of time and could be read from a distance, essential for any wall calendar. The beauty of the numbers was particularly important because, as the images became smaller with each passing month, the numbers became a more prominent part of the visuals.

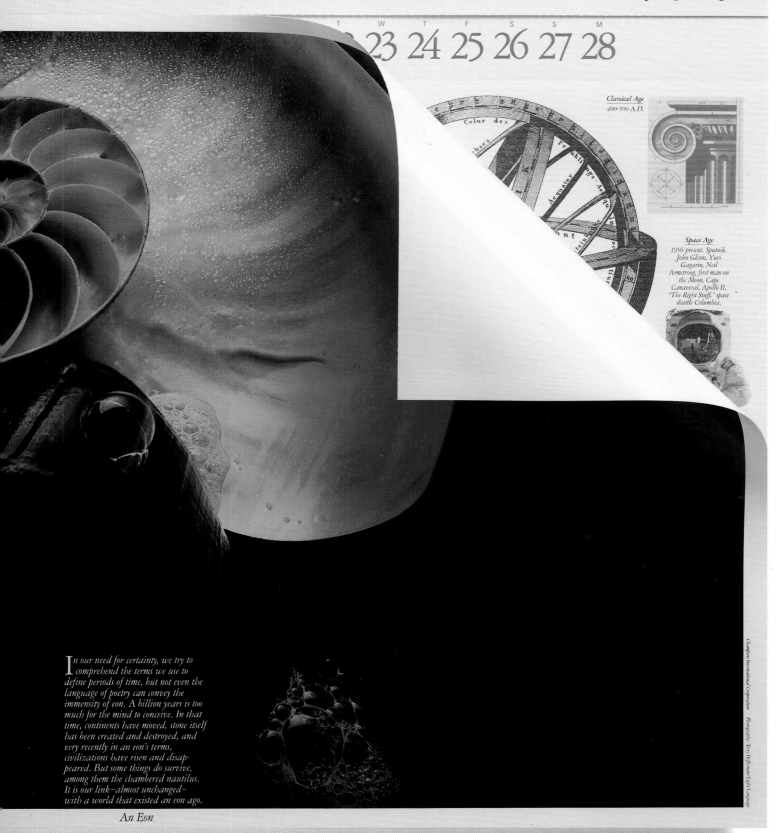

F S S M T W T F S S M T W T F S S M
14 15 16 17 18 19 20 21 22 23 24 25 26 27 28 29 30 31

T W T F S S M
23 24 25 26 27 28

Classical Age
400-500 A.D.

Colur des

Space Age
1956-present. Sputnik,
John Glenn, Yuri
Gagarin, Neil
Armstrong, first man on
the Moon, Cape
Canaveral, Apollo II,
"The Right Stuff," space
shuttle Columbia.

I*n our need for certainty, we try to*
comprehend the terms we use to
define periods of time, but not even the
language of poetry can convey the
immensity of eon. A billion years is too
much for the mind to conceive. In that
time, continents have moved, stone itself
has been created and destroyed, and
very recently in an eon's terms,
civilizations have risen and disap-
peared. But some things do survive,
among them the chambered nautilus.
It is our link–almost unchanged–
with a world that existed an eon ago.

An Eon

MCKESSON CORPORATION

McKesson Corporation (formerly Foremost-McKesson), a major pharmaceutical and retail products distribution company, wanted its 1980 annual report to focus on its plans and strategies for the coming decade. They requested a look that represented a visionary view of the future and reflected a "big picture" strategy.

Managing for Growth: Foremost-McKesson's Strategy for the '80s

The typeface choice, Remington Typewriter, came naturally. This low-tech, journalistic typography conveyed a sense of immediacy and freshness of idea that suited the text and distinguished McKesson's book from the sea of slick annual reports.

stores as families with two breadwinners seek convenience and the transportation and energy savings of buying all of their daily needs under one roof. The result is a growing number of "super-stores" or "omni stores," in some respects similar to the general store of the last century. McKesson Drug Company already is servicing a large number of these stores, with sales to its ten largest superstore customers up 38% last year alone.

In addition to the Wine & Spirits Group's emphasis on improved systems of distribution, that group's new-product and marketing programs will be given increased emphasis. Imported beer constitutes a highly attractive market, with annual volume growth in the next three years projected at 10% to 15%. We have increased sales of St. Pauli Girl, German premium-priced beer for which we are the exclusive U.S. distributor, to over one million cases in 1980 from only 35,000 years ago. Italian table wines show strong gains growth rates from 12% to 15% through have also achieved tial gains

Folonari Italian wine, currently the fifth largest selling brand of imported wine in the U.S. We expect Folonari sales to continue to grow at a rate of about 15% a year through 1985. Spirits, on the other hand, are expected to show moderate growth important exception, however, is imported rum, with term annual growth other of our propried brands, grew 15% 1981, and we expect ble its sales over five years. Through the "21" Bra Wine Compan estate-bo French a have en The gr numb fra i

We are creating a climate where creativity, intelligent risk-taking and innovation can flourish. To foster such a climate we have created a fifth major operating group whose primary focus will be to identify and develop new businesses with the potential to make an important contribution to the corporation in the next five to ten years.

A counterpoint to the typewriter type, Franklin Gothic was used for the large pull-quotes, which are effective in explaining illustrations and presenting highlights of the text.

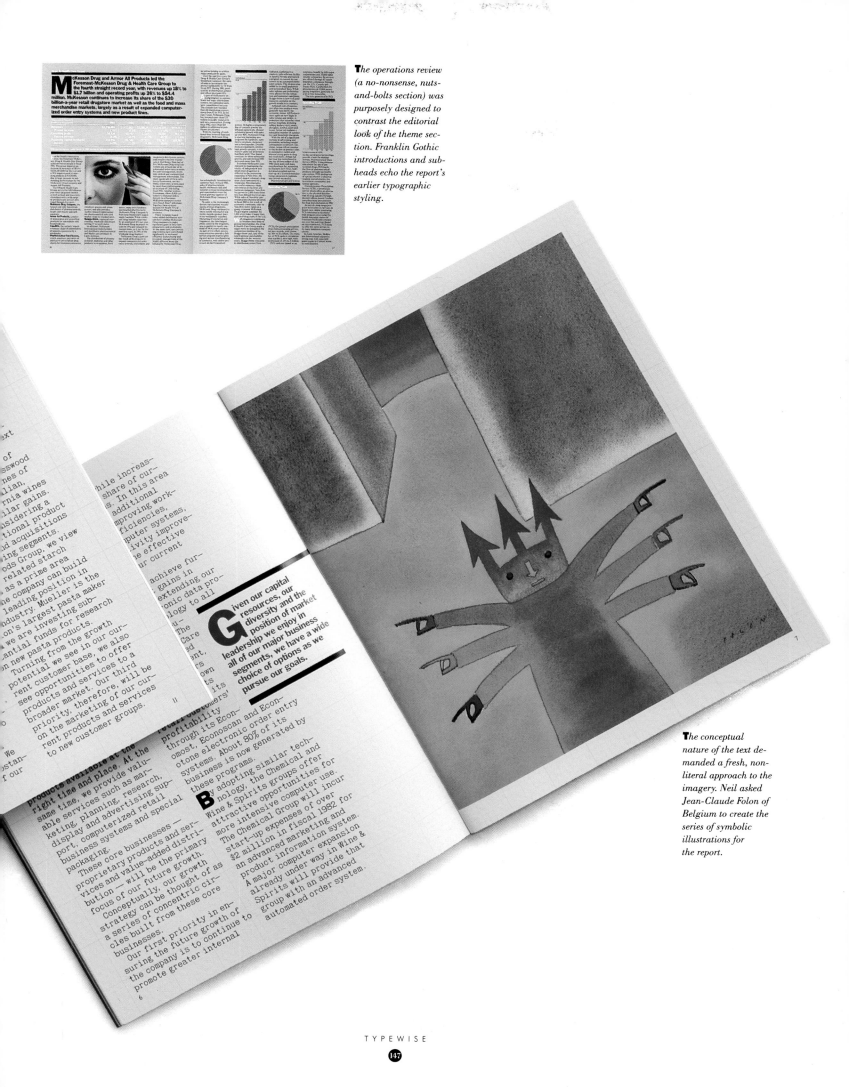

The operations review (a no-nonsense, nuts-and-bolts section) was purposely designed to contrast the editorial look of the theme section. Franklin Gothic introductions and sub-heads echo the report's earlier typographic styling.

The conceptual nature of the text demanded a fresh, non-literal approach to the imagery. Neil asked Jean-Claude Folon of Belgium to create the series of symbolic illustrations for the report.

Type can exude a youthful vitality. The latest faces are often used when presenting contemporary fashions, but even classic faces can appear provocative through spacing, color, or nontraditional organization. Bouncing letters or placing words at vertical or diagonal angles can bring an energy that would be inappropriate in another context. Mixing more than one typeface within a single word also injects a freshness in typography. An impression of youthful energy can be directed toward any age group — whether its members are ten, forty-five, or sixty. It's important to be sensitive to how each age group expresses youthful energy and to be influenced by these perceptions without mimicking them, which can appear condescending.

SHISEIDO

Shiseido, the world's third largest man-ufacturer of toiletries and cosmetics, sought a lively image for its new toiletry collection called *Trendy*, which offers a range of hair, body, and facial care prod-ucts for Japanese youth.

Kenneth and Mervyn considered contempo-rary elements — music, architecture, typography, video promotions, film and fashion — to arrive at a collage of symbols which they combined with Japanese and English lettering in bright day-glo colors. The typography, known in Japan as "scrambled communication," was used to evoke freedom, a breaking of the rules, and nonconformity.

UC SANTA CRUZ

▌n its main recruitment brochure, the
University of California at Santa Cruz
wanted to establish its position within the
world-renowned UC system and present
its own unique character and strengths.
The design had to be young and contemporary enough to appeal to teenage college applicants, yet conservative and
serious enough to meet the approval of
their parents who were likely to read the
brochure with equal interest.

*Running captions ver-
tically throughout the
book allowed an
opportunity to expose
the unexpected, adven-
turesome side of the
university, while let-
ting the dramatic pho-
tographic images
stand unobstructed.*

*A mix of warm, human-interest photographs,
vignettes of regional history, professor profiles,
student projects, and course information was
presented in a complex but expansive layout,
woven together with Bembo typography. The
cover masthead has a bit of neo-1950s
typography and adds an "old is new"
styling to the book.*

Named by Science Digest
as one of the top 100
U.S. scientists under 40,
Sandra Faber is a profes-
sor of astronomy and
astrophysics, affiliated
with Lick Observatory.
Professor Faber, who
researches the formation
and evolution of galaxies
and the formation of
structure in the universe,
was part of a group of
seven astronomers who
discovered a large flow
of galaxies called the
Great Attractor. She is a
member of the National
Academy of Sciences.

The Drift Chamber, shown here,
was jointly constructed by the Santa
Cruz Institute for Particle Physics
and Stanford Linear Accelerator
Center (SLAC) in Palo Alto. The
detector contains about 6,000 wires
that pick up signals from the passage of charged particles through
its volume. An hour's drive from
Santa Cruz, SLAC is one of three
federally funded accelerators in the
nation. UCSC maintains data links
from campus computer terminals to
large SLAC computers.

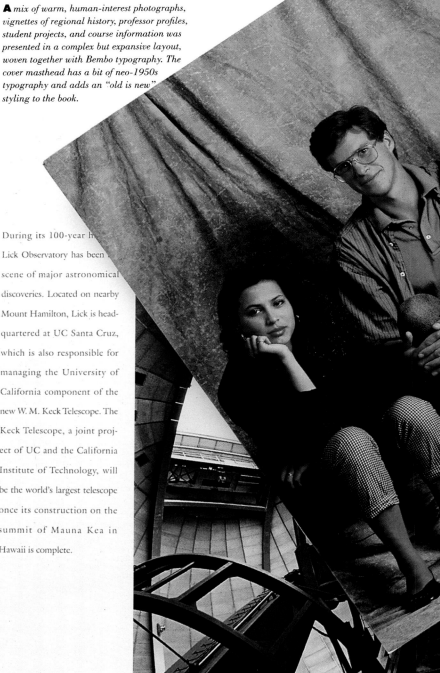

During its 100-year h[...]
Lick Observatory has been [...]
scene of major astronomical
discoveries. Located on nearby
Mount Hamilton, Lick is headquartered at UC Santa Cruz,
which is also responsible for
managing the University of
California component of the
new W. M. Keck Telescope. The
Keck Telescope, a joint project of UC and the California
Institute of Technology, will
be the world's largest telescope
once its construction on the
summit of Mauna Kea in
Hawaii is complete.

14

UC SANTA CRUZ

Linda's design for UC Santa Cruz viewbook displayed not only the usual information sought by prospective students, but the exceptional beauty of the campus and surrounding areas. The extremely leaded main text provides contrast with the photo captions.

In the 1970s, a group of Santa Cruz graduate students performed pioneer work in the new field of chaos theory, which examines the seemingly unpredictable behavior of complex systems and discerns orderly patterns within the chaos. This science has potential applications in fields as far-ranging as medicine and economics. UCSC's Center for Nonlinear Science continues research into chaotic phenomena. This computer-generated image was created by UCSC graduate Jim Crutchfield.

Professor Michael Tanner, chairman of the computer and information sciences program, is an expert on error-correcting codes that ensure the reliability of data transmissions. A consultant to Ford Aerospace and Communications, Professor Tanner has designed coding systems for NASA. He holds patents on error-correcting coding systems and fault-tolerant computer memories.

Mathematics professor Ralph Abraham, who has been at the forefront of research in dynamics, founded UCSC's Visual Mathematics Project to explore the use of interactive computer graphics in teaching math. This image is from the book Dynamics: The Geometry of Behavior, coauthored by Abraham.

15

MOCA

The Museum of Contemporary Arts in Los Angeles wanted a brochure to help guide families through its galleries and to highlight the works of some of its best-known artists. To capture the personality of the museum, the brochure had to be lively, contemporary and reflective of the diversity and experimental nature of MOCA's art collection.

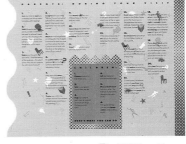

The MOCA guide was set in five languages: English, Spanish, Korean, Chinese, and Japanese. The design had to be flexible enough to allow for length variations of up to 15 percent resulting from translations.

The edges of the opening pages were die-cut to reveal the colors and patterns of the pages that followed. The die-cuts reinforced the bold geometric shapes that formed the Chermayeff & Geismar-designed MOCA logo. Futura Light with Extra Bold, a clean, modern sans-serif face, was used for the English and Spanish text.

ELCOME TO MOCA! THIS GUIDE IS WRITTEN TO INTRODUCE YOU AND YOUR FAMILY TO CONTEMPORARY ART. IT CONTAINS IDEAS TO HELP YOU LOOK AT AND THINK AND TALK ABOUT THE CONTEMPORARY ART IN THE GALLERIES. THE EXAMPLES OF THE ART WORKS IN THIS GUIDE ARE SOME OF OUR FAVORITES AT MOCA. THE GUIDE IS ONLY A SUGGESTION; THE REST IS UP TO YOU! WE WANT YOU TO ENJOY THE ART, AT YOUR OWN PACE AND WITH YOUR FAMILY.

POLAROID EUROPE

When Polaroid introduced a new camera and film throughout Europe, it asked John Rushworth to coordinate an advertising and poster campaign with its agency. The event came together as a gallery featuring the work of eighteen international designers, including Mervyn.

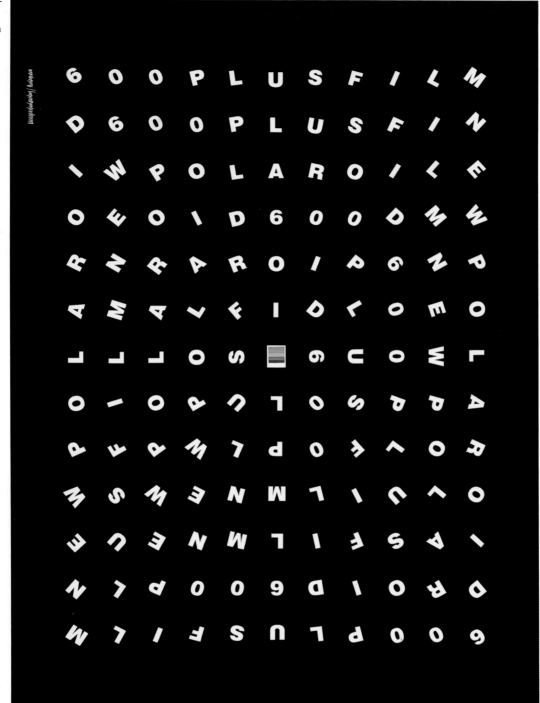

Mervyn created a poster using a spiral of words to draw the eye to the film at the center. Simply by turning in concentric circles, the unadorned typeface — Helvetica Bold — gave a sense of energy to the characters, while allowing for quick readability even without word breaks and focusing the eye to the center square.

WARNER COMMUNICATIONS

Warner Communications (now Time Warner), a company we've worked with for over fifteen years, has entertainment businesses ranging from books and magazines to records, motion pictures, and cable television. We were asked to create an ultracontemporary quarterly corporate news magazine for employees and customers. For the publication, called *Currents*, Peter designed a vital, energetic, nonconforming format, appropriate to Warner's youthful products and audiences.

WARNER

MUSIC

ELEKTRA

SPRING QUARTER

ELEKTRA

CURRENTS

This cover carries the line "With apologies to El Lissitsky," an important designer from the early days of Russian Constructivism. The strong structural organization of the page and the typography associated with this early twentieth-century designer influenced many graphic designers later in the century. The cover typography was created by scanning the type from the original El Lissitsky cover into the computer, cleaning it up, and creating new characters.

CURRENTS

With apologies to El Lissitzky

Javier Romero

From issue to issue, *Currents* is consistently inconsistent in its body text and typography; only the name remains the same. Each issue is a visual surprise. *Currents'* large tabloid size is emblematic of many music and video publications. The combination of several typefaces on a single page, as well as in a single word, is a typographic trend of the early 1990s and perfect for the totally ephemeral quality of this publication.

The same iconoclastic design and typographic approach are used throughout *Currents'* inside spreads. The freshness and vitality of this approach is normally left exclusively to the realm of record and CD jackets produced by Warner. To see this bold, graphic direction expressed in the official corporate newsletter conveys an important message to employees about being innovative, taking chances, and not being afraid to fail.

The center spread is always a surprise. In this case, the need to turn it to read involves the reader in a participatory way. The type's irregular form not only creates an interesting graphic shape, but serves as a wonderful frame for the Randy Travis photos.

The back page of each issue, like the cover, is a typographic potpourri. The mixture of various, often incongruous, typefaces, coupled with vertical headline settings and unexpected sizes and measures, conveys an extremely youthful and energetic image.

ELEKTRA

Few record companies have experienced the dramatic rise that Elektra Records has achieved in recent years. Throughout its history Elektra has been unique in the discovery and development of a wide range of artists, among them — Jackson Browne, The Cars, The Eagles and Linda Ronstadt. However, Elektra's fortune has soared recently under the astute direction of Bob Krasnow. He assumed leadership of Elektra in 1983. Elektra's biggest year, 1988, was highlighted by several popular new releases — Anita Baker, Linda Ronstadt, Tracy Chapman and Metallica among others. In 1988, Elektra's revenues increased by more than a third over the previous year. In addition, Elektra's artists won some of the industry's top honors, including eight Grammy awards. Krasnow, in a recent interview says his company's success is no surprise:

▲ It's something that we've been building towards. It's actually been the last three years that this kind of momentum has been building, and I just characterize this as the re-establishing of Elektra as one of the great companies that services the needs of the great American music public and the world's music public.

Q Elektra was in the doldrums before you took over the company, and some believed the label wouldn't survive. What was the turning point for the company?

▲ This is a business of talent. To say that Elektra wasn't in as good a shape as it is now is the understatement of the year. I think *The Los Angeles Times* characterized it best when it said Elektra Records went from being "an outhouse to a penthouse". I think *Time* magazine also characterized us as being the "Intrepid" record label. But I think that Elektra is so tied in to what it does musically, it's hard to separate.

This company puts out very few records, and each record has a very clear raison d'etre — that's the difference.

We make very specific types of recordings, whether its to work with Linda Ronstadt on her Mexican album that she did or to sign on someone with the character of Reuben Blades or choose to take the path with a Tracy Chapman, someone who is flying in the face of the Gordon Gekko, Wall Street, 'Greed is Good,' the '80s Reagan philosophy, or to choose to work with someone like Anita Baker who is not a manufactured product. Metallica is another example. We choose our product very carefully.

Q What were the building blocks which led to today's success?

▲ The artists are your building blocks. We're not chemists here. We don't manufacture anything here. We choose people to work with, that's the blocks. The quality of our artists, the fact that we were awarded 21 Grammy nominations by our own peers, I certainly think distinguishes us from anyone else. Such publications as *Time, Newsweek, The New York Times, The Los Angeles Times,* and *The London Times* — the most important and most serious newspapers and weekly newsmagazines — cover what we do on a consistent basis. They don't do that with other people. We don't put out purely pop or fluff. Again I'm not criticizing anyone else. What distinguishes us is that we have a philosophy and that philosophy is to try to be our best and to try to do the best with the best.

Q What about Nonesuch's recent critical and sales success involving such classical and contemporary artists as John Adams, Steve Reich and the Kronos Quartet?

▲ When we rebuilt Nonesuch, I brought in Bob Hurwitz. And Bob and I decided together that we would not try to compete with Deutsche-Grammophon and do some Beethoven Symphonies done by some of the greatest conductors in the world, or try to do string quartet music or chamber music by traditional people. We decided we would go into the American culture and market, and choose people like John Adams, Steve Reich, Phillip Glass and the Kronos Quartet. We would choose artists working in a contemporary field, and do contemporary music and carve our niche. We can't compete with Deutsche-Grammophon or Columbia Masterworks, the Columbia classical label. They've been doing it 50 years and they've been doing it incredibly well.

If we wanted to succeed in it, we had to find a place where first of all, we had competence, and where we had a relationship with what the musical genre was all about. Also, that we appreciated it, that we sympathized with it, and we were able to support it emotionally and in every other way. And from that philosophy, of saying yes, there are great American composers out there, they're out there, now, it's just up to us to find them. To separate the wheat from the chaff, and say, 'Hey, let's find these people. Let's record Steve Reich. Let's record John Adams. Let's support these big operas. Let's support the Kronos Quartet. Let them do unrecorded classical pieces, classic pieces. Just because somebody didn't write them two hundred years ago does not in any way make them less valuable. Let's pursue that area.' I think our success speaks for itself. Let's bring the Bulgarian Singers to America. Let's record the Gypsy Kings. Let's do something everyone in the world isn't doing. That's what I demand from myself and of everybody that's on this team. And it is a team. I am not certainly sitting in this chair doing all of this myself. We have a great staff of people here.

Q What do you look for in

ON THE MOVE

CABLE

Editor:
Lois Edwards
Director of Corporate Communications

Design:
Pentagram

Vol. 1, No. 2
Spring 1989

A Publication of Warner Communications Inc.
Corporate Public Affairs

75 Rockefeller Plaza
New York, N.Y. 10019
212 484-7895

CURRENTS

CREDITS

A story on Andy Warhol was set in typewriter type to create the feeling of a journal or diary. The same type-style used as silkscreen art is an appropriate integration of word and image. An interesting visual note is Warhol's portrait, printed like a 3-D comic, another of his many pop culture influences.

The initials WEA (Warner, Elektra, Asylum) splashed across the page would not be as effective without the contrasting restraint of the typographic columns with which it interacts.

The best definition of what the best is, is that whatever you do has some redeeming quality at the end of the day, not disposable fluff that will disappear. Whatever we do here, I hope has some staying power.

What I do is accomplished with extreme passion.

picking your team players?
▲ I think there are several qualities you look for when you hire someone.

The quality that preempts any other quality that I look for in someone I want to work with, is the ability to think on their own terms.

I don't want someone turning on the radio and after hearing Whitney Houston or Bobby Brown, approach me saying, "Hey, I've got an artist just like that." If you want to lose my interest, the best way to do that is to walk into this office and say, "Hey I've just found an artist who's a combination of Stevie Wonder and Elton John." That's the last thing this business needs. Everybody has got to think like that, for example, look at The Sugarcubes, they're a band from Iceland. We've got a new band called The Pixies that's going to take the country by storm. Again something totally unique.
● What's the significance of Elektra Records becoming Elektra Entertainment in 1988?
▲ We are certainly in the entertainment business. The records certainly bring in all the revenues as of now. But this video phenomenon is not lost on our customers. And we have been very successful in the video business. The Metallica video is close to 170,000 units, and the Motley Crue video is doing very well as is the Anita Baker video. Also, The Cure is another band. They have two videos whose combined sales are in the 100,000 unit range.

You start looking, then you say, "Hey, we sold 750,000 videos in the last year." And these videos aren't being given away. They're not $8.98, you're paying $20 to $25 for a video. There's a market out there and the film business has proven that. A major business within the film industry is their video rentals and sales. We have started our laserdisc videos; we are the only ones I'm aware of that is marketing our laserdiscs, side by side with our video-tapes. We have them man-ufactured for us. I feel the business is moving towards an audiovisual experience. I think the young people today who are growing up with MTV and seeing all of these extravaganzas, the eight-year-olds, the 12 year-olds, the 16 year olds who will be starting their bands in the next several years, they will have such an imprint of the visual capacity of music that they're going to pursue that as well as the audio.
We've started our children's line. We've joint-ventured a company with Nickelodeon. And this year we'll be putting out six to ten video-tapes and videodiscs for children. They range in audience from age four to 14, the same audience that Nickelodeon has on televi-sion. I don't think kids today are just going to go out and buy a record. And the same with Nonesuch. We will be making a video of The Nutcracker Ballet. What if you live in Iowa and you can't get here with your kids. Why should you be cheated out of that experi-ence. We're going to bring that experience to you. That's why we're in the entertainment business.

Music will always be the primary source which we will bring to the picture, but the picture will be important.
● What are your major challenges?
▲ The challenges are to find the right people to work with. That's always the challenge. The business is more competitive now because music is a way of life. You take music with you wherever you go. It's not like reading a book or seeing a film. If it's really great, you see it twice maybe. If you buy a record, it lasts a lifetime. The market is there, so the challenge is not to build the market. The challenge is to find the right people to introduce to the market. And those so-called building blocks, you talked about, that's talent.

Talent always wins.

If you choose to work with talented people, you will ultimately win.

If you're able to hang in there long enough, if you're financially able to stay with the program, you will wind up a winner providing you have the insight, the intu-ition, whatever that sixth sense is, to work with peo-ple who are quality talent.
● Any special plans for the next year?
▲ I don't think about next year. I'm thinking about three years, five years from now. Next year is already out of my hands. I've already signed the acts that we're going to be dealing with next year. When I sign an act, I'm saying, "Where is this act going?" I don't want an act to come in here

and say, "I've just written the greatest things I ever wrote in my life." Because if that's it, then there'll be a one album situation on our hands. I need to have some-one like Tracy Chapman come into my office and sit in this exact chair, and play me some songs and say, "This is what I feel right now. These are my feelings now. This is what is going through my mind, my body now." And you listen and you say to yourself, "How can a person this young, know all of this. And what is she going to know several years from now. This is someone who is obviously interested in people, inter-ested in how people treat people. Interested in the quality of life. You don't have to be a rocket scientist to say, "I want to associate myself with that."
● You've had success with breaking international or foreign acts, but do you expect more in the future?
▲ There will be more inter-national artists certainly. Absolutely. I think our A&R department does it in waves coming up on the beach. Every month someone from our A&R department is someplace else, whether it's in France, Australia, England or Italy. We're there on the scene. Look at the Gypsy Kings, the album has sold over 360,000. Can you tell me, who in the hell would sell 360,000 copies of the Gypsy Kings. We sold 150,000 of the Bulgarian Singers' releases. Somebody out there likes this music.
● Is Elektra setting a trend in music?
▲ I never think in setting trends. The last thing you want to be is cocky, "I can do this, I can do that." All

you can say is I want to be the best. Everyone defines the best in their own way. I mean I have my definition of what the best is, and everybody here has the def-inition and we're all in sync.

We're not interested in set-ting trends, starting trends, or following trends. We're interested in being the best.

Choosing the best talent.

That's the only trend we're involved in.

And certainly we didn't set that trend because a lot of great records came out before I was born. Billie Holiday set trends, Bessie Smith set trends, Mahalia Jackson set trends, Count Basie set trends, Duke Ellington set trends. The musicians set trends. We're a record company.
● How would you describe yourself?
▲ I can describe it in very simple terms: I am a guy who loves what he does, and I have very high stan-dards. It may sound like arrogance, but it's not. I feel that you have so much time each day. You have to make your own priorities. When I wake up in the morning I know what I need to do and I know what's in my way.
● What are your goals for Elektra?
▲ I want to be the best and I also want to be the biggest. I don't want to be the biggest and the best. First I want to be the best, then I want to be biggest. And I think we're well on our way.

This cover story por-trays Bob Krasnow, Elektra's president, as a revolutionary within the record business. The companion article to the El Lissitsky cover (previous page) carries more of the same Constructivist graphics of the 1920s and 1930s. Together with the "Workers Unite" illustration, the Futura typography, bold rules, and perpendicular set-ting reinforce the theme of the article.

TYPEWISE TYPOGRAPHY

This book was set in Bitstream fonts of Bodoni and Futura and was produced on a Macintosh computer with the Quark XPress program, and output on a Linotronic 300.

Bodoni was created in the late eighteenth century by Italian typographer Giambattista Bodoni, who is credited for introducing the modern Roman style of typography. Futura was designed in the late 1920s by Paul Renner, an architect associated with the Bauhaus school.

PRODUCTION CREDITS

Authors:
Kit Hinrichs
Delphine Hirasuna

Designer:
Kit Hinrichs

Design Associates:
Amy Chan
Catherine Wong
Susan Tsuchiya

Editorial Assistant:
Mary Lou Edmondson

Project Coordinator:
Gayle Marsh

Illustrator:
Regan Dunnick

Computer design
and typography:
Rick Binger

Photography:
Barry Robinson
Jim Blakely
Bill Whitehurst
Nick Turner
Corporate Images
Terry Heffernan

SPECIAL THANKS

We would also like to thank Matthew Carter, Amy Hoffman, Tobie Holden, Shelley Brosseau, Jenni Croghan, Siegfried Gatty, Gretchen Macfarlane, Randy Rocchi and Tracy Hopper.